OXFORD REFERENCE

THE OXFORD DICTIONARY OF SAINTS

David Hugh Farmer retired as Reader in History at Reading University in 1988. His books include *Magna Vita Sancti Hugonis: The Life of St. Hugh of Lincoln by Adam of Eynsham*, which he edited with Decima L. Douie for the Oxford Medieval Texts series.

THE OXFORD DICTIONARY OF SAINTS

DAVID HUGH FARMER

Third Edition

Oxford New York
OXFORD UNIVERSITY PRESS

Oxford University Press, Walton Street, Oxford OX2 6DP

Oxford New York Toronto
Delhi Bombay Calcutta Madras Karachi
Kuala Lumpur Singapore Hong Kong Tokyo
Nairobi Dar es Salaam Cape Town
Melbourne Auckland Madrid

and associated companies in
Berlin Ibadan

Oxford is a trade mark of Oxford University Press

First edition 1978
Second edition 1987
Third edition 1992

British Library Cataloguing in Publication Data
Data available

Library of Congress Cataloging in Publication Data
Farmer, David Hugh.
The Oxford dictionary of saints/David Hugh Farmer.—3rd ed. p. cm.
Includes bibliographical references and index.
1. Christian saints—Biography—Dictionaries.
2. Christian saints—Great Britain—Biography—Dictionaries.
3. Christian saints—Ireland—Biography—Dictionaries. I. Title.
BR1710.F34 1992 270'.092'2—dc20 [B] 92-6722
ISBN 0-19-283069-4 (pbk.)

3 5 7 9 10 8 6 4

Printed in Great Britain by
Clays Ltd.
Bungay, Suffolk

TO

ANN, PAUL, AND JOHN

CONTENTS

INTRODUCTION

STEADY demand for this work, first published in 1978 with a second edition in 1987, has led to this attempt to make it the standard one-volume work on its subject in English. To achieve this aim more saints have been included, principally but not exclusively from Europe and with a fuller representation of saints recently canonized. The volume now contains approximately 1,500 entries, with bibliographies as before. Some entries have been revised, but none substantially reduced. That there is need for such a volume is clear from its diffusion in the English-speaking world; and recently the second edition was translated into Italian with authorized additions and omissions: *Dizionario dei santi* (Padova, Franco Muzzio).

No one-volume dictionary of saints can be exhaustive. It required twelve large volumes of *Bibliotheca Sanctorum* (Rome, 1960–70) to include all saints in alphabetical order from all countries. French readers have for long been able to consult *Les Vies des saints et des bienheureux* (edd. Baudot and Chaussin, revised by Dom J. Dubois, 1959–) and more recently *L'Histoire des saints et de la sainteté chrétienne* (Paris, Hachette 1985–), an illustrated work based on periods in history. Both these works are likewise in twelve volumes.

This volume then, as before, is selective, not comprehensive. The criteria for inclusion are as follows:

1. All English saints, including those of English origin who died abroad and those of foreign origin who died in England.

2. All saints of whom there is or was a notable cult in England. One criterion of such a cult is the dedication of a church in his honour.[1] Another is his or her presence in an important calendar. Hence all who are venerated in the calendars of the Sarum Rite or the Book of Common Prayer or that of the Roman Church as revised in 1969 are included in this volume. So too are all saints recorded in English place-names.

3. The most important and representative saints of Ireland, Scotland, and Wales. Here especially an exhaustive coverage is impracticable except in a work concerned with nothing else. Hence numerous saints described by S. Baring-Gould and J. Fisher, *The Lives of the British Saints* (4 vols., 1907–13) or by J. O'Hanlon, *Lives of Irish Saints* (10 vols., 1875–1903) do not find a place in this volume.

[1] In this work figures for church-dedications are approximate only: they are usually based on those compiled by F. Bond, *Dedications and Patron Saints of English Churches* (1914). No account is taken of churches which have not survived.

4. Other saints have been included either because their presence was necessary to make other entries intelligible, or because of their importance in the history of the Christian Church (including that of hagiology), or because they occur frequently in calendars other than those mentioned above.

5. In this edition more space has been given to saints of Europe, from the Iberian peninsula to Russia and from Iceland to Sicily, including the most prominent saints of Eastern Rites.

6. More coverage has also been given to recently canonized saints. These include martyrs from Korea and Vietnam, a Lebanese hermit, and a missionary from Ethiopia, who now join martyrs from Canada, Uganda, Oceania, and Japan as well as saints from North and South America, already described in earlier editions.

On the other hand, the appendix on 'Some unsuccessful English candidates for canonization' has been deleted. This list was so incomplete that it would have needed very considerable augmentation to be really useful; so this task has been left to other scholars. Similarly, no attempt has been made to include in this volume worthy members of the Reformed Churches from the 16th century to the present day: a work commemorating their achievements has also been left to other, more competent hands. In spite of these limitations, however, it is hoped that this volume provides a readable and accurate account of the principal saints who are venerated in the Western Church or whose names are familiar to English-speaking Christians for one reason or another.

The saints are presented in alphabetical order: up to the end of the 15th century under their Christian names, after that time (e.g. More, Borromeo, Borgia) under their surnames.

The public veneration of saints in the Christian Church is known to have existed since the 2nd century. As will be shown below, it developed in local communities; it was based on the saint's tomb; it was a consequence of the general belief that a martyr who shed his blood for Christ was certainly in Heaven and able to exercise intercessory prayer on behalf of those who invoked him.

The belief and practice of Christians in Britain with regard to the cult of saints was no different from those of Christians elsewhere, although in Celtic lands, as will be shown below, the notion of what a saint was came to be widely extended. From Roman Britain St. Alban, venerated by Germanus at Verulamium in 429, and St. Patrick, venerated in Ireland from early times, are the best-known saints of these islands whose cults have survived continuously from their own times until the present day.

When the Anglo-Saxons were converted to Christianity by Augustine and his followers from Rome, by Aidan from Iona and Felix from Burgundy, they too shared the cults brought by their missionaries. These are known through early church dedications: unfortunately no liturgical books have survived from 7th-century England. The earliest known dedications were to SS. Peter and Paul, Mary, Michael, and Lawrence. At Canterbury there were also ancient dedications to SS. Martin, Pancras, and the Four Crowned Martyrs.

The earliest calendar to survive from Anglo-Saxon England is that of St. Willibrord, the Northumbrian missionary of Frisia in the early 8th century. Written partly in his own hand, a private calendar and hence unofficial, it testifies to his veneration of the saints of the whole Church such as St. Mary, the Apostles, and the early Roman martyrs, as well as of several English saints, such as Oswald, Cuthbert, and Chad. The Martyrology of Bede (*c.*730) and the Old English Martyrology from 9th-century Mercia show more extensive coverage but similar proportions: most of the saints venerated were of foreign origin; only a few were natives of these islands.

From the late 7th century there have been some records of the lives and actions of English saints. In hagiography as well as in history Bede was the most important pioneer: it is almost impossible to exaggerate his influence in this field. Not only did he write Lives of SS. Cuthbert, Benedict Biscop, and Ceolfrith, but he also recorded in his *Ecclesiastical History* (731) the achievements of many other saints in England, whether they worked inside or outside his native Northumbria. Almost all that can be known of such important figures as Aidan, Oswald, Theodore, Chad, Cedd, and others is to be found in the pages of Bede.

Even in his own day, however, Bede did not stand alone. A monk of Whitby had written the first Life of Gregory the Great, who was regarded as England's apostle; monks of Lindisfarne and Jarrow wrote lives of Cuthbert and Ceolfrith respectively; Eddius wrote one of Wilfrid, and later Felix one of Guthlac of Crowland. These pioneer biographies emphasized the supernatural powers of the saint, but also provided the basic facts of his life.

The Viking invasions with consequent destruction of churches and their libraries, as well as the secularization of monasteries through lay ownership, together with the widespread decline of learning so eloquently deplored by Alfred the Great, resulted in a lack of notable saints' Lives in England from *c.*800 until around the millennium. But although literary output was small, the largely illiterate laity were by no means without devotion to the saints. An anonymous writer of the early 11th century made a list of about fifty shrines in England, called *On the Resting-Places of the Saints* (hereafter *R.P.S.*). It survives both in Latin and in Old English. This short, localized Menology is precious evidence for continued interest in the often obscure Anglo-Saxon saints of the past.[1] Of only eight of them are there known written Lives: a dozen or more were mentioned or described by Bede. Some of these saints were buried in important towns like London, Canterbury, and Winchester; others in villages such as Charlbury, Congresbury, Oundle, and Wenlock. At this time towns as large as York, Chichester, Coventry, and Bath had no shrine; efforts would later be made to acquire one, either through the translation of existing saints' relics or through the recognition of holy men of the neighbourhood. The possession of a shrine visited by pilgrims brought considerable financial gain as well as spiritual lustre to the town which possessed it.

In the early 11th century too Ælfric of Eynsham provided parish priests and monks with his *Catholic Homilies* and his *Lives of the Saints*, both written in Old English. Here he described the achievements of ten Anglo-Saxon saints. None of his material was original: most was derived from Bede and other Latin writers; but it was agreeably presented and suitable for the needs of his readers. He did not, however, confine himself to English saints but also included many others.

Latin Lives of the principal saints of the monastic revival of the 10th century, Dunstan, Ethelwold, and Oswald, were written in the early 11th, but a more important series was written later in the same century or early in the 12th. These were caused by a twofold need. At this time there was a general demand for written documentation of all kinds because of the growth of the importance of law; also the Normans were suspicious, and even contemptuous, of the Anglo-Saxon saints. Sometimes when they asked for information about them, none was forthcoming; but in other cases such as those of Aldhelm, Ethelwold, Dunstan, and Alphege, suspicion about their sanctity was unjustified. In order to supply the need for documentation, to provide the old saints with their dossiers, four writers in particular went to work: one was Flemish, the other three English.

The Fleming Goscelin (*c.*1035–*c.*1107) came to England in 1058 to be a member of the household of Herman, bishop of Ramsbury and Sherborne. He was a monk of Saint-Bertin, an abbey with long-standing connections with English kings and bishops. From 1065 Goscelin was chaplain to the nuns of Wilton, but after 1080 he moved from one English monastery to another, writing Lives of the local saints at Sherborne, Barking, Ramsey, Ely, and above all Canterbury. Although uncritical and of varying quality, these Lives were the means of saving at least some saints from complete oblivion.

At Canterbury Norman disapproval was strongly felt, and the lively reaction against it was made articulate by Osbern (d. *c.*1092) the precentor, who had already suffered exile for his patriotic sympathies. His

[1] Cf. D. W. Rollason, 'Lists of saints' resting-places in Anglo-Saxon England', *Anglo-Saxon England*, vii (1978), 61–93.

works were readable Lives of Alphege and Dunstan, each of which contributed to the restoration of the cults of these saints. He was followed by Eadmer (*c.*1060–*c.*1128), who devoted his best early work to Lives of English saints such as Wilfrid, Dunstan, Oswald, and Bregwine. Later he became famous for his Life of Anselm, which marked a new type of hagiography as the first intimate portrait of a saint in our history. Other contributions he made to the cult of the saints were a treatise on the Immaculate Conception of the Blessed Virgin and a minor work on the importance of relics. In these this passionate partisan of Canterbury and Anglo-Saxon England rose above purely local interests to issues of wider significance.

Another scholar who related the lives of saints to the wider canvas of history was William of Malmesbury (*c.*1090–*c.*1143). His love of the English saints was matched by his energy in tracking down all that was known of them. Although he planned a collection of Lives of English saints, he may never have written it: it has certainly not survived. What have survived are short notices of, and frequent references to, many English saints in both the *Gesta Pontificum* and the *Gesta Regum*, two Lives of Dunstan and Wulfstan, and extended portraits of Aldhelm and Wilfrid incorporated in the *Gesta Pontificum*. William's writings may be compared with Bede's historical works and with Eadmer's biographies, even if they scarcely equalled the best qualities of each. The efforts of these four writers (and others) were crowned with success when the Normans accepted the cults of the English saints and translated their relics into shrines far more sumptuous than those in Anglo-Saxon churches. In this process there was also an element of reparation for the earlier despoliation (soon after 1066) of some Anglo-Saxon shrines.

In the Lives written in the 12th and early 13th centuries an effort was made to provide a vivid personal portrait of the saint rather than to show him as just a provider of supernatural power through miracles, visions, and prophecies, as in earlier Lives such as that of Columba by Adomnan. Although these elements could not be omitted, and miracles were demanded both by popular devotion and by the official procedure for canonization (see below), a number of writers presented the known historical facts of the saint's life and the way he acted as material for human portraiture as well as edification. Such Lives are those of Margaret by Turgot, of Anselm by Eadmer, of Wulfstan by William of Malmesbury, of Godric by Reginald of Durham, and of Hugh of Lincoln by Adam of Eynsham. The Lives of Richard of Chichester and of Wulfric of Haselbury share similar characteristics. Those of Thomas Becket and Edmund of Canterbury, however, tend to present their subject as an example of a persecuted defender of the Church's rights rather than an individual to be portrayed 'warts and all'.

In the later Middle Ages English hagiographers provided new works which were often developments of older ones. First, another list of English saints and shrines was written in the 14th century, with fuller information about the saints concerned. This *Catalogus Sanctorum Pausantium in Anglia* (hereafter *C.S.P.*) remains in manuscript, although an edition of it has been in preparation for some time.[1] Secondly, the development of drama led to new representations of miracle plays and was one factor in the writing of vernacular Lives. Thirdly, illuminated manuscripts of saints' Lives such as those by Matthew Paris of Alban, Edward, and Thomas Becket and, even more, that by John Lydgate of Edmund of Bury reflect a style and an atmosphere different from equivalent productions of the 11th and 12th centuries.[2] The rise of romance in the age of chivalry deeply influenced the production of these beautiful but quite unreal works, in which imagination and elegance were more evident than the majesty and power emphasized by earlier European taste. This can be seen above all in the *Golden Legend* of James of Voragine, archbishop of Genoa (d. 1298). This elegantly written collection of legends of the saints became immensely popular. It was translated and adapted by William Caxton; it was much read up to the Reformation.

Meanwhile in England collections of Lives of English saints had been made. The earliest known to me is that written *c.*1300 in a book which belonged to the nuns of Romsey (British Library, Lansdowne 436). It contains forty-seven Lives, most of which are abridged. Its compiler is unknown, but its purpose plain: edification through public and private reading. Similar collections had been made long before and had reached England in the 11th century; but they were of saints with a notable cult in Western Europe, especially those of French and Flemish origin. The special interest of the 14th-century English collections, however, is that in an age of growing national consciousness they contained only English saints, together with a few from Scotland, Wales, and Ireland.

The most notable of such collectors was John of Tynemouth (1290–1349), a Benedictine monk of St. Albans and probably for some time parish priest at its distant cell of Tynemouth. Like Goscelin and William of Malmesbury, he travelled over much of England in search of source material in monastic and cathedral libraries. He called his collection of 156 Lives *Sanctilogium Angliae, Walliae, Scotiae et Hiberniae.* Despite its title, the saints chosen were principally those of England. Scottish and Irish saints were represented only by those venerated in England, but those of Wales figured more prominently. This may have

[1] This work from MS. Lambeth Palace 99 (15th century) was transcribed by the late Professor F. Wormald, who kindly made it available for this Dictionary.

[2] Examples of these are the two illustrated Lives of Cuthbert: University College, Oxford 165 and British Library, Additional 39,943.

been due to John's access to a collection of Welsh saints' Lives such as the *Vitae Sanctorum Brittaniae* (British Library, Cotton Vespasian A. xiv).

John's achievement was considerable. His collection was by far the largest of its kind. He rescued from complete obscurity some saints, otherwise unknown. He abridged sources which have now been lost. But his work was open to criticism. It was uncritical compilation and he often omitted names of people and places, as well as dates. In some measure it is now possible to restore his omissions through the discovery of the *Codex Gothanus*.[1] This important English manuscript in the municipal library of Gotha enables the modern scholar to reach John's sources in a way impossible in former times.

John of Tynemouth's collection is known through its revision by the Austin Friar John Capgrave, born at King's Lynn and later provincial of his Order in England. Author of several theological and devotional works including English Lives of Catherine of Alexandria, Norbert of Magdeberg, and Gilbert of Sempringham, he edited John of Tynemouth's work under the title *Nova Legenda Angliae* (hereafter *N.L.A.*).[2] His main contribution was to alter the order of the saints from that of the calendar to that of the alphabet. Even the Introduction was added long after his death. But the whole work was, and sometimes still is, ascribed to him instead of to its rightful author John of Tynemouth.

John also compiled a martyrology, of which only a few extracts survive; like other martyrologies it included saints from the whole of Christendom. It was one of several late medieval martyrologies from England. Another, more famous one, was based on the Calendar of Sarum, which had become by the 15th century the most widely used modification of the Roman Rite in England and Wales. This martyrology was compiled by the prolific writer Richard Whytford (d. 1555), a Brigittine monk of Syon Abbey; he was the friend of More and Erasmus. The production of such works, together with the printed edition of *Nova Legenda Angliae* in 1516 and the seven printed editions of the *Golden Legend* before 1527, are substantial evidence for the continued interest in hagiography on the eve of the Reformation in England. The tradition of writing Lives of saints was continued in recusant circles by the biographers of Thomas More, by the contemporary recorders of the deaths of the Catholic martyrs, and by John Wilson's martyrologies of 1608 and 1627.

[1] P. Grosjean, 'De codice hagiographico Gothano' and 'Codicis Gothani Appendix', *Anal. Boll.*, lviii (1940), 90–103 and 177–204.

[2] Edited by C. Horstman (Oxford 1901, 2 vols.); the work of John of Tynemouth and Capgrave was to some extent complemented for Devon and Cornwall by Bishop Grandisson of Exeter (d. 1369) and later by Nicholas Roscarrock, the Cornish recusant antiquary (d. 1634). Further evidence for the cult of Celtic (and other) saints was provided by travelling antiquaries such as William Worcestre (1415–85) and John Leland (1505–52).

The cult of the saints came under widespread attack at the time of the Reformation. Abuses connected with them, including deception and fraud, were given much publicity by reformers such as Erasmus and Luther. Each was surpassed in iconoclasm by his disciples. Oecolampadius at Basle incited a mob to smash images and statues in the cathedral and other churches in 1529. Erasmus, although critical of Canterbury's and Walsingham's relics, disowned his followers' activities in Switzerland.

Luther, who had earlier commented sharply on the 5,005 relics in the chapel of Frederick the Wise at Wittenberg, returned there in later life to curb his followers who were smashing images. 'Of course there are abuses,' he said, 'but are they eliminated by destroying the objects abused? Men can go wrong with wine and women. Shall we then prohibit wine and abolish women? Such haste and violence betray lack of confidence in God.'[1]

St. Thomas More also commented adversely on popular credulity, bizarre petitions, and the cult of spurious relics. Such abuses were not approved of by Church authorities, nor did they reflect the outlook of sensible and well-informed believers. Henry VIII systematically dismantled the saints' shrines to the immense gain of the royal Treasury and even greater loss to the country's artistic and antiquarian heritage. Rood figures were demolished and burnt; images of saints were ordered to be removed from all churches in 1548; Thomas Becket, champion in his day of the 'liberties of the Church', was 'decanonized' and all mention of him was erased from liturgical books. Nevertheless, in the Book of Common Prayer saints' days were retained. They were, however, considerably reduced in number and their selection was in some ways anomalous.

While the Church of England, like the Lutherans, retained some veneration of the saints, extreme reformers wanted to abolish, not regulate, their cult. In the Lutheran and Anglican churches, future canonizations were excluded with the abolition of recognition of papal courts' decisions. In the reign of Edward VI (and later during the Commonwealth) outbreaks of iconoclasm destroyed numerous statues, stained-glass windows, illuminated manuscripts, and mural paintings of the saints. Some of the latter were covered with whitewash or plaster and have been revealed again in modern times. In Scotland and Ireland the destruction of memorials of the saints was more complete than in England, thanks to the activities of John Knox's followers in Scotland and of several English armies in Ireland. But such destruction did not

[1] Erasmus, *Pilgrimages of St. Mary of Walsingham and St. Thomas of Canterbury* (tr. J. G. Nichols, 1875); cf. R. Bainton, *Erasmus of Christendom* (1970), pp. 258 ff. See also Luther, *Works* (Philadelphia edn., 1930–43): ii. 127–32 and i. 133 and 240 are representative passages of his thoughts on saints' cults. A large proportion of the 5,005 relics came from the Holy Land and were souvenirs rather than saints' bones.

eradicate the veneration of saints from the hearts of believers. Especially in Ireland and certain parts of Wales, the 'old religion' survived many generations, and in some remote places devotion to the saints was mixed with folklore and various superstitions and it survived, as at Holywell, in pilgrimages to shrines of ancient saints.

These were principally found in Celtic areas of Great Britain. In the Middle Ages these countries had shown persistent tenacity to local tradition and had often been less susceptible to Roman influence than England, which was less geographically isolated. In their cult of saints, as in some other matters, Celtic traditions had developed somewhat differently than elsewhere in the West. At first sight, place-name evidence and the number (and obscurity) of their saints seem to indicate that a far greater proportion of the inhabitants of Ireland, Scotland, Wales, and Cornwall in the early Middle Ages were more holy than those of any other area. In fact this anomaly is due to their extended use of the term 'saint'. In these countries the word had come to mean hardly more than pious church-founder or learned ecclesiastic.[1] Some of these, no doubt, were just as genuine saints as others in Western Europe, but far too little is known about the vast majority of them to assert that all of them were. In Ireland, in particular, there were hardly any contemporary Lives written. When the writer approached his task some centuries after the death of his subject, little genuine information was to hand; but he wrote in order to glorify the monastery or diocese which the saint was believed to have founded. In recording or inventing legends, Irish writers in particular showed lively imagination and poetic sensibility, but little historical accuracy.

Owing to such uncertainty and to the widespread questioning in Reformation times concerning the nature and desirability of the cult of saints, fundamental questions were and are asked: who were the saints, how did their cult begin, what was the attitude of the Christian Church towards them?

It has often been asserted that the cult of saints was both a borrowing from and a substitute for the polytheistic cults of the ancient Graeco-Roman world. In its crude form the theory is completely unconvincing, especially when the nature of the cults is considered and placed in its context of Christian doctrine, worship, and life. But it can readily be conceded that many external elements such as anniversaries, shrines, incubation, and inconography have all been at the very least deeply influenced by pagan Mediterranean models. Nevertheless, the cults of saints originated in the beliefs and practice of Jewry and early Christianity.[2]

[1] See N. K. Chadwick, *The Age of the Saints in the Early Celtic Church* (1961).

[2] These paragraphs owe much to B. de Gaiffier, *Études critiques d'Hagiographie et d'Iconologie* (1967), pp. 7–29; see also Peter Brown, *The Cult of the Saints* (1981).

From Jewry came not only such texts as that where in a vision Judas Maccabeus saw Jeremiah 'with outstretched hands invoking blessings on the whole body of the Jews' (cf. 2 Macc. 15: 12), but also concrete examples of martyrdom in the cases of the Maccabees and of Isaiah; moreover, by the time of Christ, the Jews venerated the memory of patriarchs, prophets, or martyrs and built monuments over the places where their bones lay. As many as fifty sanctuaries in the whole Jewish world have been identified. Christians continued this practice for their own saints and venerated Jewish saints such as the prophets and the Maccabees.

The earliest Christian saints were martyrs. The word martyr means witness; the apostles were witnesses of the Resurrection of Christ (Acts 4: 33); the martyrs of the Apocalypse pray before the throne of God and receive white robes (Rev. 6: 9 ff.); these witnesses of Christ are members of the Body of Christ, specially honoured because of their close configuration to Christ, who gave his life as a witness to the Father's love for the human race, and in dying and rising again gave himself as an exemplar for the following of all Christians.

But at the very beginning of Christianity, it seems, the funeral honours of the first victims of persecution were no different from those of ordinary Christians. The ceremonies had some resemblance to those of the pagans in so far as flowers and perfumes were used and the family and friends of the dead person gathered at the cemeteries for funeral meals. Christians chose inhumation rather than cremation. The family would meet again on the anniversary of the dead person. Two differences from pagan practice showed themselves early. One was that the anniversary was not the birthday, but the death-day (the *natalis* or birthday in heaven of the martyr, reunited with Christ by his death), which was and is still commemorated; the other was that in the case of the martyrs not only the family but the whole Christian community took part in the burial and anniversary, i.e. not only the small community which had charge of the tomb, but the larger community with its official representatives.

The earliest clear witness to the cult of the martyr is the account of the martyrdom of Polycarp (*c.*156). Not only does this document preserve authentic dialogue, but it also tells us how the faithful of Smyrna collected Polycarp's bones, 'more precious than jewels of great price', buried them in a safe place, and expressed the desire to find them there again when they meet to celebrate the anniversary of his martyrdom, which will recall the memory of those who have died and prepare those who will follow. The gathering of the faithful was no doubt to offer the Eucharist, both a common meal for the believers and an appropriate 'memorial' of the sacrifice of Christ on Calvary, so vividly represented in the sufferings of the martyrs. They themselves, with St. Ignatius of

Antioch, spoke of their death being a liturgical sacrifice. Little by little the custom grew of placing the remains of the martyr under the altar as the most appropriate place: they had shared to the utmost the sacrificial death of Christ himself. In the words of St. Ambrose (following his discovery of the bodies of SS. Gervase and Protase) the prayer was made that 'the glorious victims take their place where Christ offers himself as a victim. He who was put to death for all is on the altar; those who have been redeemed by his suffering are under the altar.'[1]

As with other Christian doctrines, those on the nature and value of martyrdom and the cult of saints developed considerably over the centuries. From the texts of the Gospels which promised heavenly reward for those who confessed Christ's name, witnessing by their death both to the hope of immortality and their complete adhesion (Ignatius calls it discipleship) to Christ, the passage was easy to that of praying *to* the martyrs rather than *for* them and to the growing belief in the efficacy of their intercession for other members of the Body of Christ.

In the Gospel parable of Dives and Lazarus (Luke 16: 19–31) the poor just man is credited with being able to relieve the suffering of the rich sinner. Origen and St. Cyprian placed this doctrine in the context of the Communion of Saints and asserted more clearly the power of their intercession after death. In the growing cult of the martyrs it was left to Augustine to formulate clearly the immense difference between devotion to the martyrs and adoration of God: 'We build temples to our martyrs not like temples for the gods, but as tombs of mortal men, whose spirits live with God. We do not build altars on which to offer sacrifices to martyrs, but we offer sacrifice to God alone, who is both ours and theirs. During this sacrifice they are named in their place and order, in so far as they are men of God who have overcome the world by confessing God, but they are not invoked by the priest who offers sacrifice. He offers sacrifice to God, not to them (although it is celebrated in their memory) because he is God's priest, not the priest of the martyrs. The sacrifice is the Body of Christ.'[2]

During the 4th century devotion to the martyrs spread rapidly. Also in the 4th century came the extension of the cult to selected confessors and virgins: the ascetic, monastic life came to be regarded as something of a substitute for martyrdom, and those who pursued it faithfully as worthy of the same honour. Whilst the earliest saints to be venerated had been martyrs such as Polycarp, Ignatius, and the Martyrs of Lyons, soon Antony and Athanasius in the East, with Augustine and Martin in the West were similarly honoured soon after their death. For both categories the saint's tomb was the indispensable start of the cult.

[1] Epistola xxii. 13 (*P.L.*, xvi. 1023).

[2] *De Civitate Dei*, xxii. 10 (*C.S.E.L.*, xlviii, 828).

Soon it came to be asked how an individual should be reckoned a saint and what was the proper authority for making such a decision. In early times it was popular acclaim which led the local Christian community to venerate one who had either suffered death in persecution or been of such outstanding holiness that none could doubt his eternal destiny. The fact of true martyrdom, as distinct from either suicide by enthusiasts or the pertinacity of heretics who were not motivated by charity, needed to be established. The area in which controversy about the discernment of true from false martyrdom developed was North Africa.[1] The decisive steps in the cult were the approval by the local bishop and the 'elevation' of the saint's body to a place of veneration, where it was honoured specially on the anniversary of his death. Records or lists of martyrs were kept in some churches from the fourth century: these formed the basis of martyrologies (menologies in the East), by which martyrs of one church came to be venerated in others and eventually throughout Christendom. In this process Usuard (d. *c.*875) was the most important compiler; his influential work is a principal source of the present Roman Martyrology.

Quite early, miracles were regarded as a proof of sanctity. From Apostolic times (Acts 19: 11–12) secondary relics such as handkerchiefs and girdles were also regarded as instruments of divine healing power. The relics or bones of the saint were regarded as both a source of healing and an agent which gave protection to the church which possessed them; an increase in their number and popularity coincided with the conversion of the barbarians in the early Middle Ages. Especially when relics were moved and divided did the cult of a local saint spread to other communities and other countries. It became a distinction for a church to possess the relics of other distant churches; one would rival another in their number and quality; to acquire them, large sums of money would sometimes be spent. In the context of veneration of Christ and his life on earth the relics of saints who had been closest to him were in specially keen demand. In this unscientific age a brisk trade was carried on and fortunes were made in purveying relics of dubious authenticity. The fall of Constantinople in 1204 was the occasion for the release of further supplies.

No doubt many of the cures at the shrines were explicable in terms of faith-healing, auto-suggestion, or inaccurate diagnosis. Nevertheless, many will think that these factors do not account for the totality of cures effected. What can be safely asserted is that in an age when medical treatment was rudimentary, many sufferers regarded as incurable by ordinary means visited shrines hoping for cures, and that many did obtain relief, temporary or permanent. All classes of society and both

[1] E. W. Kemp, *Canonization and Authority in the Western Church* (1948), pp. 11–17.

sexes were represented in the records of the cures, but inevitably prominence was often given to the cures of magnates who further enriched the shrine with their thank-offerings and other benefactions.

Little by little the decision to canonize or not to canonize, that is, to declare authoritatively that a particular individual is worthy of public cult, became reserved to the papacy. There were several reasons for this. One was the conviction that owing to various abuses the earlier, more informal procedure (which still obtains in the East) was insufficient. Another was that in the growing prestige of the papacy from the 11th century a papal decision definitely enhanced the status of the local saint. The demand came from below rather than from above. Further factors included the growing need for legal processes and legal documents recording them. Without these, and where there could be doubt about the identity and even the existence of some who were claimed to be saints, more and more was the need felt to place the cults on a firm basis. Through the ages zealous bishops had intervened to suppress false cults, but only in the late 12th and 13th centuries did the authorization of new cults become juridically reserved to the Holy See. Not much could be done systematically about old cults or about the proliferation of relics by any authority except for exhortations, but at least the cult of new saints was put on to a legal basis which many of the best minds of the age helped to establish and administer. This reserve was formerly believed to be the work of Alexander III (1159–81); recent scholarship has shown it to be the work rather of Innocent III (1199–1216), who in fact built on and consolidated the work of his predecessors. The growing centralization of the Church following the Gregorian Reform was also a powerful factor in establishing the new legal requirements.

Papal commissions were appointed to investigate the life and miracles of candidates for canonization. Only if the life was seen to have been worthy were the miracles then examined. These two subjects of enquiry have remained standard from then until the present day, while the enquiries themselves have been conducted according to the best standards of the time. With the growth of scientific knowledge these have become much more searching into the nature of the cures, while the enquiry into the 'life' includes a systematic examination of the candidate's virtues. In the legal process there is a prosecuting counsel named *promotor justitiae* (popularly called the 'Devil's Advocate'), while the postulator and vice-postulator of the cause also make full use of legal advocacy, the examination of the candidate's writings, and the testimony of sworn witnesses to particular incidents in his life. The procedure was laid down by Benedict XIV in his *De Servorum Dei beatificatione et beatorum canonizatione* (1734–8), a scholarly work which owed much to his long experience as *promotor justitiae*, when his brief had been to oppose by every lawful means any canonization attempts that were made. But this is to anticipate.

From the 13th century the new processes were initiated and executed. Among the many new saints from different countries the English saints canonized between 1200 and 1457 included SS. Gilbert of Sempringham, Wulfstan of Worcester, Hugh of Lincoln, Edmund of Abingdon, Thomas of Hereford, and Osmund of Salisbury. Most of them were bishops, all men and no women, but St. Margaret of Scotland must have been canonized although vital documents have not survived. Of earlier saints Edward the Confessor and Thomas Becket had both been canonized by popes, while those of the formative years of the Anglo-Saxon period such as Augustine, Theodore, Bede, and Wilfrid had never been the object of a papal decision at all. Saints from this time, before the papal reserve became effective, had, as in the Eastern Churches today, been the objects of *local* decisions and *local* cults. Many of them achieved national or supra-national fame and cult and implicit papal approval (equipollent canonization) sometimes after the lapse of centuries. Among unsuccessful English candidates for canonization were Robert Grosseteste, Richard Rolle, and King Henry VI. The cause of the latter looked particularly promising, but failed, at least temporarily, owing to political circumstances. It must also be said that in other cases the political climate favoured the success of a petition for canonization (as in the case of Edward the Confessor); always strong support was looked for, not only within the diocese concerned, but also in other parts of the country. The intervention of the king was always desirable but not indispensable.

It was, however, one thing for legislation to be made and another for it to be always and everywhere obeyed and implemented. Unauthorized cults did not entirely cease in the later Middle Ages but in the long run they were unlikely to survive if they lacked the papal approval which they should have had. A modern authority concludes: 'In canonization as in other matters medieval theory could not always be enforced in practice, and it was not until the Roman Church had lost the Northern peoples and had undergone the counter-reformation, that the decrees of Urban VIII (1623–44) were able to bring about that complete control of the cult of the saints which had been so long desired. It is a paradox that among those who had rejected the Roman obedience were the peoples who had been foremost in acknowledging papal authority in this sphere of Christian practice.'[1]

The reform of the Roman calendar in 1969 has both regulated further the cult of the saints and introduced systematic selection of saints both

[1] E. W. Kemp, op. cit., p. 170.

for veneration throughout the Roman Church and for purely local cults.[1] The reform was part of the programme of *aggorniamento* initiated by John XXIII (1958–62) and continued by Paul VI (1963–78). It was widely held that the accumulation of saints in the calendar over many centuries had led to over-emphasis on their feastdays at the expense of the more important 'Temporal Cycle' of the calendar composed of Advent, Lent, and the Sundays throughout the year. Long before, particular Orders such as the Benedictines had enjoyed a more selective calendar than the Roman Church as a whole: it might be said that the effect of the reform was to bring the whole Church to a situation in several ways similar to that of the Benedictines. The opportunity was taken also to upgrade or downgrade certain feasts, to restore some of them to their original days, to transfer others from Lent and Advent and to omit entirely some who had previously enjoyed a considerable cult. These included SS. Philomena, Margaret of Antioch, and Catherine of Alexandria. At the same time saints were selected for universal veneration by deliberate choice from each century of the Church's history and from many countries. Examples of these include martyrs from Australasia, Uganda, Korea, and Vietnam. Their historical significance as representatives of particular types of the apostolate was duly considered. Others who had long been venerated everywhere in Christendom were approved for particular churches, countries, or religious orders. The committee charged with this selection was particularly severe on a number of early martyrs. Where historical scholarship has shown that there is no solid foundation for believing them to be martyrs, they are no longer venerated as such. The preponderance of saints of Roman origin has been ended, and the number of popes culted universally reduced to fifteen.

At the same time the ranks of feasts were substantially altered: now there are but three grades, 'solemnities' (for the greatest festivals of the liturgical year), 'feasts' (of important saints like apostles, at the rate of two or three each month), and 'memories', i.e. commemorations which are either obligatory or optional.

The result of the whole reform can be summarized as:

(1) a pruning and tidying operation which many think was overdue, which includes the elimination of dubious cults and the restoration of feasts to their appropriate day,

(2) a selection made so that the calendar has become more universal because it includes saints from all ages and many nations,

(3) a general reduction in the number of saints culted universally with greater emphasis on local cults in particular countries.

[1] *Calendarium Romanum* (1969). This book outlines the principles of reform and comments on general and particular alterations.

The decree which launched this reform gave special praise to the work of the Bollandists, who in the *Acta Sanctorum* and the periodical *Analecta Bollandiana* brought the study of hagiography to high historical standards by producing critical editions and commentaries of Saints' Lives, martyrologies, charters, and other relevant documents.[1] Also praised were the compilers of *Bibliotheca Sanctorum*, whose publication contributed to the selection of saints made. A glance at the bibliographies of this volume will indicate how deeply it depends on the researches of the Bollandists, on the other writers and collectors mentioned in this Introduction, and on the work of the late Herbert Thurston S.J., whose assiduity and accuracy matched that of the Bollandists and whose revision of Butler's *Lives of the Saints* (hereafter B.T.A., 4 vols., 1956) was crucial in making those volumes useful to scholars of the present day.

Grateful acknowledgement is here made to those who have encouraged this work: to the abbot and monks of Quarr Abbey in whose library it was begun, to the staffs of other libraries (especially the Bodleian Library) where it was completed; to the Research Board of Reading University for their financial support; above all to the late Sir Roger Mynors for his initial interest, his sustained encouragement, and his final appreciation of the completed work. The patient courtesy and the abiding confidence of the staff of the Oxford University Press have very greatly helped to bring it to a conclusion.

[1] The Bollandists, a small group of Belgian Jesuits, specially selected for this work, who have been in existence since the 17th century, can most easily be studied in D. Knowles, *Great Historical Enterprises* (1963).

ABBREVIATIONS

A.A.S.	*Acta Apostolicae Sedis* (1909–)
AA.SS.	*Acta Sanctorum* (64 vols., Antwerp, 1643–)
AA.SS. OSB.	L. D'Achéry and J. Mabillon, *Acta Sanctorum Ordinis Sancti Benedicti* (9 vols., Paris, 1668–1701)
Abh.	*Abhandlungen der (königlichen) Gesellschaft (Akademie) der Wissenschaften zu Göttingen.* Philolog.-hist. Kl., N.F. (Berlin, 1897–)
A.C.M.	H. Musurillo, *The Acts of the Christian Martyrs* (Oxford, 1972)
Alcuin, *Carmen*	P. Godman (ed.), *The bishops, kings and saints of York* (1982)
Anal. Boll.	*Analecta Bollandiana* (1882–)
Anal. Carm. discalceatorum	*Analecta Ordinis Carmelitarum discalceatorum* (1926–)
A.N.C.L.	*Ante-Nicene Christian Library* (1864–)
Antiq. Jnl.	*Antiquaries Journal* (1921–)
Arch. Ael.	*Archaeologia Aeliana* (1822–)
Archaeol. Jnl.	*Archaeological Journal* (1844–)
A.S.C.	*Anglo-Saxon Chronicle, E.H.D.*, vol. i, ed. D. Whitelock (1961)
A.S.E.	*Anglo-Saxon England* (1972–)
Auct. Ant.	*Auctores Antiquissimi*
A.V.	Authorized Version (of the Bible)
b.	born
B.A.R.	*British Archaeological Reports* (1974–)
Baring-Gould and Fisher	S. Baring-Gould and J. Fisher, *The Lives of the British Saints* (4 vols., 1907–13)
B.C.P.	Book of Common Prayer
Bd.	Blessed
Bede, *H.E.*	Bede, *Historia Ecclesiastica*, ed. B. Colgrave and R. A. B. Mynors (1969)
Beds.	Bedfordshire
Berks.	Berkshire
B.H.L.	*Bibliotheca Hagiographica Latina Antiquae et Mediae Aetatis* (1898–1901; supplement, 1911)
Bibl. SS.	*Bibliotheca Sanctorum* (12 vols., Rome, 1960–70)
B.L.	British Library
B.T.A.	*Butler's Lives of the Saints*, revised by H. Thurston and D. Attwater (4 vols., 1953–4)
Bucks.	Buckinghamshire
Bull.	*Bulletin*
c.	*circa*
c., cc.	chapter(s)
Cambs.	Cambridgeshire
C.C.	*Corpus Christianorum* (Turnhout, 1953–)
C.C.K.	*Cornish Church Kalendar* (1927)
C.H.J.	*Cambridge Historical Journal* (1923–57)
Col.	Colossians
C.M.H.	H. Delehaye, *Commentarius Perpetuus in Martyrologium Hieronymianum, AA.SS.*, vol. 65 (1931)

C.Q.R. — *Church Quarterly Review* (1875–)

C.S. — *Camden Series* (1838–)

C.S.E.L. — *Corpus Scriptorum Ecclesiasticorum Latinorum* (Vienna, 1866–)

C.S.P. — *Catalogus Sanctorum Pausantium in Anglia*, Lambeth Palace MS. 99

d. — died

D.A.C. — *Dictionary of the Apostolic Church*, ed. J. Hastings (2 vols., 1915–18)

D.A.C.L. — *Dictionnaire d'Archéologie Chrétienne et de Liturgie*, ed. F. Cabrol, O.S.B., and H. Leclercq, O.S.B. (15 vols., 1907–53)

D.C.A. — *Dictionary of Christian Antiquities*, ed. W. Smith and S. Cheetham (2 vols., 1875–80)

D.C.B. — *Dictionary of Christian Biography*, ed. W. Smith and H. Wace (4 vols., 1877–87)

D.H.G.E. — *Dictionnaire d'Histoire et de Géographie Ecclésiastiques*, ed. A. Baudrillart and others (1912–)

Dict. Bibl. — *Dictionnaire de la Bible*, ed. F. Vigouroux, P.S.S. (5 vols., 1895–1912)

Dict. Sp. — *Dictionnaire de Spiritualité*, ed. M. Viller, S.J., and others (1937–)

D.N.B. — *Dictionary of National Biography*, ed. L. Stephen and S. Lee (1885–1900)

D.T.C. — *Dictionnaire de Théologie Catholique*, ed. A. Vacant, E. Mangenot, and É. Amann (15 vols., 1903–50)

D.U.J. — *Durham University Journal* (1876–)

E.B.K. — *English Benedictine Kalendars*, ed. F. Wormald (3 vols. (H.B.S.), 1935–46)

ed. — editor, edited by

edn. — edition

E.E.T.S. — Early English Text Society

E.H.D. — *English Historical Documents*, ed. D. C. Douglas and others (1953–)

E.H.R. — *English Historical Review* (1886–)

E.O. — *Échos d'Orient* (39 vols., 1897–1942)

E.R.L. — *English Recusant Literature* (1558–1640), ed. D. M. Rogers (1970–)

Eusebius, *H.E.* — Eusebius, *Historia Ecclesiastica*, ed. K. Lake (2 vols., 1927)

G.C.S. — Die griechischen christlichen Schriftsteller der ersten drei Jahrhunderte (Leipzig and Berlin, 1897–)

Glos. — Gloucestershire

G.P. — William of Malmesbury, *Gesta Pontificum*, ed. N. E. S. A. Hamilton (*R.S.*, 1870)

G.R. — William of Malmesbury, *Gesta Regum*, ed. W. Stubbs (*R.S.*, 1887–9)

Hants — Hampshire

H.B.S. — Henry Bradshaw Society (1891–)

Herts. — Hertfordshire

H.S.S.C. — *Histoire des Saints et de la Sainteté Chrétienne* (ed. F. Chiovaro and others, 12 volumes, Paris, 1972–88)

ibid. — *ibidem*, in the same place

id. — *idem*, the same, *or* as mentioned before

I.E.R.	*Irish Ecclesiastical Record* (1864–)
I.H.S.	*Irish Historical Studies* (1938–)
Irish Saints, The	D. P. Mould, *The Irish Saints* (1964)
J.B.A.A.	*Journal of the British Archaeological Association* (3rd series, 1937–)
J.E.H.	*Journal of Ecclesiastical History* (1950–)
J.R.S.A.I.	*Journal of the Royal Society of Antiquaries of Ireland* (1849–)
J.T.S.	*Journal of Theological Studies* (1900–)
K.S.S.	*Kalendars of Scottish Saints*, ed. A. P. Forbes (1872)
Lancs.	Lancashire
Leics.	Leicestershire
Leland	*The Itinerary of John Leland*, ed. L. Toulmin-Smith (5 vols., 1907–13)
Lincs.	Lincolnshire
Macc.	Maccabees
Matt.	Matthew
ME.	Middle English
M.G.H.	*Monumenta Germaniae Historica*. The series Scriptores is split into several sub-series, of which the following contain British material: *Auctores Antiquissimi. Scriptores rerum merovingicarum*, and *Scriptores*.
M.O.	D. Knowles, *The Monastic Order in England* (2nd edn., 1963)
MS(S).	manuscript(s)
N.A.	*Neues Archiv der Gesellschaft für ältere deutsche Geschichtskunde zur Beförderung einer Gesammtausgabe der Quellenschriften deutscher Geschichte des Mittelalters* (1876; 1922–35)
N.C.E.	*New Catholic Encyclopedia* (14 vols., 1967)
n.d.	no date
N.F.	Neue Folge
N.L.A.	*Nova Legenda Angliae*, ed. C. Horstman (2 vols., 1901)
Northants.	Northamptonshire
Notts.	Nottinghamshire
N.P.N.C.F.	Nicene and Post-Nicene Christian Fathers (1887–1900)
NT	New Testament
O.D.C.C.	*Oxford Dictionary of the Christian Church*, ed. F. L. Cross and E. A. Livingstone (2nd edn., 1974)
O.D.E.P.N.	E. Ekwall, *Oxford Dictionary of English Place-Names* (4th edn., 1960)
O.D.P.	J. N. D. Kelly, *Oxford Dictionary of Popes* (1985)
OE	Old English
OT	Old Testament
Oxon.	Oxfordshire
P.B.A.	*Proceedings of the British Academy* (1903–)
Pet.	Peter
P.G.	*Patrologia Graeca*, ed. J. P. Migne (162 vols., 1857–66)
P.L.	*Patrologia Latina*, ed. J. P. Migne (221 vols., 1844–64)
Propylaeum	*Propylaeum ad Acta Sanctorum Decembris* (1940)
R.B.	*Revue Biblique* (1892–)
R.C.	Roman Catholic
Réau	L. Réau, *Iconographie d l'Art Chrétien*, 6 vols. (1955–8)
Rev.	Book of Revelation

Rev. Bén.	*Revue Bénédictine* (1885–)
R.H.E.	*Revue d'Histoire Ecclésiastique* (1900–)
R.M.	*Roman Martyrology: Martyrologium Romanum* (Torino, 1949)
R.P.S.	*'On the Resting-Places of the Saints': Die Heiligen Englands*, ed. F. Liebermann (Hanover, 1889)
R.S.	*Rolls Series* (1858–)
R.V.	Revised Version (of the Bible)
s.a.	*sub anno*, in the year
saec.	saeculum
Salop	Shropshire
S.C.	*Sources Chrétiennes* (Paris, 1940–)
Scriptores rerum merov.	*Scriptores rerum merovingicarum*
s.d.	*sub die*, under the date
S.E.L.	*The Early South English Legendary*, ed. C. Horstman (E.E.T.S., 1887)
S.H.R.	*Scottish Historical Review* (1903–)
S.J.	Society of Jesus
Som.	Somerset
SS.	Saints
S.S.	Surtees Society (1834–)
St.	Saint
S.T.	*Studi e Testi* (1900–)
Staffs.	Staffordshire
Stanton	R. Stanton, *A Menology of England and Wales* (1892)
s.v.	*sub verbo*, under the word
tr.	translated, translation
T.R.H.S.	*Transactions of the Royal Historical Society* (1871–)
vol.	volume
V.S.H.	*Vitae Sanctorum Hiberniae*, ed. C. Plummer (2 vols., 1910; 2nd edn., 1968)
Warwicks.	Warwickshire
William Worcestre	*Itineraries*, ed. J. H. Harvey (1969)
Wilts.	Wiltshire
Z.C.P.	*Zeitschrift für celtische Philologie* (1896–)
Z.K.T.	*Zeitschrift für katholische Theologie* (1877–)

An asterisk (*) preceding a word indicates a cross-reference.

A

AARON, see Julius and Aaron.

ABBO OF FLEURY (d. 1004), Benedictine monk and abbot. He was born near Orleans, became a monk at Fleury (recently reformed by Cluny), and studied at Paris and Reims. Through his writings on mathematics and astronomy, as well as on Lives of the Popes and the independence of monasteries from secular and episcopal control, he became known as one of the foremost scholars of his time. At the invitation of *Oswald of Worcester, who had become a monk at Fleury, Abbo spent two years at Ramsey Abbey (985–7). There he stimulated the monastic reform movement by his teaching and his encouragement of study: his influence is seen in the writings of Byrthferth of Ramsey. Abbo himself wrote the first Life of *Edmund of East Anglia, based on the witness of Edmund's standard-bearer, and dedicated it to *Dunstan. Abbo became abbot of Fleury in 988. During his abbacy Aristotle's *Categories* and *Analytics* were copied and studied. He died at La Réole (Gascony), a monastery which he was visiting to reform. A scuffle broke out between monks and serving-men; Abbo attempted to calm it, but was killed in the riot. Because he met a violent death, he was venerated as a martyr. Feast: 13 November.

Works in *P.L.*, cxxxix. 417–58 and *Opera Inedita* (ed. A. van der Vyer and R. Raes, 1966); contemporary Life in *AA.SS. O.S.B.*, VI (part 1), 32–52, reprinted in *P.L.*, ibid., 375–414; modern study by P. Cousin, *S. Abbon de Fleury: un savant, un pasteur, un martyr* (1954); see also H. Bradley, 'On the Text of Abbo of Fleury's Quaestiones Grammaticales', *P.B.A.*, x (1922), 173–80.

ABDON AND SENNEN, martyrs who died at Rome *c.*303 in the persecution of Diocletian. They were buried in the cemetery of Pontian on the Via Portuensis. Their early cult is recorded in the *Depositio Martyrum* (354) and in early Roman Sacramentaries. A fresco of the 6th–7th centuries near their tomb depicts them in Persian dress, serving Christ. It seems likely that they were indeed Persians, but perhaps of servile rather than noble rank, which was attributed to them by their unreliable Acts. Feast: 30 July.

AA.SS. Iul. VII (1731), 130–41; *C.M.H.*, p. 405: H. Delehaye, 'Recherches sur le légendier romain', *Anal. Boll.*, li (1933), 33–98.

ABRAHAM KIDUNAIA (sixth century), hermit. Born of a wealthy family near Edessa in Mesopotamia, Abraham agreed to his parents' wish that he should marry, but on the last of the seven-day feasting which preceded the wedding ran away to be a monk in the desert. Friends and relatives remonstrated with him in vain: he walled up the door of his cell, leaving only a small opening for food, and gave all his goods to the poor except for a cloak, a goatskin, a bowl, and a mat. Thus equipped, he led a life of penance for fifty years.

Near his cell was a pagan town Beth-Kiduna, whose citizens had hitherto resisted all attempts to convert them. The bishop of Edessa asked him to leave his hermitage and preach to the people; for this purpose he ordained him priest. Abraham had a church built and then destroyed every idol in sight. Driven out by the people, he returned during the night and again preached to the townsmen, who stoned him and left him half-dead. He returned to preach for about three years in spite of ill-treatment; suddenly there was a breakthrough: his patience convinced them of his holiness, they listened to his message and were baptized. For a year he continued to teach and then retired to his hermitage.

An attractive legend which added to his popularity relates how his orphan niece

Mary had been entrusted to his care. For her he built a cell near his own and trained her in learning and piety until she was twenty. At this point, seduced by a false monk, she ran away, longing to see the wider world, went to Troas and became a prostitute. For two years he lamented her departure in ignorance and then boldly attempted to rescue her. He disguised himself as an army officer and pretended to seek her services. At first, not recognizing him, she was uninhibited; later, holding her hand, he comforted her, appealed to her to resume her former life, and promised to take her sins on himself if only she would return. This she did and was rewarded after three years by the gift of healing.

Abraham died at the age of seventy. An immediate popular cult was manifested by local people trying to take parts of his clothing. The Life and Legend of Abraham has inspired English and other dramatists. Feast: 16 March, but in the Byzantine calendar Abraham and his niece Mary are venerated together on 29 October.

AA.SS. Mart. II (1668), 433–44; A. Lamy, 'Acta B. Abrahae Kidunaiae', *Anal. Boll.*, x (1891), 5–49; A. Wilmart in *Revue Bénédictine*, 1 (1938), 222–45; B.T.A. i. 605–6.

ACACIUS (no date), martyr, supposedly with 10,000 companions. The cult of these purely mythical martyrs seems to have begun in Armenia; their Acts closely resemble those of *Maurice and the Theban legion. The place of their death was claimed to be Mount Ararat. There is no early evidence for a cult: the Acts date from the 12th century and their popularity from the time of the Crusades. These include a story that Acacius asked God just before their death by crucifixion at the hands of a pagan army, that whoever venerated their memory would enjoy health of mind and body; for this reason, Acacius was often included among the *Fourteen Holy Helpers. His cult thrived in Switzerland and Germany; it is attested by several notable works of art from the 13th to the 16th centuries, including a 15th-century stained-glass window at Berne, which provides the most complete pictorial record of the martyrdom. Relics were claimed by Cologne, Prague, and other towns. Eventually these saints were included in R.M. on 22 June.

AA.SS. Iun. IV (1707), 175–88 with *Propylaeum*, pp. 249–50; Réau, i. 13–15.

ACCA (d. 740), Benedictine monk, bishop of Hexham 709–32. As a young man he joined the household of Bosa, bishop of York; later he became the disciple of *Wilfrid and was his constant companion for thirteen years, including those which were spent in various journeys on the Continent. When Wilfrid was ill at Meaux in 705, Acca was told the story of his vision. On his deathbed Wilfrid named Acca his successor as abbot of Hexham. In fact, Acca became bishop as well: he completed three of Wilfrid's smaller churches and adorned the principal one with altars, relics, and sacred vessels. A skilled singer himself, he entrusted his cathedral chant to Maban, a monk from Canterbury.

Acca was a notable scholar. The wide range and outstanding quality of his theological library were praised by *Bede, who dedicated several of his biblical works to Acca in language of respectful friendship. Acca, for his part, urged Bede to write a simple commentary on Luke, as that of *Ambrose was too long and diffuse. He also supplied material to Bede for the *Ecclesiastical History* and to Eddius for his *Life of Wilfrid.*

In 732 Acca either retired or was expelled from his see of Hexham for reasons unknown. The Hexham tradition, supported by two Martyrologies, asserts that he became bishop of Whithorn. Other writers connect his retirement with that of *Ceolwulf, king of Northumbria, in the same year, or with the arrival at York of Egbert as bishop.

Acca was buried at Hexham, near the east wall of the cathedral. At his tomb were placed two stone crosses, decorated with Mediterranean-style patterns of grapes and tendrils, part of which survive. In the late 11th century his relics were translated by Alfred Westow, priest of Hexham and sacrist of Durham. In the coffin was found a portable altar inscribed *Almae Trinitati, agiae Sophiae, sanctae Mariae*. His relics were translated in 1154 and again in 1240. Feast: 20 October; translation 19 February.

Bede, *H.E.*, v. 20; iii. 13; iv. 14; Symeon of Durham, *Opera* (ed. T. Arnold, *R.S.*, 1885), ii. 32–8; J. Raine (ed.), *The Priory of Hexham* (*S.S.*, 1864), i. xxx–xxxv, 31–6, 184–95; P. Hunter Blair, *The World of Bede* (1970); D. P. Kirby (ed.), *St. Wilfrid at Hexham* (1974).

ACHILLEUS, see NEREUS AND ACHILLEUS.

ADALBERT OF EGMOND (North Holland) (d. *c.*710), deacon. A native of Northumbria and disciple of *Willibrord, apostle of Frisia, Adalbert worked mainly at Egmond but possibly for a time at Utrecht. His late Life records only generalities about him together with accounts of miracles at his tomb. A Benedictine monastery dedicated to him was revived at Egmond during the first half of the 20th century. Feast: 25 June.

AA.SS. Iun. VII (1709), 94–110; W. Levison, 'Wilhelm Procurator von Egmond', *Neues Archiv*, xl (1916), 793–804; P. Andriessen, *Sint Adelbert, patroon von Egmond* (1964).

ADALBERT OF MAGDEBURG (d. 981), archbishop. Details of his early life are unknown, but he became a monk at St. Maximin of Trier. The emperor Otto the Great and his English wife Edith founded a monastery at Magdeburg to provide a base for evangelizing the Slavs: this was a policy he favoured for both religious and political reasons. At the request of *Olga of Kiev, a recently converted septuagenarian ruler, a Christian mission was sent there, headed by Adalbert. This mission ended in failure, not through Adalbert's fault, but because Olga's son Svyatoslav superseded her: he was not a Christian and some of the missionaries were killed.

Adalbert however escaped, remaining at the imperial court of Mainz until he was appointed abbot of Weissenburg. In 988 he became first archbishop of Magdeburg with papal jurisdiction over the Slavs beyond the Elbe together with the Wends whom he evangelized. In 973 Otto died; he was buried in Magdeburg cathedral by Adalbert, who outlived him for eight years. Feast: 20 June.

AA.SS. Iun. IV (1743), 30–7; Chronicle of Thietmar of Merseburg in G. Pertz, *M.G.H. Scriptores*, i. 613–29; B.T.A., ii. 590; *Bibl. SS.*, i. 183–5.

ADALBERT OF PRAGUE (956–97), bishop and missionary martyr. Born at Libice (Bohemia) of a princely family, he was educated by *Adalbert of Magdeburg. On the latter's death he returned to Prague, the proud possessor of a collection of books. In 982, although less than thirty years old, he was chosen as its bishop. Austere, zealous, and energetic, he tried to spread Christianity in Hungary as well as in half-converted Bohemia. Although he had high moral as well as intellectual standards, visiting prisoners and the poor besides dividing the revenues according to *Gregory's guidelines, he was exiled in 990 by nationalist opposition and went to Rome. There he became a monk, but was soon recalled to Bohemia by Duke Boleslas, who agreed to support him in the exercise of his authority. Adalbert soon founded the Benedictine abbey of Brevnov, helped by the influential *Maiolus of Cluny. Trouble soon returned however when a penitent adulterous noblewoman, given sanctuary in a nunnery by Adalbert, was dragged out and killed by her accusers. Excommunication and a violent reaction to this penalty obliged him to leave Prague for Rome once more in 995. This time some of Adalbert's relatives were massacred and the people of Prague refused to receive him back.

Adalbert had meanwhile become a close friend of Otto III, and his adviser on converting the Slavs. His last years were spent on a mission to convert the Prussians in

Pomerania, following successful preaching in Danzig and elsewhere on the Baltic coast, made possible by his friendship with King Boleslas of Poland. Adalbert was martyred as a suspected Polish spy, traditionally near Konigsberg. He was buried at Gniezno, but in 1039 the relics were removed to Prague. Adalbert's widespread cult, in Bohemia, Hungary, Germany, Poland, and Kiev, reflects his importance in the conversion of eastern Europe. An 11th-century sculpture survives at Rome in the church of S. Bartholomeo all'isola Tiberina, while at Gniezno he is depicted on bronze doors (*c.*1175) receiving the pastoral staff from Otto III. Adalbert is also credited with the composition of vernacular Czech and Polish hymns. Feast: 23 April.

Early Lives by John Canaparius and Bruno of Querfurt in *AA.SS.* April. III (1866), 176–207; F. Dvornik, *The Making of Central and Eastern Europe* (1949), and *The Slavs; their early History and Civilization* (1956); B.T.A., ii. 152–3; *Bibl. SS.*, i. 185–90.

ADAM, bishop of Caithness 1213–22. Adam became a Cistercian monk when a young man and was later abbot of Melrose. William, king of Scotland, appointed him as bishop in a remote area where his own power was weak and that of the Norse earls strong. Adam attempted to enforce law and order, including canon law, and the payment of tithes. The customary offering of a span of butter for twenty cows was increased by Adam to one for fifteen, then one for twelve, and finally one for ten. The people revolted, forced an entry into the bishop's house at Halkirke, and burnt him and his followers to death. His body, although 'roasted with fire and livid with bruises, was found entire under a heap of stones and buried honourably in the church'. An unofficial cult grew up. Feast: 15 September.

K.S.S., pp. 261–3; *D.N.B.*, s.v.

ADAUCTUS, see FELIX AND ADAUCTUS.

ADOMNAN (Adamnan, Adam, Eunan) (627–704), abbot of Iona. He was born in Co. Donegal and became a monk at Iona under abbot Seghine, whom he succeeded in 679. He became famous both as a writer and as a leading protagonist in Northern Ireland of the Roman system of calculating Easter. In 686 he came to Northumbria to obtain from his former pupil King Aldfrith the release of sixty Irish prisoners, captured during the reign of Egfrith (670–85). In 688 Adomnan visited *Ceolfrith of Wearmouth, who converted him from the Iona tradition of Easter calculation and other practices. In 692 he took part in Irish synods and conventions as the ruler of Iona's monasteries in Northern Ireland. Then and in 697 he met with considerable success, pleading for the acceptance of the Easter dates which were kept by Rome and virtually all the Church in the West. Only his own monasteries stood out against him.

He was also responsible for the Law of Adomnan (*Cain Adomnain*) which protected women by exempting them from going to battle and insisting that they be treated by all as non-combatants. Boys and clerics were similarly protected and provision was made for effective sanctuary. These rules came to be accepted all over Ireland.

Adomnan's principal work was the famous Life of *Columba, abbot of Iona. This influential portrait of a charismatic pioneer is one of the most vivid Lives to be produced in its time. He also wrote a work on the Holy Places of Palestine, compiled from information provided by the French bishop Arculfus, who had been shipwrecked in western Britain. *Bede knew this work, but not apparently the Life of Columba.

After Adomnan's death, Iona accepted the Roman Easter in 716. His cult flourished in both Ireland and Scotland with dedications to him in Donegal, Derry, and Sligo as well as Aberdeenshire, Banff, Forfar, and the Western Isles. In 727 the relics of Adomnan were brought from Iona to Ireland to help make peace between the tribes of Adomnan's father and mother. They were carried round forty churches which had been under Iona's rule: the people swore to obey the Law of Adomnan: His shrines were desecrated by Northmen in 830 and 1030. Feast: 23 September.

Bede, *H.E.*, v. 15–17, 21–2; A. O. and M. O. Anderson, *Adomnan's Life of Columba* (1990; previous editions by W. Reeves, 1854 and J. T. Fowler, 1920); critical edition of *De Locis Sanctis* in P. Geyer, *Itinera Hierosolymitana* (*C.S.E.L.*, xxxix. 1898, 219–97) and by D. Meehan (1958); K. Meyer, *Cain Adomnain* (1905); L. Gwynn, 'The Reliquary of Adomnan', *Archivium Hibernicum*, iv (1915), 199–214; see also D. A. Bullough, 'Columba, Adomnan and the achievement of Iona', *S.H.R.*, xliii (1964), 111–30 and xliv (1965), 17–33; J. M. Picard, 'The purpose of Adomnan's Vita Columbae', *Peritia* (1982), 160–77; M. N. Dhonnchadha, 'The guarantor list of Cain Adomnain', ibid. 178–215.

ADRIAN (Hadrian) **OF CANTERBURY** (d. 709–10), abbot. An African by birth, Adrian became a monk and eventually abbot of Nerida, near Naples. On the death of Deusdedit, archbishop of Canterbury, in 664 and of his replacement Wighard in 665, Pope Vitalian wished to appoint Adrian to Canterbury. He, however, refused, but suggested the nomination of *Theodore instead. This was agreed, but the pope asked Adrian to accompany Theodore to be his adviser and helper.

Theodore named him abbot of St. Augustine's, Canterbury, where he directed an important school, at which many future bishops and abbots were educated. Subjects taught included Greek as well as Latin, Scripture, computistics, theology, and Roman law. Students came from all parts of England and even from Ireland: *Aldhelm thought that the education offered there exceeded anything then available in Ireland. Adrian worked at Canterbury for nearly forty years, far outliving Theodore.

He died on 9 January and was buried in his monastery. His body was found incorrupt in 1091, when architectural alterations made the translation of several Canterbury saints necessary. Among the miracles recorded of him then are several accomplished in favour of the boys who studied in the monastery and were in trouble with their masters. Feast: 9 January (with an octave at St. Augustine's, Canterbury).

Bede, *H.E.*, iv. 1–4; v. 20 and 23; *N.L.A.*, i. 13–15; Goscelin's account of the translation is in *P.L.*, clv. 36–8.

ADRIAN (Hadrian) **OF MAY** (d. 875), martyr. Probably an Irish missionary bishop, Adrian was killed with many English companions, possibly disciples of *Acca after he left Hexham, by Danes on the Isle of May in the Firth of Forth. *David I, king of Scotland, built a monastery there which he gave to the Benedictine monks of Reading; later they were replaced by canons from St. Andrews. The Isle of May became a notable pilgrimage centre. Feast: 4 March.

K.S.S., pp. 266–8; B.T.A., i. 480.

ADULF (Adulph) (d. 680), supposedly the brother of *Botulf, founder of Icanho Abbey. The relics of both saints were translated to Thorney by *Ethelwold *c.*972, where they were long venerated. The hagiographer Folcard identified Adulf with a bishop of Maastricht of similar name, famous for teaching and almsgiving. This is almost certainly wrong, but it explains why Adulf is sometimes venerated as a bishop. Feast (with Botulf): 17 June.

AA.SS. Iun. III (1701), 398–406; *E.B.K. after 1100*, i. 131.

ÆBBE, see Ebbe.

AED (Aodh) **MACBRICC** (d. 588), bishop. A member of the clan Ui Neill, Aed, who was skilled in medicine, founded monasteries in Munster and Meath, where he became a bishop: his principal church was at Killare. A pilgrimage to Slieve League (Donegal), where a ruined hermitage is believed to be his, still survives. His cult also extends to Scotland. Feast: 10 November.

The Irish Saints, pp. 22–5.

AEDH, see MAEDOC.

ÆDILBURH, see ETHELBURGA.

ÆGIDIUS, see GILES.

ÆLFHEAH, see ALPHEGE (1).

ÆLFLAED, see ELFLEDA.

ÆLFRYTH, see ETHELDRITHA.

ÆLGIFU (Ælfgyva), see ELGIVA.

ÆLRED, see AILRED.

ÆTHELNOTH, see ETHELNOTH.

ÆTHELWINE, see ELWIN.

ÆTHYLFRYTH, see ETHELDREDA.

AGAPE, IRENE, AND CHIONE (d. 304), martyrs. These three young women were natives of Saloniki in Macedonia. During Maximian's persecution they left their homes and went to live on a nearby mountain to follow lives of prayer: here they were arrested under Diocletian in late 303. When they were brought with their companions before the magistrate, they refused to sacrifice, that is, eat sacrificial food. Each answered steadfastly that she would rather die than do so. The prefect summed up against them that they were guilty of treason against the emperors and Caesars; as they were obdurate, they would receive the appropriate punishment. Agape and Chione were sentenced to be burnt alive, the other because of her youth to imprisonment. After the execution of the first two, Irene was again cross-examined. She admitted that she had possessed books of the Scriptures and had taken refuge in the mountains without her father's knowledge. As she refused once again to take part in the sacrifice, she was sentenced to be sent naked into the soldiers' brothel, where she would receive daily one loaf of bread from the magistrate's residence. However, no man dared approach her. She too was eventually burnt alive. The day of her death was recorded in her Acts as 1 April, but the feast of the three martyrs together is 3 April.

A.C.M., pp. xlii–xliii, 280–93; *AA.SS.* Apr. I (1675), 245–50; H. Delehaye, *Les Passions des Martyrs* (1921), pp. 141–3; B.T.A., ii. 19–21.

AGAPITUS (date unknown), martyr of Praeneste. While details of his life are unknown, his cult at Rome and Praeneste from early times is well attested by Sacramentaries and other liturgical books, together with church dedications. His Acts describe him as a boy of only fifteen years who was killed by the sword for refusing to abjure the Christian faith. Feast: 18 August.

AA.SS. Aug. III (1737), 524–9; *C.M.H.*, pp. 448–9; A. Kellner, 'Der hl. Agapitus von Praeneste', *Studien und Mitteilungen* (1930), pp. 404–32.

AGATHA (date uncertain), virgin and martyr, died at Catania (Sicily). Her early cult is witnessed by her inclusion in the Martyrology of *Jerome, the Calendar of Carthage (*c.*530), the Canon of the Roman Mass, and *Venantius Fortunatus' *Carmina.* Two churches were dedicated to her in Rome during the 6th century, and she was depicted in the mosaics of Sant' Apolinare Nuovo, Ravenna.

Her late fictitious Acts describe her as a wealthy girl who had vowed her virginity to Christ. The consul Quintinian invoked imperial edicts against Christianity to attempt her seduction: she was handed over to 'Aphrodisia', who kept a brothel; she was tortured by rods, rack, and fire. Lastly her breasts were cut off, but she was miraculously healed by a vision of *Peter. She died in prison as the result of her sufferings.

She was invoked against fire, particularly the eruptions of Mount Etna; also against diseases of the breast; she was also the patron of bell-founders. In art her emblem is usually a dish with her breasts, sometimes mistaken for loaves blessed on her feast.

Palermo and Catania both claim to be her birthplace. Feast: 5 February.

AA.SS. Feb. I (1658), 595–656; S. Romeo, *S. Agata e il suo culto* (1922); V. L. Kennedy, *The Saints of the Canon of the Mass* (1938), pp. 169–73; English Lives in *S.E.L.* and in C. Horstman, *Old English Legendary* (1881), pp. 45–8.

AGATHONICE, see CARPUS, PAPYLUS, AND AGATHONICE.

AGILBERT, bishop of Dorchester-on-Thames 650–60; bishop of Paris 668–*c.*690. Frankish by birth, Agilbert studied in Ireland for several years under teachers of Roman sympathy and was probably consecrated bishop there. He came to Wessex in 650, where King Cenwalh (643–74) gave him the see of Dorchester, recently founded by *Birinus. Although famous for learning and industry, Agilbert did not speak the Wessex dialect. This was the ostensible reason for Cenwalh dividing his kingdom into two dioceses and establishing Wine as bishop of Winchester without consulting Agilbert. In reality, the division corresponded to the distribution of two tribes which came to Wessex from East Anglia and along the Thames on the one hand, and from the Continent via Southampton on the other. Agilbert took offence and departed: he was next heard of taking part in the Synod of Whitby (663/4) as the senior prelate on the 'Roman' side, but he invited *Wilfrid, whom he had recently ordained priest, to be the principal spokesman in his place, as his own knowledge of Old English was imperfect.

After the Synod he returned to Gaul, consecrated Wilfrid (with other bishops) at Compiègne, and became bishop of Paris. He became closely associated with Ebroin, the notorious Mayor of the Palace. But in 668–9 *Theodore spent a long time on his way to England as Agilbert's guest, learning from him much about the state of the Church in England.

Agilbert died and was buried at the monastery of Jouarre, where his sister was abbess. His fine 7th-century sarcophagus survives there. There is no liturgical evidence for an early cult. Agilbert was never formally canonized, even after an investigation of his relics in the 18th century. But some implicit approval of his cult was given, as is shown by the presence of his feast on 1 April in a calendar compiled under King James II for English Catholics in 1686.

Bede, *H.E.*, iii. 7, 25, 28; iv. 1; P. Grosjean, 'La date du Colloque de Whitby', *Anal. Boll.*, lxxviii (1960), 233–74; M. P. Helyot, 'Le Trésor et les Reliques de l'ancienne Abbaye de Jouarre d'après les inventaires', *Revue Mabillon*, xlvii (1957), 258–77; see also F. M. Stenton, *Anglo-Saxon England* (2nd edn., 1965), pp. 121–4.

AGNES (d. *c.*305), virgin martyr of Rome. The earliest surviving witness to her martyrdom and cult is the *Depositio Martyrum* (354). About the same time a basilica was built over her grave in the Via Nomentana. Her feast was kept in many churches, both East and West, from early times: its occurrence in calendars and martyrologies proves her to be one of the most famous of the early Roman martyrs. Writers who praised her include *Ambrose, *Damasus (both of whom claim reliance on authentic verbal tradition), *Jerome, and Prudentius.

Her 5th-century Acts made her a girl of only thirteen who refused marriage because of her dedication to Christ, who ultimately preferred death to any violation of her consecrated virginity. She was killed by the sword, that is, through her throat being pierced. Round this simple story arose sermons and hymns by Ambrose, early portrayals in Christian antique art, and numerous legendary accretions, such as the blinding of a man who gazed at her nakedness when she was placed in a brothel.

Through the resemblance of her name to *agnus* ('lamb'), her principal emblem since the 6th-century mosaics at San Apollinare Nuovo at Ravenna has been a lamb. On her feast at Rome lambs are blessed which produce the wool from which pallia for archbishops are woven by the nuns of St. Agnes's convent.

Varied representations of her survive from many centuries, including Renaissance paintings from Duccio to Tintoretto. She also appears frequently in late medieval stained glass, not least in England, where there are also five ancient church dedications. Perhaps the best surviving cycle of paintings of her occurs on a gold and enamel cup, which formerly belonged to the Duke of Berry and passed through the Duke of Bedford to King Henry VI: it is now in the British Museum.

Feast: 21 January. Formerly the Roman calendar had a second feast, 28 January, believed to be her birthday rather than an octave day.

AA.SS. Ian. II (1643), 350–63 with *C.M.H.*, pp. 52–3; F. de Cavalieri, *Scritti Agiographici* (2 vols., Studi e Testi, 1962); A. J. Denomy, *The Old French Lives of Saint Agnes and Other Vernacular Versions of the Middle Ages* (Harvard Studies in Romance Languages, xiii. 1938); *Bibl. SS.*, i. 382–411; *H.S.S.C.*, ii. 62–70.

AGNES OF MONTEPULCIANO (1268–1317), Dominican nun. Born at Gracchiano-Vecchio of a wealthy family, she joined the Sisters of the Sack (so called because of their rough clothes) at Montepulciano (Tuscany) in her youth. When a new foundation was made at Proceno, Agnes was sent as housekeeper; later she was bursar and superior. Meanwhile her austerities and her visions of Christ, Mary, and the angels had become known, so the citizens of Montepulciano invited her to return.

This she did and founded a convent there in premises formerly used as brothels. Meanwhile she had become convinced that, to attain permanence, the community should be aggregated to an established Order. Her choice was the Dominicans, and she was established as prioress in 1306, while the Order provided chaplains and direction. The convent grew and prospered under her rule, which lasted until her death. Prophecies and cures were attributed to her, while in character she was outstanding for ardour and simplicity. After a long and painful illness, she died at the age of forty-nine. He tomb and her incorrupt body were much visited by pilgrims, including the Emperor Charles IV and *Catherine of Siena, with whom she is often associated in Italian art. She is also represented as patroness of her town, of which she holds a model in her hand, by a Sienese painter at Montepulciano, while Tiepolo presents her as one of the saints surrounding the Madonna in the Jesuit church at Venice. Feast: 20 April.

Life by Raymond of Capua (50 years after her death) in *AA.SS.* April. II (1738), 791–817; Lives by A. Walz (1922) and P. Boitel (1929); B.T.A., ii. 135–7; *Bibl. SS.*, i. 375–81.

AIDAN (1) (Aedan) (d. 651), monk of Iona, first bishop and abbot of Lindisfarne. Nothing is known of his early life except his Irish origin; *Bede is virtually the only source. Aidan came to England in 635 when *Oswald, who had become a Christian during exile at Iona, had regained the throne of Northumbria from Mercian invaders. He looked to Iona for help in the work of conversion: first a severe monk was sent, who soon returned complaining that the Saxons were uncivilized and unteachable; he was replaced by Aidan, who enjoyed a reputation for discretion and prudence.

Oswald gave him the island of Lindisfarne, close to the royal palace of Bamburgh, better suited for evangelizing Bernicia (Oswald's power-base of northern Northumbria) than York and the southern kingdom of Deira, evangelized by *Paulinus. Aidan's evangelistic activity seems to have been principally, if not exclusively, in the Bernician kingdom. Oswald himself sometimes was Aidan's interpreter in early days; later Aidan founded churches and monasteries, liberated Anglo-Saxon slave-boys and educated them for the Church, and encouraged monastic practices among the laity, such as fasting and meditation on the Scriptures. He himself lived in poverty and detachment, which enabled him to reprove the wealthy and powerful when necessary.

After Oswald's death in 642 Aidan supported King *Oswin of Deira and enjoyed his personal friendship. Once Oswin gave him a fine horse, but soon Aidan gave it away to a poor man. During Lent he retired to the Inner Farne Island for prayer and penance; from there in 651 he saw Bamburgh being burnt by Penda, the militant king of Mercia, and prayed successfully for the wind to change. But Aidan did not long survive the death of Oswin at the hand of Oswiu, who soon reunited Bernicia with Deira. Aidan died at Bamburgh and was buried at Lindisfarne in the cemetery. Later his bones were translated into the church. Some of these were removed to Ireland by *Colman, bishop of Lindisfarne, when he retired to Ireland after the Synod of Whitby.

After the sacking of Lindisfarne by the Vikings in 793 and subsequently, Aidan's memory was somewhat eclipsed, not least by that of *Cuthbert. But in the 10th century Glastonbury monks obtained some supposed relics of Aidan; through their influence Aidan's feast appears in early Wessex calendars, which provide the main evidence for his cult after the age of Bede.

Bede himself wrote more warmly of Aidan than of any other saint. Even though he could not approve Aidan's acceptance and propagation of the Irish method of calculating Easter, he praised him eloquently for his love of prayer, study, peace, purity, and humility as well as for his care of the sick and the poor. It may well be that Bede used the example of Aidan as an implicit reproof of the bishops of his own time and that he exaggerated the extent and depth of his apostolate. For rather different reasons, both Irish and Anglican scholars of the 19th century did so even more. The parish church of Bamburgh is the only ancient English church dedicated to him. Feast: 31 August; translation, 8 October.

Bede, *H.E.*, iii. 3–6, 15–17, 26; J. B. Lightfoot, *Leaders in the Northern Church* (Sermons, 1890); E. W. Grierson, *The Story of the Northumbrian Saints* (1913); B. Colgrave, 'The Times of St. Cuthbert' in *The Relics of St. Cuthbert* (ed. C. F. Battiscombe, 1958); H. Mayr-Harting, *The Coming of Christianity to Anglo-Saxon England* (1972), pp. 94–9.

AIDAN (2), see MAEDOC OF FERNS.

AILBE (early 6th century), Irish bishop. Little is known of his life. He obtained for *Enda the gift of an Aran Island (Co. Galway) from King Angus of Munster; he is reputed to have written a monastic Rule; above all, he was a travelling evangelist who preached mainly in southern Ireland. He is the reputed founder of the see of Imlech (Emly, Co. Tipperary).

Legendary accretions credit him with having been suckled by a she-wolf, and with having retired, late in life, to the mythical Land of Promise, a blend of the Christian Paradise and the Celtic happy other-world. Feast: 12 (13) September.

V.S.H., II, xxviii–xxxi. 46–64; L. Gougaud, *Christianity in Celtic Lands* (1932); J. O'Neill, 'The Rule in Ailbe of Emly', *Eriu*, iii (1907), 92–115.

AILRED (Aelred, Ethelred) **OF RIEVAULX** (1110–67), Cistercian abbot and writer. The son of a priest of Hexham, he was educated at Durham; *c.*1130 he joined the household of *David I, king of Scotland, and became his seneschal. In 1134 he became a monk at the recently founded abbey of Rievaulx, where *Bernard had appointed his secretary William abbot over the monks from Clairvaux who formed the community. In spite of delicate health, Ailred followed the austere regime and became so esteemed in his community that he was chosen as envoy to Rome in 1142 over the disputed election of *William of York and, soon afterwards, as master of novices. In 1143 he was appointed abbot of Revesby (Lincs.); only four years later, he was recalled to be abbot of Rievaulx. Under his rule the house prospered exceedingly; it increased in numbers to 150 choir monks and 500 lay brothers and lay servants (the largest in England); it had made five foundations in England and Scotland.

Ailred's sensitive discretion and gentle holiness, with its strong emphasis on charity, inspired by the writings of *John and *Augustine, humanized the intransigence of Cistercian monasticism and attracted men of similar character to his own. Through his many friends as well as his writings he became a figure of national importance, chosen to preach at Westminster for the Translation of *Edward the Confessor in 1163. This led to his writing a Life of Edward (he had already written on *Ninian and on the saints of Hexham); other more characteristic writings included a treatise on Friendship, the *Speculum Caritatis*, and Sermons on Isaiah, often considered his finest work. A treatise on the human soul was left unfinished.

In spite of suffering agony from the stone, which obliged him to live in a hut near the infirmary towards the end of his life, he was sometimes well enough to travel. On his way to his Scottish foundations he used to visit his friend *Godric of Finchale. But in the last year of his life he could do so no longer. He died at Rievaulx on 12 January and was buried in the Chapter House. Later his relics were translated to the church. In spite of the vivid and convincing portrait of him by Walter Daniel, his friend and disciple, Ailred was never formally canonized. There was, however, a local cult, which was approved by the Cistercians, who promulgated his feast in 1476. Feast: 12 January, 3 February (for Cistercians) and 3 March.

F. M. Powicke (ed.), *The Life of Ailred of Rievaulx by Walter Daniel* (1950); *M.O.*, pp. 240–5, 257–66; A. Squire, *St. Ailred of Rievaulx* (1969); A. Hallier, *The Monastic Theology of Aelred of Rievaulx* (1969); P. Grosjean, 'La prétendue canonisation d'Aelred de Rievaulx', *Anal. Boll.*, lxxviii (1960), 124–9. Works ed. A. Hoste and C. H. Talbot in *Corpus Christianorum, Continuatio Mediaevalis* (1971) and in *P.L.*, clxxxxv. 209–796; see also A. Hoste, *Bibliotheca Aelrediana* (1962).

AILWIN, see ETHELWIN.

ALACOQUE, Margaret Mary (1647–90), Visitandine nun. Born at Janots (Burgundy) the fifth child of a notary, Margaret had an unhappy childhood, especially after the death of her father, which was followed by relatives virtually taking over her home. In 1671 she became a nun at the Visitation convent of Paray-le-Monial. As a novice she was patient and charitable, but also clumsy and impractical. She made her profession in 1672 and from 1673 to 1675 experienced a series of visions of Christ, who also, she thought, spoke to her. These experiences, although subject to human error, were valuable for reminding contemporaries and others of truths forgotten or neglected. In 17th-century France both irreligion and Jansenism had in different ways obscured the doctrine of Christ's love for all men, sinners included. John *Eudes, Margaret Mary, and others were the providential instruments of recalling this basic truth to the people. This was done in and through devotion to the Sacred Heart of Jesus, adumbrated in the Middle Ages by *Gertrude, Mechtild, and others, but made more explicit by Margaret Mary and her director, the Jesuit Claude de la Colombière, through whom her experiences became known.

Margaret Mary met with plenty of contradictions, patiently borne, from her religious superiors and others. Eventually she won the confidence of her critics and became mistress of novices and assistant-superior. Devotion to, and a feast of the Sacred Heart were eventually approved and recommended by the papacy. Margaret died at the age of only forty-three, on 17 October, which became her feast. She was canonized in 1920.

Critical edition of her Autobiography and 133 letters by L. Gauthey (3 vols., 1915), Eng. tr. by V. Kerns (1961); Lives by A. Hamon (1907), P. Blanchard (1962), and G. Tickell (1969); B.T.A., iv. 134–8; see also J. B. O'Connell, *The Nine First Fridays* (1934).

ALBAN (3rd century), soldier and protomartyr of Britain. The cult of this saint links England, as no other local cult does, with the early patristic age and with the Church of the late Roman Empire. *Gildas and *Bede attributed his martyrdom to the persecution of Diocletian (*c.*305); some modern scholars have argued more or less plausibly for that of Decius (*c.*254) or even that of Septimius Severus (*c.*209). Whatever the date, Alban is an interesting example of a martyr who suffered in the amphitheatre outside the town, whose relics were buried in a *martyrium* of a kind known on the Continent, around which the new town (St. Albans instead of Verulamium) grew up. It is also possible that Verulamium was in the Chiltern enclave which long resisted Anglo-Saxon invasion.

Few details are known about him. The legendary Acts, followed by Bede, say that Alban, a pagan soldier, sheltered a priest, was converted by him and baptized. Soldiers in pursuit of the priest, later called *Amphibalus, were sent to search his house. Alban dressed in the priest's clothes to enable him to escape. He himself was arrested and after refusing to offer sacrifice was condemned to death. One executioner was converted; Alban was beheaded by another, whose eyes (as later artists loved to depict) fell out.

He was buried nearby; the shrine, where the sick were cured, was visited by *Germanus of Auxerre and *Lupus in 429, when they removed some dust from it for their relic collection and gave other relics of apostles and martyrs in return. The shrine was in use, at least intermittently and probably continuously, to the time of Bede.

A story that the shrine was lost and then recovered by revelation at the time of Offa's supposed foundation of the monastery at St. Albans is unlikely. The relics of Alban were venerated there until the Reformation, but Ely with some plausibility claimed a rival set due to a translation under Abbot Frederick in the 11th century. St. Albans, however, alleged that the Ely relics were a false set. The St. Albans case was given further impetus by a translation in 1129 and by the discovery of Amphibalus' supposed relics at Redbourn in 1177 and of Alban's original grave in 1257. These last two claims are rightly challenged by modern historians. The cult prospered under the increasing importance of St. Albans Abbey, enhanced by the best artistic products of England's wealthiest monastery. These included the fine illustrated Life by Matthew Paris and the new shrine, part of which survives.

Alban's cult extended all over England and in parts of France influenced by Germanus. Nine ancient English churches were dedicated to him. Odensee (Denmark), founded by Evesham, also claimed his relics. Feast: 20 June (17 June in B.C.P.); translation, 2 August (15 May at Ely).

AA.SS. Iun. IV (1707), 146–70; Bede, *H.E.*, i. 7, 17–21; Matthew Paris, *Gesta Abbatum S. Albani* (*R.S.*) i. 12–18, 94; id., *Chronica Majora* (*R.S.*), ii. 306–8; v. 608–10; W. Meyer, 'Die Legende des hl. Albanus, des Protomartyr Angliae in Texten vor Beda', *Abh.* (Gott.), N.F. viii. Nr. 1 (1904); W. Levison, 'St. Alban and St. Albans', *Antiquity*, xv (1941), 337–59; J. Morris, 'The Date of St. Alban', *Hertfordshire Archaeology*, i (1968), 1–8; see also W. R. L. Lowe and E. F. Jacob, *Illustrations to the Life of St. Alban* (1924); O. Pacht, C. R. Dodwell, and F. Wormald, *The St. Albans Psalter* (1960); J. E. van der Westhuizen, *Lydgate's Life of St. Alban* (1974).

ALBERIC (d. 1109), abbot of Cîteaux. Nothing is known of his early life, but he became a hermit at Collan (near Chatillon-sur-Seine). With his companions he invited *Robert to rule them, and in 1075 they moved to Molesme with Robert as abbot and Alberic as prior. The community grew in numbers, but some of its members were unsuitable; friction developed and there was even a rebellion. After an attempt at peacemaking the former troubles returned; Robert, Alberic, and the Englishman *Stephen Harding with their followers made a fresh start at Cîteaux (near Dijon), in 1098.

From these unpromising beginnings developed the Cistercian Order. Robert went back to Molesme, so Alberic became abbot in 1099. It is almost impossible to allocate responsibility between Robert, Alberic, and Stephen for the constitutional innovations, the extended use of lay brothers and the almost puritan attitude to the Rule of St. Benedict and to customary monastic tradition as well as to Romanesque art-forms which characterized the early Cistercians. Each of them took an important part in the development of the Cistercian ideal until *Bernard of Clairvaux became their most important member. In his panegyric of Alberic, his successor, Stephen Harding called him 'a father, a friend, a fellow-soldier and a principal warrior in the Lord's battles . . . who carried us all in his heart with affectionate love'. Alberic died on 26 January, which became his feast.

AA.SS. Ian. III (1863), 368–73; J. B. Dalgairns, *Life of St. Stephen Harding* (1898); *M.O.*, pp. 197–226, 752–3; B.T.A., i. 173–4. See also J. R. Lefèvre, 'Le vrai récit primitif des origines de Cîteaux est-il l'Exordium Parvum?', *Le Moyen Âge*, lxi (1955), 79–120 and 329–62.

ALBERT OF JERUSALEM (*c.*1150–1214), patriarch. Born of a noble family of Parma, Albert became a canon regular at Montara (Lombardy) and was consecrated bishop of Bobbio in 1184. Soon translated to Vercelli, he made peace between Parma and Piacenza. In 1203 the canons of the Holy Sepulchre at Jerusalem asked Pope Innocent III to appoint him as patriarch, which he reluctantly did. As Jerusalem had fallen in 1187, the see was at Akka (Ptolemais). Again Albert exercised his skills of peacemaking, between the Frankish leaders themselves and between them and the local people. He also gained the respect of the Muslims, but his situation as western patriarch of Jerusalem was difficult and arguably untenable.

Meanwhile Brocard, prior of the hermits of Mount Carmel, invited him to codify their customary observance into a Rule. This included obedience to an elected superior, silence each day between Vespers and Terce, long fasts and perpetual abstinence, a separate house for each hermit but a common oratory, and manual work for all. Whoever may have founded the Carmelite Order, Albert was its first legislator.

Albert supported the pope's efforts to regain Jerusalem, but in vain. Summoned to the Fourth Lateran Council he met a violent death at Akka on 14 September at the hand of a hospitaller whom he had deposed from the office of Master. A cult arose soon after his death and he has been formally venerated by the Carmelites at least since 1411. Feast: 25 September.

AA.SS. April. I (1737), 769–802; *Bibl. SS.*, i. 686–90; F. Pianzola, 'S. Alberto Avogadro', *Il Monte Carmelo*, 1937–9; B.T.A., iii. 638–9.

ALBERT THE GREAT (1206–80), Dominican friar and bishop. A Swabian by birth, Albert joined the Dominicans at Padua in 1223 against the wishes of his noble family. After teaching at Hildesheim, Ratisbon, and Cologne, where *Thomas Aquinas was his student, he became a Master at Paris and organized the house of studies at Cologne in 1248. He was prior provincial for three years (1254–7) and became bishop of Ratisbon in 1260. Unsuccessful as an administrator, he resigned his see in 1262 to devote all his energies to teaching and writing. He took a prominent part in the Council of Lyons (1274) and at Paris in 1277 he staunchly defended the teaching of his disciple Aquinas.

His own pioneer scholastic writing was more diffuse and less systematic, but the two men were at one on the use to be made of Aristotle's philosophy in Christian theology. Albert was also interested in the physical sciences; his treatises, which fill thirty-eight volumes, include some on astronomy, chemistry, geography, and physiology. His main theological works were a *Summa* and a commentary on the *Sentences* of Peter the Lombard. He also wrote against the Averrhoists the treatise *De unitate intellectus.*

Commonly called the Universal Doctor and placed by Dante among the lovers of wisdom, he was beatified in 1622 and canonized as late as 1931, when he was named by Pope Pius XI both a Doctor of the Church and the patron of students of the natural sciences. Feast: 15 November.

P. de Loé, 'De vita et scriptis beati Alberti Magni', *Anal. Boll.*, xix (1900), 257–84, xx

(1901), 273–316, xxi (1902), 361–71. Works ed. A. Borgnet (1890–9); critical edition by B. Geyer and others in course of publication (Münster in Westphalia 1955–); H. Laurent and M. J. Congar, 'Essai de bibliographie albertine', *Revue Thomiste*, xxxvi (1931), 422–68; H. Wilms, *Albert the Great* (1933).

ALBURGA (d. *c.*810), foundress of Wilton nunnery. Half-sister of Egbert, king of Wessex and widow of Wolstan, called Earl of Wiltshire, Alburga is said to have changed her husband's foundation of canons at Wilton into a nunnery, which she entered and where she died. Feast: 25 December.

W. Dugdale, *Monasticon*, ii. 315; Stanton, pp. 607–8.

ALCMUND (1) (Ealhmund), seventh bishop of Hexham, ruled 767–81. He was buried beside *Acca outside the church; during the Danish invasions all trace of his grave was lost, but in 1032, following a supposed revelation, his relics were found and reburied inside the church. In 1154 the relics of all the saints of Hexham were collected into a single shrine; in 1296 they were scattered by the Scots. The date of Alcmund's death was 7 September, but no trace of a feast apart from the general one of the saints of Hexham has been found.

J. Raine (ed.), *The Priory of Hexham* (*S.S.*, 1863), pp. xxxv–xxxvi, 208–10.

ALCMUND (2), martyr of Northumbria, was the son of King Alchred (765–74). He was killed *c.*800 and King Eardwulf (796–*c.*805) was held responsible. Miracles were reported at Alcmund's tomb at Lilleshall; his body was later translated to Derby. Several churches were dedicated to him in Derbyshire and Shropshire. Feast: 19 March.

P. Grosjean, 'Codicis Gothani Appendix' (Vita S. Aelkmundi regis) *Anal. Boll.*, lviii (1940), 178–83.

ALDATE (Eldad) (d. 577?) bishop, reputedly a Briton who was killed by the Anglo-Saxons at Deorham. He is mentioned in the Sarum and other Martyrologies; his feast occurs in a Gloucester calendar (14th-century addition); churches were dedicated to him at Gloucester and Oxford, as well as a famous Oxford street. But nothing seems to be known of him: it was even suggested (unconvincingly) that his name was a corruption of 'old gate'. Feast: 4 February.

Baring-Gould and Fisher, ii. 426–8; *E.B.K. after 1100*, ii. 40.

ALDHELM (639–709), abbot of Malmesbury, bishop of Sherborne. A member of the Wessex royal family, he became a monk at Malmesbury but completed his education at Canterbury under *Adrian, companion of *Theodore. In *c.*675 he became abbot of Malmesbury and combined the skills of administrator and writer. Possibly he introduced the Rule of St. Benedict; certainly he made foundations at Frome and Bradford-on-Avon (whose surviving Anglo-Saxon church incorporates elements from his time). When the Wessex diocese was divided in 705, he became first bishop of its western half, but without ceasing to rule Malmesbury as well. He built churches at Sherborne, Warcham, Langton Matravers, and Corfe. The nearby Dorset headland, commonly called St. Alban's Head, is in reality St. Aldhelm's Head, being presumably part of his Dorset estates.

His OE verses, which were sung with harp accompaniment to draw people to church, were praised by King Alfred, but have not survived: we can judge this first notable Anglo-Saxon writer only by his Latin works. Their florid Latin style was praised but not imitated by *Bede; they influenced *Boniface and the writers of later charters. They were read on the Continent as well as in England up to the 11th century. They include treatises on Virginity in prose and verse (summaries of the Lives of biblical and early Christian saints); grammatical works, sacred poems and letters. One of these praised the school of Canterbury as superior to those of Ireland, another was written to the British King Geraint about the dating of Easter, while a third exhorted the clerics of *Wilfrid on loyalty in adversity. At least once he visited Rome, to obtain privileges for his monastery and to bring back a marble altar. A fine chasuble, woven with roundels, was kept at Malmesbury and believed to be his.

Aldhelm died at Doulting (Somerset) and was buried at Malmesbury by *Egwin; stone crosses were built at seven-mile intervals along the road between the two towns. His cult was ancient: a fine 10th-century tomb at his shrine depicted episodes from his life, and an Anglo-Saxon drawing survives of him presenting his treatises to *Hildelith, abbess of Barking. His cult was questioned and discontinued by Lanfranc, but *Osmund, bishop of Salisbury, authorized its resumption with the translation of his relics in 1078. Feast: 25 May; translation, 5 May (to commemorate a translation of 986) and 3 October (for 1078).

Bede, *H.E.*, v. 18; *G.P.*, pp. 330–443; Life by Faricius in *P.L.*, lxxxix. 63–84; see also R. S. Cook, *Sources for the biography of St. Aldhelm* (1927); M. R. James, *Two Ancient English Scholars* (1931); E. S. Duckett, *Anglo-Saxon Saints and Scholars* (1958); M. Lapidge and M. Herren, *Aldhelm: the Prose Works* (1979); M. Lapidge and J. L. Rosier, *Aldhelm: the Poetic Works* (1985); M. Lapidge and H. Gneuss, 'Learning and Literature in Anglo-Saxon England', *A.S.E.*, xiv (1985), 205–26. M. Winterbottom, 'Aldhelm's prose style and its origins', *A.S.E.*, vi (1977), 39–76.

ALDWYN (Aldwine) (early 8th century), abbot of Peartney (Lincs.). A brother of Elwin, second bishop of Lindsey, and of Ethelhild, abbess, Aldwyn's uncertain claim to sanctity is reflected in the absence of any clear feast day: he did, however, give his name to Coln St. Aldwyn, Glos.

ALEXANDER (1), with Sisinnius and Martyrius, martyred at Milan in 397. The fact of their martyrdom is certain; they were commended by *Ambrose, *Augustine, and Maximus of Turin, and they had an early cult. But the details recorded by their Acts are fictitious. Feast (in Roman and OE martyrologies): 29 May.

Propylaeum, s.d. 29 May; B.T.A., ii. 420.

ALEXANDER (2) (3rd century), one of a group of Roman martyrs, later called the *Seven Brothers. He was buried in the Jordani cemetery on the Salarian Way; his name was added to the Roman Canon by Symmachus (early 6th century). The Acts of these saints were inspired by the Book of Maccabees, who were early venerated at Rome. Feast (with Felicity): 10 July.

Propylaeum, s.d. 10 July; B.T.A., iii. 62–4.

ALEXANDER (3) (d. *c.*250), martyr of Alexandria. With his companion Epimachus, he is described by Denys of Alexandria as having endured 'numerous agonies from scrapers and whips . . . their bodies were destroyed by quicklime'. Feast: 22 August.

Eusebius, *H.E.*, vi. 41; *Propylaeum*, s.d. 22 August.

ALEXANDER NEVSKI (1220–63), prince of Novgorod, defender and protector of Russia. During his adult life Tartars invaded Russia from the south-east while Swedes, Lithuanians, and Teutonic knights did the same from the West, but with little co-ordination between them. In 1236 Alexander succeeded his father and was fortunate that the victorious Tartars turned southwards after defeating the Russian armies. In 1240 he defeated the Swedes by the river Neva (hence his name of Nevski) and in 1242 he overcame the Teutonic knights at the frozen lake of Peipous. He is said to have been a man of prayer and to have been inspired by visions of *Boris and *Gleb.

He was compromising towards the Tartars and successfully appealed to them to save his people. Shortly before his death at Gorodec on 14 November he had taken the monastic habit.

In 1381 he was canonized by Cyprian, metropolitan of Kiev and All Russia. This coincided with his return to imperial favour when Dmitri Donskoy defeated the Tartars. This emperor saw that the raising of his ancestor to the altars strengthened his own political prestige and power. The principal centre of Alexander's cult was the monastery of Vladimir-Kljazma, where he was buried. This had been the metropolitan's residence until 1323.

In 1710 Peter the Great placed St. Petersburg, his new capital, under Alexander's protection. This was considered specially appropriate after Peter's victory over the Swedes at Poltava. He built a monastery dedicated to Alexander in 1713, to which the relics were translated in 1724. To it were invited other monks whose reputation had become widespread. This policy was not entirely successful: this monastery never enjoyed the repute of Kiev or Zagorsk.

During and after the Second World War this cult became a symbol of Russian resistance to German invasion. The Russian Orthodox Church financed an armoured division called 'Alexander Nevski' and in 1942 the Order of Alexander for distinguished military service was restored. Meanwhile in 1938 Eisenstein had made a film of the saint's life, often regarded as a masterpiece. Time and again Alexander's cult has been strongly political and nationalist. It seems never to have been formally approved by the papacy, possibly in part because Alexander once replied to papal legates sent to teach him: 'We know the law of God very well and will take no lessons from you.' Feast: 23 November; translations, 23 May and 30 August.

G. P. Fedotov, *Svjayye Drevnej Rusi* (= saints of ancient Russia), 1985; J. Fennell and A. Stokes, *Early Russian Literature* (1974); J. Fennell, *The Crisis of Medieval Russia 1200–1304* (1983); *H.S.S.C.*, vi. 58–61.

ALEXIS OF ROME probably never existed, but his Legend was extremely popular in the Middle Ages. It was made by a conflation of the Life of St. John Calybita with that of the man of God Mar Riscia of Edessa. If any historical truth underlies the Legend, it is found in the life of Mar Riscia. The principal elements are that Alexis left his wife on his wedding night and went on a long pilgrimage, returning afterwards to Rome and living there unknown as a beggar in his father's house for seventeen years. He was identified after death by documents in his handwriting, by voices from heaven and by miracles. There is no mention of him in ancient martyrologies or other liturgical records; attempts to identify him with Alethius, a correspondent of *Paulinus of Nola, have failed. Apparently he was first heard of in Rome only in the late 10th century, although he was supposed to have lived in the 5th. In the 12th century the legend reached England, and is found in the Albani Psalter which probably belonged to *Christina of Markyate; it became extremely popular as the subject for vernacular Lives and dramas. Feast: 17 July.

AA.SS. Iul. IV (1725), 238–70; B. de Gaiffier, 'Intactam sponsam relinquens', *Anal. Boll.*, lxv (1947), 157–95; O. Pacht, C. R. Dodwell, and F. Wormald, *The St. Albans Psalter* (1960).

ALFREDA, see ETHELDRITHA.

ALFWOLD (d. 1058), monk of Winchester and bishop of Sherborne. William of Malmesbury recorded the following details, derived from a priest of his diocese who knew him. He was noted for his habitual abstinence at a time when self-indulgence was said to be general; he used at table common wooden platters and bowls. He was specially devoted to *Swithun, whose image he set up in the church at Sherborne, and to *Cuthbert, whose shrine he used to visit and whose antiphon he would often repeat. He quarrelled at least once with Godwin earl of Wessex, who was smitten with sudden illness and recovered only at the saint's pardon. After his death, the sees of Sherborne and Ramsbury, both poorly endowed, were reunited and in 1070 became the see of Salisbury. Feast: 25 March.

G.P., pp. 179–81.

ALGYVA, see ELGIVA.

ALKELDA (1) (Athilda) (d. *c.*800). She was patron of the church of Middleham (Yorkshire), also of Giggleswick (West Riding). Edward IV's patent survives which enabled his brother Richard (subsequently Richard III) to set up the college of

Middleham in honour of Christ, the Blessed Virgin, and St. Alkeld. Local tradition claimed that she was a Saxon princess (presumably a nun), who was strangled to death by Viking women and buried in the church at Middleham. Feast: 28 (27) March.

R. Challoner, *Memorials of Ancient British Piety* (1761), s.v.; Stanton, p. 135.

ALKELDA (2), see ARILD.

ALL SAINTS (All Hallows) is the feast of all the redeemed, known and unknown, who are now believed to be in Heaven. It has an Eastern origin, first commemorating 'the martyrs of the whole world', as witnessed by *Ephrem of Syria and *John Chrysostom. In the West, Maximus of Turin preached on the same feast on the same day, the first Sunday after Pentecost.

At Rome the Pantheon was dedicated to St. Mary and the Martyrs on 13 May 610. Many see this as the origin of the feast in the West, but the reality seems more complex.

The 7th-century lectionary called the *Comes of Wurzbourg* described the feast as one of all the saints, not only the martyrs. In the reign of Pope *Gregory III (731–41) a chapel in St. Peter's, Rome was dedicated to all the saints; Egbert of York brought the feast to England, where it is found as a marginal addition to the Martyrology of Bede under 1 November. In 799 Alcuin of York, then abbot of Tours, commended Arno of Salzburg for observing this feast on this day. Gregory IV (d. 844) encouraged Louis the Pious to extend the observance of All Saints day all through his dominions.

Meanwhile Ireland too had been celebrating 1 November as All Saints day, according to some manuscripts of *Oengus' Martyrology, together with feasts of All Saints of Europe on 20 April and All Saints of Africa on 23 December. A Northern English 9th-century calendar ranked it as a principal feast; such it has always remained. Devotional writers see in it the fulfilment of Pentecost and indeed of Christ's redemptive sacrifice and resurrection. Ancient English church dedications number 1,255, a number surpassed only by those dedicated to the Virgin Mary.

Proplyaeum, pp. 488–9; *N.C.E.*, i. 318–19; J. Hennig, 'The Meaning of All the Saints', *Medieval Studies*, x (1948), 147–61; B.T.A., iv. 232–5.

ALL SOULS (commemoration of all the faithful departed). Although prayers for the dead are inscribed in some Roman catacombs from early Christian centuries, the Church was slow to dedicate a liturgical day to offering prayers and masses to help them attain the Beatific Vision through purification later described as Purgatory. The first example of this commemoration seems to be in the time of *Isidore of Seville (d. 636): the day assigned was the Monday after Pentecost.

Dead monks were commemorated in this way: the extension to 'all the dead who have existed from the beginning of the world to the end of time' was the work of *Odilo, abbot of Cluny (d. 1049). He also appropriately decreed that the day immediately following the feast of *All Saints, 2 November, should be set aside for this purpose. The influence of Cluny was a principal reason why this practice spread to the whole Church of the West. It came to England through Lanfranc's *Monastic Constitutions*, based largely on Cluniac practice. At least four ancient English dedications are known, the most famous of which are Archbishop Chichele's foundation of All Souls College, Oxford, and the church in Langham Place, London. Christian concern for the dead is attested by very many medieval bequests and chantry foundations.

There was also widespread popular belief that souls in purgatory could appear on earth on this day to haunt, in the form of ghosts, witches, or toads, those who had wronged them in life. It was also believed that they could be helped by almsgiving in cash or in kind, such as 'soul-cakes' or fruit requested in a plaintive English folksong which survives to this day. Some of these beliefs seem to be subsumed in popular customs now associated with Hallowe'en, or the Eve of All Saints (31 October). Feast: 2 November; but in Armenian calendars on Easter Monday.

N.C.E., i. 319; H. Delehaye, *Sanctus* (1927); D. Knowles (ed.), *The Monastic Constitutions of Lanfranc* (1951), pp. 63–4; B.T.A., iv. 240–2.

ALLEN (Allun), male patron saint of St. Allens (Cornwall); otherwise unknown.

Baring-Gould and Fisher, i. 147.

ALLOWIN, see BAVO.

ALMOND, John (*c.*1577–1612), priest and martyr. Born at Allerton (Lancs.), he was educated mainly in Ireland until he became a student at the English College, Rome, in 1597. In 1601 he was ordained priest and obtained his doctorate in divinity, after showing himself exceptionally intelligent and quick in disputation. In 1602 he returned to England, where for seven years he was an energetic and successful itinerant missionary. Pursuivants captured him and he was imprisoned, first at Newgate, then at the Gatehouse. Either he escaped or he was released, for there is record of his working in Staffordshire in 1609, but in 1612 he was again arrested and imprisoned in the appalling conditions of Newgate. Because of his high reputation for holiness and learning, the archbishop of Canterbury and other divines tried to extract a recantation from him, but without success. In 1612 he was accused and convicted of being a priest, although the charge was never proved, and he was executed at Tyburn on 5 December. He was canonized by Paul VI in 1970 as one of the *Forty Martyrs of England and Wales. Feast: 25 October.

N.C.E., i. 328; B.T.A., iv. 502–3; W. J. Steele, *Blessed John Almond* (pamphlet, 1961).

ALNOTH, serf and cowherd in Werburga's monastery of Weedon (Northants), became a hermit in the woods of Stowe near by, where he was murdered by robbers (*c.*700). The only authority for this story is the late 11th-century Life of *Werburga by Goscelin. Alnoth is not mentioned in any surviving early calendars; his feast was later kept on 27 February (as in *R.M.*), or on 25 November.

AA.SS. Feb. III (1658), 684–5; Stanton, pp. 565–6.

ALOYSIUS GONZAGA, see GONZAGA.

ALPHEGE (1) (Ælfheah, Elphege) (*c.*953–1012), archbishop of Canterbury and martyr. He became a monk at Deerhurst (Glos.), but after some years retired to be a hermit in Somerset. *Dunstan appointed him abbot of Bath, a community largely composed of Alphege's former disciples. In 984 he became bishop of Winchester, in succession to *Ethelwold; he became known for personal austerity and lavish almsgiving. In 994 Ethelred the Unready sent Alphege to parley with the Danes Anlaf and Swein, who had raided both London and Wessex. The Anglo-Saxons paid tribute, but Anlaf became a Christian and promised he would never again come to England 'with warlike intent'. This promise was kept.

In 1005 Alphege succeeded Aelfric as archbishop of Canterbury and received the pallium at Rome. Meanwhile Ethelred had proved unable to defeat or even control the Danish invaders. In 1011 they overran much of southern England; the Danegeld tribute paid to them did not prevent them from further pillage and other acts of war. In September they besieged Canterbury, and captured it through the treachery of an Anglo-Saxon archdeacon Ælfmaer. For seven months they imprisoned Alphege with other magnates and demanded ransom. This was paid for the other prisoners, but the sum required for the archbishop was the enormous one of £3,000. Alphege refused to pay and forbade his people to do so. The Danes were so infuriated that, after a feast at which they got drunk, they killed him with the bones of oxen: an axeman delivered the final blow. This took place at Greenwich; Alphege was buried in St. Paul's

Cathedral, London. By his death he became a national hero.

When Cnut became king of England (1016) his policy, after a short period of violence, was one of reconciliation between Anglo-Saxon and Dane. This found expression in the endowment of the abbey of *Edmund at Bury, and in the translation of the body of Alphege to Canterbury (1023). It was buried to the north of the high altar, where the monks venerated it for long afterwards at the beginning and end of each day.

Although the feast was present in several regional calendars of pre-Conquest England, Lanfranc (archbishop of Canterbury 1070–89) questioned his cult, particularly as a martyr. He consulted *Anselm, who replied that Alphege was a martyr for justice as John the Baptist was a martyr for truth. Eventually Lanfranc confirmed the cult and commissioned the Canterbury monk Osbern to write a Life and Office in his honour.

The discovery that the body of Alphege was incorrupt (1105) led to an increase in the cult, while in his last sermon *Thomas Becket alluded to Alphege as Canterbury's first martyr, and just before his death commended his cause to God and St. Alphege. In the long run, however, the Becket cult overshadowed that of Alphege. Feasts: 19 April (all over England); Ordination (16 November) and Translation (8 June) at Canterbury.

AA.SS. Apr. II (1675), 627–41; *A.S.C.*, s.a. 984, 994, 1006, 1011–12, 1023; Osbern, *Vita S. Elphegi* in H. Wharton, *Anglia Sacra*, ii (1691), 122–47; Florence of Worcester, i. 165–6; *Chronicon Thietmari de Merseberg* (ed. F. Kurze, *M.G.H.*), viii. 42; Eadmer, *The Life of St. Anselm* (ed. R. W. Southern, 1963), pp. 50–4; R. W. Southern, *St. Anselm and his Biographer* (1963).

ALPHEGE (2), bishop of Winchester 934–51. He had been a monk before his consecration, but nobody knows where: he may have joined a monastery overseas or have been a hermit. He was important in the 10th-century monastic revival for the encouragement he gave to the pioneers *Dunstan and *Ethelwold, whom he ordained priests on the same day. This role as precursor, with his nickname 'the Bald' is virtually all that is known of his episcopate. Feast: 12 March (at Winchester and St. Albans).

AA.SS. Mar. II (1668), 225–8; *M.O.*, pp. 31–42; D. Parsons (ed.), *Tenth-Century Studies* (1975).

ALPHONSUS LIGUORI (1696–1787), bishop, founder of the Redemptorist Congregation. The son of a Neapolitan noble, he studied law and practised jurisprudence with considerable success. But his conversion to clerical life is said to have been due to his losing a case through confusing Lombard with Angevin law. He studied theology privately, was ordained priest (1726), and became famous as a preacher in and near Naples.

In 1731 he refounded a community of nuns in accordance with a revelation which he declared authentic; in 1732 he founded the Congregation of the Holy Redeemer for priests dedicated to preaching to the rural poor. This was handicapped early on by internal dissensions and later by rivalry between Church and State. Alphonsus himself was excluded from it, it is said, because he signed an important document without reading it. After his death it prospered, especially in Central Europe, and later still in England, Ireland, and the United States.

In 1745 he published his first theological and devotional works. Although the former are sometimes criticized for being too legalistic and the latter for being too exuberant, the influence of both was considerable. His most important work was the *Moral Theology*. This counteracted both rigorism and laxism by advocating that it is lawful to follow the milder of two equally probable opinions about the morality of particular actions. As in his spiritual direction, so in his preaching, he aimed at simplicity, gentleness, and intelligibility. In trying to be understood by all, he made considerable use of rhetoric, notably in his often-criticized *Glories of Mary* (1750). Similar techniques were used by his followers, whose preaching often appealed to the fear of God, and of the Day of Judgement.

Alphonsus was consecrated bishop of Sant' Agatha dei Goti (Beneventum) in 1762, but he resigned his see through ill-health in 1775. He lived for another twelve years, his last ones being saddened by divisions in his Order and by various interior afflictions. He was canonized in 1839 and declared a Doctor of the Church in 1871. Feast: 1 (formerly 2) August.

A. C. Berthe, *Life of St. Alphonsus de Liguori* (Eng. tr. 1905); R. Telleria, *San Alfonso Maria de Ligorio* (1950–1); *Opere Ascetiche* (1933–60); see also P. Pourrat, *La Spiritualité Chrétienne*, iv (1947), 449–91.

ALPHONSUS RODRIGUEZ, see RODRIGUEZ.

AMAND (*c.*584–*c.*675), monk and missionary in Flanders and Northern France. Born in Lower Poitou, he became a monk in the island of Yeu; later he moved to a cell at Bourges near the cathedral. Here he spent fifteen years under the direction of St. Austregisilus, its bishop. He was consecrated bishop in 628, but had no fixed see; he preached in Flanders and Carinthia, founded monasteries at Ghent and Elnon, later called Saint-Amand (near Tournai), and a nunnery at Nivelles. He is sometimes, inaccurately, called bishop of Maastricht; in fact, he was abbot of Elnon for at least his last four years, during which he wrote his testament, which survives.

His cult was widespread in Flanders and Picardy and reached England through visits of ecclesiastics such as *Dunstan to his monasteries at Ghent or Elnon. His name occurs in several English medieval calendars; a chapel is dedicated to him at East Hendred (Oxon.). Feast: 6 February.

AA.SS. Feb. 1 (1658), 815–904; B. Krusch, *M.G.H.*, *Scriptores rerum merov.*, V, 395–485; E. de Moreu, *Saint Amand* (1927); id., 'La Vita Amandi Prima et les Fondations monastiques de S. Amand', *Anal. Boll.*, lxvii (1949), 447–64.

AMBROSE (339–97), bishop of Milan. He was born at Trier, son of the Pretorian Prefect of Gaul; he studied Greek, rhetoric and poetry, and became a successful advocate. In 370 he became Governor of Aemilia and Liguria, at Milan. On the death of its Arian bishop Auxentius, Ambrose appealed for peace at the assembly convoked to elect his successor. During his speech a voice, often said to be that of a child, cried out: 'Ambrose for bishop.' To his astonishment (as he was not even baptized), the whole crowd took up the slogan. In vain did he plead his unsuitability: within a week he was baptized and consecrated bishop (374). He studied Scripture and the writings of Origen and *Basil with his tutor Simplicianus. He became an influential protagonist of their thought in the West; he encouraged monasticism, recommending the Virgin Mary as the patron and model of nuns; he also had an important share in the conversion of *Augustine in 386.

His daily routine as bishop combined hard work with accessibility to all. As Milan was the administrative capital of the Western Empire, he came to play an important part in politics, guiding and sometimes reproving rulers. To Gratian, a young emperor, he wrote in 377 a work *On the Faith* to warn him against Arianism, of which his uncle Valens was the protector. After Gratian's murder, Ambrose persuaded the new emperor, Maximus, to be content with a part of the Empire and leave the rest for Valentinian II. An attempt to restore the cult of the goddess of Victory came to nothing through Ambrose's intervention. He also refused to give up a church in Milan for the worship of Arians at court, and was once besieged with his people in another church, for the same reason.

He told Valentinian that the emperor is in the Church, not above it. Not long after, Valentinian fled for protection to Theodosius, emperor of the East, who defeated and killed Maximus, thus becoming the real ruler in the West as well. His enormous power did not deter Ambrose from reproving him after the infamous massacre at Thessalonica of thousands of men, women, and children in reprisal for the death of a governor. Theodosius did public penance.

Ambrose died before he was sixty. His body was translated under the high altar of his basilica in 835. His cult is ancient and well-established. In art he is often represented in episcopal vestments with the emblem of a scourge, symbolizing the penance he imposed on the emperor, or else with a beehive because a swarm of bees, symbolizing his future eloquence, settled on him when he was a child. In England there were no ancient dedications, but there are images of him as one of the four Latin Doctors (with *Augustine, *Jerome, and *Gregory).

Neither the present Ambrosian Rite nor the Ambrosian chant can be certainly traced to him, but he taught his people to sing hymns, composed by himself. Some of these survive in the Roman Breviary.

Feast: 7 December (the day of his consecration); but in B.C.P. 4 April (the day of his death).

Contemporary materials for his Life in *P.L.*, xiv. 65–114 (Life by Paulinus, tr. by F. R. Hoare, *The Western Fathers*, 1954); F. H. Dudden, *The Life and Times of St. Ambrose* (1935); J. R. Palanque, *S. Ambroise et l'empire romain* (1933); Works in *P.L.*, xiv–xvii and in *C.S.E.L.*, xxxii, lxii, lxiv, lxxiii, lxxviii–lxxix; Eng. tr. of his important catechetical works by R. H. Connolly (1952) and J. H. Srawley (1950); French tr. by G. Tissot of his influential Commentary on Luke in *S.C.* (1956–8).

AMPHIBALUS, the name given by Geoffrey of Monmouth to the cleric sheltered by *Alban. The name is said to have arisen through a mistranslation, the word for a cloak becoming the name of a saint. From the Acts of St. Alban it cannot be deduced that the cleric's name was Amphibalus, nor that he was either martyr or saint, still less that he was responsible for the conversion of huge numbers to Christianity. All these elements are derived from fictitious later legends. The cult was given impetus by the discovery in 1178 at St. Albans of his supposed body; thenceforward he was closely associated with Alban in written accounts and artistic representations of the martyrdom.

For bibliography, see ALBAN.

ANACLETUS, see CLETUS.

ANASTASIA (d. *c.*304), martyr. She has been venerated at Rome since the 5th century and is mentioned in the Roman Canon. She died at Sirmium (Yugoslavia), notwithstanding her later *Acta* which make her a Roman martyr; her relics were translated to Constantinople. At Rome there was a church near the Circus Maximus called after its owner the *titulus Anastasiae.* Here the pope sang the second Mass on Christmas Day. Perhaps the *Acta* were written to satisfy curiosity about the origin of this church. Feast: 25 December, 22 December in the East.

H. Delehaye, *Étude sur le Légendier Romain* (1936), pp. 151–66.

ANASTASIUS (d. 628), Persian monk and martyr. He was tortured and put to death at Caesarea; his relics were translated to Rome in 640. His Life was rewritten by *Bede shortly before his death: it is probable that his feast was celebrated at Wearmouth and Jarrow. Feast: 22 January.

AA.SS. Ian. III, 35–54; H. Usener, *Acta martyris Anastasii Persae* (1894); P. Meyvaert, 'Has Bede's version of the Passio S. Anastasii come down to us?', *Oxford Patristic Conference Studies*, 1978.

ANDREW (d. *c.*60), apostle and martyr, brother of Simon Peter. He was a fisherman by trade, his home was at Capernaum. He was a disciple of *John the Baptist before becoming an apostle of Christ. In all the Gospel lists of apostles his name is among the first four; he is specially mentioned for his share in the feeding of the 5,000 and in the episode of the Greeks who wished to meet Jesus (cf. John 12: 20–2).

It is not certain where he preached the Gospel, where he died or (even in Chrysostom's time) where he was buried. The most ancient written tradition links him with Greece: Scythia and Epirus both claimed him as their apostle, while Patras in Achaia claimed to be the place where he was crucified and preached to the people for two days before he died. An early medieval forgery attributed to him the founding of the Church of Constantinople. This claim was strengthened by the translation of his supposed relics from Patras; it was intended to provide some counterweight to the more solid claim of Rome to possess the relics of *Peter and *Paul.

There was also a notable cult in the West. His feast was universal from the 6th century: churches were dedicated to him from early times in Italy and France, as well as Anglo-Saxon England, where Hexham and Rochester were the earliest of 637 medieval dedications. Ancient legends include that of a journey to Ethiopia, preserved in the Old English poem *Andreas* (once attributed to Cynewulf) and, even more influential, that of a translation of his relics from Patras to Scotland by *Rule in the 8th century. He stopped at a place in Fife now called St. Andrews and built a church there, which became a centre for evangelization and eventually pilgrimage. This story, which survives in several irreconcilable forms, some of which posit angelic intervention, is the reason for the choice of Andrew as patron of Scotland.

After the fall of Constantinople in 1204, the Crusaders took his body to Amalfi. The despot Thomas Palaeologus gave his head to the pope in 1461. The latter was one of the most treasured and envied possessions of St. Peter's until it was returned to Constantinople by Paul VI.

In art Andrew is depicted with a normal Latin cross in the most ancient examples; the saltire cross (X), commonly called 'St. Andrew's Cross', which represents Scotland on the Union Jack, was associated with him from the 10th century at Autun, and became common in the 14th. His other attribute is a fishing-net. Cycles of paintings are based on his fictitious Acts, which form the basis of the Breviary Office. Andrew is also patron of Russia. Feast: 30 November; translation, 9 May.

P. M. Peterson, *Andrew, Brother of Simon Peter. His History and his Legends* (Supplements to Novum Testamentum, i. 1958); M. Bonnet, 'Acta Andreae Apostoli', *Anal. Boll.*, xiii (1894), 309–78; J. Flamion, *Les Actes apocryphes de l'apôtre André* (1911); M. R. James, *The Apocryphal New Testament* (1924); E. Mâle, *Les saints compagnons du Christ* (1957); F. Dvornik, *The Idea of Apostolicity and the Legend of the Apostle Andrew* (1958); for the Scottish connection see *K.S.S.*, pp. 436–40; W. Skene, *Celtic Scotland*, i (1876), 296–9.

ANDREW BOBOLA, see BOBOLA.

ANDREW OF CRETE (*c.*660–740), monk and archbishop. Born at Damascus, he became a monk at Jerusalem. In 685 he was sent by its Patriarch to Constantinople to attest their acceptance of the sixth ecumenical council, against monotheism. Ordained deacon at Constantinople, he was placed in charge of an orphanage and a hospital for old men. In *c.*700 he was appointed archbishop of Gortyna (Crete). After a short lapse into monotheism (see *Maximus the Confessor), he became a prolific preacher and hymnographer. Some of the *kanon* which he introduced to the Byzantine Liturgy are still sung, while some of his homilies are still read in the breviary. He died at Erisso, on the island of Lesbos. Feast: 4 July.

AA.SS. Iul. II (1747), 42–7; works in *P.G.*, xcvii. 805–1304; Eng. tr. of the 'Great Canon' by D. J. Chitty (1957); *O.D.C.C.*, p. 51; *Bibl. SS.*, i. 1142.

ANGELA MERICI (1474–1540), foundress of the Ursuline nuns. Born at Desenzano (near Lake Garda), she was orphaned in early life, but became a Franciscan tertiary and devoted herself with several companions to the education of poor girls. In 1535 they dedicated themselves to this work under the patronage of *Ursula, but they took no vows and wore lay clothes. The formal organization of this sisterhood into a Congregation came only in 1565, as the Church authorities were not prepared to approve, until then, Angela's novel concept of unenclosed and mobile religious sisters. Her Congregation flourishes today; it has been well described as 'the oldest and most considerable teaching order of women in the R.C. Church'. Angela was canonized in 1807. Feast: 27 January.

Lives by V. Postel (1878) and G. Bertolletti (1923); see also Sister M. Monica, *Angela Merici and her Teaching Idea* (1927) and P. Caraman, *St. Angela* (1963).

ANGELICO, FRA (1387–1455), Dominican priest and artist. Born Guido di Pietro at Vicchio, near Florence, he became a Dominican in 1407, spending his novitiate at Cortona in a group which included *Antoninus, the future bishop of Florence. As a young friar Angelico worked at illuminating manuscripts such as the *Dominican Diurnal 3* (in the Laurentian Library, Florence). From 1409 he continued his studies and was ordained priest at Fiesole in 1418. In the 1430s he decorated the interior of the friary of San Marco, Florence, commissioned by Antoninus. This includes his famous Annunciation, a Crucifixion, and a series of mural paintings in the cells which make this a unique religious house. Work at the Vatican followed, especially the paintings of *Stephen and *Laurence in the chapel of the scholarly and artistic pope Nicholas V. These are said to have evoked the remark from Pope John Paul II: 'Why do we need miracles? These *are* his miracles.' In 1449 he was sent to Orvieto, where he painted the vault of the chapel of St. Brice in the cathedral.

From 1449 to 1452 he was prior of Fiesole. In that year he moved to Rome, where three years later he died. He is buried in the church of S. Maria sopra Minerva. His cult was popular early on and survives today. He was beatified in 1960 and his cult further approved in 1982: he was declared patron of artists in 1984.

His many surviving paintings radiate spiritual serenity and a religious dedication achieved by few others. They reveal also a marvellous command of colour, light, and perspective. He is generally reckoned one of the greatest painters of the Quattrocento. Feast: 18 February.

Studies by J. Pope-Hennessy (1952) and S. Orlandi (1964); V. Alce, 'L'arte del Beato Angelico', *Memoriae Domenicanae*, xxxi (1955), 38–92; *Bibl. SS.*, vi. 797–805.

ANNE (Ann, Anna, Hannah) (1st century), mother of the Blessed Virgin Mary. No historical details of her life are known. She was first mentioned by name in the apocryphal gospel of James (2nd century); Epiphanius and *Gregory of Nyssa praised her. A church was built in her honour at Constantinople by Justinian; relics were taken from it to Jerusalem and Rome, where there are pictures of her at S. Maria Antiqua (8th century). In the 10th century her feast, called the 'conception of St. Anne', was kept at Naples and, soon afterwards, in England and Ireland.

The increasing cult of the Virgin *Mary in the 12th century led to new interest in her parents. Anne's feast was kept at Canterbury from *c.*1100 and at Worcester soon afterwards. Relics of her were claimed by Duren (Rhineland) and Apt-en-Provence; by Canterbury, Reading, and Durham.

In art she is often represented teaching the Virgin to read: this picture may be English in origin; there are examples of the 13th century in manuscripts at the Bodleian Library, Oxford, and in wall-paintings at Croughton (Northants). She was also represented with her husband *Joachim at their betrothal or their marriage. The most famous shrine in her honour in England was at Buxton. She was patron of various religious guilds in England from the reign of John in London, and from the 14th century in Bury, King's Lynn, Lincoln, and elsewhere.

Her cult was bitterly attacked by Luther, especially the images representing her with Jesus and Mary, favoured by Renaissance painters. This did not prevent the Holy See extending her feast to the Universal Church in 1584; it had been obligatory in England since 1382. The cult has left literary record in three ME Lives. It was, and still is, especially popular in Brittany and Canada. Feast: 26 July (with S. Joachim); in the East, 25 July.

AA.SS. Iul. VI (1729), 233–97; B. Kleinschmidt, *Die heilige Anna, ihre Verehrung in Geschichte, Kunst und Volkstum* (1930): H. M. Bannister,

'The Introduction of the cult of St. Anne into the West', *E.H.R.*, xviii (1903), 107–12; R. E. Parker, *The Middle English Stanzaic Versions of the Life of St. Anne* (E.E.T.S., 1928; reprint 1971); A. Wilmart, *Auteurs Spirituels* (1932), pp. 46–55; M. V. Ronan, *St. Anne: her Cult and her Shrines* (1927).

ANSELM (1033–1109), Benedictine monk, writer, and archbishop of Canterbury. Born at Aosta, the son of a spendthrift Lombard nobleman, with whom he quarrelled as a young man, Anselm went to live in Burgundy with his mother's family. Attracted by the reputation of Lanfranc, regarded as the foremost teacher of his time, Anselm moved to Normandy. After much hesitation he became a monk in Lanfranc's monastery at Bec (*c.*1060), studied *Augustine for ten years, but wrote nothing which has survived. Quite early he was made prior: to this period of his life belong his prayers, meditations, and *De Grammatico.* In 1077–8 he wrote the *Monologion* and *Proslogion.* The latter has been famous for centuries because of its 'ontological' proof of God's existence: it revealed Anselm's originality and prepared the way for his later theological works.

In 1078 Herluin, founder of Bec, died; Anselm was elected abbot in his place. Besides the care of his monks, for which his sensitive, intuitive mind well fitted him, he also became closely associated again with his former master Lanfranc, since 1070 archbishop of Canterbury. This brought him into contact with English ecclesiastical affairs. On Lanfranc's death in 1089 the English clergy wished Anselm to be his successor, but William Rufus kept Canterbury vacant for four years. Only when he seemed mortally ill did he agree to the appointment of Anselm, then in England for the foundation of Chester (dependent on Bec). Anselm, against his better judgement, accepted.

From then onwards he was involved in a series of disputes with William and his successor, about papal jurisdiction, investiture, and, ultimately, the primacy of the spiritual. Anselm was utterly committed to what he saw as the cause of God and the Church, to which he gave absolute obedience; he was quite out of sympathy with the world of politics and compromise. As abbot of Bec, he had already recognized Urban II as pope; hence, as archbishop of Canterbury, he was quite unable to recognize the anti-pope Wibert, supported by Rufus. The ensuing quarrel, fanned by other issues, resulted in Anselm's exile in 1097.

Now he wrote his important treatise on the Incarnation called *Cur Deus Homo?*; he also took a prominent part in the Council of Bari, when, at the pope's request, he successfully defended the doctrine of the Double Procession of the Holy Spirit against the Greeks. At a Council in Rome soon after, he whole-heartedly adopted the Gregorian view of the illegality of lay investiture.

With the accession of Henry I he returned to England in 1100, but the intransigence of both king and archbishop concerning investiture resulted in another exile in 1103. But peace was made in 1106–7, when Pope Paschal counselled some modification of Anselm's earlier positions. The resulting compromise, used as a model for settling similar disputes in other countries, gave the Church victory over the investiture of staff and ring, symbols of spiritual jurisdiction, but left the king, in practice, with undiminished control over the selection of bishops.

From then until his death Anselm remained in England, where he held councils which insisted, among other things, on stricter observance of clerical celibacy. He also established the new see of Ely. Although not conspicuous for political skill, Anselm secured a wider recognition of the Canterbury 'primacy' than his predecessor Lanfranc: Wales, Ireland, and (with important reservations) Scotland acknowledged it, while York also had to accept a papal decision favourable to Anselm and Canterbury.

He was fortunate in his biographer, Eadmer of Canterbury, who wrote an intimate, personal Life which broke fresh ground in the field of biography. But the cult grew slowly. *Thomas of Canterbury requested Anselm's canonization at Tours in 1163; Pope Alexander III referred it to a provincial council. No formal record of this survives, but a Canterbury calendar of *c.*1165 provides the earliest known evidence for two feasts of Anselm, one of them a translation. But his cult was soon overshadowed by that of Becket, while some of his works seemed to lose their popularity in the 13th century, although interest revived in the 14th and 15th. Probably through the cult in Flanders his name appeared in the Roman Martyrology (1586); in 1720 as the most important Christian writer between Augustine and *Thomas Aquinas he was named a Doctor of the Church. 'Faith seeking understanding' and the mind at faith's service were the keys to his life and teaching. Feast: 21 April; translation (at Canterbury), 7 April.

AA.SS. Apr. II (1675), 865–953; R. W. Southern (ed.), *Eadmer's Life of St. Anselm* (1962); M. Rule (ed.), *Historia Novorum* (*R.S.*, 1884), Eng. tr. by G. Bosanquet (1964); R. W. Southern and F. S. Schmitt, *Memorials of St. Anselm* (1970); A. Wilmart, *Auteurs Spirituels* (1932); Works ed. F. S. Schmitt (7 vols., 1938–70) and in *P.L.*, clviii–clix, see also *Spicilegium Beccense* (1959). Other studies include K. Barth, *Fides Quaerens Intellectum* (1931); J. MacIntyre, *St. Anselm and his Critics* (1954); R. W. Southern, *St. Anselm and his Biographer* (1963); D. P. Henry, *The De Grammatico of St. Anselm* (1964); M. J. Charlesworth, *St. Anselm's Proslogion* (1965); R. W. Southern, *St. Anselm* (1991).

ANSKAR (Ansgar) (801–65), archbishop of Bremen. Born near Amiens of a noble family, Anskar was educated at Corbie (Picardy), where he became a monk. Later he moved to Corvey (Westphalia), where he began apostolic work. Harold, king of Denmark, who had become a Christian while in exile, took back to his country Anskar, who under royal patronage evangelized the people. After a missionary journey in Sweden, he was appointed bishop of Hamburg (832) and, after the sack of Hamburg by Vikings in 845, archbishop of both Hamburg and Bremen by Pope Nicholas I, who also gave him some jurisdiction over Denmark, Norway, and Sweden.

He founded schools, was an indefatigable preacher, and was outstanding in his charity to the poor. He was also prominent in diminishing the effects of the Viking slave-trade, being powerless to abolish it. His most lasting achievements as Christian missionary were in Denmark, whose patron he is, and in north Germany; Sweden, however, relapsed into paganism and was re-evangelized by *Sigfrid and others in the 11th century.

Anskar often wore a hair shirt, lived on bread and water when his health allowed it, and added short personal prayers to each psalm in his psalter, thus contributing to a form of devotion which soon became widespread. He died and was buried at Bremen. Feast: 3 February.

AA.SS. Feb. I (1658), 391–445 for contemporary Life, also ed. G. Waitz in *Scriptores Rerum Germanicarum* (1884), Eng. tr. by C. H. Robinson (1921); modern Lives by E. de Moreau (1930) and P. Oppenheim (1931). See also C. J. A. Opperman, *English Missionaries in Sweden and Finland* (1937); B.T.A., i. 242–3 and *Bibl. SS.*, i. 1337–9.

ANTA, Cornish saint, patron of Lelant (lan-Anta). Feast day and historical information unknown.

ANTONINUS OF FLORENCE (1389–1459), archbishop. The son of a Florentine notary, Nicolo Pierozzi, he became a Dominican friar in 1405 under John Dominici, prior of Santa Maria Novella in Florence, a reformer who followed Raymond of Capua. Antoninus' novitiate was spent at Cortona, where two fellow novices were Fra Angelico and Fra Bartolomeo, the future friend of Raphael. Antoninus was assigned to the recently founded priory of Fiesole. He was soon appointed prior of Cortona, then of Fiesole (1418–28), and in turn of Naples and the Minerva at Rome (1430); here he became auditor-general of the Rota and vicar-general of the Dominicans of the Strict Observance (1432–5). He then returned to Florence and in 1436 founded the famous convent of San Marco, a Sylvestrine monastery rebuilt by Michelozzi and decorated by Fra *Angelico and his disciples with a fresco in each cell and the famous Annunciation on the main staircase. The church was rebuilt by Cosimo de' Medici. Both as host and theologian Antoninus was prominent in the Council of Florence in 1439.

His most notable writings include a highly regarded *Summa* of moral theology, treatises on the Christian life (of which one had 102 incunabula editions), and a 'world history'. He was among the first Christian moralists to teach that money invested in commerce and industry was true capital; therefore it was lawful and not usury to claim interest on it. This teaching must have been most acceptable to Medicean Florence. It must, however, be understood as but one small element in his general teaching on the Christian life.

This was revealed not only in his writings but also in his way of life when he was appointed archbishop of Florence by Eugenius IV. He observed strict personal poverty, owning neither plate nor horses, but only a single mule. He was outstandingly generous to the poor, giving away his furniture on occasion, but also founding a sodality of St. Martin for those who were ashamed to beg. Every year he visited his diocese on foot, preaching frequently and eliminating abuses such as the practice of magic and of usury. When the plague raged for a year, he personally helped its victims and encouraged the clergy to do likewise. Earthquakes in 1453–5 brought similar suffering, met by similar charity. Pope Nicholas V gave him substantial help and even declared that Antoninus was as worthy of veneration as *Bernardino of Siena whom he had canonized in 1450.

During the last years of his life Antoninus acted as a Florentine ambassador and was appointed by Pius II to a committee for reforming the Roman court. This was a fitting conclusion to a life as a friar of the reform movement, as a bishop inspired by saintly pastors, yet overall humanized by the religious art of the early Renaissance. His versatile excellence was outstanding in a milieu that badly needed the reforms he propagated.

Short of stature, his likeness was recorded by contemporary artists, as in the bust at Santa Maria Novella, Florence, and in a statue in the Uffizi. Antonio del Pollaiuolo's painting of him at the foot of the Cross survives at San Marco, as does a series of scenes from his life in its cloister of S. Antonino. He was canonized in 1523. Feast: 10 May.

AA.SS. Maii I (1680), 313–51 (contemporary Life and extracts from canonization process); works ed. P. Ballerini, *Summa Theologica* (1740 and 1958) and by R. Morçay, *Chroniques de S. Antonin* (1913); modern biographies by R. Morçay (1914), A. Masseron (1926), C. C. Calzolai (1960); see also B. Jarrett, *S. Antonino and Medieval Economics* (1914); W. T. Gaughan, *Social Theories of St. Antoninus from his Summa Theologica* (1951); J. B. Walker, *The Chronicles of St. Antoninus* (1933); *N.C.E.*, i. 646–7; *Bibl. SS.*, ii. 88–105.

ANTONY OF EGYPT (251–356), abbot. Born in Coma (Upper Egypt), he sold all his possessions at the age of twenty and lived among the local ascetics. From 286 to 306 he lived in complete solitude in a deserted fort at Pispir. Here he underwent a series of temptations usually associated with the hermit life; at the end of this period he left his solitude to guide disciples, who had gathered around him. From his monastery he went to Alexandria in 311 to encourage the confessors during the persecution of Maximinus. He lived by gardening and mat-making; in character he combined severe austerity with an emphasis on discretion and the love of God before all else. His Letters reveal him as a man whose thought was influenced by Plato and Origen.

In 355 he went again to Alexandria, this time to refute the Arians. Even the philosophers were impressed; he was reputed to be a miracle-worker and many were converted by him. His surviving letters include one to the Emperor Constantine and several to different monasteries. One conference attributed to him is preserved by *Cassian, many of his sayings by the *Vitae Patrum*, while a monastic Rule in his name contains at least some elements of his teaching.

Jerome's account of *Paul, the first hermit, describes a meeting with Antony in the desert shortly before Paul's death, at which a raven dropped a loaf of bread. Afterwards lions dug a grave for Paul, and Antony buried him in a cloak given by *Athanasius.

Antony was buried by his own choice in a place known to none. But by 561 his relics were found and translated to Alexandria. Much later, translations were claimed by Constantinople and by La Motte, where the Order of Hospitallers of Saint Antony was founded *c.*1100. This became a pilgrimage centre for those who suffered from ergotism (called St. Antony's Fire). The hospitallers, who wore black robes with a blue Tau-cross, became widespread over much of western Europe. They used to ride about, ringing little bells to attract alms; the bells were afterwards hung round the necks of animals to protect them from disease. By special privilege this Order's pigs were allowed to roam freely in the streets, whence the emblems of pigs and bells in Antony's later iconography.

The earliest representations, however, portrayed the meeting of Antony and Paul, as in the Ruthwell Cross (*c.*750) and eight Irish high crosses of before 1000, as well as in stained glass at Chartres. Illustrated Lives survive from Valetta and Florence which guided artists to paint scenes from his Life on linen cloths, hung in churches of his Order. One of these was owned by St. Antony's, Threadneedle Street, in 1499. These scenes included episodes from the Life by *Athanasius, a classic of Christian hagiography, but also apocryphal elements from a Hispano-Arabic source, among which were a journey to Barcelona and a proposal of marriage from a queenly devil. The temptations of Antony have been depicted by many artists, including Bosch and Grunewald.

Antony was an immensely popular saint in the Middle Ages. Regarded as the patriarch of monks and the healer of both men and animals, he left his trace on the English language through the word 'tantony', a diminutive applied to pigs (the smallest of the litter) and to bells (the smallest of the peal). His Legend, with English verses, can be found depicted on the backs of the stalls of Carlisle Cathedral. Feast: 17 January.

AA.SS. Ian. II (1643), 107–62; Life by Athanasius also in *P.G.*, xxvi. 835–978 with letters; ibid., xl. 977–1000 and 1065; Latin version by Evagrius of Antioch, *P.L.*, lxxiii. 125–70 with critical editions by G. Garitte (1939) and H. Hoppenbrouwers (1960). Modern studies by B. Lavaud (1943) and L. Bouyer (1950) with B. Steidle (ed.), *Antonius Magnus Eremita, 356–1956* (Studia Anselmiana, 1956). See also R. Graham, *A Picture Book of the Life of St. Antony the Abbot* (Roxburghe Club, 1937); id., 'The Order of Saint-Antoine de Viennois and its English Commandery', *Archaeol. Jnl.*, lxxiv (1927), 341–406; G. C. Harcourt, *Legends of St. Augustine, St. Antony and St. Cuthbert painted on the back of the stalls of Carlisle cathedral* (1868); P. Noordeloos, 'La translation de S. Antoine en Dauphiné', *Anal. Boll.*, lx (1942), 68–81; S. Rubenson, *The Letters of St. Antony* (1990).

ANTONY OF PADUA (*c.*1193–1231), Franciscan friar and priest. Born at Lisbon of a noble Portuguese family, at the age of about 16 he joined the Order of Austin Canons and studied at Coimbra under teachers from Montpellier, Toulouse, and Paris. The principal subject was the Bible, presented in such a way as to refute the Moors and the heretics. Impressed by some Franciscans who had visited Coimbra before being martyred in Morocco soon afterwards, he joined the friars in 1220 and sailed to Ceuta hoping to continue their mission. But he soon returned to Europe through ill-health, and took part in the General Chapter of Assisi in 1221, presided over by Brother Elias while *Francis was still alive. He was sent to a small hermitage of San Paolo near Forli, but when he preached at an ordination, his knowledge and contemplative experience were revealed. It is said that Francis himself chose him to teach theology to the friars at Bologna and Padua. A few years later he visited France, preaching and teaching in several places such as Montpellier, Toulouse, and Arles. There he was often called 'the hammer of heretics'.

Elected Provincial of northern Italy in

1227, he travelled much for the supervision of the friaries under his charge. During these three years he wrote his 'Sermons for Sundays' and became a member of a commission sent to Rome to discuss with the papacy the Rule and the Testament of Francis. At the papal court his preaching was hailed as a 'jewel case of the Bible', and he was commissioned to produce 'Sermons for Feast Days'. He returned to Padua for the last months of his life, which were devoted to preaching, hearing confessions, and working to help poor debtors. He died at Arcella, a suburb of Padua, where the friars directed a convent of Poor Clares. The latter claimed Antony's body, but it was taken to the friars' church of Our Lady in the town of Padua. Around this was built the present fine basilica in his name. His canonization took place only a year after his death.

The cult of Antony has always been strong and varied in its manifestations. Artists have depicted him preaching to the fishes (like Francis to the birds) and also represent him showing a consecrated host to a mule who immediately venerated it, rejecting a bundle of hay. These episodes remind us that although Antony was a deservedly popular preacher, whose charismatic presence attracted crowds so large that he spoke in the market-places instead of the churches, sometimes he was less successful. The point of these stories of animals is that sometimes they were more receptive than certain humans. Since the 17th century he has been frequently invoked as the finder of lost articles, because a novice who borrowed his psalter without permission was obliged to return it because of a fearsome apparition. His devotion to the poor was aptly recalled by the 19th century institution of Saint Antony's Bread. This charity, devoted to the relief of the starving and the needy, still flourishes, especially in the Third World. In Sicily huge leaves in the shape of a crown are still baked on his feast.

The popularity of this wonder-working saint is balanced by his nomination as a Doctor of the Church by Pius XII in 1946. This focused attention on the biblical and liturgical character of his preaching, based also on patristic writings. *Bernardino of Siena had given Antony's cult fresh vigour for the same reasons. The most usual post-Tridentine representations depict him with a book and a lily, together with the Infant Jesus seated on the book. Some medieval artists preferred to depict him in a nut-tree in memory of his solitude and the esteem for him on the part of *Bonaventure. Antony was above all an outstanding representative of the Franciscan pre-scholastic period, very close in spirit and outlook to Francis himself.

His relics were translated in 1263, when his incorrupt tongue and two bones were detached from the body. In 1981 his tomb was reopened and the relics were scientifically examined. Thanks to this, it can be said that Antony had a long, thin face, deep-set eyes, and long, delicate hands. He was about forty when he died and the state of his bones indicated poor feeding (through his frequent long fasts) and fatigue caused by frequent journeys on foot. Innumerable pilgrims have visited his tomb and still do so. His cult is also specially strong in France, Portugal, and Brazil (of which he is a patron), as well as in Ireland and the USA. Feast: 13 June.

AA.SS. Iun. II (1698), 703–80; A. Masseron, *La vie de saint Antoine de Padoue* (1956); W. C. Van Dyk, *L'Assidua: la vie de saint Antoine racontée par un contemporain* (1984); Biographies by C. M. Antony (1911), E. Gilliat-Smith (1926), R. M. Huber (1949), and A. Curtayne (1950); Sermons edited by A. Locatelli and others at Padua (1895–1913). See also *H.S.S.C.*, VI. 69–79; *Bibl. SS.*, ii. 156–88.

ANTONY CLARET, see CLARET.

AODH, see AED.

APPHIA, see PHILEMON AND APPHIA.

APOLLINARIS (date unknown), first bishop of Ravenna and martyr. Nothing is known of his life and actions, the best literary witness to his existence being *Peter Chrysologus. His late and unreliable Acts make him a native of Antioch and disciple of St. *Peter, who was four times expelled from his see and was stoned by a mob. His best memorials are the superb churches in Ravenna dedicated to his memory, with the fine mosaic representing him as shepherd of his flock. Feast: 23 July.

AA.SS. Iul. V (1727), 328–85; H. Delehaye, 'L'Hagiographie ancienne de Ravenne', *Anal. Boll.*, xlvii (1929), 5–30; E. Will, *Saint Apollinaire de Ravenne* (1936).

APOLLONIA (d. *c.*249), aged deaconess of Alexandria and martyr. Denis, bishop of Alexandria, described her death as follows: 'They seized that marvellous aged virgin Apollonia, broke out all her teeth with blows on her jaws, and piling up a bonfire before the city, threatened to burn her alive if she refused to recite with them their blasphemous sayings. But she asked for a brief delay and without flinching leapt into the fire and was consumed.' This happened in a riot, when many Christians were dragged from their houses and killed, while their property was looted.

Altars and churches were soon dedicated to her in the West, but there seems to have been no cult in the East. At Rome she was soon confused with another Apollonia, who suffered under Julian the Apostate. Later romancers and artists transformed her into a beautiful girl, tortured by her teeth being extracted with pincers. Other Legends were pillaged to make her a king's daughter who was tortured by her father, but who promised just before death to help all those who suffered from toothache. Artists usually depicted her holding a tooth in a pair of pincers, or else having her teeth forcibly extracted by an elaborate machine. One unexpected result of her cult is the publication of a dentist's quarterly at Boston (Mass.), called *The Apollonian.*

Apollonia's death has been much discussed by theologians concerned with the legitimacy or otherwise of her throwing herself into the flames. Feast: 9 February (since 1970 for local churches only).

AA.SS. Feb. II (1658), 278–83; Eusebius, *H.E.*, vi. 41–2; M. Coens, 'Une passio S. Apolloniae inédite', *Anal. Boll.*, lxx (1952), 138–59; H. Nux, 'Sainte Apolline, patronne de ceux qui souffrent des dents', *Revue d'odontologie, de stomachologie*, iii (1947), 113–53.

APOLLONIUS (d. 183), Roman martyr. He was mentioned by *Jerome and Eusebius; his name is in early liturgical books; more light has been shed on him by the discovery of *Acts* in Greek and Armenian. This Roman senator was denounced as a Christian to the authorities by his own slave; he made an impressive verbal and written *apologia* to the senate. This comprised a criticism of paganism as futile because its idols are human artefacts without life, autonomy, reason, or virtue: hence they should be rejected. Christianity is superior by its concepts of death and life: death is a natural necessity which has nothing frightening about it, while the true life is the life of the soul. Above all, Christianity surpasses paganism through the work of Christ, the revealing Word of God and teacher of moral life, who became man to destroy sin by his death. This last, predicted both by Scripture and by Plato, can be compared to the death of the prophets and of Socrates. In short, Christianity is the 'best bet' for his time, and if anyone is martyred, he then becomes the seed of new Christians.

Harnack and others agree that this was one of the best of early Christian apologists, but the near-contemporary sources disagree on the details of the legal process. It seems certain that Apollonius was beheaded on 21 April: his feast was kept in the Martyrology of Jerome on 18 April, but at Constantinople on 23 July.

Eusebius, *H.E.*, v. 21, 1–5; H. Delehaye, *Les passions des martyres et les genres littéraires* (1966), pp. 92–9; *H.S.S.C.*, ii. 71–3.

ARILD (Alkeld) (date unknown), virgin. The place of her death was Kingston-by-Thornbury (Glos.), the cause of it, according to Leland, was 'one Muncius a tiraunt, who cut off hir heade becawse she would not consent to lye withe hym'. After the Norman Conquest her relics were translated to Gloucester Abbey, where her shrine was famous for miracles. She was depicted in the East Window and a statue of her was on the reredos of the Lady altar. Two churches were dedicated to her: at Oldbury-on-Severn and Oldbury-on-the-Hill. Feast (at Gloucester): 20 July.

J. Leland, *Itinerary*, ii. 60; v. 156; *E.B.K. after 1100*, ii. 41–2; E. S. Lindley, 'St. Arild of Thornbury', *Trans. Bristol and Glos. Arch. Soc.*, lxx (1951), 152–3.

ARMEL (Armagilus, Ermel, Ermyn) (d. *c.*552), abbot. His earliest known cult and Life date from the 12th century. He was reputed to have been born in South Wales, was the cousin of *Samson and *Cadfan, became a monk, and then emigrated with many kinsmen to Brittany. With the help of King Childebert he founded two monasteries: Plouarmel and Ploermel. From Brittany his cult spread to Normandy, Anjou, and Touraine; in England it was encouraged by King Henry VII who believed he was saved from shipwreck off the coast of Brittany through Armel's intercession. Consequently there is a statue of him in Henry VII's chapel at Westminster Abbey, and another on Cardinal Morton's tomb at Canterbury. Other examples survive on the painted reredos of Romsey Abbey and in alabasters at Stonyhurst College (Lancs.) and St. Mary Brookfield church (London). He is generally represented in armour and a chasuble, leading a dragon with a stole round its neck. This recalls the legend that he took it to Mont-Saint-Armel and commanded it to dive into the river below. A fine 16th-century church at Ploermel contains eight stained-glass windows which depict scenes from his life. He was invoked to cure headaches, fever, colic, gout, and rheumatism; hospitals sometimes had him as their patron. Feast: 16 August (in Sarum Calendar since 1498).

A. le Grand, *Vies des Saints de Bretagne* (1901), pp. 383–7; J. Macé, *Histoire merveilleuse de saint Armel* (1909); A. R. Green, 'The Romsey painted wooden reredos, with a short account of St. Armel', *Archaeol. Jnl.*, xc (1933), 306–14.

ARNULF (1) (d. 643), bishop of Metz. He was a counsellor of King Dagobert, who promoted him to a bishopric in *c.*610. Later he resigned his see to become a monk, first as a hermit in the Vosges mountains, then in the monastery of Remiremont. Feast: 18 July.

ARNULF (2) (d. 1087), bishop of Soissons. As a young man he chose to be a soldier, but after a successful military career he became a monk at S. Médard (Soissons), where he lived as a hermit before being chosen as abbot. In 1081 he was acclaimed bishop, but was driven out by an intruder. He then founded a monastery at Aldenburg (Flanders), where he died and was enshrined. Feast: 15 August.

ARNULF (3), hermit who lived and died at Eynesbury (Cambs.), to which town he gave his name (Eanulfesbyrig). He was reputed to have been venerated here before the Danish invasions, but by *c.*1000 he seems to have been forgotten, as *R.P.S.* mentions *Neot here, but not Arnulf. Feast: 22 August.

B.T.A., iii. 139, 335–6; Stanton, pp. 405–6.

ARROWSMITH, Edmund (1585–1628), Jesuit priest and martyr. Born at Haydock (Lancs.), the son of Robert Arrowsmith, a yeoman farmer, he was educated first by an otherwise unknown elderly priest and then at the English College, Douai. He was ordained priest in 1612 and returned to Lancashire in 1613 where he became renowned for his fearless and forthright ministry. In 1622 he was arrested; after being examined by the bishop of Chester he was released, probably because King James I was then interested in a Spanish marriage for his son and it was not politic for him to appear a persecutor of the Catholics. Some years later Arrowsmith joined the Society of Jesus in their novitiate at Clerkenwell. In 1628 he was denounced by a young man whose irregular life he had reproved, and was indicted at Lancaster Assizes for being a seminary priest. He was found guilty and sentenced to death. But first he was left chained for two days without food. Until the very last moment he was promised his life if he would renounce his faith. He was executed at Lancaster on 28 August; he was canonized by Paul VI in 1970 as one of the *Forty Martyrs of England and Wales. A contemporary portrait survives, as does a hand-relic in the church of St. Oswald at Ashton-in-Makerfield, near Wigan, where cures believed to be miraculous have been reported. Feast: 25 October.

A True and False Relation of Two Catholicks who Suffered for their Religion at Lancaster in 1628 (1737), modernized in pamphlet *Blessed Edmund Arrowsmith* (1960); *N.C.E.*, i. 851; B.T.A., iii. 439–40.

ASAPH (d. early 7th century), bishop in North Wales. One of the reputed descendants of Coel Godebog and related to both *Deiniol and *Tysilio, Asaph is known largely through late Lives of *Kentigern. Asaph was his young disciple, and was reputed to have brought him live coals in his clothes without their being damaged or burnt in any way. Asaph worked principally in Flintshire with Llanasa as his centre. But he was nominated bishop of Llanelwy on the departure of Cyndeyrn to Cumbria in the late 6th century. Asaph remained, probably endowed the cathedral, and died there. His deep local influence can be deduced from the change of the placename to St. Asaph. Here the Normans established a territorial see in the 12th century, coterminous with the principality of Powys. Several churches and a few wells (including the second largest in Wales, called Ffynnon Asa) are dedicated to Asaph, and for long a fair was held on his feast in his cathedral town. Written record of his feast survives only in late Welsh calendars and in Roscarrock, also, surprisingly, in the Roman Martyrology. There was a limited Scottish cult as well. Feast: 1 May.

AA.SS. Maii I (1680), 82–3; *Propylaeum*, p. 167; Baring-Gould and Fisher, i. 177–85; A. W. Wade-Evans, *Welsh Christian Origins* (1934), pp. 191–4.

ATHANASIUS (*c.*296–373), bishop of Alexandria. Born of Christian parents and educated in Alexandria's catechetical school, Athanasius became deacon and secretary to his bishop Alexander, whom he accompanied to the Council of Nicea (325). This first General Council, in which the Alexandrians were prominent, condemned Arianism which denied the eternity of the Word of God and the Divinity of Christ in the full, proper sense of that word. The Creed there formulated, as confirmed by the subsequent Council of Constantinople (381), became part of Christian belief and liturgy to this day. A fighter all his life, Athanasius vigorously defended Christian orthodoxy and refused all compromise with Arians or semi-Arians, who were, however, strongly represented at the imperial court.

In 328 he became bishop; he made extensive pastoral visits in his province, but was soon the target of bitter attacks by Arians and Meletians. Summoned to the hostile Council of Tyre and appealing to the emperor for fair treatment, he was exiled and then restored, deposed, and then reinstated. Much of his life was spent in exile: in Trier (335–7), in Rome (339–46), in country districts near Alexandria (356–61, 362–3, 365–6). Misunderstandings, lawsuits, and persecution were his fate, but the papacy strongly supported him.

A prolific author even in exile, Athanasius contributed strongly to the theology of the Redemption. The theme of his early work *De Incarnatione* is the restoration of fallen man to the image of God in which he was created, through God the Word's union with mankind. His most important controversial work was the *Contra Arianos.* Drawing on the teaching of *Justin and *Irenaeus, who interpreted Scripture in an orthodox tradition, Athanasius further insisted that the Nicene term *Homoousios*, although not itself a Scriptural term, was necessary to formulate correctly the truth of Christ's Scriptural revelation. In 362 Athanasius returned in short-lived triumph to Alexandria, whose council condemned the semi-Arians in the same year.

For Athanasius, both asceticism and virginity are effective means of restoring the divine image in man. Several of his works were addressed to monks, to whom he also gave repeated practical help. He was the friend of *Pachomius and Serapion of Thmuis as well as the biographer of *Antony. This Life, devoted to the single combat of the hermit against the powers of evil, became a classic and was widely diffused throughout Christendom. Its Latin version was known in England from the time of *Bede and frequently inspired monastic hagiographers.

Athanasius' feast occurs frequently in calendars, but there are no known early English Church dedications. Feast: 2 May.

AA.SS. Maii I (1680), 186–258; J. H. Newman, *The Arians of the Fourth Century* (1881); F. L. Cross, *The Study of St. Athanasius* (1945); J. N. D. Kelly, *Early Christian Doctrines* (1960), pp. 243–58, 284–95; L. Bouyer, *L'Incarnation et l'Église-Corps du Christ dans la Théologie de S. Athanase;* see also *Studia Patristica*, iii (1982), 981–1045. Works in *P.G.*, xxv–xxviii and ed. H. G. Opitz for Berlin Academy (1934–); selected works ed. by F. L. Cross, *De Incarnatione* (1937), G. J. Ryan and R. P. Casey, *De Incarnatione* (1945–6), R. W. Thomson, *Contra Gentes* (1971) tr. W. Bright, *Orations against the Arians* (1873) and *Historical Writings* (1881); see also translations by various writers in *Fathers of the Church* series. Lives by G. Bardy (1914), J. M. Leroux (1956).

ATHANASIUS THE ATHONITE (*c*.925–1003), abbot of Mount Athos. Born at Trebizond on the Black Sea of wealthy parents from Antioch, he was left an orphan and was adopted first by a tax-collector and then by a general. He showed promise as a scholar and became a lecturer; he visited Athos with his guardian and met Michael Maleinos, abbot of Kymina, with his nephew, the future emperor Nicephorus Phocas. Athanasius returned with Michael and joined his monastery: after four years he became a hermit. Realizing that he might be made abbot, he fled to Mount Athos and built a hermitage, chapel, and monastery with money donated by Nicephorus. Part of it was used to pipe water from a spring eight miles away and later to build a harbour. The monastery was completed in 963.

He now wrote rules for every aspect of monastic life, making considerable use of those of *Theodore the Studite. He insisted on unity (the quarrelsome were 'tonsured with the scissors of Satan'), on study (with special coaching for the semi-literate), and on austerity of food (mainly uncooked vegetables with oil). Local opponents included hermits who resented his authority, efficiency, and new buildings which disturbed their accustomed way of life. It is even said that twice his murder was attempted. The emperor however forbade all opposition and recognized his authority over all who dwelt on Mount Athos.

In 1003 he preached to his monks for the last time, wearing a cloak given him by Abbot Michael, and went to inspect the latest building works in the church. He climbed the scaffolding in the sanctuary with several companions, but the cupola suddenly collapsed without warning. Five monks were killed instantly: Athanasius was released from the debris three hours later, but he was dead.

In former times the monks of Mount Athos have sometimes numbered several thousand: nowadays they are considerably reduced in numbers. The monasteries of Iviron (see *George the Hagiorite), Esphigmenou, and Vatopedi, all founded in Athanasius' lifetime, still exist within this most important centre of Eastern Orthodox monasticism. Feast: 5 July.

Works in P. Meyer, *Die Haupturkunden fur die Geschichte der Athoskloster* (1894), pp. 102–30; Greek Life, ed. by L. Petit in *Anal. Boll.* xxv (1906), 5–89; J. Leroy, 'Les deux vies de saint Athanase l'Athonite', *Anal. Boll.*, lxxxii (1964), 409–29; see also P. Lemerle in *Le Millénaire du Mont Athos 963–1963*, i (1963), 59–100; D.

Attwater, *Saints of the East* (1963), pp. 101–8; *Bibl. SS.*, ii. 547–9.

ATHEUS, see Tathai.

ATHILDA, see Alkelda (1).

AUBIERGE, see Ethelburga (2).

AUDE, see Juthwara.

AUDOENUS, see Ouen.

AUDOMARUS, see Omer.

AUDREY, see Etheldreda.

AUGUSTINE OF CANTERBURY (d. *c.*604), archbishop. Italian by birth, a pupil of Felix, bishop of Messana, and a companion of *Gregory, Augustine became a monk and later prior of the monastery of St. Andrew on the Celian Hill, Rome. In 596 he was chosen by Gregory, now pope, to head the mission of thirty monks whom he sent to evangelize the Anglo-Saxons. In Gaul they wished to turn back, but Gregory gave them fresh encouragement, defined Augustine's authority more clearly, and had him consecrated bishop. The party landed at Ebbsfleet (Kent) in 597. They were received cautiously by *Ethelbert, king of Kent and overlord of the other tribes south of the Humber, who gave them a house in Canterbury, allowed them to preach, but required time to consider their message before committing himself to becoming a Christian. His wife was Bertha, a Christian princess from Paris; but she and her chaplain *Liudhard appear to have taken no significant part in the conversion of Kent, then the most sophisticated of the Anglo-Saxon kingdoms.

By 601 Ethelbert and many of his people were baptized, and more clergy were sent from Rome, together with books, relics, and altar vessels. Augustine's policy was one of consolidation in a small area, rather than of dispersal of effort in a large one. He built the first cathedral at Canterbury, which included married clerks as well as priests on its staff. He founded the monastery of SS. Peter and Paul (later called St. Augustine's), just outside the walls, as well as a 'suburban' see at Rochester. In the dedications and in the style of architecture (at Reculver as well as at Canterbury) his arrangements were closely modelled on those of contemporary Rome. Later in his short episcopate he established a see at London, then a town of the East Saxons, under Ethelbert's overlordship; he also attempted to secure the co-operation of British bishops in the evangelization of the Anglo-Saxons. In this he was not successful, but there is no reason to think that the fault was exclusively his.

Early writers stressed that Gregory, rather than Augustine, was regarded as the 'apostle of the English'. Certainly the substantially authentic correspondence between them reveals Augustine as the man in the field who was executing the wishes of his superior; it also shows Gregory's wisdom and Augustine's inexperience. Gregory left him considerable freedom. He could adopt Gallican or other liturgical customs for his own use; he was independent of the bishops of Gaul, but had no control over them either; he set up his metropolitan see at Canterbury instead of London, which Gregory, using imperial records, had expected. For this he was sent the pallium, which established him in charge of the southern province, with powers to arrange for the establishment of a northern one, based at York, each of them to have twelve suffragan bishops. This plan was never fully realized, but it did make history in church organization and missionary technique. So did Gregory's Letter to *Mellitus, in which Augustine was told not to destroy pagan temples, but only the idols in them. Innocent rites could be taken over and used for the celebration of Christian feasts. Error could not be eliminated at a stroke; the policy of proceeding gradually was modelled on the development of Revelation in the Old Testament.

Augustine helped Ethelbert to draft the earliest Anglo-Saxon written laws to survive. He also founded a school at Canterbury, which both received and produced books. A 6th-century uncial manuscript, called the Gospels of St. Augustine, could well have been brought to England by him; it is now at Corpus Christi College, Cambridge, and is used at the enthronement of archbishops of Canterbury. But the so-called Charters of Ethelbert, with Augustine as witness, are spurious.

Augustine was reputed to be a miracle-worker in life, so too when his relics were transferred in 1091 to a new site in his much enlarged abbey church. No early representations of him have survived, but he is depicted in stained glass at Christ Church, Oxford (14th century), at Canterbury cathedral (1470), and in a cycle of miniatures in the breviary of the Duke of Bedford (1424). He is also in frescoes by Viviano da Urbino in the church of St. Gregory, Rome (5th century).

Feast: 26 May (certainly the day of his death, testified at Clovesho in 747), but outside England now 27 May; translation feast at Canterbury, 13 September.

AA.SS. Maii VI (1688), 373–443; Bede, *H.E.*, i. 23–ii. 3; P. Ewald and L. Hartmann (edd.), *Gregorii Papae registrum epistolarum* (*M.G.H.*); P. Hunter Blair, *The World of Bede* (1970), pp. 41–79; H. Mayr-Harting, *The Coming of Christianity to Anglo-Saxon England* (1972), pp. 51–77; R. A. Markus, 'The Chronology of the Gregorian Mission to England', *J.E.H.*, xiv (1963), 16–30; *M.O.*, pp. 750–2; P. Meyvaert, 'Bede's text of the Libellus Responsionum' in *England before the Conquest* (ed. P. Clemoes and K. Hughes, 1971); N. Brooks, *The Early History of the Church of Canterbury* (1984); F. Wormald, *The Gospels of St. Augustine* (1958).

AUGUSTINE OF HIPPO (354–430), bishop and Doctor of the Church. Born at Tagaste (Algeria) of a pagan father and a Christian mother, *Monica, Augustine was brought up as a Christian but not baptized. He studied rhetoric at Carthage to become a lawyer, but gave this up and devoted himself instead to teaching and study. His study of philosophy (mainly Plato) and later of Manichaeism for nine years resulted in his virtual renunciation of the Christian faith; he also lived for fifteen years with a mistress, by whom he had a son, Adeodatus. He moved to Rome to teach rhetoric, then to Milan. By now he was dissatisfied with Manichaeism and came under the influence of *Ambrose. After a long interior conflict, vividly described in his *Confessions*, Augustine was converted and baptized in 386. He returned to Africa in 388, established with some friends a quasi-monastic life (where study and conversation flourished as in his earlier 'school' at Cassiciacum), and was ordained priest in 391. Four years later he became coadjutor-bishop of Hippo; from 396 until his death he ruled the diocese alone.

Augustine's intellectual brilliance, wide education, ardent temperament, and mystical insight formed a personality of extraordinary quality. His understanding of Christian Revelation was shown in his voluminous writings, which have probably proved more influential in the history of thought than any Christian writer since St. *Paul. Most of his writings date from his episcopate. The most famous are the *Confessions*, the sermons on the Gospel and Epistle of John, the *De Trinitate* and, at the end of his life, the *De Civitate Dei.* This work deals with the opposition between Christianity and the 'world' and represents the first Christian philosophy of history. Many other works were occasioned by controversies with Manicheans, Pelagians, or Donatists, which led to the development of his thought on Creation, Grace, the Sacraments, and the Church.

While Augustine's massive influence on Christian thought has mainly been for the good, his teaching on Predestination has been rightly criticized. Although he has always been regarded as the Doctor of Grace, he developed an obsessive concern with the *massa peccati* and the *massa damnata* whch led to a Predestinarian pessimism which consigned unbaptized infants and others to eternal perdition. His teaching on sex and marriage has often been attacked, but in stressing the threefold good of marriage against the Manichees in the form of the family, the sacrament, and fidelity, and showing awareness of the value of companionship and intercourse, his position was more central than that of either *Jerome or Jovinian. The preamble to the marriage service in the B.C.P. is closely based on his thought. But subsequent Christian tradition rejected his view that sexual intercourse is the channel for the transmission of Original Sin or that it is sinful except for the explicit purpose of generation. On the other hand few, if any, Christian writers have written with equal depth on charity and on the Holy Trinity.

Meanwhile, Augustine lived with his clergy a community life and was actively engaged in the administration of church property, in the care of the poor, in preaching and writing, even in acting as judge in civil as well as ecclesiastical cases. As bishop, he was an upholder of order in a time of political strife caused by the disintegration of the Roman Empire. At the time of his death, the Vandals were at the gates of Hippo.

The cult of Augustine was early and widespread. His relics were translated from Sardinia to Pavia by Liutprand, king of the Lombards. The earliest surviving painting of him is in the Lateran library (6th-century fresco), while a 12th-century Canterbury manuscript (now in Florence, MS Pluto 12.17) has a fine frontispiece of him before the text of *De Civitate Dei*. Many Renaissance painters depicted him, such as Botticelli in All Saints Church in Florence, while cycles of paintings of his life survive both at Pavia (by Balduccio and Campione) and at San Gimignano (by Gozzoli) in the church of St. Augustine. Often he was depicted as one of the four Latin Doctors, as by Michael Pacher (1483) in the Brixen altarpiece, now at Munich Alte Pinakothek, and in stained glass at Beauvais cathedral (1551). There are also several English examples in screen paintings and stained glass, while a cycle of scenes from his life is painted on the Carlisle cathedral choir stalls (15th century). Many of his writings had long been known in England; King Alfred had the *Soliloquies* translated into OE in the 9th century. Feast: 28 August.

AA.SS. Aug. VI (1743), 213–460; contemporary Life by Possidius tr. by F. R. Hoare, *The Western Fathers* (1954); H. I. Marrou, *S. Augustin et la fin de la culture antique* (1938); E. Gilson, *Introduction à l'étude de S. Augustin* (1943); Lives by G. Bonner (1963), P. R. L. Brown (1967), D. Bentley-Taylor (1980), and A. Mandouze (1987). Collected works in *P.L.*, xxxii–xlvii and in *C.S.E.L.* (1887–); tr. in *Nicene and Post-Nicene Christian Fathers* (8 vols., 1887–92); particular works, such as the *Confessions* (tr. F. J. Sheed, 1944; H. Chadwick, 1991) and the *City of God* (tr. D. Weldon, 1924). See also C. Andresen, *Bibliographica Augustiniana* (1962) and T. van Bavel, *Répertoire Bibliographique de S. Augustin 1950–1960* (1963); R. A. Markus, *Saeculum* (1970); H. Chadwick, *Augustine* (1986).

AUGUSTINE (Eystein) **OF TRONDHEIM** (d. 1188), archbishop. Born of a noble family, he studied at St. Victor at Paris, returned to Norway and became the king's chaplain. In 1157 he was named archbishop of Nidaros (Trondheim), was consecrated by the pope, and in 1161 he returned with the pallium and with a legateship. This followed on the reorganization of the Church in Scandinavia in 1153 by the English legate (and future pope Adrian IV), whereby Trondheim became metropolitan of ten dioceses, which comprised not only Norway but also the Scandinavian empire of Iceland, Greenland, the Orkneys and Shetlands, with the western islands and Man.

As archbishop he encouraged neglected clerical celibacy by founding Cistercian and Augustinian monasteries and tried to ensure the policies of the Gregorian Reform. This brought him into conflict with the kings. Although he had crowned Magnus as king at Bergen in 1164 at the age of only eight, Augustine was in conflict with the child's successor Sverre, who obliged him to flee the country in 1181. He came to England, residing at the abbey of Bury St. Edmunds and helping them to obtain from Henry II the free election of Abbot Samson. In 1183 he returned to Norway and was reconciled with the king.

This enabled him to undertake the rebuilding of his cathedral, where *Olaf was buried; he employed English architects who built in the Gothic style. Of Olaf he also wrote the account of his passion and miracles, possibly during his stay in England.

Immediately after his death he was considered a saint, but various papal enquiries seem to have been unfinished. The local synod of Nidaros however declared him a saint in 1229 and Matthew Paris, who visited Norway for a few years, referred to his sanctity as being proved by many authentic miracles. Feast: 26 January.

B.T.A., i. 174–5; *H.S.S.C.*, vi, 268–9; S. Undset, *Saga of the Saints* (1934).

AUSTELL (6th century), monk. He was a disciple of *Mewan, probably coming with him from South Wales to Cornwall, and later following him and *Samson into Brittany. Austell founded the church in Cornwall at the town which takes its name from him; he died at S. Méen in Brittany and was buried in the same tomb as Mewan. Feast: 28 June.

Baring-Gould and Fisher, i. 189–90; G. H. Doble, *The Saints of Cornwall*, v (1970), 35–58.

AUXILIARY SAINTS, see FOURTEEN HOLY HELPERS.

AVELLINO, Andrew (1521–1608), Theatine priest and reformer. Born of a wealthy family at Castronuovo (Potenza) in the kingdom of Naples, he studied civil and canon law, was ordained priest and became a prominent advocate in the Church courts. He was ambitious as well as devout, but experienced a conversion *c.*1552 which resulted in his total commitment to the cure of souls and to religious education. He was commissioned to reform a decadent nunnery in 1556, where he met violent resistance, but eventually imposed strict enclosure and other monastic reforms. In the same year he joined the Theatine congregation (founded by *Cajetan) and spent the next fourteen years in their Naples house, becoming in turn novice-master and superior. In 1570 he moved to Milan to found houses there and at Piacenza at the invitation of Charles *Borromeo. Throughout his working life he propagated the decrees of the Council of Trent.

In 1582 he returned to Naples, where he remained for the rest of his life. Not outstanding as organizer or administrator, he excelled as preacher and writer for converting sinners and refuting heresies. Personal charity included forgiveness for the murderer of his nephew and the willingness to take him into his household. He died of apoplexy just before saying Mass, a scene depicted by contemporary painters. Even in lifetime miracles were attributed to him, while after death some of his hair was removed as relics. The blood consequently flowed, as it did when physicians made incisions, and subsequently liquefied like that of *Januarius. The canonization commission rejected the claim that this was miraculous, but judged Andrew worthy to be declared a saint. He was accordingly canonized in 1712. Feast: 10 November.

AA.SS. Nov. IV (1925), 609–23; devotional writings published at Naples in 1733–4, for which see B. Bas, 'Bibliografia di S. Andrea Avellino', *Regnum Dei*, xiv (1958), 303–61; A. Lechat, 'La conversion de S. André Avellin', *Anal. Boll.*, xli (1923), 139–48; B.T.A., iv. 305–6; *Bibl. SS.*, i. 1189–90.

B

BABYLAS (d. *c.*250), bishop of Antioch and martyr. Few details are known about him, although he is reckoned to be Antioch's most famous early bishop after *Ignatius. According to *John Chrysostom he refused the emperor Philip the Arabian entry to the Church in 244 until Philip had done penance for the murder of his predecessor Gordian. Babylas was executed in the persecution of Decius together with three boys whom he had instructed in the Christian faith, traditionally called Urbanus, Prilidianus, and Epolonius. But according to Eusebius he died in prison.

Babylas is the first martyr whose relics are recorded as having been translated, from Antioch to Daphne, in part to counteract the influence of the shrine of Apollo. He is also one of those described in *Aldhelm's treatise *On Virginity*. This helped his cult in England, testified by numerous early calendars. Feast: 24 January, but 4 September in the East.

AA.SS. Ian. II (1643), 569–81 and *Propylaeum*, pp. 33–4; for confusions in the tradition see H. Delehaye, 'Les deux saints Babylas', *Anal. Boll.*, xix (1900), 5–8 and ibid., xlviii (1929), 303–17.

BAITHAN, see BATHAN.

BALDHILD, see BATHILD.

BALDRED (1) (Balther), Northumbrian hermit of the 8th century, who lived at Tyningham and later on the Bass Rock. His Legend attributes to his prayers the removal of a dangerous reef between the Bass Rock and the mainland to its present site where it is known as St. Baldred's Rock. His supposed relics were discovered in the 11th century by Alfred Westow and removed to Durham, where the feasts of Balther and *Billfrith were celebrated on 6 March.

K.S.S., pp. 273–4; B.T.A., i. 502.

BALDRED (2) (early 7th century), bishop, companion, and disciple of St. *Kentigern.

B.T.A., i. 502.

BARAT, Madeleine Sophie (1779–1865), virgin, foundress of the Society of the Sacred Heart. Born at Joigny in Burgundy, the daughter of Jaques Barat, who owned a small vineyard and was a cooper by trade, she was educated largely by her brother Louis, eleven years her senior and a student for the priesthood. He seems to have combined academic ability with a rigour towards his sister both strange and abnormal. In 1793 he was arrested in Paris and imprisoned for two years because he refused to accept the civil constitution of the clergy. Later, when he was released, he continued his sister's education at Paris: Scripture and theology replaced the classics. In 1800, under the direction of l'Abbé Varin, one of a group of priests specially concerned with education, Madeleine was guided away from her intention of becoming a Carmelite lay sister into a new community founded by him for educational work among rich and poor. At the age of twenty-three she was appointed superior and retained this office for the next sixty-three years of her life. This was at Amiens, from which foundations were made at Grenoble and Poitiers in houses formerly occupied by other religious orders, and elsewhere in France and Belgium.

While she was away an attempt was made by a local superior, aided by the chaplain, to undermine her influence and, to some extent, her ideals. But by 1815 this 'palace revolution' had failed and the Society of the Sacred Heart started a period of great expansion, including the first foundations in America under Philippine *Duchesne. This was matched by a general study-plan for all their schools, drawn up at Paris, to ensure uniformity among the diversity of foundations, but the plan was flexible enough to be modifiable every six years, to take account of educational developments. The reputation of her boarding schools was so high that requests for similar ones came from all sides; she also opened day-schools for poor children whenever possible. She became a ceaseless traveller, setting up new houses and visiting old ones in France, Austria, Switzerland, and (in 1844) England.

In character she was remarkable for wisdom, insight, and a tactful prudence which knew when to wait and when to press forward. During her life the Society of the Sacred Heart was at work in eighty-six houses in twelve countries: their influence has been very great in the particular field they have chosen, not least in the English-speaking world. In 1864 Mother Barat wished to resign at the age of eighty-five; instead, a vicaress was appointed to help her. She died on 25 May, which has become her feast day. She was canonized in 1925; her largely incorrupt body rests at Jette (Belgium).

M. Monahan, *Saint Madeleine Sophie* (1925); other Lives by G. de Grandmaison (1909), A. Brou (1925), C. E. Maguire (1960), M. Williams (1965); B.T.A., ii. 392–5.

BARBARA (date unknown). The very existence of this supposed virgin-martyr is doubtful. There is no trace of an ancient cult, although Barbara was alleged to have been killed in the persecution of Maximian (*c.*303). Her Greek Acts, notoriously unhistorical, were not written until the 7th century; even more suspicious, Nicomedia, Heliopolis, Tuscany, and Rome all claimed to be the place of her death. This uncertainty did not prevent her cult becoming very popular in the later Middle Ages, especially in France.

The *Golden Legend* tells of how she was shut up in a tower by her father Dioscorus, so that no man should see her. None the less princes sought her hand in marriage. She became a Christian while her father was away and decided to live as a hermit in a bath-house he had built. Here she made the workmen add a third window in honour of the Holy Trinity. In his fury at her becoming a Christian, he nearly killed her, but she was handed over to a judge who condemned her to death. Her father was struck by lightning and died. This was the basis of her patronage of those in danger of sudden death, first by lightning, and then by subsiding mines or cannon-balls. Hence her patronage of miners and gunners.

The first known representation of her is an 8th-century fresco at S. Maria Antiqua, Rome; she is found, often with the equally mythical *Margaret of Antioch, on late medieval English screens and stained glass. Her usual emblem is a tower. The painting of her by Jan van Eyck in the Royal Museum at Antwerp is probably the most famous representation.

Feast: formerly 4 December, suppressed in the Roman calendar of 1969.

Text of her *Acts* in *P.G.*, cxvi. 301–16 and ed. A. Smith-Lewis in *Studia Sinaitica*, ix (1900), 101–10 and x (1900), 77–84 (Eng. tr.); B. de Gaiffier, 'La légende latine de sainte Barbe par Jean de Wackerzeele', *Anal. Boll.*, lxxvii (1959), 5–41.

BARBARIGO, Gregorio (1625–97), bishop of Padua. Born of a noble family and educated at Venice, he took part in the Congress of Munster (1648), which ended the Thirty Years' War through the Treaty of Westphalia. He was ordained priest in 1655 and worked heroically in the plague of 1657. Then Alexander VII promoted him to the see of Bergamo, made him a cardinal (1660), and transferred him to Padua in 1664.

Barbarigo's many-sided personality was reflected in his diverse achievements. He founded a college and a seminary; he provided a fine patristic library and a printing-press, some of whose products were distributed to Christians in Moslem countries. He also worked hard to secure reunion with the Eastern Churches. His pastoral commitment was comparable to that of Charles *Borromeo and he is said to have given at least 8,000 crowns in charity. As cardinal he took part in five conclaves and was himself considered a serious candidate for the papacy. He died on 15 June and was buried in Padua cathedral. He was beatified in 1761 and canonized in 1960. Feast: 18 June.

Works ed. by P. Uccelli (1879) and more completely by S. Serena (1963). See also C. Bellinati, *S. Gregorio Barbarigo* (1960), and *Pensieri e massime di S. Gregorio* (1962); *N.C.E.*, ii. 88; *Bibl. SS.*, vii. 387–403.

BARLOC (date unknown), hermit; feast kept at St. Werburgh's, Chester on 10 September. He also occurs in a litany in Tanner MS. 169 of the Bodleian Library, Oxford. Nothing is known about him.

E.B.K. after 1100, i. 98.

BARLOW, Ambrose (Edward) (1585–1641), Benedictine monk and martyr. Born, the son of Sir Alexander Barlow, at Barlow Hall (Lancs.) in 1585, Barlow conformed to the Church of England for some years but returned to the Roman Catholic Church in 1607 and entered the English College, Douai. He was imprisoned for unknown causes in England for a few months in 1613; on his release he became a Benedictine monk at St. Gregory's, Douai, was professed in 1614, and ordained priest in 1617. He then returned to England and worked near Manchester and Liverpool for 24 years. His principal base was Morleys Hall, near Leigh. Distinguished for his love of the poor, his wit and kindliness, he is described in a contemporary work which chronicled his long and fruitful apostolate as the man 'most likely to represent the spirit of Sir Thomas *More'. Four times he was imprisoned and four times released, but at last in 1641 he was arrested at Leigh while preaching, imprisoned in Lancaster castle, and tried. Shortly before, Charles I under extreme pressure had ordered all priests to leave the realm or incur the penalties of traitors. Barlow admitted that he was a priest, but said that the decree specified 'Jesuits and seminary priests', whereas he was neither, but a Benedictine monk; in any case, having just suffered a stroke, he was too ill to travel. He was then offered release in exchange for a promise not to 'seduce any more people'. He answered: 'I am no seducer, but a reducer of the people to the true and ancient religion . . . I will continue until death to render this good office to these strayed souls.' He was hanged, drawn, and quartered at Lancaster on 10 September. His skull is preserved at Wardley Hall (Lancs.) and his hand at Stanbrook Abbey (Worcester). He was canonized by Paul VI in 1970 as one of the *Forty Martyrs of England and Wales. Feast: 25 October.

The Apostolical Life of Ambrose Barlow (ed. W. E. Rhodes, Chetham Miscellanies, ii (1909), Chetham Society, vol. lxiii); R. Challoner, *Memoirs of Missionary Priests* (ed. J. H. Pollen 1924), pp. 392–400; B. Camm, *Nine Martyr Monks* (1931): J. Stonor, *Ambrose Barlow* (pamphlet 1961); B.T.A., iii. 535–7; *N.C.E.*, ii. 101.

BARNABAS (first century), apostle. A Jewish Cypriot and a Levite, Barnabas (the name means 'son of consolation') was an early Christian disciple but not one of the Twelve. He introduced *Paul to the other apostles; together Paul and Barnabas were sent to Antioch and undertook the 'first missionary journey' which began in Cyprus. At the council of Jerusalem Barnabas supported the Gentile Christians. Later Barnabas and Paul quarrelled and separated; Barnabas returned to Cyprus and evangelized it. Paul's references to him in Galatians and Corinthians possibly indicate a wider apostolate. However, legend claims he died a martyr at Salamis in 61. Various apocryphal writings were attributed to him.

The Order of Barnabites, founded by Antony *Zaccaria at Milan in 1530, took their name from their principal church, dedicated to Barnabas, once believed to have been Milan's first bishop. In England there were thirteen ancient church dedications and not a few modern ones. His true title to fame is the prominent part he took in the development of the infant Christian Church. Feast: 11 June.

Acts of the Apostles, especially ch. 4–15; *AA.SS.*

Iun. II (1698), 421–60; L. Duchesne, 'Saint Barnabé' in *Mélanges G.B. De Rossi*, pp. 417–71.

BARNIC, see BARRY.

BARNOC, see BRANNOC.

BARRA (Barry), see FINBAR.

BARRUC, see BARRY.

BARRY (Barnic, Barruc) (6th century), hermit. Reputedly a disciple of *Cadoc, he settled on the Glamorgan island now called Barry Island, after him. Barry, according to one tradition, died there. His chapel became a famous pilgrimage centre, mentioned by Leland. Another tradition claims that he was buried at Fowey (Cornwall): this is recorded by William Worcestre. The fact that in both places his feast is on the same day points to there being one St. Barry, not two. Feast: 27 September.

Baring-Gould and Fisher, i. 194–6; William Worcestre, p. 107; Stanton, pp. 460, 671.

BARTHOLOMEW (1st century), apostle. He was thus named by the Synoptic Gospels (the name means 'son of Tolmai'), but the Fourth Gospel speaks of Nathanael, not Bartholomew. The two are generally identified by present-day biblical scholars. Nothing is known for certain about the place of his apostolate or even of his death. Pantenus of Alexandria is said by Eusebius to have found in 'India' during the second half of the 2nd century a Gospel of St. Matthew, written in Hebrew and left behind by Bartholomew. The Roman Martyrology attributes to him an apostolate in India and Armenia, where he was said to have been flayed alive before being beheaded, the place being traditionally Derbend, on the Caspian sea.

His relics were supposed to have been translated first to the island of Lipara, then to Beneventum, and lastly to Rome, where the church of St. Bartholomew on the Tiber still claims them. An arm of St. Bartholomew was given to Canterbury in the 11th century by Cnut's wife, Queen Emma. This was regarded as a sensational acquisition, worth a fortune, and no doubt contributed to the diffusion of the cult in England, as did his appearance in the Life of *Guthlac by Felix. No fewer than 165 ancient churches were dedicated to him in England, including Crowland abbey. The method of his martyrdom appealed to the imagination of artists; his most usual emblem is the flaying-knife. By association with his own fate, he is regarded as the patron saint of tanners and all who work at skins. Feast: 24 August (Epternach and Cambrai 25 August; Persia 13 June).

AA.SS. Aug. V (1741), 7–108; B.T.A., iii. 391–2; G. F. Warner, *The Guthlac Roll* (Roxburghe Club 1928); see also E. Mâle, *Rome et ses vieilles églises* (1942), and Réau, iii. 180–4.

BARTHOLOMEW OF FARNE (d. 1193), monk and hermit. Born at Whitby of Scandinavian parents and called Tostig until he changed his name to William to avoid the ridicule it had caused, he was somewhat dissolute in his youth. But the first change in his life resulted in his refusing marriage, going to Norway, and becoming a priest there. He returned to England and spent three years in parochial ministry. In the late 1140s he became a monk at Durham and took the name Bartholomew: while he was a novice he had a vision of Christ on the Rood inclining his head towards him and stretching out his arms to embrace him. Soon after his profession he went as a hermit to the island of the Inner Farne, made famous by *Cuthbert. There he remained, except for short intervals, for his remaining forty-two years.

He practised with extraordinary perseverance the privations and penances customary to hermits, made much more arduous by the exposed site and the stormy weather. A rugged individualist, he found it difficult to live with others. A hermit called Aelwin, in possession at his arrival, soon left. Years later, the island was shared with the ex-prior Thomas, but the two could not agree about the quantity and duration of their meals. This time Bartholomew withdrew to Durham for a time; but they came to an agreement and lived afterwards in amity.

Bartholomew's more endearing traits

included continual cheerfulness, love of fishing, his fondness for his pet bird, and his generosity to his many visitors. No respecter of persons, he reproved the rich and powerful, who were sometimes so struck by his venerable presence that they abandoned oppression and took to alms-giving instead. A Flemish woman, a friend in his early life, visited him and was indignant at being refused admission to the chapel, complaining that she was treated like a dog. But when she attempted to set foot in it, she was thrown on her back 'as if by a whirlwind'. She recovered only at Bartholomew's intervention.

He passed his days in prayer and work, striding over the island, singing psalms in his splendid voice, reading and writing, milking his cow, and tending his crops. Eventually he was stricken by a painful illness with an internal abscess. Not long before his death he carved for himself a stone sarcophagus, possibly identical with the one still there, just outside the chapel where he used to pray. He experienced other visions, and miracles were reported at his tomb. His cult seems to have been confined to Durham and North-east England. Feast: 24 June.

Contemporary Life by Geoffrey of Durham in *Symeonis Dunelmensis Opera* (ed. T. Arnold, *R.S.*, 1882), i. 295–325; *AA.SS.* Iun. V (1727), 713–21; *N.L.A.*, i. 101–6.

BASIL THE GREAT (*c.*330–79), bishop of Caesarea, Doctor of the Church. He was a theologian of distinction, a monastic founder, and a diocesan bishop of extraordinary ability. He was born of a distinguished and pious family: his grandmother *Macrina the Elder, his mother and father, his sister *Macrina the Younger, his brothers *Gregory of Nyssa and Peter of Sebaste were all saints. Basil enjoyed the best education available, at Caesarea, Constantinople, and Athens. Here he became a close friend of the future saint *Gregory of Nazianzus. Basil became a monk, for a short while in Syria and Egypt, and then settled (*c.*358) as a hermit near Neo-Caesarea. Here too he enjoyed the company of Gregory; together they preached to the people as well as practising a life of contemplation. Julian the Apostate, another university friend, invited him to court. Basil refused: he left his solitude only in 364, when his bishop Eusebius of Caesarea called him to defend the Church against the persecution of the Arian emperor Valens.

He became bishop of Caesarea in 370. As such, he was also exarch of Pontus and metropolitan of fifty suffragans. The principal problem he faced was heterodoxy, both Arian and semi-Arian, with strong imperial support. Against these he opposed sound theology, vindicated after his death in the Council of Constantinople (381), combined with strong personal independence of, and even opposition to, the civil power. Like *Ambrose, Basil was regarded in later centuries as a champion of the Church's liberty against secular encroachments. But he did not neglect his people. Just before his consecration as bishop he had been conspicuous during a famine for distributing his inheritance to the poor and he organized a soup kitchen where he served out food to the hungry. As bishop he built a new town called the Basiliad, which included a church, a hospital, and a guest-house with the necessary doctors, nurses, and artisans. He would preach both morning and evening to vast congregations and organized services of psalms before daybreak. His extensive correspondence reveals other aspects of his pastoral care: the proper selection of candidates for Orders, the reform of thieves and prostitutes, the correction of ecclesiastics too closely involved in politics or simony, and of secular officials too severe in their judgements. Even more important, he advised his nephews to make full use, as he had himself done, of classical literature to prepare their minds for a deeper understanding of the Christian revelation. Unlike many other Christians, before and since, Basil was firmly on the side of a catholic, inclusive Christian outlook, which integrated all that was best in the secular culture, especially the philosophy, of the day:

without such leaders, Christian theology could have made but little progress.

Basil is also the principal monastic legislator of the East: to this day, nearly all monks and nuns of the Greek Church follow his rule. This survives in two redactions: *Regulae fusius tractatae* and *Regulae brevius tractatae*. His emphasis was on community life, liturgical prayer, and manual work rather than on individualist feats of asceticism. The rule was sufficiently flexible to allow for the development of almsgiving, hospitals, and guest-houses in which the monks worked, while it also avoided the dangers of activism by a strong contemplative emphasis.

His most important doctrinal writings are the treatise on the Holy Spirit, and the books against Eunomius. His *Philocalia* is a selection from Origen's writings. Although a champion of orthodoxy, Basil was sometimes attacked for his theological views: unlike *Athanasius, he did not enjoy the unqualified support of the papacy. In the complex matter of the Antioch succession Pope *Damasus refused to recognize Basil's candidate and friend Meletius, which led to considerable friction. His long struggle against Arianism and its political dominance was completed by the succession of Gratian as emperor on the death of the Arian Valens in battle in 378. The news reached him shortly before his death on 1 January at the age of forty-nine, when he was worn out by austerities, hard work, and disease.

The best evidence for Basil's many-sided greatness comes from his numerous letters and from the mourning, even by pagans and strangers, at his death. Eastern artists were prolific in representations of him, particularly with other Eastern Doctors such as *John Chrysostom and Gregory of Nazianzus. In Rome there are fine paintings of the 8th and 9th centuries and there is a notable 12th-century mosaic at Cefalu (Sicily). His cult spread rapidly in the West, partly through Greek monks in Italy and partly through *Benedict's recognition in his Rule of the inspiration of 'our holy father Basil'.

Feast in the West: formerly 14 June (his day of consecration), but since 1969 on 2 January with St. Gregory Nazianzen; feast in the East: 1 January.

AA.SS. Iun. II (1698), 807–959; W. K. L. Clarke, *St. Basil the Great* (1913); M. M. Fox, *Life and Times of St. Basil* (1939); G. L. Prestige, *St. Basil the Great and Apollinaris of Laodicea* (1956); works in *P.G.*, xxix–xxxii, versions in Loeb Class. Library (1926–34) and *S.C.* (1947–).

BASILIDES (date unknown), martyr. He died at Rome, perhaps in the late 3rd century and was buried about four miles outside the town on the Via Aurelia. He was venerated in Roman calendars; later he was associated with Cyrinus (= Quirinus), Nabor, and Nazarius in the Gelasian Sacramentary, possibly through a confusion of the martyrologists. It is likely that Nabor and Nazarius were Milanese. But all were venerated together, for unknown reasons, on 12 June, until 1969, when their feast was suppressed owing to its being a confusion of three different groups of martyrs, associated through unhistorical Acts.

AA.SS. Iun. II (1698), 505–15 with *C.M.H.*, pp. 315–16; *Calendarium Romanum* (1969).

BATHAN (Baithan, Bothanus), saint or saints who have been associated with place-names in Shetland and elsewhere in Scotland. Bathan, one of the addressees of a letter of Pope John IV (640) on the Easter question and the danger of Pelagianism, and described as a bishop, may well have been abbot of Bangor. A Bothanus, bishop of Dunblane, was commemorated on 18 January. Parishes of St. Bathan are found in Berwickshire and East Lothian; parishes of Bowden, Bothwell, and Ballebodan are more or less plausibly associated with a saint of this name.

K.S.S., pp. 265–6.

BATHILD (Baldhild) (d. 680), wife of Clovis II. An Anglo-Saxon slave girl who was sold into the household of the mayor of the imperial palace, Erchinoald, Bathild attracted the notice of King Clovis by her ability and beauty. In 649 they were married and had three sons, Clotaire III, Childeric II, and Thierry III. In 657 Clovis died and Bathild acted as regent, as her eldest son was only five. She founded the monasteries of Corbie and Chelles, promoted the work of *Ouen, *Leger, and others, and was especially zealous in suppressing the slave-trade and redeeming those already captured. After a palace revolution in 665 she was removed to her nunnery at Chelles where, according to her Legend, she served the other nuns and was extraordinarily obedient to the abbess. Eddius' Life of *Wilfrid unexpectedly describes her as a Jezebel for causing the assassination of ten French bishops, but almost certainly Eddius got the name wrong. Chelles was a convent destined to have notable contacts with Anglo-Saxon England: several of the more famous English nuns were trained there. Bathild, a rare example of extreme social mobility among the Anglo-Saxons, had a cult stronger in France than in Britain. She is represented in art as a crowned nun; predictably a ladder to heaven, implying the pun *échelle-Chelles*, is her emblem. Feast: 30 January, but in *R.M.* (following Usuard) on 26 January.

AA.SS. Ian. III (1643), 347–64; Life in *M.G.H. Scriptores rerum merov.* (ed. B. Krusch), ii. 475–508; references in the Life of St. Ouen, ibid., iv. 634–761; W. Levison, *England and the Continent in the Eighth Century* (1946); E. Vacandard, *Vie de Saint Ouen* (1902).

BAVO (Allowin) (d. *c.*655), hermit. A native of Brabant, Bavo was married and after the death of his wife was converted through the preaching of *Amand. He then joined the monastery at Ghent, subsequently named after him, and resolved to make expiation for past misdeeds. After joining Amand on some missionary journeys in France and Flanders he became a hermit, living for a time in a tree until he built himself a cell at Mendonck. Later he returned to Ghent and lived as a hermit on the monastic estate for the rest of his life. He is patron of the dioceses of Ghent and Haarlem (Holland); his feast was kept in the Sarum calendar as well as in his native country. Feast: 1 October.

AA.SS. Oct. I (1765), 198–303; earliest Life also in B. Krusch, *M.G.H. Scriptores rerum merov.* iv. 527–46; modern Life by R. Podevijn (1945); M. Coens, 'S. Bavon était-il évêque?', *Anal. Boll.*, lxiii (1945), 220–41; B.T.A., iv. 5–6.

BAYLON, Paschal (1540–92), Franciscan laybrother. Born at Torre Hermosa (Aragon) of a poor shepherd family, Paschal tended the flocks as a youth while also acquiring elementary education and religious awareness. As soon as he could (*c.*1564), he joined the reformed Friars Minor of *Peter of Alcantara at the convent of Loreto, where the austerity and charity were exemplary. With perpetual good humour Paschal cared for the sick and the poor. Once he shut himself in the refectory, where he was observed by another friar executing an elaborate dance before the statue of Our Lady like a latter-day *Jongleur de Notre Dame*. His devotion to Mass and the Blessed Sacrament are even better known. He would remain in deep mystical prayer before the tabernacle day after day, and would then serve one Mass after another in the early morning.

Once he was sent to France to carry important letters to the Breton Minister-General. On his way he was roughly handled by Huguenots who stoned him twice. He reached his destination but the effects of his injuries were felt for the rest of his life. He returned safely but died at the age of fifty-two in the friary of Villareal. Many cures and miracles were reported at his tomb, where also repeated knockings (*golpes*) took place, which continued at intervals for 200 years. He was beatified in 1618 and canonized in 1690. He is patron of Eucharistic devotions and congresses. Feast: 17 May.

AA.SS. Maii IV (1866), 48–131; Lives by V. Facchinetti (1922) and A. Groeteken (1929). See also B.T.A., ii. 333–7; *Bibl. SS.*, x. 358–64.

BEAN (1) (Mo-Bioc), Irish saint of Wexford, Lough Derg, or Galway, perhaps a lakeside hermit. Feast: 16 December.

BEAN (2), first bishop of Morthlach in Banff, the forerunner of the diocese of Aberdeen, in the 11th century. Feast generally, but owing to a confusion with another Bean, on 26 October. Bean is believed to have lived at Balvanie.

The two saints have often been confused; see *Propylaeum*, s.d. 16 December.

BEATRICE (more correctly Viatrix), see SIMPLICIUS, FAUSTINUS, AND BEATRICE.

BECCELIN, see BETTELIN (1).

BECKET, Thomas, see THOMAS OF CANTERBURY.

BEDE, THE VENERABLE (673–735), monk of Jarrow, biblical scholar, and first English historian. Born near Sunderland on lands afterwards owned by his monastery, Bede was educated from the age of seven, first by *Benedict Biscop at Wearmouth and then by *Ceolfrith at Jarrow, where he was a monk for the rest of his life. Ordained priest *c.*703, he devoted himself to the study of Scripture 'amid the observance of monastic discipline and the daily charge of singing in church', as he himself related, and his 'special delight was always to learn, to teach, and to write'. His impressive range of writings included works on orthography, metre, computistics, and chronology as well as lives of the saints. In his own view his 25 works of Scripture commentary were his most important, but many scholars regard his *Ecclesiastical History of the English People* (*H.E.*), finished in 731, as his most significant.

His life was externally uneventful. Apparently he travelled little, probably never outside Northumbria. He was little acquainted with courts and kings, being continually occupied with monastic duties and with his writing, made possible by the acquisition of books by Benedict Biscop and Ceolfrith, whose achievements he praised in his *Lives of the Abbots*. At the end of his life he showed himself remarkably well-informed about the Church in Northumbria; in his *Letter to Egbert* (735) he made a number of shrewd suggestions for its reform, which were not all carried out.

A moving contemporary account of his death by the monk Cuthbert survives. This reveals the veneration felt for him by his disciples and describes how he spent his last days, singing the psalms, working on his translation into Old English of the Gospel of *John and some extracts from *Isidore. Knowing he was soon to die, Bede pressed forward with his translation and finished it, dictating the last sentence to the boy who was his scribe. He also sang antiphons from the Divine Office, especially that from Ascension Day, as well as a vernacular poem about death. He died singing 'Glory be to the Father and to the Son and to the Holy Ghost'.

When news of his death reached the Anglo-Saxon missionaries, who knew and used his homely Scripture commentaries, *Boniface wrote that 'the candle of the Church, lit by the Holy Spirit, was extinguished'. His History also was widely known and appreciated from the 8th century onwards, on the Continent as well as in England. It became a classic and has been frequently translated, not least in the 20th century. Its wealth of information, its listing of authorities, its sifting of evidence, and its coherent synthesis of disparate and fragmentary sources have always appealed to scholars who, however, have not been blind to its limitations. Bede's moral qualities of modesty, humility, and disinterestedness are also apparent in his writings.

His cult as a saint was established within fifty years of his death. Alcuin claimed that his relics had worked miraculous cures. Fulda, as well as York, possessed relics of Bede in the crypt where Boniface was buried. In the 10th century Glastonbury also claimed some of his relics, but his bones were translated from Jarrow to Durham by Alfred Westow in the mid-11th century. These were translated again to the Galilee chapel of Durham Cathedral in 1370 where they rest to this day: they have some chance of being authentic. Durham and York are the main centres of his cult.

There are no extant ancient dedications to Bede in England, although William of Malmesbury described *Wulfstan of Worcester dedicating one church in his honour; there are, however, a number of modern dedications, especially of schools. Bede's life has been an inspiration to many generations of monastic scholars as well as to historians of widely different backgrounds. Several surviving medieval books have at one time or another been claimed to have been used by Bede or written in his hand. A Greek and Latin copy of the *Acts of the Apostles*, which survives in the Bodleian Library, Oxford, was almost certainly his. The Leningrad manuscript of his *Ecclesiastical History*, which is very early, contains an ancient colophon, but this was not written, as is sometimes claimed, in his own hand.

Dante, impressed by the wide diffusion of Bede's works (not least in the Breviary), named him in the *Paradiso*; centuries later, in 1899, Pope Leo XIII gave Bede the title of Doctor of the Church. Feast: originally 26 May (as in eight south English calendars before 1100), but generally 27 May (to avoid a clash with the feast of *Augustine of Canterbury); since 1969 it is on 25 May in the Roman calendar.

AA.SS. Maii VI (1690), 718–23; works ed. J. A. Giles (12 vols., 1843–4) with tr. from Paris edn. of 1521, reprinted in *P.L.*, xc-xcv; critical edn. in *Corpus Christianorum* (1955–); edns. of *H.E.* by C. Plummer (1896), B. Colgrave and R. A. B. Mynors (1970), L. Sherley-Price and D. H. Farmer (1990); studies by A. H. Thompson (ed.), *Bede; his Life, Times and Writings* (1935); P. Hunter Blair, *The World of Bede* (1970); G. Bonner (ed.), *Famulus Christi* (1976); B. Ward, *The Venerable Bede* (1990). Studies of Bede as historian by J. Campbell, 'Bede' in *Latin Historians* (ed. T. A. Dorey) and by B. Colgrave, D. Whitelock, and others in the series *Jarrow Lectures* (1960–). See also J. F. Webb and D. H. Farmer, *The Age of Bede* (1983); symposium 'Bede and his World', *Peritia*, iii (1984), 1–130.

BEGA (7th century), legendary Irish nun who lived at, and gave her name to, St. Bees (Cumbria). At her hermitage shrine was kept a bracelet, whose OE name *beag* so closely resembled hers that some suspect it gave rise to the cult. See BEGU below.

BEGU (d. 660), Anglo-Saxon nun of Hackness (N. Yorkshire) who, according to *Bede, saw in a vision the death of *Hilda, the foundress of both Whitby and Hackness. In *c.*1125 the Whitby monks, short of relics of local saints owing to the translation of Hilda to Glastonbury and the lack of interest in *Caedmon, found at Hackness a sarcophagus, supposedly by revelation, which was inscribed *Hoc est sepulchrum Begu*. The relics in it were translated to Whitby, where miracles were reported, but another set of miracles was claimed by St. Bees, one of whose monks wrote this account of the Whitby translation. The two saints, the Irish Bega and the Yorkshire Begu, were thenceforth confidently identified. The lack of literary survivals of the Whitby cult is notable. Feast: 31 October.

Life of Bega in *Registrum Prioratus de sancta Bega* (*S.S.* 1915), pp. 497–520; Stanton, pp. 519–20, 678.

BELLARMINE, Robert (1542–1621), Jesuit, archbishop of Capua, and cardinal. Born at Montepulciano (Tuscany), he became skilled in writing Latin verse, playing the violin, and speaking in debates. In 1560 he became a Jesuit, taught classics in Florence and Piedmont for several years, and was ordained priest at Ghent in 1570. He then lectured on Aquinas' *Summa Theologica* at Louvain, attacking the opinions of Baius on grace and freewill, and wrote a Hebrew grammar. In 1576 he was appointed professor of 'controversial theology' at the Roman College: his lectures were the basis of his famous *Disputations on the Controversies of the Christian Faith*. This work was a complete defence of Catholic teaching, which was so learned in Scripture, the Fathers, and Protestant theology that it was wrongly believed to be the work of a team of scholars. It had instant success, even in England, where it was banned by the Government. Other projects in which he was prominent included the revision of the Vulgate, the production of a catechism, which remained in frequent use for 300 years, and the recognition of Henry of Navarre as king of France.

He became Rector of the Roman College in 1592, provincial of Naples in 1594, and cardinal in 1598. This did not prevent him from continuing his former austerities such as living on bread and garlic, or from using the curtains of his apartment to clothe the poor. In 1602 he became archbishop of Capua: immediately he took a prominent share of pastoral and welfare work.

He resigned his see when he was recalled to Rome in 1605 to become Prefect of the Vatican Library and an active member of several Roman Congregations. His moderate views on the temporal power of the papacy lost him the favour of Sixtus V and may have delayed his canonization; but they were vindicated by later theologians. He was sympathetic to Galileo, but recommended caution to him and the need to distinguish hypothesis from proved truth.

In his old age Bellarmine withdrew from controversy and wrote books of devotion: he died at the age of seventy-nine on 17 September. Physically very small, Bellarmine had great powers of intellect and sympathy. He used to pray daily for the Protestant theologians (including King James I), whom he opposed, but never made personal, vituperative attacks on them. He was canonized in 1930 and named a Doctor of the Church in 1931. Feast: 17 September, formerly 13 May.

Works published at Cologne (1617–21) and Rome (1942–50); Lives by J. Fuligatti (1624), D. Bartoli (1678), and X. M. Le Bachelet (1911); also by J. Broderick, *Robert Bellarmine, Saint and Scholar* (1961), superseding his earlier study (1928). See also E. A. Ryan, *The Historical Scholarship of St. Bellarmine* (1936) and A. Bernier, *Un cardinal humaniste* (1939).

BENEDICT (*c.*480–*c.*550), abbot and founder of Subiaco and Monte Cassino, author of the Rule which bears his name, Patriarch of Western Monasticism; Patron of Europe. Little is known about his life, Book II of *Gregory's *Dialogues* being the only source. He was born at Nursia, and studied at Rome, which he left before completing his studies to become a hermit at Subiaco. After a time disciples joined him, whom he organized into twelve deaneries of ten and whose life was probably semi-eremitical in character. He encountered acute local jealousy *c.*525, which was said to have caused an attempt on his life. Whatever the reason, he left for Monte Cassino, near Naples, and there wrote the final version of his Rule. This incorporated much traditional monastic teaching from *Cassian, *Basil, and (very probably) the Rule of the Master, whose enactments, however, were often much modified by Benedict. His outlook was characterized by prudence and moderation realized within a framework of authority, obedience, stability, and community life.

His achievement was to produce a monastic way of life which was complete, orderly, and workable. The monks' primary occupation was liturgical prayer, complemented by sacred reading and manual work of various kinds. Benedict's own personality is mirrored in his description of what kind of man the abbot should be: wise, discreet, flexible, learned in the law of God, but also a spiritual father to his community. Gregory's *Dialogues* also attributed to him on occasion second sight and the gift of miracles. Benedict was not a priest, nor did he intend to 'found a religious Order'. His principal achievement was to write a Rule. This, both by its intrinsic qualities and by the external favour granted it by emperors and other rulers and founders, came to be recognized as the fundamental, almost the only, monastic code of western Europe in the early Middle Ages. Its flexibility enabled it to be adapted to the needs of society, so that monasteries became centres of learning, agriculture, hospitality, and medicine in a way presumably unforeseen by Benedict himself. The definitive history of the diffusion of the Rule has yet to be written: although it is very uncertain whether

*Augustine of Canterbury knew or followed it, it can safely be asserted that Englishmen such as *Wilfrid, *Willibrord, and especially *Boniface were prominent in the process. Although it was known and diffused in Gaul in the 6th–7th centuries, it obtained its predominant place in the Empire when imperial decrees (inspired by Boniface) made it obligatory in 743, 754, and 757. In Italy it seems to have been little known outside Monte Cassino until the 10th century, when Cluny reformed monasteries at Rome and elsewhere.

At first the cult of Benedict seems to have been limited in extent, but it became much more widespread under Cluniac influence. From the 7th century Fleury claimed to possess Benedict's relics, a claim which was, and is, indignantly resisted by Monte Cassino. In England the earliest clear calendar evidence for his feast comes from the 10th century.

The most notable representations of Benedict include a fresco in the crypt of St. Chrysogonus, Rome (10th century); an illustrated manuscript of his Life from Monte Cassino (11th century); a series of historiated stone capitals in the narthex of the basilica at Fleury (11th–12th century); some fine frescoes at Subiaco (13th century), and in the sacristy of San Miniato, Florence, by Spinello Aretino (1387). All these illustrate episodes from the second book of Gregory's *Dialogues*, which was very widely diffused; it was translated into OE by Bishop Werferth. Benedict's best-known iconographical attributes are a broken cup (which contained poison) and a raven which removed it at his bidding; he is also depicted wearing a monastic cowl and holding either the Rule or (less appealingly) a rod for corporal punishment.

Feast: formerly 21 March (the day of his death); translation, 11 July (and in France, 4 December). Since 1969 the Roman calendar has moved his feast permanently to be outside Lent on 11 July.

AA.SS. Mar. III (1668), 274–357; St. Gregory, *Dialogi*, *P.L.*, lxxvii. 149–430; critical edn. by A. de Vogüé (*S.C.* 1978–80); I. Herwegen, *St. Benedict* (Eng. tr. 1924); C. Butler, *Benedictine Monachism* (1924); J. Chapman, *St. Benedict and the Sixth Century* (1929); J. McCann, *St. Benedict* (1937); *M.O.*, pp. 3–30, 749–51; for the Rule, critical editions by C. Butler (2nd edn. 1935), R. Hanslik (1960), A. de Vogüé (*S.C.*, 1972–77), T. Fry (1980); facsimile editions by G. Morin (1900), and D. H. Farmer (1968, of the oldest existing copy of the Rule, Oxford, Bodleian Library, Hatton 48); tr. by J. McCann (1951) and D. Parry (1980); M. D. Knowles, *Great Historical Enterprises* (1963); also *S. Benedicti Regulae Studia*, i (1971); D. H. Farmer (ed.), *Benedict's Disciples* (1980).

BENEDICT BISCOP (628–89), founder and first abbot of Wearmouth, scholar, and patron of the arts. He was born of a noble Northumbrian family, and, as Biscop Baducing (his family name), was in the service of the Northumbrian king Oswiu until 653. He then decided to become a monk, but went first with *Wilfrid to Rome to visit the tombs of the apostles. He returned to Northumbria and soon took Alcfrith, son of Oswiu, back to Rome on his second visit. Biscop became a monk at Saint-Honorat, Lérins, on his way back, taking the name of Benedict. His third visit to Rome coincided with the presence of Wighard, archbishop-elect of Canterbury, who died in Rome before consecration. Biscop returned to England with *Theodore of Canterbury in 669, becoming abbot of St. Augustine's, Canterbury, for a short time.

Soon he wanted to make his own foundation: with the help of King Egfrith, who gave him seventy hides of land, he founded Wearmouth in 674. Within a year he had imported Frankish stonemasons who built a Romanesque church there; soon afterwards he brought in glassmakers and other craftsmen, who not only made what was necessary, but also taught local men. Books bought at Rome and Vienne were added to the endowment. He drew up a rule for his community, based on that of *Benedict and the customs of seventeen monasteries he had visited.

Soon after he visited Rome for the fifth time (679). He returned with an 'innumerable collection of books of all kinds', with relics, calendars, and service books, but above all with John, the archcantor of St. Peter's, Rome, and abbot of St. Martin's basilican monastery there, who taught the monks by word and writing the Roman liturgy and uncial script; Pope Agatho used his visit to assure himself also of the orthodoxy of the English Church. Other treasures brought by Benedict included a series of pictures (possibly on boards) of Gospel scenes, of Our Lady and the Apostles, and of incidents in the Apocalypse, to be set up in the church; and a privilege which ensured to Wearmouth the special protection of the Holy See.

In 682 Benedict founded the monastery of Jarrow with the help of Egfrith, who provided an estate of forty hides; Benedict provided twenty-two monks under *Ceolfrith. It was dedicated to St. Paul and was intended to be a sister monastery to St. Peter's, Wearmouth. In 685 Biscop made his last visit to Rome, returning with even more books and sacred images with some fine silk cloaks of exceptional workmanship, exchanged with the king for three hides of land. By this time Biscop had delegated the abbacy of Wearmouth first to *Eosterwine and then to *Sigfrid: Ceolfrith was abbot of Jarrow. But he retained a founder's interest in both. He and Sigfrid were stricken with paralysis at about the same time. Biscop's final address to his community included exhortations to keep to his eclectic rule, to keep his library together in good repair, and to elect an abbot for his manner of life and his teaching, according to the Rule of St. Benedict, rather than for his membership of a particular family; in particular, he would prefer his monastery to become a wilderness than that his own brother should succeed him as abbot. In the event Ceolfrith was his successor. Biscop's library made possible the achievements of *Bede; in script and iconography he brought England into contact with the best contemporary work on the Continent. Proof of a very early public cult of Biscop comes from a sermon of Bede on him (Homily 17) for his feast, but the cult became more widespread only after the translation of his relics to Thorney under *Ethelwold *c.*980. Glastonbury also, with less reason, claimed to possess his relics. His feast is kept on 12 January, but in different places and through various historical errors, such as confusing him with Benedict of Nursia, other days have also been assigned to him.

Contemporary Lives in *Baedae Opera Historica* (ed. C. Plummer, 1956), i. 364–404 and ii. 355–77; J. F. Webb and D. H. Farmer, *The Age of Bede* (1983); *G.P.*, pp. 328–9; *E.B.K. before 1100*; P. Hunter Blair, *The World of Bede* (1970); M. L. W. Laistner, *Thought and Letters in Western Europe* (1966); P. Meyvaert, 'Bede and the church paintings at Wearmouth–Jarrow', *Anglo-Saxon England*, viii (1980), 63–78.

BENEDICT LABRE, see Labre, B. J.

BENEDICT OF ANIANE (750–821), abbot. Born of a noble family, the son of Aigulf of Maguelone, Benedict served the emperors Pepin and Charlemagne at court. At the age of twenty, he experienced a conversion and became a monk at Saint-Seine, near Dijon. After about three years, seeking a more solitary life, he became a hermit on his own estate by the river Aniane. Here he was joined by other hermits: they worked in the fields and at other remunerative manual labour, as well as at copying books. Their food was reputed to be bread and water only except on Sundays and feasts. Extreme poverty and solitude were prominent at this stage of his monastic life, but both were somewhat modified later.

Monasteries in the empire had suffered from the twin evils of lay ownership and Viking attacks which had caused decay both internal and external. Emperors of the 8th and 9th centuries had legislated in favour of the Rule of St. Benedict as the fundamental and stable code of monastic life throughout their dominions. As *Boniface had co-operated with Carloman and Pepin, so did Benedict with Louis the Pious. All were concerned that monastic reform should be effective and permanent: to ensure this, legislation was made at the council of Aachen in 817, presided over by Benedict, who was by then established a few miles away from the emperor's court as abbot of Inde, afterwards called Cornelimunster. Already he had become prominent in the reform of many monasteries in the neighbourhood. His life-work, his biographer said, was to restore the Rule of St. Benedict in the whole kingdom of the Franks.

The legislation emphasized the fundamental guidelines of the Rule of St. Benedict, stressing individual poverty and chastity with obedience to a properly constituted abbot who was himself a monk. Under imperial pressure for uniformity in food, drink, clothing, and the Divine Office (which could be compared with Charlemagne's insistence on the Roman Rite), there was also some attempt (often exaggerated by commentators) to impose uniformity of monastic observance in less important details. Some of these were abandoned in Benedict's quest for peaceful and orderly acceptance of substantial reforms. These were summarized in the *Capitula* of Aachen which were attached to the Rule and made obligatory throughout the empire. In practice, however, complete uniformity was, at this time and given the diverse origins of many monasteries, unrealizable.

Benedict's reforms, however, substantially and permanently affected Benedictine life. He rightly insisted on its liturgical character, developed in a daily conventual Mass and, to meet benefactors' demands, by substantial additions to the basic monastic office, but he also stressed the clerical element in monasticism which led to the development of teaching and writing as opposed to 'servile' manual work, regarded as more suitable for the serfs tied to the lands given to the monasteries. His influence can be seen in the reforms of Cluny, Gorze, and in 10th-century England, where similar legislation was attempted by *Dunstan and *Ethelwold at Winchester.

Benedict's works include the *Codex Regularum* (a collection of monastic rules from East and West, beginning with *Basil's) and the *Concordia Regularum* (which assembles texts of other monastic Fathers to illustrate the text of the Rule of St. Benedict). Like his patron and namesake, Benedict of Aniane had turned away from a very austere eremitical life to a more moderate community monasticism in which there was a place for art, learning, and the sanctification of property in endowment for splendid architecture. Benedict, worn out by continual sickness in his last years, died at Inde. Feast: 11 February.

Life by his disciples Ardo in *M.G.H.* Scriptores xv (part i), 198–220, also with Benedict's writings in *P.L.*, ciii. 353–1440. Decrees of the synod of Aachen in K. Hallinger, *Corpus Consuetudinum Monasticarum*, i (1963), 451–81. J. Winandy, 'L'Oeuvre monastique de saint Benoît d'Aniane' in *Mélanges bénédictins* (1947), 235–58; P. Schmitz, 'L'influence de saint Benoît d'Aniane dans l'histoire de l'ordre de saint Benoît' in *Settimano di Studio . . . sull 'Alto Medioevo*, iv (1957), 401–15 and W. Williams, 'St. Benedict of Aniane' in *Downside Review*, liv (1936), 357–74; *M.O.*, 25–30.

BENEZET OF AVIGNON (*c.*1163–84), bridge-builder. A shepherd boy who was born at Hermillon in Savoy, he came to Avignon *c.*1178, where he was told in a vision to build a bridge over the river Rhone. First he met with incredulity from the bishop, but he made a start with some lay helpers and eventually won the bishop's support. By the time of his death the bridge was not yet complete, but it was finished a few years later. A chapel was built on it, inside which Benezet's body was buried. There it remained for nearly 500 years until in 1669, when part of the bridge was washed away, his coffin was recovered and his body was found to be incorrupt. It was subsequently translated to Avignon cathedral and in the 19th century to the Celestines' church of Saint Didier.

Contemporary evidence records the principal episodes of Benezet's life, into which an episcopal enquiry was made in 1230. From 1189 the guild of Bridge Brothers claimed him as their patron; so too did the town of Avignon. Feast: 14 April.

Documents in *AA.SS.* April. II (1675), 255–64;

H.S.S.C., vi. 269; B.T.A., ii. 93–4; *Bibl. SS.*, ii, 1099–1100.

BENIGNUS OF DIJON (2nd century), martyr. The Roman Martyrology declared him a disciple of *Polycarp, who was sent to evangelize Gaul and was put to the sword in the persecution of Marcus Aurelius. Others say that he died under Aurelian. *Gregory of Tours describes the grave at Dijon, identified in a dream as the burial-place of Benignus. After this a *Passio S. Benigni* was brought by pilgrims from Rome: in its present form, edited at Dijon, it seems worthless, like the Acts of other so-called apostles of Gaul. In reality Benignus might have been an early missionary from Lyons. Feast: 1 November.

L. Duchesne, *Fastes Episcopaux*, i. 51–62.

BENILD (1805–62), De la Salle brother. Born at Thuret (Puy-de-Dôme), Pierre Romançon was educated by the De la Salle brothers at Riom. In 1825 he joined their novitiate at Clermont-Ferrand. Given the unusual name of Benildus, he excelled both in teaching and in cooking. Only two years after his profession he was made superior of the community and school at Billom (Puy-de-Dome). Strict but fair, he made everyone work hard but also gave special encouragement to the backward.

In 1841 he was entrusted with the foundation of Saugues (Haute-Loire), where he spent the rest of his life. Like their other houses, this one provided free instruction as well as religious training, together with evening classes for adults. Benild's *forte* was religious education: his classes were followed with rapt attention. One effect of his teaching was that numerous former pupils joined the Brothers.

In 1861, after several years suffering from a hidden illness, he was struck by exceptionally severe rheumatism. He never really recovered, but prepared for death, which took place the following year. He was beatified in 1848 and canonized in 1967. Feast: 13 August.

Lives by J. Rigault (1947) and F. G. (1948); see also B.T.A., iii. 325–7; *Bibl. SS.*, ii. 1237–8.

BENIZI, Philip (1233–85), Servite friar. Born at Florence, he was educated at the universities of Paris and Padua, where he took doctorates in medicine and philosophy. Philip joined the principal house at Monte Senario as a lay brother and worked in the garden from 1255 for three years, when his talents came to light on a journey to Siena through his able contribution to a theological discussion. He was soon ordained priest, became novice-master at Siena, and later the secretary of the prior general. The latter resigned office in 1267; Philip was elected in his place. He codified the rules and constitutions which were approved in 1268 and made visitations of his order in Italy, France, and Germany. In 1274 he took part in the Council of Lyons, where he made an excellent impression. He was also skilled in peacemaking and in reconciling sinners to the Church. He sent the first Servite missionaries to the land of the Tartars and was the virtual founder of the Servite nuns. He died at the general chapter of his order at Florence, exhorting his brethren to mutual patience and love. At one time in his life he was considered a serious candidate for the papacy. He was canonized in 1671. Feast: 23 August.

AA.SS. Aug. IV (1739), 655–719; P. Soulieur, *Vie de S. Philippe Benizi* (2nd edn., 1926, Eng. tr. 1886); B.T.A., iii. 385–8.

BEOCCA AND HETHOR, monks and martyrs of Chertsey (Surrey), killed by the Danes in 870. The memory of these monks, supposed to be as many as ninety, was kept alive in fragmentary chronicles and by William of Malmesbury. Their deaths, like those of monks of Peterborough, Bardney, Ely, and Crowland, were believed to be the work of the same Danish army as that which killed *Edmund of East Anglia. It seems unlikely that the number of the monks concerned is accurate. Feast: 10 April.

G.P., p. 143; *R.P.S.*; *C.S.P.*

BEORNSTAN, see Birstan.

BEORNWALD (Berenwald, Byrnwold) of Bampton (8th century (?)), priest and possibly founder of this large Mercian minster church. His existence is proved by his presence in Latin and French versions of *R.P.S.*, in Winchester litanies of the 11th century and in Martyrologies of the 12th century (Exeter) and of the 15th (Syon Abbey), in which last he is described, probably wrongly, as martyr. There are references in an early 12th-century charter to his feast at Bampton; which the chaplain of the daughter church at Alvescot had to visit, and to his shrine, for whose repair the Dean and Chapter of Exeter assigned money. He was also mentioned in a will of 1516 in which William Wode, a Bampton clerk, bequeathed his soul 'to God, to our Lady, Sent Barnwald and all the seintes of hevyn'. The shrine was probably situated in the north transept of the church, where some remains survive; it was marked by a brass whose indent depicts a figure clothed in vestments, with a crozier but no mitre.

Bampton was not a monastic church and it seems likely that Beornwald was the ruler of an old-style secular minster. Little is known of his life or even his date, yet his memory lived on until the Reformation. Feast: 21 December.

John Blair, 'Saint Beornwald of Bampton', *Oxoniensia*, xlix (1984), 47–55.

BERCTHUN (Brithun, Bertinus) (d. 733), monk of Beverley. Disciple of *John of Beverley and Bede's informant about his master, he became the first abbot of Beverley. He died on 15 May, on which day his feast was kept locally.

Bede, *H.E.*, v. 2; *N.L.A.*, i. 160–1.

BERHTWALD (1) (Beorhtweald, Brihtwald), monk and archbishop of Canterbury 693–731. First known as abbot of Reculver, he became archbishop of Canterbury on the death of *Theodore, being consecrated at Lyons by Godwin, its archbishop. Bede describes him as learned in Scripture and ecclesiastical and monastic sciences, although far inferior to his predecessor. During his long rule he was in correspondence with *Boniface, *Aldhelm, and *Wilfrid; towards the last he was at first intransigent, but eventually agreed to the final settlement of 705. Evidence for cult is minimal, being apparently based on a single late calendar of St. Augustine's abbey, Canterbury, where, like his predecessors, he was buried. Feast: 9 January.

Bede, *H.E.* v. 8, 19, 23; *Eddius' Life of Wilfrid* (ed. B. Colgrave, 1927), cc. 46–7, 60.

BERHTWALD (2) (Brihtwald), bishop of Ramsbury 995–1045. He was one of several monks of Glastonbury who became bishops at this time; he was a generous benefactor both to his own monastery and to Malmesbury. His extraordinarily long rule seems to have earned him less fame than his prophecy and vision concerning the successor of *Edward the Confessor. He was buried at Glastonbury. Feast: 22 January, local cult only.

G.P., p. 182; F. Barlow, *Life of King Edward the Confessor* (1962), pp. lxxv–lxxvi, 8–9, 85–7.

BERIN, see Birinus.

BERNADETTE (1844–79), visionary of Lourdes and later nun. She was the daughter of François Soubirous, a miller, and was the oldest of six children, who for various reasons lived in acute poverty. At the age of fourteen, in 1858, she experienced in the space of six months a series of eighteen visions of the Blessed Virgin Mary at the rock of Massabielle, Lourdes. The Virgin described herself as 'The Immaculate Conception', ordered the building of a church, and told Bernadette to drink from a spring, which from that time until the present day produces 27,000 gallons of water a week. The content of the visions was extremely simple: they were principally concerned with the need for prayer and penance. The vast pilgrimage movement to Lourdes which developed from them is the greatest in modern Europe.

Bernadette was an undersized ailing child who suffered from asthma; her intellectual equipment was simple, and some witnesses thought her stupid. But her veracity, courage, and complete disinterestedness are beyond dispute. She was subjected to a series of searching interrogations both by the clergy and by minor state officials; from all these she emerged with her story unshaken. But she suffered considerably from publicity and curiosity; eventually in 1866 she joined the Sisters of Notre-Dame of Nevers, where she spent the rest of her life. She died at the age of thirty-five after much illness heroically borne. She was completely cut off from the development of Lourdes as a pilgrimage centre and was not present at its culmination, the consecration of the basilica in 1876. The only 'extraordinary' months in her life were those of the apparitions; before and after, her life was humdrum in the extreme.

She was canonized in 1933, not because she saw visions and experienced trances, but because of her total commitment in simplicity, integrity, and trust. For these qualities in her balanced, though limited personality, she stands almost alone among Marian visionaries of recent times. Feast: 16 April, but often in France on 18 February.

L. J. M. Cros, *Histoire de Notre-Dame de Lourdes* (3 vols., 1925–7); F. Trochu, *Sainte Bernadette Soubirous* (1957); H. Petitot, *The True Story of St. Bernadette* (1949): F. Werfel's novel *The Song of Bernadette* (1942) was criticized in some respects by B. Lebbe, *The Soul of Bernadette* (1947); see also A. Ravier, *Bernadette Soubirous* (1979).

BERNARD (*c.*1090–1153), Cistercian monk and abbot of Clairvaux. Born at Fontaines, near Dijon, the third son of Tescelin Sorrel, a Burgundian Crusader, he was educated at Châtillon-sur-Seine by secular canons. He became known as a young man of charm, wit, learning, and eloquence. At the age of twenty-two, with thirty-one companions including some of his brothers and other noblemen, he became a monk at the languishing, poverty-stricken, reformed monastery of Cîteaux. This large influx of new recruits saved it from near-extinction, but eventually under Bernard's influence, the Cistercian Order was transformed.

After a few years probation, Bernard was made abbot of Clairvaux, a new foundation. In conditions of acute poverty he was at first too severe on his community. When he realized this, he gave up preaching, improved the food (sometimes it had been barley bread and boiled beechleaves), and generally consolidated its position with the help of the local bishop. Eventually Clairvaux made numerous foundations in France and elsewhere, including Rievaulx (North Yorkshire) in 1132, Whitland (Dyfed) in 1140, Boxley (Kent) in 1146, Margam (West Glamorgan) in 1147, and Mellifont (Co. Louth) in 1142. Meanwhile, in spite of numerous other foundations, Clairvaux itself steadily increased in size until it numbered 700 monks at Bernard's death.

From an early time Bernard, although a member of an Order that purported to practise seclusion from the world in chosen obscurity, became involved in Church affairs and soon emerged as one of the most charismatic and influential personalities in the cause of reform. At the Synod of Troyes he obtained recognition for the new Order of Templars (whose rule he had written himself), which aimed at providing a respectable, dedicated body of knights to fight the Church's battles in the Crusades and elsewhere, besides devoting themselves to the care of the sick and the pilgrims. In 1130, after a disputed papal election, Bernard took sides for Innocent II against Anacletus; his ardent partisanship, together with help from *Norbert, eventually rallied the whole Church to recognize Innocent. Meanwhile, the Cistercian Order, now with strong papal support, increased even more rapidly; Cistercian influence reached its highest point when a former pupil of Bernard, Eugenius III, was elected pope in 1145. This continued until both died within a few months of each other, eight years later.

Bernard, like his knightly forebears, thrived on conflict, but his energy was directed against what he believed to be heterodoxy or monastic tepidity. He attacked both Peter Abelard and Gilbert de la Porrée, two of the best scholars of his time, for their theological opinions; he also severely criticized, not always justly, Cluny, and so, by implication, traditional Black Benedictine monasticism. He took to intervening by letter or persuasion in many episcopal elections in different parts of Europe, such as that of *William of York. Not surprisingly, he made enemies as well as friends. Perhaps the greatest failure of his life was the Second Crusade. This he had preached with immense energy and determination. Moved by the eloquence and prophetic fervour with which he identified the cause of God with this military expedition, many people of all classes had rallied to his call and taken the Cross. But this Crusade ended in disaster and some, not altogether fairly, blamed Bernard for it.

Bernard's character can best be studied in his writings. These include his Letters, which reveal his passionate eloquence and involvement, his sermons on the Canticle, which, like them, were polished and repolished, besides various treaties on theological subjects. Perhaps the most attractive, as well as one of the most simply written, is his treatise on the Love of God. This has become a spiritual classic. He was also prominent in fostering devotion to the human nature of Christ and to the Blessed Virgin. His affective approach influenced deeply the development of medieval spirituality.

His influence on monasticism has been deep and lasting. On the one hand he encouraged monks to devote themselves to mystical prayer in and through the ordinary framework of monastic observance; on the other, he modified the concepts of early Cîteaux in practice, developing the Cistercian Order into a mass movement of unprecedented expansion and renown. In this he was helped both by the genius of the earlier juridical structure of his Order and by social and economic causes which led, for example, to the enormous expansion of lay brothers. At his death the Cistercians numbered about 400 houses (over fifty in England and Wales), almost all over Europe. Whatever his failings, his influence on very many aspects of 12th-century Church life was enormous.

His cult began unofficially during his lifetime. He was formally canonized in 1174 and nominated a Doctor of the Church in 1830. Feast: 20 August.

AA.SS. Aug. IV (1739), 101–368; early Lives also in *P.L.*, clxxxv, and Eng. tr. of *Vita Prima* by G. Webb and A. Walker (1960); modern Lives by W. Williams (1935), J. Leclercq (1966). Works in *P.L.*, clxxxii–clxxxv and crit. edn. by J. Leclercq and others (1957–75), with Eng. tr. of his Letters by B. S. James (1953) and other works by American Cistercians (1970–); J. Leclercq, *Recueil d'études sur S. Bernard et ses écrits* (1962); *Bernard de Clairvaux* (1953); *Saint Bernard Théologien* (1953). See also E. Gilson, *The Mystical Theology of St. Bernard* (1940); J. Bouton, *Bibliographie Bernardine*, 1891–1957 (1958); *M.O.*, pp. 208–57, 705–9; G. R. Evans, *The Mind of St. Bernard of Clairvaux* (1983); J. Leclercq and others, *The Influence of St. Bernard* (1976), P. Riché (1989), J. Berlioz (1990).

BERNARD OF AOSTA (also called Bernard of Menthon) (d. 1081), priest. Probably of Italian rather than French parentage, he became a priest and later vicar-general in the diocese of Aosta, which for forty-two years he systematically visited, especially in its more remote areas, preaching, founding schools, building and conserving churches. He also took special care of Alpine travellers, for whom he built guest-houses on the passes later called after him the Great and the Little St. Bernard. The dangers to travellers through snowdrifts or from brigands were indeed extreme: their needs were met by the Austin Canons houses founded by Bernard as well as later by the specially trained breed of dogs named after him. Bernard died at the age of eighty-five. He was named patron of mountain-climbers by Pius XI (himself a mountaineer) in 1923. Feast: 28 May.

AA.SS. Iun. II (1698), 1071–89 contains a late Life, compiled in Savoyard rather than Italian interests; A. Colombo in *Biblioteca della società storica subalpina*, xvii (1903), 291–312; *Anal. Boll.*, lxiii (1945), 269–70; B.T.A., ii. 411–13; *Bibl. SS.*, ii. 1325–34.

BERNARDINO OF SIENA (1380–1444), Franciscan friar. Born at Massa di Carrera where his father was governor, he was left an orphan and brought up by an aunt. At the age of twenty during an outbreak of plague in Siena, Bernardino and some companions took charge of the local hospital, whose organization had all but broken down owing to the deaths of many of the staff. After the epidemic, Bernardino nursed his bedridden aunt until her death.

He then became a Franciscan in 1402, living at Colombaio near Siena and later at Fiesole near Florence, where his cell may still be seen. In 1417 he began his spectacular career as a popular preacher in Milan; later he travelled all over Italy except the kingdom of Naples, always on foot, sometimes preaching for three or four hours and often several sermons on the same day. The crowds were so large that he used a pulpit in the open air. When he started his career, his voice was weak, but with constant exercise and practice it became extraordinarily resonant. What he preached was the need for penance and voluntary poverty; he denounced gambling, usury, witchcraft, superstition, and the strife of the power-politics of Italy's city-states.

He is best remembered for his propagation of devotion to the Holy Name of Jesus. At the end of his sermons he would hold up for veneration a plaque, on which he wrote the letters IHS, surrounded by rays. So popular did these become that a former card-maker whose business was ruined by Bernardino's denunciation of gambling, more than recouped his losses through making these plaques instead. Examples of them may be seen to this day in churches and museums of Tuscany and elsewhere. The style of his sermons was lively and emotional. Like other Friars of the later Middle Ages, he made full use of a wide repertory of anecdotes, mimicry, acting, clowning, and denunciation. He moved his audiences to both laughter and tears; all over Italy he accomplished numerous conversions, the restoration of stolen or defrauded property, the reformation of morals. But his theology was attacked in some quarters, although he was finally vindicated by Martin V.

In 1437 he became vicar-general of the Observant branch of the Friars (to which he had belonged since 1403); so great was his attraction both as preacher and saint that the numbers of the Observants rose more than tenfold. The reform moved away from eremitical ideals and showed an 'image' of preachers and teachers working actively for the whole Church. Bernardino set up schools of theology at Perugia and Monteripido, as he well realized that ignorance was as dangerous as riches for the Friars. He also probably wrote the Statutes for the Observants in 1440.

In 1443 he resigned and went back to his favourite task of preaching. But his health was broken, and he journeyed on a donkey instead of on foot. In 1444, in his native town of Massa Maritima, he preached a course of fifty sermons on consecutive days, knowing that it was his last visit. He set out for Naples, preaching as he went, but died on 20 May 1444 at Aquila, where he was buried and was famous for miracles. He was canonized by Nicolas V in 1450. Medieval and Renaissance artists portray him as small and emaciated, with deep burning ēyes, generally holding the IHS tablet. Sometimes three mitres are placed at his feet, to recall the bishoprics which he refused during his lifetime, Siena, Ferrara, and Urbino. His cult was spread in England especially by the Observant Friars, who made their first foundation at Greenwich in 1482 and became a province of five houses in 1499. Feast: 20 May.

AA.SS. Maii V (1685), 257*–318*; B. de Gaiffier, 'Le mémoire d'André Biglia sur la prédication de S. Bernardin de Sienne', *Anal. Boll.*, liii (1935), 308–58; V. Facchinetti, 'Bolletino bibliographico riguardante S. Bernardino da Siena', *Aevum*, iv (1930), 319–86; A. G. Ferrers Howell, *S. Bernardino* (1913); I. Origo, *The World of San Bernardino* (1963); J. R. H. Moorman, *A History of the Franciscan Order* (1968). Works of St. Bernardino in *Opera Omnia* (Venice 1591 and 1745); modern critical edition at Quaracchi (1950).

BERTELIN (Berthelm), see BETTELIN.

BERTIN (d. 698), abbot. A monk of Luxeuil who helped *Omer to evangelize the Pas-de-Calais district in northern France, Bertin became abbot of Sithiu, called Saint-Bertin after his death, which was an important centre for missionary work and agriculture. In 663 Bertin and Omer built the church which later became the cathedral of Saint-Omer. Frequent visits by English ecclesiastics on their way to or from Rome in the late Anglo-Saxon and early Norman periods led to the introduction of the cult of Bertin into England. His relics were restored to Saint-Bertin in 1052 after being removed, like many others, to a place of safety during the invasions of the Northmen. His iconographical attribute is a boat, because Sithiu was originally accessible only by water. Feast: 5 September.

AA.SS. Sept. II (1748), 549–630; *M.G.H., Scriptores rerum merov.*, v. 729–80; L. van der Essen, *Étude sur les Vitae des saints mérovingiens de l'ancienne Belgique*, pp. 400–11.

BERTINUS, *see* BERCTHUN

BERTRAM, *see* BETTELIN (1 and 2).

BERTRAN, Luis (1526–81), Dominican priest, apostle, and patron of Colombia. Born at Valencia, he joined the Dominican Order in 1544 and was ordained priest in 1547 by *Thomas of Villanova. A man of profound prayer and austerity, Luis was appointed novice-master. This office was of critical importance in the current reform of his Order: Luis held it, on and off, for about thirty years. He also became a famous preacher and counsellor. One who asked and followed his advice was *Theresa of Avila. Luis advised her to continue her plans to reform Carmel and prophesied that her discalced nuns would become very famous after fifty years.

The main work of his life was as a missionary in Latin America. In 1562 he landed at Cartagena, where his Order already had a priory. Preaching to the Indians in Spanish and using an interpreter, he baptized many thousands in only six years at Tubara, Cipacua, Mompos, and Santa Marta, all on the mainland. He then preached with equal apparent success in the Leeward Islands, the Virgin Islands, and the Windward Islands. He insisted much on the fear as well as the love of God: his preaching, according to the canonization bull, was helped by tongues, prophecy, and miracles. The numbers and the circumstances of his apostolate recall those attributed to missionaries in Europe in the early Middle Ages.

He was one of the first to criticize the cruelty and rapacity of many Spanish adventurers, from whom he tried to obtain redress when he was recalled in 1568. He now devoted the rest of his life to training preachers for the missions. In this task he insisted on the importance both of prayer and of works that match the preaching. In 1580 he preached his last sermon in Valencia cathedral. He was taken ill immediately but lived for a further eighteen months. He was canonized in 1671. A fine painting of him by Zurbaran can be seen at Seville. Feast: 9 October.

Early Life by his disciple V. J. Antist, for which see *AA.SS.* Oct. V, 292–488; others by B. Wilberforce (1882) and R. R. Luch (1960); see also B.T.A., iv. 72–4; *Bibl. SS.*, viii. 342–8.

BETTELIN (1) (Beccelin, Bertelin, Berthelm, Bertram) (early 8th century), hermit of Crowland, disciple of *Guthlac, who lived in a nearby hermitage. Bettelin received counsel from the saint on his deathbed and witnessed his burial; he lived on for several years afterwards and died at Crowland. Later writers describe him overcoming a temptation to cut Guthlac's throat while shaving him. Feast: 9 September.

B. Colgrave (ed.), *Felix's Life of St. Guthlac* (1956).

BETTELIN (2) (Bertram) of Ilam (Stafford), where a chapel, font, and well preserve his memory and where substantial fragments of his shrine survive. Very little is known about his life. It seems likely that he was an Anglo-Saxon hermit, who lived and died in this neighbourhood and was venerated locally.

Legend supplied striking but probably fictitious details, such as that he was the son of a Mercian prince, that he fell in love with an Irish princess, brought her back to England and left her in the forest in urgent need of a midwife. When he returned, a pack of wolves was devouring her, so he became a hermit for the rest of his life. This story is borrowed from the Legend of St. Bertelme of Fécamp. Feast: 10 August.

N.L.A., i. 162–7 conflates his story with that of Bettelin of Crowland; see also B.T.A., iii. 517.

BEUNO (6th century), abbot in North Wales. The Life was written in the 14th century, but may contain genuine elements. He was supposed to have been born and educated in Herefordshire (where there is a village of Llanfeuno), but the main centre of this peripatetic monk's work was at Clynnog Fawr (Gwynedd), where he founded his principal monastery. Some of his many dedications may reflect his foundations, others those of his disciples. They are found in both central East Wales and in Clwyd, but the largest number is in the extreme north-west, including Anglesey and the Lleyn peninsula. He died and was buried at Clynnog Fawr. A stone oratory was built over his tomb; later the relics were translated to a new church (Eglwys y Bedd), where miracles were reported. He is often considered to be the most important local saint of North Wales.

His cult survived the Reformation. In the reign of Elizabeth (1589) there were complaints that lambs and calves offered at the saint's tomb were later brought back and were highly esteemed because Beuno's cattle 'prospered marvellous well'. In 1770 this custom still survived; sick children too were bathed in his holy well and left all night in his tomb. Remains of the primitive oratory were excavated in 1914. Feast: 21 April.

A. W. Wade-Evans, *Vitae Sanctorum Britanniae* (1944), pp. 16–22; id., 'Beuno Sant', *Arch. Cambrensis*, lxxv (1930), 315–41; E. G. Bowen, *The Settlements of the Celtic Saints in Wales* (1956), pp. 79–86; see also Baring-Gould and Fisher, i. 208–21.

BEUZEC, see BUDOC.

BILLFRITH (Billfrid) (8th century), hermit and goldsmith who adorned the Lindisfarne Gospels, as the inscription in it states, with gold, silver, and gems on the binding. The book survives, but the precious binding is lost. The supposed relics of Billfrith were discovered by Alfred Westow in the 11th century and removed to Durham, where the feast of Billfrith and *Baldred the hermit was celebrated on 6 March.

T. D. Kendrick and others, *Codex Lindisfarnensis* (1956, 1960).

BIRGITTA, see BRIDGET.

BIRINUS (Birin, Berin) (d. 650), apostle of Wessex and first bishop of Dorchester (Oxon.). Possibly a Lombard by birth, Birinus was sent by Pope Honorius I to continue the evangelization of Britain. He was consecrated for this task at Genoa, on his way, by Asterius, archbishop of Milan. His original plan was to penetrate into the Midlands where no preacher had been, but he found the West Saxons (Gewissae) so pagan that he decided to stay among them. This was in 635. After a period of wandering preaching, he was helped greatly by the desire of King Cynegils to be instructed in the Christian faith and by the plan of *Oswald, king of Northumbria, to marry Cynegils' daughter (later called Cyneburg). Birinus baptized Cynegils and his family, and received Dorchester as his see. This was a Romano-British town conveniently situated on road and river in the centre of an area of dense Anglo-Saxon settlement. Birinus built churches here and elsewhere in the area; none of the surviving ones are certainly his, with the possible exception of Wing (Bucks.).

Many people were baptized by Birinus; his apostolate lasted fifteen years in all. Although he was sent by the pope, there is no record of any direct contacts with the archbishops of Canterbury. Towards the end of his life Birinus dedicated a church at Winchester, whose growing importance made it inevitable that it would become the ecclesiastical centre of the kingdom. There is no record of Wessex bishops at Dorchester after 660; with part of Berkshire it was absorbed into Mercia and in the 9th century it was revived as a Mercian see. *Hedda, bishop of Winchester, translated the relics of Birinus to Winchester *c.*690. There they remained throughout the Middle Ages, being moved to fresh shrines on 4 September 980 (by *Ethelwold), and again in 1150 (by Henry of Blois). In the early 13th century the Austin Canons of Dorchester claimed to possess the relics of Birinus; an inconclusive inquiry took place in 1224, instigated by Pope Honorius III and presided over by Stephen Langton. Miracles, visions, and the body of a bishop, certainly not Birinus, were produced at Dorchester; by the early 14th century a shrine of fine workmanship was built. This Dorchester shrine has been recently restored.

The celebration of Birinus' feast was not as widespread as it deserved (it was not in the Sarum calendar): the principal centres of his cult were Winchester, Dorchester, and Abingdon, the earliest evidence for it being a Winchester calendar of the late 9th century. In the late 11th and early 12th centuries sermons and Lives were written by Goscelin and others, which survive in Abingdon and Winchester manuscripts. By this time Dorchester had become a village. Birinus' feast was added to the Roman martyrology in the late 16th century. Berinsfield, a village near Dorchester, also retains his name. Feast: 3 December; translation, 4 September.

Bede, *H.E.*, ii. 7; iv. 12; *A.S.C.* (s.a. 635, 650); *N.L.A.*, i. 118–22; J. E. Field, *Saint Berin of Wessex* (1902); T. Varley, *St. Birinus and Wessex* (1934).

BIRSTAN (Brynstan, Beornstan), bishop of Winchester 931–4. Although his feast occurs in calendars of the 11th century (Winchester) and of the 12th (West Country), the only information about this saint comes from William of Malmesbury. He stressed his personal daily service of the poor, his devotion to the dead evidenced by his frequent prayers for them in the cemetery (to which the departed souls once answered 'Amen'), his assiduous private prayer, during which he died. His memory was neglected for some years but was revived by *Ethelwold, following a vision in which it was claimed that Birstan enjoyed equal heavenly glory with the other Winchester saints *Birinus and *Swithun; therefore he should receive equal honour on earth. Feast: 4 November.

G.P., pp. 163–4; *E.B.K. before 1100*, s.d. 4 Nov.

BLAISE, one of the *Fourteen Holy Helpers. He was believed to be bishop of Sebaste in Armenia, and to have been put to death under the Emperor Licinius and the prefect Agricolaus in the early 4th century. There is no evidence of a cult in either East or West before the 8th century; there are Greek and Latin Lives of purely fictitious character. These make him the son of rich and noble Christians, very young when consecrated bishop. During persecution he hid in a cave and blessed sick or wounded animals; once a woman brought him her boy, who was at the point of death because a fishbone was stuck in his throat, and whom he healed. When he was imprisoned, the same woman brought him food and candles. Hence at the blessing of St. Blaise (still practised) sufferers from throat diseases are blessed by the application of two candles to the throat. Water with the blessing of St. Blaise is also given to sick cattle. He was believed to have been torn with wool-combs (his iconographical emblem) before being beheaded, and was for long by consequence the patron of wool-combers. Canterbury claimed relics of him, and at least four miracles were recorded at his shrine, one dated 1451. Parson Woodforde described a solemn procession in his honour at Norwich on 24 March 1783. Feast: 3 February.

AA.SS. Feb. I (1658), 331–5 (cf. *Anal. Boll.*, lxxviii (1960), 443); J. Wickham Legg and W. H. St. John Hope (edd.), *Inventories of Christ Church, Canterbury* (1902), pp. 29–30. J. Woodforde, *The Diary of a Country Parson* (ed. J. Beresford, 1956), pp. 198–200; B.T.A., i. 239.

BLANE (Blaan) (late 6th century), bishop. A native of Bute, he studied in Ireland for several years before returning home. He was then ordained priest and preached in Scotland. He founded a monastery at Kingarth (Bute), where he was buried. On the site of the monastery Dunblane cathedral was built, where a bell, reputed to be his, is still preserved. Feast: 11 or in some places 10 August.

AA.SS. Aug. II (1735), 560–1; *K.S.S.*, pp. 280–1.

BLIDA, mother of *Walstan of Bawburgh, and reputed in his Life to have been an East Anglian princess. She was buried at Martham in the late 11th century, where there was a chapel dedicated to her, to which bequests were made as late as 1522. She is represented on a screen, formerly in St. James, Norwich, crowned, holding a book and palm, and in the NE. chancel window at North Tuddenham. Like her son, she seems to have had a restricted local cult. No known feast.

M. R. James, 'Lives of St. Walstan', *Norf. Archaeol. Soc. Papers*, xix (1917), 238–67.

BLINE, see MONENNA.

BOBOLA, Andrew (1591–1657), martyr. A Polish aristocrat who became a Jesuit at Vilna in 1609, he was preacher in the church of St. *Casimir there before he was appointed superior of the house at Bobrinsk. An epidemic of plague brought out his exceptional care for the sick and the dying.

Later he resumed his missionary tasks, bringing whole villages of Orthodox Christians into communion with the papacy. This led to hatred and opposition, one form of which was for organized bands of children to follow him around and try to shout him down.

At this time rebellious Cossacks drove the Jesuits from their churches and colleges: they took refuge in marshy Podlesia, where Prince Radziwill offered them his house at Pinsk in 1652. This was attacked by Cossacks in 1657; Bobola was seized, invited to abjure catholicism, and then beaten. His firm answers under interrogation exasperated his captors further and he was killed by being scorched, flayed, mutilated, and finally beheaded. His mutilated body, found incorrupt in 1730, was removed to Moscow by Bolsheviks, but taken to Rome in 1922. Andrew was canonized in 1938. Feast: 21 May.

L. Rocci, *Vita del B. Andrea Bobola* (1924); other Lives by H. Beylard (1938) and J. Mareschini (tr. L. J. Gallagher and P. V. Donovan, 1939); B.T.A., ii. 363–4.

BOETHIUS (Severinus) (*c*.475–524), philosopher and reputed martyr. A Roman of the famous *gens Anicia*, Boethius was orphaned early in life and was brought up by Q. Aurelius Symmachus, whose daughter he married. A scholar who devoted himself to translating Plato, Aristotle, Pythagoras, and Euclid into Latin (and generations of scholars in the early Middle Ages knew these authors only through Boethius), he also wrote theological works on the Trinity and the Incarnation. His most famous work, the *Consolation of Philosophy*, written in prison at the end of his life, was the most widely diffused of all and its manuscripts provide his iconography. This work was translated into numerous vernacular languages, including Old and Middle English by King Alfred and Geoffrey Chaucer respectively. Alfred interpolated some passages to make them more explicitly Christian. Dante referred to Boethius in the *Paradiso*.

Boethius was also a statesman. Under the Ostrogoth emperor Theodoric he and his two sons became consuls. But the emperor (an Arian) suspected a political plot involving the Eastern emperor Justin and arrested a senator and ex-consul called Albinus. Boethius quite properly defended him in court, but for this he was accused of treason, also of sacrilege or studies for impious purposes, was imprisoned and eventually executed. As a victim of blatant injustice he was regarded as a martyr and his ancient cult was confirmed by Leo XIII in 1883. His feast is still kept at Pavia, where he is buried, as well as in some churches in Rome, on 23 October.

AA.SS. Maii VI (1739), 47–54; works in *P.L.*, lxiii and lxiv; V. E. Watts (ed.), *The Consolation of Philosophy* (1969); general studies of Boethius by H. M. Barrett (1940), P. Courcelle (1967), M. Gibson (1981). B.T.A., iv. 180–3; *Bibl. SS.*, iii. 218–27.

BOISIL (Boswell) (d. *c.*661), abbot of Melrose. Formed in the Irish monastic tradition by an unknown master and monastery, Boisil, when a monk of Melrose, was so esteemed for his learning, holiness, and prophecies that he attracted *Cuthbert, then a young man, to his community in 651. Boisil was also known for the preaching journeys in the neighbouring villages which Cuthbert too used to share. In *c.*659, when *Eata, abbot of Melrose, left to found Ripon, Boisil succeeded him. On Cuthbert's return from Ripon *c.*661, Boisil was stricken by the plague. Together they read the Gospel of John before Boisil died. Cuthbert also caught the disease, but recovered from it in accordance with Boisil's prophecy.

Boisil gave his name to St. Boswells (Roxburghshire), and churches were dedicated to him at Lessuden and Tweedmouth. His relics were translated to Durham in the 11th century. The Stonyhurst College manuscript of the Gospel of John, written in uncial script of the 8th century and at an early date placed in Cuthbert's coffin, probably came from Wearmouth or Jarrow, both of which were founded after Boisil's death; if so, it cannot have been Boisil's copy. A more authentic memorial of Boisil is the large fragment of his 8th-century shrine, which was brought to Jedburgh from Old Melrose. Feast: 7 July; translation, 8 June.

Bede, *H.E.*, iv. 27–8; v. 9; B. Colgrave, *Two Lives of St. Cuthbert* (1940); C. F. Battiscombe (ed.), *The Relics of St. Cuthbert* (1956); C. A. Ralegh Radford, 'Two Scottish Shrines: Jedburgh and St. Andrews', *Archaeol. Jnl.*, cxii (1955), 43–60.

BONAVENTURE (Bonaventura) (*c.*1218–74), Franciscan friar, bishop, and cardinal. The son of a physician of noble birth, he was born at Bagnoreggio, near Orvieto. He became a Franciscan in 1243; his intellectual gifts were soon recognized and he was sent to Paris to study under Alexander of Hales. In 1248 he received his licence to teach; in 1253 he became Master of the Franciscan school at Paris.

As a theologian he was more Augustinian and less Aristotelian than his contemporary *Thomas Aquinas; he stressed the importance of an affective, rather than a purely rational approach to the divine mysteries. His main theological teaching is in his commentary on Peter the Lombard's *Sentences*. While he frequently agreed with Aquinas in many conclusions, points on which they differed included Bonaventure's assertion that the creation of the world in time could be demonstrated by human reason. His other works of importance were in the field of mystical theology: they include the *Breviloquium* and the *Itinerarium mentis ad Deum*, which rapidly became a classic, much read from his own day to ours. Indeed it is often maintained that he was primarily a mystical, rather than a dogmatic theologian.

In 1257, at the early age of thirty-six, he was elected Minister-General of the Franciscan Order. He has also been called, with some justice, its second founder. He came to office at a critical time; the Friars' enormous increase in numbers, the lack of organization by *Francis, the rivalry among various factions of the Order, each of whom claimed to be heirs of the founder's thought, together with a certain decline in zeal, had made them a target for criticism. He staunchly defended Franciscan ideals, but insisted, against the teaching of Francis, on the serious need for study, and hence on the need for possessing books and buildings. He confirmed the existing practice of the Friars, studying and teaching in the universities. He saw their role in the Church as a whole as completing the work of diocesan clergy by preaching and spiritual direction, in both of which activities the other clergy were frequently deficient through poor education.

Within his Order he was the moderates'

leader; he rejected the extreme position of the Spirituals, who exalted poverty above learning and above all else, and claimed to represent the true teaching of Francis. He placed in retirement, instead of prison, his predecessor John of Parma, suspected of Joachimist heresy. His own ideals of simplicity, frugal poverty, diligence, and detachment from the rich as well as from riches were realized in his own life. He wrote a Life of Francis, which was approved as official; the Chapter of 1266 decreed the destruction of others.

As Minister-General he visited Italy, France, Germany, and England. In 1265 he was nominated archbishop of York by Clement IV; he rejected the honour. But in 1273 he was nominated cardinal-bishop of Albano by Gregory X, with a command not to refuse. When the papal messengers reached him, he was washing up the dishes in the friary of Mugello (near Florence); he told them to wait until he had finished his task.

At the Council of Lyons, summoned by the pope to effect reunion with separated churches of the East, Bonaventure took a prominent part. Thomas Aquinas had died on the way to it. Bonaventure resigned his post as Minister-General, but by conferring with the Greeks, reunion was temporarily effected. He preached at the solemn Mass of reconciliation, but did not live to see Constantinople repudiate the reunion so patiently achieved. He died at Lyons on 15 July and was buried there.

His achievements in theology and government should not blind one to his personal characteristics noted by contemporaries: gentle courtesy, compassion, and accessibility. A Life, reputedly written in 1300, was lost and there seems no trace of a very early cult. He was canonized by Sixtus IV in 1482 and declared a Doctor of the Church in 1588. He is often called the Seraphic Doctor. Notable paintings of him by Crivelli and by Zurbarán are in the Louvre at Paris. Feast: 15 (formerly 14) July.

AA.SS. Iul. III (1723), 811–60; E. Gilson, *The Philosophy of St. Bonaventure* (1938); C. H. Tavard, *Transiency and Permanence* (1954); J. Moorman, *A History of the Franciscan Order* (1968). Works in critical edn. by Franciscans of Quaracchi, 10 vols. (1882–); Eng. tr. by J. de Vinck, 5 vols. (1960–70); 'The Souls' journey into God' and other short works tr. E. Cousins (Classics of Western Spirituality, 1978); *The miroure of the Blessed Life of Christ* (1978): H.S.S.C., vi 89–95.

BONIFACE (Winfrith) (*c.*675–754), monk, apostle of Frisia and Germany, archbishop of Mainz, martyr. Born in Devon (possibly Crediton) of free, land-owning Anglo-Saxon peasants, Boniface was educated in monasteries, first at Exeter, then at Nursling (Hants) under Winbert. As a monk and schoolmaster, he wrote the first Latin grammar to be produced in England, besides some poems and acrostics in the style of *Aldhelm. At the age of thirty he was ordained priest; his knowledge of Scripture enabled him to be a successful teacher and preacher. He became known outside his monastery and was chosen by Ina, king of Wessex 688–726, and his synod, to be their envoy to Burchard, archbishop of Canterbury.

But instead of following a fruitful career in England, Boniface chose to leave it and be a missionary. He went to Frisia in 716, where *Wilfrid and *Willibrord had been the pioneers. Political conditions, however, with militant pagans in the ascendancy, made missionary work almost impossible, so Boniface returned to Nursling. He was elected abbot in 717 but refused the charge. Instead he went to Rome in 718 to receive a definite mission from Gregory II to preach the gospel. The area designated was Bavaria and Hesse. On his way there he learnt that conditions in Frisia had changed for the better, so he went to help the aged Willibrord, who wished him to be his successor, for three years. He then went to Hesse and wrote a report to the pope, who consecrated him bishop at Rome in 722.

Helped by a papal letter to Charles Martel, who gave him protection, he evangelized Hesse. One famous incident was his felling of a sacred oak at Geismar, whose pagan gods failed to protect their followers or avenge this outrage. This led to widespread conversions and Boniface moved on to Thuringia, helped by letters of guidance from the pope and from Daniel, bishop of Winchester, about techniques of evangelization. Characteristic of this period of missionary work was the use of monasteries, staffed in part by English monks and nuns and developed as centres both of Christianity and civilization; among them were Amoneburg and Fritzlar in Hesse and Ordruf in Thuringia.

In 732 *Gregory III sent him the pallium, making him archbishop with the power to consecrate bishops for Germany beyond the Rhine. He founded bishoprics at Erfurt for Thuringia, Buraberg for Hesse, and Wurzburg for Franconia, and later Eichstatt for Nordgau. Among his followers were *Lull of Malmesbury, his successor, Sturm, abbot of Boniface's most important monastery of Fulda, *Eoban, who died with him, *Burchard, and *Wigbert; the nuns included *Tecla, abbess of Kitzingen-on-Main, *Lioba, abbess of Tauberbischofsheim, and *Walburga, abbess of Eichstatt.

In 738 Charles Martel defeated the Saxons of Westphalia; this opened up new opportunities for the Anglo-Saxon missionaries. Now Boniface wrote his famous letter to the English people, asking for their prayers and help in the conversion of those who 'are of one blood and bone with you'. Although, as throughout his apostolate, English monasteries helped him with gifts of books, vestments, relics, and, above all, personnel, this particular opening was soon closed until years later Charlemagne reconquered the Saxons.

Once again Boniface visited Rome (738–9), where he was joined by new companions, Romans, Franks, and Bavarians besides the Anglo-Saxon brothers *Winnebald and *Willibald, who had just reformed St. Benedict's monastery of Monte Cassino. Using his legatine powers, he summoned a synod for all Christian Germany and established a hierarchy in Bavaria: eventually he became archbishop of Mainz while retaining legatine powers which enabled him to appoint Willibrord's successor at Utrecht. All through his apostolate Boniface had been hampered not only by pagans but also by half-converted Christians with notorious or heretical leaders: his importance lies not only in his pioneering missionary activities but also, more significantly, in his organization of the Church, inspired, in some ways, by *Theodore's work in England. His close association with the papacy was equalled by one with the emperors: he himself admitted that he could do almost nothing without their help.

His next important work was the reform of the Church in France. Here no council had been held for many years, bishoprics were often vacant, sold, or given to unsuitable laymen without training or vocation. Charles Martel, who had often helped Boniface, was largely responsible. After his death in 741 Boniface was able to make progress under his successors Carloman and Pepin. Boniface presided over reforming councils between 742 and 747, at which prevailing abuses were condemned and the Rule of St. Benedict was made the basic code for all Carolingian monasteries. Boniface's achievements made him the most important monk between *Benedict of Nursia and *Benedict of Aniane.

It was one thing to make decrees and another to have them executed. Although Boniface crowned Pepin in 751 after the retirement of Carloman to a monastery, it was probably Pepin who made some of Boniface's decrees, especially concerning bishops, ineffective. By now Boniface was nearly eighty years of age and left the leadership of the reform movement to *Chrodegang of Metz, and the care of the diocese of Mainz to Lull. He himself returned to Frisia to end his days among the people of his first missionary enterprise. He not only reclaimed the part of the country earlier evangelized, but also penetrated with some success into the pagan north-east Frisia. When he was awaiting some neophytes for confirmation, on the banks of the river Borne near Dokkum, a band of pagans attacked and killed him and his companions. His body was taken to Fulda.

Soon after his death, letters concerning him were written by Milret, bishop of Worcester, and Cuthbert, archbishop of Canterbury, to Lull. An English synod decided on the annual celebration of his feast; they regarded him as their special patron beside *Gregory and *Augustine. But he never became a principal saint in England, even in the 10th or 11th century, although his feast was widely celebrated at a comparatively low rank. His name was in the York Menology but not in the 9th-century English Martyrology: out of his numerous letters only the one describing the vision of the Monk of Much Wenlock was translated into OE. The real centre of his cult was and is Fulda, where his body rests. In present-day Germany and Holland he is widely venerated.

His ancient iconography is surprisingly slight. The oldest painting is in a 10th-century Sacramentary of Fulda (now at Bamberg), while a 12th-century Passionary of Stuttgart shows him dying, but holding in self-defence his already damaged gospel-book (such a book survives at Fulda). Later Boniface was depicted, with mitre and staff, by artists of the 16th–18th centuries.

There has been a well-deserved revival of interest in him in the 19th–20th centuries, reflected by C. Dawson's judgement that he had a deeper influence on the history of Europe than any other Englishman. This should be understood, not only in terms of Christian conversion but also in those of the alliance he made between popes and emperors, fundamental to Europe's future, and in the educational and literary influence of his monasteries. His own character, reflected in his correspondence, was notable for courage, affection, loyalty, foresight, and determination. He deserves to be better known and appreciated by his own countrymen.

Feast: 5 June; translation (at Fulda), 1 November; ordination, 1 December.

AA.SS. Iun. I (1695), 452–504; Works of Boniface, ed. J. A. Giles, 1844 and in *P.L.*, lxxxix. 597–892; his letters in *Epistulae Selectae I*, *M.G.H.*, ed. M. Tangl (1916); Eng. tr. by E. Kylie (1911) and E. Emerton (1940). Early Lives of Boniface are in W. Levison, *Vitae S. Bonifatii archiepiscopi Moguntini* (1905), tr. with selected letters by C. H. Talbot, *The Anglo-Saxon Missionaries in Germany* (1954); Modern studies by G. F. Browne, *Boniface of Crediton* (1910); G. Kurth, *S. Boniface* (1902, Eng. tr. 1935); W. Levison, *England and the Continent in the Eighth Century* (1946); E. S. Duckett, *Anglo-Saxon Saints and Scholars* (1947); T. Schieffer, *Winfrid-Bonifatius und die christliche Grundlegung Europas* (1954); C. Weber (ed.), *Sankt Bonifatius, Gedenkgabe zum zwölf-hundertsten Todestag* (1954); G. W. Greenaway, *Saint Boniface* (1955); see also M. Coens, 'Saint Boniface et sa Mission Historique', *Anal. Boll.*, lxxiii (1955), 462–95; J. M. Wallace Hadrill, *Early Medieval History* (1976); D. H. Farmer (ed.), *Benedict's Disciples* (1980); T. Reuter (ed.), *The Greatest Englishman* (1980).

BONIFACE OF SAVOY, archbishop of Canterbury 1243–70. A member of the ducal family of Savoy, Boniface was the uncle of Queen Eleanor, wife of King Henry III, and probably owed his election to her influence. In early life he had become a Carthusian at the Grande Chartreuse, but he left to become in turn prior of Mantua, administrator of the diocese of Bellay, and later of Valence. He proved to be one of the most disliked archbishops of Canterbury ever. This was due first to his financial stringency caused by the need to repay debts incurred by his predecessor *Edmund, who had suffered much loss of revenue, and by his own lavish consecration feast; secondly, to his intransigent claims of visitation as metropolitan to a number of churches which resisted. Among these were the dean and chapter of St. Paul's, the priory of St. Bartholomew in Smithfield, and the abbey of St. Albans. At St. Bartholomew's he is said to have struck the sub-prior to the ground after he had refused to receive Boniface as Visitor. A fight followed and it was noticed that Boniface wore chain mail. Appeals to Rome followed; his visitations continued but with restrictions; he had to withdraw his excommunications.

During his rule he paid off debts of

22,000 marks, founded a hospital at Maidstone, and built the great hall of his own palace. He was, however, appreciated by his own countrymen more than by the English clergy; his cult in Savoy was approved by Pope Gregory XVI in 1838. Feast: 14 July (in Savoy, Sardinia, and in the Carthusian Order).

F. A. Gasquet, *Henry III and the Church* (1905); M. Gibbs and J. Lang, *Bishops and Reform 1215–1273* (1934).

BORGIA, Francis (1510–72), Jesuit priest. The son of the duke of Gandia, the great-grandson of a pope (Alexander VI) and of a king (Ferdinand V of Aragon), Francis was educated privately and was received at the Emperor's court when eighteen years of age. The next year he married, and was made viceroy of Catalonia by Charles V. In 1543 he became duke of Gandia, but his career suffered a setback through his suppression of magistrates' corruption, and he retired to his estate, which he improved, fortified, and enriched with a Dominican foundation and the restoration of a hospital. His happy family life as the father of eight children ended when his wife died in 1546. In 1547 he secretly joined the Society of Jesus. He resigned his dukedom in favour of his eldest son, and made provision for the others. The news of this extraordinary recruit to the Society could not remain secret; although he tried hard to conceal his rank, his ability could not be hidden. He was ordained priest in 1554 and was appointed Commissary for Spain and Portugal by *Ignatius of Loyola. There he made full use of the experience he had previously acquired in governing Catalonia, and founded many colleges and other houses.

In 1561 he was called to Rome; in 1565 he was elected General of the Jesuits. For the remaining seven years of his life he was so zealous in government that he has been called the Jesuits' second founder. Both in the reform of Christian life in Europe and in its propagation overseas Francis actively inspired and supported his priests. In Rome he helped to found and direct the Roman College (later called the Gregorian University), he built the church of St. Andrew on the Quirinal, and began the famous Gesù church. He established a new province in Poland, new colleges in France, and initiated Jesuit missionary work in the Americas. In 1566, when the plague raged in Rome, he raised money for poor-relief and sent his priests to tend the sick in the hospitals. In 1571, accompanying a papal ambassador to Spain, Portugal, and France, he enjoyed great personal success, but, worn out with sickness and responsibility, he died soon after the journey was over, having blessed and prayed for all his children and grandchildren in turn. He was canonized in 1671. Feast: 10 October.

AA.SS. Oct. V (1786), 149–291; over 1,000 letters survive in *Monumenta Historica Societatis Jesu* (5 vols., 1894–1911); *Opera Omnia* were published at Brussels in 1675. The early Life by P. de Ribadeneira, *Vida del P. Francisco de Borja* (1596) is uncritical; more reliable portraits by P. Suau (1910), O. Karrer, *Der heilige Franz von Borja* (1921), and M. Yeo, *The Greatest of the Borgias* (1936). See also J. Brodrick, *The Origin of the Jesuits* (1940); id., *The Progress of the Jesuits* (1946); C. de Dalmasses and J. F. Gilmont, 'Las obras de San Francisco de Borgia', *Archiv. Histor. Societatis Iesu*, xxx (1961), 125–79.

BORIS AND GLEB (d. 1015), martyrs. Sons of *Vladimir by Anne of Constantinople, these two princes were killed at the instigation of their elder half-brother, Svyatopolk, whose aim was to 'exterminate all his brothers in order to hold all power in his own hands': Boris had been bequeathed Rostov and Gleb Muron. On returning from an expedition against the Pechenegs, Boris learned of Svyatopolk's plans. He would not allow his soldiers to fight for him against his brother, who now stood in his father's place. Instead, after much heart-searching he sent away his armed followers and passively awaited his murderers with prayer. Considering the emptiness of earthly riches and the example of the suffering Christ, whom he invoked for strength to accept his own passion, he was killed near the river Alta by spear and sword.

His younger brother Gleb was killed shortly afterwards on the river Dnieper. Invited by Svyatopolk to meet him at Kiev, Gleb suddenly met the boat which carried his murderers. He initially entreated them to spare him but at length voluntarily submitted to his fate, the final blow being a stab in the throat from his own cook. Prayers attributed to the two martyrs include a request for forgiveness for their brother, voluntary acceptance of an unjust death in imitation of Christ's passion, and acknowledgement of Christ's prophecy that his followers would be betrayed by kinsmen and friends.

In 1020, Yaroslav of Novgorod, yet another son of Vladimir, invaded Kiev and drove out Svyatopolk, who died in flight to Poland. Yaroslav translated the bodies of Boris and Gleb, reputedly incorrupt, to the church of St. Basil at Vyshgorod, near Kiev; miracles were reported and pilgrimages began. The Greek metropolitan of Kiev hesitated to canonize them: they were neither ascetics nor teachers, neither bishops nor martyrs in the sense of being killed for the faith. They were seen, however, as 'passion-bearers', innocent men who had renounced violence and accepted death as a sacrifice in the unresisting spirit of Christ. They were accordingly canonized and Pope Benedict XIII approved their cult as martyrs in 1724. In the West they are sometimes called Romanus and David. Feast: 24 July.

Bibl. SS., iii. 356–9; B.T.A. iii. 175–6; C. de Grunwald, *Saints of Russia* (1960), pp. 31–8.

BORROMEO, Charles (1538–84), archbishop of Milan. Born of an aristocratic and wealthy family in the castle of Arona on Lake Maggiore and related through his mother to the Medicis, he was educated at Milan and Pavia. He was intelligent and devout, but suffered a speech-impediment. He had, however, an enormous capacity for hard work.

From the age of twelve he had received both the clerical tonsure and the revenues of the commendatory abbacy of Arona, long enjoyed by his family. At the age of twenty-two he took his doctor's degree, by which time his uncle, Cardinal de Medici, had become pope as Pius IV. He heaped honours on his nephew, including legations, protectorates, the administration of the diocese of Milan and appointment as cardinal, and in practice Secretary of State. This required residence in Rome; Charles delegated the government of his diocese to deputies. He kept a large household and entertained in a manner suitable to his rank. But he desired to leave the papal court and perhaps become a monk. He was advised, however, to continue in his present position and to reside in his diocese as soon as an opportunity offered.

He energetically supported Pius IV in reopening the Council of Trent for its last and final session. Charles's outstanding energy, diplomacy, and vigilance were to a great extent responsible for its continuance and conclusion. Many of the doctrinal and disciplinary decrees were passed at this session; Charles was specially prominent in drafting the Catechism. He was also responsible for reforming liturgical books and church music, in which he was a patron of Palestrina.

In 1564 he was ordained priest and consecrated as bishop. As papal legate for all Italy, he held a provincial council at Milan, which promulgated the Tridentine decrees of reform. He was summoned to the pope's deathbed in 1565 and obtained from his successor *Pius V the opportunity to reside in his diocese. In 1566 he began its reform, being the first resident bishop there in 80 years.

He started by adopting a very simple standard of living and giving away to the poor much of his considerable revenue. He held councils, synods, and regular visitations, and reorganized the administration. He was very concerned with clerical education, for which he founded seminaries which were much copied elsewhere; he insisted on the moral reform of the clergy already in office and founded a confraternity to teach Christian doctrine to children in Sunday school. Religious Orders who helped his work of reform included the Jesuits (founded by *Ignatius of Loyola) and the Barnabites (founded by Antony *Zaccaria). He gave very generous help to the English College at Douai, while his own confessor was a Welshman, Dr. Griffiths Roberts. He also venerated John *Fisher, whose picture he always had with him. He visited distant Alpine valleys in his diocese, removing ignorant and unworthy clergy, preaching and catechizing everywhere, and reconciling some of those who had adhered to Zwinglianism.

His reforms met vigorous opposition in some quarters, manifested by conflict with the civil authority and even in an attempt by a discontented friar to assassinate him (1569). In 1570 and again in 1576 he was conspicuous in helping his city; in the first case feeding many during a famine, and in the second nursing the plague-stricken. On both occasions he not only organized the relief-work, but also took a prominent personal part in it.

In 1580 he was visited at Milan by a party of young Englishmen on their way back to their native country. These included Ralph *Sherwin and Edmund *Campion. In 1583 he was appointed apostolic visitor in Switzerland, where he had to deal with witchcraft and sorcery as well as the consequences of the teaching of Calvin and Zwingli. Tireless, energetic, always on the move, he was worn out by the time he was forty-six. He died at Milan on the night of 3 November; he is buried in Milan cathedral. A spontaneous cult arose immediately and he was canonized in 1610. His influence in the Counter-Reformation, comparable to that of Ignatius of Loyola or Philip *Neri, was immediate and profound, particularly in the field of clerical education and in catechizing. Above all he gave a conspicuous example of an utterly devoted, reforming pastor in an important diocese at the very time it was most needed. A fine portrait, by G. B. Crespi, survives in the Ambrosian Gallery, Milan. Feast: 4 November.

Lives by A. Valiero (1586), J. P. Giussano (1610, Eng. tr. 1884), L. Cellier (1912), A. Deroo (1963). See also M. Yeo, *A Prince of Pastors* (1938), B.T.A., iv. 255–62, *N.C.E.* and *Bibl. SS.*, iii. 812–50.

BOSA, bishop of York 678–86 and 691–705. This monk of Whitby was consecrated by *Theodore bishop of Deira (the southern half of Northumbria, roughly the equivalent of modern Yorkshire) when *Wilfrid had been expelled from Northumbria following his quarrels with King Egfrith. Bosa ruled his diocese until his death except for the years of Wilfrid's restoration. *Bede praised his 'singular merit and holiness'; one of his disciples was *Acca, later the follower and successor of Wilfrid at Hexham. Feast: 9 March.

Bede, *H.E.*, iv. 12; v. 19–20.

BOSCARDIN, Maria Bertilla (1888–1922), nun. Born of a poor family at Brendola (Vicenza), she attended primary school intermittently largely because her father was jealous, violent, and not infrequently drunk. She was considered stupid (called a 'goose' by the local clergy); but she joined the sisters of St. *Dorothy at Vicenza. In 1904 she took the habit and worked in scullery, bakehouse, and laundry until her profession in 1907. Promoted to the children's diphtheria ward, she became a devoted nurse, but incurred an infection which ultimately proved fatal.

The most exciting years of her short life were during the First World War. After the disastrous battle of Caporetto, the hospital at Treviso was attacked in air raids. Although frightened, she used to bring coffee and marsala to the patients who were too ill to be moved to safety. Evacuated with others to a military hospital at Viggiú (near Como), she proved an excellent nurse for soldiers and was admired by the chaplain on this account. The superior, however, banished her to the laundry. Four months later the Mother-General (who esteemed her highly) withdrew her from Viggiú and restored her to Treviso, where she had the charge of the children's isolation ward.

Her health deteriorated in 1922 and a serious operation failed to save her. She died on 20 October. A memorial plaque described her as a 'chosen soul of heroic goodness . . . an angelic alleviator of human suffering in this place'. Her tomb at Vicenza was the centre of pilgrimage and miracles. She was beatified in 1952 and canonized in 1961. She resembled *Theresa of Lisieux, whose spiritual teaching she followed, in having good judgement, a strong will, and unobtrusive perseverance in humdrum duties. Feast: 20 October.

A.A.S., liii (1961), 278–95; P. G. di S. M. Maddalena, *Diario spirituale della B. Bertilla Boscardin* (1952); Lives by L. Caliaro (1952) and E. Federici (1961). See also B.T.A., iv. 161–2.

BOSCO, John (Don Bosco) (1815–88), founder of the Salesian Order. Born in Piedmont, he was the youngest son of a peasant farmer, who died when John was only two years old. He was brought up by his mother in extreme poverty; when he entered the seminary in 1831 his clothes and shoes were provided by charity. He was ordained priest in 1841 and soon settled into his life work, the education and apostolate of boys and young men, especially of the working class. Turin was the principal place of his activity. Persuaded by St. Joseph *Cafasso, rector of a seminary in Turin, to abandon his dream of foreign missionary work, and introduced by him both to wealthy benefactors and to the slums and prisons which would gain most from his ministry, John was appointed a chaplain of a refuge for girls. He devoted himself also to the needs of young men. His attractive charismatic personality soon drew many to his oratory and his evening classes.

Soon he resigned his post as chaplain and lived in poverty with his mother and about forty destitute boys in the Valdocco area: later he opened workshops for training shoemakers and tailors. By 1856 their number had grown to 150 resident boys with four workshops: there were also 500 children attached to the oratories and ten priests to help teach them. An eloquent preacher and a popular writer of great skill and diligence, John Bosco also had a reputation as a visionary, a wonder-worker, and one with an extraordinary gift for handling difficult youths without punishment but with a gentle and effective firmness.

Don Bosco often used to take boys on Sunday expeditions in the country, with Mass to start with, followed by breakfast and open-air games, a picnic, catechism-class, and Vespers to conclude. He believed in the value, especially for deprived urban boys, both of contact with natural beauty and the uplifting power of music. In 1859 he began to organize a Congregation which was formally approved in 1874; at the founder's death fourteen years later it numbered 768 members in sixty-four houses in both the Old and the New World. Now it numbers many thousands and specializes in pastoral work and schools of all kinds, including technical, agricultural, and ecclesiastical seminaries. As a church-builder he achieved the apparently impossible by heroic trust in Providence to provide necessary finance. One of his triumphs in this regard is the church of Sacro Cuore, Rome, completed shortly before his death. Another achievement was the foundation of an Order for nuns to do work for girls similar to that achieved for boys by his own Institute. It was called the Daughters of Our Lady, Help of Christians, and spread to most of the countries where the Salesian Fathers were at work. Its foundress was Maria *Mazzarello.

The funeral of John Bosco in 1888 seems to have been followed by a large proportion of the city of Turin: 40,000 people visited his body as it lay in state. He was canonized in 1934. Feast: 31 January.

G. B. Lemoyne and E. Ceria, *Memorie biografiche di don Giovanni Bosco* (19 vols., 1898–1939; Eng. tr. 1964–); E. Ceria (ed.), *Epistolario* (1955–); Lives by A. Auffray (1929, Eng. tr. 1930), H. L. Hughes (1934), H. Ghéon (1935, Eng. tr. 1935), and L. C. Sheppard (1957). See also articles in *N.C.E.* and *Bibl. SS.*, vi. 968–95.

BOSTE, John (1543–94), seminary priest and martyr. Born at Dufton (Cumbria),

Boste was educated at Queen's College, Oxford. In 1576 he was converted to the R.C. Church and entered the English College, Reims. He was ordained priest in 1581 and returned to England soon afterwards to an active apostolate of over ten years, mainly in the northern counties. He was sometimes disguised as a liveried servant of Lord Montacute. Eventually he was betrayed by an apostate and arrested near Durham in 1593. He was imprisoned and tortured in the Tower of London and sent back to Durham for trial in 1594. He refused to plead to the indictment that he was ordained abroad and had returned to England to extend the Catholic faith, and he also denied all involvement in political plots: 'our function', he said, 'is to invade souls, not to meddle with these temporal invasions'. He was found guilty of high treason and was hanged, drawn, and quartered at Dryburn, near Durham, on 24 July. He was canonized by Paul VI in 1970 as one of the *Forty Martyrs of England and Wales. Feast: 25 October.

J. Morris (ed.), *The Troubles of our Catholic Forefathers Related by Themselves* (1872–7), iii. *passim;* R. Challoner, *Memoirs of Missionary Priests* (ed. J. H. Pollen, 1924).

BOSWELL, see Boisil.

BOTHANUS, see Bathan.

BOTULF (Botolph) (d. 680), abbot of Icanho. He was born in East Anglia and started to build his monastery in 654 on land given by a king of East Anglia (Ethelhere, 654 or, more likely Ethelwold, 654–64). Hence it is much more probable that Icanho is Iken (Suffolk) than Boston (Lincs.), which is sometimes claimed as the site. Botulf had previously been chaplain to a nunnery where two of the king's sisters were inmates (possibly Chelles). Liobsynde, the first abbess of Wenlock (Salop), was from this convent; Wenlock was initially dependent on Icanho, clearly a very famous monastery in its time. One of its visitors, attracted by the teaching and observance of Botulf, was *Ceolfrith, who went there *c.*670 before joining *Benedict Biscop at Wearmouth.

Nothing more is known of Botulf's life. His church was destroyed in the Danish invasions. *Ethelwold sent his disciple Ulfkitel to collect the relics of Botulf and his brother *Adulf for his monastery at Thorney. The bones of Botulf could not be moved without those of Adulf as well. Eventually the head of Botulf was given to Ely, the rest was shared by Thorney, Bury St. Edmunds, and, later, Westminster, while Adulf's body went intact to Thorney. Sixty-four ancient churches were dedicated to Botulf, sixteen of them in Norfolk, and three (all rebuilt by Wren) in the city of London. Feast: 17 June; translation, 1 December.

AA.SS. Iun. III (1701), 398–406; C. Plummer (ed.), *Baedae Opera Historica*, i (1956), 389; H. P. R. Finberg, *The Early Charters of the West Midlands* (1961), pp. 197–224; F. S. Stevenson, 'St. Botulf', *Proc. of Suffolk Inst. of Archaeol. and Nat. Hist.* (1922), pp. 29–52.

BOTVID (d. 1100), martyr. A Swedish layman from Sodermannland, Botvid became a Christian in England and then returned to Sweden to help spread Christianity in his native country, where already English missionary monks were at work. Following the policy of *Gregory and *Aidan, he bought a Finnish slave, instructed and baptized him. He then set him free by rowing him with a companion across the Baltic sea. The freed slave, however, murdered them both and sailed the boat away. According to the legend, a search-party was guided by a bird, singing on the boat until the bodies were found. Botvid was buried at Botkyrka: the Life written by a monk of Bodensee claims him as an apostle of Sweden. Feast: 28 July.

AA.SS. Iul. VI (1729), 635–8; *Scriptores rerum Suevicarum*, II (part i), 377–87.

BOURGEOYS, Marguerite (1620–1700), foundress of the Sisters of Notre Dame de Montréal. Born at Troyes (Aube), the daughter of a prolific wax-chandler, she tried to be a nun at the local convents of Carmelites and Poor Clares. Both refused her. After this she joined a local unenclosed community of active nuns, but this venture came to nothing.

In 1652 the governor of Montréal visited Troyes and recruited her as schoolmistress: she landed at Québec in 1653 and went to the fort of Ville-Marie (Montréal), where she taught the children and helped in the hospital and general life of the tiny outpost. In 1658 the first school at Montréal was opened under her charge, but realizing that it would expand, she returned to France and brought back four more helpers. This process was repeated in 1670–2. By this time she had decided to found a Congregation and in 1676 it was canonically established by the bishop of Québec.

Difficulties abounded, but so also did opportunities. Schools for Indian children were begun; education for French children expanded under Marguerite's care to Québec and Trois Rivières. There were various disasters such as fires and massacres by neighbouring Iroquois. In face of them all she continued with indomitable courage through the hardships of poverty, pioneering, and the misunderstandings of bishops. In 1698 twenty-four sisters made their professions, but by then she had resigned from being their superior. Her health and strength diminished until she died on 12 January 1700. The 200 convents of her congregation today are evidence for her wisdom and sheer goodness described by contemporaries. She was beatified in 1950 and canonized in 1982. Feast: 19 January.

Lives by A. Jamet (1942), Y. Charron (Eng. tr. 1950); B.T.A., i. 125–7; *Bibl. SS.*, iii. 375–6.

BRANDON, see BRENDAN THE NAVIGATOR.

BRANNOC (Barnoc) (date unknown). He is the titular saint of Braunton (Devon), where William Worcestre and Leland say he was buried. Some identify him with Brynach, the Welsh missionary of the 6th century. Feast (at Exeter and according to William Worcestre): 7 January, while the feast of Brynach is 7 April. This makes the identification of the two unlikely.

W. G. Hoskins and H. P. R. Finberg, *Devonshire Studies* (1952); William Worcestre, p. 115; Baring-Gould and Fisher, i. 325–6.

BRANWALADER (Branwalator, Brelade, Breward) (6th century), monk and ? bishop. Of Celtic, perhaps, Welsh, origin, he worked with *Samson in Cornwall and the Channel Islands, and possibly in Brittany. The Exeter martyrology describes him as a son of a Cornish king, Kenen. He gave his name to St. Brelade (Jersey). In the early 10th century King Athelstan obtained his relics from Breton clerics in flight from the Northmen and gave them to his monastery of Milton (Dorset). It was not a whole body but either an arm (Milton charter) or his head (*R.P.S*). William Worcestre claimed that the body was at Branston (Devon), and Leland referred to a chapel of St. Breward near Seaton.

If there is uncertainty about his life and about his relics, at least his cult was clear from the 10th century. His name is found in litanies; his feast was kept at Winchester and Exeter, but on a different day in Cornwall. Feast: usually 19 January, but Whytford says this was a translation; in Cornwall both 9 February and 6 June are found as his day. Confusion in Brittany with *Brendan or *Brannoc have sometimes caused other days to be considered his.

G. H. Doble, *The Saints of Cornwall*, iv (1965), 116–27; Baring-Gould and Fisher, i. 227–8.

BRAY, see BREAGE.

BREACA, see BREAGE.

BREAGE (Breaca, Bray), obscure Cornish woman saint possibly of Irish origin, presumably the foundress of the church of Breage (Cornwall). Leland made short extracts from her Life, kept in her church. According to this, she was a native of Lagonia (= Laois?), became a nun at St. *Brigid's foundation at 'Campus Breacae' in Ireland, and came to Cornwall in the company of many saints, among them Sinwin, *Germoe, Elwen, *Crowan, and *Helen. Breage came first to Pencair, then to Trenwith and Talmeneth, where she built churches. Feast-day not known.

J. F. Kenney, *Sources for the History of Ireland*, i. 181; J. Leland, *Itinerary*, i. 187.

BRÉBEUF, Jean de (1593–1649), Jesuit priest and martyr of Canada. Born in Normandy, Brébeuf became a Jesuit at Rouen in 1617. His health was so affected by tuberculosis that he could neither study nor teach for the customary periods. But he offered himself for the Canadian mission and sailed in 1625. He worked among the Huron Indians, unsuccessfully at first, but with considerable reward from 1633 until his death. At their request he lived among them, sometimes with companions and sometimes alone, preaching and catechizing in their own language. Superstition, violence, and cannibalism were among the obstacles to the apostolate; equally important was the fact that Brébeuf and his companions, however disinterested and spiritual, belonged to an alien, conquering race. He founded schools and baptized over 200 neophytes in one year. Once he was condemned to death, but spoke so eloquently about the afterlife that he was reprieved. In 1646 his companion, Isaac *Jogues, was killed by Iroquois tomahawks. In 1649 the Iroquois, deadly enemies of the Hurons, attacked the village where Brébeuf and his companion Gabriel Lalemant were. They were captured, mutilated, tortured, burnt, and eventually eaten. Their passion was one of the most horrifying in the records of martyrdom.

These Canadian Jesuit martyrs were canonized in 1930; their cult was extended world-wide in 1969 as the proto-martyrs of North America. Feast: 19 October (formerly 26 September).

R. G. Thwaites, *Jesuit Relations* (1897–1901); H. Fouqueray, *Martyrs du Canada* (1930); R. Latourelle, *Étude sur les Écrits de S. Jean de Brébeuf* (1953).

BREGOWINE (d. 764), archbishop of Canterbury. Reputedly a Continental Saxon who became a monk in England after attending the school founded by *Theodore, he became archbishop in 761. He received the pallium from Pope Paul I. The only recorded act of his episcopate is an attempt to recover the monastery of Cookham (Berks.) from Cynewulf, king of Wessex. But there are also later references to a synod held by him. A letter of his to *Lull, archbishop of Mainz, survives. This reminds him of their friendship during a visit to Rome, regrets the loss of contact due to war, and refers to the present of a reliquary.

Like his predecessor *Cuthbert he was buried in the baptistery of Canterbury cathedral, to the intense indignation of the monks of St. Augustine's, whose ancient privilege it was to bury the archbishops in their own church. When the baptistery was destroyed by fire in 1067, the relics of Bregwine and other archbishops buried there were placed together over the vault of the north transept.

In 1121–2 a German monk named Lambert, who had friends in high places, came to Canterbury and obtained permission from the dying archbishop Ralph to transfer Bregwine's body to a monastery he planned to build in his own country. But Lambert died soon afterwards, supposedly through the saint's displeasure, and was buried at Canterbury. Bregwine's relics were translated, not to his native Germany, but to the altar of St. Gregory in the south transept of Canterbury Cathedral: this event was the occasion for the short Life by Eadmer. There is no surviving record of an early feast: Florence of Worcester placed his death on 24 August, while some 15th-century calendars record his feast on 26 August.

Life by Osbern in H. Wharton, *Anglia Sacra* (1691), i, 75–7; B. W. Scholz, 'Eadmer's Life of Bregwine, archbishop of Canterbury 761–4', *Traditio* xxii (1966), 127–48; N. Brooks, *The Early History of the Church at Canterbury* (1984) 80–5, 103.

BRELADE, see BRANWALADER.

BRENDAN OF BIRR (d. 573), Irish abbot. Friend and disciple of *Columba, his eminence was shown both in his title of chief of the prophets of Ireland and in his intervention at a synod at Meltown (Meath) which ended Columba's excommunication.

At the death of Brendan, Columba saw a

vision in Iona of angels receiving his soul, so he ordered a special Mass to be said in his honour. From Brendan's monastery at Birr later came the MacRegol Gospels, now in the Bodleian Library, Oxford. Feast: 29 November.

A. O. and M. O. Anderson (edd.), *Adomnan's Life of Columba* (1961), bk. III, cc. 3, 11; *The Irish Saints*, pp. 35–6.

BRENDAN (Brandon) **THE NAVIGATOR** (*c.*486–*c.*575), abbot of Clonfert. Born probably near Tralee, fostered by *Ita and educated by *Erc, bishop of Kerry, Brendan became a monk and later abbot. His main centre of activity was western Ireland, where several place-names and landmarks (including Mount Brandon in the Dingle peninsula) are called after him. His most important monastic foundations were Clonfert (founded ?559), Annadown (Co. Galway), Inishadroum (Co. Clare), and Ardfert (Co. Kerry). Like many other Irish monks, he was a great traveller: he is said by *Adomnan to have visited *Columba at Hinba (Argyll); others claim that he founded a Scottish monastery, became abbot of Llancarvan (Wales), or that he went to Brittany with *Malo. In fact very few details about his life can be asserted with certainty. His cult, however, was certainly strong in Ireland (from the 9th-century martyrologies onwards), and in Wales, Scotland, and Brittany.

The cult owed much to the famous *Navigation of St. Brendan*. This visionary romance of the 9th–10th centuries transformed the historical, seafaring abbot into a mythical adventurer, who accomplished incredible exploits. Written by an expatriate Irish monk, it tells of a sea voyage with a band of monks to an island of promise in the Atlantic Ocean. This quest for a happy other-world has some features derived from early apocryphal Christian writings, others from Irish folklore. Its immense popularity is proved from the survival of 116 medieval Latin manuscripts of the text, and of versions in Middle English, French, German, Flemish, Italian, Provençal, and Norse. Various attempts have been made to identify the itinerary, but it is more likely that the whole story is a delightful fiction. Matthew Arnold recounted the story in verse in 'Saint Brandan'. Feast: 16 May.

P. F. Moran, *Acta Sancti Brendani* (1872); W. W. Heist, *Acta Sanctorum Hiberniae* (1965), pp. 56–81, 324–31; P. Grosjean, 'Vita S. Brendani Clonfertensis e codice Dubliniensi', *Anal. Boll.*, xlviii (1930), 99–123; C. Selmer, *Navigatio Sancti Brendani Abbatis* (1959); J. F. Kenney, *The Sources for the Early History of Ireland* (1929), i. 406–20; id., 'The Legend of St. Brendan', *Trans. Roy. Soc. of Canada*, xiv (1920), 51–67; R. H. Bowers, 'The Middle English St. Brendan's Confession', *Archiv für das Studium der neueren Sprachen*, clxxv (1939), 40–9; E. G. R. Waters, *The Anglo-Norman Voyage of St. Brendan by Benedict* (1928); G. A. Little, *Brendan the Navigator* (1945); T. Severin, *The Brendan Voyage* (1978); J. F. Webb and D. H. Farmer, *The Age of Bede* (1983).

BREWARD, see BRANWALADER.

BRIANT, Alexander (*c.*1556–81), priest and martyr. Born in Somerset, Briant was educated at Hart Hall, Oxford; while an undergraduate he returned to the R.C. Church in 1574 and entered the English College, Douai, in 1577. He was ordained priest in 1578 and returned to Somerset in 1579, where he reconciled many to the Church, including the father of the famous Robert Persons, S.J. In the outcry for the arrest of the latter in 1581 (see CAMPION, Edmund) Alexander Briant was taken by pursuivants in London from the very next house to that in which Persons was hiding. Briant was imprisoned in the Tower and savagely tortured by starvation, the rack, the thumbscrew, needles under his nails, and the 'scavenger's daughter'. All these failed to elicit from him the wanted information, especially the whereabouts of Persons. One of his torturers described him as a miracle of pertinacity. News of his treatment shocked contemporaries and elicited a reply from the government in 1583. From prison he applied for admission to the Society of Jesus but, although his formal entry could not be arranged, he is often claimed as a Jesuit. On 21 November he was tried at Westminster Hall and found guilty of a fictitious plot. He suffered with Edmund *Campion and Ralph *Sherwin the usual execution on 1 December. He was canonized by Paul VI in 1970 as one of the *Forty Martyrs of England and Wales. Feast: 25 October.

H. Foley, *Records of the English Province of the Society of Jesus* (1877–82), iv (2), 343–67; P. de Rosa, *Blessed Alexander Briant* (pamphlet 1961); B.T.A., iv. 469–70; *N.C.E.*, ii. 795.

BRIAVEL (date unknown), patron of St. Briavels (Glos.), of whom the first written record goes back to 1130. He seems to have been a Celtic saint, whose name, according to Ekwall, dates from the Old Celtic Brigomaglos. Stanton says he was a hermit in the Forest of Dean, who gave his name to this place, but whose life is unknown. Feast: 17 June.

Stanton, p. 271.

BRICE (Britius) (d. 444), bishop of Tours. Educated at *Martin's monastery of Marmoutier, Brice became a critic of his master, but eventually his successor. While he was a deacon he said Martin was crazy; but when called on to justify his criticism, withdrew it. Another time he said Martin was falling into superstition in his old age, but again asked his pardon. He must, however, have been reasonably able, because he was elected bishop on the death of Martin in 397. This, it was said, fulfilled Martin's own prophecy.

But if Martin's episcopate had been long, Brice's lasted longer still. Although he was difficult, he had considerable powers of survival. He was accused of various faults, sometimes justly, at other times unjustly. In the thirty-third year of his episcopate his enemies accused him of adultery. Brice went to Rome and was eventually vindicated by the pope. After this incident he was comparatively subdued; he returned to Tours, having suffered exile for seven years, and spent his remaining years in energetic apostolic activity. It is thought that this implied expiation for his earlier shortcomings, and when he died he was soon venerated as a saint.

By 470 his cult was firmly established at Tours; soon it spread to Italy and England through his association with Martin. In English monastic calendars before 1100 it was almost universal and his feast was also in the Sarum calendar. But, like his life, so also his feast was controversial; in 1002 King Ethelred the Unready ordered the Danes in England to be massacred on St. Brice's Day. This misguided attempt was the occasion for Swein's invasion of England in 1003. Feast: 13 November.

Sulpicius Severus, *Vita S. Martini* (*P.L.*, xx. 159–222 and *C.S.E.L.*, i. 108–216); H. Delehaye, 'S. Martin et Sulpice Sévère', *Anal. Boll.*, xxxviii (1920), 1–136; letters of Pope Zosimus in *P.L.*, xx. 650–63; C. Stancliffe, *St. Martin and his Hagiographer* (1983).

BRIDE, see BRIGID OF IRELAND.

BRIDGET, see BRIGID OF IRELAND.

BRIDGET (Birgitta) **OF SWEDEN** (1303–73), foundress and visionary, patron of Sweden. The daughter of Berger, the rich governor of Upland, she married Ulf Gudmarrson at the age of fourteen. For many years, she lived as chatelaine on his estates and bore him eight children, one of whom was St. *Catherine of Sweden. In 1335 she was summoned to court to be the principal lady-in-waiting to the queen, Blanche of Namur, wife of King Magnus II. She now began to experience supernatural revelations; the king and queen respected her but did not reform their lives; the courtiers gossiped about her. Bridget made pilgrimages: one to St. *Olaf's shrine at Trondheim (Norway), another (with her husband) to St. *James at Compostela (Spain). Her husband died soon afterwards at the Cistercian monastery at Alvastra, where Bridget then lived as a penitent (1343–6).

Having recovered from her husband's death, and now more clear about what she should do, she founded a monastery in 1346 at Vadstena (on Lake Vattern) for sixty nuns and twenty-five monks, who lived in separate enclosures but shared the same church. In temporal matters the abbess was supreme, but in spiritual ones the monks. All superfluous income was given to the poor; luxurious buildings were forbidden, but all the inmates could have as many books for study as they wished. In some respects the Brigettine Order was modelled on Fontevrault; like it, Vadstena enjoyed the generous patronage of royalty, in this case, King Magnus.

In 1349 Bridget went to Rome to obtain approval for her Order, as well as the jubilee indulgence of 1350. She never returned to Sweden but spent the rest of her life in Italy or on various pilgrimages, including one to the Holy Land. Her austerity of life, her devotion both in visiting shrines and in serving pilgrims, the poor, and the sick were impressive. Meanwhile her visions continued. Some of these were of the Passion of Christ; others, underlined by comminatory prophecies, were concerned with political and religious events of her own day. She tried to dissuade King Magnus from a so-called crusade against pagans of Estonia and Latvia; like other visionaries she also warned Pope Clement VI to return to Rome from Avignon and to make peace between England and France. Threats of punishment for persistent wrongdoing feature fairly prominently in her writings.

Unfortunately, her experiences can be known only through the editions published by her directors. These imply the work of one or two editors, recording and sometimes interpreting the message. Her original perception too was human and fallible. She was canonized for her virtue, not her revelations.

Her Order was approved by the Holy See. It once numbered seventy houses, but now there are only twelve Brigettine nunneries in the world; one, at South Brent (Devon), has unbroken continuity with Syon Abbey, Isleworth, founded by King Henry V. The Brigettine monks, in spite of an attempt to revive them by an Englishman of the 20th century, are now extinct.

Feast: 23 July, formerly 8 October, which was both the day of her canonization (1391) and the day her relics were translated to Vadstena Abbey. There they remain and part of her nunnery has been restored.

AA.SS. Oct. IV (1780), 368–560; Lives also in *Scriptores Rerum Suevicarum Medii Aevi* (1871), pp. 185–206; I. Collijn, *Acta et Processus canonizationis beatae Birgittae* (1924–31): id. *Iconographica Birgittina* (1915); modern Lives by H. Redpath (1947), and J. Jorgensen (Eng. tr. 1954); E. Graf, *Revelations and Prayers of St. Bridget* (1928); A. Butkovich, *Revelations: Saint Birgitta of Sweden* (1972); B.T.A., iv. 54–9.

BRIEUC, see Brioc.

BRIGID (Brigit, Bridget, Bride) **OF IRELAND** (d. *c.*525), abbess of Kildare. Historical facts about her are extremely rare; some scholars have even doubted her existence altogether; her Lives are mainly anecdotes and miracle stories, some of which are deeply rooted in Irish pagan folklore.

She is believed to have been born near Uinmeras about 5 miles from Kildare, of parents of humble origin, baptized by *Patrick; to have become a nun at an early age; to have founded the monastery of Kildare and so contributed notably to the spread of Christianity. Her miracle stories portray her almost as a personification of compassion. Some emphasize the theme of multiplication of food: either of butter to the poor, or of changing her bath-water into beer to satisfy the thirst of unexpected clerical visitors. Even her cows gave milk three times the same day to enable some bishops to have enough to drink. Other legends make her a personification of the Blessed Virgin ('Mary of the Gael'); this is based on a vision of bishop Ibor the night before an assembly addressed by Brigid. When she arrived she corresponded exactly to his vision of Mary. The same Ibor is said to have consecrated Brigid a bishop, but this seems impossible, and the preposterous claims that bishops and abbesses of Kildare were supreme over others in the whole of Ireland were a principal reason for the existence of early

Lives, such as that by Cogitosus (*c.*650). This was written ignoring Armagh and Patrick. The later development of Kildare into an important double monastery, with shrines of Brigid and *Conleth in the elaborately decorated wooden church, should not lead us to suppose that it was equally developed in Brigid's own lifetime.

But if there is much uncertainty about her life, there is none about the extension of her cult, especially in Ireland and in churches of Irish origin on the Continent, where it was second only to that of Patrick. Many manuscript copies were made of her Lives, translations were made into Old French, Middle English, and German. In England there were at least nineteen ancient church dedications in her honour (the most famous is St. Bride's, Fleet Street), and almost as many in Wales. The name of St. Bride's Bay, Dyfed, emphasizes the strong connection between Irish and Welsh Christianity, while several places in Wales are called Llansantaffraid (= St. Bride's Church). She is still venerated in Alsace, Flanders, and Portugal.

Brigid is patron of poets, blacksmiths, and healers. Her most usual iconographical attribute is a cow lying at her feet, which recalls her phase as a nun–cowgirl. An interesting relic of her shoe, made of silver and brass, set with jewels, survives in the National Museum at Dublin.

Folkloric elements have been important not only in her Lives, but also in her cult. Gerald of Wales (d. *c.*1220) described a fire kept burning continuously at her shrine for centuries, tended by the twenty nuns of her community. The fire was surrounded by a circle of bushes, which no man was allowed to enter. Such details, added to the facts that the name *Brig*, meaning valour or might, was personified as a goddess, whose fire-cult took place on 1 February, has led some critics to identify Brigid unconvincingly with this heathen goddess.

Principal feast: 1 February; translation, 10 June. Another feast on 24 March commemorated the discovery by *Malachy in 1185 of the supposed bodies of Patrick, *Columba, and Brigid at Downpatrick. This feast was kept in Ireland, but also some English centres such as Chester, while the principal feast was almost universal. Her tunic, supposedly given by Gunhilda, sister of King Harold II, survives at St. Donatian's, Bruges.

AA.SS. Feb. 1 (1658), 99–185: Latin Lives also in J. Colgan, *Trias Thaumaturga* (1647); Irish Lives in W. Stokes, *The Book of Lismore* (1890, with Eng. tr.) and in C. Plummer, J. Fraser, and P. Grosjean, 'Vita Brigitae', *Irish Texts*, i (1931); also M. A. O'Brien, 'The Old Irish Life of St. Brigid', *I.H.S.*, i (1938–9), 121–34, 343–53; M. Esposito, 'On the Earliest Latin Life of St. Brigit of Kildare', *P.R.I.A.*, xxx (1912); J. Kenney, *The Sources for the Early History of Ireland*, i (1929), 356–63; F. O'Briain 'Brigitana', *Z.C.P.*, xxxvi. 112–37; 'The Hagiography of Leinster' in J. Ryan (ed.), *Essays and Studies presented to Prof. Eoin MacNeill* (1940); L. Gougaud, *Les Saints irlandais hors d'Irlande* (1937); R. Sharpe, 'Vitae S. Brigitae: the Oldest Texts', *Peritia*, i (1982), 81–106; K. McCone, 'Brigid in the Seventh Century: a Saint with Three Lives', ibid. 107–45; S. Connolly, 'The Authorship and manuscript tradition of Vita I S. Brigitae', *Manuscripta*, xvi (1972), 67–82.

BRIHTWALD, see BERHTWALD.

BRIOC (Brieuc), Celtic saint of the 6th century who has given his name to St. Breock (Cornwall) and Saint-Brieuc (Brittany). He was probably born in Cardigan where he founded a monastery. Whether or not he was educated in France, as his 12th-century Life claims, he died in Brittany in another of his monastic foundations. It is not certain that he was a bishop: more likely he was an abbot of the Celtic type who kept a bishop in his monastery as one of his subjects. No legend claims that anyone was the successor of St. Brioc in the see of Saint-Brieuc. As Saint-Brieuc is near the sea, it was very vulnerable to Norse invasions. Therefore, the relics of Brioc were taken to Angers in the middle of the 9th century. In 1166 there was a translation, at which Henry II was present. In 1210 one arm, two ribs, and part of the neck bones were given back to Saint-Brieuc. On account of legends of his great charity he is the patron of purse-makers. Feast: 1 May; translation, 18 October.

G. H. Doble, *The Saints of Cornwall*, iv (1965), 67–104.

BRITHUN, see BERCTHUN.

BRITIUS, see BRICE.

BRUNO (*c.*1032–1101), founder of the Carthusian Order. Bruno was educated at Reims and Cologne and became a canon at St. Cunibert's, Cologne, from which in 1056 he returned to Reims as a lecturer in grammar and theology in the cathedral school. This post he kept for 18 years and among the many gifted young clerics he taught was the future Pope Urban II. He was appointed chancellor of the diocese of Reims by its archbishop, Manasses, who turned out to be a person of notoriously scandalous life. Bruno acted with prudence and decision in a council which resulted in Manasses' deposition, followed by his plundering the houses of his accusers and selling their prebends. Manasses was eventually reinstated, but by then Bruno had left for Cologne and decided to become a monk. He lived as a hermit under the direction of *Robert of Molesme, but soon moved to the diocese of Grenoble whose bishop, St. *Hugh, helped Bruno and his six companions to live in solitude. In 1084 Hugh gave them by an extant charter the forest-covered, mountainous land of the Chartreuse, where they built an oratory with cells round it. Their form of monasticism was eremitical, emphasizing poverty, solitude, and austerity, and inspired by the primitive monks of Egypt and Palestine rather than by the Rule of St. Benedict. Their regime consisted of prayer (Vespers and Matins only in the church, with Mass on Sundays and feasts), reading, and manual work, which, once the agricultural work was deputed to lay brothers, consisted largely in copying books. Three volumes survive of a Bible written in this first monastery, soon destroyed by an avalanche. But monastic life continued in a new monastery further down the mountain.

After only six years Pope Urban summoned him to Rome to advise him about the state of the Church. Bruno settled in a hermitage among the ruins of the baths of Diocletian, but his influence cannot be explicitly proved in particular items of the Gregorian Reform. It is likely that he was influential in the papal efforts for clerical reform. Urban offered Bruno the archbishopric of Reggio (Calabria), but he refused. Instead, with some new disciples from Rome, he founded another hermitage at La Torre (Calabria) on land given by Roger, brother of Robert Guiscard, who became Bruno's close friend. From Calabria he wrote to his Carthusians at Grenoble; with their prior Landuin, who visited him, he helped to organize more fully their way of life, a process completed by the *Consuetudines* of Guigo I in the early 12th century.

Bruno died at La Torre on 6 October 1101. The mortuary roll sent out from there survives with 178 notices. Although the Holy See never formally canonized Bruno, it did so equivalently by approving his cult for the Carthusians in 1514 and extending it to the Universal Church in 1623. Carthusian monks came to England in 1173 (see HUGH OF LINCOLN) and remained, as elsewhere in Europe, a spiritual force out of all proportion with their small numbers; there were nine houses in late medieval England. Some of their monks, especially from London, provided the papacy with some of its most impressive witnesses (see *FORTY MARTYRS OF ENGLAND AND WALES). A Charterhouse, founded in the 19th century, survives in Sussex. Feast: 6 October.

Bruno's writings (Scriptural treatises and letters) in *P.L.*, clii–cliii; contemporary testimonies and a 13th-century Life in *AA.SS.* Oct. III (1700), 491–777; B. Bligny, *Saint Bruno* (1984); *La Grande Chartreuse par un Chartreux* (1984).

BRYCHAN (no date), legendary Welsh king with many saintly children who appear in varying forms in Celtic hagiology. One version stresses the connection of Wales with Ireland, while another claims Brychan was buried in Scotland. Several manuscript Lives of Welsh saints mention him, as do William Worcestre, Leland, and Roscarrock. The number of children attributed to him varies from twelve to sixty-three, the number most frequently encountered being twenty-four. The genealogy is obscure and saints most frequently claimed as his children (descendants through three marriages or several generations?) include *Nectan, *Endellion, *Morwenna, *Clether, etc. Most of them came from Brecon to Cornwall or Devon, where they were venerated.

A 16th-century stained-glass window at St. Neot, Cornwall, depicts Brychan, seated and crowned, holding in his arms ten children. This, however, has been described by a standard modern guide as 'God the Father with souls in his lap'. Roscarrock gives 6 April as his feast.

A. W. Wade-Evans, *Vitae Sanctorum Britanniae* (1944), pp. 313–17; Baring-Gould and Fisher, i. 303–31; William Worcestre, pp. 63–5.

BRYNSTAN, see BIRSTAN.

BUDOC (Buoc, Beuzec) (6th century), Celtic saint, patron of Budock and Budoc Vean (Cornwall) and St. Budeaux (Devon). Budoc was honoured also in Pembrokeshire (Dyfed) in and near Steynton; to him was dedicated a Tironian monastery at Pill in 1200. An Oxford church (near the castle) was also dedicated to Budoc; it may well have been of pre-Conquest date.

Budoc is also venerated in Brittany. The 9th-century Life of *Winwaloe describes him as a teacher living in the island of Laurea. The Life of *Maglorius, written *c.*900, and the 11th-century Chronicle of Dol, make him Maglorius' successor as bishop of Dol. He is the local saint of Plourin, where his relics are still preserved. There is a cult and no place-names at Dol, but place-names without a cult in Cornouaille. Whether this Breton bishop is the same as the abbot venerated in Pembrokeshire and Cornwall it is impossible to determine. The date of the Breton feast (9 December) is sufficiently close to the Exeter martyrology entry to favour an identification; it is a curious fact also that Budock faces St. Mawes across Falmouth harbour, while *Mawes was abbot of an island monastery in Brittany close to that of Budoc. The main centres of the cult(s) of Budoc are all close to the sea.

The most picturesque legend of Budoc concerns his birth at sea in a barrel. His mother Azenor had been falsely accused of infidelity to her husband by her jealous stepmother who had her thrown pregnant into the English Channel in a barrel. Fortified by visions of *Brigid she reached Ireland and became the washer-woman of the monastery of Beau Port, near Waterford, where her son was brought up. This story is derived from Greek mythology; with other late accretions it has done nothing to help unravel the tangled skeins of this saint's life and cult. Feast: 8 December; Glastonbury claimed to possess a relic.

G. H. Doble, *The Saints of Cornwall*, iii (1964), 3–14; Albert Le Grand, *La Providence de Dieu sur les Justes en l'Histoire admirable de Saint Budoc, Archevesque de Dol* (1640).

BUGGA, see EDBURGA OF MINSTER.

BURCHARD (d. 754), bishop of Wurzburg. A Wessex man, Burchard was one of many English people who offered their services to *Boniface in the evangelization of Germany. Burchard joined him in 732 and became the first diocesan bishop of Wurzburg, in which area the Irish *Kilian had worked fifty years before and whose relics he translated to his own cathedral. Burchard was an energetic bishop: he founded both a school and an abbey in his cathedral town. Like Boniface he worked in close concert with the emperors; he led a mission to the papacy in 749 which resulted in a decision about the succession to the Frankish imperial throne favourable to Pepin the Short. He retired from his bishopric *c.*753 and died some months later at Homburg-on-Main. Feast: 14 October.

AA.SS. Oct. VI (1794), 557–94; F. J. Bendel, *Vita S. Burkardi* (1911); see also *Archiv des Hist.*

Vereins für Unterfranken und Aschaffenburg, xlv. 1–61; lxviii. 377–85.

BURYAN (Burien), Cornish saint who gave her name as titular of a church to the village of the same name. The first written record is in an Anglo-Saxon charter in 943. Nothing is known of this saint except her name.

BYRNWOLD, see BEORNWALD.

C

CABRINI, Frances Xavier (d. 1917), nun and foundress. The youngest of thirteen children of an Italian farmer who lived near Pavia, Frances was strictly brought up, but in 1870 both her parents died. Two years later she tried to become a nun at the convent school where she was educated, but was refused for health reasons. She applied to another Order, but was refused a second time for the same cause. Now a schoolteacher, who had taken a private vow of virginity, she was called in by the parish priest of Codogno to reorganize an orphanage. This was badly mismanaged by its foundress, who made things so impossible for Frances and her companions that the bishop closed the orphanage and encouraged her to be a missionary. Prioress over seven companions from the orphanage at Codogno from 1880, she made foundations at Grumello, Milan and in 1887 at Rome. Papal approval for her 'Missionary Sisters of the Sacred Heart' was now obtained and although her first idea had been to work in China, she was advised by several prelates to devote herself instead to the Italian immigrants in the USA, of which she became first a citizen and later the first canonized saint.

In New York, whose archbishop Corrigan had invited her to found schools and orphanages, it has been estimated that in 1889 (when she arrived) there were 50,000 Italians, of whom only 1,200 were churchgoers: most lived in conditions of extreme poverty. No adequate arrangements had been made for her nuns: the orphanage plan had fallen through, and she was presented with plenty of pupils but no school building. Undeterred by the archbishop's recommendation to return to Italy, she got the orphanage under way and in 1890 moved it to West Park on the river Hudson, where she established the novitiate and most important house of her congregation in the USA. Foundations followed at New Orleans, Managua (Nicaragua), and New York (the Columbus hospital). Later foundations included Chicago, Buenos Aires, and Brockley (Kent). In 1917 her congregation numbered over 1,500 nuns in eight countries: there were sixty-seven houses in all devoted to education, nursing, and the care of orphans, their scope far transcending the original plan of ministry to Italian immigrants. In character she was strict, but just and loving: sometimes her actions reflected the limitations of her early education, as in her rejection of illegitimate children from some of her schools, and her lack of understanding and sympathy for American Protestants. Against these stand the extraordinary and permanent achievement of herself and her nuns. She died of malaria in Chicago on 22 December 1917; she was canonized by Pope Pius XII in 1946. Her body rests in Mother Cabrini High School, New York. Feast: 22 December.

E. de Sanctis Rosmini, *La beata Francesca Saverio Cabrini* (1938); A Benedictine of Stanbrook, *Frances Xavier Cabrini: the Saint of the Emigrants* (1944); other Lives by C. C. Martindale (1931), E. J. McCarthy (1937), and T. Maynard (1948): Her writings include *Escortationi della Cabrini* (1954) and *Diario spirituale* (1957); canonization documents are summarized in *Novissima positio super virtutibus* (1937). See also articles in *N.C.E.*, ii. 1039 and *Bibl. SS.*, v. 1028–45.

CADARN, see DERFEL.

CADFAN (Catamanus, Catman) (5th century), abbot. Breton in origin he migrated to Wales, gathered numerous disciples, and founded the church of Towyn (Gwynedd) and the large, famous monastery of Bardsey Island, both of which claimed to be the place of his death. From Towyn he used to travel to Llangadfan (named after him) through Pistyll Gadfan, Eisteddfa Gadfa, and Llwbyr Gadfan. A chapel of St. Cadfan used to exist in the churchyard at Towyn with his holy well close by, reputedly the cause of cures from rheumatism and scrofulous and cutaneous illnesses; well after the Reformation it attracted many visitors; baths and changing-rooms were added until in 1894 it had become disused and was converted to other purposes. An ancient inscription on a stone pillar in Towyn church, called the Cadfan stone, and possibly genuine, records his burial place: 'Beneath a similar mound lies Cadfan, sad that it should enclose the praise of the earth. May he rest without blemish.' In Brittany there is also a cult of Cadfan in Finistère and Côtes du Nord; he is patron of a church at Poullan, near Douarnenez and a statue of him in military costume survives at Briec. His identification with Cadfan of Wales, however, remains problematical. Feast: 1 November.

Baring-Gould and Fisher, ii. 1–9; A. W. Wade-Evans, *Welsh Christian Origins* (1934), pp. 161–4; G. H. Jones, 'Celtic Britain and the Pilgrim Movement', *Y Cymmrodor*, xxiii (1912), 354–62; E. G. Bowen, *The Settlements of the Celtic Saints in Wales* (1956), pp. 92–6; B.T.A., iii. 239–40.

CADOC (1) (Sophias) was a leading figure among the monks of South Wales in the early 6th century and founder of the church of Llancarfan. He was probably the contemporary of *David and *Gildas and the master of *Finnian, through whom he was known in Ireland. Dedications to him are common in S. Wales (fifteen), very rare elsewhere (one chapel in Cornwall). Over 500 years after his death two Lives were written by Lifris and Caradoc. Lifris of Llancarfan pieced together legends which revealed the past grandeur and the present power of Cadoc in a long, ill-digested mass. The purpose was to glorify Cadoc at all costs and show him as one who would always defend his property, his subjects, and his name. In both the Lives Cadoc ends as bishop and martyr in Benevento: no access is allowed for British pilgrims to his grave for fear they steal the relics! The difference between the two biographers is that Lifris transports Cadoc in a white cloud to Benevento and makes him a martyr, while Caradoc takes him there by road and makes him die a natural death. These extraordinary stories may be explained by the fact that the Welsh had hidden his relics, whereas both the biographers represent the Anglo-Norman conquest of Glamorgan, in which Llancarfan was given to St. Peter's, Gloucester. This Cadoc is distinct from a Scottish and a Breton saint of the same or similar name. Feast: 25 September.

The Life by Lifris is edited by A. W. Wade-Evans, *Vitae Sanctorum Britanniae* (1944), pp. 24–141; the Life by Caradoc by P. Grosjean, 'Vie de S. Cadoc par Caradoc de Llancarfan', *Anal. Boll.*, lx (1942), 35–67; critical assessment by C. N. L. Brooke, 'St. Peter of Gloucester and St. Cadoc of Llancarfan' in *Celt and Saxon* (ed. N. K. Chadwick, 1963). See also H. D. Emanuel, 'An analysis of the . . . Vita Cadoci', *Nat. Lib. of Wales Jnl.*, vii (1952), 217–27; G. H. Doble, *The Saints of Cornwall*, iv (1965), 55–66.

CADOC (2), Scottish saint commemorated on 24 January, to whom Cambusland is dedicated. *C.S.P.* (and others) confuse him with the more important Welsh Cadoc whose feast is 25 September.

W. I. Watson, 'St. Cadoc', *Scottish Gaelic Studies*, ii (1927), 1–12.

CADWALADR (d. 664), Welsh king. Son of Cadwallon, who with Penda of Mercia defeated and killed *Edwin, king of Northumbria, in 633, Cadwaladr was a peaceful, pious prince, who earned the nickname of 'battle-shunner', led his people in 658 against the Wessex army at Peonne (Somerset), and suffered a terrible defeat. Several churches are named after him and may have been his foundations; they are called Llangadwaladr (in Anglesey, Denbighshire, and Monmouthshire). Welsh calendars of the 15th and 16th centuries give 12 November as his feast.

Baring-Gould and Fisher, ii. 43–6.

CAEDMON (d. 680), monk of Whitby. All that we know of him comes from

*Bede. He was a herdsman of Whitby, who as an adult suddenly discovered within himself a gift for both song and poetry. He became a monk there and devoted much of his time to the composition of vernacular poems about the Creation and the Genesis stories, about the Exodus and the entry of the Jews into the promised land, about the birth, passion, and resurrection of Christ, about the Last Judgement, Heaven, and Hell. He died in holiness and perfect charity to all, after showing that he knew his end was near, although he was not in a state of serious illness. Unfortunately none of his poems has certainly survived, except for the nine lines recorded by Bede in Latin and in the vernacular in an early manuscript of the *Ecclesiastical History*. His gift must have been of enormous value in propagating Christianity in vernacular poetry and song, in an age when few knew how to read or write and fewer still could understand Latin. Feast (at Whitby): 11 February.

Bede, *H.E.*, iv. 24.

CAEDWALLA (d. 689), king of Wessex 658–88. A descendant of Ceawlin, king of Wessex, the Saxon Caedwalla, whose name indicates some British blood connection, became king by conquest. His notorious violence was to some extent tamed by *Wilfrid, to whom he gave 300 hides of the conquered Isle of Wight. He was a successful ruler but abdicated in order to go to Rome and become a Christian. He was baptized on Holy Saturday 689 and given the name of Peter by Pope Sergius. Soon afterwards he was taken ill and died, still wearing his white baptismal robes. He was buried in the crypt of St. Peter's: his epitaph, written by Crispus, archbishop of Milan, is reproduced by Bede. There is no clear evidence of an ancient liturgical cult: his reputed sanctity is accounted for partly by Bede's account of him and partly by the belief that the sacrament of Baptism remits all sin and makes the recipient, if he commits no subsequent sin, worthy of immediate heavenly reward. Caedwalla was the first of four Anglo-Saxon kings to end his days in Rome. He was aged about thirty and died on 20 April.

Bede, *H.E.*, iv. 15–16; v. 7; W. J. Moore, *The Saxon Pilgrims to Rome* (1937).

CAENTIGERN, see KENTIGERNA.

CAESARIUS OF ARLES (*c.*470–542), bishop. Born at Chalons-sur-Saône (Burgundy) of a noble Gallo-Roman family, Caesarius became a monk at Lérins in 489. After an unsuccessful spell as cellarer, he was seconded to Eonus, bishop of Arles, who ordained him priest and appointed him abbot of a relaxed monastery, which he reformed, giving the monks a Rule and presiding over them for three years. On the death of Eonus, Caesarius was chosen as his successor at the early age of thirty-three.

As a pastor he was remarkable for his preaching and for his regulation of the Liturgy. This he ordered to be celebrated publicly not only on Sundays and feasts as before, but on every day; furthermore he always insisted that it should be a real raising of the mind and heart to God, not a mere external observance. 'Match your behaviour to the words you sing', he would often say.

He founded a nunnery at Arles, for which he wrote a Rule and which was governed by his sister. His two monastic Rules became famous after his death. Like *Benedict he emphasized stability; for the nuns he insisted on enclosure. He is rightly reckoned an important predecessor of the Benedictine Rule. As archbishop of Arles he presided over the council of Orange in 529, which condemned both those who asserted that God predestines any man to damnation and those who denied that God inspires the first acts of faith and love.

Arles was under the rule of Alaric II, king of the Visigoths, who exiled Caesarius for a time to Bordeaux for his Burgundian sympathies. These were manifested when prisoners were taken at the siege of Arles, whom Caesarius fed thanks to melting down church plate. Not long afterwards Theodoric, king of Italy, seized Languedoc and had Caesarius brought to Ravenna as a prisoner. But when he met him, he recognized his sanctity at once and gave him a silver basin and 300 pieces of gold, much of which Caesarius devoted to redeeming captives. He then received the pallium from Pope Symmachus, possibly the first recorded example of this distinction.

When the Franks took Arles in 536, Caesarius retired to the nunnery, made a will in its favour and died soon afterwards, with a fine reputation as teacher, scholar, and pastor. Feast: 27 August.

Lives ed. B. Krusch in *M.G.H. Scriptores rerum Merov.*, iii. 457–501; his Will ed. G. Morin, *Rev. Bén.*, xvi (1899), 97–112; Works ed. G. Morin (2 vols., 1937–42); Eng. tr. of sermons by M. M. Mueller (*Fathers of the Church*, 1956 ff.) and of the Rule by M. C. McCarthy (1960); modern Life by A. Malnory (1934); see also W. E. Klingshirn in *Rev. Bén.*, Tome c (1990), 441–81; *N.C.E.*, ii. 1046–8; B.T.A., iii. 418–21.

CAFASSO, Joseph (1811–60), diocesan priest. Born at Castelnuovo d'Asti (Piedmont) of a wealthy peasant family, he was educated in the seminary of Chieri and ordained priest for the Turin dioceses in 1833. After three years' further study he was appointed lecturer in moral theology. Undersized (like *Bellarmine) and called 'The little one', he made his mark both as preacher and spiritual director. In 1848 he became superior of the Institute of St. Francis at Turin which housed sixty young priests from different dioceses and of diverse political opinions. He also directed a retreat house at Lanzo, while his special apostolate for prisoners and convicts, including preparing the condemned for execution, was widely admired.

From 1827 he directed John *Bosco into an apostolate for boys, helped him to settle in Turin, introduced him to wealthy patrons, and came to be regarded as the second founder of the Salesian congregation. In 1860, still under fifty but ill with pneumonia, he knew that death was near and made a will in favour of the foundations of Joseph *Cottolengo and John Bosco. His funeral was attended by large crowds and Bosco was the preacher. His cause was begun in 1895: he was canonized in 1947. Feast: 23 June.

F. Accornero, *La dottrina spirituale di S. Giuseppe Cafasso* (1958); G. Bosco, *Biografia del sacerdote Giuseppe Cafasso* (1960); other Lives by L. N. de Robilant, G. Bitelli, and C. Salotti (all 1960); see also B.T.A., ii. 628–31; *N.C.E.*, ii. 1049–50; *Bibl. SS.*, vi. 1317–21.

CAIN, see KEYNE.

CAINNECH, see CANICE.

CAJETAN (1480–1547), founder of the Theatine Order. Born at Vicenza and educated at Padua University, Cajetan distinguished himself in theology and law, but gave up the worldly career which his noble birth and ability could have won for him and became a priest in 1516. At Rome, Vicenza, and Venice he founded confraternities of clergy and laity for the service of the sick and the poor. At Rome in 1523 he founded, with Pietro Caraffa (afterwards the fanatically intransigent Pope Paul IV), a congregation of clergy bound by vows. The inspiration of the project was that of restoring true apostolic life among the clergy in an age of notorious corruption. Study of the Bible and Christian doctrine, restoration of the dignity and spirituality of worship, care for the sick and poor, preaching and pastoral care with complete disinterestedness were some of the characteristic marks of the new Order. Cajetan, who was Provost-General for three years, worked in Verona, Venice, and Naples. Here he founded the pawnshops called *Monts de Piété* which were designed to help, not exploit, their users. In 1547 the Englishman Thomas Goldwell, later a Marian bishop of St. Asaph's (1555–9), became a Theatine at Naples. The Order was famous as a spearhead of reform, although it was in some ways eclipsed by the better organized and more famous Order of Jesuits, founded by *Ignatius of Loyola. No doubt it also suffered from the unpopularity of its co-founder Caraffa. Cajetan was canonized in 1671. Feast: 7 August.

AA.SS. Aug. II (1735), 282–301; modern Lives

by P. Chiminelli (1948), S. da Valsanzibio (1949), A. V. Ballester (1950), and P. H. Hallett, *Catholic Reformer* (1959). See also B.T.A., iii. 272–4 and *Bibl. SS.*, v. 1345–9.

CALASANZ, Joseph (1556–1648), founder of the Clerks Regular of the Christian Schools. Born at Peralta de la Sal, the youngest son of an Aragonese nobleman, he was educated at Estadilla, Lerida, and Valencia. In 1583 he was ordained priest; a few years later he was appointed vicar-general of the diocese and was sent to re-establish religious standards in the inaccessible valleys of Andorra. For some time, however, he had believed himself called to the work of educating the urban poor, so in 1592 he resigned his office and prospects of preferment, divided his patrimony, and left for Rome.

There he nursed the sick and the dying during the plague of 1595 with his friend *Camillus of Lellis, but he returned to educating children, especially the homeless and neglected, of whose ignorance and degradation he had learnt by experience. As other religious Orders were unable or unwilling to help, he started a free school with three other priests in 1597. Soon there were 100 pupils which caused a move to larger quarters; in 1602 numbers had risen to 700. A few years later, with papal help and protection, the whole institute with Calasanz as superior, with numerous priests, and with a school of 1,200 pupils, was housed in 1611 in a *palazzo* near the church of St. Pantaleon. Other schools were soon opened, the Institute expanded, and obtained recognition as a religious congregation with Calasanz as superior general.

Now aged sixty-five, Calasanz faced the most severe trial of his life. Mario Sozzi, a priest of his congregation, had been appointed provincial in Tuscany, where he proved overbearing and devious. He denounced Calasanz to the Holy Office on false charges, some grave, some concerned with his alleged senility. Calasanz was arrested by the Holy Office, led through the streets like a criminal, and only escaped imprisonment through the intervention of Cardinal Cesarini. Calasanz was suspended from office; an apostolic visitor was put in control: Sozzi was unpunished and continued intrigues until his death in 1643. In 1645 a commission of cardinals appointed to investigate recommended Calasanz's reinstatement; but this too was frustrated by further intrigues, and in 1646 his congregation was reduced to being a society of priests under the rule of diocesan bishops.

Now aged ninety, Calasanz died at Rome after bearing all these trials with heroic patience. The sordid story reflects little credit on the authorities. Only in 1656 was the congregation reconstituted and only in 1669 was it made into a religious Order, called the Piarists, which flourished specially in Italy, Spain, and South America. It was particularly useful when the Jesuits were suppressed in 1773.

Calasanz was canonized in 1767 and in 1948 Pius XII declared him patron of Christian schools. A fine painting by Goya of his death is in the Collegio S. Antonio, Madrid. Feast: formerly 27 August, now 25 August.

Letters ed. by L. Picanyol (9 vols, 1950–6); Lives by C. Bau (1949 and 1967), F. Giordano, *Il Calasanzio* (1960); Eng. tr. of an Italian Life in F. W. Faber, *The Saints and Servants of God* (1850); L. Picanyol (ed.), *Florilegium Calasantianum* (1958); B.T.A., iii. 413–16; *Bibl. SS.*, vi. 1321–30.

CALLISTUS (Callixtus) (d. 222), pope and martyr. A rare example of a pope who had been born a slave, had served a sentence as a convict, was the champion of forgiveness, and died for the Christian faith. Much of the available information about him comes from hostile sources, viz. *Hippolytus, his rival, and Tertullian, his severe critic.

The Christian master of Callistus named Carpophorus put him in charge of a bank, but Callistus lost the money deposited by other Christians. He fled from Rome, was caught at Porto, and sentenced to the treadmill. His creditors obtained his release; he tried to collect debts from the Jews and was soon arrested again for brawling in a synagogue. Sentenced to work in the mines in Sardinia, he was released with other Christians through the intervention of Marcia, mistress of Emperor Commodius. Pope Zephyrinus made Callistus (now freed) manager of what is now called the Cemetery of Callistus, a burial ground with crypt where most of the previous bishops of Rome were buried. This he administered well and became a deacon.

Eighteen years later, in 217, Callistus was elected pope, and had a short but controversial reign. For his attempt at mediation between two parties with rival theories of the Incarnation, he was labelled a Sabellian by Hippolytus (the unsuccessful candidate for the papacy), and because he allowed the readmission to communion of those who repented of murder and adultery, he was accused of laxity. Furthermore he wanted to recognize the validity of marriages between free people and slaves against Roman civil law. He was particularly concerned with the marriages of wealthy Christian women, who, if they did not find suitable Christian husbands of their own class, would be likely either to marry pagans and risk apostasy for themselves or their children, or else contract illicit unions with Christian slaves. The result of all this controversy was a schism in the Roman Church led by Hippolytus. Callistus died during a popular riot, but the details of his passion, incorporated in the entry of *R.M.*, including his being killed by being thrown down a well, are unhistorical. Feast: 14 October.

AA.SS. Oct. VI (1794), 401–48; J. J. I. von Dollinger, *Hippolytus and Callistus* (1853, Eng. tr. 1876); L. Duchesne, *Le Liber Pontificalis*, i. 141–2 (1886-92); A. D'Alès, *L'Edit de Calliste* (1914); B. Altaner and C. B. Daly, 'The Edict of Callistus', *Studia Patristica*, iii (1961), 176–82.

CAMILLUS OF LELLIS (1550–1614), founder of the Ministers of the Sick. Born at Bocchianico in the Abruzzi, he joined the Venetian army to fight against the Turks. An exceptionally big man (6′ 6″ tall), hasty in temper and an inveterate gambler, he contracted an incurable disease of the leg. In 1574–5 he lost everything in gambling, experienced a religious conversion, and tried to be a Franciscan, but his health prevented him from being professed. Instead he joined the hospital of San Giacomo, Rome, where he eventually became bursar.

In association with his adviser Philip *Neri, Camillus, now a priest, founded in 1585 a congregation of male nurses, who bound themselves to serve the plague-stricken, the sick in hospitals or their homes, and the prisoners. In 1595 and 1601 some of them served on the battlefield in Hungary and Croatia, the first recorded examples of a 'military ambulance unit'. In Rome and Naples they founded hospitals and served the galley-slaves; in both places some of them lost their lives through contracting the plague from their patients.

He was a pioneer in insisting on fresh air, suitable diets, and isolation of infectious patients, and lived to see his institute number fifteen houses and eight hospitals. In spite of suffering a variety of serious illnesses himself, he spared no effort in tending the sick personally right up to the end of his life. He died at Genoa and was canonized in 1746. He is patron both of nurses and of the sick. Feast: 14 July.

M. Vanti, *S. Camillo de Lellis* (1929); C. C. Martindale, *St. Camillus* (1946); B.T.A., iii. 134–6; *Bibl. SS.*, iii. 707–22.

CAMPION, Edmund (1540–81), Jesuit priest and martyr. Campion was the son of a London bookseller, was educated at Christ's Hospital, and won a scholarship to St. John's College, Oxford, where he became Junior Fellow in 1557. His exceptional brilliance and popularity made him one of the most notable figures of his time in Oxford and won him the patronage of the Earl of Leicester. When Queen Elizabeth visited Oxford in 1566, Campion was chosen by the University as orator to welcome her. He was ordained deacon of the Church of England in 1569, but was openly uncertain of his religious future. To try and solve this difficulty he went to Ireland to help found a University at Dublin (later Trinity College) and wrote a stimulating *History of Ireland*, later incorporated, much altered, in Holinshed's *Chronicle* (1587). He returned to England in 1571, but soon crossed the Channel for the English College, Douai, where he formally rejoined the R.C. Church and was ordained subdeacon in 1573. He left for Rome the same year to join the Society of Jesus. After his novitiate at Brünn (Moravia) he taught rhetoric and other subjects in the Jesuit school at Prague, where also he was ordained priest in 1578. The following year, at the suggestion of Dr. (later Cardinal) Allen, Edmund Campion and Robert Persons were chosen to start a Jesuit mission in England. Campion set out from Rome in 1580, visited Charles *Borromeo at Milan, and landed at Dover disguised as a jewel merchant. He ministered to Catholic prisoners in London and wrote a challenge to the Privy Council (called *Campion's Brag*), which described his mission as one 'of free cost to preach the Gospel, to minister the Sacraments, to instruct the simple, to reform sinners, to confute errors; in brief to cry alarm spiritual against foul vice and proud ignorance, wherewith many of my dear countrymen are abused'.

His eloquence, learning, attractive personality, courage, and daring gave new heart to the dispirited English Catholics; his printing-press and his preaching together disseminated an up-to-date, vigorous catholicism, which the Government could not ignore. Campion was elusively mobile: he worked in Lancashire, Yorkshire, and the Midlands, often in disguise; at Stonor (Oxon.) he wrote and printed his most famous work, the *Decem Rationes*, an open and reasoned challenge to Protestants to debate with him the foundations of catholicism. Four hundred copies of this booklet were secretly distributed before Commemoration service at St. Mary's University Church, Oxford. A few weeks later he was arrested at Lyford Grange (Berks.) and imprisoned in the Tower. Bribes, torture, and theological debate all failed to induce him to conform.

On 14 November he was indicted with others in Westminster Hall on the fabricated charge of having plotted rebellion abroad and come to England to implement it. In spite of his able defence which demolished the evidence and discredited the witnesses, the packed jury found him guilty and he was condemned to death. On this occasion he said: 'In condemning us you condemn all your own ancestors, all the ancient bishops and kings, all that was once the glory of England . . . posterity's judgment is not liable to corruption as that of those who are now going to sentence us to death.' His loyalty to the Queen was clear; his only offence his religion. With Alexander *Briant and Ralph *Sherwin he was hanged, drawn, and quartered at Tyburn on 1 December. By his death was lost a brilliant thinker and literary stylist comparable to any in the Elizabethan age, one who might have contributed no less effectively to his cause by the spoken and written word than by heroic suffering. He was canonized by Paul VI in 1970 as one of the *Forty Martyrs of England and Wales. Feast: 25 October.

R. Persons, *On the Life and Martyrdom of Father Edmund Campion* (facsimile edn., ed. T. Alfield, 1970); W. Allen, *Martyrdom of Father Campion and his Companions* (1908); R. Simpson, *Edmund Campion* (1867); E. Waugh, *Edmund Campion* (1935); E. E. Reynolds, *Campion and Parsons: the Jesuit Mission of 1580–81* (1980); for Campion's works see E. Campion, *A historie of Ireland* (1571, facsimile edn., ed. M. Hamner, 1971); *Ambrosia* (ed. J. Simons, 1970); *Decem Rationes* (1581, *E.R.L.* i (1971), with tr.).

CANADA, Martyrs of, see BRÉBEUF and JOGUES.

CANDIDA, see WHYTE.

CANICE (Cainnech, Kenneth, Canicus) (*c.*525–*c.*600), Irish abbot. Born the son of a bard in Co. Derry, he was educated by *Finnian at Clonard, and became a friend of *Columba, whom *Adomnan mentioned several times. When plague scattered his community of Glasnevin, he went to Llancarvan in Wales for a time but returned to Ireland, where he founded monasteries in the north and the south, the principal one being Aghaboe in Laois, which became the most important church of Ossory. Other foundations included Drumahose in Derry and Cluain Bronig in Offaly.

In Scotland his principal church was Inchkenneth in Mull; other churches which bear his name include Kilchennich in Tiree, Kilchainie in South Uist, and the abbey of Cambuskenneth. He visited Columba at Iona fairly frequently; both a church and a cemetery were dedicated to him there.

Like other Irish monastic saints Canice lived as a hermit for certain periods of his life, enjoying close communion with nature and with wild animals, especially on deserted islands. Stories told of him include his expulsion of mice for nibbling his shoes and his admonition to the birds to cease their noise on Sundays. He also copied books in solitude, especially a manuscript of the Four Gospels. He was on occasion an effective preacher and he told Columba that this was due to divine illumination.

His journeys in Scotland include one with Columba to King Brude at Inverness; some churches in Kintyre and Fife also claimed to be founded by him. Feast: 11 October, in *R.M.*, Scottish and Irish calendars.

AA.SS. Oct. V (1786), 642–6; J. F. Kenney, *Sources for the Early History of Ireland*, i. 305–7, 394–5, 437–9; *K.S.S.*, pp. 295–7; C. Plummer, *V.S.H.*, i. 152–69; *The Irish Saints* (1964), pp. 52–6; A. O. and M. O. Anderson, *Adomnan's Life of Columba* (1961).

CANISIUS, Peter (1521–97), Jesuit priest, writer, and educator. Born at Nijmegen (Holland) (his father was tutor to the sons of the duke of Lorraine and became burgomaster of his native town), Peter was educated at Cologne University and at Louvain, where he studied canon law. He soon found that the legal career and marriage which his father had intended for him would not satisfy him, he took a vow of celibacy, returned to Cologne, attended a retreat at Mainz given by Peter Favre, one of the first companions of *Ignatius of Loyola, and decided to join the Society of Jesus. His novitiate was spent at Cologne where he spent much time in prayer, study, teaching, and the care of the sick. His first publications were editions of the works of *Cyril of Alexandria and *Leo the Great. After his ordination he became a prominent preacher, attended two sessions of the Council of Trent, was sent to teach in the first Jesuit school at Messina, and was recalled to Rome to work beside Ignatius.

He was sent to Ingoldstadt, where he became in turn rector and vice-chancellor of the University, which he successfully reformed, making his mark as a preacher and catechizer at the same time. But in 1552 he was sent to undertake a more general task of reform in Vienna. Here there were many parishes without clergy, there had been no ordinations for twenty years, monasteries were deserted, and many people had abandoned religious practices. His energy was almost incredible and he won the esteem of the Viennese by looking after the sick during the plague. The king and the nuncio both wished him to become archbishop of Vienna; instead he consented to administer it for a year, but without becoming a bishop. In 1555 he published his famous Catechism (*Summa Doctrinae Christianae*), which was in some ways the Catholic equivalent of Luther's famous work. It was translated into fifteen languages during Peter's lifetime and became a model for other similar works. In 1556 he was appointed provincial of a new Jesuit province for Austria, Bavaria, and Bohemia. Resident in Prague, he established a college which became famous for its religious and academic standards. From 1559 to 1565 he lived at Augsburg, repeating his earlier achievements of reclaiming those lapsed from religion, converting Protestants, and encouraging the Catholics. Once again he insisted on the importance of schools and writing for publication by the now flourishing printing presses. Later at Dillingen he taught in schools and universities.

He then took a leading part in founding Fribourg university which has become one of the most important of its kind since. He suffered a paralytic seizure in 1591, but continued writing, with the help of a secretary, until his death six years later on 21 December. He is generally reckoned the principal theologian and writer of his generation in central Europe, to whose influence much of the success of the Counter-Reformation in that area is due. In dealing with Lutherans he always distinguished between those who had deliberately propagated heresy and those who had been brought up in, or had drifted into it, whose errors, as he thought, came from ignorance rather than malice. Always courteous in controversy, he nevertheless thought that discussions between Catholic and Protestant theologians on doctrine were often useless because they widened the gulf between them. He preferred to stress basic Christian doctrine rather than controversial matters like indulgences, purgatory, or pilgrimages. He was canonized and declared a Doctor of the Church in 1925. Feast: 21 December (formerly 27 April).

Lives by J. Broderick (1935), J. H. M. Tesser (1932), W. Reany (1931). Peter's works ed. O. Braunsberger, *Beati Petri Canisii societatis Iesu Epistolae et Acta* (8 vols., 1896–1923) and *Meditationes seu Notae in Evangelicas Lectiones* (3 vols., 1957–63); *Bibl. SS.*, x. 798–814.

CANUTE (Cnut) (d. 1086), king of Denmark and martyr, patron of Denmark. An illegitimate son of Swein Estrithson, who was the nephew of Cnut, king of England 1016–35, Canute became king of Denmark in 1081 in succession to his brother Harold. By now Denmark, largely evangelized by Englishmen, was nominally Christian: Canute promulgated laws which restrained the power of the *jarls* (or earls), protected the clergy, and exacted the payment of tithes for their upkeep, and in fact made some of them powerful temporal lords. He also built and endowed churches lavishly such as Lund. Roskilde (to which he gave his crown) became the burial place of Danish kings.

Twice he attempted unsuccessfully to invade England: first in 1075, when the three earls who rebelled against William the Conqueror asked for his help. His fleet of 200 ships achieved only a raid on York before the rebellion was suppressed. Again in 1085 Canute renewed his claim to the English throne, and started to assemble a huge fleet with his allies of Norway and Flanders. The threat was so serious that William the Conqueror imported numerous mercenaries, removed supplies from the coast, and soon instituted the famous Domesday Survey. In the event the attack came to nothing because Canute's subjects, led by the *jarls*, rebelled against his taxation, tithes, and 'new order', took his brother Olaf as their leader, and besieged Canute in the church of St. Alban at Odensee. After receiving the sacraments of Penance and the Eucharist, Canute was killed kneeling in front of the altar with eighteen followers. His biographer, the English monk Aelnoth of Canterbury, an exile for twenty-four years, attested both to the miracles of Canute which led to his relics being enshrined and to the disaffection of the Anglo-Saxons in England which led, he says, to their support for Canute. However that may be, Pope Paschal II approved the cult of Canute in 1101, although his claim to be a martyr is perhaps equivalent to those of several Anglo-Saxon kings, such as *Oswin and *Ethelbert. Feast: 19 January, although the day of his death was 10 July, when Evesham, the mother-house of Odensee, where his body still rests, celebrated his feast.

AA.SS. Iul. III (1723), 118–49; Life by Aelnoth also in J. Langebek, *Scriptores rerum Danicarum*, iii. 373 *et seq.*; C. Gertz, *Vitae Sanctorum Danorum*, pp. 27–168, 531–58; F. M. Stenton, *Anglo-Saxon England* (2nd edn. 1946), pp. 603–9; B.T.A., i. 121; *Knuds-bogen*, Studie over Knud den Hellige (1986).

CANUTE LAVARD, martyr (*c.*1096–1131). Born at Roskilde, the second son of Eric the Good, king of Denmark, Canute stayed at the Saxon court for some years. When he returned with ideals of feudalism and military organization, his uncle King Niels appointed him duke of southern Jutland to rule from Schleswig (which he fortified) and defend the whole territory against the Wends. Canute, committed to peace and justice, also encouraged *Vicelin in his efforts to convert them; but when Emperor Lothair recognized him as king of the Western Wends, King Niels was furious and regarded him as a rival. Two of Canute's cousins murdered him in the forest of Haraldsted (near Ringsted). When Canute's son, Valdemar I, became king of Denmark he requested his father's canonization at Rome. The archbishops of Lund and Uppsala presented evidence about Canute's life and miracles and Alexander III canonized him in 1169. His relics were enshrined at Ringsted in 1170. He was regarded as a martyr in Denmark, presumably for justice. Feast: 7 January; translation, 25 July.

M. C. Gertz, *Vitae sanctorum danorum* (1912); E. W. Kemp, *Canonization and Authority in the Western Church* (1948), pp. 79–86; B.T.A., i. 49; *Bibl. SS.*, iii. 753–5.

CAPITANIO, BARTOLOMAEA (1807–33), co-foundress of the Sisters of Charity of Lovere (Lombardy). She was born there, the daughter of a corn merchant, took a private vow of chastity, became a teacher and devoted herself in an ascetical personal regime to the apostolate of youth. Seeing the need to make her work permanent, she associated herself from 1829 onwards with the older Catherina *Gerosa, who was specially interested in nursing. Together they founded a congregation dedicated both to teaching and nursing, for which the rule of the Sisters of Charity of St. *Vincent de Paul was adapted. Political realities prevented them from being ruled from outside Austria and they were independent from the start. The Sisters received papal approval in 1840.

In character Bartolomaea was simple, tactful, and strong: she influenced many people by her conversation, teaching, and writings, which include 300 letters. She died of consumption at the age of twenty-six. She was canonized in 1950. Feast: 26 July.

Lives by L. I. Mazza (2 vols. 1905), C. Carminati (1934), and A. Stocchetti (1950), also E. Belgari, *Il profilo di una maesta santa* (1951); see also B.T.A., iii. 191–2; *Bibl. SS.*, ii. 849–52.

CARADOC (Caradog) (d. 1124), Welsh monk. Born at Brycheiniog of moderately wealthy parents, he lived as a young man at the court of Rhys ap Tewdwr (prince of South Wales 1077–93) where he was a harper. After neglectfully losing Rhys's greyhounds and consequently his favour as well, he broke off the head of his lance and, using the shaft as a walking-stick, went to Llandaff where he was tonsured and entered the service of the bishop. A few years later he became a hermit in Gower at the ruined church of St. *Kyned (Llangenydd). Again he moved, this time to Menevia, where he was ordained priest before retiring to an island off the Pembrokeshire coast with some companions. Here they suffered harassment from Vikings, which resulted in his moving once more, this time to the cell of St. *Ismael (St. Isell's, Haroldston), where he died. He was buried at his own request in the cathedral of St. David's; his body was claimed to be incorrupt. William of Malmesbury tried unsuccessfully to take away a finger. Part of his shrine survives. Gerald of Wales attempted to have him canonized and a letter of Innocent III survives which ordered an enquiry to be made into his life and miracles. Although never formally canonized, Caradoc was venerated from the early 13th century on 14 April, but Roscarrock in the 16th century said his feast was on 13 April. The church of Lawrenny is dedicated to him.

AA.SS. Apr. II (1675), 150–2; *N.L.A.*, i. 174–6; Giraldus Cambrensis, *Itinerarium*, i. 11 (Gerald also wrote a Life of Caradoc, which has not survived); Baring-Gould and Fisher, ii. 75–8.

CARANTOC (Carannog, Carentoc), Celtic saint, patron of Crantock (Cornwall), Llangranog, and Carhampton

(Somerset). Carantoc was probably of Welsh origin: he built a monastery in Somerset, was the leader of the group of monks who evangelized central Cornwall in the 6th or 7th century, and went from there to Brittany, where he was known as Caredec. William Worcestre mentions a 'Sanctus Cradokus' in a church or chapel near Padstow 'on account of his destroying worms when people drink the water of a well there'. It is uncertain whether Carantoc or Cadoc was intended. His biographer attributed to him also a fruitful missionary visit to Ireland. The Cornish antiquary Roscarrock mentions a Cornish church dedicated to him which formerly had seven churchyards belonging to it. Seven parishes from these seven churches used to come each year and bring relics to the mother church, placing them on special stones like altars. Feast: 16 May; cult in S. Wales, Somerset, Cornwall, and Brittany.

AA.SS. Maii III (1680), 584–7; *N.L.A.*, i. 177–9; J. A. Robinson, 'St. Carantoc in Somerset', *Downside Review*, xlvi (1929), 234–43; G. H. Doble, *The Saints of Cornwall*, iv (1965), 31–52; A. W. Wade-Evans, *Vitae Sanctorum Britannae et Genealogiae* (1944), pp. 142–50; William Worcestre, p. 73.

CARPUS, PAPYLUS (Pamfilus), **AND AGATHONICE** (d. *c.*170), martyrs. The Acts of these martyrs who died at Pergamum (Asia Minor), were used by Eusebius. Their deaths are usually dated to the reign of Marcus Aurelius, but some scholars prefer that of Decius. Carpus was a bishop, Papylus a deacon, and Agathonice his sister. The proconsul Optimus ordered them to sacrifice in the name of the emperor. Carpus answered: 'The living do not sacrifice to the dead . . . (the gods) look like men, but they are unfeeling. Deprive them of your veneration . . . and they will be defiled by dogs and crows.' When the proconsul insisted that he must sacrifice, Carpus said: 'I have never before sacrificed to images which have no feeling or understanding . . . I have pity on myself, choosing as I do the better part.' After this exchange, Optimus ordered him to be hung up for torture by being scraped with claws. In torment Carpus said: 'I am a Christian and because of my faith and the name of our Lord Jesus Christ I cannot become one of you.' Ultimately the pain was so great that he could no longer utter a sound.

Papylus' turn came next. He admitted to being a wealthy citizen and to having many children. At this point a bystander shouted: 'He means he has children in virtue of the faith of the Christians.' And indeed Papylus agreed that he had spiritual children in every province and city. Like Carpus he steadfastly refused to sacrifice, with the same result. He too was hung up and scraped with claws. Three pairs of torturers were employed but he did not cry out. A little later he said: 'I feel no pain because I have someone to comfort me: one whom you do not see suffers within me.' Both were then sentenced to be burnt alive.

At this point Agathonice was interrogated. She too confessed that she was a Christian and that she had never sacrificed to demons, but only to God. 'If I am worthy,' she continued, 'I desire to follow the footsteps of my teachers.' On being called on to have pity on her children, she replied: 'My children have God, who watches over them; but I will not obey your commands nor will I sacrifice to demons.' She was then sentenced to the same death as Carpus and Papylus. When she was led to the place of execution, she removed her clothes and gave them to the servants. When the crowd saw how beautiful she was, they grieved and lamented. The servants hung her over the fire, and she cried out three times: 'Lord Jesus Christ, help me because I am enduring this for your sake.' She died soon after. Feast: 13 April.

A.C.M., pp. xv–xvi, 22–37; Eusebius, *H.E.*, iv. 15; *Propylaeum*, pp. 136–7; B.T.A., ii. 83–4.

CARTHACH, see MOCHTA.

CASIMIR (1458–84), prince of Poland. Born at Cracow he was the third son of Casimir IV, king of Poland. At the age of thirteen he was sent by his father to the Hungarian border with a large army, as the

Hungarian nobles wished to have Casimir as their king in place of Matthias Corvinus. His own soldiers, however, deserted because their pay was in arrears and the Hungarian king had assembled an army to fight them. So Casimir went home, but was banished by his father to the castle of Dobzki. He also refused to take up arms again against any Christian country at a time when Christians were in great danger from the Turks, and refused to marry a daughter of Emperor Frederick III, preferring a life of celibacy, devotion, and austerity. This was one result of his early education by John Dlugosz, canon of Cracow. He died of tuberculosis at the age of twenty-six and was buried at Vilna. Miracles were soon reported at his tomb and he was canonized by Leo X in 1521. The hymn sometimes called St. Casimir's, *Omni die dic Mariae*, was not composed by him but by Bernard of Cluny in the 12th century; Casimir, however, frequently said it and a copy of it was buried with him. In the 16th to 17th centuries his supernatural help was claimed by Lithuanians, whose patron he became, in conflicts against the Russians. Feast: 4 March.

AA.SS. Mar. I (1668), 837–57; B.T.A., i. 478–9; *Bibl. SS.*, iii. 859–906.

CASSIAN (John Cassian) (*c.*360–433), abbot. Born probably in Romania, Cassian became a monk at Bethlehem, but left in *c.*385 with his friend Germanus to study monasticism in Egypt. Here he was influenced by the teaching of Evagrius Ponticus. In *c.*400 he was in Constantinople, where he was ordained deacon and became the fervent disciple and defender of *John Chrysostom, who had favoured and promoted Origenist monks. For a time Cassian seems to have shared the charge of the cathedral treasury. A few years later, however, when Chrysostom was deposed at the Synod of the Oak, his disciples, Cassian included, left Constantinople for Italy, where he pleaded Chrysostom's cause with the pope, Innocent I. From then onwards his life was spent in the West.

Ordained priest probably at Marseilles, Cassian founded two monasteries there in *c.*415: one for men (at the tomb of *Victor), the other for women. At this time Provence was overrun by refugees from the barbarian invasions; the monastic movement, approved by some and attacked by others, both Christian and pagan, needed leadership, example, and an interpreter of the Egyptian tradition to Gaul. This Cassian became through his monastic writings, the *Institutes* and the *Conferences*.

The *Institutes* were concerned with life in community, the *Conferences* are supposedly sermons of Egyptian hermits, but inevitably there is much overlap between the two treatises. Cassian insisted that monastic life was apostolic in origin, based on the practice of the early Church of the Acts of the Apostles. He recognized the theoretical superiority of the hermit life, but seemed in practice to dissuade anyone 'imperfect' from undertaking it. According to some scholars the solitude which was higher than the community was 'not naked solitude but the society of hermits with a common worship and discipline'. This, however, was not how his teaching was always understood. It does seem certain that Cassian's own monasteries were, like *Benedict's, schools for beginners or cenobites. It was through Benedict's recommendation of Cassian as a spiritual guide to his monks that Cassian's writings attained very wide diffusion. With *Augustine and *Gregory he was a standard monastic guide throughout the Middle Ages and beyond.

Cassian's other works include a treatise on the Incarnation, requested by *Leo to acquaint Western readers with the teaching of Nestorius. More damaging to his posthumous reputation was his teaching on Grace. Here he reacted so strongly against what he saw as Augustine's excesses on predestination that he is sometimes called the founder of semi-Pelagianism. A well-meant reaction led to his falling into error, teaching that the first steps towards the Christian life were taken by the human will which only later was helped powerfully by divine grace.

There are no Acts of Cassian, no record of miraculous cures at his tomb in Marseilles. But his body, that of a big man, was kept in the later Middle Ages (and probably before), in a marble tomb on four pillars. Urban V, an Avignon pope and formerly abbot of Marseilles, caused his head to be enclosed in a silver casket and engraved 'Head of St. Cassian'. In the diocese of Marseilles but not outside it his feast was kept on 23 July. He does not appear in the Roman Martyrology; he was regarded as a writer for monks, to be read with caution. The Greeks, however, culted him on 29 February.

Works in *P.L.*, xlix–l and in *C.S.E.L.* (ed. M. Petschenig), xiii and xvii; Institutes in J. C. Guy, *Institutions Cenobitiques* (*S.C.* 1965), tr. E. C. S. Gibson in *Nicene and Post-Nicene Fathers* (1894) and in O. Chadwick, *Western Asceticism* (1958). Studies by J. C. Guy (Paris 1961), L. Cristiani (2 vols., 1946), and O. Chadwick, *John Cassian* (2nd edn., 1968); see also P. Rousseau, *Ascetics, Authority and the Church* (1978), pp. 169–239.

CASSYON (Cassian), of Autun 314–50, bishop with one English church-dedication, at Chaddesley Corbett (Worcs.). Feast: 5 August.

F. Bond, *Dedications of English Churches* (1914).

CATALD (Cathal) (7th–8th century), Irish saint. His cult is centred in Taranto (S. Italy) and extends over Italy, Sicily, and Malta; it can be traced back as far as 1071 when his relics were discovered at Taranto. Inside the coffin was the head of a pastoral staff of Irish workmanship with the inscription *Cathaldus Rachau*: all attempts to discover this last place-name have so far failed. The cult flourished under Norman and Benedictine influence: a painting of Catald survives in the basilica of the Nativity at Bethlehem and 12th-century mosaics in Palermo and Monreale. No doubt Catald is an example of the many Irish monks, otherwise unknown, who chose exile for the love of Christ in the early Middle Ages. He is invoked against plagues, drought, and storms. Feast: 10 May.

AA.SS. Maii II (1680), 569–78; J. Hennig, 'Cathaldus Rachau', *Medieval Studies* (1946), pp. 217–44; *The Irish Saints*, pp. 61–2.

CATAMANUS (Catman), see CADFAN.

CATHAN, see CHATTAN OF KINGARTH.

CATHERINE (Katharine) **OF ALEXANDRIA** (supposedly 4th century). There is no ancient cult of this saint, no mention in early Martyrologies, no early works of art. The cult began in the 9th century at Mount Sinai, to which her body was supposed to have been transported by 'angels', though this may have been a misinterpretation of 'monks', often described in antiquity as living an 'angelic' life. The details of her mythical Legend make her a noble girl, persecuted for her Christianity, who despised marriage with the Emperor because she was a 'bride of Christ', who disputed successfully with fifty philosophers who were called in to convince her of the errors of Christianity. Her protests were against the persecution of Christians by Maxentius; her tortures consisted of being broken on a wheel (later called Catherine wheel), but the machine broke down injuring bystanders; Catherine was beheaded.

The cult built on this legend, which strongly appealed to the imagination of artists, flourished exceedingly throughout Europe in the Middle Ages under the influence of the Crusaders and later of the *Golden Legend*. Her intercession was valued because she was considered to be (*a*) the bride of Christ, (*b*) the successful advocate who triumphed over the philosophers, (*c*) the protectress of the dying. Hence she was the patron of young girls, of students (and hence the clergy), especially philosophers and apologists, of nurses (because milk instead of blood flowed from her severed head), and of craftsmen whose work was based on the wheel, such as wheelwrights, spinners, and millers.

In England her cult was as widespread as anywhere in the West. Sixty-two churches were dedicated to her and 170 medieval bells still bear her name. The earliest English Life was written in the 13th century;

Capgrave, Bokenham, and Archbishop Langham also wrote Lives or poems in her honour. The earliest recorded example of a miracle play was one in her honour in Dunstable, *c.*1110: Gorran, who directed it, borrowed some copes from St. Albans which were accidentally burnt and he became a monk there in reparation, but remained Catherine's devotee all his life. Mural paintings were frequent: the earliest (*c.*1225) is at Winchester cathedral in the chapel of the Holy Sepulchre, the most complete cycle is in Little Missenden (Bucks.), *c.*1270. Other notable examples are at Castor (Northants.), Sporle (Norfolk), Pickering (N. Yorkshire), and Great Chalfield (Wilts.) with single figures at Cold Overton (Leics.) and Eton College chapel. In all at least fifty-six English murals of her are known to have existed, of which thirty-six survive. Cycles of her life in stained glass survive in whole or in part at York Minister, Clavering (Essex), Combs (Suffolk), and Balliol College, Oxford. There are also plenty of examples of her depiction in manuscripts, ivories, panel paintings, and embroidery. Sinai, Cyprus, Venice, and France are places where her cult specially flourished, while in Germany she was regarded as one of the *Fourteen Holy Helpers. Feast: 25 November, suppressed by the Holy See in 1969.

Propylaeum, pp. 543–4; Baudot and Chaussin, *Vies des Saints*, xi. 854–72; A. Poncelet, 'S. Catharinae translatio et miracula Rotomagensia', *Anal. Boll.*, xxii (1903), 423–38; A. Fawtier, 'Reliques rouennaises de Ste. Catharine', *Anal. Boll.*, xli (1923), 357–68; G. B. Bronzini, *La Leggenda di S. Caterina d'Alessandria: Passioni greche e latine* (1960); E. C. Williams, 'Mural Paintings of St. Catherine in England', *J.B.A.A.*, xix (1956), 20–33. English versions of the Legend include: *Seinte Katerine* (ed. S. R. d'Ardenne and E. J. Dobson, E.E.T.S. 1981); by Clemence of Barking, ed. W. MacBain (Anglo-Norman Texts xviii, 1964); by Capgrave (ed. C. Horstmann, E.E.T.S. 1893); and by O. Bokenham (ed. M. Serjeantson, E.E.T.S. 1936); *Bibl. SS.*, iii 954–78.

CATHERINE OF GENOA (1447–1510), widow. Born of the noble Ligurian family of Fieschi, Catherine was married at the age of sixteen to Julian Adorno for family, not personal, reasons. He proved to be spendthrift, inordinately pleasure-loving, bad-tempered, and frequently unfaithful: for the first five years of their marriage he was hardly ever at home. She persisted in a life of devotion: this, together with external misfortunes, effected his conversion. They moved to a small house in 1473, agreed to live in continence, and devoted themselves to the care of the sick in the hospital of Pammatone. From this time onwards Catherine combined an intense life of prayer with extreme practical efficiency in the administration of the hospital where she became matron, and in tireless care for others in need of help. In 1493 she nearly died of the plague; in 1496 her health broke down again; in 1497 her husband died. Thenceforward her spiritual life was even more intense, but she did not join a 'Third Order' for the laity. Remaining independent, she wrote her treatise on Purgatory and a Dialogue between the soul and the body. She also underwent various contemplative and visionary experiences. For the last three years of her life she suffered grave illness, which remained undiagnosed even by John-Baptist Boerio, the principal doctor of King Henry VII. Catherine was beatified in 1737 and equipollently canonized by Pope Benedict XIV a few years later. Feast: 15 September.

AA.SS. Sept. V (1755), 123–95; English tr. of Catherine's *Treatise on Purgatory and the Dialogue* by H. D. Irvine and C. Balfour (1946). The most notable study of her in English is F. von Hugel, *The Mystical Element of Religion as studied in St. Catherine of Genoa and her Friends* (2 vols., 1908 and 1961); the extent to which her writings were altered before they reached their present form is much disputed, see Umile Bonzi da Genoua, *S. Caterina Fieschi Adorno* (1961–2), and the same writer's article s.v. in *Dict. Sp.*, ii (1938), 290–325; see also L. Sertorius, *Katherina von Genua* (1939) and L. de Lapérouse, *La vie de ste. Catherine de Gênes* (1948); *Bibl. SS.*, iii 983–90.

CATHERINE OF SIENA (1347 [1333?]–1380), virgin, member of the Dominican Third Order. The youngest of the twenty or more children of a Sienese dyer, Giacomo Benincasa, Catherine from an early age was devoted to a life of prayer and penance, which she led at home in spite of strong but intermittent parental opposition. She steadfastly refused to consider marriage, became a Dominican tertiary, and, after years of solitude and preparation, began to mix with other people, first through nursing the sick in hospital and then by gathering a group of disciples, men and women, including Dominicans, Augustinians, and an English Austin Friar, William Flete. These accompanied her in her frequent journeys; their influence was manifested in some spectacular conversions and in their call to reform and repentance through a renewal of total love of God. Catherine tried to express her ideals in her Dialogue and in her letters, both of which were dictated by her, as she never learnt to write. Her personal holiness, enhanced rather than diminished by frequent and strong criticism, together with these writings, made her a very influential spiritual leader of the late Middle Ages.

In the last five years of her life she became involved with the politics of both State and Church. The importance of these interventions has sometimes been exaggerated. Her attempts to make peace between Florence and the papacy (then in Avignon) were disclaimed by the Florentines, while the papacy imposed harsh terms on them for their revolt. Later she added her voice to the many who urged Gregory XI to return to Rome from Avignon and end the so-called Babylonish Captivity and with its excessive French influence in the Curia. In 1376, on the same day that Gregory left Avignon by water for Rome, Catherine and her followers began the same journey by road. The two parties met in Genoa, but Catherine then went to Florence, still rent by factions and violence.

In 1378, after the death of Gregory XI, occurred the Great Schism, when Urban VI was elected pope in Rome and a rival set up in Avignon. Catherine wrote frequent letters both to Urban to moderate his harshness and to various European rulers and cardinals urging them to recognize him as the genuine pope. In spite of her reproofs Urban invited her to Rome, where she soon wore herself out working for his cause. She suffered a stroke on 21 April 1380 and died eight days later. Her friend and biographer, Raymond of Capua, later Master General of the Dominican Order, wrote her Life, which was influential in leading to her canonization in 1461 by the Sienese Pope Pius II. The quality of her writings and her membership of the Dominican Order gave her cult considerable diffusion. She became not only Siena's principal saint, but also a figure of international importance whose influence, it was popularly believed, was decisive in bringing about the return of the papacy to Rome. Like *Bernard, Catherine had prophetic vision and personal intransigence; these led both of them to identify God's cause with their own. Her house and an early portrait survive at Siena, where her head is also kept, but her body lies at S. Maria sopra Minerva at Rome, close to that of Fra *Angelico. She is depicted on two Devonshire church screens in Dominican habit, holding a heart and a book, and wearing a crown of thorns. Her more common emblem is a lily. Catherine was declared a Doctor of the Church in 1970. Feast: formerly 30 April, but since 1969, 29 April.

AA.SS. Apr. III (1675), 853–959 which reprints the *Legenda Maior* of Raymond of Capua (English version by Caxton *c.* 1493 and by G. Lamb, 1960) and the *Legenda Minor* of Thomas Caffarini; these sources have been radically criticized by R. Fawtier, *Sainte Catharine de Sienne* (2 vols., Bibl. des Écoles françaises d'Athènes et de Rome, cxxi and cxxxv, 1921–30), who suggests an earlier date for her birth, but see E. Jordan, 'La date de naissance de Ste. Catherine de Sienne', *Anal. Boll.*, xl (1922), 365–411; H. M. Laurent and F. Valli, *Fontes Vitae S. Catharinae Senensis historici* (1935); biographies by A. Curtayne (1929), A. Lennoyer ('Les Saints', 1934), M. de la Bedoyère (1947), and S. Undset (1951, Eng. tr. 1954). See also R. Fawtier and L. Canet, *La Double Expérience de Catherine Benincasa* (1948) and A. Dondaine, 'Sainte Catharine de Sienne et

Niccolo Toldo', *Archiv. Fratrum Praedicatorum*, xi (1949), 169–207. Catherine's dialogue is edited by I. Taurisano (1947), also extant in a 15th-century Eng. tr. *The Orchard of Syon*, ed. P. Hodgson and G. M. Liegey (E.E.T.S. cclviii. 1966) and a modern version by A. Thorold (1925). Her Letters are edited by N. Tommaseo and P. Miscatelli (6 vols., 1939–47); see V. D. Scidder, *Saint Catherine of Siena as seen in her letters* (1905); see also: G. Caratelli, *S. Caterina da Siena* (1962), G. Kaftal, *Saint Catherine in Tuscan Painting* (1949), T. Burckhardt, *Siena: City of the Virgin* (1962); *Bibl. SS.*, iii (1963), 996–1044.

CATHERINE OF SWEDEN (Vadstena), abbess (1331–81). The fourth of eight children of Ulf of Godmarsson and *Bridget of Sweden, Catherine married Eggard Lydersson, an invalid whom she nursed devotedly: some claim that the marriage was never consummated. With his consent she joined her mother in Rome and Jerusalem from 1349 onwards. Returning to Sweden, she again looked after her husband until his death. From then onwards she was even more closely associated with her mother's religious activities and particularly with her convent of Vadstena, where Catherine became abbess, and where her cell survives, with a window on to the church's sanctuary. Catherine was important in the history of the Brigittine Order, as she obtained papal approval for it in 1376. She also worked hard to secure the canonization of Bridget, which was finally achieved in 1381. The approval of her own cult followed in 1484. Feast: 24 March.

I. Collijn, *Processus Canonizationis b. Katerinae de Vadstenis* (1942–46); J. Jorgensen, *St. Bridget of Sweden* (2 vols. 1954).

CEADDA, see CHAD.

CECILIA (Cecily, Celia), Roman martyr of the 3rd century, of whom almost nothing is known for certain. Her great popularity is largely due to the late 5th-century Legend. According to this, she was a young Christian patrician, betrothed to a pagan called Valerian. But she had already vowed her virginity to God and refused to consummate the marriage. Both her husband and his brother, *Tiburtius, became Christians, were arrested, and martyred. Soon afterwards Cecilia buried the two martyrs and was brought before the prefect. She refused to sacrifice, converted her persecutors, and was sentenced to be suffocated in her bathroom. This plan failed and a soldier was sent to behead her. Three blows failed to kill her and she survived half-dead for three days. Later her house was dedicated as a church by Pope Urban who had encouraged her in her resolve.

Unfortunately this story is unsupported by any near-contemporary evidence. There is no mention of Cecilia in the 4th-century *Depositio Martyrum* nor in the writings of *Jerome, *Ambrose, *Damasus, or Prudentius, all of whom were specially interested in the martyrs. Many similar Legends embellish the memory of some historic person, but in the case of Cecilia a church in the Trastevere, Rome, founded by a certain Roman matron called Cecilia, is at the base of the story. It does seem, however, that the martyrs associated with Cecilia were indeed historical persons.

Her relics, with those of her companions, were translated by Pope Paschal I *c.*820 to her church. When it was rebuilt in 1599, the tomb of Cecilia was opened and the body was found incorrupt, but it quickly disintegrated through contact with the air. The sculptor Maderna, however, made a life-size marble statue of the body 'lying on the right side, as a maiden in her bed, her knees drawn together and seeming to be asleep'. A replica of this statue occupies Cecilia's supposed original tomb in the cemetery of Callistus.

Cecilia has been most famous as the patron of musicians since the 16th century. The origin of this seems to be found in the antiphon taken from her Acts: 'as the organs (at her wedding feast) were playing, Cecilia sung (in her heart) to the Lord, saying: may my heart remain unsullied, so that I be not confounded.' At the foundation of the Academy of Music in Rome in 1584 she was chosen as its patroness. Dryden wrote a 'Song for St. Cecilia's Day' and Pope an 'Ode for Music on St. Cecilia's Day'. The traditional account of her life is famous as the Second Nun's Tale in Chaucer's *Canterbury Tales*.

Cecilia is the patron of Albi cathedral and of a few English churches and convents; in art her principal emblem since the 16th century is an organ (as in Raphael's painting at Bologna) or some other musical instrument such as a lute; but she appears without emblem in ancient representations such as the mosaic in S. Apollinare Nuovo, Ravenna (6th century), and in Roman frescoes in the catacomb of Callixtus and in the church of S. Maria Antiqua. There are also cycles of her Life in stained glass at Bourges (13th century) and in frescoes at the Carmine church in Florence (15th century). Feast: 22 November.

H. Delehaye, *Étude sur le légendier romain* (1936), pp. 77–96; V. L. Kennedy, *The Saints of the Canon of the Mass* (Studi di Antiquita Cristiana, xiv. 1938); Baudot and Chassin, *Vies des Saints*, xi (1954), 731–59; H. Quentin in *D.A.C.L.*, ii. 2712–38 (who questions the usual account of Maderna's sculpture and other elements in the traditional account); see also *Bibl. SS.*, iii. 1064–86.

CEDD (d. 664), bishop of the East Saxons. Almost all we know of him comes from *Bede. Cedd and his three brothers, *Chad, Cynebill, and Caelin, were Anglian boys educated at Lindisfarne by *Aidan and *Finan: all became priests and two of them bishops. When Peada, king of Mercia, became a Christian in 653, he invited Cedd and three other priests to evangelize his people. Soon after, *Sigebert, king of the East Saxons, became a Christian through the influence of Oswiu of Northumbria, then his overlord, who sent Cedd to evangelize Essex. His mission was so successful that Finan of Lindisfarne consecrated him bishop. Cedd worked especially in the neighbourhood of Bradwell-on-Sea and Tilbury, where he founded monasteries. On one of his visits to Northumbria in 658 he was given land for the foundation of a monastery at Lastingham (N. Yorkshire) by Oethelwald, Oswiu's son, and fasted forty days before consecrating it. At the Synod of Whitby in 663/4 Cedd acted as interpreter; after it he accepted its decisions for his own diocese. Soon after, he died of the plague at Lastingham, where he was buried, first outside the walls and later in the sanctuary of the church of St. Mary.

Lastingham was less successful in spreading his cult than Lichfield was in glorifying his brother Chad; but by the 11th century Cedd's relics were venerated at Lichfield with Chad's. Cedd is the best-known example of a Lindisfarne monk of Irish training who worked at a great distance from his monastery; but it is interesting to note the strongly Roman character of his building at Bradwell, which closely resembles early Christian churches in Kent. The day of his death, according to Florence of Worcester, was 26 October, which is his usual feast; the alternative day, 7 January, presumably commemorates a translation.

Bede, *H.E.*, iii. 22–6; H. M. and J. Taylor, *Anglo-Saxon Architecture* (1965).

CEIN, see KEYNE.

CELESTINE V, see PETER CELESTINE.

CELIA, see CECILIA.

CELSUS (Cellach Mac Aodh), archbishop of Armagh 1105–29. The last of a long line of archbishops of Armagh, chosen as laymen by hereditary succession, Celsus proved a notable reformer. He is known mainly through the Lives of his protégé and successor, *Malachy. As co-arb of *Patrick he travelled over many parts of Ireland, collecting dues, finding out the general state of the Church and implicitly asserting the rights of Armagh. He presided over the reforming Synod of Rath Bresail in 1111 with Gilbert of Limerick, the papal legate, when normal diocesan and metropolitan organization was set up and various liturgical reforms promulgated. This council, whose conclusions were not always well received, aimed at bringing the Irish Church into line with others in western Europe. Celsus rebuilt Armagh cathedral, and was often in demand as a peacemaker between warring Irish kings. He promoted Malachy, first as his own archdeacon, later as bishop of Connor, and finally as archbishop of Armagh, thus breaking the line of hereditary succession. Feast (in *R.M.*): 1 April; more generally in Ireland, 7 April.

AA.SS. Apr. I (1675), 619–20; *The Irish Saints* (1964), pp. 62–7; H. S. Lawlor, *St. Bernard of Clairvaux's Life of St. Malachy of Armagh* (1920).

CENYDD, see KYNED.

CEOLFRITH (Ceufroy) (d. 716), abbot of Wearmouth and Jarrow. A noble Northumbrian by birth, Ceolfrith became a monk at Gilling (North Yorkshire), but a few years later moved to Ripon, founded by *Wilfrid. Here he was ordained priest at the early age of twenty-seven. After visits to Canterbury and to Icanho, made famous by *Botulf, he became 'most learned in ecclesiastical and monastic practices', but his practical ability caused him to be appointed baker (presumably caterer) of his monastery at Ripon. Here the Rule of St. Benedict was followed: to increase its influence at Wearmouth, perhaps, *Benedict Biscop asked Ceolfrith to join him there. Soon Ceolfrith became prior and in 676 superior of the community while Biscop was in Rome. At this point the opposition of certain monks of noble birth caused his temporary return to Ripon, but his future lay with Wearmouth. In 682 the monastery of Jarrow was founded from Wearmouth with Ceolfrith as its first abbot. Although a plague soon killed most of the monks who could sing or read (only Ceolfrith and the boy *Bede were left), Jarrow soon recovered and prospered considerably.

On the death of Biscop in 689 Ceolfrith became abbot of both Wearmouth and Jarrow, still regarded as one community. During his energetic but kindly rule the number of monks increased to 600, the library was doubled, the endowments and treasure increased, the papal privileges of protection renewed. He wrote (or caused Bede to write) an important letter on Easter dates to Nectan, king of the Picts. He also commissioned from his own scriptoria three Pandects (i.e. complete bibles in single volumes), written in uncial script. One was for Jarrow, one for Wearmouth, and the third a present for the pope. The last survives as the *Codex Amiatinus*, an enormous volume in the Biblioteca Laurenziana at Florence. It is the oldest surviving complete Latin Bible in one volume, is the work of at least seven English scribes, and represents, on the whole, a sound text of the Vulgate; it has important affinities with Cassiodorus' monastery and plan of studies. Its authenticity was brilliantly demonstrated in the 19th century when ultra-violet light revealed the partially altered inscription at the beginning of the volume which corresponds exactly with Bede's record of its dedicatory verses. When Ceolfrith resigned from the abbacy in 716, he took this book with him. In his farewell address he exhorted his monks to keep to the rule, he asked and granted forgiveness for all frailties, and urged them to persevere in unity, charity, and peace. He then confirmed the election of Hwaetbert as his successor and left for Gaul by sea on his way to Rome. But on 25 September he died at Langres in Burgundy and was buried there. His relics were soon translated to Wearmouth where they were enshrined until the Viking invasions. Glastonbury monks claimed to have obtained them in the 10th century. Feast (at Wearmouth, Glastonbury, and in Burgundy): 25 September.

Contemporary Lives by an anonymous monk of Jarrow and by Bede in *Baedae Opera Historica* (ed. C. Plummer, 1956) with Eng. trs. in J. F. Webb and D. H. Farmer, *The Age of Bede* (1983) and in *E.H.D.*, i. 697–708; R. L. S. Bruce-Mitford, *The Art of the Codex Amiatinus* (Jarrow Lecture, 1969); E. A. Lowe, *English Uncial* (1960). See also J. McClure, 'Bede and the Life of Ceolfrid', *Peritia*, iii (1984), 71–84. A few leaves of one of Ceolfrith's other bibles survive in the British Museum.

CEOLWULF (d. 764 [760?]), king of Northumbria. He became king in 729, was deposed by being captured and forcibly tonsured in 731, was released the same year, and continued to rule until 737. He then abdicated and became a monk at Lindisfarne. *Bede dedicated the *Ecclesiastical History* to him and highly praised his piety, while also expressing reserve about his ability to rule. Once at Lindisfarne Ceolwulf endowed the community with a generosity which enabled them to drink beer or wine, whereas formerly they used to drink only water or milk, like many Irish and Welsh ascetics. Ceolwulf was buried near *Cuthbert at Lindisfarne, where miracles were believed to prove his sanctity. His relics were translated in 830 to Egred's new church at Norham-on-Tweed with those of Cuthbert; later Ceolwulf's head was translated to Durham. Feast: 15 January.

Bede, *H.E.*, preface and v. 23, also *Letter to Egbert*, §9 in *Baedae Opera Historica* (ed. C. Plummer, 1956), i. 5, 349–50, 412; ii. 336, 340; Symeon of Durham, i. 47, 52, 201 and ii. 32, 42, 375.

CERAN, see CIARAN OF CLONMACNOISE.

CETT, in the words of the 11th-century *Resting-Places of the Saints*, lies buried in the monastery called *Undola* (= Oundle), by the river Nen. Nothing seems to be known of him.

CEUFROY, see CEOLFRITH.

CHAD (Ceadda) (d. 672), first bishop of Mercia and Lindsey at Lichfield. Brother of *Cedd, whom he succeeded as abbot of Lastingham (N. Yorkshire), and disciple of *Aidan, who sent him to Ireland for part of his education, Chad was chosen by Oswiu, king of Northumbria, as bishop of the Northumbrian see, while *Wilfrid, who had been chosen for Deira by the sub-king Alcfrith, was absent in Gaul seeking consecration, soon after the Synod of Whitby (663/4). Faced with a dearth of bishops in England, Chad was unwise enough to be consecrated by the simoniacal Wine of Dorchester, assisted by two dubious British bishops. Wilfrid, on his return to England in 666, found that Alcfrith was dead or exiled and retired to Ripon, leaving Chad in occupation. But in 669 *Theodore, archbishop of Canterbury, restored Wilfrid to York and deposed Chad (who retired to Lastingham), but soon reconsecrated him to be bishop of the Mercians. This unusual step was due both to a new opening for Christianity in Mercia and to the excellent character of Chad himself, whom both Eddius and *Bede recognized as humble, devout, zealous, and apostolic. Chad's episcopate of three years laid the foundations of the see of Lichfield according to the decrees of the council at Hertford. Wulfhere, king of Mercia, gave him fifty hides of land for a monastery at Barrow (Lincs.); he also established a monastery close to Lichfield cathedral. Chad died on 2 March and was buried in the church of St. Mary. At once, according to Bede, he was venerated as a saint and his relics were translated to the cathedral church of St. Peter. Cures were claimed in both churches. Bede described his first shrine as 'a wooden coffin in the shape of a little house with an aperture in the side through which the devout can . . . take out some of the dust, which they put into water and give to sick cattle or men to drink, upon which they are presently eased of their infirmity and restored to health'. A vernacular Life also survives.

His relics were translated in 1148 and moved to the Lady Chapel in 1296. An even more splendid shrine was built by Robert Stretton, bishop of Lichfield (1360–85), of marble substructure, with the feretory adorned with gold and precious stones. Rowland Lee, bishop of Lichfield 1534–43, pleaded with Henry VIII to spare the shrine: this was done, but only for a time. At some unknown date the head and some other bones had been separated from the main shrine. Some of these, it was claimed, were preserved by recusants, and four large bones, believed to be Chad's, are in the R.C. cathedral of Birmingham. A fine Mercian illuminated Gospel Book of the 8th century called the Gospels of St. Chad was probably associated with his shrine, as the Lindisfarne Gospels were associated with the shrine of *Cuthbert; it is now in Lichfield cathedral library. The 11th-century shrine list mentions the relics of Cedd and *Hedda resting at Lichfield with Chad. Thirty-three ancient churches and several wells were dedicated to him, mainly in the Midlands. There are also several modern dedications. Feast: 2 March.

Bede, *H.E.*, iii. 28, iv. 3; *Eddius' Life of Wilfrid* (ed. B. Colgrave, 1928), cc. 14–15; *AA.SS.* Mar. I (1668), 143–6 and *Propylaeum*, p. 83; *N.L.A.*, i. 185–8 (cf. *Anal. Boll.*, lviii (1940), 96; R. V. Vleerskruyer, *The Life of St. Chad* (1953); R. H. Warner, *The Life and Legends of St. Chad* (1871); J. Hewitt, 'The Keeper of St. Chad's Head', *Jnl. of Arch. Inst.*, xxxiii (1876), 72–82; *R.P.S.* and *C.S.P.*

CHANEL, Peter (1803–41), Marist priest and martyr. Born of peasant stock near Cras in the diocese of Belley (Ain, France), Peter was chosen as a pupil by his parish priest, the Abbé Trompier, for his unusual intelligence and piety. He went to the local seminary and was ordained priest: a year later he became pastor of the unsatisfactory parish of Crozet, which he revived in three years. In 1831 he joined the Marist missionary congregation, recently founded by Jean Colin at Lyons, hoping to work on the foreign missions. Instead he taught for five years as a lecturer in the seminary of Belley, but in 1836 he was sent to preach the Catholic faith in the islands of the southern Pacific ocean with a few companions. With one colleague he went to the Islands of Futuna (1837), one of a group under French sovereignty near Fiji, where cannibalism had formerly flourished. There they were given a friendly welcome by the people, whose confidence they won by healing the sick. The missionaries then learnt the local language and began to teach Christianity. The chief's son asked to receive baptism, but this so incensed his father that he sent a group of warriors with orders to kill. One of them clubbed Peter to the ground and the others cut up his body with knives and axes. But less than a year later the whole island became Christian. Peter was canonized in 1954 by Pius XII. Feast: 28 April. This feast was formerly celebrated only in New Zealand and Australia, of which he is regarded as the protomartyr, but recently it has been included in the universal Roman calendar.

Lives by C. Nicolet (1920), and W. Symes (1963); see also J. Hervier, *Les missions maristes en Océanie* (1902). Works edited by C. Rozier (1960).

CHANTAL, Jane Frances de (1572–1641), widow and foundress of the Order of the Visitation. Born of the noble Burgundian family of Frémyot, she married Baron Christophe de Chantal at the age of twenty; three children died in infancy but four survived. Jane was a faithful wife, devoted mother, and efficient housekeeper, but after only nine years of married life she was left a widow when her husband was killed in a shooting accident in 1601. She took a vow of chastity the same year and in 1604 met *Francis of Sales, who became her director: until his death in 1622 she benefited greatly from his wise guidance. He stressed at the beginning the duties of her state, as daughter, mother, and member of society.

Later she wished to become a nun; with Francis she founded a new Order, whose special purpose was to enable women of delicate health to live the religious life and to work *outside* the cloister. In fact the latter characteristic was altered by the prelates, who withheld approval unless it were changed. This attitude had been caused by Lutheran attacks on the laxity of certain convents; Roman authorities found it almost impossible to admit the respectability of 'unenclosed' nuns. *Angela Merici and Mary Ward were two other foundresses who faced similar difficulties at this time, but with more success in retaining their original ideals.

Francis of Sales inaugurated the convent at Annecy in 1610 with Jane as superior and about a dozen other nuns. Francis had to agree to the Visitation nuns being enclosed; this did not prevent its rapid expansion to eighty-six houses in just over thirty years. This was due to Francis's teaching and writings *On the Love of God*, his insistence on the importance of humility and meekness rather than corporal austerity, and the prudence and dedication of Jane. The foundation of a house at Paris in 1619 was a turning-point and brought her into contact with *Vincent de Paul, who later described her as 'one of the holiest souls I have ever met'. All this time Jane had been also concerned with her own family. When she became a nun, two of her daughters were married but her son was only fifteen. Later he married, but was killed fighting against the Huguenots and the English at the Isle of Rhé in 1627. His infant daughter later became Madame de Sévigné. Other bereavements followed. In 1628 there was a severe outbreak of plague: Jane wholeheartedly devoted her convent of Annecy to the ill, and inspired the local rulers to make adequate provision for the sick and the bereaved. In later years she made systematic visits of all the houses in her Order; in 1641 she was in Paris as the guest of Anne of Austria. She died on the return journey at Moulins on 13 December, at the age of sixty-nine. She was beatified in 1751 and canonized in 1767. Her body had been buried in Annecy and was translated to a new tomb in 1912. Feast: 12 December.

F. M. de Chaugny, *Mémoires sur la vie et les vertus de sainte Jeanne-Françoise Frémyot de Chantal* (1874–9, 8 vols.); L. V. E. Bougaud, *Histoire de sainte Chantal et des Origines de la Visitation* (2 vols., 1861; Eng. tr. 1895); A. Gazier, *Jeanne de Chantal et Angélique Arnauld d'après leur correspondance* (1915). Lives by H. Bremond (1912), E. K. Sanders (1918), E. C. V. Stopp (1962); *Bibl. SS.*, vi. 581–6.

CHARLES (1), see BORROMEO.

CHARLES (2), see LWANGA.

CHATTAN (Cathan) **OF KINGARTH** (6th century). Irish by birth, Chattan migrated to the Clyde area, founded several churches there, and later the monastery of Kingarth on the Isle of Bute. He was the uncle of *Blane, whom he sent to be educated by *Comgall of Bangor before succeeding his uncle at Kingarth. Chattan died and was buried in Northern Ireland.

E. G. Bowen, 'The travels of the Celtic Saints', *Antiquity*, xviii (1944), 16–28.

CHILIAN, see KILIAN.

CHIONE, see AGAPE, IRENE, AND CHIONE.

CHRISTIAN (d. 1186), Irish Cistercian monk and abbot and bishop of Lismore. The confusing legends and traditions about him make it difficult to establish biographical details. It seems that he was born in Bangor (Ulster), and was the disciple and later archdeacon of *Malachy. He stayed behind at Clairvaux when Malachy returned from Rome to Ireland, became a monk there under *Bernard, and was chosen first abbot of Mellifont, Ireland's first Cistercian monastery, in 1142. He supported Malachy's policy of reforming the Irish Church and ruled the see of Lismore (1151–79); later he acted as papal legate. Feast: 18 March.

J. O'Hanlon, *Lives of Irish Saints*, iii. 839; B.T.A., i. 630.

CHRISTINA (4th century?), virgin and martyr. There are two claimants to this title who have come to share the same Acts: Christina of Tyre (Phoenicia) and Christina of Bolsena in Tuscany. It would seem that the former never existed, while the latter, probably a genuine martyr with a surviving shrine and catacomb, was not called Christina. Both Eastern and Western churches had a cult of Christina on 24 July; the Legend which does duty for both made her the heroine of a series of unlikely tortures endured for refusing to sacrifice to the pagan gods: eventually she was shot to death with arrows. The Legend seems to be a conflation of those of *Barbara, *Catherine of Alexandria, and *Ursula. Her iconography begins with a mosaic at Ravenna (6th century) in which she has no special attributes. In the 15th and 16th centuries there are notable paintings by Cranach and Paul Veronese, her attributes being a millstone, a wheel, pincers, and arrows.

AA.SS. Iul. V, 495–534; *C.M.H.*, p. 394; *Propylaeum*, p. 304; C. Ricci, *Santa Christina e il lago de Bolsena* (1928); art. Bolsena in *D.A.C.L.*; B.T.A., iii. 173–4.

CHRISTINA (Theodora) **OF MARKYATE** (*c.*1097–*c.*1161), virgin. Christina came of a noble Anglo-Saxon family in Huntingdon, the daughter of Autti, a rich and influential guild merchant in the town. In 1112, on a visit to St. Albans abbey, she made a private vow of virginity, which was intended to be fulfilled in some form of public dedication. It was not, however, acceptable to her parents. Ralph Flambard (after he became a bishop) attempted to seduce her in 1114; bishop Robert Bloet of Lincoln first agreed that she should not marry Burhtred, the man of her parents' choice, but was later bribed to give judgement against her. So after a year's virtual imprisonment, and having been both betrothed and married but retaining her virginity, she was helped to escape by the hermit Eadwin who had consulted Ralph, archbishop of Canterbury, about her case. She took refuge at Flamstead with an anchoress named Alfwen for two years and in 1118 moved to a hermitage at Markyate, where the elderly recluse Roger protected and instructed her. In 1122 both her betrothal and her marriage were annulled by Thurstan, archbishop of York, and Burhtred was free to marry again. This decision was reached in view of the unconsummated marriage being cancelled by her earlier vow of virginity and of it being undertaken under duress from her parents. Her return to Markyate was made possible by the death of Bloet in 1123. There, apart from short intervals, she remained for the rest of her life, attracting disciples as her fame spread far and wide. The house became a regular priory of nuns. In 1130 archbishop Thurstan invited Christina to become abbess of his nunnery of St. Clement at York; Fontevrault and Marcigny nunneries also asked her to join them, but she was persuaded by Geoffrey, abbot of St. Albans, to remain at Markyate. Until his death in 1147 he guided her and she deeply influenced him away from the worldly success of administration towards prayer, solitude, and poverty. Hermits and recluses in the neighbourhood gained from his generosity. Christina, who was a skilful needlewoman, embroidered for the English pope Adrian IV (educated at St. Albans) a present of mitres and sandals. She probably owned the sumptuous St. Albans Psalter, a masterpiece of Romanesque illumination which contains unusual elements such as the Legend of *Alexis, who left his wife on their wedding-night to pursue a life of devotion and voluntary poverty.

Christina seems to have been a well-balanced and able person, highly strung but not hysterical, who experienced visions on occasion, but was not given to excessive mortifications. There are some traces of a cult. There was a feast at St. Albans of her companions, Roger and Sigar, on 5 December, and a Christina is mentioned on the same day in some Parisian calendars and in the *English Martyrologe* of 1608. A modern Bollandist conjectures that the feast of 5 December was the feast of the whole group, including Christina, while on the rood-screen at Gately (Norfolk) among other saints is a 'puella de Ridibowne', probably intended for Christina of Redburne or Markyate. Markyate continued as a nunnery until 1537.

C. H. Talbot, *The Life of Christina of Markyate* (1959); O. Pächt, C. R. Dodwell, and F. Wormald, *The St. Albans Psalter* (1960); *N.L.A.*, ii. 532–7; P. Grosjean in *Anal. Boll.*, lxxvii (1960), 197–206; C. J. Holdsworth in D. Baker (ed.), *Medieval Women* (1978).

CHRISTOPHER (3rd century?), martyr. Nothing is known of his history except the record of his death in Asia Minor. A church was dedicated to him in Bithynia in 452 and there are 8th-century Legends in both Greek and Latin. These were augmented, especially in 12th-century Germany, until they reached the final form in the *Golden Legend*, which inspired innumerable artistic representations all over Europe and assured Christopher a place among the *Fourteen Holy Helpers. The name

Christopher (Christ-bearer) is made the basis for the Legend: 'he bare him on his shoulders by conveying and leading, in his body by making it lean, in mind by devotion and in his mouth by confession and preaching.' Christopher, supposedly a Canaanite, was a giant of fearsome appearance, who first decided to serve the Devil, but finding that the latter was afraid of Christ and his Cross, decided to serve Christ instead. A hermit instructed him in the Christian faith, and assigned to him as his Christian service residence near a river and helping travellers to cross it. Once a child asked Christopher to carry him across, but Christopher found him so heavy that he was bowed down with the weight. The child then told him that he was Jesus Christ and that he had carried the weight of the whole world and 'him that created and made all the world upon thy shoulders'. He told Christopher to plant his staff in the ground: the next day it would bear flowers and dates as a sign of the truth of the message he had received. Later he was said to have preached Christianity in the city of Lycia with enormous success, but was imprisoned when in persecution (under Decius?) he refused to sacrifice to the gods. Two women who were sent to seduce him in prison were converted instead; Christopher was beaten with rods of iron; shot with arrows, one of which injured the king in the eye, later healed by Christopher's blood; finally he was beheaded.

Many English wall-paintings of Christopher have survived. Mostly they were placed on the north wall opposite the porch so that he would be seen by all who entered the church. This was because he was not only the patron of travellers, but also was invoked against water, tempest, and plague and especially against sudden death. It was popularly believed that whoever saw an image of Christopher would not die that day. Hence in modern times he is invoked as the patron of motorists (a church in the Javel area of Paris, where Citroën cars are made, is dedicated to his patronage), and the motorists' plaques often bear the ancient inscription 'Behold St. Christopher and go thy way in safety'. The surviving paintings vary in elaboration. In most of them he is depicted as a giant, carrying the Infant Jesus on his back. From the 14th century the picturesque element is more in evidence, with the hermit, the river, the flowering staff, boats, fishes, and the arrow wounding the king. The two temptresses and even a mermaid are also sometimes found. Examples may be seen at Shorwell (I.W.), Aldermaston (Berks.), Little Missenden (Bucks.), Impington (Cambs.), Breage and St. Keverne (Cornwall), Haddon Hall (Derbyshire), Little Baddow (Essex), and many other places. There are also notable examples in stained glass (e.g. Great Malvern Priory) and sculpture (e.g. Terrington St. Clement, Norfolk). Nine English churches have ancient dedications to him.

The cult of Christopher was severely criticized by Erasmus in his *Praise of Folly*; his popularity suffered both from the Reformation and the Counter-Reformation, so that from the 17th century (in contrast to earlier times) it is hard to find notable examples of images of him. But in modern times his popular cult has revived with the increase in travel by air and motorway. As travelling becomes (or is believed to become) more dangerous, so does devotion to Christopher flourish. When in 1969 the Holy See reduced his feast to the dimension of a merely local cult, there was a sharp reaction in various countries, led in Italy by popular film stars. It seems likely that this medieval legend and cult will never completely lose its popularity. Feast: 25 July.

AA.SS. Iul. VI (1729), 125–49 with *Anal. Boll.*, i (1882), 121–48 and x (1891), 393–405; H. Usener, *Acta S. Marinae et S. Christopori* (1886), 54–76; W. Morris and F. S. Ellis (edd.), *The Golden Legend* (1892); H. C. Whaite, *St. Christopher in English Medieval Wallpainting* (1929); H. F. Rosenfeldt, *Der hl. Christophorus* (1937); C. Johnson, *St. Christopher* (1938); A. Masseron, *Saint Christophe, patron des automobilistes* (1933); A. Caiger-Smith, *English Medieval Mural Paintings* (1963); G. McN. Rushforth, *Medieval Christian Imagery* (1936), pp. 221–4; *Bibl. SS.*, iv 349–64.

CHRODEGANG OF METZ (d. 766), bishop. Born near Liège and educated at the abbey of Saint-Trond, he was appointed in turn secretary, chancellor, and principal minister by Charles Martel. He became bishop of Metz in 742 and acted as ambassador of Pepin to Stephen III, working for the coronation of the emperor in 754 and helping to establish Frankish rule in Italy through the defeat of the Lombards.

His political achievements were matched by equally important ecclesiastical ones. In 748 he founded the abbey of Gorze which became a prominent reforming monastery, in some ways comparable to Cluny. But Chrodegang was best known as the author of a Rule for canons, written for those of his own cathedral. Under it they lived a community life devoted to the public prayer of the Church, but in close association with diocesan personnel and with full authorization to own property individually. This attracted the attention of Charlemagne who enacted that all clerics living in community should follow the Rule of *Benedict or else that of Chrodegang. His Rule spread to Germany, Italy, and England, where it was translated into OE and was used in some cathedral chapters which were not monastic.

Chrodegang also founded a school of Church music at Metz, which became long famous for Gregorian Chant. Feast: 6 March.

Life ed. G. H. Pertz, *M.G.H. Scriptores*, x (1852), 552–72; John the Deacon, *Liber de Episcopis Mettensibus*, ed. G. H. Pertz, ibid., ii (1829), 267 et seq.; Rule in *P.L.*, lxxxix. 1057–96 with OE version by A. S. Napier (E.E.T.S. 1916 and 1971); see also R. Folz, *Saint Chrodegang* (1967).

CHRYSOGONUS (d. *c.*304), martyr of Aquileia. According to the Passion of St. *Anastasia, he was a Roman official who was imprisoned under Diocletian and beheaded at Aquileia, and whose body was recovered from the sea by Christians. His cult spread to Rome where the church founded by another Chrysogonus was dedicated to him. He was mentioned in the Roman Canon. Feast: 24 November, the dedication day of the Roman Church.

Propylaeum, s.d. 24 November; H. Delehaye, *Étude sur le légendier romain*, pp. 151–71.

CIARAN (Ceran, Kieran, Queran) **OF CLONMACNOISE** (Cluain Mocca Nois) (*c.*512–*c.*545), abbot. The son of a travelling carpenter of Connaught, Ciaran studied under *Finnian of Clonard, taking a cow to supply himself with milk. Later he went as a monk to *Enda on Aran island (*c.*534), where he was ordained priest, and then to Senan on Scattery island (*c.*541). He finally settled at Clonmacnoise, on the Shannon (Co. Meath), and founded a monastery on a fine site with about ten companions. He worked at the first buildings but died within a year, supposedly at the early age of thirty-three.

Various legends are attached to Ciaran: that when he was a student a tame young fox used to take his writings to his master until it was old enough to eat the satchel; that the other 'saints of Ireland' were so jealous of him that all of them except *Columba prayed and fasted so that he would die young; that soon before his death he told his disciples to leave his bones on the hilltop 'like a stag's' and preserve his spirit rather than his relics. At Clonmacnoise the succession of abbots was not hereditary: this unusual state of things recalled the humble origins of the founder. Clonmacnoise became one of the most important monasteries and centres of learning in Ireland. It survived many Viking raids and plunderings in various Irish and Anglo-Norman wars, continuing as a monastery until 1552. Notable ruins survive from its early days. Although Ciaran's shrine was plundered several times in the early Middle Ages, the Clonmacnoise crozier in the National Museum, Dublin, is believed to belong to it. Feast: 9 September.

AA.SS. Sept. III (1750), 370–83; *V.S.H.*, i. 200–16; R. I. Best and E. Macneill, *Annals of Innisfallen* (1933), s.a. 930, 1018, 1021, 1130, 1155; R. A. S. MacAlister, *The Latin and Irish Lives of Ciaran* (1921), P. Grosjean, 'Notes d'Hagiographie Celtique', *Anal. Boll.*, lxix (1951),

102–6; R. I. Best, 'The graves of the kings of Clonmacnois', *Eriv*, ii (1905), 163–71; J. Ryan, 'The Abbatial Succession at Clonmacnois', *Feil-Sgribbin Eoin Mic Neill* (1940), pp. 490–507; J. McNawse, 'The Chronology of the life of St. Ciaran of Clonmacnois', *Jnl. of Ardagh and Clonmacnois Antiquarian Soc.* (1945), pp. 2–16.

CIARAN OF SAIGHIR (5th–6th century), bishop and monk. Born in West Cork of an Ossory family, Ciaran went to Europe as a young man, was baptized and ordained. He returned to Ossory and settled at Seirkieran (= Saighir) near Birr (Co. Offaly), first as a hermit, and later as abbot of a large monastery. He may have been consecrated bishop by *Patrick.

Many legends are told of him, especially of his influence over wild animals. A wolf, a badger, and a fox together worked for him and his monks, helping them to cut woods and build huts. Eventually the fox stole Ciaran's shoes and fled to his lair. The wolf and the badger were charged by the saint to bring him back; the badger bound the fox from ear to tail and delivered him unwillingly. Ciaran reproved the fox, told him to fast and do penance like a monk, and to continue work as before.

Ciaran's monastery became the burial-place of the kings of Ossory; notable ruins remain. The site may have been pre-Christian; as in some other Irish sanctuaries, perpetual fire is said to have burnt there. His other site, the island of Cape Clear (Cork), was probably his hermitage at or near his birthplace. Here a ruined church and well survive of great antiquity. From medieval times this Ciaran was identified wrongly with the Cornish *Piran; he must also be distinguished from his younger namesake, *Ciaran of Clonmacnoise. Feast: 5 March.

W. W. Heist, *Vitae Sanctorum Hiberniae* (1965), pp. 346–52; P. Grosjean, 'Vita S. Ciarani, Episcopi de Saighir', *Anal. Boll.*, lix (1941), 217–71, *The Irish Saints*, pp. 76–9.

CISSA (early 8th century), monk. He was a disciple of *Guthlac at Crowland and provided the biographer Felix with much of his material. Cult at Crowland only, with no official feast-day.

CITHA, see ZITA.

CIWA, see KEW.

CLARE (1194–1253), virgin, foundress of the Minoresses or Poor Clares. She was born at Assisi of the Offreduccio family, but nothing is known of her early life. When she was eighteen, she was so moved by the preaching of *Francis of Assisi that she joined him at the Portiuncula, where she renounced all her possessions and took the habit of a nun. She was then formed in the religious life at the Benedictine convents of Bastia and Sant'Angelo di Panzo until Francis was able to offer her and her companions a small house adjacent to the church of San Damiano, Assisi, which he had restored. There she became abbess in 1215 of a community of women who wished to live according to the rule and spirit of Francis: it soon included among its members Clare's mother and two sisters, and some members of the wealthy Ubaldini family from Florence. The way of life was one of extreme poverty and austerity, believed to be harder than that of any other nuns of the time: this was safeguarded as far as communal possessions were concerned by the papal 'Privilegium paupertatis' of 1228 for three convents, including San Damiano, to live entirely by alms, renouncing all rents and other common property. Like the Franciscan friars, Clare's nuns soon spread to other parts of Europe, especially Spain (47 convents in the 13th century), Bohemia, France, and England, where four convents were founded in the late 13th and 14th centuries.

Clare never left her convent at Assisi: she was distinguished as one of the great medieval contemplatives, devoted to serving her community in great joy, practising Franciscan ideals, including Francis' love of the world of nature, long after his death in 1226. For the last twenty-seven years of her life she suffered various illnesses, being sometimes bedridden, but she was always devoted to her nuns and to the town of Assisi. This was expressed not only by her sewing altar cloths and corporals for its churches, but also by prayer and penance on its behalf in times of crisis. Twice Assisi was in danger of being sacked by the armies of the Emperor Frederick II, which included a number of Saracens. Clare, although ill, was carried to the wall with a pyx containing the Blessed Sacrament, at which, say her biographers, the armies fled. This is why in art she is often depicted with a pyx or a monstrance, as on the D'Estouteville Triptych of English origin *c.*1360. She was canonized only two years after her death by Alexander IV in 1255. Among her nuns, as among the Franciscan friars, controversies about poverty continued as a divisive force until *Colette reformed the Poor Clares in the 15th century. They continue today in many countries as a contemplative Order, comparatively few in number but still distinguished by the same ideals as those which inspired Francis and Clare. Feast: 11 (formerly 12) August. Recently she has been named patron of television.

Five letters of Clare survive, together with her Rule and her Testament; the earliest Life (before 1261) is by Thomas of Celano in *AA.SS.* Aug. II (1735), 754–67 (Eng. tr. by P. Robinson, 1910); Z. Lazzeri, 'Il processo di canonizzazione di S. Chiara d'Assisi', *Archivum Franciscanum Historicum*, xiii (1920), 403–507; P. Robinson, 'St. Clare' in A. G. Little, *Franciscan Essays* (1913), pp. 31–49; *Santa Chiara d'Assisi*: Studi e cronaca del VII centenario 1253–1953 (1954); E. Gilliat Smith, *St. Clare of Assisi* (1914); R. M. Pierazzi, *Sainte Claire* (1937); M. Fassbinder, *Die hl. Klara von Assisi* (1934); N. de Roebeck, *St. Clare of Assisi* (1951); F. Casolini, *S. Chiara* (1953); R. B. and C. N. L. Brooke in D. Baker (ed.), *Medieval Women* (1978); *Bibl. SS.*, iii. 1201–17.

CLARE OF MONTEFALCO (Chiara della Croce) (d. 1308), Augustinian nun. At an early age she joined a community of Franciscan hermits, whom the bishop of Spoleto refounded as Augustinians. In 1291 she became abbess. She was famous for her total devotion to the Passion of Christ, manifested in extreme austerities, ecstasies, miracles, and infused knowledge.

After death and to this day she is famous also for the incorruption of her body, for her heart, where she claimed the marks of the Passion would be found, and for the liquefaction of her blood. Her relics, very impressive to some, are still shown. Her cult began immediately after her death; Urban VIII authorized her Office and Mass; she was canonized in 1881. Feast: 17 August, subsidiary feast: 30 October.

A. N. Merlin, *Une grande mystique ignorée* (1930); A. Semenza, *Vita S. Clarae de Cruce Ordinis Eremitarum S. Augustini* (1944); D. Sox, *Relics and Shrines* (1985), pp. 127–30; *Bibl. SS.*, iii. 1217–24.

CLARET, Antony (1807–70), archbishop of Cuba, founder of the Claretian congregation. Born at Sallent in northern Spain, Antony followed his father's trade of weaving before going to a seminary at Vich. He was ordained priest in 1835, went to Rome, and joined the Jesuits to devote himself to missionary work overseas. But his health broke down and he returned to Spain. For ten years he preached tirelessly in Catalonia, founding the congregation of Missionary Sons of the Immaculate Heart of Mary, commonly called Claretians. Soon afterwards he was appointed to the turbulent see of Cuba, where he encountered all kinds of opposition, even attempted assassination. But in 1857 he resigned, returned to Spain to be the confessor of Queen Isabella II, and devoted himself to preaching and writing, especially in Catalan. A special feature of his apostolate was his emphasis on the printed as well as the spoken word: he is reputed to have published 200 books or pamphlets. His considerable cultural interests are also evidenced by his establishing, while Rector of the Escorial, a science laboratory and a natural history museum, with schools of music and of languages. At the revolution of 1868 he went into exile with Queen Isabella and died in the Cistercian monastery of Fontfroide, near Narbonne. He was canonized in 1950 by Pius XII. Feast: 24 October.

B.T.A., iv. 195–6; J. Echevarria, *Reminiscences of*

Antony Claret (1938); D. Sargent, *The Assignments of Antonio Claret* (1950); see also the summary of his life in decree of canonization, *Acta Apostolicae Sedis*, xliv (1952), 345–58.

CLAVER, Peter (1580–1654), Spanish Jesuit priest, apostle of the Negroes. He was born at Verdu (Catalonia), was educated at Barcelona university, and became a Jesuit in 1600 at Tarragona. He was sent to the college of Palma (Majorca), where he met Alphonsus *Rodriguez, who encouraged his desire for missionary work in the New World. He studied theology at Barcelona and was sent to Cartagena (now in Colombia) in 1610, where he was ordained priest five years later.

At this time Cartagena was one of the principal centres of the flourishing but iniquitous slave-trade in Negroes from Angola and elsewhere in western Africa, who were shipped in large numbers and often unspeakable conditions across the Atlantic. Cartagena was a convenient clearing-house; it has been estimated that 10,000 reached it every year. Peter devoted himself to them under Fr. Alfonso de Sandoval, who had already spent forty years looking after them. Peter both imitated and surpassed the achievements of his predecessor. When a slave-ship arrived in the port, the slaves were shut up in yards, herded together in the heat without care or medical attention of any kind. Peter would visit them with medicine, food, brandy, lemons, and tobacco. His band of helpers assisted in this distribution and acted as interpreters. With their help and with the use of pictures he would teach the principal truths of Christianity and prepare the slaves for baptism. He also inspired them with some idea of their dignity and worth as men who were redeemed, in contrast with their appalling state of present misery. Eventually the slaves were sent to the mines (where the work was too hard for the native Indians) and to the plantations, which he visited every spring, not always with the approval of their masters. He would also nurse the slaves in conditions which nobody else could endure: he used to call himself 'the slave of the Negroes for ever'. This, however, did not prevent him from caring also for the souls of the more well-to-do members of society and for the traders and visitors (including Moslems and English Protestants) to Cartagena, or for condemned criminals, many of whom he prepared for death. He was also a frequent visitor to the city's hospitals. His apostolate included an annual mission to traders and seamen in the port every autumn. Miracles, prophecies, the gift of reading hearts, and the practice of severe personal penance were all ascribed to him. In 1650 he was taken ill while preaching to the Negroes. Although he recovered, he suffered from paralysis for the remaining four years of his life, broken in health, neglected by the young man who was responsible for looking after him, able to leave his cell only for short visits to the hospital or to friends. He lived long enough to welcome his successor in his apostolate. At his death the civil authorities and the clergy who had thought him indiscreet or misguided united in his praise; he was given a civic funeral while Negroes and Indians arranged for a Mass of their own. He was canonized in 1888 and declared patron of all missionary enterprises among the Negroes. His feast, 9 September, is on the day after his death; his cult is particularly strong in the United States and Latin America.

AA.SS. Sept. III (1750), 205 ff., J. Fernandez, *Apostolica y penitente vida de el V.P. P. Claver*, (1666); other Lives by G. Ledos (1923) and A. Valtierra (1954; Eng. tr. 1960); see also M. D. Petre, *Aethiopum Servus* (1896); A. Lunn, *A Saint in the Slave Trade* (1935).

CLEER (Clarus), see CLETHER.

CLEMENT (d. *c.*100), pope and martyr. Bishop of Rome after *Peter, *Linus, and *Cletus, Clement is known today mainly for his Epistle to the Corinthians of *c.*96, an exceptionally early and significant witness to the function and authority of the ministers of the Christian Church. It also shows for the first time a bishop of Rome intervening effectively in the affairs of another church, and provides evidence for the residence and martyrdom of Peter and *Paul at Rome. Other writings ascribed to Clement, including the so-called Second Epistle to the Corinthians (an early sermon on the quality of Christian life and the need for penance), are spurious. Although his genuine epistle was read at the Liturgy at Corinth in *c.*170 and a copy of it was added to the *Codex Alexandrinus* of the New Testament, it was less well known in the Middle Ages. Then Clement was thought of primarily as an early martyr. His *Acta* (of the 4th century) are of slight historical value, although they abound in picturesque detail. According to this source, Clement was exiled to the Crimea for the skill and extent of his apostolic activities in Rome. While in exile he was compelled to work in the mines, he opened a miraculous supply of water, he preached with such effect that again he made innumerable converts so that there was need for seventy-five churches. He was killed by being thrown into the sea with an anchor round his neck: angels were said to have made him a tomb on the sea-bed, which was uncovered once a year by an exceptionally low tide.

Seven centuries later, the missionary brothers *Cyril and Methodius, who were apostles of the Slav countries, 'miraculously recovered', they claimed, the body of Clement, piece by piece, together with the anchor. These relics were translated to Rome *c.*868 and buried in the fine church of San Clemente, built on the site of the *titulus Clementis*, a pastoral centre of the 3rd century which grew out of a place of worship of the 1st century in the house of one Clement, probably different from the saint. Fine frescoes of the 9th century survive at San Clemente, depicting the Legend and Translation of the saint. His usual emblem in art is an anchor; sometimes he is represented with a tiara and a cross with three branches. Representations of him survive at Chartres, Cologne, and Stara Boleslav in Bohemia, but also in England, especially on painted screens in East Anglia. The most famous of the forty-three churches dedicated to him in this country is St. Clement Danes, London, whose parish emblem is an anchor. Clement is also patron of the Guild of the Glorious and Undivided Trinity of London, i.e. Trinity House, the authority responsible for lighthouses and lightships. Feast in the West: 23 November; in the East, 24 November.

C.M.H., pp. 615–16; J. B. Lightfoot, *Apostolic Fathers*, part i, vol. I, pp. 148–200, with Eng. version of the epistle, also in K. Lake, *The Apostolic Fathers* (1930), and J. A. Kleist in *The Epistle of St. Clement and St. Ignatius* (1946); H. Delehaye, *Étude sur le Légendier romain* (1936), pp. 96–116; L. Boyle, *St. Clement's Rome* (pamphlet, 1960).

CLEMENT OF OKHRIDA, see SEVEN APOSTLES OF BULGARIA.

CLETHER (Cleer, Clarus), hermit of the 6th(?) century, probably of Welsh origin and of the family of *Brychan. After living in Wales by the river Never, he settled in N. Cornwall in later life in the remote and beautiful Inny valley at the place which still bears his name. His original oratory and well, the finest example of its kind, were rebuilt in the 15th century; the 11th-century parish church had been built in his honour a small distance away. Nothing is known of the details of Clether's life; he has often been identified with St. Cleer, who gave his name to another village a few miles to the south. Feast: 4 November.

Baring-Gould and Fisher, ii. 149–51; *C.C.K.*, pp. 30, 38; G. H. Doble, *St. Clether* (pamphlet, 1930); A. H. Malan, 'St. Clether's Chapel and Holy Well', *Jnl. of Royal Inst. of Cornwall* (1898).

CLETUS (Anacletus), traditionally bishop of Rome after *Peter and *Linus but before *Clement, and a martyr of the late 1st century. Nothing is known of him for certain, but the division of Rome into twenty-five parishes is dubiously ascribed to him. Formerly mentioned in the Roman Canon, his feast, with that of Marcellinus, was kept until 1969 on 26 April.

L. Duchesne, *Liber Pontificalis* (2 vols., 1886–92),

especially i. lxix–lxx; B.T.A., ii. 163–4; *O.D.C.C.*, s.v.

CLITAUCUS, see CLYDOG.

CLITHEROW, Margaret (1556–86), martyr. Born in York, the daughter of Thomas Middleton, a chandler who later became sheriff of York, Margaret was brought up as a Protestant and in 1571 married John Clitherow, a prosperous butcher of York. Three years later she became a Catholic, but her husband, a kindly and easygoing man, and now a chamberlain of York, remained a resolute Protestant both before and after her death. She became known as an active and outspoken Catholic: she was imprisoned for two years for not attending the parish church. During this time she learned to read; after her release she organized a small school for her own and her neighbours' children in her own house. Here, too, she used to harbour priests against the penal laws, hiding them in a specially built room with a narrow secret access. Her husband used to turn a blind eye to these activities, but in 1586 he was summoned before the court to explain his son's absence abroad, due in fact to his being at a Catholic college. At the same time his house was raided, but no trace was found of priest, vestments, or chalice. A searching interrogation followed, in which the Clitherow children gave nothing away, but a Flemish boy under threats revealed the hiding-place and the Mass vestments.

Margaret was arrested, imprisoned, and charged with harbouring priests and attending Mass. She steadfastly refused to plead, saying: 'Having made no offence, I need no trial.' Her purpose was to avoid the necessity of friends, servants, and her own children giving evidence against her. The penalty for refusing to plead was the *peine forte et dure* which resulted in the victim being crushed to death. The judge reluctantly sentenced Margaret and she was executed in the Tollboothe, York, on 25 March. She was dead after only fifteen minutes.

Margaret Clitherow was described by contemporaries as good-looking, witty, and merry: 'everyone loved her and would run to her for help, comfort and counsel in distress'. Although her refusal to pray with those who did not share her beliefs hardly accords with present-day ecumenical ideals, Margaret Clitherow is one of the most notable and attractive of the Forty Martyrs. Her house was in the Little Shambles, York, but was not, it seems, the one claimed as such. The place of her trial (Guildhall) and imprisonment (Castle) can be seen at York; a relic of her hand is at the Bar Convent. She was canonized by Paul VI in 1970 as one of the *Forty Martyrs of England and Wales. Feast: 25 October.

Anonymous contemporary Life (by her confessor John Mush) in J. Morris, *The Troubles of our Catholic Forefathers*, iii (1872–7), 333–440; M. T. Monro, *Blessed Margaret Clitherow* (1947); B.T.A., i. 679–82.

CLYDOG (Clodock, Clitaucus) (6th(?) century), king and martyr. He was of the family of *Brychan who ruled in Ewyas (Hereford and Monmouth area). His Legend, first recorded in the *Book of Llan Dav* about six centuries after his death, relates that a nobleman's daughter fell in love with him and said she would marry nobody but him. One of Clydog's comrades who had himself decided to marry her, killed the king with his sword while hunting. The body was placed on a cart and driven to a ford in the river Monnow, but then the yoke broke, the oxen refused to be driven further, and a church was built on the spot, ever since called Clodock or Merthir Clitauc (Hereford and Worcester), where the king was buried. Whytford described him as 'a kynges son of strayte iustyce, a louer of peace, and of pure chastite, and of strayte and perfyte life y[t] was cruelly slayne by a fals traytour at whose death were shewed many myracles and at his tombe after many moo'. He is represented in art wearing a crown and bearing a sword and a lily. But some modern scholars maintain that the title of martyr was given to a hermit and confessor through 'Merthir' being understood as 'martyrium', when it simply meant 'shrine'. Feast: 3 November.

N.L.A., i. 190–1; *AA.SS.* Aug. III (1737), 733; F. G. Llewellin, *The History of St. Clodock* (1920); Baring-Gould and Fisher, ii. 153–4.

CNUT, see CANUTE.

COAN, see COMGAN.

COEMGEN, see KEVIN.

COENBURGA, see QUENBURGA.

COLETTE (1381–1447), Franciscan nun and reformer. Born at Calcye in Picardy, where her father was a carpenter at Corbie abbey, she was christened Nicolette. She grew up with a notable taste for prayer and solitude. Both her parents died in 1398: under the direction of the abbot of Corbie she lived as a hermit close to the abbey church and became a Franciscan tertiary. A reputation for austerity and holiness resulted in numerous visitors seeking her advice. Dreams and visions followed, she believed she was called upon to restore the Rule of *Francis and *Clare to existing convents of Franciscan nuns. The anti-pope Benedict XIII (Peter de Luna), recognized by France and some other countries, encouraged her by professing her as a Poor Clare and by placing her in charge of all convents which she might found or reform.

At first she met with rejection in several convents but reformed the nunnery at Besançon in 1410 and eventually founded seventeen new convents as well as reforming several old ones. Perhaps the most famous is that of Le Puy (Haute-Loire), which has enjoyed unbroken continuity. Her convents were established mainly in France, Flanders, and Savoy.

Like Francis she combined a deep devotion to Christ's Passion with appreciation and care for animals. She died at Ghent; under Joseph II her body was translated to Poligny (Jura). She was canonized in 1807. Feast: 6 March.

U. d'Alençon, *Les vies de sainte Colette Boylet de Corbie* (1911); J. Goulven, *Rayonnement de Sainte Colette* (1952); S. Roisin in *D.H.G.E.*, xiii (1856), 238–46; a fine illuminated manuscript of her Life, commissioned by Margaret of Burgundy (sister of Edward IV of England) survives in the convent of Poor Clares at Ghent, ed. C. van Corstanje, *Vita sanctae Coletae* (1981). See also B.T.A., i. 506–8; *Bibl. SS.*, iv. 76–81.

COLLEN (Colan), patron and founder of Llangollen church (Clwyd) and of Colan (Cornwall), and perhaps of Langolen in Finistère (Brittany). Nothing is known of this saint, but a Life in Welsh survives in two MSS. of the 16th century. This farrago makes Collen fight a duel with a pagan Saracen in the presence of the pope, go to Cornwall and Glastonbury, and deliver the people in the Vale of Llangollen from a fierce giantess by slaying her. Feast: 21 May.

Baring-Gould and Fisher, ii. 157–61.

COLMAN. There are about 300 saints of this name mentioned in Irish martyrologies: for the purposes of this work it seems sufficient to mention four, those of Cloyne, Dromore, Kilmacduagh, and Lindisfarne.

1. **COLMAN OF CLOYNE** (*c.*530–*c.*606), bishop. Born in Munster, he became a poet and royal bard at Cashel and was about fifty years old when he became a Christian, supposedly as a consequence of *Brendan discovering the bones of *Ailbe at Cashel. After being ordained priest and consecrated bishop he worked in Limerick and Cork, where he built the first church at Cloyne and another at Kilmaclenine. In both places are the remains of churches; at Cloyne there was also a holy well. Feast: 24 November.

B.T.A., iv. 419; *The Irish Saints*, pp. 84–5.

2. **COLMAN OF DROMORE**, bishop of the 6th century. Born in Ulster, he spent much of his working life in Co. Down and was founder of the monastery at Dromore where he was also bishop. There he is reputed to have taught *Finnian of Moville. He was venerated in both Scotland and

Ireland from early times on 7 June: the Scottish cult being possibly due to his disciples or to another tradition of his birth, viz. in Dalriada (Argyllshire). The churches of Llangolman and Capel Colman in Dyfed are also sometimes attributed to him, but whereas the date of the feast in Scotland and Ireland is constant, that of the founder of these Welsh churches is 20 November.

B.T.A., ii. 493–4; Baring-Gould and Fisher, ii. 162–4. *AA.SS.* Iun. II (1698), 25–9.

3. **COLMAN OF KILMACDUAGH** (d. *c.*632), bishop. Born at Corker in Kiltartan in the mid 6th century, he became a monk at Aranmore and later lived at Burren (Co. Clare) where, having been unwillingly consecrated bishop, he lived with only one disciple on a diet of vegetables and water. He later founded a monastery at Kilmacduagh on land given him by King Guaire of Connaught and was venerated as its first bishop. Like other monastic saints he was reputed to have a special affinity with animals: a cock used to wake him before the night-office, a mouse prevented him from going to sleep after it, and a fly kept the place in his book. Part of his crozier is in the National Museum, Dublin. Feast: 29 October.

AA.SS. Oct. XII (1867), 880–92.

4. **COLMAN OF LINDISFARNE** (d. 676), bishop 661–4. A monk of Iona and Irish by race, Colman was the successor of *Aidan and *Finan as bishop-abbot of Lindisfarne. This was the most important monastery in Northumbria, sited close to the royal castle of Bamburgh, and the home of a number of monks who evangelized other English kingdoms. But a crisis arose concerning the date of Easter, the style of tonsure, and eventually the role of the bishop, between the Irish, led by Colman, and those of Roman formation, led by *Ronan, *Agilbert, and *Wilfrid. This was resolved at the Synod of Whitby (663/4), convened and presided over by Oswiu, king of Northumbria, who favoured the Irish view, and in which various ecclesiastics from elsewhere in England took part. Colman was the main spokesman for the Irish side, for an ancient but insular tradition, while Wilfrid spoke for the practice of Rome and Western Europe. Neither side could prove their claims historically, but the appeal to the practice of the rest of the known contemporary Church was decisive. The king ruled in favour of the Roman calculation of Easter, thereby bringing about unity of observance in Northumbria and eventually in all England. Colman resigned and went back to Iona with all the Irish and about thirty English monks from Lindisfarne, taking with him some of the bones of Aidan. They then migrated to Ireland where Colman founded a monastery on the isle of Inishbofin (Co. Galway) *c.*667. Even here, however, there was discord because the Irish monks, according to *Bede, left the monastery in the summer when the harvest had to be gathered in, but returned in the winter expecting an equal share with the English monks who had provided it. Colman tried to solve this dispute and eventually settled the English monks at Mayo, while the Irish remained at Inishbofin. 'Mayo of the Saxons', as it was called, flourished greatly, was praised by Bede for living under a Rule and an abbot canonically elected (i.e. it was not a Celtic 'hereditary' monastery), and in frugality through living by the labour of their own hands. Alcuin also praised them for leaving their homeland in voluntary exile, where they shone by their learning among a 'very barbarous nation', and exhorted them to regard their bishop as their father. The date of Colman's death is variously given by chronicles as 672, 674, and 675. Feast: 18 February; but in some parts of Ireland on 8 August.

AA.SS. Feb. III (1658), 82–8; Bede, *H.E.*, iii. 25–6; iv. 4; P. Grosjean, 'Débuts de la controverse pascale chez les Celtes', *Anal. Boll.*, lxiv (1946), 200–44; P. Grosjean, 'La date du Colloque de Whitby', *Anal. Boll.*, lxxviii (1960), 233–55; H. Mayr-Harting, *The Coming of Christianity to Anglo-Saxon England* (1972), pp. 94–116.

COLUMBA (date unknown), Cornish saint. Patron of St. Columb Major and St.

Columb Minor (Cornwall), usually called Columba the Virgin, from medieval records. But Baring-Gould conjectures that this Columba was an Irishman, identical with Columba of Tir-da-Glas. The Cornish Church Calendar assigns no day to this saint.

O.D.E.P.N., s.v.; Baring-Gould and Fisher, i. 164–9.

COLUMBA (Colum-cille) **OF IONA** (*c.*521–97), abbot. Born at Gartan (Donegal) in the royal Ui Neill clan, he was trained as a monk first by *Finnian of Moville and then by *Finnian of Clonard. He founded the monasteries of Derry (546), Durrow (*c.*556), and probably Kells. But in 565 he left Ireland with twelve companions for Iona, an island off SW. Scotland given to him for a monastery by the ruler of the Irish Dalriada. His motives have been variously explained: voluntary exile for Christ, an attempt to help overseas compatriots in their struggle for survival, or even a punishment for his responsibility for a battle between monasteries, supposedly over a psalter which he had copied and refused to give up. Whatever the reason, Columba remained for the rest of his life in Scotland, mainly Iona, returning to Ireland only for occasional, but important, visits.

Our principal source is the famous Life by *Adomnan, one of the most influential biographies of the early Middle Ages. Disappointing as a historical document, it is a portrait of a charismatic personality, which skilfully describes miracles, prophecies, and visions from Iona tradition. From it Columba emerges as a tall, striking figure of powerful build and impressive presence, who combined the skills of scholar, poet, and ruler with a fearless commitment to God's cause. Able, ardent, and sometimes harsh, Columba mellowed with age. Most of his activity concerned the building of his monastery, the training of its members (among whom were some Anglo-Saxons), the imparting of spiritual counsel, and the solution of the problems of neighbouring rulers.

He converted Brude, king of the Picts, and in 574 the Irish king, Aidan of Dalriada, was consecrated by him. He also founded two churches in Inverness. But his missionary work in Scotland has been much exaggerated. Like *Patrick and *David of Wales he was once believed to have evangelized enormous areas with total success and to have founded personally very many churches. Many of these are now believed to be the work of his later followers or of a near-namesake such as Colm of Buchan. No ancient churches in Strathclyde, SE. Scotland, or Northumbria are certainly his. Most of his foundations are in the Irish part of Scotland such as the Western Islands, Hinba, Mag-lunge (Tiree), and Diuni (near Loch Awe). In general it seems more accurate to regard him as leader of the Irish in Scotland than as simply the apostle of Scotland. Even *Bede seems to have exaggerated his apostolic influence, but scholars are divided on how to interpret his text.

Columba retained some sort of overlordship over his monasteries in Ireland. In *c.*580 he took part in the assembly of Druim-Cetta, where he mediated about the obligations of the Irish in Scotland to those in Ireland. It was decided that they should furnish a fleet, but not an army, for the Irish high-king. The same assembly also dealt with the social position of bards. Columba, who was a bard himself, saved their order from extinction and assured the presence of educated laity in Irish Christian society.

Three surviving Latin poems, including the *Altus Prosator*, may well be his. Its theme is the Christian view of the future life; its finest passages describe the Last Judgement. But no surviving vernacular poem is Columba's. His skill as a scribe can be seen in the *Cathach* of Columba, a late 6th-century psalter in the Irish Academy, which is the oldest surviving example of Irish majuscule writing. It was later enshrined in wood, and then in silver and bronze, sculptured with figures of the saints. It was venerated in churches, but also used both at visitations and in battles as a reminder of Columba's power.

Four years before his death Columba's strength began to fail. He spent much time in transcribing books, but his end was foreseen by his community and even sensed, if we are to believe Adomnan, by his favourite horse. He died in the church just before Matins. But his memory lived on in his monasteries and more generally in Ireland, Scotland, and Northumbria. His traditions were upheld by his followers for about a century, not least in the Synod of Whitby and in Irish monasteries on the continent of Europe. His feast occurs in the Calendar of *Willibrord and in other ancient records.

After four Viking raids on Iona his relics were translated to Dunkeld in 849, where they were visited by pilgrims, including Anglo-Saxons of the 11th century, guided there by the writer of the *Resting-Places of the Saints* (*R.P.S.*). Feast: 9 June.

AA.SS. Iun. II (1698), 180–236; Bede, *H.E.*, iii. 4 and 25; v. 9; A. O. and M. O. Anderson, *Adomnan's Life of Columba* (1990); other editions by W. Reeves (1857) and J. T. Fowler (1894); G. Bruning, 'Adamnans Vita Columbae und ihre Ableitungen', *Z.C.P.*, xi (1917), 213–304; J. M. Picard, 'The purpose of Adamnan's Vita Columbae', *Peritia*, i (1982), 160–77; H. Lawlor, 'The Cathach of St. Columba', *P.R.I.A.*, xxxiii (1916), 241–443; J. F. Kenney, *The Sources for the Early History of Ireland*, i (1929), 263–5, 422–42; W. D. Simpson, *The Historical Saint Columba* (2nd edn., 1963); id., *The Celtic Church in Scotland* (1935); D. P. Kirby, 'Bede and the Pictish Church', *The Innes Review*, xxiv (1973), 6–25; K. Hughes, *Early Christian Ireland* (1972) and *Early Christianity in Pictland* (Jarrow Lecture, 1970); N. Chadwick, *The Age of the Saints in the early Celtic Church* (1961); P. Grosjean, in *Anal. Boll.*, xlv (1927), 75–83; xlvi (1928), 197–9; lv (1937), 96–108; lxiii (1945), 119–22; D. A. Bullough, 'Columba, Adomnan and the Achievement of Iona', *S.H.R.*, xliii (1964), 111–30 and xliv (1965), 17–33. See also A. D. S. MacDonald, 'Aspects of the monastery and monastic life in Adomnan's Life of Columba', *Peritia*, iii (1984), 271–302, R. Sharpe, *ibid.*, 230–70.

COLUMBANUS (Columban) (*c.*543–615), abbot. He was born in Leinster, probably of a noble family, and was well educated before becoming a monk. This he did, according to his biographer, through following the advice of a woman hermit after severe carnal temptation, and completely against his mother's wishes. His first teacher was Sinell, a disciple of *Finnian; later he became the disciple of *Comgall of Bangor with whom he stayed for many years until *c.*590, when with twelve companions he left for Gaul, choosing 'voluntary exile for Christ'.

He founded the monastery of Annegray in a disused Roman fort, given him by King Childebert II of Austrasia, whose court Columbanus had visited on his way. Soon he attracted numerous followers and founded the monastery of Luxeuil, also in the Vosges. There his monks lived according to Irish tradition, keeping the Irish date of Easter, having a bishop who was subordinate to the abbot promulgating Irish penitential practice. In all these ways Columbanus' monasteries differed from the rest of the Frankish church and friction was almost inevitable. After the death of Childebert the attack on Columbanus was centred on the date of Easter. But he wrote directly to *Gregory the Great (and later to Boniface IV), affirming his loyalty to the successor of St. Peter, but at the same time asserting that the Irish had maintained ancient Christian tradition, pure and unsullied, in contrast to other nations. A few years later, when attacked by the archbishop of Lyons, he wrote to the Synod of Chalon, asking simply for toleration for his own communities to live according to the monastic traditions of Ireland.

A turning point in the opposition to Columbanus came when he refused to bless the illegitimate sons of Theuderic II and thus incurred the hatred both of the king and of the queen-grandmother Brunhild. Columbanus and his monks were then taken under military escort to Nantes to be deported back to Ireland. But scarcely had his ship left port when it was forced back by a storm. Columbanus then went to the court of King Clotar II of Neustria and later to Metz in Austrasia, where, at King Theudebert's court, he met again some of his monks from Luxeuil. They then rowed up the Rhine, hoping to settle at

Bregenz on Lake Constance. Here also they met with fierce opposition, while the victory of Theuderic over Theudebert made their situation untenable. They moved into the Lombard duchy, settling at Bobbio in the Apennines, in territory ruled over by the Arian Duke Agilof, whose wife and sons were Catholics, but divided from the Holy See over the vexed question of the Three Chapters condemnation. Columbanus wrote to the pope in a way which combined deep respect, plain speaking, and insufficient understanding of the issues involved. He settled at Bobbio *c.*613, founding a new monastery where there was only a ruined church and taking part himself in the actual work of building. He died in 615 on 23 November.

His principal writings are letters, a Rule, a Penitential, and several poems, among which a boating-song is perhaps the most famous. His style varies in accordance with the needs of each subject and is of high quality. Bobbio, famous for its large library and the richness of its insular manuscripts, and Luxeuil both had long and important histories. Columbanus' Rule, although influential, was too severe for many, especially in its harsh insistence on corporal punishment, and was largely superseded by the Rule of St. Benedict. But for his example, inspiration, and pioneering achievements he is generally reckoned to be the greatest of Ireland's many apostles to the Continent of Europe. Feast: 21 (in Ireland 23) November.

G. M. S. Walker, *Sancti Columbani Opera* (1957); *Ionae Vitae Sanctorum Columbani, Vedasti, Iohannis* (1905), pp. 1–294, also in B. Krusch, *M.G.H. Scriptores Rerum Merov.*, iv (1902), i–156 and vii (part 2, 1920), 822–7; G. Metlake, *The Life and Writings of St. Columban* (1914); M. M. Dubois, *Un Pionnier de la civilisation occidentale* (1950; Eng. tr. 1961); F. Macmanus, *Saint Columban* (1963); L. Bieler, *Ireland: Harbinger of the Middle Ages* (1963), pp. 25–94; J. Laporte, *Le Pénitentiel de S. Columban* (1958); L. Gougaud, *Les saints irlandais hors d'Irlande* (1936), pp. 51–62; J. F. Kenney, *The Sources for the Early History of Ireland*, i (1929), 186–209; *San Colombano e la sua opera in Italia* (1953); A Maestri, *Il culto di San Colombano in Italia* (1955); P. Grosjean, 'Débuts de la controverse pascale chez les Celtes', *Anal. Boll.*, lxiv (1946), 200–15; T. O'Fiaich, *Columbanus* (1974).

COMGALL (d. *c.*601), founder and first abbot of Bangor (Northern Ireland). After being trained by *Fintan at Clonenagh and ordained priest, he lived as a hermit in Lough Erne in conditons of extreme austerity. Later he founded Bangor (*c.*555), which became the largest monastery in Ireland with several daughter houses, whose total population (presumably including families of the clan) is reputed to have reached 3,000. Comgall is also important because he trained *Columbanus and was associated with *Columba, whom he visited on Iona. Comgall and Columba together preached the Gospel in Inverness to the chieftain Brude according to a hagiographical tradition not entirely accepted by Columba's biographer *Adomnan. Also attributed to Comgall is a remark about the death of his director: 'My soul-friend has died and I am headless; you too are headless, for a man without a soul-friend is a body without a head.' Feast (throughout Ireland): 11 May; elsewhere 10 May. His relics, kept at Bangor, were 'desecrated by foreigners' in 822.

AA.SS. Maii II (1680), 580–8; *V.S.H.*, ii. 3–21; P. Grosjean, 'S. Comgalli Vita Latina; Accedunt Duae Narrationes Gadelicae', *Anal. Boll.*, lii (1934), 343–56. His supposed Rule is edited by J. Strachan in *Eriu*, i (1904), 191–208; ii (1905), 58 ff. See also J. Ryan, *Irish Monasticism* (1931) and L. Gougaud, *Christianity in Celtic Lands* (1933).

COMGAN (Congan, Cowan, Coan) (8th century), abbot. Traditionally an Irish chieftain, son of Kelly, prince of Leinster, whom he succeeded, Comgan was driven out by a coalition of neighbouring tribes, wounded in battle, and exiled to Scotland with his sister and her children, one of whom was *Fillan. He settled in Lochalsh, near Skye, founded a small monastery, and lived devoutly for many years. Fillan buried Comgan's body in Iona and built a church in his honour. The place-names Kilchoan and Kilcongen are believed to record his memory, as do several church dedications in Scotland. Feast: 13 October.

AA.SS. Oct. VI (1794), 223–6; *K.S.S.*, pp. 310–11; B.T.A., iv. 104.

CONALL, Irish saint of unknown date whose bell with its shrine survives in the British Museum.

CONAN (Conon) (d. 648), bishop. Traditionally an abbot who helped educate *Fiacre, Conan seems to have become a bishop and to have lived and worked in the Hebrides and the Isle of Man where various places bear his name. Anachronistically he is sometimes called first bishop of Sodor, but this term is a Viking one denoting 'southern islands' as distinct from the Shetlands and Orkneys which were 'northern islands'. Feast: 26 January.

K.S.S., pp. 307–8; O. Kolsrud, 'The Celtic Bishops in the Isle of Man', *Z.C.P.*, ix (1913), 357–79. B.T.A., i. 172–3.

CONDEDUS (Conde, Condede) (late 7th century). An English 'exile for Christ', Condedus settled in France at Fontaine-Saint-Valery, became a monk at Fontenelle (Saint-Wandrille) for a short time, but soon returned to a hermit's life. He settled on an island called Belcinac in the middle of the Seine, near Caudebec, given by King Thierry III together with other land as an endowment. He built two churches on the island which attracted many visitors. After his death there he was buried at Fontenelle; his island has disappeared, submerged by the river Seine. Feast: 21 October.

The Life, written about a century after the death of Condedus, is in *AA.SS.* Oct. IX (1858), 351–8 and in W. Levison, *M.G.H. Scriptores rerum Meroving.*, v. 644–51.

CONGAN, see COMGAN.

CONGAR (1) (Cungar, Cyngar, Docco) (6th century), eponym of Congresbury (Somerset). Probably of Pembrokeshire origin (Llanwngar near St. David's), Congar was one of the Welsh missionaries who founded Christian communities in Somerset and Devon. A Winchester litany of *c.*1060 contains his name. Congresbury claimed to have his body enshrined during the Middle Ages (it is mentioned in 11th- and 14th-century pilgrim guides), most Somerset calendars have his feast, and there seem to have been no rival claimants to his relics. Late medieval wills include legacies for lights at his shrine. Congresbury is first mentioned in Asser's *Life of Alfred* as a derelict Celtic monastery which was assigned to Asser, bishop of Crediton. A 12th-century Life was concocted at Wells: this consists of a hotch-potch of hagiographical and folkloric elements mainly drawn from Lives of other Welsh saints. Feast: 27 November.

CONGAR (2) (date unknown), Welsh saint. He is honoured at Llangefni, Anglesey; near Criccieth (Gwynedd) is Ynys Gyngar. In Clwyd Congar is patron of Hope, formerly called Llangyngar. Feast, in these two towns and in late medieval Welsh calendars: 7 November.

CONGAR (3) (date unknown), Breton saint. He is patron of several Breton churches and his name forms part of several place-names there such as Saint-Congard, Roscongar, Lescongar. Feasts of Congar in Brittany are kept on 13 February and 12 May. This makes it unlikely that he is to be identified with either of the others, but Doble identifies the Breton Congar with the St. Ingonger of Lanivet (Cornwall), and suggests that *Petroc, Congar, and *Cadoc were 'brothers' in a great missionary enterprise.

G. H. Doble, *The Saints of Cornwall*, v. 3–29 (and 'St. Congar', *Antiquity*, xix (1945), 32–43, 85–95); P. Grosjean, 'Cyngar Sant', *Anal. Boll.*, xlii (1924), 100–20; J. A. Robinson, 'A fragment of the Life of St. Congar', *J.T.S.*, xx (1919), 97–108, 'The Lives of St. Cungar and St. Gildas', ibid., xxiii (1922), 15–22, 'St. Cungar and St. Decuman', ibid., xxix (1928), 137–40. See also *AA.SS.* Nov. III (1910), 403–7. B.T.A., s.v.

CONLETH (Conleat) (d. *c.*520), Irish monk and bishop of or at Kildare. According to the Life of *Brigid by Cogitosus, Conleth was a hermit who lived at Old Connell (Co. Kildare) on the Liffey and who was a skilled metalworker. Brigid invited him not only to make sacred vessels for Kildare but also to be pastor of the people near by. Traditionally he was the sculptor of the crozier of St. Finbar of Termon Barry, now in the Royal Irish Academy. A gloss in an Irish martyrology says that he was devoured by wolves on his journey to Rome, undertaken against the wishes of Brigid. This might be an attempt to explain his name, i.e. *coin* 'to wolves' and *leth* 'half'. Feast (nowadays with *Catald): 10 May.

The Irish Saints, p. 132; B.T.A., ii. 266–7.

CONON (3rd century), martyr. According to his Acts, Conon came from a long-established Greek Christian family of Nazareth. In his old age he settled at Carma (in Phrygia or Pisidia), where he was employed on an imperial estate maintaining the irrigation canals. The prefect was stationed in the town of Magydos (Pamphilia), where he summoned the people by herald to hear the details of the imperial decrees against the Christians. These, however, had all fled from the city and its surrounding lands. An auxiliary soldier went to seek the people but found only Conon, watering one of the imperial gardens. He was summoned to the prefect, who cross-examined him about his name, origin, and religion. 'If you have recognized Christ', he said, 'then recognize our gods too . . . Simply take a little incense, wine and a branch and say: "Zeus all highest, protect this people." . . . Why do you all continue to err, saying that a man, and indeed one who died as a criminal, is God? For I have learnt from the Jews what was his family . . . and how he died on a cross . . . So cease this foolishness and be of good cheer with us.'

Conon answered: 'Most impious of men, I wish that you too could share this foolishness and were not destroying souls that should not be lost, paying heed to lifeless stones that can neither see nor hear and are merely men's handiwork. How can you blaspheme thus against the God of all things when your breath is in his hands? May it be my lot . . . ever to hymn and praise him who is the God and saviour of all.' The prefect then threatened tortures, regarding him as a representative of the numerous absent Christians; but Conon remained constant in the profession of his faith.

The prefect ordered spikes to be driven into Conon's feet and made him run ahead of his own chariot. He was driven on by two men with whips until he reached the market-place where he was faint with exhaustion. Soon afterwards he died. Feast: 6 March.

Some details of these Acts may be fictional, but there seems no reason to doubt the substance of the story: see *A.C.M.*, pp. xxxii–xxxiii, 186–93; *Propylaeum*, pp. 86–7; R. van Doren in *D.H.G.E.*, 13 (1956), 460–1.

CONRAD OF PARZHAM, Franciscan laybrother (1818–94). Born in Parzham (Bavaria), the ninth and youngest son of a peasant family, he became a Capuchin laybrother after his parents' death in 1849. Professed in 1852, he was sent to Alltötting, a famous Marian shrine, where for forty years he was porter of his friary and devoted himself to the numerous pilgrims. Charitable, patient, and tactful, he was also reputed to have read the secrets of hearts and to have exercised the gift of prophecy. He fell ill in 1894 and died on 21 April. He was beatified in 1930 and canonized in 1934, a rapid procedure by the standards of that time. Feast: 21 April.

A.A.S. xxii (1930), 319–23; Fr. Dunstan, *St. Conrad of Parzham* (1934).

CONRAN (7th century (?)), bishop. Although he is often believed to have been the apostle of the Orkneys and especially of Kirkwall, there are no place-names or dedications connected with him there, although there are several to Colm. The Bollandists numbered him among the *praetermissi . . . et rejecti*, and several standard Scottish reference books, have nothing to say about any evidence for him working in the Orkneys. His existence must be considered doubtful. Feast: 14 February.

AA.SS. Feb. II (1658), 741 and *Anal. Boll.*, lxix (1951), 168–9; B.T.A., i. 336.

CONSTANTINE (date unknown), Cornish chieftain and martyr (?). The Cornish tradition is that he was converted by *Petroc, became a monk, and founded churches in Devon and Cornwall. These are recalled by two places in Cornwall called Constantine: one near Padstow, the other on the banks of the Helford river in SW. Cornwall. This was the larger of the two and survived as a monastery until the 11th century. He was also patron of the Devon churches of Milton Abbot and Dunsford.

There are also confused traditions in both Scotland and Ireland concerning Constantine, a king who became a monk. The Scottish tradition says that he was martyred at Kintyre in 576.

Feast in Cornwall and Wales: 9 March; in Scotland, 11 March.

G. H. Doble, *The Saints of Cornwall*, ii (1962), 15–24.

CORENTIN (date unknown), Cornish founder and patron of Cury in the Lizard. He was a Celtic hermit who later became a bishop in Brittany. An ancient cross stands near his church; in 1890 a fresco was discovered in Breage (the mother-church of the Lizard), which depicts him in cope and mitre with a pastoral staff. Beside him is a fish, from which he was reputed to have cut and eaten one slice each day, without any diminution in the size of the fish.

His name occurs in a Winchester missal of the 10th century and a Canterbury litany of the 11th. An ancient Breton cult in his honour was revived by a private revelation in the 17th century, when several old shrines there were restored. His feast (translation?) at Quimper is the occasion for presents of blessed cakes. Ancient feast: 1 May.

G. H. Doble, *The Saints of Cornwall*, ii (1962), 45–53.

CORNELIUS (d. 253), pope and martyr. Nothing is known of his early life, but after a vacancy of a year due to the persecution of Decius, Cornelius, a member of the *gens Cornelia*, was chosen bishop of Rome by the clergy and people in 251. The main problem of his pontificate was not persecution but dissension within the Church concerning the reconciliation of those who had lapsed. Novatian, a gifted Roman priest, opposed his policy of leniency, maintaining that the Church had no power to pardon those who had lapsed during persecution, nor those who had committed murder and adultery, nor even, apparently, those who contracted second marriages. Novatian then set himself up as a rival bishop of Rome. Cornelius, strongly supported by *Cyprian of Carthage, asserted that the Church indeed does have the power to forgive apostates and other sinners, and to admit them to communion after suitable penance has been done. A few letters of Cornelius to Cyprian survive with Cyprian's answers, some of which date from the time when Cornelius was banished to Civita Vecchia (Centumcellae), when the persecution was renewed in 253. Cornelius died soon after, probably through the hardships endured there; Cyprian called him a martyr; later accounts say that he was beheaded. He was buried at Rome in the crypt of Lucina, where his tomb can still be seen with the inscription 'Cornelius Martyr'. A painting of Cyprian was added to the wall of the crypt in the 8th century: Cornelius and Cyprian are associated in the *R.M.*, in the Canon of the Mass, and in their common feast in the Western Church, formerly on 14 September, now on 16 September. At the church of Portlemouth (Devon) there is a screen painting of Cornelius, vested as a pope, holding a triple cross and a horn.

AA.SS. Sept. IV (1753), 143–91; Letters of Cornelius are 49–50 in the collected letters of Cyprian; also extracts in Eusebius, *H.E.*, vi. 43; see also A. d'Alès, *Novatien* (1925); J. Chapman, *Studies in the Early Papacy* (1928). For his death, burial, and inscription with the fresco see A. Wilpert, *La cripta dei Papi e la cappella di santa Cecilia* (1910, cf. *Anal. Boll.*, xxix (1910), 185–6).

COSMAS AND DAMIAN (date unknown). They were martyred at Cyrrhus, where a famous basilica was built in their honour and whence their cult spread throughout the Christian world. Other notable churches built in their honour were at Constantinople (5th century) and Rome, where a 6th-century example survives near the Forum, with mosaics of the saints inside. Their names are in the Roman Canon of the Mass.

Their late and historically worthless Legend made them twin brothers and doctors who practised their art without asking for fees: extremely numerous cures of healing were claimed at their intercession. They are the patron saints of doctors; their Acts recount their skill in healing both men and animals. These stories appealed to artists, who depicted not only individual portraits but also whole cycles of their Lives. One of the most notable was painted by Fra Angelico, another is in a 15th-century North Italian antiphoner at the Society of Antiquaries, London. This includes their most picturesque medical achievement: the grafting of a new (white) leg on to the (live) body of a cancerous Negro. The cult was given encouragement and patronage by the Medici, a number of whom were called Cosmo, unexpectedly in view of the saints' reputation for disinterestedness about financial gain. Feast: in the West 26 (formerly 27) September, in the East 1 July or 1 November.

AA.SS. Sept. VII (1760), 430–77; H. Delehaye, 'Les recueils antiques de Miracles des Saints', *Anal. Boll.*, xliii (1925), 8–18; M. L. David-Danel, *Iconographie des saints médecins Côme et Damien* (1958); A. Wittmann, *Kosmas und Damian* (1967).

COTTOLENGO, Joseph (1786–1842), priest and founder of the Societies of the Little House of Divine Providence. Born at Bra (Piedmont) of a middle-class family, he was educated in the seminary of Turin, was ordained priest in 1811, and became a canon in 1818. There he spent the rest of his life caring for the poor and catering for nearly every human need. This he did by founding a variety of religious institutes. Inspired by the example of Vincent *de Paul, he first provided for a small hospital of five beds: this had been occasioned by the death of a sick family in the slums without adequate care. The hospital grew rapidly: its staff became the nucleus of the Brothers and Sisters of St. Vincent. During the cholera epidemic of 1831 the local authority closed this hospital, so the Vincentians nursed the poor in their own homes instead.

Later the Cottolengo hospital was moved to Valdocco: homes for epileptics, the deaf and dumb, orphans, the elderly, and the mentally handicapped grew around it. These were followed by a rescue home for girls. Thus the 'little House' became a 'town of charity' or, more accurately, a street of charities within the town of Turin. He also founded communities of prayer for the dying and those in grave moral danger: his aim throughout was to provide not only for physical needs, but also for the good of souls.

His trust in Providence was complete, even when money ran out. Sometimes he seemed imprudent: it is said that he spent all he was given as soon as it arrived, without keeping accounts. However this may be, at the age of fifty-six he handed over to his successor the whole administration of his institutes. A week later he died of typhoid fever in his brother's house at Chieri. He was beatified in 1917 and canonized in 1934. Feast: 29 April.

Lives by P. Gastaldi (1910), J. Guillemin (1917), and S. Ballario, *L'apostolo della carità* (1944); V. di Meo, *La spiritualità di S. Giuseppe B. Cottolengo* (1959); B.T.A., ii. 191–2; *Bibl. SS.*, vi. 1310–17.

COWAN, see COMGAN.

CRADOC(K), see CARANTOC.

CREDA, see CRIDA.

CREDAN (1) (Credus, Credanus), obscure Cornish saint who founded the church of Sancreed. According to Roscarrock, he 'Killed by misfortune his owne father, with which he was so moved as abandoning the world he became a hogherd, and lived so exemplary as he was after esteemed a saint'. There is also a trace of a Credan in Co. Moyne and Wicklow in Ireland with feast on 11 May.

Baring-Gould and Fisher, ii. 187–8.

CREDAN (2) (8th century), abbot of Evesham in the time of Offa, king of Mercia (757–96), in some of whose charters his name appears. Virtually nothing is known of his life, but a cult flourished. This, like that of other obscure Anglo-Saxon saints, was an object of suspicion to Lanfranc and to Norman bishops and abbots. At Evesham his relics, with those of other local saints, were put to an ordeal by fire in 1077. From this they emerged, we are told, quite unscathed, and at the translation which followed soon after they seemed to shine like gold. It was also regarded as a miracle that his shrine escaped all damage when the church tower fell in 1207. His name is found in two Litanies from Evesham. Feast: 19 August.

W. D. Macray (ed.), *Chronicon Monasterii de Evesham* (*R.S.*, 1863), pp. 323–4, 335–6; Stanton, pp. 399–400.

CRESCENTIA, see VITUS.

CREWYN (Crewenna, -us), see CROWAN.

CRIDA (Creda) (7th century), widow, patron of Creed (Cornwall). Of Irish origin, supposedly the daughter of Senach Ron, king of Leinster, who was a friend of *Canice, Crida was raped by a robber and gave birth to the future St. Boethin. But she persevered in the religious life and founded churches at Kilcredy (Upper Ossory). She presumably came to Cornwall with *Finbar or other missionaries of his period, rather than with the earlier group of Sennan, *Ia, *Erc, etc. A fresco of Crida, who wears a crown and holds a sceptre, much restored, survives at Lanivet church. Feast in Cornwall 'on the Sunday nearest 30 November'.

Baring-Gould and Fisher, ii. 185–7.

CRISPIN AND CRISPINIAN (d. *c*.285), martyrs. They were probably of Roman origin, although the centre of their cult, due to translation of their relics, was at Soissons from the 6th century or earlier. Only one writing of poor quality claims that they died there, but it was popularly believed that they were of local origin. French hagiographers made them noble Romans and brothers who preached in Gaul and exercised their trade of shoemaking so as to avoid living from the alms of the faithful. Their shrine was later rebuilt by *Eloi.

An unlikely English tradition claimed that they fled to Faversham during the persecutions and plied their trade at a house on the site of the Swan Inn in Preston Street, visited by English and foreign pilgrims as late as the 17th century. An altar in their honour is in Faversham parish church. This tradition makes more intelligible Shakespeare's sixfold mention of them in Henry V's famous speech on the eve of Agincourt (*Henry V*, IV. iii), fought on their feast day. Crispin and Crispinian are the patrons of cobblers, shoemakers, and leather-workers. Feast: 25 October.

AA.SS. Oct. XI (1864), 495–540; H. Delehaye, *Étude sur le légendier romain* (1936), pp. 126–35; B.T.A., iv. 197–8; M. I. Allen, 'The metrical Passio SS. Crispini of Crispiniani et Henry of Avranches', *Anal. Boll.*, cviii (1990), 357–86.

CRISPINA OF TAGORA (d. 304), martyr. Her Acts record that she was interrogated at Tebessa (Africa) by the proconsul Annius Anullinus, who tried unsuccessfully to persuade her to 'offer sacrifice to all our gods for the welfare of the emperors in accordance with the laws of the *Augusti* Diocletian and Maximian'. She answered: 'I have never sacrificed and I shall not do so save to the one true God and to our Lord Jesus Christ, his Son, who was born and died.' Later she added: 'I am ready to undergo any tortures . . . rather than defile my soul with idols which are stones and the works of men's hands.' Anullinus then ordered the court notary to have her 'hair cut and her head shaved with a razor until she is bald, that her beauty might first thus be brought to shame'. When this proved ineffectual, and the minutes of the trial were read, Anullinus said: 'Seeing that Crispina has persisted in infamous superstition and refuses to offer sacrifice to our gods in accordance with the heavenly decrees of the Augustan law, I have ordered her to be executed with the sword.' Crispina replied: 'I bless God who has so deigned to free me from your hands. Thanks be to God.' She was then executed by beheading on 5 December, her feast day. *Augustine frequently praised her in his writings.

A.C.M., xliv, 302–9; B.T.A., iv. 497–9; *Propylaeum*, pp. 567–8; H. Delehaye, *Les passions des martyrs et les genres hagiographiques* (1921), pp. 110–14; Augustine, *De sancta Virginitate*, 44 (*P.L.*, 40, 422).

CROSS. Dedications of churches to St. Cross or Holy Cross are mentioned in this work only to remove misconceptions. These churches are dedicated not to a saint but to Christ in the Cross, the instrument of his humiliation, which has been venerated in Christian tradition as the object most closely associated with his redemptive death. It was believed to have been discovered at Jerusalem in 335 in the course of excavations for the foundations of Constantine's basilica of the Holy Sepulchre on Mount Calvary. Details about his mother *Helen's share in the find, together with some cures associated with it, may be apocryphal. *Cyril of Jerusalem wrote in 346 that 'the saving wood of the Cross was found at Jerusalem in the time of Constantine and that it was disturbed fragment by fragment from this spot'. The stem and title of the Cross were venerated at Jerusalem before the end of the 4th century, described by the pilgrim Etheria and others. From there it spread to Rome, where the basilica of S. Croce was built to house relics of the Passion and Cross, and thence to other churches in the West.

One sign of Anglo-Saxon veneration of the Cross is the fine poem *The Dream of the Rood*, which unites patristic theology with heroic ideals. Part of it was written in runic characters on the Ruthwell Cross (*c.*700) and part on the 10th-century Brussels reliquary, which contains a piece of the Cross given to King Alfred by Pope Marinus in 885. Later evidence for its veneration is found in the poem *Elene*, in calendars, martyrologies, and at least 106 ancient dedications, including those of Holyrood Abbey (Scotland) and St. Cross (Winchester). Later legends about the Cross were recorded in the *Golden Legend* and illustrated by artists such as Piero della Francesca in the church of San Francesco, Arezzo (Tuscany).

Feasts of the Holy Cross are the Exaltation on 14 September (which commemorates its restoration to Jerusalem by the Emperor Heraclius) and the Finding on 3 May. The latter was suppressed in the 1969 revision of the Roman calendar, but the former retained.

O.D.C.C., s.v.; M. Swanton, *The Dream of the Rood* (1970).

CROWAN (Crewyn, Crewennus, Crewenna), Cornish saint of undetermined sex, whom a 16th-century tradition makes a companion of *Breage. Feast day unknown. Some identify this saint with Crozon of Brittany.

G. H. Doble, *History of the parish of Crowan* ('Cornish Parish Histories', no. 5, 1939); cf. *Anal. Boll.*, lix (1941), 323–4.

CUNEGUND (*c.*978–1033), empress. The child of Siegfried and Hedwig of Luxemburg, she married the Emperor *Henry II, was crowned with him by the pope in 1014, and influenced him in his ecclesiastical endowments, especially of Bamberg. The couple were childless, a fact mistakenly interpreted by later hagiographers as evidence that their marriage was virginal: a similar tendency can be seen in the case of *Edward the Confessor. At the time of a dangerous illness Cunegund vowed to found a convent at Kaufungen, near Cassel (Hesse). The buildings were nearly finished when her husband died (1024); on his first anniversary the church was dedicated. After the Gospel she offered at the altar a relic of the Cross; then she exchanged her imperial robes for a Benedictine nun's habit and spent the rest of her life in prayer, reading, and the care of the sick.

The 12th-century biography prepared for her canonization relates that she once asked to undergo the ordeal of walking on hot ploughshares to clear herself of an accusation of infidelity to her husband. This incident is depicted among other scenes of her life in a 16th-century relief in Bamberg cathedral. Another story is that the first abbess of Kaufungen, Cunegund's niece Judith, was frivolous and lax, preferring to be feasting with some young sisters at the time she was supposed to be at the Sunday procession. Cunegund, not for the first time, admonished her without much effect until, exasperated, she slapped her face. The finger marks were said to have remained on the abbess's face until her death and served as a perpetual warning to the community.

Cunegund was buried with her husband Henry in Bamberg Cathedral. She was canonized by Innocent III in 1200; the bull of canonization survives and is interesting as the first example of the technical phrase *plenitudo potestatis* being used in connection with canonization, whose process had been begun under Celestine III. Feast: 3 March.

AA.SS. Mart. I (1668), 265–82; E. W. Kemp, *Canonization and Authority in the Western Church* (1948), pp. 104–5; B.T.A., i. 470–1; *Bibl. SS.*, iii. 393–9; R. Klauser, *Der Heinrichs- und Kunigundenkult in mittelalterlichen Bistum Bamberg* (1957).

CUNGAR, see CONGAR (1).

CUBY, see CYBI.

CURY, see CORENTIN.

CUTHBERT (*c.*634–87), monk and bishop of Lindisfarne. Not only his personal achievements but also the incorruption of his body apparently for several centuries powerfully contributed to the popularity of his cult, so that he became Northern England's most popular saint. His bones have rested for centuries, and still rest, with the unique secondary relics associated with him, at Durham Cathedral.

Born of a fairly well-to-do Anglo-Saxon family, Cuthbert became a monk at Melrose in 651. With abbot *Eata he moved to Ripon to start a monastery on estates given by Oswiu's son Alcfrith; Alcfrith, however, insisted on the adoption of Roman customs; the Melrose monks retired and were succeeded by *Wilfrid. Cuthbert became prior of Melrose *c.*661; during the next few years he undertook missionary journeys for a week or a month at a time in the neighbourhood. After the Synod of Whitby (663/4) he adopted Roman customs and became prior at Lindisfarne, where by his patient persistence he gradually won over the monks to his own point of view. He lived as a hermit for a time on St. Cuthbert's Isle adjacent to Lindisfarne, and in 676, relinquishing the office of prior, he withdrew to Inner Farne, where *Aidan used to spend Lent, in order to live in almost complete solitude. However, by 685, through visitors to Inner Farne from Lindisfarne and elsewhere, his holiness and other qualities had become so famous that he was chosen by King Egfrith and Archbishop *Theodore as bishop of Hexham. Almost immediately he exchanged this see with Eata for that of Lindisfarne. His zeal was expressed in preaching, teaching, and visiting his diocese; he was also reputed to have gifts of prophecy and of healing. His extraordinary charm and ability can be inferred from the contemporary Lives. He died on Inner Farne on 20 March 687 and was buried at Lindisfarne. Eleven years afterwards, when his body was elevated to a new shrine, its incorruption was discovered. From that time onwards it was the object of special veneration.

After the Vikings destroyed Lindisfarne in 875, several members of its community travelled round northern England and SW. Scotland with the shrine and relics, seeking a safe home for them. Places where they rested include Norham-on-Tweed, Ripon, and Chester-le-Street, where King Athelstan offered 96 lb. of silver, two gospel books, and a book of his Life to the shrine (now MS. Corpus Christi College, Cambridge 183). Their permanent home was Durham, reached in 995. A Saxon church was built over the shrine: Cuthbert's relics were translated into it in 999.

Under William of St. Carilef, Durham became a monastic see in 1083: the monks who formed its chapter were drawn from the revived monasteries of Wearmouth and Jarrow and were mainly Anglo-Saxon in race and outlook. Cuthbert's relics were translated to the new Norman Cathedral in 1104. Once again the body was examined and pronounced incorrupt even by observers originally sceptical. It remained in the shrine until this was dismantled at the Reformation; then the Commissioners, impressed by its extraordinarily lifelike condition, wrote back to London for special instructions. Eventually the relics were buried under their original site. There they remained until 1828 when they were re-examined: the bones were reburied, but the secondary relics such as cloths, vestments, and the contemporary coffin, portable altar, and pectoral cross are housed in the monastic buildings at Durham. Important manuscripts connected with Cuthbert include the Lindisfarne Gospels and the uncial Gospel of St. John at Stonyhurst College (Lancs.). These near-contemporary works were associated with the shrine at an early date.

The cult of Cuthbert was well established in the late 7th century. An anonymous Life by a monk of Lindisfarne and another by *Bede were both written soon after the translation of 698. Both were soon in demand on the Continent as well as in England: the abbot of Wearmouth, Cuthbert, sent Bede's Life to *Lull, archbishop of Mainz. During the Danish invasions the cult had spread to Wessex and Kent. But the most important period for its development was 1000–1200. Miracle stories were collected, manuscripts of his Lives produced; especially important was MS. University College, Oxford, 165, which was the first fully illustrated Life of a saint to be produced in England. Another one of the late 12th century is at London, B.L. Yates Thompson M.S. 26.

The translation of 1104 and the verification of incorruption gave an immense stimulus to the cult. The Durham community fostered it and lost no chance to gain temporal advantage from the Patrimony of St. Cuthbert, an extensive set of lands supposedly given to him during his life or dedicated to him after his death by kings and magnates. From Durham as its centre the cult spread over much of England and Scotland. No fewer than 135 churches are dedicated to Cuthbert in England, besides seventeen in Scotland. Most are in the six northern counties and the remainder as far afield as Cornwall, Somerset, and East Anglia. Calendars and martyrologies tell the same story. Cuthbert is in the Martyrology of Bede and early continental ones, and in the Calendar of *Willibrord. In 819 a chapel in the crypt was dedicated to him at the consecration of Fulda. By the late 12th century Reginald of Durham claimed that the three most popular English saints were Cuthbert, *Edmund, and *Etheldreda. This was probably true, as each of the three is found in most medieval calendars and each had a story of incorruption (of which Cuthbert's is the best documented). Other notable examples of Cuthbert iconography in the later Middle Ages are the Cuthbert window in York Minster and the rather crude paintings on the backs of the stalls at Carlisle cathedral.

Place-names such as Kirkcudbright (Galloway), Cotherstone (N. Yorkshire), and Cubert (Cornwall) recall his name, as do various geographical features of the Inner Farne, where he died. This was used as a hermitage by Durham monks. Appropriately all the Farne Islands, once believed to be specially under Cuthbert's protection, are now a sanctuary for birds, seals, and other wild life under the care of the National Trust. Feast: 20 March: translation 4 September.

Bede, *H.E.*, iv. 27–32; W. Jaager (ed.), *Bedas Metrische Vita sancti Cuthberti* (1935); B.

Colgrave, *Two Lives of St. Cuthbert* (text and translation) (1940); Bede's Prose Life also in J. F. Webb and D. H. Farmer, *The Age of Bede* (1983); Symeon of Durham, *Opera* (ed. T. Arnold) (*R.S.*, 1882–5); Reginald of Durham, *De admirandis virtutibus B. Cuthberti* (S.S. 1835); Sir E. Craster, 'The Miracles of St. Cuthbert at Farne', *Anal. Boll.*, lxx (1952), 5–19 (English translation in *Arch. Aeliana*, xxix (1951), 93–107). The most comprehensive studies are C. F. Battiscombe (ed.), *The Relics of St. Cuthbert* (1956) and G. Bonner and others, *St. Cuthbert, his cult and his community* (1989).

For particular aspects see H. H. E. Craster, 'The Patrimony of St. Cuthbert', *E.H.R.*, lxix (1954), 177–99; A. Hamilton Thompson, 'Churches dedicated to St. Cuthbert', *Trans. Arch. and Archaeol. Soc. of Durham and Northumberland* (1936), 151 ff.; B.Colgrave, 'Post-Bedan Miracles and Translations of St. Cuthbert' in *The Early English Culture of North-West Europe* (ed. C. Fox and B. Dickins, 1950). For Cuthbert's iconography W. Forbes-Leith, *The Life of St. Cuthbert* (1888), reproducing 45 pictures from B.M. Yates Thompson M.S. 26; B. Colgrave, 'The St. Cuthbert Paintings on the Carlisle Cathedral stalls', *Burlington Magazine*, lxxiii (1938), 17–21; M. Baker, 'Medieval Illustrations of Bede's Life of St. Cuthbert', *Jnl. of the Warburg and Courtauld Institutes*, xli (1978), 16–49. See also R. B. Dobson, *Durham Priory, 1400–1500* (1975).

CUTHBURGA (d. *c.*725), first abbess of Wimborne. She was the sister of Ine, king of Wessex (688–726), and was married to Aldfrith, king of Northumbria (685–704), who was famous for his learning and favour to the Church. But after a few years Cuthburga was separated from him and became a nun at Barking under *Hildelith. Soon after 705 with her sister *Quenburga she founded the double monastery at Wimborne. Like others of its kind at this time it was predominantly a nunnery, and enclosure was rigorously observed: even prelates were forbidden to enter the nuns' quarters and Cuthburga communicated with them through a little hatch. These details are gleaned from the Life of *Lioba, abbess of Bischofsheim, who was formed in the monastic life by Cuthburga. The hagiographers describe her as austere to herself but kindly to others and assiduous in prayer and fasting. Feast: 31 August.

AA.SS. Aug. VI (1743), 696–700; *G.R.*, i. 935; *G.P.*, p. 379; C. H. Talbot, *The Anglo-Saxon Missionaries in Germany* (1954); *R.P.S.* and *C.S.P.*

CUTHFLEDA, virgin, local saint of Leominster (Hereford and Worcester), presumably abbess of the nunnery endowed by Leofric, Earl of Mercia (11th century). Mentioned in *C.S.P.*

CUTHMAN (d. 8th century), Anglo-Saxon hermit saint, associated with Steyning (West Sussex), where he died and was buried. His name appears in a few early calendars, and in *R.P.S.*, which clearly indicate a pre-Conquest cult. However, Edward the Confessor gave Steyning church to Fécamp, which monastery established a cell of monks on the site of his old wooden church. After the Conquest a stone church was built by them, but Cuthman's relics were transferred to Fécamp. The Lives preserved there may contain some genuine material. They say he was born *c.*681 probably at Chidham, near Bosham, which was the centre of early missionary work. After his father's death he looked after his paralysed mother, for whom he made a wheelbarrow couch; with the help of a rope over his shoulders he used to wheel her wherever he went, travelling as a mendicant hermit. He finally settled at Steyning, where he built a hut for his mother and himself and later a church. Feast: 8 February.

AA.SS. Feb. II (1658), 197–9; *R.P.S.*; *C.S.P.*; G. R. Stephens and W. D. Stephens, 'Cuthman; a neglected saint', *Speculum*, xii (1938), 448–53; F. W. Cox, 'St. Cuthman; what is known of him', *Sussex Notes and Queries*, iv (1933), 204–7: P. Grosjean, 'Codicis Gothani appendix', *Anal. Boll.*, lviii (1940), 197–9.

CYBI (Cuby) (6th century), abbot, founder of a monastery at Holyhead (called in Welsh Caer Gybi, 'Cybi's Fort') in Anglesey, the small island on which it stands being called Holy Island or Ynys Gybi. With his friend *Seiriol he is generally regarded as the most important saint of Anglesey. There are, however, other traces of Cybi in Welsh and Cornish place-names. Llangybi, near Pwllhelli (Gwynedd), had a well and half-ruined 'beehive' cell still called St. Cybi's Well which could date back to his time. This is situated in a valley on the edge of a wood, about a quarter of a mile from the parish church, which has in its graveyard a very ancient carved cross. The well, used for baptism and healing, is a most impressive early Christian monument. There is another Ynys Gybi, an islet off the north coast of Dyfed, and another Llangybi in the valley of the Teifi river.

A dedication to Cybi at Llangibby-on-Usk, together with Cornish dedications at Cuby, Tregony, and Landulph, have helped to establish the view of Cybi as a Cornish saint who travelled by sea and river, living as a hermit and/or evangelist in the various places which bear his name and finally settling on Anglesey, where his most important work was achieved. This is much less fanciful than the 13th-century Life which makes him go to Jerusalem, stay with St. Hilary (d. 449) for fifty years and be consecrated by him as bishop, and then go to Ireland via Menevia for several years before arriving in Anglesey. The claim, however, that he was given the site of his monastery there by the Welsh prince Maelgwn Gwynedd of Cunedda may well be correct. It is an interesting, almost unique Welsh example of a church being situated in the enclosure of a Roman fort, presumably a coastguard station. Feast in Cornwall and Wales generally on 8 November; other dates in Wales 5, 6, 7 November, but in Cornwall (Roscarrock) 13 August.

E. G. Bowen, *The Settlements of the Celtic Saints in Wales* (1956), pp. 118–20; A. W. Wade-Evans, *Vitae Sanctorum Britanniae et Genealogiae* (1944), pp. 234–51; G. H. Doble, *The Saints in Cornwall*, iii (1964), 105–32.

CYNFARCH, see KINEMARK.

CYNGAR, see CONGAR (1).

CYNHELM, see KENELM.

CYNIBURG (Kineburga). There are reputed to have been three Anglo-Saxon saints of this name:

1. A Mercian princess, daughter of Penda, who married Alcfrith, the son of Oswiu, king of Northumbria. She was foundress and abbess of the convent of Castor (Northants.). She died *c.*680 and was succeeded by her sister Cyneswith. The relics of these two sisters, together with those of their kinswoman *Tibba, were translated to Peterborough and later to Thorney. Feast: 6 March, the day of their translation.

2. Cyniburg of Gloucester, to whom a chapel was dedicated there in 1147. Her Legend made her a princess who fled there to escape marriage and took employment as a baker's servant. His wife, motivated by jealousy, murdered her and threw her body into a well. She was taken up and buried near by; a church was built and miracles reported. For a long time, however, miracles ceased, supposedly because of the custodian's irreverence. Archbishop Courtenay ordered a fresh translation in 1390, accomplished by Henry of Wakefield, bishop of Worcester, on 10 April that year, after which miracles were renewed. Feast: 25 June.

3. Cyniburg, supposedly first abbess of Gloucester (according to the *Gloucester Annals*), claimed with other Mercian princesses as *alumnae* and benefactresses. If she ever existed (which seems doubtful), she should be identified with the abbess of Castor above. Or, more likely, her story could have been caused by confusing the other two Cyniburgs.

P. Grosjean in *Anal. Boll.*, lxxiii (1955), pp. 350–1 and lxxix (1961), p. 168.

CYPRIAN (Thasius Cecilianus Cyprianus) (*c.*200–58), bishop of Carthage and martyr. Born at Carthage, Cyprian became an orator, a teacher of rhetoric, and an advocate in the courts before being converted to Christianity *c.*245. His conversion was very thorough: he gave up all pagan writings and concentrated his studies exclusively on Scripture and the Christian commentaries, especially those of Tertullian, his compatriot, whom he regarded as his master. Within a few years of his conversion he became a priest, and in 248 bishop of Carthage by the choice of the people, the clergy, and the consent of the neighbouring bishops. A small clique refused to recognize his election. Almost immediately he was faced by the Decian persecution. He fled to safety but ruled and encouraged his flock by letter. During the persecution a number of Christians had apostatized by sacrificing to idols or lapsed by buying certificates which stated falsely that they had sacrificed. Cyprian reconciled these *Lapsi* after a suitable time of penance: his priest Novatus readmitted them without any penance at all, while Novatian the anti-pope was far too severe and taught that the Church could not absolve an apostate at all. Throughout Cyprian insisted on discreet compassion, on the unity of the Church, and the need for obedience and loyalty. His recommended treatment of the lapsed was approved by the Council of Carthage in 251.

From this controversy arose another concerning the validity of baptism given by schismatics, heretics, and apostates. Here Cyprian was in conflict with Pope Stephen II, but was supported by other African bishops in rejecting the validity of these baptisms. The controversy became acrimonious and was settled only after the death of the two protagonists by the Church's acceptance of the Roman tradition in favour of their validity. In the words of *Augustine he atoned by his glorious martyrdom for his passion in this controversy. Under the persecution of Valerian, which required bishops, priests, and deacons to take part in official pagan worship, Cyprian was exiled in 257 and condemned to death and executed after a second trial in 258. A contemporary *passio* survives, as does the biography by Pontius, which portrays a devoted pastor who enjoyed great personal prestige. His ideals are best seen in his writings, the most important of which are his *De Catholicae Ecclesiae Unitate* (251), *De Lapsis, De Habitu Virginum*, sermons and letters. His feast is kept in the Roman calendar on 16 September (14 September is the day of his death) together with *Cornelius, the pope whom he actively supported; but in the Book of Common Prayer his day is 26 September, through confusion with the convert magician of Antioch of the same name.

AA.SS. Sept. IV (1753), 191–348; *A.C.M.*, pp. xxx–xxxi, 168–75; for the trustworthy but not primitive *passio* see H. Delehaye, *Les passions des martyrs et les genres littéraires* (1921), pp. 82–104; standard biographies by E. W. Benson, *St. Cyprian* (1897), P. Monceaux, *Saint Cyprien* (1914), and J. H. Fichter, *St. Cecil Cyprian* (1942); on his doctrine see A. d'Alès, *La Théologie de S. Cyprien* (1922) and H. Koch, *Cyprian und der römische Primat* (T.U. xxxv. 1. 1910) and *Cyprianische Untersuchungen* (1922); works of Cyprian ed. W. Hartel in *C.S.E.L.* (3 vols., 1868–71), English tr. by R. E. Wallis in *A.N.C.L.* (2 vols., 1868–71) and T. A. Lacey, *Select Epistles of St. Cyprian* (1922); see also M. Bevenot (ed.), *St. Cyprian: the Lapsed, the Unity of the Catholic Church* (1957); G. S. M. Walker, *The Churchmanship of St. Cyprian* (Ecumenical Studies in History, ix. 1968); P. Hinchcliff, *Cyprian of Carthage* (1974).

CYPRIAN AND JUSTINA, martyrs of Antioch, *c.*300, whose supposed relics are in the baptistery of St. John Lateran. A worthless Legend made Cyprian a magician who tried to seduce the Christian Justina, but was converted by her: he later became a bishop and she an abbess; both were beheaded at Nicomedia, and sailors brought their relics to Rome. Feast: 26 September, suppressed by the Holy See in 1969.

AA.SS. Sept. VII (1760), 195–262; H. Delehaye, 'Cyprien d'Antioche et Cyprien de Carthage', *Anal. Boll.*, xxxix (1921), 314–32.

CYRICUS (Cyriacus, Quiriac, Quiricus, Cyr) **AND JULITTA**, martyrs, supposedly *c.*304. The Legend of Cyricus and Julitta which survives in several versions, but which was proscribed by pseudo-Gelasius, made Julitta a widow of Iconium, who took her three-year-old son Cyricus to Tarsus to escape persecution. Here, however, she was recognized and accused, suffered with her child a series of tortures which rebounded in some way against the persecutors, whom Cyricus attacked; eventually Julitta and her son were executed and their relics saved by other Christians.

Cyricus occurs in many place-names and church dedications in countries of Europe and the Near East, without his mother Julitta. He was supposed to come from Antioch and was a child-martyr of immense popularity. The oldest known representation of him is a series of frescoes at S. Maria Antiqua, Rome (8th century), while a 12th-century antependium at the Museum of Barcelona represents scenes from his Legend, as does a series of 15th-century stained-glass windows at Issoudun. His connection with France was strong, partly because some relics were brought back from Antioch by Amator, a 4th-century bishop of Auxerre, partly through a Nivernaise story (reproduced in the *Golden Legend*), according to which Charlemagne in a dream was saved from death by a wild boar on a hunt by the appearance of a child, who promised to save him from death if he would give him clothes to cover himself. The bishop of Nevers interpreted this to mean that he wanted the emperor to repair the roof of the cathedral, dedicated to St. Cyr. Hence his iconographical emblem of a naked child riding on a wild boar.

There are at least three churches in England dedicated to Cyricus including Newton St. Cyres (Devon). He was patron of children. Feast: 16 June (15 July in the East).

AA.SS. Iun III (1701), 15–37; H. Delehaye, *Les Origines du culte des Martyrs* (1933), pp. 167–8; A. Crosnier, *Notice historique sur saint Cyr et sainte Julitte* (1868).

CYRIL OF ALEXANDRIA (*c.*376–444), bishop. Traditionally regarded as the most outstanding theologian of Alexandria, Cyril presented against Nestorius of Constantinople the classical doctrines of the Trinity and the Person of Christ based on the work of *Athanasius, *Basil, and *Gregory of Nazianzus. Little is known of his early life. He was born at Alexandria and first became known as a young priest who was the nephew of the patriarch of Alexandria, Theophilus, whom he succeeded in 412. His intransigent vigour was soon expressed in attacks on the Novatians, the Neoplatonists, the Jews, and the imperial governor Orestes. The latter was believed to have been influenced by the philosopher Hypatia against him: Cyril's followers lynched her without his knowledge. His controversy with Nestorius was the most important of his life. The different exegetical traditions of Constantinople and Alexandria, sharpened by rivalry between the two sees for pre-eminence, embittered the quarrel. Nestorius was believed to have taught that there were two distinct persons in Christ who were joined by a merely moral union: consequently the Blessed Virgin Mary should not be called Theotokos or Mother of God. Cyril certainly and Nestorius probably appealed for support to Pope Celestine, who, after examining the question in a council at Rome, condemned Nestorius' teaching, excommunicated and deposed him unless he retracted, and appointed Cyril to carry out the sentence. Nestorius refused to submit; the Council of Ephesus (431) was summoned; 200 bishops took part. Cyril presided and condemned Nestorius, who refused to appear, before the arrival of the bishops of the patriarchate of Antioch. They in their turn condemned Cyril first but later reached agreement with him. The emperor upheld the condemnation of Nestorius and the word Theotokos became a touchstone of orthodoxy. The precision, accuracy, and skill of Cyril as a theologian has often been remarked and his intransigence and even misunderstanding of his opponents' thought is often criticized by modern scholars. Traditionally he was regarded as the fearlessly outspoken champion of orthodox thought on the Person of Christ. In addition to this, his writings contain some fine passages on the Real Presence of Christ in the Eucharist and the place of Mary in the Incarnation. His works include sermons and letters besides more formal theological treatises. As the moving spirit of the third Ecumenical Council of the Church he is of great importance in the development of Christian Doctrine. His feast in the East is 9 June, in the West formerly 9 February (or 28 January), now 27 June. He was declared a Doctor of the Church by Leo XIII in 1882.

AA.SS. Ian. II (1643), 843–54; Works in *P.G.*, lxviii–lxxvii: *Kyrilliana:* Études variées à l'occasion du XVe centenaire de saint Cyrille d'Alexandrie (1947); J. Liebaert, *La Doctrine christologique de saint Cyrille d'Alexandrie avant la Querelle Nestorienne* (1951); A. Kerrigan, *St. Cyril of Alexandria, Interpreter of the Old Testament* (1952); *O.D.C.C.*, s.v. with further bibliography.

CYRIL OF JERUSALEM (*c.*315–386), archbishop, Doctor of the Church. Born in or near Jerusalem and educated there, he became a priest and was entrusted by St. Maximus with the instruction of catechumens. These catechetical discourses, delivered both to those preparing for, as well as those who had just received Baptism, form his most famous work. He became bishop *c.*349; in the first year of his episcopate strange lights were reported to appear over the city. He soon became involved in determining the precise status of his see in view of a claim by the metropolitan of Caesarea, Acacius, to precedence and jurisdiction over him; he also accused him of heresy. Cyril refused to appear before a council of bishops who charged him both with contumacy and with having sold church goods to relieve the poor. The emperor was brought into the dispute; Cyril was exiled in 357, recalled in 359, and banished again later twice. His own orthodoxy had been questioned, both by the 'homoousians' and by the Arians: some writers see him as on the left wing of orthodoxy or on the right wing of the semi-Arians, others insist that although afraid of the word homoousios earlier, he took a full part and consented to the conclusions of the Council of Constantinople (381). Earlier he had been reinstated in his see by the Council of Seleucia which deposed his accuser Acacius; he was probably orthodox throughout in intention, if not always in language. He died at the age of about seventy after being bishop for 35 years, of which about 16 were spent in exile. He was named a Doctor of the Church in 1882. Feast: 18 March.

AA.SS. Mart. II (1668), 625–33; A. Fortescue, *The Greek Fathers* (1908), pp. 150–68; works ed. W. K. Reischl and J. Rupp (1848–60), catechetical discourses by F. L. Cross (1951); see also W. J. Swaans, 'A propos des catéchèses mystagogiques attribuées à S. Cyrille de Jérusalem', *Le Museon*, xl (1942), 6–43 and J. Lebon, 'La position de S. Cyrille de Jérusalem dans les luttes provoquées par l'arianisme', *R.H.E.*, xx (1924), 181–210 and 357–86.

CYRIL (826–69) **AND METHODIUS** (*c.*815–85), brothers, Apostles of the Slavs. Born of a senatorial family in Thessalonica, they both became priests and went to Constantinople, where the younger of them, Constantine (who was called Cyril only when he became a monk much later), was librarian at Santa Sophia. In *c.*863 the Emperor sent them to Moravia as Christian missionaries at the request of the local ruler Rostislav, who wanted them to teach in the vernacular. They accepted with enthusiasm, translated some of the Scriptures and the Liturgy into Slavonic and even invented the Glagolithic alphabet (from which the 'Cyrillic' was derived later) in which to write them. For this reason they are regarded as the founders of Slavonic literature. In their apostolate they encountered German missionaries, to whom Rostislav had wanted them to provide an alternative, as he preferred to be aligned with Byzantium rather than Germany. Not altogether surprisingly they met with non-co-operation or even opposition from the German bishops, who refused to ordain them or their followers, so they returned towards Byzantium, reaching Venice just at the time of the Photian schism. The pope sent for them and they brought with them to Rome the alleged relics of *Clement, one of the early popes. They were received with great honour; Cyril became a monk, but died soon afterwards. He was buried in the beautiful church of San Clemente, where an ancient fresco depicts his funeral.

Methodius was consecrated archbishop of Sirmium (Pannonia) by the pope and returned to Moravia. Once again the bishops opposed him and he was imprisoned for two years. The pope secured his release, but told him to cease the use of a vernacular liturgy. In 879 he was called to Rome to answer charges of heterodoxy and disobedience. He was cleared of both charges, returned confirmed as archbishop of Moravia, and died at Velehrad in Czechoslovakia. In modern times his cult has received new extension, as he is regarded as a pioneer of the use of the vernacular in the Liturgy and as a patron of ecumenism, whom both Eastern and Western Christians venerate. Pope John Paul II nominated Cyril and Methodius as joint patrons of Europe together with *Benedict. Feast in the East: 11 May; in the West, 14 February (formerly 9 March or 7 July).

Greek Life in *P.G.*, cxxvi. 1194–1240; F. Dvornik, *Les Légendes de Constantin et de Méthode vues de Byzance* (1933); P. Meyvaert and P. Devos, 'Trois énigmes cyrillo-méthodiennes de la Légende italique résolues', *Anal. Boll.*, lxxiii (1955), 375–461; id., 'La Légende morave de SS. Cyrille et Méthode et ses sources', ibid., lxxiv (1956), 441–69; P. Duthilleul, *L'Évangélisation des Slaves* (1963); A. E. N. Tachiaos, *Cyril and Methodius of Thessalonica* (1989); see also *N.C.E.* and *Bibl. SS.*, iii. 1328–38.

D

DADO, see Ouen.

DA LUA, see Molua.

DAMASUS (*c.*304–84), pope. Born in Rome, Damasus was of Spanish extraction, his father was a priest. Damasus became a deacon under Pope Liberius and succeeded him in 366. A minority of the Roman clergy, however, elected Ursinus: a violent struggle ensued, the Emperor Valentinian supported Damasus and exiled Ursinus. Damasus' pontificate was notable for several reasons. The Emperor Theodosius proclaimed that the Christianity of Rome and Alexandria was the religion of the Roman State; Damasus proceeded energetically against heretics, mainly Arians, Macedonians, and Donatists; he promulgated the Canon of Scripture and commissioned *Jerome to revise the Latin text of the Bible by producing a single 'Vulgate' to replace the many different versions then in existence. He also saw to the collection and housing of papal archives and took a keen interest in the Roman martyrs, whose relics formed a unique collection and made Rome especially glorious. This was manifested by his famous collection of inscriptions and epigrams in their honour, mainly composed by himself. Some modern scholars believe that this activity was inspired by political and propaganda motives against Constantinople as well as by religious ones. He built the churches of S. Lorenzo in Damaso and of SS. Marcus and Marcellianus on the Via Ardeatina, where he was buried with his mother and sister: his tomb was embellished with his own epitaph affirming his belief in the Resurrection of Christ and of his own. Feast: 11 December.

Liber Pontificalis (ed. L. Duchesne), i. 212–15; works in *P.L.*, xiii. 109–424; A. Ferrua, *Epigrammata Damasiana* (1942); C. H. Turner, 'Latin Lists of the Canonical Books, I, The Roman Council under Damasus, A.D. 382', *J.T.S.*, i (1899–1900), 554–60; E. M. Shepherd, 'The Liturgical Reform of Damasus I' in P. Granfield and J. A. Jungmann, *Kyriakon* (1970), pp. 847–63; A. Van Roey in *D.H.G.E.*, xiv (1960), 48–53.

DAMIAN, see Cosmas and Damian.

DAMIAN, P., see Peter Damian.

DANIEL, see Deiniol.

DANIEL THE STYLITE (409–93), hermit. Born of devout parents at Maratha, near Samosata in Mesopotamia, Daniel left home at the age of twelve and offered himself to a nearby monastery. After consulting his parents, the abbot received him. Some years later Daniel travelled with him to Antioch, where a visit to *Simeon Stylites inspired him with an example to follow for life. The abbot died soon afterwards; the monks wished Daniel to succeed him but he refused. Instead he visited Simeon again, stayed for a fortnight in the monastery built close to his pillar, and climbed a ladder to receive spiritual direction from the holy man.

Daniel then set out on pilgrimage to Palestine, but was dissuaded because of political unrest. Instead he settled near Constantinople; first he spent seven days in the oratory of St. Michael at Anaplus, then he made his hermitage in a disused temple, reputedly inhabited by devils, at Philempora (Roumeli-Hissar). These were believed to be responsible for losses of ships at sea and repeated attacks at night on passers-by. Daniel locked himself in and communicated with the outside world only through a small window. Hideous noises and apparitions, with attacks by phantoms carrying swords, were experienced by Daniel as part of the single combat with devils expected of hermits. He stayed there for nine years, helped by the patriarch Anatolius, who was healed from serious illness reputedly by Daniel's prayers.

After the death of Simeon Stylites (459), Daniel inherited both his cloak and his way of life. Other relics of Simeon reached Constantinople some years later. Daniel with friends' help set himself up on a pillar overlooking the Bosphorus a few miles from the city. He nearly froze to death one night, after which the Emperor built him a better home of two pillars fastened together, on top of which were a balustrade and a shelter. Even this was in danger of being destroyed in storms until it was strengthened after swaying dangerously. Here Daniel was ordained priest by the patriarch Gennadius, who read the prayers beneath the pillar and then climbed the ladder to lay hands on him and give Communion.

Daniel's long life in his extraordinary regime was mainly uneventful. He was often visited by troubled people in search of his advice and prayers, especially the sick who were sometimes cured by his laying hands on them or anointing them with the oil which burnt before his icons and relics. He preached regularly in the afternoon, his theme frequently being the love of God and of one's neighbour, especially shown in almsgiving, as well as 'the everlasting condemnation which is the lot of sinners'.

In 465 Daniel foretold that there would be a disastrous fire: it destroyed several regions of the city. This event brought Daniel into contact with the Emperor Leo I, who visited him frequently and gave him relics. He also used to show him off to visitors as one of the wonders of the empire. Leo died in 474. His successor Zeno appreciated Daniel no less. But Basiliscus, brother of the dowager empress, usurped the throne and protected the heretics, especially the Euthychians. Daniel said that God would overthrow this government and added other messages too inflammatory to be passed on.

Hoping to discredit him, Daniel's heretical enemies bribed a notorious prostitute called Basiane to say that she had seduced Daniel when his disciples brought her up the ladder to be healed of a simulated illness. Much controversy followed which was ended only when she was 'possessed by a devil' and revealed the names and ranks of those who had bribed her. Meanwhile the patriarch Acacius persuaded Daniel to 'come to the rescue of the Church'. He came down from his pillar, was carried in a chair as he was unable to walk, and went to visit Basiliscus, who refused to see him. The reign of Basiliscus was soon ended by the return of Zeno, who promptly revisited Daniel.

Daniel's last discourse seven days before his death was impressive. Strong biblical inspiration pervaded his summary on the Creation and Redemption. He promised his disciples that God would strengthen them and keep them from evil: 'He will keep your faith in him firm and immovable if you continue in unity with each other and in perfect love . . . Do not neglect hospitality: never separate yourselves from your holy mother the Church; turn away from all causes of offence and from the tares of heretics . . . and now I bid you farewell.' The noise of the monks' lamentation sounded 'like a clap of thunder'. The patriarch Euphemius climbed the ladder, announced that Daniel was still alive and gave him the viaticum. Soon afterwards he died. His hair was four cubits long and his beard three. His knees were drawn up to his chest and his heels and legs to his thighs. When his body was straightened, his bones cracked so loudly that an accident was feared. His body, attached to a plank, was shown to the faithful before being buried in the chapel at the foot of his column.

In life and death Daniel was an outstanding example of the holy man in antiquity. He spent twenty-five years in a monastery and thirty-three on a series of columns. He prayed for all men, instructed them in what was necessary for salvation, counselled them not to be covetous, showed hospitality to all, yet refused all presents. All in all, however, the comment of monastic writers on other practices as 'worthy of admiration, not imitation' seems appropriate for Daniel's chosen way of life. Feast: 11 December.

Text of full and accurate contemporary Life in H. Delehaye, *Les Saints Stylites* (1923) and in *Anal. Boll.*, xxxii (1913), 121–229; tr. E. Dawes and N. H. Baynes, *Three Byzantine Saints* (1948); Life by Metafrastes in *P.G.*, cxvi. 969–1037; for political incidents in the Life see *E.H.R.*, xl (1925), 397–402; B.T.A., iv. 539–41.

DARERCA, see MONENNA.

DAVID OF SCOTLAND (*c.*1085–1153), king. The sixth and youngest son of King Malcolm III of Scotland and his wife *Margaret, he was educated for some years at the Anglo-Norman court, became prince of Cumbria (including Lothian) on the accession of his brother Alexander in 1107, and married Matilda, daughter of *Waldef, the Anglo-Saxon patriot earl of Northampton and Huntingdon. He thus became himself an English earl and had a strong claim to the earldom of Northumberland. He became king of Scotland in 1124. With his ancestry, upbringing, and social position he was inevitably involved with English politics and furthered his claim to Northumbria by every means at his disposal. In 1127, like other English barons, he bound himself to recognize Henry I's daughter Matilda (his own niece) as successor to the English throne. In 1135, when Stephen became king instead, David captured nearly all the border castles: the price of peace was for his son Henry to be granted Carlisle, Doncaster, and the honour of Huntingdon. In 1136 David also claimed Northumberland and invaded the north of England in 1138, helped by miscellaneous allies from Norway, Denmark, Germany, and especially the Picts of Galloway, whose barbarism and atrocities (which included the murder and enslavement of women) were long remembered with horror. Even though the army of the English North, aided by Thurstan, archbishop of York, and carrying a consecrated host in a pyx as well as banners of the Northern saints, defeated David's army at the battle of the Standard (near Northallerton), David obtained favourable terms: Northumberland and Cumberland were ceded, and David held court at Carlisle, but he took little further part in the civil war.

Instead he devoted himself to the improvement of Scotland. He instituted a feudal system of land tenure which replaced the Celtic tribal one; he introduced Norman colonists and an Anglo-Norman judicial system and encouraged the development of towns such as Edinburgh, Berwick, and Perth with trade practised by merchants of many races. Above all, he reorganized the Church in Scotland. Contact with Rome was close and more effective, both through visits from papal legates and the issue of numerous decretals, but he opposed Canterbury's primatial claims. He founded the bishoprics of Brechin, Dunblane, Caithness, Ross, and Aberdeen and numerous churches and monasteries. These included houses for Austin Canons at Holyrood, for Cistercians at Melrose, Kinloss, Newbottle, and Dundrennan, and the increase of endowments for the Benedictines of Dunfermline. *Ailred of Rievaulx, who had been steward (*dispensator*) at David's court when a young man and the close friend of the king's son Henry, gave a eulogistic portrait of David in his panegyric. This tells of his reluctance to become king, his justice in administration, his accessibility to all and his conversation about gardens, orchards, and buildings. His one fault was his failure to control his soldiers when they invaded England, which was punished by the loss of his son and the defeat of his armies. His chastity in marriage and widowerhood were exemplary, he said the divine office, confessed and communicated weekly, and gave abundant alms, often in person, like his mother. His death also was worthy of her: after viaticum he said numerous psalms; when asked to rest, he replied: 'Allow me rather to think about the things of God, so that my soul may be strengthened . . . when I stand before God's judgment-seat, none of you shall answer for me, none of you protect me or deliver me from his hand.' He died on 24 May and was buried at Dunfermline where his cult continued until the Reformation. Later it was revived when Archbishop Laud inserted his name in the calendar of the Prayer-book for Scotland. His name also appears in medieval Scottish calendars and he is the titular of several churches. His historical importance is that he founded the Scotland which defied Edward I; it has also been claimed that at no period of its history has Scotland stood so high in its national reputation. Feast: 24 May.

Ailred of Rievaulx, *De Bello Standardii* and *Genealogia regum Anglorum* in *P.L.*, 195, 701–38: Richard of Hexham, *Chronicles of Stephen, Henry II and Richard I* (ed. R. Howlett, R.S., 1886) iii. 151–78; A. L. Poole, *Domesday Book to Magna Carta* (1964), pp. 269–75; M. Morgan, 'The Organization of the Scottish Church', *T.R.H.S.* (4th ser.), xxix (1947), 135–49: G. W. S. Barrow, 'Scottish Rulers and the Religious Orders 1070–1153', *T.R.H.S.* (5th ser.), iii (1953), 77–100 and *David of Scotland: The Balance of New and Old* (Stenton lecture, 1984); *M.O.*, pp. 239–49.

DAVID OF SWEDEN (also called David of Munkthorp) (d. *c.*1080), bishop. An English monk, he was attracted to the Scandinavian apostolate by the example of *Sigfrid, bishop of Vaxio (Sweden), whom he joined, and then worked in Vastmanland, building a monastery at Munkthorp. He is usually described as the first bishop of Vasteras. He worked long and hard in his missionary work and died peacefully in old age, whereas he had hoped for martyrdom like Sigfrid's nephews. Miracles were reported at his tomb. Feast 15 July, or in some calendars 25 June (translation).

Scriptores Rerum Suevicarum, vol. ii, part 1, 408–11; C. J. A. Oppermann, *English Missionaries in Sweden* (1937), pp. 112–17; B.T.A., iii. 111.

DAVID (Dewi) **OF WALES** (d. 601 or 589), monk and bishop of the 6th century. From the 12th century he has been regarded as the patron of Wales; he is also the only Welsh saint to be canonized and culted in the Western Church. It is regrettable that very few details about his life are known.

What seems certain is that he was primarily a saint of Pembrokeshire (Dyfed), whence his cult spread through South Wales by dedications well before the 12th century; there are almost none in North Wales, but some are found as far afield as Brittany, Cornwall, and Herefordshire. The oldest written evidence about him, however, comes from Ireland where the Catalogue of the Saints (*c.*730) says that they 'received the Mass from bishop David and the Britons Gillas (= *Gildas) and *Teilo', and the earliest Irish Martyrologies (*c.*800) place the feast on 1 March and locate his monastery at 'Menevia', i.e. St. David's. On this firm but rudimentary basis is built later information, such as his nickname *Aquaticus* as the leader of reformed monks who drank neither wine nor beer but only water (from the 9th-century Life of St. *Paul Aurelian), that calendars and litanies of 10th–11th century Wessex mention him (following the spread of his cult by Alfred's bishop Asser), and that Glastonbury claimed him as its patron. It may well be too that his original monastery, inherited from his father, was at Henllan from where he removed to Menevia; from there he could have made foundations in an eastward direction and may have travelled to Brittany (and Cornwall) after the plague of 547.

The earliest Life of David was written by Rhygyvarch, son of Julien, bishop of St. David's *c.*1090; its motive was to further Welsh independence of Canterbury. Hence it should be treated as propaganda, which may, however, contain some elements of true tradition. According to this David was educated first at Hen Vynyw, then for ten years as a priest in Scripture studies on an island under Paulinus the scribe. After this he founded ten monasteries, among them Menevia and Glastonbury, where the monks lived in extreme hardship, imitating the monks of

Egypt in their regime of heavy manual labour and study, sustained by a diet of bread, vegetables, and water. David devoted himself to works of mercy and practised frequent genuflexions and total immersion in cold water as his favourite austerities. He was called to the Synod of Brevi where he preached to such effect that 'with the consent of all he was made archbishop and his monastery was declared the metropolis of the whole country, so that whoever ruled it should be accounted archbishop'. This latter claim and the story that he was consecrated bishop at Jerusalem are pure fables.

The cult was approved by Callistus II in 1120: two pilgrimages to St. David's were worth one to Rome. The relics were translated in 1131, and again in 1275 by Richard Carew, bishop of St. David's, who rebuilt the cathedral largely from offerings at the shrine. English kings who made this pilgrimage include William I and later Henry II on his way to and from Ireland.

David is usually depicted in episcopal vestments, standing on a mound with a dove at his shoulder, in memory of his share in the Synod of Brevi. The custom of Welshmen wearing leeks or daffodils on St. David's Day is described by Shakespeare as 'an ancient tradition begun upon an honourable request', but no satisfactory explanation of it has yet been made. His name is often spelled Dafydd, whence 'Taffy', colloquial for any Welshman. Feast: 1 March.

Rhygyvarch's Life of St. David was edited by J. W. James (1967) in Latin and English; also in *N.L.A.*, etc., i. 254–62 and in A. W. Wade-Evans, *Vitae Sanctorum Britanniae et Genealogiae* (1944), pp. 150–70. See also [W. Morgan], *Catalogue of Manuscripts, Book Engravings etc. relating to St. David* (1927); S. M. Harris, *St. David in the Liturgy* (1940); C. N. L. Brooke, 'The Archbishops of St. Davids, Llandaff and Caerleon-on-Usk' in *Studies in the Early British Church* (ed. N. K. Chadwick, 1958). For the canonization cf. M. R. Toynbee, *St. Louis of Toulouse and the process of canonization in the XIVth century* (1929), pp. 239–40 and *Anal. Boll.*, xlix (1931), 211–13; S. M. Harris, 'Was St. David ever canonized?' in *Wales* (June 1944); E. G. Bowen, *The Settlements of the Celtic Saints in Wales* (1956), esp. pp. 50–65; Baring-Gould and Fisher, ii. 285–322; P. Grosjean, 'Notes d'hagiographie celtique', *Anal. Boll.*, lxxv (1957), 413–18.

DAVID THE BRUCE (d. 1402), duke of Rothesay. According to William Worcestre, he was 'brother of King James of Scotland who was with King Henry V of England'; this St. David lies buried in Lindores Abbey near Newburgh in Scotland. He died a martyr, starved to death for lack of food in Falkland castle. There seems to have been no official cult.

William Worcestre, p. 7.

DAY (Dei, Thei), very obscure patron of the mining village of St. Day, near Redruth, Cornwall, possibly to be identified with the Breton Dei or Thei, said to be a monk of Landevennec and abbot. There is no evidence of liturgical cult on either side of the Channel and consequently no feast day. The chapel of St. Day was dedicated to the Holy Trinity before 1269.

G. H. Doble, *Saint Day* (*Cornish Saints*, no. 32), 1933. Baring-Gould and Fisher, ii. 322–3.

DE BRITTO, John (1647–93), Jesuit martyr. He joined the Jesuits from his noble family in 1662, was ordained priest in 1673, and left for Goa soon afterwards with sixteen companions. He spent virtually all the rest of his life in southern India. He followed the example of the famous Jesuit Fr. de Nobili in living, as far as possible, in an Indian way, wearing Indian robes, abstaining from animal food, and respecting (except for sin) the varied taboos of caste.

He was placed in charge of the Madura mission in Madras, where he long laboured in the intense heat. Contemporaries testified to his austerity and courage which bore fruit in numerous conversions. The turbulence of the area was a further hazard and at least once he and his companions were tortured for refusing to pay honour to the god Siva. Recalled to Lisbon, he was exhorted to remain in Europe, but chose instead to return to Madura.

A convert to Christianity who had formerly been polygamous, put away his wives. One of them complained to her uncle who was Rajah of Marava, blaming John for her misfortune. A persecution of Christians followed and John was imprisoned. He wrote to his superior: 'I await death and await it with impatience . . . It forms today the most precious reward of my labours and sufferings.' On the following day he was beheaded at Oriur because he had taught 'what was subversive of the worship of gods of the country'. He was canonized in 1947, a pioneer of missionary techniques which have been followed in our own day. Feast: 4 February.

J. Bertrand, *La Mission du Madure* (1850), of which vol. 3 contains several of De Britto's letters. Lives by A. Bessières (1947) and M. Trullas (1950); see also B.T.A., i. 254–5; *Bibl. SS.*, vi. 989–93.

DE JACOBIS, Justin (1800–60), missionary bishop in Ethiopia. Born at San Fele (Basilicata) of a large family which soon emigrated to Naples, he joined the congregation of the Mission in 1818. Ordained in 1824, he excelled at preaching, especially to the rural poor. After helping to set up a foundation at Monopoli he soon became superior at Lecce (Apulia). His special gift was to make religion attractive both to the scholar and to the ignorant. In 1836–7 he served the sick with heroic charity in the cholera epidemic in Naples. In 1839 he was appointed to take charge of the missions at Godar and Adua in Ethiopia.

The situation was bleak. Following Portuguese intransigence in the 16th century, all Catholic missionaries had been excluded for 200 years. Most of the population were Muslim or else Coptic Christians who had been in schism for many centuries. Justin tried to bridge the cultural gap by studying the country, its inhabitants, and languages for two years. He hoped to break down prejudice by understanding and humility, showing the dissident clergy that he wished to help and to serve. Progress however was painfully slow.

Unexpectedly in 1840 Justin was invited to take part in a deputation to the Coptic Patriarch of Alexandria, who appointed one of his monks to be primate of Ethiopia. Justin persuaded some of the delegation to accompany him to Rome, to seek reunion with the Holy See. The venture failed, but Justin gained credit and confidence.

At last the numbers of native Catholics increased; a college for future clergy was established at Massawa, an island in the Red Sea. In 1846 Justin asked the pope to send a bishop as vicar-apostolic. The Capuchin William Massaia was chosen, but persecution greeted his arrival, and he was obliged to withdraw to Aden. Meanwhile instructions were issued, apparently by Negus and Patriarch, to kill Abba Jacob and all his people . . . 'to kill one who follows their religion is to earn seven heavenly crowns hereafter'. Some believers were heroic; others were not; but by 1853 there were 20 Ethiopian Catholic priests and 5,000 laity.

Meanwhile Justin was consecrated bishop in 1849. Persecution flared up again: he was imprisoned in Gondar for several months, but then allowed to escape. He tried to return to his flock in Tigrai, but had to remain on the coast of the Red Sea. Imprisoned again, this time for giving hospitality to a French political mission, he endured forced marches, rapid changes of climate, and a fatal fever. He returned towards Halai on horseback, but could ride no further than Alghedien. Knowing that death was near, he was anointed by a companion, his head supported by a rock in the desert, and there he died. He was buried at Hebo, where his shrine has always attracted pilgrims. He was beatified in 1939 and canonized in 1975, an impressive pioneer of ecumenism as well as missionary achievement. Feast: 31 July.

D. Matthew, *Ethiopia* (1937); D. Attwater, *Christian Churches of the East*, vol. i (1947); Lives by S. Arata and J. Baeteman (1939); B.T.A., iii. 230–5; *E.C.*, iv. 1337.

DE PAUL, see VINCENT DE PAUL.

DECLAN (d. early 5th century), Irish bishop. There is much confusion about the chronology of this saint, but it seems most likely that he was a bishop in the Waterford area, one of the four who lived before *Patrick organized Irish Christianity. Declan, according to his Life, was of noble blood, his home was near Lismore, he studied at home and abroad (probably in Wales or Gaul), and founded the church of Ardmore when he had been consecrated bishop. Ancient buildings there indicate the sites both of a monastery and a hermitage: in addition there is both a holy well (restored in 1951) and an ancient St. Declan's stone on the beach. The week in the year nearest his feast on 24 July is known at Ardmore as 'Pattern week' and still attracts numerous pilgrims.

AA.SS. Iul. V (1727), 590–608; *V.S.H.*, ii. 32–59; P. Power, *Life of St. Declan of Ardmore* (1914). *The Irish Saints*, pp. 137–42.

DECUMAN, patron of Watchet and St. Decumans (Somerset), was probably a 6th-century Welsh monk who came from Rhoscrowther (=Llandegyman) in Pembrokeshire (Dyfed) and settled in North Somerset, near Dunster. The 15th-century Life in *N.L.A.* says that he lived as a hermit there and met an entirely unprovoked death by decapitation at the hand of an assassin while he was at prayer. After this, the body carried the head to a nearby well (like *Nectan and others). His cult was firmly established at Wells and Muchelney; dedications to him in Cornwall, Wales, and Somerset are more probably due to disciples than to his own itinerary. The usual day for his feast is 27 August, but Norwich (and Roscarrock) kept his day on 30 August.

N.L.A., i. 263–5; G. H. Doble, *The Saints of Cornwall*, ii (1962), 25–33; *C.S.P.*

DEI, see DAY.

DEICOLA (1) (Dicul, Dicuill) (late 7th century), Irish abbot of Bosham. This devout but uninfluential abbot with five or six monks was found by *Wilfrid when he evangelized Sussex (681–6). Nothing is known of him, but his name occurs in a few ancient martyrologies. Challoner's *Memorial* (for convenience only) places him on 18 April with *Deicola of Lure.

Bede, *H.E.*, iv. 13; R. Challoner, *Memorial*, p. 21.

DEICOLA (2) (Deicolus, Desle) (d. *c.*625), Irish monk, disciple of *Columbanus at Luxeuil, founder of the abbey of Lure.

J. Mabillon, *AA.SS.O.S.B.*, ii. 102–16; *M.G.H.*, *Scriptores*, xv. 675–82; B.T.A., i. 116.

DEINIOL (Daniel) (d. *c.*584), monk and bishop. Reputedly a descendant of Coel Godebog, a Celtic chieftain of North Britain, Deiniol founded the two monasteries of Bangor Fawr (on the Menai Straits) and Bangor Iscoed (Clwyd), which became, according to Bede, the most famous monastery of British Christianity and came to number over 2,000 monks before they were routed at the battle of Chester by the pagan Æthelfrith, king of Northumbria. Later Deiniol was regarded as 'first bishop of Bangor' (Gwynedd) and his reputed area of influence was consolidated in the Norman (and modern) diocese. There are, however, in the Flintshire (Clwyd) area Deiniol dedications at Marchwiail and Worthenbury which perhaps inspired the dedication of W. E. Gladstone's famous library at Hawarden; also (according to Baring-Gould) at Llanuwchllyn and Llanfor, near Bala. There are a few dedications in S. Wales and one in Gwent at Itton (formerly called Llandeiniol). In the Life of *David by Rhygyvarch, Deiniol and *Dyfrig were the two bishops who finally persuaded David to take part with them at the famous Synod of Brefi (*c.*545). Whether this was concerned with Pelagianism or (more likely) with penitential discipline, it is significant that Deiniol was considered comparable to the other two Welsh bishops. Feast: 11 September.

E. G. Bowen, *The Settlements of the Celtic Saints in Wales* (1956); Baring-Gould and Fisher, ii. 325–31; T. F. Tout in *D.N.B.*, s.v. 'Daniel'.

DEL BUFALO, Gaspare (1786–1837), founder of the Missioners of the Precious

Blood, priest. Born in Rome the son of a chef, he was educated at the Collegio Romano and ordained priest in 1808. When Napoleon took Rome, Gaspare with most of the Roman clergy refused to renounce his allegiance to the Holy See and went into exile for five years. When he returned, he was faced with a decline in religion owing to the lack of priests and sacraments. He hoped to arrest this by preaching missions and founding a congregation devoted to this work. The pope gave him a church and palazzo in Giano for this work. Other foundations followed in towns with the worst reputations, six of which were in the kingdom of Naples.

His training of young clergy (begun in 1824) included the encouragement of devotion to Jesus and to Mary. But devotion was not enough: study of Scripture, theology, and foreign languages were also necessary. 'Missioners', he would say, 'must be ready for anything: like soldiers and sailors, they must never surrender.' Always on the move from one town to another, they preached missions which were often dramatic: Vincenzo *Strambi described them as a spiritual earthquake. The priests would take the discipline in public, they would burn firearms, obscene books, and anything else which they thought might offend Almighty God.

In Rome he founded charitable institutions for young and old, men and women. Here he died during the cholera epidemic; he is buried at S. Maria in Trivio. Miracles were reported during his life and after his death. He was canonized in 1954. Feast: 2 January.

Live by G. de Libero, *San Gaspare del Bufalo romano* (1954); B.T.A., i. 25–6; *Bibl. SS.*, vi. 40–3.

DENYS (Dennis, Dionis, Dionysius) (d. *c.*250), bishop of Paris, patron of France. According to *Gregory of Tours, Denys was born in Italy and sent to convert Gaul with five other bishops. He reached Paris, preached with great success, and established a Christian centre on an island in the Seine. His companions, Rusticus a priest and Eleutherius a deacon, were imprisoned and beheaded with him. Their bodies were recovered from the Seine; over their tomb was built the abbey of Saint Denis, later the burial-place of French kings. In the 9th century the cult received enormous impetus from the false identification, propagated by Hilduin, abbot of St. Denis, of this martyr with Pseudo-Denys the Areopagite, the influential Christian neo-Platonist of the 5th century. This writer claimed to be Dionysius the disciple of St. Paul, who came to the Christian faith after Paul's discourse at Athens on the 'Unknown God' (Acts 17: 13–34). This conflation of three individuals into one led to a revision of the Legend of Denys, which made *Clement of Rome responsible for sending him to France and anticipating the founding of Christianity in France to apostolic times. It also helped the cult of Denys, bishop of Paris, which resulted in England in the dedication of no fewer than forty-one ancient churches in his name. Four Benedictine abbeys kept his translation feast, including Wilton, where *Edith built a chapel in his honour decorated with murals of his martyrdom. Feast: 9 October; translation, 21 (22) April.

AA.SS. Oct. IV (1780), 865–987; S. McK. Crosby, *The Abbey of St.-Denis 475–1122*, i (1942), esp, pp. 24–52; P. Peeters, 'La Vision de Denys l'Aréopagite à Héliopolis', *Anal. Boll.*, xxix (1910), 301–22; R. J. Loenertz, 'La Légende parisienne de S. Denys l'Aréopagite', *Anal. Boll.*, lxix (1951), 217–37; R. Bossuat, 'Traditions populaires relatives au martyre et à la sépulture de Saint Denis', *Le Moyen-Âge*, lxii (1956), 479–509; E. Colledge and J. C. Marler, 'Céphalogie, a recurring theme in classical and medieval lore', *Traditio*, xxxvii (1981), 11–26 and 418–19.

DERFEL (often called Cadarn (i.e. mighty) or Gdarn) (d. 6th century), confessor. In early life he was a soldier and distinguished himself at the battle of Camlan (537). He was the founder and patron of Llanderfel (Gwynedd), where there was a famous wooden statue of him, mounted on a horse and holding a staff. In 1538 Dr. Ellis Price, Cromwell's agent for the diocese of St. Asaph, wrote to him for special instructions in its regard because 'the people have so much trust in him that they come daily on pilgrimage to him with cows or horses or money, to the number of five or six hundred on 5th April. The common saying was that whoever offered anything to this saint would be delivered out of hell by him.' Cromwell's instruction was to send the image to London; in spite of a £40 bribe by the local people this was done. On 22 May 1538 a Franciscan Observant friar from Greenwich, John Forest, confessor to Queen Catherine of Aragon, was burnt at Smithfield for denying Henry VIII's claim to be Supreme Head of the Church in England. A little before his execution a 'huge and great image' (Derfel's) was brought to the gallows. The Welsh 'had a prophecy that this image should set a whole forest afire; which prophecy now took effect, for he set this friar Forest on fire and consumed him to nothing'. Remains of Derfel's wooden horse and staff survive at Llanderfel. Late Welsh writers state that Derfel became a monk, and abbot at Bardsey. Feast: 5 April, as in early Welsh calendars.

T. Wright, *Three Chapters of Letters relating to the suppression of Monasteries* (*C.S.*, xxvi. 1843), p. 190; Baring-Gould and Fisher, ii. 33–6; E. Hall, *Chronicle* (ed. C. Whibley, 2 vols., 1904).

DERMOT (Diarmaid) (6th century), Irish abbot. Said to have been of royal blood and a native of Connacht, Dermot was the founder of the monastery on the island of Inchcleraun (Innis Clothran) in Lough Ree, and was associated with *Senan. Ruins of six churches survive on his island, which was both his burial place and a centre of pilgrimage. Feast: 10 January.

The Irish Saints, pp. 142–3.

DESLE, see DEICOLA (2).

DEUSDEDIT (Frithona), archbishop of Canterbury 655–64, was the first Anglo-Saxon to occupy the see. Few details are known about his life. He had some share in the foundation of the monastery of Medehamstede (Peterborough) in 657, he founded a nunnery in the isle of Thanet, and he consecrated Damian bishop of Rochester. He died of the plague on 14 July 664 on the same day as King Erconbert of Kent and was buried in the monastery church of SS. Peter and Paul (later St. Augustine's) Canterbury. His shrine remained until the Reformation. Feast: 14 July.

Bede, *H.E.*, iii. 20, 27; iv. 1–2; *A.S.C. s.a.* 655–657 ('E' version), 664; *N.L.A.*, i. 265–7; *AA.SS.* Iul. IV (1725), 48–50; P. Grosjean, 'La date du Colloque de Whitby', *Anal. Boll.*, lxxviii (1960), esp. 260–4.

DEVEREUX, see DYFRIG.

DEWI, see DAVID OF WALES.

DIARMAID, see DERMOT.

DICUILL (Dicul), see DEICOLA (1).

DINGAD (Digat), Welsh church-founder of the tribe of *Brychan, patron of Llandingat, i.e. Llandovery (Dyfed). Like other foundations of his tribe his churches are in S. Wales and seem to presuppose a westward migration along the Roman roads. The patron of Dingestow (Gwent) may be this Dingad or Dingad ab Nudd Hael, king of Bryn Buga. Feast: 1 November.

E. G. Bowen, *The Settlement of Celtic Saints in Wales* (1956), pp. 27–32; Baring-Gould and Fisher, ii. 343–4.

DINO, see DONATUS.

DIONIA, see DIUMA.

DIONIS (Dionysius), see DENYS.

DISIBOD (7th century), Irish bishop. Discouraged by apparent failure to reform his compatriots, he went to Germany 'in exile for Christ' and founded the monastery known later as Disibodenberg (Diessenberg or Mount St. Disibod), near Bingen. There he met with greater success and died peacefully. In 1170 a Life of Disibod was written by the visionary *Hildegard: although this was attributed to a revelation, the few 'facts' are simply the traditions then current. Virtually no details are known about him. Feast: 8 September, although he is not mentioned in either the early Irish or Roman martyrologies.

AA.SS. Iul. II (1721), 581–99, which prints Hildegard's Life; B.T.A., iii. 509.

DISMAS, the Good Thief (d. *c.*30). The words of Christ on the Cross to the good thief, crucified with him, 'Today thou shalt be with me in Paradise' (cf. Luke 23: 39–43) were traditionally regarded as meaning that his salvation was assured and he could therefore be invoked as a saint. Nothing is known about him: the very name Dismas comes from the Greek dysme (dying) in the Gospel of Nicodemus. An Arabic 'Gospel of the Infancy' embroiders the story further by positing that the Good Thief was identical with Titus, one of a band of robbers who waylaid the Holy Family during the Flight into Egypt, but subsequently released them. The words of Dismas, 'Lord, remember me when you come into your kingdom', are given prominent place in the Byzantine Mass. Dismas came to be regarded in the Middle Ages as the special patron of prisoners and thieves. He is commemorated in the Roman Martyrology on 25 March.

A. Bessières, *Le Bon Larron, Saint Dismas* (1937); art. 'Larrons' in *Dict. Bibl.*; B.T.A., i. 676–7.

DIUMA (Dimma) (d. 658), bishop of the Middle Angles and Mercians. Of Irish origin, Diuma was one of the four priests sent by *Finan, bishop of Lindisfarne, to evangelize Mercia after the baptism of Peada, son of Penda *c.*652. The others were *Cedd, Betti, and Adda, of whom nothing is known. Their apostolate in Mercia, according to *Bede, was most successful. When Penda died in 654, the Christian King Oswiu of Northumbria ruled Mercia for a few years; during this time Diuma was consecrated bishop by Finan over the peoples of the Mercians and Middle Angles. It seems that he worked mainly among the latter and died in a district called *Infeppingum*. The 11th-century Anglo-Saxon saints' list (*R.P.S*) says that he lies buried at Charlbury (Oxon.); the form of his name led to a belief that Dimma (Diuma) was a woman. Feast 7 December.

Bede, *H.E.*, ii. 21: *R.P.S.*

DOCCO, see CONGAR (1).

DOGMAEL (Dogfael, Dogwel) (d. early 6th century), Welsh monk. The place-names and dedications to this saint point clearly to Pembrokeshire (Dyfed) as his main area of influence, but there was also one parish in Anglesey dedicated to him. It is likely, but not certain, that he moved to Brittany where a St. Dogmeel or Toel has had a considerable cult, and is invoked to help children to learn to walk. Feast: 14 June.

Baring-Gould and Fisher, ii. 349–51; B.T.A., ii. 542–3.

DOMHNALL, see DONALD.

DOMINIC (*c.*1170–1221), founder of the Order of Friars Preachers or Black Friars. Born at Calaruega (Castile), Dominic Guzman was the youngest of four children of the warden of the town. He was educated by his uncle, the archpriest of Gumiel d'Izan, and later at Palencia. During this time he became an Austin canon of Osma cathedral. As a priest he led an outwardly uneventful life for seven years, devoted to prayer and penance. In 1201 he became prior of the community. In 1204, on his way to Denmark, Dominic first met Albigensian heretics at Toulouse, whose reconciliation to the Church was to be a principal element of his apostolate. For this work he trained religious women in communities who lived lives as austere and devoted as those of the *perfecti* of the Cathars. The first house was the nunnery at Prouille (founded 1206), near which was one for preachers who by persuasion, poverty, and learning would convert the Cathars and silently reprove the standards of the Cistercians sent to preach against them. In 1208 the murder of the papal

Legate, Peter of Castelnau, led to the declaration of a 'crusade' or holy war against the Albigensians. Dominic had no share in the violence and massacres then perpetrated, but used only the peaceful instruments of instruction and prayer. Three times he refused a bishopric, believing himself to be called to other work.

This was the foundation of the Friars Preachers, which occupied the last seven years of his life. Dominic's plan was to provide communitites which were centres of sacred learning, whose members would be devoted to study, teaching, and preaching as well as prayer. He retained the Divine Office, but it was chanted more simply and expeditiously than by monks. These members would be trained men whose contemplation would bear fruit in the communication of the word. They would be mobile and specially devoted to poverty, but in a less total and romantic way than the followers of *Francis of Assisi, whom Dominic knew and respected. Unlike Francis, he was an excellent organizer, and a pioneer in representative government. His Order was also the first formally to abandon manual labour. Papal approval was obtained for it, but only on condition that it should follow one of the already existing rules. Dominic chose the short and flexible rule of *Augustine, but was able to add detailed Constitutions to ensure its smooth day-to-day running. It rapidly spread all over Western Europe and became a pioneering missionary force in Asia and (much later) in the Americas.

Dominic spent the next few years (1216–20) in continual travels to Italy, Spain, and Paris. In 1220 the first General Chapter was held at Bologna; the following year Dominic died there after attempting a preaching tour in Hungary. At the time of his death there were five provinces: Spain, Provence, France, Lombardy, and Rome. In six other countries, including England, there were smaller groups of Dominican friars already at work. At Rome Dominic was given the old churches of S. Sisto for the nuns and S. Sabina for the Friars.

His preaching against the Albigensians seems to have met with only limited success, but the foundation of communities dedicated to sacred learning and sound teaching fulfilled an acutely felt need in the medieval church and subsequently the work of *Albert the Great and especially *Thomas Aquinas represented the fulfilment of Dominic's ideals.

Popular devotion to Dominic sprang up soon after his death and he was canonized in 1234. His tomb at Bologna, built thirty years later by Nicolas Pisano and embellished by Michelangelo among others, is a more sumptuous and less authentic memorial than the earliest portrait, an anonymous Sienese primitive, in the Fogg Art Museum of Harvard University. His usual attributes in art are a lily and a black and white dog, a pun (*Domini canis*) on the name of Dominic and the Dominicans, which holds a torch in his mouth as herald of the truth; there are also fine cycles of his life by Fra Angelico at Fiesole and Florence, based closely on the tomb-sculpture at Bologna. Later artists depicted him with a rosary, which devotion he was erroneously believed to have invented. Feast: first 6, then 4, now 8 August.

AA.SS. Aug. I (1733), 358–658; M. H. Laurent, *Monumenta Historica S.P.N. Dominici* [Monumenta Ordinis Fratrum Praedicatorum Historica xv] (1933–5); French tr. of primary documents by M. H. Vicaire, *Saint Dominique de Caleruega d'après les documents du XIIIe siècle* (1955); Eng. tr. of primary documents by E. C. Lehner, *Saint Dominic: Biographical Documents* (1964). Biographies by B. Jarrett (1924), P. Mandonnet (1937, Eng. tr. 1944); but earlier works are largely superseded by the work of M. H. Vicaire, *Histoire de Saint Dominique* (2 vols., 1957, Eng. tr. 1964). See also G. R. Galbraith, *The Constitution of the Dominican Order 1216–1360* (1925); W. A. Hinnebusch, *The History of the Dominican Order* (1966); G. Kaftal, *St. Dominic in early Tuscan painting* (1948).

DOMINIC OF SILOS (*c.*1000–73), abbot. Born at Cañas in Rioja (Navarre) of a free peasant family, he worked on the family farm for some years before becoming a monk at S. Millan de la Congolla. Ordained priest, he became novice-master and then prior. After a dispute over property rights with Garcia III of Navarre, he was exiled with two companions. But Ferdinand I of Old Castile welcomed these monastic refugees and in 1041 gave them the monastery of St. *Sebastian at Silos (near Burgos), which was then in a critical state. Most of its buildings were in ruins and it had but six monks. Dominic was chosen as abbot and rescued it. Inspired by Cluniac ideals, he rebuilt the church, planned the cloisters, and established a notable scriptorium, one of whose products was the magnificent Apocalypse now in the British Library. The fame of Dominic's holiness and learning soon spread: numerous miracles were attributed to him in life and after death, including healings of all kinds and the liberation of captives from the Moors. At his death the monastery numbered over forty monks: its resources included a flourishing gold and silver workshop, which made possible extensive charity to the local community. Three years after his death, Dominic's body was translated into the church, this being the equivalent of local canonization. Churches and monasteries were dedicated to him from 1085 onwards.

Dominic's caring and curing powers were traditionally associated with pregnancy. Jane of Aza, the mother of the Dominicans' founder, gave him Dominic's name after a fruitful pilgrimage to his shrine some months before his birth. Dominic's pastoral staff was used to bless queens of Spain and it remained by their bedside until they had a safe delivery. Silos was revived as a monastery by Solesmes in the 19th century and flourishes today: its fine double Romanesque cloisters and extensive library are specially notable.

Feast: 20 December; translation, 5 January.

Three ancient Lives in S. de Vergara, *Vita y milagros del . . . santo Domingo Manso* (1763); M. Ferotin, *Histoire de l'Abbaye de Silos* (1897); Life by A. Ruiz (1950); *D.H.G.E.*, xiv. 623–7; B.T.A., iv. 588–9; *Bibl. SS.*, iv. 736–7.

DOMINIC SAVIO, see SAVIO.

DOMNEVA, see ERMENBURGA.

DONALD (Domhnall) (d. early 8th century). He was a Scot who lived at Ogilvy (Forfarshire), married, and had nine daughters, with whom, after his wife's death, he led a religious life. After his death they moved to Abernethy. They are generally known as the Nine Maidens, a name often applied also to natural features in the areas such as hills and wells. Feast: 15 July.

K.S.S., pp. 324–5, 395–6.

DONAN (Donnan) **AND COMPANIONS** (d. 618), monks and martyrs. An Irish monk of Iona under *Columba, Donan founded a monastery at Eigg (Inner Hebrides). While the monks were celebrating Mass on Easter night, a gang of robbers (possibly Vikings) arrived on the island, herded the monks into the refectory, and set fire to it. Those who tried to escape were killed by the sword. One story placed responsibility on a woman who had lost her pasture rights on the island and instigated the attack to recover them. The Martyrology of Tallacht says that his companions numbered fifty-two. At least eleven Scottish churches bear his name, among them St. Donan's (Uig), Kildonnan (S. Uist). Kildonan (Sutherland, Arran, and Eigg). Feast: 17 April.

AA.SS. Apr. II (1675), 483–5; *K.S.S.*, p. 325; P. Grosjean, 'Notes d'hagiographie celtique', *Anal. Boll.*, lxiii (1945), 119–22; A. B. Scott, 'St. Donnan the Great', *Trans. Scottish Ecclesiol. Soc.*, i (1906), 256–67; see also *Scottish Notes and Queries* (1935), 161–5, 177–80; *Annals of Ulster* (ed. W. M. Hennessy and B. MacCarthy, 1887–1901), *s.a.* 618.

DONATUS (Donat, Dino) (d. 876), Irish monk, bishop of Fiesole. He left his Irish homeland, went on pilgrimage to Rome, and on his way back happened to arrive at Fiesole when a new bishop was being chosen: as soon as he entered the cathedral the bells rang, the lamps were lit, and he was acclaimed (*c.*829). He served under Lotharius and Louis the Pious, which meant among other duties leading his troops against the Saracens, and obtained the right to hold his own court and levy taxes. He was also a scholar and teacher: his works include a Life of *Brigid, a poem in praise of Ireland, and his own epitaph. He founded a hospice for Irish pilgrims dedicated to St. Brigid, and took part in the Roman Council of 861. He died and was buried at Fiesole: his relics were translated to the present cathedral in 1817. Feast: 22 October.

AA.SS. Oct. IX (1858), 648–62 and *Propylaeum*, p. 470; L. Traube, *M.G.H.*, *Poet. lat. aevi carol.*, iii. 692; *The Irish Saints*, pp. 143–6.

DONWEN (Donwenna), see DWYN.

DOROTHEUS, see GORGONIUS, PETER, AND DOROTHEUS.

DOROTHY (Dorothea) (d. *c.*313), virgin martyr. The early martyrologies place her death at Caesarea in Cappadocia during the persecution of Diocletian. There are no historical details of her life; her surviving Acts are legendary but influential. They tell of a young lawyer called Theophilus who jeered at her on her way to execution for refusing to marry or to worship idols. He asked her to send him fruits from the garden (of paradise) where she was going. She agreed to do so and prayed just before her execution. An angel then appeared and gave Theophilus a basket containing three apples and three roses. He was converted and was martyred, also under Diocletian. Her popularity is Western rather than Eastern, centred in Italy and Germany. In England she seems to have been less prominent than some of the other legendary virgin-martyrs, but she does figure in stained glass and in screen-paintings especially of the 15th century. Her legend was known in Anglo-Saxon England to *Aldhelm; in later centuries it inspired *The Virgin Martyr*, a tragedy by John Massinger and Thomas Dekker (1622), as well as poems by Swinburne and G. M. Hopkins. Dorothy's body is believed to rest at the church in Rome dedicated to her. Her usual attribute in art is a basket of heavenly fruit and flowers. Feast: formerly 6 February.

AA.SS. Feb. I (1658), 772–6 and *Propylaeum*, p. 51; *O.D.C.C.*, s.v.; see also G. Keller, *Sieben Legenden* (1872), pp. 123–35; C. Woodforde, *Stained Glass in Somerset, 1250–1830* (1946).

DOTHOW, see DUTHAC.

DRITHELM (Drythelm) (d. *c.*700), monk of Melrose. When Drithelm was a married layman living at Cunningham (now Ayrshire, then in Northumbria), he fell ill and apparently died, but was revived a few hours afterwards. The mourners fled in terror, but he went to pray in the village church until daylight. He then divided all his wealth into three, giving one third to his wife, another third to his sons, and the remainder to the poor. The reason for his change of life was a vision of the next life he had seen. Accompanied by a celestial guide, he had been shown souls in torment in hell (the pains were of alternating extreme heat and extreme cold), others in purgatory, others in paradise, and lastly a glimpse of heaven which he was not allowed to enter. For the rest of his life Drithelm lived as a monk at Melrose and would often stand in the cold waters of the Tweed reciting psalms, even when there was ice in the river. Those to whom he told his story included Aldfrith, king of Northumbria, *Ethilwald, bishop of Lindisfarne, and an Irish monk called Haemgisl. Alcuin mentions Drithelm in his poem on the saints of York; Challoner includes him in his *Memorial of British Piety*, but no trace has been found of a formal cult. *Bede's detailed account of him is the only source of authentic information; his assurance of the quality of Drithelm's life and death is the reason why his name is found in Lives of the Saints. His Vision was the first example of this kind of literature from England: it certainly contributed considerably to the popularity both here and on the Continent of Bede's History. Drithelm can be considered a remote precursor of Dante: it is significant that so full a statement of the variety of life beyond the grave can be found in Anglo-Saxon England of the late 7th century. Feast: 1 September.

Bede, *H.E.*, v. 21 (with commentary in Plummer's edn. ii. 294–8); Homily by Ælfric (ed. B. Thorpe, ii (1846), 348–56); S. J. Seymour, *Irish Visions of the Other World* (1930), pp. 154–6.

DROSTAN (d. early 7th century), abbot and founder of the monastery of Deer (Aberdeenshire). This became an important centre for the foundation of churches on both sides of the Moray Firth. Being in a distant part of hostile Pictland, it is most unlikely that it was ever founded, as is sometimes claimed, by *Columba. There are several dedications to Drostan in NE. Scotland. Feast: 11 July. The old church at Aberdour claimed his relics, and St. Drostan's Well is near by.

AA.SS. Iul. III (1723), 198–200; W. D. Simpson, *The Historical St. Columba* (3rd edn., 1963), pp. 48–53; A. B. Scott, 'St. Drostan', *Trans. Gaelic Soc. Inverness*, xxvii (1908–11), 110–25.

DRYTHELM, see DRITHELM.

DUBRICIUS, see DYFRIG.

DUBTACH, see DUTHAC.

DUCHESNE, Philippine (1769–1852), nun of the Society of the Sacred Heart and missionary. Born at Grenoble of a merchant family, she was educated by the Visitation nuns there. In 1786 she wished to join this community, but her father refused his consent to her profession owing to the political situation. In 1791 the Visitation nuns, like others, were expelled; during the Revolution Philippine rejoined her family and devoted herself to good works. In 1802 she bought the convent buildings and tried to revive the religious life there, but this failed. She offered herself and the buildings to Madeleine Sophie *Barat, the foundress of the Society of the Sacred Heart. Philippine and four companions were professed in 1805. She wished to be a missionary in America. This idea was accepted in principle, but it was fulfilled only in 1818 when the bishop of Louisiana initiated a foundation.

Philippine and four other nuns sailed to New Orleans and travelled up the Mississippi to St. Louis (Missouri), to the west of which they established a free school in pioneering conditions. They moved into a brick building at Florissant, received the first American postulants in 1820, made another foundation in 1821, and two more in 1826: these were all in the Mississippi valley. Such progress was however modified by other events. Slander and misrepresentation, ill-health and intrigues, one school reduced to five pupils, all contributed to the increasing strain born by Philippine. Never perhaps entirely sympathetic to the North Americans, she resigned her office in 1840 at a visitation. Now aged seventy-one, she agreed to set up a school for the Indians at Sugar Creek (Kansas). The conditions however were too severe for one of her age and she could not speak their language. She retired to Saint Charles (Missouri), the place of their first log-cabin school, living in conditions of extreme personal poverty for another ten years. These years of suffering and prayer, during two of which her letters to Mother Barat were never delivered, may well have been the most difficult of all in the life of this courageous pioneer. She died at the age of eighty-three on 18 November. She was beatified in 1940 and canonized in 1988. Feast: 17 November.

Lives by M. Baumard (Eng. tr. 1879), M. Erskine (1926); M. Symon (1926); see also L. Callan, *The Society of the Sacred Heart in America* (1937), and M. K. Richardson, *Redskin Trail* (1952); B.T.A., iv. 378–81; *Bibl. SS.*, iv. 847.

DUNCHAD (d. 716), abbot of Iona. He was of the family of Conall Gulban, and became a monk and abbot at Killochuir (SE. Ulster), and later at Iona. Under his rule, by the persuasion of Egbert, Iona at last adopted the Roman calculation of Easter. For *Bede this was the final sign of unity from diversity which was the main theme of his History. Dunchad died on 24 March, his usual feast, but in Donegal it was on 25 May. He was the patron of sailors in Ireland.

Bede, *H.E.*, v. 22; J. Colgan, *Acta Sanctorum Hiberniae*, i (1645), p. 745; *K.S.S.*, p. 328.

DUNSTAN (909–88). Benedictine monk and reformer, archbishop of Canterbury.

Born at Baltonsborough, near Glastonbury, of a noble family with royal connections, he was educated at Glastonbury, joined the household of his uncle Athelm, archbishop of Canterbury, and then the court of King Athelstan. In 935, accused of 'studying the vain poems and futile stories of the pagans and of being a magician', he was expelled from court. He now nearly got married, but instead made private monastic vows and was ordained priest by Elphege, bishop of Winchester, on the same day as his friend *Ethelwold. He then returned to Glastonbury, living as a hermit and practising the crafts of painting, embroidery, and metalwork. In 939 Edmund became king of Wessex, recalled Dunstan to court, and after a narrow escape from death while hunting near Cheddar Gorge, installed him as abbot of Glastonbury, endowing the monastery generously. The Danish invasions and the hostility of the local magnates had previously extinguished monastic life in England. This restoration, under the Rule of St. Benedict, was to be one of Dunstan's principal achievements: it began in 940; from that date until 1539 Benedictine life in England continued without interruption. Dunstan attracted disciples, enlarged the buidings, and gave new life to an establishment of great antiquity.

Under King Edred (946–55) Dunstan was entrusted with part of the royal treasure, which he kept at Glastonbury, and was left £200 in the king's will for the people of Somerset and Devon. Edred, like Edmund, was buried at Glastonbury. With the accession of Edwy in 955 Dunstan's fortunes changed again. His enemies at court contrived his exile: he went to Mont Blandin (Ghent) and there saw for the first time a monastery of the reformed continental type, of which he had heard at Athelstan's court. He was recalled by King Edgar, who made him in 957 bishop of Worcester, in 959 bishop of London, and in 960 archbishop of Canterbury. Thus began the fruitful collaboration between king and archbishop which reformed the Church in England largely through the monastic Order, and was regarded after the Conquest as a 'golden age'. Dunstan was personally responsible for the reform of Glastonbury, Malmesbury, Bath, Athelney, Muchelney, and Westminster; his friends Ethelwold and *Oswald were made bishops; and the promulgation of the *Regularis Concordia* in *c.*970 marked the success of the movement he had started at Glastonbury years before. Important features of this monasticism were its close dependence on the royal power for protection, not least against the local lay lords, its liturgical additions, including prayers for the royal family, and its insistence on the importance of the scriptorium and the workshops.

Dunstan's influence spread far wider than the monastic Order. He was a zealous diocesan bishop; he insisted on the observance of marriage laws and on fasting; he built and repaired churches and often acted as judge; he also inspired some of Edgar's laws, especially the codes of Wihtbordecctan and of Andover. The former contains a passage in which the archbishop and the king together command the payment of tithes. The laws of Andover command Peter-pence and other church taxes to be paid with heavy fines for neglecting them, and enjoin the practice of some handicraft on every priest. Dunstan had a considerable personal influence on Edgar, deferred his coronation for fourteen years (possibly for scandalous conduct, see WULFHILDA) and modified the coronation rite, some of which survives to the present day.

On Edgar's death his elder son *Edward, Dunstan's protégé, succeeded to the throne. His assassination in 978 was connected with the anti-monastic reaction which followed Edgar's death. Dunstan presided at the translation of Edward's body to Shaftesbury in 980. During Ethelred's reign Dunstan's name still appeared on charters, but with increasing age he spent more of his time at Canterbury with the monks in his household, occupied with teaching, correcting manuscripts, and administering justice. Both now and earlier, visions, prophecies, and miracles were attributed to him; he was also specially devoted to the Canterbury saints, whose tombs he would visit at night. Dunstan remained active until his death: he preached three times on Ascension Day 988; two days later, on 19 May, he died, aged nearly eighty. It has been well said that the 10th century gave shape to English history, and Dunstan gave shape to the 10th century.

After his death his cult sprang up spontaneously and increased rapidly. Already before 999 Ethelred's confirmation of Æthelric's will, drawn up by a monk of Canterbury, recognized him as the 'chief of all the saints who rest at Christ Church'. His feast appears in several pre-Conquest calendars. During Lanfranc's pontificate, however, he was in eclipse: in the *Monastic Constitutions* there is no mention of Dunstan's feast even in the third rank, whereas *Gregory and *Alphege are in the second. But under Anselm's rule his cult increased: his feast was celebrated with an octave; the altars of Dunstan and Alphege stood on either side of the high altar, on a beam over it the figure of Christ in majesty was flanked by statues of these two saints. By then his cult had become nationwide. Canterbury possessed his body, though Glastonbury too claimed it: the controversy was only finally settled when the Canterbury tomb was opened in 1508.

Hagiographical tradition made Dunstan a painter, musician, and metalworker; these claims have some foundation. Bells and organs were attributed to him. Some metalworker's tools of the 10th century survive at Mayfield convent (East Sussex) and are claimed to be his. Artists sometimes depicted him holding the devil by the nose with a pair of tongs. The most interesting surviving relic of him is MS. Auct. F. IV. 32 in the Bodleian Library, Oxford. This Glastonbury book contains scriptural extracts in Latin and Greek, an Anglo-Saxon homily on the Cross, and some extremely ancient Welsh glosses, besides a portrait of Dunstan prostrate at the feet of Christ. This could well be Dunstan's own work, as a 13th-century inscription claims. Two other MSS. at Oxford probably once belonged to him. The tradition which attributes to him *Kyrie rex splendens* (Kyrie VII in Vatican Gradual) is a later development of a statement of his first biographer, and must be considered doubtful. None of the literary works attributed to him are genuine: a Penitential, a commentary on St. Benedict's Rule, a treatise on alchemy called *On the philosopher's stone*. But contemporary letters, such as *Abbo of Fleury's, are witness to the esteem in which he was held.

Goldsmiths, jewellers, and locksmiths claim him as their special patron. Feast: 19 May; ordination feast at Canterbury, 21 October.

The ancient Lives are in W. Stubbs, *Memorials of St. Dunstan* (*R.S.*, 1874), which also contains letters and documents on the saint and his cult. See also *G.R.*, nos. 141–64; *G.P.*, nos. 17–19 and 91: D. Whitelock (ed.), *E.H.D.*, i (1968), 43–51, 94–100, 200–12, etc.; T. Symons, *The Regularis Concordia* (1953). For his portrait see F. Wormald, *English Drawings of the Tenth and Eleventh Centuries* (1952) and M. T. D'Alverny, 'Le symbolisme de la Sagesse et le Christ de Saint Dunstan', *Bodleian Library Record*, v (1956), 232–44; R. W. Hunt, *St. Dunstan's Classbook from Glastonbury* (1963). For a general picture see J. A. Robinson, *The Times of St. Dunstan* (1923); E. S. Duckett, *St. Dunstan of Canterbury* (1955); *M.O.*, pp. 31–82, 695–701 and D. Parsons (ed.), *Tenth-Century Studies* (1975). Cf. also E. John, 'The beginning of the Benedictine Reform in England', *R.B.*, lxxiii (1963), 73–87 and *Orbis Britanniae* (1966), pp. 154–264; for his cult, R. W. Southern, *St. Anselm and his Biographer* (1963), pp. 250–2; and (with reservations) A. Gasquet and E. Bishop, *On The Bosworth Psalter* (1908); M. Korhammer, 'The Origin of the Bosworth Psalter', *Anglo-Saxon England*, ii (1973), 173–88.

DUNWEN, see DWYN.

DUTHAC (Dothow, Dubtach) (d. 1065), bishop. Of Scottish origin, Duthac studied for some years in Ireland; on his return he was consecrated bishop. He worked mainly in Ross. He died on 8 March and was buried at Tayne. After seven years his body was found to be incorrupt and was translated to a more splendid shrine. William Worcestre describes him as 'the saint reckoned to be most venerated in the land of Ross'. Some of his miracle stories are picturesque. A guest at a party, who drank too much and had a headache, sent some pork to Duthac asking to be cured. His disciple left it on a grave with a gold ring while he prayed. A kite stole them both, but Duthac conjured back the kite, returned the ring, but let the kite eat the pork. There are dedications at Arbroath, Kilduich, and Kilduthie; his shrine was visited by King James IV and many others. Feast: 8 March.

William Worcestre, p. 7; *K.S.S.*, pp. 328–9; B.T.A., i. 526.

DWYN (Donwen, Donwenna, Dunwen, Dwynwen) (5th–6th century), virgin. One of the children of *Brychan, Dwyn settled in Anglesey, where her name is retained in Llanddwyn and Porthddwyn. Her church was the goal of the sick and especially young men and maidens, as she is the Welsh patron of lovers. The Legend explaining this tells of a certain Maelon who wished to marry her, but she rejected him and prayed to be delivered. She dreamt that she was given a drink which cured her, but the drink turned Maelon to ice. Then she made three requests: that Maelon be unfrozen, that all true-hearted lovers should either succeed in their quest or else be cured of their passion, and that she should never wish to be married. Accordingly she became a nun. In the Middle Ages Llanddwyn was one of the richest prebends in Wales, largely due to the offerings at the shrine and at the holy well, where the movements of fishes were believed to indicate the destiny of those who consulted it. This practice and the invocation of Dwyn for curing sick animals long survived the Reformation: the remote situation of Llanddwyn, perhaps formerly an island, near Newborough, enabled the popular superstitions to survive. Feast: 25 January.

Baring-Gould and Fisher, ii. 387–92; William Worcestre, p. 66.

DYFRIG (Dubricius, Devereux) (d. *c.*550), monk and bishop who worked mainly in the Hereford–Gwent area. He was one of the earliest and most important of the saints of South Wales, but there is very little early and authentic information about him. Madley (near Hereford) is claimed as his birthplace, and his earliest foundation was at Ariconium (= Archenfield, Hereford); he was also reputed to own land at Caerleon. These facts point to his close connection with Romano-British Christianity. Other places associated with him, either because he founded monasteries there or because the churches are dedicated to him, include Hentland, Whitchurch, Madley, and Moccas, in the Wye valley.

The 7th-century Life of *Samson testifies to his importance and to his activity far outside his principal sphere of influence. He is called bishop, even *papa* by some MSS. of this Life, which also attributed to him the ordination of Samson, his appointment as abbot (of Caldey?) and his consecration as bishop. At Caldey survives an ancient uncompleted inscription *Magl Dubr* (the tonsured servant of Dubricius). A church dedication to Dyfrig at Gwenddwr (Powys), and another at Porlock (Somerset) suggests that he or his disciples were active in the expansion of Christianity to the West and the South-West, possibly in association with the children of *Brychan. Dyfrig retired to Bardsey Island in old age and died there.

Later tradition, represented by the *Book of LlanDav* and the Life by Benedict of Gloucester, claimed that he was a disciple of *Germanus of Auxerre and that he conceded to *David at the Synod of Brevi the 'metropolitan' status of archbishop of Wales. This is, of course, anachronistic, and the claims that he owned extensive properties claimed as part of the territory of the 12th-century bishops of Llandaff are also highly suspect. But the translation of Dyfrig's relics there in 1120 gave the cult new life.

The unreliable Geoffrey of Monmouth said that he crowned Arthur 'King of

Britain' while Tennyson made him 'high saint' in his *Coming of Arthur*. Feast: 14 November.

N.L.A., i. 267–71; W. Davies, *The Llandaff Charters* (1979); H. Wharton, *Anglia Sacra* (1691), ii. 654 *et seq.*; Baring-Gould and Fisher, ii. 359–82; G. H. Doble, *Lives of the Welsh Saints* (1971); E. G. Bowen, *The Settlements of the Celtic Saints in Wales* (1954), pp. 33–48; S. M. Harris, 'Liturgical Commemorations of Welsh Saints: "St. Dyfryg" ' in *Faith in Wales*, xix. 4.

DYMPNA (7th century (?)), martyr. Her cult is an excellent example of the relics and shrine of considerable antiquity of a saint, under whose patronage admirable work for the unfortunate has been and still is accomplished. But this is linked with an almost complete dearth of historical knowledge. The Legend of Dympna seems almost pure folklore. According to this source she was the daughter of a Celtic or British king; her mother died when she was a child; when she grew up she looked extremely like her mother; her father fell in love with her, and to escape his incestuous intentions she fled with her confessor St. Gerebernus to Antwerp and then to Gheel (twenty-five miles away). Her father pursued them, tracing them by coins they had used, and found them living as solitaries. When they refused to return, the attendants killed the priest and the king killed his daughter. Both bodies were buried on the spot: they were translated in the 13th century, an event marked by numerous cures of epileptics and lunatics. This was the reason why she became patroness of the insane. From then onwards the town of Gheel has had a splendid record in the care of the mentally ill; in modern times it has been among the pioneers of their residence and supervision in the homes of farmers and other local residents. Feast: 15 May.

AA.SS. Maii III (1680), 477–97; H. Delehaye, *The Legends of the Saints* (1962), pp. 8, 77, 124; B.T.A., ii. 320–1.

E

EADBERT (Eadbeorht), see EDBERT.

EADBURH, see EDBURGA.

EADFRITH, see EDFRITH.

EADGYTH (Eadida), see EDITH.

EADMUND, see EDMUND.

EADNODUS, see ETHELNOTH.

EADWOLD, see EDWOLD.

EANFLAED, see ENFLEDA.

EANNA, see ENDA.

EANSWYTH (Eanswida, Eanswitha) (d. *c.*640), virgin. The daughter of Edbald, king of Kent and the granddaughter of *Ethelbert, Eanswyth refused to marry a Northumbrian prince; instead she founded a nunnery at Folkestone, which she entered and where she died at an early age. It seems likely that she was trained in France and that hers was the first nunnery in England. This was destroyed in Viking raids and the church, but not the convent, was restored by King Athelstan. In 1095 a monastery of Black Benedictine monks was founded on the same site, but the cliff became unsafe and eventually fell into the sea. A new church was built for them in the early 12th century, which is substantially the present parish church of SS. Mary and Eanswythe. Here, according to *N.L.A.* and *C.S.P.*, was the shrine of the saint. In 1885 a Saxon coffer was found in the north wall containing the bones of a young woman. It was assumed that these were the bones of Eanswyth, although there is no certain record of a genuine translation. Feast (in two 13th-century calendars and several medieval martyrologies): 31 August (St. Augustine's, Canterbury and Durham) or 12 September. Eanswyth is depicted on the seals of Folkestone.

Stanton, pp. 429–32; B.T.A., iii. 545–6; A. Cockayne, *Leechdoms* (*R.S.*), iii. 422: *N.L.A.*, i. 296–9.

EARCONWALD, see ERKENWALD.

EATA (d. 686), bishop of Hexham. He was one of the twelve English boys educated by *Aidan at Lindisfarne. He became a monk, and eventually abbot, at Melrose; one of the monks he trained there was *Cuthbert, who arrived in 651. Several years later, Alcfrith, sub-king of Deira, gave Eata lands at Ripon for a monastery. Eata, Cuthbert, and others went there to make a start, but returned in 661 rather than accept the Roman calculation of Easter. But after the Synod of Whitby (663/4), both accepted it: Eata, at the request of *Colman, became abbot of Lindisfarne, with Cuthbert as his prior.

When *Theodore of Canterbury divided the vast diocese of Northumbria in 678, Eata became bishop of Bernicia, its northern half. Three years later this too was divided into the dioceses of Hexham and Lindisfarne; Eata ruled Lindisfarne from 681 to 685. In this year Theodore deposed Tunbert, bishop of Hexham, apparently for disobedience; Cuthbert was chosen to succeed him, but by mutual agreement Eata returned to Hexham, while Cuthbert became bishop of Lindisfarne.

Eata died of dysentery only a year later. Like Aidan, he was a man of peace and simplicity; his acceptance of the Roman Easter, together with the other decisions of the Synod of Whitby and of Theodore's councils, contributed considerably to the unity of the Church in Northumbria. He was buried to the south of *Wilfrid's church at Hexham; a chapel was later built over his tomb. In the 11th century his body was translated inside the church. In 1113 Thomas II, archbishop of York, disappointed that his town had no shrine of a local saint, tried unsuccessfully to obtain Eata's relics for York. He was discouraged effectively, Eata's late biographer tells us, because the saint appeared to him in a dream and vigorously belaboured him with his pastoral staff.

The church of Atcham (Salop) is dedicated to Eata. Feast: 26 October.

Bede, *H.E.*, iii. 26; iv. 12, 25–6; v. 2, 9; J. Raine (ed.), *Miscellanea Biographica* (S.S., 1838); *N.L.A.*, i. 300–2; B. Colgrave (ed.), *Two Lives of St. Cuthbert* (1940).

EBBE (Æbbe, Ebba) (d. 683), first abbess of Coldingham (Berwickshire). Daughter of Ethelfrith, king of Northumbria, she fled to Scotland on his death in 616, when *Edwin conquered Northumbria. Later she became a nun at Coldingham and subsequently abbess of this double monastery. In 672 *Etheldreda was separated from her husband, King Egfrith, with the counsel of *Wilfrid, and became a nun under Ebbe (who was her aunt) before founding her own monastery at Ely. In 681 Egfrith visited Coldingham with his second wife Ermenburga, who was then seized with some kind of sudden illness. Ebbe, now famous for wisdom, interpreted this as a punishment for the imprisonment of Wilfrid, disobedience to Roman decisions in his favour, and the theft of his relics and reliquaries by Ermenburga. Egfrith released Wilfrid; Ermenburga restored the relics and soon recovered.

Not long afterwards, the aged Ebbe was warned by the priest Adomnan of the relaxed state of her community. The nuns were said to spend their time weaving fine clothes, to adorn themselves like brides or to attract the attention of strange men; while both monks and nuns alike neglected vigils and prayers. In spite of Adomnan's threat of divine punishment, the community mended its ways only for a little while. A few years after Ebbe's death, the monastery was burnt down (686). These failures of Ebbe's community did not destroy her reputation for holiness. Her name was given to Ebchester and to St. Abb's Head, where the remains of a fort possibly indicate the site of her monastery. Interest revived in her during the 12th century, following the discovery of her relics in the late 11th. At this time, according to an account attributed to Reginald of Durham, she was known from York to Lanark. Calendar evidence for her feast comes from Durham, Aberdeen, and Winchcombe, while Durham and Coldingham shared her relics. She is also the titular of a church and street in Oxford. The present church at Coldingham (part of the priory founded by Durham) is more than a mile away from Ebbe's monastery.

Feast: 25 August; translation, 2 November.

Bede, *H.E.*, iv. 19, 25; B. Colgrave (ed.), *Two Lives of St. Cuthbert* (1940), pp. 79–80, 189–90, 318; id., *Eddius' Life of St. Wilfrid* (1927), p. 79; *N.L.A.*, i. 303–7 (abridged from the Life in Bodleian Library, MS. Fairfax 6, attributed to Reginald of Durham); *E.B.K. after 1100*, pp. 161–6.

EBBE THE YOUNGER, according to Matthew Paris, perhaps using an older, lost source from Tynemouth, was martyred with her community at Coldingham by the Vikings in 870. The Viking invaders, with a record of massacre and rape, arrived at the monastery shortly after Ebbe had warned her community. Her method of preserving her virtue, imitated by her community, was to cut open her nose and lips with a razor. The raiders were so disgusted by the spectacle that they kept their distance, but returned soon afterwards and burnt the monastery with all its inhabitants. There is no surviving record of this Ebbe older than Matthew Paris, and no ancient cult, but there was a shrine in the 13th century and a curious feast of a dedication of the altar of St. Ebbe on 22 June in a Coldingham manuscript may refer to this Ebbe or to her namesake.

Matthew Paris, *Chronica Majora* (ed. H. R. Luard, *R.S.*, 1872), i. 391–2. *C.S.P.; N.L.A.*, i. 307–8. *E.B.K. after 1100*, i. 161–79.

EBRULF, see Evroul(t).

ECGWINE, see Egwin.

ECHA OF CRAYKE (North Yorkshire) (d. 767). He was a hermit renowned for his holiness and gift of prophecy. Feast: 5 May.

Symeon of Durham, ii (S.S.), 22; J. Raine, *Historians of the Church of York* (*R.S.*), i. 390.

EDBERT (Eadbert, Eadbeorht), bishop of Lindisfarne 688–98. All that we know of him comes from *Bede, who described him as a priest of great biblical learning, famous also for his generosity: he used to give to the poor each year a tenth of his livestock, grain, fruit, and clothing. While bishop of Lindisfarne he roofed with lead the wooden church built by *Finan of Lindisfarne. Each year, like his predecessor *Cuthbert, he retired for Lent to St. Cuthbert's Isle, off Lindisfarne. During Lent in 698 some monks, whom he had authorized to inspect Cuthbert's body, reported to him there that it was incorrupt and brought him some of the clothes in which the body was wrapped. He told them to make a new shrine for Cuthbert and decided to be buried himself in the tomb just vacated. Soon after, he was struck down with a mortal illness and died on 5 May. The miracles which took place at his tomb led to his being considered a saint at Lindisfarne; after 875 his relics were carried with those of Cuthbert through Northumbria. Feast: 6 May (in Old English and Roman Martyrology), but there seems no Durham evidence for an individual feast. See EDFRITH.

Bede, *H.E.*, iii. 25; iv. 27–8; *AA.SS.* Maii II (1680), 107–8.

EDBURGA (Eadburh) **OF BICESTER** (or Aylesbury) (d. *c.*650). Claimed to be a daughter of Penda, king of Mercia (although her name is absent from the usual lists), this Edburga, who helped to train *Osith in the religious life, was a nun and perhaps abbess of Aylesbury, although the Legend states that she lived at Adderbury (Oxon.), some thirty miles away, a place-name which means 'Eadburg's burh'. Edburga's relics were translated to Bicester (Oxon.), a house of Austin Canons founded in 1182, which was dedicated to Our Lady and St. Edburga. The splendid base of the shrine, made in 1320, survives in the church of Stanton Harcourt (Oxon.). Feast: 18 July, which by an unfortunate coincidence is also the translation feast of Edburga of Winchester. Edburga of Bicester also appears in litanies and, possibly in the *Liber Vitae* of Durham.

Stanton, pp. 346–7, 662 (confused); C. Hohler, 'St. Osyth and Aylesbury', *Records of Bucks*, xviii, part 1 (1966), 61–72; E. A. G. Lamborn, 'The Shrine of St. Edburg', *Reports of Oxford Archaeol. Soc.*, lxxx (1934), 43–52. J. Leland, *Itinerary*, v. 167–72.

EDBURGA (Eadburh, Bugga) **OF MINSTER** (d. 751), abbess. She was a disciple of *Mildred, of whose nunnery of Minster-in-Thanet she became abbess in 716. Most of what we know of her comes from the Letters of *Boniface. To her he addressed the famous account of the monk of Much Wenlock's vision of the afterworld. He also asked her, as she was a skilled scribe, for a copy of the Acts of the Martyrs and later for the Epistles of St. Peter, written in letters of gold. Her gifts to him included fifty pieces of gold and a carpet, examples of munificence which accord well with the claim that she was a princess of Wessex (although some mistakenly claimed her for the royal house of Kent). At Minster she built a church where she translated the relics of Mildred; she also built a monastery there for her nuns. Her church was consecrated by Cuthbert, archbishop of Canterbury 741–58. *Lull, the helper and successor of Boniface, sent her a present of a silver stylus and some spices. Edburga was buried at Minster, where cures were claimed at her tomb. Lanfranc's hospital of St. Gregory, Canterbury, was endowed with relics of both Mildred and Edburga, but rival shrines of both these saints were maintained. Feast: 13 December (at Christ Church, Canterbury), later 12 December (12 November at St. Gregory's Canterbury, according to *C.S.P.*).

M. Tangl (ed.), *Die Briefe des Heiligen Bonifatius and Lullus* (*M.G.H.*, 1916), nos. 29, 30, 35, 65; O. Cockayne, *Leechdoms etc.* (*R.S.*), iii. 422–33;

N.L.A., i. 308–11; K. Sisam, 'An Old English translation of a letter from Wynfrith to Eadburga', *Modern Language Review*, xviii (1923), 253–72, which concerns the vision of the monk of Wenlock.

EDBURGA OF REPTON (*c.*700). She is mentioned by *R.P.S.* as 'resting at Southwell-on-Trent' and should probably be identified with Edburga, abbess of Repton, who occurs in Felix's Life of *Guthlac. There appears to be no record of an ancient feast.

B. Colgrave (ed.), *Felix's Life of Guthlac* (1956); *R.P.S.*

EDBURGA (Eadburh) **OF WINCHESTER** (d. 960). She was a daughter of Edward the Elder, king of Wessex (900–25), and his third wife Eadgifu. She was educated in the abbey of St. Mary at Winchester (also called Nunnaminster), founded by her father. She remained there as a nun, distinguished for gentleness and humility, but never became abbess. She died young, aged forty or less. There was a considerable cult both before and after the Norman Conquest in the monasteries of Winchester and Wessex and in those founded by *Ethelwold. Pershore abbey, refounded *c.*972, obtained some relics and was dedicated to SS. Mary, Peter and Paul, and Edburga. Hence a cult at Westminster also. Feast: 15 June; translation feast (at Winchester): 18 July.

G.R., i. 268–9; *G.P.*, pp. 174, 298; unpublished Life by Osbert of Clare in MS. Laud Misc. 114, fos. 85–120 in Bodleian Library, Oxford; E. W. Williamson, *The Letters of Osbert of Clare* (1929), p. 26; *E.B.K. after 1100*, ii. 60.

EDFRITH (Eadfrith) (d. 721), monk and bishop of Lindisfarne. Little is known of Edfrith before he became bishop in 698, except that he studied in Ireland, and was a well-trained scribe, artist, and calligrapher, for it seems almost certain that he alone wrote the Lindisfarne Gospels, a masterpiece of Northumbrian illumination, now in the British Library, in honour of *Cuthbert, before and perhaps during his episcopate. In the planning and execution of this task, which must have taken at least two years, he showed extraordinary scholarly as well as artistic qualities. He welcomed the new text of the Gospels and the new lay-out, both of which came from Wearmouth–Jarrow and eventually Italy; he provided Evangelist portraits as a creative artist in a field of Mediterranean expertise, but he also excelled in insular majuscule script and Irish geometric and zoomorphic decoration of extraordinary delicacy and accuracy. The uniting of all these elements in a single manuscript is a testimony not only to Edfrith's all-round ability as 'the first personality in English art-history' but also to the fusion of Roman and Irish elements in Northumbria less than thirty-five years after the Synod of Whitby.

Edfrith's known achievements as bishop of Lindisfarne are largely associated with Cuthbert. To him was dedicated the Anonymous Life of Cuthbert and it was he who invited *Bede to write his Prose Life of Cuthbert also. He restored Cuthbert's oratory on the Inner Farne Island for the use of *Felgild. Some time during the reign of Osred (705–16) Eanmund, a Northumbrian monastic founder, consulted Edfrith about his monastery and borrowed from him a priest to draw up a rule and instruct the monks. He may too have been the Edfrid to whom *Aldhelm addressed a letter. When Edfrith died he was buried near Cuthbert's tomb: his relics, with those of *Aidan, *Edbert, *Ethilwald, etc., were taken with Cuthbert's in their wanderings through Northumbria from 875 to 995, when they reached Durham. When Cuthbert's body was translated to the new cathedral in 1104, Edfrith's relics were buried there too, but in a different site. His cult, with those of the other early bishops of Lindisfarne, was commemorated in a Durham feast of 4 June 'Translacio episcoporum Dunelmensium', dating from the 14th century, or before.

C. Plummer (ed.), *Baedae Opera Historica*, i (1896), pp. cv, cxlviii; ii. 297–8; B. Colgrave (ed.), *Two Lives of St. Cuthbert* (1940), pp. 310–11: Symeon of Durham, *Opera* (*R.S.*), i. 57, 252, 265–94; *Aldhelmi Opera* (ed. R. Ehwald), *M.G.H.*, *Auct. Ant.* (1919), 486–7; T. D. Kendrick and others, *Codex Lindisfarnensis*, ii (1960), 16–20, 288–95; F. Henry, 'Codex Lindisfarnensis', *Antiquity*, xxxvii (1963), 100–10.

EDGAR (943–75), king of England. He was the son of Edmund, king of Wessex, and the brother of Edwy, whom he succeeded in 959, after being chosen king of Mercia and Northumbria in 957. He was educated by *Dunstan and *Ethelwold and became king of all England at the age of only sixteen. His early life was not beyond reproach. He was so fond of two young nuns of Wilton, *Wulfhilda, whom he tried to seduce, and Wulfthryth, by whom he had a daughter, *Edith, that it would have seemed unlikely to contemporaries that his reign would be regarded as a golden age by later monastic writers. These irregularities may well have been the reason why he was crowned only in 973.

They must not be allowed to obscure his real achievements as a ruler. The key to his reign was the very close co-operation between Church and State. He promoted justice, and his four Law-codes are important in the history of Anglo-Saxon legislation, not least for the use made of them by his successors. The recognition of his royal power in 973 by rulers of Wales, Scotland, and the English Danelaw marked the apogee of the power of Wessex 10th-century kings. During his reign about thirty monasteries were founded, several of them on extensive lands given or sold by Edgar; he and his queen were their protectors and in practice chose their rulers, who acted prominently in local government on the king's behalf, while the monasteries were also notable educational and artistic centres.

Edgar married twice. His first wife was Æthelflaed (daughter of Ordmaer), by whom he had a son, *Edward the Martyr. His second was Ælfthryth (daughter of Ordgar of Devon), by whom he had another son, Ethelred the Unready. By comparison with the violent reigns of his predecessors and successors Edgar's was regarded as a model of peaceful government. This, with his close association with the 10th-century monastic revival, earned him the praise of 12th-century historians. King Cnut, however, referring to *Edith, thought that no child of so scandalous a king could be considered a saint.

Edgar was buried at Glastonbury, the cradle of the monastic revival. Here it was claimed that his body was incorrupt and emitted blood when cut at the opening of the tomb in 1052. His relics were enshrined with those of *Apollinaris and *Vincent; only Glastonbury, it seems, culted him, on 8 July.

G.R., i. 164–81; W. Stubbs (ed.), *Memorials of St. Dunstan* (*R.S.*, 1874); E. John, *Orbis Britanniae* (1961), pp. 154–264; D. Parsons (ed.), *Tenth-Century Studies* (1975).

EDILTRUDIS, see ETHELDREDA.

EDITH (Eadgyth, Eadida, Edyva) **OF WILTON** (961–84), virgin. Born in Kemsing (Kent), the daughter of *Edgar and Wulfthryth, his concubine, a novice at Wilton, Edith was brought up from infancy at Wilton, where her mother returned after her birth. Two chaplains of this royal convent undertook her education, Radbod of Reims and Benno of Trèves. This comprised not only letters but also script and illumination, sewing and embroidery. Edith also knew *Dunstan, *Ethelwold, and *Elstan of Ramsbury. As the king's daughter she could have attained an important position in society three times, but three times she refused, preferring the obscurity of the cloister. Once, at her profession, her father, King Edgar, tried to remove her; another time she was nominated abbess of Winchester, Barking, and Amesbury, but over all three she appointed superiors and remained with her mother, now abbess of Wilton; in 978 after the murder of her half-brother *Edward the Martyr, certain magnates wished her to become queen, but she refused.

Instead she built an oratory in honour of *Denys, which was decorated by Benno with murals of the Passion of Christ and the martyrdom of Denys. At the dedication Dunstan was supposed to have prophesied her approaching death and the incorruption of her thumb. Edith was conspicuous for her personal service of the poor and her familiarity with wild animals. She died at the age of only twenty-three; miracles at her tomb helped to establish her cult. Neither her apparently illegitimate birth nor King Cnut's scepticism about any child of Edgar attaining holiness prevented her feast spreading to many monasteries and the Sarum calendar; three ancient church dedications are known. Her relics were translated in 997; from then on she was, with *Iwi, Wilton's principal saint. Feast: 16 September; translation, 3 November.

AA.SS. Sept. V (1755), 364–72; *G.R.*, i. 269–70; *N.L.A.*, i. 311–15; *R.P.S.; C.S.P.;* A. Wilmart, 'La légende de Ste Édith en prose et vers par le moine Goscelin', *Anal. Boll.*, lvi (1938), 5–101, 265–307; C. Horstmann, *S. Editha sive Chronicon Vilodunense* (1883).

EDMUND (Eadmund) (841–69), king of East Anglia and martyr. Born of Saxon stock, Edmund was brought up as a Christian and became king of the East Angles before 865. In 869–70 the Great Army of the Vikings, under Ingwar, invaded East Anglia. Edmund led his army against them, but was defeated and captured. He refused to deny the Christian faith or to rule as Ingwar's vassal. He was then killed, whether by being scourged, shot with arrows, and then beheaded, as the traditional account relates, or by being 'spread-eagled' as an offering to the gods in accordance with Viking practice elsewhere. His death took place at Hellesdon (Norfolk); his body was buried in a small wooden chapel near by. In *c.*915 his body was discovered to be incorrupt and was transferred to Bedricsworth (later called Bury St. Edmunds). In 925 King Athelstan founded a community of two priests and four deacons to take care of the shrine. The landing of another Danish army at Ipswich in 1010 placed it in danger, so its custodian removed it to London, where it remained for three years. In spite of local resistance it was returned to Bury.

By now the cult, which, like those of *Oswald and *Ethelbert, fulfilled the ideals of Old English heroism, provincial independence, and Christian sanctity, had grown considerably. The earliest evidence for it is on 9th-century East Anglian coins inscribed 'Sc Eadmund rex', while the Life by *Abbo of Fleury based on the memoirs of Edmund's armour-bearer transmitted by *Dunstan, was written at Ramsey in the 10th century. King Cnut in 1020 ordered a stone church to be built at Bury and the clerks to be reformed by Benedictine monks. His policy of reconciliation between Danes and Anglo-Saxons through reparation for his compatriots' misdeeds found expression in 1028, when he gave his abbey a charter of jurisdiction over the town which was growing up around the abbey, together with notable land endowments. *Edward the Confessor continued this policy and extended the jurisdiction over most of West Suffolk in 1044. Bury soon became one of the most important and powerful of the English Benedictine abbeys.

In 1095 Edmund's body was translated to the large new Norman church; in 1198 it was re-enshrined, as was vividly described by Jocelin of Brakelond. By the 11th century Edmund's feast figures prominently in monastic calendars in southern England and later in that of Sarum. More than sixty churches in England are dedicated to Edmund.

His cult has left notable artistic record. A fine illustrated Life, written at Bury *c.*1130, survives at New York (J. P. Morgan Library, MS. 736). A later verse Life, written and illustrated by John Lydgate, monk of Bury, is in the British Library (MS. Harley 2278); it was presented to King Henry VI in 1439. There are also notable paintings of Edmund in the Albani Psalter and the Queen Mary Psalter, but the most famous representation of him is in the Wilton Diptych (National Gallery, London), where he and *Edward the Confessor are depicted as two royal patrons of England who present King Richard II to the Virgin and Child. In East Anglia ten screen-paintings of Edmund survive, as do several mural paintings in different parts of England. His most usual emblem is an arrow, the supposed instrument of his passion, or else a wolf, who was believed to have guarded his head after death. It was also claimed that his head and body were miraculously rejoined, but if he was never beheaded there is no extraordinary phenomenon to explain.

After the battle of Lincoln in 1217, the defeated French soldiers claimed to have removed his body to France. This set of relics (now at Saint-Sernin, Toulouse) was offered to Westminster Cathedral in 1912. M. R. James and other scholars protested that these relics were not authentic and that Edmund's body remained at Bury until the Reformation, where it was reburied on a site at present unknown. The proposed translation was therefore abandoned. There are no clear Bury documents about his body after 1198: the cult at Toulouse is supported by documents from the 15th century onwards. Feast: 20 November; translation, 29 April.

A.S.C., *s.a.* 870; Life by Abbo of Fleury with later Legends in T. Arnold (ed.), *Memorials of St. Edmund's Abbey*, i (*R.S.*, 1890), 3–209; Life by Ælfric in W. W. Skeat (ed.), *Lives of the Saints*, ii (E.E.T.S., 1900), 958–64; texts and versions of the principal sources in Lord Francis Hervey, *Corolla S. Eadmundi* (1907); id., *The History of King Edmund the Martyr and of the early years of his Abbey* (1929); M. Winterbottom (ed.), *Three Lives of English Saints* (1972). For the translation H. E. Butler (ed.), *The Chronicle of Jocelin of Brakelond* (1949), pp. xv–xxiv, 109–16; for the development of the legend, G. Loomis, 'The growth of the St. Edmund Legend', *Harvard Studies and Notes in Phil. and Lit.*, xiv (1932), 83–113 and especially D. Whitelock, 'Fact and Fiction in the Legend of St. Edmund', *Proc. Suffolk Inst. of Archaeology*, xxxi (1969), 217–33 and A. Gransden, 'The legends and traditions concerning the origins of the Abbey of Bury St. Edmunds', *E.H.R.*, xcix (1985), 1–24; examples of his iconography in O. Pächt, F. Wormald, and C. R. Dodwell, *The St. Albans Psalter* (1960) and Sir G. F. Warner, *The Queen Mary Psalter* (1912); R. M. Thomson, 'Geoffrey of Wells. De Infantia S. Edmundi', *Anal. Boll.*, xcv (1977), 25–34; id., 'Two Versions of a Saint's Life from St. Edmund's Abbey', *Rev. Bén.*, lxxxiv (1974), 383–408. See also A. P. Smyth, *Scandinavian Kings in the British Isles, 850–880* (1977), pp. 201–13.

EDMUND OF ABINGDON (Edme) (*c.*1175–1240), archbishop of Canterbury. The eldest son of Reginald Rich, a merchant who later became a monk, Edmund, who was notably devout all his life, was educated at Oxford University in grammar and then took the Arts course at Paris. He returned to Oxford and taught in the Arts faculty 1195–1201 at a time when the new logic was becoming known. He subsequently studied theology at Paris, where he probably wrote his *Moralities on the Psalms*. After living for a year with the Austin Canons at Merton (Surrey), he incepted in theology at Oxford in 1214. A pioneer of Scholasticism, he gave great importance both to the literal sense and historical context of the Bible, as well as to its spiritual sense, which was a vehicle for his theological thought. In 1222 he became Treasurer of Salisbury: he continued lecturing in the cathedral school, but his administrative duties were no sinecure as the cathedral was then being built. His almsgiving too was particularly generous: to recover he sometimes retired to Stanley (Wilts.), a Cistercian monastery whose abbot, Stephen of Lexington (a monk of Quarr), was a former pupil of his.

In 1233 he was appointed archbishop of Canterbury by the pope after three elections had been quashed. Although he found administration and politics distasteful, he became a notable and effective reforming bishop. He chose for his household men of outstanding talent, such as *Richard of Chichester; he claimed and exercised the right of metropolitan visitation; when this was challenged he resorted to litigation, not least with his own monastic chapter at Canterbury. Although the presence of Cardinal Otto as papal legate diminished his exercise of metropolitan power, his relation to the legate was more friendly than is often supposed. He resisted royal interference and mismanagement; in 1234–6, mediating between king and barons, he united the Church in England in political action, and civil war was averted.

He also resisted some papal appointments to English benefices, but this did not prevent him from invoking the pope's help in his disputes with the king. On his way to see him, Edmund died at Soissy on 16 November 1240. He was buried at Pontigny, in the abbey of the Cistercians, who, with the Friars, were his favourite Orders. His body was never translated to Canterbury, whose Black Benedictine community had resented what they regarded as Edmund's attacks on their independence.

The papal commission for inquiry into his Life and miracles in view of canonization included both Grosseteste (bishop of Lincoln 1235–53), and Alexander of Hales, the Franciscan theologian; further to their favourable report, Edmund was canonized in 1246. For the first celebration of his feast, Henry III offered a chalice, a white samite vestment, and 20 marks for candles at his shrine. In 1254 he made the pilgrimage there: although this was popular for a time, pilgrims dwindled by the end of the 13th century. But at Salisbury a collegiate church and an altar in the cathedral were dedicated to him, while his cult became, through the Sarum calendar, widespread in England, particularly at his birthplace Abingdon (Oxon.) and at Catesby (Northants.), where his sisters Margaret and Alice were nuns.

The first Oxford master to be officially canonized, Edmund is also the first of whom anything considerable is known. St. Edmund Hall at Oxford takes its name from him.

Edmund's writings are mainly Scripture commentaries and works of devotion. The most notable of these was the *Speculum Ecclesiae*, widely read in England and elsewhere in the 13th and 14th centuries. Written primarily for monks and nuns, it was revised later by Edmund for the needs of the secular clergy and the laity. In simple language it provided a comprehensive plan for achieving spiritual perfection; not particularly original, it restated for its own time traditional monastic teaching on the contemplative life. Feast: 16 November; translation, 9 June; feast at Abingdon on 30 May (dedication of the chapel which had been his birthplace).

Critical study of the four contemporary Lives and of the canonization by C. H. Lawrence, *St. Edmund of Abingdon: a study in hagiography and history* (1960); id., 'St. Edmund' in J. Walsh (ed.), *Pre-Reformation English Spirituality* (1964), pp. 104–20; A. B. Emden, *An Oxford Hall in Medieval Times* (1927); W. A. Pantin, *The English Church in the Fourteenth Century* (1955), pp. 222–4. Other Lives by W. Wallace (1893) and F. Paravicini (1898). Edmund's works are in M. de la Bigne, *Bibliotheca Patrum et Veterum Auctorum Ecclesiasticorum* (1610), v. 983–1004; versions in ME. in C. Horstmann, *Yorkshire Writers: Richard Rolle* (1895), i. 219–61; in French in H. W. Robbins, *La Merure de Seinte Eglise* (1925); see also H. P. Forshaw, *Edmund of Abingdon: Speculum Religiosorum and Speculum Ecclesiae* (1973).

EDMUND CAMPION, see CAMPION.

EDNOTH, see ETHELNOTH.

EDWARD THE CONFESSOR (1003–66), king of England. Son of King Ethelred the Unready and his second, Norman wife Emma, he was educated first at Ely, then in Normandy. This exile was necessary because the Scandinavian leaders Sweyn and Cnut became in succession kings of England. Nevertheless, in 1041 Edward was chosen as his successor by Harthacnut and was acclaimed king in 1042. His personality and reign have been variously assessed by historians: some see him as a weak, vacillating individual who paved the way for the Norman Conquest; others stress his tenacity and cunning which enabled him in a situation of near-isolation to preserve peace for over twenty years, while Danish and Norman magnates struggled for power. His reputation for holiness, which began during his life, was based on his accessibility to his subjects, his generosity to the poor, and his supposedly unconsummated marriage with Edith, the daughter of Godwin, earl of

Wessex. He was also reputed to have seen visions and cured scrofula (the King's Evil) by his touch. He strengthened the close links between the Old English Church and the Papacy: he sent bishops to *Leo IX's councils in 1049–50 and received papal legates in 1061. He promoted secular clerks, sometimes from abroad, to bishoprics, thus diminishing the near-monopoly of monastic bishops.

This did not imply lack of esteem for monasticism. On the contrary he was the virtual founder of Westminster Abbey, to which he devoted at one time as much as one-tenth of his income. He generously endowed it with many grants of land in different counties and built a huge Romanesque church, 300 feet long, with a nave of twelve bays. This was destined to be the place of coronation and burial of kings and queens of England. It was finished and consecrated just before his death, when he was too ill to attend. But he was buried there and his relics are undisturbed to this day.

Divergent contemporary sources claimed that he recognized William of Normandy as his heir and nominated Harold (by sign, if not by word) as his successor on his death-bed. After a period of uncertainty caused by political circumstances, the cult became acceptable to Normans and Anglo-Saxons alike; for the former because William claimed to be Edward's rightful heir, and for the latter because Edward was the last king of the Old English line.

In 1102 the body was found to be incorrupt. Under Stephen in 1138 an attempt was made to obtain formal papal canonization, supported by a new Life by Osbert of Clare. Pope Innocent II delayed a decision, but encouraged the monks of Westminster to collect more information. In 1160 Henry II, related by blood to Edward through his great-grandmother, *Margaret of Scotland, again pressed for canonization; by supporting Alexander III against an anti-pope he obtained it in 1161. On 13 October 1163 the relics were solemnly translated. This was a national event; the sermon was preached by *Ailred of Rievaulx who wrote another Life of Edward; this day became the principal feast of Edward.

When Henry III rebuilt the choir and sanctuary of Westminster Abbey, yet another translation to a new shrine took place in 1269. It had taken over twenty-five years to build and decorate; the most skilled Italian workmen had been employed, and this shrine was of unparalleled magnificence. It was despoiled at the Reformation but the body remained. Under Queen Mary Westminster was restored as a monastery; Abbot Feckenham also restored the shrine. The gilded wooden feretory, usually attributed to him, probably dates from the reign of Henry VII and may be the work of Torrigiano.

In the Middle Ages Edward was a very popular saint: with *Edmund of East Anglia he was widely considered to be England's patron. Thus at the siege of Calais in 1351 English troops, according to William Worcestre, invoked saints Edward (although no soldier himself) and *George together before making their final assault. In the Wilton Diptych (*c.*1380) Edward and Edmund are depicted presenting the young King Richard II to the Madonna and Child. The high altar, however, of the chapel of Windsor Castle was rededicated to St. George *c.*1400. At the battle of Agincourt (1415), as described by Shakespeare, St. George appears to be regarded as England's main intercessor, but without excluding Edward; by *c.*1450 George was regarded as patron of England in the same way as *Denys was of France.

The important iconography of Edward is closely connected with his Legend. From the Bayeux Tapestry and his earliest Life there is a constant tradition of his physical appearance: he was a tall man with a long face, ash-blond hair and beard, ruddy complexion and long, thin fingers. Coins and seals of Edward survive (with many writs); there are six scenes from his Life appropriately recorded in the abbreviated Domesday Book (13th century) in the Public Records Office, London. From about the same time dates Matthew Paris's illustrated *La Estoire de Seint Ædward le Rei*: this is the fullest surviving record of his Life and cult, and includes excellent pictures of the shrine. From it were derived the series of fourteen scenes on the cornice of the screen (*c*.1441) which separates the presbytery at Westminster Abbey from the chapel of Edward. There are shorter but notable series of Edward paintings in MSS. at Trinity College, Cambridge, both dating from the 15th century: one in an Apocalypse, the other in a Brut Chronicle.

The most famous incident represented is the story of his ring. This legend relates that Edward gave a ring to a beggar near Westminster. Two years later some English pilgrims in the Holy Land (or in India) met an old man who said he was *John the Apostle. He gave them the ring and told them to return it to Edward, whom they were charged to warn of impending death in six months' time. The best surviving example is in stained glass (15th century) in the church of Ludlow (Salop). It is also represented on tiles at Westminster Abbey, in the St. John window at York Minster (*c*.1400), in murals at Faversham (Kent), and in many other places.

Edward also figures frequently in screen-paintings in East Anglia and Devon; both royal patronage and popular devotion contributed to the extension of his cult. At least seventeen ancient churches were dedicated to Edward. His original feast was 5 January (the day of his death), but this was overshadowed by his translation feast of 13 October, which replaced it as his principal feast. Medieval Ely had a subsidiary commemoration on 8 January.

A.S.C., *s.a.* 1042–66; *G.R.*, i. 271–80; F. Barlow (ed.), *The Life of King Edward who rests at Westminster* (1962); this and other Lives in H. R. Luard (ed.), *Lives of Edward the Confessor* (*R.S.*, 1858); M. Bloch, 'La vie d'Edouard le Confesseur par Osbert de Clare', *Anal. Boll.*, xli (1923), 5–132; Ailred's Life in *P.L.*, cxcv. 757–90. Vernacular Lives in M. R. James, *La Estoire de S. Aedward le Roi* (facsimile edn. by Roxburgh Club, 1920); O. Sodergaard, *La Vie d'Edouard le Confesseur, poème anglo-norman du XIIe siècle* (1948); G. E. Moore, *The Middle English Life of Edward the Confessor* (1942); C. E. Fell, 'The Icelandic Saga of Edward the Confessor', *Anglo-Saxon England*, i (1972), 247–58. F. Barlow, *Edward the Confessor* (1970); id., *The English Church, 1000–66* (1965); F. M. Stenton, *Anglo-Saxon England* (1943), pp. 555–71; F. E. Harmer, *Anglo-Saxon Writs* (1952); R. W. Southern, 'The First Life of Edward the Confessor', *E.H.R.*, lviii (1943), 385–400; B. W. Scholz, 'The Canonization of Edward the Confessor', *Speculum*, xxxvi (1961), 38–60; L. E. Tanner, 'Some Representations of St. Edward the Confessor', *J.B.A.A.*, xv (1952), 1–12; M. Harrison, 'A Life of St. Edward the Confessor in early 14th century stained glass at Fécamp in Normandy', *Jnl. of the Warburg and Courtauld Institutes*, xxvi (1963), 22–37.

EDWARD THE MARTYR (*c*.962–79), king of England. He was the son of King Edgar and his first wife Æthelflaed: his succession to the throne had been disputed, but he was chosen by the witan in 975 under the preponderant influence of *Dunstan. His violent death at the hand of an assassin at Corfe was connected with a struggle for power among the magnates; the anti-monastic party in Mercia wanted his half-brother Ethelred, who was even younger than Edward, as king. The Anglo-Saxon Chronicle describes his death: 'King Edward was slain at eventide at Corfe gate and was buried at Wareham without any kingly honours.' But miracles soon followed and his relics were translated to Shaftesbury by Dunstan in 980. In a charter of Ethelred of 1001 he was called saint and martyr; in 1008 the laws of Ethelred ordered the observance of his feast all over England; calendar and litany evidence reveal a widespread cult from the early 11th century.

William of Malmesbury, writing in the 12th century but using the 11th-century *Passio*, provided further details. The villain of the piece was Ælfthryth, Ethelred's mother and Edward's stepmother, who wanted power for herself and her son. Edward came to Corfe from a hunt, and while his attendants were seeing to the dogs she 'allured him to her with female blandishment and made him lean forward, and after saluting him while he was eagerly drinking from the cup which had been presented, the dagger of an attendant pierced him through'. He clapped spurs to his horse, but one foot slipped and he was dragged by the other through the wood, his blood leaving a trail until he was dead. The wicked stepmother, who was very beautiful, expiated her crime by eventually becoming a nun at Wherwell.

This view of the responsibility for the crime gained credence and is reflected by *C.S.P.* describing Edward as 'killed by the guile of his stepmother'. Edward is sometimes represented in screen paintings holding a dagger in his left hand. Evidence for the continued popularity of the cult is provided by an indulgence for visitors to his shrine, granted by Robert Hallum, bishop of Salisbury (1407–17), in a sermon on his feast which 'portrays his ideal of a Christian prince in elegant diction'. Five ancient churches were dedicated to him. Some of his relics are now in an Eastern Orthodox church at Brookwood (Surrey). Feast: 18 March; translation, 20 June.

A.S.C., *s.a.* 979; *G.R.*, i. 181–5; C. E. Fell, *Edward, King and Martyr* (1971); *AA.SS.* Mar. II (1668), 638–44; *E.B.K. before 1100;* s.d. 18 March, 20 June. D. J. V. Fisher, 'The Anti-Monastic Reaction in the reign of Edward the Martyr', *C.H.J.*, x (1952), 254–70; W. H. Hutton, *The Lives and Legends of English Saints* (1903), pp. 167–80; C. E. Wright, *The Cultivation of Saga in Anglo-Saxon England* (1939). See also C. E. Fell, 'Edward, king and martyr and the Anglo-Saxon hagiographic tradition', in D. Hill (ed.), *Ethelred the Unready: papers from the Millenary Conference* (*B.A.R.*, lix. 1978); S. J. Ridyard, *The Royal Saints of Anglo-Saxon England* (1988).

EDWIN (584–633), king of Northumbria. A prince of the dynasty of Deira, whose territory was in the Yorkshire area, he was obliged to spend many of his early years in exile in Wales and East Anglia from Ethelfrith, king of Northumbria, of the rival tribe of Bernicia in the Northumberland area. Early in life he married Cwenburg of Mercia by whom he had two sons. In 616, with the help of Redwald, king of East Anglia, his host in exile who had steadfastly refused to betray him, Edwin defeated and killed Ethelfrith at the battle of the river Idle and so became king of Northumbria.

Cwenburg had presumably died and Edwin sought to marry *Ethelburga, a Christian princess from Kent. His embassy met with an initial rebuff because he was not a Christian, but the marriage was eventually agreed on condition that Ethelburga would be free to practise her own religion and that Edwin would seriously consider joining it. *Paulinus was consecrated bishop and sent to York *c.*625 as the queen's chaplain, but with a view to the spread of Christianity in the North. As in Kent, there was an interval of some years before the king decided to become a Christian. Edwin was a thoughtful and melancholy man and not inclined to hurry important decisions; he naturally wished to take his followers with him when and if he decided to change his religion. Three events led up to his conversion: an unsuccessful assassination attempt by West Saxons; the pagan high priest, Coifi, deciding to abandon his old religion; and a reminder by Paulinus of a mysterious experience Edwin had undergone when in exile some years before. Edwin was baptized at Easter 627, after the birth of a daughter. Many thanes and others, in Yorkshire and Lincolnshire, followed his example.

Edwin continued the expansionist policies of his predecessor, extending his territory to the north at the expense of the Picts, to the west at the expense of the Cumbrians and the Welsh, from whom he captured Anglesey and Man; he also absorbed the British enclave of Elmet (near Leeds) into his kingdom. He became the first Northumbrian to be overlord of the southern kingdoms as well as the first Christian king of Northumbria. But the king whom he could not conquer, Penda of Mercia, eventually conquered and killed him. This was at the battle of Hatfield Chase in 633. Aided by the Christian Welsh king Cadwallon, Penda decisively defeated the Northumbrians: the massacres and disorders which followed were ended only by the accession of *Oswald the following year.

Like Oswald, Edwin was regarded by his people as a tribal hero as well as a model Christian king. The cult was centred on York where the church he had built contained his head, and on Whitby, which had a shrine of his body, supposedly discovered by revelation and brought there from Hatfield Chase. The abbey of Whitby, ruled in turn by Edwin's daughter *Enfleda and granddaughter *Elfleda, was a burial-place for the royal house of Deira and the home of the writer of the first biography of *Gregory the Great. Unfortunately its early liturgical books like those of other centres in Northumbria were lost, so there is no early calendar evidence for Edwin's feast. There was, however, at least one ancient church dedication and, centuries later, his cult was approved by Gregory XIII implicitly through his being included among the English Martyrs in the famous wall-paintings at the English College, Rome. Feast: 12 October.

Bede, *H.E.*, ii. 5, 9–18, 20; iii. 1; *N.L.A.*, i. 352–61; B. Colgrave (ed.), *The Earliest Life of Gregory the Great* (1968); for other interpretations of the evidence see D. P. Kirby, 'Bede and Northumbrian Chronology', *E.H.R.*, lxxviii (1963), 514–27 and N. K. Chadwick, *Celt and Saxon* (1963).

EDWOLD (Eadwold) **OF CERNE** (9th century), hermit. Reputedly a brother of *Edmund, king of East Anglia, he left his homeland to live as a hermit on a hill about four miles from Cerne (Dorset). He was said to have lived on bread and water, to have worked many miracles, and to have been buried in his cell. Later a monastery, dedicated to St. Peter, was built near by, to which Edwold's body was translated. Feast: 29 August; translation, 12 August.

G.P., p. 185; *N.L.A.*, i. 362–4; unpublished Life in B.L., MS. Sloane 1772.

EDYVA, see EDITH.

EGBERT (d. 729), monk and bishop. A Northumbrian of noble birth, Egbert became a monk at Lindisfarne. When he was studying in Ireland at an unidentified monastery called Rathmelsigi, his companion Æthelhun was killed by the plague of 664. He also was struck by the same disease and vowed voluntary exile for life if he recovered. In 684 he tried unsuccessfully to dissuade King Egfrith from invading Ireland. Egbert inspired the Anglo-Saxon missionaries on the Continent such as *Wigbert, *Wilfrid, and *Willibrord. He was prevented from going himself, according to *Bede, by a monitory vision, in which he was instructed to go to Iona instead. There he lived for the last thirteen years of his life and succeeded where *Adomnan had failed, in persuading the Iona community to adopt the Roman calculation of Easter. On the very day that he died, 24 April, the Iona monks were celebrating Easter for the first time on the same day as the rest of the Western Church. Feast: 24 April; mentioned in Roman and Irish martyrologies and in the metrical calendar of York.

AA.SS. Apr. III (1675), 313–15 and *Propylaeum*, pp. 154–5; Bede, *H.E.*, iii. 4, 27; iv. 3, 29; v. 9–10, 22–4; W. Levison, *England and the Continent in the Eighth Century* (1956), pp. 52–6.

EGBIN, see ETHBIN.

EGELWIN, see ETHELWIN.

EGWIN (Ecgwine) (d. 717), bishop of Worcester 693–711, founder of Evesham abbey. The translation of his relics in 1039 by Ælfward, bishop of London (formerly abbot of Evesham), was the occasion of the first Life of Egwin, which claimed to incorporate older elements. According to this he was of royal blood, related to Ethelred, king of Mercia. During his episcopate he incurred the enmity of a faction who denounced him to the king and the archbishop of Canterbury and obliged him to withdraw from his diocese. Wishing to vindicate himself at Rome (here the writer modelled himself on Germanic and Hellenic folklore), he locked his feet in fetters and threw the key into the Avon. Later, on pilgrimage to Rome, he bought a fish in the market and found the key inside. The pope vindicated him of the unspecified charges and he returned to his diocese. These fabulous elements may be compared to those in the Life of *Aldhelm; Egwin's connection with Malmesbury was further emphasized by his conducting the funeral of Aldhelm in 709. Some connection with *Wilfrid over the foundation of Evesham is possible, but unsupported by contemporary evidence, but Evesham could have been one of Wilfrid's seven unnamed Mercian monasteries.

In the late 11th century, when some of the Anglo-Saxon saints' cults were questioned by Lanfranc and the Normans, Egwin's sanctity was vindicated by an ordeal through fire, by miracles, and by a successful fund-raising tour of southern England, undertaken by monks of Evesham, carrying Egwin's relics with them. This was in order to buy wood and stone for the new church needed by a rapidly growing community. Miracles were recorded on this journey (1077) as far afield as Dover, Oxford, and Winchester; at least once the party crossed the Trent. Feast: 30 December; translation feasts 10 September and 11 January. Two ancient churches were dedicated to him.

AA.SS. O.S.B., saec. III, 330–8; *R.P.S.* and *C.S.P.*; W. D. Macray, *Chronicon Abbatiae de Evesham* (*R.S.*, 1863); Florence of Worcester, *Chronicon de Chronicis*, i. 43–9; *G.P.*, pp. 296–7, 383–6; *N.L.A.*, i. 370–8; A Benedictine of Stanbrook, *St. Egwin and his Abbey* (1904); J. C. Jennings, 'The Writings of Prior Dominic of Evesham', *E.H.R.*, lxxvii (1962), 298–304 (this establishes Dominic's authorship of the Life printed by Macray). See also P. Grosjean, 'De codice hagiographico gothano', *Anal. Boll.*, lviii (1940), 90–103.

EILWIN, see ETHELWIN.

ELDAD, see ALDATE.

ELEN OF LUYDDOG, see HELEN OF CARNARVON.

ELEUTHERIUS, see DENYS.

ELEVEN THOUSAND VIRGINS, see URSULA.

ELFLEDA (Ælflaed) (653–714), abbess of Whitby. Her father, Oswiu, king of Northumbria, and her mother *Enfleda vowed to consecrate her in infancy to the religious life if he were successful in battle against Penda, the heathen king of Mercia. He won the battle of the Winwaed (654); accordingly, he entrusted her to *Hilda, abbess of Hartlepool. A few years later, both went to Whitby, a double monastery ruled by Hilda, and later a mausoleum of the Northumbrian royal family. Enfleda and Elfleda became abbesses in turn; during Elfleda's abbacy the earliest Life of *Gregory the Great was written there.

She was the friend of both *Cuthbert and *Wilfrid. In 684 she met Cuthbert on Coquet Island; he told her that her brother, King Egfrith, would die within a year and that her half-brother Aldfrith would succeed him. Later she was cured of paralysis by Cuthbert's girdle. Her skill as mediator was exercised in Wilfrid's favour at the synod of the river Nidd (705), when he was reconciled to both Canterbury and the church in Northumbria. She asserted that Aldfrith on his death-bed had promised to obey the commands of the papacy concerning Wilfrid and had enjoined his heir, Osred, to do the same. This earned the praise of Wilfrid's biographer as the 'comforter and best counsellor of the whole province'.

Her relics were discovered and translated at Whitby *c.*1125; her cult is attested only by late martyrologies. Feast: 8 February.

Bede, *H.E.*, iii. 24; iv. 26; B. Colgrave (ed.), *Eddius Stephanus' Life of Wilfrid* (1927); id., *Two Lives of St. Cuthbert* (1940); *G.P.*, pp. 242, 254.

ELFSTAN, see ELSTAN.

ELGIVA (Ælgifu, Algyva, Ælgytha). Both *R.P.S.* and an 11th-century calendar of Hyde testify to the cult of Elgiva at Shaftesbury. Most probably she should be identified with the wife of Edmund, king of Wessex (921–46). She was the mother of Kings Edwy and Edgar and died in 944. William of Malmesbury called her the foundress (or the second foundress after

Alfred) of the Shaftesbury nunnery, and said that she died there. He praised her for generosity, wise counsel, and the gift of prophecy; he also wrote some verses in honour of her miracles. Later, as in *C.S.P.*, she was called abbess of Wilton. Feast: 18 May.

R.P.S.; *C.S.P.*; *G.P.*, pp. 186–7.

ELIAS (Elijah), Old Testament prophet of 9th century BC who upheld the worship and service of God by moral practice against the Canaanites and Phoenicians. His only claim to a place in this book comes from the assertion, persistently maintained by certain Carmelite writers, that he was their founder and consequently that they were (and are) the most ancient Religious Order in the Church. Other writers (Carmelites included) rightly insisted that they were founded in the 13th century by the organization and amalgamation of already existing groups of hermits. His shrine survives on Mount Carmel. Feast (in Carmelite Order): 20 July.

B. Zimmermann, *Les saints Déserts des Carmes déchaussés* (1927); id., 'De sacro scapulari Carmelitano', *Anal. Carm. discalceatorum* (1927).

ELIDIUS (Eliud), see TEILO.

ELIGIUS, see ELOI.

ELIZABETH, see ZACHARY AND ELIZABETH.

ELIZABETH OF HUNGARY (Elizabeth of Thuringia) (1207–31), queen. Born at Pressburg, the daughter of King Andrew II of Hungary, she was brought up in Thuringia and in 1221 married its Landgrave, Louis IV. Ardent, passionate, and handsome, she enjoyed a married life of extraordinary happiness, bore three children, and was generous to a fault, spending enormous sums on almsgiving, founding hospitals, and providing for helpless children, especially orphans. But in 1227 Louis went on a Crusade under Frederick II; less than three months after he died of the plague. Elizabeth was first incredulous, then distraught almost to insanity; Louis' death was the turning-point in her life.

Her brother-in-law Henry drove her from the court; some advisers wished her to marry again but she refused; in 1228 she settled at Marburg under the spiritual direction of her confessor, Conrad of Marburg, whom she had known since 1225. She became a Franciscan tertiary, expressing her ardour in love of poverty, the relief of the sick, the poor, and the elderly through building, and working in, a hospital close to her very modest house. Conrad's direction seems to have been domineering, severe, and insensitive. Elizabeth provided for others to educate her children. Conrad made her dismiss her favourite ladies-in-waiting for whom he substituted two harsh companions, and would punish her with slaps in the face and blows with a rod. She refused an offer to return to Hungary, preferring to live out her days in good-humoured and resilient exile. She would occupy herself with menial tasks like spinning and carding, or cleaning the homes of the poor and fishing to help feed them. Her new regime lasted only two or three years: she died at the early age of twenty-four, her life shortened by her own austerities and the almost sadistic direction of one who had been a successful inquisitor of heretics.

She was canonized in 1235 by Gregory IX; in 1236 her relics were translated to the church of St. Elizabeth at Marburg where they remained as the object of enthusiastic popular pilgrimage until 1539, when they were removed to an unknown place by the Lutheran Philip of Hesse. She is depicted on a screen at Tor Brian (Devon) of *c.*1500 holding a double crown, and in a 20th-century stained-glass window at Eversley (Hants). Feast: 17 (formerly 19) November.

Early Lives by Theodoric of Apolda (ed. H. Canisius, *Antiquae Lectiones*, v (1604), 147–217), by Caesarius of Heisterbach (ed. A. Huyskens in *Annalen des historischen Vereins für den Niederrhein*, lxxxvi (1908), 1–59) and by Conrad of Malburg, ed. by id., *Quellenschriften zur Geschichte der hl. Elisabeth Landgräfin von Thuringen* (1908), pp. 110–40, also id., *Libellus de dictis Quattuor Ancillarum Sanctae Elisabeth* in *N.A.*, xxxiv (1908), 427–502; for these cf. *Anal. Boll.*, xxvii (1908), 493–7 and xxviii (1909), 333–5. Modern Lives by

C. R. F. Montalembert (1836, Eng. tr. 1904), W. Canton (1913), and J. Ancelet-Hustache (1946, Eng. tr. 1963), who also wrote in *D.H.G.E.*, xv (1963), 225–8; see also the stimulating essay of I. Coudenhove, *The Nature of Sanctity* (1932); B.T.A., iv. 386–91.

ELIZABETH (Isabel) **OF PORTUGAL** (1271–1336), queen. The daughter of Peter III, king of Aragon, and named Elizabeth after her distant relative *Elizabeth of Hungary, she married King Denis of Portugal at the age of twelve and bore him two children about eight years later. Denis was a strong ruler but a bad husband; Elizabeth pursued a life of prayer and piety and founded hospitals, orphanages, and homes for fallen women. In addition she provided hospitality for pilgrims and the poor. A peacemaker all her life, she reconciled her son with her husband after he had taken up arms, and, at the end of her life, prevented a war between Portugal and Castile. Her husband fell ill in 1324 and died the following year after being devotedly nursed by Elizabeth and giving clear signs of repentance. Elizabeth then went on pilgrimage to Compostela and wanted to become a Poor Clare nun, but was dissuaded. Instead she retired to a small house near the monastery she had founded, became a Franciscan tertiary, and lived in great simplicity like Elizabeth of Hungary. Her last peacemaking enterprise exhausted her and she died at Estremoz on 4 July. She was buried in the Poor Clares' convent at Coimbra. Many miracles followed; Leo X authorized the celebration of her feast locally in 1516; Urban VIII canonized her in 1626. Feast: 4 July.

AA.SS. Iul. II (1721), 169–213; A. G. Ribeiro De Vasconcellos, *Evolucão do culto de Dona Isabel de Aragão* (2 vols., 1894); P. de Moucheron, *Ste. Elisabeth d'Aragon* (1896); V. McNabb, *St. Elizabeth of Portugal* (1937).

ELLEN, see HELEN.

ELMO, see ERASMUS.

ELOI (Eligius, Loy) (*c.*588–660), bishop of Noyon. Born at Chaptelet (Haute-Vienne), he became a goldsmith and entered the service of Bobon, the royal treasurer. His reputation was based not only on excellent design, but also on economical use of materials. When he made two golden thrones out of metal allocated for one, Clotar II (d. 629) took him into his own service and commissioned him, as did his successor Dagobert I, to decorate tombs and shrines and make chalices, crosses, and plaques. Eloi became a priest, then bishop of Noyon in 641.

He became a very successful preacher and founded monasteries at Noyon, Paris, and Solignac. He was especially active in the Tournai area and was a pioneer apostle in much of Flanders. Of his supposed surviving homilies one is specially notable for his warnings against pagan superstitions such as fortune-telling, watching the omens, and keeping Thursday holy in honour of Jupiter. Instead of these Christians should arm themselves with the sign of the cross, with prayer, and the Eucharist. Late in life he became a counsellor of *Bathild, the queen-regent, an Anglo-Saxon who had been liberated from slavery and subsequently made good. To their influence may be traced the decree of the Council of Chalon, which forbade the sale of slaves out of the kingdom and insisted on their freedom to rest on Sundays and holy days.

It seems that no surviving piece of goldsmith's work is certainly Eloi's, although shrines of *Quentin, *Julian, *Germanus, *Brice, and *Martin were attributed to him; his plaque above the altar of St. Denis was admired in the Middle Ages, and his chalice at Chelles, which disappeared during the French Revolution, is known from surviving drawings. His reputation both as an apostolic bishop and as a distinguished craftsman who became the patron of goldsmiths, blacksmiths, and farriers ensured the diffusion of his cult from Picardy and Flanders over most of Europe. In England, where only one ancient church was dedicated to him, he was so well known through his feast, legends, and representations, such as that at Shorthampton

(Oxon.), that Chaucer's Prioress's strongest oath was 'by St. Eloi'. His principal emblem is a horseshoe; like *Dunstan he is depicted holding the devil by the nose with a pair of pincers (13th-century glass at Angers). Perhaps his most picturesque representation (14th century) is that of him shoeing a horse whose leg he first removed and then restored. He is a good example of a genuine saint of antiquity whose cult attained its widest popular diffusion in the later Middle Ages. Feast: 1 December; translation (Ely), 25 June.

AA.SS. Belgii III, 194–331; near-contemporary Life based on one by St. Ouen, his friend, ed. B. Krusch in *M.G.H.*, *Scriptores rerum meroving.*, iv (1902), 634–761 (also in *P.L.*, 87, 481–94 with homilies attributed to him, 593–654); see also 'Inventio reliquiarum S. Eligii anno 1183', *Anal. Boll.*, ix (1890), 423–36; P. Parsy, *Saint Eloi* (1907); S. R. Maitland, *The Dark Ages* (1889), pp. 101–40; E. Vacandard in *D.T.C.*, iv (1908), 340–9.

ELPHIN (date unknown). He is the patron of the parish church of Warrington (Lancs.); he has been conjectured to be Irish or British, but nothing is known of him.

ELSTAN (Elfstan) (d. 981), bishop of Ramsbury. A monk of Abingdon who was trained by its founder, *Ethelwold, he became the community cook as a young man and reputedly plunged his hand, unscathed, into boiling water at Ethelwold's command. He later became abbot of Abingdon. In 970 he was promoted to Ramsbury (Wilts.), then the poorest of the Wessex sees, which needed the support of extra endowments. Possibly its poverty was a partial cause of the sparse evidence for his cult: neither Abingdon, where he was buried, nor Winchester, nor other centres of Wessex, provide clear calendar evidence of his feast. The date of this, 6 April, depends on Wilson's *Martyrologe* (1608), which may record an earlier tradition.

G.P., p. 181; Florence of Worcester, i. 146; J. Stevenson (ed.), *Chronicon Monasterii de Abingdon* (*R.S.*), i. 128; ii. 259; Stanton, pp. 145–6.

ELTUT, see ILLTUD.

ELWIN (Æthelwine), bishop of Lindsey 680–92. He studied in Ireland and was consecrated by *Theodore at the request of Ethelred, king of Mercia. *Bede calls him a *uir sanctus*: there seems to have been no early cult. Wilson's *Martyrologe* mentions him under 29 June; Challoner seems to have invented 3 May as his feast, with his brother *Aldwyn, abbot of Peartney, and two other brothers, Edilhun and Egbert.

Bede, *H.E.*, iii. 11, 27. Stanton, p. 193.

EMERENTIANA (d. *c*.304), virgin and martyr. A martyr of this name, buried in a Roman cemetery a little way from the church of St. Agnes on the Via Nomentana, suffered probably with the martyrs Victor, Felix, and Alexander on 16 September. But her Legend, followed by the Roman Martyrology, makes her a foster-sister of *Agnes, stoned to death while praying at her tomb. This connection ensured her popularity and may have determined the date of her feast on 23 January, two days after that of Agnes.

AA.SS. Ian. II (1643), 458; *Propylaeum*, p. 32: B.T.A., i. 152–3.

ENDA (Eanna) (d. *c*.530), abbot. The son of Ainmire and born in Meath, Enda became a soldier in early life and then a monk. He was trained in *Ninian's monastery of Whithorn (Galloway). He returned to Drogheda, founded monasteries in the Boyne valley, and finally settled in Inishmore in the Aran Islands. This became his principal monastery, to which be brought his numerous disciples, one of whom was reputed to be *Ciaran of Clonmacnoise.

Enda was the earliest organizer of Irish monasticism; his work preceded that of the more influential *Finnian of Clonard: hence he was the pioneer of a very important movement which affected many in Ireland, England, and on the Continent. His Legend abounds in unreliable information about his early life, attributing to his sister Fanchea a preponderant role in his every important decision and claiming that he made a journey to Rome to be ordained.

More authentic memorials of him survive at Tighlagheany at Inishmore, where he was buried, and where there are notable monastic remains, some of which date to his time. Feast: 21 March.

AA.SS. Mart. III (1688), 267–74; *V.S.H.*, ii. 60–75; *The Irish Saints*, pp. 147–9.

ENDELLION (Endelient) (6th century (?)), virgin, one of the children of *Brychan. Virtually nothing is known of her life. She gave her name to St. Endellion (Cornwall), where part of her tomb survives and two wells are named after her. A chapel was also dedicated to her at Tregony, where she was reputed to have lived. Roscarrock records the legend that she lived there on the milk of one cow only, which was killed by the lord of Tregony because it strayed into his grounds. Her godfather, a great man, he says, caused the lord to be slain, but she miraculously revived him. At Lundy Island (opposite her brother *Nectan's settlement at Hartland) another chapel was dedicated to her. Feast: 29 April.

Baring-Gould and Fisher, ii. 452–5.

ENFLEDA (Eanflaed) (d. *c.*704), abbess of Whitby. The daughter of *Edwin, king of Northumbria, and his wife *Ethelburga, a Kentish princess, Enfleda was baptized by *Paulinus at Pentecost 626. This marked the beginning of his fruitful apostolate in Northumbria and was the expression of Edwin's gratitude at being delivered from the hand of an assassin. After Edwin's defeat and death at the battle of Hatfield Chase (633), Ethelburga and Enfleda (now aged seven) returned to Kent with Paulinus. In 642 Enfleda married Oswiu of Bernicia: this marriage to the princess of the Deiran line was planned to unite the two sections of Northumbria into one coherent kingdom. Enfleda, however, was faithful to her Roman-trained teachers: she was the patron of *Wilfrid when he was a young man, and her adhesion to the European calculation of Easter while her husband followed the Northern Irish system helped to bring about the Synod of Whitby (663/4), which decided on the single Easter for the whole kingdom. Soon after this Pope Vitalian wrote to Oswiu and sent her a present of a gold cross with a key made out of the links of what were believed to be St. Peter's chains.

After Oswiu's death in 670 Enfleda became a nun at Whitby which she ruled with her daughter *Elfleda. This was not the first time she had shown interest in the monastic life, for in 651, after her husband had murdered his brother *Oswin, she had persuaded him to found the monastery of Gilling in reparation. Oswiu was buried at Whitby, and during Enfleda's rule the relics of her father, Edwin, were translated there and buried in the chapel of St. Gregory. Whitby fostered the cult of Edwin as Bardney (Lincs.) promoted that of *Oswald. Both Edwin and Oswald had been killed by the heathen Penda of Mercia and both, it was thought, could be accounted martyrs. The destruction of Whitby and its records by the Danes has removed all trace of an early liturgical cult of Enfleda, but Glastonbury claimed to have her relics, with those of some other Northumbrian saints, in the 11th century. A late Welsh tradition that Enfleda and Edwin were baptized by a certain Rum map Urbgen is unworthy of credence. Feast: 24 November (in Wilson's *Martyrologe* of 1608, followed by Challoner).

Bede, *H.E.*, ii. 9; iii. 15, 24–5, 29; iv. 26; v. 19; B. Colgrave (ed.), *The Earliest Life of Gregory the Great* (1968); Stanton, pp. 564–5.

ENODER, an otherwise unknown Cornish saint who gave his name to the town called after him.

ENODOC (Guinedocus), a Welsh hermit who settled on the north coast of Cornwall, where a church, close to St. *Minver and made famous by Sir John Betjeman, bears his name. Feast (according to William Worcestre): 7 March; dedication day (since 1434): 13 July.

EOBAN (d. 754), bishop, companion of *Boniface in his last apostolate and death at Dokkum (Frisia). He was probably English and figures among the English martyrs in the 16th-century paintings of them by Circiniani at the English College, Rome. Feast: 5 June.

EORMENBURGH, see ERMENBURGA.

EORMENHILDE, see ERMENGILD.

EOSTERWINE (650–86), abbot of Wearmouth. Of noble birth, he joined the service of Egfrith, king of Northumbria, and fought in his army. At the age of twenty-four he became a monk at Wearmouth, the monastery just founded by his cousin *Benedict Biscop. Here he followed all the regular observance, taking his full share in the menial tasks. He milked the cows and the sheep, he worked in bakehouse, garden, and kitchen, he shared in the harvesting and winnowing. In 679 he was ordained priest and in 682 he was appointed abbot by Biscop to rule during his own absence. As abbot, he was kind and accessible to all, just as he had been before his promotion. He had the same food and sleeping accommodation as the rest of his community and joined in the manual work. He died at the early age of thirty-six, on 6 March, while the community were at Matins. He was buried by the church-door, but his relics, with those of Benedict Biscop and *Sigfrid, were translated by *Ceolfrith to a shrine close to the high altar. His cult was mainly local but his name also occurs in the OE martyrology from Mercia. Feast: 7 March.

C. Plummer (ed.), *Baedae Opera Historica* (1956), i. 364–404; ii. 355–77; J. F. Webb and D. H. Farmer, *The Age of Bede* (1983).

EPIMACHUS, see GORDIAN AND EPIMACHUS.

EPHREM OF SYRIA (*c.*306–73). A native of Nisibis (Mesopotamia), he was baptized *c.*324 and joined the cathedral school there, of which he later became the head. After the Persians captured Nisibis in 363, Ephrem became a monk, living in a cave near Edessa. There he wrote exegetical works and hymns which were later incorporated into the Liturgy and translated into several languages. In 370 he visited *Basil whose brother, *Gregory of Nyssa, wrote in his praise. In 372 he organized charity to victims of famine and died soon afterwards in his cave. His voluminous works earned him the title of Doctor of the Church in 1920. Feast: 9 (formerly 18) June.

Works ed. J. S. Assemani (1732–46) and E. Beck (1953–9); Lives by E. Emereau (1919) and A. Vööbus (1958).

ERASMUS (Elmo, Telmo) (d. *c.*300), bishop of Formiae in the Campagna, martyr. His name occurs in the Martyrology of Jerome, in early Irish and Anglo-Saxon ones also. *Gregory the Great referred to his relics being venerated at Formiae, but when this town was sacked by Saracens in 842, Erasmus' body was translated to Gaeta whose patron he became. Although he existed, almost nothing is known about him. Hagiographers and artists attempted to supply this deficiency with such effect that his cult spread through most of the Western world until in the 15th century he was invoked as one of the *Fourteen Holy Helpers.

His Legend makes him a Syrian bishop (based on an Erasmus of Antioch) who fled the persecution of Diocletian to be a hermit on Mount Lebanon, where he was discovered, beaten, and rolled in pitch which was then set alight. Cast into prison, he was released by an angel to Illyricum, where he was again tortured until an angel took him to Formiae, where he died. Curiously this gives no clue to his usual emblem of a windlass. This association apparently arose because his Legend described him preaching during a thunderstorm, undeterred by a thunderbolt near by, whence he became the patron of sailors, who had good reason to fear the effect of sudden storms. The lights sometimes seen at mastheads after storms called St. Elmo's Fire (or, less correctly, St. Helen's Fire) were believed to be a sign of his protection. The windlass, it is thought, was chosen for his emblem as the sailors' patron. Later this was misunderstood as being an instrument of torture, and it was thought that he was martyred through having his intestines removed. Hence his secondary patronage of all, especially children, who suffer from colic or similar diseases. The parish church of Faversham (Kent) used to have an altar of St. Erasmus, where lights were provided by frequent legacies in the later Middle Ages. Paintings of Erasmus by Grünewald, Cranach, and Dirk Bouts survive; so also does a sculpture in the chapel of Henry VII, Westminster Abbey, and several medieval English alabasters. Feast: 2 June.

AA.SS. Iun. I (1695), 211–19; R. Flahault, *S. Erasme* (1895); Réau, i. 437–40; B.T.A., ii. 453–4; *Bibl. SS.*, iv. 1288–93.

ERC (Ercus, Ercius, Erth) (no date), patron of St. Erth, Cornwall. He occurs in Irish martyrologies of the 9th century under 2 November; the 12th-century martyrology of Gorman calls him 'Erc of Slane, bishop of Lilcach and from Ferta Fer Feic beside Sid Truim from the West'. *C.C.K.* gives his feast as 31 October. A distich ascribed to *Patrick runs:

Bishop Erc,
Whatever he judged was rightly judged:
Whosoever gives a just judgment
Shall receive the blessing of bishop Erc.

William Worcestre said his relics were in St. Paul's, London, confusing him with *Erkenwald.

G. H. Doble, *The Saints of Cornwall*, i (1960), 95–6.

ERCONGOTA, see Erkengota.

ERKENGOTA (Ercongota) (d. *c.*660), virgin. She was a daughter of Erconbert, king of Kent, and his wife *Sexburga, later abbess of Ely. She became a nun with her aunts *Ethelburga of Faremoutier and *Saethrith in the double monastery of Faremoutier-en-Brie. Unlike them she never became abbess, but died comparatively young. Bede narrates traditions of her visions and prophecies: how she visited the aged nuns to say farewell and ask their prayers, and how angelic visitors arrived in the monastery at the moment of her death. She was buried in the church of St. Stephen near by: the balsam-like scent from her grave three days later was believed to attest to her sanctity.

At Faremoutier and Ely her feast was on 21 February, while the diocese of Meaux celebrated it on 26 February. The more usual, but apparently incorrect, date is 7 July.

Bede, *H.E.*, iii. 8; *N.L.A.*, ii. 542; Stanton, pp. 79, 319, 630, 657–8; *E.B.K. after 1100*, ii. 4.

ERKENWALD (Earconwald) (d. 693), bishop of London, was London's most important diocesan between *Mellitus and *Dunstan, and its principal saint in the Middle Ages. Reputed to be of royal blood he was certainly rich; he founded the monasteries of Chertsey (Surrey) and Barking (Essex). He ruled the former, while his sister *Ethelburga was abbess of the latter. Even before being consecrated bishop by *Theodore in succession to the simoniacal Wine, Erkenwald was reputed to be holy. His diocese of the East Saxons extended over Essex and Middlesex: in the preamble to the Laws of Ina of Wessex he is called 'my bishop'. He helped Theodore and *Wilfrid to be reconciled shortly before the former's death in 690. In *Bede's time miracles were reported as caused by the couch in which Erkenwald used to be carried in his declining years.

He died at Barking on 30 April 693: his relics were claimed by the nuns there, by the monks of Chertsey, and by the clergy of London. The claim of the last was successful, and Erkenwald was buried in the cathedral of St. Paul which he had enlarged. The relics escaped the fire of 1087 and were placed in the crypt; on 14 November 1148 they were transferred again to a new shrine behind the high altar; on 1 February 1326 there was a further translation to yet another shrine, which was constantly enriched by canons and merchants of London until well into the 15th century. Vernacular literature about the saint and his shrine was also written. Miracles were reported there until the 16th century. Feast: 30 April; translation feasts, 1 February and 13 May.

Bede, *H.E.*, iv. 6. B. Colgrave (ed.), *Eddius Stephanus' Life of St. Wilfrid* (1927), p. 87; W. Dugdale, *History of St. Paul's Cathedral* (1658); W. R. Matthews and W. M. Atkins, *A History of St. Paul's Cathedral* (1957). See also H. L. Savage, *St. Erkenwald: a Middle English Poem* (1926); I. Gollancz, *St. Erkenwald* (1932); E. G. Whatley, *The Saint of London* (1989).

ERME, see HERMES.

ERMEL, see ARMEL.

ERMELANDUS, abbot, commemorated in the St. Albans calendar under 25 March: otherwise unknown.

ERMENBURGA (Eormenburh, also called Domneva) (d. *c.*700), abbess. She was the daughter of Ermenred, brother of Erconbert, king of Kent (640–64). She married Merewald, said by later writers to have been a son of Penda, king of Mercia, and had four children: *Mildred, abbess of Minster, *Milburga, abbess of Wenlock, *Mildgyth, nun in Northumbria, and a son, Merefin, who died young. Ermenburga's younger brothers were *Ethelred and Ethelbricht; when they were murdered by Thunor, Egbert's counsellor, Ermenburga received the *wergild* and asked for this to take the form of land in Kent for the foundation of a nunnery at Minster, in the isle of Thanet, where she became first abbess (*c.*670). Her daughter Mildred, after being formed at Chelles, succeeded her. Although called 'saint', no evidence has survived of Ermenburga's early liturgical cult. Feast: 19 November, in Wilson's *Martyrologe* (1608), followed by Challoner and Stanton.

Fragments of biography in O. Cockayne (ed.), *Leechdoms etc.* (*R.S.*), iii. 423–31; *G.R.*, pp. 78, 261–2, 267. Symeon of Durham, *Opera* (*R.S.*), ii. 11–13; Stanton, pp. 557–8.

ERMENGILD (Ermenhilda, Eormenhilde, Hermynhild) (d. *c.*700), queen of Mercia, abbess of Ely. She was the daughter of Erconbert, king of Kent, and of his wife *Sexburga, who was sister of *Etheldreda. Ermengild married Wulfhere, king of Mercia (657–74) and son of Penda. She converted her husband and bore him two children, Coenred, king of Mercia 704–9, and *Werburga. After Wulfhere's death she became a nun at Minster-in-Sheppey, founded by her mother Sexburga. When the latter resigned this abbacy and went to Ely, Ermengild succeeded her at Minster; when Sexburga died at Ely twenty years later, Ermengild became Ely's third royal abbess in succession. Nothing is known of her rule there, not even the day of her death. Her daughter Werburga succeeded her as abbess of Ely. Ermengild's cult was extensive, but several pre-Conquest calendars wrongly describe her as a virgin. Feast: 13 February; Ely kept the feast of her translation on 17 October.

O. Cockayne (ed.), *Leechdoms etc.* (*R.S.*), iii. 431–3; E. O. Blake (ed.), *Liber Eliensis* (*C.S.*, 1962); *G.R.*, i. 77–8, 267; *G.P.*, pp. 308, 323; F. Wormald, 'The English Saints in the Litany in Arundel MS. 60', *Anal. Boll.*, lxiv (1946), 82; *N.L.A.*, i. 405–6.

ERMYN, see ARMEL.

ERNIN (Ernan) (1) (6th century), monk. Ernin came from North Wales, the son of Helig whose territory on the mainland opposite Anglesey was permanently flooded by the sea. Ernin, on losing his lands, became a monk at Bardsey.

ERNIN (2) (6th century), Breton hermit. He was reputedly a native of Britain who settled on land at Duault, near Carhaix, where, the local tradition says, a stag took refuge and hounds did not dare attack it. Ernin died and was buried at Locarn. Count Conmore (later of Domnonia) ordered a chapel to be built there; this was on the site of the present church at Locarn where Ernin's head and arm are enshrined. Invoked as a patron to cure headaches, his feast is on 2 November. It is possible, but not certain, that the two Ernins are really one and the same.

Baring-Gould and Fisher, ii. 464–5.

ERTH (1), see Erc.

ERTH (2), see Urith.

ESKIL (d. *c.*1080), bishop and martyr. This Englishman, who was a relative of *Sigfrid of Sweden, helped him reconvert the Swedish people who had lapsed into paganism after the death of *Anskar. He worked mainly in Södermanland, and was consecrated bishop at Strangnas, of which he was later believed to have been the first diocesan. The murder of the friendly King Inge, as so often with similar assassinations in Scandinavia, caused another reaction: Eskil was stoned to death after a violent storm had destroyed a pagan altar and its sacrifices. Feast (mainly in northern Europe): 12 June.

AA.SS. Iun. II (1968), 598–600; C. J. A. Oppermann, *English Missionaries in Sweden* (1937), pp. 103–11; B.T.A., ii. 533.

ETHBIN (Egbin) (6th century), monk and hermit. He was born in Britain of a noble family; his father died when he was only fifteen, and his mother entrusted him to *Samson to be educated. Later Ethbin became a monk in Brittany under *Winwaloe. When the monastery was destroyed by the Franks, Ethbin went to Ireland and lived for twenty years as a hermit in a woodland called *Nectensis* (unidentified). Here he died, but there was no Irish cult, although his name appears in the Roman and other late Martyrologies. The relics are claimed by Montreuil and Pont-Mort (Eure) in France. In his Legend there are several persons and places which are suspiciously unidentifiable: P. Grosjean suggested that the wood (*silva*) called *Nectensis* could be a corruption of Silvanectensis (i.e. of Senlis, dep. Oise), but does not explain how this could be in Ireland. What seems certain is that Ethbin's name is Anglo-Saxon, not Celtic. Feast: 19 October.

N.L.A., i. 368–70; Baring-Gould and Fisher, ii. 466–7; *Propylaeum*, p. 463.

ETHELBERT (1) (Æthelberct, Edilbertus) **OF KENT** (560–616), the first Christian Anglo-Saxon king. Although he had been defeated by Ceawlin of Wessex at the battle of Wimbledon in 568, Ethelbert became the third *bretwalda* of England, exercising overlordship, if not effective rule, over all the country south of the Humber. Under his rule Kent was the most cultured of the Anglo-Saxon kingdoms; it was closely associated with the Frankish Rhineland; and Ethelbert had married the Christian Bertha, daughter of Chilperic's brother Charibert, king of Paris, before 588. She brought with her as chaplain *Liudhard, but their role in the conversion of Kent has often been exaggerated: as late as 601 *Gregory the Great reproached her for not having converted her husband. Although he had received *Augustine and his monks in 597 in a friendly way in Thanet, he was nevertheless reserved, insisting on a conference in the open air, according to *Bede, through fear of magic. After giving them a fair hearing, he declared himself unable to accept Christian teaching and abandon the age-old beliefs of his nation. But recognizing their sincerity, he gave them a house in Canterbury and allowed them to preach. They used a Romano-British church, dedicated (perhaps by Liudhard) to St. Martin. In July 598 Gregory wrote to Eulogius, patriarch of Alexandria, that 10,000 English had been baptized. Even if the number is exaggerated it seems clear that large numbers of Ethelbert's subjects became Christian before he did. In 601 Gregory wrote an encouraging letter to Ethelbert, congratulating him on becoming a Christian: his conversion was certainly decisive in the Christianization of Kent, and later England. Augustine restored an old church which he dedicated to Christ and made his cathedral; Ethelbert had the monastery of SS. Peter and Paul (later St. Augustine's) built outside the walls of Canterbury; Augustine received the pallium and reinforcements of personnel; with Ethelbert's strong support he established sees at Rochester and at London, then the principal town of the East Saxons.

Ethelbert was the first Anglo-Saxon king to leave a code of laws: it includes one which protected the clergy and the churches by exacting very high compensation for damage done to them or their property. In spite of Bede they seem nearer the Salic law of Clovis than to Roman law, but Roman influence, probably through Augustine, is evident in the oldest Canterbury charters.

Ethelbert died on 24 February 616 and was buried beside his first wife Bertha in the *porticus* (side-chapel) of St. Martin in the church of the monastery of SS. Peter and Paul. *C.S.P.* noted that he was 'the first Anglo-Saxon king to receive faith in Jesus Christ through the preaching of Augustine. From his stock there has arisen a numerous and holy race, which shines with virtue through the whole world.' There seems to have been an unofficial cult at Canterbury from early times, but his feast is found in calendars only from the 13th century, and generally on 25 or 26 February because St. Matthias occupied 24 February.

Bede, *H.E.*, i. 25–6, 32–3; ii. 2–3, 5. *A.S.C.*, *s.a.* 565, 618; *G.R.*, i. 13–21; *N.L.A.*, i. 409–11. For his laws, F. Liebermann, *Die Gesetze der Angelsachsen*, i (1903), 3–8 and D. Whitelock, *E.H.D.* i. 357–9. For his charters, W. Levison, *England and the Continent in the Eighth Century* (1946), pp. 174–233; for the cult, E. M. Thompson, *Customary of the Benedictine Monasteries of St. Augustine, Canterbury and St. Peter, Westminster* (1904), ii. 289, 294, 303. See also F. M. Stenton, *Anglo-Saxon England* (1943), pp. 54–61, 109–12; S. Brechter, *Die Quellen zur Angelsachsenmission Gregors des Grossen* (1941), pp. 241–8; R. A. Markus, 'The Chronology of the Gregorian Mission to England', *J.E.H.*, xiv (1963), 16–30; N. Brooks, *The Early History of the Church of Canterbury* (1984), pp. 3–14.

ETHELBERT (2) (d. 794), king of the East Angles. He was venerated as a martyr because of his violent death for political reasons at the hand of Offa, king of Mercia, whose daughter Ælfthryth he visited, with a view to marriage, at Sutton Walls (Hereford and Worcester). There he was assassinated in 794, presumably on 20 May. The body was buried by the river Lugg at Marden and later translated to Hereford, where it remained until the Danes burnt it in 1050. His head was buried at Westminster. William of Malmesbury, however, said that Ethelbert's relics were still at Hereford; he clearly felt some misgiving about his cult as a martyr and invoked the authority of *Dunstan as well as the witness of miracles in favour of its continuance. Ethelbert is titular of Hereford cathedral, of churches at Marden (Herefordshire), Little Dean (Glos.), and of eleven others in East Anglia. The cult flourished in medieval England: Hereford was reckoned as second only to Canterbury as a pilgrimage centre; fragments of the shrine remain. Feast: 20 May.

A.S.C., *s.a.* 792 in D. Whitelock, *E.H.D.*, i. 167; *G.P.*, p. 305; Florence of Worcester, *Chronicon ex chronicis*, i. 62–3; M. R. James, 'Two Lives of St. Ethelbert, King and Martyr', *E.H.R.*, xxxii (1917), 214–44; *AA.SS.* Maii V (1685), 72*–76*; *N.L.A.*, i. 412–18; A. T. Bannister, *The Cathedral Church of Hereford*, pp. 109–14; R. M. Wilson, *The Lost Literature of Medieval England* (1952), pp. 106–8; C. E. Wright, *The Cultivation of Saga in Anglo-Saxon England* (1939).

ETHELBRICHT, see ETHELRED AND ETHELBRICHT.

ETHELBURGA (1) (Ædilburh) (d. 675), abbess of Barking. Of a wealthy (possibly royal) family and sister of *Erkenwald, Ethelburga was quite likely the owner, as well as the ruler, of Barking. A late tradition says that Erkenwald invited *Hildelith from Chelles to be prioress and future abbess of Barking: her difficult task was to teach Ethelburga monastic traditions while retaining a subordinate role.

*Bede devoted several chapters to marvellous events just before Ethelburga's death, such as the death of a three-year-old boy after calling 'Edith' three times for his favourite nun, and the cure of the nun *Tortgith after a vision of Ethelburga. Feast: 11 October; Barking had translation feasts on 7 March, 4 May, and (with those of Hildelith and Wulfrida) 23 September.

Bede, *H.E.*, iv. 6–10; *N.L.A.*, i. 419–23; P. Grosjean, 'De Codice hagiographico Gothano', *Anal. Boll.*, lviii (1940), esp. p. 101.

ETHELBURGA (2) (Ædilburh, Aubierge) **OF FAREMOUTIER** (d. 664). Daughter of Anna, king of East Anglia, she became a nun at Faremoutier-en-Brie and eventually succeeded her half-sister *Saethrith as abbess. She started to build an abbey church, but it was uncompleted at the time of her death. Her body was buried there, but was translated seven years later to the church of St. Stephen as it was found to be incorrupt. She is mentioned in the Roman and French Martyrologies as well as the English ones. Feast: 7 July.

Bede, *H.E.*, iii. 8 (with Plummer ii. 144, 149–50).

ETHELBURGA (3) (Ædilburh, Tata) (d. 647), princess of Kent, abbess of Lyming. She was the daughter of *Ethelbert, king of Kent, and married *Edwin of Northumbria. After his death she returned to Kent with *Paulinus and founded the nunnery of Lyming, which she ruled until her death. There is no ancient calendar evidence of a feast, but Wilson (1608) gives 8 September.

Bede, *H.E.*, ii. 9, 11, 20.

ETHELDREDA (Æthelthryth, Ediltrudis, Audrey) (d. 679), queen, foundress and abbess of Ely. She was the daughter of Anna, king of East Anglia, and was born probably at Exning (Suffolk). At an early age she was married (*c*.652) to Tondberht, ealdorman of the South Gyrwas, but she remained a virgin. On his death, *c*.655, she retired to the Isle of Ely, her dowry. In 660, for political reasons, she was married again, this time to Egfrith, the young king of Northumbria, then only fifteen years old and several years younger than her. He agreed that she should remain a virgin, as in her previous marriage. But twelve years later he wished their marital relationship to be normal; Etheldreda, advised and aided by *Wilfrid, bishop of Northumbria, refused. Egfrith offered bribes in vain. Etheldreda left him, became a nun at Coldingham under her aunt *Ebbe (672), and founded a double monastery at Ely in 673. Egfrith married again: Wilfrid, some years later, was exiled from Northumbria.

Etheldreda meanwhile restored an old church at Ely, reputedly destroyed by Penda, the pagan king of Mercia, and built her monastery on the site of the present Ely cathedral. For seven years she lived an austere life of penance and prayer, eating only one meal a day, wearing woollen clothes instead of linen, watching each morning between Matins and dawn. In this wealthy family monastery, where she was joined or succeeded by sisters and nieces, she died of a tumour on the neck, interpreted as a divine punishment for her vanity in wearing necklaces in her younger days. It was the result of the plague, which also carried off several other nuns in her community.

Seventeen years later her body was found incorrupt: Wilfrid and her physician Cynefrid were among the witnesses. The tumour on her neck, which had been cut by her doctor, was found to be healed. The linen cloths, in which her body had been wrapped, were as fresh as the day when she was buried. Her body was placed in a stone sarcophagus of Roman workmanship found at Grantchester and translated by *Sexburga on 17 October 695. Her shrine was much frequented and she became the most popular of the Anglo-Saxon women saints.

Ely was refounded by *Ethelwold in 970 as a monastery for monks only; it was so lavishly endowed by him and King Edgar that it became the richest abbey in England except Glastonbury. Etheldreda's shrine remained and was presented by Emma, wife of King Cnut, with a purple cloth, richly worked with gold and jewels. After the Norman Conquest a new choir was built, which made necessary a new translation. This was eventually accomplished in 1106 and involved the relics of the other Ely saints Sexburga, *Ermengild, and *Werburga also. Ely became a bishopric in 1109, and the shrine was rich enough for it to be stripped in 1144 by bishop Nigel to pay a fine of 300 marks. It was restored by bishop Geoffrey in 1225 and yet another translation took place in 1252, with some supposed relics of *Alban, when the cathedral was consecrated. The shrine was destroyed in 1541, but some relics are claimed by St. Etheldreda's church, Ely Place, London, and her hand, discovered in 1811 in a recusant hiding-place near Arundel, is claimed by St. Etheldreda's R.C. church at Ely.

Etheldreda is usually represented in art as an abbess, crowned, with a pastoral staff and two does, who were said to have supplied the Ely community with milk during a famine. The Society of Antiquaries of London has a fine painting of scenes from her life and her first translation. This was almost certainly part of the retable for her shrine-altar; its date of *c.*1455 was recently confirmed by dendrochronology. Other series of incidents from her life are carved on the capitals round the interior of the Ely Lantern Tower. Etheldreda is also depicted on six rood-screens of East Anglia and one in Devon. Besides Ely, twelve ancient churches are dedicated to her.

At St. Audrey's Fair necklaces of silk and lace were sold; these were often of so poor a quality that the word tawdry (a corruption of St. Audrey) was applied to them. Feast: 23 June; translation, 17 October.

Bede, *H.E.*, iv. 19–20; B. Colgrave (ed.), *Eddius Stephanus' Life of Wilfrid* (1927); E. O. Blake (ed.), *Liber Eliensis* (*C.S.*, 1962); E. Miller, *The Abbey and Bishopric of Ely* (1951); C. W. Stubbs, *Historical Memorials of Ely Cathedral* (1897); T. D. Atkinson, *An Architectural History of the Benedictine Monastery of St. Etheldreda at Ely* (1933).

ETHELDRITHA (Alfreda, Ælfryth) (d. *c.*835), recluse. The daugher of Offa, king of Mercia, Etheldritha was sought in marriage by *Ethelbert, king of the East Angles. On his death, through her father's treachery, she became a hermit at Croyland *c.*793. There she remained for the rest of her life and was famous for her prophecies. Her tomb was among those of Croyland saints arranged round that of *Guthlac, but her relics were lost in 870 when the Danes destroyed the monastery. Such is the Croyland tradition about her, but it lacks any supporting evidence from elsewhere. Feast at Croyland: 2 August.

AA.SS. Aug. I (1733), 173–5.

ETHELFLEDA (Elfleda) (fl. *c.*960), abbess of Romsey. Daughter of Ethelwold of Wessex who founded Romsey, Ethelfleda joined the community at an early age under *Merewenna and eventually became abbess.

Her Legend tells that she was brought to the notice of the king and queen and stayed at court, where her habit, for ascetical reasons, of bathing in the nude at nighttime was the occasion of the queen's nervous illness, caused by her indiscreet curiosity when she followed her to see where she went. The queen was afterwards cured by the abbess's intercession. Ethelfleda died at an advanced age. Feast: 23 October.

AA.SS. Oct. XII (1867), 925–6; *N.L.A.*, i. 379–81.

ETHELHARD (Æthilheard) (d. 805), archbishop of Canterbury. Abbot of Louth (Lincs.), he was placed in the see of Canterbury (793) just after the southern province had been divided by King Offa and the pope, and a second metropolitan see set up at Lichfield. This had coincided with Mercian domination over Kent, so at first Ethelhard was not very acceptable to his own flock. On the death of Offa in 796 Kent revolted against Mercian supremacy; Ethelhard fled, but through Alcuin's intervention returned the following year. Already the re-establishment of Canterbury's former status had been discussed; attempts by Mercia to have the metropolitan at London instead were set aside; in 802 Pope Leo III restored Canterbury to the *status quo* before Lichfield had become a metropolitan, and this archbishopric was abolished. One important consequence of Ethelhard's Synod of Clovesho in 803 was the custom of each newly elected bishop making a written profession of his ortho doxy, and a promise of obedience to his metropolitan. Ethelhard died at

Canterbury and was buried in the cathedral; he was venerated for his notable part in the recovery of Canterbury's primatial power and prestige. He was also one of the Anglo-Saxon saints whose cult was suppressed by Lanfranc because of lack of documentation. No writer of the 11th or 12th century made good this deficiency and the cult seems to have died. Feast: 12 May.

Letters to Ethelhard from Alcuin and Pope Leo III are printed with other relevant texts in *E.H.D.*, i. 788–800; *G.P.*, 17–19 (but errs in making him bishop of Winchester first); Florence of Worcester, *s.a.* 805.

ETHELNOTH (Ednoth, Eadnodus, Æthelnoth) (d. 1038), monk of Glastonbury, archbishop of Canterbury. William of Malmesbury called him dean (i.e. cathedral prior) of Canterbury and praised his outstanding wisdom and guidance of King Cnut. He became archbishop in 1020, received the pallium at Rome, presided at the translation of the relics of *Alphege, but also bought for one golden talent and 100 silver ones the arm of *Augustine of Hippo which he gave to Coventry. He obtained for his old monastery, of which he was the seventh monk to become archbishop, some important benefactions from Cnut, whom he also persuaded to help finance the rebuilding of Chartres cathedral. He died full of merit on 30 October, but there seems no evidence from Canterbury and other calendars for a formal cult. But both Mabillon and the Bollandists devoted an entry to him.

AA.SS. Oct. XIII (1893), 451–6; *G.R.*, i. 224–6; J. Mabillon, *AA.SS. O.S.B.*, VI (part i), 394–7; B.T.A., iv. 222–3.

ETHELRED, see AILRED.

ETHELRED AND ETHELBRICHT (Ethelbert), princes of the royal house of Kent and martyrs. They are not mentioned by Bede: *A.S.C.* records their death, but not their names, in 640. Their Legend places this about 30 years later. They were the sons of Ermenred and great-grandsons of *Ethelbert of Kent: their uncle Erconbert ruled from 640 and his son Egbert succeeded in 664. Egbert's counsellor Thunor murdered the princes and buried them at Eastry. Egbert was held responsible, and in expiation founded the monastery of Minster, where the princes' sister *Ermenburga was first abbess. Their bodies were translated outside Kent for political reasons to Wakering (Essex) and later to Ramsey Abbey by *Oswald of Worcester on 17 October, the day when their feast was kept both there and at St. Augustine's, Canterbury. The Legend was fully developed only in the 11th century.

A.S.C., *s.a.* 640; *G.R.*, i. 261–2, 267; *N.L.A.*, i. 429–31.

ETHELWIN (1) (Ailwin, Egelwin) (7th century), monk and hermit. Reputedly the brother of Cenwalh, king of the West Saxons 643–74, Ethelwin was a hermit-founder of the abbey of Athelney (Somerset). He was reputed to have suffered ill-health all his life, but to have been a marvellous posthumous healer of others' infirmities. Athelney was the centre of his cult. There seems no ancient authority for the date of his feast: Challoner gives 29 November.

G.P., p. 199; Stanton, p. 569.

ETHELWIN (2), bishop of Lindsey, died *c.*700. Brother of Edilhum (friend of Egbert and of Aldwin), abbot of Peartney (Lincs.) and also of abbess Ethelhild nearby, Ethelwin was consecrated by *Theodore in 680. His diocese (roughly modern Lincolnshire) had formerly been part of Northumbria, but was later under the rule of kings of Mercia. Little is known of his achievements or even the place of his seat (see *Herefrith), but *Bede mentions him and his family. Feast: 3 May (or 29 June in Wilson's *Martyrologe*).

Bede, *H.E.*, iii. 11, 27; Stanton, p. 193.

ETHELWOLD (*c.*912–84), Benedictine monk and reformer, bishop of Winchester. Born at Winchester, he served at the court of King Athelstan (924–39), but became a priest, being ordained by *Alphege on the same day as his friend *Dunstan. Not long afterwards he decided to join Dunstan at Glastonbury in his plan of reviving monastic life in England under the Rule of *Benedict (*c*.941). Although he became prior, he was not, it seems, completely satisfied with Glastonbury, and asked if he could go to France to study the new reformed monasticism of Cluny. Instead, King Edred gave him the derelict abbey of Abingdon, which he restored with monks from Glastonbury and clerics from elsewhere; he sent his disciple Osgar to study at Fleury in his place. He built a new church (incorporating older elements) in the form of a double rotunda. When Dunstan was exiled by King Edwy (*c*.956), Ethelwold became the most important figure in the Reform and also was tutor to the future king, Edgar.

In 963 he became bishop of Winchester, the principal town of Wessex. The next year King Edgar and Ethelwold replaced the cathedral canons with monks from Abingdon, thus founding the first monastic cathedral, a specifically English institution which remained until the Reformation. From this change the monastic reform both gained momentum and changed direction. It became closely associated with the king, whose principal palace was but a stone's throw away from Winchester cathedral, but also with the diocesan and parochial needs of the Church. Strongly supported by the king, Ethelwold restored old monasteries such as Milton (Dorset) in 964, New Minster, and Nunnaminster in Winchester itself in 965, while new monasteries were founded and richly endowed at Peterborough (966), Ely (970), and Thorney (972), where he sometimes spent Lent living as a hermit and where he built a church with an apse at each end. His charter for the endowment of Peterborough with land, serfs, cattle, church plate, and twenty manuscripts survives.

In character Ethelwold was austere, able, and dynamic. The scribe of his *Benedictional* called him a *Boanerges* (= son of thunder). When he was prior at Glastonbury he used to urge the brethren to greater effort in their monastic observance; he never slept after Matins and would eat meat only once in three months, at Dunstan's express command. He also possessed considerable practical and artistic gifts. At Glastonbury he had been cook; at Abingdon he worked at the building until he broke his ribs falling off a scaffold; at Winchester he set the monks to work with the masons in the cathedral and built the most powerful organ of its time in England. It was played by two monks and had 400 pipes and 36 bellows. Bells and a crown of metal for candles in the sanctuary at Abingdon were also attributed to him. Even more important was the appearance in Ethelwold's monasteries of the new influential Winchester style of illumination, which soon surpassed in excellence the products of many scriptoria of continental monasteries. His school of vernacular writing at Winchester, of which Ælfric is the most famous example, was the most important of its time; its accurate translations, linguistically significant, were designed to meet the needs of bishops and clergy who were not themselves monks. In music Ethelwold's Winchester had the distinction of producing the first English polyphony in the *Winchester Troper*. His monastery at Winchester must have been large in personnel and outstanding in achievement. The rebuilt cathedral, which awkwardly incorporated older elements, was the setting for a wonderfully rich and varied liturgy. Nor were the needs of the town forgotten: Ethelwold built an aqueduct for it.

Three important events marked his episcopate. One was the Congress of *c*.970 when the *Regularis Concordia*, the characteristic statement of the monastic revival's observance, was promulgated as the norm of the thirty reformed monasteries in the southern half of England. Based on the practices of Ghent, Fleury, and Glastonbury, it was probably compiled by Ethelwold himself, who was also responsible for an important vernacular account of the aims of the reform and an OE version of the Rule of St. Benedict. The second event was the translation of the relics of *Swithun of Winchester in 971. The third was the consecration of the cathedral in 980. Each occasion was marked by a large concourse of clergy and laity and was a sign of the success of the monastic reform movement, of which Dunstan and Ethelwold had been the pioneers. Their monasteries provided about three-quarters of the bishops of England until the Norman Conquest and a number of missionaries to Scandinavia; they were themselves centres of OE art and letters for many years to come.

Ethelwold was described by contemporaries as an outstanding counsellor of the king and as the benevolent bishop, the father of monks. These characteristics need to be recalled, as well as his ability and intransigence, for any final assessment of his personality. Feast: 1 August (2 August at Abingdon); translation, 10 September; Ely had a *commemoratio* on 8 October: Deeping and Thorney an *exceptio* on 23 October.

Life by Wulfstan ed. and trs. by M. Lapidge and M. Winterbottom (OMT 1991); that by Ælfric in J. Stevenson (ed.), *Chronicon Monasterii de Abingdon* (*R.S.*, 1858), i. 253–66 and both in M. Winterbottom, *Three Lives of English Saints* (1972); T. Symons (ed.), *The Regularis Concordia* (1953); E. John, 'The Beginnings of the Benedictine Reform in England' in *Orbis Britanniae* (1966); D. Parsons (ed.), *Tenth-Century Studies* (1975); see also *M.O.*, pp. 31–56, 448–52, 528–37. For his artistic, literary, and musical importance see G. F. Warner and H. R. Wilson, *The Benedictional of St. Ethelwold* (facsimile edn., 1919) and F. Wormald, *The Benedictional of St. Ethelwold* (1958); H. Gneuss, 'The Origin of Standard Old English and Æthelwold's school at Winchester', *A.S.E.*, i (1972), 63–83; M. Gretsch, 'Æthelwold's translation of the Regula Sancti Benedicti and its Latin exemplar', ibid., iii (1974), 125–52; W. H. Frere, *The Winchester Troper* (1894) and J. Handschin, 'The Two Winchester Tropers', *J.T.S.*, xxxvii (1936), 34–9, 156–72. See also B. Yorke (ed.), *Bishop Ethelwold: His Career and Influence* (1988).

ETHILWALD (1) (Æthelweald) (d. 740), monk, bishop of Lindisfarne. A Northumbrian who became a monk at Melrose, Ethilwald was a disciple of *Cuthbert and became prior and later abbot of Melrose. On the death of *Edfrith, bishop of Lindisfarne, and scribe of the Lindisfarne Gospels, Ethelwald was chosen as his successor. His interest in Edfrith's work is shown by his patronage of the hermit *Billfrith, who made at his request a binding for it of gold and precious stones (now lost). His reputation for sanctity is shown by his relics being removed from Lindisfarne with those of St. Cuthbert, whose peregrinations they shared. A stone cross with his name on it also came from Lindisfarne eventually to Durham. A compilation by him called *Ymnarius Edilwaldi* is a source of the *Book of Cerne*, of which work he was at least a part-author. Feast: 12 February; translation (to Westminster by King Edgar) 21 April.

Bede, *H.E.*, v. 12 (and Plummer, ii. 297); B. Colgrave, *Two Lives of St. Cuthbert* (1940), pp. 13–14, 331–2; T. D. Kendrick and others, *Codex Lindisfarnensis* (1960); A. B. Kuypers, *The Book of Cerne* (1902).

ETHILWALD (2) (Oidilwald) **OF FARNE** (d. 699), hermit. He was a monk and priest of Ripon, who succeeded *Cuthbert in the Inner Farne hermitage in 687. Almost nothing is known of him. Once Guthrid, the future abbot, with two monks of Lindisfarne, visited him by boat; on the return journey they were saved from shipwreck in a sudden storm by his prayers. The day of his death is usually recorded as 23 March, but he is mentioned in the Calendar of *Willibrord under 21 April. He was buried at Lindisfarne next to Edbert and Cuthbert; his relics shared the wanderings of Cuthbert's body until both finally rested at Durham. Florence of Worcester reported many miracles due to his intercession.

Bede, *H.E.*, v. 1; *Bedas Metrische Vita sancti Cuthberti* (ed. W. Jaager, 1935) *c.*45; Florence of Worcester, *Chronicon*, i. 40.

EUDELME (Ethelina?), patroness of Little Sodbury (Glos.). Nothing is known of her.

Stanton for unstated reasons gives 18 February as her day.

EUDES, John (1601–80), founder of the Congregation of Jesus and Mary (Eudists). Born of a farming family at Ri (Normandy), he was educated by the Jesuits at Caen. In 1623 he joined the French Oratorians, inspired by Philip *Neri, and stayed with them for twenty years, being zealous in preaching, especially missions, and the care of the sick during epidemics. By some good judges he was reckoned as the preacher in the France of his day who most touched the hearts of his hearers.

In 1643 he founded his new congregation for the education of priests in seminaries; foundations were made at Coutances, Lisieux, and Rouen. Eudes also founded refuges for fallen women. After his death his work prospered and the houses became much more numerous.

In the field of devotion he gave impetus to the spread of devotion to the Sacred Heart by providing a firm doctrinal basis for it. This completed the revelations made to Margaret Mary *Alacoque. He died at Caen, and was canonized in 1925. Feast: 19 August.

Lives by H. Joly (1907, Eng. tr. 1932), D. Sargent (1949), and P. Herambourg (1960). Works published in Paris (12 vols., 1905–9); selected letters (ed. C. Berthelot du Chesnay, 1958). See also E. Georges, *La Congrégation de Jésus et Marie, dite des Eudistes* (1933).

EULALIA OF MERIDA (Spain) (d. *c.*304), virgin and martyr. The existence and cult of this martyr are known from the Calendar of Carthage and the Martyrology of Jerome. There are also hymns in her honour by Prudentius and *Venantius Fortunatus and a sermon of *Augustine. Her martyrdom was known to *Bede (in his hymn to Etheldreda), *Aldhelm, and the OE martyrology; it inspired too the oldest surviving French poem, the *Cantilène de Sainte Eulalie.* Her Acts of the 6th century are unreliable. These make her a girl of twelve who, when the edicts of Diocletian were published obliging everyone to offer sacrifice to the gods, came to the judge at Merida and reproached him with trying to destroy souls through obliging them to deny the one true God. The judge Dacian tried to flatter, bribe, and lastly terrify her, but she trampled on the sacrificial cake and spat at the judge. Executioners then tortured her and she was burnt alive.

Snow covered her body until it was buried by Christians near by. The oven in which she was believed to have been burnt is incorporated into her shrine at Merida.

Later, a very similar story was developed concerning a supposed Eulalia of Barcelona, but the Bollandists and other scholars are convinced that there was only one martyr Eulalia, that of Merida. Oviedo, however, also claims her relics. Feast: 10 December.

Propylaeum, pp. 60, 576; *C.M.H.*, pp. 642–3; H. Quentin, *Les martyrologes historiques du moyen âge* (1908), pp. 162–4; B.T.A., iii. 530–1; R. Collins in *Visigothic Spain* (ed. E. James, 1980), pp. 189–219.

EULOGIUS OF CORDOBA (d. 859), theologian and martyr. One of a large and wealthy family which had owned land nearby since Roman times, Eulogius is an example of a Christian who lived under Islamic occupation for many years and who would have become a bishop if he had not been martyred first. Most of his life was spent in this wealthy and populous Moorish capital. Extra tax was paid by Christians for freedom of worship, but the conversion of Mohammedans to Christianity was punishable by death.

Eulogius was educated by priests and by abbot Sperandeo. He too became a priest, but his friend and future biographer Alvarez married and became a writer. Meanwhile Eulogius's youngest brother became an important official in the local Islamic court. Eulogius, described as devout, restrained, learned, and kindly, was in the habit of visiting hospitals and monasteries; for the latter he drew up new rules, based in part on those in Navarre and Pamplona.

In 850 there was a persecution of Christians in Cordoba, due probably to indiscreet attacks on Mohammed or attempted proselytism. An Andalusian bishop Reccared seems to have caused the imprisonment of the bishop and priests of Cordoba, including Eulogius, who read the Scriptures to the others and wrote his *Exhortation to Martyrdom* for two young women, who were executed by the sword. Soon afterwards the other captives were released.

In 852 others were martyred in spite of the Council of Cordoba's decree forbidding provocation. Meanwhile Eulogius wrote a *Memorial of the Saints* which described their suffering and death in persecution: he followed this up with an *Apologia* in their favour.

On the death of the archbishop of Toledo, Eulogius was chosen as his successor, but did not live long enough to be consecrated. He had befriended and hidden Leocritia, a Christian convert of Islamic parentage. Her hiding-place was discovered; all involved were arrested; Eulogius boldly proclaimed the Christian Gospel and was struck for speaking against Mohammed. He refused blandishments and was indifferent to threats: he was led out from his trial to be beheaded. Buried at Cordoba, his relics were translated to Oviedo cathedral in 883 and are still there. Feast: 11 March.

Life by Alvarez in *AA.SS.* Martii II (1735), 88–97; works in *P.L.*, cxv. 705–870; J. Perez de Urbel, *A Saint under Moslem Rule* (1937); B.T.A., i. 561–3; *Bibl. SS.*, v. 218–19.

EUNAN, see ADOMNAN.

EUNY (Ewin, Uny, Euninus), patron of Lelant, Crowan, and Redruth (Cornwall), appears in no ancient calendars or Lives of the Saints. William Worcestre in 1478 noted: 'Saint Uny, the brother of St. Herygh [and of St. Ia] lies in the parish church of St. Uny near the town of Lallant, on the northern sea three miles from Mont-Myghell, his day is kept on the first day of February.' At Maroony (= Merther Uny) farm in the parish of Wendron a fine Celtic cross was discovered on the site of a chapel of St. Euny. In the parish of Sancreed near Land's End there was a 'Chapel Euny' with a sacred well, still reputed to have healing properties in the 18th and 19th centuries.

G. H. Doble, *The Saints of Cornwall*, i (1960), 79–88.

EUSEBIUS OF VERCELLI (d. 371), bishop. Sardinian by birth, of a family who had suffered persecution for their Christianity, Eusebius was educated in Rome and then served the Church in Vercelli (Piedmont), first as lector and later as its first bishop. Here he instituted a rule for his clergy, living with them a semi-monastic regime similar to that of *Augustine, with whom he is often reckoned the founder of the Austin Canons.

That he was a serious scholar is clear from his surviving letters, and from the attribution to him (in neither case certain) of the writing of the Vercelli Gospel Book (the earliest existing manuscript of the Old Latin version) and the composition of the Athanasian Creed. From 354 onwards his life and activity were concerned with the wider field of doctrinal orthodoxy. Pope Liberius sent him to the Emperor Constantius to negotiate for the convoking of a council, which took place in Milan in 355. At this he refused to sign a condemnation of *Athanasius and insisted on all signing their adherence to the Nicene Creed before proceeding further; in the consequent quarrel he insisted that Athanasius should not be condemned unheard and that secular force should not influence ecclesiastical decisions. He was then exiled, first to Palestine, then to Cappadocia, then to Egypt. On the death of Constantius in 361 Eusebius and other exiled bishops were allowed to return to their sees. Again he was called elsewhere: first to Alexandria to concert plans with Athanasius, then to Antioch in the vain hope of ending the schism, then to work with *Hilary against an Arianizing bishop of Milan. Nothing is known of his last years but he died presumably at Vercelli on 1 August, on which day he is eulogized in the Roman and OE martyrologies: his feast of 16 December marks the anniversary of his consecration. He is sometimes called a martyr, but for his sufferings, not for violent death.

He should not be confused with other men of the 4th century called Eusebius, such as Eusebius of Caesarea, the church historian, Eusebius of Nicomedia, the Arian court bishop, or St. Eusebius of Samosata, who was killed by an Arian woman who threw a brick at his head and whose feast is on 21 or 22 June. Eusebius of Vercelli's feast is now on 2 August.

The *Clavis Patrum Latinorum* (1951) attributes to him a treatise *De Trinitate* (*P.L.*, lxii. 237–88) as well as three letters (*P.L.*, xii. 947–54); see also V. Bulhart in *C.C. Series Latina*, ix (1957), 1–205, and V. C. De Clercq in *D.H.G.E.*, xv (1963), 1477–83; B.T.A., iv. 569–71.

EUSTACE (Eustachius, Eustathius), martyr of unknown date and quite probably of no historical existence, patron of hunters and one of the *Fourteen Holy Helpers. There are churches dedicated to Eustace in Rome (from the 8th century) and Constantinople; also three ancient dedications in England. He is probably most familiar from pictures of him meeting a stag between whose antlers was a crucifix (an incident which also figures in the Legend of *Hubert). There is no early cult nor clear place of origin, which may well be Eastern.

The historically worthless legend tells of a Roman general called Placidas under Trajan, who was converted through seeing the stag with the crucifix, changed his name and that of his wife and children, lost his fortune and his family, was recalled to command the army at a critical time, was reunited with his family, and with them suffered martyrdom through being roasted to death in a brazen bull after refusing to sacrifice.

In England, as elsewhere in Christendom, Eustace was a popular saint. At Wells cathedral (NW. tower of West Front) he is depicted carrying his children across a river (sculptured *c.*1240), while in the British Museum is a head-reliquary of him which contained a head-bone and various other relics with labels in a 12th-century hand. These were all restored to the Swiss cathedral from which they were originally looted by the armies of Napoleon. Feast: 20 September (suppressed by the Holy See in 1969); in the East, 2 November.

AA.SS. Sept. VI (1757), 106–37; *Propylaeum*, pp. 407–8; H. Delehaye, 'La Légende de S. Eustache' in *Mélanges d'hagiographie grecque et latine* (*Subsidia Hagiographica*, xlii, 1966), pp. 212–39; B.T.A., iii. 606–7; *Bibl. SS.*, v. 281–91.

EUSTOCHIUM CALAFATO (1434–68), Franciscan abbess of Messina. Daughter of Bernard, a rich merchant of Messina and his wife, she was christened Smeralda (= Emerald). After experiencing a vision of Christ crucified, she entered the Poor Clare convent of S. Maria di Basico in 1446. In 1457, disillusioned by its supposed laxity, she was authorized to found a community of strict observance nearby, under the care of Franciscan Observants: this community was transferred to Montevergine in 1463. By then it included some of her close relatives.

Her love of Christ in poverty and penance were outstanding; she wrote a treatise, now lost, on the Passion, and her devotion to the Holy Places (which she never visited) in some ways recalls that of *Bridget of Sweden. Elected abbess at the age of thirty, she suffered many exterior and interior trials, dying at the age of only thirty-five. She was buried at Montevergine. The state of her incorrupt body was described in great detail by the then archbishop of Messina in 1690. The cult was formally approved in 1782 and she was canonized in 1988. In art she is represented with a cross in her hand or kneeling before the Blessed Sacrament. Feast: 20 January.

AA.SS. Ian. II (1643), 251; Lives by R. G. Nuti (1925), M. Catalano (1942), and [Clarisse di Montevergine] *Vita della B. Eustochia* (1961); see also *Bibl. SS.*, iii. 660–2.

EVANS, Philip (d. 1679), Jesuit priest and martyr. A Welshman born at Monmouth and educated at St. Omer, Evans joined the Society of Jesus in 1665 and was ordained priest in 1675. He was then sent to work in South Wales, but his apostolate lasted only three years. Following the scare of the 'Popish Plot' invented by Titus Oates, a reward of £250 was offered for the capture of Evans. He was arrested at Skier (Glamorgan) and imprisoned at Cardiff for five months, while the country was scoured for witnesses who would testify that they had seen him minister as a priest. Eventually a poor woman and a dwarf testified, whereupon the jury were instructed to find him guilty.

But his execution was delayed and his imprisonment somewhat mitigated. From these last few weeks of his life comes evidence of his skill at both tennis and music. While he was playing tennis he was told that his execution would take place the following day; this did not deter him from finishing the game and he spent some of his last hours playing the Welsh harp. He was executed on 22 July at Cardiff; in his final sermon on the scaffold he declared: 'I die for God and religion's sake; and I think myself so happy that if I had never so many lives, I would willingly give them all for so good a cause.' He was canonized by Paul VI in 1970 as one of the *Forty Martyrs of England and Wales. Feast: 25 October.

R. Challoner, *Memoirs of Missionary Priests* (ed. J. H. Pollen, 1924), pp. 544–7; T. P. Ellis, *Catholic Martyrs of Wales* (1933), pp. 119–25; H. Foley, *Records of the English Province of the Society of Jesus* (1877–82), v (2), 882–91; J. Stonor, *Six Welsh Martyrs* (pamphlet 1961).

EVERILD (Everildis, Averil) (d. *c.*700), virgin. All that we know of her comes from the York breviary. According to this source she was of a noble Wessex family; she went to the north of England to become a nun with her companions Bega and Wulfreda. They settled on land owned by *Wilfrid called Bishop's Farm, which he gave them. The nunnery grew until, we are told, it numbered eighty; Everild died peacefully when her mission was accomplished. It was believed that this saint gave her name to Everingham (now Humberside) but E. Ekwall gives as its derivation 'The ham of Eofor's people'. Feast: 9 July, in medieval calendars of York and Northumbria and two martyrologies.

AA.SS. Iul. II (1721), 713; Stanton, pp. 328–9. *York Breviary*, s.d. 9 July.

EVROUL(T) (Ebrulf) (626–706), abbot. Evroul, a Bayeux noble, was a married man at the Merovingian court, his wife became a nun and he joined a monastery near Bayeux. Later he became a hermit at Ouche (Normandy) with a few companions who lived in very primitive conditions. He converted a band of robbers who helped to swell the numbers of his community which made foundations elsewhere. Both by exhortation and example he emphasized the importance of manual work for monks, both in order to earn their living and as a means of serving God. Four abbots from the monastery of Saint-Evroul ruled English monasteries in the 11th and 12th centuries, who both brought relics of, and fostered interest in, the saint. The calendar of Deeping and Thorney testifies to this with feasts on 29 December (the usual day) and 30 August (a translation feast, called *exceptio*, which presumably commemorated the arrival of relics from Saint-Evroul to Thorney, very likely under Robert de Pruniers, abbot of Thorney 1113–51). A translation had already taken place at Saint-Evroul in 1130. The Anglo-Norman historian, Ordericus Vitalis, was a monk of Saint-Evroul and described monastic life there in his time and this particular translation. In England the cult of Evroul was soon eclipsed by that of *Thomas of Canterbury on the same day, 29 December, but Deeping venerated him on 30 August.

Ninth-century Life in *AA.SS. O.S.B.*, i. 354–61; Ordericus Vitalis, *Historia Ecclesiastica* (ed. M. Chibnall), iii (1972), 264–302. French verse Life ed. J. Blin, *Bulletin de la soc. hist. arch d. de l'Orne*, vi (1887), 1–83; *E.B.K. after 1100*, i. 129–32; B.T.A., iv. 639–40.

EVURTIUS (Evortius, Enurchus) (4th century), bishop of Orléans, who might possibly be identified with an Eortius who took part in the council of Valencia (374). Nothing is known about him, not even the date of his death. In 1604 his name was added to the calendar of the Book of Common Prayer from the York Breviary to distinguish the birthday of Queen Elizabeth I. Feast: 7 September.

AA.SS. Sept. III (1750), 44–58; *Propylaeum*, p. 385; V. Staley, *The Liturgical Year* (1907), pp. 43–5. F. Bond lists his artistic presentation, surely in error, as: 'Cook with apron; dove on his head.'

EWALD, see HEWALD.

EWE, patron of St. Ewe (Cornwall). Nothing certain is known about this saint. There have been tentative efforts to identify him (or her) with the Welsh Yw or the Breton Theo. Believed to be a woman (Ewa) in the Middle Ages.

G. H. Doble, *The Saints of Cornwall*, v (1970), 30–2.

EWIN, see EUNY.

EYSTEIN, see AUGUSTINE OF TRONDHEIM.

F

FABIAN (d. 250), pope and martyr. He became pope in 236, chosen, according to Eusebius, in spite of being a layman and a stranger. *Cyprian praised him as 'an incomparable man, the glory of whose death corresponded with the holiness of his life'. The *Liber Pontificalis* ascribed to him the division of Rome into seven deaconries. When the persecution of Decius began, he was its first victim in Rome. His body was buried in the catacomb of Callistus and later moved to the church of St. Sebastian, with whom he shares his feast. The original slab which covered his first tomb survives; his body was rediscovered in 1915. Feast: 20 January.

AA.SS. Ian II (1643), 252–6; Cyprian, *Epistola ix* (ed J. Hartel, *C.S.E.L.*, iii. 488–9); F. Grossi-Gondi, *S. Fabiano papa e martire, la sua tomba e le sue spoglie attraverso i secoli* (1916); B.T.A., i. 128.

FAELAN, see FOILLAN.

FAITH (Foy) (3rd century?), virgin, martyr. The Martyrology of *Jerome records her death at Agen in Gaul, so it is likely that she really existed. But her Legend is quite unhistorical; she was further confused with the mythical sisters Faith, Hope, and Charity and their mother Sophia. The diffusion of her cult in the Middle Ages was remarkable. Her body was translated to Conques, where the justly famous reliquary from the 10th century survives, a masterpiece of barbaric Dark Age art. Here both Crusaders and pilgrims to the shrine of St. James at Compostela invoked her intercession and took back the memory of her to their own countries. In many districts of France are found place-names and church dedications to Sainte Foy. In England a shrine of the saint was set up at Horsham St. Faith, near Norwich. Her fame passed not only to Italy and Spain, but also eventually to South America, especially Bogotá. In England fifteen Black Monk abbeys celebrated her feast, which passed into the Sarum Missal. Chapels were dedicated to her in Westminster Abbey and St. Paul's cathedral; no fewer than twenty-three ancient English churches also were consecrated in her name. Her Acts make her a young girl who was put to death by being roasted on a brazen bed and then beheaded. This inspired numerous artistic representations of her, in which a sword or a bundle of rods is her emblem. She was not so much a healing saint as one whose patronage was invoked by soldiers, prisoners, and pilgrims. Feast: 6 October; translation, 14 January.

AA.SS. Oct. III (1770), 263–329; Réau, i. 513–16; A. Fabre, *La chanson de sainte Foy de Conques* (1940); B.T.A., iv. 45.

FARA (Burgundofara), foundress and abbess of the double monastery of Faremoutier-en-Brie (d. 657). During her rule of 37 years several English nuns such as *Saethrith, *Ercongota, and *Ethelburga were trained by her, some of whom later set up monasteries in England. Feast: 7 December.

Life by Jonas of Bobbio in B. Krusch, *MGH Scriptores Meroving*, iv; Bede, *HE*, iii 8; H. M. Delsart, *Sainte Fare: sa vie et son culte* (1911).

FAUSTINUS, see SIMPLICIUS, FAUSTINUS, AND BEATRICE.

FECHIN (Vigean, corrupted to Virgin) (d. 665), Irish abbot. Born at Bile Fechin (Connacht), he was trained by Nathy at Achonry (Co. Sligo) and made his first foundation at Fore (Westmeath). Later he founded Ballysadare, Cong, Imaid Island, Omey, and Ard Oilean, another island monastery, whence came the oldest MS. of his Life. In most of these places are some ruins, of which a small part may go back to Fechin's time. Like several other Irish saints, Fechin had a cult in Scotland, due perhaps to the journeys of his disciples; there is a parish of St. Vigean near Arbroath, where a fair was held on his feast, 20 January.

V.S.H., ii. 76–86; *The Irish Saints*, pp. 151–4; W. Stokes, 'Life of St. Fechin of Fore', *Revue Celtique*, xii (1891), 318–53; R. A. S. Macalister, 'The Antiquities of Ard Oilean, Co. Galway', *J.R.S.A.L.*, xxvi (1896), 196–210; *K.S.S.*, pp. 456–8.

FELGILD (Feleogild) (d. *c.*725), hermit of Farne. He is described by *Bede as the third hermit who lived on the Inner Farne, succeeding *Cuthbert and *Ethilwald, as an 'athlete of Christ', who was aged seventy when Bede was writing (*c.*721). The hermitage had become very draughty and Felgild was cured of sores on his face by applying to it a calf-skin previously used to seal the holes. There is no known cult or feast, but only a mention in Durham's *Liber Vitae*.

B. Colgrave, *Two Lives of St. Cuthbert* (1940), pp. 300–7; J. Raine, *Miscellanea Biographica* (S.S., 1844), p. 116.

FELICIAN, see PRIMUS AND FELICIAN.

FELICITAS (Felicity) **OF CARTHAGE**, martyr; see PERPETUA AND FELICITAS.

FELICITY (Felicitas) **OF ROME**, martyr; see SEVEN BROTHERS.

FELIX OF DUNWICH (d. 647), bishop of the East Angles. A Burgundian by birth and education, Felix was consecrated bishop at an unknown date and came to Honorius, archbishop of Canterbury, with the intention of building up the Church among the Angles. In 630 the Christian King *Sigebert returned from exile to rule the East Angles, so Honorius sent Felix to evangelize his people. How long Felix had been a bishop, how long he had stayed at Canterbury, and whether or not he had known Sigebert in Gaul before coming to England are alike uncertain. In East Anglia he made Dunwich the centre of his see and established a school on the Gaulish model with teachers from Canterbury. During his episcopate the Irish monk *Fursey founded a monastery at Burgh Castle; there is no record of any conflict between the two. Felix is a good example of the Gaulish contribution to the conversion of the Anglo-Saxons; his fruitful episcopate of seventeen years in close collaboration both with the king of East Anglia and with the see of Canterbury resulted in the stability of his see. He also founded the monastery of Soham where he was buried, and from where his relics were translated to Ramsey abbey. The oldest surviving calendar evidence for his cult dates from *c.*1000, at Bury, Croyland, and Ely. Six ancient English churches are dedicated to Felix; he has given his name and patronage to Felixstowe (Suffolk) and possibly, but less likely to Felixkirk (N. Yorkshire). Feast: 8 March.

Bede, *H.E.*, ii. 15; iii. 18–20; *AA.SS.* Mar. I (1668), 779–81; J. M. Wallace-Hadrill, 'Rome and the Early English Church', *Settimano di Studio del Centro Italiano di Studi sull'alto medioevo*, viii (1960), 519–48; P. Hunter Blair, *The World of Bede* (1970), pp. 107–9.

FELIX OF NOLA (d. 260), confessor. As his compatriot Paulinus relates, he was tortured but not killed in time of persecution, and afterwards enjoyed a fruitful apostolate, notable for conversions and miracles. *Bede wrote a summary of this work. His cult is witnessed by the Martyrologies of Jerome and of Carthage and by many ancient sacramentaries. His church at Nola, decorated by murals of Old Testament subjects, was a notable pilgrimage centre from the 4th century. The hagiographers, however, confused the issue by either making several Felixes out of one, or else identifying several separate ones. It seems most likely that the basilica of Felix on the Pincian Hill, Rome, was built to honour the *martyr* Felix on the Via Portuensis. There are sixty-six saints of the name of Felix listed in the Roman Martyrology alone. Felix of Nola occurs in the Sarum calendar and in fifteen English Benedictine calendars. Feast: 14 January.

AA.SS. Ian I (1643), 937–50 and *Propylaeum*, pp. 20–1; B.T.A., i. 80–1. Bede, *H.E.*, v. 24; see also *P.L.*, xciv. 789–98.

FELIX OF THIBIUCA (247–303), bishop and martyr. Nothing is known of his early life, but he was one of the first martyrs of Diocletian's persecution. The cause of his martyrdom was his persistent refusal to hand over the sacred Scriptures to be burnt. This had been ordered in Diocletian's first edict of 23 February 303, which was promulgated in Thibiuca on 5 June. Not only were all copies of the Scriptures and liturgical books to be surrendered but Christian worship was also forbidden and the churches ordered to be destroyed. A preliminary examination of a local priest and two lectors resulted in the matter being referred to the bishop, then absent in Carthage. On his return to his diocese Felix was arrested and interrogated. For Felix the conflict was clearly between the commandments of God and those of men. He was given three days' grace to change his mind: when he refused, he was referred to the proconsul. Felix admitted that he had the Scriptures, but refused to give them up. For this he was ordered to be beheaded. His last words were: 'God, I thank you. I have passed fifty-six years in this world. I have preserved my chastity; I have observed the Gospels; I have preached the faith and the truth. Lord God of heaven and earth, Jesus Christ, I bend my neck as a sacrifice for you, who abides for ever.' He was condemned to be beheaded at Carthage on 15 July, which is his true feast day. Later interpolations of the authentic Acts, however, claimed that he died at Venosa in Apulia: the comparative success of this fiction resulted, through confusion with another saint of the same name, in his feast being recorded on 24 October in the Roman Martyrology.

A.C.M. pp. xl and 266–71; H. Delehaye, 'La Passion de S. Felix de Thibiuca', *Anal. Boll.*, xxxix (1921), 241–76; B.T.A., iv. 188.

FELIX AND ADAUCTUS (d. *c.*304), martyrs of Rome. Buried in the cemetery of Commodilla on the Ostian Way, they must be among the most solidly attested of all Roman martyrs, with feasts in the early Roman Sacramentaries, inscriptions from the pontificates of Siricius and Damasus, and a church built over their tomb, uncovered in 1905. Felix, a Roman priest, suffered in the beginning of Diocletian's persecution. On his way to execution he was joined by a stranger, who also confessed that he was a Christian and suffered with Felix. As his name was not known he was called Adauctus (= the one added). Feast: 30 August.

AA.SS. Aug. VI (1743), 545–51 with *C.M.H.*, pp. 476–8 and *Propylaeum*, p. 369; B.T.A., iii. 446.

FERDINAND III (1199–1252); king of Castile and Leon. Born near Salamanca, the son of Alfonso IX of Leon and Berengaria of Castile, he became king of Castile in 1217 and of Leon in 1230. His definitive union of these two kingdoms made possible the principal achievement of his reign: the recovery from the Moors of most of Andalusia and its assimilation into the Christian State. In this way Ferdinand's series of victories over twenty-seven years was of more than local importance. They included Ubeda (1234), Cordoba (1236), Seville and Cadiz (1249). At the battle of Xeres, where only twelve Spaniards were killed, *James was reputed to have led the army in person. Appropriately Ferdinand restored to the cathedral of Santiago de Compostela the bells previously removed by the Moors. In thanksgiving for his deliverance of Christians from the power of Moslems he rebuilt Burgos cathedral and converted an important mosque at Seville into a church. But once Moslems and Jews submitted, he was politically tolerant, while encouraging the Friars to convert them. He was also prominent in the foundation of Salamanca university and possibly Valladolid.

He administered impartial justice and chose wise counsellors such as Rodrigo Ximenes, archbishop of Toledo, whose chronicle is a principal source for his achievements.

Ferdinand's first wife was Beatrice of Swabia, by whom he had seven sons and three daughters; his second was Joan of Ponthieu, by whom he had two more sons and a daughter, Eleanor the future wife of Edward I of England.

Ferdinand was buried in Seville cathedral, dressed not in royal robes but in the habit of a Franciscan. The widespread popular cult of this warrior king arose soon after his death; he was formally canonized in 1671. His emblem in art is a greyhound. Feast: 30 May.

AA.SS. Maii VII (1688), 281–414; L. F. De Retana, *San Fernando III y su época* (1941); J. Laurentie, *Saint Ferdinand III* (1910); other Lives by F. Maccono (1924) and J. R. Coloma (1928); J. N. Hillgarth, *The Spanish Kingdoms 1250–1516* (1976); D. W. Lomax, *The Reconquest of Spain* (1978); B.T.A. (1688), ii. 426; *N.C.E.*, v. 886–7.

FERGHIL, see VIRGIL.

FERGUS (Fergusianus) (early 8th century), bishop. An Irish bishop called 'the Pict' in his own country, Fergus was the apostle of substantial areas of Scotland, according to the Aberdeen Breviary, whose conclusions accord well with the evidence of dedications and place-names. Fergus founded three churches in Strogeth, then went to Caithness (where he presumably founded Wick and Halkirk), then to Buchan, where the place formerly called Lungley is now St. Fergus and the churches of Inverugy, Banff, and Dyce may have been his. He died at Glamis, where a well and a cave both bear his name. Fergus may be identical with the *Fergustus episcopus Scotiae Pictus* who took part in the council of Rome in 721 which condemned irregular marriages of various kinds, sorcerers, and clerics who grew their hair long. Fergus's relics were kept at Glamis until an abbot of Scone in the time of James IV (1488–1513) removed the head while providing a more splendid marble tomb for the body. Aberdeen had an arm relic. Feast: 27 November.

K.S.S., pp. 336–8; *D.C.B.*, ii. 505–6.

FEUILLAN, see FOILLAN.

FIACRE (d. *c.*670), hermit. One of the many Irishmen who sought 'exile for Christ', Fiacre came to Meaux, where its bishop, St. Faro, gave him land for a hermitage at Breuil, a few miles away. Here he settled and lived as a hermit until his death. His cult flourished in France rather than Ireland, where his name did not come into the Martyrologies until the late 12th century. The presence of his Life in *N.L.A.* reveals that he was known in late medieval England. He is a patron of horticulturists because of his skill in this craft during his life. His Legend also made him a misogynist both in life and after death: possibly this is connected with his patronage of those who suffer venereal disease. His relics were translated to Meaux, where they still rest; this was the centre of devotion to Fiacre which flourished in the 17th and 18th centuries; his clients included Anne of Austria, Bossuet, and *Vincent de Paul. The place where the saint lived is now called Saint-Fiacre (Seine-et-Marne); the hackney carriages which were let for hire were called *fiacres* because they plied their trade from the hotel Saint-Fiacre in Paris. The name remains for taxi-cabs. Feast: 30 August; 1 September (in France and Ireland), but 18 August in *N.L.A.*

AA.SS. Aug. VI (1743), 598–620 and *Propylaeum*, p. 370; *N.L.A.*, i. 441–3; L. Gougaud, *Les Saints irelandais hors d'Irlande* (1936), pp. 86–92; B.T.A., iii. 460–1.

FIDELIS OF SIGMARINGEN (1577–1622), Franciscan friar and martyr. Born at Sigmaringen (Hohenzollern), he was educated at Freiburg-in-Breisgau, receiving doctorates in philosophy and law. From 1604 to 1610 he was tutor to some Swabian young men on their travels. Soon afterwards he was ordained priest and joined the reformed Capuchin branch of the Franciscan Order. He was superior of three houses in succession (1618–22), and became famous as a preacher and for his care of the sick. He was sent to preach among the Zwinglians of the Grisons area with the purpose of reconciling them to the

Church of Rome. He was killed by enraged peasants at Zwinglian instigation in the church at Seewis (Switzerland). He was canonized in 1746. Feast: 24 April.

Lives by L. da Lavertazzo (1922) and B. Gossens (1933); see also B.T.A., ii. 156–7 and *N.C.E.*, s.v.

FILLAN (Fillan, Foelan, Fulan) (early 8th century), abbot. Of Irish extraction, he was the nephew of *Comgan. He became a monk perhaps in Taghmon (Wexford) and a solitary at Pittenweem (Fife), and was chosen as abbot of the neighbouring monastery. But he resigned after some years and retired to Glendochart (Perthshire), where place-names and dedications recall his memory. Further north, in Ross-shire, there are dedications to Fillan and his uncle Comgan close by (Kilkoan and Killellan). He was buried at Strathfillan. He was recorded in the earliest Irish and Scottish martyrologies. His cult was sufficiently important for Robert the Bruce to take his arm relic to the battle of Bannockburn and to attribute his victory to the saint's intercession. The bell and staff of St. Fillan still survive. In the pool of Strathfillan the mentally ill used to be dipped and then left all night, tied up, in a corner of Fillan's ruined chapel. If they were found loose, they were considered cured. This practice continued until the early 19th century. Feast: 9 (or 19) January.

K.S.S., pp. 341–6; B.T.A., i. 120.

FINAN CAM (d. *c.*600), founder and abbot of Kinnity (Co. Offaly). Feast: 7 April.

FINAN LOBUR (6th century), abbot. Although of Munster descent he was born in Leinster. He suffered from a skin disease (described as 'leprosy'). He ruled over the monastery of Swords (north of Dublin) and possibly over Clonmore at the end of his life, where he was buried. Feast: 16 March.

B.T.A., i. 606–7; *The Irish Saints*, pp. 159–60.

FINAN OF ABERDEEN (6th century), disciple of *Kentigern. He first worked in Anglesey (place-name Llanffinnan), then went to Scotland *c.*573 and built several churches near Aberdeen between the rivers Dee and Don. Feast: 18 March.

FINAN OF LINDISFARNE, bishop and abbot 651–61. Irish and from Iona, this successor of *Aidan resembled him in character and policy. Zealous, learned, and prudent, he worked in close co-operation with Oswiu, king of Northumbria (d. 670). He built the wooden church at Lindisfarne; he defended Irish customs against the Roman cleric *Ronan, yet agreed to *Wilfrid going from Lindisfarne to Rome. He sent Northumbrian and Irish missionaries to Mercia and Essex, when an opening had been made through the baptism of their kings and through Northumbrian predominance. Feast: 17 February.

Bede, *H.E.*, iii. 21–2, 25; P. Grosjean, 'La date du Colloque de Whitby', *Anal. Boll.*, lxxviii (1960), 233–55.

FINBAR (Findbarr, Barra, Barry) (*c.*560–*c.*610), bishop, patron of Cork and of Barra, Outer Hebrides. Of the clan of Ui Briuin Ratha from West Connacht, Finbar was born at Lisnacaheragh (Co. Cork). His father, of illegitimate birth, was a metal-worker who married a slave-girl. Finbar studied under bishop MacCuirp at Achad Durbcon (Macroom). Later he became a hermit at lake Gougane Barra. Soon disciples gathered round him: the monastery at Etargabail on the east bank of the lake became a famous school which attracted students from southern Ireland. Several other churches in the neighbourhood claimed to be founded by him, but the greatest work of his life was the foundation of the monastery at Cork, round which the town developed.

Traditionally he was consecrated bishop *c.*600. The year of his death has been variously calculated as 610, 623, and 630. The Irish cult was founded on his reputation as teacher and saint and was strictly local: no foreign disciples or overseas missionary journeys were claimed for him. But there is also a Scottish cult, based on calendars and place-names, though almost devoid of hagiographical literature. His patronage of Barra, with his feast on the traditional day, is more probably due to journeys by men of Cork than by Finbar. The cult in Caithness and Sutherland (especially at Dornoch) is probably due to a confusion with Finbar of Moville.

Although Cork was Finbar's burial-place, the real centre of his cult in penal times and today is his monastery at Gougane Barra, still a place of pilgrimage. Feast: 25 September.

AA.SS. Sept. VII (1760), 130–9; *V.S.H.*, i. 65–74; P. Grosjean, 'Les Vies de S. Finbarr de Cork, de S. Finbarr d'Écosse et de S. MacCuilinn de Lusk', *Anal. Boll.*, lxix (1951), 324–47; T. A. Lunham, 'The Life of St. Finbarre', *Jnl. Cork Historical and Archaeol. Soc.* (1906), 105–20.

FINGAR, see Gwinear.

FINGAR AND PIALA (Guigner and Ciara), obscure Irish saints supposedly martyred at Hayle (Cornwall) *c.*455. Brother and sister, children of an Irish king, they were converted by *Patrick, driven into exile by their father, and landed first in Brittany, where they were well received, before moving on to Cornwall where they died at the hand of Tewdrick, king of Dumnonia. The feast of Fingar is kept in Brittany on 14 December.

Stanton, p. 600.

FINNIAN (Vennianus, Vinniaus) (d. 549), abbot of Clonard. The 10th-century Life stresses his Leinster birth and education, probably at Idrone (Co. Carlow), near which he made his first three foundations: Rossacurra, Drumfea, and Kilmaglush. After these beginnings he went to Wales and studied the traditional monasticism of *David, *Cadoc, and *Gildas. When he returned to Ireland, he made foundations at Aghowle (Co. Wicklow) and Mugna Sulcain. Having visited Kildare, he moved on again to the most important achievement of his life, the foundation of Clonard (Co. Meath) in a strategically central geographical position. Here he gathered numerous disciples (3,000 are claimed for his whole period there); its special characteristic was to unite study, especially of Holy Scripture, with the Welsh (and ultimately the Eastern) form of monastic life. Finnian personally had the reputation of 'Master' or 'Teacher of the Saints of Ireland', in particular of the *Twelve Apostles of Ireland, some of whom, however, are anterior in date. When his monks left Clonard, they took with them a gospel-book, a crozier and a reliquary, round which they later built their churches and monasteries. Finnian died of the plague on 12 December: 'As Paul died in Rome for the sake of the Christian people lest they should all perish in Hell, so Finnian died at Clonard for the sake of the people of the Gael, that they might not all perish of the yellow pest', said the writer of the Irish Life.

The Penitential of Finnian is probably his: it is based on Welsh and Irish sources, and on *Jerome and *Cassian, but is in large part original and influenced that of *Columbanus. It is the oldest surviving example of its kind and spread the influence of Clonard in penitential discipline and Scripture studies.

Finnian's relics were enshrined at Clonard until their destruction in 887. His feast is testified by a Spanish Martyrology of the early 9th century. After his death his monastery came under the power of the northern half of Ireland, ruled by the Ui Neill, and it built up a *paruchia* in Connacht rather than in Leinster as Finnian had done. It came to share an abbot with Kildare or with Clonmacnoise. Later still it was refounded as a house of Austin Canons, from whom there survives an Office of St. Finnian, some of whose elements were taken from a source, otherwise unknown. Feast: 12 December.

Irish Life in W. Stokes, *Lives of Saints from the Book of Lismore* (1890), pp. 75–83 and 222–30; Latin Life in W. W. Heist, *Acta Sanctorum Hiberniae* (1965), 96–106; R. A. S. Macalister, *The*

Latin and Irish Lives of Ciaran (1921): K. Hughes, 'The nistorical value of the Lives of St. Finnian of Clonard', *E.H.R.*, lxix (1954), 535–72; id., 'The cult of St. Finnian of Clonard from the eighth to the eleventh century', *Irish Historical Studies*, ix (1954), 13–27; L. Bieler, *The Irish Penitentials* (1963); J. T. Macneill and H. Gamer, *Medieval Handbooks of Penance* (1965).

FINNIAN OF MOVILLE (d. 579), abbot. Said to be of the royal race of Dal Fiatach, he was educated first at Dromore and later at *Ninian's monastery of Whithorn. He then returned to Ireland, possibly bringing from Rome a biblical manuscript. He founded one monastery at Moville (Co. Down) *c.*550 and another at Dromin (Louth) and became famous as a scholar and teacher: among his pupils was *Columba. It is possible that some Scottish dedications to Finnian are his, but little can be safely asserted about him, as he has been confused with either *Finnian of Clonard or with Frigidian of Lucca. The Penitential of Vinnian has been sometimes claimed as his. Feast: 10 September.

B.T.A., iii. 531–2; *The Irish Saints*, pp. 169–71.

FINTAN OF CLONENAGH (d. 603), abbot. Born in Leinster and educated by St. Colum of Terryglass, he founded Clonenagh which was famous for great austerity: he himself was reputed to live on a diet of barley bread and clayey water. This, however, did not prevent him from establishing a milder regime for some neighbouring monks. When some of his monks left the monastery without permission he received back at least one of them. When some soldiers came to the monastery bearing the severed heads of their enemies, Fintan had these buried in the monks' cemetery in the hope that by Doomsday they would have benefited from the prayers of generations of monks; 'since the principal part of their bodies rest here, we hope they will find mercy'. Feast (all over Ireland) 17 February.

V.S.H., ii. 96–106; J. Ryan, *Irish Monasticism* (1931), pp. 127–8; B.T.A., i. 356–7.

FINTAN OF RHEINAU (d. 879), hermit. Born in Leinster, captured and enslaved by Vikings who took him to the Orkneys, Fintan escaped and was protected by an unnamed Scottish bishop. He made a pilgrimage to Rome; on his way back he joined a group of hermits on an island in the Rhine near Schaffhausen, where he spent the rest of his life. The Sacramentary of Zurich (Kantonsbibl. 30) of 'Gelasian' type, which contains a calendar with Irish saints, may have been his. His relics at Rheinau, enshrined in 1446, still survive. Feast: 15 November.

Early Life in *M.G.H., Scriptores*, xv. 503–6; L. Gougaud, *Les Saints irlandais hors d'Irlande* (1936), pp. 95–6; B.T.A., iv. 350; *The Irish Saints*, pp. 173–4.

FINTAN MUNNU (Mundus, Munnu) (d. 635), abbot of Taghmon (Wexford). The son of Talchan of the Ui Neill clan, Fintan was trained in monastic life under *Comgall of Bangor, under Sinell at Cleenish on Lough Erne, and in one of *Columba's monasteries at Kilmore. This was the regime he liked best, so he decided to join Columba at Iona. When he arrived (597), Columba had just died; his successor, Baithene, refused to receive him as a monk, claiming an instruction from Columba soon before his death that Munnu was coming but should not be any abbot's monk, but rather an abbot himself. Accordingly Fintan returned to Ireland and founded the monastery of Taghmon, which soon became famous enough for its founder to be mentioned in the Lives of *Canice, *Mochua, and *Molua.

Towards the end of his life Fintan took part in the synod of Magh Lene, at which he strenuously defended the Irish calculation of Easter, opposing *Laserian and others, whose views ultimately prevailed, bringing Ireland into line with the rest of western Europe in this matter. Fintan suffered from a skin disease, probably leprosy. Hagiographers did not claim that he cured this by miracle, but that he voluntarily prayed to be afflicted by it, so that he could at least equal the merit and the heavenly reward of Molua. There is a cult in Scotland based on a series of dedications of local churches to him. These may be due to disciples or to a saint of similar name. He is sometimes identified with the Scottish saint Mundus. Feast: 21 October.

Latin Lives in *AA.SS.* Oct. IX (1858), 325–42; A. O. and M. O. Anderson, *Adomnan's Life of Columba* (1961), 206–15; *V.S.H.*, ii. 226–39; *K.S.S.*, pp. 414–16; *The Irish Saints*, pp. 174–7.

FIRMIN (Firminus) (4th century), bishop and martyr. He was probably a missionary bishop who died at Amiens, over whose tomb a later bishop of Amiens, St. Firmin the confessor, built the church now called St. Acheul. The martyrologies and the liturgical books of the 10th–11th centuries from different places mention one or the other Firmin of Amiens, but on different dates: Firmin the martyr on 25 September; Firmin the confessor on 1 September. Firmin the martyr is titular of two ancient English churches.

AA.SS. Sept. VII (1760), 24–57 and *Propylaeum*, p. 415; B.T.A., iii. 632–3; for Firmin the Confessor, *AA.SS.* Sept. I (1746), 175–99; J. Corblet, *Hagiographie du diocèse d'Amiens* (1870), ii. 31–216.

FISHER, John (1469–1535), bishop and martyr. Born at Beverley (Humberside), the son of a mercer, Fisher was educated at Cambridge University from the age of fourteen. He became a distinguished scholar, was elected a Fellow of Michaelhouse (now Trinity College), was ordained priest in 1491, and became in turn senior proctor, doctor of divinity, Master of Michaelhouse in 1496, and Vice-Chancellor in 1501. In 1502 he resigned the Mastership and became chaplain to the king's mother, Lady Margaret Beaufort, and in the same year he became the first Lady Margaret professor of divinity. Together they reformed and re-endowed Cambridge University, he guiding her to make good use of her considerable fortune, she respecting his scholarship and sanctity. His own academic reforms included the reintroduction of Greek and Hebrew into the curriculum, the invitation to Erasmus to lecture, and the endowment of scholarships. He was such a famous preacher that he was chosen as the panegyrist of both King Henry VII and Lady Margaret Beaufort.

Some years earlier, in 1504, he became both Chancellor of Cambridge University and bishop of Rochester. His lack of personal ambition made him refuse wealthier sees: his duties as diocesan of England's smallest see, even when scrupulously performed, left him free also for his academic pursuits. He built up a fine library, reputedly one of the best in Europe, and he strongly upheld traditional doctrine on the Real Presence and the Eucharistic Sacrifice against Protestant protagonists in English universities. He also wrote four volumes against Luther. There was no doubt of his high reputation. Henry VIII claimed that no other prince or kingdom had such a distinguished prelate, while the ambassador of Charles V declared him a paragon of Christian bishops for learning and holiness. He was an obvious choice as confessor to Henry VIII's queen Catharine of Aragon.

When the king started to plan divorce, Fisher, as one of her counsellors in the nullity suit of 1529, clearly demonstrated the validity of the marriage and showed it could not be legally dissolved by any power on earth. A few years later he became the champion of the supremacy of the Church and of the pope. In Convocation in 1531 he had protested against the new title of 'Head of the Church of England' for Henry VIII and inserted the all-important qualification, rejected by the king, 'so far as the law of Christ allows'. From then on, or even earlier, he lost the king's favour and was a marked man. In 1534 whether justly or not, he was condemned to perpetual imprisonment and loss of property for supposed encouragement of Elizabeth Barton, a young nun of Kent, whose visions included threats of divine punishment on the king if he did not repudiate Anne Boleyn. In fact the sentence was commuted to a fine because of his poor health. When he was tendered the oath of Succession in 1534, he refused to take it in the wording presented because this was tantamount to an oath of Supremacy, although, like his friend Thomas *More, he would have agreed to the succession itself. He was then arrested and imprisoned in the Tower of London, where he wrote a treatise on prayer for his sister, a Dominican nun. Two acts of attainder were passed against him: he was declared by the king to be deposed from his office and his see was considered vacant.

The recently elected pope, Paul III, nominated him a cardinal, to which Henry VIII replied that even if he sent him a red hat, Fisher would have no head to put it on. It is often said that a personal messenger from the king visited him in the Tower to declare in strict confidence for him alone his opinion of the royal supremacy, and that because his opinion went against Henry's wishes he was condemned to death as a traitor. The trial took place on 17 June 1535, and his execution by beheading five days later. Already contemporaries had wondered how one who was aged sixty-six, but looked more like eighty-six, could have endured ten months' imprisonment in the Tower. But his physical weakness caused by ill-health, austerity, and strain did not affect his heroic demeanour on the scaffold. Fortified by reference to the words in John 17: 3–4, he pardoned his executioner, declared in a clear voice that he was dying for the faith of Christ's holy Catholic Church, asked the people to pray for him, and recited the *Te Deum* and a psalm. His body was buried in the churchyard of All Hallows, Barking, without rites or shroud; his head was displayed on London Bridge for a fortnight before being thrown into the Thames.

Inevitably Fisher's life was controversial. He has been criticized for political indiscretion, as shown in his dealings with the Spanish ambassador and Elizabeth Barton, and for having a medieval theological outlook, although he was one of the finest scholars and humanists of his day; he is also a less humanly attractive figure than his friend Thomas More, and so has less often attracted biographers. Even if his austerity (exemplified by his keeping a skull on his table as a reminder of death) does not appeal to all tastes, his courage and integrity, like his outstanding academic achievements and his devotion to the welfare of his diocese, deserve to be better known. His theological works influenced the Council of Trent. He was canonized in 1935. Feast: with Thomas More, 22 June (formerly 9 July).

Latin works in *Fisheri Opera* (1597 and 1967): English works ed. J. E. B. Mayor, *E.E.T.S.*, 1876 and 1935; letters to and from Erasmus in J. Rouschasse, *Erasmus and Fisher* (1968); critical edn. of his *Sacri Sacerdotii Defensio contra Lutherum* by H. K. Schmeink (*Corpus Catholicorum*, 1925); devotional works ed. A. R. (1640 and 1969). The earliest Life was by T. Bailey, *The Life and Death of John Fisher* (1655), re-edited by F. van Ortroy, 'Vie du B. martyr Jean Fisher', *Anal. Boll.*, x (1891), 121–365 and xii (1893), 97–281; also ed. R. Bayne in *E.E.T.S.*, 1921; modern tr. by P. Hughes (1935). Modern Lives by T. Bridgett (1881), E. E. Reynolds (1955), and M. Macklem (1967); for his influence see E. L. Surtz, *The Works and Days of John Fisher* (1967). See also J. Rouschasse (ed.), *Erasmus and Fisher: their Correspondence* (1968); J. B. Mullinger, *The University of Cambridge from Earliest Times* (1873).

FLANNAN (7th century), bishop. There are cults of St. Flannan in both Ireland and Scotland; the fact that the feast-day is the same in the two countries makes it likely that they refer to the same person. In Ireland Flannan is closely connected with Killaloe, whose cathedral formerly housed his relics and besides which a stone oratory survives, believed to be his. According to the late and unreliable Legends Flannan was the disciple and successor of *Molua, founder of the monastery of Killaloe. Like other Irish monks he was both a wanderer and a preacher. His Legend attributes to him churches at Lough Corrib and at Inishbofin and an incident on the Isle of Man. In Scotland the Flannan islands, to the west of Lewis and Harris, are named after him; on one of these there are monastic remains called the chapel of Flannan. As late as 1678–9 there is record of men visiting these islands for the sake of killing the numerous birds and regarding it as a sacred place. Feast: 18 December.

W. W. Heist, *Vitae Sanctorum Hiberniae* (1965), pp. 280–301; P. Grosjean, 'Catalogus codicum hagiographicorum latinorum bibliothecarum Dubliniensium', *Anal. Boll.*, xlvi (1928), 124–41; *K.S.S.*, p. 350; *The Irish Saints*, pp. 177–80; H. G. Leask, 'The Church of St. Lua', *J.R.S.I.A.*, xl (1930), 130–6.

FLORENTIUS, martyr, whose relics were bought from the monks of Bonneval by Abbot Ælfsi of Peterborough in 1016 and venerated there (as *R.P.S.* testifies) with those of Cyneswith and *Cyniburg, is not easy to identify. His feast on 27 September might suggest that he was in reality Florentinus of Sedun, who suffered in the Vandal persecution.

Propylaeum, pp. 418–19; *R.P.S.*; W. T. Mellows and A. Bell, *The Peterborough Chronicle of Hugh Candidus* (1949).

FOILLAN (Faelan, Feuillan) (d. *c.*655), Irish monk. Foillan was the brother of *Fursey, who came with him to East Anglia where they established the monastery of Cnobheresburg (Burgh Castle). After East Anglia was ravaged by Penda, king of Mercia, Foillan followed his brother to Neustria, where he was well received by Clovis II. Foillan founded a monastery at Fosses on land given to him by Ita, abbess of Nivelles. He was also a notable missionary in Brabant. He was killed by outlaws at Serette while on a visitation to various Irish monasteries including Lagny and Péronne; he was buried at Fosses. Feast: 31 October.

AA.SS. Oct. XIII (1883), 370–445; B. Krusch, 'Vita S. Foillani' in *M.G.H. Scriptores rerum merov.*, iv. 449–51; P. Grosjean, 'Notes d'hagiographie celtique', *Anal. Boll.*, lxxxv (1957), 379–419.

FORTUNATUS, see VENANTIUS.

FORTY MARTYRS OF ENGLAND AND WALES, a group of representative English and Welsh Roman Catholics who were martyred between 1535 and 1679; they were selected from 200 already beatified by earlier popes. The forty were canonized by Paul VI on 25 October 1970. Thirteen were seminary priests, ten were Jesuits, three Benedictine, and three Carthusian monks, one Brigettine, two Franciscans, and one Austin Friar: the remaining seven were lay folk, four men and three women. The cult of some of these was spontaneous and contemporary: it is exemplified by a famous series of paintings in the English College, Rome, by Circiniani. This series included, by express papal permission, martyrs of England from 1535 to 1583, who were accorded the same veneration as that given to earlier martyrs such as Alban, Boniface, Edmund, and Thomas of Canterbury. The forty include those who were executed for refusing to take the Oath of Supremacy, or simply for being priests or because they harboured priests. *See* John Almond, Edmund Arrowsmith, Ambrose Barlow, John Boste, Alexander Briant, Edmund Campion, Margaret Clitherow, Philip Evans, Thomas Garnet, Edmund Gennings, Richard Gwyn, John Houghton, Philip Howard, John Jones, John Kemble, Luke Kirby, Robert Lawrence, David Lewis, Anne Line, John Lloyd, Cuthbert Mayne, Henry Morse, Nicholas Owen, John Paine, Polydore Plasden, John Plessington, Richard Reynolds, John Rigby, John Roberts, Alban Roe, Ralph Sherwin, Robert Southwell, John Southworth, John Stone, John Wall, Henry Walpole, Margaret Ward, Augustine Webster, Swithun Wells, Eustace White. Feast: 25 October.

J. H. Pollen, *Acts of English Martyrs* (1891); R. Challoner, *Memoirs of Missionary Priests* (ed. J. H. Pollen, 1924); *Lives of the English Martyrs* (vol. i, ed. B. Camm, 1904; vol. ii, ed. E. H. Burton and J. H. Pollen, 1914); T. P. Ellis, *The Catholic Martyrs of Wales* (1933); C. Tigar, *The Forty Martyrs of England and Wales* (1961); G. F. Nuttall, 'The English Martyrs 1535–1680: a statistical review', *J.E.H.*, xxii (1971), 191–7.

FORTY MARTYRS OF SEBASTE (d. 320). These soldiers of the 'thundering Legion' were the victims of a persecution by the Emperor Licinius, which required repudiation of Christianity under pain of death. The local governor of Sebaste (now Sivas in Turkey) tried persuasion, promises, and torture to obtain their apostasy. When all these failed, he ordered them to be exposed naked all night on a frozen lake outside the city. A fire and a warm bath were prepared on the bank to tempt them further. Out of the forty, thirty-nine were constant and died of exposure rather than deny their faith, while the remaining one who conformed was replaced by another soldier, so at the end they were still forty in number. Their cult was extremely widespread in the East, being celebrated in sermons by *Basil, *Ephrem, *John Chrysostom, and *Gregory of Nyssa. The relics went to both Annesis (Caesarea) and to Constantinople. There is some variation in the details of the story, but substantial agreement among the panegyrists. A possibly contemporary 'Testament of the Forty Martyrs of Christ' survives, which records their last messages to friends and relations. There is, however, some doubt about the historicity of some details of their Acts. Feast: in the East, 9 March; in the West, formerly 10 March, suppressed in 1969.

AA.SS. Mar. II (1668), 12–29; H. Delehaye, *Les passions des martyrs et les genres littéraires* (1921), pp. 210–35; P. F. de Cavalieri, 'I quaranta martiri di Sebastia' in *Note agiographice*, *Studi e Testi*, xlix (1928), 155–84.

FOSTER, see VEDAST.

FOUR CROWNED MARTYRS (Quattuor Coronati) (early 4th century). Two groups of early martyrs venerated at Rome on 8 November are called the Crowned Martyrs: one of five Persian stonemasons, the other of four Roman soldiers. H. Delehaye opts firmly for the sole authenticity of the Persians whose relics were translated to Rome, where a fine basilica on the Celian Hill is dedicated to them. Their names, according to their Legend, were Claudius, Nicostratus, Simpronian, and Castorius, while the fifth who suffered with them but seems for some reason to have been dropped out of popular accounts, Simplicius, became a Christian because he thought that the others' skill in carving was due to their religion. Their Acts describe the imperial quarries and workshops at Sirmium, and Diocletian as an unstable character who had a passion for building. Claudius and his companions are said to have made a number of carvings for the emperor, but refused to make a statue of Aesculapius. Eventually they were imprisoned for refusing to sacrifice to the gods: Lampadius, the officer of Diocletian who conducted the enquiry, died suddenly and the stonemasons were held responsible by his relatives. Partly owing to their intervention, Claudius and his companions were killed by drowning.

The alternative, and inferior, version of their Legend makes them four Roman soldiers who under Diocletian refused to sacrifice to the god Aesculapius, for whom the emperor built a temple in the Baths of Trajan. They were beaten to death with leaden scourges and although their bodies were thrown into the drains, they were later reburied by Pope Miltiades on the Via Lavicana.

*Bede records that Canterbury in the early 7th century had a church dedicated to the Four Crowned Martyrs, which probably contained relics of them. Most of the early Canterbury dedications were to Roman saints; the site of the Roman basilica of these martyrs is very close to the monastery in Rome from which Augustine came to England. The dedication could be due to him; their relics could be among those sent from Rome to England in 601.

These saints kept their popularity in medieval England, being recorded in fifteen English Benedictine calendars. They were also the patrons of guilds of stonemasons, whose articles direct the reader to find out more about them in the *Golden Legend*. The English Freemasons' journal is called *Ars Quatuor Coronatorum*. Feast: 8 November.

AA.SS. Nov. III (1910), 748–84; *C.M.H.*, pp. 590–1; H. Delehaye, *Étude sur le Légendier romain* (1936), pp. 64–73 and 'Le culte des Quatre Couronnés à Rome', *Anal. Boll.*, xxxii

(1913), 63–71; L. Duchesne in *Mélanges d'archéologie et d'histoire*, xxxi (1911), 231–46; Bede *H.E.*, ii. 8.

FOURTEEN HOLY HELPERS (Fourteen Auxiliary Saints), a group of saints who enjoyed a collective cult in the Rhineland from the 14th century. From Ratisbon and Bamberg this devotion spread to the rest of Germany, Hungary, and Sweden; but it had little following in France and Italy. Its apogee was reached in the 15th century; in the 16th it was attacked by the reformers and discouraged by the Council of Trent. It enjoyed, nevertheless, a certain revival in the baroque abbeys of Bavaria and Swabia.

The names of the fourteen saints concerned varied somewhat from place to place, but the main principle of their selection seems to have been the efficacy of their intercession against various diseases, and especially at the hour of death in view of supposed revelations that their clients would thus obtain salvation. Most, but not quite all, were venerated as martyrs; several are of doubtful historicity. The list generally comprises the following saints: *Acacius, *Barbara, *Blaise, *Catherine of Alexandria, *Christopher, *Cyricus, *Denys, *Erasmus, *Eustace, *George, *Giles, *Margaret of Antioch, *Pantaleon, and *Vitus. For one or other of these were sometimes substituted *Antony, *Leonard, *Nicolas, *Sebastian, or *Roch.

There are several notable artistic representations, particularly on retables and predellas of altars. Examples include the work of Grünewald at Lindenhardt (1503) and of Cranach at Hampton Court. Sometimes the saints are grouped round the Virgin or the Child Jesus on the shoulders of St. Christopher.

Réau, ii. 680–3.

FOY, see FAITH.

FRANCES OF ROME (1384–1440), widow. Born in the Trastevere of a wealthy but pious family, Frances was married to Lorenzo Ponziano at the age of thirteen, although she really desired to be a nun. In the same house lived her husband's brother and his wife: the latter, Vanozza, shared her ideals: together the two young wives devoted themselves to relieving the distress of Rome's poor, especially in the hospitals. In 1400 she bore the first of her six(?) children, to whom she was constantly devoted; the next year she took over the charge of the whole household.

In 1408 Ladislas of Naples captured Rome; the Ponziano household and property in the Campagna were singled out for attack as they were prominent supporters of the popes, but Frances continued in difficult circumstances and much suffering to minister to the poor. In 1425 after the death of two of her children she founded a society of devout women, under the Rule of St. Benedict but not under vows, to carry out these works. First they were known as Oblates of Mary, later as Oblates of Tor de Specchi. After her husband's death in 1436 Frances entered this community and became its superior for the four remaining years of her life. She was buried in the church of Santa Maria Nuova (now called Santa Francesca Romana), where her relics still rest; her house (now Casa degli Esercizi Pii) is a well-equipped pilgrimage centre. She was canonized by Paul V in 1608. Various revelations, visions, and strange illnesses are recorded of this particularly gentle saint, the most famous of which was her continuous vision for several years of her guardian angel. Possibly for this reason she was named patron of motorists by Pius XI. Feast: 9 March.

AA.SS. Mar. II (1668), *88–*216 and *Propylaeum*, pp. 90–1; P. T. Lugano (ed.), *I processi inediti per Francesca Bussa dei Ponziani* (*Santa Francesca Romana*), 1440–63 (*S.T.*, cxx; 1945): Lives by Lady Georgiana Fullerton (1855) and Berthe Bontoux (1931); see also E. Vaccaro in *Bibl. SS.*, v. 1011–21.

FRANCIS OF ASSISI (1181–1226), confessor, founder of the Franciscan Order. Born the son of a wealthy cloth-merchant of Assisi, Francis was originally christened John, but called Francesco, i.e. the Frenchman, because his mother was

Provençal and he was born while his father was in France. As a youth he assisted his father in running his business, but was also a leader of society in the town. In a war between Assisi and Perugia Francis was taken prisoner for a year and was seriously ill. Soon after, riding fully equipped, he turned back from the war, risking the accusation of cowardice. Already his regard for the poor and for lepers was conspicuous. A little later he heard a voice which seemed to come from the Byzantine-style crucifix in the small, semi-derelict church of San Damiano of Assisi: 'Go and repair my house, which you see is falling down.' Francis set about the task, having sold some of his father's cloth to pay for the materials. This led to a prolonged conflict with his father which was only resolved when Francis dramatically renounced his inheritance and even his clothes. The bishop of Assisi provided him with simple garments and Francis began his new life.

The inspiration of this was religious, not social; the object of his quest the Crucified Christ rather than Lady Poverty, to whom he later declared himself espoused, following the vocabulary of courtly love. Nevertheless, he did now experience extreme and deliberately chosen poverty. He rebuilt San Damiano with money begged from his townsmen; he also travelled as a pilgrim, identifying himself with the penniless and tending those who suffered from 'leprosy' (as then understood). For two or three years he lived alone, wandering and mendicant. Later seven disciples gathered round him, some of them mature, middle-aged men; together they lived a communal life at the Portiuncula in Assisi near a leper colony; when the appropriate time had come they went out on preaching tours, meeting a mixed reception which gradually became more favourable, especially for Francis himself. One of the things which distinguished them from other bands of Italian poor preachers of the time was their respect for, and obedience to, the Church authorities, and their doctrinal orthodoxy. Francis's *Regula Prima* (*c.*1210) begins with a promise of obedience and reverence to Pope Innocent III and his successors; most of it is a gloss on the passages of the Gospels which refer to renunciation and to the conditions of life of the followers of Christ, but it continues: 'all the brothers shall be catholic and live and speak as catholics. If any shall err from the catholic faith and life either by word or deed and shall not mend his way, let him be expelled from the brotherhood.' This primitive Rule was approved at Rome in 1210. Later the apostolate increased in size and extent; Francis's sermons received popular acclaim. When the preaching tours were finished, the brethren would return to their convent and perform liturgical and private prayer, living in the poverty of labourers, supplemented, when necessary, by begging. Their buildings were simple wattle and daub huts; their churches modest and small; they slept on the ground, had no tables or chairs, and very few books. Only later did they become an Order whose theologians won fame in the Universities. *Bonaventure both exemplified and approved this development.

Francis had longed for a wider field of preaching and looked towards the conversion of the Saracens. In 1212 he set off eastwards, but was driven on to the Dalmatian coast. In 1214 he left for Morocco through Spain but became so ill he had to return home. In 1219, with a dozen friars, he sailed from Ancona for Acre and Damietta. Here his illusions about Crusaders were rudely shattered: he denounced the loose-living adventurers, 6,000 of whom were killed in an attack on the city. Somehow or other Francis passed through the enemy lines and met the Sultan who was deeply impressed but remained unconverted. Francis refused all the rich presents offered and returned to the Christian armies. He then spent a few months on pilgrimage in the Holy Land, until he was recalled urgently by news of changes which had taken place in the Order he had founded.

This had suffered from its own success. The numbers had become large, foundations had been made outside Italy, there was no proper novitiate, no organization, and only the simplest of rules. Their protector, Cardinal Ugolino, wished the whole Church to benefit from their ideals and example, and even for some friars to become bishops. He wished the Order (now 5,000 strong) to become a well-organized body devoted to reform. Francis, having upbraided his friars at Bologna who were living in a stone house and were planning to open a school connected with the University, resigned his office of Minister-General at the General Chapter of 1220, realizing that he was not the administrator or organizer which the Order now needed. He was succeeded by Brother Elias of Cortona. In 1221 Francis drew up another Rule; after certain modifications it was approved in 1223 as the *Regula Bullata* by Honorius III. This now canalized the Franciscan Order into the Church, but contained concessions which Francis regretted but could not effectively resist. In 1221 he also drew up instructions for 'Tertiaries', laymen who followed Franciscan ideals but remained with their families, outside the life of the vows of religion.

To his later years, while he held no official position in the Order, belong some of the most famous incidents of Francis's life: the inauguration of the Christmas crib at Grecchio, prepared by friar John, at which Francis, a deacon until his death, read the Gospel with such devotion that men wept; the canticle of the Sun (1224), written when he visited *Clare at Assisi in conditions of extreme illness and discomfort; above all, the experience of the Impression of the Stigmata on Mount La Verna (also in 1224). The scars of these wounds, received in ecstasy, remained on his body, hidden until death. Soon after this experience, he fell ill and the next year became blind. He endured agonies from primitive surgery and other medical treatment and died at last, aged only forty-five, at the Portiuncula, Assisi. He was canonized in 1228 by his old friend Gregory IX, formerly Cardinal Ugolino. Francis was buried in the church of S. Giorgio, Assisi; his relics were translated to the New Basilica, built by Elias to contain them in 1230 and later decorated with Giotto's frescoes. They were rediscovered in 1818 and reburied, first in an ornate tomb, and then, in 1932, in a very simple one. Assisi is a pilgrimage centre for Franciscan devotees from all over the world.

Francis's close rapport with the animal creation, based on episodes in the *Fioretti*, has often inspired artists. His preaching to the birds was and is a favourite scene from his life. The wolf of Gubbio, tamed by Francis's words, was apparently buried in the church there. This affinity, believed to represent the saint's return to a state of innocence enjoyed by Adam in Eden, is not unique to Francis (examples are found in Lives of several English and Irish saints). They rightly emphasize his consideration for, and sense of identity with, all elements of the physical universe, as seen in his *Canticle of the Sun*. It is this which makes him an apt patron of natural conservation.

Francis has always had a widespread cult, fostered in the Middle Ages by his friars who came to England in 1224. They soon established houses in the principal towns, supported by, and recruited from, the merchant class to which Francis had belonged and whose way of life he had rejected. Within 100 years they established fifty houses with 1,350 friars. They were a powerful influence for reform and exercised a unique apostolate in towns, universities, and through missions in parishes. Later this was partly marred by internal divisions concerning poverty and by quarrels with the diocesan clergy.

The 20th century has witnessed a widespread revival of interest in Francis, but also a tendency to see in him only those traits which appealed to individual writers (or film-makers). This resulted in caricatures of a sentimental nature-lover or a hippy 'drop-out' from society, which omit the real sternness of his character and neglect his all-pervasive love of God and identification with Christ's sufferings, which alone make sense of his life. Francis, depicted in life by Cimabue, is one of the most attractive and best-loved saints of all time.

Two ancient and many modern English churches are dedicated to him; his feast is in the calendars of York and Hereford. Feast: 4 October; Impression of the Stigmata, 17 September.

AA.SS. Oct. II (1768), 545–1004; A. van Ortroy, 'Traité des miracles de S. François d'Assise par le B. Thomas de Celano', *Anal. Boll.*, xviii (1899), 81–176; id., 'La Légende de S. François d'Assise dite Legenda trium sociorum', ibid., xxii (1900), 119–97; id., 'S. François d'Assise et Frère Elie de Cortona', ibid., xxii (1903), 195–202; id., 'S. François et son voyage en Orient', ibid., xxxi (1912), 451–62. Works ed. L. Wadding (1623) and in *Bibliotheca Franciscana Ascetica Medii Aevi* (1904, 1949) with Eng. tr. by P. Robinson (1906), L. Sherley-Price (1959), and B. Fahy (1964). Lives by Thomas of Celano and St. Bonaventure in *Legendae S. Francisci Assisiensis saeculis XIII et XIV conscriptae* (Analecta Franciscana 1926–41); see also R. B. Brooke, *Scripta Leonis* (1970); id., 'The Lives of St. Francis of Assisi' in T. A. Dorey, *Latin Biography* (1967), pp. 177–98; id., *Early Franciscan Government* (1959); J. R. H. Moorman, *The Sources for the Life of St. Francis of Assisi* (1940); id., *St. Francis of Assisi* (1963). Other Lives by P. Sabatier (1893, Eng. tr. 1894), M. de la Bedoyère (1962); pictorial Life by L. von Matt and W. Hauser (1952, Eng. tr. 1956) and X. Schnieper, *St. Francis of Assisi* (1981). See also *The Little Flowers of St. Francis* (Everyman edition, 1975); R. Brown and M. A. Habig, *St. Francis of Assisi: writings and early biographies* (1979); R. B. Brooke, 'Recent work on St. Francis of Assisi', *Anal. Boll.*, c (1982), 654–76.

FRANCIS OF PAOLA (1416–1507), founder of the Franciscan Minim Friars. Born at Paola (Calabria), he lived in a neighbouring Franciscan friary for a year when he was thirteen, went on pilgrimage to Assisi and Rome, and then became a hermit near his home town in a cave overlooking the sea. When he was twenty he was joined by two companions, for whom a chapel and three cells were built by the neighbours. Later others came and new foundations were made. These Friars were called Minims through humility and were approved by the Holy See in 1474. They underlined the monastic elements of the Franciscan ideal; their charity and extreme austerity attracted many; there was usually only one priest in each community, most of whom were of very limited education.

Francis became famous for prophecy and miracles even during his life. His last 25 years were spent in France. Louis XI, mortally ill, specially requested his presence. Francis was sent by the pope and prepared Louis for death. He also helped to restore peace between France and Brittany and between France and Spain. For a time he was tutor to the future king, Charles VIII.

He died at Tours and was canonized in 1519. Artists who depicted him include Murillo, Velazquez, and Goya. Because many of his miracles were connected with the sea, he was declared patron of seafarers in 1943. He is particularly popular in Italy, France, and Mexico. Feast: 2 April.

F. Russo, *Bibliografia di S. Francesco di Paola* (1957); G. M. Roberti, *S. Francesco di Paola* (1963); *N.C.E.*, s.v.

FRANCIS OF SALES (1567–1622), bishop of Geneva. Born in Savoy at the Château de Sales, he was delicate as a boy. He was educated privately at first and then at the University of Paris where he studied rhetoric, philosophy, and theology. In 1591 he became a Doctor of Law at Padua; although opportunities were available both for a brilliant marriage and a worldly career through becoming a senator of Savoy, he refused both, because he wished to become a priest more than anything else. Through the influence of a cousin he was offered the provostship of Geneva, to which he was eventually nominated by the pope: this, it was hoped, would reconcile his father to the prospect of his son devoting his life to the service of the Church. On obtaining his father's consent, Francis was ordained priest in 1593; soon he was distinguished for service to the poor and skill as a preacher. The next year he undertook the daunting task of converting the Chablais country from Calvinism. In spite of danger to his life from both assassins and wolves, he survived; he eventually succeeded simply by preaching Catholic doctrine with great love and understanding, with persistent patience and gentleness. These were to be his main characteristics for the rest of his life.

After undergoing a severe examination in theology at Rome in the presence of the pope, cardinal Baronius, *Bellarmine, and others, he was nominated coadjutor-bishop in 1599, and became bishop of Geneva in 1602. He excelled in administrative work, in preaching, spiritual direction, and catechizing. His most famous writings, the *Treatise of the Love of God* and the *Introduction to the Devout Life*, belong to these years. The latter was written for layfolk and was instantly acclaimed as fulfilling a long-felt need and was soon translated into several languages. One of his better-known friends was Jane Frances de *Chantal, whom he first knew as a widow and who founded the Order of the Visitation in 1610 under his direction. Extremely influential as a director and writer, he excelled in gently leading ardent souls to the extremes of self-sacrifice and the love of God: one of his favourite sayings was that more flies are attracted by a spoonful of honey than by a whole barrel of vinegar. Nevertheless, the pleasant style of his direction should not blind the reader to the stern ideals which he propagated. He died at Lyons in a Visitandine convent on 28 December. His body was translated to Annecy in January 1623 and again to a new shrine in 1912. He was canonized in 1665, declared a Doctor of the Church in 1877, and named patron saint of writers in 1923. He was specially influential in the revival of French Catholicism in the 17th century, but his works have appealed to Christians of many generations and many countries. Feast: 24 (formerly 29) January.

Work of St. Francis of Sales in 26 volumes (1892–1932; Eng. tr. by H. B. Mackey and others, 6 vols., 1883–1908); selected letters tr. by E. Stopp (1960). The most important early Life is by Ch. Aug. de Sales, his nephew, *De Vita et rebus gestis . . . Francisci Salesii* (1634); see also J. P. Camus, *L'esprit du Bienheureux François de Sales* (6 vols., 1639–41; abridged in 1727, Eng. tr. 1910 and 1952). Modern studies include F. Trochu, *Saint François de Sales* (2 vols., 1946) and E. J. Lajeunie, *Saint François de Sales* (2 vols., 1966) and English biographies by E. K. Sanders (1928), M. de la Bédoyère (1960), M. Trouncer (1963), and R. Murphy (1964). See also R. Kleinman, *Saint François de Sales and the Protestants* (1962) and M. Henry-Couannier, *Francis de Sales and his Friends* (1964).

FRANCIS XAVIER, see XAVIER.

FREMUND (d. 866), martyr. Reputedly a relative of Offa, king of Mercia, and of *Edmund, king of East Anglia, he became a hermit. But as he had royal blood, he was a possible claimant to the throne of Mercia and was killed by an apostate kinsman Oswy, with the help of some of the same Danish army who slew Edmund. He was buried at Offchurch (Warwickshire); his relics were translated to Dunstable in 1212, where miracles attested his sanctity. Cropredy (Oxon.) also claimed to possess his body. Little reliance can be placed on the details of this traditional account; he may have been a purely fictional character. Feast: 11 May, in three medieval calendars, including Syon Abbey.

N.L.A., i. 450–6; metrical Life ed. Lord Francis Harvey in *The Pinchbeck Register*, ii (1925), 365–78; William Worcestre, p. 165; Stanton, pp. 207, 645.

FRIDESWIDE (*c.*680–727), virgin, patron of Oxford. There is no early Life, but recent historical and archaeological research has clarified the background and some details of the traditional Legend. Frideswide was almost contemporary with *Bede, but much less is generally known of the Wessex–Mercia border than of Northumbria. It now seems that a territory of west Oxfordshire was ruled in the late 7th century by a sub-king under Mercian overlordship called Dida of Eynsham. Here and at Bampton and Oxford he endowed minster churches. His daughter Frideswide was first abbess of the Oxford double monastery. This was on the site of Christ Church and it became the nucleus of the town of Oxford.

The Legend, recorded by William of

Malmesbury from a version attributed to Robert of Cricklade (then prior of Oxford) makes her the intended victim of seduction by Æthelbald of Mercia. She escaped his attentions by flight into a forest retreat at Binsey and then to Oxford. He was temporarily blinded, but was cured at Bampton by her intercession. It is noteworthy that Oxford, Bampton, and Binsey are all on the river Thames. The Thames valley in her lifetime was under the control of Mercia in spite of the early importance of Dorchester (a Wessex border-town) evangelized by *Birinus. Frideswide's monastery at Oxford, where she died and was buried, became early an important landowner in the area. Unfortunately most of its early records were destroyed in 1002 when the church was set on fire with Scandinavians inside it in the attempted massacres triggered by the notorious decree of Ethelred II.

The existence of her shrine is formally attested by *R.P.S.* in the 11th century: in the early 12th century her monastery was refounded as a house of Austin Canons. Her relics were translated in 1180 and in 1289. Her cult was strengthened by her being formally adopted as patron of Oxford University in the early 15th century. Twice a year her shrine was solemnly visited, and perhaps this academic connexion inspired the choice of St. Hilda and St. Catherine as subjects of the stained glass in her shrine chapel.

Before the general dissolution of English monasteries Cardinal Wolsey suppressed Frideswide's monastery to provide revenues for his Cardinal College (now Christ Church), built on the same site. To achieve this, two bays of the west end of the nave were demolished, but Frideswide's shrine was left undisturbed. In 1538, however, it was despoiled by Henry VIII's commissioners. In 1546 this church became (and still remains) the cathedral church of the new diocese of Oxford. The shrine was restored under Queen Mary, but in 1558 it was desecrated by Frideswide's relics being inextricably mixed with those of Catherine Dammartin, wife of the Zwinglian theologian Peter Martyr Vermigli, formerly an Austin Canon and subsequently Regius professor of Divinity. This was achieved by James Calfhill, a Calvinist divine, intent on the suppression of the cult.

In modern times part of the shrine has been reconstructed from remains discovered in a well at Christ Church and it still attracts pilgrims, especially on her two feasts of 19 October and 12 February (translation).

AA.SS. Oct. VIII (1853), 533–90; *G.P.*, pp. 315–16; J. Blair, 'Saint Frideswide Reconsidered', Oxoniensia lii (1987), 71–127; F. M. Stenton, 'St. Frideswide and her Times' in *Preparatory to Anglo-Saxon England* (1970), pp. 224–33, E. F. Jacob, *St. Frideswide, the patron saint of Oxford* (pamphlet); H. M. Mayr-Harting, 'Functions of a Twelfth-Century Shrine: the miracles of St. Frideswide', in *Studies in Medieval History presented to R. H. C. Davis* (1985).

FRIDOLIN (6th century(?)), abbot, founder of Sackingen. There was a notable cult in Austria, southern Germany, and Switzerland; pilgrims came from the British Isles. His unreliable Life described him as an Irishman who had nephews in Northumbria who joined him in France, where he was a wandering monk and preacher. He joined a monastery at Poitiers, where he discovered the relics of *Hilary and built a church to house them. Guided by a revelation, he moved on to an island in the Rhine, pausing only to build a few more churches on the way; at Sackingen he built a church and monastery for monks and a nunnery not far away. He encouraged sport in the monastery school and took part himself. Feast: 6 March.

B.T.A., i. 499–500.

FRITHEBERT, bishop of Hexham 734–66. The successor of *Acca, he is also mentioned as the administrator of Lindisfarne while its bishop, Cynewulf, was in prison. No other details are known of his life. His bones were discovered at Hexham in 1154. Feast: 23 December.

J. Raine, *Memorials of Hexham Abbey*, i (S.S., 1864), pp. 199–200; *D.C.B.*, ii. 566.

FRITHESTAN (d *c.*932), bishop of Winchester 909–31. Very little is known of this saint. William of Malmesbury records that he was one of seven bishops consecrated on the same day by Plegmund, archbishop of Canterbury, that several of his books survived, and that his unknown tomb could not hide his holiness. Other traces of his cult survive from the 13th century only in two martyrologies and a late entry in one Winchester calendar. Feast: 10 September.

G.P., pp. 162–3; F. Wormald, *E.B.K. before 1100*, p. 164.

FRITHONA, see DEUSDEDIT.

FRUCTUOSUS, AUGURIUS, AND EULOGIUS (d. 259), martyrs. Fructuosus was bishop of Tarragona; Augurius and Eulogius, his deacons, were arrested and imprisoned with him. The governor Aemilianus presided at their examination. He asked if they knew of the emperor's orders to worship the gods. Fructuosus answered: 'I worship the one God who has made heaven and earth.' On being asked if he knew that the gods exist, he answered: 'No, I do not.' The governor replied: 'These are obeyed, these are feared and these are adored; if the gods are not worshipped, then the images of the emperors are not adored.' He then told Augurius not to listen to Fructuosus and asked Eulogius if he worshipped Fructuosus. He answered: 'No, but I worship the one whom he worships.' Aemilianus then asked Fructuosus if he was a bishop. 'Yes, I am', said Fructuosus. 'You were', replied Aemilianus, and sentenced him to be burnt alive.

As he was being taken to the place of execution, both Christians and pagans showed him sympathy; some offered him drugged wine. But he jokingly refused it because Wednesday was a fast day. One of his readers asked if he could take off his sandals for him, but again he refused. One Felix came to shake hands with him and ask his prayers. He answered aloud: 'I must have in mind the whole Catholic church both east and west.' The three martyrs were burnt alive: the writer of their Acts said that to each at his post the Father was present, the Son gave help, and the Holy Spirit walked in the midst of the fire. They knelt down and spread their arms in memory of the crucifixion, 'in joy assured of the resurrection'.

At nightfall the Christians went to the amphitheatre, quenched the smouldering bodies with wine and each kept some of the ashes for themselves. But Fructuosus was said to have appeared to them and asked them to restore the relics to one place. Feast: 21 January.

A.C.M., pp. xxxii, 176–85; P. Delehaye, *Origines du culte des martyrs* (1933), pp. 66–7; *Propylaeum*, p. 30; Augustine, *Sermo 273* (*P.L.*, xxxviii. 1250); B.T.A., i. 137–8; *H.S.S.C.*, ii. 158–60.

FURSEY (Fursa) (d. 650), Irish Abbot. He became a monk in Ireland but left it as a 'pilgrim for Christ', coming to East Anglia *c.*630. King *Sigebert received him and his companions, especially *Foillan, kindly and gave them the old fortress of Cnobheresburg (Burgh Castle, Suffolk) with adjacent lands for a monastery. On the death of Sigebert in battle against Penda, king of Mercia, Fursey left for France. Again he was helped by a ruler, Erchinoald, mayor of Neustria, who gave him land for another monastery, which he built at Lagny-sur-Marne. He died at Mezerolles (Somme); his body was buried at Péronne (Picardy), afterwards called *Perrona Scottorum*, in another Irish monastery.

In 654 his relics were translated to a shrine 'in the shape of a little house', supposedly made by *Eloi. Another translation took place in 1056. Most of the relics remained until the French Revolution; a head reliquary survived even the Prussian bombardment of 1870. French, Irish, and

English calendars (especially Canterbury, which claimed head-relics) attest his cult.

This was assisted by Bede's account of his vision of the after-life, one of the earliest of its kind. During a state of trance he saw visions of heaven and hell, angels and devils; on recovering he described his experiences and warned against future and detailed punishments for sins. Feast: 16 January.

AA.SS. Ian. II (1643), 35–55; Bede, *H.E.*, iii. 19; *Vita Prima S. Fursei* in *M.G.H.*, *Scriptores rerum merov.*, iv. 423–49; W. Stokes, 'Betha Fursa', *Revue Celtique*, xxv (1904), 385–404; J. Hennig, 'The Irish Background of St. Fursey', *I.E.R.* (1952), 18–28.

G

GABRIEL, archangel. Mentioned in the OT as the angel who helped Daniel understand his visions (Dan. 8: 15 and 9: 21), Gabriel appears in the NT as the prophet of the birth of *John the Baptist to his father Zachariah (Luke 1: 11–20), but above all as the angel who brought the tidings to Mary of the future birth of Jesus (Luke 1: 26–38). Gabriel's name was first invoked in the Liturgy in the Litany of Saints, which according to E. Bishop dates in substance from the pontificate of Sergius (687–701). Representations of the angels in art, however, and of Gabriel in particular, go back even further: an ancient chapel in Rome on the Appian Way has frescoes so prominent that a Gabriel dedication is likely; medieval representations were frequent. In England six ancient churches were dedicated to Gabriel. He was declared the patron of post office, telephone, and telegraph workers by Benedict XV in 1921.

Appropriately, his feast was closely connected with that of the Annunciation: in the West on 24 March, in the East, 26 March. Since 1969, however, his feast is kept with that of *Michael and All Angels on 29 September.

E. Bishop, *Liturgica Historica* (1918), pp. 142–51; *O.D.C.C.*, s.v.; B.T.A., i. 667–8 and iii. 680.

GABRIEL of Our Lady of Sorrows, see POSSENTI.

GALGANI, Gemma (1878–1903), virgin. Born at Borgo Nuovo di Camigliano near Lucca of pious parents, Gemma was orphaned at the age of eighteen and joined the household of Matteo Giannini at Lucca. She ardently desired to be a nun of the Passionist Congregation, to which her spiritual director belonged, but was prevented by a series of illnesses, the worst being tuberculosis of the spine.

From 1899 to 1901 she experienced periodically the stigmata of Christ as well as marks of the scourging in prayer. There were also visions of Christ, the Blessed Virgin, and her Guardian Angel. On the other hand, she also appeared to suffer diabolical possession, on occasion spitting on a crucifix and breaking a rosary. When she spoke in ecstasy her voice was unusual and bystanders recorded her words. Throughout these years she was outstanding in obedience and patience in acute suffering as well as in the practice of heroic poverty. For these reasons, not the preternatural phenomena, she was beatified in 1933 and canonized in 1941. The popular cult which arose soon after her death was increased when in 1943 her correspondence with her director was published. The choice of Gemma as a Christian name, not only by Italian but also British and American parents in recent years, is in part due to the life and example of this saint. Feast: 14 May.

Germano of St. Stanislas, *Estasi, diario, autobiografia, scritti vari di S. Gemma Galgani* (1943; American tr., 1947); Sr. St. Michael, *Portrait of St. Gemma, a stigmatic* (1950); see also Lives by Fr. Germanus (1914) and P. Coghlan (1949); B.T.A., ii. 75–6; *N.C.E.*, xii. 1104–5.

GALGANO (*c.*1140–81), hermit at Monte Siepi (Tuscany). Born at Chiusdino, near Siena, of a noble family, he gave himself up to hunting and other pleasures as a young man. But after experiencing visions of the archangel *Michael he became a hermit and built a cell on a steep mountain near a monastic community founded by *William of Malavalle. Disciples joined him, but he found that ruling them was troublesome. In 1181 he visited Alexander III to discuss this problem, but he did not live long enough to solve it.

He died at Monte Siepi on 30

November. A round church was built over his tomb, where pilgrims came in large numbers and miracles were claimed. A papal commission of enquiry was set up in 1185; it is probable that Galgano was canonized in 1190. In that year Cistercian monks took over Monte Siepi at the request of Hugh, bishop of Volterra, but most of Galgano's monks left, scattered over Tuscany, and became Augustinian hermits. By 1220 a large Cistercian monastery was built below Galgano's hermitage: they then claimed him as a Cistercian saint. His cult was lively in Siena and Volterra, where numerous representations survive. The ruins of his hermitage can still be seen, while his cloak is kept in the church of Santuccio at Siena. Feast: 5 December.

R. Arbesmann, 'The three earliest Vitae of S. Galganus' in *Didascaliae: Studies in Honour of A. M. Albareda* (1961), 3–37; *H.S.S.C.*, vi. 271; *Bibl. SS.*, vi. 1–6.

GALL (Gallech, Gilianus) (d. *c.*630), Irish monk and hermit. Probably from Leinster, Gall became a monk at Bangor under *Comgall and *Columbanus. With the latter he went to Gaul where they founded monasteries at Annegray and Luxeuil. Exiled from that area they preached around Tuggen, by Lake Zurich, and later were given land for hermitages and as a base for evangelization at Bregenz and later at Arbon (Switzerland). The local king, Sigebert, offered Gall a bishopric, and the monks of Luxeuil on the death of Columbanus' disciple, Eustace, elected Gall as their abbot; but he refused both offices and lived out his days as a hermit and occasional itinerant preacher. There are various legends which tell of some disagreement with Columbanus; however, his monks at Bobbio after his death sent his pastoral staff to Gall as a sign of forgiveness for not going with him to Italy. Gall did not found the Benedictine monastery which bears his name, which (with the town around it) grew up on the site of one of his hermitages, about a century after his death. However, Gall was a principal pioneer of Christianity in Switzerland, although he was a hermit and never bishop or abbot. His cult is very ancient, his name is in early 9th-century martyrologies. His shrine remained until the Reformation: when it was rifled, his bones were seen to be unusually large. His abbey survived until 1805 and the church is now a cathedral. Beside it there remain many manuscripts of the famous abbey library, one of the most notable in Europe and including several early and important manuscripts of Gregorian Chant. Feast: 16 October, but in some ancient martyrologies 20 February (probably an early translation feast).

Three early Lives of Gall, one anonymous, one by Wetting, and the third by Walafrid Strabo, are edited by B. Krusch, *M.G.H.*, *Scriptores rerum merov.*, iv. 251–337 (tr. of the third by M. Joynt, *The Life of St. Gall*, 1927); see also *AA.SS.* Oct. VII (1845), 856–909; J. M. Clark, *The Abbey of St. Gall* (1926).

GALLWELL, see GUDWAL.

GARMON, see GERMANUS.

GARNARD (Garnat), see GERARDIN.

GARNET, Thomas (*c.*1575–1608), Jesuit priest and martyr. Born in Southwark, Garnet was educated at Horsham grammar school. His father was imprisoned for his religious beliefs and his uncle was the more famous Henry Garnet, S.J., who was prominent in organizing and deploying the English Catholic clergy and who died on the scaffold in 1606 for alleged complicity in the Gunpowder Plot. Thomas Garnet became Lord William Howard's page and entered the Jesuit College at St. Omer, whence he moved to the English College at Valladolid in 1596, where he was ordained priest in 1599. After a short spell of work as a priest in England he became a Jesuit in 1604. After the discovery of the Gunpowder Plot he was arrested, imprisoned, and rigorously examined about his own and his uncle's supposed involvement; when he proved his innocence he was banished with other priests in 1606.

After his novitiate in Louvain, he

returned in defiance of the law in 1607. A few weeks later he was arrested and again imprisoned, this time in the Gatehouse and at Newgate. He was tried at the Old Bailey, condemned to death for being a priest ordained overseas who had returned to England, and was executed at Tyburn on 23 June. He is the protomartyr of the College of St. Omer (now at Stonyhurst, Lancs.). He was canonized by Paul VI in 1970 as one of the *Forty Martyrs of England and Wales. Feast: 25 October.

H. Foley, *Records of the English Province of the Society of Jesus* (1877–82), ii (2), 475–505; J. H. Pollen, *Acts of the English Martyrs* (1891); R. Challoner, *Memoirs of Missionary Priests* (ed. J. H. Pollen, 1924).

GDARN, see DERFEL.

GEMINIANUS, martyr, whose feast on 16 September was kept in numerous English Benedictine calendars, is mentioned in *R.M.* together with a St. Lucy of Chalcedon; Geminianus was reputed to have died by the sword in Rome. It seems that the feast commemorates the dedication of a church in his honour.

AA.SS. Sept. V (1755), 286–92 and *Propylaeum*, p. 399.

GEMMA, see GALGANI, GEMMA.

GENESIUS (Gennys) **OF ARLES** (d. *c.*303), martyr. This saint is mentioned in the Martyrology of Jerome, in the writings of Prudentius, *Venantius Fortunatus, *Hilary, and *Gregory of Tours, and there can be little doubt that he was a genuine martyr during the persecution of Maximian and Diocletian. His Legend calls him a notary who made shorthand summaries of judicial proceedings for the public archives. One day, while performing his duties in the presence of the judge, Genesius, who was a catechumen, was so offended by the edict of persecution which was read out that he threw down his register and quitted his profession. He then fled from the town and sought out a bishop who would baptize him; but the bishop, perhaps fearing a trap, put him off and told him that if he shed his blood for Christ, this would have the same effect as Baptism. Genesius was eventually captured by the persecutors and beheaded.

His cult spread to Narbonne, Spain, and eventually Rome, where also a church was built in his honour. It was wrongly assumed that he was a Roman martyr whose body was buried there; hence he is often (as in OE Martyrology) wrongly described as Genesius of Rome. Later his Legend was transformed still further: this made Genesius a comedian who, while acting an anti-Christian satire on the stage, was suddenly converted and confessed Christ with such constancy that he suffered the rack and was eventually beheaded. It seems that this legend is at least as old as the 6th century, for the calendar of Carthage of that date commemorates Genesius the actor. Feast: 25 August, dedication of his basilica at Arles on 16 December.

There are two ancient English churches dedicated to Genesius. Bond, however, attributes these to Genesius of Clermont, a French bishop who died *c.*660, also called Genet. His episcopate seems to have been peaceful and successful; he built a church in honour of St. Symphorian (later called St. Genesius) and a monastery called Grandlieu. Feast: 3 June.

For Genesius of Arles *AA.SS.* Aug. V (1741), 119–36 with *C.M.H.*, pp. 464–5 and H. Quentin, *Les Martyrologes Historiques du moyen âge* (1908), pp. 533–41; B.T.A., iii. 398–400; S. Cavallin, *Saint Genès le Notaire* (1945). For Genesius of Clermont *AA.SS.* Iun. I (1695), 322–4; B.T.A., ii. 46.

GENEVIEVE (Genofeva) (d. *c.*500), virgin, patroness of Paris. Born at Nanterre, Genevieve took the veil at the age of about fifteen; on the death of her parents she moved to Paris, where she continued her chosen life of prayer and austerity. She was supported by *Germanus of Auxerre, who had apparently known her from childhood. When the Franks under Childeric besieged Paris, Genevieve is said to have personally made a sortie with an armed band to obtain provisions by river from Arcis and Troyes. She won Childeric's respect, however, and she built a church in honour of *Denys. Clovis also, we are told, venerated her and released prisoners at her request. She is also said to have encouraged the Parisians to avert the coming of Attila and his Huns by the frequent use of fasting and prayer: in the event they changed the route of their march and Paris was spared.

After her death Genevieve was enshrined in the church of SS. Peter and Paul (later St. Genevieve's), built by Clovis, where her miracles made it famous. The fabric eventually decayed and a new church was begun in 1746, but was secularized at the Revolution and is called the Pantheon, a burial place for the worthies of France. During the Middle Ages the feretory of Genevieve was carried in procession at times of disaster: her most famous cures were from an epidemic of ergotism in 1129, but over and over again Parisians have invoked her in times of national crisis. Several churches were dedicated to her there and two in medieval England, where at least five abbeys celebrated her feast. Her cult also spread to SW. Germany in the Middle Ages. Her shrine and relics were largely destroyed at the Revolution, but this by no means finished her cult in France. Many of the most notable artistic representations of her, continuing traditions from the late Middle Ages, date from the 17th–19th centuries, including the frescoes of Puvis de Chavannes in the Pantheon. Her most usual emblem is a candle, with or without the devil, who was reputed to have blown it out when she went to pray at night in the church.

Her name is in the Martyrology of Jerome, so her cult is ancient, but the Life which purports to be contemporary was written some centuries after her death. Consequently little can be asserted about her with certainty, but her cult has flourished on civic and national pride. Feast: 3 January.

AA.SS. Ian. I (1643), 137–53; Text 'A' edited by B. Krusch in *M.G.H.*, *Scriptores rerum merov.*, iii (1896), 204–38; text 'B' by C. Kohler, *Étude critique sur le texte de la vie latine de Sainte Généviève* (1881); text 'C' by C. Kunstle, *Vita Sanctae Genofevae* (Teubner edn. 1910). Some scholars maintain the traditional date and value of the Life, see G. Kurth, 'Étude critique sur la Vie de sainte Généviève' in *Études Franques*, ii (1919), 1–96; see also Lives by C. H. Lesêtre (1900) and M. Reynès-Monlaur (1924); N. Jacquin, *Sainte Généviève, ses images et son culte* (1952); Réau, ii. 563–8; *Bibl. SS.*, vi. 157–64.

GENNARO, see JANUARIUS.

GENNINGS, Edmund (1567–91), priest and martyr. Born at Lichfield, Gennings was brought up as a Protestant but became a Catholic under the influence of Richard Sherwood, whose page he became in 1583. He entered the English College at Reims in 1584 and, in spite of interrupting his studies for suspected tuberculosis, was ordained priest in 1590. He returned to England the same year, landing at Whitby, but went to Lichfield hoping to convert his brother; he was, however, unsuccessful and returned to France. In 1591 he returned to London. He soon met a fellow priest, Polydore *Plasden; together they decided to say Mass at the house of Swithun *Wells in Gray's Inn Lane the next day. Here they were captured by the notorious pursuivant Topcliffe during Mass, with the congregation of ten, on 8 November. The two priests were tried and executed together at Gray's Inn Fields on 10 December. They were canonized by Paul VI in 1970 among the *Forty Martyrs of England and Wales. Feast: 25 October.

The Life and Death of Edmund Gennings by his Brother John Gennings (1614; 1887 and 1961); J. H. Pollen, *Acts of English Martyrs* (1891), pp. 98–127; B.T.A., iv. 532–4.

GENNYS, patron of St. Gennys (Cornwall) is sometimes identified with *Genesius of Arles, but the fact that his feast is kept in Cornwall in 2 May (and not on 25 August) probably points to the cult of an obscure local founder, later identified with the more famous *Genesius. The confusion is worse confounded by William Worcestre's entry: 'There were three brothers of the name of Genesius, each one of whom carried his head and one was archbishop of Lismore.' Each of these statements is false. The head-relics enshrined in the canons' church at Launceston were identified with those of 'Genesius the Martyr', and were commemorated in their calendar under the Translation of the head of Genesius on 19 July. If the patron of St. Gennys was distinct from the famous martyr, nothing seems to be known of him.

G. H. Doble, *St. Gennys* (Cornish Saints, no. 38); William Worcestre, pp. 84–5.

GENOFEVA, see GENEVIEVE.

GEORGE (d. *c.*303), martyr, patron of England. He suffered at Lydda (= Diospolis) in Palestine, where his tomb was shown. It is likely but not certain that he was a soldier. The cult was both ancient and widespread, with feasts in the East, where he was called 'megalomartyros', and in the West, where he occurs in the Martyrology of Jerome and the Gregorian Sacramentary. Churches were dedicated to him in Jerusalem and Antioch in the 6th century and from early times he was invoked as patron of the Byzantine armies. The record and the cult of George considerably *precede* the Acts which, derived from Pasicrates, who mendaciously claimed to be a witness, survive in Greek, Latin, Armenian, Coptic, Syriac, Ethiopian, and Turkish.

The famous story of George and the Dragon is by no means primitive, but became immensely popular in the West through the *Golden Legend*, translated and printed by Caxton. The dragon, a local pest which terrorized the whole country, poisoned with its breath all who approached it. Every day it was appeased with an offering of two sheep, but when these grew scarce, a human victim, chosen by lot, was to be substituted instead. The lot had fallen on the king's daughter, who went to her fate dressed as a bride. But George attacked the dragon, pierced it with his lance, and led it captive with the princess's girdle, as if it were completely tame. George told the people not to be afraid: if they would believe in Jesus Christ and be baptized he would rid them of this monster. The king and people agreed; George killed the dragon and 15,000 men were baptized. George would take no reward, but asked the king to maintain churches, honour priests, and show compassion to the poor. The Legend continued with an account of the sufferings and death of George in the persecution of Diocletian and Maximian, this last point being probably the only historical element in the story.

George has been known in England since the 7th–8th centuries, evidenced by the Martyrology of *Bede, and the OE Martyrology. He is also recorded in the Irish Martyrology of *Oengus. Ælfric also repeated the Legend.

The cult of George took on new dimensions for England during the Crusades. A vision of SS. George and Demetrius at the siege of Antioch preceded the defeat of the Saracens and the fall of the town on the first Crusade. The author of the *Gesta Francorum* claimed that George's body was in a church near Ramleh. Richard I placed himself and his army under George's protection. By now he was the special patron of soldiers. At the Synod of Oxford (1222) his feast was made a lesser holiday. Edward III (1327–77) founded under his patronage the Order of the Garter, for which the fine chapel of St. George at Windsor was built by Edward IV and Henry VII. Meanwhile, in 1415 archbishop Chichele had George's feast raised in rank to that of one of the principal feasts of the year: this was after the battle of Agincourt, when Henry V's famous speech invoked St. George as England's patron. But even then, *Edward the Confessor and *Edmund of East Anglia were not entirely displaced. The cult of George reached its apogee in the later Middle Ages: by then not only England, but Venice, Genoa, Portugal, and Catalonia regarded him as their patron: for all he was the personification of the ideals of Christian chivalry. He was also numbered in Germany among the *Fourteen Holy Helpers while Russia and Ethiopia also venerated him. With the invention of gunpowder and the consequent diminution of the importance of sword and lance his popularity faded, a process largely completed by the Reformation. In England, however, he retained his popularity: the most complete surviving cycle of his Legend (with even more fantastic elements) survives in the early 16th-century glass at St. Neot's Cornwall, while Spenser declared:

Thou, among those saints which thou
 doest see,
Shalt be a saint, and thine own nation's
 friend
And patron; thou Saint George shalt
 called be,
St. George of merry England, the sign of
 victory.

Elsewhere Renaissance artists of many countries had painted or sculptured his image, the most famous being Uccello's painting in the National Gallery, London, and Raphael's in the National Gallery of Art, Washington. There are also notable cycles of murals at the cathedral of Clermont-Ferrand and the chapel of San Giorgio at Padua. Dedications were frequent; there are famous churches of St. George at Rome, Constantinople, Venice, and Verona; in England over 160 ancient churches and not a few modern ones are dedicated to him. His patronage extends to soldiers, knights, archers, armourers, and through a pun on the Greek form of his name, to husbandmen also. He was also invoked against the plague, leprosy, and syphilis. It is one of the more unexpected destinies of Palestinian soldier-saints that George, of whom so little is known, should be regarded as the symbol of English nationalism and prowess in war. The name of St. George's Channel applied to the Irish Sea is due to a very late form of the Legend which made him travel to England by sea, approaching it from the West. Feast: 23 April; but his cult was reduced to a local one in the reform of the Roman calendar in 1969; 18 April in the Coptic Church.

AA.SS. Apr. III (1675), 100–63 with *C.M.H.*, pp. 205, 209; H. Delehaye, *Les Légendes grecques des saints militaires* (1909), pp. 45–76; on the versions of the Legend see K. Krumbacher, 'Der heilige Georg', *Abhandhungen der K. bayerischen Akademie*, xxv (no. 3), 1911 and E. A. W. Budge, *St. George of Lydda* (1930) for the Ethiopic version and E. W. Brooks in *Museon*, xxxviii (1925), 67–115 for the Syrian. See also F. Cumont, 'La plus ancienne Légende de saint Georges', *Revue d'Histoire des Religions*, cxiv (1936), 5–51 and for popular accounts G. J. Marcus, *Saint George of England* (1939); I. H. Elder, *George of Lydda* (1949). See also *Bibl. SS.*, vi. 512–21.

GEORGE THE HAGIORITE (1009–65), monk. Born of a pious aristocratic family in Tao-Klardzheti (Georgia), he was educated at Constantinople in religious and secular subjects. Desiring to be a monk, he returned home for his consecration in 1034. In 1036 he visited the Holy Land and became the disciple of George the Recluse, a Georgian monk of Antioch, who gave him the mission of translating the principal Greek religious treatises into Georgian. For this purpose he went to Mount Athos, where among other monasteries was a Georgian one called Iviron. Here he was ordained priest in *c.*1045 and became its abbot.

He established the cults of the monastic founders, reorganized the scriptorium to produce translations, and became a principal propagator of orthodoxy with its integral elements of theology, liturgy, and canon law. After some years the administrative aspects of his office became wearisome and in 1056 he resigned his abbacy, retired to the monastery of the Black Mountain, near Antioch, and there continued his literary work. Some years later he was drawn into controversy about Georgian orthodoxy. They claimed to have been evangelized by the apostle *Andrew and Antioch had conceded them autocephalous status. George himself was recognized as completely orthodox. In spite of the East–West schism of 1054 he developed the idea that the same Christian faith can inspire different liturgical practices, and he also recognized the pre-eminence of Rome. Above all he wished his fellow countrymen to be completely dissociated from Armenian Monophysites.

At the urgent appeal of both king and archbishop he returned to Georgia in 1060. He stipulated that he should not be consecrated a bishop, but for five years worked for the recognition of basic principles later promoted by the council of Ruis-Urbnisi. These included the acceptance by the rich for the support of the poor, respect for justice in the law-courts, the observance of canon law, the submission of the clergy to the bishops, and the rejection of all contacts with heretics. At this very time Georgia was suffering grievously from Turkish invasions. George, believing his end was near, left for the Holy Mountain (Athos) with 24 orphans to whom he had taught Greek and Georgian for them to enter the monastery of Iviron. He never reached his destination as he died at Constantinople. His body, however, was translated to the Holy Mountain (which gives him his name of Hagiorite), the millenary of whose foundation was celebrated in 1982 at Tbilisi. Feast: 30 June; translation, 24 May.

P. Peeters, 'Histoires monastiques géorgiennes', *Anal. Boll.*, xxxvi–xxxvii (1917–19), 69–159; J. Lefort, *Actes d'Iviron I: des origines au milieu du XIe siècle* (1985); *H.S.S.C.*, vi. 159–63.

GERALD OF AURILLAC (855–909), confessor. Gerald had poor health from an early age and gave much time to prayer and study instead of martial pursuits; when he became count of Aurillac on his father's death, he continued to lead a devout life with almsgiving, fasting, and prayer. He founded a monastery and built a church at Aurillac, thought of becoming a monk there, but was dissuaded by Gausbert, bishop of Cahors, who told him he would be more useful devoting himself as a layman to his neighbours and dependants. He became blind for the last seven years of his life. Feast: 13 October, at Gloucester.

Good contemporary Life by Odo of Cluny in *AA.SS.* Oct. VI (1794), 277–332 (Eng. tr. G. Sitwell, *Lives of Odo of Cluny and Gerald of Aurillac* (1958) and French summary in Baudot and Chassin, *Vies des Saints*, x (1952), 413–26); A. Poncelet, 'La plus ancienne Vie de S. Géraud d'Aurillac', *Anal. Boll.*, xiv (1895), 88–107; B.T.A., iv. 104–5.

GERALD OF MAYO (d. 732), abbot. An Englishman who become a monk at Lindisfarne and probably migrated with *Colman of Lindisfarne to Inishbofin (Galway), Gerald became abbot of the English part of this community, which became known as Mayo of the Saxons. This flourished greatly and was known as a centre of study, sufficiently important for Alcuin to correspond with its abbot and monks. Gerald is sometimes described as a bishop, but this seems incorrect; he is also believed to have founded the abbeys of Tempul-Gerald (Connacht) and Teaghna-Saxon. Feast: 13 March.

AA.SS. Mar. II (1668), 288–93; also in *V.S.H.*, ii. 107–15; B.T.A., i. 584; *The Irish Saints*, pp. 191–2.

GERARD MAJELLA, see MAJELLA.

GERARD SAGREDO (d. 1046), bishop of Csanad and martyr. A Venetian by birth, Gerard became a monk and later prior at San Giorgio Maggiore. On a pilgrimage to Jerusalem by a circuitous route, he travelled through Hungary, whose king *Stephen invited him to be his son's tutor. Not long afterwards the see of Csanad was established with Gerard as its first bishop: he pioneered against the twin problems of paganism and imperfectly converted Christians, as *Willibrord and *Boniface had done elsewhere. On Stephen's death in 1038 there was a revolt against Christianity. At Buda Gerard was attacked by pagans, stoned, and transfixed with a lance: his body was thrown from the Blocksburg cliff into the river Danube. In 1083 his relics were enshrined with those of Stephen, but in 1333 Venice obtained a share of them and translated them to the island of Murano. There he is venerated as Venice's first martyr. Feast: 24 September.

AA.SS. Sept. VI, 722–4; C. A. Macartney, *Medieval Hungarian Historians* (1953); E. Pasztor, 'Problemi di datazione della Legenda maior S. Gerhardi episcopi', *Bull. del l'Instituto Storico . . . e Archivio Muratoriano*, lxxxiii (1961), 113–40; B.T.A., iii. 629; *Bibl. SS.*, vi. 184–6.

GERARDIN (Garnard, Garnat, Gernardius, Gervardius) (d. *c.*934), monk and hermit. An Irishman who came to Morayshire, he lived first at Kenedor and then at Holyman Head near Elgin, where his cave survived until the 19th century. Gerardin's Legend claimed for him some contact with the English soldiers sent by King Athelstan in 934, besides the providential arrival of wood for his church by a river swollen in the storm. His cave is mentioned in Elgin charters. Feast: 8 November.

K.S.S., pp. 354–5.

GERENT (Geraint, Gerontius), patron of Gerrans (Cornwall). There is considerable uncertainty about his identification. The Exeter Martyrology (*c.*1100) refers to the son of a King Gerent being cured by the Irish saint Berriona, while a St. Gerontius occurs in an Exeter litany attributed to bishop Leofric. A famous letter of *Aldhelm was addressed to a Geraint, king of Dumnonia, concerning the paschal question. There is also a Welsh saint of this name honoured at Magor (Gwent) and mentioned in the Book of Llan Dav. The difficulty is to determine whether all, or some of these, should be identified. A modern Bollandist believes that Gerent was a 'local saint of the usual type . . . whom later hagiographical writers have arbitrarily made a king'. There certainly was at least one king of this name, but there seems no compelling reason to identify him with the patron of Gerrans, of whom moreover there is no known feast-day.

G. H. Doble, *The Saints of Cornwall*, iii (1964), 74–88.

GEREON (Geron) and companions (d. 304(?)), martyrs of Cologne. According to *Gregory of Tours, these fifty martyrs were soldiers of the Theban Legion who were put to death for the name of Christ. Because of the rich mosaics with which their chapel was decorated they were called the Golden Saints: a splendid Romanesque church survives there, dedicated in their honour. Although they are sometimes said to be purely local saints of Cologne, they are mentioned in the Martyrology of *Bede, and their feast was celebrated in the Sarum calendar and in those of Durham and Barking. The martyrology entries are confusing: from being fifty in number they became 392; 330 more were commemorated at Xanten, and there are entries under 9, 10, and 15 October which very likely refer to the same group of martyrs. A 13th-century Cistercian, Helinand, wrote a Legend for them. In art Gereon is represented either as a Roman legionary or as a medieval knight wearing a cross on his chest and bearing lance and shield. As a soldier he was presumably patron of knights from the Cologne area and like other saints who were beheaded, he was invoked against headaches and migraine. See also URSULA for a similar Legend, also from Cologne. Feast: usually 10 October.

AA.SS. Oct. V (1786), 14–60 which *C.M.H.*, pp. 547–8, 550, 557; B.T.A., iv. 78–9; Réau, ii. 581–2. *E.B.K. after 1100.*

GERMANUS OF AUXERRE (d. 446). He was born of Romano-Gallican parents, was trained as an advocate in Roman law, married, and became governor of the Armorican border province. On the death of Amator, bishop of Auxerre, in 418, Germanus was chosen as his successor. Meanwhile the Pelagian heresy had become rife in Britain. At the request of the British, the bishops of Gaul sent Germanus with *Lupus of Troyes across the Channel to refute the heretics. This they did at a conference at Verulamium, thereby giving new heart to the British Christians. On this occasion Germanus visited the grave of *Alban and exchanged some relics of the apostles and martyrs for earth from Alban's tomb. About 447 Germanus revisited Britain after a revival of Pelagianism, which he again refuted with success, obtaining the banishment of its leaders. Soon afterwards he directed British forces in battle, when they won the famous 'Alleluia victory' against a combination of Picts and Saxons, apparently without bloodshed. A year later he was in Ravenna, pleading the cause of the rebellious Bretons to the emperor. There he died on 31 July. His body was translated to Auxerre for a magnificent funeral; his shrine was a famous pilgrimage centre. St. Germans (Cornwall) is named after him. Feast: 31 July: translation, 1 October. Fifteen ancient English churches are dedicated to him; his feasts were very widely celebrated in England.

Bede, *H.E.*, i. 17–21; *AA.SS.* Iul. VII (1731), 184–304; near-contemporary Life by Constantius is also printed by W. Levison in *M.G.H.*, *Scriptores rerum merov.*, vii. 229–83 (tr. by F. R. Hoare, *The Western Fathers*, 1954); metrical Life, ed. L. Traube, in *M.G.H.*, *Poetae Latinae*, iii (1896), 428–517. See also R. W. Mathisen, 'The last year of St. Germanus of Auxerre', *Anal. Boll.*, xcix (1981), 151–9; L. Prunel, *Saint Germain d'Auxerre* (1929); G. le Bras, *Saint Germain d'Auxerre et ses Temps* (1950).

GERMANUS (Garmon, German) **OF MAN** (*c.*410–*c.*475), bishop. The presence of a number of dedications in North Wales and Cornwall, sometimes wrongly attributed to *Germanus of Auxerre, together with references to German in Lives of Celtic saints which are chronologically impossible for Germanus, has led Celtic scholars to seek at least one other German to explain them. Baring-Gould summarizes the life of Germanus of Man as follows. He was born in Brittany *c.*410; went to Ireland to stay with *Patrick in *c.*440; came to Wales and lived in the monastery of *Brioc and *Illtud *c.*450; left Gaul to meet Patrick in Britain *c.*462, where he engaged in a magic contest with Gwrtheyrn; returned to Ireland and became bishop of Man *c.*466. These dates are highly conjectural. The areas of Garmon dedications are Caernarvonshire, Denbighshire, Montgomeryshire, and Radnorshire. Leland mentioned a pilgrimage to Garmon ('Armon') at Llanarmon yn Ial, where offerings were made to a statue in sacerdotal vestments. Feast: (in Man) 3 July, but in Wales 31 July or 1 October, through confusion with Germanus of Auxerre.

Baring-Gould and Fisher, iii. 60–79; J. Leland, *Itinerary in Wales*, pp. 70–1.

GERMIN, see JURMIN.

GERMOE (Germoc, Germanus Mac Guill) (date unknown), bishop. Patron of Germoe (Cornwall), he was probably one of a party of Irish monks who settled in Cornwall before most of them moved on to Gaul. But Germoe, says Leland, was buried at Germoe; his chair was in the churchyard and his well a little outside it. The Legend of *Breage, however, makes Germoe a king; a 15th-century fresco representing him with crown and sceptre survives in Breage church. Baring-Gould identifies him with the founder of a chain of churches in Brittany. Germoe's feast-dates correspond to his historical uncertainty: William Worcestre dates his feast as on 'die S. Johannis in festo natalis', leaving it to the reader to interpret this as either 24 June or 27 December; Irish martyrologies commemorate him on 30 July, but *The Cornish Church Kalendar* places his feast on the 'Sunday after the first Saturday in May'.

J. Leland, *Itinerary*, i. 188; William Worcestre, pp. 28–9; Baring-Gould and Fisher, iii. 80–1.

GERON, see GEREON.

GERONTIUS, see GERENT.

GERTRUDE (d. 1302), Benedictine nun and visionary, called 'the Great'. Nothing is known of her parents or her place of origin. From the age of five she was educated in the nunnery of Helfta (Thuringia) under Mechtild (d. *c.*1285). There she made her profession and spent the rest of her life, undergoing a deep conversion at the age of twenty-five and various mystical experiences throughout her remaining twenty years. These were based on the Liturgy and many of her visions actually took place during the singing of the Divine Office. This needs to be stressed because much of her writing seems emotional and individualist in tone. She was a child of her age in so far as her piety expressed contemporary insistence on devotion to Christ's humanity: she is often regarded as a pioneer of the devotion, which later became popular, to the Sacred Heart of Jesus. From the time of her conversion

Gertrude lost interest in secular studies, in which she had been well grounded, and concentrated entirely on Holy Scripture, the Liturgy, and the Fathers. Her own writings include the 'Legatus Divinae Pietatis' (usually called *The Herald of God's Loving-Kindness* or the *Revelations of St. Gertrude*), of which, however, only the second book (out of five) was actually penned by her, the others being based on her notes. The *Book of Special Grace* contains the Revelations of Mechtild, but were written by Gertrude; while the collection of prayers, usually attributed to Gertrude and Mechtild in the 17th century, are probably not theirs at all. Other collections of their prayers, extracted from their genuine works, have, however, been made.

Gertrude is usually regarded as one of the most important medieval mystics. She was never abbess, although this title has been claimed for her by confusion with another Gertrude, who was abbess of Helfta when Gertrude entered it as a child. She was never formally canonized but her fame was diffused through the printing of her works in Latin in 1536: in 1677 Pope Innocent XI added her name to the Roman Martyrology and in 1738, at the request of the king of Poland and the duke of Saxony, her feast of 15 November was extended to all countries. Later it was moved to 16 November (in the Benedictine Order 17 November).

Works edited by the Benedictines of Solesmes, *Revelationes Gertrudianae et Mechtildianae* (1875); new improved edn. with French tr. by J. Hourlier, A. Schmitt, and P. Doyère, *Oeuvres Spirituellés* (*S.C.*, 1967 ff.); several Eng. trs. Lives by G. Ledos (1901) and anon., *St. Gertrude the Great* (1912); M. Jeremy, 'Similitudes in the Writing of Saint Gertrude of Helfta', *Medieval Studies*, xix (1957), 48–54. See also arts. in *Dict. Sp.*, vi (1967), 331–9; *N.C.E.*, vi (1967), 450 ff. and *Bibl. SS.*, vi. 277–87.

GERTRUDE OF NIVELLES (626–59), abbess. Daughter of Pepin of Landen and his wife Itta, she was born at Landen and was brought up religiously. Her mother, having consulted *Amand of Maastricht, built a double monastery at Nivelles where Gertrude became abbess and Itta herself one of the nuns. Notable for her hospitality to pilgrims and her generous benefactions to Irish monks such as *Foillan, brother of *Fursey, who founded a monastery at Fosses on land given by her, Gertrude at the age of thirty resigned her office to her niece. She was weakened by many austerities and wished to devote herself more completely to prayer and reading. She died a few years later.

Her cult was strong in the Low countries and spread to England and elsewhere. She is represented in art with mice as her emblem. This has never been convincingly explained, but there is some possibility of transference from pagan myths. However this may be, she was invoked against pests of rats and mice as recently as 1822, when offerings to her shrine at Cologne were made in the form of gold and silver mice. She was also invoked by travellers as well as pilgrims, who used to drink a stirrup-cup in her honour before setting out. As an extension of this patronage she was also invoked as a patroness of the recently dead, who were popularly supposed to experience a three-day journey to the next world, spending the first night under the care of Gertrude and the second under that of *Michael. Fine weather on her feast was regarded as the signal for beginning garden work. Feast: 17 March, the day of St. *Patrick, whose protection on the day of her death was assured by Foillan. She is mentioned in the Martyrology of *Bede.

Life edited by B. Krusch in *M.G.H. Scriptores rerum meroving*, ii. 447–74; *AA.SS.* Mart. II (1663), 592–604; B.T.A., i. 620–1.

GERVASE AND PROTASE (of unknown date), protomartyrs of Milan. Their bodies were discovered by *Ambrose in 386 on the eve of the dedication of the basilica, which still bears his name. His secretary and biographer Paulinus, together with *Augustine, were there at the time and testified to the miracles, especially the restoration to sight of a blind butcher, which accompanied the removal of the relics from the church of Nabor and

Felix to the cathedral. No historical details are known of the lives of these saints: in Milan there were only vague memories of their existence; the later *Acta* are spurious. J. Rendel Harris asserted that Gervase and Protase were identical with Castor and Pollux, but most hagiographers regard them as genuine martyrs, possibly of the 2nd century, whose memorials had been lost. Ambrose chose to be buried beside them; in the 9th century the relics of all three were placed in a sarcophagus of porphyry, rediscovered in 1864, and still on view today. Feast in many early calendars and martyrologies: 19 June. Church dedication at Little Plumstead (Essex).

AA.SS. Iun. III (1701), 817–46; H. Delehaye, *Les Origines du culte des Martyrs* (1912); id., 'Castor et Pollux dans les légendes hagiographiques', *Anal. Boll.*, xxiii (1904), 427–32; see also ibid., xlix (1931), 30–5; J. R. Harris, *The Dioscori in the Christian Legends* (1903).

GIANELLI, Antonio Maria (1789–1846), bishop of Bobbio, founder of the Missioners of St. Alphonsus. Born in Cereta (eastern Liguria) of a middle-class family, he was specially intelligent and industrious. Consequently he was sponsored by a benefactress for his education at the seminary at Genoa. He was ordained priest in 1812. Notable for his educational work, he became in turn parish priest and archpriest of Chiavari (1826), as well as a preacher and confessor in great demand. In 1827 he founded the Missioners of St. Alphonsus and in 1829 a congregation of nuns called Sisters of S. Maria dell 'Orto. These were devoted to teaching the poor and nursing the sick.

In 1838 he was appointed bishop of Bobbio. He ruled prudently and firmly, helped by the priests of his congregation. He also restored the cult of *Columbanus. He died on 8 June. He was beatified in 1925 and canonized in 1951. The congregations which he founded have prospered in Italy and elsewhere since his death. Feast: 7 June.

Decree of beatification in *A.A.S.*, xvii (1925), 176–9; Lives by L. Rodino (1896), L. Sanguinetti (1925), G. Frediani (1951); see also B.T.A., ii. 500–1; *Bibl. SS.*, ii. 211–15.

GILBERT OF CAITHNESS (d. 1245), bishop. The son of William de Moravia, lord of Duffus and Strabrok, who owned immense estates in northern Scotland, Gilbert became archdeacon of Moray, being appointed by King Alexander II with responsibilities for secular and religious government in a notoriously turbulent area. His enemies there set fire to his account-books; their survival was believed to be a miracle. In 1223, after the violent death of *Adam of Caithness and the punishment of his murderers and their kin by the king, Gilbert was appointed bishop to succeed him. Notable achievements of his episcopate were the building of the cathedral of Dornoch, whose statutes were modelled on those of Moray and Lincoln, and the provision of several hospices for the poor. He enjoyed a reputation as a fine preacher and administrator who, in his twenty years of peaceful rule, did much to civilize his diocese. He became the patron saint of his cathedral and diocese; his relics were venerated until the Reformation and were used for the swearing of oaths until 1545. There is no evidence that he was, as is sometimes asserted 'high steward to several monarchs', nor can he be identified with the Gilbert who, at the council of Northampton in 1176, made an impassioned speech in favour of Scots' ecclesiastical independence of the see of York. Feast: 1 April.

K.S.S., pp. 355–6; *D.N.B.*, s.v.

GILBERT OF SEMPRINGHAM (*c.*1083–1189), founder of the Gilbertine Order. His father was a Norman knight, Jocelin; his mother was Anglo-Saxon. Gilbert suffered physical deformity from birth, which made him unfit for knightly pursuits. He became a cleric, studied in France, and was named a Master. On returning home he started a school for both boys and girls; he also received from his father the churches of Sempringham and West Torrington (Lincs.), built on his own demesne.

As he was still not a priest, he appointed a vicar for the church services, lived in poverty in the vicarage, and by teaching and example made his parish a model of devout and temperate behaviour. Robert Bloet, bishop of Lincoln, made Gilbert his household clerk in 1122. Bloet, formerly chancellor and later justiciar, died the next year, but Gilbert stayed on in the court of his successor Alexander, living as a devout but unordained pluralist, who devoted his revenues of West Torrington entirely to the poor. Alexander ordained him priest, offered him a rich archdeaconry, which Gilbert refused, and allowed him to return to his parish before 1131. By this time his father had died, and Gilbert was squire as well as parson of Sempringham.

Among his parishioners was a group of seven devout young women, who lived under his direction in a house he had built for them adjacent to the church. Gilbert's rule for them was based on the Rule of St. Benedict, with the usual emphasis on seclusion and the virtues of the cloister. By the advice of the Cistercian William, first abbot of Rievaulx, Gilbert added some lay sisters to their community. Little by little the Order spread: to safeguard and develop their possessions, regular labour was needed, which was provided by the third element in the Order, lay brothers. With their rapid growth it became clear that stable, experienced government was needed: in 1147 Gilbert went to Cîteaux hoping to persuade the general chapter to rule his Order through English Cistercian abbots. But Eugenius III was present in chapter; the Savignac Order was aggregated to the Cistercian, and the Chapter refused Gilbert's request. Instead *Bernard helped him draw up the Institutes of the Order of Sempringham, of which Eugenius made him Master. To help him with the direction, Gilbert added canons to his institute, modelling the whole thing on Fontevrault; but the canons followed the Rule of St. Augustine and the lay brothers that of Cîteaux. But the nuns always formed the backbone of the Order; the men both governed them and ministered to their needs, temporal and spiritual. As Master, Gilbert continued his austere way of life, travelling frequently from house to house (mainly in Lincolnshire and Yorkshire). He would work at copying manuscripts, making furniture, or building.

In 1164 the Gilbertines incurred Henry II's displeasure because they had helped *Thomas of Canterbury escape to the Continent after the council at Northampton (1163). Thomas had eluded the king's officers, dressed as a Sempringham lay brother; he went north to their houses in the Lincolnshire Fens before doubling back on his tracks south to Kent. Gilbert made no secret of his support for Becket; although summoned to the king's presence to answer for his conduct, he obtained pardon and immunity for himself and his Order. This, however, was later disturbed by internal dissensions. Gilbert, at the age of nearly ninety, was faced by a rebellion of the lay brothers, whose main grievances were that there was too much work and not enough food. They were led by two skilled craftsmen among their number, who slandered Gilbert, obtained funds and support from magnates in church and state, and went to Rome. Gilbert, however, was upheld by the papacy and received back the rebels; the lay brothers' food and dress were somewhat improved. He delegated much of the government because of increasing age to Roger of Malton; on 4 February 1189 he died, blind but unbowed in spirit, at Sempringham, where he was buried.

He had built thirteen monasteries, of which nine were double monasteries, the other four for canons only. The aggregate of personnel was about 1,500. He also founded orphanages and leper-hospitals. Contemporary chroniclers highly praised both Gilbert and his nuns. His cult was spontaneous and immediate: he was canonized by Innocent III at Anagni in 1202. Hubert Walter ordered the English bishops to celebrate his feast. His name was added to the calendar on the wall of the Roman church of the *Four Crowned Martyrs soon afterwards. His Order remained in existence until the Reformation, the only one founded by an Englishman, which, although inspired largely by continental movements, never made an overseas foundation. Some relics are claimed by the church of S. Sernin, Toulouse. Feast: 4 February.

AA.SS. Feb. I (1658), 567–73, *N.L.A.*, i. 470–2; *M.O.*, pp. 205–7; R. Graham, *St. Gilbert of Sempringham and The Gilbertines* (1901); D. Knowles, 'The Revolt of the Lay Brothers of Sempringham', *E.H.R.*, l (1935), 465–87; R. Foreville, *Un procès de canonisation à l'aube du xiii*e *siècle. Le livre de saint Gilbert de Sempringham* (1943); id., *The Book of St. Gilbert* (1986); J. J. Munro, *John Capgrave's Lives of Saint Augustine and Saint Gilbert of Sempringham* (E.E.T.S., 1910).

GILDAS (*c.*500-*c.*570), abbot. Born probably near the Clyde, he became a monk at Llaniltud in S. Wales, perhaps after being married and widowed. He was a most notable figure in Welsh monastic life. Famous Irish monks became his disciples for a time; he himself visited Ireland and wrote letters to distant monasteries. In *c.*540 he wrote his famous work *De excidio Britanniae*, cited by *Bede, which gives a vivid picture of the decadence of contemporary British secular rulers and clerics, and blames their own sins for the victory of the Anglo-Saxon invaders. This work shows rhetorical power as well as considerable knowledge of Holy Scripture, Virgil, and the Letters of *Ignatius of Antioch. For some years he lived as a hermit on Flatholm Island in the Bristol Channel, but he ended his days in Brittany on an island near Rhuis (Morbihan). Here he had founded a monastery which became the centre of his cult. Gildas's chronology has been much disputed; it has also been asserted that there were in reality two men of this name who have been confused. Gildas's writings were widely known and used by Wulfstan, archbishop of York, in the early 11th century, in his famous *Sermon of the Wolf* to the English people during the calamitous reign of Ethelred the Unready. Feast: 29 January. Some early Irish Martyrologies commemorate him on this day, as does the Leofric Missal (*c.*1050) and various other Anglo-Saxon calendars of 9th–11th centuries.

Works and Life of Gildas ed. T. Mommsen in *M.G.H.*, *Auctores Antiquissimi*, xiii (1896), 3–110; *N.L.A.*, i. 468–9; M. Winterbottom (ed.) *Gildas, the Ruin of Britain and other works* (1978); F. Lot, 'De la valeur du *De excidio* . . . de Gildas' in *Medieval Studies in Memory of Gertrude Loomis* (1927); C. E. Stevens, 'Gildas Sapiens' in *E.H.R.*, lvi (1941), 353–73; P. Grosjean, 'Notes d'Hagiographie celtique', *Anal. Boll.*, lxxv (1957), 185–226; id., 'Remarques sur le *De excidio*', *Bull. Du Cange*, xxv (1955), 155–87. H. Williams, *Christianity in Early Britain* (1913); J. F. Kenney, *Sources for the Early History of Ireland*, i (1929), 176–9; M. Lapidge and D. Dumville (ed.), *Gildas: New Approaches* (1984).

GILES (Aegidius) (d. *c.*710), hermit. All that is known of this saint, who became immensely popular in the Middle Ages, is that he was born in the early 7th century and founded a monastery at the place later called Saint-Gilles (Provence) on land given by a King Wamba. His shrine became an important pilgrimage centre on the route for both Compostela and the Holy Land as well as in its own right. The 10th-century Legend, a tissue of borrowing from other Lives, was most influential. This made him an Athenian by birth, who became a hermit near the mouth of the Rhône not far from Nîmes, attracted to the area by the renown of *Caesarius of Arles. While out hunting King Wamba was in pursuit of a hind; he shot an arrow at it which wounded and crippled Giles, with whom the hind had taken refuge. Another legend made an emperor (wrongly identified as Charlemagne) seek forgiveness from him for a sin he did not dare confess, but while Giles said Mass next day he saw in a chart written by an angel the nature of the sin in question: the letters disappeared as Giles's prayers were so efficacious. Towards the end of his life Giles went to Rome and offered his monastery to the pope (thereby acquiring privileges and protection); the pope gave him two doors of cypress wood which the saint threw into the sea but which were transported to a beach near his monastery.

From Provence (called *provincia sancti Aegidii*) his cult spread, partly through Crusaders, to other parts of Europe. His patronage of cripples, lepers, and nursing mothers (based on the story of his giving shelter to the hind), aided by the belief that the invocation of Giles was so effective that his clients did not need full auricular confession, contributed powerfully to his popularity. In England 162 ancient churches were dedicated to him and at least twenty-four hospitals. The most famous in Britain are St. Giles at Edinburgh and St. Giles, Cripplegate, London. His feast was celebrated by all English Benedictine monasteries and the Sarum rite, as elsewhere in Europe. His artistic representations are either of a simple abbot with staff (as on Norfolk screens at Hempstead and Smallburgh), or of cycles of his life (as in 13th-century glass at Chartres and Amiens or the frescoes in the crypt of Saint-Aignan-sur-Cher), or of the incidents mentioned above of his protecting the hind (misericord of Ely Cathedral), or of the Mass of St. Giles (National Gallery, London).

The diffusion of his cult did not save its centre from becoming poverty-stricken in the late Middle Ages when offerings at his shrine, on which the monks had depended too exclusively, were greatly reduced, and the community looked to special exhibitions of the relics, aided by papal indulgences, to restore their income. At least two famous fairs in England are connected with St. Giles' Day: one in Winchester, no longer extant; the other at Oxford, which has lost its original purpose of buying and selling local produce, but survives as a funfair. Late in the Middle Ages Giles was reckoned in Germany as one of the *Fourteen Holy Helpers. His churches are often found at road junctions, which travellers could visit while their horses were being shod in smithies near by, of which Giles was also patron. Feast: 1 September.

AA.SS. Sept. I (1746), 284–304 with *Propylaeum*, p. 373; G. Paris (ed.), *La Vie de Saint Gile* (metrical Life by William of Barnwell) (1881); *Liber Miraculorum S. Aegidii* (ed. P. Jaffé), *M.G.H., Scriptores*, xii (1861), 316–23, also in *Anal. Boll.*, ix (1890), 393–422; E. E. Jones, *Saint Gilles* (1914); F. Brittain, *Saint Giles* (1928); J. Sumption, *Pilgrimage* (1975).

GILIANUS, see GALL.

GIULIANI, Veronica (1660–1717), Franciscan nun. Born at Mercatello of an affluent family, she showed precocious devotion and in 1617 became a Capuchin nun against her father's wishes. Her novitiate at Città di Castello was difficult. After her profession she experienced mystical union with Christ in his Passion which resulted in her receiving the stigmata. Visions of Christ bearing his cross and offering her a chalice of suffering followed: in 1697 a crown, as of thorns, appeared on her forehead. The local bishop examined these phenomena, devised a special, fraud-excluding regime for her, and became convinced that they were genuine. Throughout he was impressed by her obedience and humility. After a favourable report to the Holy Office, Veronica resumed normal community life.

She was mistress of novices for 34 years and insisted on the fundamental virtues fostered by reading Rodriguez's *Christian and Religious Perfection*, excluding works of advanced mysticism at the early stages. Elected abbess in 1716, she not only improved the spiritual life of the community but also installed piped water and enlarged its buildings.

At her confessor's command she left a spiritual diary in ten volumes, carefully examined in her canonization process and since published. Among other things she claimed that the instruments of Christ's Passion were imprinted on her heart: after her death reliable witnessess saw small objects in her right ventricle corresponding to a plan she had drawn. Levitations, stigmata which ceased bleeding at a word of command, and other phenomena reveal her as one of the best documented examples of how prolonged and intense consideration of Christ's Passion can have extraordinary effects in the devotee. She was beatified in 1804 and canonized in 1839. Feast: 9 July.

Works ed. Prof. Buccioni (1927); Life by R. Cioni (1965); B.T.A., iii. 57–9; *Bibl. SS.*, xxi. 1050–6.

GLEB, see BORIS AND GLEB.

GLYWYS (Gluvias) (date unknown), monk and possibly martyr. Of Welsh origin and sometimes said to be the nephew of *Petroc, he is the patron of St. Gluvias (Cornwall). He should probably be identified with Glywys, patron of Coedkernew (Gwent) and with Clivis, whose Glamorgan shrine, Merthir Glivis, is mentioned in the Book of Llan Dav. In some 15th-century wills he is called a martyr. Feast: (in Cornwall) 3 May.

G. H. Doble, *The Saints of Cornwall*, iii (1964), 15–19; Baring-Gould and Fisher, iii. 131–2.

GOBNET (5th century), virgin. Born in County Clare, she is said to have fled to the Aran Islands to escape a family feud. She built a church but was instructed in a vision that this was not to be the 'place of her resurrection', but rather another place, where she would find nine white deer grazing. So she came to southern Ireland, founded the church of Kilgobnet (near Dungarvan), and eventually settled at Ballyvourney. There she built a nunnery and was guided by St. Abban, who was buried there. She was a skilful bee-keeper and is represented as such by artists. She is said to have prevented a robber from building himself a castle by throwing a stone ball across the glen.

The pilgrimage was approved by indulgences issued by Clement VIII in 1601; it survives today as visits to some buildings and a holy well of uncertain date. The round stone associated with her is still preserved. Feast: 11 February.

The Irish Saints, pp. 192–5; see also W. W. Heist, 'Vita S. Abbani' in *Vitae Sanctorum Hiberniae* (1965), pp. 256–73.

GODELIVA (Liva) (d. 1070), martyr. Born near Boulogne, she was married when young to Bertulf of Ghistelles, a Fleming. He soon tired of her and never consummated the marriage. Godeliva was maltreated by her stepmother so she fled to her family and made complaints to the count of Flanders and the bishop of Tournai. Bertulf was exhorted to take her back and treat her well; he accepted the first recommendation but rejected the second. Simulating reconciliation, he had her seized by two servants who drowned her in a pond while a noose had been tied round her neck. They then replaced her in bed, hoping that her death would be attributed to natural causes. Meanwhile Bertulf had gone to Bruges to escape suspicion: he then married again almost at once.

In 1084 Godeliva's body was enshrined in the church of Ghistelles following reports of miracles. This is still a place of pilgrimage where water drunk from her well cures sore throats. One of her miracles resulted in the cure from blindness of Bertulf's daughter. An early Life of Godeliva survives, as does the document verifying her relics in 1084. Her cult was popular in Boulogne and Flanders: artists from the 15th to the 18th century (and possibly earlier) depicted her being strangled with a scarf by the two servants. Feast: 6 July.

Lives in *AA.SS.* Jul. II (1747), 409–36; M. Coens, 'Vie ancienne de Ste Godelive par Drogon', *Anal. Boll.*, xliv (1926), 102–37; M. English, *Les quatre couronnes de sainte Godelive de Gistel* (1953); see also B.T.A., iii. 26–7; *H.S.S.C.*, vi. 272; *Bibl. SS.*, vii. 70–6.

GODRIC (*c.*1069–1170), hermit. Born of Anglo-Saxon parents in Walpole (Norfolk), he became a pedlar in Lincolnshire from *c.*1085 to 1089; he then made a pilgrimage to Rome. Soon he went to sea, trading in Flanders, Denmark, and Scotland. Later he bought a half-share in one ship, a quarter-share in another, and became the captain. In 1101 he made a pilgrimage to Jerusalem, but he might be identical with the Godric, an 'English pirate', who took Baldwin I from Arsuf to Jaffa in 1102. On his return to England through Compostela he became a bailiff, but soon left to make more pilgrimages to

Rome and Saint-Gilles in Provence. Soon afterwards he made a third pilgrimage to Rome, accompanied this time by his aged mother.

In *c.*1105 he sold all his goods, left home, and tried to be a hermit, inspired perhaps by visits in seafaring days to the island of the Inner Farne, once the home of *Cuthbert. For a time he lived in forests near Carlisle with the *Psalter of St. Jerome* as his prayer-book; then he joined the hermit Ælric at Wulsingham (Durham) until his death in 1108. A few months later Godric made another penitential pilgrimage to Jerusalem: he visited the Holy Places, he lived with other hermits in the desert of *John the Baptist, and worked in a hospital for several months.

On returning to England, he resumed his old trade of pedlar to enable him to settle in a deserted hermitage at Eskedale Side near Whitby. A year later he arrived at Durham, acted as sexton in the church of St. Giles, and went to school with the choirboys at St. Mary-le-Bow. Now over forty, he settled finally at Finchale on the bishop of Durham's land; first at St. Godric's Garth, finally on the beautiful site now occupied by Finchale Priory.

His regime was one of 'almost superhuman' austerity and penance for his past sins, as sailor and merchant, of impurity and dishonesty. At first, without a director, he lived on roots and berries; later he grew vegetables and both milled his barley and baked it into loaves. He felled trees to make a hut and a wooden oratory (dedicated to St. Mary), in a corner of which he had a covered bath of cold water. Later a small stone church of St. John the Baptist was built, joined to St. Mary's with a cloister of wattle and mud. He wore both a hairshirt and a metal breastplate. Roger, prior of Durham, eventually gave him a rule of life and confraternity with the Durham community. His life was generally uneventful, but twice he was nearly killed: once by the Wear in flood and once (1138) when Scottish soldiers killed his cow and beat him severely, believing he had hidden treasure.

His holiness, clairvoyance, and prophetic gifts attracted visitors, among whom were *Ailred of Rievaulx, *Robert of Newminster, the two Laurences (of Durham and Westminster), William of Newburgh, and, above all, his future biographer, Reginald of Durham. Geoffrey of Coldingham knew him as a boy and described him: 'He had a broad forehead, sparkling grey eyes, and bushy eyebrows which almost met. His face was oval, his nose long, his beard thick. He was strong and agile, and in spite of his small stature his appearance was very venerable.' William characterized him as 'eager to listen, but slow to speak; always serious, and sympathetic to those in trouble'. Another pleasing trait of his character was his care for animals. In snow and ice he would bring rabbits and field-mice to his hut, warm them by the fire, and set them free. Once a stag took refuge in his hermitage (Finchale was the bishop of Durham's hunting-land), and when the huntsmen asked where it was, Godric answered: 'God knows where it is.' They, impressed by his radiant appearance, rode off, apologizing for disturbing him.

Godric was the author of the earliest surviving Middle English verse, which he himself set to music. The most famous is a hymn to the Blessed Virgin. There is also his hymn to St. Nicholas, and an air, sung in a heavenly vision by his sister Burchwen, accompanied by a choir of angels. The music of all three survives. Burchwen had been a solitary with Godric at Finchale for a time, but left to become a 'sister' in the hospital at Durham, where she died.

Towards the end of his life preternatural phenomena, believed to be of diabolic origin, increased; some of them, perhaps due to poltergeists, are remarkably similar to those recorded of the Curé d'Ars seven centuries later. Godric received messengers from *Thomas of Canterbury whom he encouraged; Pope Alexander III wrote to him from Beneventum, commending his way of life, asking his prayers for himself and the whole Church, and making him a sharer in the pope's own prayers. After a long illness, in which he was nursed by Durham monks, he died on 21 May 1170.

His liturgical cult seems to have been confined to Durham and Finchale and some calendars of the Cistercians, who claimed him (wrongly) as of their Order, but manuscripts of his life, notices by the chroniclers, and above all his hymns gave him a wide reputation. Around his body at Finchale a priory was built, which after a period of prosperity became a holiday-house for Durham monks in the later Middle Ages. Among paintings of him may be mentioned that in MS. Cotton Faustina B. VI, part ii, fo. 16v, which depicts Godric dressed in white, kneeling on grass and holding a rosary, while above the Blessed Virgin and her Son appear, teaching him her song. It is a manuscript of *c.*1400 containing a poem about the contemplative life, illustrated by pictures of hermit saints. Feast: 21 May.

Exceptionally full, contemporary Life by Reginald of Durham, ed. J. Stevenson, *Vita S. Godrici* (*SS.*, 1838) with Norman-French version, unprinted, in Paris, Bibl. Nat., MS. Mazarine 1716; shorter Life by Geoffrey of Coldingham in *AA.SS.* Maii V (1685), 70–85; see also *N.L.A.*, i. 475–500; William of Newburgh, *Historia* (*R.S.*), i. 149–50. For Godric's songs, J. W. Rankin, 'The Hymns of St. Godric', *Pubs. Mod. Lang. Ass. of America*, xxxviii (1923), 193–220; J. B. Trend, 'The First English Songs', *Music and Letters* (1928), 111 *et seq.* Letter of Pope Alexander III to Godric in W. Holtzmann, *Papsturkunden in England*, iii. 303. For Finchale see J. Raine, *The Priory of Finchale* (*SS.*, 1843) and C. R. Peers, 'Finchale Priory', *Arch. Aeliana* (1927), 193–220. See also V. M. Tudor in D. H. Farmer (ed.) *Benedict's Disciples* (1980), 195–211.

GODWALD, see GUDWAL.

GONAND, patron of Roche (Cornwall), venerated there in the 13th century as a male saint, appears in no calendar or martyrology. Possibly to be identified with St. Conan in Brittany.

G. H. Doble, *The Saints of Cornwall*, iv (1965), 128–31.

GONZAGA, Aloysius (1568–91), Jesuit. Son of the marquis of Castiglione and his wife, who was lady-in-waiting to the queen of Spain, Aloysius was destined for a military career. As a small boy he took part in military parades with a pike on his shoulder, and once fired off a real cannon, unauthorized. His piety was precocious. While he was a page at the court of Francesco de' Medici at Florence, he suffered from kidney disease, which gave him leisure for prayer and reading the Lives of saints. His family accompanied the empress of Austria to Spain (1581–3), where to his father's intense indignation, he decided to become a Jesuit. His family's return to Italy in 1584 did nothing to alter his decision, in spite of pressure from other magnates and the attraction of life at court.

He entered the novitiate in 1585; obedience curbed his excessive desire for austerity, only his weak health prevented him from being an ideal novice. He was professed in 1587. He nursed the sick in a plague hospital in 1591, caught the disease, and nearly died. He partially recovered, but his health was undermined and he lived only until 21 June.

In his last years he had been directed by Robert *Bellarmine, to whose guidance he owed the development of a courageous, single-minded devotion to God and his neighbour and the shedding of naïve, even priggish, attitudes to human affection and imitation of the saints. In his defence some have urged that the corrupt, immoral milieu in which he was brought up needed a completely uncompromising, if angular, example, comparable with the single-mindedness of Renaissance politicians.

The cult was approved in 1621; he was canonized in 1726 and declared patron of youth in 1729. Feast: 21 June.

AA.SS. Iun. IV (1707), 847–1169; contemporary Life by V. Cepari (1606), ed. A. Schroeber (Eng. tr. 1891); C. C. Martindale, *The Vocation of Aloysius Gonzaga* (1927); Writings ed. A. Hauser (1850).

GORAN (Goron, Gorran), patron of Gorran (Cornwall). Probably identical with the hermit Vuron (Wron), who lived at Bodmin and departed 'to a place about a day's journey south and ended his days there' after

*Petroc arrived at Bodmin. The reason for his departure is unknown. At Gorran the cave and well believed to be his survive. Feast: 7 April.

G. H. Doble, *The Saints of Cornwall*, v (1970), 33–4.

GORDIAN AND EPIMACHUS (d. *c.*250), Roman martyrs. Gordian, according to his funeral inscription, was a boy: it contrasts his tender years with the maturity of his Christian witness. Epimachus suffered some time before: the body of Gordian was buried in the church of Epimachus; henceforth they were venerated together. The body of an Alexandrian martyr Epimachus was translated to Constantinople; there has been some confusion between these two saints. Gordian is mentioned in the Martyrology of *Bede; the feast of Gordian and Epimachus was in the Sarum calendar. The late Acts are worthless and make Gordian a minister of the Emperor Julian. Part of the relics of these martyrs were given by Charlemagne's wife to the abbey of Kempten (Bavaria). Feast: 10 May (or 6, 9 May).

AA.SS. Maii I (1680), 551–5 *C.M.H.*, p. 244; *Propylaeum*, p. 182; B.T.A., ii. 265.

GORETTI, Maria (1890–1902), virgin and martyr. Born near Ancona, the eldest daughter of a peasant, she was a devout but cheerful girl. Her father died in 1900; her mother went out to work while Maria took care of the house. A young man of the neighbourhood first made advances to her, then pestered her, and finally attempted to rape her, threatening to kill her if she resisted. She repelled him with all her strength, he repeatedly stabbed her, and she died the next day. Her killer was sentenced to life imprisonment: after eight years he repented, after twenty-seven he was released, a new man. He lived to see his victim canonized in 1950, a martyr for chastity and for the Christian life, who had died at about the same age as *Agnes. In canonizing Maria Goretti, the Roman Church also honours innumerable others who, in similar circumstances, preferred death to dishonour. Feast: 6 July.

C. Marini, *L'eroica fanciulla Maria Goretti* (1904); M. C. Buerhle, *Saint Maria Goretti* (1950).

GORGONIUS, Roman martyr of early date, buried on the Via Lavicana. Feast: 9 September in Roman and Sarum missals.

GORGONIUS, PETER AND DOROTHEUS, martyred at Nicomedia in 303, as described by Eusebius (*H.E.*, viii. 6) with a well-attested cult in East and West on 12 March, but not, it seems, in England. The two Gorgonii have been wrongly identified.

B.T.A., i. 573–4, iii. 512.

GORKUM, MARTYRS OF (d. 1572). These were a group of nineteen religious, including eleven Franciscans, two Premonstratensian canons, and some diocesan priests, who were hanged by militant Calvinists at Briel. Gorkum had just been captured by the Gueux, an extremist group of Dutch Calvinists who had continued a war of independence from Spain after practising piracy.

The priests were arrested and imprisoned from 26 June to 6 July. They were then taken on a ship to Briel, half-naked and the butt of mob insults. They were then interrogated in front of Admiral Lumey and were offered their freedom in return for denying Catholic teaching on the Eucharist and the papal primacy. This they refused to do. They were then joined in prison by three other priests, especially John of Cologne, the Dominican parish priest, who suffered with them.

William of Orange ordered their release and the Gorkum magistrates deplored their arrest, but they were hanged regardless of these authorities in a deserted monastery at Ruggen, near Briel. At this point the courage of a few failed, although of apparently blameless life, while others, who had previously lived scandalously, atoned for this by courageous constancy. Their bodies were mutilated before or after death and buried in a ditch until they were translated to the Franciscan church in Brussels in 1616. Vivid portrayals of their deaths survive in paintings by Jan van

Sande and Cesare Fracassini. These martyrs were beatified in 1675 and canonized in 1867. Feast: 9 July.

AA.SS. Iul. II (1721), 736–847; Lives by H. Meuffels and D. De Lange (1954); see also B.T.A., iii. 56–7; *Bibl. SS.*, vii. 111–12.

GOTHIAN, see GWYTHIAN.

GOVAN (Gowan) (6th century), hermit. This saint gave his name to a headland and a chapel on the south coast of Pembrokeshire (Dyfed), where he spent the last few years of his life. The ruined buildings are of great interest, especially to readers of Bede's Life of *Cuthbert, with its description of the hermit's cell from which only the sky is visible, as the Govan cell reproduces this feature exactly. Govan is said to have been a disciple of the Irish saint *Ailbe. Feast: 26 March in Irish martyrologies. Other saints of this name include a disciple of *Fursey who eventually settled at Laon. Feast: 20 June.

Baring-Gould and Fisher, iii. 143–7.

GREGORY THE GREAT (*c.*540–604), pope, apostle of the English, one of the most important popes and influential writers of the Middle Ages. Gregory was the son of a Roman senator and entered the service of the State as a young man. But in 573 he sold his enormous properties, founding six monasteries in Sicily and a seventh in Rome, and giving generously to the poor. The next year he entered his own monastery of St. Andrew's on the Celian Hill as a monk and was distinguished for his austere life, which both filled him with nostalgia in later years and caused some of the ill-health which he suffered so constantly. Pope Benedict I, however, called him out of the monastery to become one of the seven deacons of Rome, and his successor, Pelagius II, made him *apocrisiarius* (ambassador) in Byzantium. After six years of distinguished service Gregory returned to Rome to become abbot of St. Andrew's, seemingly convinced that the future of Christianity lay with monasticism rather than with the declining Eastern Empire. But his own choice of monastic life was destined to be frustrated. He had hoped to lead some missionaries to bring the Gospel to the Anglo-Saxons—he had been specially impressed by some Anglo-Saxon slaves on sale in the Roman market—but he was elected pope during an outbreak of plague. Reluctantly he accepted and was confirmed by the emperor.

He was at once faced with a state of crisis. Floods, famine, plague, a Lombard invasion, all called for urgent attention, while in the longer term there were the dominance of Byzantium in Church affairs and the need of barbarian peoples to be converted to Christianity. His care for other Western churches was matched by few popes before his time and contributed to the emergence of the medieval papacy.

In 592–3 he concluded a separate peace with the Lombards, virtually ignoring the exarch of Ravenna, who was the emperor's representative in Italy. He also appointed governors to Italian towns, administered the vast estates of the Church with prudence and skill, and in the breakdown of imperial authority assumed many of the roles of a civil ruler.

One of the most notable initiatives of his pontificate was the conversion of the Anglo-Saxons. In the whole process Gregory personally took the lead; he had corresponded in advance about it, he had arranged for the liberation of some Anglo-Saxon slaves, and he sent *Augustine and his monks on this hazardous but imaginative undertaking. After their initial success Gregory still directed by giving guidance in matters that perplexed Augustine, by sending reinforcements in 601, and by writing to the king and queen of Kent. This policy was continued by Gregory's successors: as a consequence the Church in England was in many ways closer to the papacy than that in Gaul. In England was written the first Life of Gregory: from *Bede at Wearmouth, *Aldhelm at Malmesbury, and the anonymous biographer from Whitby come eulogies of Gregory as the 'apostle of the

English', 'our father and apostle in Christ', 'he from whom we have received the Christian faith, he who will present the English people to the Lord on the Day of Judgment as their teacher and apostle'. Later devotion to Augustine and *Aidan have obscured this earliest realization of Gregory's personal importance as apostle of the English. By choosing the personnel of the mission and by his direction, encouragement, and support he was both pioneer and continuator in the work. After his death his influence continued by his writings.

These were remarkable for quantity, quality, and their suitability for the readers of his own and future generations. His principal achievement was to pass on to converted barbarians the wisdom of the Fathers of the Graeco-Roman world, such as Origen, *Augustine of Hippo, and *Ambrose of Milan. This was particularly true of his Homilies on the Gospels and the *Moralia* on the book of Job, written in Constantinople at the request of *Leander. His more original works such as the *Pastoral Care* (later translated into OE. by King Alfred) and the *Dialogues* (or Lives of the saints) also enjoyed great popularity: one formed the episcopate of the Middle Ages more deeply than any other book, while the other both reflected and encouraged the preoccupation of contemporaries for the miraculous, before the role of secondary causes in the Christian world-view was properly understood. Both books were standard works in most Anglo-Saxon libraries; their popularity did not cease at the Norman Conquest. Gregory's 854 Letters are perhaps his most interesting work for historians of today. They reveal his wisdom, prudence, and preoccupation with the problems of both Church and State, including monasticism, the missionary role of the Church, the legitimacy of icons, the integrity of catholic doctrine, and the reproof of prelates who gave themselves grandiloquent titles. He preferred to be known as the 'servant of the servants of God', a title retained by his successors to the present day.

His role in the development of the Roman Liturgy was considerable, but disputed. He certainly modified various minor features and composed a number of prayers which formed the kernel of the Gregorian Sacramentary, even if this reached its final form after his death. Many prayers in it also were inspired by his thought and terminology if not actually written by him. His name has always been associated with Church music and especially Gregorian Chant: he probably took a prominent part in the gradual codification and adaptation of at least four pre-existing forms of plainsong. Although he wrote the earliest Life of *Benedict of Nursia in book II of his *Dialogues* and showed great appreciation of his Rule, it seems that his own monastery was not formally 'Benedictine' but rather basilican in character. Nevertheless, his writings reveal much influence of the Rule, and the traditional image of him as a Benedictine, even if juridically incorrect, still stands as a description of his spirit and outlook. It would be hard to name anyone more influential in forming the spirit of medieval monasticism. Indeed, in the wider sphere of the life of the Church as a whole, Gregory's reign of only thirteen years is rightly seen as decisive in the development of the medieval papacy; he thoroughly deserved the title of 'the Great'.

During much of his life he suffered from both gout and gastritis, but these afflictions seldom affected his judgement. Even when reduced in health just before his death, he dictated letters and cared for the needs of the churches. He must have been sixty-five or seventy when he died. He was soon acclaimed a saint.

In England thirty-two ancient and many modern churches are dedicated to him and his principal feast was given a high rank from early times and celebrated universally. The earliest pictures of Gregory show him as pope, writing, with the Holy Spirit in the form of a dove dictating what he should write: these survive especially in liturgical books of the early Middle Ages. Later he figures (as on Norfolk screens and pulpits) as one of the Four Latin Doctors (with SS. Ambrose, *Jerome, and Augustine). Later again the pictures stress his role as teacher of the efficacy of prayer and the sacrifice of the Mass in freeing souls from the pains of Purgatory, either the emperor Trajan, delivered by the prayers of Gregory himself, or the monk unfaithful to poverty who was freed by thirty masses said on successive days (still called a gregorian trental). Luigi Capponi especially developed these themes in the 15th-century sculptures in the church of St. Gregory at Rome. In the 15th and 16th centuries (but not afterwards) the 'Mass of St. Gregory' paintings were popular, especially but not exclusively in Germany and Flanders. These depict him saying Mass while the suffering Christ appears above to confirm the faith of the ministers in the Real Presence. This is not based on any incident in Gregory's life, nor does it appear in the account in the *Golden Legend*. Gregory was also highly esteemed in the East and in ancient Ireland, where he was even provided with an Irish royal genealogy and an apocryphal *Liber de Gradibus Coeli* attributed to him. Feast: 3 September; ordination, 29 March.

Early Lives by the *Liber Pontificalis* (ed. Duchesne), i. 312; by the Monk of Whitby, ed. B. Colgrave, *The Earliest Life of Gregory the Great* (1968); by Bede, *H.E.*, ii. 1; by Paul the Deacon (late 8th century), ed. H. Grisar in *Z.K.T.*, xi (1887), 158–73 and in expanded form in *P.L.*, lxxv. 41–60; by John the Deacon (9th century) in *P.L.*, lxxv. 59–242. Modern Lives by F. H. Dudden, *Gregory the Great* (2 vols., 1905); P. Battifol (1928; Eng. tr. 1929), Abbot Snow (1932). Gregory's works are in *P.L.*, lxxv–lxxviii; critical editions of some of his Scriptural works in *C.C.*, *Series Latina*, vols. cxliv (1963) and cxlii (1971) and of his *Registrum Epistolarum* (ed. P. Ewald and L. M. Hartmann) *M.G.H.*, *Epistolae*, i and ii (1891–9), for which see D. Norberg, *In Registrum Gregorii Magni Studia Critica* (2 vols. 1939). For his spiritual teaching see C. Butler, *Western Mysticism* (1922, 1966) and V. Recchia, *L'esegesi di Gregorio Magno al Cantico dei Cantici* (1967); for his monasticism K. Hallinger, 'Papst Gregor der Grosse und der hl. Benedikt' in *Studia Anselmiana*, xlii (1957), 231–319 and G. Ferrari, *Early Roman Monasteries* (1957); for other aspects L. Weber, *Hauptfragen der Moraltheologie Gregors des Grossen* (1947); E. Spearing, *The Patrimony of the Roman Church in the Time of Gregory the Great* (1918); E. H. Fisher, 'Gregor der Grosse und Byzanz', *Zeitschrift der Savigny-Stiftung fur Rechtsgeschichte*, lxvii (1950), 15–144. See also J. Ryan, 'The Early Irish Church and the See of Peter' in *Medieval Studies presented to Aubrey Gwynn* (1961); J. Richards, *Consul of God* (1980); W. D. McCready, *Signs of Sanctity* (1989); R. Godding, *Bibliografia di Gregorio Magno* (1990).

GREGORY II (d. 731), pope. Born in Rome, Gregory became a subdeacon under Pope Sergius; later he was treasurer and librarian and, in 710, now a deacon, accompanied Pope Constantine to Constantinople to help settle certain doctrinal and disciplinary difficulties. On Constantine's death Gregory was chosen bishop of Rome. He proved an energetic and apostolic ruler. In Rome he held synods to enforce discipline and morality, he rebuilt old churches and established new hospitals and monasteries, including St. Paul's-outside-the-Walls, and encouraged the revival of Monte Cassino under Petronax. He fought constantly for the independence of Rome from the emperors, the Saracens, and the Lombards. He vigorously opposed the iconoclasm of Emperor Leo III, but at the same time insisted that the Italians keep their allegiance to the emperor. His interest in the Anglo-Saxons was shown by his encouragement and direction of *Boniface, whom he consecrated bishop and to whom he gave both name and mission; he also helped *Nothelm with his researches in the papal archives to provide material for *Bede's *Ecclesiastical History*. He received at Rome the Wessex king Ina, who became a monk there in 726. Feast: 11 (or 13) February.

AA.SS. Feb. II (1658), 692–705; *Liber Pontificalis* (ed. Duchesne), i. 396–414; W. Levison, *England and the Continent in the Eighth Century* (1956), pp. 72–4; *O.D.P.*, pp. 86–7.

GREGORY III (d. 741), pope. A Syrian by birth, able and learned as well as holy, he was acclaimed as pope by the people after the funeral of *Gregory II (731). The

Liber Pontificalis described him as a man of deep humility and true wisdom, learned in the Scriptures, who knew the Psalms by heart. He was an eloquent preacher, skilled in Latin and Greek, a strong upholder of the faith; a lover of poverty and the poor, protector of widows and orphans, a friend of monks and nuns. This picture needs completion by reference to current controversies.

When he became pope, the iconoclastic dispute was at its height as Emperor Leo III had forbidden sacred images and their veneration in the east. When Gregory received no answer to his request to the emperor to think again, he held a council which denounced iconoclasm and excommunicated all who destroyed images. In reply the emperor sent an armed fleet to Italy, which was wrecked, and sequestered the papal patrimonies in Sicily and Calabria.

When the Lombard king Liutprand had invaded the duchy of Rome and threatened the city itself, Gregory appealed for help from the Frankish Charles Martel, mayor of the palace (716–41), imploring him to defend the Church and God's particular people, offering sumptuous gifts and patrician rank. Charles, unlike some of his successors, was unwilling to help, but Gregory had seen the importance of a pact with the Franks to assure the papacy's independence.

In ecclesiastical matters he was more successful. He fully backed *Boniface's missionary work, giving him the pallium and authority to establish bishoprics (732); six years later he made him 'legate of the apostolic see' with full powers to organize the Church in Bavaria, Alemannia, Hesse, and Thuringia, supporting him with letters to lay and ecclesiastical magnates. He also gave the pallium to Egbert of York in 735, thus completing *Gregory the Great's plan for two ecclesiastical provinces in England.

In his ten years' rule he improved the churches of Rome, enriching the shrine of St. Peter with six onyx columns, a present from the exarch Eutychius. He also supported existing monasteries and founded new ones. An oratory in St. Peter's, dedicated to Christ, the Virgin Mary, and All the Saints was built by him for housing relics of the saints; here he was buried among splendid images, which affirmed the belief of the pope and the Western Church in the value of icons. His cult is witnessed by Ado's Martyrology (9th century). Feast: 28 November.

Liber Pontificalis i. 415–25; *O.D.P.*, pp. 88–9; M. Tangl, *Bonifatii Epistulae Selectae* (*M.G.H.*, 1916).

GREGORY VII (Hildebrand) (*c.*1021–85), pope. Of plebeian origin, born at Soano (Tuscany), he went to Rome when very young, became a monk probably at St. Mary on the Aventine, and was chosen by Pope Gregory VI as his chaplain, in which capacity he shared the pope's exile in 1046. Hildebrand, as he was generally known, retired to a monastery (Cluny?) on Gregory VI's death in 1047, returned to Rome in 1049 with *Leo IX (just elected pope), and under him and his successors occupied important financial and other offices. He came to formulate papal policy in a way not unlike that of a modern Secretary of State, except that Hildebrand's influence was both more theoretical and more thoroughgoing. He was elected pope in 1073; although he began his work for Church reform, like his predecessors, by decrees against simony and the incontinence of the clergy, he went on to a more comprehensive quest for the liberty of the Church in practice, by forbidding lay investiture of ecclesiastical offices.

This stand aroused much hostility during and after Gregory's lifetime and affected most of western Europe, including England. Here William I refused to obey, but escaped condemnation because he generally supported the pope's other reforming policies; *Anselm, however, vigorously opposed William II and Henry I on this very issue. In France the reforms were eventually carried through, although many bishops lost their sees in the process. But in Germany the issue was fought out with great bitterness on both sides. The emperor Henry IV, who was threatened with deposition, declared Gregory deposed himself. He replied by freeing Henry's subjects from their oath of allegiance, after excommunicating the emperor. German magnates then agreed that Henry should lose his crown unless he received absolution in a year. This led to the famous confrontation at Canossa when Henry spent three days in the snow at the castle gate, accused himself, and received absolution. Although this is often seen as the triumph of Church over State, in fact it was a triumph for the emperor, who never gave up his claims to investiture but caused extreme discomfiture to the pope, who as spiritual guide had no alternative to absolving him as a private penitent. Henry was excommunicated again in 1080 as he had not kept his promises made at Canossa; but in reply he set up Wibert of Ravenna as anti-pope and took Rome after a siege of more than two years. Gregory called in the Normans under Robert Guiscard to rescue him. This they did, but the Norman soldiers so oppressed the Romans that they rejected Gregory, who fled to Monte Cassino and lastly to Salerno, where he died.

Historians, like contemporaries, were divided in their estimate of Gregory: he has been considered by some an ambitious tyrant, 'Holy Satan', an unscrupulous and intransigent pope who deformed the papacy. Others make a more favourable estimate: one who devoted his life to reforming and strengthening the Church, to which he was utterly devoted, partly because he saw himself as being the Vicar of St. Peter and, lacking any worldly position by birth, he was detached from the temporal involvements of most ecclesiastics. What is certain is that the Gregorian Reform, which owed more to him than to any other individual, was a successful revolutionary movement which has profoundly modified the relation between Church and State, the nature of the clerical and monastic orders, and the involvement of Christianity in society ever since. Gregory's name was added to the Roman Martyrology in 1583: he was canonized in 1606; his feast was extended to all countries by Pope Benedict XIII in 1728. Feast: 25 May.

AA.SS. Maii VI (1688), 101–59; E. Caspar, *Registrum Gregorii VII Papae* in *M.G.H.*, *Epistolae Selectae*, ii (1920–3), tr. of selected letters by E. Emerton (1932); for other letters of Gregory, P. Jaffé, *Monumenta Gregoriana* (1865); H. E. J. Cowdrey, *Epistolae Vagantes* (with Eng. tr., 1972); A. Murray, 'Pope Gregory VII and his Letters', *Traditio*, xxii (1966), 149–201; A. Fliche, *S. Grégoire VII* (1921); id., *La Réforme Grégorienne* (1924–7); H. X. Arquillière, *Saint Grégoire VII* (1934); E. Caspar, 'Studien zum Register Gregors VII' in *Neues Archiv.*, xxxviii. 143–226; A. J. Macdonald, *Hildebrand* (1932); W. Ullmann, *The Growth of Papal Power in the Middle Ages* (2nd edn., 1962), pp. 262–309; E. John, *Holy Satan*; *O.D.P.*, pp. 154–6; L. F. J. Meulenberg, *Der Primat der römischen Kirche im Denken und Handeln Gregors VII* (1965); *Bibl. SS.*, vii. 294–379.

GREGORY OF NAZIANZUS (329–89), monk and bishop. The son of the bishop of Nazianzus (Cappadocia), Gregory received the best education available, at the University of Athens, where *Basil, his lifelong friend, and Julian, the future emperor (the 'Apostate'), were fellow-students. In 359 he left Athens and became a monk, leading a solitary life with Basil as his companion in beautiful surroundings at Pontus. Their frequent discussions on theology and monasticism bore fruit in the active organization of Basil and the theological depth and penetration of the contemplative Gregory. After two years Gregory went home to help his father (then aged eighty) to manage his diocese and estates. Against his own inclination he was ordained priest. He fled to Basil for 10 weeks, but eventually returned to his new duties; he wrote an *apologia* for his flight, which became a classic on the nature and duties of the priesthood.

Meanwhile Basil had become archbishop of Caesarea. Faced with a rival at Tyana, he had Gregory consecrated bishop of Sasima, an unhealthy border-town, in order to maintain his own influence in a disputed area. This episode caused a quarrel between the two: Basil accused Gregory, who never visited Sasima, of slackness, while Gregory was not prepared to live in a hostile and unpleasant town, still less to become a pawn in ecclesiastical politics. Later Basil and Gregory were reconciled, but their friendship never quite recovered its former warmth. Meanwhile, Gregory continued as coadjutor at Nazianzus to his father, who died in 374. But he always desired the solitary life and his health broke down in 375. He lived in Seleucia for the next five years.

After the death of the persecuting emperor Valens, peace returned to the Church, but much reconstruction was necessary, especially at Constantinople itself. For over 30 years the capital had been dominated by Arians; orthodox believers even lacked a church. Neighbouring bishops sent for Gregory to restore its Christian community. Once again he protested, but finally consented, although the intrigue and violence of Constantinople were utterly repugnant to this scholarly contemplative. In spite of his evident poverty and premature old age, the next few years were the most important in his life.

He transformed his house into a church; there he preached the famous sermons on the Trinity which gave him the surname of Theologian, i.e. one who penetrates in faith and understanding to the Divinity of Christ. Through his skilful and profound teaching his reputation spread, his audience increased. Arians attacked him by slander, insults, and violence but he persisted in preaching the faith and doctrine of Nicea. In 381, under the emperor Theodosius, the Council of Constantinople finally established and confirmed the conclusions of Nicea as authentic Christian doctrine. Both in this and in its other doctrinal conclusions Gregory played an important part. During this council he was appointed bishop of Constantinople and installed in the basilica of Santa Sophia. Opposition to him, however, did not cease; he soon resigned for the sake of peace, his most important work of restoring orthodoxy in the capital was done.

He returned to his home town of Nazianzus, still without a bishop, and administered the see until a successor was appointed. In *c.*384 he retired to his estates and spent his time reading and writing, enjoying his garden with its fountains and shady groves. To these years belong his religious poems and his autobiography. He died at Nazianzus. His relics were translated, first to Constantinople and later to St. Peter's Rome. As one of the four great Eastern Doctors his cult has been universal. Feast: In the East, 25 and 30 January; in the West, formerly 9 May (translation on 11 June); but since 1969, with Basil, on 2 January.

AA.SS. Maii II (1680), 369–459: works in *P.G.*, xxxv–xxxviii, *Theological Orations* (ed. A. J. Mason, 1899); Letters ed. P. Gallay (2 vols., with French tr., 1964–7) and Eng. tr. in *Post-Nicene Christian Fathers*, ser. II, vol. vii (1894). French biographies by A. Benoit (1885) and P. Gallay (1943); see also J. H. Newman, *Historical Sketches*, iii (1903), 50–94 and R. R. Ruether, *Gregory of Nazianzus: Rhetor and Philosopher* (1969).

GREGORY OF NYSSA (*c.*330–*c.*395), bishop. Born at Caesarea (Cappadocia), the younger brother of *Basil, he was given an excellent education at Athens, became a rhetorician, and married. After some disillusionment with his post of professor of rhetoric, he was ordained priest (*c.*362). It is not certain when he became a monk, whether his wife died or became a nun. In 371 he was chosen as bishop of Nyssa, a remote outpost of Basil's province near Armenia; but Gregory seems to have lacked skill and diplomacy in supporting Basil's cause. Gregory was an intellectual and his writings against Arianism in ardent defence of Nicea, as well as his ascetical works, such as the Life of Moses and his sermons on the Song of Songs, are his chief title to fame. He took a prominent part in the Council of Constantinople (381) with *Gregory of Nazianzus, and later travelled much as a preacher. He is nowadays reckoned as an important link in the transmission of the thought of Origen to later ages and as a spiritual writer of great authority and depth. Feast: 9 March.

AA.SS. Mar II (1668), 4*–10*; works ed. W.

Jaeger (1921–60); id., *Two Rediscovered Works of Ancient Christian Literature: Gregory of Nyssa and Macarius* (1954); J. Daniélou, *Platonisme et Théologie Mystique* (1944); H. U. von Balthasar, *Présence et Pensée* (1942); *Bibl. SS.*, vii. 205–10. See also MACRINA.

GREGORY OF TOURS (539–94), bishop. Born at Clermont-Ferrand, the most important town in the Auvergne, of a distinguished senatorial family which also numbered several bishops and saints among its members, Gregory was educated in the household of his uncle Gallus, bishop of Clermont-Ferrand. Meanwhile, his father had died and his mother had moved to Burgundy. Gregory paid frequent visits to the bishops of Lyons and of Tours, both of them relatives. He was ordained deacon in 563 and was elected bishop of Tours in 573.

In a turbulent and violent age bishops of Merovingian Gaul were expounders and defenders of the faith and of public morality; they practised charity and compassion on a large scale, were responsible for the building and repair of churches including the tombs of martyrs and other saints; they were visitors of monasteries and nunneries, founders of schools, and administrators of vast estates. In all these things Gregory had a fine record; in addition he was a voluminous and articulate writer. Most of what we know about his life comes from his own works, which include his famous *History of the Franks* in ten books, seven books on miracles of the saints including *De gloria Martyrum*, *De gloria confessorum* as well as those of *Martin and *Julian, one book on the Lives of the Desert Fathers, one commentary on the Psalms, and one on the Offices of the Church. Out of all these the first is easily the most famous, while those on the saints have recently and rightly attracted more interest than formerly. In them Gregory reveals himself as a substantially accurate and acute observer, with a sense of both humour and irony, who was neither more nor less credulous than most of his contemporaries.

What distinguishes him from *Bede and many medieval historians is that he had first-hand experience of the court life of his time. The rulers of Merovingian Gaul indeed were often both a trial and a challenge to conscientious bishops.

The life at court was frequently violent, treacherous, and dangerous. Assassination, torture, and despoliation were by no means rare. Elsewhere there were looting, floods, famine, and epidemics. Through all these a bishop had to survive with consience intact as best he could. Gregory had to deal with four civil rulers of Tours during his twenty-one years' episcopate: Sigibert, Childeric, Childebert II, and Gunthar, with all of whom he was closely, if not always amicably, associated. He was often sent on diplomatic missions to other Frankish kings and he travelled widely over many parts of Gaul but not, it seems, outside it.

At the end of his *Historia Francorum*, however, Gregory did not list his diplomatic successes but rather his achievements as bishop of Tours and as a writer. Although he was modest about his style, he adjured his successors to pass on his writings in their entirety. His work as bishop included the rebuilding of Tours cathedral, destroyed by fire, on a larger scale than before, and the refurbishing of St. Martin's church with paintings and decorations. Gregory also built a new baptistery and enriched this, the old baptistery, and many other churches and oratories which he dedicated, with relics of the saints. He was indeed a devotee of, as well as successor to, the great St. Martin of Tours and recorded with devotion the history of his see and especially the numerous fasts and vigils instituted by his predecessor Perpetuus, its sixth bishop. Gregory was also an important witness to the growing cult of the Virgin Mary, especially through belief in her Assumption.

Gregory was buried in his cathedral. In the seventh century *Ouen built a rich tomb for him beside that of Martin. In the 9th century it was destroyed by the Vikings, in the 11th it was restored, and in 1562 it was destroyed again by the Huguenots. The Life attributed to *Odo of Cluny describes the miracles at his tomb. Feast: 17 November.

Works in *M.G.H. Scriptores rerum meroving*, i (1884–5), and in *P.L.*, lxxi; *History of the Franks*, tr. O. M. Dalton (1927 and 1971) also L. Thorpe (1974), selections of his minor works tr. by W. C. MacDermott (1949); also E. James, *Gregory of Tours: Life of the Fathers* (1985); J. M. Wallace Hadrill, *The Frankish Church* (1983), esp. chs. III–V, *The Long Haired Kings and other Studies* (1962), pp. 49–70; G. Vinay, *San Gregorio di Tours* (1940); P. Brown, 'Relics and Social Status in the age of Gregory of Tours' in *Society and the Holy in Late Antiquity* (1982), id., *The Cult of the Saints* (1981). See also H. Delehaye, 'Les recueils antiques de miracles des saints', *Anal. Boll.*, xliii (1925), 305–25 and J. Verdon, *Grégoire de Tours, 'le père de l'Histoire de France'* (1989).

GREGORY THE WONDERWORKER (Thaumaturgus), (*c.*213–*c.*270), bishop. This important and charismatic bishop, who links the time of the persecutions with that of the Cappadocian Fathers, has no satisfactory Life and few authentic works. From the sparse surviving evidence it appears that he was born of noble pagan parents at Neo-Caesarea (Pontus). He then studied law and rhetoric before going to Caesarea in *c.*233 to complete his education. Here he became a Christian under the influence of Origen and stayed for five years. Soon after his return to Neo-Caesarea he became its bishop, although there were only seventeen Christians in the town. He took lodgings with the magnate Musonius, preached in the streets, and before nightfall had a small congregation. Next day a crowd of sick people arrived, many of whom he cured. Soon he built a church thanks to the money and labour contributed.

Both *Basil and *Gregory of Nyssa give examples of his supposed miracles: these included altering the course of a river, drying up a swamp, and moving a mountain. Evidently such stories have lost nothing in the telling; more credible are his success in converting the pagans and his skill in clear exposition of the Christian faith, memorized by *Macrina the Elder and passed on to her children and grandchildren. Basil also described Gregory's characteristics: reverence and recollection in prayer, simplicity and modesty in speech, and the elimination of lies, falsehood, anger, and bitterness.

The problems faced by this pioneer bishop were manifold. When the persecution of Decius broke out in 250, he advised the Christians to flee rather than risk apostasy; he himself retired into the desert. After persecution came the plague and then an invasion of Goths; later still he defended the orthodox faith against Paul of Samosata and others at the first Synod of Antioch (265).

Shortly before his death he asked how many unbelievers remained in his city. He was told that there were but seventeen, exactly the same number as that of the Christians at the start of his episcopate. He then prayed for their conversion and asked his followers not to arrange any special place of burial for him. Eventually his body was translated to Calabria, which accounts for his cult in southern Italy and Sicily, where he is invoked in time of earthquake and flood.

His authentic works include a panegyric on Origen, a treatise on the Creed, a canonical epistle (mainly about penance in the early Church) and a dissertation to Theopompus on the impassibility of God. Feast: 17 November.

Panegyric by Gregory of Nyssa in *P.G.*, xlvi. 893–958; works ed. H. Crouzel (*S.C.*, 1969) and F. Froidevaux, 'Le symbole de Saint Grégoire le Thaumaturge', *Recherches de Sciences Religieuses*, xix (1929), 193–247. See also A. Poncelet, 'La vie latine de S. Grégoire le Thaumaturge', *Anal. Boll.*, i (1910), 132–60; W. Telfer, 'The Cultus of St. Gregory Thaumaturgus' in *Harvard Theological Review*, xxix (1936), 225–344; B.T.A., iv. 362–4; *N.C.E.*, s.v.

GRIMBALD (*c.*825–901), monk of Saint-Bertin, dean of New Minster (Winchester). Born at Thérouanne (Pas-de-Calais), he joined the community of Saint-Bertin *c.*840 and was ordained priest *c.*870. Grimbald became a notable scholar; he went to Reims in 886; through Fulk of Reims he was invited to England by King Alfred in 887. Here he lived in a small Winchester 'monastery', becoming a court-scholar who assisted Alfred with his translations of Latin works into OE, notably *Gregory's *Pastoral Care*. Alfred wished him to become archbishop of Canterbury in 889, but Grimbald refused. Instead he became dean at Winchester of the secular canons of the New Minster. This was a town-church, where prominent Winchester citizens had burial-rights; it was distinct from the cathedral and probably absorbed the small community which Grimbald had previously ruled. There Grimbald died and was buried; his relics, with those of *Judoc, were the most notable in this church. There were translations in 938, *c.*1050, and again in 1110, when the whole establishment was moved out to Hyde. Grimbald's cult centred at Winchester, was extended to Malmesbury and at least nine other Benedictine abbeys; his feast was in the calendars of York and Hereford.

The extent of Grimbald's achievements is partly disputed. It seems probable that he brought to England the 9th-century MS of Prudentius, now at Corpus Christi College, Cambridge; it has also been conjectured that he brought the famous Utrecht Psalter. His interpolated Legend (from Hyde) provides the earliest legendary account of the foundation of Oxford University. Feast: 8 July.

AA.SS. Iul. II (1721), 651 ff.; *N.L.A.*, i. 500; P. Grierson, 'Grimbald of St. Bertin's', *E.H.R.*, lv (1940), 529–61; id., 'The Relations between England and Flanders before the Norman Conquest' in R. W. Southern (ed.), *Essays in Medieval History* (1968), 61–92; M. Biddle, 'Felix Urbs Wintoniae' in D. Parsons (ed.), *Tenth-Century Studies* (1975); J. B. L. Tolhurst, *The Monastic Breviary of Hyde Abbey*, s.d. 8 July (H.B.S., 1939).

GUARDIAN ANGELS. Their existence was at least suggested in various OT texts and explicitly taught by Christ concerning children (Matt. 18: 10), and accepted by the early Christians concerning St. Peter (Acts 12: 15). This fundamentally Jewish belief has also some analogies in the writings of Plato (*Phaedo* 108B): it was made explicit by the *Shepherd* of Hermas (2nd century); patristic opinion was divided about it, but very early collects from the feast of *Michael in the Leonine Sacramentary refer to the angels as individual guardians. In England devotion to the angels, both in Anglo-Saxon times and later, was strong. Alcuin wrote of them as intercessors (his text is in the 11th-century Leofric Missal); Herbert of Losinga, bishop of Norwich (d. 1119), specially praised them, while his contemporary, Reginald of Canterbury (like some Anglo-Saxon nuns of the 9th century), wrote prayers in their honour. Honorius Augustodunensis (d. 1151) clarified the exisiting belief by asserting that each human soul, when infused into the body, is entrusted to the particular care of a single angel, who protects both body and soul and offers prayers to God.

For many centuries Christendom was satisfied with the feast of St. Michael (and all Angels), but a special feast of the Guardian Angels was introduced in Austria, Spain, and Portugal in the 15th–16th centuries, whether as guardians of particular towns or regions, or of each individual. There is a record of a feast of the latter at Cologne in 1521. Paul V extended the authorization of this feast in 1608 and Clement X made it universal in 1670, fixing its date to 2 October, which replaced various earlier dates such as 28 September.

AA.SS. Sept. VIII (1762), 7–8, 29–38 with *Propylaeum*, pp. 430–1; A. Wilmart, *Auteurs spirituels* (1932), pp. 537–58; J. Duhr in *Dict. Sp.*, i (1937), 586–98; *N.C.E.*, and *O.D.C.C.*, s.v.

GUDULE (Gudula) (*c.*648–712), virgin, patron of Brussels. Her mother Amalberga was a niece of the emperor Pepin. Gudule was educated by her cousin *Gertrude of Nivelles, after whose death she lived in Brabant, consecrating her life to prayer, fasting, and almsgiving. Although the church at Moorsel was two miles from her home, she used to pray there regularly in the early morning. She died in her hometown of Hamme and was buried in front of the church door. From there her relics were moved first to Moorsel, then to Brussels in 978 (to S. Gery's church), lastly in

1047 to the large collegiate church of S. Michel (later called S. Gudule). There they remained until the Calvinists scattered them in 1579. In art she is usually represented with a lantern or a candle, which it was said the devil extinguished, but was subsequently reignited by divine power. The context of this story is the saint's early morning visits to Moorsel. There are several 16th-century examples of these paintings in or near Brussels. Feast: 8 January.

AA.SS. Ian. I (1734), 513–30 and R. Podevijn in *Revue Belge de Philologie et d'Histoire*, ii (1923), 619 ff. and xv (1936), 489–96; see also E. de Moreau, *Histoire de l'Eglise en Belgique* (1945) i. 197–200; B.T.A., i. 54; *Bibl. SS.*, vii. 440–3.

GUDWAL (Godwald, Gurval, Gallwell) (6th century), obscure Celtic abbot. He was an early pioneer of Christianity in Brittany, where the islands of Locoal and Guer (Morbihan) are the probable sites of his hermitage and monastery as well as the main centres of his cult. He is sometimes, but incorrectly, claimed as first bishop of Saint-Malo. During the Viking invasions his relics were moved to St. Peter's, Ghent, whence presumably his cult came to England; he is patron of Finstall (Worcester) and Worcester celebrated his feast at a fairly high rank. The church of Gulval (Cornwall) is also claimed to be dedicated to him.

For long he was thought to have been British. Whytford described him as a bishop born of the noble blood of England, who resigned his bishopric and lived on a desolate rock where he built a monastery and gathered 188 monks '. . . he went to the sea at lowest ebb and charged it to keep that place and never flow nearer the monastery . . . he healed the sick, raised the dead and had revelations of angels'. It is possible, but not very likely that he came from Wales or Cornwall. Feast: 6 June (in Cornwall, 4 or 7 June).

AA.SS. Jun I (1695), 715–36; *N.L.A.*, 501–4; G. H. Doble, *The Saints of Cornwall*, i (1960), 61–78.

GUERIR, mysterious saint known only through a reference in Asser's *Life of Alfred* to a visit by Alfred to Cornwall, during which he turns aside to pray in the church where 'St. Guerir lies buried'. A later scribe added: 'and where St. Neot now rests.' Guerir may be a misreading for *Gwinear or a corruption of *Goran, a saint who left Bodmin at *Petroc's arrival. Egbert, king of Wessex, had subdued at least part of Cornwall, allowing some Saxon penetration there, and Cornish estates were among those given by Alfred to Asser. But Guerir's identity remains a mystery.

Asser's Life of King Alfred (ed. W. H. Stevenson) (1959), c. 74; D. Whitelock, *The Genuine Asser* (1968).

GUIGNER, see GWINEAR.

GUIGNER AND CIARA, see FINGAR AND PIALA.

GUINOCH (Guinochus) (d. 838), Scottish saint. Honoured specially in Buchan, he was believed to have been a counsellor of King Kenneth and to have aided by the efficacy of his prayers the annihilation of the Picts in seven skirmishes in one day. Feast: 13 April.

K.S.S., p. 358.

GUNDLEUS, see GWYNLLYW.

GUTHLAC (*c.*673–714), hermit of Crowland (Lincs.). Of royal blood from the Mercian tribe of Guthlacingas, he became a soldier (*C.S.P.* called him *robustus depraedator*) from the age of fifteen, but after nine successful years gave up warfare to be a monk at Repton, a double monastery where some Mercian kings were buried, ruled by abbess Ælfrith. He was rather unpopular at first because of his total abstinence from intoxicating drink; later he was better appreciated. In about 701 he moved on to the solitary life at Crowland on a site accessible only by boat. Here his life resembled the regime of the Desert Fathers; annoyances included attacks by Britons who had taken refuge in the Fens, and violent temptations by devils; consolations were visions of angels and of his patron *Bartholomew the Apostle. After fifteen years as a hermit, he knew that his death was near. Edburga, abbess of Repton, sent him a shroud and a leaden coffin. His sister *Pega, an anchoress at Peakirk, came to his burial with his disciples *Cissa, *Bettelin, Egbert, and *Tatwin, who occupied cells near by. A year later the grave was opened and the body found incorrupt. The Guthlac cult began, centred on his shrine at Crowland, to which Pega had given his psalter and scourge. It soon became popular, with Wiglaf, king of Mercia (827–40), and Ceolnoth, archbishop of Canterbury (who was cured of ague by the saint in 851), among its devotees. The feast soon spread through Mercia to Westminster, St. Albans, and Durham and eventually became general.

Besides the near-contemporary Latin Life by Felix, vernacular ones were written in OE prose and verse; at least nine ancient churches were dedicated to him. The cult flourished also in the 12th century. His relics were translated in 1136 in the abbey church built on the site of his cell and the shrine was embellished with gold, silver, and jewels. Yet another translation took place in 1196. A magnificent pictorial record of his life survives in the late 12th-century Harleian Roll Y.6 at the British Museum, usually called the Guthlac Roll. This is a series of eighteen roundels, which are cartoons for stained-glass windows. The scenes in it are based on Felix's Life of Guthlac and, to a lesser extent, on pseudo-Ingulph's history of Crowland. The style is especially vivid and no other comparable example survives in this country from the same date. Some 13th-century sculptures of his Life also survive at Crowland. A seal of Henry de Longchamp, abbot of Crowland 1191–1236, depicts St. Bartholomew giving Guthlac a scourge. This was not for self-flagellation but for use as a defensive and offensive weapon against diabolical attacks. Guthlac, after *Cuthbert, must be reckoned England's most popular pre-Conquest hermit saint, but it must be admitted that a number of incidents in the Life by Felix are closely modelled on episodes in the life of *Antony the Hermit. Feast: 11 April; translation, 30 August; commemoration, 26 August.

B. Colgrave (ed.), *Felix's Life of St. Guthlac* (1956); W. de Gray Birch, *Memorials of St. Guthlac of Crowland* (1881: this includes the metrical Life by William of Ramsey, *c.*1200); C. W. Goodwin (ed.), *The Life of St. Guthlac* (1848), an OE prose Life, commented on by P. Gonser *Das angelsachsische Prosa-Leben de hl. Guthlac* (Anglistische Forschungen xxvii, 1909); for the OE poem *Guthlac, The Exeter Book* (ed. G. P. Krapp and E. V. K. Dobbie, 1936). Abridged Life in *N.L.A.*, ii. 698–719. See also J. Roberts, 'An Inventory of Early Guthlac Materials', *Medieval Studies*, xxxii (1970), 193–233; B. P. Kurtz, 'From St. Antony to St. Guthlac: a study in biography', *Univ. of California Publications in Modern Philology*, xii (1925–6), 133–46; G. F. Warner, *The Guthlac Roll* (Roxburghe Club, 1928); see also N. Adkin, 'The proem of Henry of Avranches' Vita S. Guthlaci', *Anal. Boll.* cviii (1990), 349–55.

GUY, see Vitus.

GWEN OF CORNWALL (Wenn) (date unknown), sister of *Non. She was married to Selyf, king of Cornwall, was the mother of *Cybi and foundress of the church of St. Wenn. A few other churches may have been dedicated to her in Devon and Cornwall. Feast: 18 October.

GWEN TEIRBRON OF BRITTANY (date unknown). She was reputedly married twice and the mother of *Winwaloe, Gwethenoc, and James. Called three-breasted, she was represented as such in Breton folk-art. It has been conjectured that she should be identified with *Whyte (or Candida). The word Gwen means 'white', Athelstan gave relics of various Breton saints to English churches; sculptures at Whitchurch (meaning 'the Church of Wite') represent a ship, pike, and axe, which may refer to characteristic elements in he incredible legend. Feast: 1 June (Roscarrock).

Baring-Gould and Fisher, iii. 166–71.

GWENFAEN (date unknown), saint of Rhoscolyn (Anglesey), titular of the parish church there. About half a mile away are substantial remains of his well, contained inside a small square stone building. This probably represents, like the examples of *Seiriol and *Cybi, the primitive settlement of a hermit who later founded the local church, perhaps in the 7th century. A later dedication to an early saint is another possible explanation.

An Inventory of the Ancient Monuments in Anglesey (1937), p. 146.

GWENFREWI, see WINEFRIDE.

GWENGUSTLE, see NINNOC.

GWENNARTH, see WANNARD.

GWINEAR (Guigner, Fingar) (date unknown), patron of Gwinear (Cornwall). He seems to have been a Welsh missionary like his companion *Meriasek, who with him evangelized the district of Gwinnear and Camborne, and later went to Brittany, where also their cults are found side by side. At Pluvigner, in the diocese of Vannes, there is a stained-glass window of Gwinear hunting a stag with a cross between its antlers (through confusion with the legend of *Eustace), and a well near the church to which processions go on the day of the Pardon. Guigner was supposed to have struck the ground with his lance, while thirsty, out hunting: three fountains sprang up, one for himself, one for his horse, and one for his dog. A Life was written by Anselm, perhaps a Cornish canon, *c.*1300. According to this, Gwinear and his companions were martyred by Theodoric, king of Cornwall. Among the miracles recorded was one of two lovers who embraced while seated on the tomb of a bishop, one of Gwinear's companions, and could not be disentangled until they were brought to Gwinear's tomb. Feast: 23 March.

G. H. Doble, *The Saints of Cornwall*, i (1960), pp. 100–10; *AA.SS.* Mar. III (1668), 455–9.

GWITHIAN, see GWYTHIAN.

GWYN, Richard (*c.*1537–1584), martyr. Born at Llanidloes (Montgomeryshire, now Powys), he was educated mainly at St. John's College, Cambridge. He then returned home and became a schoolmaster at Overton (Flintshire, now Clywd), where he married and eventually had six children, of whom three survived. As a recusant he was threatened with imprisonment by the bishop of Chester if he did not attend his local church: for a time he conformed but later repented, moved to Overstock, and opened another school. One day he was recognized in Wrexham, was arrested, but soon escaped. The next year (1580) the Privy Council told the bishops to be more vigilant against all recusants, especially schoolmasters. Only a month later, Gwyn was arrested again and imprisoned in Ruthin Castle. On his repeated refusal to conform, he was placed in irons; once he was forcibly taken to church in Wrexham, where he rattled his chains so loudly that the preacher could not make himself heard. He was released, then fined for recusancy and fined again: when he could no longer pay, he was imprisoned and placed in the stocks.

At his eighth assize in Wrexham he was accused of treason for reconciling one man to the Catholic Church (the evidence was both false and bought), and for maintaining the supremacy of the pope. He was finally condemned to death for refusing to recognize the queen as Head of the Church in England. On the scaffold he acknowledged Elizabeth as the lawful queen of England, denied all treason, but still refused to admit she was Head of the Church. He was hanged, drawn, and quartered on 15 October, the protomartyr of Welsh recusants. He was canonized by Paul VI in 1970 as one of the *Forty Martyrs of England and Wales. Feast: 25 October.

R. Challoner, *Memoirs of Missionary Priests* (ed. J. H. Pollen 1924), pp. 102–5; T. P. Ellis, *Catholic Martyrs of Wales* (1933); B.T.A., iv. 202–4; *Blessed Richard Gwyn* (pamphlet, 1960).

GWYNLLYW (Gundleus, Woolos) and **GWLADYS** (6th century), traditionally the parents of *Cadoc. Gwynllyw was a chieftain of SE. Wales: Gwladys was one of the twenty-four children of *Brychan. Much of their life was given over to armed violence, but their son Cadoc converted them to a devout life. They settled at Stow Hill, near Newport (Gwent), where they lived austerely like monks; but their ascetical practice of cold-water bathing in the Usk, winter and summer alike, preceded and followed at night-time, it appears, by a mile-long walk in the nude, was brought to an end by Cadoc, who persuaded his parents to separate. Gwladys moved eventually to Pencanau in Bassaleg. Gwynllyw was visited on his death-bed by *Dyfrig: he died on 29 March. All these details come from a Life dating in its present form from the 12th century: it includes some interesting miracle stories from the times of *Edward the Confessor and William I. Several place-names and church dedications in the districts associated with these saints preserve their memory. Feast: (together) 29 March.

A. W. Wade-Evans, *Vitae Sanctorum Britanniae et Genealogiae* (1944), pp. 173–93; *N.L.A.*, i. 504–6.

GWYTHIAN (Gwithian, Gothian), patron of the parish of this name in N. Cornwall and of an ancient ruined chapel in the sands near by, was probably associated with *Winwaloe, who settled near by at Towednack. Feast: 1 November.

Baring-Gould and Fisher, iii. 249–51.

H

HADRIAN, see Adrian.

HAEDDI, see Hedda.

HALLVARD (d. 1043), martyr and patron of Oslo. The son of a noble landholder of Husaby (Norway), he spent his youth in Viking activities.

One day, crossing the Drammenfiord by boat, he was accosted by a woman who appealed to him to take her with him, as she was falsely accused of stealing and was in danger of death. Her pursuers then arrived and called on him peremptorily to give her up. He refused as he believed her to be innocent; whereupon they were both shot dead with a bow. Hallvard's body was thrown in the sea with a stone attached, but it floated: he was revered as a martyr for defending an innocent person. His body was enshrined in a stone church in Oslo, whose patron he became and still remains. Feast: 15 May.

B.T.A., ii. 322; S. Undset, *Saga of Saints* (1934), pp. 149–62; *Bibl. SS.*, i. 894.

HANNAH, see Anne.

HARDING, see Stephen Harding.

HARDULPH (date unknown). Titular saint of the church of Breedon (Leics.) whose feast was also kept by the Augustinians of Nostell. He may, perhaps, be identified with the hermit of Breedon who appears in the Life of *Modwenna. Feast: 6 August (?).

Stanton, p. 404.

HEDDA (Haeddi) **OF PETERBOROUGH** (d. 870), abbot and martyr. Together with all his community, supposedly eighty-four in number, Hedda was killed by the same Danish army which had killed *Edmund of East Anglia the same year. While the monastic chroniclers regarded these Danish armies as militant pagans, killing the Christians for their religion, some modern historians assert that it was rather love of booty which motivated them.

In the later Middle Ages the 'Hedda stone' stood in the cemetery over the grave of Hedda and his companions; holes were cut to place candles for saying Mass on it, a custom supposedly started by abbot Godric. Seventeenth-century visitors used to put their fingers in these holes, perhaps to take dust as a souvenir. Feast: 10 April.

A.S.C., *s.a.* 870 ('E' version); B.T.A., ii. 62; Stanton, pp. 150–1.

HEDDA (Haeddi) **OF WINCHESTER** (d. 705). He was educated at Whitby and was consecrated by *Theodore in 676. He was the first bishop of the West Saxons to reside at Winchester instead of Dorchester-on-Thames, founded by *Birinus. This change corresponded to the emergence of Southampton-based Saxons as more powerful than the settlers of the Thames Valley. His episcopate spanned the reigns of Centwine, Caedwalla (who expelled him but died at Rome 689), and Ina (d. 726), who explicitly acknowledged Hedda's help in framing his laws.

*Bede remarked on Hedda's prudence and innate wisdom. Little is known of his episcopate except his translation of the relics of Birinus to Winchester and the high esteem he enjoyed from contemporaries. This was reflected in the reports of cures at his tomb and the practice of taking dust from it, mixed with water, to heal sick men and animals. His relics are still in Winchester cathedral. He was culted in Wessex monasteries, but also at Crowland, where he was believed to have ordained *Guthlac; in the 16th century his name was added to *R.M.* by Baronius. Feast: 7 July.

Bede, *H.E.*, iii. 7; iv. 12; v. 18; *G.P.*, p. 159;

AA.SS. Iul. II (1721), 482–3 and *Propylaeum*, p. 275; *E.B.K. before 1100*, pp. 120, 134, 148, 162, 260.

HEDWIG (Jadwiga) (*c.*1174–1243), duchess of Silesia. Born at Andechs (Bavaria), the daughter of count Berthold, she lived as a child in the monastery of Kitzingen. At the age of twelve she married Henry, future duke of Silesia, then eighteen years old, who succeeded his father in 1202. By him she had seven children, from whose quarrels she suffered much.

She was prominent in founding religious houses, notably those of Friars, and a Cistercian nunnery at Trebnitz (near Breslau), the first convent of women in Silesia. Convict labour was employed to build it. After 1209, from which time she and Henry lived in continence, she made her home nearby and took the Cistercian habit after his death in 1238.

Henry was involved in wars, notably in 1227–8 against Swatopluk of Pomerania and Conrad of Masovia. When he was captured, she acted as peacemaker; the two dukes were reconciled and her two granddaughters were betrothed to Conrad's sons.

In 1240 her son Henry led his troops against the Tartar invaders and died at the battle of Wahlstadt. She comforted her daughter and daughter-in-law, knowing of the death by prophecy long before it was announced. Her biographers claimed other prophecies and miracles for her while still alive. She died and was buried at Trebnitz and was canonized in 1267. Feast: 16 October.

AA.SS. Oct. VIII (1853), 198–270; modern Lives by K. and F. Metzger (1927) and H. Quillus (1938); see also B.T.A., iv. 124–5 and *Bibl. SS.*, iv. 933–4.

HELEN (Helena, Ellen) (*c.*250–330), empress. She was born at Drepanum (later Helenopolis) in Bithynia, possibly an innkeeper's daughter; *c.*270 she married the Roman general Constantius Chlorus. When he became emperor in 292 he divorced her. But her son, later the Emperor Constantine, greatly honoured and respected her. In about 312, aged over sixty, she became a Christian, but was so devout that contemporaries thought she had been so since childhood. She dressed quietly, gave generously to churches, to the poor, and prisoners, and made a pilgrimage to the Holy Land, where she died. Coins were minted in her honour (330); she was buried at Rome.

Geoffrey of Monmouth (d. 1154) claimed she was of British origin and the daughter of Coel, legendary king of Colchester; this was widely believed in England, but Trier also was claimed as her birthplace. She won renown as the mother of the first Christian emperor, but also because of her share, claimed by *Ambrose, in the Finding of the True Cross with its attendant miracles (see CROSS). This story is the subject of Cynewulf's finest poem, *Elene* (9th century).

Helen's feast was kept in several southern English monasteries, but dedications to her, 135 in all, were more frequent in the north-east, possibly because of Constantine's connection with York. Various place-names such as St. Helens (Lancs.) and St. Helens (I.W.) reflect the development of a town around her churches. But the Atlantic island of St. Helena was so called because it was discovered by Spanish sailors on her feast.

In art she is depicted as a principal figure in the many representations of the Finding of the Cross; at Ashton-under-Lyne (Lancs.) there survives a series of eighteen stained-glass panels which depict her life.

Feast: in the East (with Constantine), 21 May; in the West, 18 August.

AA.SS. Aug. III (1737), 548–654; P. Grosjean, 'Codicis Gothani Appendix', *Anal. Boll.*, lviii (1940), 199–203; *C.S.P.;* R. Couzard, *Sainte Hélène d' après l'histoire et la tradition* (1911); J. Maurice, *Sainte Hélène* (1929); F. Nau, 'Les Constructions palestiniennes dues à Sainte Hélène', *Revue de l'Orient Chrétien*, x (1905), 162–88.

HELEN OF CARNARVON (Elen Luyddog), princess, wife of Magnus

Clemens Maximus, emperor in Britain, Gaul, and Spain 383–8, when he died trying to obtain Roman recognition. Apparently she accompanied her husband, staying some time at Trier before his death in Aquileia. Welsh tradition attributes to her the making of roads (Sarn Elen or Fford Elen) and leading a military expedition into North Wales. She was reputed to have five children, one of whom was called Constantine. She may be the patroness of some Welsh churches dedicated to Helen, and of Llanelen in West Gower. Feast: 22 May or 25 August. See previous entry.

Baring-Gould and Fisher, iii. 255–60; B.T.A., iii. 346.

HELEN (Helan) **OF CORNWALL** (date unknown), priest. Brother of *Germoe who in the company of *Breage first came to Cornwall, then crossed to Brittany, he was well received at Reims and finally settled at Bucciolus, near Biscuil, where he died and was buried. He is probably the titular of Cornish churches dedicated to Helen. Feast: 7 (or 8) October.

Baring-Gould and Fisher, iii. 253–4.

HELEN (Elin) **OF SKOVDE** (d. *c.*1160). She was of aristocratic birth from Vastergötland, was married young and widowed soon afterwards. She then devoted her wealth and work to the cause of religion and the service of the poor. On her return from a pilgrimage to the Holy Land she was killed by the relatives of her son-in-law for supposedly conniving at his death. Her body was buried at Skovde in the church which she had built. On the strength of the miracles claimed there Alexander III authorized her cult as a saint. Like some others who met a violent death in Scandinavia she was venerated as a martyr. Her cult was widespread in medieval Sweden and parts of Denmark such as Tusvilde (Zeeland), which claimed some relics: it is attested by surviving paintings and sculptures. She was regarded as the patron of Vastergötland and even of all Sweden. Feast: 31 July.

AA.SS. Iul. VII (1759), 343: *Scriptores rerum Sueciarum*, iii (part 2), 135–8; B.T.A., iii. 228; *Bibl. SS.*, iv. 996–7.

HELIER (6th century), martyr, first saint of Jersey (C.I.). He was a hermit from Tongres (Belgium) who lived in a cave in Jersey above the town which bears his name. He was killed by pagans or robbers to whom he tried to preach the Gospel. He was associated with, and visited by, *Marcoul. Feast: 16 July (in England and the diocese of Coutances).

AA.SS. Iul. IV (1868), 145–52; E. A. Pigeon, *Vies des Saints du diocèse de Coutances*, ii. 136–45; B.T.A., iii. 118.

HENRY (d. 1127), hermit of Coquet Island. A Dane by birth, Henry became a hermit abroad rather than marry unhappily at home. He then went to Tynemouth and agreed with the prior to settle on Coquet, an island which had had a community of monks in the age of *Bede and where *Cuthbert used to meet *Elfleda, abbess of Whitby. He lived in the simplest way, earning subsistence by looking after a garden, pursuing his chosen austerities in spite of discouragement from the monk who looked after the island. After some years a party of Danes tried to persuade him to return to his own country, where there was no lack of sites suitable for hermits. But after a night in prayer and the experience of a locution from the figure of Christ crucified, he decided to stay on. As his holiness became known, visitors became more numerous, attracted by his special gifts of prophecy, telekinesis, and reading the secrets of hearts. One interesting example of the last was his reproof and punishment of a man who had refused his wife sexual intercourse during Lent.

Henry fell ill; with lack of care his illness increased, but so also did his cheerfulness in enduring it alone. Finally, he rang his hermit's bell for help; when the monk arrived Henry was dead, holding the bell-rope in one hand and a candle in the other. In spite of strong resistance from the islanders, the monks of Tynemouth took back his body to their monastery and buried it in the sanctuary, near their patron

*Oswin. Feast: 16 January. His name occurs in later martyrologies but there is no surviving early record of his feast.

AA.SS. Ian. II (1643), 424–6; *N.L.A.*, ii. 22–6.

HENRY II (973–1024), Holy Roman Emperor. Born in Bavaria and educated at Hildesheim, he succeeded his father, Henry the Quarrelsome, as duke of Bavaria in 995 and became emperor in 1002. His main political aim was to unify and consolidate the German Empire. This was largely achieved through wars in the East and in Lombardy. He used the Church for his political ends, but, after being crowned by the pope in 1014, he restored property and wealth in several sees and founded that of Bamberg, where he built both the cathedral and a monastery. He became the friend of *Odilo of Cluny and promoted the movement of reform. Later legend claimed that his childless marriage to *Cunegund was a virgin marriage and that he pursued other ascetical ideals for which there is little contemporary evidence. He was canonized in 1146. Feast: 13 (formerly 15) July.

AA.SS. Iul. III (1723), 711–93; Lives also in G. Waitz, *M.G.H.*, *Scriptores*, iv (1841), 679–95 and 789–816; Lives by H. Lesêtre (1899), H. Gunter (1904), and C. Pfaff (1963). See also R. Klauser, *Der Heinrichs und Kunigundenkult im mittelalterlichen Bistum Bamberg* (1957).

HENRY OF FINLAND (d. 1156), bishop and martyr; patron saint of Finland. English by birth, he was consecrated bishop by Nicholas Breakspear, papal legate to Scandinavia and later Pope Adrian IV, at the council of Linköping in 1152. Previously Henry seems to have belonged to Nicholas's household. Warlike expeditions of the Finns into Swedish territory provoked a punitive expedition led by King Eric IX in 1154; Henry accompanied him and the project was called a crusade. Eric offered peace and the Christian faith to the Finns, who refused both. The Swedes won the ensuing battle.

Henry baptized the defeated Finns in the spring of Kuppis near Abo and stayed behind to continue missionary work, while Eric returned to Sweden. Henry built a church at Nousis and made it the centre of his work. After a few years he met a violent death. Lalli, a convert Finn, murdered a Swedish soldier and was excommunicated by Henry. He was so furious that he killed Henry with an axe, traditionally on Kirkkosaari (Church Island) in Lake Kjulo. Henry was buried at Nousis; miracles followed at his tomb.

On 18 June 1300 his body was translated to Abo cathedral; in 1370 a magnificent Flemish sepulchral brass was placed on his original tomb, vividly depicting his life, death, and miracles. This unique monument still survives. In medieval Finnish churches Henry was frequently depicted in wall-paintings, panel paintings, and statues, often represented as treading on his murderer, Lallis. These are said to be Finland's main contribution to medieval iconography. The cult of St. Henry spread to Sweden and Norway; at least one English chapel was dedicated to him: that in the Carmelite church at Great Yarmouth, seen by William of Worcester. He also has a place in the important series of paintings of the English martyrs, executed in 1582 for the Venerable English College, Rome, by Niccolo Circignani. Henry's relics were removed from Abo by the Russians in 1720. He was specially invoked in storms by the local seal-fishers. The union of Finland and Sweden accomplished by Eric and Henry lasted until the 14th century. Feast: 19 January; translation, 18 June.

AA.SS. Ian. II (1643), 613–14; T. Borenius, 'St. Henry of Finland: an Anglo-Scandinavian saint', *Archaeol. Jnl.*, lxxxvii (1930), 340–56; M. R. James, 'The sepulchral brass of St. Henry of Finland', *Cambridge Antiq. Soc. Proceedings*, x (1901–2), 215–22; C. J. A. Oppermann, *English Missionaries in Sweden and Finland* (1937); A. Malin, *Der Heiligenkalender Finlands* (1925).

HENWYN, see Hywn.

HERBERT OF DERWENTWATER (d. 687), priest and hermit. A close friend of *Cuthbert, Herbert used to visit him at Lindisfarne every year. In 686 Cuthbert was in Carlisle and they met there instead;

Cuthbert prophesied that they would both die soon on the same day. In fact both died on 20 March 687. Cuthbert's feast was by far the more popular of the two and Herbert was largely forgotten. In 1374 Thomas Appleby, bishop of Carlisle, ordered the vicar of Crosthwaite to celebrate a sung Mass on St. Herbert's Isle each year on his feast, and granted forty days' indulgence to all who visited it on this day. Ruins of a circular stone building there may be connected with him. The Martyrology of Tallaght describes St. Herbert, like St. Cuthbert, as a 'Saxon'. Feast: 20 March.

Bede, *H.E.*, iv. 27; B. Colgrave (ed.), *Two Lives of St. Cuthbert* (1940), pp. 15, 125, 249–51, 326; P. Grosjean, 'The supposed Irish origin of St. Cuthbert' in *The Relics of St. Cuthbert* (ed. C. F. Battiscombe, 1956).

HEREFRITH (Herefrid) of Louth (d. *c.*873), bishop and possibly martyr. With those of other saints his relics were translated by *Ethelwold to Thorney; the record of this event describes him as bishop of Lincoln. Lincoln probably here means Lindsey (the county of Lincolnshire). Herefrith may well have been the last bishop of Lindsey before the Danes wintered at Torksey in 872–3, after which the episcopal succession ceased. Herefrith, like *Edmund, could have been killed by the Danes.

At Louth there was a church of St. Herefrith mentioned in several records of the 13th–15th centuries. An ivory comb 'that was saynt Herefridis' belonged to its parish church of St. James in 1486. It seems likely but not certain that this church was originally dedicated to Herefrith, but when the cult of *James had increased and that of Herefrith been largely forgotten, especially as his relics were at Thorney, the dedication was changed. Feast at Thorney, Deeping, and Bury St. Edmunds on 27 February; translation, 21 August.

A. E. B. Owen, 'Herefrith of Louth, saint and bishop; a problem of identities', *Lincs. History and Archaeology*, xv (1980), 15–19; *R.P.S.; E.B.K. before 1100*, p. 241; *E.B.K. after 1100*, p. 131.

HERMES (Erme) (3rd century), martyr. This famous Roman martyr died in one of the early persecutions and his early cult is well established by entries in the *Depositio Martyrum* (354), the Martyrology of Jerome, and the early sacramentaries. The large basilica of *c.*600 over his tomb in the cemetery of Basilla on the Old Salarian Way was also mentioned in various pilgrim guides. But there were no authentic Acts, only fabulous details in the legendary Acts of *Alexander. His relics, however, have a history: some secondary ones were given by *Gregory the Great to Spoleto, and churches were dedicated to him in Italy, Sicily, and Sardinia. Later his body was given by Pope Leo IV to the Emperor Lothair, who translated it first to Cornelimunster and then to Renaix (Flanders) in 860, where it still remains as a centre for pilgrimage and for cures of lunatics. In England his feast was quite widely celebrated and there are three Hermes dedications in Cornwall (at St. Erme, St. Ervan, and Marazion), but none elsewhere. Feast: 28 August.

AA.SS. Aug. VI (1743), 142–51 with *C.M.H.*, pp. 472–3; G. H. Doble, *St. Hermes* (1935); B.T.A., iii. 434.

HERMYNHILD, see ERMENGILD.

HERWALDUS, see HEWALD.

HETHOR, see BEOCCA AND HETHOR.

HEWALD (Ewald, Herwaldus) **THE BLACK** and **HEWALD THE WHITE**, Anglo-Saxon priests and missionaries among the Old Saxons, were martyred on 3 October *c.*695. According to *Bede they shared the same name and the same zeal, but were called 'Black' and 'White' because of the colour of their hair. They had for long lived in exile in Ireland, before joining the missionary enterprise of *Willibrord in Frisia. Both men were devout and religious, but Hewald the Black was more learned in Scripture.

When they arrived among the Old Saxons they said Mass each day on a portable altar and devoted themselves to the Divine Office. The people realized that they belonged to a different religion; fearing that they would convert their chief, they seized them and put them to death: Hewald the White immediately by the sword, and Hewald the Black by long torture. Their bodies were thrown into the Rhine, but were later recovered. Pepin had them enshrined in the church of St. Cunibert at Cologne, where they still remain. Some of their relics were given to *Norbert: churches at Xanten and Gorze also claim to possess their relics. The traditional place of their martyrdom is Aplerbeke on the Embscher, one of the Rhine's tributaries, near Dortmund. The Calendar of St. *Willibrord records them under 4 October, but the Fulda Martyrology, English Calendars, and Bede place their feast on 3 October.

Bede, *H.E.*, v. 10; *AA.SS.* Oct. II (1768), 180–207.

HEWYN, see HYWN.

HIBALD (Higbald), see HYBALD.

HIERITHA, see URITH OF CHITTLEHAMPTON.

HIERONYMUS, see JEROME.

HILARION (*c.*291–*c.*371), abbot, monastic pioneer of Palestine. According to *Jerome, whose Life of Hilarion is based on lost writings of Epiphanius, who knew Hilarion, he was the son of pagan parents from Gaza. He studied at Alexandria, where he became a Christian. He visited *Antony, then at the height of his fame, but returned to Palestine, found his parents were dead, gave all his goods to his brothers and to the poor, and became a hermit at Majuma (*c.*306). His regime was based on Antony's: he lived on figs, bread, vegetables, and oil. First, he made a shelter of reeds, later a cell of about five feet by four, which survived until Jerome's time. Disciples of both sexes came to learn from him; so also did the crowds, attracted by his austerities and miracles. For the sake of his monks he had come to own household goods and a farm: to escape these responsibilities and the crowds, he left Palestine, first for Egypt, then for Sicily (where his disciple Hesychius found him), and eventually for Epidaurus in Dalmatia. Once more his miracles attracted publicity and he fled to Cyprus. He settled near Paphos, but later retired to a more remote site twelve miles away, where Epiphanius, bishop of Salamis (d. 403), visited him. Here he died at the age of eighty. He was buried near Paphos, but his relics were translated to Majuma.

Jerome's Life (some of whose details are unreliable) was the basis of the Greek, Armenian, and Coptic Acts. Hilarion is mentioned in *Bede's Martyrology and appears frequently in Pre-Conquest English monastic calendars, but later his feast was ousted in England by those of *Ursula and *Dunstan's Ordination, which fell on the same day. His cult, however, remained strong elsewhere as that of a primitive monk like Antony, who was not martyred, but was venerated from early times in East and West as an example of monastic holiness. Feast: 21 October.

AA.SS. Oct. IX (1858), 16–59; Jerome's Life also in *P.L.*, xxiii. 29–54; Sozomen, *H.E.*, iii. 14; v. 10; vi. 32; E. Coleiro, 'St. Jerome's Lives of the Hermits', *Vigiliae Christianae*, xi (1957), 161–78; J. N. D. Kelly, *Jerome* (1975).

HILARY (*c.*315–*c.*368), bishop of Poitiers. Born at Poitiers of pagan, wealthy parents, Hilary became an orator, married, and had a daughter, Afra. In 350 he became a Christian through a long process of study. This led him to the convictions that man is in the world for the practice of the moral virtues which must be rewarded hereafter, that there is only one God, the eternal and creative first cause, and that the Word of God who became incarnate in Jesus Christ is likewise eternal and of one substance with the Father. In *c.*353 he was chosen bishop; for the rest of his life he was the outspoken champion of orthodoxy against the Arians. He was praised by *Augustine and *Jerome as 'the illustrious teacher of the churches' and as 'a fair cedar transplanted out of this world into the Church'. He has also been described as the 'Athanasius of the West'. This reputation was based on his defence of orthodoxy at the Synod of Bitterae in 356 and the council of Seleucia in 359, and by his exile for four years to Phrygia under the Emperor Constantius (356–60). He returned to Gaul amid great rejoicing; discipline and orthodoxy were restored; Hilary went to Milan in 364 to refute successfully its Arian bishop, Auxentius. In character Hilary was gentle, courteous, and friendly, although his writings could be sometimes severe in tone: his style is difficult and involved, sometimes to the point of obscurity. His principal works are *De Trinitate* (against the Arians), *De Synodis*, and Commentaries on the Psalms and on Matthew's Gospel. The influence of Origen is strong in his writings. His feast began the Hilary Term at the Law Courts and in some Universities. Hilary as a Christian name has been used for women as well as men both in the Middle Ages and in the 20th century. There are three churches dedicated to him in England. He was named a Doctor of the Church by Pius IX in 1851. Feast: 13 (formerly 14) January.

AA.SS. Ian. I (1643), 782–802, which includes the Life and Miracles by Fortunatus; works in *P.L.*, ix–x, also in *C.S.E.L.* (1891 ff.); the *Tractatus Mysteriorum* is edited by J. P. Brisson in *S.C.*, xix (1947); Eng. tr. of *De Trinitate* by S. McKenna (1954); studies include J. Daniélou and others, *Hilaire de Poitiers, évêque et docteur (Études Augustiniennes*, 1968); E. R. Labande (ed.), *Hilaire et son temps* (Centenary Studies, 1969); biographies by A. Largent (1902) and P. Galtier (1960); see also D. H. Williams's reassessment in *J.E.H.*, xlii (1991), 202–17.

HILDA (Hild) (614–80), abbess of Whitby. Related to the royal families both of Northumbria and East Anglia, Hilda, whose parents had lived in exile in the British enclave of Elmet (N. Yorkshire), became a Christian with *Edwin, being baptized by *Paulinus. For the first thirty-three years of her life she lived a secular life; the remaining half was dedicated to God in the monastic life. She first planned to join the nunnery of Chelles from East Anglia, like her sister, but was called back to Northumbria by *Aidan, who gave her a small plot of land (one hide) on the north bank of the Wear, whose exact location is unknown. She soon moved to Hartlepool where she succeeded Heiu as abbess and organized community life according to the rule she learnt from mainly Irish sources, based perhaps in part on the Rule of Columbanus. In 657 she founded (or refounded) the abbey of Whitby, a double monastery like Gaulish examples, which became famous for its learning, for training at least five bishops, and for being the site of the famous Synod of Whitby of 663/4. Hilda was hostess to this gathering and supported the Irish party in the discussion over the date of Easter, but she accepted its decision in favour of Rome. Later (678) she supported *Theodore's division of *Wilfrid's Northumbrian see, for *Bosa and *John of Beverley, educated at Whitby, were among the bishops who replaced Wilfrid.

Her zeal for education was not confined to building up libraries and instructing clerics in Latin language and literature. Under her rule the Anglo-Saxon cowherd and poet *Caedmon was encouraged to produce vernacular poems about Christian doctrine. Hilda enjoyed great personal prestige; not only did religious and learned men value her wisdom, but kings, rulers, and common people would ask her advice. She was an excellent example of how in the Anglo-Saxon Church an able woman could attain to great influence and authority without, however, there ever being question of her being ordained.

The last six years of her life had been spent in chronic illness, which, however, scarcely diminished her activity. She died on 17 November. While the main influences on her own religious life seem to have been Irish and Frankish, her monastery later became more 'Roman' in sympathy under *Elfleda and *Enfleda: in it was written the first Life of *Gregory the Great about twenty-five years after her death.

Whitby was very thoroughly sacked by the Danes *c.*800: Hilda's supposed relics were translated to Glastonbury under King Edmund (d. 946), but Gloucester also claimed them. Fifteen ancient English churches were dedicated to her, eleven in Yorkshire and two in Durham; her cult was strong in the North. Evesham kept her feast at a high rank because of its connection with the refounding of Whitby as an abbey for monks in the 11th century. The most ancient and interesting witness to her cult is the entry in the Calendar of St. *Willibrord, written in the early 8th century. Feast: 17 November; translation, 25 August.

Bede, *H.E.*, iv. 23; *N.L.A.*, ii. 29–33; *C.S.P.* (under Glastonbury); P. Hunter Blair, *The World of Bede* (1970), pp. 145–8; H. Mayr-Harting, *The Coming of Christianity to Anglo-Saxon England* (1972), pp. 150–2; B.T.A., iv. 369–70.

HILDEBRAND, see GREGORY VII.

HILDEGARD (1098–1179), Benedictine nun and visionary. Born at Bokelheim (West Germany), she was educated from the age of eight by a recluse called Jutta, became a nun at fifteen, and led an uneventful, studious life for seventeen years until her visions and revelations began. In 1136 she succeeded Jutta as abbess of Diessenberg and was told to write down the content of her visions, which in the work *Scivias* (i.e. 'sciens vias Domini', the one who knows the ways of the Lord) were approved first by the archbishop of Mainz and in a more reserved way later by Pope Eugenius III at the suggestion of *Bernard. Meanwhile, her community had grown too large for its convent and Hildegard moved it to Rupertsberg, near Bingen, whence she reformed several other convents and made a foundation at Eibingen.

Like several other visionaries she felt called upon to reprove rulers; her correspondents included Henry II of England, the Emperor Frederick Barbarossa, Pope Eugenius III, and various other prelates. In addition to this, she showed herself remarkably versatile in other fields. She wrote poems, hymns, and a morality play, besides works of medicine and natural history. These last comprised studies on the elements, plants, trees, minerals, fishes, birds, quadrupeds, and reptiles, a remarkable achievement for its time, especially for a cloistered nun. The medical work treats of the circulation of blood, headaches, vapours and giddiness, frenzy, insanity, and obsessions. Other works include commentaries on the Gospels, on the Athanasian Creed, and on the Rule of St. Benedict as well as some Lives of Saints. She was also a musician and artist. The illustrations of her *Scivias* have been reproduced in modern times and have been compared with the work of William Blake.

Towards the end of her life she and her convent were in trouble with the chapter of Mainz and placed under interdict for burying an excommunicate in their cemetery; but she successfully appealed to the archbishop. She died at the age of nearly eighty: although miracles were reported during life and after death, attempts to secure her formal canonization in the 13th–14th centuries were unsuccessful. But her name was inserted in the Roman Martyrology in the 15th century and her cult was approved for German dioceses: the cult, it seems, can be traced back to the 13th century. Feast: 17 September; translation, 25 August.

AA.SS. Sept. V (1755), 629–701; P. Bruder, 'Inquisitio de virtutibus et miraculis S. Hildegardis', *Anal. Boll.*, ii (1883), 116–29; S. Hilpisch, 'Der Kult de hl. Hildegard', *Pastor Bonus*, xlv (1934), 118–33; Lives by P. Franche (1903) and F. M. Steele (1914). See also C. J. Singer, *Studies in the History and Method of Science* (1917), pp. 1–55; H. Leibenschutz, *Das allegorisches Weltbild der heiligen Hildegard von Bingen* (Studien der Bibliothek Warburg, xvi; 1930); H. Schipperges, *Die Welt der Engel bei Hildegard von Bingen* (1963); L. Baillet, 'Les Miniatures du "Scivias" de Sainte Hildegarde conservé à la Bibliothèque de Wiesbaden', *Monuments et Mémoires publiés par l'académie des Inscriptions et Belles-Lettres*, xix (1911), 49–149. Articles by M. Schrader in *Dict. de Spiritualité*, vii (1969), 505–21 and in *Bibl. SS.*, vii. 761–6.

HILDELITH (Hildelida) (d. *c.*712), abbess of Barking. According to *Bede,

Hildelith was the successor of *Ethelburga, first abbess of Barking and sister of *Erkenwald; she ruled for many years, well into old age, with firmness and the discipline of the rule; she enlarged the rather cramped monastic buildings and translated the relics of nuns with a reputation for holiness from the cemetery into the church. She was also known personally to both *Aldhelm and *Boniface; Aldhelm dedicated to her and her nuns his treatise on Virginity, whose elaborate language presupposed advanced Latin reading skills, while Boniface praised her highly in his letters and mentions one of her visions which she had described to him. Barking was probably founded *c.*666: Hildelith, according to Florence of Worcester, succeeded in 675. Later writers state that she was trained at Faremoutier or Chelles (which is likely enough), that she was a princess (less likely), and that she trained Ethelburga before becoming a nun under her rule. Possibly this story arose because Barking was a family monastery which belonged to Erkenwald, so his sister would have been the first abbess. Hildelith's rule, however, seems to have been more important in the history of the house. Feast: usually 24 March, but also 22 December or 3 September. Barking had translation feasts on 7 March and 23 September.

AA.SS. Mar. III (1865), 483–5; Bede, *H.E.*, iv. 10 and v. 18; W. F. Bolton, *A History of Anglo-Latin Literature* (1967), pp. 87–93.

HILDUTUS, see ILLTUD.

HIPPOLYTUS (1) (d. 235), martyr. A Roman priest, of whose early life nothing is known, Hippolytus was probably the most important writer of his time in Italy, but he opposed the bishops of Rome, *Zephyrinus and *Callistus, whom he accused of insufficient zeal against the heresy of Sabellius and excessive leniency to sinners. He went into schism under Callistus, apparently as an 'anti-pope', but with Pontianus (bishop of Rome 230–5) he was exiled to Sardinia during the persecution of Maximinus; there he was probably reconciled to the Church and with Pontianus died a martyr. Their bodies were brought to Rome under *Fabian (236–50): Hippolytus was buried in the cemetery on the Via Tiburtina. His cult is attested by the Liberian Catalogue, the *Liber Pontificalis*, and the Leonine, Gelasian, and Gregorian Sacramentaries. But his identity became much confused. Prudentius perhaps began the process by confusing him with another martyr of the same name. He placed his martyrdom at the mouth of the Tiber, attributing his death to wild horses (the name Hippolytus means 'loosed horse'). The Legend of *Lawrence, buried near by, made him a prison officer converted by the saint and sentenced to be torn asunder by horses (like Hippolytus, the son of Theseus). The connection with horses is also clear in the place-name Ippollits (Herts.), one of the two places in England where a church was dedicated to Hippolytus: sick horses were formerly brought to his shrine there through the north door of the church.

In 1551 Hippolytus, whose works had been largely forgotten in the West, was rediscovered as a theologian. This was due to the excavation in his cemetery of a 3rd-century statue, which portrayed him seated on a chair, on whose sides are a list of his works and his tables for calculating Easter. This is now in the Lateran museum. More recently the discovery of some of these works has further increased his reputation. The most important are the *Philosophoumena*, a refutation of all heresies through tracing them back to erroneous systems of philosophy; commentaries on Daniel and the Canticle of Canticles, and probably the *Apostolic Tradition*, whose account of the Canon of the Mass, formerly believed to be Egyptian, forms the basis of one of the new texts of the Roman Canon. Feast: in the West, 13 August; in the East, 30 January. His feast was kept in sixteen English Benedictine calendars.

AA.SS. Aug. III (1737), 4–15 with *C.M.H.*, pp. 439–40 (and cf. *Anal. Boll.*, li (1933), 58–66); J. B. Lightfoot, *The Apostolic Fathers*, i (2), 317–477; A. d'Alès, *La Théologie de saint Hippo-*

lyte (1906); G. Bovini, *Sant' Ippolyto della Via Tiburtina* (1934); works of Hippolytus in *G.C.S.* (4 vols., 1897–1955) and with French tr. in *S.C.* (1949–50); Eng. tr. in *A.N.C.L.* (vi and ix); R. H. Connolly, *The So-Called Egyptian Church Order* (1916); critical editions of the Apostolic Tradition by G. Dix (1937) and H. Chadwick (1968); see J. M. Hanssens, *La Liturgie d'Hippolyte* (1965); B.T.A., iii. 315–16; *Bibl. SS.*, vii. 868–79.

HIPPOLYTUS (2) **AND COMPANIONS**, see TIMOTHY, HIPPOLYTUS, AND SYMPHORIAN.

HOFBAUER, Clement-Mary (1751–1820), Redemptorist priest, apostle and patron of Vienna. Born at Tasswitz (Moravia), the youngest son of a Slavonic butcher, he became a baker's apprentice and then worked in a monastery at Klosterbruck. He tried to become a hermit, but soon found he was more fitted to an active life. After two pilgrimages to Rome he returned to Vienna, where Joseph II ruled. During all Clement's life the influence of the 'Enlightenment' and Joseph II's anti-papal Erastianism were at their height.

Clement was sponsored and educated for the priesthood in Rome. He joined the Redemptorist congregation in 1784, while Alphonsus *Liguori was still alive. In 1785 he returned to Vienna to found a Redemptorist house, but this proved impossible under the Josephite legislation. So in 1787 he opened the house of St. Benno in Warsaw, which took special but not exclusive care of German speakers. He stayed in Poland until 1808, founding other houses, initiating many charitable and educational enterprises, preaching so effectively that both Jews and Protestants were converted. Napoleon's invasion brought this work to an end, so Clement returned to Vienna.

He worked unobtrusively in the Italian quarter and later was chaplain to Ursuline nuns and rector of their church. Again he became widely known as preacher and director of souls: his clientele included princes, academics, artists, writers, and others. He helped to thwart a plan to set up a German Church independent of the papacy at the congress of Vienna. He was accused of being a Roman spy, but the archbishop of Vienna supported him, knowing the value of Hofbauer's contribution to the Catholic revival. This was shown also in his tireless care for the sick and the dying and by his sensitive consideration for devout and conscientious Protestants.

In 1819 he was mortally ill of several diseases and after taking part in the funeral of a notable benefactor, early the next year he died. His funeral at Vienna cathedral was attended by thousands. Soon afterwards the cause for which he had long laboured, the founding of Redemptorist houses in Austria, was achieved. He was canonized in 1909 by *Pius X, who named him patron of Vienna. Feast: 15 March.

Lives by M. Haringer (1877; Eng. tr. by Lady Herbert of Lea); J. Hofer (1920; Eng. tr. New York, 1926); J. Carr (1939), and E. Hosp (1951); *Monumenta Hofbaueriana* (15 vols. 1915–51); B.T.A., i. 601–4; *Bibl. SS.*, iv. 49–51.

HOLY INNOCENTS, the children of Bethlehem, two years old and under, who were massacred by the Idumean, Herod the Great. Told by the Magi of the birth of a new king, he tried in this way to eliminate all possible rivals (Matt. 2: 1–18). Commentators estimate their number as between six and twenty-five. Their feast has been kept in the West from the 4th century: they were considered to be martyrs because they not only died for Christ, but instead of Christ. In the Martyrology of Jerome they are called 'the holy babes and sucklings', in the Calendar of Carthage, simply 'the infants'.

Poets such as Prudentius, preachers such as *Augustine, and artists such as Masaccio developed both the theological and the human elements of the cult. In honouring the Innocents, the Church honours all who die in a state of innocence and consoles parents of dead children with the conviction that these also will share the glory of the infant companions of the infant Jesus. *Bede too wrote a hymn in their honour; in England their feast was called Childermas. Relics of them were claimed by English and French churches.

Feast: in the East, 29 December; in the West, 28 December.

Propylaeum, p. 605; B.T.A., iv. 626–7; *D.A.C.L.*, vii. 608–16.

HOMOBONUS (d. 1197), merchant of Cremona. His name, given at baptism, means 'good man'. Homobonus was trained by his father to follow his own profession with diligence, honesty, and exactitude. In due course he married a wife, who matched his prudence and generosity. He was notable both for his frequent prayers in the church of St. *Giles and for his extraordinarily generous almsgiving. On 13 November he stretched out his arms in the form of a cross during the *Gloria* at Mass, fell on his face, and died. Sicard, bishop of Cremona, vigorously requested his canonization: this was granted by Innocent III only two years after his death, as he was satisfied with the official inquiry into the life and miracles of Homobonus. He is an interesting example of a lay saint at the end of the 12th century, whose cult was approved not only by local bishops but also by the papacy at the very time that the papal reserve became effective. He deserves to be better known as one who attained sanctity by doing 'ordinary things extraordinarily well' at a time when few who were neither martyrs, bishops, monks, nor kings attained the full honours of canonization. Homobonus is the patron of tailors and clothworkers, in which field he exercised his profession. Feast: 13 November.

Propylaeum, pp. 520–1; G. Balladori, *Il trafficante celeste* (1674); B.T.A., iv. 334–5.

HONORIUS (d. 653), archbishop of Canterbury. He came to England in 601, one of the second band of Roman missionaries to Kent. He succeeded *Justus as archbishop in 627, being consecrated at Lincoln by *Paulinus. He received the pallium from Pope Honorius with the instruction that when one archbishop died, the other would consecrate his successor. During his twenty-five years' rule he consolidated the work of conversion by sending the Burgundian *Felix to evangelize East Anglia. He received the exiled Paulinus to the see of Rochester after the disastrous battle of Hatfield Chase (634). He lived to see the apostolate of *Aidan in Northumbria, the replacement of *Birinus of Wessex by *Agilbert, the conversion of Peada and the Middle Angles, and the arrival of the young *Wilfrid in Kent on his way to Rome. Honorius, like his predecessors, was buried at Canterbury in the monastery of SS. Peter and Paul (later St. Augustine's), the centre of his cult. He is mentioned in the Roman and other martyrologies. Feast: 30 September.

Bede, *H.E.*, ii. 15–18; iii. 14, 20, 25; v. 19.

HOUGHTON, John (1487–1535), Carthusian monk and martyr. A member of a family of Essex gentry, Houghton studied Law at Christ's College, Cambridge, and then became a secular priest through the usual medieval method of living with and learning from another priest in the neighbourhood. After four years of ministry, he became a Carthusian at Smithfield in 1515. In 1522 he became sacristan and in 1527 procurator. In 1531 he was elected prior of Beauvale (Notts.), but after a few months he was recalled by unanimous vote to be prior of the London Charterhouse. As prior of this young community (half were less than thirty-five years of age), highly esteemed and much visited for the sake both of its dignified liturgy and its spiritual direction, Houghton acquired a reputation for sanctity long before the conflict which made him famous. Notably abstemious, but accessible to all his community, zealous for the Divine Office and for sacred learning, Houghton was small in stature, 'graceful and modest in appearance'. His community, belonging to an Order which frequently won the praise of even antimonastic contemporaries, must have been one of the most distinguished in England at the time.

Like other subjects of Henry VIII, the Carthusians were required to take the Oath of Succession in 1534, which implied a recognition of the invalidity of Henry's marriage to Catherine of Aragon and of the legitimacy of his marriage to Anne Boleyn with their daughter's right of succession to the throne. First Houghton and his procurator asked to be left in peace as it was no concern of theirs, then they said they could not see how such a long-standing marriage as that of Henry and Catherine could be invalid. They were then committed to the Tower, where Edward Lee, archbishop of York, persuaded them that the Act (whose preamble they never saw) was not contrary to the Faith, so they agreed to take it 'in so far as it was lawful'. But with the passing of the Act of Supremacy in 1534, the underlying doctrinal conflict could no longer be evaded. In 1535 commissioners were appointed to administer an Oath of acknowledgement that the king was Supreme Head on earth of the Church in England: in due course they visited the London Charterhouse, where the community had spent three days in prayer and preparation for their ordeal. The priors of Beauvale and Axholme (Robert *Lawrence and Augustine *Webster) now joined Houghton; together they went to see Thomas Cromwell, the king's Vicar-General, trying without success to negotiate for their communities an acceptable form of the oath 'so far as the Law of God might allow'. Cromwell refused all such qualifications, said that 'he cared naught for the Church and Augustine might hold as he pleased'; all he wanted to know was whether they would swear a direct oath or not. On their refusal, due to their belief that a matter of faith was at stake, they were committed to the Tower.

At their trial in Westminster Hall they pleaded not guilty of treason (recently defined as including mere words, or even refusing to acknowledge that the king was Supreme Head of the Church in England). The jury deliberated long and were browbeaten by Cromwell to produce a verdict of guilty. The Carthusians were executed at Tyburn on 4 May, after being dragged on hurdles in their religious habits through the streets and refusing a pardon offered at the foot of the gallows if they would recant. They were hanged, drawn, and quartered; Houghton's arm was hung up over the gate of the London Charterhouse. Thomas *More, imprisoned in the Tower, saw the Carthusians going to their death and remarked to his daughter Margaret: 'Do you not see that these blessed fathers be now as cheerfully going to their deaths as bridegrooms to their marriage?' The three priors suffered together on the same day, but the rest of the London Carthusian community endured persecution of various kinds for two years more. Some were sent elsewhere, some conformed, but ten remained steadfast; these were imprisoned at Newgate and starved to death. Houghton, Lawrence, and Webster are among the *Forty Martyrs of England and Wales canonized by Paul VI in 1970. Feast: 25 October.

E. M. Thompson, *The Carthusian Order in England* (1930), pp. 371–485; M. Chauncy, *The Passion and Martyrdom of the Holy English Carthusian Fathers* (1935); D. Knowles, *The Religious Orders in England*, iii (1961), 222–40 and 471–2; R. W. Chambers, *Thomas More* (1935), pp. 320–32; F. van Ortroy, 'Opusculum Mauritii Chauncy de BB. martyribus anglicis O. Cartus', *Anal. Boll.*, vi (1887), 36–51; xxii (1903), 54–75; D. Knowles and W. F. Grimes, *Charterhouse* (1954). See also L. E. Whatmore, 'The Carthusians under King Henry VIII', *Anal. Cartusiana*, cix (1983).

HOWARD, Philip (1557–95), earl of Arundel and martyr. Born in London, the eldest son of the duke of Norfolk, heir to the premier earldom and five baronies besides the dukedom, his status was inferior to that of royalty alone. On Elizabeth's accession his father conformed to the Church of England: Philip was brought up a Protestant with John Foxe the martyrologist as his tutor. But when the duke proposed marriage to Mary, Queen of Scots, he was found guilty of high treason and executed in 1572. His family was therefore disgraced, but Lord Burghley was appointed Philip's guardian and sent him to Cambridge. Later he was presented at court and enjoyed the favour of the queen, which, however, came to an end when he became reconciled to his wife, Anne Dacres, whom he had married when only twelve years of age and had afterwards neglected.

In 1581 he was present at a disputation between some Protestant theologians and Edmund *Campion: the latter so impressed him that he left court and planned to live on the Continent with his wife, both now reconciled to the R.C. Church. But Philip was arrested at sea and sent to the Tower. A charge of treason failed, but lesser charges resulted in a fine of £10,000 and imprisonment during Her Majesty's pleasure. In 1589 he was again accused of high treason, on the ground that he had prayed for the Armada's success. Although this story was proved to be a fabrication and the judges ruled that prayer could not constitute treason, he was found guilty and sentenced to death. The sentence was not carried out, but he remained in prison for the rest of his life; his wife and son (whom he had never seen) were not allowed by the queen to visit him. He was consoled to some extent by translating devotional works and by reading Robert *Southwell's *Epistle of Comfort*. Worn out by over ten years' continuous imprisonment, he died at the age of thirty-eight. 'The Catholic and Roman faith', he wrote, 'which I hold is the only cause . . . why either I have been thus long imprisoned or why I am now ready to be executed.' Inscriptions written by him on the wall of Beauchamp Tower in the Tower of London survive, as do his relics in Arundel cathedral and a contemporary portrait in Arundel Castle. He was canonized by Paul VI in 1970 as one of the *Forty Martyrs of England and Wales. Feast: 25 October.

H. G. F. Howard (ed.), *The Lives of Philip Howard and of Anne Dacres, His Wife* (1857 and, ed. F. W. Steer, 1971); *Catholic Record Society Publications*, xxi (1919), *passim*; M. Creighton in *D.N.B.*, x. 52–4; B.T.A., iv. 152–4; Philip Howard's translation of J. J. Lanspergius, *An Epistle of Jesus Christ* (ed. by a monk of Parkminster, 1926).

HUBERT (d. 727), bishop of Maastricht and Liège. Details of his early life and conversion are unknown. He became the pioneer evangelist of the Ardennes district of Belgium and the successor of *Lambert in the see of Maastricht in 705. In 716 he translated Lambert's relics to a church in Liège which he had built and later made his cathedral. He is therefore venerated as first bishop of Liège, while two orders of chivalry (in Lorraine and Bavaria) also claim him as their patron.

His miracles and the translation of his relics in 743 to Andain (now called Saint-Hubert) contributed to the diffusion of his cult, clearly witnessed by many calendars of the 9th century. Two churches were dedicated to him in England and the Sarum calendar eventually included his feast.

The famous episode of his conversion while hunting on Good Friday through seeing an image of the crucified Christ between the antlers of the stag is borrowed from the Acts of *Eustace and is unknown before the 14th century. But from then onwards it became frequent in paintings of Hubert, as by the Master of Werden in the National Gallery, London, or in several English examples which depict him holding a book, on which (or at his feet) is a miniature stag. He is patron of huntsmen, and his supposed hunting-horn is in the Wallace Collection, London. Feast: 30 May; translation, 3 November.

AA.SS. Nov. I (1887), 759–930; T. Rejalot, *Le culte et les reliques de S. Hubert* (1928); M. Coens, 'Notes sur la Légende de S. Hubert', *Anal. Boll.*, xlv (1927), 345–62; id., 'Une relation inédite de la conversion de S. Hubert', ibid., 84–92; other studies by F. Pény (1961) and A. Paffrath (1961).

HUGH OF CLUNY (1024–1109), abbot. The eldest son of Dalmatius, count of Semur (near Autun), related to the dukes of Aquitaine and to several Burgundian noblemen, Hugh seemed destined to a notable worldly career. But he was both too studious and too clumsy as a youth to be a knight and, in defiance of his father's wishes, was professed as a monk at Cluny in *c.*1040. About four years later he was ordained priest. Promotion came very early, for *Odilo, then abbot, appointed him as prior in 1048. By then he had become tall and handsome, able and sympathetic; his achievements revealed him as single-minded and detached, with wonderful interior order and balance.

On the death of Odilo in 1049 he was elected abbot of Cluny. Already this was a very important monastery with as many as sixty dependencies, but its expansion in Hugh's abbacy of sixty years may be gauged from the fact that at his death these dependent monasteries (with very various forms of association) numbered about 2,000. They were situated in Italy, Spain, England, and France. Indeed the expansion of Cluny in the 11th century was comparable with that of Cîteaux in the 12th. His abbacy was also marked by the development of constitutional and administrative procedures, by the widespread endowments and the construction of the new and enormous church and monastery. The former, consecrated by Urban II in 1095, was the biggest in Christendom.

His influence was also very great outside the monastic Order. He became an important adviser to as many as nine popes, and Cluny was a staunch supporter of the programme of Reform initiated by *Leo IX and *Gregory VII. Hugh personally took part in such varied events as the condemnation of Berengarius in 1050, the reforming councils of 1055 and 1060, and was papal legate in Hungary (1051–2), Toulouse (1062 and 1068), and Spain (1073). He also mediated between pope and emperor at Canossa (1077) and set in hand the foundation of the priory of St. *Pancras at Lewes (Sussex) *c.*1078. He also helped to initiate the first Crusade at the Council of Clermont (1095).

Few of his writings survive, but he must be reckoned as one of the most influential figures of the second half of the 11th century. He was canonized in 1120. Feast: 29 April.

AA.SS. Apr. III (1675), 641–78; A. L'Huillier, *Vie de Saint Hugues* (1888); N. Hunt, *Cluny under Saint Hugh* (1967); H. E. J. Cowdrey, *The Cluniacs and the Gregorian Reform* (1970); F. Barlow, 'The Canonization and the Early Lives of Hugh I, abbot of Cluny; *Anal. Boll.* xcviii (1980), 297–334.

HUGH OF GRENOBLE (1052–1132), bishop. Born at Châteauneuf (Dauphiné) the son of a knight called Odilo, he was educated in the cathedral school of Valence, where he became a canon. Talented and learned, good-looking yet very bashful, he was appointed by Hugh, bishop of Die and papal legate, as his secretary. In 1080 he took him to the synod of Avignon, which reviewed the deplorable state of the diocese of Grenoble, where simony and usury, lay intrusion, and clerical unchastity were rampant. Hugh of Grenoble was elected bishop, was consecrated at Rome by *Gregory VII, and returned to his diocese.

He began his episcopate as a living embodiment of the principles of the Gregorian Reform. He fought vigorously and with success against the abuses described. He sustained the papacy in its dispute against the emperor Henry V although at the cost of persecution. Grenoble was in the emperor's territory, but his people rallied to the bishop's support. He had built a bridge, a market-place, and three hospitals for his city besides restoring the cathedral and the church of St. Laurence. He founded houses of canons regular, but above all he is known as the virtual co-founder of the Carthusian Order.

His charter which gave to *Bruno the mountainous estate of the Grande Chartreuse still exists: his encouragement and support were decisive in the difficult early days. His own father died as a Carthusian monk at the age of a hundred; he himself delighted in the monks' company and stayed in their monastery for retreats. His own close relationship with them ensured that the diocesan bishop was always expected (contrary to other monastic orders) to guide and cherish Charterhouses in their dioceses.

Hugh repeatedly tried unsuccessfully to resign his see, but the papacy regularly refused it. Right at the end of his long life he supported Pope Innocent II with *Bernard against the anti-pope Anacletus. During his last few weeks of life, he seemed to forget everything except the Lord's Prayer and the psalms; he died surrounded by Carthusian monks, who treasured his memory and fostered his cult. He was canonized only two years after his death, in 1134. Zurbaran gave him a prominent place in his paintings of the early Carthusians in the museum of Seville. Feast: 1 April.

Life by Guigo, prior of the Grande Chartreuse in *AA.SS.* April. I (1737), 36–46; B. Bligny, *Saint Bruno, le premier chartreux* (1984); see also B.T.A., ii. 3–5; *H.S.S.C.*, vi. 274–5; *Bibl. SS.*, xii. 759–64.

HUGH OF LINCOLN (1) (*c.*1140–1200), Carthusian monk and bishop. Born at Avalon near Grenoble, in Imperial Burgundy, he was educated and made his profession in the priory of Austin Canons at Villarbenoît. At the age of about twenty-five he became a monk at the Grande Chartreuse. He became its procurator *c.*1175 and was invited by King Henry II to become prior of his languishing Charterhouse at Witham (Somerset), founded in reparation for the murder of *Thomas of Canterbury, but insufficiently endowed and ruled by two unsuitable priors in succession. Under Hugh it soon flourished rapidly and attracted several distinguished monks and canons as its inmates.

In 1186 Henry chose him as bishop of Lincoln, but he refused to accept because he believed the election was uncanonical. Eventually he undertook to rule this, the largest diocese in England, only in obedience to the prior of the Grande Chartreuse. To help him in the task, he carefully chose worthy and learned men as his canons, to several of whom, as archdeacons, he delegated much government.

Reputedly the most learned monk in the country, he revived the Lincoln schools, considered by Gerald of Wales to be second only to Paris. He extended his cathedral, damaged by an earthquake; sometimes he worked on it with his own hands; part of his choir and transepts survive. He held synods and visitations; he travelled ceaselessly to consecrate churches, confirm children, and bury the dead. His justice was proverbial: three popes made him judge-delegate for some of the most important cases of his time, and the king also appointed him to act in his court. Always a friend of the oppressed, he tended lepers and risked his life in riots to save some Jews from death.

He was the friend, but also the critic, of three Angevin kings. He excommunicated royal foresters and refused to appoint courtiers to church benefices. He overcame Henry's anger on this occasion by an impudent joke. Later, a playful shaking dissolved the anger of Richard I, caused by Hugh's refusal to provide knight-service overseas at the Council of Oxford (1197), the first recorded instance of its kind. His admonitions of John at the beginning of his reign, however, had little effect, although he did help to carry Hugh's coffin at his funeral.

Hugh witnessed the treaty of Le Goulet but, after visiting his home and various French monasteries, fell mortally ill in his London house. On his death-bed he gave clear instructions about completing the cathedral and about his own funeral arrangements. He also refused to abandon the opposition he had made to Hubert Walter, archbishop of Canterbury. He died on 16 November.

One of his sermons (on care for the dead) has survived and several of his sayings. One of these was that laity who practised charity in the heart, truth on the lips, and chastity in the body would have an equal reward in heaven with monks and nuns. Austere but gentle, intransigent but tender, he was considered by Ruskin as 'the most beautiful sacerdotal figure known to me in history'.

In 1220 he was canonized by Pope Honorius III, the first Carthusian to receive this honour. His feast became one of the highest rank in Charterhouses from 1339. This fostered interest in him in Flanders and the Rhineland, in France, Italy, and Spain as well as in England. His principal cult was at Lincoln, where the rose window called the Dean's Eye records his funeral and where his relics were translated to a new shrine in the famous Angel Choir in 1280. His shrines here attracted many pilgrims; his feast was kept in the Sarum calendar.

His usual iconographical attribute is his tame swan (from his manor at Stow) or a chalice with the infant Jesus on it, as on the altarpiece from the Charterhouse at Thuison and in Zurbaran's portrait at Cadiz. A picture of him in the Paris Charterhouse became a centre of pilgrimage for mothers with sick children.

His shrine was dismantled at the Reformation, but searches for his body in 1887 and in 1956 proved unsuccessful. His white linen stole, formerly at the Grande Chartreuse, survives in the Charterhouse at Parkminster (West Sussex). Feast: 17 November; translation, 6 October.

D. L. Douie and D. H. Farmer, *Magna Vita S. Hugonis* (1985); R. M. Loomis, *Gerald of Wales' Life of Hugh of Avalon* (1985); C. Gorton, *Metrical Life of St. Hugh* (1986); for the canonization report, D. H. Farmer in *Lincs. Arch. and Archaeol. Soc. Papers*, vi (1956), 86–117. Lives by H. Thurston (1898), R. M. Woolley (1927), and D. H. Farmer (1985); see also *M.O.*, pp. 375–91 and C. R. Cheney, *Hubert Walter* (1967).

HUGH OF LINCOLN (2) (Little St. Hugh) (d. 1255), 'martyr'. He was a boy of only nine years old who met a violent death at the hands of persons unknown; his body was discovered in a well and buried in the cathedral near the tomb of Grosseteste. But the story circulated and became immensely popular that his death was due to ritual murder practised by the strong and wealthy Jewish community in Lincoln. It was asserted that the Jew Koppin enticed the boy into his house on 31 July and kept him there until 27 August, when he was scourged, crowned with thorns, and finally crucified. They tried to bury the body, but the earth refused to receive it and it was thrown down a well. Koppin is supposed to have confessed: he and eighteen other Jews were executed, while others were imprisoned in London and released by the intervention of the Friars and fined heavily. It is likely that the cult of 'Little St. Hugh' was the expression of anti-Semitic envy and that the story had little, if any, foundation in fact. The general charge of ritual murder on the part of the Jews has many times been refuted by Christian as well as Jewish writers. But the calumny stuck in the Middle Ages, perhaps because it was what people wanted to believe, and the Legend of 'Little St. Hugh' is best known through the Prioress's Tale in Chaucer's *Canterbury Tales*. The cult was never official, although miracles were claimed at his intercession. Feast: 27 August.

H. R. Luard (ed.), Matthew Paris, *Chronica Majora* (*R.S.*, 1880), v. 516–19; B.T.A., iii. 421–2; G. Longmuir in *Speculum*, xlvii (1972), 459–82.

HUNA (7th century), priest and monk. He lived under *Etheldreda, whom in fact he buried. He retired soon afterwards to the life of a hermit at Huneya in the Fens. Here he died; later his relics were translated to Thorney, where they were venerated in the 11th century or before. Feast: 13 February.

Stanton, p. 67; *R.P.S.*

HWAETBERT (Huaetberct) (716–*c.*747), abbot of Wearmouth and Jarrow. Like *Bede, Hwaetbert had been offered to the monastery in childhood and educated there in ecclesiastical and monastic learning. He had been ordained priest before he was unanimously chosen as abbot and confirmed by *Acca. Letters to him from Pope *Gregory II and from *Boniface survive, the latter being a request for the works of Bede and for a bell, accompanied by a gift of a goat's hair bed-covering. A letter of Hwaetbert to Gregory commending his predecessor *Ceolfrith also survives: earlier he had visited Rome, presumably with Ceolfrith or *Benedict Biscop. To Hwaetbert were dedicated Bede's commentary on the Apocalypse and his *De Temporum ratione*, concerned with chronology. He was called 'Eusebius' because of his holiness. No record of a feast-day or of a liturgical cult seems to have survived.

C. Plummer, *Baedac Opera Historica*, i. 364–404 for the Lives of the abbots of Wearmouth and Jarrow by Bede and the anonymous writer; the latter work is also translated in *E.H.D.*, i. 697–708. Letter from Boniface to Hwaetbert in M. Tangl, no. 76 and *E.H.D.*, i. 759.

HYA, see IA.

HYACINTH, see PROTUS AND HYACINTH.

HYACINTH (Iazech) **OF CRACOW** (1185–1257), Dominican friar and apostle of Poland. Born of a noble Silesian family at Kammien (Grosstein), he was educated at Prague and Bologna. His uncle, who was bishop of Cracow, appointed him a canon and took him to Rome on church business in 1220. Here Hyacinth met *Dominic, by whom he was dramatically converted. He received the Dominican habit from the Order's founder at Santa Sabina, Rome. As a first-generation friar he was specially important in the Order's expansion, in his case to eastern and northern Europe.

He preached the Gospel with effective eloquence like Dominic's own at Cracow and elsewhere in Poland, where he founded five houses of his Order. These became centres of both learning and preaching in the towns. From them Dominican missionaries went north to Gdansk and eastwards along the Vistula. Hyacinth is claimed to have evangelized also in Scandinavia, Lithuania, and Russia, but the saga-like accounts do not inspire confidence. All efforts of the Christian apostolate in this area were hindered by Mongol invasions in 1238 and later.

Hyacinth died on 15 August and is buried in the Dominican church at Cracow. He was canonized in 1594. Feast: 17 August.

Oldest but unreliable Life by Stanislas of Cracow in *Monumenta Poloniae Historica*, IV (1884), on which see R. J. Loenertz in *Archiv. Fratrum Praedicatorum*, xxvii (1957), 5–38; B. Alataner, *Die Dominikaner Missionen des 13. Jahrhunderts* (1924); see also B.T.A., iii. 338–9; *Bibl. SS.*, vi. 326–31.

HYBALD (Hibald, Higbald) (7th century), abbot in Lincolnshire. He is mentioned by Bede as being very holy and abstemious in connection with a vision of the death of *Cedd by Egbert. Four Lincolnshire churches were dedicated to him and Hibaldstow takes its name from his grave there, also recorded by *R.P.S.* His name occurs in the Durham *Liber Vitae*; it has been conjectured by *D.C.B.* that his monastery was Bardney. Feast: 14 December (in 11th-century martyrology of Exeter).

Bede, *H.E.*, iv. 3; Stanton, pp. 451, 688; *R.P.S.*

HYDROC (Hydoc), Cornish saint, possibly a hermit, and titular of Lanhydrock. Feast: 5 May. Attempts to identify him with the Irish Huydhran or Odran lack plausibility.

Baring-Gould and Fisher, iii. 286–8.

HYWN (Henwyn, Hewyn), Welsh monk and possibly bishop. Trained at Llantwit, he eventually became abbot of Bardsey. He is the patron of Aberdaron on the Lleyn peninsula, where pilgrims used to embark for Bardsey. His feast is in no ancient calendars known to Baring-Gould, but wakes were held in his honour at Aberdaron on 1 or 6 January. Churches in Bristol, Gloucester, and Hereford, dedicated to Ewen, have been dubiously claimed as his.

Baring-Gould and Fisher, iii. 263–5.

I

IA (Hya, Ives), patron of St. Ives, Cornwall, according to local tradition was an Irish virgin who sailed across the Irish Sea on a leaf. She was said to be a sister of *Euny. Leland saw a Life of her at St. Ives which made her a noble of St. Barricus; a church was built at her request by Dinan, a great lord of Cornwall. Breton tradition, however, makes her a convert of Patrick the Older: she came to Armorica with 777 disciples and was martyred there. She is the eponym of Plouyé, near Carhaix. She should not be confused with *Ives of St. Ives, Hunts. Feasts: 3 February and 27 October.

G. H. Doble, *The Saints of Cornwall*, i (1960), 89–94. William Worcestre, p. 115.

IDE, see ITA.

IGNATIUS OF ANTIOCH (d. *c*.107), bishop and martyr. Of Syrian origin, Ignatius became bishop of Antioch *c*.69. Nothing is known of his early life or even of his episcopate before his last journey from Antioch to Rome, which took place under military guard because he had been condemned to death in Trajan's persecution for being a Christian. On this journey he wrote seven revealing letters, which make him a significant witness to Christianity in sub-apostolic times. Four of them were written at Smyrna, where he had been received with great honour by *Polycarp and many other Christians. They were addressed to the churches of Ephesus, Magnesia, Tralles, and Rome. At Troas he wrote his remaining letters to Polycarp and to the churches of Philadelphia and Smyrna.

The letters show their author as ardently devoted to Christ, whose Divinity and Resurrection from the dead they clearly affirm. They urge unity, in and through the Eucharist and its president, the local bishop. Ignatius described the Church of Rome as the one founded by *Peter and *Paul, and therefore worthy of special reverence. He called himself both a disciple and the 'bearer of God' (theophoros), so convinced was he of the presence within him of Christ whom he longed to see soon after death.

Describing himself as the 'wheat of Christ', he was thrown to the lions in the Colosseum and died almost at once. His works were soon translated into Latin and some Oriental languages; one was cited by *Gildas.

Antioch kept his feast on 17 October as the Roman Church has done since 1969. Formerly his feast in the West was on 1 February, but *Bede, the Roman Martyrology, and B.C.P. keep 17 December, his translation day. The Eastern Churches generally prefer 20 December.

AA.SS. Feb. I (1658), 13–37, J. B. Lightfoot, *The Apostolic Fathers* (part II, 1885); J. H. Srawley, *The Epistles of St. Ignatius* (1935); C. C. Richardson, *The Christianity of St. Ignatius of Antioch* (1935); B. H. Streeter, *The Primitive Church* (1929).

IGNATIUS OF LACONI (1701–81), Capuchin laybrother. Born at Laconi (Sardinia) of a poor but devout family, Ignatius became a laybrother at Buoncammino, near Cagliari, after a shock caused by his horse bolting, although it left him unharmed. This was in 1721. In 1741, known for love of prayer, solitude, and silence, he was appointed *questor* (begging for alms): he travelled on foot in all weathers. He held this office for the rest of his life, meeting sometimes with refusals and contradictions; but it gave him scope to exercise his gentle love of children, the poor, and the sick.

An unusual legend relates that he would never ask for alms from an unscrupulous moneylender, who complained of this neglect. The local Guardian told Ignatius to call on him and he returned with a sack of food. When it was opened, it dripped with blood.

More authentic is a contemporary description (confirmed by a surviving portrait at Cagliari) of him as of medium height with slight features, with white hair and beard, upright in gait and easy in manner. Other accounts tell of levitations and miracles of healing. He was canonized in 1951. Feast: 11 May.

Letters concerning Ignatius ed. by J. Fues (1899); Lives by S. da Chiaramonte (1940) and F. Majella (1946); see also B.T.A., ii. 281–3; *Bibl. SS.*, vii. 672–4.

IGNATIUS OF LOYOLA (1491–1556), founder of the Jesuits. The youngest of eleven children of a Basque nobleman, he was brought up to be a soldier. He fought the French in Castile, but was wounded at the siege of Pamplona in 1521. His broken leg was badly set, was broken again, and reset: the impact of the cannon-ball, made worse by bad surgery, left him deformed and with a limp for the rest of his life. During his convalescence he asked to read knightly romances; instead he was given a Life of Christ and some Legends of the Saints. His conversion followed; he lived for a year in prayer and penance at Manresa, close to the famous abbey of Montserrat. Here he experienced both desolation and consolation, and wrote the first draft of his famous *Spiritual Exercises*, which incorporated some of the traditional teaching of Montserrat. In 1523 he made a pilgrimage to Jerusalem, begging his way like many before him. Franciscans there persuaded him to renounce a project for converting the Muslims, so he returned to Spain, still without a clear plan for his life.

He decided to study Latin in order to work for souls. He went to Barcelona, Alcala, Salamanca, and lastly Paris (1528), where he also studied philosophy for three years, graduating in 1534 as master of arts. He had lived in austere holiness and, although still a layman, had given direction to those in trouble, especially women of varied backgrounds. In Spain this had led to his imprisonment as a suspected heretic. In Paris he gathered six disciples, to whom he gave the *Spiritual Exercises*; together they took vows of poverty and chastity and promised to serve the Church either by preaching in Palestine or in other ways that the pope thought fit. In 1537 they met in Venice: unable to reach the Holy Land, they went to Rome and resolved to become a new religious Order. By now, they had all been ordained priests. Vows of obedience and readiness to go anywhere the pope sent them were added to the others. Works of charity such as teaching the young and uneducated, as well as missionary enterprises, were among their earliest ideals. The choral celebration of the Divine Office was abolished so as to leave them free for these works. This was a revolutionary step, but the whole package won papal approval in 1540. Ignatius was chosen, predictably but unwillingly, as the first General. For the rest of his life he stayed at Rome, directing the Society he had founded.

For fifteen years he inspired, counselled, and directed his subjects with prudence and understanding. His iron will and determination did not make him unlovable or impatient. But the way of total obedience, made by the aspirant during the Spiritual Exercises, was insisted upon; it has often been compared to a military commitment and the Society of Jesus to an army. Perhaps it is more accurate to consider the Jesuits as analogous to the Friars in the Middle Ages, but bound by a tighter organization more appropriate to the crisis situation of the 16th century.

The papacy directed them to meet this in Germany. Here Peter *Canisius, supported by the German College at Rome, also directed by the Jesuits, effected a notable counter-attack to the diatribes of Lutherans and Calvinists. Fundamental to the whole enterprise of the Counter-Reformation in many countries was the unobtrusive educational work of the Jesuit schools. Their education was 'modern' and 'progressive' in so far as it made use of the classics and critical scholarship; it stimulated competition as well as interest; but it also tended to be authoritarian.

The Jesuits were prominent in the foreign missions. The pioneer work of Francis *Xavier in the Far East was emulated by others later in India and China, Ethiopia and the Congo, South America, and Canada. Ignatius and his successors were generous in their allocation of personnel, money, and time to their enterprises. Among Ignatius' personal foundations at Rome were houses for convert Jews and hostels for fallen women. Spiritual direction, which was to complete rather than replace the work of parish priests, was undertaken by Jesuits; but not, in their early days, the actual charge of parishes.

The first Jesuits to reach England arrived in 1542. More famous were those of the Elizabethan age like Edmund *Campion and Robert *Southwell, whose education, humanism, courage, and resourcefulness made them an inspiration to many English Catholics.

Ignatius died suddenly on 31 July 1556. By then the Jesuits numbered over 1,000 members in nine European provinces besides those working in the foreign missions. He was canonized in 1622 and declared patron of spiritual exercises and retreats by Pius XI. He is also patron of many schools, churches, and colleges. Feast: 31 July.

AA.SS. Iul. VII (1731), 409–853; *Monumenta Ignatiana* (1903–65) contain the Life, Letters, Spiritual Exercises, and other writings: Eng. tr. of his *Letters to Women* (1960), *Constitutions* (ed. G. N. Ganss, 1970), and the *Exercises* (ed. T. Corbishley, 1963). Lives by P. van Dyke (1926), C. Hollis (1931), J. Brodrick (1956), H. Boehmer (1951), and V. Larranaga (1956). See also J. Brodrick, *The Origin of the Jesuits* (1940); G. R. Elton, *Reformation Europe 1517–1559* (new edn. 1974), F. Wulf and others, *Ignatius von Loyola . . . 1556–1956* (1957); J. F. Gilmont and P. Daman, *Bibliographie Ignatienne, 1894–1957* (1958); B.T.A., iii. 221–7; *Bibl. SS.*, vii. 674–705.

ILDEPHONSUS OF TOLEDO (*c.*607–77), archbishop. Born of a noble Spanish family, he may have been educated in part by *Isidore. He became a monk at Agalia in his youth, was ordained priest *c.*637 and was appointed abbot in *c.*650. He took part in councils at Toledo (653 and 657) and was appointed archbishop also in 657. He was not only a devoted pastor but also a notable writer. His treatise on Baptism was followed up by one on the spiritual journey of the soul after Baptism; he also wrote a *De viris illustribus*, short biographies of worthies of the 7th-century Church in Spain. He is also specially remembered for his treatise on the Virginity of Mary, whose exuberant enthusiasm (said to be a Spanish symptom) was imitated later by others. A story related of her appearing to him on his episcopal throne and giving him a chasuble is found in most collections of *Mary-Legends* which were widely diffused from the 12th century onwards. This scene was painted by Velazquez, El Greco, and others. Feast: 23 January.

AA.SS. Ian. II (1734), 535–9; works in *P.L.*, xcvi. 9–330; A. Braegelmann, *The Life and Writings of St. Ildephonsus of Toledo* (1942); J. M. C. Davila, *Doctrina Mariana de S. Ildefonso de Toledo* (1958); *Bibl. SS.*, vii. 756–60.

ILLTUD (Illtyd, Eltut, Hildutus) (d. early 6th century), founder and abbot of Llanilltud Fawr (Llantwit Major). The early Life of *Samson claims that Illtud was a disciple of *Germanus of Auxerre, that he was the most learned Briton in the study of Scripture and philosophy, and that he was the abbot of his monastery in Glamorgan. The earliest Life of Illtud, full of implausible legends, was written *c.*1140. From it may perhaps be retained the claim that he sailed to Brittany with some corn ships to relieve the famine: some Breton churches and villages certainly bear his name. The same Life (abridged in *N.L.A.*) tells of Illtud's bell being recovered from King Edgar's armies and of Illtud's protecting his people against the people of North Wales in the time of King William. A 9th-century inscription on a cross at Llantwit mentions 'Illtet, Samson, and Ebisar', but there is no formal evidence for a cult surviving from before the 11th century. Many churches in Wales, however, are dedicated to him, while his monastery, reputed to contain hundreds of monks, was one of the most influential in South Wales. Feast: 6 November.

N.L.A., ii. 52–6; A. W. Wade-Evans, *Vitae Sanctorum Britanniae* (1944), 194–233; *Vita Samsonis* (ed. R. Fawtier, 1912; Eng. tr. by T. Taylor, 1925); G. H. Doble, *Lives of the Welsh Saints* (1971); Baring-Gould and Fisher, iii. 303–17.

INDRACT (d. *c.*700), martyr. He is described in the Martyrology of Tallaght (*c.*800) as a martyr for the faith at Glastonbury, and his name also occurs in an 11th-century litany. William of Malmesbury portrayed him as the son of an Irish king, who, with his nine travelling companions, was set upon and killed by brigands: 'credulous antiquity regarded them as martyrs.' Another Life says that Huna, the king's thane, murdered them, believing that they carried gold. The place of their death is believed to be Huish Episcopi. Ina, king of Wessex (688–726), translated the relics to Glastonbury, where they were buried beside the high altar of the Old Church, destroyed by fire in 1184. William Worcestre mentions that his body lay at Shepton Mallet in 1478: by then his companions were estimated at one hundred. Feast 8 May, but the Bollandists list him under 5 February.

G. H. Doble, 'St. Indract and St. Dominic', *Som. Rec. Soc.*, lvii (1942), 1–24; M. Lapidge, 'The cult of St. Indract at Glastonbury' in *Ireland in Early Medieval Europe* (ed. D. Whitelock, 1981), pp. 179–212.

INNOCENTS, see HOLY INNOCENTS.

IRENAEUS OF LYONS (*c.*130–200), bishop. Of Eastern origin, perhaps from Smyrna whose bishop *Polycarp, disciple of *John the Apostle, he had known as a boy, Irenaeus studied at Rome and then became a priest of Lyons, at the invitation of its first bishop Pothinus. This city was a flourishing trade-centre, which soon became the most important of its kind in the West, and the principal bishopric of Gaul. During a sudden persecution, which caused the imprisonment of many of its members, the church of Lyons sent Irenaeus to Rome with a letter for the pope. This urged leniency towards the Montanists in Phrygia, a sect of enthusiasts with whom Irenaeus had little sympathy; but he acted, as his name implies, for peace and unity. On his return *c.*178 he was appointed bishop, as *Pothinus had been killed in the persecution. He acted as peacemaker again in 190. Pope Victor III had excommunicated the Quartodecimans of Asia Minor, who celebrated Easter on the day of the Jewish Passover instead of on the following Sunday with all other Christians. As a result of Irenaeus' intervention, good relations were restored; some centuries later they conformed on their own accord.

Irenaeus was also an important theologian, whose significance has been fully realized only in the 20th century. His principal works, the *Adversus Haereses* and the *Demonstration of Apostolic Preaching* (discovered in 1904) effectively refuted Gnosticism. His principal points were a clear reassertion of Christian monotheism, emphasizing the identity of the God of the Old Testament with that of the New, and the unity of the Father and the Son in the work of Revelation and Redemption. His special contribution to the theology of the Incarnation consists in his theory of the 'recapitulation' of human nature in Christ. He also strongly emphasized the importance of Tradition, realized in the apostolic succession of the episcopate and in the formation of the Canon of Scripture, in which the authority of the Four Gospels, which complete each other, is supreme.

Irenaeus died at Lyons and was buried in the crypt of the church of St. John (now Saint-Irenée), where his shrine remained until it was destroyed by Calvinists in 1562. Although he is usually venerated as a martyr, the evidence for his martyrdom is late and unsatisfactory. Feast: in the East, 23 August; in the West, 28 June.

AA.SS. Iun. V (1709), 335–49 with *C.M.H.*, pp. 341–2; *A.C.M.*, pp. 294–301; J. Lawson, *The*

Biblical Theology of St. Irenaeus (1948); A. Benoit, *Saint Irénée: Introduction à l'Étude de sa théologie* (1960); works ed. A. Stieren (1848–53) and W. W. Harvey (1857); the *Demonstration* ed. J. A. Robinson (1920) with Eng. tr.; French tr. by F. M. Sagnard and A. Rousseau in *S.C.* (1952–69).

IRENAEUS OF SIRMIUM (d. 304), bishop and martyr. A comparatively young man, whose youth and good looks are referred to in his Acts, Irenaeus suffered under the emperors Diocletian and Maximian at Sirmium, a town now in ruins near Sremska Mitrovica in Yugoslavia. When called on by the prefect Probus to sacrifice to the gods, he answered (as in Exod. 22: 20) 'Whoever sacrifices to the gods and not to God, will be utterly destroyed. My duty', he continued later, 'is to undergo torture rather than deny my God and sacrifice to demons.' In spite of the weeping and mourning of his relatives, servants, and friends, he persisted; so he was imprisoned and tortured. When recalled for a final interrogation he again refused and was sentenced to be beheaded, and then thrown in the river Sava. Irenaeus' final words were: 'Lord Jesus Christ, who deigned to suffer for the world's salvation, let your heavens open that your angels may take up the soul of your servant Irenaeus, who suffers all this for your name and for the people formed of your catholic church of Sirmium. I ask and implore your mercy to receive me and to strengthen them in your faith.' He was then beheaded and his body was thrown in the river. Feast: originally 6 April, his day of death, but on 25 March erroneously in the Roman Martyrology.

A.C.M. xliii–iv, 294–301; *AA.SS.* Mart. III (1668), 555–7.

IRENE, see AGAPE, IRENE, AND CHIONE.

ISABEL, see ELIZABETH OF PORTUGAL.

ISIDORE OF SEVILLE (*c.*560–636), archbishop. Born at Seville of a noble family from Cartagena, Isidore was educated mainly by his brother Leander, a monk, but did not become one himself. From this monastic formation he acquired and communicated an encyclopedic knowledge in his books, which became most influential in medieval clerical and monastic education. His importance as archbishop was also considerable. He ruled for thirty-six years, succeeding his brother Leander, and energetically completing his work of converting the Visigoths from Arianism and organizing the Church in Spain through synods and councils. The most notable were the councils of Seville (619) and Toledo (633), over both of which he presided in person; one of their achievements was the decree (centuries before Charlemagne's similar one) that a cathedral school should be established in every diocese. Besides being a successful and influential educator, Isidore completed the Mozarabic missal and breviary and was notable for his abundant charity to the poor. Soon before his death, he had himself clothed in sackcloth and ashes. Isidore was formally canonized only in 1598 and declared a Doctor of the Church in 1722.

His reputation is due principally to his writings. *Bede, at the time of his death, was working on a translation of extracts from Isidore's book *On the Wonders of Nature* (*De natura rerum*), but the *Etymologies* is his most famous work. This is a kind of encyclopedia which contains elements of grammar, rhetoric, theology, history, mathematics, and medicine, presented in the form of etymologies, which are in fact often erroneous. His *Chronica Majora*, which covers the years from the Creation to 615, is an influential compilation from various other church historians, but with special information on Spanish history. Other works include biographies of famous men (completing *Jerome's work), a summary of Christian doctrine, rules for monks and nuns, and the History of the Goths. From the time of Bede onwards the writings of Isidore figure in medieval library lists almost as frequently as those of *Gregory the Great, with whom he shares the unofficial title of 'Schoolmaster of the Middle Ages'. Feast: 4 April.

AA.SS. Apr. I (1675), 327–64; P. Séjourné, *Le dernier Père de l'Eglise. Saint Isidore de Séville* (1929); E. Bréhaut, *An Encyclopaedist of the Dark Ages, Isidore of Seville* (1912); M. L. W. Laistner, *Thought and Letters in Western Europe* (1966); P. Hunter Blair, *The World of Bede* (1970), pp. 132–7, 291–5; *Miscellanea Isidoriana* (1936); M. C. Diaz y Diaz (ed.), *Isidoriana* (1961); works of Isidore in *P.L.*, lxxxi–lxxxiv; crit. edn. of *Etymologiae* by W. M. Lindsay (1911), of historical works by E. Waitz in *M.G.H., Auctores Antiquissimi*, xi (1894), 241–506 and of *De Natura Rerum* by J. Fontaine (1960): *Bibl. SS.*, vii 973–82.

ISIDORE THE FARMER (*c.*1080–1130), patron of Madrid. Few details of his life survive through a biography written 150 years after his death. Born of devout parents, he worked as a farm labourer at Torrelaguna near Madrid to the same employer, John de Vergas, all his life. He married S. Maria de la Cabeza; they had a son who died young, after which the couple lived in perfect continence. Isidore would rise early to visit a church, he would pray for long periods while guiding the plough; he would often spend holidays on pilgrimage to local shrines.

Delightful legends about him include his employer seeing a second team of white oxen led by angels who ploughed alongside Isidore, who had been accused of arriving late for work. On another occasion, in deep mid-winter, Isidore saw a number of disconsolate hungry birds perching on a branch, while he was carrying a sack of corn. In spite of his companion's jeers he gave half the corn to the birds, while the remainder yielded a double amount of flour.

Miracles and a cult followed his death, and his body was translated in 1170. In 1211 he is said to have guided King Alphonsus of Castile in a vision to an unknown path, which enabled him to make a successful surprise attack on the Moors. In about 1615 King Philip III of Spain was cured of a mortal fever through Isidore's relics being moved into the sick king's bedroom. This led to the Spanish king's petitioning the Holy See for Isidore's formal canonization. This was achieved in 1622, when at one ceremony four other Spanish saints, *Ignatius, Francis *Xavier, *Theresa and Philip *Neri, were thus honoured with Isidore. He is an interesting example of a lay saint of humble origin, comparable to *Homobundus, *Godric, or *Walstan, who attained sanctity in life through humdrum occupations, but who posthumously became famous. His emblem is a sickle. His body is reputedly incorrupt. Feast: 15 May.

AA.SS. Maii III (1738), 512–50; B.T.A., ii. 323–4; *Bibl. SS.*, vii. 953–7.

ISMAEL (Ysfael, Osmail) (6th century), Welsh bishop. According to the Life of Oudoceus he was the son of Budic, a prince of Cornouaille, forced into exile in Dyfed, whence he returned to Brittany, but his sons, including Ismael, later returned to Wales. Here it is claimed that the three brothers were disciples of *David, *Dyfrig, and *Teilo, and that Ismael was consecrated by Teilo and became 'bishop of Menevia' after St. David. There are several dedications to Ismael in Pembrokeshire and one in Carmarthenshire. Feast: 16 June.

Baring-Gould and Fisher, iii. 323–4.

ISTVAN, see STEPHEN OF HUNGARY.

ITA (Ide) (d. *c.*570), Irish nun. Apart from *Brigid, Ita is probably the most famous woman saint of Ireland. Her Life was written centuries after her death. She is said to have been of royal origin, born near Waterford, and called Deirdre; later she migrated to Killeedy (Limerick) where she founded a small nunnery and lived for the rest of her life. Her spiritual life was like that of other Irish ascetics, with much prayer and fasting; in her case it is claimed that devotion to the indwelling Holy Trinity was her characteristic. An Irish lullaby for the Infant Jesus is also attributed to her. Further, although her own Life says nothing of this, she is called 'foster-mother of the saints of Ireland', especially of *Brendan, although the chronology seems scarcely possible. He is supposed to have asked her what three things God specially loved, to which she answered: 'True faith in God with a pure heart, a simple life with a religious spirit, and open-handedness inspired by charity.' It is probable that she educated some young boys who later became famous and that her nuns helped to treat the sick of the neighbourhood. Like other monastic figures of Ireland, she spent considerable time in complete solitude and was also much in demand for advice and help. There are church dedications and place-names which recall her both in her place of origin and around her monastery; she is also mentioned in Alcuin's poem on the Irish saints. Her cult is still alive today. Feast: 15 January.

Life in *V.S.H.*, ii. 116–30; R. Flower, *The Irish Tradition* (1947), esp. p. 56; J. Ryan, *Irish Monasticism* (1931), pp. 138–40; *The Irish Saints*, pp. 196–9.

ITHAMAR (Ythamar) (d. *c.*660), bishop of Rochester. He was a man of Kent, whose learning was considered equivalent to that of *Justus and *Paulinus. When he was consecrated by *Honorius in 644, he became the first Anglo-Saxon to occupy an English see. Later he consecrated the first Anglo-Saxon archbishop of Canterbury, *Deusdedit. The precise date of his death is unknown, but he was buried at Rochester.

The appointment of Gundulf as bishop of Rochester in 1077, and its revival as a monastic chapter, led to extensive rebuilding. This caused a translation of Ithamar's relics and the recording of miracles at his tomb. Another translation was accomplished by bishop John, who was cured of severe pain in the eyes by Ithamar's intercession. Feast: 10 June.

Bede, *H.E.*, iii. 14, 20; *N.L.A.*, ii. 83–5; T. D. Hardy, *Catalogue of Materials* (*R.S.*), i. 251–2.

IVES (1), patron of St. Ives, Cornwall, see Ia.

IVES (2) (Yves), patron of St. Ives (Huntingdon), a village formerly called Slepe. According to Goscelin (d. *c.*1107) the cult had been extant for a century. Four bodies were discovered to 1001, one of which had episcopal insignia buried with it. Following a peasant's dream this was unhesitatingly identified as that of a Persian bishop, Ives (or Ivo), who was supposed to have come to England and lived and died there as a hermit. The bodies were translated to Ramsey Abbey: miracles followed, mainly operated through a spring of water which flowed close to the relics and was believed to have medicinal powers. About a century later, light appeared at night reaching from Ramsey to Slepe which was interpreted as meaning that the companions of Ives should be translated back to Slepe, where a new foundation from Ramsey could enjoy this subsidiary shrine as a useful source of revenue, while that of Ives could continue at the mother-house. Feast: 24 April (at Ramsey, Ely, and St. Albans).

Goscelin, *Vita S. Yvonis* in *P.L.*, clv. 84 ff; *G.P.*, p. 320; Stanton, pp. 180–1.

IVO OF BRITTANY (*c.*1235–1303), lawyer and patron of lawyers and judges. Sometimes called Ivo Helory or Ivo of Kermartin, he was born at Kermartin, near Tréguier (Brittany). His father, the lord of the manor, sent him to study canon law and theology at Paris for 10 years and then he studied civil law at Orléans under Peter de la Chapelle. As a student he was reputed to have practised monastic austerities of fasting and abstinence. On his return to Brittany in 1262 he was appointed by the archdeacon of Rennes as judge ('official') of the church courts.

Soon the bishop of Tréguier reclaimed him for the same office, in the exercise of which he won a reputation for complete impartiality, special care for poor litigants, and absolute incorruptibility. He repeatedly tried, often with success, to persuade litigants to settle out of court, thus avoiding expensive and sometimes unnecessary lawsuits.

Only in 1284 was he ordained priest and appointed parish priest of Tredrez. In 1287 he resigned his legal appointments and devoted himself to his parishioners, first at Tredrez and from 1292 at Lovannec. There he built a hospital where he tended the sick in person, and would give beggars his clothes or let them use his bed. Although he was no longer an official judge, he often acted as an unofficial arbitrator. Fluent in Latin and French as well as Breton, he was much in demand as a preacher outside his own neighbourhood. He died after an illness which lasted from the beginning of Lent to Ascensiontide. He was canonized in 1347. Feast: 19 May.

AA.SS. Maii IV (1866), 538–614: A. de la Borderie, *Monuments Originaux de l'Histoire de S. Yves* (1887); Lives by C. de la Roncière (1925); A. Masseron, *S. Yves d'après les témoins de sa vie* (1952). See also B.T.A., ii. 351–3; *Bibl. SS.*, vii. 998–1002.

IWI (Ywi) (7th century), Northumbrian monk and deacon. A disciple of *Cuthbert at Lindisfarne who wished to follow the Irish ideal of 'exile for Christ', he took ship with some sailors for whatever their destination. This turned out to be Brittany, where he lived austerely as a hermit, accomplished miracles of healing, and died on 6 October.

About 250 years later, a group of wandering Breton clerics arrived at Wilton Abbey, carrying the relics of Iwi. They were met in solemn procession by the abbess, Wulftrudis, and left the relics on the altar of *Edith. After enjoying the hospitality of the abbess, they found the reliquary was immovable. Their tears and cries, rending of clothes, and blows at the feretory were alike unavailing: they were quite unable to remove the relics. So the abbess gave them 2,000 *solidi* to console them for their loss. They then departed for Brittany, leaving the relics behind.

Iwi's feast was celebrated at Wilton, Winchester, Worcester, and elsewhere in SW. England. The date was 8 October, presumably commemorating the translation rather than the death of the saint.

N.L.A., ii. 91–2; A. Wilmart, 'La légende de Ste Édith en prose et vers par le moine Goscelin', *Anal Boll.*, lvi (1938), esp. pp. 273–4.

J

JADWIGA, see HEDWIG.

JAMBERT (Jaenbeorht) (d. 792), archbishop of Canterbury. Of Kentish origin, he became a monk, later abbot, of St. Augustine's, Canterbury. Consecrated in 765, he ruled his see at a time when Offa, king of Mercia, had reduced the status of Kent to that of a dependent sub-kingdom. Partly through a quarrel with Jambert, Offa asked and obtained from the pope that Lichfield should become a metropolitan see: this meant that Jambert lost about half his province. During his successor's tenure of office the pope restored the *status quo ante*, which Canterbury never lost again. Possibly Jambert was regarded as a saint for his stand in the matter. His feast on 12 August is testified by a calendar of St. Augustine's, Canterbury, where he was buried.

F. M. Stenton, *Anglo-Saxon England*, pp. 205–17; *E.B.K. after 1100*, i. 47–62.

JAMES OF THE MARCHES (1394–1476), Franciscan priest and preacher. Born at Montebrandone (Marches of Ancona) of a poor family, he joined the Franciscans at Assisi, studied under *Bernardino at Fiesole, and later read law at Perugia. He was ordained priest in 1423. He adopted a very penitential life-style and became a most effective preacher in and outside his homeland. His frequent fasting, denial of sleep, and wearing a threadbare habit were joined with an extreme zeal for souls.

His life was controversial. He was involved in disputes between branches of the Franciscan Order, exacerbated by the addition of heretical elements to the Fraticelli who had already been condemned by the papacy. Some criticized James for being too severe and ruthless against them. Later he preached against the Bogomils in Bosnia and the Hussites in Hungary. To the latter, however, now less intransigent, he offered the practice of communion under both kinds at the council of Basle (1431), while at that of Florence (1438) he took part in the reunion with the Greeks. In several of these controversies he had assisted *John Capistrano, whom he succeeded as papal legate in Hungary in 1456. Four years later he was offered but refused the see of Milan: itinerant preaching was essential to his way of life. Among other enterprises to help the poor, he set up *montes pietatis* (embryo pawnshops) to enable them to avoid financial disaster through loans at reasonable rates.

His later years were clouded by his being denounced to the Inquisition at Brescia in 1462 for holding unorthodox views on the precious blood of Christ. Controversies between Dominicans and Franciscans followed, until the Holy See, after an inconclusive disputation, imposed silence on both parties. In 1473 James was moved to Naples. Here he died, and was buried in the church of S. Maria Nuova. Crivelli's fine portrait of him in the Louvre depicts him as austere, emaciated, and ethereal. James was canonized in 1726. Feast: 28 November.

Life by his travelling companion V. de Fabriano (ed. T. Somigli) in *Archivum Franciscanum Historicum*, xvii (1924), 378–414; more recent Lives by S. Candela (1962) and G. Caselli (2 vols., 1926). For his writings see D. Paccetti in *Studia Franciscana*, 1942–4. See also B.T.A., iv. 440–1; *Bibl. SS.*, vi. 388–402; *N.C.E.*, vii. 811–12.

JAMES THE DEACON (d. late 7th century). His origin and nationality are unknown, but he was probably from Italy, like *Paulinus, whom he constantly assisted during the Northumbrian pioneering apostolate which lasted from

625 until the battle of Hatfield, when King *Edwin was killed in 633. Paulinus now retired to Kent with King Edwin's widow and daughter, but James stayed behind in Northumbria, braving the hostile regime of Penda of Mercia and Cadwallon of Gwynedd and continuing Paulinus' work of preaching and baptizing near Catterick (N. Yorkshire). As an old man he took part in the Synod of Whitby in 663–4, where he supported the Roman calculation of Easter which he had followed in Northumbria for nearly forty years. *Bede praised his constancy and nobility of soul and described him as a pioneer also in the Roman method of chanting, later taught in England by Eddius Stephanus and John the Archcantor. The date of his death is unknown and his cult seems to have been informal. Not being a monk he had no community to provide a centre for his memory.

Bede, *H.E.*, ii. 16, 20; iii. 25; iv. 2; H. Mayr-Harting, *The Coming of Christianity to Anglo-Saxon England* (1973), p. 42.

JAMES THE GREAT (d. 44), apostle and martyr. Described in the Gospels as the son of Zebedee and the brother of *John, James was one of the three witnesses of the Transfiguration of Christ and his agony in the garden of Gethsemane. He was also the first apostle to die for the Christian faith, being put to the sword at Jerusalem by King Herod Agrippa (Acts 12: 2). The word Boanerges, used by the evangelists to describe James and John, means 'sons of thunder', indicating impetuous character and fiery temper.

No early documents claim either that James preached the Gospel in Spain or that he was buried there. Of the two claims the former is the earlier (7th century), the latter (9th century) the less unlikely; neither nowadays commands much credence outside Spain. The heyday of Santiago de Compostela was from the 12th to the 15th century: the cult was fostered by kings, popes, and bishops and flourished on the concept of James as the powerful defender of Christianity against the Moors, as testified by many miracle stories of varying degrees of antiquity and credibility. This military aspect of James's posthumous reputation coincided with the more general Crusading Movement and does not, it seems, antedate it. However that may be, the pilgrimage to Compostela, was one of the most important of medieval Christendom: Cluniac and Augustinian monasteries were built along the roads especially in northern Spain, to provide hospitality for the pilgrims. These came from most countries in western Europe: Cluny was prominent in support of the pilgrimage, while Reading Abbey, to which the Empress Matilda gave the hand-relic of James, enjoyed several privileges connected with the cult and the pilgrimage.

Although in its fullest form the James Legend is unconvincing, it has none the less certain authentic elements. The shrine of Compostela is on the site of an early Christian cemetery, where a *martyrium* testifies to the cult of a saint of early patristic times: his identity is, however, unknown. A conjectural claim has been made to identify him with Priscillian. The earliest *documentary* evidence for the translation of James's relics from Jerusalem to Spain occurs in the Martyrology of Usuard (865). This is subsequent to the existence of the local cult a century earlier. But St. Mary's church at Merida possessed relics of James and other apostles and early martyrs before the Islamic conquest and perhaps as early as 627. The cults and relics moved northwards; the Asturian kings Alphonso II and especially III (866–910) fostered the cult of James, which was already flourishing (like that of *Martin of Tours) well before the Crusades brought further developments.

The pilgrimage to Compostela was so popular and important that it eventually transformed the iconography of James. His own emblems became the pilgrim's hat and the scallop-shell associated with Compostela. In England over 400 churches are dedicated to him. Feast: 25 July.

AA.SS. Iul., VI (1729), 5–124; T. D. Kendrick, *St. James in Spain* (1960); L. Duchesne, 'Saint Jacques en Galice', *Annales du Midi*, xii (1900), 145–79; B. de Gaiffier, 'Le Breviarium Apostolorum: tradition manuscrite et œuvres apparentées', *Anal. Boll.*, lxxxi (1963), 89–116; J. S. Stone, *The Cult of Santiago* (1927); Y. Bottineau, *Les chemins de Saint-Jacques* (1964); R. A. Fletcher, *St. James' Catapult* (1985). See also J. Sumption, *Medieval Pilgrimage* (1975); H. Chadwick, *Priscillian of Avila* (1976).

JAMES THE LESS (1st century), apostle. The son of Alphaeus is often but not certainly identified with the James whose mother stood by Christ on the Cross, and also with James, the 'brother of the Lord', who saw the risen Christ and is often called the first bishop of Jerusalem. He is also sometimes identified with the author of the Epistle of St. James. If none of these identifications is correct, we know practically nothing about James the Less. His traditional iconographic emblem is a fuller's club because he was believed to have been beaten to death with it, after being sentenced by the Sanhedrin in AD 62 to be stoned. In England only twenty-six churches are dedicated to James the Less, often together with *Philip. Feast: with the Apostle Philip, 1 May, but 3 May since 1969 in the Roman calendar.

O.D.C.C., s.v.; W. Patrick, *James, the Lord's Brother* (1906); R. P. Bedford, *St. James the Less: a study in Christian Iconography* (1911).

JAMES, martyr, see MARIAN AND JAMES.

JANE FRANCES DE CHANTAL, see CHANTAL.

JANUARIUS (Gennaro) (d. *c.*305?), bishop of Benevento, martyr. His martyrdom somewhere near Naples is testified in early 5th-century writings and pictures of him with a nimbus of the same date, and by the presence of his name in early calendars of East and West. But the details given by his Acts are suspect. Early in the 5th century Naples obtained his relics from the church dedicated to him near the Soltfara. During the Norman wars they were translated to Benevento and Monte Virgine but returned to Naples later. They are specially famous because of the alleged liquefaction of his blood which is claimed to take place every year in connection with his three feasts. This was first recorded in 1389. Often attacked by sceptics, some of whom claim that there is a mixture of wax in the blood which is melted by the heat, the prodigy does still take place, whatever its explanation may be. In fact there is no correlation between the temperature and the variable speed of the liquefaction, but there is variation in weight and in the apparent bulk of the blood in the glass phial. It also sometimes behaves unpredictably: there are recorded examples of liquefaction taking place during repairs and several times it has not taken place for the December feast, to the intense consternation and anger of his devotees. Unexpectedly the blood liquefied at Cardinal Cooke's visit in 1978; the last time the expected prodigy did not occur is said to have been when Naples elected a Communist mayor. Some other less famous blood relics in Naples are also claimed to liquefy. Feast: 19 September, translation of relics on first Saturday in May; the feast of 16 December marks his patronage of Naples and the anniversary of a threatened eruption of Mt. Vesuvius in 1631.

AA.SS. Sept. VI (1757), 761–891 with *C.M.H.*, p. 517; H. Thurston in *Catholic Encyclopedia*, viii. 295–7 and id., 'The Blood-Miracles of Naples', *The Month*, cxlix (1927), 44–55, 123–35, 236–47 and id., 'The "Miracle" of St. Januarius', ibid., clv (1930), 119–29; H. Delehaye, 'Hagiographie napolitaine', *Anal. Boll.*, lix (1941), 1–33; see also *Bibl. S.S.*, s.v. Gennaro and D. Sax, *Relics and Shrines* (1985), pp. 158–60.

JAPAN, Martyrs of, see MIKI.

JARLATH (d. *c.*550), Irish monk and bishop(?). Very little is known of this saint. He is said to have belonged to a noble family in Galway and to have been a disciple of *Enda. He founded a monastery at Cluain Fois; later he moved two miles away to Tuam, of which he is asserted to have been bishop. His monastery had a high reputation for learning: *Brendan of Clonfert and Colman of Munster are claimed as disciples. His shrine was kept at a chapel in Tuam until 1830. Feast: 6 June.

The Irish Saints, p. 199; B.T.A., ii. 489.

JEROME (Hieronymus) (*c.*341–420), monk and Doctor of the Church. Born at Strido, near Aquileia, in Dalmatia, Jerome was well educated, first by his father, then by the grammarian Donatus at Rome. After this he studied rhetoric with such success that it is evident in all his writings. Meanwhile he used to visit the churches and especially the catacombs of Rome and was baptized some time before 366. He travelled in Gaul, Dalmatia, and Italy. While at Trier he decided to become a monk; this he did with like-minded friends in Aquileia until, after a quarrel caused by some real or supposed scandal, Jerome left for Palestine. He reached Antioch in 374: two of his companions died, Jerome too was seriously ill. In this state he dreamt that he appeared before God's judgement-seat and was condemned for being a Ciceronian rather than a Christian. For several years he took this experience very seriously. He became a hermit in the desert of Chalcis in Syria for five years, gave up the classics he knew and loved so well, and learnt Hebrew instead to study Scripture in its original language. Already he had learnt Greek, so that, with his mastery of style and rhetoric, he was equipped for his future achievements as writer and translator. Unfortunately Jerome also had a difficult, cantankerous temperament and a sarcastic wit which made him enemies.

After being ordained priest in Antioch, although he had no wish for orders and in fact never said Mass, he studied in Constantinople under *Gregory of Nazianzus; no doubt Jerome found himself more at home in the sophisticated capital than among the rustic Syrian monks. There he translated Eusebius' Chronicle from Greek into Latin, and a number of Origen's homilies; to these he added his first original Scriptural work on the Vision of Isaiah, addressed in its later form to *Damasus. He returned to Rome to act as interpreter to Paulinus, one of the claimants to the See of Antioch.

Once there, he was retained as his 'secretary' by Damasus, then a very old man; he produced other scriptural *opuscula*, mainly translations. He then embarked on the enormous task of producing a standard Latin text of the Bible, revised according to the meaning of the original texts, but not, apparently, an entirely new translation. He began on the Gospels and the Psalter; eventually he produced all, or nearly all, the Bible in what was later called the Vulgate version. He also wrote a number of influential commentaries on particular books such as the Prophets and the Epistles; that on Matthew's Gospel became a standard work.

His stay in Rome lasted only three years, but during it he became the guide of a group of dedicated Christian ladies, *Paula, Marcella, Eustochium, and others, most of whom had been living a semi-monastic life in their widowhood. He gave them much help in their study of Scripture and in their pursuit of a more perfect Christian life apart from the worldly conditions of Rome. His relationship with them gave rise to scandalous gossip, largely unjust. But Jerome made enemies wherever he went: his aggressive sarcasm and readiness to equate himself with authentic tradition were often counter-productive. He paid the price for being a brilliant controversialist for good causes by arousing jealousy and animosity. He left Rome in 385, as he had left Syria and Constantinople before, under something of a cloud; he resolved to start again, this time at Bethlehem, where Paula established a convent of nuns and Jerome one of monks. There he spent the rest of his life, teaching, writing, and studying.

The causes for which he fought were three: the provision of as accurate a text as possible of the Bible through recourse to the original languages and previous translations. The biblical text should be illuminated by sound exegesis. Monastic life should be based on a systematic *lectio divina*, a prayerful but serious study of Scripture and the Fathers. This life is derived from the counsels of the Gospel and *Paul; it finds its best exemplar in the life of the Virgin *Mary, especially in her perpetual virginity. In the welter of conflicting theological opinions of his time he believed the See of Rome was the surest guide. His achievement as scholar and controversialist was somewhat marred by his jealousy or his self-centredness, seen in his quarrel with his old friend Rufinus. But his immense learning was unmatched by other Christian writers except *Augustine, while his passionate devotion and the asceticism which he believed necessary in the following of Christ are manifest. His works in favour of Christian monasticism such as the Lives of *Paul of Thebes, *Hilarion, and *Malchus, and the works against Jovinian were especially influential. His Letters are the finest of Christian antiquity.

Jerome died at Bethlehem and was buried under the church of the Nativity there, close to the graves of Paula and Eustochium, close also to the traditional site of the birth of Christ. Later his body was translated to the basilica of St. Mary Major, Rome. In art Jerome is often represented (anachronistically) as a cardinal, sometimes in his monastic cave with a lion at his feet. One Renaissance pope, looking at his portrait, said it was well for him that he held his stone, which was a sign of his voluntary penance, for without this he could scarcely be considered a saint. Such paintings were common from the 15th to the 17th centuries, but the earliest representation of him seems to be one in the 9th-century Bible of Charles the Bald, where he sets out for the Holy Land and expounds the Scriptures to Paula and Eustochium. As one of the four Latin Doctors he is depicted on East Anglian screens and elsewhere. Feast: 30 September.

Works in *P.L.*, xxii–xxx and *C.S.E.L.*, liv–lvi, lix; *Corpus Christianorum*, lxxii and lxxviii; tr. in *S.C.* and *Ancient Christian Writers.* Studies by G. Grutzmacher, *Hieronymus; Eine biographische Studie* (3 vols., 1901–8); F. Cavallera, *Saint Jerome* (2 vols., 1922); I. d'Ivray, *Saint Jérôme et les dames de l'Aventin* (1938); D. Gorce, *Saint Jérôme et la Lectio Divina* (1952); A. Penna, *S. Gerolamo* (1949); id., *Principi e carattere dell'exegesi di S. Gerolamo* (1950); F. X. Murphy (ed.), *A Monument to St. Jerome* (1952); H. F. D. Sparks, 'Jerome as Biblical Scholar', in *The Cambridge History of the Bible*, i (1970), 510–41; J. N. D. Kelly, *Jerome* (1975); E. D. Hunt, *Holy Land Pilgrimage in the later Roman Empire* (1982).

JEROME EMILIANI (1481–1537), priest and founder of the order of the Somaschi. Born at Venice, Jerome became an officer of the Venetian army and was appointed to command the fortress of Castelnuovo (Treviso) against the League of Cambrai. He was taken prisoner, but escaped from his dungeon; he was ordained priest in 1518 and devoted himself entirely to the relief of the suffering. From 1531, when he recovered from the plague, he founded orphanages, hospitals, and houses for repentant prostitutes. To look after them he also founded a small congregation of clerks regular, called the Somaschi after their place of origin. Out of all these good works his favourite was the care of the orphans, in whose education he is believed to have been the first to make use of catechism technique. He died at the age of fifty-six on 8 February and was canonized in 1767. He was declared the patron of orphans and abandoned children by Pius XI in 1928, and as a typical representative of this type of charitable work has his place in the revised Roman calendar of 1969. Feast: 8 February (formerly 20 July).

AA.SS. Feb. II (1658), 220–74; S. Raviolo, *San Girolamo Emiliani* (1947); G. Landini, *S. Girolamo Miami* (1947); see also *L'Ordine dei Chierici Regolari Somaschi 1528–1928* (1928).

JESTIN, see JUSTINIAN.

JOACHIM (1st century), husband of *Anne and father of the Blessed Virgin *Mary according to the 2nd-century apocryphal 'Gospel of James'. Neither Joachim nor Anne are mentioned in Holy Scripture. The 'Gospel of James', though ancient, is not trustworthy: the story of the Virgin's birth is closely modelled on that of the conception of Samuel (1 Sam. 1) with its emphasis on the childlessness of Joachim, considered a reproach, and angelic intervention to both Joachim and Anne which preceded the conception of Mary. The cult of Joachim began in the East with artistic representations as on the columns of St. Mark's, Venice (6th century), but only became notable in the West in the later Middle Ages, helped by the cult of the Blessed Virgin, with her miracles. In the West, the cult of Anne seems much more ancient than that of Joachim. Perhaps the most famous cycle of paintings of them both is that by Giotto in the Arena Chapel at Padua, but some scenes such as the marriage of Joachim and Anne were also quite well known in England (as in the stained glass at Great Malvern Priory, Hereford, and Worcester) and elsewhere. The hesitancy of the Roman Church in allowing an official cult (no older than the 15th century) of Joachim can be seen in the authorization of the feast by Julius II, its suppression by *Pius V, and its restoration by Gregory XV. Clement II placed it in August and Leo XIII raised its rank. In the East the feast of Joachim and Anne together has been on 9 September for many centuries; in the West Joachim is in the Roman Martyrology on 20 March, but his feast was on 16 August but is now with St. Anne on 26 July. He was reputedly buried at Jerusalem.

AA.SS. Mar. III (1668), 77–80; E. Amann, *Le protévangile de Jacques et ses remaniements latins* (1910), pp. 45–51; L. Cré, 'Tombeau de S. Joachim et de Ste Anne', *Revue Biblique*, ii (1893), 245–74; H. Vincent, 'La crypte de S. Anne à Jerusalem', ibid., xiii (1904), 228–41; G. McN. Rushforth, *Medieval Christian Imagery* (1936), pp. 272–5; É. Mâle, *L'Art Religieux du XIIIIe siècle en France* (1931).

JOAN OF ARC (1412–31), virgin. Born at Domrémy (Champagne), the daughter of a peasant farmer, Joan was a pious girl brought up during the Hundred Years War: she was three years of age when the battle of Agincourt took place and only nine when Henry V of England and Charles VI of France died. After this the English armies under the duke of Bedford fought a successful campaign and took numerous fortified towns. Intelligent but illiterate, Joan first heard her famous voices when only fourteen; these she identified as belonging to *Michael and the dubious *Catherine of Alexandria and *Margaret of Antioch; they told her to save France. At this time the military situation looked almost hopeless, and she had no success in persuading the commander of the French forces, but her voices persisted and gave her no rest. Her credibility was increased when some predictions and prophecy of further defeat were fulfilled. Eventually she was sent to the Dauphin (later Charles VII), who was impressed by her recognizing him in disguise and to whom she is said to have given some secret sign (never divulged) which attested the supernatural origin of her message. Theologians then gave her a searching examination for three weeks at Poitiers, found there was no reason for disapproval, and advised the Dauphin to make good use of her abilities.

She asked for troops to relieve Orléans; in April 1429 they left Blois with Joan riding at their head wearing white armour. Orléans was saved; English forts around it were captured; there can be no doubt that her presence and belief in her mission had enormously strengthened the morale of the troops. Her wound in the breast by an arrow enhanced rather than diminished her reputation. With the duke of Alençon she took part in a short campaign on the Loire which led to the victory of Patay. In July the Dauphin was crowned at Rheims with Joan standing at his side with her standard. This completed her mission; her voices had warned her that she would not live for very long. She found it impossible to withdraw at the moment of success, even though she was the object of suspicion, misunderstanding, and jealousy in the predominantly male world of the court, the army, and the Church.

An attack on Paris was a failure and an inactive winter was followed by her relief of Compiègne, then besieged by the Burgundians who were allies of the English. She led a sortie from the gates but was cut off from the main body of troops and captured. The duke of Burgundy imprisoned her; Charles made no attempt to save her; the Burgundians sold her to the English, who attributed her success to witchcraft and spells. She was imprisoned at Rouen and was tried for witchcraft and heresy by the court of the bishop of Beauvais, Pierre Cauchon, who carefully chose her judges. She was examined repeatedly, but made a spirited and shrewd defence single-handed. Inevitably her simple upbringing and ignorance of theological terms led her into mistakes. The judges declared that her visions were false and diabolical, and the summary of her statements was also condemned by the University of Paris. If she refused to recant, she would be handed over to the secular arm for punishment as a recalcitrant heretic. She was brought into the cemetery of St. Ouen and before a large crowd was intimidated into making some sort of recantation, the exact terms of which are a matter of dispute. Imprisoned once more, she resumed the male clothes which she had previously promised to abandon; after another visit from Cauchon she was declared a lapsed heretic, handed over to the secular arm, and burnt at the stake in the market-place at Rouen on 30 May. She died with fortitude, looking at a cross and calling on the name of Jesus. Her ashes were then thrown into the Seine.

About twenty years later, Joan's family asked for the case to be reopened: Callistus III appointed a commission which in 1456 quashed the verdict and declared her innocence. She was beatified by *Pius X and canonized by Benedict XV in 1920. She is not venerated as a martyr but as a virgin who responded with complete integrity and courage to what she believed to be the revelation of God's will for her, and endured persecution and death with heroic fortitude. In England there has been considerable interest in her shown by the dedication of some churches in her honour, by the placing in Winchester cathedral of a statue of her opposite the splendid tomb of Cardinal Beaufort who took part in her condemnation, and in the play by G. B. Shaw and the study by V. Sackville-West. Interpretations of her character, governed by authors' presuppositions, have made her a patriot, a lesbian feminist, or even the first Protestant. What seems certain from the story of her condemnation is that neither the Burgundians nor the French nor the English authorities can be considered guiltless, nor can the Church in so far as it provided a legal framework for a political murder. It is to the credit of the Holy See that it carried through the process of rehabilitation to its ultimate conclusion. Her military importance has sometimes been exaggerated: the English reverses were also due to war-weariness, lack of financial support, incompetent leadership, and natural hazards such as disease; but there can be no denying Joan's immense success in boosting the morale of her compatriots, from whom she certainly deserved a better fate. Nowadays she is France's second patron. Feast: 30 May.

P. Tisset and Y. Lanhers, *Procès de Jeanne d'Arc* (Société de l'Histoire de France, 3 vols., 1960–71); Eng. tr. of the trial documents by J. P. Barrett, *The Trial of Joan of Arc* (1931); P. Doncoeur and Y. Lanhers, *Documents et Recherches relatives à Jeanne la Pucelle* (5 vols., 1952–61); studies by J. B. J. Ayrolles (1890), P. H. Dunand (3 vols., 1898–9), A. Lang (1908), G. Goyau (1920), A. B. Paine (1925), V. Sackville-West (1936), R. Pernoud (1954; Eng. tr. 1961), M. Warner (1980).

JOAVAN (d. *c.*562), Irish monk and bishop. He became a monk at Landevenic (Brittany), the disciple of *Paul Aurelian, and came with him to Britain. Later he succeeded him as bishop in Brittany. Joavan was buried at Plougen, where his tomb has survived, but not his relics. At least two Breton churches are dedicated to him. Feast: 2 March.

Stanton, pp. 95–8, which cites Lobineau, *Saints de Bretagne*, i. 177 and a calendar of St. Paul's cathedral as sources for his cult.

JOGUES, Isaac (1607–46), Jesuit missionary and martyr in Canada. Born at Orléans, he became a Jesuit at Rouen in 1624, after which he was educated at La Flèche. In 1636 he was sent to Canada and preached the Gospel to the Mohawks, travelling as far as Lake Superior. In 1624 Jogues set out from Quebec on a mission of mercy to the Hurons, who were suffering from famine and disease. The expedition reached its destination, but on the return journey it was ambushed by the Iroquois, enemies of the Hurons. Jogues and his assistant were beaten with knotted sticks, had their hair, beards, and nails torn out and their fingers mutilated. Jogues remained a slave for some time, but managed to escape with Dutch help from Fort Orange. He then returned to France.

In 1644 he returned to Canada and worked near Montreal. He was sent on a peace mission to the Iroquois at Ossernenon (now Auriesville, NY), where he had been captured earlier. He left a box of religious objects behind him. This, however, was wrongly believed by the Indians to be the cause of crop failure and sickness which happened to ensue soon after. The Bear clan of the Mohawks invited him to a meal and killed him with tomahawks: they cut his head off and set it up on a pole. This took place on 18 October. His feast is kept with his friend Jean *Brébeuf and their companions on 19 October.

B.T.A., iii. 645–52; see also under BRÉBEUF, Jean.

JOHN THE APOSTLE (d. late 1st century). He was a son of Zebedee who with his brother *James and *Peter belonged to the small group of Apostles of Christ, who were privileged witnesses of special events such as the raising of Jairus' daughter and especially the Transfiguration and the Agony in the Garden. James and John were called by the Lord 'Boanerges' or 'sons of thunder'; their ardent temperament was revealed both in their wishing to call down fire from Heaven on the Samaritans who rejected Christ and in their willingness to drink of the cup of suffering as witnesses to the Lord. This was verified in the case of James by his early martyrdom and in that of John by his suffering (according to ecclesiastical tradition) under Domitian's persecution, from which, however, he escaped alive and ended his days at an advanced age at Ephesus.

The tradition that identifies John as the author of the Fourth Gospel goes back to the 2nd century. It is certain, thanks to the discovery of the Chester-Beatty fragment, that this Gospel was in writing in the early 2nd century or earlier. This fragment is far older than that of any extract from the synoptic gospels. Although the Johannine authorship has been much disputed over the last century or more, it is strongly supported by internal as well as external reasons. There seems no compelling reason for rejecting the identification of John with the beloved disciple of the Gospel who was a witness of the events he describes. But he wrote about them in a contemplative way, emphasizing the theological reality and presupposing in his readers a knowledge of Christ's life, portrayed by the synoptic gospels. Above all he clearly stressed the Divinity of Christ, who is both Light and Life, and the importance of Charity (*agape*) which is the bond between Father and Son and between Christ and his disciples, as well as between the disciples themselves. Traditionally he wrote his Gospel towards the end of his life at the end of the 1st century, including within it inspired meditation on the truths he had witnessed. In this case it would have been written after the three epistles also contained in the New Testament. The Revelation or Apocalypse, however, although also ascribed to him, is so different in thought, style, and content from the genuine Johannine writings that John's personal authorship of it in any normally accepted sense seems unlikely.

After the Resurrection John, who had taken the Blessed Virgin Mary, following Christ's words on the Cross, as his adopted mother, was prominent in the early Church. Not only was he among the earliest witnesses of the Risen Lord, but he also shared in the preaching, organization, and even imprisonment of Peter, towards whom he was subordinate. Later he settled at Ephesus. Various anecdotes are related of him there by Clement of Alexandria and others, such as his recorded fear that the baths at which the heretic Cerinthus was bathing would fall down because he was in them, or again his repeated exhortation to his followers to love one another, which, often repeated, caused them tedium, but which he emphasized because 'it is the word of the Lord and if you keep it, you do enough'.

Other traditions have had a more direct influence on artistic representations. These include a cup with a viper in it as his emblem, in memory of the challenge to him by a high priest of Diana at Ephesus to drink a poisoned cup. Another symbol is a book, while in evangelist portraits his emblem appropriately is an eagle. One hundred and eighty-one ancient churches and not a few modern ones are dedicated to him. He must have been a very familiar figure to medieval people through being represented on rood-screens, while the iconography of medieval apocalypses often include a series of pictures of his life. He is often represented in the West with *John the Baptist, as on the stole of *Cuthbert, embroidered at Winchester during the 9th century. A copy of the Gospel of John, written in uncials at Wearmouth–Jarrow in the 7th century and placed in *Cuthbert's tomb, is now in the British Library. John is patron of theologians, writers, and all who work at the production of books.

Feast: in the East, 26 September; in the West, 27 December and 6 May, the Dedication of the church of St. John before the Latin Gate, which also commemorates his legendary escape from being plunged into a cauldron of boiling oil under Domitian. But in early times there was some confusion in the date of his feast: in some places it was kept with that of St. James the Less, in others there seems to have been some confusion with St. John the Baptist; but the feast of 27 December is very ancient, appropriately close to Christmas Day. In England both feasts were kept almost universally in the Middle Ages.

F. M. Braun, *Jean le Théologien et son évangile dans l'Église ancienne* (1959), pp. 301–93; F. L. Cross (ed.), *Studies in the Fourth Gospel* (1957); id., 'St. John on Patmos', *New Testament Studies*, ix (1963), 75–85; recent studies of the fourth Gospel include those by C. H. Dodd (1953 and 1963), C. K. Barrett (1955), M. J. Lagrange (1924), R. H. Lightfoot (ed. C. F. Evans, 1956), E. Malatesta, *St. John's Gospel 1920–65;* a cumulative and classified bibliography (1967). See also B.T.A., ii 240–2 and iv. 620–3 and *Bibl. SS.*, vi. 757–97.

JOHN OF AVILA (1500–69), priest, writer, and mystic. Born at Almodovar-del-Campo (New Castile) of wealthy parents of Jewish extraction, he studied law at Salamanca, but then renounced it. He gave himself to prayer and penance at home for three years, and then studied philosophy and theology at Alcalà under Dominic de Soto for six years until 1526. Ordained in 1525, he gave away most of his inheritance to the poor and intended to join the missions in Mexico. The archbishop of Seville however persuaded him to re-evangelize Andalusia instead. This southernmost province had been ruled by the Moors and needed the Gospel message to be preached again. John won almost universal acclaim: the Inquisition however accused him in 1531–3 of teaching rigorism and the exclusion of the rich from heaven. These accusations were never proved: when John was released, he received strong popular support.

He was also highly esteemed by some of the most notable saints of the time. *Theresa of Avila chose him as her counsellor, Francis *Borgia and *John of God owed their conversions to him. John's writings, mainly letters and sermons, are substantial in quantity and notable for their spiritual depth. The most famous is *Audi filia*, a treatise on Christian perfection written in 1530 for Donna Sancha Carillo, who had renounced wealth and status to lead a life of prayer and solitude.

John suffered much illness in his last fifteen years. His admiration for Ignatius *Loyola inclined him to join the Jesuits, but he was dissuaded by the Provincial of Andalusia. He was, however, buried in the Jesuit church at Montilla. Long esteemed as a spiritual writer, he was canonized in 1970. Feast: 10 May.

Works ed. by L. Sala Balust (Biblioteca de Autores Cristianos, 2 vols., 1952–3; *Audi Filia* (Espirituales Espagnoles, 1963); Spiritual

Letters, ed. V. Garcia de Diego (Classicos Castellanos, 1912, Eng. tr. by a Benedictine of Stanbrook, 1904). Life by Luis of Granada, ed. L. Sala Balust (Espirituales Espagnoles 1964); other Lives by M. Ruiz (1618) and L. degli Oddi (1754). See also the specialist review *Maestro Avila* (Montilla, 1946–), *O.D.C.C.*, p. 745; B.T.A., ii. 268–9; *Bibl. SS.*, ii. 649–56.

JOHN I (d. 526), pope. Tuscan by birth, John joined the clergy of Rome and held the important office of archdeacon. Friend and confidant of *Boethius, in 523 he was chosen bishop of Rome in succession to Hormisdas in spite of advanced years and failing health. His short episcopate was mainly filled by the embassy which the Arian Emperor Theodoric the Goth compelled him to make to Byzantium. The object of this was to obtain toleration for the Arians in the East; if he failed, there would be reprisals against the orthodox Catholics in the West. John was received with immense enthusiasm and respect by the Greeks, but obtained only minor concessions from the Eastern Emperor. When he returned to Ravenna, then Theodoric's capital, he was imprisoned because Theodoric suspected him of betrayal and of siding with the Eastern Emperor against him. John died in prison shortly afterwards. He was responsible for introducing to the West the Alexandrian calculation of Easter. Feast: 18 May.

AA.SS. Maii VI (1688), 702–10; L. Duchesne, *Le Liber Pontificalis*, i. 276; *O.D.P.*, pp. 54–5.

JOHN THE BAPTIST (d. *c.*30), precursor of Jesus Christ. All that is certainly known about him comes from the Gospels. He was the son of Zachariah, a Temple priest, and his wife Elizabeth, who was a cousin of the Blessed Virgin *Mary. He was born when his mother was comparatively advanced in years, after the foretelling of his birth and the choice of his name by an angel. Nothing more is heard of him until he began his mission of preaching and baptizing in the river Jordan *c.*27. His way of life and style of preaching closely resembled those of some OT prophets: his diet was locusts and wild honey, his message one of repentance and preparation for the coming of the Messiah and his Kingdom. Among his disciples were the future apostles *Peter and *Andrew. He himself baptized Christ and recognized him as the Messiah when he saw the Spirit come down upon him. Later Christ praised him, saying that none among the sons of women had arisen who was greater than him.

John also denounced the incestuous union of Herod Antipas with his niece and brother's wife, Herodias, and was imprisoned for doing so. His death was brought about by the hatred of Herodias and the weakness of Herod. When Salome, her daughter, had greatly pleased the king with her dancing at his birthday feast, he promised she could have from him whatever she liked 'even if it is half my kingdom'. Instigated by her mother, she demanded the head of John the Baptist on a dish. Herod, without a trial of any kind, dispatched an executioner to John's prison (identified as Machaerus by the Dead Sea) and had his head presented to Salome, who passed it on to her mother.

John the Baptist was believed to have been buried at Sebaste (Samaria) where he was honoured in the 4th century, but the tomb was desecrated by Julian the Apostate. Various relics of the head of John the Baptist are claimed at Rome and elsewhere, but there seems little likelihood of any of them being authentic. His cult, however, is exceedingly ancient both in East and West: the Martyrology of *Jerome, the Calendar of Carthage, and the sermons of *Augustine all emphasize that his principal feast of 24 June is that of his earthly birthday, calculated from the Gospels as being six months before the birth of Christ (25 December = *octavo kalendas Januarii*, while 24 June = *octavo kalendas Julii*). This led to a belief that he was sanctified in the womb and never committed sin.

John the Baptist has always been held in high repute of the Monastic Order: by his solitary and austere life in the desert he was considered to have been a monk himself. His intercession was believed to lead to the coming of Christ within the souls of the devout, just as his work in history had been to prepare the Jews for his earthly coming.

In England, as elsewhere, John the Baptist was immensely popular in the Middle Ages: no fewer than 496 ancient churches were dedicated in his honour, a total exceeded only by SS. Mary, Peter, Michael, Andrew, and All Saints. Another of his many patronages was of the Knights Hospitallers, whose principal work was to guard the Holy Sepulchre at Jerusalem and protect pilgrims to and from the Holy Land. Several of their round churches survive in England.

In art John is represented both as prophet and baptizer: his association with Baptism especially made him familiar to the medieval laity. His image could also be frequently seen on wall-paintings, stained-glass windows, bench-ends, and statues, dressed in skins and pointing to the lamb (or *Agnus Dei*) lying on a book; he also carries a long cross in his other hand. Sometimes the Gospel text was interpreted as meaning that he was dressed in the entire skin of a camel. This may have had its origins in medieval drama and it seems especially popular in York representations of the 14th–15th centuries (examples in stained glass both in the Minster and the parish churches). Other notable examples include the paintings in the Byward Tower of the Tower of London, at Chalgrove (Oxon.), Piccott's End (Herts.), Cerne Abbas (Dorset), Idsworth (Hants), and Trimingham and Horsham (Norfolk). Also in the 15th century alabaster heads of John the Baptist were manufactured in quantity at and near Nottingham.

Various attempts to link the historical John the Baptist with either the Mandeans (a Gnostic sect tinged with Manichaeism) or with the Essenes (Jewish ascetics of the 1st–2nd century) are most implausible. Feast: in the East, Conception, 23 September, John as baptizer, 7 January, birthday (as in the West), 24 June, and day of his death (as in the West), 29 August.

Luke 1, John 1; Matthew 14, Mark 1 and 6: 14–29; for his influence at Ephesus see Acts 19: 1–7. *AA.SS.* Iun. IV (1707), 698–705 with *C.M.H.*, s.d. 24 June and 29 August; D. Buzy, *The Life of St. John the Baptist* (1947), C. H. Kraeling, *John the Baptist* (1951); C. H. H. Scobie, *John the Baptist* (1964): J. Daniélou, *Jean-Baptiste témoin de l'Agneau* (1964); W. Wink, *John the Baptist in the Gospel Tradition* (1968), A. Schuster, *The Sacramentary*, iv. 265–71; *Lexicon der Christlichen Ikonographie*, s.v.; G. McN. Rushforth, *Medieval Christian Imagery* (1936), 234–5.

JOHN-BAPTIST DE LA SALLE, see La Salle.

JOHN OF BEVERLEY (d. 721), bishop of York. Born at Harpham (Humberside), he studied at Canterbury under *Adrian; on returning to Yorkshire he became a monk at *Hilda's double monastery of Whitby. In 687 he was consecrated bishop of Hexham in succession to *Eata. He was reputed to have shown special care for the poor and the handicapped, including one young man whom he taught to speak. He also used to retire to a hermitage for periods of prayer; it was he who ordained *Bede both deacon and priest.

On the death of *Bosa in 705, John became bishop of York. At the same time, *Wilfrid, now an old man, succeeded him at Hexham as part of the final settlement of his prolonged dispute with Northumbrian kings. John, however, never incurred the enmity of Wilfrid or his followers. As bishop of York he founded the monastery of Beverley, then in a forest. He retired there in 717, about four years before his death there on 7 May.

Both Bede and Alcuin recorded his miracles. King Athelstan (d. 939) invoked his intercession for victory against the Scots. Early calendars record his feast. In 1307 his relics were translated; this was the occasion for a Life by Folcard. Other devotees include the anchoress Julian of Norwich, King Henry V, who ascribed the victory of Agincourt on his translation feast to his intercession, and John *Fisher, who was born at Beverley. Some of the relics were discovered in 1664. Feast: 7 May; translation, 25 October.

Bede, *H.E.*, v. 2–6; *AA.SS.*, Maii II (1680), 166–94; *N.L.A.*, ii. 59–63; J. Raine (ed.), *Historians of the Church of York* (*R.S.*), i. 239–91.

JOHN OF BRIDLINGTON (d. 1379), Austin Canon. Born at Thwing near Bridlington, he studied at Oxford University and became a canon at St. Augustine's monastery, Bridlington. Eventually he was in turn precentor, cellarer, and lastly prior (1362). In an age when monastic slackness was fairly widespread, John gave an example of complete fidelity in small things as well as great. Some of his words have been preserved, among them a special recommendation to study the Fourth Gospel. As superior he was prudent, wise, and greatly loved: he united a fervent life of prayer with the practical duties of his office with exceptional success. Miracles were reported at his tomb; after the usual inquiries he was canonized by Boniface IX in 1401. Richard Scrope, archbishop of York, translated his relics on 11 March 1404. The English success at the battle of Agincourt was attributed by Henry V to the intercession of the two Yorkshire saints, *John of Beverley and John of Bridlington. There is a 15th-century stained-glass window of him in Morley (Derbyshire). Feast: 21 October.

AA.SS. Oct. V (1868), 135–44; *N.L.A.*, ii. 64–78 (near contemporary but verbose and empty production ascribed to George Riplay); J. S. Purvis, *St. John of Bridlington* (1924); P. Grosjean, 'De S. Iohanne Bridlingtoniensi collectanea', *Anal. Boll.*, liii (1935), 101–29.

JOHN OF CAPISTRANO (1386–1456), Franciscan preacher. Born at Capistrano in the Abruzzi, he studied law at Perugia with conspicuous success, married, and became governor of Perugia in 1412. He was separated from his wife, presumably by mutual consent, and became a Franciscan at the age of thirty. He was ordained priest in 1420 and combined extreme austerity of life with unremitting effort in studying theology under *Bernardino of Siena. He then became a successful preacher in Italy, attracting huge crowds and using the same techniques as Bernardino. He also worked hard at the reform and reorganization of the Franciscan Observant friars and of the nuns who were inspired by *Colette.

Papal confidence in him was shown by his appointment as inquisitor-general to Vienna in 1451. Here his presence was greeted with immense enthusiasm, but his zeal against the Hussites was criticized by later historians. Contemporaries, however, claimed that he worked frequent miracles and described him as a small man, withered and emaciated, who was cheerful, strong, and strenuous.

The Fall of Constantinople in 1453 led to his being called on by Pius II to preach a new crusade against the Turks. This met with little support from Bavaria and Austria, but Hungary, faced by a direct threat of a Turkish army to Belgrade, responded generously. The exhortations of John and the military skill of the Hungarian general, Hunyady, resulted in a complete victory for their army at Belgrade. But the neglect of unburied corpses around the city caused the deaths of both through disease in the same year. He was canonized in 1724. Feast: 23 October (formerly 28 March).

AA.SS. Oct. X (1861), 269–552, 915–16; J. Hofer, *St. John Capistran, Reformer* (1943); B.T.A., i. 692–5; *Bibl. SS.*, vi. 646–54.

JOHN CASSIAN, see CASSIAN.

JOHN CHRYSOSTOM (347–407), archbishop of Constantinople. Born the son of an army officer at Antioch, John was brought up by his widowed mother and received the best education which Antioch could offer, both in oratory and law. From *c.*373 he became a monk in a mountain community not far from the city and nearly ruined his health through austerities and the damp conditions of his cave hermitage. He returned to Antioch in 381, was ordained deacon, and served the local church until his ordination as priest in 386. He then became the bishop's special assistant, particularly for the temporal care and the spiritual instruction of the numerous Christian poor of the city. He soon became famous as a preacher and commentator on the Epistles of Paul and the Gospels of Matthew and John. He insisted in the Antiochene tradition on the literal meaning of Scripture and its practical application to the problems of the time. Hence much of his work has relevance today also.

He obtained political fame too in his twenty-one sermons on 'The Statues' (387): these had been broken in a riot against the emperor's taxes, and they represented the Emperor Theodosius himself and his father, sons, and dead wife. Reprisals were expected, but an amnesty was obtained by the aged bishop Flavian; Chrysostom's sermons also were important in furthering the cause of peace and understanding.

In 397 after the death of the archbishop of Constantinople, Emperor Arcadius wished John Chrysostom to be chosen in his place and sent an envoy to detach him from Antioch, secretly for fear of popular opposition. Theophilus, archbishop of Alexandria (uncle of the future *Cyril of Alexandria), a disappointed rival, consecrated him in 398. At once he started to reform the corrupt morals of court, clergy, and people. He reduced the customary spending of his own household in favour of the poor and the hospitals. He enacted severe discipline for the clergy; this and his attacks on the Jews have been rightly criticized. He also attacked the behaviour, the clothes, and the make-up of the women at court and those Christians who had been to the races on Good Friday and to the games in the stadium on Holy Saturday. The Empress Eudoxia regarded his drive for moral reform as a personal attack on herself: matters were not improved when a silver statue of her was set up outside his cathedral of Santa Sophia and dedicated with public games, an occasion for superstition and immorality. Meanwhile Theophilus made common cause with the empress and organized a cabal of bishops which assembled at Chalcedon, condemned Chrysostom unheard on a series of more or less false charges, accused him also of treason for calling Eudoxia 'Jezebel', and asked for his banishment. Chrystostom was exiled, but an earthquake in Constantinople terrified Eudoxia and he was recalled. He resumed his plain speaking which again enraged her; Theophilus intrigued against him with appeals to an Arian council of Antioch, and Chrysostom was again banished, this time for resuming the duties of a see from which he had been 'lawfully deposed'. This took place in 404; although his own people, the pope, and many western bishops supported him, he was exiled, first to Cucusus in Armenia and then to Pontus where he was killed by enforced travel in bad weather, on foot and in spite of repeated pleas of exhaustion. The date of his death was 14 September.

Thirty-one years later his body was taken back to Constantinople and reburied in the church of the Apostles. In the West he is invoked as one of the Four Greek Doctors (with *Athanasius, *Basil, and *Gregory of Nazianzus), in the East as one of the Three Holy Hierarchs and Universal Teachers. The exegetical works and the treatise on the Priesthood are his most famous: the establishment of the 'Liturgy of St. Chrysostom' is most probably not due to him; its general use is caused by the influence of Constantinople and its present form is much more recent than his time. Feast: in the West, 13 September (formally 27 January, the day of his translation to Constantinople); in the East, 13 November.

AA.SS. Sept. IV (1753), 401–709; Life by Palladius also in critical edn. by P. R. Coleman-Norton (1928); see also Socrates, *H.E.*, vi. 2–23 and vii. 25–45, Sozomen, *H.E.*, viii. 2–28. Modern Lives by A. Moulard (1941), D. Attwater (1959), and especially C. Baur (2 vols., 1929–30, Eng. tr. 1959–60); see also B. H. Vandenberghe, *Saint Jean Chrysostome et la parole de Dieu* (1961). Works in *P.G.*, xlvii–lxiv, in *S.C.* (1966–); Eng. tr. in N.P.N.C.F., first series ix–xiv. See also J. D'Alton, *Selections from St. John Chrysostom* (1940); F. Halkin, *Douze récits byzantins sur S. Jean Chrysostome* (1977).

JOHN CLIMACUS (d. 649), monk and abbot of Mount Sinai. A native of Palestine, he was married in early life and became a monk on the death of his wife. After some years in community, John became a hermit for the greater part of his life, living at Thole like the Egyptian monks, coming with other solitaries to church on Saturday and Sunday, but spending the rest of the week in almost complete solitude. There he wrote the work which gave him his name 'Climacus' (= ladder), usually called *The Ladder to Paradise.* This influential treatise of monastic spirituality deals with vices and virtues, community and eremitical life, and the pursuit of *apatheia* (passive disinterestedness) which was regarded as a perfect state. At the age of seventy he was chosen as abbot of Sinai and ruled for four years before retiring to his hermitage. He died at the age of about eighty. His concept of the spiritual life as a ladder inspired artists to develop interesting pictorial conventions as illustrations, while his own emblem is also a ladder. Feast: 30 March.

AA.SS. Mar. III (1668), 834–7; works in *P.G.*, lxxxviii. 585–1248 (Eng. tr. by L. Moore, *The Ladder of Divine Ascent*, 1959); W. Volker, *Scala Paradisi* (1968); J. R. Martin, *The Illustration of the Heavenly Ladder of John Climacus* (1954); B.T.A., i. 703–4 and L. Petit in *D.T.C.*, vii. 690–2.

JOHN DAMASCENE (John of Damascus) (*c.*657–*c.*749), monk and theologian. His whole life was spent under Muslim rule: his father, a wealthy Damascus Christian, held the office of chief of the revenue and was also the principal representative of the Christians in his city. Already John had been extremely well educated by Cosmas, a Sicilian monk skilled in both science and theology, for whose liberation John's father paid a large sum of money. John succeeded him, but in 716 became a monk and later a priest at the abbey of St. Sabas, near Jerusalem. John was soon very busy as a writer both of hymns and of theological works. The most important of these is called 'The Fount of Wisdom', which deals in turn with philosophy, heresy, and the orthodox faith. The last part, called *De Fide Orthodoxa*, had immense influence for centuries in the East and the West; it is a summary of the teaching of the Greek Fathers on the principal mysteries of the Christian faith, such as the Trinity and the Incarnation (including notable elements on the Blessed Virgin such as the Assumption and her preservation from all sin) and the Real Presence in the Eucharist. He also wrote three important and topical tracts against the iconoclasts. These brought him the extreme displeasure of the iconoclastic Christian emperors, who were unable to proceed against him because he resided in Muslim territory. An almost exact contemporary of *Bede, and like him both a monk and an assiduous writer, John Damascene was declared a Doctor of the Church in 1890 (or just nine years earlier than this title was granted to Bede). Feast: 4 December (formerly in the West, 27 March).

Works in *P.G.*, xciv–xcvi and critical edn. by B. Kotter in *Patristische Texte und Studien*, 1969 ff.; Eng. tr. of *De Fide Orthodoxa* by S. D. F. Salmond (N.P.N.C.F., 1899); M. Jugie, 'La Vie de S. Jean Damascène', *E.O.*, xxiii (1924), 137–61 and 'Une nouvelle Vie et un nouvel écrit de saint John Damascène', ibid., xxviii (1929), 35–41; modern Lives by J. H. Lupton (1883) and J. Nasrallah (1950); B.T.A., i. 689–91; *Bibl. SS.*, vi. 732–40.

JOHN FISHER, see FISHER.

JOHN GUALBERT (*c.*995–1073), founder and abbot of the Vallombrosian monks. Although he was a member of the noble Florentine Visdomini family, only one detail of his early life is known. This was an unexpected meeting with his brother's murderer one Good Friday. Custom required that John should kill him in revenge, but the defenceless murderer asked for pardon and crossed his arms. Faithful to Christ's teaching, John forgave his enemy and spared his life. Soon afterwards he became a monk at San Miniato, Florence.

Several years later after a disputed abbatial election John left this monastery with one companion in search of a more austere and contemplative life, untouched by current abuses in the Church. These included clerical concubinage, nepotism, and simony, of which last the archbishop of Florence was a notorious example. John visited *Romuald's monastery at Camaldoli, but set up his own at Vallombrosa, about twenty miles east of Florence. Here silence, poverty, and enclosure safeguarded the observance of St. Benedict's rule. On ground donated by a local abbess they built a small monastery of wood. To prevent the choir monks being overburdened with manual work, John instituted lay-brothers: a concept developed with notable success by the Cistercians a century later.

Vallombrosa provided inspiration also for other communities with hospices for the poor and the sick: these became part of his new Order under his rule, in spite of rival claims to jurisdiction. In this and other ways John became involved in current reform movements in the Church, for which he was commended by popes *Leo IX and Alexander II.

John never became a priest. He had a reputation for prophecy, healing, and feeding the hungry poor even by miracle. He died at the age of about eighty and his Order expanded considerably in the Middle Ages. Like the Carthusians of *Bruno, it was reduced considerably in numbers in later centuries, but still survives today. John was canonized in 1193. A fine altarpiece in Santa Croce, Florence, depicts four scenes from his life. Feast: 12 July.

AA.SS. Iul. III (1723), 343–82 contains early Lives: modern ones by E. Lucchesi (1959) and A. Salvini (1961). See also A. Wilmart, 'Le manuel des prières de saint Jean Gualbert', *Rev. Bén.* xlviii (1936), 259–99 and R. Duvernay, 'Cîteaux, Vallombrose et Étienne Harding', *Anal. S.O. Cist.* viii (1952), 379–495; *Bibl. SS.*, vi. 1012–29.

JOHN OF GOD (1495–1550), founder of the Brothers Hospitallers. Born at Monte Mor il nuovo (Portugal), he joined the mercenaries of the Count of Oroprusa (Castile) in 1522 and fought for Spain against the French and the Turks, notably in Hungary. In the army he gave up all practice of religion. On the disbandment of his troop, he went to Andalusia and worked as a shepherd. At the age of about forty, he was converted to a life of dedication to the service of God in compassion to the poor extending, he thought, to martyrdom in North Africa through helping Christian slaves. He was strongly advised against this. In Gibraltar he became a pedlar who sold sacred books and pictures so successfully that he opened a shop in Granada in 1538. He then suffered a period of apparent madness, running aimlessly through the streets, tearing his hair, and giving away his stock of books. *John of Avila, a famous visiting preacher, calmed him and persuaded him to devote his energies in future to the care of the sick and the poor.

He left hospital in 1539, rented a house in Granada and filled it with sick poor people. Both his efficiency and his devotion astonished the townsfolk; the bishop gave him a religious habit. For over ten years he worked with the utmost devotion for the physical and spiritual well-being of his patients. His ceaseless energy was balanced by prayer and austerity. His final illness was brought on through rescuing a drowning man in a flood; he died before the altar of his hospital chapel at the age of fifty-five. After his death rules were drawn up for his followers, who took vows and became a Religious Order, which claimed him as their founder. He is patron of hospitals and the sick, but also of booksellers and printers. Feast: 8 March.

AA.SS. Mar. I (1668), 814–60; modern Lives by I. M. Mangnin (1931, Eng. tr. 1936) and N. McMahon (1952); B.T.A., i. 517–20; *Bibl. SS.*, vi. 740–8.

JOHN OF KANTI (1390–1473), priest. Born at Kanti, near Oswiecim (Poland), of a fairly affluent country family, he was educated at the University of Cracow. He was ordained priest soon after completing his course and was appointed lecturer. He was notably successful as both teacher and preacher, but for some reason he was removed from his post and appointed to the parish of Olkusz. Although single-minded and energetic, he was not altogether successful and he was recalled to the Chair of Theology at Cracow after a few years.

He became famous not only for his academic excellence, but also for his own extreme poverty and austerity, as well as for his almsgiving. He told his students to fight all false opinions, but to do so with moderation and courtesy. He was held in such high esteem that his gown was used, on degree days, to vest each new doctor of the University. He died on 24 December at the age of eighty-three. He was canonized in 1767. Feast: 23 December (formerly 20 October).

AA.SS. Oct. VIII (1853), 1042–73; A. Arndt, 'De loco et anno nativitatis . . . S. Iohannis Kant', *Anal. Boll.*, viii (1889), 382–8; *Propylaeum*, pp. 464–5; B.T.A., iv. 154–5; *Bibl. SS.*, vi. 644–5.

JOHN OF NEPOMUK (Nepomucen) (*c.*1345–93), priest and martyr. Born at Pomuk (Nepomuk) in Bohemia, John Wolflin was educated at Prague University, was ordained priest, and after many years of ministry became vicar-general of the bishop of Prague, John of Genzenstein. The latter became involved with a long and bitter struggle against Wenceslas IV, king of Bohemia, over ecclesiastical rights and over property.

In 1393 Wenceslas, in order to reward a favourite with a new bishopric, planned to confiscate the abbey of Kladruby as soon as its aged abbot died. In order to frustrate this plan, John Nepomuk and the monks colluded to appoint a new abbot so quickly that news of the old abbot's death and the election of his successor reached the king simultaneously. He was so furious that he is said to have attacked the dean with his sword-hilt and the vicar-general by setting his clothes alight. John was nearly burnt to death; but he was then tied to a wheel and thrown into the river Moldau. The drowned body was recognized next day: it was translated into St. *Vitus's cathedral, Prague, where it still rests.

John's cult flourished as a patron of Bohemia and a counterpart to the memory of John Hus. He was also later regarded as a martyr for the seal of confession because of an unlikely story that he incurred the king's anger for refusing to reveal the contents of the queen's confession. This and some other details of his life-story have been long disputed. He was canonized in 1729. Feast (for local churches): 16 May.

AA.SS. Maii III (1680), 668–80; P. de Vooght, 'Jean de Pomuk', *R.H.E.*, xlviii (1953), 777–95, and 'S. Jean Nepomucène: un problème d'Hagiographie' in *Ami du Clergé*, lxxii (1962), 735–6; Lives by W. A. Frind (1929) and J. Weisskopf (1931); see also B.T.A., ii. 332–3; *Bibl. SS.*, vi. 847–55.

JOHN OF THE CROSS (1542–91), Carmelite friar and virtual founder of the Discalced Carmelite friars. He was also one of Spain's foremost poets, mystics, and mystical theologians. Born of a noble but impoverished Toledan family, Juan de Yepes was brought up by his widowed mother, went to a poor-school at Medina del Campo, and was apprenticed to a silk-weaver. But he showed no aptitude for this trade, went to a Jesuit college, and joined the Carmelite Order in 1563; he studied theology at Salamanca and was ordained priest in 1567. At this time he thought of becoming a monk of the Carthusian Order, then flourishing. Instead he was persuaded by *Theresa of Avila to join the Discalced Reform, which she had initiated for the nuns and which she had been authorized to make available for two houses of friars. One of these was the poverty-stricken house of Duruelo, where John began the reformed way of life. In 1571 he became rector of Alcala, a study house attached to the University, and from 1572 to 1577 confessor to the nuns of Avila, the mother-house of Theresa's reform.

But in 1575 he had been seized and imprisoned by the Calced Carmelite friars following a General Chapter in Piacenza, which both rejected the reform and refused to give its houses independence. The place of his confinement was Toledo, its conditions appalling, yet it was there that he wrote some of his finest poetry. He escaped after nine months; a little later the Discalced were separated from the Calced and in 1579 John founded a college at Baeza and was rector for three years. Prior at Granada from 1582 (the year of

Theresa's death) and at Segovia from 1588, he suffered at the end of his life harsh treatment from Nicholas Doria, the Discalced Carmelites' vicar-general. He was deprived of his offices and banished to Ubeda, in the province of Andalusia, where he died in 1591. This bare recital of the external events of John's life gives no idea of the warmth of this wonderful mystic, so much admired by his disciples and by Theresa, yet also the victim of jealousy and power-politics in a religious order during one of the most repressive periods of the Church's history.

A man of very small physical stature, John, as poet and mystic, is among the giants. What was rare about him was the combination of deep poetic sensitivity and articulateness with the rigorous thought-training of Thomist philosophy and theology. Written as commentaries on his poems, his spiritual works stress the need for active asceticism as well as the far deeper purification of the soul by divine grace and by the unsought humiliations of external agents. Through a life of pure faith and love of God, the soul eventually attains the deepest mystical union. John's writings are theologically substantial and that is why he is regarded not only as a mystic but also as a supreme Doctor of Mystical Theology. He was beatified in 1675, canonized in 1726, and declared a Doctor of the Church in 1926. The cult of John was not confined to his own Order, whose persecution reflects little credit on either branch of it, but has spread not only throughout the R.C. Church but also wherever the contemplative life is valued. Feast: 14 December (formerly 24 November).

Lives by Bruno de Jésus-Marie, *Saint Jean de la Croix* (1929, revised 1961; Eng. tr. 1932) and Crisogono de Jesus (revised by Matias del Nino Jesus, 1964); E. A. Peers, *Handbook to the Life and Times of St. Theresa and St. John of the Cross* (1954); A Benedictine of Stanbrook, *The Mediaeval Mystical Tradition and St. John of the Cross* (1954); E. A. Peers, *Studies of the Spanish Mystics* (2nd edn. 1951), pp 227–88. Works of St. John of the Cross, ed. Silverio de Santa Teresa (1929–31) and Luciano del SS. Sacramento (1946); English translations by E. A. Peers (3 vols., revised edn. 1953) and K. Kavanaugh and O. Rodriguez (1966). Poems translated by Roy Campbell (1951). See also J. Baruzi, *Saint Jean de la Croix et le problème de l'expérience mystique* (2nd edn. 1931) and E. W. T. Dicken, *The Crucible of Love* (1963).

JOHN THE ALMSGIVER (*c.*620), patriarch of Alexandria. Born at Amathus (Old Limassol) in Cyprus, of a noble and wealthy family, he married and fathered several children. But all of them died young, as did his wife; at the age of over fifty he was chosen as patriarch of Alexandria by his adopted brother Nicetas, who had helped the Emperor Heraclius to come to power. Two near-contemporary Lives were written to demonstrate the power of almsgiving by which, rather than by theological refutation, John came to attract the believers back to orthodoxy away from the currently dominant Monophysitism. Both the wealth of the see of Alexandria and John's generosity seem almost incredible.

His own living standards were extremely simple and he was known to give away his own bedding to the poor. These he called his 'masters'; they numbered 7,500 in his city; he showed his interest in them by ordering the use of just weights and measures, by forbidding his officials to take presents, and by sitting in the open in front of the church on Wednesdays and Fridays to ensure that everyone had free access to him.

On becoming patriarch, he distributed 80,000 pieces of gold in his church treasury to hospitals and monasteries. He also founded new ones as well as poor-houses and hostels for strangers and seven maternity hospitals of forty beds each. Although not a monk himself, he came to respect them and founded two new monasteries in his city. When the Persians under Chosroes sacked Jerusalem, he came to the rescue by providing large sums of money, plenty of wine, corn, oil, and clothes, besides many beasts of burden for transporting these goods to where they were most needed. He also spent immense sums rescuing captives, especially nuns. Nor were the refugees who poured into Egypt from Jerusalem forgotten. His almsgiving in fact was both individual and collective: some was directed to specific Christian purposes, at other times all benefited, whatever their creed or race.

Individuals he helped included a merchant twice ruined by shipwreck, whom John provided with a ship full of corn which was sold at great advantage during a famine in the British Isles. Sometimes he was deceived by impostors who kept on asking for alms in disguise when he had already helped them generously: even when he knew he was imposed on, he still gave again and again. Once a young monk begged alms for several days, accompanied by an attractive young woman; as a result of the consequent scandal John had the woman beaten and separated from the monk, who was scourged and placed in solitary confinement. That night John dreamt that he saw the monk who told him that for once he had made a mistake. He called for the monk who was so badly lacerated and injured that he could scarcely walk; he told John that he was a eunuch and that the young woman was a Jewess who wished to become a Christian. John apologized for his mistake, offered the monk 100 *numismata* (which he refused), and gave him an admonition saying it was not right for those who are clad in angelic robes to wander about unguardedly in cities and, above all, they should not take women round with them to the scandal of the beholders. Thenceforth John showed special honour and hospitality to monks and built them a hostel for their exclusive use called The Monks' Inn.

John was not exclusively concerned with almsgiving: he also gave much thought and care to the Liturgy. When some of the congregation developed a habit of leaving the church after the Gospel to chatter instead of praying, he several times left the church too and joined them, saying: 'Where the sheep are, there also the shepherd must be. Come inside and I will come in; stay here and I will stay too.' They soon reformed their conduct. He also forbade meeting in the sanctuary, saying: 'If you come here to pray, occupy your mind and heart with that, but if you come merely to meet someone, remember it is written that the house of God shall be called a house of prayer; do not turn it into a den of thieves.' He also insisted that believers should never under any circumstances take Holy Communion with heretics. 'Communion', he said, 'is so called because he who has communion has things in common and agrees with those with whom he has communion; therefore I implore you never to go near the oratories of heretics in order to communicate there.'

Nicetas persuaded John to visit Emperor Heraclius with him at Constantinople when the Persians were near in 619. But at Rhodes John realized that death was approaching and sailed back to Cyprus, where he died at his birthplace Amathus. His body was long kept at Constantinople, but a Turkish sultan presented it to King Matthias of Hungary. In 1530 it was translated to Tall, near Bratislava, and in 1632 to Bratislava, which still claims it. John was the special patron of the Knights of Malta. Feast in the East: 11 November, but in the Roman Martyrology 23 January (translation feast).

Two near-contemporary Lives, one by John Moschus and Sophronius, the other by Leontius of Cyprus, were early conflated into a single text, ed. H. Delehaye, 'Une vie inédite de Saint Jean l'aumonier', *Anal. Boll.*, xlv (1927), 5–74 and 'Les saints de Chypre', ibid., xxvi (1907), 161–301; English tr. in E. Dawes and N. H. Baynes, *Three Byzantine Saints* (1948), pp. 195–270; *AA.SS.* Ian. II (1643), 495–535; *Propylaeum*, pp. 32–3; B.T.A., i. 153–5.

JOHN THE DWARF (5th century), hermit. When young he went to the Egyptian desert of Skete to become a hermit. He believed that monastic perfection consists in keeping to the cell and having God continually present in his mind. Indifferent to 'news' and phenomenally absent-minded, he seems to have had no idea of time. He was highly reputed by his fellow monks and helped to train the great Arsenius, a former courtier who became a monk, by treating him with near-contempt. The story that John, when a novice, watered a dead stick every day under obedience until it brought forth fruit in the third year is very likely a story invented in monastic circles to illustrate the principle of obedience. His last words are said to have been: 'I never followed my own will, nor did I ever teach another what I had not practised first myself.' He fled in the Berber invasions across the Nile and died in the place hallowed by *Antony. Feast: 17 October.

AA.SS. Oct. VIII (1853), 31–48; *Apothegmata Patrum* in *P.G.*, lxv. 125–8; B.T.A., iv. 138–9; *Bibl. SS.*, vi. 666–9.

JOHN THE SAGE, mentioned in *R.P.S.* (11th century) as resting at Malmesbury with Maedub and *Aldhelm. He should probably be identified with the John whose tomb William of Malmesbury described and whose epitaph he transcribed. He believed that this was John Scotus Erigena, the Irish philosopher of the 9th century, and that he was killed by the pens of his students after settling at Malmesbury. It seems certain that this is due to confusion with another John and that the manner of John's death is borrowed from the Acts of St. Cassian of Imola. Feast: (at Malmesbury), 28 January.

William of Malmesbury, *G.P.*, pp. 393–4; *E.B.K. after 1100*, pp. 75–6, *R.P.S.*; for John Scotus Erigena see *O.D.C.C.*, s.v.

JOHN AND PAUL, Roman martyrs of the 4th century. Although their cult is both early and well established in all the Roman sacramentaries, their identity is much disputed. Their worthless Acts are entirely borrowed from those of other martyrs. The fine church dedicated to them in Rome is the *titulus Pammachii*, to which the relics of these saints, supposedly brothers, were brought. It is not even certain that they were Roman by birth or that they suffered at Rome. But hypotheses about their really being identical with the Apostles or with John the Baptist are even less likely. Little can be known about them with certainty. William of Malmesbury and other English writers mention their church in the guide to Rome, and the Council of Oxford in 1222 made their feast a day when the faithful should attend Mass before going to work. Their feast is recorded both in the Martyrology of *Bede and in the Sarum calendar. The popularity of their Acts must have helped the diffusion of their cult. These make them brothers and soldiers of the Emperor Constantine, who on a campaign against the Scythians in Thrace assured their commander Gallicanus of victory if he became a Christian. Angels obligingly then put the enemy to flight. Later Julian the Apostate summoned them to court but they refused to obey. They were given ten days' grace and were then executed in their own house on the Celian Hill and their bodies buried in the garden. Several internal implausibilities make the whole tale highly suspect and it seems better to conclude that all details of their life have been irretrievably lost. A fine church dedicated to them in Venice is the burial-place of several of the Doges. Feast: formerly 26 June, suppressed in the Roman calendar of 1969.

AA.SS. Iun. V (1709), 158–63 with *C.M.H.*, pp. 336–7; H. Delehaye, *The Legends of the Saints* (1962), pp. 178–9; B.T.A., ii. 645–6.

JONES, John (Buckley) (1559–98), Franciscan priest and martyr. Born at Clynog Fawr (Caernarvonshire), he joined the Franciscan Order at Pontoise (France) *c.*1590, presumably as a priest. He was professed in Rome at the Ara Coeli church in 1591 and returned to England to work in and near London the following year. He became closely associated with Henry Garnet, S.J. In 1597 he was arrested and kept in prison for a year, pending the collection of evidence. The charge was that as a priest ordained abroad he had returned to minister in England. He was found guilty on his own admission and was executed on 12 July at St. Thomas Waterings on the Old Kent Road, Southwark. During an hour's delay on the scaffold because the executioner had forgotten his rope, Jones asserted that he had never entertained even the thought of treason. He was canonized by Paul VI in 1970 as one of the *Forty Martyrs of England and Wales. Feast: 25 October.

R. Challoner, *Memoirs of Missionary Priests* (ed. J. H. Pollen, 1924), pp. 234–9; *Catholic Record Society Publications*, v. 362–75; J. E. Paul, *Blessed John Jones* (pamphlet, 1960).

JOSAPHAT (1580–1623), archbishop and martyr. Born at Vladimir of a wealthy merchant family, he was educated locally and was apprenticed to a merchant in Vilna. In 1604 he became a monk there and was soon ordained priest. He was famous as a popular preacher in the cause of extending the union with Rome of the province of Kiev, which had taken place in 1595. In 1614 he became abbot of Vilna; soon afterwards he took part in an abortive attempt to reform the large but relaxed monastery of The Caves at Kiev.

In 1617 he became archbishop of Polotsk. In a few years he had reduced the ecclesiastical power of local landowners, had held synods and published catechisms, and distinguished himself by his tireless pastoral activity. But in 1620 a rival hierarchy was set up and Josaphat had the added problem of widespread schism to contend with. In the complex situation of conflicting interests, affected by nationalism, long-standing custom, and Eastern dislike of Rome, Josaphat stood firm as the proponent of union with Rome, but at the same time maintained the right of Byzantine clergy, with their local customs, to equal consideration with those of Rome. Tragically suffering misrepresentation by both sides, Josaphat was eventually the victim of a murder-plot, instigated by the violent and uncontrolled supporters of his rival to the see of Polotsk. He clearly foresaw his own death through violence; in response to his plea that his servants should not suffer, he was stunned by a halberd and shot. He was canonized in 1867 and could well be considered as a patron, in spite of different historical circumstances, of ecumenical endeavour today. Feast: 12 (formerly 14) November.

Propylaeum, pp. 516–17; A. Guépin, *Un apôtre de l'union des Églises au xviie siècle: Saint Josaphat* (2 vols., 1898); B.T.A., iv. 337–40; *Bibl. SS.*, vi. 545–8.

JOSEPH, foster-father of Christ and husband of the Blessed Virgin *Mary, died in the 1st century. All that is known of him for certain is contained in the Gospels: Matt. 1–2 and 13: 55; Luke 1–2 and 4: 22. He was of Davidic descent, but his trade of carpenter shows that he was impoverished. He was betrothed to Mary at the time of the Virgin Birth: his doubts about her conception, the decisions to go to, and return from, Egypt were all the objects of angelic admonitions in sleep. It can be said that broadly Matt. 1–2 represents Joseph's point of view and Luke 1–2 that of the BVM concerning the events connected with the birth of the Lord.

The apocryphal Protevangelium of James makes him an old man at the time of his betrothal to Mary, but the duties implied in the protection of the Holy Family and in the upbringing of Jesus Christ make this unlikely. A Greek document called the *History of Joseph the Carpenter* (5th–6th century) was influential in creating a liturgical cult of Joseph, which probably originated in the East but reached its full development in the West much later. Martyrology entries date from the 8th century (Rheinau) and the slightly later Irish martyrologies of *Oengus and of Tallacht, but the feast of Joseph was celebrated in England before 1100 at Winchester, Worcester, Ely, and other centres. It seems that insular devotion long preceded any general cult of Joseph, although later medieval saints such as *Vincent Ferrer, *Bridget of Sweden, and *Bernardino of Siena all propagated his devotion, partly in reaction against medieval mystery plays, in which he is a channel for comic relief. Carmelite breviaries of 1480 onwards give his feast, as does the Roman breviary of 1482 and the Roman Missal of 1505. But the diffusion and popularity of his feast at a high rank in the Roman Church was due in great part to *Theresa of Avila, who dedicated the mother-house of her reformed Carmelite convents at Avila to the saint and frequently recommended devotion to him in her writings. *Ignatius of Loyola also propagated his cult. Gregory XV made his feast a Holiday of Obligation, but this is not widely observed today. In 1714 Clement XI composed a new office for his feast; in 1870 he was declared 'Patron of the Universal Church' by Pius IX who also encouraged his 'Patronage' (later 'Solemnity') feast on the third Wednesday after Easter. This feast was replaced by that of 'St. Joseph the Worker' on the significant day of 1 May by Pius XII. His name was added to the Canon of the Mass by John XXIII in 1962.

Joseph is patron of fathers of families, of bursars and procurators, of manual workers, especially carpenters, and of all who desire a holy death. This last devotion, which has become widespread since the 17th century, is probably based on the imaginary account of Joseph's own death in the *History of Joseph the Carpenter.* This document makes Joseph fearful of death and filled with self-reproach, comforted by the words of Mary and Jesus, who promised protection and life to all who do good in the name of Joseph. Many churches, hospitals, and religious congregations are dedicated to Joseph; the very frequent use of Joseph as a Christian name is some evidence of his widespread popularity. In medieval art he seldom appears alone, but nearly always with Mary or Jesus: later Murillo and Zurbaran produced the most famous paintings of him. In the New World, Canada (especially Montreal) is the most notable centre of devotion of Joseph. Feast: 19 March and 1 May.

AA.SS. Mar. III (1668), 4–25; A. H. Lépicier, *Tractatus de S. Ioseph* (1908); C.A. 'Le Développement historique du culte de S. Joseph', *Rev. Bén.*, xiv (1897), 104–14, 145–55, 203–9; P. Grosjean, 'Notes d'Hagiographie celtique', no. 26, *Anal. Boll.*, lxxii (1954), 357–62; U. Holzmeister, *De sancto Ioseph quaestiones biblicae* (1945); F. L. Filas, *The Man nearest to Christ* (1947); B. Llamera, *Teologia de San José* (1953, Eng. tr. 1962); B.T.A., i. 631–3; Réau, ii. 752–60.

JOSEPH OF ARIMATHEA (1st century). All that is certainly known about him is in the Gospels: that he was a Jewish councillor, a disciple of Jesus in secret, who had taken no part in his condemnation and who, after the death of Jesus, asked Pilate for his body and buried it in a tomb newly hewn out of the rock.

The accretions of legend soon began. The apocryphal 'Gospel of Nicodemus' gave him an important share in founding the first Christian community at Lydda. But a French legend connecting him with the Holy Grail (the cup believed to have received the blood of Christ at Calvary) was given great prominence, with local variations, by Glastonbury Abbey. William of Malmesbury's treatise on the *Antiquity of Glastonbury* (*c.*1125) was interpolated a century after his death with a fictitious chapter which described *Philip the Apostle preaching the Gospel in Gaul together with Joseph of Arimathea, whom he sent to England with twelve disciples. The king who received them would not become a Christian but gave them the island of Yniswitrin, later called Glastonbury, where they built a wattle church in honour of St. Mary, which, it was claimed, had been dedicated by the Lord himself.

Part of the Glastonbury Legend of its foundation by Joseph arose through a competition in antiquity with Westminster, and a rival claim to Canterbury to possess *Dunstan's relics. Some further incentive was given by the difficulties which the abbey experienced in the late 12th century after the destruction by fire of the old church, a prolonged struggle with King Richard I about their exemption, and the attempt by Savary, bishop of Bath, to take the double title of bishop of Bath and Glastonbury by annexation. The dispute was not settled until 1219. The Joseph of Arimathea and the Arthur legends at Glastonbury (Arthur's body was 'discovered' in 1191) both arose during a period of crisis. They were (and are) passionately believed in by some, but all the early sources, including William of Malmesbury, are silent about them. The Legend, as presented by John of Glastonbury *c.*1400, does not mention the Grail: later artists depict instead two silver cruets, supposedly containing the blood and sweat of Christ from the Cross and brought by Joseph to England. Examples are on the painted rood-screen at Plymtree (Devon) and in the stained glass at Langport (Devon); the arms of Richard Bere (abbot of Glastonbury 1494–1524) with blood-drops and two cruets are in the early 16th-century glass of St. John's, Glastonbury.

This legend had other effects: first, it helped to foster growing devotion to the physical details of Christ's Passion which characterized the later Middle Ages: secondly, the claim to antiquity resulted in Glastonbury demanding seniority among the English Black Benedictine abbeys and the English clergy at the Councils of Constance (1414–18) claiming that England had received Christianity before any other western country. At Glastonbury itself the pilgrims' attention was drawn to the Joseph of Arimathea legend both by a column to the north of the Lady Chapel, on which an inscription recorded the main points of the Glastonbury case and claimed to mark the original eastern limit of the old church, and by the *Magna Tabula.* This was a large wooden frame covered with extracts from John of Glastonbury's *History*, which told all who read it of Joseph, King Arthur, St. Patrick and his charter, the alleged translation of St. Dunstan, and so forth. Only in 1502 was a poem called *The Lyfe of Joseph of Arimathia* written, based on John of Glastonbury but also containing a series of miraculous cures said to have been accomplished by Joseph on sick people from Wells, Ilchester, Yeovil, and other West Country towns. It also contains the first mention of the Holy Thorn, which flowers at Christmas and was reputed to have sprung from Joseph's staff. The grave of Joseph was believed to be at Glastonbury but, despite a royal authorization to look for it and an East Anglian claim that it had been found in 1367, the silence of Glastonbury itself is strong evidence that it was never found. The abbey of Moyenmoutier in the Vosges, however, also claimed to possess his relics. Feast: in the East, 31 July; in the West, formerly 17 March.

AA.SS. Mar. II (1668), 507–10; J. A. Robinson, *Two Glastonbury Legends* (1926); W. Newell, 'William of Malmesbury and the Antiquities of Glastonbury', *Pubs. of the Modern Language Association of America*, xviii (1903), 459–512; R. F. Treharne, *The Glastonbury Legends* (1967); Réau, ii. 760–1; B.T.A., i. 617–19; T. D. Kendrick, *British Antiquity* (1950).

JOSEPH OF COPERTINO (1603–63), Franciscan priest. He was born of poor parents, at Copertino near Brindisi, in a garden shed because his father, a carpenter, had had to sell his house to pay debts. Resented by his mother, who was soon widowed, he had an unhappy childhood; he was nicknamed 'the Gaper' for his habit of wandering about open-mouthed. This was combined with a hot temper and an exemplary performance of religious duties. Attempts to join the Franciscan conventuals and Capuchins in this poverty-stricken area were alike unsuccessful: after eight months with the Capuchins when he forgot to do what he was told, dropped piles of plates and dishes on the floor, and neglected to tend the all-important kitchen fire, he was dismissed. A wealthy uncle failed to come to the rescue; his mother wanted to be rid of him and arranged for him to work as a servant for the Franciscan conventuals at Grottella. There he quickly grew in efficiency and in religious spirit to such an extent that he was admitted as a novice in 1625.

Although very backward in his studies, his extreme good luck in examinations enabled him to be ordained priest in 1628. His life thenceforward was distinguished by extreme austerity, many ecstasies and apparently supernatural healings. They were witnessed by men of unchallenged integrity, as the 'Devil's Advocate' against his canonization (subsequently Pope Benedict XIV) admitted. Perhaps the most famous are his repeated levitations, i.e. the raising and movement through the air of his body by no apparent physical force, of which seventy instances were recorded during his seventeen years at Grottella. The most spectacular were his flying to images placed high above the altars and helping workmen to erect a Calvary Cross thirty-six feet high by lifting it into place in mid-air 'as if it were straw'. Ten men had previously failed to lift it. Such feats earned him the nickname 'the Flying Friar'. His affinity with birds and animals was equal to that of *Francis of Assisi; while when he was in ecstasy, blows, burning, and pinpricks failed to 'awake' him.

These phenomena were so disturbing to his superiors that for thirty-five years he was not allowed to celebrate a public Mass or attend choir and refectory with his community. After some time Neapolitan Inquisitors accused him of 'drawing crowds after him like a new Messiah through prodigies accomplished on the ignorant who are ready to believe anything'. The charge was not proven; Joseph was sent to see Pope Urban VIII, at the sight of whom he went into ecstasy. His apparently incurable hypersensitivity to religion resulted in his being sent first to Assisi in 1639, where he remained for thirteen years in complete spiritual aridity; later, following the Inquisition of Perugia's intervention, to a lonely friary of Capuchins in Pietrarossa, where he lived in a prison-like seclusion until pilgrims discovered his presence; he was then removed to Fossombrone. The Lutheran Duke of Brunswick became a Catholic after twice seeing him in ecstasy at Mass. In 1655 the conventuals petitioned for the return of Joseph to Assisi; two years later he was restored to their house at Osimo in strict seclusion. Here he died and was buried, the object of both official reserve and popular veneration. In 1767 he was canonized, not for his levitations, but for his extreme patience and humility. Certain features of his life resemble in different ways those of *John of the Cross and of Padre Pio in our own day. Baroque artists painted pictures of him and a drawing by Cades survives in the Ashmolean Museum, Oxford. Feast: 18 September.

AA.SS. Sept. V (1755), 992–1060; A. Pastrovicchi, *St. Joseph of Copertino* (tr. F. Laing, 1918); G. Parisciani, *San Giuseppe de Copertino alla luce dei nuovi documenti* (1964); H. Thurston, *The Physical Phenomena of Mysticism* (1952); B.T.A., iii. 587–91; *Bibl. SS.*, vi. 1300–3.

JOSSE, see JUDOC.

JUDE (1st century), apostle and martyr. He is usually identified with Thaddaeus and Jude, the brother of James, one of the 'brethren of the Lord' and the author of the Epistle of Jude. Little is known of his life after Pentecost. According to Western tradition he joined with *Simon in preaching the Gospel in Persia, where both were martyred. In modern times Jude has acquired considerable popularity as 'patron of hopeless cases' whose efficacy is testified even in the personal columns of *The Times.* This patronage is said to have originated because nobody invoked him for anything since his name so closely resembled that of Judas who betrayed the Lord; consequently he favours even the most desperate situations of his clients. There are at least three ancient English dedications to SS. Simon and Jude, but none to either of them alone. The relics of SS. Simon and Jude are believed to have been translated to St. Peter's, Rome, in the 7th–8th century: Reims and Toulouse also claimed notable relics. In art Jude's usual emblem is a club, the instrument of his death; otherwise (as often on East Anglian screens) he holds a ship, while Simon holds a fish, possibly because they were believed, as cousins of Zebedee, to follow the same calling as him. Feast: (with Simon) in the West, 28 October; in the East, Jude alone on 19 June.

NT passages are Luke 6: 16; John 14: 22; Acts 1: 13; Jude 1 (which was an important source of 2 Peter); *AA.SS.* Oct. XII (1867), 421–67; R. A. Lipsius, *Die apokryphen Apostelgeschichten*, ii (2), 142–200; see also arts. in *D.C.A.*, i (1875), 891–3.

JUDITH AND SALOME (9th century), anchoresses of Ober Altaich (Bavaria). Salome was reputedly an English princess, whom Judith, her aunt, was sent from England to find. The only possible English princess identifiable with Salome is Edburga, daughter of Offa of Mercia. This beautiful but wicked wife of Beorhtric, king of the West Saxons (786–802), was reputed to have murdered some of his noblemen and accidentally killed her husband, who drank some poison intended for a young favourite. Rumour of her misdeeds led to her exile: Charlemagne gave her a rich monastery to rule, but deposed her for scandalous behaviour soon after. She then led a wandering life with a maidservant as her companion: Asser said that people had seen her begging at Patavium (Pavia). But if this is a mistake for Patavia (Passau), it would provide a vital link with Salome; for it was from Passau that the Altaich biographer said that Salome had come. The identity of these two recluses, however, is by no means certain. There is no contemporary Life, but Asser, from whom William of Malmesbury drew part of the story, is contemporary. This may be a case of a lost saga of Anglo-Saxon England receiving unexpected confirmation from a German source. Feast: 29 June.

AA.SS. Iun. V (1709), 492–8; W. Holder-Egger in *M.G.H.*, *Scriptores*, xv. 847 ff.; *G.R.*, i. 118; B.T.A., ii. 673; R. M. Wilson, *The Lost Literature of Medieval England* (1952).

JUDOC (Josse) (d. *c.*668), prince and hermit. A son of Juthael, king of Brittany, Judoc renounced his position and wealth *c.*636, was ordained priest, went on pilgrimage to Rome, and then became a hermit in Ponthieu in the place later called Saint-Josse-sur-Mer (near Étaples) where he died. His body was claimed to be incorrupt, his beard and hair were trimmed from time to time by his followers (as was claimed for *Cuthbert). Charlemagne gave this hermitage to Alcuin to be used as a guest-house for English travellers; Judoc's connection with England was substantially strengthened when *c.*902, while the New Minster at Winchester was being built, there arrived some refugees from Saint-Josse who brought with them the relics of their founder. *Grimbald enshrined them in the new church. Consequently feasts of Judoc were kept at a high rank at Winchester; Winchester influence is inferred when they occur elsewhere in English calendars.

His popularity in England may be deduced from the frequent Christian name Joyce (for both men and women) and from the use of his name in oaths by the Wife of Bath in Chaucer's *Canterbury Tales* ('by God and by Seint Joce'). The cult of Judoc also spread partly through the discovery of a rival set of relics at Saint-Josse in 977 from northern France to Flanders (where he is sometimes called Joost), Germany, Alsace, Switzerland, and Austria, where he is represented on the mausoleum of Maximilian at Innsbruck. In art his usual emblem is a pilgrim's staff, with a crown at his feet symbolizing his renunciation of royal power and honour. There seem to have been no ancient English church dedications but there were plenty abroad in the areas mentioned. Feast: 13 December; translation, 9 January.

Propylaeum, p. 581; J. Mabillon, *AA.SS. O.S.B.*, ii. 542–7; for other lives see *B.H.L.*, 4504–11; M. Chibnall (ed.), *Ecclesiastical History of Orderic Vitalis*, ii (1969), 156–66, 366–7; J. Trier, *Der heilige Jodocus* (1924); B.T.A., iv. 550; *D.C.B.*, iii. 467–8.

JULIAN OF BRIOUDE (3rd century), martyr. The details of his life are obscure; his cult ancient and strong, so that he became patron saint of the Auvergne. His Acts say that he was a soldier who was also a devout Christian; when Crispin, governor of Vienne, decided on a policy of persecution, Julian withdrew to the Auvergne. Later, learning that he was being sought out by the persecutors, he gave himself up and was beheaded.

The church built over his tomb at Brioude became an important pilgrimage centre; others were built at Tours, Reims, Paris (S. Julien-le-pauvre), and elsewhere. *Gregory of Tours helped to propagate his cult and described how he moved some of his relics by night into a church he consecrated in Julian's honour. The many miracles which the saint accomplished concerned not only healing but also control of the weather, avenging of robbery, and other actions of anger, protection, and destruction as well as of benevolence. In these ways Julian was a characteristic saint of the early Middle Ages with a strong local presence and power; woe betide those who questioned or disdained it. Sidonius Apollinaris and *Venantius Fortunatus also referred to Julian and his cult. Feast: 28 August.

AA.SS. Aug. VI (1743), 169–88; *Propylaeum*, p. 365; Gregory of Tours; *De virtutibus S. Juliani* in *M.G.H. Scriptores rerum meroving*, i. 562–84; J. M. Wallace Hadrill, *The Frankish Church* (1983), pp. 75–93.

JULIAN OF LE MANS (4th century(?)), bishop. Almost nothing is known of his life: breviary lessons claim him as a Roman nobleman who became first bishop of Le Mans and apostle of the neighbourhood. Plenty of churches are dedicated to him there (and a few in England) of which the oldest dates from the 7th century. Julian was formerly venerated in the church of Saint-Julien-du-Pré, now Notre-Dame-du-Pré (Le Mans); his relics were translated to the cathedral in 1254. His feast was kept in the Sarum rite and in at least nine Black Benedictine English monasteries. The cult was probably encouraged by Henry II, who was born at Le Mans and baptized in the church of St. Julian. Attempts to identify him with Simon the Leper or with one of the seventy-two disciples of Christ are characteristic of French attempts to assert apostolic origins of their sees. Julian does, however, appear first in the episcopal lists of Le Mans, where there are stained-glass windows of the 12th–13th century and a tapestry of the 16th which illustrate episodes of his Legend. Feast: 27 January.

AA.SS. Ian. II (1643), 761–7; A. Ledru, *Les premiers temps de l'Église du Mans* (1913), 55–238; B.T.A., i. 183.

JULIAN THE HOSPITALLER, almost certainly an entirely mythical saint, who was falsely associated with one or more genuine saints of this name. He has no date, no country, no tomb: his feast on 29 January in the *Acta Sanctorum* seems an arbitrary date. But seven ancient English churches were dedicated to him besides others elsewhere; there are important cycles of his Legend in the 13th-century stained glass at both Chartres and Rouen besides notable paintings elsewhere in the later Middle Ages, especially in Flanders; Wiggenhall St. Mary Magdalen (Norfolk) has a stained-glass picture of him and Suffield (Norfolk) a screen-painting. His story was widely diffused in the *Golden Legend* of James of Voragine, in the sermons of Antoninus of Florence, and in the 19th century by Gustave Flaubert in one of his *Trois Contes*. It is, however, found even earlier in the works of Vincent of Beauvais (13th century).

According to this romance he was a young nobleman who, when hunting, came upon a hart which said to him: 'You are hunting me and you will kill your father and your mother.' To avoid such a terrible destiny he went to a far country and served the king so well that he was knighted and given a rich widow in marriage with a castle for her dowry. Later his father and mother went to find him, but he was out; his wife gave them her own bed to sleep in. Next day her husband returned while his wife was at church, entered his bedroom, and found a man and a woman asleep there. He jumped to the conclusion that his wife was committing adultery and killed both of them in the bed. He then went out and met his wife coming home from church. Struck with grief and remorse he left that country, came with his wife to an important river-crossing and built a hospital for the poor. Like *Christopher he also acted as a guide for travellers to cross the river. Once, at midnight, he heard cries for help, rescued a traveller half-dead with cold and placed him in his own bed. Later this man, who seemed to be a leper, died; Julian saw him go to heaven, saying: 'Julian, our Lord sent me here and tells you that he has accepted your penance.' Soon afterwards Julian and his wife died. Many hospitals were dedicated to him, especially in the Netherlands;

he was the patron of innkeepers, boatmen, and travellers; trade guilds were partly responsible for the works of art which honour him.

B. de Gaiffier, 'La Légende de S. Julien l'Hospitalier', *Anal. Boll.*, lxiii (1945), 144–219; G. Flaubert, *La légende de S. Julien l'Hospitalier* (1874); A. M. Gossez, *Le Saint Julien de Flaubert* (1903); M. Oberziner, *La leggenda si S. Giuliano il Parricida* (1933); B.T.A., i. 314–16; Réau, ii. 766–9.

JULIANA (early 4th century), virgin and martyr. She probably suffered at Cumae or Naples; Gregory the Great requested relics of her from Fortunatus, bishop of Naples, for an oratory which a lady had built on her estate in Juliana's honour. The principal episode of her unreliable Legend is a long verbal contest between her and the Devil, who tried to persuade her to obey the wishes of her father and her suitor to get married. Thus she is represented in art with a winged devil or dragon at her feet (as in stained glass at Martham and on screens at Hampstead and North Elmham, Norfolk). Her cult in England goes back to the Martyrology of *Bede and her feast, on 16 February, was in the Sarum Calendar.

AA.SS. Feb. II (1658), 868–84; B.T.A., i. 349–50; C. Woodforde, *The Norwich School of Glass-Painting in the Fifteenth Century* (1950), pp. 178–9.

JULIANA FALCONIERI (1270–1341), foundress of the Servite nuns. Her parents built the fine Annunziata church in Florence, her uncle Alexis was one of the *Seven Servite Founders, while Juliana at the age of fifteen became a Servite tertiary. In 1304, on her mother's death, she moved to another convent of nuns popularly called *Matellate*, became superior, and wrote constitutions for them. Ultimately they were recognized as full Servite nuns and Juliana was recognized as their foundress. Austere and zealous, she was also charitable and sympathetic to all. Few details are known of her life, but miracles and an immemorial cult were claimed when she was canonized in 1737. A few convent churches in England are dedicated to her. Feast: 19 June.

Lives by M. Conrayville (1951) and A. M. Rossi (1954); B.T.A., ii. 581–3; *Bibl. SS.*, vi. 1184–8.

JULIOT, very obscure Cornish woman saint of very early times. She is probably one of the daughters of *Brychan, also called Ilud or Juliana; her church and cross are at Luxulyan (Cornwall). She is said to have suffered a violent death at the hands of a robber who had already stolen from her. She had often been confused with *Julitta; for example Tintagel is listed as dedicated to Julitta, although the original dedication may have been to Juliot. Her feast-day is 'not certainly known'; her parish feast is on the Sunday nearest 29 June.

Baring-Gould and Fisher, iii. 333–5; *C.C.K.*

JULITTA, see Cyricus and Julitta.

JULIUS AND AARON, British martyrs of Caerleon, *c.*304. These are mentioned by *Gildas and *Bede. Nothing is known of them except their martyrdom, which has been called into question because there is doubt about Diocletian's persecution being carried out in Britain. However, there are dedications to these saints in and near Caerleon, testified by Gerald of Wales and the Book of Llan Dav. Feast: 1 July.

Bede, *H.E.*, i. 7 (citing Gildas, *De Excidio*, 10–11); B.T.A., iii. 11–12; Baring-Gould and Fisher, i. 101–3.

JULIUS THE VETERAN (d. 304), martyr. A soldier of twenty-seven years' service on seven military campaigns, the inferior of no man in battle and with an unblemished military record, Julian declared at his interrogation by the prefect Maximus that he must be faithful to higher orders. On being asked about his military service, Julian said that he had been in the army and had re-enlisted as a veteran: all this time he worshipped in reverence the God who made heaven and earth, and he served him right up to the present day. Maximus praised him as a wise and serious man, offered him a generous ten-year bonus if only he would sacrifice to the gods, and offered to take the blame himself if Julius would give the impression of acting voluntarily. Julius steadfastly refused all such subterfuges. When asked why he feared a dead man more than living emperors, he answered: 'It was he who died for our sins to give us eternal life. This same man, Christ, is God and abides for ever and ever. Whoever believes in him will have eternal life; whoever denies him will have eternal punishment.' Maximus' reply counselled him out of pity to sacrifice and continue to live. 'To live with you', said Julius, 'would be death for me . . . I have chosen death that I might live with the saints for ever.'

On his way to execution at Durostorum in Moesia Inferior (now Silistria in Bulgaria) he was greeted by a man called Isichius, another Christian soldier who was in prison. 'Take the crown', he said, 'which the Lord has promised to give to those who believe in him, and remember me for I too will follow you. Give my warmest greetings to the servant of God, our brother Valentio who has already gone before us to the Lord by his loyal confession of faith.' When Julius took the blindfold before being beheaded, he said: 'Lord Jesus Christ, I suffer this for your name. I beg you to receive my spirit together with your holy martyrs.' The executioner then ended Julius' life by the sword. Feast: 27 May.

Propylaeum, pp. 211–12; *A.C.M.*, pp. 261–5; H. Delehaye, 'Saints de Thrace et Mésie', *Anal. Boll.*, xxxi (1912), 259–390; B.T.A., ii. 405.

JURMIN (Germin) (7th century), prince of East Anglia. According to the *Liber Eliensis* he was a son of Anna, king of the East Angles (634–54), and was buried at Blythburgh (Suffolk) before being translated to Bury St. Edmunds in 1095. William of Malmesbury mentions his tomb at Bury (with Botulf's) but says he could find out nothing about him except that he was a brother of *Etheldreda, herself a daughter of Anna. But modern historians doubt if Anna had any sons; some suggest that Jurmin was the son of Æthelhere, the brother and successor of Anna. Feast: 23 February in a late Bury calendar.

Stanton, p. 82; *Liber Eliensis* (ed. E. O. Blake, C.S., 1962), pp. 12, 18; *G.P.*, p. 156.

JUSTIN (*c.*100–65), philosopher and martyr. Born at Nablus (= Shechem), Samaria, of parents of Greek origin, he was well educated in rhetoric, poetry, and history before he turned to philosophy, which he studied at Ephesus and Alexandria. He joined in turn the schools of the Stoics, the Pythagoreans, and the Platonists, but became a Christian *c.*130 and is commonly regarded as the first Christian philosopher. His search for truth was satisfied by the Bible and above all by Christ, the Word of God, but he did not cease to wear the philosopher's cloak. He held disputations with Jews, pagans, and heretics, particularly at Rome, which he reached *c.*150.

His surviving writings, which comprise the two Apologies and the Dialogue with Trypho, are among the earliest products in the sub-apostolic age which reflect the outlook of a Christian intellectual. They tell of the faith of the Christians, the rite of Baptism and the Eucharist, and the distribution of alms. They refute accusations of immorality and atheism and show that loyalty to the Emperor is based on the teaching of Christ and Paul. Justin's aim was apostolic; he thought that pagans would become Christians if they were made aware of Christian doctrine and practice through articulate, well-presented writings.

His death took place in the reign of Marcus Aurelius. At his trial, whose authentic record survives, he clearly confessed his Christian beliefs, refused to sacrifice to the gods, and accepted suffering and death as the means of salvation. Feast: 1 June (formerly 14 April in the West).

AA.SS. Apr. II (1675), 104–19 and Iun. I (1695), 16–22; authentic Acts of his trial and martyrdom are also in *A.C.M.*, pp. 42–61, and other collections; for his works see *P.G.*, vi, modern edn. of *Apologies* by A. W. F. Blunt (1911) and of *Dialogue with Trypho* by A. L. Williams (1930). Modern Lives by M. J. Lagrange (1914), C. C. Martindale (1923), and L. W. Barnard (1967). See also H. Chadwick, 'Justin Martyr's Defence of Christianity', *Bull. of John Rylands Library*, xlvii (1965), 275–97.

JUSTINA, see CYPRIAN AND JUSTINA.

JUSTINA OF PADUA (*c*.300), virgin and martyr. She was one of the many victims of persecution in the Roman Empire, probably under Maximian, but little is known of her life and death. In the 6th century a church was dedicated to her in Padua, while *Venantius Fortunatus, who had seen her depicted in the Ravenna mosaics, ranked her among the most notable saints of her time: by making Padua famous, she had done for her town the same as *Euphemia for Chalcedon and *Eulalia for Merida.

In the 10th century the monastery attached to her church was extremely generously endowed with property within the province, protected by papal and imperial privileges. In the eleventh it was reformed according to the Rule of St. Benedict and acquired considerable relics including some claimed to be of *Luke the evangelist. Following the destruction of the basilica by earthquake in the early 12th century, Justina's relics were translated in 1117. At this time a legendary Life was written, supposedly based on information given by Prosdocimo, first bishop of Padua and a disciple of St. Peter.

After some years of decline the monastery was reformed again by Lodovico Barbo from 1408 onwards. It became the centre of the reformed Cassinese Congregation of St. Benedict's Order. Justina was their patron and they rebuilt her church lavishly from 1521 till 1587. Feast: 7 October.

AA.SS. Oct. III (1770), 790–826; Anon., 'Passio S. Iustinae martyris Patavii', *Anal. Boll.*, x (1891), 467–70; A. Barzon, 'S. Giustina vergine e martire di Padoua', *Boll. Dioc. di Padoua*, xxxiv (1949), 269–314; *Bibl. SS.*, vi. 1345–49.

JUSTINIAN (Jestin) (6th century), hermit and martyr of Ramsey Island (off Pembrokeshire, now Dyfed). The only information about him comes from the Life in *N.L.A.*, copied presumably from a St. David's manuscript of the 12th century or later, since lost. According to this source Justinian was a Breton of noble birth and good education who became a priest and then left his country to follow Christ's teaching more completely. He eventually settled at Ramsey and found another devout man, Honorius, already in occupation there with his sister and her maid. Honorius invited him to settle there but he would only agree if the women were sent away. At first incredulous, Honorius later agreed; the two men then lived in amity: *David heard of Justinian, invited him to visit him, and was so impressed that he gave him houses on the island and the mainland. Later some sailors told him that David was ill and offered to take Justinian to see him; when they were well on their way to the mainland, Justinian realized from their ugliness that they were devils, said Psalm 79, and at the appropriate verse they 'flew away like black crows'. The boat landed safely; David was in perfect health and the devils, temporarily foiled, tried again.

This time they attacked him through his three servants: when Justinian told them to work hard, they flew into a rage, threw him on to the ground, and cut off his head; from the place where it fell a spring of water sprang up and cured the sick. The murderers were struck with leprosy and lived out their days in isolation on a crag called 'the Lepers' rock'. Justinian's body carried its head to the place where he wished to be buried and where a church was built. After many miracles there, David translated his body to a new tomb in his own church.

This story is a tissue of impossible commonplaces quite readably assembled with some local knowledge; it may well be almost entirely fictional. But the feast of Justinian is consistently attested by Welsh calendars, by William Worcestre, and Roscarrock, while the church of Llanstinan (near Fishguard) is dedicated to him. The cult is probably far older than the Life. Feast: 5 December.

N.L.A., ii. 93–5; Baring-Gould and Fisher, iii. 339–42.

JUSTUS (1) (Just) (d. 627), archbishop of Canterbury. He was one of the Roman missionaries sent in 601 by *Gregory the

Great to reinforce *Augustine. He was consecrated first bishop of Rochester in 604. Together with *Laurence of Canterbury and *Mellitus of London, Justus wrote to both the Irish and the British Christians asking them to conform their customs to those of the Roman see: the extract of the letter in Bede is not tactfully worded and it seems to have been largely ignored. In 616 there was a pagan reaction in Kent and Essex after the death of *Ethelbert: without support from the pagan King Edbald, Justus and Mellitus thought the situation untenable and retired temporarily to France. But they returned after the conversion of the king; Justus became archbishop of Canterbury in 624 and received from Boniface V both the pallium and the power to consecrate bishops in England. Justus was buried like other early archbishops of Canterbury at St. Augustine's monastery. When the church was rebuilt in the 11th century his relics were translated with those of other archbishops to a site behind the high altar. Goscelin now wrote his Life. Justus and the writers of the letter to the Irish are mentioned in the diptychs of the Irish Stowe Missal. Feast: 10 November.

Bede, *H.E.*, i. 29–ii. 9; *AA.SS.* Nov. IV (1925), 533–7, W. St. John Hope, *Recent Discoveries in the Abbey Church of St. Austin at Canterbury* (1916).

JUSTUS (2) (Just), patron of St. Just in Penwith and St. Just in Roseland (Cornwall), described as martyr in a document of 1140 (perhaps mistakenly). The day of his feast is unknown.

JUSTUS OF BEAUVAIS (3rd century?), martyr. This boy-saint was very popular in France, Belgium, and Switzerland, but also at Winchester where the cathedral claimed important relics of him, at least from the 11th century. His incredible Legend is partly borrowed from that of St. Justin of Paris; the diffusion of his cult may be due to confusion with saints of the same or similar name. His Acts make him a boy of nine years old who declared himself a Christian in the persecution of Diocletian under the mythical Rictiovarus; his head was struck off by a soldier but he nevertheless continued to speak. He was a static rather than a mobile *céphalophore*, who had given his life to avoid disclosing the hiding-place of his father and uncle. Feast: 18 October.

AA.SS. Oct. VIII (1866), 323–43; M. Coens, 'Aux origines du céphalophore', *Anal. Boll.*, lxxii (1954), 269 ff.; B.T.A., iv. 143–4.

JUTHWARA (Aude) (date unknown), virgin (and martyr?), was British, perhaps from Cornwall. Her brother was said to be *Paul Aurelian and her sisters *Sidwell of Exeter and Wulvela of Cornwall. Her relics were translated to Sherborne under Ælfwald II (1045–58). These seem to be the most certain facts about her: her Legend in *N.L.A.* is a farrago of impossibilities. According to this story, as in the Legend of Sidwell, she was the victim of a jealous stepmother. Juthwara, a pious girl who practised much prayer, fasting, and almsgiving, suffered after her father's death from a pain in the chest, brought on perhaps by her sorrow and austerities. The stepmother recommended as a remedy two cheeses applied to her breasts; meanwhile, she told her own wicked son called Bana that Juthwara was pregnant. He accused her, found her underclothes were moist, and struck off her head there and then. The usual spring of water then appeared; Juthwara carried her head back to the church; Bana repented, became a monk, and founded a monastery of Gerber (later called Le Relecq) on a British battlefield. The place of Juthwara's death may have been Lanteglos by Camelford (Cornwall), where the church, now St. Julitta's, may originally have been Juthwara's. The neighbouring parish of Lancast is dedicated to her sisters. She is depicted with her sister Sidwell on the screens of Hennock and Ashton (Devon); her usual emblem is a cream-cheese or a sword. A late medieval statue at Guizeny (Brittany) shows her holding her head in her hand.

Feast: 28 November, translation, 13 July. Roscarrock gives 6 January.

N.L.A., ii. 98–9; C. H. Talbot, 'The Life of St. Wulsin of Sherborne by Goscelin', *Rev. Bén.*, lxix (1959), 68–85 (completed by P. Grosjean in *Anal. Boll.*, lxxviii (1960), 197–206); Baring-Gould and Fisher (s.v. Aude), i. 185–8.

K

KATHARINE, see Catherine of Alexandria.

KEA (Ke, Quay), monk and bishop, who worked in Devon and Cornwall, where Landkey (Devon) and Kea (Cornwall) bear his name. He is identical with Breton Quay (Saint-Quay in North Brittany) and Saint-Quay-Portrieux near Saint-Brieuc), whose Legend survives. It seems likely that Kea, Fili, and *Rumon came from Glastonbury; as they travelled into Devon and Cornwall they founded Christian centres. Noble parentage is claimed for Kea and some association with *Gildas, who is brought into the story as a bellfounder. He is also associated with stags in his Legend and in Breton pictures of him. It is probable that Kea migrated to Brittany and died there. He is invoked for the cure of toothache. Feast: 5 November.

G. H. Doble, *The Saints of Cornwall*, iii (1964), 89–104.

KEMBLE, John (1599–1679), seminary priest and martyr. Born at St. Weonards (near Hereford) of a Wiltshire family, Kemble was educated at the English College, Douai, where he was ordained priest in 1625. Soon afterwards he returned home for his apostolate, making his brother's house, Pembridge Castle, the headquarters from which (with Jesuit help) mission centres were set up in Herefordshire and Gwent. His extraordinarily long apostolate of fifty-four years makes him unique among recusant priests of his time. During the reign of Charles I and even the Commonwealth he was comparatively safe and unmolested, when he founded centres at the Llwyn, the Craig, Hilston, and Codanghred. But after the Popish Plot (1678) priests were arrested in different parts of the country and brought to London to be confronted by Titus Oates. At the age of eighty Kemble was arrested, imprisoned at Hereford for three months, and tried for being a seminary priest. He was sentenced to be hanged, drawn, and quartered. But first he was taken to London, strapped to a horse, and offered release if he would reveal details of the non-existent plot. He was then sent back to Hereford prison. On 22 August the under-sheriff came to take him to execution: Kemble asked for time to pray, to smoke a last pipe, and take a last drink; together the two men shared a cup of wine and a pipe. The hangman also venerated the courageous priest and showed his esteem by making sure that he was dead after hanging before carrying out the rest of the sentence.

Kemble's room can still be seen at Pembridge Castle: his altar and missal are at the R.C. Church at Monmouth. A sketch of him drawn from life survives. The Herefordshire expression 'Kemble pipe' signifies the last one in a sitting. Kemble was canonized by Paul VI in 1970 as one of the *Forty Martyrs of England and Wales. Feast: 25 October.

R. Challoner, *Memoirs of Missionary Priests* (ed. J. H. Pollen, 1924), pp. 555–7; B. Camm, *Forgotten Shrines* (1910), pp. 333–42; M. V. Lovejoy, *Blessed John Kemble* (pamphlet, 1960).

KENED, see Kyned.

KENELM (Cynhelm) (d. 812 or 821), prince of Mercian royal family. The historical Kenelm was the son of Coenwulf, king of Mercia 796–821. Kenelm signed a number of charters from 803 to 811; already in 798 Pope Leo III had confirmed to him the ownership of Glastonbury. But Kenelm died before his father, possibly in battle against the Welsh, and was buried at Winchcombe Abbey. When *Oswald revived Winchcombe in the second half of the 10th century, Kenelm was regarded as a martyr and figured as such in liturgical books, including a sacramentary, written at Winchcombe and presented to Fleury, where he ranks next to *Stephen.

The next stage was the development of a Kenelm Legend. This took place in the 11th century; it was used by William of Malmesbury and is represented in abridged form in *N.L.A.* According to this, Kenelm was only seven years old and reigned for a few months as his father's successor, but was put to death by his tutor at the instigation of his jealous sister, the princess Quendreda. The chapel of St. Kenelm at Clent near Halesowen (Hereford and Worcester) was believed to mark the site of his murder. Even more astonishing, the body was discovered by an Anglo-Saxon document being dropped by a dove on to the high altar of St. Peter's, Rome; it was duly deciphered by English pilgrims. The body was accordingly translated to Winchcombe and while the evil Quendreda was reciting a psalm backwards (presumably for magical purposes), her eyes fell out.

In fact the historical Quendreda was abbess of Minster (Kent). The Legend of Kenelm is a good example of how a writer with a vivid imagination and some half-understood historical data produced a completely fictitious account of a prince who certainly existed but of whom virtually nothing is known. The crypt of the church of St. Pancras at Winchcombe has been recently identified as the shrine of Kenelm, buried there with his father. Feast: 17 July.

G.R., i. 94–5, 262–3; *G.P.*, pp. 294–5; *N.L.A.*, ii. 110–13; W. Levison, *England and the Continent in the Eighth Century* (1956), pp. 249–59; G. T. Haig, *History of Winchcombe Abbey* (1948); B.T.A., iii. 127–8; E. S. Hartland, 'The legend of St. Kenelm', *Trans. Bristol and Glos. Arch. Soc.* xxxix (1916), 13–65; S. R. Bassett, 'A probable Mercian royal Mausoleum at Winchcombe', *Antiq. Jnl.*, lxv (1985), 82–100.

KENETH, see KYNED.

KENNETH, see CANICE.

KENNOCH, see MOCHOEMOC.

KENTIGERN (Mungo) (d. 612), monk and bishop, evangelist of Strathclyde and Cumbria. There are many legends but few known facts about Kentigern: all the sources date from the 11th and 12th centuries and most of them are from the North. They contain various folkloric elements which are considerably older than the 11th century, but have no historical value. From these traditions it may be assumed that he was the grandson of a British prince (Urien?) and of illegitimate birth; that he was educated by *Serf at Culross; that he was a monk of the Irish tradition who practised the customary austerities, that he was consecrated bishop of the Strathclyde area by an Irish bishop; that he suffered from the political disorder of his kingdom and was exiled to Cumbria (and much less likely to Wales). Then he returned to Strathclyde and lived at Hoddam (Dumfries) and especially at Glasgow, as before; here he died and was buried: his relics are claimed by Glasgow cathedral.

Some of the more incredible elements of the Legends include his mother being thrown off a cliff in a wagon and being set adrift in a coracle before Kentigern's birth; Kentigern in later life telling the queen who had given her husband's ring to her lover not to worry, as one of his monks extracted it from a salmon which he caught (after the king had thrown the ring out to sea and told her to find it in three days). This story is the cause of the presence of the ring and the fish on the arms of the city of Glasgow. One of his biographers made him 185 years old when he died: perhaps he really lived to be eighty-five.

There are several ancient Scottish dedications to Kentigern under his pet-name of Mungo and nine in England, mainly in Cumbria. The story that he founded a large and important monastery in North Wales numbering nearly 1,000 monks and that he became first bishop of St. Asaph's is exceedingly unlikely. It depends on only one late Welsh source and is unsupported by any trace of a liturgical cult in N. Wales or by church dedications. Less unlikely is the story that he exchanged pastoral staffs with *Columba near the end of that saint's life. Feast: 13 January.

The best modern critical study is by K. H. Jackson, 'The Sources for the Life of St. Kentigern' in N. K. Chadwick, *Studies in the Early British Church* (1958), pp. 273–357. The sources themselves are in A. P. Forbes, *Lives of St. Ninian and St. Kentigern* (1874; 'The Historians of Scotland', vol. v), in *AA.SS.* Ian II (1643), 98 ff. and *N.L.A.*, ii. 114–27. See also: J. MacQueen, 'Yvain, Ewen and Owein ap Urien', *Transactions of Dumfriesshire and Galloway Nat. Hist. and Antiq. Society*, xxxiii (1956), 107 ff.; J. Carney, *Studies in Early Irish Literature* (1955) and J. W. James, *A Vindication of St. Kentigern's Connection with Llanelwy* (pamphlet, Bangor, 1960).

KENTIGERNA (Caentigern, Quentigerna), anchoress who died on Inch Cailleach in Loch Lomond *c.*733. According to the Aberdeen Breviary she was of Irish royal blood, her father being Cellach, prince of Leinster; she married a neighbouring prince and had a son Fillan. After her husband's death she left Ireland, lived as a nun in Scotland, and eventually settled on Loch Lomond, where the island church of Inch Cailleach, of which ruins remain, was dedicated to her. Feast: 7 January.

K.S.S., p. 373; B.T.A., i. 120

KERRIAN (Keriane), a British male saint culted in Cornwall, Brittany, and at Exeter (Leofric Psalter and church dedication). Once wrongly identified with the Irish *Ciaran. Feast unknown.

G. H. Doble, *The Saints of Cornwall*, ii (1962), 56–8.

KESSOG (Mackessog) (6th century), bishop. Born at Cashel of the royal family of Munster, Kessog went to Scotland, became a monk and eventually a bishop in the area around Loch Lomond. Luss was the principal centre of his cult with a sanctuary granted by Robert Bruce, his traditional residence was the Monks' Island in the Loch. Kessog is said to have been murdered by assassins at Bandry, where a heap of stones known as St. Kessog's Cairn once stood. Part of this was removed during road-making in the 18th century and a stone statue of Kessog was found inside it. Several churches in different parts of Scotland are dedicated to him. Feast: 10 March.

K.S.S., pp. 373–4; B.T.A., i. 546.

KEVERNE (date unknown) was the founder of a large parish in the NE. of the Lizard peninsula called Meneage (= Monks' Land). He was formerly wrongly identified with the Irish *Ciaran. Feast unknown.

G. H. Doble, *The Saints of Cornwall*, ii (1962), 54–6.

KEVIN (Coemgen) (d. *c.*618), founder and abbot of Glendalough (Co. Wicklow). The Latin and Irish Lives all date from at least 400 years after his death, tell little about the saint, and were written to further the claims of Glendalough, by then an important monastery and diocese.

Kevin was traditionally of a noble Leinster family which was ousted from the kingship. From childhood he was educated by monks. After ordination he settled as a hermit at Glendalough, most probably by the Upper Lake, marked by the cave called 'St. Kevin's Bed' and the Teampull na Skellig (the rock church), the former being a Bronze Age rock tomb, re-used by the saint. As disciples gathered round him, these premises became too small and the monastery was moved down near the Lower Lake after his death. Later again, perhaps in the time of *Laurence O'Toole, more churches were built even further to the east. But out of all the surviving buildings at Glendalough only those by the Upper Lake can be certainly associated with Kevin.

There are a number of Legends about him, but almost no historical facts. He is said to have fed his community for some time on salmon brought to him by an otter. It is also claimed that he went to see *Ciaran of Clonmacnoise just before his death and that Ciaran gave him his bell. Artists have represented a blackbird who is supposed to have laid one of her eggs in his hand outstretched at prayer, the saint remaining in this position until it was hatched. Kevin was reputed to have died at the age of one hundred and twenty. Glendalough eventually founded other monasteries and became an important pilgrimage centre. Feast: (all over Ireland), 3 June.

Latin Lives in *V.S.H.*, i. 234–57 and in W. W. Heist, *Vitae Sanctorum Hiberniae* (1965), pp. 361–5; Irish Lives in C. Plummer, *Bethada Naem nErren*, i (1922), 125–67 (Eng. tr. in ii. 121–61); see also P. Grosjean, 'Relations mutuelles des Vies latines de S. Caemgen de Glenn Da Locha', *Anal. Boll.*, lxiii (1945), 122–9; *The Irish Saints*, pp. 79–83; B.T.A., ii. 473–5.

KEW (Ciwa, Kuet, Kywere) (?5th century), virgin, patron of St. Kew (Cornwall). This place was formerly called Docco after the saint also known as *Congar, but Congar's monastery came to an end well before 1000 and by the 14th century (or earlier) Kew had replaced him as patron. According to Roscarrock she was his sister; but when she visited her brother in his hermit's cell, 'he would not receive her until such time as he sawe a wild boare miraculously obeye her, after which time he conversed with her, who proved of such rare vertue and holiness as she was after her death reputed a saint and the Church of the parish called after her'. Feast: in the Exeter Martyrology and in Welsh calendars, 8 February.

G. H. Doble, *The Saints of Cornwall*, i (1965), 105–9; Baring-Gould and Fisher, ii. 139–46 wrongly identify her with Cuach, the nurse of the Irish Ciaran.

KEYNE (Cain, Ceinwen) (?6th century), patron of St. Keyne (Cornwall) and possibly of Llangeinor (Mid Glamorgan), but not, according to Ekwall, of Keynsham (Somerset), which means 'Ceagin's (Caega's) hamm'. There was no ancient cult of Keyne in Somerset, which also militates strongly against the attribution of Keynsham to Keyne by Camden and other antiquaries. Traditionally Keyne was one of the daughters of *Brychan, the Welsh patriarch whose children were Christian pioneers of South Wales and Cornwall. She was outstandingly beautiful but refused all offers of marriage, became a solitary on the other side of the Severn (location unspecified), migrated to Cornwall, met *Cadoc at Mount St. Michael, and was persuaded by him to return to Wales, where she died. Haddan and Stubbs, however, consider that she is among the saints 'of whom no reliable evidence can be found that they ever existed at all'. A popular legend about her has been given literary expression in a ballad by Southey called *The Well of St. Keyne*: the tradition is that if the husband or the wife is the first to drink of its waters, he or she will thereby 'get the mastery'. A Cornishman left his bride at the church porch in order to be the first at the well, but he was outwitted by her as she already had taken a bottle of the well-water to church. Feast: 8 (or 7) October.

N.L.A., ii. 102–4 (late and of little value); Baring-Gould and Fisher, ii. 52–5; G. H. Doble, *St. Nectan, St. Keyne* ('Cornish Saints', no. 25) and in *Downside Review* (1931), 156–72; B.T.A., iv. 63–4.

KIDUNAIA, Abraham, see ABRAHAM KIDUNAIA.

KIERAN, see CIARAN.

KILDA (Kilder), supposedly titular of an island west of the Outer Hebrides, never existed. The name is a corruption of 'Skildir', a Norse word meaning 'shields', which was given to a group of these islands to the west of Harris. Later it was transferred to the island Hirta, which by the late 16th century, through orthographic and cartographic error, became known as 'St. Kilda'.

A. B. Taylor, 'The name St. Kilda', *Scottish Studies*, xiii (1969), 145–58.

KILIAN (Chilian) (d. *c.*689), bishop at Wurzburg and martyr. An Irishman, possibly from Mullagh, he set out, perhaps already a bishop, with eleven companions for Germany arriving at Ascaffenburg on the Rhine and then sailing up this river and the Main to Wurzburg. Here he converted the local ruler from paganism. He then visited Pope Conon (686–7), who is said (anachronistically) to have given him a mission to Thuringia and Eastern Franconia. On returning from Rome he found that King Gozbert had married his brother's widow, who, when Kilian attempted to separate them, had him murdered.

It seems clear that he met a violent death, but the details may not be historical. His cult was early and important. His relics were translated in 752 by *Burchard and he is found with *Boniface in the calendar of Godescale (*c.*782). There are also records of him in the early 9th-century Irish martyrologies. Kilian is the principal patron of Wurzburg; his figure appears on seals and coins. The Kilianifest every year is the occasion of an annual mystery play of his life. Some old hymns in Latin and German survive in his honour. Feast: 8 July, especially celebrated in Wurzburg, Vienna, and Ireland.

AA.SS. Iul. II (1721), 599–619: *Herbipolis Iubilans* (1952); A. Gwynn, 'Ireland and Wurzburg in the Middle Ages', *I.E.R.*, lxxxiii (1952), 401–11; id., 'New Light on St. Kilian', *I.E.R.*, lxxxviii (1957), 1–16; J. Hennig, 'Ireland and Germany in the Tradition of St. Kilian', *I.E.R.*, lxxxiii (1952), 21–33.

KINEMARK (Cynfarch Oer) (5th century). According to the Book of Llan Dav he was a disciple of *Dyfrig and gave his name to Llangynfarch, which is St. Kinmark, near Chepstow. Another Cynfarch has church dedications in N. Wales and at Llanfair Dyffryn, Clwyd there was once a *sanctus Kynvarch* represented in a stained-glass window. Feast: 8 September.

Baring-Gould and Fisher, ii. 241–2.

KIRBY, Luke (*c.*1548–82), seminary priest and martyr. Born at Richmond (N. Yorkshire), Kirby received a university education before going to the English College, Douai, where he was received into the R.C. Church and was ordained priest in 1577. He continued his studies in Rome for three years until he set out for England in 1580 with Edmund *Campion. Immediately he landed at Dover he was arrested and was imprisoned in London at the Gatehouse, and tortured by the 'Scavenger's Daughter' at the Tower. In November 1581 he was tried together with Edmund Campion, Ralph *Sherwin, and Alexander *Briant for alleged complicity in a fictitious plot against the queen. He was sentenced to be hanged, drawn, and quartered, but the execution was delayed until 30 May 1582. Relics survive at Stonyhurst College (Lancs.). He was canonized by Paul VI in 1970 as one of the *Forty Martyrs of England and Wales. Feast: 25 October.

R. Challoner, *Memoirs of Missionary Priests* (ed. J. H. Pollen, 1924); B. Camm, *Lives of the English Martyrs*, ii (1914), 500–22; B.T.A., ii. 415–16; M. T. H. Banks, *Bd. Luke Kirby* (pamphlet, 1961).

KOLBE, Maximilian (1894–1941), Franciscan priest. Born at Zdunska Wola near Lodz, he was the second son of devout parents who worked in a cottage weaving industry. Under Russian government the family were impoverished and the parents became Franciscan tertiaries. In 1907 Maximilian joined the junior seminary at Lwow; in 1910 he entered the Franciscan Order. His parents then separated and became religious: his mother a Benedictine and later a Felician lay sister, his father a Franciscan until he left the Order to direct a bookshop at Czestochowa, the national shrine of the Blessed Virgin. After enlisting with Palsudski's patriots, he was wounded fighting the Russians: as one of their subjects he was hanged as a traitor in 1914, aged forty-three.

Maximilian studied at Rome. After his ordination in 1919 tuberculosis was diagnosed and he returned to Poland, where his main work was teaching Church history in a seminary. After a nearly fatal attack he determined to launch his militant sodality and found a magazine for Christian readers in Cracow who needed effective apologetics. Soon the obsolete presses were moved to Grodno, circulation was increased to 45,000, new machinery was installed, which was worked by priests and lay brothers alone. Another attack of tuberculosis was followed by the re-establishment of his printing presses at Niepokalanow near Warsaw. Here Maximilian founded a Franciscan community which combined prayer with cheerfulness and poverty with modern technology: daily as well as weekly newspapers were now produced.

After founding another community at Nagasaki in Japan, he was recalled in 1936 as superior of Niepokalanow, which grew to number 762 friars. When the Germans invaded Poland in 1939, Kolbe, realizing that his monastery would be taken over, sent most of the friars home, warning them not to join the underground resistance. Maximilian and others were taken away for internment, but were soon released, returning to their monastery which became a refugee camp for 3,000 Poles and 1,500 Jews. For some time the papers continued publication, taking a patriotic, independent line, critical of the Third Reich. Kolbe, who had refused German citizenship, was arrested as a journalist, publisher and 'intellectual'. Gestapo officers were shown round the whole monastery and were astonished at the small amount of food prepared for the brothers. They took away Maximilian and four companions to Auschwitz in May 1941, then both a labour camp and a death camp. Names were exchanged for tattooed numbers; the heavy work of moving loads of logs of double weight and at double speed, was enforced by kicks and lashes. Maximilian also moved the bodies of the tortured. He continued his priestly ministry, hearing confessions in unlikely places and smuggling in bread and wine for the Eucharist. He was conspicuous for sympathy and compassion towards those even more unfortunate than himself.

If anyone attempted to escape from the camp, men from the same bunker were selected for death by starvation. Near the end of July, following an escape, men from Kolbe's bunker were paraded, knowing what to expect. One man from each line was selected including a sergeant, Francis Gajowniczek. When like the others he shouted out in despair, Kolbe stepped forward, saying: 'I am a Catholic priest. I wish to die for that man. I am old; he has a wife and children.' The officer, keen to liquidate the old and the weak, changed the numbers. Maximilian went to the death chamber of Cell 18, preparing the others to die with dignity by prayers, psalms, and the example of Christ's Passion. Two weeks later only four were left alive: Maximilian alone was fully conscious. He was injected with phenol and died on 14 August, aged forty-seven.

He was beatified by Paul VI in 1971 and canonized in 1982 by Pope John Paul II, formerly archbishop of Cracow, the diocese which contains Auschwitz, in the presence of the sergeant whose life had been saved. Maximilian was a characteristic figure of Polish religion: his energy, poverty and patriotism, culminating in his death as a martyr to charity, make him an example of unsung heroism among detainees in concentration camps and other prisons. Feast: 14 August.

D. Dewar, *Saint of Auschwitz* (1982); G. Bar, *The Death of Blessed Maximilian Kolbe in the Light of Canon Law* (1972); S. C. Lorit, *The Last Days of Maximilian Kolbe* (1981).

KOREA, MARTYRS OF (1839). Christianity first came to Korea through Christian books sent from China, and the first Korean Christian was baptized in Peking in 1784. A Chinese priest in 1794 found 4,000 Christians; but he was killed in 1801 and the Koreans were without a priest for 30 years. Pius VII sent a bishop, Laurence Imbert, who arrived in disguise in 1837, preceded by two other priests of the same Paris Missionary Society. Christianity was forbidden and for two years they worked in complete secrecy, rising at 2.30 a.m. and ministering at unusual times in conditions of extreme poverty. The growing numbers of Christians (estimated at 9,000) could not for ever remain hidden. Violent persecution followed and the three French priests allowed themselves to be taken, to avert massacre and apostasy. They were beheaded at Seoul on 21 September 1839. No fewer than 78 Koreans were martyred in the same persecution, either like Agatha

Kim or John Ri in the same year, or, a few years later, in 1846, when the first Korean priest to be martyred was Andrew Kim. Beatified in 1925, they were canonized in 1984. Feast: 20 September.

C. Dallet, *L'Histoire de l'Eglise de Corée* (1874), ii. 118–85; A. Launay, *Martyrs français et coréens* (1925); B.T.A., iii. 611–13.

KOSTKA, Stanislaus (1550–68), Jesuit novice. Born at the castle of Rostkovo (Poland) of a noble and wealthy family, he was educated first by a private tutor and then, with his older brother Paul, at the Jesuit college in Vienna. He suffered bullying from his brother, misunderstanding from the family tutor who accompanied them, and unsatisfactory lodgings in a Lutheran household: Stanislaus consequently fell ill. On his recovery he decided to become a Jesuit, but the Austrian Provincial did not dare to receive him, so Stanislaus set out on a 350-mile walk to Rome to put his case before the General. On his way he saw Peter *Canisius who encouraged him, but also tested him by assigning him menial tasks. When he reached Rome, Francis *Borgia admitted him to the Society of Jesus at the age of seventeen. During the remainder of his life he showed himself a model religious in all respects, experienced both ecstasy and visions, but died after only nine months. His brother Paul became a Jesuit also but not until the age of sixty. Stanislaus was canonized in 1726. Feast: 13 November.

AA.SS. Aug. III (1737), 146, 200; U. Ubaldini (ed. Arndt), 'Vita S. Stanislai Kostkae', in *Anal. Boll.*, ix (1890), 360–78, xi (1892), 416–67, xiii (1894), 122–56, xiv (1895), 295–318, xv (1896), 285–315, xvi (1897), 253–96; C. C. Martindale, *Christ's Cadets* (1913); J. Broderick, *St. Peter Canisius* (1935), pp. 674–6.

KUET, see KEW.

KYNEBURGA, see CYNIBURG.

KYNED (Kened, Keneth, Cenydd) (6th century?), according to Welsh tradition, was a son of *Gildas who married and had at least one son and then became a monk under St. Illtud and the founder of Llangenydd in Gower. He later went to Brittany where Ploumelin is the centre of his cult. There is an extraordinary Legend, collected from Welsh sources by John of Tynemouth for *N.L.A.*, which makes him a native of Brittany who was born a cripple, placed in a cradle of osiers, and dropped into a stream which brought him to the island of 'Henisweryn', where a series of miracles and angelic intervention assured his survival and education in the Christian faith. He became a hermit and was joined by a servant. This man stole the lance of some robbers whom Kyned received hospitably. Later *David cured Kyned of his deformity, but he was displeased and asked for it to be retored as before. In all this farrago a breast-shaped bell, on which oaths were taken, figures prominently; but the tale breaks off abruptly, unfinished. The calendar and place-name tradition points to the historical existence of Kyned, but the Legend seems to be pure invention. Feast: in Brittany, Wales, and England, 1 August; translation, according to William Worcestre, 27 June.

N.L.A., ii. 105–9; Baring-Gould and Fisher, ii. 107–15.

KYWERE, see KEW.

L

LABOURÉ, Catherine (1806–76), Sister of Charity. Born at Fain-les-Moutiers (near Dijon) of a large farming family, she looked after her widowed father for several years, then worked as a waitress in her uncle's café at Paris. She joined the Sisters of Charity at Châtillon-sur-Seine in 1830. She made her novitiate at Paris (rue du Bac) and was professed there. She lived inconspicuously for 46 years in her community at Reuilly (Paris) as portress, looking after the elderly in a rest-home and tending the poultry. Superiors described her as 'matter of fact, unexcitable, insignificant, cold, and apathetic'. Until a few months before her death hardly anyone knew about the visions she had experienced as a young nun.

These had several saints as their subject, including the founder *Vincent de Paul. Most famous however were visions and dialogues with the Blessed Virgin, whose content included world-wide disasters, the violent death of a future archbishop (possibly Mgr. Darboy in 1871), and Catherine's future difficulties. Once Mary appeared as in a picture standing on a globe with shafts of light coming from her hands: an inscription surrounded her: 'Mary conceived without sin, pray to us who have recourse to thee.' On the reverse side was a capital 'M' with the cross above and two hearts below. Catherine believed she was ordered to have this produced as a medal: 1,500 were minted in 1832, authorized by the archbishop. In 1834 an account of its origins and efficacy was published: 130,000 copies were soon sold. In 1836 a canonical enquiry into the visions declared them authentic. This judgment seemed to be confirmed when Alphonse Ratisbonne, an Alsatian Jew, was converted to Christianity in 1842, became a priest, and founded the Fathers and Sisters of Sion. From that time onwards this 'Miraculous Medal' and the associated devotion has been very widely propagated.

Catherine died on 31 December and her body remains incorrupt in the convent chapel at rue du Bac, Paris. Miracles were reported at her tomb. She was beatified in 1933 and canonized in 1947. Feast: 28 November.

C. Yves, *La vie secrète de Catherine Labouré* (1948); O. Engelbert, *Catherine Labouré and the Modern Apparitions of Our Lady* (1959); B.T.A., iv. 443–5; *N.C.E.*, viii. 301–2; *Bibl. SS.*, iii. 1045–7.

LABRE, Benedict Joseph (1748–83), confessor. Born at Amette near Boulogne, the oldest of fifteen children of a shopkeeper, he tried to be a Cistercian, then a Carthusian monk, but without success. He was too eccentric for community life and at last accepted the fact, setting out on pilgrimage to Rome. The life of a pilgrim suited him and he made this his way of life, visiting numerous shrines in western Europe: Loreto, Assisi, Bari in Italy, Einsiedeln in Switzerland, Compostela in Spain, and Aix-en-Provence with Paray-le-Monial in France. He practised to an extreme degree the evangelical counsels, wandering in acute poverty, seldom begging, but accepting food from the kindly, although he often gave away money offered to him. Perhaps unconsciously he resembled in his way of life the calling of the Eastern wandering holy man.

In 1774 he settled in Rome, sleeping rough in the Colosseum, spending his days in prayer in the churches, especially during the Forty Hours devotion. Growing infirmities, aggravated by his verminous state, obliged him to accept the shelter of a hospice for poor men, where however he would often give away his portion of soup to those even less fortunate. During Holy Week in 1783 he collapsed in his favourite

Roman church, Santa Maria dei Monti, and died in the house of a friendly butcher. Popular acclaim that a saint had died, enhanced by a biography written by his confessor, led to the introduction of his cause for canonization. This was finally achieved, after rigorous scrutiny, in 1881. He is the patron saint of tramps and the homeless; an authentic portrait, painted by A. Cavalucci while Benedict was in prayer, survives in the Galleria Nazionale d'Arte Antica, Rome. Feast: 16 April.

Life by G. L. Marconi (his confessor), *Ragguaglio della vita del servo di Dio, Benedetto Labre Francese* (1783, Eng. tr. (abridged) 1786); modern Lives by F. Gaguère (1936), A. de la Gorce (Eng. tr. R. Sheed, 1952), P. Doyère (1964); B.T.A., ii. 106–8; *N.C.E.*, s.v.; *Bibl. SS.*, ii. 1218–20.

LAMBERT (*c.*635–*c.*705), bishop of Maastricht and patron of Liège. Born at Maastricht of a noble family, he was educated by its bishop, Théodard, who was murdered for political reasons in 670. Lambert was chosen to succeed him. In the revolution which followed the death of Childeric II in 674, Ebroin resumed power as mayor of the palace and attacked the supporters of Childeric. Lambert, who was one of these, was exiled from 675 to 682 in a monastery at Stavelot. Following the assassination of Ebroin (681), Pepin restored Lambert and the other exiled bishops and expelled the intruders in their sees.

Lambert then worked as a missionary in Kempenland and Brabant, still largely pagan. He met a violent death, probably the outcome of a blood-feud, though his later biographers attributed it to his reproof of Pepin for adultery with his sister-in-law Alpais, mother of Charles Martel.

Because of his violent death Lambert was venerated as a martyr. His successor, *Hubert, translated his relics to a church built over the house where he died. Around this church grew the city of Liège, which became the centre of the diocese. Two ancient English churches are dedicated to him, his feast was kept before and after the Norman Conquest in English monasteries and in the Sarum calendar. Feast: 17 September; translation, 31 May.

Early Lives in *AA.SS.* Sept. V (1755), 518–617 and in B. Krusch, *M.G.H.*, *Scriptores rerum merov.*, vi (1913), 299–429; J. Demarteau, *Vie la plus ancienne de S. Lambert* (1890); G. Kurth, 'La Vita Sancti Lamberti et M. Krusch', *Études Franques*, ii (1919), 319–47.

LA SALLE, John-Baptist de (1651–1719), founder of the Brothers of the Christian Schools. Born at Reims of a noble family, de la Salle was early destined for the Church. He was tonsured at eleven years of age and became a canon of Reims at sixteen. Three years later he went to study at Saint-Sulpice and was ordained priest in 1678. In collaboration with a layman, Adrian Nyel, he opened two schools for poor boys in a society in which there were few such schools and fewer opportunities for social mobility. First, he rented a house for them and later invited them to share his own home; this caused the departure of two of his own brothers, but five of the schoolmasters soon left as well. They were gradually replaced; de la Salle gave up his canonry, sold all his goods, and devoted the proceeds to famine-relief in Champagne and dedicated his life to education.

He opened four schools in spite of the difficulty of finding suitable teachers, but twelve of these eventually joined a religious community under his direction, which soon grew and prospered, partly owing to youths of fifteen to twenty years of age, whom de la Salle set up in a 'junior novitiate' under his own supervision. Soon parish priests sent him young men to train as teachers before returning to schools in their own villages: to meet this need he established the first training-college for teachers at Reims in 1686, which was followed by others at Paris and Saint-Denis. At Paris also he established two free schools which proved remarkably successful.

Later he accepted an invitation from James II, king of England, then in exile in France, to start a school for fifty young gentlemen. This brought his ideas and techniques into contact with a more influential sector of society. These included the replacement of individual instruction by class teaching in the vernacular (instead of Latin), the insistence on the silence of the pupils while the teaching took place, and providing on Sundays religious instruction combined with technical education for artisans. Yet another innovation of de la Salle was the foundation of reformatories for disturbed boys: the present-day activity of his Order in the 'approved schools' has been a direct development of his ideals and practice.

One characteristic of his Order, which remains today, is that no member of it can ever be ordained a priest and no priest can become a member. His Order suffered from internal conflict during his lifetime as well as external opposition, partly from those who rejected all education for the poor except in manual skills. He drew up a Rule in 1695, but suffered some sort of deposition in 1702, which, however, was allowed to lapse because of strong opposition to it inside his Order: in fact he remained in charge until his resignation in 1717. He died on 7 April 1719, aged sixty-eight. He was canonized in 1900 and declared patron of all school-teachers in 1950. His relics were translated to Rome in 1937.

His two principal works reflect his life's main achievements: *The Conduct of Christian Schools* explains his widely praised educational methods and ideals, while his *Meditations for Sundays* reproduces his teaching on prayer, much influenced by Bérulle and other French writers of his time. Nowadays his Order (frequently called the 'Christian Brothers' or 'De la Salle Brothers') numbers about 20,000 members. It has been very influential in the English-speaking world as well as in France and many other countries. He was a notable pioneer in education for the working classes, in the training of teachers, and in the rehabilitation of delinquents. Feast: 7 April (formerly 15 May).

Contemporary Life by J. B. Blain (1733); in English the standard works are by W. J. Battersby, *De La Salle* (3 vols., 1945–52) and a single-volume biography, *St. John Baptist de la Salle* (1957); see also Lives by J. Guibert (1900), A. Delaire (1902), F. Thompson (1911), and G. Rigault, *Histoire Générale de l'institut des Frères des Écoles Chrétiennes* (9 vols., 1937–53).

LASERIAN (Laisren, Molaise) (d. 639), monk and perhaps bishop. Born in Ireland, he is venerated in both Ireland and Scotland. Little is known of his life. He was abbot of Old Leighlin (Co. Carlow), founder of Inishmurray (Co. Sligo), and propagated the Roman calculation of Easter. His Life claims improbably that he was consecrated bishop at Rome and was even a 'papal legate'. A legend that he voluntarily accepted illness caused by thirty diseases at once, in expiation for his sins and to avoid purgatory after death, partly accounts for his present-day cult. This is centred on Inishmurray, where there are notable monastic remains and a series of praying-stations. In Scotland a cave hermitage which bears his name is on Holy Island in Lamlash Bay, off Arran. Feast: 18 April.

K.S.S., pp. 407–9; *The Irish Saints*, pp. 203–4.

LAUDUS (Lo), bishop of Coutances, 6th century. He took part in councils at Orléans in 533, 538, and 541; in 549 he buried *Paternus. Otherwise nothing is known of him. But his name was given to Saint-Lo (Manche), as well as to a college and railway-station at Angers. His feast was kept in the Sarum calendar and elsewhere on 22 September.

AA.SS. Sept. VI (1756), 438–48 with *Propylaeum*, pp. 410–11; *Bibl. SS.*, vii. 1121–2.

LAURENCE (d. 258), deacon and martyr of Rome. His existence and his martyrdom are witnessed by the very ancient *Depositio Martyrum*, but few details of his life are historical. He was a Roman deacon, closely associated with Pope *Sixtus II, who was martyred a few days before him in the persecution of Valerian; he was also prominent in almsgiving, which was part of his duties.

But other details, including the famous

roasting on the gridiron, are quite unhistorical, as the contemporary instrument of capital punishment was the sword. The gridiron story was probably derived from a Phrygian source through the Acts of *Vincent of Saragossa. Laurence's own Acts, with vivid dialogue and imaginary details, powerfully contributed to the cult of Rome's most famous post-apostolic martyr; so did the writings of Prudentius, *Ambrose, and *Augustine.

In Rome five ancient basilicas are dedicated to him, including that built over his tomb called St. Laurence-outside-the-walls. His name is in the Canon of the Roman Mass, and wherever the Roman calendar penetrated, so did the cult of Laurence. Pope Vitalian sent relics of Laurence to King Oswiu of Northumbria (7th century); there are several early English dedications to Laurence, such as that of the Anglo-Saxon church at Bradford-on-Avon. Before the Reformation English dedications numbered 228. Scandinavia too had important early dedications, such as Lund Cathedral, while Spain, which claimed him as a native, had a strong cult revealed by the dedication of the Escorial.

In the Ravenna mosaics (mausoleum of Galla Placidia) Laurence is depicted carrying a long cross on his shoulder and a gospel book in his hand; he walks towards the fire and the gridiron. The gridiron is his usual emblem, but occasionally a purse of money, to recall his almsgiving. Often he forms a pair with *Stephen, the two patrons of deacons. The most complete cycle of his life was painted by Fra Angelico for the chapel of Nicholas V in the Vatican; there are notable stained-glass windows of his life in the cathedrals of Bourges and Poitiers.

His intercession was believed to have caused the victories of Christian armies in the battle of Lechfeld against the Magyars (955) and of Saint-Quentin in 1557. Feast: 10 August.

AA.SS. Aug. II (1735), 485–532; H. Delehaye, 'Recherches sur le légendier romain', *Anal. Boll.*, li (1933), 34–98; Bede, *H.E.*, iii. 29 and *Historia Abbatum*, c. 17; Ambrose, *De Officiis*, i. 41, ii. 28; Epistola xxxvii; *P.L.*, xvi. 84–5, 141, 1093.

LAURENCE GIUSTINIANI (1381–1455), archbishop of Venice. Born of a noble Venetian family, Laurence lived devoutly at home for several years before he renounced wealth and honours to join the Augustinian monastery of San Giorgio on the island of Alga. This became a congregation of canons regular in 1404. Laurence was ordained priest in 1406, became prior in 1407 and again 1409–21, and then general of the congregation 1424–31. During these years he wrote notable ascetical and mystical works, based on his perception of Eternal Wisdom. Early works treat the contemplative, later ones the apostolic life. The most important is *De casto connubio Verbi et animae* (1425).

In 1433 he was appointed bishop of Castello, which included part of Venice, by Eugenius IV. In 1451 Nicholas V reorganized the whole area by suppressing Castello, reconstituting Grado at Venice, and making Laurence its first bishop. As he was first in line of the new organization, he is often but incorrectly called Patriarch of Venice.

As bishop, Laurence was famous for personal austerity and generosity to the poor. He generally preferred to give food and clothes rather than money, as he had learnt by experience how easily cash handouts could be abused. So he gave money in small quantities only, specially to those too shy or too proud to ask for help. He generally preferred to delegate finances to his steward and to reserve his time and strength for the spiritual aspects of his office. This included peacemaking and other pastoral work, of which he was reckoned to be a model by contemporaries.

In his last illness very many clergy and layfolk came to see him, among them the beggars and the destitute. He died on a bed of straw on 8 January. Canonized in 1690, his feast is on the day of his consecration as bishop: 5 September. Paintings of him by Bellini and Segala survive at Venice.

Life by his nephew in *AA.SS.* Ian. I (1643), 551–63; other Lives by D. Rosa (1914), P. La Fontaine (1960), and S. Giuliani (1962); see also *San Lorenzo Giustiniani nel V centenario della morte, 1456–1956* (1959); *N.C.E.*, viii. 567–8; *Bibl. SS.*, viii. 150–9.

LAURENCE LORICATUS (*c.*1190–1243), hermit of Subiaco. Born at Facciolo (Apulia), he killed a man accidentally in his youth and decided to expiate for it, first by a pilgrimage to Compostella and then by becoming a hermit at Subiaco, hallowed by *Benedict long before. Discovered by shepherds and pilgrims, he received and trained disciples into a small community. He himself habitually wore not a hairshirt but a coat of chain-mail next to the skin (hence his name), and also practised the strictest poverty, giving away to the poor the offerings made by visitors.

A book of prayers written by him survives. His fame attracted a visit from Cardinal Hugolino (later Pope Gregory IX) who in 1224 persuaded him to abandon his breastplate. He died in 1243 after 34 years of eremitical life. He was succeeded by his disciple Amico de Canterano, who had shared his way of life for 24 years.

An enquiry into his life and miracles initiated by Innocent IV in 1244 did not lead to an immediate formal canonization, but a popular cult flourished which was approved by Pius VI in 1778. Laurence's relics, including a manuscript in his own hand and his breastplate, are enshrined in St. Benedict's Cave at Subiaco. Feast: 16 August.

H.S.S.C., vi. 277; B.T.A., iii. 337; *Bibl. SS.*, viii. 136–41.

LAURENCE OF BRINDISI (1559–1619), Capuchin Franciscan. Born at Brindisi (near Naples) of a wealthy Venetian family, Laurence became a Franciscan at Verona at the age of sixteen. He soon developed an extraordinary gift for learning languages, both ancient and modern, and for the study of the text of the Bible. These aptitudes were used at Rome, where he was deputed by Clement VIII to work specially for the conversion of the Jews. He was then sent to establish the Capuchin reform in Germany and founded houses at Prague, Vienna, and Gorizia. He became minister-general in 1602, but refused re-election in 1605; later he was commissary-general (1606–10) and definitor-general (1613, 1618).

He also acquired some political and even military importance. Rudolf II, the emperor, gave him the mission of uniting the German princes against the Turks. As chaplain-general he exhorted the troops and rode in front of them, armed only with a crucifix, in the striking victory of Szekes-Fehervar (1601). Later he persuaded Philip III of Spain to join the Catholic League and founded a Capuchin house at Madrid. Soon after he became nuncio at Munich, both co-ordinating the efforts of the League and being active in preaching and peacemaking.

In 1618 he retired to Caserta for a life of contemplative devotion, from which he was sent to Spain and Portugal to persuade Philip III to replace the viceroy of Naples. He died at Lisbon and was buried in a Poor Clare cemetery at Villafranca. He was canonized in 1881 and declared a Doctor of the Church by John XXIII in 1959. His works include sermons, a commentary on Genesis, and some controversial works against the Lutherans. Feast: formerly 23 July, now 21 July in the Roman calendar.

Life by A. Brennan (1911) and A. da Carmignano (Eng. tr. 1963); works published at Venice (1928–55); see also Capuchin Educational Conference, *St. Lawrence of Brindisi* (1960); *Bibl. SS.*, viii. 161–80.

LAURENCE OF CANTERBURY (d. 619), archbishop. He was one of *Augustine's companions in the mission to England in 596–7. He was sent back to Rome to tell *Gregory of the early conversions in Kent and brought back (in 601) Gregory's answers to Augustine's questions about the organization of the Church in Canterbury. Augustine chose him as his successor during his lifetime, an irregular but not unprecedented procedure.

Archbishop of Canterbury from *c.*604, Laurence followed Augustine's policy of consolidation in the south-east of Britain and attempted co-operation with the British bishops in the conversion of the Anglo-Saxons. British intransigence and racial antipathy made this last impossible. When *Ethelbert's son Edbald married his stepmother and refused to give the Christians the same support in Kent as his father, the very existence of the Church in Canterbury seemed in danger. *Mellitus and *Justus retired temporarily to Gaul and Laurence thought of following them. He was deterred, according to *Bede, by a vision in sleep of *Peter, who beat him black and blue for cowardice. This story seems to be a conflation of the *Quo Vadis?* legend of St. Peter and a famous letter of *Jerome. Whether or not Bede gives the true explanation, Edbald became a Christian, favoured Laurence and his companions, and enabled the Church to expand more rapidly.

Laurence was buried in the monastery church of SS. Peter and Paul (later called St. Augustine's), Canterbury, which he had consecrated himself. His body and those of other early Canterbury saints were translated in 1091. His tomb was opened in 1915. The Irish Stowe missal, depending perhaps on a Canterbury list of the 7th century, records his feast. This was on 3 February. A translation feast of Augustine and his companions, including Laurence, was kept at Canterbury on 13 September.

Bede, *H.E.*, i. 27, 32; ii. 4–5; Goscelin, *Historia Translationis S. Augustine; P.L.*, clv. 14–46; W. H. St. John Hope in *Archaeol. Cantiana*, xxxii (1916), 1–26; N. Brooks, *The Early History of the Church of Canterbury* (1984).

LAURENCE O'TOOLE (Lorcan Ua Tuathail) (1128–80), archbishop of Dublin 1162–80. Born in Co. Kildare of a marriage between the chieftain families of O'Toole and O'Byrne, Laurence spent part of his childhood as the hostage of Dermot McMurrogh, king of Leinster. He became a monk at Glendalough and was elected abbot at the age of twenty-five. His duties included not only the government of his monastery but also the relief of famine and the suppression of brigandage (some of it due to apostate monks) in the vicinity. In 1162 he was elected archbishop of Dublin. To ensure a supply of good pastoral clergy he introduced Austin Canons of Arrouaise into the principal churches, wearing their religious habit himself and following their community life. His nephew became bishop of Glendalough, replacing an unworthy intruder, supported by the local chieftain; Laurence retained contact by living there from time to time in *Kevin's cell above the principal lake. He was also outstanding for his relief of the poor in his diocese, sometimes sending them, later in his life, to England for rehabilitation.

When the English invaded Ireland in 1170, Laurence acted as peacemaker between Strongbow and the Irish. He took part in various synods including Cashel (1172), convened by Henry II, where Adrian IV's Bull imposing clerical celibacy and the Sarum Rite was accepted. In 1172 he negotiated a treaty between Henry II and Rory O'Connor, high-king of Ireland. On this occasion he visited *Thomas Becket's shrine at Canterbury and narrowly escaped violent death at the hand of a mad assassin.

Inevitably Laurence had become involved in affairs of State as well as those of the local church. In 1179 his activities widened: with five other Irish bishops he went to Rome for the third Lateran Council, where he gave Alexander III a full report on the Church in Ireland and became papal legate. On their way to Rome they had been obliged by Henry II to swear not to injure his rights as ruler of Ireland when they were in Rome; this did not prevent Laurence obtaining papal protection for the properties of the see of Dublin and its five suffragans, especially Glendalough. Also in 1179 was held a council at Clonfert which deposed seven 'lay bishops', prevented priests' or bishops' sons from receiving holy orders, and above all forbade any layman to have 'the rule of any church or church matters'. These decrees show that the success of *Malachy in fighting the same battles had been partial only. The growing power of Dublin was made clear in 1180 when Laurence promoted a Connacht bishop to the primatial see of Armagh.

Also in 1180 Laurence again visited Henry II on behalf of Rory O'Connor to negotiate tribute and other matters. But Henry, incensed by Laurence's use of the papal bulls in property disputes with Norman settlers near Dublin, refused to see him, keeping him waiting at Abingdon for three weeks. Laurence followed him to Normandy and obtained his permission to return to Dublin. But on the way Laurence died at Eu (Seine-Inférieure) on 14 November 1180, where his relics survive and where his Life was written.

Laurence was canonized by Honorius III in 1225; his relics were translated 10 May 1226. He has a place in the painted calendar of saints canonized in the 13th century in the basilica of the *Four Crowned Martyrs at Rome. Feast: 14 November; translation, 10 May.

C. Plummer, 'Vie et miracles de S. Laurent, archevéque de Dublin', *Anal. Boll.*, xxxiii (1914), 121–86; M. V. Ronan, 'St. Laurentius, Archbishop of Dublin: Original Testimonies for Canonization', *I.E.R.*, xxvii (1926), 347–64; xxviii (1926), 246–56, 467–80, 596–612; 'St. Lorcan Ua Tuathail', *I.E.R.*, xxxviii (1936), 369–86, 486–509; A. Gwynn, 'St. Laurence O'Toole as Legate in Ireland', *Anal. Boll.*, lxviii (1950), 223–40; J. F. O'Doherty, 'St. Laurence O'Toole and the Anglo-Norman Invasion' *I.E.R.*, l (1937), 449–77, 600–25; li (1938), 131–46; J. Hennig, 'The place of the archdiocese of Dublin in the hagiographical tradition of the Continent', *Repertorium Novum*, i (1955–6), 45–63; J. Ryan, 'The ancestry of St. Laurence O'Toole', ibid., pp. 64–75.

LAWRENCE, Robert (d. 1535), Carthusian monk and martyr. He became a monk of the London Charterhouse and some years after his profession became prior of Beauvale (Notts.). In February 1535 he visited the London Charterhouse with his fellow prior, Augustine *Webster of Axholme, to consult the prior of London, John *Houghton, about the Carthusian attitude to the religious policies of King Henry VIII, soon to be imposed on the whole country and consequently on all the religious, including monks. After the three priors' visit to Thomas Cromwell, their fate was exactly the same; together they suffered martyrdom at Tyburn on 4 May: all three are among the *Forty Martyrs of England and Wales canonized by Paul VI in 1970. Feast: 25 October.

For further information and bibliography see John HOUGHTON.

LAZARUS OF BETHANY (1st century), brother of Martha and Mary. The account of his being raised from the dead by Jesus (John 11: 1–44) was the reason for widespread veneration in Jerusalem (witnessed by the Spanish pilgrim Etheria in *c.*390) and elsewhere. The New Testament writings say nothing about his life after the Resurrection. An Eastern tradition relates that he was placed in a leaky boat with his sisters by the Jews at Jaffa and that they all landed safely at Cyprus, where Lazarus became bishop and died peacefully thirty years later. His relics were translated to Constantinople in 890.

The famous legend connecting him with France originated in the 11th century. According to this, Lazarus and his sisters were placed in a boat without oars or rudder, from which they landed in the south-east of Gaul. They made many converts at and around Marseilles, where Lazarus became bishop and was eventually martyred under Domitian (81–96). It was believed that he was buried in a cave, over which the abbey church of St. *Victor was later built: this may be due to confusion with a 5th-century bishop of Aix, also called Lazarus, who was buried in the crypt of this church. Later in the Middle Ages an account of a vision of the next world was attributed to Lazarus.

Both the military Order of Knights Hospitallers and many medieval lepers and leper-hospitals claimed Lazarus as their patron, but this was the fictitious Lazarus in Christ's parable of Dives and Lazarus recounted by Luke (16: 19–31).

The more recent Order of Lazarists, founded by *Vincent de Paul, took its name from the Paris church dedicated to Saint-Lazare.

Feast: 17 December; but 4 May in the East for the translation to Constantinople. Chichester cathedral has a fine 11th-century sculpture of the Raising of Lazarus.

Bibl. SS., vii. 1135–52; H. Thurston in *Studies*, xxiii (1934), 110–23; G. Morin, 'Saint Lazare et saint Maximin', *Mémoires de la Soc. des Antiquaires de France*, lvi (1897), 27–51; M. Voigt, *Beitrage zur Geschichte der Visionenliteratur in M.A.*, ii (1924); B.T.A., iv. 576–7.

LEANDER (*c.*550–600), bishop of Seville. The son of Severian, duke of Carthagena, and the older brother of *Isidore, Leander became a monk at Seville and was consecrated bishop *c.*584 after having been on an embassy to Constantinople, where he met *Gregory the Great and suggested to him that he should write his famous *Moralia* on Job.

On his return he started his life-work of propagating Christian orthodoxy against the Arians in Spain. His arduous labours were eventually crowned with success. The third Council of Toledo (589) declared the consubstantiality of the three Persons of the Holy Trinity and initiated moral reforms also. By his wisdom and reasoning he obtained the conversion to orthodoxy of both the Visigoths and the Suevi and was rewarded by Gregory both with affectionate congratulation and with the pallium.

Leander also wrote an influential Rule for Nuns and introduced into the West the custom of singing the Nicene Creed at Mass, later adopted by Rome and other Western centres. Feast: 27 February.

AA.SS. Mar. II (1668), 275–80; works in *P.L.*, lxxii. 869–98; modern edn. of his Rule by A. C. Vega (1948); J. Madoz, 'Libellus de Institutione Virginum', *Anal. Boll.*, lxvii (1949), 407–24.

LEBUIN (Liafwine) (d. *c.*775). An Anglo-Saxon who became a monk at Wilfrid's monastery of Ripon, Lebuin joined his compatriot missionaries in Germany and Frisia in 754, the year of the death of *Boniface. His Frankish disciple Gregory, then at Utrecht, received Lebuin gladly and sent him to the eastern Netherlands, where he worked in the dangerous border area of Franks and Saxons near the river Ysel. The main centre of his work was Deventer, where he built a church, subsequently burnt down and then rebuilt, and where he died and was buried. He was not a bishop and should not be identified with the bishop Leofwine who wrote with Boniface to Ethelbald, king of Mercia. Lebuin's preaching at Marklo, where the Saxons held an annual secular assembly, is described in the 9th-century Life. Holding a cross and a gospel-book he proclaimed that the Lord alone, the Creator, is the only true God, that their heathen gods were dead and powerless, that he himself had been sent to bring them peace and salvation through baptism, and that if they refused they would be destroyed by a king who would be sent against them. Although some of the Saxons cut stakes to kill him, others honoured him as an 'ambassador from God', and he was allowed to travel and preach wherever he wished. Feast: 12 November, mainly in Holland.

Life by Hucbald in *P.L.*, cxxxii. 877–94; second Life, ed. A. Hofmeister in *M.G.H.*, *Scriptores*, xxx (part 2), 789–95 (Eng. tr. in C. H. Talbot, *Anglo-Saxon Missionaries in Germany*, 1954); see also F. Hesterman, *Der hl. Lebuin* (1935), and W. Levison, *England and the Continent in the Eighth Century* (1956), pp. 108–10.

LEGER (Ledger, Leodegar, Leodegarius) (*c.*616–79), bishop of Autun and martyr. He was educated at the court of King Clotaire II and by a priest of Poitiers, chosen by Dudon, Leger's uncle and bishop of that city; he became a deacon at twenty and archdeacon soon after. Once ordained priest he became abbot of Saint-Maixent, which he reformed by introducing the Rule of St. Benedict. He was chosen as bishop of Autun by *Bathild, the regent, of Anglo-Saxon origin. His appointment followed a long vacancy and put an end to the strife and bloodshed caused by rival candidates; he ruled as a reforming bishop: building churches, caring for the poor, holding synods, but also, like other bishops of his time, fortifying the town and becoming involved in secular and court affairs. In 673, on the death of Clotaire III, he supported Childeric II against the intrigues of Ebroin, the Neustrian palace-mayor. For a time all went well, but Childeric married a near-relative against his advice and without ecclesiastical approbation. Leger fell from favour and was banished to Luxeuil. Theoderic, however, restored Leger to Autun, but Ebroin pursued him with an army. Leger surrendered to avoid bloodshed, was blinded, mutilated, and finally beheaded.

Although his death was for political reasons, he was regarded as a martyr and his cult, centred on his tomb at 'Sarcingum' (= Saint-Léger in the Pas-de-Calais) and on Saint-Maixent, to which his relics were translated in 682, rapidly spread in France, came to England before the Norman Conquest, and became well established in monastic calendars and in the Sarum Rite. Five ancient English churches are dedicated to him. He is represented on screens at Ashton and Wolborough (Devon). But the famous horse-race is named not after him, but after an 18th-century Colonel St. Leger. Feast: 2 October.

AA.SS. Oct. I (1765), 355–491 (contains two early but not contemporary Lives, based on a lost original, provisionally reconstituted by B. Krusch, *M.G.H.*, *Scriptores rerum merov.*, v (1910), 249–362); F. Camerlinck, *Saint Léger* (1910) and A. Lesage, *Le Fondateur de Liège* (1919); B.T.A., iv. 9–11; *N.C.E.*, viii. 654–5.

LEO THE GREAT (d. 461), pope. He was probably born in Rome of Tuscan parentage; of his early life there is no record. Under Celestine I and Sixtus III he was at least a deacon and sufficiently important to correspond with *Cyril of Alexandria, and for a treatise of John *Cassian on the Incarnation to be dedicated to him. He was also employed as a peacemaker between two generals whose differences endangered the safety of Gaul from the barbarians. Leo was still in Gaul when messengers arrived in 440 to tell him that he had been elected bishop of Rome.

Leo's twenty years' pontificate was important in several ways. His statement of the doctrine of the Incarnation of Christ, acclaimed at the Council of Chalcedon (451), has often been regarded as one of the highlights of Christian history; he also acted energetically to free Rome from the power of the barbarians and to restore the spiritual and material damage they perpetrated; in his writings and actions shone a deep conviction that the doctrinal primacy of Rome was of divine and scriptural authority: throughout his reign he consolidated and increased the influence and prestige of the papacy.

His 143 surviving letters, although less numerous than those of *Gregory the Great, reveal a similar care for the Church in Spain, Gaul, and Africa. In different places the errors of Manichaeism, Priscillianism, and Pelagianism reappeared and required vigilant and determined treatment. On occasion he had to reassert the ancient tradition whereby bishops had a right of appeal to Rome: he found that *Hilary had exceeded his powers as metropolitan and so Leo overruled some of his decisions. In all his guidance and intervention he was conscious of his authority, or rather, that of Peter in his successors.

Leo's political importance was also considerable. In 452 Attila with the Huns sacked Milan and caused terror by his violence far and wide. He moved against Rome and was met by Leo, who persuaded him to accept tribute instead of sacking Rome. Later the Vandal Genseric came with a large army: again Leo went out to meet him. This time Rome was almost without defence, but although Leo again tried to save the city, it was plundered for fourteen days. Many captives were taken to Africa, but some ecclesiastical treasures were restored. Leo sent priests and alms to the captives, and to Sicily.

The greatest triumph of his life was the acceptance of his dogmatic letter (or Tome) at the Council of Chalcedon. As in his other writings, so in this one, he showed remarkable clarity of thought and felicity of wording. Jesus Christ, he taught, is one Person, the Divine Word, in whom the two natures, human and divine, are permanently united without confusion or mixture. When the council heard this document read by Leo's legates, they cried 'Peter has spoken by Leo'. It became thenceforth the official teaching of the Christian Church. But the same council enhanced the status of the see of Constantinople, and in spite of the legates' protests made it a patriarchate, mainly for political reasons. So here, as with the fall of Rome to the barbarians, Leo's success was mixed with failure. Jalland described Leo's character as one of indomitable energy, magnanimity, consistency, and devotion to duty. He died on 10 November and was buried at St. Peter's, Rome. His relics were translated on 28 June 688.

Some of the collects in the Leonine Sacramentary are inspired by his thought and may be his own work. His principal writings to survive are ninety-six sermons and letters. He was declared a Doctor of the Church in 1754. His feast was formerly kept on 11 April, following the *Liber Pontificalis*, and on 28 June in the Sarum calendar and numerous monastic calendars; now it is on 10 November in the West and 18 February in the East.

AA.SS. Apr. II (1675), 14–22; *C.M.H.*, pp. 183, 593–4; L. Duchesne, *Liber Pontificalis*, i. 239; T. G. Jalland, *The Life and Times of St. Leo the Great* (1941); A. Regnier, *Saint Léon le Grand* (1910); S. Brezzi, *S. Leone Magno* (1947); P. Stockmeier, *Leo I der Grosse* (1959); W. Ullmann, 'Leo I and the Theme of Papal Primacy', *J.T.S.*, xi (1960), 25–51; Leo's works are in *P.L.*, liv–lvi (from Ballerini's edn. of 1753–7); Eng. tr. of his letters by C. L. Feltoe (1896); French tr. of the sermons by R. Dolle (*S.C.*, 1947 ff.); see also E. Dekkers, 'Autour de l'oeuvre liturgique de S. Léon le Grand', *Sacris Erudiri*, x (1958), 363–98; D. M. Hope, *The Leonine Sacramentary* (1971). See also *O.D.P.*, pp. 43–5.

LEO III (d. 816), pope. A Roman priest who became cardinal-priest of St. Susanna, Leo was chosen as pope in 795. From the beginning of his reign a faction surrounding his predecessor's disappointed nephew bitterly opposed him, even attempting to blind and mutilate him in 799. Leo retired to Paderborn where Charlemagne was; he was given an escort and returned to Rome amid great rejoicing. But his enemies made serious charges against him of perjury and adultery, of which Leo purged himself in a synod. Leo's reliance on the emperor was similar to that of his predecessor, but it was Leo's achievement to cement the alliance between papacy and empire by crowning Charlemagne in St. Peter's on Christmas Day, 800. This symbolic act inaugurated the Christian empire of the West, believed to be equal to the Eastern empire of Constantinople and to realize Augustine's ideal of the City of God. On this alliance was founded the unity of medieval Christendom; but opinions differ about the precise significance of the coronation and whether pope or emperor gained most from it in authority and protection. Leo gained security against his enemies and greater ability to intervene effectively outside the papal states, but he resisted imperial pressure to impose the *Filioque* clause in the Creed because of the risk of alienating Greek Christians. Leo was concerned with English affairs through Offa's requests to his predecessor to set up Lichfield as a metropolitan see, which had been granted. But after Offa's death Leo in 803 restored the previous status of Canterbury; Lichfield reverted to being one of its suffragans. He also helped to settle differences between archbishops of Canterbury and kings of Kent. The death of Charlemagne in 814 was the occasion for renewed plots against Leo; at the same time there was a Saracen invasion of the Italian coast. Leo restored order but his health gave way: he died on 12 June after a reign of twenty years. His cult dates from the 10th century, but he was canonized only in 1673. A restored near-contemporary mosaic survives in the Lateran depicting St. Peter giving the pallium to Leo and a standard to Charlemagne. Feast: 12 June.

AA.SS. Iun. II (1698), 572–90; L. Duchesne, *Le Liber Pontificalis*, ii. 1–48; Letters and other documents in *P.L.*, cii. 1023–72; P. Jaffé, *Regesta Pontificum Romanorum*, i (1885), 307–16; L.

Wallach, 'The Genuine and Forged Oath of Pope Leo III', *Traditio*, xi (1955), 37–63; id., 'The Roman Synod of December 800 and the alleged trial of Leo III', *Harvard Theol. Rev.*, xlix (1956), 123–42; see also H. K. Mann, *The Lives of the Popes in the Middle Ages*, ii (1906), 1–110; W. Ullmann, *The Growth of Papal Government in the Middle Ages* (2nd edn., 1962) and *O.D.P.*, pp. 97–9.

LEO IX (1002–54), pope. Born of noble, bilingual parents in Alsace, he was educated at Toul, mainly by Adalbert, later bishop of Metz. As a deacon of the pre-Gregorian unreformed Church he was given command of troops provided by the bishop to put down a Lombard rebellion. He was most successful and gained a reputation for handling men skilfully. In 1027 he was chosen bishop of Toul. He reformed the canons who served the cathedral, and the monasteries of Moyenmoutier and Saint-Dié. He also held many synods and visitations. In 1048 the Emperor Henry III chose him as pope, and Leo was acclaimed by the Roman clergy and people.

Once pope, he travelled through Italy, Germany, and France, holding twelve reforming synods. This process was a useful innovation which greatly helped to eliminate simony and nepotism, long taken for granted, and clerical marriage. At Reims, for example, his synod led to the deposition of certain bishops, while others, including the host-bishop of the assembly, had to make their peace privately with the pope by resigning their charge and accepting it again from him, significantly with a new crozier. The movement spread through Europe, obtaining English participation and support through delegates sent to the councils. It was paradoxical that Leo IX, usually regarded as the initiator of the Gregorian Reform which liberated the Church from both the emperors and the Roman nobility, owed his appointment to both. The ideal of independence from the secular power emerged later; in its early days the Gregorian papal reformers were ready to work with and through the kings. So close was their partnership that at the end of his life Leo tried to form a political and military alliance against the Norman invaders of southern Italy. He led an army against them, but was defeated and captured at Civitella. *Peter Damian and others criticized severely this military involvement: battles should be fought by emperors, not popes.

Another important setback just before his death was the breach with Constantinople, which eventually led to the Eastern Schism. He sent legates to Constantinople to deal with accusations of heresy which came from Michael Cerularius, the patriarch: he did not live to see the full conflict unfold of mutual accusation and separation. Leo placed his bed and his coffin side by side in St. Peter's and died there on 19 April. Within forty years, it is said, seventy cures, believed to be miraculous took place; Leo was acclaimed as a saint; in 1087 his relics were enshrined. Another link between Leo IX and England was his friendly relationship with *Edward the Confessor. Edward had vowed to go on pilgrimage to Rome but found himself unable to do so. Instead Leo accepted his plan to refound Westminster Abbey. Feast: 19 April.

AA.SS. Apr. II (1675), 642–74; A. Poncelet, 'Vie et miracles de S. Léon IX', *Anal. Boll.*, xxv (1906), 258–97; A. Fliche, *La Réforme grégorienne*, i (1924), 129–59; H. Tritz, 'Die hagiographischen Quellen zur Geschichte Papst Leos IX', *St. Greg.*, iv (1952), 191–364; R. Mayne, 'East and West in 1054', *C.H.J.*, xi (1953–5), 133–48; D. M. Nicol, 'Byzantium and the Papacy in the 11th century', *J.E.H.*, xiii (1962), 1–20. See also *O.D.P.*, pp. 147–8.

LEODEGAR (Leodegarius), see LEGER.

LEONARD, hermit of the 6th(?) century. There seems to be no trace of any cult in liturgical books, church dedications, or inscriptions earlier than the 11th century, but he became one of the most popular saints of western Europe in the later Middle Ages. His most notable patronages were of pregnant women and captives such as prisoners of war: the former was based on an episode recounted in his quite unhistorical Life (of *c.*1025), the latter was partly due to the release of Bohemond, the crusading prince of Antioch, in 1103 from a Moslem prison, who subsequently visited Noblac (now Saint-Léonard, near Limoges), the site of the saint's monastery and shrine, where he made an offering in gratitude for his release.

According to the Life Leonard was a Frankish noble, converted to Christianity by *Remigius. His godfather was Clovis who offered Leonard a bishopric. This he refused; he became a monk at Micy and later a hermit at Noblac, where he built himself a cell and lived completely alone. Clovis hunted in the forest one day, accompanied by his wife, who was safely delivered of a child there by the help and prayers of Leonard. Clovis was so grateful that he gave him as much land as he could ride around on a donkey in one night. With this endowment he founded the abbey of Noblac, where he died and was buried. If this Life did not create the cult, it powerfully transformed it. The cult spread from France to England, Italy, and especially Bavaria. In England no fewer than 177 churches are dedicated to him; towns in Sussex and Roxburgh bear his name. Feast: 6 November, in Sarum calendar and elsewhere. Leonard's historical existence is probable, but unproved.

AA.SS. Nov. III (1910), 139–209; A. Poncelet, 'Boémond et S. Léonard', *Anal. Boll.*, xxxi (1912), 24–44; F. Arbellot, *Vie de S. Léonard* (1883); J. A. Aich, *Leonard, der grosse Patron des Volkes* (1928); B.T.A., iv. 273–4; *Bibl. SS.*, vii 1198–1208.

LEONARD OF PORT MAURICE (1676–1751), Franciscan priest. Baptized Paul Jerome Casanova in his native town of Porto Maurizio (Liguria), he was educated by the Jesuits in Rome, but joined the Franciscan Order as a young man. He completed his studies at St. Bonaventure's College on the Palatine and was ordained priest in 1703. In 1709 he restored the Florentine friary of San Francesco del Monte to a state of austere fidelity to Francis's teaching on poverty. Soon its denizens increased in numbers and they preached with success throughout Tuscany. Soon Leonard became Guardian and established a mountain hermitage at Incontro, where the friars retired twice a year to live in solitude, fasting, and silence like primitive monks.

In 1730 he was appointed Guardian at St. Bonaventure's, Rome: for six years he preached to soldiers, sailors, convicts, and galley-slaves as well as giving parish missions. From 1736 he preached in Umbria, Genoa, and the Marches of Ancona, often in the open air as the churches were too small. Frequently he preached the Way of the Cross and set up about 500 sets of Stations of the Cross in Italy. This devotion is still popular today.

In 1744 he was sent to Corsica in the hope that his energetic preaching would restore peace and order there. The problems he faced were feuds, vendettas, lawlessness, ignorance, and neglect of religion. Some men came to his sermons fully armed. Unfortunately he was regarded as an emissary of Genoa, whose government sent a ship to rescue him after six months. Even the pope recognized that it was inadvisable for him to return.

In 1750, a Jubilee year, he set up Stations of the Cross in the Colosseum. After preaching extensively in Lucca the following year, his strength failed and he died at Rome.

Writer as well as preacher, he composed numerous devotional treatises and letters: his most famous work is his *Resolutions*. Cardinal Henry of York helped to further his cause: Leonard had been his mother's spiritual director. He was beatified in 1796 and canonized in 1867. He is patron of popular missionaries. Feast: 26 November.

Works ed. by B. Innocenti (1915); Lives by L. de Cherance (1903), G. Cantini (1936), and F. M. Pecheco (1963). See also B.T.A., iv. 429–32; *Bibl. SS.*, vii. 1208–21.

LEONARDI, John (*c.*1542–1609), founder of the Clerks Regular of the Mother of God. Born at Lucca, he became an apothecary and then studied to become a priest. He was ordained *c.*1572 and founded a confraternity for teaching

Christian doctrine. In 1574 he founded his congregation of diocesan priests living under vows and dedicated to the much-needed reform of clerical life. He was appointed by Clement VIII to reform the monks of Vallombrosa and Monte Vergine in 1595 and shared in the foundation of the Roman College called Propaganda. His congregation remained small by deliberate choice; it is almost unknown outside Italy. He died through nursing the plague-stricken on 9 October. He was canonized in 1938. Feast: 9 October.

Propylaeum, p. 446; B.T.A., iv. 65.

LESTONNAC, Jeanne de (1556–1640), foundress. Born at Bordeaux of a religiously divided family and the niece of Montaigne, Jeanne in her youth resisted maternal pressure to become a Calvinist and married in 1573 Gaston de Montferrand, related to the kings of France. This happy marriage ended on his death in 1597; of their four children two became nuns and two subsequently married. In 1603, in spite of family opposition, she became a Cistercian nun at Les Feuillantes, Toulouse, but had to leave as her health was not sufficient for the austere regime. Two quiet years were spent in the country before she returned to Bordeaux, where she devotedly nursed the victims of plague. She now came under the influence of Jean de Bordes, a Jesuit priest who saw the need for a group of dedicated women to educate girls as his own Order educated boys. This accorded with her own plans and a start was made with several companions at Bordeaux in 1608. Other foundations rapidly followed and the schools prospered.

Meanwhile the Bordeaux community suffered divisions. The archbishop of Bordeaux resented attempts to gain extra-diocesan freedom and Blanche Hervé, a middle-class but illiterate nun, was preferred as superior. Once in power, she oppressed and humiliated Jeanne who showed heroic humility. This regime lasted for three years, after which Jeanne in 1625 visited the other 26 houses in turn, returning to Bordeaux only in 1631. Two of her daughters and at least one granddaughter had by now joined the Company of Mary, as her Congregation was called, for which the revised rules and constitutions were drawn up in 1638. Meanwhile the foundress's health was failing and she died on 2 February. Miracles of different kinds were reported at her tomb. After many delays she was beatified in 1900 and canonized in 1949. Her nuns number about 2,500 and serve in seventeen countries. Feast: 2 February.

Life by Paula Hostel (1949), tr. in 1951 *In the Service of Youth*.

LETARD, see LIUDHARD.

LEUFRED (Leufroy, Leutfridus) (d. 738), abbot. Born near Évreux, he studied locally, then at Chartres, decided to teach other boys, but changed his mind and became a hermit, and then a monk under the Irish St. Sidonius of Rouen. He eventually returned to his own country and built a monastery, first called La-Croix-Saint-Ouen and later La-Croix-Saint-Leufroy. He is said to have been abbot for forty-eight years. The Life on which the above details depend was written more than 100 years after his death and has little authority. His relics were translated first in 851 and later to Saint-Germain-des-Prés. In 1222 they were returned to their first resting-place. Feast: 21 June, as in the calendars of southern monasteries, Hereford, and York.

AA.SS. Iun. V (1709), 91–100; critical edn. by W. Levison, *M.G.H.*, *Scriptores rerum merov.*, vii(i), 1–18; B.T.A., ii. 610; J. B. Mesuel, *Saint Leufray, abbé de la Croix* (1918).

LEVAN, see SELEVAN.

LEWINNA (d. *c.*685), hermit and martyr. There is no contemporary record of her life, but her relics were discovered in a Sussex church which belonged to Bergues (near Dunkirk) and translated to another church, variously identified as Seaford or Alfriston. Feast: 24 July.

AA.SS. Iul. V (1727), 608–27; B.T.A., iii. 174–5; *Bibl. SS.*, vii. 1354–5; L. E. Whatmore, *St. Lewinna: East Sussex Martyr* (1979).

LEWIS, David (also called Charles Baker) (1616–79), Jesuit, priest, and martyr. Born in Monmouthshire in 1616 of a Protestant father and a Catholic mother, David Lewis was educated at Abergavenny Grammar School and at the Middle Temple. In 1635 he joined the household of the Comte Savage as tutor, was received into the R.C. Church at Paris, and soon afterwards entered the English College, Rome. He was ordained priest in 1642 and became a Jesuit in 1644. After his profession he became Spiritual Director to the English College, but returned to Herefordshire in 1648 and worked there for the rest of his life. The main centre of his activity was Llanrothal, where a large farmhouse was used as a mission centre, Lewis being twice superior during its fifty years' existence.

During the persecution after the 'Popish Plot' of Titus Oates, the farmhouse was sacked, its library was given to Hereford Cathedral, and Lewis was arrested. He was imprisoned at Monmouth, tried at Usk, and condemned for his priesthood. He rode with John *Kemble to London for questioning and on his return was executed at Usk, on 27 August. On this occasion the official hangman refused to perform his task and fled; a convict was offered his freedom if he would take his place, but he was stoned by the bystanders and likewise fled; a blacksmith was finally induced to carry out the sentence. On the scaffold Lewis spoke at length in Welsh, summarizing his convictions and describing why he was to suffer. His grave in Usk is still visited by pilgrims. He was canonized by Paul VI in 1970 as one of the *Forty Martyrs of England and Wales. Feast: 25 October.

Lewis's own account of his arrest, imprisonment, and trial survive with a copy of his last speech: R. Challoner, *Memoirs of Missionary Priests* (ed. J. H. Pollen, 1924), pp. 557–61; J. Foley, *Records of the English Province of the Society of Jesus*, v. 912 et seq.; *Catholic Record Society Publications*, xlvii (1953), 299–304; T. P. Ellis, *Catholic Martyrs of Wales* (1932), 129–40.

LIAFWINE, see LEBUIN.

LIDE (Elid, Elidius), Celtic hermit saint of the Isles of Scilly, who settled on and gave his name to the island now called St. Helen's, where remains, both of his buildings and of his tomb, have been found. A small community lived on this island in the Middle Ages: like Tresco it became subject to Tavistock, whose calendar includes a feast of St. Lide, adding that he was a bishop buried on the Isles of Scilly. In 1461 all pirates who raided the Isles of Scilly were excommunicated, and as the much-visited chapel of St. Elidius was in great need of repair and new furnishings, an indulgence of seven years and seven quarantines was granted to all who visited it at the feasts of Christmas, St. John Baptist, and St. Elidius. Leland mentioned 'Saynct Lide's Isle, where in times past at her [*sic*] sepulchre was gret superstition'. St. Lide's dates are most uncertain: the earliest pottery found in the ruins dates from the 11th century. It is tempting to identify him with the seer at Scilly visited by Olaf Tryggvason. Feast: 8 August.

A. B. Taylor, *Orkeneyinge Saga* (1938), pp. 149–50; Mrs. H. E. O'Neill, 'Excavation of a Celtic hermitage on St. Helens, Isle of Scilly 1956–8', *Archaeol. Jnl.*, cxxi (1964), 40–69.

LINE, Anne (*c.*1565–1601), martyr. Born at Dunmow (Essex) of ardent Calvinist parents, Anne Heigham, with her brother William, joined the R.C. Church before the age of twenty, with the result that they were disinherited and driven from home. In 1585 she married Roger Line, also a disinherited convert, who, after being imprisoned for attending Mass, was eventually exiled to Flanders where he died in 1594. He left Anne more or less destitute and she became the housekeeper of Fr. John Gerard S.J. who kept a large house in London as a place of hospitality for priests. Although frail in health, Anne proved herself capable, discreet, and kindly: in her spare time she taught children and worked at embroidery. After Gerard's famous escape from the Tower in 1597 she had to move to another house. In order to make her dedication more permanent and complete, she took vows of poverty, chastity, and obedience. On 2 February an unusually large number of recusants assembled for Mass at her house. Pursuivants soon arrived and, although the priest escaped, Anne was arrested and imprisoned. On 26 February she was tried under the statute of 27 Elizabeth for harbouring a priest, the principal evidence being the altar found in her house. She was found guilty and was sentenced to death: her execution took place the next day. She might well be considered the model and patron of the demanding profession of priest's housekeeper. She was canonized by Paul VI in 1970 as one of the *Forty Martyrs of England and Wales. Feast: 25 October.

J. Gerard, *The Autobiography of a Hunted Priest* (ed. P. Caraman, 1952); R. Challoner, *Memoirs of Missionary Priests* (ed. J. H. Pollen, 1924), pp. 257–9; M. O'Dwyer, *Blessed Anne Line* (pamphlet, 1961).

LINUS (d. *c.*80), pope. Early episcopal lists name Linus bishop of Rome after St. Peter, but virtually nothing is known about him. *Irenaeus and others identify him with the Linus mentioned in 2 Tim. 4: 21. His name is in the Canon of the Roman Mass. An 11th-century fresco at S. Piero a Grado, near Pisa (probably based on lost paintings from St. Peter's, Rome), depicts him burying *Peter. In the West he was venerated as a martyr, but historians have pointed out that there was no known persecution during his tenure of office. Consequently his feast has been suppressed in the Roman calendar since 1969. Feast: formerly on 23 September.

AA.SS. Sept. VI (1757), 539–45; Irenaeus, *Adversus Haereses*, III. iii. 13; Eusebius, *H.E.*, ii. 3; v. 6.

LIOBA (Liobgytha) (d. 782), abbess of Bischofsheim. Born of a noble Wessex family (her mother was a relative of *Boniface), Lioba was educated first at the nunnery of Minster-in-Thanet and then at Wimborne (Dorset), where she became a nun under abbess Tetta. After some years correspondence Boniface asked in 748 and obtained that she should be sent to help him in the evangelization of Germany by establishing convents. About thirty nuns were sent in all; they were settled at Tauberbischofsheim, possibly in Boniface's own previous residence, under Lioba as abbess. The Life by Rudolf of Fulda, written about fifty years after her death and based on the testimony of four companions, paints an attractive portrait. Lioba was both beautiful and accessible, intelligent and patiently kind. Her community was so highly esteemed that abbesses for other houses were taken from it, while Lioba's advice was sought by magnates of both Church and State. Her monasteries followed the Rule of St. Benedict: all the nuns had to learn Latin: manual work in scriptorium, kitchen, bakery, brewery, and garden was assiduously practised, but all was subordinate to the public prayer of the Church.

Before his final mission to Frisia in 754 Boniface said goodbye to her, recommended her care both to *Lull and to the monks of Fulda, and said that he would like her body to be buried near his. After his death she used to visit Fulda on privileged terms. When she had been abbess for twenty-eight years, she resigned and retired to Schornsheim, but once visited Charlemagne's court at the invitation of his queen Hildegard. Lioba died soon afterwards and was buried near Boniface's tomb at Fulda. Her relics were translated in 819 and again in 838, this time to the church of Mount St. Peter. Hrabanus Maurus inserted her name into his martyrology *c.*836; it also occurs in litanies of the 9th century. Her cult has always been centred in Germany, but seems surprisingly to have been little known in England. Feast: 28 September.

Life by Rudolph of Fulda in *AA.SS.* Sept. VII (1757), 748–69; Eng. tr. by C. H. Talbot, *Anglo-Saxon Missionaries in Germany* (1954); M. Tangl, *Die Briefe des heiligen Bonifatius und Lullus*

(*M.G.H.*, 1916); W. Levison, *England and the Continent in the Eighth Century* (1946); B.T.A., iii. 668–71. See also T. Schieffer, *Winfrid-Bonifatius und die christliche Grundlegung Europas* (1954), pp. 162–6.

LIUDGER (Ludger) (d. 809), bishop of Munster. Frisian by birth, Liudger was closely associated with the Anglo-Saxon mission on the Continent through his education at Utrecht under Gregory, the friend of *Boniface, and at York under Alcuin (767–81). He then returned to Utrecht and rebuilt the church at Deventer, destroyed by pagans, where *Lebuin was buried. He then preached in remote areas of Frisia and despoiled pagan shrines of considerable wealth, some of which was given to the Church by Charlemagne. In 777 he was ordained priest and then built several churches, including that at Dokkum, where Boniface died, for whose dedication Alcuin wrote some verses. But when the Saxons under Widekund invaded this district in 784 they drove out the priests, destroyed the churches, and tried to restore paganism.

Liudger took the opportunity to visit Rome and Monte Cassino, where he stayed for two years, planning to found a Benedictine monastery of his own, which he later achieved at Werden. In 786 he returned to Westphalia, where he rebuilt the ruined churches and where his gentle persuasiveness achieved far more for Christianity than Charlemagne's harsh repression had done. About 804 he was consecrated bishop of Munster, where he built a monastery for canons, following the Rule of St. *Chrodegang of Metz. Although he was denounced to Charlemagne for excessive almsgiving to the detriment of the ornamentation of churches, and kept the emperor waiting for an explanation until he had finished his devotions, he did not lose his favour. Liudger died at Werden after a long illness; most of his relics remain there today. His feast is recorded in liturgical books from the 9th century. Feast: 26 March.

AA.SS. Mar. III (1668), 626–65; W. Levison, *England and the Continent in the Eighth Century* (1946); H. Schrade, *Die vita des heiligen Liudger und ihre Bilder* (1960).

LIUDHARD (Letard) (d. *c.*603), bishop, chaplain of Queen Bertha. Ethelbert king of Kent (560–616) married the Frankish Christian princess Bertha some time before 597, but on condition that she should be free to practise her religion and bring her bishop with her. But the Frankish Liudhard seems to have taken little part in the conversion of Kent except the possible, but unproved role of preparing the king's mind for the acceptance of Christianity. But there are no letters of *Gregory to him; that to Bertha of June 601 rather reproaches her for her failure to achieve her husband's conversion. Liudhard, however, had restored an ancient Romano-British church at Canterbury for Bertha's use and had very likely dedicated it to the Gaulish *Martin. He died presumably at Canterbury, was buried in the *porticus* of St. Martin in the abbey of SS. Peter and Paul (later called St. Augustine's), Canterbury, where his feast was kept on 7 May. Goscelin wrote a short Life of him in the late 11th century. But in some 9th-century martyrologies a false identification was made with Liephard, whose feast is kept at Cambrai and who was called 'archbishop of Canterbury and martyr' with a feast on 4 February. Liudhard was neither a martyr nor archbishop of Canterbury.

Bede, *H.E.*, i. 25–6; Goscelin, *Vita et miracula S. Letardi* in *P.L.*, clv. 45–6; B.T.A., ii. 246; Stanton, pp. 51–2, 200–1.

LLOYD, John (*c.*1630–79), seminary priest and martyr. Born at Brecon, he entered the English seminary at Valladolid in 1649 and was ordained priest in 1653. The next year he returned to Wales and exercised his ministry for over twenty years without any recorded molestation. In the scare following the 'Popish Plot' of Titus Oates, Lloyd was arrested in Glamorgan (1678) and charged with having said Mass at Llantilio, Penrhos, and Trievor. He was imprisoned at Cardiff castle with Philip *Evans who was tried with him on 3 May:

both were condemned for their priesthood. They were hanged, drawn, and quartered on 22 July. Lloyd and Evans are among the *Forty Martyrs of England and Wales canonized by Paul VI in 1970. Feast: 25 October.

R. Challoner, *Memoirs of Missionary Priests* (ed. J. H. Pollen, 1924), pp. 544–7; J. Stonor, *Six Welsh Martyrs* (pamphlet, 1961).

LO, see LAUDUS.

LOMAN (Lonan) (d. *c.*450) was traditionally a nephew of *Patrick who became bishop of Trim (Co. Meath), where he was succeeded by Fortchern, who with his family had been baptized by Patrick. But it has also been claimed that Loman did not live in the time of Patrick, but is rather a 7th-century bishop of Trim of the same name. Feast: 17 February.

B.T.A., i. 356: the story occurs in the Tripartite Life of Patrick; see also P. Grosjean, 'S. Patrice d'Irlande et quelques homonymes', *J.E.H.*, i (1950), 151–71.

LONGINUS, the name traditionally given to the soldier who pierced the side of the crucified Christ with a lance. The name is almost certainly derived from the Greek word '*longche*' which means a lance. Earlier he was identified with the centurion who at the Passion declared Christ to be the Son of God. Extravagant stories grew up around him, exemplified by the *Golden Legend.* According to this the blood of Christ immediately healed him of incipient blindness, which led him to leave the army and become a monk at Caesarea (centuries before there were any known Christian monasteries). He was later brought to trial, refused to sacrifice to the pagan gods, was condemned to have his teeth knocked out and his tongue cut off. He took hold of a convenient axe and smashed the idols, whence came some devils who possessed the governor, who became mad and blind. Longinus told him that he would be healed only after his own death. This soon followed and the governor instantly returned to normal and ended his life in good works. Earlier Longinus' cult had been strengthened by the discovery of the Holy Lance on the First Crusade in a church at Antioch, which had transformed the morale of the Christian soldiers. Feast: in the East, 16 October; in the West (including England), 15 March.

AA.SS. Mar. II (1668), 376–90: Greek account of the martyrdom in *P.G.*, xciii. 1546–60; the cult is mentioned by Gregory of Nyssa, *Epistola xvii* (*P.G.*, xlvi. 1061). See also Rose Peebles, *The Legend of Longinus in Ecclesiastical Tradition and in English Literature and its Connection with the Grail* (Bryn Mawr College Monographs ix. 1911) and Malory, *Morte d'Arthur*, II. xvi.

LORCAN UA TUATHAIL, see LAURENCE O'TOOLE.

LOUIS (Lewis) **IX** (1214–70), king of France. Born at Poissy, the son of Louis VIII and the half-English Blanche of Castile, Louis reigned from his father's death in 1226, but his mother was regent during his minority. In 1234 he married Margaret of Provence and thus became brother-in-law to King Henry III of England. In many respects Louis was a model Christian king, but his lively biographer the Sieur de Joinville (a soldier, not a cleric) portrays him as a human being with faults as well as virtues. His long reign was not an unqualified success: his crusading expeditions were both disastrous, while his arbitrations between Henry III and his barons were not always efficacious. But he ruled France at a time of great cultural achievement, revealed by the building of Gothic cathedrals and the development of universities. *Thomas Aquinas and other friars were guests at his table; the founder of the Sorbonne was a personal friend. Louis was also prominent in almsgiving, in founding a hospital for the poor and blind, called Quinze-Vingts (for 300 inmates), while his justice was famous for its impartiality. He also forbade private wars of feudal lords and was well known for keeping his word in treaties and other undertakings. The most famous church he founded was the Sainte-Chapelle at Paris, built to house what was believed to be the relic of Christ's Crown of Thorns, a present from Baldwin, the crusading Latin emperor at Constantinople. His monastic foundations included Royaumont, Vauvert, and Maubuisson.

In 1244 after a serious illness he decided to take the Crusader's cross, but the expedition could not start until 1248 after ecclesiastical benefices had been taxed at the rate of five per cent for three years. Louis sailed to Cyprus with his army (joined there by 200 English knights); in 1249 they took Damietta, but Louis was unable to control the violence and injustice which followed. Disease struck the crusading army which has heavily defeated at Marsuna (1250), when Louis was taken prisoner. He obtained his own release and that of other prisoners, in return for the surrender of Damietta and a large sum of money. He then sailed to Palestine (without the sick and wounded crusaders, who had been massacred), visited those few of the Holy Places which were accessible, fortified the Christians in Syria, and returned to France in 1254. The next fifteen years were notable both for internal reforms and for various political activities concerning England.

From 1267 another crusade was planned. It got under way in 1270 and a landing was made near Tunis. But this expedition also ended in almost total disaster. Louis and his son Philip caught typhoid fever soon after landing; Louis died on 24 August, after strongly urging the Greek ambassadors to seek reunion with the Church of Rome. He was canonized by Pope Boniface VIII in 1297. It is difficult to detect any ancient cult of St. Louis in England, partly no doubt because his political activities were sometimes hostile to English interests, but his feast is in the Roman calendar. In France he is traditionally regarded as the patron and example of the monarchy, although it is perhaps a matter of regret that French royalists often looked for inspiration to the reign of Louis XIV rather than to his. Feast: 25 August.

Contemporary Life by J. de Joinville, ed. N. de Wailly (1874) with his other works; Eng. tr. by Joan Evans (1938), and by M. R. B. Shaw (1963) in *Chronicles of the Crusades*; other Lives in *AA.SS.* Aug. V (1741), 275–758; Louis' instructions to his son are called *Les Établissements de saint Louis* (ed. P. Viollet, Soc. de l'Histoire de France, 1881–6); G. de Saint-Pathus, *Les miracles de Saint Louis* (ed. P. B. Fay, 1932); H. Wallon, *S. Louis et son Temps* (1875); modern Life by M. W. Labarge (1968). See also J. R. Strayer, 'The Crusades of Louis IX' in *A History of the Crusades* (ed. K. M. Setton, 1955–) and Sir S. Runciman, *History of the Crusades* (3 vols., 1951–4).

LOUIS GRIGNION DE MONTFORT, see MONTFORT.

LOUIS OF TOULOUSE (1274–97), Franciscan friar and bishop. Born Louis d'Angio at Brignolles (Provence), the son of Charles II of Naples and his wife Mary, princess of Hungary, he was a relative of both *Louis IX and *Elizabeth of Hungary. His father was taken prisoner by the king of Aragon in a sea-battle in 1284: Louis became a hostage and spent seven years in or near Barcelona. During this time he studied hard under the direction of Franciscans. In 1295 he was set free and James II of Aragon wished his sister to marry Louis.

He, however, was convinced that he should become a Franciscan, so he refused this offer and renounced all claim to the kingdom of Naples. He entered the Order at Rome, was professed in 1296, and ordained priest in 1297. Pope Boniface VIII had decided to promote him at once, so he was consecrated bishop of Toulouse only a few days later.

As bishop, he lived in a poverty worthy of *Francis. He refused to use silver plate and jewelled cups; he wore an old patched habit in silent reproach to his wordly clergy. He said Mass every day and preached frequently. In spite of this promising start, he asked to resign his bishopric within only a few months. Whether he suspected he was ill, or whether he needed more time to adjust to his sudden promotion, we do not know. He certainly regarded the episcopate as a heavy burden. Before his petition could be answered, he fell ill at Brignolles and died there at the age of only twenty-three. He was buried in the Franciscan church at Marseilles, but his relics were later translated to Valencia by Alphonso V. One of his surviving sayings was: 'Jesus Christ is my kingdom. If I possess him alone, I shall have all things; if I have him not, I lose all.' He was canonized in 1317. A fine series of paintings by Simone Martini of scenes from his life is in the national museum of Naples. Feast: 19 August.

AA.SS. Aug. III (1952), 775–822; A. Van Ortroy, 'Vita S. Ludovici episcopi Tolosani', *Anal. Boll.*, iv (1890), 278–353; M. R. Toynbee, *St. Louis of Toulouse and the Process of Canonization* (1929); *Bibl. SS.*, viii. 300–7.

LOUISE DE MARILLAC, see MARILLAC.

LOY, see ELOI.

LUA, see MOLUA.

LUCIAN OF ANTIOCH (d. 312), martyr. Born at Samosata (Syria), he became a priest at Antioch; he was specially interested in emending the corrupt texts of Scripture then current, and in propagating its literal sense. He also founded an important theological school, one of whose members was Arius, whose followers sometimes called themselves Lucianists. Although he was involved in the schism of Antioch and although his orthodoxy was highly suspect, he made his peace with the Church in 285 and died in full communion at Nicomedia. His body was taken to Drepanum (renamed Helenopolis by Constantine in memory of his mother); firm evidence of his cult is provided by Eusebius and *John Chrysostom, and by church dedications. A later Legend of which he is the hero has been claimed as one evolved from pagan myth. Feast: in the West, 7 January; in the East, 15 October.

Eusebius, *H.E.*, VIII. xiii. 2 and IX. vi. 3; St. John Chrysostom in *P.G.*, l. 519 ff.; *AA.SS.* Ian. I (1643), 357–64; G. Bardy, *Recherches sur S. Lucien d'Antioche* (1936); H. Delehaye, *The Legends of the Saints* (1962), pp. 147–50.

LUCIAN OF BEAUVAIS, martyr, who is said to have preached the Gospel in Gaul in the third century and to have died at Beauvais. His relics were discovered in the 7th century and were famous for miracles 100 years later. With his two companions he is culted in the Sarum calendar and one English church is dedicated to him. Feast 8 January, the day after that of *Lucian of Antioch, with whom he is sometimes confused. Some scholars, such as L. Duchesne, consider the whole story of Lucian as unhistorical.

AA.SS. Ian. I (1643), 640 ff.; L. Duchesne, *Fastes Episcopaux*, iii. 141–52; H. Moretus, *Les Passions de S. Lucien et leurs dérivés céphalophoriques* (1953).

LUCIUS (1), see MONTANUS AND LUCIUS.

LUCIUS (2), see PTOLOMAEUS AND LUCIUS.

LUCY (d. 304), virgin and martyr. She died at Syracuse in the persecution of Diocletian. Her cult was both early and widespread: an inscription of *c.*400 referring to her survives at Syracuse; her name is included in the Canons of the Roman and Ambrosian rites and occurs in the oldest Roman sacramentaries, in Greek liturgical books, and in the marble calendar of Naples. Churches were dedicated to her in Rome, Naples, and eventually Venice. Here, in a church near the railway station, survives a partially incorrupt body claimed to be hers. Two ancient churches were dedicated to her in England, where she has been certainly known from the time of *Aldhelm, who praised her in his treatises on Virginity in the late 7th century.

Her historically valueless Acts make her a wealthy Sicilian, who refused marriage offers, gave her goods to the poor, and was accused by her suitor to the persecuting authority. The judge ordered that she should be violated in a brothel, but she was made miraculously immovable; he then tried to have her burnt, also unsuccessfully; so she was finally killed by the sword. Her iconography is based on these Acts, her usual emblem being her eyes, which were reputed to have been torn out and miraculously restored. This element occurs especially in late medieval representations: the earliest surviving image is a simple one without attributes in the frieze of virgins in the 6th-century mosaics of S. Apollinare Nuovo, Ravenna. Especially in Sweden her feast on the shortest day of the year has become a festival of light: the youngest daughter, dressed in white, wakes the rest of the family with coffee, rolls, and a special song. There and in Sicily the song 'Santa Lucia' remains popular. Feast: 13 December.

C.M.H., p. 647; Greek Acts ed. G. R. Taibbi (Istituto Siciliano di Studi Byzantini, Testi vi, 1959) and Latin Acts by A. Beaugrand, *Sainte Lucie* (1882); see also Aldhelm in R. Ewald, *M.G.H.*, *Auctores Antiquisiimi*, xv (1919), 293–4; O. Garana, *S. Lucia nella tradizione, nella storia, nell'arte* (1958) and M. Capdevila, *Iconographia de Santa Lucia* (1949); D. Sox, *Relics and Shrines* (1985).

LUDGER, see LIUDGER.

LUDWAN (Ludan, Ludgvan, Ludjan), patron and presumably church-founder of Ludgvan (Cornwall), where there is also a holy well. His feast, according to the Cornish Kalendar, is not 'certainly known'. Baring-Gould, however, on the flimsiest evidence, identifies him with St. Lithgean of Clonmore, whose feast is on 16 January. He also asserts that Ludwan's feast was on 27 January. It seems much safer to say that nothing is known about him.

C.C.K.; Baring-Gould and Fisher, iii. 362–4.

LUKE (1st century), evangelist. Almost all that we know of him comes from the New Testament. He was a Greek physician (Col. 4: 14), a disciple of St. Paul, and his companion on some of his missionary journeys (Acts 16: 10 ff.; 20: 5 ff., 27–8) and the author of both Acts and the third gospel, which he describes in his idiomatic Greek as 'the former treatise which I wrote' (Acts 1: 1). The traditions that he was one of the first members of the Christian community at Antioch, testified by Eusebius, and a physician by profession, may well be correct: less certain is the claim that he lived to the age of eighty-four and died unmarried. Much can be gleaned about his character from his writings. In his Gospel the elements proper to him include much of the account of the Virgin Birth of Christ (Luke 1–2), some of the most moving parables such as those of the Good Samaritan and the Prodigal Son, with the words of Christ in the Passion to the women of Jerusalem and to the Good Thief. All these elements underline the compassion of Christ, which together with Luke's emphasis on poverty, prayer, and purity of heart make up much of his specific appeal to the Gentiles, for whom he wrote this Gospel of the Saviour of the world. Women figure more prominently in Luke's gospel than in any other, for example, *Mary, *Elizabeth, the widow of Nain, and the woman who was a sinner. In the Acts of the Apostles Luke shows himself a remarkably accurate observer, concerned with making necessary links between sacred and profane history. Many of his details have been strikingly confirmed by archaeology. Luke also showed himself an artist with words, which perhaps was the base of the tradition that he was a painter and made at least one icon of the Blessed Virgin; but none of those claimed to be his can be authentic. This has not prevented Luke becoming the patron of artists as well as of doctors and surgeons. Where he is represented with the other evangelists, his symbol is an ox, sometimes explained by reference to the sacrifice in the Temple at the beginning of his Gospel. In England twenty-eight ancient churches were dedicated to him and his feast was celebrated from very early times. The earliest representations of him show him as an evangelist writing, but Flemish painters of the 15th–16th centuries show him painting the blessed Virgin.

Translations of the relics of Luke are claimed by Constantinople and by Padua. Feast: 18 October.

AA.SS. Oct. VIII (1853), 282–313; R. A. Lipsius, *Die apokryphen Apostelgeschichten*, ii. 2, pp. 354–71; commentaries on his Gospel by M. J. Lagrange (Études Bibliques, 1921), W.

Manson (1930), and A. R. C. Leaney (2nd edn. 1966). See also A. Harnack, *Luke the Physician* (1907); A. T. Robertson, *Luke the Historian in the Light of Research* (1920); H. J. Cadbury, *The Making of Luke–Acts* (1927); C. K. Barrett, *Luke the Historian in Recent Study* (1961); P. Esler, *Community and Gospel in Luke–Acts* (1987).

LULL (Lul) (*c.*710–86), archbishop of Mainz. Born in Wessex, Lull became a monk of Malmesbury, but joined his cousin *Boniface in his missionary work in Germany while still a young man. He spent the rest of his life as Boniface's assistant and eventually his successor. In 751 Boniface sent him to consult with Pope Zachary at Rome; on his return he was consecrated bishop (752). When Boniface left for Frisia in 754, Lull became bishop of Mainz. He received the pallium only in 781. This delay was partly the result of a long struggle between Lull and Sturm, abbot of Fulda, concerning this monastery's exemption from episcopal jurisdiction, which Lull claimed. He even deposed Sturm who, however, appealed to Pepin and was restored. Lull himself made monastic foundations at Bleidenstadt (Nassau) and Hersfeld, where he died and was buried. Lull's correspondence reveals his appreciation of books from England, his zeal for the observance of the canons, and his concern that prayers and fasts should be offered both for better weather for harvests and for the repose of the soul of a deceased pope. His episcopate was distinguished by energetic organization and the propagation of learning; he also took part in numerous councils in the Empire. In most of his policies he continued the plans of Boniface; his cult flourished in Germany rather than in Britain. Feast: 16 October.

Life by Lambert of Hersfeld (11th cent.) in *AA.SS.* Oct. VII (1845), 1050–91; Letters in M. Tangl, *Bonifatii et Lullae Epistolae* (*M.G.H.*, 1916); H. Hahn, *Bonifatius und Lull* (1883); W. Levison, *England and the Continent in the Eighth Century* (1946); T. Schieffer, *Angelsachsen und Franken* (1950).

LUPUS OF TROYES (d. 478), bishop. He is known and culted in England because of his association with *Germanus of Auxerre, who preached effectively against the Pelagians on his two visits to Britain. Lupus was born in the late 4th century at Toul, married a sister of *Hilary, but after six years they separated by mutual consent. Lupus sold his estates, became a monk at Lérins, and bishop of Troyes *c.*426. In 429 he came to Britain with Germanus. Later, when Attila the Hun was ravaging Gaul, Lupus went out to meet him and persuaded him to spare the province, but at the cost of himself becoming his hostage. When Attila was defeated, Lupus was accused of helping him to escape and had to retire to the mountains as a hermit. But after some years he resumed the rule of his diocese until his death.

Most of these details come from an unreliable Life, believed to have been written to further the interests of the see of Troyes during the 8th century. Feast: 29 July.

AA.SS. Iul. VII (1731), 51–82; B. Krusch, 'Vita S. Lupi' in *M.G.H.*, *Scriptores rerum merov.*, vii. 284–302; B.T.A., iii. 207–8.

LWANGA, Charles and Companions, martyrs of Uganda (d. 1885–7). This group of twenty-two Africans who died for their faith includes Joseph Mkasa, who reproached the ruler Mwanga for debauchery and for murdering a Protestant missionary bishop, James Hannington (1885), Charles Lwanga, who was in charge of the royal pages and had baptized four of them, and Kizito (aged thirteen), who was one of the pages, whom Lwanga had saved from the ruler's paederasty. The day after the chieftain had killed another page, Denis Sebuggwawo, for catechizing, all the pages were assembled; Christians were ordered to separate themselves from the others; fifteen at once did so (all under twenty-five years old), and they were later joined by two others already under arrest and by two soldiers. They were asked if they wished to remain Christians and they answered: 'Until death.'

By this time Mkasa had been beheaded;

the others were led out to Namugongo, thirty-seven miles away, were wrapped in mats of reeds and burnt alive. Their exemplary courage and cheerfulness were comparable with those of the early Christian martyrs.

The persecution, instigated by a tyrant who was fanatically opposed to Christianity, also claimed Protestants as well as Catholics. Further victims were Matthias Murumba, a judge, and Andrew Kagwa, a prominent catechist. All these martyrs of Uganda were canonized in 1964; their feast was included in the Roman calendar in 1969 as the protomartyrs of Black Africa. Feast: 3 June.

Apostolic Letter of Benedict XV, with details of their martyrdom in *A.S.S.*, xii (1920), 272–81; J. P. Thoonen, *Black Martyrs* (1941); J. F. Faupel, *African Holocaust* (1962); *Bibl. SS.*, xii. 746–8.

M

MABYN, one of the many daughters of *Brychan, who came to Cornwall from Wales in the 6th(?) century. She was presumably a nun who founded the church of, or lived close to, the present town of St. Mabyn. She is depicted in stained glass (the Wives Window of 1523) in the church of St. *Neot (Cornwall). Episcopal registers of the 13th century describe her church as *Sancte Mabene*, but the Feet of Fines (1234) refer to *Sancto Malbano*, a male saint. Feast (according to Roscarrock): 18 November.

Baring-Gould and Fisher, iii. 390; *O.D.E.P.N.*, p. 401.

MACANISIUS (Oengus Mac Nisse) (d. *c.*514), bishop. He was one of the earliest and least-recorded saints of Ireland, reputed to be a disciple of *Patrick. He became a hermit at Kells and later bishop of his own clan in the district. The Life is a late compilation of unreliable material, but it preserves the quaint legend that he had such veneration for Scripture that he would not, like other Irish monks, carry his Gospel-book in a leather satchel, but bore it on his shoulders hunched up or on all fours. Feast: 3 September, in Ireland.

Life in W. W. Heist, *Vitae Sanctorum Hiberniae* (1965), pp. 404–7; *The Irish Saints*, p. 214.

MACARIUS THE GREAT (Macarius of Egypt), monk (*c.*300–90). A native of Upper Egypt, he founded *c.*330 a monastery in the desert of Scetis. About 340 he was ordained priest. He knew and followed the teachings of *Antony of Egypt. Various anecdotes concerning him are to be found in the *Apothegmata Patrum* and in the Lausiac History: there is no need to think that all of them are authentic, still less that the many writings, including homilies traditionally ascribed to him, are actually his work.

During his lifetime he was certainly highly esteemed in monastic circles; his counsel was greatly appreciated not least by Evagrius, more famous in our own day. At this distance it seems almost impossible to separate the authentic from the apocryphal sayings and deeds. Feast: 15 January.

H.S.S.C., iii. 278; Palladius, *Lausiac History*, c. 17; J. C. Guy, *Les Apothegmes des Pères du Désert* (1966), pp. 166–82; Writings attributed to him are in H. Dorries, E. Klostermann, and M. Kroeger, *Patristiche Texte und Studien*, iv (1964) with Eng. tr. by A. J. Mason (1921); see also W. Jaeger, *Two Rediscovered Texts of Ancient Christian Literature: Gregory of Nyssa and Macarius* (1954); *Bibl. SS.*, viii. 425–9.

MACARTAN (Aedh Mac Cairthinn) (d. *c.*505), bishop. Reputedly consecrated bishop of Clogher by *Patrick, Macartan was one of the earliest Irish saints with a reputation as a miracle-worker. Nothing is known of his life, but his grave at Clogher was venerated and earth was taken from it, as Bede records of others. The liturgical office in his honour is the only one to survive from an Irish source. A reliquary called the Great Shrine of St. Mac Cairthinn, intended to contain relics of the Cross as well as of his bones, has been much altered over the centuries but survives as the 'Domnach Airgid'. Feast: 24 March.

The Irish Saints, p. 213; E. C. R. Armstrong and H. J. Lawlor, 'The Domnach Airgid', *P.R.I.A.*, xxxiv (1917–19), 96–126; fragmentary Life in W. W. Heist, *Vitae Sanctorum Hiberniae* (1965), pp. 343–6.

MACHABEES (Maccabees) (*c.*168 BC), martyrs. The cult of these Old Testament martyrs (cf. 2 Macc. 6–7) in the Christian Church is both ancient and widespread; it originated perhaps in Antioch, and was the subject of homilies of both Eastern and Western Fathers. They are believed to typify the Christian martyrs who found themselves in similar circumstances and the cult may be held to reveal the close connection between Jewry and early Christianity and to show Christian sympathy for the sufferings of Jewish martyrs in the Roman Empire. The rebellion of the Machabees had been brought about by the efforts of Antioches Epiphanes to impose Hellenistic paganism on the Jews, especially at Jerusalem. Eleazar, a chief scribe, refused to eat pig-meat (forbidden by Jewish law) or to simulate having eaten it, which was a test of Jewish constancy and obedience to the Law. He was impervious to bribery, threats, and violence to make him apostatize, implicity or explicitly. His execution was followed by those of the seven brothers and their mother, who remained alike constant in their beliefs. Later the Acts of the *Seven Brothers seem to have been modelled on the story of the Machabees. With the *Holy Innocents, they are the only personages of the pre-Christian era to enjoy a general cult in the West, while in the East both patriarchs and prophets were honoured in this way. The history of the supposed relics of the Machabees is obscure: it is not known either when or by whom they were brought to Rome, where they were housed in the church of St. Peter's Chains. Modin and Antioch, according to Jerome, also claimed their relics. In the 1930s it was discovered that the bones at Rome believed to be theirs were in reality canine remains; so they were immediately withdrawn from the veneration of the faithful. Their feast, formerly on 1 August, was suppressed in the revision of the Roman calendar (1969).

B.T.A., iii. 237–8; H. Bévenot, 'The Holy Machabees', *The Month*, cl (1927), 107–14.

MACHALUS (Machella, Maccul, Maghor, Maughold) (d. 498), bishop of the Isle of Man. Nothing is known of him beyond a legend which makes him a pirate in Ireland, who was told by *Patrick to put to sea in a coracle without oars as a penance for his misdeeds. He landed on the Isle of Man where, after suitable reparation, he was made bishop. He is described in the Martyrology of *Oengus as 'a rod of gold, a vast ingot, the great bishop MacCaille'. One church in Scotland is dedicated to him at Castletown. William Worcestre said he was a native of the Orkneys, and that his shrine was on the Isle of Man. Feast: 27 April.

B.T.A., ii. 172; J. M. Mackinlay, *Ancient Church Dedications in Scotland* (1914), p. 104; William Worcestre, p. 73.

MACHAN (Manchan) (6th century). Traditionally regarded as a Scottish disciple of *Cadoc (2), he was trained in Ireland before returning to Campsie (Scotland) where he worked, died, and was buried. Over his tomb a church was built, later given to Glasgow cathedral, which had a fine altar in his honour. He was said to have been consecrated bishop at Rome. Feast: 28 September.

K.S.S., pp. 380–1.

MACHAR (Mochumma) (6th century), bishop. Of Irish origin, he came to Iona with *Columba, evangelized Mull and, later, the Picts around Aberdeen. For this reason he is often described anachronistically as first bishop of the see of Aberdeen. His Legend, however, in the Aberdeen breviary makes him 'Archbishop of Tours', appointed by *Gregory the Great for the last few years of his life. This story deserves no credence. Water from his well was used for baptism in Aberdeen cathedral. A few dedications survive from this area. Feast: 12 November.

K.S.S., pp. 393–4; C. Horstmann, *Altenglische Legende* (1881).

MACHUTUS, see MALO.

MACKESSOG, see KESSOG.

MACLOU, see MALO.

MACRINA THE ELDER (d. 340). A disciple of *Gregory the Wonderworker, she was a Christian witness to the faith who went into exile during persecution. There in Pontus she and her husband suffered hunger, deprivation, and loss of property. She was the grandmother of *Basil, *Gregory of Nyssa, and *Macrina the Younger: to each of these she passed on the ideals and teaching from the age of the persecutions. She died at Neo-Caesarea. Feast: 14 January.

See following entry.

MACRINA THE YOUNGER (*c.*327–79), virgin. The oldest of ten children of Basil the Elder and Emmelia and the sister of *Basil and *Gregory of Nyssa, who wrote her life, Macrina was a fine example of how, in her own right, a woman of a distinguished family contributed powerfully to the achievements of the Christian Church in 4th-century Cappadocia. She was educated by her mother, who used the Sapiential Books of the Bible for reading practice rather than the current classical poems, and also taught her household management as well as spinning and weaving. At the age of twelve she was betrothed, but her fiancé died suddenly. After this, although exceptionally beautiful, she steadfastly refused all other suitors and devoted herself wholeheartedly to the duties of the Christian life. Initially these consisted of educating her younger brothers and sisters, later of living a monastic life. Gregory relates how her brother Basil returned from Athens University 'puffed up beyond measure with the pride of oratory . . . excelling in his own estimation all the local dignitaries'. Macrina took him in hand with such effect that he renounced his property and prospects to become a monk. Another brother, Naucratius, handsome, sporting, and versatile, became a hermit and supported the poor by going on fishing expeditions. Tragically he died young; Macrina strongly sustained her mother in her grief. Eventually both voluntarily adopted the standard of living of their servants before retiring to Annesi, an estate in Pontus by the river Iris, where they lived as nuns with other women under the general direction of Basil.

Basil died in 379 and Macrina fell ill nine months later. Gregory of Nyssa visited her after the synod of Antioch; this was his first visit for eight years owing to heretics having driven him out of his bishopric. He found his sister very weak, lying on the floor with two planks to support her. Although she found it difficult to talk, her discussion of the future life was developed by Gregory into his treatise *De Anima et Resurrectione* (On the Soul and the Resurrection). Her poverty was absolute, her preparation for death complete. Her last prayer was barely audible, but impressive: 'Thou hast freed us from the fear of death. Thou hast made the end of this life the beginning of true life. . . . One day thou wilt take again what thou hast given, transfiguring with grace and immortality our mortal and unsightly remains. . . . May my soul be received into thy hands, spotless and undefiled, as an offering before thee.' She died at the time of Vespers and was buried amid widespread lamentation. Feast: 19 July.

Life by Gregory of Nyssa in *P.G.*, xlvi. 959–1000 and in V. W. Callahan, *Gregorii Nysseni Opera*, viii, part 1 (1952), 347–414; Latin version in *AA.SS.* Iul. IV (1725), 589–604; Eng. tr. by W. K. L. Clarke (1916) and V. W. Callahan, *St. Gregory of Nyssa, Ascetical Works* (1967), 159–91; A. E. D. van Loveren, 'Once again: The Monk and the Martyr; St. Antony and St. Macrina', *Studia Patristica*, ii (1982), 528–38; J. Daniélou 'La résurrection des corps chez Grégoire de Nysse', *Vigiliae Christianae*, vii (1953), 154–70. See also B.T.A., iii. 145–6.

MADRON (Madern), monk of the 6th(?) century after whom the Cornish town Madron is called. Who he was is far from clear. Some identify him with *Paternus, others with Medran, disciple of *Ciaran of Saighar, others with *Piran, others with Matronus, disciple of *Tudwal, who lived and died with him in Brittany. The well and chapel of Madron were a pilgrimage centre for miraculous cures both before and after the Reformation. Joseph Hall, bishop of Exeter, examined in 1641 the cure of a cripple who had walked on his hands for sixteen years, who was 'suddenly so restored to his limbs that I saw him able to walk. . . . I found here was no art nor collusion: the thing done, the author invisible.' Francis Coventry (Christopher Davenport) gave further details: the cripple was twenty-eight years old, he spent the night at the altar of the ruined church and washed in the stream which flowed from the well through the chapel. After sleeping on St. Madron's bed for an hour and a half, he felt pain in nerves and arteries, and walked better. After two more visits he was completely cured. He later enlisted in the royalist army but was killed at Lyme (Dorset) in 1644. Methodists and Anglicans still hold services in the chapel at Madron. Feast: 17 May.

H. R. Jennings, *Historical Notes on Madron* (1936); J. Hall, *On the Invisible World* (1641); F. Coventry, *Paralipomena Philosophica de Mundo Peripatetico* (1652); Baring-Gould and Fisher, iii. 396–8; B.T.A., ii. 337–9.

MADRUN (Materiana) (5th century). She was reputedly the daughter of Vortimer and wife of Ynyr Gwent, ruler of the area around Caerwent (Monmouthshire). She was the mother of three children; in the fighting in which Vortigern was killed, described by Nennius, Madrun fled with her infant son, Ceidio, first to Carn Fadryn and then to Cornwall, where she died. Churches are dedicated to her at Tintagel, and Minster (near Boscastle) where she was buried. The whole story is of doubtful authority. Feast: 9 April and 19 October.

Baring-Gould and Fisher, iii. 398–9.

MAEDOC (Aedh, Aidan) **OF FERNS** (d. 626) bishop. Born in Connacht, educated in Leinster and in St. *David's school in Pembrokeshire, Maedoc returned to Ireland and founded a monastery on land given by Brandrub, prince of Leinster, at Ferns (Co. Wexford). He also founded monasteries at Drumlane and Rossinver, which disputed Ferns' claim to be his burial-place. The late Lives, written to further the claims of particular monasteries some centuries after his death, contain few historical details. One says that he bequeathed his staff, bell, and reliquary to his three monasteries. All survive; the first in the National Museum (Dublin), the others in the Library of Armagh cathedral. The Lives also attribute him incredible feats of austerity such as fasting on barley bread and water for seven years, as well as reciting daily 500 psalms. Less conventional is the story of how some spurious beggars, who hid their clothes and dressed in rags, asked for his help; knowing what they had done, he gave away their clothes to some more deserving poor, and sent off the impostors with neither clothes nor alms. Feast: 31 January.

V.S.H., ii. 142–63, 295–311; Irish Lives in *Bethada Naem nErenn*, i (1922), 183–290; *The Irish Saints*, pp. 214–19.

MAELRUAIN (d. 792), Irish abbot. Founder of the monastery of Tallaght (Co. Wicklow) on land given by Cellach mac Dunchada, king of Leinster, in 774, Maelruain became the most influential figure in the reform movement of the Culdees (Celi-Dé). Little is known of his life, but several important writings survive: *The Teaching of Mael-ruain*, the *Rule of the Celi-Dé*, and *The Monastery of Tallaght*. The movement was necessary because the Irish monasteries had not maintained their traditional ascetical practices. The Culdees restored the primacy given to community prayer, with its repetitions of psalters and genuflexions; they also insisted on the continuous practice of 'enclosure' with the consequent exclusion of 'pilgrimage' with its implication of wandering exile and sometimes settlement in other countries. They insisted too on the practice of celibacy, both by monks and the other clergy.

In these ways their programme was similar to those of Carolingian and English reformers of the 9th–10th centuries, but their presentation of it was marked by a characteristic extremism. Women were spoken of as 'men's guardian devils', ascetic practices included total abstinence from alcohol; Sunday was observed like a Jewish sabbath; while vigils in cold water or with the arms in the form of a cross and flagellation were recommended. Although their strictures on the decadence of contemporaries cannot always be believed, they had no scruples about collecting from them tithes to which they believed themselves entitled. In general they revived traditional ascetic observances, but lacked all constitutional means of making their reform permanent.

This led, however, to the compilation, under Maelruain's direction, of the oldest Irish Martyrologies, those of *Oengus and of Tallaght, also to the production of his Stowe Missal, formerly enshrined, which is a unique record of early Irish liturgy. Like other Irish reformers, he attached great importance to spiritual direction and to the confession of sins: he laid down rules for both. His monastery's devotional life was distinguished by emphasis on both the Blessed Virgin and *Michael as its heavenly protectors.

Intellectual and manual work were integral elements of its life. There are, he said, 'three profitable things in the day: prayer, labour and study, or it may be teaching or writing or sewing clothes or any profitable work that a monk may do, so that none may be idle' . . . Or again: 'Labour in piety is the most excellent work of all. The kingdom of heaven is granted to him who directs study, him who studies and him who supports the student.'

On the site of Maelruain's monastery at Tallaght a church was built in 1829, partly from medieval remains. A long-standing custom of holding on his feast a house-to-house procession, which included dancing jigs in the day and drinking at night, was suppressed by the Dominicans in 1856. Feast: 7 July.

K. Hughes, *The Church in Early Irish Society* (1966), pp. 173–93; E. J. Gwynn, 'The Teaching of Mael-ruain', *Hermathena*, 2nd suppl. vol. (1927), pp. 1–63; id., 'Rule of the Celi Dé', ibid., pp. 64–87; E. J. Gwynn and W. J. Purton, 'The Monastery of Tallaght', *P.R.I.A.*, xxix (1911), C, 115–79; *The Irish Saints*, pp. 228–41.

MAELRUBBA (Malrubius) (*c.*642–*c.*722), apostle of the Picts. Born in Ireland, he became a monk at Bangor (Co. Down) *c.*671; later he founded a monastery at Applecross (Ross and Cromarty) on the west coast of Scotland. From there he evangelized Skye and penetrated as far north as Loch Broom. He also built a church on an island in Loch Maree, where his spring was famous for its healing properties. Place-names such as Mulruby, Mury, and Summuruff also testify to his memory. Feast: 21 April (or 27 August).

W. Reeves, 'St. Maelrubba, his History and Churches', *Proc. of Soc. of Antiquaries of Scotland*, iii (1861), 258–96; A. B. Scott, 'St. Maolrhuba', *S.H.R.*, vi (1909), 260–80; W. J. Watson, *History of the Celtic place-names of Scotland* (1926).

MAFALDA OF PORTUGAL (1184–1257), princess. Daughter of Sancho I, king of Portugal, she was married in 1215 to her young cousin Henry I, king of Castile. In 1216, however, this marriage was annulled on grounds of consanguinity. Mafalda returned to Portugal and took the veil in 1222 at Arouca, a nunnery which became Cistercian at her suggestion. The austerity of her life was revealed by sleeping on the ground or spending whole nights in prayer. She devoted her considerable fortune to restoring Oporto cathedral, founding a hospice for pilgrims, and a hospital for twelve widows at Arouca as well as building a bridge over the river Talmeda. She ended her life on sackcloth and ashes. When her body was exhumed in 1617, it was found flexible and incorrupt. Her cult was confirmed in 1793. Feast: 2 (or 13) May.

AA.SS. Maii I (1737), 170, 787–91: Life by Fortunato di S. Bonaventura (1814); *Bibl. SS.*, viii. 490–1.

MAGHOR, see MACHALUS.

MAGI, the wise men described in Matt. 2: 1–12 as the first Gentiles to believe in Christ, were venerated as saints in the Middle Ages. The evangelist numbered their gifts not the givers, but from the time of Origen they traditionally numbered three, subsequently called Casper (Jasper), Balthasar, and Melchior. Their relics, enshrined in a fine casket in Cologne cathedral, were given by Frederick Barbarossa in 1164. He obtained them from Milan and they were believed to have been brought there from Constantinople in the 5th century. The cult was fostered by keen demand for relics of people closely associated with Christ's earthly life and by the mystery plays which frequently depicted their coming. In their rich and varied iconography they are sometimes depicted as one old man, one middle-aged, and one youthful, but the practice of painting one of them as a negro, entirely appropriate for the theme of Epiphany, dates from the 15th century. They were naturally regarded as the patrons of travellers before *Christopher became more popular. Feast: 23 July.

O.D.C.C, p. 858; B.T.A., iii. 168–9; *Bibl. SS.*, viii. 494–528.

MAGLORIUS (d. *c.*575), abbot. Of Irish origin, he was educated at Llantwit Major by *Illtud. With *Samson he went to Brittany and founded monasteries under the protection of King Childebert. Maglorius became abbot of one of them near Dol. After some years he retired to Sark, where he founded a monastery and died. A connection with Jersey is also claimed by his late Life: his removal of a tiresome dragon was rewarded by gifts of land.

His relics were translated, first to Lehon (near Dinant) in 857 and later to Paris at the time of the Viking invasions. They are still claimed by the church of Saint-Jacques. His cult is witnessed by additions to the Martyrologies of *Bede and Ado, by Breton calendars, *N.L.A.*, and Richard Rolle. Feast: 24 October.

AA.SS. Oct. X (1861), 772–93, *N.L.A.*, ii. 156–7, *D.N.B.*, x.v.; F. Duine, *Mémento des sources hagiographiques de Bretagne* (1918), pp. 49–51.

MAGNUS (*c.*1075–1116), earl of Orkney, martyr. The son of Erling, one of two Vikings who ruled the Orkneys, Magnus became a pirate in early life but was converted to Christianity. He was captured by Magnus Barefoot, king of Norway, and compelled to take part in raids along the west coast of Britain. At Anglesey he refused to fight and stayed in his ship reading the psalter. He soon escaped to the court of Malcolm III, king of Scotland, and lived as a penitent in a bishop's house. When Magnus Barefoot died, he returned to the Orkneys to share the government with his cousin Haakon. This arrangement proved impractical: Haakon and his followers killed Magnus at Egilsay. Magnus, according to the Saga, accepted violent death as a sacrifice, praying for his murderers.

Like some other princes who met a violent death for political more than religious reasons, he was venerated as a martyr. His miracles resulted in his becoming the principal saint of Orkney, Shetland, and North Scotland. Kirkwall cathedral, where he was buried and where his relics were discovered in 1919, and several other churches, including some in the City of London, rebuilt by Wren, were dedicated to him. He is said to have appeared to Robert Bruce on the eve of the battle of Bannockburn (1314) and promised him victory. Feast: 16 April.

AA.SS. Apr. II (1675), 438–41; J. Mooney, *St. Magnus, Earl of Orkney* (1935); S. Cruden, 'The cathedral and relics of St. Magnus, Kirkwall' in M. R. Apled (ed.), *Ancient Monuments and their Interpretation* (1977); *Orkneyinga Saga. The History of the Earls of Orkney* (ed. H. Pálsson and P. Edwards, 1978).

MAIEUL (906–94), monk and abbot of Cluny. Born at Avignon, he studied at Lyons and became archdeacon of Macon. Heir to large estates near Riez in Provence, overrun by the Saracens, he was apparently destined for high office in the Church, but Maieul refused to be consecrated to the see of Besançon and became a monk instead. His father had been a notable benefactor of Cluny, where Maieul received the monastic habit and eventually became librarian and bursar. These appointments made him important in both the studies and the administration of estates. Later, when Abbot Aymard became blind, Maieul was appointed coadjutor abbot, and succeeded in 965. A handsome man with a fine presence, he inspired respect and affection, emphasizing specially the eminence of charity.

Under his rule Cluny went from strength to strength. Maieul built the church later called Cluny II; he obtained papal privileges for his monastery and reformed others, especially at Ravenna and Pavia. He enjoyed the favour and protection of the Ottonian emperors and was even requested to become pope. This, however, he refused in 974. When he became old, he chose *Odilo as his successor and retired to a life of contemplation and penance. He died at the abbey of Souvigny on his way to reform the abbey of S. Denis, near Paris, a task urgently requested by Hugh Capet, king of France. The later achievements of Odilo and *Hugh were in part due to his example and ideals. His relics were translated in 1095 by Pope Urban II. Feast: 11 May.

AA.SS. Maii II (1680), 657–700; K. J. Conant, *Cluny* (1968); N. Hunt (ed.), *Cluniac Monasticism in the central Middle Ages* (1971); J. Evans, *Monastic Life at Cluny* (1968); B.T.A., ii. 272–3; *Bibl. SS.*, viii. 564–6.

MAINCHIN, see MUNCHIN.

MAJELLA, Gerard (d. 1755). Redemptorist lay brother. Born at Muro Lucano, fifty miles south of Naples, the son of a tailor, Gerard was a devout child who, on his father's death, was apprenticed to a tailor and then became a servant to the bishop of Lacedogna. In both these occupations he encountered considerable personal difficulties. He then returned home to live with his mother and three sisters, was notable for his extreme generosity, and spent long hours in prayer. He had already tried to join the Capuchin branch of the Franciscan Order but was refused because of weak health. The Redemptorists, however, accepted him with some misgivings at Deliceto (Foggia); following the direct intervention of the founder *Alphonsus Liguori, Gerard was professed as a lay brother in 1752. After three eventful years during which stories of clairvoyance, prophecy, the gift of reading the secrets of hearts, charity to the poor, and supposedly miraculous healings were related of him, he died of consumption at the age of twenty-nine, in the monastery of Caposele, Avellino. The marvels related of him must not obscure the fact that most of his time was spent in humdrum duties as porter, tailor, and gardener. He was beatified by Leo XIII in 1893 and canonized by Pius X in 1904. He was praised as the patron and model of lay brothers in their humble, hidden lives, but paradoxically he has also been acclaimed as the 'most famous wonder-worker of the 18th century'. Feast: 16 October.

Propylaeum, pp. 458–9; *Compendium vitae, virtutum et miraculorum necnon actorum in causa canonizationis B. Gerardi Majella* (1904); contemporary Life by A. M. Tannoia, *Vita del servo di Dio Fr. Gerardo Majella* (1811), Eng. tr. in *Lives of the Companions of St. Alphonsus* (1849), pp. 243–453; O. Vassall-Phillips, *Life of St. Gerard Majella* (1914); J. Carr, *To Heaven Through a Window* (1946); B.T.A., iv. 131–4; *Bibl. SS.*, vi. 192–6.

MALACHY (Maol Maedoc) (1094–1148), archbishop of Armagh. This most famous pioneer of the Gregorian Reform in Ireland was the son of Mughron Ua Morgain, a teacher, and called 'Irish of the Irish'. He was educated at Armagh and became a monk there under abbot Imar when he was about twenty. In 1119 he was ordained priest. Soon after, while Cellach of Armagh occupied Dublin, Malachy ruled Armagh diocese as his vicar. His policy, based on the synod of Rath Bresaill (1111), was to insist on canon law as the norm of government, to restore marriage as a stable, legal contract, to renew the practice of confession and confirmation, and to introduce Roman chants and ceremonies in the liturgy. All of these had previously been neglected owing to insular traditions and repeated Viking invasions. In 1121 Malachy studied the Gregorian Reform programme more completely and monasticism as an integral part of it under Malchus, archbishop of Cashel and formerly a monk of Winchester.

In 1123 his uncle gave him the famous, but deserted, abbey of Bangor (Co. Down). Malachy accepted it, but refused most of its lands and revenues. He restored it with the help of ten monks from Armagh and built a wooden church. In 1124 he was consecrated bishop of Connor (and Down), but he still lived at Bangor. His principal problems were a severe shortage of priests, neglect of the sacraments, rejection of canon law in favour of Irish customs, and the non-payment of tithes. For three years Malachy worked at transforming his diocese until he was driven out by a local chieftain. He retired to found the monastery called *Ibracense* (perhaps Ballinskelligs, Co. Kerry), which became the centre of one of his most important achievements, the propagation of the Order of Austin Canons in many parts of Ireland. Their blend of pastoral and educational work in community provided a much-needed regular way of life. Eventually they had houses in many cathedral towns.

In 1129 Cellach, archbishop of Armagh, died. He left the succession to his see not to a blood relation but to Malachy, who was, however, supplanted by a rival candidate, Muirchertach, who was supported by both the local chieftain and Cellach's clan. For three years Malachy, to avoid bloodshed, made no attempt to occupy his see until Gilbert of Limerick, papal legate, overcame his reluctance. For a time Malachy exercised jurisdiction in part of his diocese, but not the town or cathedral of Armagh. An armed peace followed until Muirchertach's death in 1134. But his successor Niall, although he left Armagh to Malachy, retained the crozier called the Staff of Jesus and the Book of Armagh. These assured him some recognition in the north, but the south was solidly for Malachy. This long dispute, a test-case for the old custom of hereditary succession, only ended with Malachy's resignation in 1137 and the consecration of Gilla, abbot of Derry, whom all parties agreed to accept.

Malachy then returned to his own diocese, reserving Down for himself and consecrating another bishop for Connor. Soon after he went to Rome (via Scotland, York, and Clairvaux) to secure confirmation of the changes made by the reformers, and pallia for the archbishops of Armagh and Cashel. One result of this journey was the meeting with *Bernard, which led to the foundation of Mellifont in 1142. This Cistercian abbey became the 'parent' of many others, including several of the ancient but disorganized Irish ones. At the synod of Innishpatrick (1148) formal application for the pallia was made by the Church in Ireland: once again Malachy was sent to obtain them; eventually four metropolitan sees were set up instead of two. Malachy, however, did not live to see this, as he died in the arms of St. Bernard at Clairvaux on his way to Rome.

His cult sprang up at Clairvaux, fostered by Bernard. In 1170 his name appears in the Irish Martyrology of Gorman. In 1190 Clement III approved the cult among the Cistercians, thus equivalently canonizing him. The feast was moved from 2 November to 3 November to avoid All Souls' Day; there is also some early evidence for 5 November.

The so-called Prophecies of St. Malachy, a series of symbolical titles of the popes from 1143 until the supposed end of the world, are not by Malachy but are a late 16th-century compilation published by Dom Arnold de Wyon in 1595. The choice of Malachy as their supposed author is evidence for his fame in Renaissance Rome.

Contemporary Life by St. Bernard, also letters concerning Malachy (nos. 341, 356–7, 374) and sermons in *AA.SS.* Nov. II, i (1894), 135–66 and *P.L.*, clxxxii. 1073–118; clxxxiii. 481–90. All these documents translated with introduction by H. J. Lawlor, *St. Malachy of Armagh* (1920), and P.-Y. Emery (*S.C.*, 367, 1990). More recent studies include A. Gwynn, 'St. Malachy of Armagh', *I.E.R.*, lxx (1948), 961–87; lxxi (1949), 134–48 and 317–31; J. Leclercq, 'Documents on the Cult of St. Malachy', *Seanchas Ardmacha*, iii (1959), 318–32; P. J. Dunning, 'The Arroasian

Order in Medieval Ireland', *I.H.S.* (1945), 297–315; A. B. Scott, *Malachy* (1976). For the Prophecies of Malachy see H. Thurston, *The War and the Prophets* (1915), pp. 120–61; also P. Grosjean, 'La prophétie de S. Malachie sur l'Irlande', *Anal. Boll.*, li (1933), 318–24.

MALCHUS (d. *c.*390), monk. Born at Nisibis (Nysaybia) in Mesopotamia, he was the only son of wealthy parents who wished him to marry, but he ran away to join some Syrian hermits in the desert near Khalkis. Having heard of his father's death, he returned home against his abbot's will to comfort his mother and collect his legacy to found a monastery. He joined a caravan for the hazardous journey, but it was attacked by Bedouin who carried off Malchus and a young woman beyond the Euphrates. For some time he lived among these Nomads, working as a shepherd and goatherd, living on dates, cheese, and milk.

His master wanted him to improve his status by marriage: in Bedouin tradition an unmarried man was not a full man but one who had to live in dependence on another, sharing his tent. The lady chosen was his fellow-captive, already married to another, but she was ready to accept the new plan. But Malchus, conscious of his monastic vows, refused. All he would accept was for them to live together in perfect continence under the appearance of marriage. This was agreed, but he later said: 'I loved this woman as a sister, but never quite trusted her as a sister.'

Eventually they decided to run away together: he to his monastery, she to her husband. They took food in goatskins, which they inflated to float across the Euphrates and hid in a cave. Their master and his companion caught up with them but were killed by a lioness. Malchus and his lady mounted the camels and escaped to safety through Edessa. The lady never found her husband, but settled down to live near Malchus and died at a great age. He first rejoined his hermits at Khalkis, but ended his days at Maronia, where he met *Jerome who wrote the semi-fictional Life on which this notice is based. This Life was soon translated into Greek and Syriac (35 manuscripts of it survive in the Vatican Library alone). A verse Life by Reginald of Canterbury is based on Jerome's work. Feast in the West: 21 October; in the East: 20, 26 March, 16 April.

Jerome's Life in *AA.SS.* Oct. IX (1869), 59–69, and in *P.L.*, xxiii. 55–62; Reginald of Canterbury's Life in *Classical Bulletin* (1946), 31–60; D. Attwater, *Saints of the East* (1963), 55–8; *Bibl. SS.*, viii. 585–7; J. N. D. Kelly, *Jerome* (1975).

MALLONUS, see MELLON.

MALO (Machutus, Maclou) (6th–7th century), bishop. Possibly of Welsh origin, Malo is mainly known as an apostle of Brittany, who founded the church of Aleth (Saint-Servan), with the town now called Saint-Malo as its main centre. A primitive Life, now lost, was the basis for two more of the 9th century which survive, but are not of great value. They do, however, provide some kind of portrait of a rugged pioneer, who sang psalms in a loud voice as he travelled on horseback, who made enemies as well as friends in the districts where he preached until he was driven out. This caused his removal to Saintes until a deputation asked him to return, but his death came first. His feast was widely celebrated in England both in a number of southern monasteries and in the calendars of Sarum, York, and Hereford. It has been asserted that his cult was encouraged by bishops of Winchester because the Latin word for Gwent closely resembles that for Winchester. Whether or not this was so, relics of Malo were claimed by Bath and other churches, while geographical contacts with his town must also have been close. Feast: 15 November; translation, 11 July.

AA.SS. Iun. III (1701), 178 ff.; Lives edited by F. Plaine in *Bulletins et Mémoires de la Soc. archéol. du département d'Ille-et-Vilaine*, xvi (1883), 167–256 and by A. de la Borderie, ibid., 267–93; F. Lot, 'Les diverses redactions de la vie de saint-Malo', *Mélanges d'Histoire bretonne* (1907), pp. 97–206; L. Duchesne, 'La Vie de saint Malo: étude critique', *Revue celtique*, xi (1890), 1–22; A. Poncelet, 'Une source de la vie de S. Malo par Bili', *Anal. Boll.*, xxiv (1905), 483–6; R. Brown and D.

Yerkes, 'A sermon on the birthday of St. Machutus', *Anal. Boll.*, lxxxix (1981), 160–4.

MALRUBIUS, see MAELRUBBA.

MANACCA, abbess of 5th–6th century (?), who gave her name to the Cornish village of Manaccan, was possibly of Irish origin and believed to be the sister of *Selevan. Feast: 14 October.

Baring-Gould and Fisher, iii. 434–5.

MANACCUS (Mancus), bishop, titular of Lanreath church (Cornwall), where, according to William Worcestre, his body rested. He is depicted in St. *Neot's church (Cornwall) in the 16th-century stained glass called the Young Women's Window. Feast: 3 August.

Baring-Gould and Fisher, iii. 435.

MANCHAN, see MACHAN.

MANCHEN, see MUNCHIN.

MAOL MAEDOC, see MALACHY.

MARCELLIAN, see MARK AND MARCELLIAN.

MARCELLINUS AND PETER (d. 304), Roman martyrs. The evidence for their cult is early and strong, consisting of feasts in the sacramentaries and calendars, the survival of their tombs, and some verses by *Damasus. They are also mentioned in the Roman Canon. Marcellinus was a priest, Peter an exorcist. Their unreliable Acts say that they made converts of the gaoler and his family while they were in prison, that the place of their execution was called the Black Wood, but afterwards the White Wood, that the magistrate who condemned them was called Severus. They were buried in the catacomb of Tiburtius on the Via Lavicana, over which a church was later built. In 827 Pope Gregory IV sent their relics to Einhard, former secretary and biographer of Charlemagne, to enrich his monastery at Seligenstadt; records of the miracles which then took place survive. Feast: 2 June.

AA.SS. Iun. I (1695), 170–209; *C.M.H.*, pp. 293–4; B.T.A., ii. 452; Eng. tr. of the account of the translation by B. Wendell (1926).

MARCELLUS (d. 309), pope. He succeeded Pope Marcellinus in 308; he became unpopular because he enforced the canons on penance and was exiled for treating an apostate with severity. He died in exile, but not apparently by a violent death. But he is called a martyr in early liturgical books. His body lies under the Roman church dedicated to his name. Feast: 16 January.

L. Duchesne, *Liber Pontificalis*, i. xcix and 164.

MARCELLUS THE CENTURION (d. 298), martyr. The authentic Acts of this martyr survive in two recensions which disagree about the place of his death; one places it at Leon (Spain), the other more convincingly at Tingis (Tangier). During the celebration of the birthday of the emperors Diocletian and Maximian, Marcellus the centurion threw off his soldier's belt in front of the legion's standards and said publicly: 'I am a soldier of Jesus Christ, the eternal king. From now on I cease to serve your emperors and I despise the worship of your gods of wood and stone, for they are deaf and dumb images.' The soldiers who heard this outburst were dumbfounded; they arrested and imprisoned him and reported the matter to the governor, Fortunatus. When called upon to give an account of his actions, Marcellus replied: 'On 21 July, when you were celebrating the emperor's feast day, I declared publicly and openly that I was a Christian and said that I could not serve under this military oath, but only for Christ Jesus, the son of God the Father Almighty.' Fortunatus said that he could not conceal this rash action, but would have to report it to the emperors and Caesar: Marcellus would be handed over to Agricolanus, deputy for the praetorian prefects.

On 30 October the official report was read. Marcellus was asked if in fact he said what was reported, was he serving as a regular centurion, first class, and did he throw away the badges of allegiance, and indeed his arms. To all these questions he replied in the affirmative. The explanation he added was that it is not fitting for a Christian, who fights for Christ his lord, to fight for the armies of this world.

Agricolanus said that Marcellus' actions deserved punishment according to military rules. 'And so, whereas Marcellus, who held the rank of centurion, first class, has confessed that he has disgraced himself by publicly renouncing his military oath and has further used expressions lacking in self-control as recorded in the report of the prefect, I hereby sentence him to death by the sword.' As he was being led out to execution, he said: 'Agricolanus, may God reward you.' Like *Maximilian, he judged that military service was incompatible with the practice of the Christian religion. This seems to have been a minority view, overlooked by the many who admired their religious motivation. Feast: 30 October.

A.C.M., xxxvii–xxxix, 250–9; H. Delehaye, 'Les Actes de S. Marcel le Centurion', *Anal. Boll.*, xli (1923), 257–87; B. de Gaiffier, 'S. Marcel de Tanger ou de Léon?', *Anal. Boll.*, lxi (1943), 116–39; *Propylaeum*, pp. 484–5; B.T.A., iv. 220–1.

MARCOUL (Marculf) (d. *c.*558), abbot. Born at Bayeux of a wealthy family, Marcoul became a priest at Coutances and preached the gospel in its neighbourhood. But he longed for a more solitary life, became a hermit on an unidentified island, and later founded a monastery at Nanteuil. From this came several famous disciples, including *Helier, who also lived as an island hermit.

Marcoul was invoked against skin diseases; the kings of France used to venerate his relics at Corbeny immediately after their coronation at Reims. It was popularly believed that through him came the royal power to 'touch for the king's evil'. His shrine survived until the French Revolution. Feast: 1 May (2 May at Malmesbury).

AA.SS. Maii I (1680), 70–82; B.T.A., ii. 210.

MARGARET OF ANTIOCH (Marina) (no date). Very popular in the later Middle Ages in England and elsewhere, Margaret probably never existed as a historical person, but only as a character in pious fiction.

Her Legend was declared apocryphal by Pope Gelasius in 494; there was no ancient liturgical cult. Her name first appeared in the West in the Martyrology of Rhabanus Maurus (9th century). Some supposed relics were translated from the East to San Pietro della Valle (near Lake Bolsena) in 908, and thence to Montefalcone cathedral in 1145 and to Venice in 1213. She became famous in the time of the Crusades.

According to her Legend she was the daughter of a pagan priest, Aedisius of Antioch. She became a Christian, was turned out of home, and lived as a shepherdess. Olybrius, governor of Antioch, carried her off to his palace and tried to seduce or marry her. She proclaimed herself a Christian and refused. She was then tortured and tempted in various incredible ways. She was even swallowed by a dragon which later burst asunder. Through her preaching she converted immense numbers to Christianity. They were beheaded in the persecution of Diocletian; so was she.

At the end of her life she promised, as the Sarum breviary relates: that those who write or read her 'history' will receive an unfading crown in heaven, that those who invoke her on their death-beds will enjoy divine protection and escape from the devils, that those who dedicate churches or burn lights in her honour will obtain anything useful they pray for, and that pregnant women who invoke her will escape from the dangers of childbirth, as will their infants. These apocryphal promises contributed powerfully to the spread of her cult.

This can be traced back before the Norman Conquest in England, when the first of seven vernacular Lives were written. Well over 200 ancient English churches were dedicated to her, including fifty-eight in Norfolk. She was frequently depicted in wall paintings and stained-glass windows, often transfixing a dragon with a spear or else emerging unharmed from inside it. Wace, Bokenham, and Lydgate were among those who wrote her Life. *Joan of Arc believed that she heard the voice of Margaret of Antioch encouraging her in her mission to the French king.

Patroness of childbirth, she became recognized as one of the *Fourteen Holy Helpers. Feast: in the East, 13 July; in the West, 20 July. Her cult was suppressed by the Holy See in 1969.

AA.SS. Iul. V (1727), 22–44 with *Propylaeum*, p. 297; H. Delehaye, *Les Légendes hagiographiques* (1905), pp. 222–34; G. H. Gerould, *Legends of the English Saints* (1918); F. M. Mack, *Sainte Margarete virgin and martyr* (E.E.T.S., 1934); N. R. Ker, *Facsimile of MS. Bodley 34* (E.E.T.S., 1960).

MARGARET OF CORTONA: (*c.*1247–97), Franciscan penitent. Born at Lavinio (Tuscany), the daughter of a small farmer, she lost her mother in childhood and suffered from an unsympathetic stepmother. She was seduced by a knight of Montepulciano, lived openly as his mistress for nine years, and bore him a son. But her lover was murdered by persons unknown; Margaret gave up all her goods and returned home with her young son to her father's house, asking for forgiveness. He, however, at his wife's instigation refused. Margaret asked the Franciscan friars for help. Two ladies took her and her son into their home; she led a life of public penance, somewhat dramatically manifested and, in abhorrence for her former life, tried to undertake bizarre mortifications which included self-mutilation, and even some ill-treatment of her son. In spite of these excesses and after several years probation, she was admitted to the Third Order of St. Francis; from that time onwards and with the departure of her son, first to school in Arezzo and later to the Franciscan novitiate, she advanced steadily in prayer and holiness. Margaret devoted herself to nursing the sick poor, first in her own house and later in a community which she founded at the Spedale di Santa Maria della Misericordia at Cortona. Her personal austerities were extreme: a starvation diet and little sleep, the wearing of haircloth in expiation; to these sufferings were added those of calumny, misrepresentation, and contempt. But in obedience to a revelation she undertook to call others to repentance: by attacking vice, she converted sinners from Cortona; her reputation, fostered by cures believed miraculous, attracted visitors from other parts of Italy and even further afield. She died at the age of fifty, after spending twenty-nine years in penance. She was formally canonized in 1728, but from 1515 her feast on 22 February had been approved for the diocese of Cortona. Her incorrupt body rests in the church at Cortona.

AA.SS. Feb. III (1658), 298–357; Fr. Cuthbert, *A Tuscan Penitent* (1907); F. Mauriac, *Margaret of Cortona* (1948); *Bibl. SS.*, viii 759–73.

MARGARET OF ENGLAND (d. 1192), Cistercian nun. Possibly Hungarian by birth but with an English mother, or else, as popularly reputed, an Englishwoman, Margaret took her mother on pilgrimage to Jerusalem and Bethlehem, where they both led an austere life of penance for some years. Her mother died in the Holy Land, but Margaret made other pilgrimages to Montserrat and Puy before she became a Cistercian nun at Sauve Benite. There she died; miracles followed at her tomb; her shrine became a principal feature of the church and crowds came there to invoke 'Margaret the Englishwoman', whose feast was kept on 3 February. The local tradition that she was English was accepted by the Maurists and *Gallia Christiana.*

B.T.A., i. 243–4; *Gallia Christiana Nova*, ii. 777; P. Mongour, *Sainte Marguerite de la Séauve: son histoire et sa légende* (1954).

MARGARET OF HULME (d. 1170), i.e. Hoveton St. John, near St. Benet's Hulme (Norfolk), venerated as a martyr. She was buried in the abbey church. Feast: 22 May.

William Worcestre, pp. 228–9.

MARGARET OF HUNGARY (1242–70), princess and Dominican nun.

The daughter of King Bela IV and his wife Mary Lascaris, Margaret was born in the castle of Turoc. The Tartar invasions made this a critical time and at the age of three she was offered to the Dominican nuns at Vesprem. Some years later the king built a convent on an island in the Danube near Buda, where Margaret was professed in 1255 and took the veil in 1261. She had previously refused to marry Ottokar, king of Bohemia.

The rest of her short life was spent in prayer, extreme penance, and menial work. Just because she was privileged, she chose the most repulsive tasks in caring for the sick. She also identified with the poor by following their standards of hygiene. Intellectually limited, she centred her devotional life on the Eucharist and on the Passion of Christ. Hence every Lent she fasted very strictly, went without sleep, and performed austerities with long prayers, sometimes accompanied by visions.

Prematurely worn out, she died on 18 January, aged only twenty-eight. An unofficial cult began at once, and pilgrims visited her tomb. In 1277 her cause was begun, the evidence of whose witnesses form the principal source for her life. Her cult was approved in 1789; she was canonized in 1943. Feast: 26 January.

AA.SS. Ian. II (1643), 897–909; G. Frankoi, *Monumenta Romana Episcopatus Vesprimiensis*, i (1896), 163–383; S.M.C., *Margaret, Princess of Hungary* (1945); B.T.A., i. 176–8; *Bibl. SS.*, viii. 768–801.

MARGARET OF SCOTLAND (1046–93), queen. Grand-daughter of Edmund Ironside and daughter of Edward the Atheling (d. 1057), Margaret was well educated, mainly in Hungary, where her family was exiled during the rule of Danish kings in England. As one of the last members of the Anglo-Saxon royal family, she was in danger after the Norman Conquest and took refuge at the court of Malcolm III, king of Scotland. Intelligent, beautiful, and devout, with a keen taste for fine clothes, Margaret married him in 1069. This union was exceptionally happy and fruitful for the Scottish court and nation; and through Margaret and her daughter Matilda the English royal family of today can trace their descent from the pre-Conquest kings of England.

Her biographer Turgot, prior of Durham and bishop of St. Andrews, stressed both her public and private achievements. Through her the Scottish court achieved a higher standard of civilization; consequently its reputation was improved. She was also a principal agent in the reform of the Church in Scotland, then at a low ebb. Councils propagated the practice of Easter communion and abstinence from servile work on Sundays, while she took a prominent part in the foundation of monasteries, churches, and hostels for pilgrims. She revived the abbey of Iona, made famous by *Columba and *Aidan, and built Dunfermline to be like a Scottish Westminster Abbey as a burial-place for its royal family. In the fields of both politics and religion her reign brought strong English influence; her achievements are therefore both praised and criticized.

Her private life was devoted to prayer and reading, lavish almsgiving (including the liberation of Anglo-Saxon captives), and to ecclesiastical needlework. Her influence over the king was considerable. Initially rough in character, he came through love for her to value what she valued. He 'saw', as her biographer wrote, 'that Christ truly dwelt in her heart . . . what she rejected, he rejected . . . what she loved, he for love of her loved too'. Although he could not read, he liked to see the books she used at prayer and would have them embellished with gold or silver binding. One such book, certainly hers, a pocket Gospel book with fine Evangelist portraits and gold initials, survives in the Bodleian Library at Oxford. A psalter at Edinburgh University Library may well have been hers: so too a famous illustrated Life of *Cuthbert (Oxford, University College, 165).

Of Margaret's eight children two (Alexander and *David) became kings of Scotland; her daughter Matilda married Henry I of England. She herself lived just long enough to learn of the tragic death of her husband and one of her sons on a military expedition against William Rufus, who had confiscated Edgar Atheling's estates. Worn out with her austerities and childbearing, Margaret died at the age of forty-seven.

She was buried beside her husband at Dunfermline: her body was translated on 19 June 1250 following a papal inquiry into her Life and miracles. The document of her canonization, however, does not survive. But an indulgence of forty days for visiting Dunfermline on her feast dates from 1249. At the Reformation the bodies of Margaret and Malcolm were translated to a chapel in the Escorial, Madrid, specially built for the purpose, while her head was obtained by the Jesuits at Douai. She was named patron of Scotland in 1673, and is Scotland's only saint to enjoy a universal cult in the Roman calendar. Feast: 16 November; translation, 19 (or by Baronius' error, 10) June.

AA.SS. Iun. II (1698), 320–40; *Proplyaeum*, p. 231; Life by Turgot also in Symeon of Durham's *Opera* (S.S.), i. 234–54 and in J. Pinkerton, *Lives of the Scottish Saints*, ii (1889), 159–82, tr. W. M. Metcalfe, *Ancient Lives of Scottish Saints* (1895), pp. 298–321. Modern studies by T. R. Barnett (1926), L. Menzies (2nd edn. 1960), and D. McRoberts (1960). See also G. W. S. Barrow, 'Scottish Rulers and the Religious Orders', *T.R.H.S.*, 5th ser. iii (1953), 77–100; id. 'From Queen Margaret to David I. Benedictines and Tironians', *Innes Review*, xi (1960), 22–38; D. Baker (ed.), *Medieval Women* (1978), pp. 119–42.

MARIA GORETTI, see GORETTI.

MARIAN AND JAMES (d. 259), martyrs. James was a deacon, Marian a lector. They died at Cirta Iulia (later Constantina), the chief city of Numidia. They were condemned to death by the *legatus* of Numidia, probably C. Macrinius Decianus. Their Acts, somewhat rhetorical, borrow something from those of *Perpetua and Felicitas, and record visions as well as tortures. They were written by an anonymous friend of the martyrs who was arrested with them, but subsequently released. They were known in their final form to *Augustine (Sermon 284).

In the course of this particular persecution two bishops named Agapius and Secundinus suffered first, having called in at the writer's house on their way to martyrdom. Not only their example but also their positive encouragement helped to inspire Marian and James. A large band of centurions surrounded the house and made several arrests. Marian and James both openly confessed their faith and acknowledged their holy orders; they were then subjected to tortures of the rack and imprisoned. This was the point when they experienced visions, including one of *Cyprian, who invited them to come and sit with him and gave them a drink of pure water to encourage them.

The place of the martyrs' execution was in a river valley with high banks on each side. A number of others unnamed suffered with Marian and James. The martyrs were arranged in rows and blindfolded, then beheaded. Their bodies were thrown in the river Rummel. Marian prophesied that epidemics, famine, earthquakes, and poisonous flies would soon afflict the neighbourhood. His mother Mary was present and embraced his lacerated body, but through their suffering, said the writer, they were 'at last restored to the patriarchs in glory and delivered from the distress of this world'. Feast: 6 May, but 30 April in Roman Martyrology. Gubbio cathedral claims their relics.

A.C.M., xxxiii–xxxiv, 194–213; Augustine, *Sermo* 284; *Propylaeum*, pp. 163–4; B.T.A., ii. 198–9.

MARILLAC, Louise de (1591–1660), widow, foundress of the Sisters of Charity. Born of an aristocratic country family, Louise was educated by nuns at Poissy and by her own father, especially after her mother's early death. Her father died when she was only fifteen; although she experienced some attraction towards the cloister, she married Antony Le Gras. They had one son and lived happily together for twelve years. He died in 1625, although nursed most devotedly by Louise. Certain that she wanted to devote herself entirely to God's service, but uncertain in what way, she met *Vincent de Paul, who became her director. At this time he was organizing devout, wealthy ladies into helping the poor and the sick in often appalling conditions. It soon became clear that many of the ladies were unfitted to cope with the actual conditions. The practical work of nursing the poor in their own homes, caring for neglected children and dealing with often rough husbands and fathers, was best accomplished by women of similar social status to the principal sufferers. The aristocratic ladies were better suited to the equally necessary work of raising money and dealing with correspondence. Vincent, however, recognized Louise as a woman of clear mind, great courage, endurance, and self-effacement. He chose her to train and organize girls and widows, mainly of the peasant and artisan classes, for the service of the sick and poor. In 1633 four candidates started work in Louise's Paris home in the Rue des Fosses-Saint-Victor. From this humble beginning grew the world-famous institute of the Sisters of Charity. Vincent had not intended to found a religious order. The sisters, he said, should consider themselves simply as Christian women devoted to the sick and the poor: 'your convent will be the house of the sick, your cell a hired room, your chapel the parish church, your cloister the city streets or the hospital wards, your enclosure obedience, your grill the fear of God, your veil modesty.' Until 1642 they took no vows at all; to this day they take vows for a year only, which may, however, be renewed year after year until death. Louise's Sisters took charge of the Hôtel-Dieu hospital in Paris, of orphanages, and even of schools; Louise herself nursed those ill with the plague in Paris and reformed a neglected hospital at Angers. Her son, married and with a small family, visited her at the end of her life in 1660. She died the same year, exhorting her Sisters to be diligent in serving the poor 'and to honour them like Christ himself'. She was canonized in 1934. Her Sisters have always been held in high repute and have made foundations in all parts of the world. Their distinctive habit, a grey wool tunic with a large head-dress or *cornette* of white linen, was the usual dress of Breton peasant women of the 17th century and later. In recent times it has been replaced by dress more in accordance with the sartorial customs of the 20th century. Feast: 15 March.

P. Coste, *S. Vincent de Paul et les Dames de la Charité* (1937); J. Calvet, *Louise de Marillac: a Portrait* (Eng. tr. 1959); other Lives by E. de Broglie (Eng. tr. 1933); M. V. Woodgate (1942); M. Flinton (1957); B.T.A., i. 598–601.

MARINA, see MARGARET OF ANTIOCH.

MARINUS OF CAESAREA (d. *c.*260), martyr. Eusebius recorded his death and other details. Marinus, both noble and wealthy, had made a fine career in the Roman army. An important post fell vacant and by seniority Marinus should have filled it. But a disappointed candidate denounced him as a Christian, saying that Marinus would not sacrifice to the emperors and therefore he himself should receive the appointment.

The magistrate interrogated Marinus, who persistently confessed he was a Christian, so he was given three hours to reconsider his position. Theoctenus, bishop of Caesarea, led Marinus to the church and then to the altar. He pointed to Marinus' sword and had a Gospel book brought to the altar; he then asked him which he preferred. Without hesitation Marinus chose the Gospel book with his right hand. 'Hold fast,' said the bishop, 'hold fast to God: with the strength he has given you, may you obtain what you have chosen. Now go in peace.'

When the allotted time was over, Marinus was summoned before the tribunal. Here he showed even greater loyalty to the faith and was led off to execution. Feast: 3 March.

A.C.M., xxxvi, 240–3; Eusebius, *H.E.*, vii. 15–16; B.T.A., i. 466–7; *Propylaeum*, p. 83.

MARK (d. *c.*74), evangelist. He is usually, but not invariably, identified with John Mark whose mother's house in Jerusalem was a meeting-place for the Apostles and with the young man, described in Mark 14: 51, who followed Christ after his arrest and then escaped capture. He was later the companion of both *Paul and *Peter. Paul and *Barnabas (Mark's cousin) took him with them on the first missionary journey, but Mark turned back at Perga (Pamphylia) for Jerusalem. Paul was not satisfied; the ensuing quarrel with Barnabas led to Barnabas and Mark together preaching in Cyprus (Acts 13 and 15). Later, when Paul was captive at Rome, Mark was with him, helping (Col. 4: 10). Peter also referred to him affectionately as his 'son' (1 Pet. 5: 13), which accords well with the traditional ascription to Mark of a gospel which represented the teaching and memoirs of Peter, whose 'interpreter' Clement of Alexandria and Papias say he was. It is likely that the Gospel of Mark was written in Italy, perhaps at Rome.

The assertion that Mark went to Alexandria (of which he is reckoned the first bishop) was recorded by Eusebius, but neither Clement of Alexandria nor Origen mentions it. This persistent tradition, however, together with unreliable details about his martyrdom which is placed in 'the eighth year of Nero' is virtually the only information about him not contained in the NT writings.

The history of his relics is notable. Early in the 9th century his body was brought to Venice, whose patron he became and has remained to this day. Although the original church of St. Mark there was burnt in 976, the rebuilt basilica contains both the relics from Alexandria and the magnificent series of mosaics on Mark's life, death, and translation. These date from the 12th–13th centuries and form a unique record of him. The symbol of Mark as an evangelist, the lion, is also much in evidence at Venice, as it is elsewhere in portraits of the evangelists.

Feasts: 25 April; in the East, formerly 23 September; the translation feast to Venice, 31 January.

AA.SS. Apr. III (1675), 344–58 and Sept. VII (1760), 379–90; G. Pavanello, 'San Marco nella legenda e nella storia', *Rivista della citta di Venezia* (1928), pp. 293–324; G. Musolino, *La Basilica di San Marco in Venezia* (1955); for St. Mark's Gospel, the commentary by Bede (ed. D. Hurst, *C.C.*, cxx, 1960) is the standard one of Christian antiquity, while modern ones are by M. J. Lagrange (*Études Bibliques*, 1911), R. H. Lightfoot, *The Gospel Message of Mark* (1950), A. M. Farrer, *A Study in St. Mark* (2nd edn. 1966); N. R. Telford, *The Interpretation of Mark* (1985).

MARK AND MARCELLIAN (d. *c.*290), Roman martyrs. These martyrs are commemorated in the ancient Roman sacramentaries; their tomb, with frescoes of them and their companions, has been identified in the catacomb of St. Balbina. For the details of their Lives the only source is the unreliable 5th-century Acts of *Sebastian. This makes them twin brothers of noble birth, converts to Christianity in youth; both were married. In Diocletian's persecution they were condemned to death. Thirty days' stay of execution procured by their friends, and the entreaties of their parents, wives, and children, failed to make them change their resolve, in which they were encouraged by Sebastian, an army officer. They were eventually executed; their relics were translated from the catacombs first to the church of SS. Cosmas and Damian and then to that of St. Praxedes. Feast: 18 June.

AA.SS. Iun. III (1701), 568–71 and *C.M.H.*, pp. 324–5.

MARTHA (1st century). The sister of *Lazarus and of Mary who is usually identified with *Mary Magdalene, Martha received Christ in their household at Bethany, which was specially loved by him (Luke 10: 38–42), on which occasion he gently reproved her for her complaint that her sister Mary did not help her sufficiently in the necessary preparations. The words of Christ were traditionally represented as indicating the excellence of the contemplative life (represented by Mary) over the cares of the active life, represented by Martha. In the Gospel of John, Martha also appeared on the occasion of the Raising of Lazarus (John 11: 1–46), when her faith in Christ and his divine power was the occasion for the famous words 'I am the resurrection and the life', and for the miracle of Lazarus' return to life. It was also recorded that Christ once again had supper at Bethany, where Martha served him six days before the passover (John 12: 1–2). This is all that can be known of her from the New Testament; there is no early tradition about her death.

But a medieval legend arose which connected her, Mary Magdalene, and Lazarus with the evangelization of Provence: Martha's supposed relics were discovered and enshrined in 1187 at Tarascon. Her iconography depends both on the authentic data of the Gospel and on the historically worthless Provençal legends. She is invoked as the patron of housewives and lay sisters, and her attributes are a ladle, a broom, or a bunch of keys; but she is also represented with a dragon, which she was supposed to have tamed at Tarascon by aspersing him with holy water and wrapping her sash round his neck, before leading him to Arles, where he was killed. She is also represented in scenes of the Raising of Lazarus, as in the fine Romanesque sculptures at Chichester cathedral.

Feast: 29 July in the West. There is much divergence about her feast in antiquity: an interpolator in the Martyrology of Jerome places her with her brother and sister on 19 January; Ado on 17 October; while the Greeks cult her on 6 June among the holy women who brought spices to anoint Christ's body.

AA.SS. Iul. VI (1729), 4–13; E. Vacandard, 'La Venue de Lazare et Marie-Madeleine en Provence', *Revue des Questions Historiques*, c (1924), 257–305.

MARTIN OF TOURS (*c.*316–397), monk bishop. One of the most popular saints of the Middle Ages, Martin was born in Pannonia (now Hungary); his father was a pagan officer in the Roman army; Martin too joined the army for some time, probably as a conscript. He intended to become a Christian from an early age and was enrolled among the catechumens. He became convinced that his commitment to Christ prevented him from continuing to serve as a soldier. After making a protest that could be considered an early example of 'conscientious objection' to military service, he was imprisoned and, at the end of hostilities, was discharged. It is to this period of his life that belongs the episode, made famous by artists, of his cutting his cloak in half to clothe a nearly naked beggar at Amiens, which episode was followed by a dream in which Christ appeared to him, wearing the cloak he had given away. He then became a disciple of *Hilary at Poitiers, was baptized, and travelled to Pannonia, Milan, and Illyricum.

On Hilary's return to Poitiers in 360 from banishment, Martin rejoined him and became a solitary monk at Ligugé on land given by Hilary. Here disciples joined him in this first monastery in the whole of Gaul and here Martin remained as pioneer of western monasticism until he became bishop of Tours in 372, at the acclamation of clergy and people. As bishop he continued to live as a monk, first in a cell near his cathedral and later at the monastery of Marmoutier, which soon numbered eighty monks. He also founded other monasteries, which he saw as a potent means of achieving his other pioneer activity, the conversion of the rural areas. Until now Christianity had been largely confined to the urban centres of population (the word *pagani* meaning primarily 'country-men'): to Martin are attributed the destruction of heathen temples and sacred trees, the rudimentary 'visitation' of the outlying centres of his diocese on foot, by donkey, or by boat. His twenty-five years' episcopate was marked both by his growing reputation as a wonder-worker in healing lepers and even raising a dead man to life, and by his involvement in doctrinal disputes.

The most famous of these concerned the Priscillianists. This Gnostic sect appealed to the Emperor Maximus against the Synod of Bordeaux in 384 which condemned them, as Pope *Damasus and *Ambrose had done already. But Priscillian was accused of sorcery, a capital offence, at Maximus' court at Trier in 386.

Martin pleaded in his favour, not defending his teaching but maintaining that such matters should be dealt with by the Church and not by the emperor. His stand met much opposition from contemporaries, but when Priscillian was executed, the first example of a death penalty for heresy, the Priscillian sect increased in Spain. It continued to exist there, a distant precursor of Catharism, until the 6th century.

In old age Martin had a presentiment of his approaching death, which was shared by others, who asked him not to leave them. In answer to this he prayed: 'Lord, if your people still need me. I do not refuse the work; let your will be done.' He died on 8 November at Candes and was buried at Tours on 11 November. His cult spread rapidly not only because of his reputation as a miracle-worker in life and after death, but also because of the Life written by his friend Sulpicius Severus. This became one of the most popular of the Middle Ages, comparable in influence with *Athanasius' Life of *Antony, as a model for medieval hagiographers. His cult in France is reflected in the 500 villages and 4,000 parish churches which are dedicated to him; his tomb was the principal place of pilgrimage for the Franks. Churches were soon consecrated in his honour at Rome, Ravenna, and later Chioggia. Spain, Germany, and the Low Countries too all culted him widely. In Britain, from early times, he was a patron of churches: those at Canterbury (under *Augustine) and at Whithorn (under *Ninian) being the most ancient examples. At least four more were dedicated to him before the end of the 8th century, while by 1800 173 ancient churches bore his name.

In art the most popular scene was that of dividing his cloak to clothe a beggar; but there are also innumerable other representations in illuminated books and in stained glass at Tours, Chartres, Beauvais, and Bourges. In England the most complete cycle in stained glass is at St. Martin's church, York (15th century); the churches of Chalgrave (Beds.) and Nassington (Northants.) have surviving mural paintings. His emblems are either a globe of fire over his head seen while he said Mass, or (from the 15th century) a goose, whose migration often coincides with his feast. In England this was the usual time for hiring servants and for killing cattle for salting during winter. St. Martin's Summer is a spell of fine weather which sometimes occurs around his feast. This is on 11 November (12 November in the East); a feast on 4 July of his Ordination and Translation is retained in B.C.P.

Life by Sulpicius Severus with three Letters and other documents ed. C. Halm (*C.S.E.L.*, 1866) and *P.L.*, xx. 159–222; also with Fr. tr. by J. Fontaine (*S.C.*, 1967–9); Eng. tr. by F. R. Hoare, *The Western Fathers* (1954); Gregory of Tours, *Historia Francorum*, i. 36–8, 43; and *de Libri IV S. Martini* (*P.L.*, lxxi. 911–1008). H. Delehaye, 'S. Martin et Sulpice Sévère, *Anal. Boll.*, xxxviii (1920), 1–136; N. K. Chadwick, *Poetry and Letters in Early Christian Gaul* (1955), pp. 89–121; J. Fontaine, 'Sulpice Sévère, a-t-il travesti S. Martin en martyr militaire?', *Anal. Boll.*, lxxxi (1963), 31–58; *Saint Martin et son Temps* (16th centenary, 1961). Other Lives by P. Monceaux (1926, Eng. tr. 1928) and especially C. Stancliffe, *St. Martin and His Hagiographer* (1983).

MARTIN I (d. 655), pope and martyr. Born at Todi (Umbria), he became a deacon at Rome. His conspicuous intelligence and charity resulted in his being sent as *apocrisiarius* ('nuncio') to Constantinople. In 649 he was elected pope. He soon held a council at the Lateran which condemned the error of Monothelitism (which denied that Christ had a human will) together with the *Typos* and the edicts of Constans II, the reigning emperor, which favoured it. Martin was supported by the bishops of Africa, England, and Spain, but was arrested by Constans and taken to Constantinople. The long voyage and dysentery, he told in his letters, weakened him; he was jailed for three months, not having been allowed to wash, even in cold water, for forty-seven days; the food he was given made him sick. Eventually he was tried on a charge of 'treason', while his real offence had been his refusal to accept the *Typos*. He was condemned unheard. Public insults, flogging, and imprisonment followed; at the intercession of the Patriarch of Constantinople his life was spared, but he was exiled to Chersonesus in the Crimea. From there he wrote of the famine and neglect be suffered; he blamed the Romans for forgetting him, while he had prayed steadily for their faith to be preserved inviolate. He died in exile on 13 April, the last pope to be venerated as a martyr.

His name was recorded in the Bobbio Missal (8th century). Feast: in the East, 20 September; in the West, 13 April has been restored as his feast since 1969; formerly it was on 12 November (10 November at York).

Letters and other writings in *P.L.*, lxxvii. 119–211 and in Jaffé–Wattenbach, *Regesta Pontificum Romanorum*, i (1885), 230–4; L. Duchesne *Liber Pontificalis* i (1886), 336–40; P. Peters, 'Une vie grecque du pape S. Martin', *Anal. Boll.*, li (1933), 225–62; *O.D.P.*, pp. 73–5.

MARTIN DE PORRES, see PORRES.

MARTINIAN, see PROCESSUS AND MARTINIAN.

MARTYRS OF CANADA, see BRÉBEUF, Jean, and JOGUES, Isaac.

MARTYRS OF ENGLAND AND WALES, see FORTY MARTYRS.

MARTYRS OF JAPAN, see MIKI, Paul.

MARTYRS OF KOREA, see KOREA.

MARTYRS OF ROME. The feast of the protomartyrs of the Roman Church commemorates those who died in the persecution of Nero in the late 1st century. *Peter and *Paul suffered in this persecution; appropriately this feast has been held since 1969 on the day following theirs, viz. 30 June. It compensates in some degree for the several names of Roman martyrs no longer (i.e. since 1969) culted universally by the Roman Church.

MARTYRS OF SCILLIUM (Scillitan Martyrs) (d. 180). The early and authentic Acts of these twelve martyrs have always been highly esteemed, but the place of Scillium has not been definitively identified. It was somewhere in North Africa; a basilica was built over the martyrs' tomb, where *Augustine preached three sermons in their honour.

Their interrogation took place at Carthage. The pro-consul P. Vigellius Saturninus (mentioned by Tertullian) presided. Speratus was the principal spokesman for the Christians, supported vocally by other men and women. Saturninus opened the proceedings by telling them that if they returned to their senses, they could still obtain the emperor's pardon. Speratus answered: 'We have never done wrong, we have never lent ourselves to wickedness; we have never uttered curses, but when we are unjustly treated we have given thanks because we honour our own emperor.' Later he said: 'I do not recognize the empire of this world. Rather do I serve God whom no man has seen . . . I have not stolen; on any purchase I pay tax because I acknowledge my lord as emperor of kings and of all nations.' To the others Saturninus said: 'Have no part in this folly of his!' Cittinus said: 'We have no one else to fear but our Lord God who is in heaven.' Donata added: 'Pay honour to Caesar as Caesar, but reverence only to God.' Vestia said: 'I am a Christian.' Secunda said: 'I wish to be what I am.' Secundinus asked Speratus again: 'Do you persist in remaining a Christian?' He answered: 'I am a Christian.' And all the others agreed with him. They were then granted a reprieve of thirty days.

Saturninus again examined them; again Speratus said: 'I am a Christian', again all the others agreed. Saturninus then read his decision: 'Whereas these have confessed that they have been living in accordance with the rites of the Christians, and whereas though given the opportunity to return to the usage of the Romans they have persevered in their obstinacy, they are hereby condemned to be executed by the sword.' Speratus answered: 'We thank God.' Nartzalus added: 'Today we are martyrs in heaven; thanks be to God.' Straightaway they were beheaded for the name of Christ. Feast: 17 July.

A.C.M., pp. xxii–xxiii, 86–89; *AA.SS.* Iul. IV (1725), 204–16; H. Delehaye, *Les passions des martyrs* (1921), pp. 60–3: B.T.A., iii. 124–6; 'Passio martyrum Scillitanorum, *Anal. Boll.*, viii (1889).

MARTYRS OF UGANDA, see Lwanga.

MARTYRS OF VIETNAM, see Vietnam.

MARY, THE BLESSED VIRGIN (1st century), mother of Jesus Christ. In both East and West Mary is accounted pre-eminent among all the saints. The unique privilege of being the mother of one who was, according to Christian belief, both God and Man is at the heart of the special honour paid to Mary, described by *Thomas Aquinas as 'hyperdulia', i.e. a veneration which exceeds that paid to other saints, but is at the same time infinitely below the adoration ('latria') due to God alone, which it would be blasphemous to attribute to any creature.

Of her early life Scripture tells us nothing, but in the Gospels Mary figures most prominently in Christ's infancy narratives of Matt. 1–2 and Luke 1–2. It has often been observed that Luke's account gives the story from Mary's viewpoint, while Matthew's gives more prominence to Joseph. In both, the virginal conception of Christ is clearly, but equivalently stated. During Christ's public life Mary occasionally appears (e.g. at the marriage feast of Cana), but remains habitually in the background. She reappears in John's gospel at the foot of the cross, where the beloved disciple received Christ's injunction to treat her as his mother; thenceforth presumably she lived in his household.

In the early chapters of the Acts of the Apostles she was with the Apostles and received the Holy Spirit with them on Whitsunday. But her role was not the active one of teaching and preaching; in the early church, as in Christ's ministry, she remained so much in the background that it is difficult to know where she lived or even where she died. Both Ephesus and Jerusalem claimed to be the place of her death, with the Eastern Fathers generally supporting Jerusalem. From the 6th century or earlier, in both East and West *John Damascene, *Gregory of Tours, and others clearly formulated the doctrine of her corporal Assumption into Heaven, earlier asserted in some apocryphal writings. Side by side with this development went an increasing emphasis on her power in Heaven.

Meanwhile the significance of Mary's role in the Redemption had become clarified through the Trinitarian and Christological controversies of the early Christian centuries. *Justin and *Irenaeus had developed the theme of Mary as the New Eve, whose obedience in some ways cancelled the disobedience of Eve; Mary's perpetual virginity was also taught from early centuries and formulated with characteristic energy by *Jerome, as by *Athanasius before him. But it was especially with the Council of Ephesus (431) that the full implication of Mary's role in the Redemption was formulated, whereby the title *Theotokos* (*Deipara*, or Mother of God), of Alexandrian origin, became recognized as orthodox because of the hypostatic union of Divinity and humanity in the single person of Christ.

In England the faith and doctrine were the same as that of the rest of the Christian Church, testified from early times by *Mellitus, *Theodore, and *Wilfrid. So also presumably were the liturgical books and the feasts devoted to Mary. The most important feasts were the Annunciation (25 March), the Nativity (8 September), and the Assumption (15 August) which was the Marian feast *par excellence* which corresponded most closely to that of the *Natalis* (or birthday in Heaven, i.e. the day of death) of the martyrs. About twenty English churches are known to have been dedicated to Mary by the end of the 8th century; by the Reformation the number had risen to well over 2,000. In England too, before the Norman Conquest, there was a feast of the Conception, sometimes called the Conception of St. Anne, but not fully and explicitly declaring the Immaculate Conception as it was later formulated. Eadmer (d. *c.*1110), however, wrote a treatise in its favour, which was influential in its development by Duns Scotus and the Franciscan school. But in medieval times this was still disputed by *Bernard, Thomas Aquinas, and the Dominicans. The doctrine of the Assumption, however, was not only unopposed, but testified to by sermons and numerous works of art which depict the Coronation of the Virgin.

The development of Marian devotion in England took another step forward in the 12th century with the collection of stories of Miracles of the Blessed Virgin by William of Malmesbury, Dominic of Evesham, and others. These stressed the intercessory power of Mary in saving sinners: they emphasized her role in providing hope for those who would have despaired if they had to face the Divine Judge alone. This went together with an increased awareness of the humanity of Christ, soon to be manifested in a more tender portrayal of Christ and his mother in the 13th and subsequent centuries. The later Middle Ages were the time when, again with increased awareness of the human and emotional stress of the Passion, the Blessed Virgin was invoked as Our Lady of Pity and the devotion to the Seven Sorrows of the Blessed Virgin (a pendant to the earlier Seven Joys of Mary) was developed.

Medieval devotion to Our Lady also left its trace in English episcopal and conciliar decrees and in art and architecture. Reforming bishops like Grosseteste insisted on all the faithful knowing the Hail Mary as well as the Our Father and the Creed: it was also recommended in the Durham statutes of 1220 and other later ones.

In the 13th and 14th centuries Lady Chapels were built in cathedral, abbey, and other churches, often but not invariably at the east end. Frequently these were structures of considerable importance and beauty, as at Winchester, Ely, Long Melford, and elsewhere. In very many churches there were shrines of the Blessed Virgin with a statue or painting of her as at Caversham (Oxon.), Westminster, Willesden, Aylesford (Kent), Cardigan, Eynsham, King's Lynn, and elsewhere. Some of these have been revived in modern times, as has England's principal place of Marian pilgrimage, Walsingham (Norfolk). Here was built a replica of what was believed to be the Holy House of Nazareth as early as the 11th century. Less admirable features of this shrine were the claim to possess a phial of Mary's milk as well as the practices caricatured and condemned by Erasmus.

Anglo-Saxon images of Mary are rare and unfamiliar, but plenty survive from the 12th century onwards in many media. The hieratic type of Madonna is represented in a famous illumination from Eynsham, which may be a representation of the local shrine-statue, while the more tender 13th-century example of the Chichester Roundel from the bishop's chapel reminds us that the human traits of Mary were a favourite feature of that time. But the more ancient depiction of Mary, crowned and sceptred as queen, based on Byzantine and Roman examples, was humanized into examples such as that of the Malvern stained glass. Representations of the Annunciation were also very popular, as in the sculpture at Wells cathedral of the 14th century or in the mural of Great Hockham (Norfolk) of the 15th century. Also in the later Middle Ages were developed series of paintings based on the apocryphal Gospels, sometimes representing the Life of Christ and the life of Mary in parallel, as at Croughton (Northants.). Other apocryphal elements in the Virgin's Life are featured at Chalgrove (Surrey), while series on the Miracles of the Virgin occur both at Eton College and at Winchester cathedral. In the later medieval centuries representations of the Virgin in scenes of the Passion were more frequent; that of Our Lady of Pity at Durham, for example, was much appreciated for its presentation of the human sufferings of Mary at the Passion of her Son. Such medieval works in England

and the Continent were precursors of Michelangelo's famous *pietàs*.

During the Reformation both in England and on the Continent many images of Mary were destroyed, particularly from rood-screens and shrines; but the principal feasts of Mary were retained in the Book of Common Prayer, with the exception of the Assumption which was removed in 1549, but retained at Oxford University and other places. Also at Oxford Laud installed the statue over the porch of the church of St. Mary. The feasts of the Visitation (2 July), Nativity (8 September), and Conception (8 December) were never dropped, still less the Annunciation (25 March) and Purification (2 February), the latter sometimes called the Presentation of Christ in the Temple.

Since 1969 in the new Roman calendar New Year's Day has been explicitly devoted to Mary's role in the Incarnation and the Redemption, in accordance with ancient Roman custom. The feast of the Visitation has also been moved to 31 May, and various feasts which commemorated apparitions of the Blessed Virgin (e.g. Our Lady of Lourdes) or particular aspects of her intercession (Mediatrix of All Graces) have been either suppressed or reduced to the rank of local observance.

The Second Vatican Council made an extended statement of Catholic doctrine on Mary, added to the Constitution on the Church, which treats of her relationship both to Christ and to the Church. It stresses her complete dependence on her Son, regards her as a model of the Church, and in emphasizing the Scriptural and Patristic elements in the cult of Mary, exhorts theologians and preachers to explain rightly the offices and privileges of the Blessed Virgin, always related to Christ, and to avoid all words and deeds which could lead 'separated brethren and anyone else into error regarding the true doctrine of the Church'. Among Anglicans, although the Thirty-Nine Articles forbade the invocation of Saints (Mary included), in recent times a number of theologians have adopted positions little if at all different from those of moderate Roman Catholics. In the Eastern Churches, untroubled by the controversies of the Reformation in the West, there has always been deep and universal veneration of the Blessed Virgin, and the Greek prayer *Sub tuum praesidium* is the oldest and perhaps the most beautiful expression of belief in the efficacy of Mary's intercession. The feast of the Dormition is equivalent to the Western one of the Assumption, but is less explicit in its formulation of this doctrine. In popular devotion the ikons of the Blessed Virgin are extremely important. Islamic authors too have always had a high regard for Mary as the mother of one whom they believe to have been a great prophet. Perhaps the 20th century will witness some reconciliation of Christians among themselves and towards others on the role of the Blessed Virgin in the life of Christ and of those who believe in him.

Principal Marian shrines of today include Lourdes (France), Fatima (Portugal), Walsingham (England), Loreto (Italy), Czestochowa (Poland), and Guadalupe (Mexico).

The Documents of Vatican II (ed. W. M. Abbot, 1966); H. du Manoir, *Maria* (8 vols., 1949–71); K. McNamara (ed.), *Mother of the Redeemer* (1959); H. C. Graef, *Mary* (2 vols., 1963–5); R. Laurentin, *La Question mariale* (1963, Eng. tr. 1965); id., *La Vierge au Concile* (1965). E. L. Mascall and H. S. Box (edd.), *The Blessed Virgin Mary* (1963): C. Miegge, *La Vergine Maria* (1950, Eng. tr. 1955); arts. in *O.D.C.C.*, *N.C.E.*, *Bibl. SS.*, *D.T.C.*

MARY MAGDALENE (1st century). This follower of Christ, 'out of whom he had cast seven devils', who stood by his cross, went to anoint his body at the tomb and to whom the risen Christ appeared on Easter Sunday morning, has often, but not universally in the West, been identified both with Mary the sister of *Martha of Bethany and with the woman who was a sinner, who anointed Christ's feet in the house of Simon (Luke 7: 37). This identification, propounded by *Gregory the Great, but now rejected by the Roman Calendar, was accepted in the traditional cult of Mary Magdalene and by the artists who depicted her.

Legend in both East and West added apocryphal details to the simple data of the Gospels. In the East she was said to have gone to Ephesus with the Blessed Virgin and *John the Apostle (of whom a later tradition made her the rejected fiancée when Christ called him; there she died and was buried; there the English *Willibald saw her supposed tomb in the 8th century. In the West Vézelay claimed her relics from the 11th century, and a legend arose that she, her brother *Lazarus, and her sister Martha had all evangelized Provence, where Mary lived as a hermit in the Maritime Alps before dying at Saint Maximin. In spite of immense popular support for this legend it is rejected by practically all modern scholars.

Her feast has been kept in the West since the 8th century. In art Mary Magdalene is usually represented with the emblem of a pot of ointment, or is depicted in Gospel scenes of the Passion and Resurrection. Her popularity in England is reflected in the 187 ancient dedications of churches and in her universal appearance in medieval calendars. Both Oxford and Cambridge have a College dedicated to her. A late Middle English *Play of Mary Magdalene* survives, which presents her both in Palestine and in Provence. Mary Magdalene is patron both of repentant sinners and of the contemplative life; this, together with her close association with Christ, explains her immense popularity through the ages. Feast: 22 July; translation, especially in the East, 4 May.

AA.SS. Iul. V (1727), 187–225; M. J. Lagrange, 'Jésus, a-t-il été oint plusieurs fois et par plusieurs femmes?', *Revue Biblique*, ix (1912), 504–32; H. M. Garth, *Saint Mary Magdalene in Medieval Literature* (1950); V. Saxer, *Le Culte de Marie Madeleine en Occident des origines à la fin du moyen-âge* (1959).

MARY MAGDALENE DE' PAZZI, see Pazzi.

MARY OF EGYPT (5th century(?)), penitent. A certain Mary lived the life of a hermit in Palestine according to John Moschus, and her tomb was visited by Cyril of Scythopolis, who in his Life of Cyriacus related how two of his disciples had met a woman hermit in the desert beyond Jordan, and on a second visit found her dead and buried her. There is no record of a public cult.

According to this popular and agreeably written source, Mary was an Egyptian, who left home at the age of twelve and went to live in Alexandria, where she became a prostitute for seventeen years. At the age of twenty-nine through curiosity she joined a pilgrimage to Jerusalem, paying for her passage by offering herself to the sailors. Once at Jerusalem, she was held back from entering the church with the other pilgrims by an invisible and irresistible force. Lifting her eyes to an icon of the Blessed Virgin, she was told to go over the Jordan where she would find rest. She bought three loaves and went to live in the desert, where for the rest of her long life she lived on dates and berries. Her clothes wore out, but her hair grew long and took their place. She could not read, but was divinely instructed in the Christian faith. A devout monk called Zosimus met her by chance in the desert, covered her with his cloak at her own request, and heard her story. He promised to meet her in the same place next Maundy Thursday to bring her holy communion. This was done and arrangements made for another meeting. But when he came, he found her dead body, which a lion helped him to bury. This story was popular in the East, but it was also known in the West, as by Ælfric in his *Lives of the Saints*, and artists depicted it from the 12th century on carved capitals, in stained glass in the cathedrals of Chartres, Bourges, and Auxerre (13th century), and in paintings and sculptures of the later Middle Ages. She is often confused with *Mary Magdalene (also depicted as a hermit) and occurs in Books of Hours and elsewhere clothed with her long hair and carrying with her three loaves as her emblem, as on a screen at Kenn (Devon). Feast: usually 2 April (as in most English monasteries) but sometimes on 9 or 10 April.

AA.SS. Apr. I (1675), 67–90; A. T. Baker, 'Vie de Sainte Marie l'Égyptienne', *Revue des langues romanes*, lix (1916–17), 145–401; 13th-century Life by Rutebeuf ed. B. A. Bujila (1949); K. Kunze, *Studien zur Legende der heiligen Maria Aegyptiaca im deutschen Sprachgebiet* (*Philologische Studien und Quellen*, xlix, 1969); B.T.A., ii. 14–16.

MATERIANA, see MADRUN.

MATTHEW (1st century), apostle and evangelist. Called Levi by Mark and Luke, Matthew was a publican, i.e. a tax-collector of Jewish race who worked for the Romans, before he left all at the call of Christ (Matt. 9: 9). From very early times he has been regarded as the author of the first of the four Gospels, to which both *Irenaeus and Papias are witnesses. Written in the second half of the 1st century and commonly, though not universally, believed to be dependent on Mark, Matthew's Gospel is in correct, concise style, suitable for public reading. His usual emblem as an evangelist is a man, because his genealogy emphasized the family ties of Christ.

Christian traditions differ about the mode and place of his martyrdom: some with the Roman Martyrology place it in Ethiopia, others with the Martyrology of *Jerome at Tarrium in Persia, others at Tarsuana, east of the Persian Gulf. His supposed relics were translated to Salerno by Robert Guiscard from Finistère (Brittany), to which they were reputed to have come from Ethiopia. In art, Matthew is represented as either an evangelist or as an apostle. In the first case he sits at his desk, writing his gospel with an angel either guiding his hand or holding the inkwell; in the second he holds the emblem of his martyrdom (a spear, a sword, or a halberd) or else a money-bag, or, a money-box sometimes with a slot in the top, in memory of his former profession. In the later Middle Ages he is sometimes depicted with spectacles, presumably to help him read his account-books. Feast: in the West, 21 September; in the East, 16 November.

AA.SS. Sept. VI (1757), 194–227; B. de Gaiffier, 'Hagiographie salernitaine: la translation de S. Matthieu', *Anal. Boll.*, lxxx (1962), 82–110; Patristic commentary by Jerome, modern ones by M. J. Lagrange (1948), F. W. Filson (1960), J. C. Fenton (1963), and J. D. Kingsbury (1986).

MATTHIAS (1st century), apostle. The qualifications required for an apostle to take the place of the suicide Judas were (Acts 1: 15–26) to have been a follower of Christ from the Baptism to the Ascension, and a witness of the Resurrection. In the event the choice was made between two: Joseph Barsabas and Matthias; the latter was chosen by lot. Like the other apostles he received the gift of the Holy Spirit at Pentecost, but authentic details of the places and dates of his apostolate are hard to find. He is said to have preached first in Judaea, which is likely enough, but later, according to the Greeks, he worked in Cappadocia and near the Caspian Sea; there is also a tradition which links him with Ethiopia, while the fictitious Acts of *Andrew and Matthias in the city of the Cannibals was very popular from early times and versions were made in several Eastern languages. But sometimes the stories were related of Matthew and Andrew, as is the case in the Anglo-Saxon poem *Andreas.* There was also some confusion in art between *Matthew and Matthias, the latter's usual emblem being an axe or halberd, regarded as the instrument of his martyrdom. His supposed relics were translated from Jerusalem to Rome by the empress *Helen, and some of these were moved to Trèves in the 11th century. Feast: traditionally 24 (25) February in the West, but since 1969 14 May in the Roman Church: 9 August in the East.

AA.SS. Feb. III (1658), 431–54; J. Renié, 'L'élection de Matthias', *Revue Biblique*, lv (1948), 43–53; B.T.A., i. 407–8.

MAUDEZ, see MAWES.

MAUGHOLD, see MACHALUS.

MAUNANUS, see MAWNAN.

MAURICE AND COMPANIONS (d. *c.*287), martyrs. The details of the Legend of this popular soldier saint are unhistorical, but reduced to credible proportions may well embody genuine tradition. Maximian the Emperor marched against rebellious Gauls (Bagaudae) with an army which included the Theban Legion, recruited in Egypt and composed exclusively of Christians. At Martigny, near the lake of Geneva, he ordered the whole army to join in sacrifice to the gods for military success. The Theban Legion refused to do so and withdrew to Agaunum (now Saint-Maurice-en-Valais). Maurice was their *primicerius* or principal officer, the spokesman of the dignified protest which, as Eucherius of Lyons (5th century) tells the story, was a profession of faith in the one true God joined with a refusal to renounce Him or take part in the killing of innocent Christians, who were not the emperor's enemies at all. The least credible part of the story is the order to decimate the Theban Legion and then, at their continued refusal to sacrifice, to butcher every one of them, unresisting to the end. The incredible numbers claimed for this massacre are 6,600 or, according to another source, 6,666. There seems to have been a genuine martyrdom at the base of this story, but the numbers, as in the case of *Ursula, have been enormously exaggerated. These saints became very popular in the West: Maurice's patronage includes the countries of Piedmont, Savoy, and Sardinia, and the professions of soldiers (especially the papal Swiss Guards), weavers, and dyers (especially of the Gobelins tapestry manufacture). In art he is usually represented as a Negro foot-soldier; eight ancient English churches are dedicated to him. Feast: 22 September.

AA.SS. Sept. VI (1757), 308–403, 895–926; L. Dupraz, *Les Passions de S. Maurice d'Agaune* (1961); B. Krusch, 'Passio Acaunensium Martyrum' in *M.G.H.*, *Scriptures rerum merov.*, iii (1896), 20–41; see also M. Besson, *Monasticon Acaunense* (1913).

MAURUS (6th century), monk. A nobleman's son who was entrusted to *Benedict by his father to be educated and to become a monk at Monte Cassino, Maurus, according to *Gregory the Great, was notable for obedience, and once at Benedict's command rescued the boy *Placid from drowning by walking, without realizing it, on the water. Nothing more is known of him afterwards. Later he was identified by pseudo-Faustus (Odo, abbot of Glanfeuil) with another Maurus, founder of the abbey of Glanfeuil, who was supposed to have died in 584 on 15 January. This identification is almost universally rejected nowadays. Its uncritical acceptance in the 17th century led to the adoption of Maurus as the patron of the famous learned French Benedictine Congregation of Saint-Maur. In their reformed calendar the Benedictines now celebrate the feast of Maurus and Placid together on 5 October (formerly 15 January).

AA.SS. Ian. I (1643), 1038–62; *AA.SS. O.S.B.*, I (1668), 275–98; J. McCann, *St. Benedict* (1938), pp. 274–81; H. Bloch in *Traditio*, viii (1950), 182–221.

MAWES (Maudez) (5th century(?)), bishop. Cornish tradition makes him the founder and patron of the fishing village near Falmouth which bears his name; Leland said he was a bishop in Brittany and is 'painted as a schoolmaster'. Topographical evidence points to a close association with *Budoc; Doble thinks that both of them were monks and missionaries from Wales who founded monasteries in Cornwall and Brittany, perhaps at Dol. The cult of Mawes in Brittany has always been much more notable than in England or Wales. He settled with some disciples on an island, Île Modez, near the coast of Léon and had the reputation of being a famous teacher, who was also popularly invoked against headaches, worms, and snake-bite. About sixty churches and chapels in Brittany are or were dedicated to him; his relics were venerated at Quimper, Treguier, Lesneven, and other places, especially Bourges, which claimed that his body had been translated there during the Viking invasions of the 10th century. Feast: 18 November.

G. H. Doble, *The Saints of Cornwall*, iii (1964), 57–73; Baring-Gould and Fisher, iii. 441–9.

MAWGAN, patron of two Cornish parishes of this name. No Life of this saint has survived and only the most meagre liturgical evidence. Saints of similar name were venerated in Wales and Brittany, but there is no proof that either should be identified with the other or with the patron of the Cornish parishes. Mawgan *may* have been abbot of Demetia (Pembrokeshire, now Dyfed) who shared with other 6th-century Welsh saints in the migration over Cornwall and Brittany. Roscarrock makes him bishop of the Isles of Scilly. *Sancte Maucanne* was invoked in an 11th-century Exeter litany.

G. H. Doble, *The Saints of Cornwall*, ii (1962), 34–44.

MAWNAN (Maunanus) (date unknown), Cornish saint who gave his name to the town of this name. Baring-Gould identifies him with Magnenn of Kilmainham, an Irish roving bishop who had a pet ram, was given to cursing his enemies, and favoured bizarre austerities. He once asked counsel from *Maelruain who roundly refused to administer reconciliation to a man who did not work for his daily bread but lived on alms. The prophecy was attributed to him that 'A time shall come when girls shall be pert and tart of tongue; when there will be grumbling and discontent among the lower classes and lack of reverence to elders; when churches will be slackly attended and women shall exercise wiles.' It must be said that this identification is far from certain; Mawnan may well be a local founder of whom nothing is known; the Cornish Church calendar lists him as a saint whose 'day is not certainly known'. Feast: 18 (or 26) December, in Ireland.

Baring-Gould and Fisher, iii. 453–7.

MAXIMILIAN (d. 295), martyr. The Acts of this martyr are ancient and authentic; they provide an early example of a Christian conscientious objector, who can be compared with soldier saints such as *Marinus or *Julian the Veteran. In 295 the proconsul Dion went to Tebessa (Algeria) to recruit soldiers for the third Augustan legion stationed there. At this time the Roman army was recruited mainly from volunteers, but sons of veterans were obliged to serve. Through the *advocatus* Pompeianus, Fabius Victor presented his son Maximilian, twenty-one years old, to the recruiting agent. Pompeianus, seeing he would make an excellent recruit, asked for him to be measured: he was five foot ten tall. When asked his name, Maximilian replied: 'Why do you wish to know my name? I cannot serve because I am a Christian.' In spite of this, orders were given for him to be measured and given the military seal (or badge). He answered: 'I will not do it: I cannot be a soldier.' When told he must either serve or die, he said: 'You may cut off my head, but I will not be a soldier of this world because I am a soldier of God.' Dion then said to Victor: 'Speak to your son.' He answered: 'He knows what he believes and can take his own counsel on what is best for him.' 'Agree to serve,' insisted Dion to Maximilian, 'and receive the military seal.' 'I will not accept the seal', he replied, 'I already have the seal of Christ my God . . . I will not accept the seal of this world; if you give it to me. I will break it for it is worthless. I cannot wear a piece of lead round my neck after I have received the saving sign of Jesus Christ my Lord, the son of the living God. You do not know him; yet he suffered for our salvation; God delivered him up for our sins. He is the one whom all Christians serve; we follow him as the prince of life and author of salvation.' Dion threatened a miserable death if he would not serve and told him to have regard for his youth; serving in the army was suitable for a young man. When Maximillian answered: 'My service is for the Lord: I cannot serve the world', Dion then said: 'There are soldiers who are Christian who serve in the bodyguard of our lords Diocletian and Maximian.' Maximilian answered: 'They know what is best for them. I am a Christian and I cannot do what is wrong.' Dion continued: 'What wrong do those commit who serve in the army?' Maximilian answered: 'You know very well what they do.' The final alternative was then presented: military service or death. 'I shall not perish', he said, 'and if I do depart from this world, my soul shall live with Christ my Lord.'

When Maximilian's name was struck off, he was condemned: 'Whereas Maximilian has disloyally refused the military oath, he is sentenced to die by the sword.' Just before execution he encouraged his companions to perseverance and asked his father to give his new clothes to the executioner. A devout woman called Pompeiana obtained his body, brought it to Carthage and buried it close to that of *Cyprian. Maximilian's father Victor died soon afterwards. Feast: 12 March.

A.C.M., xxxvii. 245–9; *Propylaeum*, p. 94; H. Delehaye, *Les passions des martyrs* (1921), pp. 104–10; C. J. Cadoux, *The Early Christian Attitude to War* (1919); B.T.A., i. 571–3.

MAXIMILIAN KOLBE, see KOLBE.

MAXIMUS OF TURIN (*c*.350–*c*.415), bishop. Little is known about his life: he became Turin's first bishop in 397 and held a council of Gaulish bishops there in 398. More than 100 of his sermons survive which reveal him as an evangelist in Piedmont in conflict with rural paganism, stressing the importance of the Christian liturgy. Feast: 25 June.

AA.SS., Iunii V (1744), 48 ff.; Works ed. A. Mutzenbecher, *C.C.S.L.*, xxiii (1962); *N.C.E.*, ix. 516; *Bibl. SS.*, ix. 68–72.

MAXIMUS THE CONFESSOR (*c*.580–662), abbot. Born of a noble family in Constantinople, he excelled in philosophical and theological studies and became chief secretary to the Emperor Heraclius. In about 616 he resigned this post to become a monk at Chrysopolis (Scutari); here he soon became abbot. During the Persian invasion of 626 he took refuge in Alexandria. Here he continued his notable theological writings on biblical difficulties, on the liturgy as mystically understood, and on the Incarnation of Christ, which with its consequent divinization of man he saw as the purpose of human history. He is best known however for his works against Monothelitism (the attribution to Christ of only one will, the divine one). Here he continued the teaching of Sophronius of Alexandria and closely supported Pope *Martin I, who condemned this heresy at the Lateran council of 649. The emperor Constans however had long supported this heresy: he imprisoned and exiled Martin and arrested Maximus, now aged seventy-five, in Rome. In order to obtain his recantation, a bishop was sent to offer him favour and honours; he refused. For six years he was imprisoned; he was sentenced to be flogged and for his tongue and his right hand to be amputated. He died soon afterwards, exiled in the Caucasus.

His writings have long been appreciated in the East; in recent years they have become more widely known in the West. Feast: 13 August.

R. Devresse, 'La vie de S. Maxime le Confesseur', *Anal. Boll.*, xlvi (1928), 5–49; Works in *P.G.*, xc–xci; Eng. tr. of *Liber Asceticus* and *Capita de Caritate* by P. Sherwood (1955), author also of *An Annotated Date-List of the Works of Maximus the Confessor* (1952); L. Thunberg, *Microcosm and Mediator* (1965); *O.D.C.C.*, p. 895; D. Attwater, *Saints of the East* (1963), 80–8: *Bibl. SS.*, ix. 41–7.

MAYNE, Cuthbert (*c*.1543–77), seminary priest and martyr. Born at Youlston (N. Devon) and educated as a member of the Church of England at Barnstaple Grammar School, he was given the living of Huntshaw parish at the age of seventeen through an uncle's influence and was later ordained in the Anglican church. He took a degree in arts at Oxford, being a member of St. Alban's Hall (later Merton College). Here he was influenced by Edmund *Campion and after some indecision was received into the R.C. Church and joined the English College, Douai, in 1573. He was ordained priest in 1575 and became a Bachelor of Theology in 1576. The same year he returned to Cornwall and joined the household of Francis Tregian disguised as a steward, but actually engaged in ministry to the recusants of the neighbourhood. His short apostolate ended on 8 June 1577 when Richard Grenville and 100 armed men arrested him and most of

Tregian's household at Golden Manor. A waxen *agnus-dei* was found on his person and he was imprisoned at Launceston castle.

His trial attracted special attention because (1) he was the first seminary priest to be tried; (2) the evidence presented was circumstantial only; and (3) one of the justices, unsatisfied, sent a report of the proceedings to the Privy Council. Whereas the bench of judges had been divided, Grenville had browbeaten the jury to bring in a verdict of guilty. The Council, however, ordered the execution to be carried out 'as a terror to the papists'. This took place after he had refused to acknowledge the queen's ecclesiastical supremacy on 30 November. Mayne's skull survives at the Carmelite monastery of Lanherne (Cornwall); a contemporary portrait is in the Ashmolean Museum, Oxford. He was canonized by Paul VI in 1970 as one of the *Forty Martyrs of England and Wales. Feast: 25 October.

W. Allen, *A Briefe Historie of the Glorious Martyrdom of Twelve Reverend Priests* (1582; 1908); B. Camm, *Lives of the English Martyrs*, ii (1914), 204–21; R. A. McElroy, *Blessed Cuthbert Mayne* (1929); P. A. Boyan and G. R. Lamb, *Francis Tregian* (1955).

MAZZARELLO (1837–81), Maria-Domenica, foundress of the Salesian Sisters. Born of a large farming family at Mornese (Piedmont), she worked hard in field and vineyard until 1860, when she caught typhoid fever nursing her relatives. Weakened by this disease, she became a professional dressmaker and employed several girls in this enterprise. Meanwhile she had become most devout and was a member of a sodality founded by the parish priest. In 1864 John *Bosco, hoping to found a boys' school, visited Mornese. His plans were frustrated, but aware of the need for nuns to do similar work for girls, he established this sodality, with Maria as first superior, as the Salesian Sisters. Eleven sisters were professed that year and another fifteen received the habit.

In spite of her limited education Maria was successful in government. The sisters aimed at encouragement, not repression in their teaching; they shared Bosco's characteristic charity and joy. Maria's fidelity and humility led to her election in 1874 as superior-general, with the mother-house at Nizza Monferrato. In 1876 she sent six nuns to found a house in Argentina. Nowadays her congregation has 1,400 houses in 54 countries.

In 1881 she had to return suddenly from Marseilles owing to illness. John Bosco comforted her, but she said it was time for her to go as she now had her passport. Aged only forty-four she died soon after; her body is enshrined beside that of Bosco in Turin. She was canonized in 1951. Feast: 14 May.

Lives by H. L. Hughes (1933), F. Maccono (1947), and G. Favini (1951); see also B.T.A., ii. 313–15; *N.C.E.*, ix. 523; *Bibl. SS.*, viii. 1062–3.

MEBER, see Meubred.

MÉDARD (*c.*470–*c.*560), bishop of Vermandois. He was born at Salency (Picardy) of a Frankish noble family, was educated at Saint-Quentin, and was ordained priest *c.*505. Much later he was consecrated bishop. He gave the veil to *Radegund and is credited with removing his see to Noyon and ruling it together with that of Tournai. But these latter details are suspect through lack of contemporary evidence.

His cult dates from the 6th century and is attested by *Venantius Fortunatus and *Gregory of Tours. Popular tradition attributes to him, like *Swithun, the determination of the weather for forty days after his feast, in accordance with that prevailing on his day. On his feast also the most exemplary girl in the neighbourhood is escorted to the church, crowned with roses, and given a purse of money. Médard was also invoked for toothache. Feast: (in Sarum calendar and elsewhere), 8 June.

Early Life ed. B. Krusch, *M.G.H.*, *Auctores Antiquissimi*, iv (part 2), 67–73; B.T.A., ii. 502–3.

MÉEN, see MEWAN.

MEINRAD (d. 861), hermit and martyr. Born at Sulichgau (near Wurtemberg) of a free peasant family, he became a monk and a priest at Reichenau (Switzerland). In 829 he moved to Einsiedeln to be a hermit and remained there for 25 years, practising the traditional eremitical austerities. In 861 he courteously received two visitors, who searched for treasure but found none. Angrily they then battered him to death with clubs. The murderers were executed: Meinrad's body was enshrined at Reichenau. In the 10th century Einsiedeln was refounded as a regular Benedictine monastery: such it has remained in unbroken continuity until the present day. Feast: 21 January.

Early Life in *M.G.H. Scriptores*, xv. 445–8; *Bibl. SS.*, ix. 273–8.

MEL (d. 488), bishop of Ardagh. Supposedly a Briton and a disciple of *Patrick who consecrated him, Mel was closely associated with the evangelization of the district of Ardagh, but is otherwise unknown. Feast: 6 February.

B.T.A., i. 262; *The Irish Saints*, p. 245.

MELAINE (Melanius, Mellion) (d. *c.*535) has been patron of Mullion, on the Lizard peninsula, and of St. Mellyan (Cornwall) since the early Middle Ages. He succeeded *Amand as bishop of Rennes and was an adviser of Clovis. His cult spread very rapidly in Brittany. One of his letters survives, requiring Breton priests to renounce the abuse of 'wandering from cabin to cabin, celebrating Mass on portable altars, accompanied by women who administered the chalice to the faithful'. The abbey of St. Melaine at Rennes was built round his tomb, described by *Gregory of Tours. His fame probably caused him to supplant the primitive patron of these two parishes who had a similar name, perhaps that of the Breton Mollien, a Celtic missionary monk. Feast: 6 November.

G. H. Doble, *The Saints of Cornwall*, ii (1962), 109–19.

MELLITUS (d. 624), first bishop of London, third archbishop of Canterbury. A Roman abbot of noble birth, he was sent to England by *Gregory the Great at the head of a group of missionaries in 601 to reinforce *Augustine of Canterbury. After he had left, Gregory sent him a famous letter which modified his previous ruling to Augustine. He now told Mellitus to tell Augustine not to destroy the temples of the Saxons but only their idols: on the contrary, the temples should be converted into churches and their feasts taken over and directed to Christian purposes such as dedications. This directive was important in the whole history of missionary activity.

In 604 Augustine consecrated Mellitus bishop of the East Saxons, with his see at London, where Ethelbert (king of Kent and overlord of Southern England) had built the first church of St. Paul. As bishop of London, Mellitus went to Rome to consult with Pope Boniface IV about the Church in England; while there, he took part in a synod of Italian bishops concerning the life of monks and (presumably) their peaceful relations with bishops. He brought the decrees back to England, together with papal letters to archbishop Laurence and King Ethelbert. When Saeberht, the Christian king of the East Saxons, died, his three pagan sons succeeded him and soon expelled Mellitus. The occasion for this was said to be Mellitus' refusal to give holy communion ('the white bread') to the unbaptized princes. But with this reverse in Essex corresponding to a greater setback in Kent, the bishops decided to retire to Gaul for the time. Mellitus and Justus departed but were soon recalled by *Laurence, archbishop of Canterbury. Lacking the support of a strong Christian ruler like the recently dead Ethelbert, Mellitus was unable to return to London and the East Saxons. In 619 he succeeded Laurence as archbishop of Canterbury and ruled actively and well in spite of suffering from gout. *Bede attributed the change of wind which saved the Canterbury church of the *Four Crowned Martyrs from being destroyed by fire to Mellitus' being carried into the path of the flames to pray.

Mellitus died on 24 April, thenceforth

kept as his feast in numerous English calendars before and after the Norman Conquest. With *Laurence and *Justus, Mellitus is mentioned in the commemoration of the dead in the Stowe Missal. He was buried near Augustine in the abbey church of SS. Peter and Paul, Canterbury.

AA.SS. Apr. III (1675), 280–3; Bede, *H.E.*, i. 29–ii. 7; H. Mayr-Harting, *The Coming of Christianity to Anglo-Saxon England* (1972).

MELLON (Melanius, Mallonus) (4th century), bishop. Traditionally he was first bishop of Rouen and a native of Llanlleurog, near Cardiff, now called Saint Mellons, and where the church is dedicated to him. There are three late Legends of the 12th century which deserve little credence. Feast: 22 October.

AA.SS. Oct. IX (1858), 554–74; E. Vacandard, *Vie de S. Ouen* (1902).

MELLOR (Melar), see MYLOR.

MEN(N)AS (d. *c.*300), martyr. This very famous saint was Egyptian by birth; he was killed in Egypt for his Christian faith, perhaps under Diocletian; he was reputed to be a soldier in the Roman army, but this detail, like others of his Legend, may have been borrowed from that of St. Gordius. His shrine at Bumma (near Alexandria) was a principal pilgrimage centre until the Arab invasions of the 7th century; from it came phials of well-water which bore his name. The whole complex of church, monastery, baths, and other buildings was excavated at the beginning of the 20th century. After the battle of El Alamein in 1943 the patriarch of Alexandria attributed the saving of Egypt to the intercession of Mennas and initiated a project for restoring his shrine near Alamein. His popularity in the East is seen from the numerous versions of his Acts. He was patron of merchants and caravans of the desert; his emblem has been a pair of camels at least since the 6th century, probably because of his patronage of pilgrims to his shrine who arrived on camels. In the West his feast was kept at Rome and elsewhere, including York and Hereford, on 11 November.

'Acta S. Menae', *Anal. Boll.*, iii (1884), 258–70; H. Delehaye, 'L'invention des reliques de S. Menas à Constantinople', *Anal. Boll.*, xxix (1910), 117–50; P. Devos, 'Un récit des miracles de S. Menas en copte et en éthiopien', *Anal. Boll.*, lxxvii (1959), 154–60 and lxxviii (1960), 275–308; C. M. Kaufmann, *Die Menasstadt und das Nationalheiligtum der altchristlichen Aegypter* (1910); id., *Ikonographie der Menas-Ampullen*: M. A. Murray, 'St. Menas of Alexandria', *Proc. of the Society of Biblical Archaeology*, xxix (1907), 25–30, 51–60, and 112–22; R. Miedema, *Der heilige Menas* (1913).

MENEFREDA, see MINVER.

MEREWENNA (10th century), abbess of Romsey. When King Edgar refounded Romsey nunnery in 967, Merewenna was its first abbess; under her guidance the house prospered and princesses were later among its inmates. Among her disciples was *Ethelfleda; the two saints were buried close to each other in the abbey church. Merewenna's original feast was 10 February; the translation of Merewenna and Ethelfleda on 29 October was also kept.

R.P.S.; *AA.SS.* Oct. XII (1867), 918; Stanton, p. 209.

MERIASEK (Meriadoc) (6th century(?)), bishop, patron of Camborne (Cornwall). His name indicates a Welsh origin; he seems to have founded at least one church in Cornwall, he went to Brittany, where he founded monasteries and became a regional bishop who worked in and near Vannes. His feast is kept in various Breton dioceses, but not elsewhere in France, probably because his relics remained in Brittany at the Viking invasions. He seems to have been a companion of *Gwinear in both areas of his apostolate. The Cornish miracle-play *Beunans Meriasek*, written in the vernacular, is a unique survival, but contains many legendary and few historical elements. It and the various breviary lessons all depend on a 12th-century Life of little value. Wells named after him survive in Brittany and Cornwall. Feast: 7 June (*C.C.K.*, however, gives 3 June, Roscarrock 9 June).

G. H. Doble, *The Saints of Cornwall*, i (1960),

111–45; W. Stokes, *Beunans Meriasek* (1872); extracts from the same edn. by R. M. Nance and A. S. D. Smith (1949); the play was revived at Redruth in 1924.

MERRYN (date unknown), monk. Patron of St. Merryn (Cornwall), he is probably identical with the Breton saint honoured at Lanmerin and Plomelin. In the Middle Ages the legendary saint Marina (who was supposed to have lived as a monk for years in disguise and even to have been falsely accused of fathering a child) was believed to be the patron of St. Merryn. For this reason the Cornish church held the feast on 7 July, whereas the Breton feast was on 4 April.

G. H. Doble, *The Saints of Cornwall*, iv (1965), 53–4; Baring-Gould and Fisher, iii. 475–6.

METHODIUS, see CYRIL AND METHODIUS.

MEUBRED (Meber, Mybard) (5th–6th century). Virtually nothing is known of his life. William Worcestre called him a hermit, son of a king of Ireland, whose body lay in a shrine in the church of Cardyngham (Cornwall). His companion in the hermit life was called *Manaccus. Cardyngham church is still dedicated to him; he is figured in a stained-glass window at St. Neot, made in 1529. William Worcestre says his feast was kept on the Thursday before Whitsun; he has no day in the Cornish Church calendar.

William Worcestre, pp. 97–9; G. H. Doble, *History of the Church and Parish of St. Mewbred, Cardyngham* (1939).

MEWAN (Méen) (6th century), abbot. Born in South Wales, he was a disciple of *Samson and a companion of *Austell, who migrated from Wales to Brittany through Cornwall, where they founded churches in the same neighbourhood. Mewan founded one monastery in the forest of Broceliande and another in the place now called Saint-Méen, where his Life was written about 500 years after his death. The cult of Mewan spread all over France and pilgrimages to his shrine at Saint-Meén were formerly numerous. In England he is the patron of St. Mewan and perhaps Mevagissey (Cornwall). Glastonbury claimed some of his relics; his feast was kept at Exeter, as well as in Cornwall, on 21 June.

G. H. Doble, *The Saints of Cornwall*, v (1970), 35–58.

MICHAEL, archangel. His name means 'Who is like unto God?' He appears in the Book of Daniel as 'one of the chief princes' of the heavenly host and as the special guardian or protector of Israel (Dan. 10: 13 ff. and 12: 1). In the Book of Revelation he is the principal fighter of the heavenly battle against the devil (or dragon), 'who was cast unto the earth and his angels were thrown down with him' (Rev. 12: 7–9). In the Epistle of Jude (9) he disputes with the devil about the body of Moses and says: 'May the Lord rebuke you.' It seems likely that this passage cites a lost passage of the *Assumption of Moses*, an apocryphal Jewish work. In this and similar writings he is 'the great captain, who is set over the best part of mankind'. The early Christian *Shepherd of Hermas* (2nd century) depicts Michael as an angel of majestic aspect, who presides over the awards when the willow twigs, some of which grow and others wither away, are brought for inspection and judgement. He had authority over 'this people and governs them, for it was he who gave them the law . . . and superintends those to whom he gave it to see if they kept it'. In *The Testament of Abraham* (also 2nd century) Michael is the principal character whose intercession is so powerful that souls can be rescued even from Hell. Perhaps this passage inspired the offertory antiphon formerly used in the Roman Liturgy for the dead: 'May Michael the standard bearer lead them into the holy light, which you promised of old to Abraham and his seed.'

It seems that the formal cult of Michael began in the East, where he was invoked for the care of the sick: Constantine built a church in his honour for this purpose at Sosthenion, near Constantinople: hot springs were also dedicated to him in

Greece and Asia Minor. A famous apparition of Michael on Monte Gargano (SE. Italy) in the late 5th century was important in spreading the cult to the West; the feast of 29 September commemorates the dedication of his basilica on the Salarian Way near Rome.

From early times his cult was strong in the British Isles. There were known dedications of churches at Malmesbury (Wilts.), Clive (Glos.), and Stanmer (East Sussex), besides that of the cemetery-oratory near Hexham mentioned by *Bede. According to Eddius' Life, *Wilfrid had a vision of Michael shortly before his death. Many high places were associated with his cult, one of the most spectacular being the Great Skellig (Skellig Michael, Co. Kerry), while St. Michael's Mount (Cornwall) was believed to commemorate a vision there in the 8th century. Often he was chosen as patron of cemeteries. His cult became popular in Wales in the 10th–11th centuries, while in England by the end of the Middle Ages, his church dedications numbered as many as 686.

In art he was represented in at least two ways. Sometimes he is depicted slaying the dragon, as on an 11th-century English bronze crucifix at Copenhagen, or in 14th-century East Anglican psalters, or in Epstein's famous sculpture at Coventry cathedral. Less familiar nowadays, but frequent in medieval art, were paintings of him weighing souls, either as part of a Doom or separately. Examples survive from the 13th century at Chaldon (Surrey), from the 14th at Swalcliffe (Oxon.), and from the 15th at South Leigh (Oxon.). Stained-glass examples survive at Eaton Bishop (Hereford and Worcester) and Martham (Suffolk). Certain iconographical links with ancient Egyptian paintings are commonly claimed in this type of representation.

The most famous shrine in western Europe is Mont-Saint-Michel (Normandy), where a Benedictine abbey was founded in the 10th century to commemorate an earlier apparition. After the Norman Conquest some abbots and monks came to England, who presumably further emphasized devotion to Michael.

His principal feast is on 29 September. This is often called 'St. Michael and All Angels'; since 1969 the Roman calendar has included *Gabriel and *Raphael under this feast. Local feasts which commemorated the apparitions at Monte Gargano and at Mont-Saint-Michel were kept on 8 May and 16 October.

AA.SS. Sept. VIII (1762), 4–123; O. Rojdestvensky, *Le Culte de Saint Michel et le moyen âge latin* (1922); A. M. Renner, *Der Erzengel Michael in der Geistes- und Kunstgeschichte* (1927); J. Lemarié, 'Textes liturgiques concernant le culte de S. Michel', *Sacris Erudiri*, xiv (1963), 277–85; see also J. Daniélou, *Les anges et leur mission* (1952).

MIKI, Paul, **AND COMPANIONS** (d. 1597), martyrs in Japan. The first Christian apostle of Japan was Francis *Xavier, who landed in 1549; when he left a few years later the Christians numbered perhaps 2,000. Nearly fifty years afterwards they were even more numerous and the Japanese ruler Hideyoshi, incensed by their increase and by the boasting of a Spanish sea-captain, embarked on a policy of persecution. This extended according to Japanese custom to the dependants of the victims. They were twenty-six in all: Paul Miki was Japanese, of aristocratic family, a Jesuit priest, and a notable preacher. Two were Jesuit lay brothers. The others comprised six Franciscans, of whom four were Spanish, one from Mexico City, and one from Bombay. The other seventeen were all Japanese layfolk, except one Korean; they included catechists, interpreters, a soldier, a physician, and three young boys. The martyrs had part of their left ears cut off and were displayed in various towns to terrify the others. They were crucified near Nagasaki, being bound or chained to the crosses on the ground first; these were then planted in a row, and each martyr was dispatched by a separate executioner, who stood by the cross with his lance at the ready. After their death their clothes and their blood were treasured by their fellow Christians. These martyrs were canonized in 1862. For a long time their feast was celebrated principally in Japan and by the Franciscans and Jesuits, but in 1970 it was included in the revised Roman calendar, as the first martyrs of the Far East. Feast: 6 February. Other Japanese martyrs, some hundreds in number, suffered in 1617, 1622, 1624, 1626, 1629, and 1632.

AA.SS. Feb. I (1658), 729–70; C. M. Cadell, *The Cross in Japan* (1904); B.T.A., i. 259–60; *N.C.E.*

MILBURGA (Milburh) (d. 715), abbess. Daughter of Merewald, king of Mercia, and *Ermenburga, princess of Kent, Milburga was the sister of *Mildred and *Mildgyth. Merewald founded the nunnery of Wenlock *c.*670 and placed it under the direction of *Botulf of East Anglia. Its first abbess was Liobsynde, a French nun from Chelles; its second abbess was Milburga. Goscelin's Life of her (late 11th century) said she was consecrated as a virgin by *Theodore, had miraculous healing powers, and lived and died in a conspicuously saintly way. During her abbacy occurred the famous Vision of the Monk of Wenlock, described by *Boniface. Goscelin also preserved her testament, which is an apparently authentic list of lands which belonged to her at her death. Her tomb was long venerated, but its site was unknown when Cluniac monks from La-Charité-sur-Loire refounded Wenlock in 1079. The church had a silver casket which contained relics of Milburga and documents describing the site of her grave, near an altar then unknown. After consulting *Anselm, the monks excavated an old, disused church. Some boys playing on the site fell into a tomb, where bones were found with the remains of a coffin and an altar. Details of this discovery and of cures in 1101 were described by Otto, cardinal-bishop of Ostia, the next year. These included the healing of lepers and the blind, also the vomiting of an extraordinary worm, which had caused a wasting disease. The distinction of this writer contributed to the diffusion of Milburga's cult, which resulted in five ancient churches being dedicated to her. Her feast was common in English calendars from the Bosworth Psalter (*c.*1000) onwards. Feast: 23 February; translation (according to Goscelin), 25 June.

AA.SS. Feb. III (1658), 388–91; *G.P.*, pp. 305–6; *N.L.A.*, ii. 188–92; A. Edwards, 'An early twelfth century account of the Translation of St. Milburga', *Trans. Shropshire Archaeol. Soc.*, lvii (1962–3), 134–51; H. P. R. Finberg, *The Early Charters of the West Midlands* (1962), pp. 197–224; P. Grosjean, 'Saints anglo-saxones des Marches Gauloises', *Anal. Boll.*, lxxix (1961), 163–6.

MILDGYTH (7th century). She was the youngest and least famous of the three daughters of Merewald, king of Mercia, and *Ermenburga, princess of Kent; her sisters were *Mildred and *Milburga. According to one tradition she became a nun in Northumbria and was buried there; the Thanet tradition, however, made her a nun of Eastry, and the successor of Mildred, abbess of that monastery, and claimed that both of them were buried there. When the Danes destroyed Thanet, the bones of both of them were hidden at Lyming until Lanfranc translated them to his hospital of St. Gregory, Canterbury, in 1085. This tradition is represented by *C.S.P.*, a 13th-century saints' list. Feast: 17 January.

C.S.P.; Stanton, pp. 24, 623.

MILDRED (d. *c.*700), abbess. A daughter of Merewald, king of Mercia, and *Ermenburga, princess of Kent, she was educated at the convent of Chelles, near Paris, to which she had retired to avoid the attentions of an unwelcome suitor. She then returned to become a nun at Minster-in-Thanet. This abbey had been founded by Ermenburga on land provided by Egbert of Kent in compensation for the murder of her brothers *Ethelred and Ethelbricht. She became abbess before 694, when she attended a council in Kent. Goscelin (late 11th century) attributed to her the conventional virtues of tranquillity of temper and generosity to the poor, especially widows and children. She died after a long illness; her tomb became a place of pilgrimage. In

1035 her relics were translated to St. Augustine's Abbey, Canterbury, whence some of them were given to Deventer (Holland). However, a rival set of relics was given by Lanfranc to his hospital of St. Gregory, Canterbury. In modern times a Benedictine nunnery has been revived at Minster by the Benedictines of Eichstatt (Bavaria), founded by *Walburga. Feast: 13 July; translation, 18 May; also 20 February.

AA.SS. Iul. III (1723), 512–23; *N.L.A.*, ii. 193–7; *G.R.*, i. 267; M. L. Colker, 'A hagiographic polemic', *Medieval Studies*, xxxix (1977), 60–108; D. W. Rollason, *The Mildrith Legend* (1983).

MINDRED, East Anglian female saint of whom nothing is known. Her well at Exning, Suffolk, contains water said to be good for ailments of the eyes. She may be identical with *Wendreda, patroness of the church at March (Cambs.).

M. R. James, *Suffolk and Norfolk* (1930), pp. 14, 32.

MINVER (Menefreda) (6th century(?)), virgin. Often called a daughter of *Brychan, but probably his grand-daughter and the daughter of Brynach, she seems to have originated in South Wales (possibly at Minwear, Dyfed), and lived as a nun at Tredresick, near Padstow (Cornwall). There a church and well bear her name; nearby Lundy Hole was traditionally the place where the devil fled, discomfited when Minver threw her comb at him, after he tempted her while she was combing her hair at the well. Feast: 24 (or 23) November.

Baring-Gould and Fisher, iii. 474–5, William Worcestre, pp. 63, 89.

MIRIN (Merinus, Meadhran) (7th century(?)), an Irish abbot who worked in Scotland. Reputedly a disciple of *Comgall, he became a monk at Bangor (Co. Down) and founded the monastery of Paisley, where he died, was buried, and where his shrine was the object of pilgrimage. A chapel dedicated to him is in ruins at Inch Murryn, the largest island in Loch Lomond. Feast: 15 September.

K.S.S., pp. 397–8.

MO-BIOC, see BEAN (1).

MOCHOEMOC (Mo-Chaomhog, Kennoch) (7th century), abbot. He was the nephew of *Ita who fostered and educated him; later he became a monk at Bangor (Co. Down) under *Comgall, who sent him to found a monastery at Arderin. Finally, he founded the abbey of Liathmor, now Leamokevoge (Co. Tipperary), which was the principal achievement of his life. The supposed Scottish Kevoca, titular of the church of Quivox, is really the Irishman Mochoemoc. Feast: 13 March.

V.S.H., ii. 164–83; *AA.SS.* Mar. II (1668), 280–8; B.T.A., i. 583–4.

MOCHTA (Mochteus, Mochuta) (5th century(?)), abbot. Reputed to be of British origin and to have become a disciple of *Patrick in Ireland, he is supposed to have been educated and consecrated bishop in Rome. On his return to Ireland he first settled with some disciples at an unidentified 'Kell Mor Ydan' (Co. Meath). After some years, because of local opposition, he moved north to Louth, where he founded a large monastery which soon enjoyed a nationwide reputation, and where he is claimed as its first bishop.

Legendary elements in his Life include a mutual agreement with Patrick that each would look after the other's community after the founder's death; that he lived for 300 years because he doubted the ages of the Old Testament patriarchs, and even that he had 200 bishops as his disciples. Feast: 19 August.

W. W. Heist, *Vitae Sanctorum Hiberniae* (1965), pp. 394–400; B.T.A., iii. 356.

MOCHUA (d. *c.*657), Irish monk. His home was in the Achonry district of Connacht; his father was called Lonan. He became a successful soldier who was converted to monasticism in his early manhood. His principal foundation was

Timahoe (Co. Laois), but he died at another of his monasteries at Derinish (Co. Cavan). Some monasteries in Scotland also claimed him as their founder. There are said to be more than fifty saints called Mochua; Mochua of Timahoe has his feast on 24 December.

The Irish Saints, pp. 248–9.

MOCHUMMA, see MACHAR.

MODAN (6th century), abbot. He worked at Stirling and Falkirk and used to retire to solitude in the mountains near Dumbarton. Churches at Stirling, Roseneath (Dunbartonshire), and Falkirk are dedicated to him. Feast: 4 February. There is another Scottish Modan, sometimes confused with him, who was a bishop in the 8th century. Feast: 14 November, especially at Philorth (Fraserburgh) where his silver head-relic was formerly carried in procession to bring down rain or improve the weather in other ways. His principal foundation was Timhood.

K.S.S., pp. 400–3.

MODOMNOC (6th century), abbot. Supposedly of the royal O'Neill family of Ireland, he studied under *David in his Pembrokeshire monastery of Menevia. One of his duties was bee-keeping: according to his Legend, a swarm of his bees settled on his ship when it was time for him to return to Ireland, whereby apiculture was introduced there. This is supported by his entry in the Martyrology of *Oegus the Culdee (*c.*800): 'in a little boat from the east over the pure-coloured sea my Domnoc brought . . . the gifted race of Ireland's bees.' Modomnoc settled at Tibberaghny (Co. Kilkenny); some writers claim that he became bishop of (or at) Ossory. Feast: 13 February.

C. Plummer, *Miscellanea Hagiographica Hibernensis*, p. 217; B.T.A., i. 322.

MODWENNA (7th century(?)), virgin, lived as a hermit at Andressey near Burton-on-Trent. Her shrine was at Burton. Some writers identify her with the Irish *Monenna; in its final form her Legend is perhaps a conflation of three different saints. *C.S.P.* summarizes it, saying that she was 'born in Ireland, died in Scotland and was buried in England: first at Andressey on a small island where she had been an anchorite for seven years, but now at Burton, where she is famous for miracles'. One tradition made a king of Mercia give her lands at Trensall (Staffs.) for a nunnery, where she trained Edith of Polesworth before that house was ready for her. The Scottish saint of the same or similar name seems distinct. There was confusion over the relics, which seems clear from the detail in the Legend that the Irish, the English, and the Scots all wanted her body. An Anglo-Norman text of her Life has little historical value, as do the Latin Lives of the 12th century. Feast: 5(6) July; translation, 9 November.

A. T. Baker and A. Bell, *St. Modwenna* (1947): the Lives in *AA.SS.* Iul. II are of Monenna and of Irish origin.

MOLAISE, see LASERIAN.

MOLING (Mullins) (d. 697), bishop. He was a Leinster man who became a monk at Glendalough. Later he founded his monastery of St. Mullins (Co. Carlow) beside the river Barrow whose ferry-service (which continues to this day) he reputedly founded. He also lived for a time in a nearby hermitage. He is said to have become bishop at (or of) Ferns after the death of Aidan and to have obtained remission from a heavy tribute of many oxen to the local king.

The Book of Mulling is a 9th-century Gospel Book, probably copied from Moling's autograph, as its colophon suggests. It was described by Gerald of Wales (*c.*1200) and survives to this day in a splendid jewelled shrine in the library of Trinity College, Dublin. It is specially famous for its plan of Moling's monastery; some crosses in it probably indicate areas of sanctuary. Moling's pet fox gave rise to many legends; his cult was early and widespread. Feast: 17 June.

H. J. Lawlor, *Chapters on the Book of Mulling* (1897); W. Stokes. 'The Birth and Life of Moling', *Revue Celtique*, xxvii (1906), 256–312; *The Irish Saints*, pp. 252–7.

MOLUA (Lua, Da Lua) (d. *c.*609), abbot and founder of Killaloe (Co. Clare). Almost nothing is known of him except that he was a monk, a builder, and perhaps a hermit, whose oratory on Friars' Island, a few hundred yards from the cathedral, was re-erected before the area was submerged by the Shannon hydro-electric works in 1929. Molua's principal disciple was *Flannan, who succeeded him. Feast: 4 August.

AA.SS. Aug. I (1733), 342–52; *V.S.H.*, ii. 206–25; H. G. Leask, 'The Church of St. Lua or Molua, Friars' Island near Killaloe', *J.R.S.A.I.*, lx (1930), 130–6.

MOLUAG (Lugaid, Molloch), abbot (*c.*530–92) was born in northern Ireland, became a monk at Bangor and went to Scotland where he founded the island monastery of Lismore *c.*562. Later, churches were founded from it in E. Scotland, Skye, and the outer Hebrides. In Lewis he was invoked for cures from madness. A pastoral staff of blackthorn, enshrined in gilded copper, reputedly his, survives. Feast: 25 June.

The Irish Saints, pp. 259–61; W. D. Simpson, *The Celtic Church in Scotland* (1935).

MONENNA (Darerca, Bline) (d. *c.*518), abbess and foundress of Killeevy (Co. Armagh). She was closely associated with *Patrick and *Bridget, and founded her nunnery with eight virgins and one widow. The latter's child, Luger, was fostered by her and later became a bishop. Their regime was so poor that they lived at subsistence level. At least one of her community was sent to Whithorn in SW. Scotland, *Ninian's foundation, for further monastic formation. Various miraculous powers were claimed for Monenna. Later, she was hopelessly confused with *Modwenna of Burton-on-Trent by hagiographers. Feast: 6 July.

AA.SS. Iul. II (1721), 297–312; W. W. Heist, *Vitae Sanctorum Hiberniae* (1965), pp. 83–95; M. Esposito, 'The sources of Conchubranus' Life of St. Monenna', *E.H.R.*, xxxv (1920), 71–8; id., 'Conchubrani Vita Sanctae Monennae', *P.R.I.A.*, xxviii C (1910), 202–46.

MONICA (332–87), widow. Born probably at Tagaste, North Africa. Monica was married to Patricius, described variously as a pagan or as a nominal Christian, but who was certainly dissolute and violent in temper. Her mother-in-law lived in the house with them and added to her difficulties. Monica, who had earlier overcome a tendency to heavy drinking, by her patient persistence won over both her mother-in-law and her husband, who although frequently unfaithful, never struck her or physically ill-treated her. He was baptized in 370 and died the following year. Monica was the mother of three children: *Augustine, Navigius, and Perpetus. As the mother of Augustine she is especially famous; in her patient treatment of him over many years of anxiety ended by his conversion, she is seen as the model of Christian mothers. Most of our information about her comes from Augustine's *Confessions* (Book IX). When he was young, she had enrolled him as a catechumen according to contemporary custom, but his irregular life caused her so much suffering that she once refused to allow him to live in her house. But she soon relented; realizing (through a priest) that the time for his conversion had not yet come, she gave up arguing with him (or asking others to do so) and turned instead to prayer, fasts, and vigils, hoping that they would succeed where argument had failed. Eventually Augustine went to Rome, deceiving her about the time of his departure in order to travel alone. He went on to Milan, but Monica followed him. She was highly esteemed by its bishop, *Ambrose, who also helped Augustine towards a deep moral conversion besides acceptance of the Christian faith. This took place in 386. As a consequence Augustine renounced also his mother's plans for his marriage, deciding to remain celibate; with Monica and a few chosen friends he went away for a period of preparation for Baptism. The dialogues of this little group of friends were recorded by Augustine in his *De Beata Vita* and other opuscules. Augustine was baptized in 387; Monica and his friends set out on the journey to Africa with him, but she died on the way at Ostia. Just before her last illness she said to him: 'Nothing in this world now gives me pleasure. I do not know what there is left for me to do or why I am still here, all my hopes in this world are now fulfilled. All I wished to live for was to see you a Catholic and a child of Heaven. God has granted me more than this in making you despise earthly happiness and consecrate yourself to his service.' She died at the age of fifty-five and was buried at Ostia. There seems to have been no early cult of her, but in 1162 her relics were translated to Arrouaise, where the Austin Canons kept her feast on 4 May, the day before the conversion of St. Augustine. From this house the cult spread to others of the same Order. In 1430 it received fresh impetus from the translation of other relics from Ostia to Rome, where they rest in the church of S. Agostino. In the reformed Roman calendar her feast is on 27 August.

AA.SS. Maii I (1680), 473–91; Augustine, *Confessions*, Book IX; modern Lives by E. H. Bougaud (1865, Eng. tr. 1894) E. Procter (1931) and L. Cristiani (1959). See also P. Henry, *La Vision d'Ostie* (1938), and, for a less favourable view of Monica, P. L. R. Brown, *St. Augustine of Hippo* (1965).

MONTANUS AND LUCIUS (d. 259), martyrs. Their sufferings are recorded in a letter from martyrs in prison to the church of Carthage, written by at least two authors in rhetorical African style. In this persecution of Valerian nine named martyrs suffered, including two catechumens. There are several accounts of visions in prison. Montanus had 'had words with Julian over a woman who had slippen into our communion but did not partake with us'. He maintained a certain coolness because of this quarrel. In his vision (or dream) Montanus saw centurions who conducted them to a huge field where they were joined by *Cyprian and others. Their clothes began to glow and their bodies became even brighter. 'Looking into my bosom I saw some stains and then in my vision I awoke. I told Lucian of my vision and said: "Those stains are there because I did not at once make up with Julian." '

This story of human weakness among future martyrs is completed by the account of their sufferings. After several months in prison they all confessed that they were Christians and were led out to execution. Lucius, in poor health and of retiring temperament, died first. Montanus, sturdy in mind and body, cried out repeatedly: 'He who sacrifices to the gods will be utterly destroyed, save to the Lord only' (Exod. 22: 20). He also vigorously attacked heretics, saying they should learn the truth of the Church from the abundance of martyrs and that they should return to her. He then attacked apostates for hasty desertion, but urged the believers to hold their ground with courage and perseverance. 'You have good models', he said. 'Let not the treachery of apostates lead you to ruin but rather let our endurance strengthen you for the crown.' Just before he was beheaded he prayed so loud that pagans as well as Christians heard him. He asked that his blindfold should be given to one Flavian, still in prison and that space should be reserved for him in the cemetery. Feast in the calendar of Carthage 23 May, but in Roman Martyrology erroneously 24 February.

A.C.M., xxxiv–xxxvi, 214–39; *Propylaeum*, p. 75; B.T.A., i. 408–11.; H. Delehaye, *Les passions des martyrs* (1921), pp. 72–8.

MONTFORT, Louis Grignion de (1673–1716), priest and founder of the Company of Mary and of the Daughters of Wisdom. Born at Montfort (Brittany) and educated by the Jesuits at Rennes, he went to Paris in 1693 to start his studies for the priesthood. After experience of poverty-stricken and badly run students' hostels which caused him serious illness, he entered the seminary of Saint-Sulpice and was ordained in 1700. He decided to devote himself to the spiritual care of the poor and the sick in a society where the gulf between rich and poor was immense; he taught the roughest children in Paris their catechism and founded at Poitiers an institute of sisters for improving the care of the sick in hospitals. Opposition to him, however, became so strong that he was forbidden to preach in the diocese of Poitiers: but armed with papal authority which made him a 'missionary apostolic', he spent the rest of his life preaching popular missions, mainly in Poitiers and Brittany. Although much of the appeal of his preaching was emotional, it sometimes bore permanent results in the restoration of churches, almsgiving, and spiritual revival. He composed verses and hymns, some of which are still sung today, propagated the use of the rosary, and sometimes used dramatic 'revivalist' techniques to appeal to his audience. He organized bonfires of irreligious books under an effigy of the devil dressed as a woman of high society: at other times he would act the part of a dying sinner, whose soul was being claimed both by a devil and a guardian angel, whose parts were acted by other priests. Perhaps his greatest success was the reconciliation of numerous Calvinists at La Rochelle. In 1712 he founded the Company of Mary, an association of missionary priests who shared his ideals. Since then, they and his order of sisters have spread to other countries, including the English-speaking world, and are active in the field of education. His principal writing is called *True Devotion to the Blessed Virgin*; although often criticized by both Catholics and Protestants for its rhetorical and exaggerated language, it has proved very influential in certain circles. It seems likely, however, that its popularity will sharply decline in the post-Vatican II era of the Roman Church. Montfort was canonized in 1947; feast 28 April.

Contemporary Lives by J. Grandet and P. de Clorivière and recent ones by G. Bernoville (1946), F. Morineau (1947), and Cardinal E. Tisserant (1943), and E. C. Bolger (1952), in English. See also A. Laveille, *Le bienheureux L. Grignion de Montfort d'après des documents inédits* (1907); D. Cruikshank, *Bd. Louis Marie Grignon de Montfort and His Devotion* (1892); E. Tisserant, 'Le Testament de Louis M. Grignion de Montfort', *Anal. Boll.*, lxviii (1950), 464–74; B.T.A., ii. 184–5.

MORE, Thomas (1478–1535), martyr. The son of Sir John More, barrister and judge, Thomas More at the age of thirteen joined the household of John Morton, archbishop of Canterbury (1486–1500), who sent him to Canterbury College, Oxford, where he stayed for only two years on a very restricted allowance from his father, who called him home. In 1496 he entered Lincoln's Inn and was called to the Bar in 1501. In 1504 he entered Parliament (his constituency is unknown). For four years he had lived at the London Charterhouse, uncertain in his own mind whether to join it or the Friars Minor or to become a diocesan priest. In the event he did none of these things but decided to pursue his legal career and get married. But from these years date his lifelong habit of wearing a hairshirt, the daily recitation of the Little Office, and the use of the discipline. If some reaction against clerics and clerical life is seen in this decision, it would be quite untrue to assume on Thomas's part any rejection of asceticism. In 1505 he married Jane Colt of Netherhall (Essex), the eldest daughter of John Colt. Although More had originally found her younger sister more attractive, the marriage was a happy one; three daughters and a son were born, but Jane More died in 1511. Already More had made friends with and been deeply influenced by some of the leading men of the New Learning, especially Erasmus, but also Linacre, Grocyn, and Colet. More's many-sided personality, made up of intellectual sophistication and simple moral honesty, brilliance and receptivity, loyalty to his king and affection to his wife, friends, and children, was becoming known. Henry VIII, who became king in 1509, early recognized his worth and integrity; he promoted him to a whole series of public offices: Under-Sheriff of London (1510), envoy to

Flanders (1516), Privy Councillor and Master of Requests (1518), Speaker of the House of Commons (1523), High Steward of Oxford University (1524), High Steward of Cambridge University, and Chancellor of the Duchy of Lancaster (1525). Meanwhile his reputation as a man of letters and a wit was helped by his publications, the most notable of which was *Utopia*, written in Latin in 1516, but soon translated into the principal European languages. This is an ironical political essay describing a society in which there is no private property but where there is universal religious toleration and free education for both men and women. Other writings include his *Life of John Picus* (1510), *History of Richard III* (printed 1543, a pro-Lancastrian tract later used by Shakespeare) and controversial works against Tyndale such as the *Dialogue* (1528), the *Confutacyon of Tyndale's Answere* (1528–32), and his own *Apologye* (1533).

A few weeks after the death of his first wife More married again. His second wife was a widow, Alice Middleton; she was an experienced housewife, full of common sense, and a good stepmother for his children. In 1523 he had undertaken a defence, written against Luther, of Henry VIII's book on the Seven Sacraments, which had earned Henry the title of Defender of the Faith from the papacy. More wrote under the name Gulielmus Rosseus. In 1524 he moved to Chelsea, where his famous household was painted by Hans Holbein (*c.*1526). His cultured and delightful family life, which included the education of his daughters (especially Margaret Roper) to a level far surpassing that currently available to most women, was often commented on by contemporaries. Devotional elements included the reading of passages from Scripture at table and family prayers every night, but the general culture, fed in part by his early study of the classics and by a scientific curiosity which led him to keep unusual pets such as a monkey, was of a particularly high level and seasoned by More's wit. His realism about clerical scandals or superstition in the invocation of the saints was matched by his assessment of the king's favour for him: 'If my head would win him a castle in France, it should not fail to go.'

In the late 1520s Henry (who used to visit More's house informally, arriving by barge) consulted him about the supposed invalidity of his marriage to Catherine of Aragon. More first excused himself for lack of expert knowledge, but when pressed again made it clear that he did not share the king's opinion. This, however, did not prevent the king choosing him as Lord Chancellor in succession to Cardinal Wolsey in 1529. As judge he was famous for fairness, promptitude, and incorruptibility, which could not be said of many contemporaries in similar offices. But his tenure of office was too short to be profoundly influential on English history. He initiated, speaking for the king, the programme of the reform of the clergy, which had results even he would not have foreseen. But the cloud of doubt about Henry's marital plans hung over the friendship between More and the king, as did another caused by the king's plans to take to himself the powers over the Church of England held by the pope, according to traditional Christian belief the successor of St. Peter, prince of the Apostles. Only little by little did the king's intentions become clear. His imposition on the clergy of the acknowledgement of himself as 'Protector and Supreme Head of the Church of England' was accepted by Fisher and others only 'so far as the law of Christ allows'. More at first wished to resign his office at this point, but was persuaded to accept the oath with John *Fisher's proviso. Further measures inhibiting the liberty of the clergy and refusing 'firstfruits' of bishoprics to the Holy See were opposed by More, but in vain. As the king's intentions became increasingly clear, More found his situation impossible and resigned the chancellorship.

The final crisis came over the Act of Succession with its inescapable implications. While the nullity case of Henry's marriage with Catherine of Aragon was still being decided at Rome, Henry married Anne Boleyn, who was then crowned Queen. More refused to attend her coronation. In 1534 the Act of Succession required the king's subjects to recognize the offspring of the marriage of Henry and Anne as successors to the throne; also that the union with Catherine of Aragon was no true marriage, but that the union with Anne was a true marriage and that the authority of any foreign prince or potentate should be repudiated. To the first part of the oath More was ready to agree, but he could not accept the other propositions, especially as only a little while before Clement VII had at last pronounced the marriage of Henry and Catherine to have been valid. Opposing the Act had been declared high treason, so after a second refusal More and John Fisher, bishop of Rochester, were committed to the Tower. This was on 13 April 1534. More was imprisoned for the remaining fifteen months of his life. Many efforts were made to induce him to conform but in vain; he forfeited all his lands and his family shared his poverty. In 1535 the Act of Supremacy which gave to the king the title 'only supreme head of the Church in England' came into force. John *Houghton and the other London Carthusian monks were executed for 'treason' on 4 May and were watched by More on the way to their death. On 22 June, Fisher, More's friend and adviser, was beheaded on Tower Hill; on 1 July More, weak from illness and imprisonment, was tried in Westminster Hall. His defence was that his indictment was based directly on an Act of Parliament repugnant to the laws of God and the Church; that no temporal prince can presume by any law to take upon himself a spiritual pre-eminence given by Christ to St. Peter and his successors in the See of Rome; that a particular country could no more make laws against the general law of the Church than the City of London could make a law against Parliament to bind the whole country; that the new title was contrary to the king's coronation oath. Further, although bishops and universities had agreed to this Act, More had not found in seven years' special study of the subject a single ancient writer or doctor that advocated the supremacy of any secular and temporal prince. In Christendom itself learned bishops and virtuous men still alive, not to mention the saints who were dead, agreed with More; therefore he was not obliged to prefer the council of one realm against the General Council of Christendom or one Parliament ('God knows what manner of one') to all the Councils made these thousand years. Nevertheless, he was condemned to death. Characteristically he then expressed the hope that he and his judges may 'hereafter in heaven all meet merrily together, to our everlasting salvation'. A last affectionate meeting with his daughter Margaret followed on his way back to the Tower; she and other members of his family had taken the oath which he refused. He was executed on Tower Hill on 6 July, his last words being that he died for the faith of the Holy Catholic Church and was 'the king's good servant, but God's first'.

His body was buried in the church of St. Peter ad Vincula inside the Tower; his head was first exhibited on Tower Bridge and then buried in the Roper vault at St. Dunstan, Canterbury. His death, with that of Fisher, shocked many in Europe. More and Fisher were beatified in 1886 and canonized in 1935. The assertion which they refused to accept was neither conciliarist nor Gallican but, in their view, heretical and therefore unacceptable. Their memory was hallowed in recusant circles for centuries, but in the case of More there has been an enormous proliferation of studies during the 20th century in America, Germany, France, and the Low Countries, as well as in England. He ranks high as a writer of English prose in spite of his prolixity; the spiritual depth of his later works, written in the Tower, such as the *Dialogue of Comfort against Tribulation* and his *Treatise on the Passion of Christ* forms a suitable climax to a long literary career, whose earlier products reveal a humanist and a wit rather than a saint. Many modern churches and schools are dedicated to

Thomas More (with or without John Fisher); authentic portraits by Holbein survive. The feast of More and Fisher, formerly on 9 July, is now on 22 June: they are among the few English saints now culted by the whole Roman Church.

Earliest Lives by William Roper and Nicholas Harpsfield (ed. E. V. Hitchcock (E.E.T.S., 1932 and 1935)); by Thomas Stapleton (ed. P. E. Hallett, 1928); by Ro. Ba. (ed. E. V. Hitchcock and P. E. Hallett, E.E.T.S., 1950), and Cresacre More (1630); modern Lives by T. E. Bridgett (1891), R. W. Chambers (1935), E. E. Reynolds (2nd edn. 1968), A. Prévost (1969) and A. Fox (1982). For a less favourable view see R. Marius, *Thomas More* (1984) and B. Bradshaw in *J.E.H.* xxxvi (1985), 535–69. See also A. Kenny, *Thomas More* (1984). More's Works were first edited by W. Rastell (1557); Latin works published at Louvain (1565) and Frankfurt (1689); English works ed. W. E. Campbell (1931, two vols. only); Yale edition of complete works (ed. G. L. Carroll and J. B. Murray, 1963–). Other studies on More include G. Marc'Hadour, *Thomas More et la Bible* (1969); id., *L'Univers de Thomas More* (1963); R. W. Gibson, *St. Thomas More* (1961). The periodical *Moreana* (ed. by G Marc'Hadour) 1963 onwards, records current research into More's life and times.

MORSE, Henry (1595–1645), Jesuit, priest, and martyr. Born at Brome (Suffolk), Morse studied Law at Barnards Inn (London), was later converted to Catholicism and joined the English College, Douai, in 1614. He returned to England, was in prison for four years in London and then banished. He entered the English College, Rome, was ordained priest and in 1624 returned to England. In 1626 he was arrested again and imprisoned for four years in York. Here he was able to complete his year's novitiate as a Jesuit. In 1633 after a spell as military chaplain in Holland to Spanish troops he was sent back to London where, during the plague of 1636, he ministered to the sick with conspicuous courage and devotion: he appealed successfully for alms for food and medicine, but caught the plague himself. His unexpected recovery was regarded by some as miraculous. At this time the penal laws against Catholics were often ignored, but in 1638 an informer made it his business to tell the authorities that Morse was a priest ordained overseas who seduced the king's subjects from their faith and allegiance. He was tried and found guilty on the first count and imprisoned at Newgate. Queen Henrietta Maria, however, persuaded King Charles I to release him. Morse then had another spell as military chaplain (to Gage's regiment fighting for the Spanish against the Dutch). Then came a period of ministry to recusants in both Cornwall and Cumberland which ended in arrest, escape, and rearrest by Parliamentarian troops at Newcastle. After trial and imprisonment at Newgate he was executed at Tyburn on the strength of his previous conviction nine years earlier. The French, Spanish, and Portuguese ambassadors with their suites were present at the execution of one of the most colourful and adventurous of the English Martyrs, who asserted to the end that he was dying for his religion and that he knew nothing about plots against the king. He died on 1 February 1645 and was canonized by Paul VI in 1970 as one of the *Forty Martyrs of England and Wales. Feast: 25 October.

P. Caraman, *Henry Morse* (1957); R. Challoner, *Memories of Missionary Priests* (ed. J. H. Pollen, 1928); H. Foley, *Records of the English Province of the Society of Jesus* (1877), vol. i; B. Camm, *Forgotten Shrines* (1910).

MORWENNA (Mwynen) (6th century?), patron of Morwenstow (Cornwall), named after her. Her identity is difficult to establish through confusion with *Modwenna. It seems that Morwenna was of Irish–Welsh family, descended from *Brychan, whose family settled in North Cornwall. Legend related that when the people built a church, Morwenna carried a stone on her head up from beneath the cliff; when she put it down to rest, St. Morwenna's well sprang up; when she finally deposited it in the place she wanted, the church was built there, although the first choice for its site was elsewhere. Feast: ?5 July.

Baring-Gould and Fisher, iii. 490–7.

MOSCATI, Giuseppe (1860–1927), scientist and doctor. Born of a noble Beneventan family, he showed extraordinary promise as a student at Naples University, where he joined the medical faculty and came to be reckoned a precursor of modern biochemistry. His religious commitment was shown in both a vow of chastity and whole-hearted care of incurables at Santa Maria del Populo. The eruption of Vesuvius in 1906 and an outbreak of cholera in 1911 proved his charity still further. His scientific research continued, he exercised his medical profession to relieve suffering, not to make profits, and he used to retire regularly for long periods of prayer. Three years after his death his relics were translated to the church of Gesu Nuovo. He was beatified in 1975 and canonized in 1987. Feast: 16 November.

Lives by G. Papasogli (1959) and F. Bea, *Storia di un medico* (1961); *Bibl. SS.*, ix. 602–4.

MULLINS, see MOLING.

MUNCHIN (Mainchin, Manchen) (7th century), Irish abbot or bishop. He is mentioned in three early Irish martyrologies and called 'The Wise', traditionally he is associated with Limerick, whose principal patron and first bishop he is claimed to be. But little can be known of him with certainty. He belonged to the clan of the Dal Cais, who lived near the west coast of Co. Clare (Ennistimon area); a ruling prince gave him the island of Limerick possibly in exchange for his claim to supremacy over his own people. Feast: 2 January.

M. Moloney, 'Limerick's Patron', *North Munster Antiquarian Journal*, vii (1957), 11–14; B.T.A., i. 21–2.

MUNDUS (Munnu), see FINTAN MUNNU.

MUNGO, see KENTIGERN.

MURA (Muranus, Muru), Irish abbot of early 7th century. He was the founder of Fahan (Innisowen, Co. Donegal). Both his crosier and his bell-shrine survive: the former in the Royal Irish Academy and the latter in the Wallace Collection, London. His cross is preserved at Fahan as a National Monument. Feast: 12 March in early Irish martyrologies.

Bibl. SS., ix. 681.

MURIALDO, Leonard (1828–1900), founder of the Congregation of St. Joseph. Born and educated in Turin, he was ordained priest in 1851 and then devoted himself to the education of working-class boys through directing the Oratory of St. Louis, fostered by John *Bosco. After visiting Saint-Sulpice (Paris) in 1865 he returned to Turin to become rector of a Christian College of further education and technical training. This achieved a high reputation.

To make this work permanent, he founded his Congregation and promoted the Catholic Workers' Movement through the newspaper *La voce dell'Operario*, supported later by the monthly *La buona Stampa*. He also established a nationwide federation to improve the standards of the press. He died peacefully and is buried in the church of Santa Barbara, Turin. At his canonization in 1970 Pope Paul VI stressed that not only his personal virtues were honoured, but also the social activities which these virtues clothed. Feast: 30 March.

Lives by J. Cottino (1963) and F. Bea (1963); A. Marengo, *Contributi per uno studio su L. Murialdo educatore* (1964); *N.C.E.*, x. 83: *Bibl. SS.*, ix. 679–81.

MURTAGH (Muredach) (6th century)(?), Irish bishop. Two traditions concerning this saint make him respectively a convert of *Patrick or a contemporary of *Columba. One or the other must be wrong, probably the first. He is venerated as the first bishop of Killala and as the founder of Innismurray, a fertile monastic island in complete contrast to the famous Skellig Michael. On Innismurray (Co. Sligo) are notable remains of a secular fort, oratories, and beehive cells, some of which may date back to the founder. Feast: 12 August.

The Irish Saints, pp. 264–5.

MURU, see Mura.

MWYNEN, see Morwenna.

MYBARD, see Meubred.

MYLOR (Melor, Melar), martyr of unknown date, titular of Amesbury Abbey which claimed his relics, and probably of three churches in Cornwall, Mylor, Merther Mylo, and Linkinhorne. This very obscure saint's life has been obfuscated by hagiographers who have confused names, dates, and places almost irretrievably. It seems probable that he was a saint of Brittany rather than of Britain, whose Legend was worked over in the later Middle Ages (possibly by Bishop Grandisson). Cornwall was substituted for Cornouaille and Devon introduced. According to the Legend, which has several Celtic folkloric elements, he was a prince of seven years old when his father was killed by his uncle; the uncle Rivoldus wished to kill the child also but was dissuaded by a council of bishops, at whose intervention he agreed to maim him instead, cutting off his right hand and left foot. These were replaced by a silver hand and a bronze foot. Mylor was sent to a remote monastery to be educated, but by the time he was fourteen, his artificial limbs had begun to work as though they were natural; so Rivoldus induced Mylor's guardian Cerialtanus to kill him. This was done by decapitation. Rivoldus touched the severed head and died three days afterwards. The body was brought to Amesbury, placed on the altar, and was prevented by Mylor's power from being removed. This picturesque story was probably invented to explain the presence of Mylor's relics at Amesbury and the dedication. It seems likely that Mylor, like *Branwalader, was a Breton saint whose relics were collected by King Athelstan and given to churches such as Milton and Amesbury in which he was specially interested. Amesbury later became one of England's most famous medieval Benedictine monasteries, but even William of Malmesbury could find out nothing about its patron saint. Feast: 1 October.

Life in *N.L.A.*, ii. 183–5; G. H. Doble, *The Saints of Cornwall*, iii (1964), 20–52.

N

NATHALAN (d. *c*.678), Scottish saint of the Aberdeen district. He was believed to have been born in Tullicht and to have built churches there and at Bothelim and Colle; he is recorded in early Irish martyrologies such as that of Aengus. His Legend in the Aberdeen breviary makes him a nobleman who decided to cultivate the earth in order to devote himself to God, who fed the people near by in times of famine. Folklore influence is evident in the story of his locking his hand and leg together, throwing away the key, and recovering it in Rome from the inside of a fish. Feast: 8 January.

K.S.S., pp. 417–19.

NATHANAEL, see BARTHOLOMEW.

NECTAN (Nighton) (6th century), Welsh hermit who settled near Hartland (N. Devon), where he was killed by robbers. The fullest surviving Life from the 12th century in the Gotha manuscript, says that he was the eldest and most illustrious of the twenty-four children of *Brychan. Already a monk, he sailed from South Wales to N. Devon, followed by his many relatives. He settled in the dense forests which provided him with solitude. His family would meet him at his hermitage on the last day of each year. After several years spent in solitude in a beautiful but remote valley, provided with a spring, he helped a swineherd find his pigs and was later rewarded with a present of two cows from his master. These, however, were soon stolen by thieves. Nectan found them, remonstrated with them, took the opportunity to attempt to convert them to the Christian faith, but was rewarded for his pains by being beheaded. According to the same authority, after his death he carried his head for half a mile to the spring by his hut. This legend made Nectan comparable with *Denys and *Decuman.

The medieval cult was considerable in the West Country. Lyfing, bishop of Crediton 1021–46, who had at first refused to translate Nectan's body, approved of it as an accomplished fact and provided treasures for the church at Hartland which included bells, lead for the roof, and a sculptured reliquary. Nectan's staff was decorated with gold, silver, and jewels; the church was also endowed with manors to strengthen it against pirates from the Viking settlements in Ireland. Benefactors to Hartland are said to have included King Harthacnut, Earl Godwin, and his wife. In the early 12th century the Austin Canons restored the church and shrine at Hartland which remained in their care until the Reformation. Five churches are dedicated to Nectan in Devon and Cornwall and possibly two Breton place-names may be connected with him. William Worcestre asserts that Nectan was the most important of the children of Brychan in Devon and Cornwall, which may well be correct. His feast was kept at Launceston, Exeter, Wells, and elsewhere, usually on 17 June, the day of his death. Roscarrock gives 18 May, but the Gotha text gives 4 December as his translation day. The fair in his honour at St. *Winnoc was, however, on 14 February, which Wilson's Martyrology (1640) gives as his feast.

G. H. Doble, *The Saints of Cornwall*, v (1970), 59–79; P. Grosjean, 'Vie de S. Nectan', *Anal. Boll.*, lxxi (1953), 359–414; F. Wormald, 'The seal of St. Nectan', *Jnl. of the Warburg and Courtauld Institutes*, ii (1938), 70–1.

NEOT (d. *c*.877), monk and hermit, who gave his name to St. Neot (Cornwall) and St. Neots (Cambridgeshire). He joined the community of Glastonbury in early life; from there he settled as a hermit near

Bodmin Moor at the place later called Neotstoke (St. Neot), where he founded a small monastery. He was buried in this church, where his relics were enshrined after translation on the north side of the sanctuary.

In 972–7 Earl Alfric (or Leofric) founded a monastery at Eynesbury (Cambridgeshire) with monks from Thorney. From the warden of Neot's Cornish shrine they obtained by gift or theft the greater part of his relics. The town of Eynesbury was then called St. Neots. This priory was refounded from Bec *c.*1086. Its relics were inspected by *Anselm, who declared them authentic and also complete except for one arm left in Cornwall. Anselm himself gave to Bec a relic of Neot's cheekbone, presumably from the Eynesbury shrine, described in the relic-list of 1134. This shrine was sufficiently important to be mentioned in the saints' lists of both the 11th and the 13th centuries (*R.P.S.* and *C.S.P.*).

There are three Latin Lives and one Old English Life, which preserve some details of interest. Royal blood was claimed for Neot, either from the East Anglian dynasty or that of Wessex. Alfred visited him and sought his counsel; Neot is said to have suggested to him the revival of the 'English School' at Rome. Neot, like *Cuthbert, is said to have appeared to Alfred on the eve of the battle of Ethandun against the Danes. He was so small in stature that he needed to stand on a stool in order to say Mass. The Life, written at Bec in the 12th century, relates incidents borrowed from Lives of Irish saints, such as that of stags being yoked to a plough to take the place of oxen stolen by robbers and that of a fish which was repeatedly eaten but never diminished. This Life was the source of the fine stained-glass window at St. Neot, donated by the young men of the parish in 1528.

John Leland, travelling through England in the 1540s, saw the tunic of the saint at St. Neots and his comb 'made of a little bone of two fingers' width, into which were inserted small fishes' teeth, the whole having the appearance of a pike's jaw'.

Some recent scholars claim unconvincingly that Neot was a Celtic, not an Anglo-Saxon, saint. Feast: 31 July.

AA.SS. Iul. VII (1731), 314–29; *N.L.A.*, ii. 213–18; W. H. Stevenson, *Asser's Life of Alfred* (1959), pp. 256–61. E. C. Axford, *Some Notes on St. Neot, Cornwall* (1976); M. P. Richards, 'The Medieval Hagiography of St. Neot', *Anal. Boll.*, lxxxxix (1981), 259–78; M. Chibnall, 'History of the Priory of St. Neots', *Cambridge Antiq. Soc. Proceedings*, lix (1966), 60 ff.

NEREUS AND ACHILLEUS, Roman martyrs of the (?)2nd century. Their cult centred on their relics in the cemetery of Domitilla, is very ancient and well testified. From an inscription of Pope *Damasus (late 4th century) it can be learnt that they were soldiers, used to executing through fear the orders of a cruel tyrant; that they were suddenly converted to Christianity, left the military life and threw away their arms, confessed the faith of Christ, and were martyred. Over the cemetery of Domitilla a church was built in the 4th century in which their now empty tomb was discovered by archaeologists in 1874. Another church was built in their honour by *Leo III *c.*800.

Their legendary Acts make these martyrs eunuchs of the lady Flavia Domitilla, a relative of the emperor Domitian; they shared her exile to Ponza and then to Terracina where, during Trajan's reign, Nereus and Achilleus were beheaded and Domitilla burnt to death for refusing to sacrifice to idols. Feast: 12 May with *Pancras and formerly Domitilla.

AA.SS. Maii III (1680), 4–16 and *C.M.H.*, pp. 249–50; A Guerrieri, *La chiesi dei SS. Nereo ed Achilleo* (1951); P. F. de Cavalieri, *Note agiographice*, ii (*S.T.*, xxii, 1909), 43–55.

NERI, Philip (1515–95), priest, founder of the Congregation of the Oratory (Oratorians). He was the son of a Florentine notary, Francesco Neri. His mother died when he was a child, but his stepmother brought him up admirably. He was educated by the Dominicans in the famous convent of S. Marco (Florence), then for a short time took a business appointment in a firm run by his uncle, who planned to make him his heir. But he soon gave it up after experiencing a deep conversion, went to Rome without either plans or money, and lived in an attic in extreme poverty, paying his rent by giving lessons to his landlord's two sons. He lived almost like a hermit for two years, spent another three studying philosophy and theology, but then gave up his studies and sold some of his books. He turned instead to the apostolate, first in an informal way, talking to young Florentines employed in banks and shops. His extraordinarily attractive personality quickly won him friends, whom he encouraged to abandon evil practices and instead to serve the sick in the hospitals and visit the churches of Rome with him. Sometimes he would spend the night in a church or in the catacombs in prayer. In 1544 he experienced in a vision that a globe of fire entered his mouth and dilated his heart: it seems that this experience left permanent physical effects which were verified after his death. In 1548 he founded a confraternity to look after the numerous pilgrims who flocked to Rome and later to take care of poor convalescents. In 1551 he was ordained priest and went to live among a community of priests at San Girolamo della Carita. Here he spent long hours directing souls through the confessional, through spiritual discussions or conferences followed by Vespers, Compline, or visits to the seven churches. He had extraordinary powers of reading the secrets of hearts. At one time, inspired by the achievements of Francis *Xavier, he wanted to be a missionary abroad, but a Cistercian told him that Rome was to be his Indies; hence he was often called the Apostle of Rome.

This apostolate proved very fruitful; from it developed the Congregation of the Oratory, so called because Philip and his five priest-disciples used an oratory built over the nave of S. Girolamo, to which they would call the faithful by ringing a small bell. The priests shared a common life and were obedient to Philip, but were not bound by vows, nor did they renounce their property. The congregation was approved in 1575, by which time Philip's personal following, mainly made up of those whom he had helped by his kindly advice and direction, had reached immense proportions. He still lived on at S. Girolamo at the top of the house; his veranda commanded a fine view over the city rooftops. He received cardinals, foreigners, the poor, and the troubled in an almost unending stream. Meanwhile he experienced ecstasy in prayer so often that when he was saying Mass, the server sometimes used to absent himself for two hours and then come back when the saint returned to normal. In 1575 the pope gave to the congregation the church of S. Maria in Vallicella, which was small and dilapidated. Philip, without any funds, decided to pull it down and rebuild a larger one. This Chiesa Nuova was occupied by the Oratorians in 1577, but Philip went to live there only in 1584. The building was paid for by donations from rich and poor. In 1593 Philip resigned as superior in favour of Baronius, the patristic scholar and later cardinal; in the same year he averted a conflict between France and the Holy See by decisive influence in favour of absolving the former Protestant Henry IV (of Navarre). Always apparently happy and considerate, he sometimes indulged in practical jokes; but this did not prevent him from being regarded as a saint during his lifetime. He died on 25 May, after a normal day of seeing visitors, at the end of which he said: 'Last of all, we must die.' At midnight he suffered a haemorrhage and died soon after. His body rests in the church of S. Maria in Vallicella; he was canonized in 1622. St. Philip's Oratorians gave their name to a musical art-form, the Oratorio, which developed from their services and conferences in which the resources of art and music were fully used. In England the Oratorians are best known through the work of John Henry Newman, their most eminent representative, who founded the Birmingham Oratory and the London Oratory. The latter was developed by F. W. Faber in the Brompton Road; it closely resembles a medium-sized Roman Renaissance church, although built in the second half of the 19th century. Feast: 26 May.

Early Lives in *AA.SS.* Maii VI (1688), 460–656; L. Ponnelle and L. Bordet, *Saint Philippe Néri et la société romaine de son temps* (1928, Eng. tr. 1932 and 1979). Other Lives by P. J. Bacci (1622 and 1837, Eng. tr. by F. W. Faber, 1847), R. F. Kerr (2nd edn. 1927), V. J. Matthews (1934), A. Baudrillart (1939), M. Jouhandeau (1957, Eng. tr. 1960), and M. Trevor (1966).

NEUMANN, John (1811–60), Redemptorist priest, bishop of Philadelphia. Born at Prachatitz (Bohemia) of a German father and a Czech mother, who owned a small stocking factory, John studied at Budweis seminary and at Prague University. He spoke eight languages and was especially interested in botany and astronomy besides the usual ecclesiastical subjects. His ordination was delayed by the Austrian government and he decided to work on the North American mission. He arrived in Manhattan in June 1836; he was warmly welcomed, although unannounced, by John Dubois, bishop of New York. He ordained him priest and sent him to minister to the German-speaking immigrants, who were clearing forests by Niagara Falls.

After four years of pioneer missionary work he joined the Redemptorist Congregation, founded by *Alphonsus Liguori. He was sent as a travelling mission-preacher to the east coast; eventually he became parish priest in Baltimore. For his outstanding pastoral work he was consecrated bishop of Philadelphia in 1852. He worked prodigiously, having 100 churches and 80 schools built, and spent much time visiting the remote and hitherto neglected areas of his diocese.

In 1860, worn out with his labours, he dropped dead on Vine Street, Philadelphia. Popular devotion preceded official investigation and approval of the cult. After over 100 years, with the continued support of both his diocese and his order for the cause of canonization, this was accorded in 1977 at immense financial cost over the years.

Diminutive in stature, lacking 'presence' and majesty, he spent much time and energy encouraging layfolk to lives of hidden sanctity. Ultimately, this work achieved the recognition which was its due. He was also the author of catechisms, published in 1852; these were widely used in the USA for the rest of the century. Feast: 5 January.

F. X. Murphy, 'Sainthood and Politique', *The Tablet*, 18 June 1977. See also M. Walsh (ed.), *Butler's Lives of the Saints* (concise edn., 1985), pp. 5–6.

NEWLYN (Newelina), female saint of Cornwall who has given her name to this town, whose church is dedicated to her and where a well also bears her name. Her feast is not certainly known, according to *C.C.K.*; but Roscarrock ascribed it to 27 April. She may be the same as the Breton Noyala, whose story is based on Winefride's and who was supposed to have been killed by a king. Feast: 6 July.

Baring-Gould and Fisher, iv. 10–14; *C.C.K.*, p. 48.

NICASIUS (Nichasius) (5th century), bishop of Reims and martyr. Tenth in the list of bishops of Reims (coming after Severus), Nicasius was faced with victorious barbarians at the gates and even in the streets of his city. Trying to save the lives of his people, he stood at the door of his cathedral, where soldiers cut off his head. With him died a deacon and a lector, together with his sister Eutropia. The barbarians who killed him were more likely the Huns (451) rather than the Vandals (407). Feast: 14 December.

Propylaeum, p. 582; Flodoard, *Historia Remensis Ecclesiae* in *M.G.H.*, *Scriptores rerum merov.*, xiii. 417–20; B.T.A., iv. 558.

NICHOLAS (4th century), bishop of Myra. Nicholas's life, although he was one of the most universally venerated saints in both East and West, is virtually unknown. His see of Myra is in Lycia, south-western Turkey and called Mugla. Attempts to make him one of the fathers at the Council of Nicea (325), who had previously been in prison during the persecution of Diocletian, have failed through lack of evidence. But there can be no doubt about the antiquity of his cult, which was clearly established in the East from the 6th century, increased by a fictitious biography by Methodius (d. 847), and became widely known in the West in the 10th century. But when Myra and its shrine were taken by the Moslems, the relics were translated to Bari (1087), where there were many Greek immigrants. Here a new church was built to house them and Pope Urban II, who held a council at Bari (which *Anselm attended) in 1095, was present at the inauguration. From this time onwards Nicholas's cult became almost universal in the West.

His reputation as a thaumaturge was both cause and effect of his many patronages. Countries such as Russia, towns such as St. Nicholas at Wade (Kent), children, sailors, unmarried girls, merchants, pawnbrokers, apothecaries, and perfumiers all claimed him as their patron. Some of these patronages are linked with episodes in his legendary Acts. He was reputed to have given three bags of gold to three girls for their marriage dowries in order to save them from prostitution. It seems that this is the basis for the use of three gold balls as the pawnbroker's sign. The number three appears several times in his legend, as in the case of three boys whom he is said to have raised to life after they were murdered in a brine-tub by a butcher, and in his saving three unjustly condemned men from death and three sailors near the coast of Turkey. From his shrine at Bari there came a substance sometimes called 'manna' or else a fragrant 'myrrh' which explains his patronage of perfumiers; whatever it may have been it attracted numerous pilgrims to his shrine.

In England about 400 churches were dedicated to Nicholas; in England also there survive two important iconographical cycles of his life, on the font at Winchester cathedral and on an ivory crozier-head at the Victoria and Albert Museum, both of the 12th century. The latter, a masterpiece of fine carving, includes several scenes, one of which is a lively depiction of the infant Nicholas refusing his mother's breast on Wednesdays and Fridays, in accordance with his Legend. Other examples include a fine late medieval window at North Moreton (Oxon.), entirely devoted to his life, and windows in the Jerusalem Chamber, Westminster, at Great Malvern (Hereford and Worcester), and Hillesden (Bucks.). Further afield the frescoes (8th century) at S. Maria Antiqua, Rome, mosaics at S. Sophia, Istanbul (10th century), at St. Mark's, Venice, and Monreale, Sicily (both 12th century) should be mentioned, together with stained-glass cycles of his life at Chartres, Le Mans, and Tours. Renaissance painters also depicted him: all in all, he was probably the most frequently represented saintly bishop of all for many centuries.

Perhaps the most popular result of his cult is the institution of Santa Claus. Based ultimately on Nicholas' patronage of children with its attendant custom in the Low Countries of giving them presents on his feast, it attained its present form in North America, where the Dutch Protestants of New Amsterdam united to it Nordic folkloric legends of a magician who both punished naughty children and rewarded goods ones with presents.

The name Nicholas has been in use in England from Anglo-Saxon times and became very popular in the 12th century. It gave rise to numerous names such as Colin, Nicolson, Nixon, Nicola, Nicolette, and others. He was an extremely popular figure in medieval drama, a tradition continued by Benjamin Britten's *Saint Nicholas*. Prayers to him were composed by *Anselm, *Godric, and others. Feast: 6 December; translation, 9 May.

N. C. Falconius, *Sancti Nicolae Acta Primigenia* (1751); G. Anrich, *Hagios Nikolaos* (1913–17); F. Nitti di Vito, *La leggenda della translazione di S. Nicola da Mira a Bari* (1937); K. Meisen, *Nikolauskult und Nikolausbrauch in Abendlande* (1931); modern studies by J. Laroche (1893), E. Crozier (1949), A. D. de Groot (Eng. tr. 1965); B.T.A., iv. 503–6; Réau, ii. 976–88; K. Young, *The Drama of the Medieval Church* (1933); C. W. Jones, *St. Nicholas of Myra, Bari, and Manhattan* (1978).

NICHOLAS OF FLUE (1417–87), hermit and patron saint of Switzerland. Born at Flueli, near Sachseln (Unterwalden), of a family of farmers who owned the estate of Flueli, Nicholas was a member from an early age of the lay association called the Friends of God. By living strict lives and meditating on the Passion of Christ, they aimed to achieve the Imitation of Christ. Although he could neither read nor write, he early developed judgement and wise counsel, for which he was much esteemed. Both he and his father were prominent in public service and twice Nicholas fought in the army, first in 1439 against Zurich and again in 1453 in Thurgau, where he prevented the destruction of a nunnery. In 1447 he had married Dorothy Wissling, by whom he had ten children, one of whom became a governor of a province and another a priest. Nicholas himself acted as magistrate and judge; meanwhile he also followed a life of prayer, especially at night, experiencing visions and revelations.

In 1467, with his wife's consent, he resigned his offices, left his wife and children, and set out to be a hermit near Strasbourg, the headquarters of the Friends of God. Deterred by a severe thunderstorm and by reports that the Swiss were unpopular in Alsace, as well as by severe gastric pains (possibly caused by an ulcer), he decided to stay in Switzerland and lived for twenty years at Ranft, not far from his home. In a lonely cottage, situated above a narrow gorge within earshot of the mountain stream, he spent the hours from midnight to midday mainly in prayer and contemplation, but in time many visitors used to come and see him in the afternoons, seeking his advice on both religious and worldly matters. His reputation was enhanced by the belief that he never ate or drank.

Near the end of his life he exercised an important role in the history of Switzerland. Just after they had fought successfully for their independence from Charles the Bold of Burgundy in three battles, the Swiss suffered acute internal divisions over sharing the spoils, over whether to include Fribourg and Soleure in the confederation, and on the sharing of power between urban and rural interests. Most of the differences were resolved by the Edict of Stans, which, however, did not settle the destiny of Fribourg and Soleure. The deputies, when passions were running very high, sent a priest to obtain Nicholas' advice. This was decisive in obtaining a unanimous decision within the hour in favour of the two provinces. Indeed, some suggest that the Edict of Stans itself was inspired by Nicholas and may even have been drafted under his direction. What seems certain is that this saintly hermit, detached from all worldly interests, mediated effectively in a crisis which was resolved in such a way as to lead to the permanent achievement of national unity. Nicholas died on 21 March after eight days' severe illness. He was immediately honoured as patriot and saint; the cult was approved in 1669 and he was canonized in 1947. Several accounts survive of visitors' memories of him: one described him as tall, brown, and wrinkled with thin grizzled locks and a short beard, bright eyes, white teeth, and a shapely nose. This corresponds closely with a Fribourg portrait of 1492. Just as he had exhorted the Confederates to peace, so also did he recommend peace and obedience to all his visitors. He was buried at Sachseln, where his tomb survives. Feast: 21 March, but in Switzerland, 25 September.

Lives by R. Durrer (2 vols., 1917–21), K. Vokinger (1947), C. Journet (1947), and G. R. Lamb (1955). See also M. L. von Franz, *Die Visionen des Niklaus von Flue* (1959); *Bibl. SS.*, ix. 914–17.

NICHOLAS OF TOLENTINO (1245–1305), Austin friar. Born at Sant' Angelo in the march of Ancona, Nicholas was named after *Nicholas of Myra, at whose shrine his middle-aged and hitherto childless parents had prayed for a son. When he was eighteen he joined the Austin friars, was ordained priest in 1269, and lived in various friaries for different periods, holding at one time the office of novice-master and acquiring the reputation of a wonder-worker. He finally settled at

Tolentino, a town much disturbed by developments in urban life and by Guelf and Ghibelline factions with consequent civil and moral disorders. Nicholas met immediate spectacular success as a popular preacher, as a confessor, and as a visitor of the sick and the dying, especially the poor and the destitute. He also achieved the conversion of some notorious sinners. After nearly a year's serious illness, he died on 10 September; immediately enquiries were set on foot to lead to his canonization. This, however, was delayed until 1446 owing to the Great Schism.

Paintings of him by Piero della Francesca, Raphael, and Zurbarán and others survive; his usual attribute is a basket of rolls of bread, which were called St. Nicholas's Bread and were distributed to the sick or to women in labour, to be swallowed soaked in water. His church and relics, rediscovered in 1926, survive at Tolentino. His cult is widespread in Europe and America. Feast: 10 September.

AA.SS. Sept. III (1750), 636–743; Lives by E. Foran (1920), E. Eberhard (1952), D. Gentili (1966); *Bibl. SS.*, ix. 953–68.

NICOMEDES, Roman martyr of unknown date, buried in the catacomb on the Via Nomentana, whose cult is well testified by ancient liturgical books. A Roman church was dedicated to him on 1 June, his feast in the Sarum calendar and B.C.P., but his usual feast is on 15 September.

AA.SS. Sept. V (1755), 5–12; *C.M.H.*, p. 510; B.T.A., iii. 555.

NIGHTON, see NECTAN.

NILUS OF ROSSANO (*c.*910–1005), abbot. Born of a Greek family settled in Calabria, he became an official of the treasury. Before he was thirty, he suffered the loss both of his mistress and of their daughter. He became a monk in a Greek monastery nearby, lived in several as hermit or cenobite, and became abbot of St. Adrian's, near San Demetrio Corone. During most of his life both Saracens from Sicily and mercenary soldiers were a repeated threat to peace.

Nilus became reputed for his austerity and holiness as well as for his knowledge of Greek and Latin literature and for his composition of hymns. He seems to have believed that the numbers of the saved were extremely small; on the other hand, he did not easily grant monastic status to powerful laymen: 'Your baptismal promises are quite sufficient without your taking monastic vows: these are not required for repentance, but only a sincere determination to change your way of life.'

In 981 he fled with his community of 60 monks from the Saracen armies, travelling north to Monte Cassino, where they were warmly welcomed by the successor of *Benedict. They were given hospitality and sung the Greek Liturgy in the abbey church until they moved to the empty monastery of Vallelucio, where they lived for 15 years. From there they moved on to Serperi (near Gaeta), where the Emperor Otto III visited them in 999 and was astounded by their primitive conditions of life. He offered to rebuild the monastery but Nilus refused, accepting instead a purse of money.

In 1004 he visited Grottaferrata (near Rome), where he was assured in a vision that this would be his community's permanent home. Before the building was completed he died, but he is reckoned as this monastery's founder. For nearly 1,000 years this Byzantine-rite abbey has flourished as a place of holiness and learning, formerly devoted to the production of manuscript books, but nowadays to their conservation by the most modern scientific techniques. Feast: 26 September.

AA.SS. Sept. VII (1867), 262–319; Lives by A. Rochi (1904) and G. Giovanelli (1966); see also D. Attwater, *Saints of the East* (1963), pp. 118–24; *Bibl. SS.*, ix. 995–1008.

NINE MAIDENS, see DONALD.

NINIAN (Nynia) (5th century), British bishop and apostle in Whithorn and Galloway, traditionally also apostle of the Picts. Our principal information comes from *Bede, whose source and accuracy have been much discussed recently, but without any final conclusion being generally accepted. Archaeology at Whithorn, however, has tended to confirm Bede's statements, in so far as remains have been found there of an early church, whose masonry was in fact painted white, which could have given Bede's name for it *Ad Candidam Casam*. A number of inscribed Christian stones were also found, which confirm the existence of a monastery near by. The dedication to St. Martin mentioned by Bede has been much contested. It has been suggested that Ninian brought a relic of *Martin to Whithorn, perhaps for a subsidiary chapel, in or near the monastery, and that Ninian's monasticism was inspired by that of Martin at Tours, whom, however, he did not necessarily visit. Bede also stressed Ninian's formation at Rome, his shrine at Whithorn and the presence of other relics there.

The extent of his apostolate among the 'southern Picts' has also been much disputed. The first problem is to identify these people. It seems likely that Bede means those in Forfar, Perth, Sterling, and Fife but not the people living in Galloway. Some confirmation of this is seen in the place-name St. Ninians near Stirling, but the use of this evidence is uncertain because of the unknown date of many place-names; it would also be unwise to assert that St. Ninian's Isle represents the furthest point of his own personal apostolate. It seems safer to stress Ninian's influence in and around Whithorn and to say that the extent of his apostolate in Pictish territory is unknown. There are, however, many Ninian dedications in different parts of Scotland, and three in northern England.

Ninian was sufficiently important to attract later biographers, such as an anonymous 8th-century writer, whose work, now lost, is believed to be the source of an 8th-century poem on Ninian. In the 12th century Ailred of Rievaulx also wrote a Life which can be regarded as a standard statement of how Ninian was traditionally regarded when *Ailred lived in Scotland. His shrine was a popular pilgrimage-place and survived until the 16th century. By this time his cult had spread to Kent and Denmark. Feast: 26 August.

Bede, *H.E.*, iii. 4; W. Levison, 'An Eighth-Century Poem on St. Ninian', *Antiquity*, xiv (1940), 280–91; Ailred's Life in A. P. Forbes, *The Historians of Scotland* (1874) and A. O. Anderson, *Early Sources of Scottish History* (1922); W. D. Simpson, *Saint Ninian and the Origins of the Christian Church in Scotland* (1940), but see A. O. Anderson, 'Ninian and the southern Picts', *Scottish Hist. Review*, xxvii (1948), 25–47 and E. A. Thompson, 'The origin of Christianity in Scotland', ibid., xxxv (1958), 17–22; J. Macqueen, *St. Nynia* (1961); id., 'History and Miracle Stories in the biography of Nynia', *Innes Review*, xiii (1962), 115–29; A. Boyle, 'Saint Ninian: some outstanding problems', ibid., xix (1968), 57–70; D. P. Kirby, 'Bede and the Pictish Church', ibid., xxiv (1973), 6–25: see also A. B. Scott, 'The Brito-Celtic church on the northern mainland and islands', *Gaelic Soc., Inverness Trans.*, xxxiii (1932), 327–55; F. T. Wainwright, *The Problem of the Picts* (1955). R. P. C. Hanson, *St. Patrick* (1968); G. Hay, 'A Scottish Altarpiece in Copenhagen', *Innes Review*, vii (1956), 5–10.

NINNOC (Ninnocha, Gwengustle), one of the women of the tribe of *Brychan, who migrated to Brittany and was a nun, perhaps abbess there. Here memory is kept alive by various images of her and by her feast on 4 June. There is also a worthless legendary Life.

Baring-Gould and Fisher, iv. 16–19.

NON (Nonna, Nonnita) (5th century), mother of *David of Wales. Almost all that is known of her comes from Rhygyfarch's Life of David. According to this source (11th century), she was a nun at Ty Gwyn, near Whitesand Bay (Dyfed), who was seduced by a prince called Sant: David was their son. Others reject this story in favour of Non being the daughter of a Pembrokeshire chieftain, who was married to Sant. However this may have been, it seems that Non settled first in Cornwall at Altarnon, where there is a church and well in her honour, and died in Brittany, where her fine tomb survives at Dirinon (Finistère). She may have become a nun in her widowhood rather than before David's birth. In the Middle Ages Altarnon claimed her relics; a medieval chapel and well of hers also survive near St. David's. There are also dedications at Pelynt (Cornwall) and at Bradstone (Devon), besides several in Wales. Feast: 3 March, but at Altarnon, 25 June (3 July at Launceston, according to William Worcestre).

A. W. Wade-Evans, *Vitae Sanctorum Britanniae et Genealogiae* (1944), pp. 150–70; G. H. Doble, *St. Nonna* (1928); for the Breton play 'Buhez Santes Nonn' see *Revue Celtique*, viii (1887).

NORBERT (*c.*1080–1134), archbishop of Magdeburg and founder of the Premonstratensian or white canons. Born at Xanten of a noble family related to the Emperor, Norbert led a worldly life, but became a subdeacon and canon at Xanten. This did not immediately lead to a conversion; for some years he led the life usual for one in his station, in comparative opulence and ease. His biographers attribute his conversion to an escape from sudden death in a thunderstorm in 1115. He took priest's orders, exchanged wealth for poverty by resigning his canonry, selling his estates, and giving away the proceeds, went to see Pope Gelasius II at Saint-Gilles, confessed his misdeeds, and undertook to perform penance for them. The pope authorized him instead to preach the gospel wherever he chose, so he became an itinerant preacher in northern France and quickly acquired a reputation for eloquence and miracles.

Earlier he had failed in his attempts to reform the canons of Xanten; in 1119 the bishop of Laon invited him to reform his canons of St. Martin. Again the canons refused to accept him, so he made a fresh start with thirteen disciples in the valley of Prémontré. They soon increased to forty in number in spite of the poor location; they made their professions according to the rule of St. Augustine in 1121, choosing a very austere regime, and they became known not so much as a 'new order' as a reforming movement among the canons regular. In their acceptance of preaching and pastoral work they presented a more active form of life than the monks, but their austerity owed much to the example of the Cistercians and *Bernard, with whom Norbert came to be closely associated. The Premonstratensians received formal approval from the papacy in 1126, but in the same year Norbert was appointed archbishop of Magdeburg. Already his canons had been a considerable influence in the reform of the conventual clergy of both France and Germany: this appointment gave Norbert even more influence in the cause of reform in the Church at large.

One abuse against which he fought long and hard was the alienation of church property; he took energetic action against lay intruders, as he regarded them as little better than robbers. Another cause he vigorously supported was that of the celibacy of the clergy. In doing so, he inevitably made enemies. These even attempted to assassinate him. The emperor's favour, however, led the people of Magdeburg to ask for Norbert's return.

In the schism which followed Honorius II's death, Bernard, Norbert, and Hugh of Grenoble effectively secured the recognition of Innocent II. Although exiled from Rome, he held a council at Reims; after this Norbert championed his cause in Germany. One important effect of this was that the emperor Lothair marched to Italy against Anacletus II. He was accompanied by Norbert, who attempted to win over the anti-pope by persuasion.

Norbert returned to Magdeburg in 1134, now a sick man; he died on 6 June and was buried there in the church of his canons. In 1582 he was formally canonized; in 1627 his relics were translated to Strahov, near Prague. Feast: 6 June.

AA.SS. Iun. I (1695), 819–58; Lives also in *M.G.H. Scriptores*, xii. 663–706 and *P.L.*, clxx. 1253–1344; C. L. Smetana, *The Life of St. Norbert by John Capgrave* (1977); G. Madelaine, *Histoire de S. Norbert* (3rd edn. 1928); E. Maire, *Saint Norbert* (1932); P. Lefevre, 'L'épisode de la conversion de S. Norbert et la tradition hagiographique de la *Vita Norberti*', *R.H.E.*, lvi (1961), 813–26.

NOTHELM (d. 739), archbishop of Canterbury. A priest of the diocese of London, Nothelm was a correspondent of both *Bede and *Boniface. His researches in the papal chancery and in the Canterbury archives were warmly acknowledged in the preface to Bede's *Ecclesiastical History*. He also sent thirty questions to Bede about the Books of Kings; these were the occasion of Bede's treatise. To Boniface he sent a copy of *Gregory's replies to *Augustine of Canterbury. He became archbishop in 735; but little is known of his episcopate. He received the pallium from Pope Gregory III in 736, consecrated at least three bishops, and held a synod, which agreed to the division of the Mercian diocese.

Nothelm was buried in the *porticus* of St. Gregory in the church of St. Augustine, Canterbury; his cult seems to have been confined to Canterbury. In 1091 his body was translated to the new apse with those of other archbishops, grouped round the body of Augustine.

In recent years some scholars have asserted that Gregory's replies to Augustine are forgeries and that Nothelm was responsible for them. Neither accusation has been proved. Unless and until this happens, the confidence of Bede and Boniface with the cult at Canterbury seems sufficient to maintain the traditional, favourable opinion of Nothelm's character. Feast: 17 October.

Bede, *H.E.*, preface (with notes by C. Plummer), ii. pp. 2–3, 13–14, 45–7; Boniface, *Epistolae* (ed. M. Tangl, *M.G.H.*, 1916), p. 158; S. Brechter, *Die Quellen zur Angelsachsenmission Gregors des Grossen* (1941); M. Deanesly and P. Grosjean, 'The Canterbury Edition of the Answers of Pope Gregory I to St. Augustine', *J.E.H.*, x (1959), 1–49; P. Meyvaert, 'Les responsiones de S. Grégoire le Grand à S. Augustin de Cantorbéry', *R.H.E.*, liv (1959), 879–94.

NYNIA, see NINIAN.

O

ODA (Odo) (d. 958), archbishop of Canterbury. Born in East Anglia of Danish parents, he became a Christian in early life, then a priest. He was appointed bishop of Ramsbury (Wilts.) *c.*925. He became a counsellor of King Athelstan (924–39), who sent him in 936 to France to negotiate the restoration of Louis, then exiled in England, who was the son of the Emperor Charles the Simple. Oda was present at the battle of Brunanburgh in 937, when Athelstan decisively defeated a combined army of Northumbrians, Vikings from Ireland, and Scots, thereby establishing the supremacy of Wessex kings over northern England.

In 942 Oda was appointed archbishop of Canterbury. About this time he had taken the monastic habit at Fleury, through sympathetic identification for the monastic order rather than an intention of living the normal cloistered life of a monk. He encouraged the monastic revival in England by supporting *Dunstan, who reformed Glastonbury in 940, and helping his own nephew, *Oswald of Worcester, to become a monk at Fleury. By now Oda was a principal adviser to the kings Edmund and Edred.

In his own lifetime he was called 'Oda the Good' for his devoted pastoral activities. These included the restoration of churches, the raising of moral standards among the clergy, and the patronage of monks and scholars such as *Abbo of Fleury and Frithegod, to whose verse Life of *Wilfrid Oda contributed an elaborate preface. He also arranged the translation of relics of saints, such as *Ouen and Wilfrid, to Canterbury. In all these ways he was a precursor and model of Dunstan (d. 988), who indeed never passed Oda's tomb without kneeling.

Later legends about Oda attribute to him the miraculous repair of Athelstan's sword at Brunanburgh and a eucharistic miracle whereby the host dripped with blood to strengthen the faith of bystanders. Feast: 2 June (at Canterbury); later calendars give 29 May or 4 July.

Eadmer, 'Vita S. Odonis' in H. Wharton, *Anglia Sacra* (1691), ii. 78–87 and in *P.L.*, cxxxiii. 933 ff., abridged in *N.L.A.*, ii. 224–8; see also the Life of Oswald in J. Raine, *Historians of the Church of York* (*R.S.*, 1879), i. 399–475; *G.P.*, pp. 20–6; J. A. Robinson, *St. Oswald and the Church of Worcester* (1919); R. W. Southern, *St. Anselm and his Biographer* (1963), pp. 279–81.

ODGER (8th century), deacon and monk. He was the companion of the Northumbrian saints *Wiro and *Plechelm both on a pilgrimage to Rome and in their missionary work in Holland. Pepin of Herstal gave them land at Odilienberg, where they built a church and a small monastery, and from which they evangelized the lower Meuse valley. They also built a church at Roermond, where Wiro and Plechelm's bodies were translated, but Odger's relics remained where they were buried at Odilienberg. Feast: 8 May.

B.T.A., ii. 252–3; Stanton, pp. 443–4.

ODILO (*c.*962–1049), Benedictine monk and abbot of Cluny. Born of an aristocratic family, he became a Cluniac monk as a young man, coadjutor to abbot Maieul in 991 and abbot of Cluny in 994. For the previous thirty years it had been ruled by *Maieul, for the next fifty-five Odilo was its head; it is arguable that under him it became the most important abbey in western Europe. Called by Fulbert of Chartres the 'archangel of monks', Odilo united in his character gentleness with firmness, organizing power with peace-making ability. In Burgundy, Provence, Auvergne, and Poitou monasteries joined the Cluniac reform, whether directly (about thirty during his abbacy) or indirectly by association, especially in Italy and Spain. Odilo was also a great builder, and his example at Cluny was imitated by many reformed monasteries. Above all he sought to promote the spirit of true monasticism and to remove abuses: in this task, the Rule of St. Benedict, as understood by Black Monk tradition, was all-important. During his long reign he constantly strove to promote the close union of Cluny and the Holy See. The exemption granted from the claims of the bishop of Macon was effectively maintained when the papacy was strong, but when it was weak Odilo had to cede some ground to the bishop.

He became also an important figure in the political world. Not only was he on cordial terms with emperors such as Henry III (who visited Cluny during Odilo's rule), but he also effectively promoted the *pactum Dei* or protection of ecclesiastical persons and property against attack in official or unofficial warfare, and also the *Treuga Dei*. This sought to limit the actual fighting through both sides agreeing to a cessation of hostilities from Fridays to Mondays as well as during Advent and Lent. Although the idea met with much opposition, it was ultimately received in many French provinces.

The mystery of the Incarnation was the favourite subject of his sermons and poems. The place of *Mary in this mystery was also worked out by Odilo, to whose writings the Mariology of St. *Bernard owed much. He also made at least one important liturgical innovation: the institution of *All Souls day to be observed by his monasteries primarily for dead monks and by extension later for all the dead. He was also famous for his generosity to the poor in times of famine and scarcity from 1028 to 1033, when he sold or melted down much of the treasure of Cluny to relieve them. Perhaps his most famous saying was that he would prefer to be damned for being too merciful than for being too severe. He died at the age of eighty-seven at Souvigny; he was canonized in 1063. Feast: 1 (2) January or 29 April.

AA.SS. Ian I (1643), 65–77; J. Mabillon, *AA.SS. O.S.B.*, vi (part 1), 631–701; *P.L.*, cxlii. 831–1038; J. Hourlier, *Saint Odilon, abbé de Cluny* (1964); N. Hunt, *Cluny under St. Hugh* (1967); J. Leclerq, 'Pour une histoire de la vie à Cluny', *R.H.E.*, lvii (1962), 385–408, 783–812; H. E. J. Cowdrey, *The Cluniacs and the Gregorian Reform* (1970).

ODO, see ODA.

ODO OF CLUNY (879–942), Benedictine monk and abbot. Born at Tours, the son of a knight, Abbo of Maine, Odo was brought up in the household of William of Aquitaine, the future founder of Cluny. He became a canon of Tours, studied for some years at Paris, was specially interested in music and read the Rule of St. Benedict for the first time. This led to his resigning his canonry at Tours and becoming a monk at Baume under the first abbot of Cluny, St. Berno. Meanwhile Cluny, founded in 909, began its life as a reformed monastery following St. Benedict's Rule in comparative obscurity; few would have prophesied its rapid rise to become the most important abbey in Europe.

A considerable share in this development belongs to Odo. He was soon put in charge of the monastic school at Baume; when he succeeded Berno as abbot of Cluny in 927, he continued and transformed the founding abbot's achievements. One of the most important of these was the obtaining of papal and royal charters which recognized Cluny's immunity and freedom from all secular interference and domination. For the internal regime of Cluny and the dependencies which it soon attracted, Odo insisted much on silence, abstinence, and the exact observance of authentic inherited custom in the interpretation of the Rule. The fundamental points of the reform were the common life of poverty and the exact observance of chastity. These were in contrast to the practice of many clerics of the time; through them the Monastic Order helped the formation of clerical ideals which were to be realized later through the Gregorian Reform.

Odo's influence and jurisdiction extended far beyond Cluny itself. Monasteries in France like Fleury (important for England) and Bourg-Dieu were ruled directly by him, while his reforms were promulgated in many other monasteries in south-east and central France under papal influence. At Rome itself Odo reformed St. Paul's-outside-the-walls and deeply influenced both Monte Cassino and Subiaco. His withdrawal from the world led to his being invited to act as an impartial mediator in political matters, particularly between Hugh 'king of Italy' and the Patrician Alberic of Rome. By the end of his life Odo had become extremely influential and much respected. Stories were told of his generosity to the poor and of his compassion to prisoners. He died at the monastery of St. Julian at Tours, a few days after taking part in the feast of his patron, *Martin of Tours, on 11 November. His own death and feast were on 18 (19) November.

J. Mabillon, *AA.SS. O.S.B.*, v, 150–99. Life by John of Cluny with works ascribed to Odo in *P.L.*, cxxxiii. 105–845; G. Sitwell, *St. Odo of Cluny* (1958), which includes tr. of John's Life and of the Life by Odo of Gerald of Aurillac, see also *À Cluny* (1950); N. Hunt, *Cluny under St. Hugh* (1967); H. E. J. Cowdrey, *The Cluniacs and the Gregorian Reform* (1970); J. Leclercq, 'Pour une histoire de la vie à Cluny', *R.H.E.*, lvii (1962), 385–408 and 783–812.

ODRAN (Otteran) **OF IONA** (d. *c.*563). British by birth, Odran was one of *Columba's first companions on Iona, who died not long after his arrival. Columba saw in a vision Odran's soul ascending to heaven, after being fought over by angels and devils. The cemetery at Iona was called *Reilig Orain* in his memory.

Irish tradition makes him abbot of Meath and founder of Latteragh (Co. Tipperary). It is probable, but not certain, that the two traditions refer to the same person. Feast: 27 October.

A. O. and M. O. Anderson, *Adomnan's Life of Columba* (1961), p. 477; *K.S.S.*, p. 426; B.T.A., iv. 209.

ODULF (d. 855), monk and missionary in Frisia. Born at Oorschot (North Brabant) and outstanding in his youth both for intelligence and piety, he became a priest. After a few years he was sent by St. Frederick of Utrecht to minister to the partially converted Frisians. He made his base at Stavoren, where he built both church and monastery; he worked for many years in the same area, retired to Utrecht in old age, and died there on 12 June. His body was enshrined, his cult grew, and a number of churches were dedicated to him in Holland and Belgium. His connection with England came by the theft of his relics in the early 11th century by Viking pirates who brought them to London. Aelfward, bishop of London, bought them for the large sum of 100 marks and gave them to Evesham abbey, over which he still ruled. Their presence in the abbey church gave it lustre and prestige. But later a Norman abbot of Evesham, Walter, tried to remove them to Winchcombe. The Evesham chronicler related that the shrine became so heavy for the bearers that they were quite unable to continue, but when they turned back to Evesham, it seemed as light as a feather. This, like the blindness suffered earlier by Queen Edith, who wished to take some of his relics for her private collection, was interpreted as meaning that Odulf disapproved of such removals and wanted to be left undisturbed in his adopted home of Evesham. But the fact that the Evesham relics were stolen from Stavoren, while the Utrecht tradition was that Odulf was buried at Utrecht itself without any translation to Stavoren, makes the Evesham claim very dubious. This did not prevent Odulf's feast being celebrated on 12 June, with one translation feast on 10 October and yet another on 24 November.

AA.SS. Iun. II (1701), 591–5; *N.L.A.*, ii. 229–30; W. D. Macray, *Chronicon de Evesham* (*R.S.*, 1863), pp. 313–20; J. C. Jennings, 'The Writings of Prior Dominic of Evesham', *E.H.R.*, lxxvii (1962), 298–304; B.T.A., ii. 532–3.

OENGUS THE CULDEE (d. *c.*824), author of the earliest Irish martyrology, called the Felire. Born of a kingly Ulster family and educated at the monastery of Clonenagh (Co. Laois), he lived as a hermit at Disertbeagh and later at Dysert Enos, where he practised the usual Irish austerities of frequent genuflections, daily recitation of the psalter (a third of it while immersed in cold water), and fasting. Later he joined the monastery of Tallacht (near Dublin), where he concealed both his identity and his scholarship and was allocated menial work. His identity was discovered through his coaching an unsuccessful student and the abbot, *Maelruain, recognized and venerated him. Here Oengus completed his martyrology and helped Maelruain compile the Tallacht Martyrology also. He is reputed to have been chosen as abbot and bishop before he died. Feast: 11 March, but he is not venerated in Ireland at the present time.

W. Stokes, *Felire Oengusso Celi De: the Martyrology of Oengus the Culdee* (*H.B.S.*, 1905); *AA.SS.* Mar. II (1668), 85–8; J. O'Hanlon, 'The Life and Works of St. Aengusius Hagiographus, or St. Angus the Culdee', *I.E.R.*, v (1869), 1–29, 73–81, 97–108: P. Grosjean, 'Le Martyrologe de Tallacht', *Anal. Boll.*, li (1933), 117–30.

OENGUS MAC NISSE, see MACANISIUS.

OFFA OF ESSEX (d. *c.*709), king. Son of Sighere, king of the East Saxons, and of *Osith, Offa became king *c.*707, and was, according to *Bede, a lovable, handsome, and popular prince. But in 709 he left 'his wife, his lands, his kinsmen and his fatherland for Christ', abdicated, went to Rome where he was tonsured, and died a monk soon afterwards. His betrothal to Cyneswith, daughter of Penda of Mercia, claimed by Florence of Worcester and William of Malmesbury, is chronologically impossible. It must also be remembered that at this period the abdication and tonsuring of kings was sometimes the result of palace revolutions both in Gaul and in Britain. No record of an official cult of Offa has survived; Stanton assigns his feast to 15 December.

Bede, *H.E.*, v. 19; *G.R.*, i. 99; *G.P.*, p. 317; Florence of Worcester, i. 46–7. Stanton, pp. 600–1.

OGILVIE, John (1580–1615), Jesuit priest and martyr. Born at Drum-na-Keith (Banffshire), he was brought up as a Calvinist. Sent to be educated in France, he decided to join the R.C. Church, into which he was received at Louvain in 1596. He then studied at Regensburg and joined the Society of Jesus at Brno in 1599. For ten years he worked in Austria, mainly at Graz and Vienna. He was then assigned to the French province and was ordained at Paris in 1610. From this time he desired to return to Scotland, but was allowed to do so only in 1613.

Owing to the penal laws he travelled as a horse-dealer or as a soldier. He found that most of the Scottish Catholic noblemen had conformed, at least in appearance, and were unwilling to help a proscribed priest. Unable to make much impression, he went to London to contact one of the king's ministers and then to Paris for consultation. He was told sharply to return to Scotland, which he did.

In Edinburgh he stayed at the house of William Sinclair, an advocate. He became his son's tutor and ministered to a congregation besides visiting Catholics in prison. He also ministered in Glasgow and Renfrewshire, reconciling, counselling, and preaching. He was arrested in Glasgow, was interrogated by the archbishop, but refused to incriminate himself. He explicitly recognized James as king of Scotland and detested the attempt to kill him in the Gunpowder Plot. He was then tortured by deprivation of food and sleep, by having his hair torn out, and by being repeatedly thrown on to the floor. The purpose of these tortures, repeated until the doctors said their continuation would be fatal, was to obtain the names of his co-religionists.

He was tried in Edinburgh for high treason and a questionnaire was drawn up for him, supposedly by James I himself. To these five questions on Church and State he answered according to his conscience, but even so, every effort was made to induce him to conform. Meanwhile, he had managed to write an account of his arrest and treatment in prison, which was smuggled out by visitors.

At his trial he declared his readiness to shed his blood in defence of the king's temporal power, but could not obey in matters of spiritual jurisdiction unjustly seized. He was condemned for high treason, but was offered both his freedom and a rich benefice if he would abjure his religion. This he refused and was hanged for defending the spiritual supremacy of the pope. He was canonized in 1976. Feast: 10 March.

N.C.E., s.v.; B.T.A., i. 552–6; W. E. Brown, *John Ogilvie* (1925).

OLAF (Olave, Ola, Tola) (995–1030), king of Norway 1016–29, and its patron saint. He was the son of a Norwegian lord named Harold Grenske; after a career of war and piracy in the Baltic and Normandy, where he became a Christian, he fought for Ethelred II in England against the Danes in 1013. A few years later he returned to Norway; partly through his military prowess, aided by his eloquence, partly through the flight of his rivals, he seized power and ruled as king. Unexpectedly he gave his subjects peace and security, remaking old laws and insisting on their just execution unaffected by bribes or threats. His principal work for Norway was to make her Christian, for which end, like several other rulers, he used force as well as persuasion. This harshness contributed to a rebellion against him, fostered by Cnut, king of England and Denmark. Olaf was exiled in 1029; the following year he tried to regain his throne with Swedish help, but was defeated and killed at the battle of Stiklestad, 29 July 1030.

From his grave springs of water with healing properties flowed and miracles were reported. Grimkell, the English bishop of Nidaros (Trondheim), one of the missionaries who had helped Olaf establish the Church built a chapel on the site of his grave and declared him a saint. The next year Olaf's body, reputedly incorrupt, was enshrined. His cult was aided by the unpopular rule of Swein, Cnut's son; Cnut's death in 1035 resulted in the flight of many Danes from Norway and the accession of Olaf's son Magnus. Thereafter the cult spread rapidly: Adam of Bremen (*c.*1070) wrote of his feast being celebrated by all the Scandinavian nations.

The cult was strong in England too, especially in the Viking areas. There are over forty ancient church dedications in Britain mainly in Yorkshire, Lincolnshire, East Anglia, the Isle of Man, the Hebrides, Orkney, and Shetland. Others are in mercantile centres such as London, Chester, Waterford, and Dublin. His feast occurs in calendars of London, Norwich, Exeter, Winchester, and York; and in monastic ones of Ramsey, Sherborne, Abbotsbury, Launceston, and Syon. Possibly founders or benefactors of Viking origin may account for some of these.

English iconography of Olaf includes representations on the seals of Grimsby Abbey and Herringfleet Priory (Suffolk), on the 15th-century screen at Barton Turf (Norfolk), on an ivory crozier in the Victoria and Albert Museum, in glass at York Minster. He usually carries emblems of a battle-axe and loaves of stone. The most complete example, with six medallions from Olaf's life, occurs in the *Beatus* initial of the 13th-century Carrow Psalter, written in East Anglia and now in the Walters Art Gallery, Baltimore.

The name Olaf was used in England before the Conquest as a Christian name. In Gaelic it became Amlaibh (Aulag), whence the Hebridean surname Macaulay. In England the name became corrupted by the addition of initial 't' from the final letter of 'saint'. As such it survives, e.g. in Tooley Street, Southwark, in whose neighbourhood schools, libraries, and a dock are named after this saint.

Olaf is a good example of a patriot who met a violent death being accorded the title of martyr, even in the Roman Martyrology. As in the case of *Oswald, dynastic and patriotic considerations greatly helped his cult. Olaf's shrine in Trondheim cathedral remained until the Reformation, when his body was reburied. Feast: 29 July; Grimkell's translation took place on 3 August 1031.

AA.SS. Iul. VII (1731), 87–120; Life by Richard of Fountains in *Anecdota Oxoniensia* (1881); Saga by Snorri Sturlason in *Saga Olafs konungs ens helga* (ed. P. A. Munch and C. R. Unger, 1853) and by O. A. Johnsen and J. Helgason (1941): Eng. tr. by E. Monsen and A. H. Smith (1932); B. Dickins, 'The Cult of St. Olave in the British Isles', *Saga-Book of the Viking Society*, xlii (1945), 53–80; F. M. Stenton, *Anglo-Saxon England*, pp. 396–400; G. Turville-Petre, *Origins of Icelandic Literature* (1953), pp. 175–90; Gwyn Jones, *A History of the Vikings* (1968), pp. 375–85.

OLGA (*c.*879–969), grand-duchess and widow. Most of her long life was spent in ruling her people: after the assassination of her husband, Prince Igor of Kiev, in 945, she ruthlessly punished his murderers and their followers and ruled the country in his stead. In about 957 she became a convinced Christian and made strong but largely unsuccessful attempts to introduce Christianity among her people: she also failed to convert her son Syvatoslav. However, she continued her efforts and requested missionaries from the emperor Otto I. Her grandson *Vladimir brought her aspirations to fulfilment: she is usually associated with his achievements as a precursor. The Russian council of 1574 confirmed a popular cult: her feast is observed by Russian and Ukrainian churches on 11 July.

Bibl. SS., ix. 1149–52.

OLIVER PLUNKET, see PLUNKET.

OMER (Audomarus) (d. *c.*699), bishop of Therouanne. Born near Coutances, he became a monk at Luxeuil. In *c.*637 he was appointed by King Dagobert as a missionary bishop in the Pas-de-Calais. He founded the monastery of Sithiu (now Saint-Omer) and preached the gospel eloquently and with insistence on disinterested service and reconciliation. He died and was buried in his monastery. Feast: 9 September.

AA.SS. Sept. III (1868), 384–417; B.T.A., iii. 516–17.

OSANNA (date unknown). According to Gerald of Wales (d. *c.*1220) she was a woman saint buried at Howden (Humberside) and venerated there. He calls her the sister of King Osred, but modern historians seem to know nothing of any sister of either Osred I (d. 716) or Osred II (d. 792). There is no known cult. Gerald asserts that a priest's mistress who sat on Osanna's tomb was immovably fixed until she had been severely punished.

Giraldus Cambrensis, *Itinerary in Wales*, bk. i, ch. ii; *AA.SS.* Iun. I (1695), p. 551.

OSBURGA (d. *c.*1018), abbess of Coventry. This nunnery, founded by Cnut before he was recognized as king of England (1016–35), was ruled by Osburga from its inception. Nothing is known of her life. Her shrine became the place of many miracles, so the clergy and people of Coventry in 1410 asked for a feast in her honour to be established. This was granted by a synod to the archdeaconry of Coventry. Feast: 30 March.

B.T.A., i. 705; Stanton, p. 137.

OSITH (Osgyth, Osyth) (d. *c.*700) f Chich (Essex), was an obscure Anglo-Saxon princess. Her tribe was that of the Hwiccas; she was married to Sighere, king of the East Saxons (*c.*664–83), at the instigation of his overlord Wulfhere, king of Mercia (656–75). One purpose of the marriage may have been to consolidate Christianity in Essex, whose state was precarious owing to Sighere's apostasy; *Bede has nothing to say of Osith, but does recount the reconversion of Sighere by bishop Jaruman. The son of Sighere and Osith, called *Offa, became king of the East Saxons but abdicated in 709. Osith meanwhile had founded a convent at Chich, died there, and was venerated as a saint.

Bede's silence and the lack of corroborative evidence to support these details from her late Legend make the story suspect. Its more picturesque details include the appearance of a large and aggressive white stag whenever Sighere tried to consummate the marriage (ignoring the fact that they had a son), Osith's flight to some East Anglian bishops who accepted her vow of chastity and persuaded her husband to give her land for her nunnery, her violent death at Chich at the hands of pirates because she refused to commit idolatry, and her carrying her severed head after death to a church three miles away, where she was buried.

Her body, we are told, was translated to Aylesbury (Bucks.) during the Danish invasions, but if this ever happened, it was returned to Chich by *c.*1000, when the treatise 'On the Resting-Places of the Saints' (*R.P.S.*) mentions her shrine. The bishops of London favoured the cult: Maurice (1085–1107) translated her body to a new shrine behind the high altar of the church at Chich, while his successor, Richard de Belmeis (1108–27), founded the monastery of Austin canons there, both to restore the shrine and to give thanks for his recovery from a stroke, supposedly caused by Osith's vengeful anger for his alienating her lands to provide a pleasure park.

Osith was sometimes erroneously identified with *Zita; she was also invoked, like *Agatha, against fire; arm relics were claimed by St. Paul's, London, and by Canterbury Cathedral. Her principal feast was on 7 October, with translation feasts(?) on 27 April, 3 June, and 2 October. Her cult flourished at Hereford, Worcester, and Evesham because of her supposed origin among the Hwiccas.

Beside her principal shrine at Chich, there was one at Aylesbury (Bucks.), which attracted devotees until 1502, when concerted action by the bishops of Lincoln and London put an end to this cult. It seems likely if not certain that in reality there were two Osiths, of Chich and of Aylesbury, represented by the feasts of 7 October and 3 June, in the liturgical traditions of London and Hereford. These were conflated by mistaken hagiographers into a single person. *C.S.P.* also is a witness of medieval confusion about this saint: it calls her a native of Aylesbury who was 'beheaded in the Danish persecution and so was called the daughter of Paul'. Four ancient churches were dedicated to Osith.

AA.SS. Oct. III (1770), 942–3; *N.L.A.*, ii. 232–6; A. T. Baker, 'An Anglo-French Life of St. Osith', *Mod. Languages Review*, vi (1911), 476–502; H. P. R. Finberg, *Early Charters of the West Midlands* (1961), pp. 182–3; D. Bethell, 'The Lives of St. Osyth of Essex and St. Osyth of Aylesbury', *Anal. Boll.* lxxxviii (1970), 75–127; C. Hohler, 'St. Osyth and Aylesbury', *Records of Bucks.*, xviii (1966), 61–72; *R.P.S.* and *C.S.P.*

OSMAIL, see ISMAEL.

OSMANNA (no date), virgin. Of supposed Irish royal origin and pagan upbringing, she left her country rather than marry a man of her parent's choice. She then became a solitary in a wood near the river Loire with a maid called Aclitenis. She was discovered through a wild boar taking refuge with her during a hunt. The bishop arrived, persuaded her to receive Christian instruction and baptism, and be consecrated as a virgin. A rustic was deputed to make her a garden to provide subsistence; but he was led astray by a devil, who entered a pact with him to tempt Osmanna into sin. But by her prayer she healed the blindness with which he had been stricken. She also cured the wife and daughter of the king of Spain who happened to be in the neighbourhood. Osmanna died on 9 September, her feast. This tale finds a place in *N.L.A.* (and so in this volume), presumably because of the saint's Irish origin. There seems no sure guarantee of Osmanna's historical existence.

AA.SS. Sept. III (1750), 422 ff.; *N.L.A.*, ii. 237–9.

OSMUND (Osmer) (d. 1099), bishop of Salisbury. Norman by birth, Osmund was the son of Henry, count of Séez; he followed William the Conqueror into England. Here he became royal chaplain, until he was promoted to be chancellor in 1072. In this office he wrote royal letters and charters, besides obtaining useful experience of administration.

In 1078 he succeeded Herman as bishop of Salisbury. This see had been formed by uniting those of Sherborne and Ramsbury and making the new centre at Old Sarum, where the cathedral was built in the same enclosure as the royal castle. Osmund completed and consecrated this cathedral, and formed a chapter with its own constitution, which became a model for other English cathedrals later. Formerly he was thought to have initiated the Sarum Rite, a local variant of the Roman rite which became very widespread in medieval England; it reached its definitive form under Richard le Poore, bishop of Salisbury 1198–1228.

Osmund loved books as well as administration. He liked to copy them himself and bind them with his own hands. Other qualities, according to William of Malmesbury, were purity and learning, strictness both with himself and others, and a commendable lack of avarice and ambition. William was also grateful for Osmund's approval of the cult of *Aldhelm, the Anglo-Saxon abbot of Malmesbury and bishop of Sherborne, whose translation was accomplished by Osmund in 1078. This event marked the end of the period in which, like other Anglo-Saxon saints, Aldhelm had been under attack by the Normans and by Lanfranc, who had questioned his sanctity. Osmund was even credited with a Life of Aldhelm, which has not, however, survived.

His promotion to the episcopate did not bring to an end his share in royal administration. He certainly took part in the preparation of the Domesday Book, but his precise share is difficult to identify. Some attribute to him the important survey of Grantham, which included most of the Danelaw together with Lancashire and Westmorland. He was certainly present at the council of Sarum, when the results of the Domesday inquiry was presented to William in April 1086.

Towards the end of his life he took part in summoning William of St. Calais, bishop of Durham, to the king (1088) and a few years later was present at the council of Rockingham (1095), on the king's side. For this, however, he asked and obtained absolution from *Anselm, who later consulted him in 1097.

Osmund died on 4 December 1099 and was buried in his cathedral at Old Sarum. His chasuble and staff were among the treasures there in 1222; but in 1226 his body and its tomb were translated to the new cathedral of Salisbury. In 1228 Gregory IX authorized preliminary inquiries into his life and miracles with a view to canonization. But the cause hung fire, and was destined to be one of the longest and most expensive of medieval England. Further attempts to obtain the canonization were made in 1387 and 1406. In 1412 Robert Hallam, bishop of Salisbury, took up the cause with his usual energy and in 1416 his canons allocated a tenth of their income for seven years for this purpose. Further petitions were made, supported by Henry V and Henry VI; further commissions investigated more miracles, and the canonization was finally pronounced by Callistus III in 1456. Surviving accounts and receipts reveal that it cost the large sum of £731 13*s.* 0*d.*

A new shrine was set up in the Lady Chapel of Salisbury cathedral in 1457, parts of which, as well as the original tomb, still survive. Osmund's miracles gave rise to his being invoked against toothache, rupture, paralysis, and madness. Three ancient, and a few modern, churches are dedicated to him. Feast: 4 December; translation, 16 July.

G.P., pp. 183–4, 424–8; *N.L.A.*, ii. 239–52: some charters of his are in the *Register of St. Osmund* (ed. W. H. R. Jones, *R.S.*, 1883–4); A. R. Malden, *The Canonization of St. Osmund* (1901); W. J. Torrance, *St. Osmund of Salisbury* (1920); F. J. E. Raby, 'The tomb of St. Osmund at Salisbury', *Archaeol. Jnl.*, civ (1947), 146–7; *D.N.B.*, s.v.

OSTRYTHE (d. 697), queen of Mercia. Daughter of Oswiu, king of Northumbria

(641–70), Ostrythe married Ethelred, king of Mercia *c.*679. Together they founded and enriched the monastery of Bardney (Lincs.), where Ostrythe received the relics of her uncle *Oswald in spite of the Mercian monks' initial reluctance to venerate a Northumbrian saint. Ostrythe was murdered, presumably for political reasons; but her cult continued round her shrine at Bardney, as is testified by the 'Resting-Places of the Saints', a late Saxon document of *c.*1000. The day of her feast is unknown.

Bede, *H.E.*, iii. 11 (with Plummer's notes); *R.P.S.*

OSWALD (1) (d. 642), king of Northumbria and martyr. The son of Ethelfrith, king of Northumbria, Oswald fled to Scotland when Edwin seized the kingdom in 616, and became a Christian at Iona. On Edwin's death in 633 he and his family, like other royal exiles, returned to Northumbria. Osric and Eanfrid, his brother, were soon killed by the British king, Cadwalla, who ruled Northumbria as a tyrant for a year before Oswald, with a much smaller army, defeated and killed him at Hevenfelt, near Hexham. Before the battle Oswald had set up a wooden cross and assembled his army to pray for victory around it. Not more than a small proportion could have been Christian, but soon after the battle he sent for a bishop from Iona to preach the Gospel in Northumbria. First a severe bishop was sent, who met with no success among people whom he considered barbarous and obstinate. He was soon replaced by the kindly *Aidan, whose sermons Oswald himself interpreted and to whom he gave the island of Lindisfarne for a monastery and episcopal seat, close to the royal residence of Bamburgh. Aidan met with great success; numerous Northumbrians became Christians and Christianity was established.

Oswald united both parts of Northumbria (Bernicia and Deira) under his rule; the other Anglo-Saxon kings acknowledged his overlordship: he married Cyneburga, daughter of Cynegils, king of Wessex, to whom he stood as godfather at his baptism. But his reign did not last long; after only eight years he was killed by the pagan king Penda of Mercia in the battle of Maserfield (Salop) at the age of only thirty-eight, praying with his last breath for the souls of his bodyguard who died with him. His body was sacrificially mutilated to Woden by order of Penda, the head, arms, and hands being hung up on stakes. The members were recovered and venerated in different places, which led to the diffusion of his cult.

The head was buried at Lindisfarne; from 875 it shared the wanderings of St. *Cuthbert's body and was found when the tomb was opened at Durham in 1827. But Epternach also claimed to possess his head (*Willibrord took *some* relics of Oswald to Frisia): a splendid octagonal German casket of *c.*1180 survives at Hildesheim cathedral treasury, which encloses a 'head of St. Oswald': other kings represented on it include *Edward and Cnut.

The arms were deposited at Bamburgh: one was later stolen by a monk of Peterborough and subsequently transferred to Ely. Durham and Gloucester both claimed another arm. Swartreband, an old monk of Durham in the 12th century, told Symeon he had often seen the hand of Oswald which Aidan had prophesied would remain incorrupt because of the generous charity it wrought, but he did not say where.

The body was buried at Oswestry, then translated to Bardney, by Ostryd, Oswald's niece and queen of Mercia, and in 909 to Gloucester by Ethelfleda, Lady of the Mercians. The monastery of St. *Winnoc's at Bergues (Flanders) also claimed to have been given the whole body by Harold Harefoot: this was burnt by Protestants in 1558. Other churches which claimed some of his relics were Trèves, Tergensee, Prufening, Ramshoven, Wettingen, Sauris, and Tai. Willibrord told *Wilfrid and *Acca about the miracles accomplished by his relics in Ireland and Frisia. *Bede recounted these and others. The term 'relics' included fragments of his wooden cross and earth taken from his grave.

Seventy churches were dedicated to him

in England, including Hexham, Carlisle, Oswestry, Bardney, Paddlesworth (Kent), and Winwick (Lancs.): important places on the Continent with chapel or altar dedications include Bamberg, Prague, and St. Emmeran, Ratisbon.

His feast on 5 August (or 8th or 9th) was kept from the late seventh century. It is in the Calendar of St. Willibrord and in many monastic calendars and martyrologies. His cult eventually extended to Scotland, Ireland, Portugal, Bohemia, Holland, Germany, Austria, and Switzerland. He was remembered as one of England's national heroes; his bravery and military skill, his generosity and piety, together with a sacrificial death in battle for country and faith, combined Anglo-Saxon hero and Christian saint. It was commonly said that whoever fasted on his vigil (4 August) would have foreknowledge of his death. A translation feast was kept on 8 October at Evesham and Gloucester.

Bede, *H.E.*, iii. 1–6, 9–13; iv. 14; Alcuin, *Carmen*, vv. 275 ff. Later Lives by Drogo in *AA.SS.* Aug. II (1735), 94–103 and by Reginald of Durham in *Symeonis Dunelmensis Opera* (ed. T. Arnold, *R.S.*, 1882), i. 326–85. Abridgement in *N.L.A.*, ii. 261–7; Icelandic saga of the 15th century in *Annaler for Nordisk Oldkyndighed* (1854). Modern Studies by E. W. Grierson, *The Story of the Northumbrian Saints* (1913), pp. 3–41; B. Colgrave, 'The Times of St. Cuthbert' in C. F. Battiscombe (ed.), *The Relics of St. Cuthbert* (1956), pp. 116–18; E. P. Baker, 'St. Oswald and his church at Zug', *Archaeologia*, xciii (1949), 103–23 and 'The Cult of St. Oswald in North Italy', ibid., xciv (1951), 167–94; W. Bonser, 'The Magic of St. Oswald', *Antiquity*, ix (1935), 418–23; R. Folz, 'Saint Oswald roi de Northumbrie', *Anal. Boll.*, xcviii (1980), 49–74.

OSWALD (2) (d. 992), Benedictine monk and bishop of Worcester from 961, archbishop of York from 972. Of a Danish military family and related to the two archbishops, *Oda of Canterbury and Oskytel of York, Oswald was a canon of Winchester for some years before becoming a monk. He was educated at Fleury-sur-Loire (which claimed the relics of St. Benedict and was a Cluniac house with a considerable intellectual tradition) and returned to England as a priest in 958/9. King Edgar, on *Dunstan's recommendation, appointed him bishop of Worcester. He founded the monastery of Westbury-on-Trym (near Bristol) in 962, reformed his own cathedral chapter in 969 (according to Worcester tradition), supposedly acting more gently than *Ethelwold in similar circumstances at Winchester in 964. But his largest and most famous monastery was founded outside his diocese at Ramsey by Aethelwine by 971; into it were incorporated most of the Westbury monks and from it were founded the Severn valley monasteries of Evesham and Pershore (972–5). At Ramsey, where his biographer tell us that he liked best to live, he introduced the scholarly *Abbo of Fleury for some years, whose stay was beneficial for the monastic formation of the new community and left concrete results in the Life of *Edmund of Bury and in the later work of Byrhtferth, whose mathematical, scientific, and homilectic writings made him one of the most notable Anglo-Saxons of the 11th century. He may well have been also the author of the Life of Oswald. This source stresses Oswald's fine physique, magnificent singing voice, attractive and accessible character, and special love of the poor.

But other sources reveal other characteristics. Oswald's close co-operation with the king led to his acquiring for his bishopric or his monasteries very considerable quantities of land. Leases with 'feudal' implications for a number of these survive, but the supposed foundation charter of Edgar called *Altitonantis* is a later forgery. Oswald helped the king by keeping in his hands much of the local government in the areas of his territory near the Welsh border. Another sign of his close dependence on the king was his acceptance of the see of York in plurality with that of Worcester. Admittedly this had some precedents in its favour and was alleged to be necessary because of the loss of lands by York in the Danish wars, but the York territories, especially in Nottinghamshire, were still considerable. It seems more likely due to political than economic reasons as Anglo-Saxon kings were weak in the north. Oswald failed in his attempt to revive Ripon as a monastery; this meant that the monastic revival, for which he had laboured long and hard with Dunstan and Ethelwold, was largely confined to Wessex and Mercia: only long after Oswald's death did monks from his western monasteries refound monasteries north of the Humber.

In the anti-monastic reaction which followed Edgar's death in 975, a movement concerned with local power rather than with monastic life in itself, Elfhere of Mercia dispersed temporarily some of Oswald's monasteries, but Ramsey was left untouched. Oswald remained an influential diocesan bishop until his death, administering his two dioceses, building churches, acting as judge, visiting his monasteries. In 991 he visited Ramsey for the last time to reopen the church which had been damaged by the fall of the tower. Both the Mass and the banquet which followed were memorable; two days later there were mutual farewells which he realized were final. He spent the winter at Worcester, the cathedral he loved best, and began Lent with his usual ascetic practices, including washing the feet of twelve poor men each day. As he completed this task on 28 February, reciting the Gradual Psalms, he died. Oswald's memory and example lived on at Worcester after him, inspiring his successors, especially *Wulfstan, who translated his body to a new shrine *c.*1086.

Some recent historical work has questioned the traditional account of St. Oswald replacing the Worcester canons gradually by building a church of St. Mary for monks which so outshone that of the canons that it was deserted by the townsfolk, so that the canons eventually joined the monks. It has been asserted from the titles of charter-witnesses that the change was so gradual as not to be a change at all; that some of the charters concern leases of lands to men supposed to be monks; and that the witnesses sign as clerics rather than monks. While these are at present largely unsolved problems, they must be set against the formal claims, both of Oswald's biographer and of 'Florence of Worcester', that he was indeed responsible for the change to monastic status of the Worcester chapter. Perhaps more surprising is this reformer's pluralism in holding the sees of both Worcester and York and his prolonged residence as abbot-founder at Ramsey, which was outside either of his dioceses. But there can be no doubt of the impression his sanctity made on contemporaries, or of the popularity of his cult. Feast: 28 February; translation, 15 April; ordination, 1 June.

Contemporary Life in J. Raine, *Historians of the Church of York*, i (*R.S.*, 1874), 399–475; another Life by Eadmer, ibid., ii (1886), 1–59, abridged in *N.L.A.*, ii. 252–60; J. A. Robinson, *St. Oswald and the Church at Worcester* (British Academy Suppl. Papers, 1919); E. H. Pearce, *St. Oswald of Worcester and the Church of York* (1928); Sir Ivor Atkins, 'The Church of Worcester from the Eighth to the Twelfth Century', *Antiquaries Journal*, xvii (1937), 371–91; *M.O.*, pp. 31–56; E. John, 'St. Oswald and the Tenth Century Reformation', *J.E.H.*, ix (1958), 158–72; D. Parsons (ed.), *Tenth Century Studies* (1975), pp. 84–93; D. J. V. Fisher, 'The anti-monastic reaction in the reign of Edward the Martyr', *C.H.J.*, x (1952), 254–70.

OSWIN (Oswini) (d. 651), king of Deira in Northumbria 644–51 and venerated as a martyr. When Oswin's father Osric, king of Deira (i.e. roughly the territory of the former county of Yorkshire), was killed by the pagan king Cadwalla in 634, Oswin went to the kingdom of Wessex (in southern England) for safety. After the death in battle in 634 of his cousin *Oswald (1), who had united the two parts of Northumbria (Bernicia and Deira) into a single kingdom, Oswin returned to the North to be king of Deira, while his cousin Oswiu, who could not live peacefully with him, became king of Bernicia. Oswin's short reign and premature death were due to treachery and dynastic struggles; he was in fact the last king of Deira. All that we know of his life comes from *Bede. Greatly loved by all, he ruled his province most successfully. But Oswiu, wishing to regain the land and power held by Oswald, quarrelled with

Oswin and they raised armies against each other. Instead of adding one more battle to the long tale of violence in 7th-century Northumbria, Oswin, realizing that he was outnumbered, disbanded his army to avoid bloodshed, hoping to make good his claim at some future date. Accompanied by a single trusted soldier, he hid in the house of his best friend Hunwald. This earl, however, treacherously betrayed him to Oswiu, who ordered Oswin and his soldier to be put to death. This was on 20 August 651. Oswin was a devoted friend of *Aidan, apostle of Northumbria, who died only twelve days after him. Bede described him as 'a man of handsome appearance and great stature, pleasant in speech and courteous in manner. He was generous to high and low alike and soon won the affection of all by his kingly qualities of mind and body so that even men of very high birth came from nearly every province to his service.'

In expiation for his crime, Oswin built a monastery at Gilling, where Oswin was killed. But he was buried at Tynemouth. Later this church was vulnerable to Viking raiders; the tomb was largely forgotten until its rediscovery in 1065, when the relics were translated. Tynemouth became a cell of St. Albans; Durham tried hard but unsuccessfully to recover it in the 12th century. Like some other Anglo-Saxon kings such as *Kenelm and *Ethelbert who met a violent death, Oswin was culted as a martyr, because he died, 'if not for the faith of Christ, at least for the justice of Christ', as a 12th-century homilist explained. Feast: 20 August; translation, 11 March (kept at Durham, St. Albans, and Tynemouth).

Bede, *H.E.*, iii. 14 (with Plummer's notes); *N.L.A.*, ii. 268–72; J. Raine (ed.), *Miscellanea Biographica* (*S.S.*, 1850); B.T.A., iii. 366–7.

OSYTH, see Osith.

O'TOOLE, Laurence, see Laurence O'Toole.

OTTERAN, see Odran.

OUDOCEUS (Oudaceus, Odoceus) (d. *c.*615), bishop. All that we know of him comes from a Life in the Book of Llan Dav (*c.*1150), which may incorporate some older material. According to this, Oudoceus came from a princely Breton family, which migrated to Wales *c.*545, where Oudoceus was born soon after. During his early manhood Anglo-Saxon invaders penetrated into western Britain and the battle of Dyrham (577) separated the Welsh from Devon and Cornwall, leaving the Severn valley open to invasion and settlement. Oudoceus was a monk in Llandogo (where he became bishop *c.*580), having persuaded the abbots of Llancarfan, Llantwit, and Llandough to combine against a corrupt local chieftain. In this respect he may be perhaps considered as a distant precursor of the formation of the see of Llandaff. The presence of Oudoceus in numerous English calendars, including Sarum, York, and Hereford, with several monastic examples too, is probably due to the legend that he presented himself to *Augustine of Canterbury for consecration. His shrine remained at Llandaff until 1540. Feast: 2 July.

AA.SS., Iul. I (1719), 284–5; *N.L.A.*, ii. 273; Baring-Gould and Fisher, iv. 28–36; G. H. Doble, *Lives of the Welsh Saints* (1971).

OUEN (Audoenus, Dado), (*c.*600–84), bishop of Rouen. Born at Sancy near Soissons, Ouen was brought up at the court of Clotaire II in the company of *Eloi, *Wandrille, and Didier. He became chancellor of Dagobert I and Clovis II, founded the monastery of Rebais, and received Holy Orders rather late in life, when at the height of his secular career. In 641 he became bishop of Rouen, while his friend Eloi became bishop of Noyon. As bishop he sent missionaries to parts of his diocese which were still infected with paganism and superstition, he founded monasteries as centres of piety and learning; he also combated simony, then rife. He was a counsellor of Thierry III and supported the policies of Ebroin, mayor of the palace. He died at Clichy-la-Garenne, near Paris, later called Saint-Ouen, 24 August 684. This has constantly remained his feast day. Canterbury claimed to possess his body, although a more plausible set of relics existed at Rouen, where there is still a fine flamboyant church in his honour, as well as forty church dedications in the diocese, and twenty-nine in that of Evreux. The Canterbury claim, as expounded by Eadmer, was that during the reign of Edgar four unknown clerics arrived at his court, bearing the bones of Ouen. Edgar's suspicions of their authenticity were allayed by the miraculous cures, which were approved by *Oda, archbishop of Canterbury (940–60). The clerks brought the relics to Canterbury and became monks there. The bones were placed in a *confessio* with those of *Blaise and *Wilfrid, and a chapel in the SE. transept of the crypt at Canterbury was dedicated in his honour. The Canterbury cult of Ouen thus dates from the 10th century; after 1100 his feast was almost universal in English Benedictine calendars. Other places which claimed relics were Boursies, near Cambrai (a head), and Clichy (a finger). Feast: 24 August.

AA.SS. Aug. IV (1739), 794–840: *Vita S. Audoeni* (ed. W. Levison), *M.G.H.*, *Scriptores rerum merov.*, v. 536–67; E. Vacandard, *Vie de saint Ouen* (1902); A. Wilmart, 'Les Reliques de Saint Ouen à Cantorbéry', *Anal. Boll.*, li (1933), 285–92; N. R. Ker, 'Un fragment des Miracles de S. Ouen', *Anal. Boll.*, lxiv (1946), 50–3.

OWEN, Nicholas (*c.*1550–1606), Jesuit lay brother and martyr. He was born of an Oxfordshire recusant family and was trained in early life as a carpenter and builder. This enabled him to construct hiding-places for priests in various country houses with extraordinary skill and ingenuity over a period of twenty-six years. Thus he helped to save the lives of many priests and the fortunes of many recusant families. Examples of his work survive at Sawston Hall (Cambs.), Hinlip Hall and Huddington Court (Hereford and Worcester), Harrowden (Northants.), Coughton Hall (Warwicks.), and Broadoaks (Essex), most of which were built single-handed, at night, in complete secrecy.

Three times Owen was imprisoned: once after the arrest of Edmund *Campion, whom he served and praised, again after the imprisonment of John Gerard, whose escape he planned and executed, and again, while serving the Provincial Henry Garnet, at Hinlip Hall. Here Owen, after a fortnight without food in his own hiding-hole, gave himself up to the pursuivants in the hope that they would call off the pursuit of the priests. He was taken to the Tower and mercilessly racked, although legally exempt from this torture owing to a rupture. As he constantly refused to give information about the whereabouts of priests, he was again racked, until on 2 February he died in agony after his vital parts had burst out under torture. The Council asserted that he had committed suicide, but few contemporaries believed it. He was canonized by Paul VI in 1970 as one of the *Forty Martyrs of England and Wales. Feast: 25 October.

J. Morris, *The Condition of Catholics under James I* (1871); P. Caraman, *The Autobiography of Father John Gerard* (1951); H. Foley, *Records of the English Province of the Society of Jesus*, iv. 245–67; M. Hodgetts, 'Elizabethan Priest-Holes', in *Recusant History*, xiii (1975–6), 18–55, 254–79.

OWIN (Owini) (d. *c.*670), monk, known only through *Bede. He was born in East Anglia, became master of *Etheldreda's household and went with her to Northumbria for her marriage to King Egfrith. When she became a nun at Coldingham, Owin joined the monastery at Lastingham under *Chad. He arrived in poor clothes, carrying an axe, his intention being to 'work hard rather than pursue idleness in monastic life', as some did. What he lacked in meditation on the Scriptures he made up for by manual work. When Chad became bishop of Mercia and Lindsey in 669, Owin went with him to Lichfield as a member of his household monastery. One day he experienced an audition of heavenly voices, which presaged Chad's forthcoming death. Owin died at about the same time; his feast is traditionally 4 March, but there seems no surviving trace of cult except the dedication of ancient churches at Gloucester and Bristol.

Bede, *H.E.*, iv. 3 (with Plummer's notes); *AA.SS.*, Mar. I (1668), 313.

P

PACHOMIUS (d. 346), founder of Christian community monasticism. Born in Upper Egypt of pagan parents, he was conscripted into the army and became a Christian on his release in 313. For a few years he lived as a hermit, but then organized monastic life for the many, using to the full his exceptional powers of administration. His first monastery was founded in 320, but others followed until at his death he ruled over nine monasteries for men and two for women. These are reputed to have been very large in size. Their internal organization was based on a division into houses, according to the particular craft practised by the monks, such as agriculture, tailoring, baking; they also sold their produce to Alexandria. Pachomius' military training influenced the organization of his monasteries: he himself, like a general, could transfer monks from one monastery to another: there were also local superiors and deans in charge of the houses. All in authority met at Easter and again in August for presenting the annual accounts. This centralized rule, which emphasized total obedience, was matched by an austere regime, in which food, drink, and sleep were carefully regulated, but whose standard was both less severe and less erratic than that of some of the hermits. His Rule, which survives in Jerome's Latin translation, influenced those of *Basil and *Benedict; in the latter, thirty-two passages can be attributed to Pachomian influence. In recent years much work has been done on Pachomian sources in Eastern languages. Feast: 14 May in the West; 15 May in the East, but 9 May in the Coptic Church. His feast was kept in medieval St. Albans.

A. Boon, *Pachomiana Latina* (1932); F. Halkin, *S. Pachomii Vitae Graecae* (1932); T. H. Lefort, *Oeuvres de S. Pachôme et de ses disciples* (1965); A. J. Festugière, *Les Moines d'Orient*, vi. 2 (1965); L. T. Lefort, *Les vies coptes de saint Pachôme et de ses premiers successeurs* (1943); Rule and letters of Pachomius translated by St. Jerome in *P.L.*, xxiii. 61–99; see also *Pachomiana* (1955), A. Veilleux, *La liturgie dans le cénobitisme pachomien au quatrième siècle* (1968); A. de Vogüé, 'Études récentes sur S. Pachôme', *R.H.E.*, lxix (1974), 425–53; F. Halkin, 'Une vie inédite de saint Pachôme', *Anal. Boll.*, lxxxvii (1979), 5–55 and 241–79; P. Rousseau, *Pachomius* (1985).

PADARN, see PATERNUS OF WALES.

PAINE, John (*c*.1550–82), seminary priest and martyr. Born at Peterborough, Paine was brought up as a member of the Church of England, but joined the R.C. Church at an unknown place and date. In 1574 he entered the English College at Douai and served for some time as bursar before being ordained priest in 1576. He soon returned to England with Cuthbert *Mayne: while Mayne ministered in Cornwall, Paine went to Essex and made Ingatestone Hall, the home of the Petre family, his principal base. Here he ministered to the scattered recusants while apparently working as an estate steward. In 1577 he was imprisoned for a short time and then returned to Douai; in 1578 he returned to Ingatestone and worked there until he was betrayed in 1581. He was then arrested and imprisoned at Greenwich by Walsingham. He was charged with conspiracy against the Queen, was twice racked in the Tower, and was sentenced to be hanged, drawn, and quartered. On the scaffold at Chelmsford on 2 April he was offered pardon if he would conform to the Church of England, but he refused, protesting that 'his feet did never tread, his hands did never write, nor did his wit ever invent any treason against Her Majesty'. He was so well known and loved in the neighbourhood that the crowd compelled the hangman to wait until he was dead before cutting him down.

An interesting relic survives in private hands. The Bosworth Burse has a representation of Christ rising from the Sacrament during the Elevation at Mass and is based on a vision experienced at Douai by John Paine. He was canonized by Paul VI in 1970 as one of the *Forty Martyrs of England and Wales. Feast: 25 October.

W. Allen, *A Briefe Historie of the Glorious Martyrdom of Twelve Reverend Priests* (ed. J. H. Pollen, 1908); B. C. Foley, *Blessed John Paine* (pamphlet, 1961).

PALLADIUS (5th century), apostle of Ireland. Under the year 431 the contemporary Chronicle of Prosper of Aquitaine records that Palladius was sent by Celestine, bishop of the Roman Church, to the Irish believers in Christ, to be their first bishop. Already he had mentioned him under the year 429 as one who had persuaded Pope Celestine to send *Germanus of Auxerre to extirpate the Pelagian heresy in Britain. It is likely but not absolutely certain that they were one and the same person. It is disputed whether Palladius was a deacon of Auxerre or of Rome. It seems probable that he was a deacon from Auxerre who went to Rome to gain papal approval for Germanus' visit to Britain. This mission needed some wider authority if it was not to seem to be mere interfering with the needs of another local church. Palladius probably accompanied Germanus to Britain, reported the results to Rome, where he was kept by the pope, and sent to Ireland not long afterwards. Christianity had presumably reached there, as it had elsewhere in the West, through migrant traders, but a definite organization of Christianity by a bishop was necessary if it were to survive and prosper. Palladius seems to have landed and worked mainly in Wicklow, where three places, Tigroney, Donard, and Cilleen Cormac (near Dunlavin), claim to be churches founded by him. His apostolate was not of long duration and was soon forgotten; it was in the interest of those emphasizing the role of *Patrick that it should be. It seems likely that Palladius went from Ireland to Scotland, whether from distaste for his task or from the hostility which he encountered, or both, is not clear. He died there and the place of his death is claimed to be Forddun and there is still a cult of him in Aberdeen. It seems certain that Palladius and not Patrick was the first bishop to work in Ireland, that he is not to be identified with Patrick, that the evidence for a papal mission of Palladius is stronger than that for Patrick, and that a Scottish tradition that he preached in Scotland for twenty-three years is unreliable. Feast: 7 July.

AA.SS. Iul. II (1721), 286–90; J. B. Bury, *St. Patrick and his Place in History* (1905), pp. 342–4; R. P. C. Hanson, *Saint Patrick* (1968), pp. 52–6, 192–4; *K.S.S.*, pp. 427–30; L. Bieler, 'The Mission of Palladius', *Traditio*, vi (1948), 1–32; P. Grosjean, 'Notes de'hagiographie celtique', *Anal. Boll.*, lxiii (1945), 73–86, 112–19. See also PATRICK.

PALLOTTI, Vincent (1795–1850), priest and founder of the Society of the Catholic Apostolate. The son of a Roman grocer, Vincent was educated for the priesthood and ordained in 1817. He obtained a doctorate in theology, which he taught at the Sapienza College, but soon resigned this post to devote himself entirely to pastoral work through the influence of *Caspar del Bufalo. He then became confessor of several Roman colleges, including the English, Scots, and Irish.

He developed a lay apostolate in spite of clerical hostility, anticipating the later Catholic Action movement and the teaching of Vatican II on an apostolic role for all Christians. In 1835 he founded his Society from a group of clergy and laity, who were committed to conversion and social justice. He organized schools and evening classes for workers to improve professional standards and general education. These policies resembled those of John *Bosco.

He practised exorcism and had the gift of prophecy: more important were his charity and fidelity in the confessional and his repeated habit of giving away his clothes to the destitute. He died of pleurisy at the age of fifty-five. His Congregation (as well as the Pallottini sisters, founded in 1843) has flourished in Italy, Brazil, Australia, and the USA, where it has specialized in care for the immigrants and, like their founder, in promoting ecumenical contacts with Eastern Orthodox Christians. He was canonized in 1963. Feast: 22 January.

[J. Hettenkofer] *Historia Piae Societatis Missionum* (1935) and *Historia Societatis Apostolatus Catholici* (1950); Lives by F. Frank (2 vols., 1962–3), D. Pistella (1963): see also B.T.A., i. 148–9; *Bibl. SS.*, xii. 1781–6.

PANCRAS OF ROME (d. early 4th century), martyr. Beyond the well-attested fact of his martyrdom which led to a notable cult centred on his body in the fine church on the Via Aurelia in Rome, almost nothing is known of him. The legendary Acts make him a Phrygian orphan brought by his uncle to Rome, where both were converted and Pancras suffered as a martyr at the early age of fourteen. *Gregory the Great dedicated a monastery at Rome to Pancras and *Augustine a church in Canterbury. Relics of Pancras were sent to Oswiu, king of Northumbria, by Pope Vitalian *c.*664. Partly for this reason Pancras appears in the Martyrology of *Bede, in the OE Martyrology, and in most English calendars including Sarum. Six ancient churches in England were dedicated to Pancras, including one in North London, from which the cemetery and the railway station take their name. Feast: 12 May, often with Nereus and Achilleus.

AA.SS. Maii III (1680), 17–22; Bede, *H.E.*, iii. 29; B.T.A., ii. 285. P. Franchi de'Cavalieri, *Hagiographica* (1908), pp. 77–105.

PANCRAS OF TAORMINA (1st century), martyr. He is reputed to have been sent by St. *Peter to evangelize Sicily, where after a career of preaching and miracle-working he suffered martyrdom through being stoned to death by brigands. He was immensely popular in Sicily; there are ten English churches (according to Bond) dedicated to him, though whether through the influence of ancient calendars or through the close contact between England and Sicily in the 12th century is not clear. The cult was early and even spread to Georgia. Feast: 3 April, or sometimes 8 July.

AA.SS. Apr. I (1675), 237–43; B.T.A., ii. 18; F. Bond, *Dedications of English Churches* (1914), p. 326.

PANDONIA (Pandwyna) (d. *c.*904), virgin, to whom the church of Eltesley (Cambs.) is dedicated. All that we know about her comes from Leland, according to whom she was 'a king of Scots' daughter and after fleeing them that would have deflowered her, she came to a kinswoman of hers, prioress of a nunnery at Eltesley in Cambridgeshire, four miles from St. Neots, and after dying was buried in Eltesley by a well called S. Pandonia Well. She was translated into Eltesley church in 1344, as it appeareth by the lessons of her translation made by one Sir Richard, parish priest there'. This Life is no longer extant, but the date of her death seems to be derived from it. She is included in a Litany of Saints in a Book of Hours, made in Flanders for English use, at St. Peter Hungate Museum, Norwich; *C.S.P.* makes her a virgin martyr. Feast: 26 August.

J. Leland, *Itinerary*, v. 218; Stanton, pp. 413–14; *C.S.P.*

PANTALEON (Panteleimon) (d. *c.*305), doctor and martyr. His name means 'all-compassionate': his cult was well established from an early date in both East and West, particularly in Nicomedia and Bithynia. According to his Legend he was the son of a pagan father and a Christian mother, Eubula, who brought him up as a Christian. But he later relapsed into paganism until he was reconciled to the Church through a fellow-Christian, Hermolaos. By this time he was a successful physician who numbered the Emperor Galerius among his patients. When the persecution of Diocletian began in Nicomedia in 303 he was denounced as a Christian by his colleagues, was arrested, tortured in various ways, and ultimately beheaded. In the East he is venerated as a great martyr and wonder-worker and as one of the holy men who looked after the sick without being paid. In the West he was considered (in Germany and the Low Countries) as one of the *Fourteen Holy Helpers; his blood at Ravello is believed to liquefy like that of *Januarius. Churches were dedicated to him in Constantinople and Rome. Feast: 27 July.

AA.SS. Iul. VI (1729), 397–426; H. Delehaye, *Les Origines du culte des Martyrs* (1912), pp. 181 ff.; I. R. Grant, *The Testimony of Blood* (1929), pp. 17–44. The liquefaction is also described by J. H. Newman in a letter to H. Wilberforce of August 1846.

PAPYLUS (Pamfilus), see CARPUS, PAPYLUS, AND AGATHONICE.

PARAGUAY, MARTYRS OF (d. 1628). These were three Jesuits: Roque Gonzalez, Alonso Rodriguez, and Juan de Castillo, all deeply involved in the foundation of the famous 'Reductions' of Paraguay. These were settlements of Christian Indians run by the missionaries, not as conquerors but as guardians and trustees of native people and their ancient traditions. Their opposition to Spanish colonialism and to the Inquisition contributed to their suppression in the 18th century.

Roque Gonzalez was born in Asunción in 1576 of a noble Spanish family: he was ordained priest in 1599, appointed vicar-general in 1608, and devoted himself more than most to the religious instruction of the Indians. In 1609, looking for more missionary work, he joined the Jesuits. For the rest of his life he worked in the Reductions, first in that of St. Ignatius, then founding six more to the east of the Parana and Uruguay rivers. This led him into suffering extreme hunger, cold, exhaustion, and insect bites. These however were more than offset by the admiration of the Indians, but his work was hampered by the Spanish insistence on the presence of sometimes brutal Europeans in their midst.

In 1620, joined by his two colleagues, he founded a new Reduction near the Ijuhi river. Juan de Castillo was left in charge, while the others went on to Caaro (now in Brazil), where they were directed to found yet another Reduction in strange country. This time a powerful medicine-man opposed them and incited others to attack them. As Gonzalez was hanging a church bell, he was attacked from behind with tomahawks. Rodriguez came to investigate the commotion, but was knocked down and then killed. The chapel was set alight and the two bodies were burnt inside it. This was on 15 November and on 17 November Castillo was seized, beaten, and stoned to death.

Although evidence was at once collected and recorded, the documents were lost. Over 200 years later, they were discovered in Argentina. This made these beatifications possible; they were completed in 1934. These martyrs were canonized in 1988. Feast: 17 November.

J. M. Blanco, *Historia documentada de la Vida y gloriosa Muerte de los PP. Roque Gonzalez . . .* (1929); see also H. Thurston, 'The first beatified martyr of Spanish America', *Catholic Historical Review*, xx (1935), 371–83; *N.C.E.*, vi. 611; B.T.A., iv. 376–7.

PATERNUS OF AVRANCHES (Pair) (d. 564), bishop. Born at Poitiers, the son of a civil servant. Paternus became a monk at Ansion (Poitou), but after some time he was a hermit near Coutances, settling with St. Scubilio in Scissy. Later a monastery was built there called Saint-Pair. Paternus became abbot and founded other monasteries near by. At the age of seventy he became bishop of Avranches, attended a council at Paris, and ruled for thirteen years. He died on the same day as Scubilio; both were buried at Scissy. This saint and the following one, of the same name and nearly the same date, are frequently confused in Martyrologies and calendars. Feast: 16 April (23 September at Abingdon and Malmesbury: 27 September at Gloucester).

AA.SS. Apr. II (1675), 425–30; Life by Venantius Fortunatus, ed. B. Krusch in *M.G.H.*, *Auctores Antiquissimi*, iv (part 2), 33–7; see also P. Grosjean, as below.

PATERNUS (Padarn) **OF WALES** (5th–6th century), monk and bishop, probably from SE. Wales in birth and education. Padarn is principally famous as the founder of Llanbadarn Fawr (Dyfed) of which he was both abbot and bishop for twenty years and from which he evangelized the neighbouring countryside. He seems to have been more closely associated with Roman civilization than some other early Welsh saints. His dedications to the west, Llanbadarn Fach (= Trefeglwys) and Llanbadarn Odwyn and Pencarreg, are closely connected with one Roman road, and his eastern dedications in the former county of Radnorshire (Llanbadarn Fawr, Llanbadarn Fynydd, and Llanbadarn Garreg) with another. Padarn was formerly much honoured in Wales; the Book of Llan Dav testifies to the importance of his Cardiganshire monastery and from there in *c.*1120 was written a Life of Padarn which conflates two different saints into one: this Welsh saint and a Breton one who was bishop of Vannes. Feast: 15 April (including Gloucester and Malmesbury).

A. W. Wade-Evans, *Vitae Sanctorum Britanniae* (1944), pp. 252–69; G. H. Doble, *St. Patern* (1940); E. G. Bowen, *The Settlements of the Celtic Saints in Wales* (1956), pp. 50–6; P. Grosjean, 'S. Paterne d'Avranches et S. Paterne de Vannes', *Anal. Boll.*, lxvii (1949), 384–400.

PATRICK (*c.*390–461(?)), bishop, apostle of Ireland. Much controversy has surrounded the details of Patrick's life and achievements. The exaggerated popular view of him as the only true apostle of Ireland who converted the whole country single-handed (based on a conflation of late Lives and the primatial claims of the see of Armagh) has given place to a widespread conviction that nearly all that can be known of Patrick comes from his authentic writings: his *Confessio* (or autobiography), the Letter to Coroticus (protesting against British slave-traders), and the *Lorica* (or 'Breastplate'). Patrick was British by birth, the son of a *decurio* (town councillor) who was a deacon, while his grandfather was a priest. The place of his birth was somewhere in the west between the mouth of the Severn and the Clyde, called Bannavem Taburniae. While still a youth, he was captured by Irish pirates and reduced to slavery for six years. The location of his service (mainly in tending his master's herds) is not certainly identified, but he used the time to pray, in contrast to his earlier years in Britain when he 'knew not the true God' and did not heed clerical 'admonitions for our salvation'. After six years he was told in a dream he would soon go to his own country. He either escaped or was freed, made his way to a port 200 miles away (perhaps on the SE. coast), and eventually persuaded some sailors to take him with them. After various adventures in a strange land, including near-starvation, Patrick returned to his family, much changed. He received some form of training for the priesthood, which included the Latin Bible which he came to know well; but it was not a 'higher education', the lack of which he regretted, and for which he was criticized. His own Latin writings are certainly inelegant, even at times rustic.

There was some contact with Gaul at this time and perhaps with the papacy, which had sent *Palladius to be the 'first bishop of the Irish who believe in Christ'. Palladius' mission does not seem to have lasted long and Patrick was in fact his successor. There was some opposition to his appointment, probably from Britain, but Patrick made his way to Ireland *c.*435. He worked principally in the North, setting up his see at Armagh and organizing the Church on the lines of territorial sees, as elsewhere in the West (and East). While Patrick encouraged the Irish to become monks and nuns, it is not certain that he was a monk himself; it is even less likely that in his time the monastery became the principal unit of the Irish church. The choice of Armagh seems determined by the presence nearby of a most powerful king; there Patrick had a school and presumably a small *familia* in residence; from this base he made missionary journeys. There seems to have been little contact with the Palladian Christianity of the south-east.

Patrick's writings are the first literature certainly identified from the British Church and reveal a scale of values and a type of activity which are full of interest. Although he had little learning and less rhetoric, Patrick had sincere simplicity and deep pastoral care. He was concerned with abolishing paganism, idolatry, and sun-worship; he made no distinction of classes in his preaching and was himself ready for imprisonment or death in the following of Christ. In his use of Scripture and in his eschatological expectations (and presumably in much else besides) he was a typical but very individual 5th-century bishop. One of the traits which he retained as an old man was a consciousness of his being an unlearned exile and formerly a slave and fugitive, who learnt to trust completely in God.

The historical Patrick is much more attractive than the Patrick of legend, the thaumaturge who expelled snakes from Ireland or 'explained' the Trinity by reference to the shamrock, or accomplished single-handed immense missionary tasks of conversion which actually took many evangelists and several generations to accomplish. Places sometimes associated with him in the past, such as Lérins (Côte d'Azur), Croagh Patrick, even Saul and Downpatrick, cannot be proved to have the significance in his life which they were once believed to have. Even the place of his death and burial are not known for certain. This was how it became possible for Glastonbury to claim that the relics of Patrick the Older, which had long been there, were those of the historical St. Patrick. Eight ancient English churches were dedicated to Patrick, as were several chapels in Pembrokeshire (Dyfed). He remains the most popular of the saints of Ireland (of whom he is the patron) to this day. In art he is usually depicted in bishop's vestments, treading on snakes, but there seem to be no early notable examples. In the National Museum at Dublin shrines survive of his bell and his tooth (12th and 14th centuries): they presumably derive from the Downpatrick shrine. The cult of Patrick spread from Ireland to the numerous Irish monasteries in Europe in the early Middle Ages; the Normans encouraged it in Ireland and elsewhere, while in modern times it has spread to the United States and Australia, where it flourishes especially among families and churches of Irish origin. The principal cathedral of New York is dedicated to him, as are numerous modern parish churches in the English-speaking world. His feast is constant in calendars and martyrologies for 17 March: a subsidiary feast of the finding of the bodies of Patrick, *Columba, and *Brigid in 1185 by *Malachy was kept in Ireland and some places in England such as Chester on 24 March. There was also a translation feast on 10 June; but Glastonbury's Patrick had 24 August as his feast.

Works printed by L. Bieler, *Libri Epistolarum sancti Patricii Episcopi* (1961); translation and commentary by the same in *The Works of St. Patrick* ('*Ancient Christian Writers*', 1953). The later Lives are in W. Stokes, *The Tripartite Life of Patrick and other documents relating to that Saint* (2 vols., 1887). For the Book of Armagh: J. Gwynn, *Liber Ardmachanus: the Book of Armagh* (1913) (and cf. P. Grosjean, 'Analyse du Livre d'Armagh', *Anal. Boll.*, lxii (1944), 32–41). Modern studies on Patrick are numerous: D. A. Binchy, 'Patrick and his Biographers', *Studia Hibernica*, ii (1962), 7–173; R. P. C. Hanson, *St. Patrick: his Origins and Career* (1968) and *The Life and Writings of the Historical St. Patrick* (1983). J. B. Bury, *St. Patrick and his Place in History* (1905); L. Bieler, *The Life and Legend of St. Patrick* (1948); E. Macneill, *St. Patrick* (1964); J. Ryan (ed.), *St. Patrick* (1958). Special mention should be made of articles by P. Grosjean, 'Patriciana', *Anal. Boll.*, xliii (1925), 241–60; 'Notes sur les documents anciens concernant S. Patrice', ibid., lxii (1944), 42–73; 'Notes d'hagiographie celtique', ibid., lxiii (1945), 65–130; 'S. Patrice d'Irlande et quelques homonymes dans les anciens martyrologes', *J.E.H.*, i (1950), 151–71: 'Les Pictes apostats dans l'épître de S. Patrice', *Anal. Boll.*, lxxvi (1958), 354–78. See also: J. Toynbee, 'Christianity in Roman Britain', *J.B.A.A.*, xvi (1953), 1–24; K. Hughes, *The Church in Early Irish Society* (1966), M. W. Barley and R. P. C. Hanson, *Christianity in Early Britain* (1968); E. A. Thompson, *Who was St. Patrick?* (1985); R.

Sharpe, 'Some problems concerning the Organization of the Church in early medieval Ireland', *Peritia* iii (1984), 230–70.

PAUL (1) (d. *c*.65), apostle of the Gentiles. A Jew, born at Tarsus and brought up by Gamaliel as a pharisee, Saul was first a persecutor of Christianity, who took part in the stoning of *Stephen, sought out Christians and had them imprisoned, but on his way to Damascus experienced a vision of Christ which was to be decisive in determining the future course of his life. The substance of the experience caused a conviction that Jesus was in some way identified with the Christian Church and that Paul was to bring the Christian faith to the Gentiles. He was then baptized, retired to Arabia for about three years of prayer and solitude, and returned to Damascus. There his Jewish enemies were so hostile that he escaped by night, lowered in a basket over the city wall, and went to Jerusalem where he was received with some hesitation until *Barnabas quelled the doubts of the community. Some years later he worked at Antioch and its vicinity, where he reproved *Peter for appearing to compromise with the Jews. The three missionary journeys followed, first to Cyprus, then to Asia Minor and eastern Greece, lastly to Ephesus where he made a prolonged stay and wrote I Corinthians, then to Macedonia and Achaia, where he wrote Romans, before returning to Jerusalem. There he was attacked and beaten by a mob for preaching against the enactments of the Jewish Law, but Paul invoked his privileges as a Roman citizen and eventually appealed to Caesar for a trial at Rome, as his life was in danger from religious extremists. On the voyage to Rome he suffered shipwreck at Malta; when he reached it, he was under house-arrest for two years, during which he wrote the four 'captivity' epistles. Presumably he was acquitted at his trial, for he probably revisited Ephesus and may even have gone to Spain. According to tradition he was martyred at Rome during the persecution of Nero, being beheaded (as a Roman citizen) at Tre Fontane and buried where the basilica of St. Paul 'outside the walls' now stands. The belief that Peter and Paul died on the same day was caused by their sharing the same feast of 29 June.

Paul was not only a tireless missionary: he was also a powerful thinker, saturated in the Mystery of Christ; his epistles, most of which were written for particular practical needs, led to the development of Christian theology on them as one of its principal foundations. His key ideas included that of Redemption through faith in Christ who abrogated the Old Law and began the era of the Spirit; Christ is not only Messiah, but the eternal Son of God, pre-existing before the Incarnation and exalted after the Resurrection to God's right hand; the Church is the (mystical) Body of Christ, and the believer lives in Christ and will eventually be transformed by the final resurrection. It is difficult to overemphasize the influence of Paul on Christian thought and history, through *Augustine, *Thomas Aquinas, Luther, Calvin, and other writers as well in conciliar documents.

The apocryphal *Acts of Paul and Thecla* say that he was small in stature, bald and bandy-legged, with a long nose and eyebrows meeting; many representations of Paul depict a fairly constant image of a long face and long beard with a bald head and deep-set eyes. His usual emblems are a sword and a book. Never quite as popular as Peter, he nevertheless appears in art frequently with him or among the twelve apostles (where Paul often displaces *Matthias). Ancient English churches dedicated to Paul alone number only forty-three, but there were 283 which were dedicated to Peter and Paul. Like Peter, his name has attracted numerous apocryphal writings, such as the *Acts of Paul*, the *Apocalypse of Paul*, the *Martyrdom of Paul*, and the *Acts of Paul and Thecla*, which date from the 2nd to the 4th centuries. As with the apocryphal gospels, the best way to judge their worth is to compare them with the canonical writings. They did, however, enjoy a certain uncritical popularity.

The colourful and adventurous preaching career of Paul described in the Acts of the Apostles provided artists with material for his representation. Famous English examples include the fresco in St. Anselm's Chapel, Canterbury Cathedral (late 12th century), an enamel in the Victoria and Albert Museum, and innumerable initial miniatures in the famous Bibles of the 12th century. Statues and stained-glass representations must be even more numerous. Besides the usual joint feast on 29 June, there are subsidiary feasts of Paul on 25 January (Conversion) and (until 1969) 30 June (Commemoration).

Acts of the Apostles and *Epistles of Paul* (Galatians is important for the chronology; Romans and Ephesians for the doctrine). Innumerable studies include W. M. Ramsay, *St. Paul the Traveller* (1908); A H. McNeile, *St. Paul* (1920); G. Ogg, *The Chronology of the Life of Paul* (1966); F. Prat, *The Theology of St. Paul* (Eng. tr., 2 vols., 1927–34); A. Schweitzer, *The Mysticism of St. Paul the Apostle* (1931); L. Cerfaux, *La Théologie de l'Église suivant S. Paul* (1942); id., *Le Christ dans la théologie de S. Paul* (1951); *Studia Paulina* (1953); *Studiorum Paulinorum Congressus Internationalis* (*Analecta Biblica*, 1963).

PAUL (2), see JOHN AND PAUL.

PAUL AURELIAN (Paulinus), patron of Paul (Cornwall), is better known as Saint Pol (Paul-de-Léon), who came from Wales to Brittany in the 6th century and worked as bishop in the neighbourhood called after him. The *Vita* by Wrmonoc, a 10th-century monk of Landevennec, makes him a hermit, a disciple of *Illtud, who left his country as *peregrinus pro Christo*, stayed with his sister (in Cornwall?), landed at Ushant, built a monastery at Ploudalmezau, was consecrated bishop, and himself consecrated two coadjutors, dying at the age of 104. His body was translated to Fleury *c.*960 and remained there until 1562; his head, arm-bone, and bell are in the cathedral of Saint Pol-de-Léon. He is probably to be identified with the Welsh St. Paulinus, who lived for some years as a hermit near Llandovery and founded a monastery at Llanddeusant. An inscribed stone of the 6th century from Cynwyl Caeo survives and there are a few Welsh dedications. The original feast on 12 March was overshadowed by the subsidiary one on 10 October, which arose through a confusion with *Paulinus of York. His feast was well established in Brittany and the Loire valley, but appears in no English calendar.

G. H. Doble, *The Saints of Cornwall*, i (1960), 10–60; id., *St. Paulinus of Wales* (Welsh Saints no. 1), 1942.

PAUL OF THE CROSS (1694–1775), priest, founder of the Passionist Congregation. Paul Danei was born at Ovada, near Genoa, being the eldest son of an impoverished business man of noble ancestry. Brought up devoutly from an early age, he refused the opportunity both of a rich inheritance and an advantageous marriage. After a year's trial as a volunteer in the Venetian army to fight the Turks in 1714, he spent several years in prayer and retirement before he decided in 1720 to found in response to a vision, a new congregation which was duly tested and approved. With his younger brother John, who was to be his lifelong companion and helper, and a few other companions he started the new congregation at Monte Argentaro in 1727 after being ordained priest at Rome. The main features of this form of religious life were to combine an austere monastic penitential regime with intense devotion to the Passion of Christ, which should be communicated to others by mission work in the parishes. The aim was thus to combine the active and contemplative lives at the deepest level. So outstanding was their ministry to the sick and the dying, and in reconciling the sinners and the lapsed that they were soon in demand in many parts of Italy. Meanwhile many novices left, finding the regime too austere, but the work continued with the foundation of three houses by 1747. Papal approbation had been obtained on condition that some of the severest features were mitigated.

Paul was an extremely effective preacher, especially on the subject of Christ's Passion; he was also endowed with gifts of prophecy, healing and reading the secrets of hearts. Much of his correspondence is concerned with ascetical and mystical theology. From early times he had been specially interested in the reconciliation of England to the Holy See, an aim vigorously pursued by his disciples in the 19th century, who included Dominic Barberi, who received John Henry Newman into the R.C. Church. Final papal approbation was given to the Passionists in 1769, after which time Paul resided mainly at Rome by the basilica of SS. John and Paul, which Clement XIV had given them after Paul's brother John had died in 1765. Near the end of his long life Paul founded a convent of enclosed Passionist nuns at Corneto in 1771. He died at the age of eighty on 18 October and was buried in the church of SS. John and Paul. He was canonized in 1867; his feast, formerly on 28 April, is now on 19 October.

Lives by V. M. Strambi (1786, Eng. tr. 1853); by Edmund Burke (1946), C. Almeras (1957, Eng. tr. 1960), and E. Zoffoli (1963). Letters ed. Amadeo della Madre del Buon Pastore (4 vols., 1924). See also Basilio de San Pablo, *La espiritualidad de la Passion en el magisterio de S. Pablo de la Cruz* (1961); B.T.A., ii. 178–80; *O.D.C.C.*, s.v.

PAUL THE FIRST HERMIT (Paul of Thebes, d. *c.*345), traditionally the first Christian hermit, visited and later buried by *Antony of Egypt. He had fled to the desert in persecution (perhaps of Decius) and was reputed to have lived there ever since to well over a hundred years of age. *Jerome's Life of Paul, based on a Greek original and almost the only authority for these details, is a baffling mixture of fact and fantasy. Paul is represented in art usually with two lions, who traditionally burrowed the ground at Antony's request for Paul's grave, or else with a palm tree, which provided him with food and shelter during his long life as a hermit. Scenes from his life, especially the meeting with Antony, are depicted on the Ruthwell cross (*c.*700) and on some Irish crosses. He also appears on the 15th-century painted rood-screen of Wolborough (Devon) with other monastic saints. Feast (kept in several medieval monasteries): 10 January in the West (suppressed 1969): 5 or 15 January in the East.

AA.SS. Ian. I (1643), 602–9; Life by Jerome also in *P.L.*, xxiii. 17–28 (tr. in H. Waddell, *The Desert Fathers* (1936), pp. 35–53); J. Bidez, *Deux versions grecques inédites de la vie de Paul de Thèbes* (1900); F. Nau, 'Le texte grec originale de la Vie de S. Paul de Thèbes', *Anal. Boll.*, xx (1901), 121–57; H. Delehaye, 'La Personnalité historique de S. Paul de Thèbes', *Anal. Boll.*, xliv (1926), 64–9.

PAUL OF LÉON, see PAUL AURELIAN.

PAUL MIKI AND COMPANIONS, see MIKI.

PAULA (d. 404), widow. Related to the noblest Roman families of the Scipios and the Gracchi, Paula was happily married until her husband died when she was thirty-two. A period of extreme sorrow, prolonged by the death of her eldest daughter Blesilla, was followed by a religious conversion, which took the form of penance expressed by an austere regime of eating, drinking, and sleeping, by the renunciation of all amusements and social life, and in generous gifts to the poor. At this point she came under the influence of *Jerome and decided to leave Rome. With her daughter Eustochium and other companions she made a long pilgrimage to the Holy Land and to Egypt, where they visited the hermits; eventually they settled at Bethlehem under the direction of Jerome. They built a monastery for men and a convent for women with a guest-house for pilgrims, all of which were of modest dimensions and simply furnished. There Paula lived for the rest of her life, helping Jerome in his studies through her wealth and her knowledge of Greek, and being helped by him in other ways, including the education of her grand-daughter, Paula the younger. She died at the age of fifty-six on 26 January, on which day her feast has been kept from ancient times. A famous English 12th-century initial to Jerome's Commentary on Isaiah depicts her burial, under the church of the Nativity at Bethlehem. Jerome's epitaph letter is probably the finest he ever wrote.

AA.SS. Ian. II (1643), 711–22: Jerome, *Epistola 108* in *P.L.*, xxii. 878 ff.; F. Lagrange, *Histoire de Sainte Paule* (1868); R. Genier, *Sainte Paule* (1917); J. N. D. Kelly, *Jerome* (1975).

PAULINUS, see PAUL AURELIAN.

PAULINUS OF NOLA (d. 431), bishop. Born at Bordeaux of a very wealthy family (his father was prefect of Gaul and owned lands in Italy, Spain, and Aquitaine), Paulinus was educated by the poet Ausonius, practised as a lawyer and held public office probably in Campania, travelled extensively, and married a Spanish wife, Therasia. Some years later after a period of agreeable and sophisticated leisure, they both became Christians. They lived in Spain *c.*390, where a son was born, but he died in infancy. Soon after they began to distribute much of their immense wealth to the poor and to the Church. In response to popular insistence the bishop of Barcelona ordained Paulinus a priest, although he was not a deacon at the time. But he had decided to settle at Nola (Campania); having sold most of his estates in France he settled down, built a church at Fondi, an aqueduct at Nola, and a guest-house for pilgrims, debtors, and the like, who lived on the ground-floor of his house while he with a few friends followed a semi-monastic regime on the upper floor. There he wrote his poems and letters to some of the most eminent Christians of the day, such as *Ambrose, *Jerome, *Augustine, and *Martin; the divine office was recited daily and Therasia was the housekeeper of the little community. One subject of great interest to him was the cult of the saints: every year he wrote a poem in honour of *Felix of Nola, who was buried in the church very close to Paulinus' house. He later built another church there which he decorated with mosaics and described in another poem.

About 409 he was chosen bishop of Nola, but little information has survived about his pastoral ideals and achievements. Perhaps it was for the needs of his flock that he wrote to Jerome about difficult passages of Scripture and obtained from Augustine the treatise on the Care for the Dead. Paulinus' own work was steeped in classical forms and ideas but he skilfully transformed them with the Christian ideals of hope and of love and he is generally reckoned as comparable to Prudentius as a Christian poet. His attractive personality, which represented much that was best in Roman and early Christian civilization, won him many friends in his own day and the esteem of scholars in our own. He died on 22 June at the time of Vespers, having recently celebrated the Eucharist with two visiting bishops and given his last present to the poor of fifty silver pieces. He was buried in his own church at Nola; later his relics were translated to Rome, but they were restored to Nola by Pius X in 1909. Feast: 22 June.

AA.SS. Iun. IV (1707), 193–237; works ed. W. von Hartel, *C.S.E.L.*, xxix–xxx (1894); F. de Labriolle, *La correspondance d'Ausone et de Paulin* (1910); P. Fabre, *Essai sur la chronologie de l'oeuvre de Saint Paulin de Nole* (1948); id., *Saint Paulin de Nole et l'amitié chrétienne* (1949); R. C. Goldschmidt, *Paulinus's Churches at Nola* (1940).

PAULINUS OF YORK (d. 644), monk and first bishop of York. He was one of the second group of monks sent to England by *Gregory the Great in 601 and became through a favourable political opening the first apostle of Northumbria. This was the request by *Edwin, king of Northumbria, to marry *Ethelburga, the Christian sister of Edbald, king of Kent. The first answer was that a Christian woman could not be given in marriage to a pagan husband. But when Edwin answered that he would give complete freedom of conscience to Ethelburga and her household, and might even become a Christian himself, consent was given to the marriage. Paulinus was consecrated bishop and went to the north as Ethelburga's chaplain, but with a hope that the conversion of the Northumbrian king and people would follow. After some years Paulinus baptized Edwin and his infant daughter at Easter 627/8 in a wooden church at York. This had been preceded by the decision of the pagan high-priest Coifi to abandon the service of the pagan gods and was followed by many nobles and others seeking baptism. This was administered by Paulinus in the river Swale, near Catterick and the Glen, near Yeavering with its royal palace, and elsewhere in Yorkshire and Lincolnshire. With the deacon, *James, he baptized in the Trent at Littleborough, built a church at Lincoln of stone, and consecrated in it Honorius, archbishop of Canterbury (628).

Paulinus' northern apostolate was cut short by the death of Edwin in the battle of Hatfield Chase in 633 at the hand of the pagan Penda of Mercia and his Welsh Christian ally Cadwallon. Ethelburga returned to Kent; Paulinus, thinking there was no future for Christianity in Northumbria without the king, went with her and, now aged about sixty, acted as bishop of Rochester for the rest of his life. Pope Honorius had sent him the pallium, but Paulinus was already in Kent when it arrived. *Bede, on whom we depend for most of our information, described Paulinus as a 'tall man with a slight stoop, who had black hair, a thin face and a narrow, aquiline nose, his presence being venerable and awe-inspiring'. He died on 10 October, the day observed as his feast, especially in monasteries and in the North. Five ancient churches were dedicated to him. There was also a cult of him at Canterbury and Rochester. The dates of his apostolate are disputed, the latest suggestion being that it began as early as 619 instead of the traditional 625. Attempts have also been made unconvincingly to assert that Edwin was baptized not by Paulinus but by a Welsh bishop; but this story is contradicted by the independent and far more ancient witness both of Bede and of the earliest biographer of Gregory the Great.

Bede, *H.E.*, ii. 9–20, iii. 1 and 14; B. Colgrave, *The Earliest Life of Gregory the Great* (1968); F. M. Stenton, *Anglo-Saxon England* (1943), 113–16; D. P. Kirby, 'Bede and Northumbrian Chronology', *E.H.R.*, lxxxviii (1963), 514–27; N. K. Chadwick, *Celt and Saxon* (1963).

PAZZI, Mary Magdelene de' (1566–1606), Carmelite nun and mystic. She was born in Florence of a wealthy family closely associated with the Medicis. Two contemporary portraits show that she was strikingly beautiful, but she renounced everything to become a Carmelite nun there in spite of strong family opposition. She was professed in 1584, became novice-mistress in 1598, and later subprioress. From 1604 onwards she was bedridden and suffered much pain and aridity.

Her spiritual life was extraordinary and included many visions and ecstasies. During these she sometimes seemed lifeless, but at others she conversed with Christ and the saints. Her words then spoken were recorded in detail and form an important component of her seven volumes of writings. She sometimes prophesied future events and could read the secrets of hearts.

These favours were balanced by acute sufferings, based on sharing in the sufferings of Christ for sinners, heretics, and infidels. Violent headaches and hyperacute sensitivity were accompanied by paralysis. Knowing that death was near, she exhorted the sisters to love Jesus alone, to trust in him implicitly, and encourage each other constantly to suffer for love of him. She died on 25 May. A cult began almost at once and is centred on her still incorrupt body at S. Maria degl'Angeli, Florence. She was canonized in 1669. Feast: 29 May.

AA.SS. Maii VI (1688), 177–351; writings ed. F. Nardoni (7 vols., 1960 ff.); Ermanno del SSmo Sacramento, 'I manuscritti originali di S. Maria Maddalena de'Pazzi', *Ephemerides Carmeliticae*, vii (1956), 323–40; Lives by V. Cepari (Eng. tr. by F. W. Faber, 1849), Sr Maria Minima (1941; Eng. tr. 1958), and A. Ancilli (1967); see also B.T.A., ii. 416–19; *Bibl. SS.*, viii. 1107–31.

PECHTHELM, see PLECHELM.

PEGA (d. *c.*719), virgin, sister of *Guthlac. She lived as an anchoress at Peakirk (i.e. 'Pega's church') in Northamptonshire, not far from Guthlac's hermitage at Crowland. When he realized that his end was near (714), he invited her to his funeral. For this she sailed down the Welland, curing a blind man from Wisbech on the way. She inherited Guthlac's psalter and scourge, both of which, it was claimed, she later gave to Crowland. She went on pilgrimage to Rome and died there *c.*719. Ordericus Vitalis claimed that her relics survived in an unnamed Roman church in his day, and that miracles took place there. Feast: 8 January.

AA.SS. Ian. I (1643), 532–3; B. Colgrave, *The Life of St. Guthlac by Felix* (1956); G. F. Warner, *The Guthlac Roll* (Roxburghe Club, 1928); E. Clive Rouse, 'Wall paintings in the church of St. Pega, Peakirk, Northamptonshire', *Archaeol. Jnl.*, cx (1953), 135–49.

PELAGIA (1) (5th century?), actress of Antioch, penitent at Jerusalem. Her Legend has been immensely popular in East and West. It was written by someone well versed in the writings of the Desert Fathers, who purported to be James the deacon of bishop Nonnus. According to this fictional account, Pelagia was a beautiful but dissolute actress of Antioch, at the height of her renown, with many lovers, jewels, and servants. When some bishops were seated at the tomb of St. Julian, listening to a sermon from Nonnos, she passed by, provocatively dressed, surrounded by her 'fans'. All the bishops turned away shocked, except Nonnus, who was moved to tears by her zeal and success in her profession (regarded as Satan's) compared with the tepidity and slowness of his own and others' progress in holiness.

After a dream-troubled night Nonnos preached in the cathedral of Antioch and Pelagia walked in again, was converted on the spot, and asked for baptism. A deaconess Romana was deputed to be her sponsor and Pelagia was duly instructed and baptized. Soon afterwards she gave away all her ill-gotten gains, left her life of comfort and luxury, and went to live as a hermit, dressed as a man, on the Mount of Olives (Jerusalem). There the deacon James visited the beardless recluse 'Pelagius'; only after her death not long afterwards were her identity and her sex discovered.

The whole story, whose phrases and situations recall the writings of the Desert Fathers, is a product of that same monastic milieu, spread over Egypt, Palestine, and Antioch. It served as an exemplary story of repentance and perseverance, giving, like the Legends of *Mary Magdalene and *Mary of Egypt, an imaginative glamour to relieve the monotony of monastic life. It was probably written in the 5th century; Eastern manuscripts of it survive from the eighth and western ones from the 12th. But abridged versions occur as early as the *Anglo-Saxon Martyrology* (9th century), while a longer version, including speeches attributed to Satan, became popular through the *Golden Legend* (*c.*1263), widely diffused up to the Reformation. Artists ancient and modern have illustrated the Legend, while writers have retold the story with embellishments suitable to their times. Critical scholars of hagiography regard the whole story as a fiction, but in *John Chrysostom's 67th homily on Matthew's Gospel there is a story of an actress of Antioch, who underwent a sudden conversion and spent the rest of her days in a convent, refusing to see her former friends. This may be the factual basis of the story. Feast: 8 October.

H. Delehaye, *The Legends of the Saints* (1962), pp. 150–5; *H.S.S.C.*, iii. 241–6; *Bibl. SS.*, x. 432–7.

PELAGIA (2) **OF ANTIOCH** (d. *c.*311), virgin and martyr. This saint occurs in the Ambrosian Canon: both *Ambrose and *John Chrysostom preached sermons in her honour. She really existed; was a girl of fifteen, who in time of persecution was arrested by soldiers. Asking and obtaining permission to change her clothes, she went upstairs and then jumped off the roof into the river to escape dishonour. She died in the process and was venerated as a martyr. Feast: in the East, 8 October; in the West, 9 June.

B.T.A., ii. 510–11; *O.D.C.C.*, p. 1058.

PELLEGRINO LAZIOSI (1265–1345), Servite friar and priest. Born at Forli (Romagna), he became very active in politics, strongly supporting the Ghibelline (anti-papal) party. At one meeting tempers became so heated that he physically attacked *Philip Benizi, the Servite General Superior, who however literally turned the other cheek. This caused Pellegrino to repent. He joined the Servites in *c.*1292 at Siena, where he devoted himself to prayer, reading, penance, and almsgiving.

In 1322 he founded a new friary at Forli, near Ravenna. His reputation as preacher and director grew, so did his special reverence in saying Mass. Many miracles were attributed to him; of one he himself was the beneficiary. For many years he had suffered from severe varicose veins in the right foot; doctors decided to amputate it the next day as all other remedies had failed. He prayed long that night and woke up on the morrow completely healed.

He died on 1 May, aged eighty, and miracles were reported at his tomb. The immemorial cult was approved by the Holy See in 1609; he was canonized in 1726. Feast: 3 (formerly 1) May.

Life by Niccolo Borghese (15th century) for which see A. M. Serra, *Niccolo Borghese e i suoi scritti agiografici servitani* (1966); other Lives by G. M. Albarelli (1943) and P. M. Armadori (1930); see also B.T.A., ii. 211–12; *Bibl. SS.*, x. 468–80.

PEREGRINE OF AUXERRE (d. *c.*261), bishop and martyr. The fact of his martyrdom is testified by the Martyrology of Jerome, which places it at Bouhy, where he was buried. Legend makes him Auxerre's first bishop, consecrated by *Sixtus II and sent by him to Gaul. His death was occasioned by his appealing to the people of Entrains (Intaranum) to reject idolatry on the occasion of a dedication of a temple of Jupiter in the town. Feast: 16 May.

AA.SS. Maii III (1680), 561–4; L. Duchesne, *Fastes épiscopaux*, ii. 431–4.

PERPETUA AND FELICITAS (Felicity) (d. 203), martyrs of Carthage. Perpetua was a young married woman of twenty-two who had given birth to a son a few months before being arrested with other African catechumens in the persecution of Septimius Severus, who had forbidden fresh conversions to Christianity. This rendered catechumens liable to the death penalty. With Perpetua were a pregnant slave, Felicitas, and her husband Revocatus, also Saturninus and Secundulus; but the excellent contemporary account of the martyrdom concentrates on the women rather than the men. This was written up largely in the martyrs' own words, possibly by Tertullian, and greatly influenced other accounts of Christian martyrdom. It also contains accounts of visions and apocalyptic elements, but its possibly Montanist origin and feminist slant did not prevent it being used with enthusiasm by *Augustine and other Christian writers.

After their arrest, the Christians were kept under guard in a private house where Perpetua spoke to her father; later they were imprisoned. Perpetua with her baby, concerned at her family's anxiety for her, said: 'my prison became a palace to me and I would rather have been there than anywhere else.' There she experienced various visions while awaiting the day of the Games at which they were to suffer. Perhaps the most remarkable of them is that of her being led out to the arena, where she was stripped, transformed into a man, and had unarmed single combat with an Egyptian (typifying the devil), whom she overthrew. She then trod on his head.

Meanwhile Felicitas gave birth to a girl in prison and the confessors enjoyed a last *agape* together. On the day of the Games they left the prison for the amphitheatre 'joyfully as though they were on their way to heaven'. Perpetua refused to wear the dress of Ceres and sang a hymn of praise. Animals were prepared for killing the prisoners: leopards and bears for the men, a mad heifer for the women. Saturninus was unhurt by a wild boar but, as he foretold, was 'finished with one bite of the leopard'. The heifer tossed Perpetua, but she got up and raised Felicitas to her feet. Perpetua had been so absorbed in ecstasy that she seems to have been unaware of what had happened, for on her return to the gate of the amphitheatre she said: 'When are we going to be thrown to that heifer or whatever it is?' She refused to believe she had already suffered until she was shown the marks on her dress and on her body. Saturninus, mangled by the leopard, went with the other martyrs to the place where the mob asked to see them despatched. They exchanged a final kiss of peace; Perpetua then guided the erring and pain-causing gladiator's knife to her throat; 'it was as though so great a woman . . . could not be despatched unless she herself were willing.'

The feast of these martyrs soon became very famous in the whole Christian Church and was recorded in the earliest Roman and Syriac calendars as well as in the Martyrology of Jerome. In 1907 an inscription in their honour was discovered at Carthage in the Basilica Majorum where they were buried. Their feast was constantly on 7 March for centuries but was moved for some time to 6 March to allow room for the feast of *Thomas Aquinas. In 1970, however, it was restored to its original day. One ancient English church was dedicated to Perpetua. She is depicted in the Ravenna mosaics (6th century); eight episodes of her life are represented on a 14th-century altar frontal at Barcelona.

Latin text of the Acts ed. by J. A. Robinson (Texts and Studies, 1891) and with Eng. tr. by W. H. Shewring (1931) and *A.C.M.*, pp. 106–31; the Greek version ed. with the Latin text by C. I. van Beek (1938). See also H. Delehaye, *Les Passions des martyrs et les genres littéraires* (1921), pp. 63–72 and A. Fridh, *Le Problème de la Passion des saintes Perpetue et Felicité* (1968) with V. L. Kennedy, *The Saints of the Canon of the Mass* (1938) and P. Monceaux, *Histoire Littéraire de l'Afrique chrétienne*, i (1901), 70–96.

PERRAN, see PIRAN.

PETER (1) (d. *c.*64), leader of the apostles. Most of what we know of him comes from the New Testament. He was called Simon, a native of Bethsaida, near the Sea of Galilee, and a brother of *Andrew, who introduced him to Christ, who gave to him the name of Cephas (Peter) which means rock. Andrew and Peter, who was married, were fishermen by profession; Peter may have been the leader of a 'co-operative' which included the sons of Zebedee. In the list of the apostles he is always in the first place; he was one of the three apostles who were privileged to witness the Transfiguration, the raising of the daughter of Jairus, and the Agony in the Garden. The meaning of the name Peter was further explained by Christ when, in answer to Peter's famous confession of faith, recognized by Jesus as the result of revelation by the Father, Christ told him that he would be the rock on which his Church would be built, that the 'gates of hell' would never prevail against it, and that Peter would have the power of 'binding and loosing' (like the other apostles), but that he personally would be given 'the keys of the kingdom of heaven'. The strongly Aramaic character of this passage, together with the fact that it is present in all the earliest manuscripts of the Gospels, makes varied attempts to explain it away as an interpolation completely unconvincing. Christ also prophesied Peter's betrayal and subsequent strengthening of the other apostles; after the Resurrection Christ appeared to Peter before the other apostles and gave him later the mission to feed both the lambs and the sheep of Christ's flock. In the early chapters of the Acts of the Apostles Peter took the lead in deciding what should be done: he designated the successor to Judas; he preached authoritatively at Pentecost; he was the first apostle to work a miracle and soon became the most notable miracle-worker; he justified the apostles' teaching to the sanhedrim, condemned Ananias and Sapphira, admitted gentiles into the church with Cornelius; later he took a prominent part in the council at Jerusalem. Later still he was rebuked by *Paul at Antioch for temporizing about eating with gentiles.

The venerable and early tradition which links Peter with an apostolate and martyrdom at Rome is not explicitly affirmed in the New Testament, but it is quite consistent with it, especially in view of Peter's first epistle mentioning 'Babylon', which is usually identified with Rome; Paul's preaching at Rome had been long delayed because it was his usual policy not to preach where other apostles were at work. But Peter's presence in Rome is explicitly affirmed by many early witnesses such as *Clement of Rome, *Ignatius of Antioch, and *Irenaeus. The same passages imply that he was the founder, instituted the episcopal succession, and suffered martyrdom. Tradition affirms that he suffered under Nero and was crucified head-downwards (Origen), but the claim that his apostolate there lasted twenty-five years appears first in Jerome and is less convincing. Recent excavations at the Vatican, while of very great interest, do not conclusively prove that Peter's relics are under St. Peter's, although it is probable that the tomb is authentic. It is also most significant that Rome is the only city that ever claimed to be Peter's place of death.

Among various writings of apostolic or sub-apostolic times ascribed to St. Peter or his influence are the Gospel of Mark, usually agreed to represent his own catechesis; the First Epistle of Peter, although its authenticity has often been questioned, is very probably his. But the Second Epistle of Peter, which calls Paul's epistles 'scripture' and depends heavily on the epistle of Jude in crucial passages, is almost certainly much later than Peter's death. Other works called the Gospel of St. Peter, the Preaching of St. Peter, the Apocalypse of St. Peter, and the Acts of St. Peter are all documents of the 2nd century or later. They do, however, testify to the enormous importance attached to St. Peter in the early Church.

The history of the relics of Peter and Paul is uncertain. It seems that Peter was buried at the Vatican and Paul on the Ostian Way under his basilica; that both were venerated from very early times both in the Liturgy and in private invocation, testified by Greek and Latin graffiti in the catacombs of the early 3rd century. The alleged translation of the relics of both apostles in 258 to the catacombs is regarded by Delehaye and others as the initial date of their public, liturgical commemoration. Others place this, by conjecture, at the Peace of the Church in 313. If there is some doubt about the origin of the cult, there is none about its diffusion. From very early times Peter was invoked as a universal saint, as the heavenly doorkeeper, as the patron of the Church and the papacy, as one who was both powerful and accessible. In England there were important dedications to Peter from early times: monasteries such as Canterbury, Glastonbury, Malmesbury, Peterborough, Lindisfarne, Whitby, Wearmouth, and especially Westminster; cathedrals such as York, Lichfield, Worcester, and Selsey. The total of pre-Reformation churches dedicated to Peter in England has been calculated as 1,129 as well as another 283 dedicated to SS. Peter and Paul together. His name is constant in all the calendars, with the principal feast with St. Paul on 29 June and a subsidiary feast on 1 August of St. Peter's Chains, commemorating his escape from prison. Images of Peter are innumerable, but his portraiture (possibly an early tradition) remains curiously constant, of a man with a square face, a bald or tonsured head, and a short square, curly beard. His principal attribute is a set of keys, sometimes with a ship or fish, or even a cock in memory of his denial of the Lord. Sometimes he is dressed in a toga; at other times vested as pope or bishop, with or without tiara or mitre. He is also portrayed crucified upside down. The cycles of his life mainly follow the incidents of his life in the Gospels and the Acts of the Apostles (Masaccio's frescoes in the Carmine church at Florence being outstanding). In England St. Peter was a familiar figure in the Middle Ages, appearing frequently in screen paintings (with the other apostles, in East Anglia), sculptures, or stained-glass windows. From the Norman Conquest to the 16th century it was an immensely popular Christian name, as it is also in the 20th century.

AA.SS. Iun. VII (1717), 1–174; F. J. Foakes Jackson, *Peter, Prince of the Apostles* (1927); R. Aigrain, *S. Pierre* (1948); O. Cullmann, *Petrus* (1952, Eng. tr. 1953); C. H. Turner, 'St. Peter in the New Testament', *Theology*, xiii (1926), 66–78 (reprinted in his *Catholic and Apostolic*, 1931). On his connection with Rome H. Lietzmann, *Petrus und Paulus in Rom* (2nd edn. 1927); D. W. O'Connor, *Peter in Rome: the literary, liturgical and Archeological Evidence* (1969); O. Karrer, *Peter and the Church* (1963); see also A. A. de Marco, *The Tomb of Saint Peter* (1964); J. Toynbee and J. W. Perkins, *The Shrine of St. Peter and the Vatican Excavations* (1956); also J. Dauvillier, *Les Temps apostoliques* (1970).

PETER (2), see MARCELLINUS AND PETER.

PETER (3), see GORGONIUS, PETER, AND DOROTHEUS.

PETER OF ALCANTARA (1499–1562), Franciscan priest. This future founder of a reformed branch of the Franciscan Order came from Estremadura (Spain), where his father was a lawyer and its governor. He was educated at Salamanca university, but became an Observant Franciscan in 1515 at Manjaretes, an extremely strict house, where he began the life of asceticism which was to equal that of some of the Desert Fathers. Although not yet a priest, he was sent as guardian to a new foundation at Badajoz; three years later, in 1524, he was ordained. His example of extreme penitence and poverty was matched by his skill as a preacher, which depended on infused as well as acquired knowledge of God. At Lapa, a remote contemplative house of which he became guardian, he later wrote a book on prayer (*c.*1556), which may have been derived from Luis of Granada's similar work. It won instant acclaim and was translated into several European languages. In 1538 he became a provincial of the strict Estremaduran province, tried unsuccessfully to reform it still further, and then retired to Arabida, near Lisbon, where he inspired a community of Franciscan hermits.

This led to the foundation of a new province later called the Alcantarines, based on Pedrosa, where the surviving miniature monastery, built to his own specifications, had cells only seven feet long; the number of friars was never more than eight and they practised three hours' mental prayer a day besides the usual liturgy and austere practices. These he described to *Theresa of Avila, whom he first met in 1560 and strongly encouraged in her Carmelite reform. 'He told me', she wrote, 'that he slept but one hour and a half in twenty-four hours for forty years together . . . that he never put up his hood, however hot the sun or heavy the rain; nor did he wear any other garment than his habit of thick coarse cloth or anything upon his feet . . . It was usual for him to eat but once in three days. One of his companions told me that sometimes he ate nothing at all for eight days; but that perhaps might be when he was in prayer, for he used to have great raptures and vehement transports of divine love, of which I was once an eye-witness . . . When I came to know him, he was very old and his body so shrivelled and weak that it seemed to be composed as it were of the roots and dried bark of a tree rather than flesh. He was very pleasant but spoke little unless questions were asked him; he answered in a few words, but in these he was worth hearing, for he had an excellent understanding.' She later testified that he had done more to help her nascent reform than anyone else. A few months after her convent of St. Joseph at Avila was opened, Peter fell ill and died in his convent at Arenas, kneeling. He was canonized in 1669 and made patron of Brazil in 1826 and of Estremadura in 1962. Feast: 19 October.

Earliest Life with testimony of St. Theresa etc. in *AA.SS.* Oct. VIII (1866), 623–809; *Estudios sobre San Pedro de Alcantara en el IV centenario de su muerte, 1562–1962* (Archivo Ibero-Americano, 1962). Other Lives by F. Marchese (1667, Eng. tr. 1856) and J. Piat (1959). His treatise on prayer was translated into English by D. Devas (1926); see also E. A. Peers, *Studies of the Spanish Mystics*, v. 2 (1930); *Bibl. SS.*, x 652–62.

PETER OF CANTERBURY (d. 607), abbot. First abbot of St. Augustine's (then called SS. Peter and Paul), Peter was probably the monk of that name who was sent by *Augustine to give news of the first

Anglo-Saxon conversions to *Gregory the Great and who brought back to England Gregory's replies to Augustine's questions. Peter was sent later on a mission to Gaul, but was drowned in the English Channel in the bay of Ambleteuse (Amfleet). The local inhabitants, according to Bede, buried him in an 'unworthy place' but, as the result of a prodigy of mysterious light appearing over his grave at night, translated his relics to a church in Boulogne with suitable honour. At St. Augustine's, Canterbury, his feast was kept on 30 December; other authorities give 6 January.

Bede, *H.E.*, i. 27, 33; *AA.SS.* Ian. I (1643), 334.

PETER OF TARENTAISE (*c.*1102–1174), Cistercian monk and archbishop. Born near Vienne of a free and devout family, he became a Cistercian monk at nearby Bonnevaux *c.*1122; about ten years later he was elected abbot of Tamié, where with the help of Amadeus III, count of Savoy, he built a guest-house and hospital for travellers from Geneva to Savoy who passed very close to the abbey. In 1142 he was elected archbishop of Tarentaise, where he took a difficult succession owing to the neglect and corruption of his predecessor, who had been deposed. *Bernard was insistent that Peter accept this charge.

He appointed Austin canons to his cathedral and worthy priests to his parishes. He visited his diocese regularly, made educational and charitable foundations, recovered alienated property, and provided for the reverent performance of the Liturgy. Both as abbot and bishop he delighted in taking an active personal share in charitable works; he was also believed to work miracles of healing and of the multiplication of food. Perturbed by the acclaim for his miracles and longing for his initial monastic solitude, he suddenly disappeared in 1155. A year later he was discovered in a Swiss Cistercian abbey, living as a lay-brother. On returning to his diocese he rebuilt the guest-house at the Little St. Bernard pass and founded the custom of distributing free soup and bread from May onwards before harvest time in his largely mountainous diocese. As a reforming bishop he supported Pope Alexander III against the antipope Victor, who was the protégé of the emperor Frederick Barbarossa. Peter laboured long and hard for Alexander, preaching in Alsace, Burgundy, and Italy and openly supported his cause in several councils, even in the presence of the emperor himself who was his sovereign. Peter's words were confirmed by many cures.

In his old age he used to visit the Grande Chartreuse, near Grenoble, where he met and was looked after by the young Hugh of Avalon, later *Hugh of Lincoln, whose policies as a bishop seem to resemble closely those of Peter. Both were conspicuous for courageously withstanding kings and emperors, as Alexander III and his English predecessor Hadrian IV had done.

Towards the end of his life Peter was sent by Alexander to make peace between Henry II of England and Louis VII of France. He was well received by both kings. Walter Map, then in attendance at Henry's court, helped to entertain Peter and wrote warmly of his sanctity, miracles, and love of the poor. He also described his character as being joyful, modest, and humble. Map's witness is all the more impressive as he was cynical and no lover of the Cistercians. Peter died on 14 September at Bellevaux Abbey, near Besançon on his way back to his diocese. He was canonized in 1191; his relics were divided between France and Savoy: Tarentaise, Tamié, and Cîteaux obtained the largest portions. Feast: 8 May.

Contemporary Life by Geoffrey, abbot of Hautecombe in *AA.SS.* Maii II (1680), 320–48; anonymous modern Life by a monk of Tamié, *S. Pierre de Tarentaise* (1935) and by H. Brultey (1945); see also Walter Map, *De nugis curialium* (O.M.T., 1983), pp. 134–41; B.T.A., ii. 253–5.

PETER CANISIUS, see CANISIUS.

PETER CELESTINE (Celestine V) (1215–96), monk and founder of the Celestine Order and pope. As the only pope in history who voluntarily abdicated, at the age of over eighty and after a reign of only a few months, he has a unique place in the history of the papacy. The eleventh child of a peasant family, born at Isernia, Peter of Morrone was intelligent and devout, became a hermit in the mountains, was ordained priest, and then resumed his eremitical life, this time under Benedictine patronage from Faizola and eventually on Monte Majella. Several times his solitude had been interrupted by others who wished him to be their guide and ruler; in the end he agreed to be abbot of a monastery of hermits at Monte Morone, where the life was based on the Rule of St. Benedict but also encouraged the practice of solitary life. There he lived for about forty years, obtaining approval for his Order, called the Celestines, in 1274; he was widely revered and had some contact with the Franciscan Spirituals and the movements which looked for inspiration in the writings of Joachim of Fiore. In 1294, because of a complete deadlock in the election by the cardinals of a successor to Nicholas IV which resulted in a very long vacancy, Peter, then in charge of twenty monasteries, sent them a message threatening them with divine retribution if they continued to endanger the state of the Church by further delay. To end the deadlock, they chose Peter himself as the new pope (Celestine V).

Immediate acclaim greeted this holy and unworldly abbot as he rode on a donkey to Aquila flanked by the kings of Hungary and Naples. But his reign was a disaster. His simplicity, his ignorance of canon law, and his desire to please all and give offence to none were exploited by the king of Naples, who persuaded him to live in his own city, to create thirteen new cardinals in the interests of Naples and France, and to make a number of unsuitable appointments. Indeed he sometimes bestowed the same benefice several times on different candidates. Completely unworldly, he gave away treasure and positions of influence for which he had no use himself, regardless of the difficult political situation in which Christian rulers were at war with each other and each looked for support from the successor of St. Peter, who had rights of intervention and arbitration. As Advent came, Peter, miserable with the cares of office and the confusion and disorder which his own actions had caused, decided to retire into complete solitude, asking for a cell to be made inside the palace. Warned that his plan of leaving the rule of the Church to three cardinals could result in the appearance of three rival popes, he consulted the able canonist cardinal Gaetani about the possibility and the legality of his resigning his office. Gaetani replied after consultation that it was permissible, and sometimes advisable, to resign. In spite of an outcry from those in favour of his continuing in office, some of whom were spiritual men who looked to him for renewal, he read a solemn declaration of his abdication on the grounds of age, incapacity, and lack of knowledge. He asked pardon for his many mistakes and exhorted the cardinals to choose a worthy successor.

He retired to a monastery and the cardinals elected Gaetani as Pope Boniface VIII. Celestine tried to escape from Italy across the Adriatic; Boniface, who brought the papacy back to Rome out of the power of Naples, had political enemies who continued to use Celestine as a figure-head and declared Boniface's election invalid; Boniface accordingly captured Celestine and enclosed him at Fumome, near Anagni, with a few other monks in honourable captivity. 'I wanted nothing in this world but a cell, and a cell they have given me', said Celestine. He died on 19 May 1296. His canonization in 1313 by Clement V, the first of the Avignon popes, was part of a movement instigated by Philip the Fair, to discredit Boniface VIII. Feast: 19 May, from 1668 in the universal calendar until 1969. Celestine's body rests at S. Maria del Colle at Aquilia, where he was consecrated bishop.

AA.SS. Maii IV (1685), 419–536; 'Vita et miracula S. Petri Caelestini', *Anal. Boll.*, ix (1890), 147–98 and x (1891), 386–92; A. Van Ortroy, 'S. Pierre Celestin et ses premiers biographes', *Anal.*

Boll., xvi (1897), 365–487 and 'Vies primitives de S. Pierre Celestin', *Anal. Boll.*, xviii (1899), 34–42; F. X. Seppelt, *Monumenta Caelestiniana* (1921); A. Frugoni, *Celestiniana* (1954); H. K. Mann, *The Lives of the Popes in the Middle Ages*, xvii. 247–341.

PETER CHRYSOLOGUS (d. *c.*450), archbishop of Ravenna. A native of Imola (about 30 miles west of Ravenna), Peter was a deacon there when chosen bishop of Ravenna by Valentinian III and his mother Galla Placidia, who helped him in his reforming and building projects, particularly at the port of Classis, but he cannot be certainly associated with any of the surviving mosaics at Ravenna. He also enjoyed the confidence of *Leo the Great, whose teaching on the Incarnation he strongly supported, urging on Eutyches the need to acquiesce in the teaching of the Roman Church. His reputation as a preacher was very high: many of his sermons, but few other works, survive. As bishop he was concerned with both the survival of paganism and the growth of abuses. He received hospitality from *Germanus of Auxerre and presided at his funeral in August 450. He himself died at Imola on 31 July. He was declared a Doctor of the Church in 1729 by Benedict XIII. Feast: 30 July (formerly 4 December).

The earliest Life was written in 836 and reveals some confusion between two different bishops of Ravenna, both called Peter; it is printed in *P.L.*, lii. 9–680 with his sermons; critical edn. by A. Olivar, *Los sermones de San Pedro Crisologo* (1962); Eng. tr. of selected writings by G. E. Ganss (*Fathers of the Church*, vol. xvii, 1953, pp. 3–287); monographs by G. Bohmer (1919) and D. L. Badisserri (1920); see also J. H. Baxter, 'The Homilies of St. Peter Chrysologus', *J.T.S.*, xxii (1920–1), 250–8; C. Jenkins, 'Aspects of the Theology of St. Peter Chrysologus', *C.Q.R.*, ciii (1927), 233–59; and R. H. McGlynn, *The Incarnation in the Sermons of St. Peter Chrysologus* (1956).

PETER CLAVER, see CLAVER.

PETER DAMIAN (1007–72), bishop, monk, and cardinal. Born at Ravenna of a large and comparatively poor family, Peter lost both his parents in childhood and was oppressed by one brother but adopted by another who was archpriest of Ravenna, and gave him the best education he could provide. This comprised grammar, rhetoric, and law, studied at Faenza and Parma; afterwards he became a teacher at Ravenna. Already he lived an austere life, and he decided to become a monk. This he accomplished in 1035 when he joined the Camaldolese Benedictine monastery of Fonte Avellana reformed by Romuald. This was a community of hermits who lived two in a cell, following a very austere regime of fasting, abstinence, and vigils, which for Peter resulted in a temporary breakdown of health. His studies now consisted of Scripture and patristic theology, which he pursued with the same zeal and thoroughness which he had previously devoted to secular studies. Some of the time devoted to manual labour was spent in transcribing manuscripts; liturgical and private prayer with sacred reading were the other occupations of the monks. Some of them lived in complete solitude. In 1043 he was elected abbot of this poor and small community. Insisting on solitude and charity with fidelity to the founding fathers, he eventually made five foundations. Ardent, energetic, intransigent, Peter was also kind to his monks and could be indulgent to penitents. But his writings reveal rather his strictness and severity: reproofs of bishops for playing chess match those of wandering wealthy monks. The state of the Church was so critical at this time that he was soon called on to direct his energies into a wider field. First his eloquent voice was heard at the synods of Italy held by reforming popes like *Leo IX, preaching against simony and clerical marriage and in favour of the reformed papacy which he saw as the key to the whole future of the Church. He was also severe about laxity of all kinds in the monastic Order.

In 1057 he was appointed bishop of Ostia and cardinal. For several years he took a prominent part in the Gregorian Reform, acting energetically against various antipopes, going on diplomatic and ecclesiastical missions to Milan, Germany, and France, preaching and writing in the cause of reform. In 1059 he took part in the Lateran synod which proclaimed the right of the cardinals alone to elect the future bishops of Rome. In 1069 he managed to dissuade the emperor Henry IV from divorcing his wife Bertha. Meanwhile he had remained a monk at heart and repeatedly asked successive popes to be relieved of his episcopal duties. This was eventually granted by Nicholas II, and Peter returned to his monastery at Fonte Avellana, practising the austerities which he had recommended for others. An interesting occupation of his old age was making wooden spoons and other artefacts. The last mission he accomplished was to his native town of Ravenna, whose archbishop had been excommunicated; as a result the town was divided into factions. When he arrived the archbishop had died, but he settled matters satisfactorily by punishing his accomplices and restoring peace and order. On his way back to Rome he died in a monastery at Faenza on 22 February. Important as an ecclesiastical statesman and reformer, he also made a significant contribution to monastic thought, in so far as he regarded the eremitic life as the best for everyone and community life as a rather poor second. But he also advocated regular canonical life for cathedral clergy, and was a precursor of devotional development to the Passion of Christ and the Blessed Virgin. He was also a notable poet, perhaps his best-known hymn being that in honour of St. Gregory, beginning '*Anglorum iam Apostolus*'. Feast: 21 February.

Life by his disciple John of Lodi in *AA.SS.* Feb. III (1658), 416–27 and in *P.L.*, cxliv. 113–46; modern Lives by R. Biron (1908), F. Dressler (*Studia Anselmiana*, 1954), J. Leclercq (1960), and O. J. Blum (1947). See also A. Fliche, *La Réforme grégorienne* (vol. i, 1924) and J. P. Whitney, *Hildebrandine Essays* (1932), pp. 95–120. Works in *P.L.*, cxliv and cxlv; in *M.G.H.*, 'Libelli de Lite Imperatorum et Pontificum in Saeculis XI et XII', i (1891), 15–75; opuscula ed. P. Brezzi-Nardi (1943) and poems by M. Lokrantz (1964). Eng. tr. of *Selected Writings on the Spiritual Life* with useful Introduction by P. A. McNulty (1959). See also J. J. Ryan, *Saint Peter Damiani and his Canonical Sources* (1956); J. Gonsette, *Pierre Damien et la culture profane* (1965); *Studi su san Pier Damiano in onore del Cardinale Cicognani* (1961).

PETER NOLASCO (*c.*1182–1256), founder of the Mercedarian Order. Much uncertainty surrounds the details of his life owing to legends and spurious documents. He was born in Barcelona of a merchant family. He became procurator of *Raymond of Pennafort's lay confraternity for ransoming slaves from the Moors. This became the Mercedarian Order in 1234, following the Rule of St. Augustine and approved by Gregory IX in 1235. Peter was its Master-General until 1249. During a visit to Valencia and Granada it is claimed that he redeemed 400 Christians. His Order spread through most of Spain and was closely associated with *Ferdinand III's reconquest of the southern provinces.

In 1628 the papacy confirmed Peter's cult and extended it to the universal church in 1664. A fine series of paintings by Zurbarán survives at the Prado, Madrid. Feast: 28 January.

N.C.E., xi. 225; *Bibl. SS.*, x. 844–52; *H.S.S.C.*, vi. 281.

PETER THE MARTYR (Peter of Verona) (1205–52), Dominican friar and priest. He was born of Cathar parents at Verona, but at the age of fifteen as a student at Bologna University he received the habit from *Dominic and made his profession at Bologna. Zealous in his monastic duties and his studies, he was soon destined for promotion. He became prior of various houses of Dominicans (still in their early formative period) and was famous for his preaching in Lombardy. He won an immense personal following, helped both by his reputation as a wonder-worker and by his vindication from a false charge that he had admitted strangers and women into his cell. In 1234 he was appointed inquisitor for the Milan area, and in 1251 his jurisdiction was extended to most of northern Italy, including Venice,

Genoa, Bologna, and the Marches of Ancona. The heretics with whom he argued and whom he reconciled to the Church or denounced as contumacious were mainly Cathars, in whose beliefs he had himself been brought up. He was also a firm and discreet director of nuns; zealous for biblical study and the spiritual life, he regretted that he had to leave his cell too often. He realized that his work of preaching and disputation, although less violent than the Albigensian crusades, aroused the same hostility. His life was often in danger from assassins and his end came at the early age of forty-seven. On his way from Como to Milan he was ambushed by two assailants, of whom one split his head open with an axe and stabbed his companion, a friar called Dominic. Peter commended himself to God in the words of *Stephen, but the tradition which asserts that he wrote the words *Credo in Deum* in his own blood before his death from another blow is somewhat dubious. He died on 6 April; his murderer, Carino, abjured his heresy and became a Dominican lay brother who after many years died with a reputation for sanctity. Peter was canonized in 1253. He was regarded as the first martyr of the Dominican Order; his tomb at Milan became an important pilgrimage centre, and several notable artists, especially Fra Angelico, depicted him with a wound in his head, a dagger in his shoulder, and his fingers on his lips. There are English examples at Long Melford (stained glass) and at Thornham Parva (Suffolk) on the retable. Feast: 29 April (in England at St. Augustine's, Canterbury, Barking, and Muchelney), especially in Dominican churches.

AA.SS. Apr. III (1675), 678–719; another 13th-cent. Life in B. M. de Reichert, *Vitae Fratrum Ordinis Praedicatorum* (1897), 236–48; A. Dondaine, 'Saint Pierre Martyr', *Archivum Fratrum Praedicatorum*, xxiii (1953), 66–162; S. Orlandi, *S. Pietro martire da Verona* (1952).

PETROC (6th century), abbot, Cornwall's most famous saint. The sources for his Life are late and unsatisfactory. He came from South Wales, landed at Haylemouth, and founded a monastery in succession to Wethinoc at Lanwethinoc, now called Padstow (= Petroc's Stow). About 30 years later, he founded another monastery at Little Petherick (Nanceventon), where he also built a mill and a chapel. He later lived as a hermit on Bodmin Moor, where the hermit *Goran met him, but departed southwards soon afterwards. Petroc built a cell for himself by the river, and a monastery on the hilltop for the twelve disciples who had followed him. At the end of his life he visited the other monasteries he had founded, but died at Treravel on his way. He was buried at Padstow, which became the centre of his cult. Like several other hermit saints, he had a special affinity with wild animals and is generally portrayed with a stag as his emblem, in memory of the one whom he sheltered from huntsmen.

His cult was diffused partly through the activities of his disciples and partly through the theft, and subsequent restoration, of his relics. Churches were dedicated to him in Cornwall, Devon (18), South Wales, and Brittany. Padstow became the Cornish see, but *c.*1000 the shrine and relics (including his staff and bell) were translated to Bodmin. There too went the community which claimed him as their founder, although they were by then canons rather than monks.

In 1177 Martin, a malcontent Bodmin canon, stole the relics and took them to Saint-Méen (Brittany). Bartholemew, bishop of Exeter, investigated the matter and brought it to the attention of the king. Henry II intervened; a rib was left at Saint-Méen; the remaining relics were restored to Bodmin; Walter of Coutances (his Cornish seal-bearer and future archbishop of Rouen and Justiciar of England) gave for a head-reliquary a fine ivory casket of Sicilian–Islamic workmanship. This was hidden at the Reformation, was discovered over the Bodmin porch in the 19th century, and remains in the parish church; it belongs to Bodmin's Town Council and is one of the finest reliquaries in England.

Petroc's feast occurs in several early West Country calendars as well as the Canterbury books of the 11th century, such as the Bosworth Psalter and the Missal of Robert of Jumièges. It eventually reached the Sarum calendar and even the Hours of Gregory XIII and a 15th-century Italian Franciscan psalter. York, Ely, and Bury were other churches which venerated him, while both Exeter and Glastonbury claimed relics. Feast: 4 June, 1 October (first translation), and 14 September (*Exaltatio*, which celebrated the return of the relics in 1177); a Truro calendar also gives 23 May.

R.P.S.; *C.S.P.*; *N.L.A.*, ii. 317–20; P. Grosjean, 'Vie et Miracles de S. Petroc', *Anal. Boll.*, lxxiv (1956), 131–88, 470–96; G. H. Doble, *St. Petroc* (1938); id., 'The Relics of St. Petroc', *Antiquity*, xiii (1939), 403–15; R. H. Pinder-Wilson and C. N. L. Brooke, 'The Reliquary of St. Petroc and the Ivories of Norman Sicily', *Archaeologia*, civ (1973), 261–306; see also J. Stonor, 'St. Petroc's Cell on Bodmin Moor', *Downside Review*, lxvi (1948), 64–74.

PETRONILLA, an early Roman martyr, the date and details of whose death are unknown. She belonged to the family of Domitilla, in whose catacomb she is described as a martyr. Her fictitious 6th-century Acts make her a daughter of *Peter, who refused marriage to a Count Flaccus; he threatened to have her killed, but she died after three days' fasting. Her sarcophagus was moved to St. Peter's in the 8th century and her chapel there became that of the kings of France. Charlemagne and Carloman were considered St. Peter's adopted sons, and his supposed daughter became their patroness. The chapel was embellished by kings of France and by later popes who employed Michelangelo and Bramante. Mass on her feast day, 31 May, is offered for France and attended by French residents. St. Petronilla occurs fairly frequently in English late medieval stained glass and painted screens, and her usual emblem is a set of keys, presumably borrowed from St. Peter.

AA.SS. Maii VII (1688), 420–2; *C.M.H.*, pp. 280, 285; H. Delehaye, *Sanctus* (1927), pp. 118–20.

PHILEAS (d. 306), bishop of Thmuis and martyr. Learned and eloquent, Phileas became a Christian in adult life, was chosen as bishop of his city in the Egyptian Thebaid and was arrested soon after his consecration at Alexandria under the edicts of Diocletian. This was in *c.*303; during his long imprisonment he wrote a moving letter about the tortures of Christian martyrs in his diocese. The Greek Acts of his martyrdom survive in a fragmentary manuscript written within about fifteen years of his death. This document records the fifth and last interview between the bishop and the prefect Culcianus. It reveals genuine, if ironic, interest in Christian doctrines such as the resurrection of the body and the role of conscience by the prefect and the cool but inflexible rationality of Phileas.

To the question 'Can you now be reasonable?' Phileas answered: 'I am always reasonable and I exercise myself in good sense.' In answer to repeated demands that he offer sacrifice, Phileas answered that the sacrifices which God asks are 'a pure heart, a spotless soul, and spiritual perceptions which lead to deeds of piety and justice'. To the direct question 'Was Jesus God?' Phileas answered: 'Yes . . . he did not say of himself that he was God because he performed the works of God in power and actuality . . . he cleansed lepers, made the blind see, the deaf hear, the lame walk, the dumb speak . . . he drove demons from his creatures at a command; he cured paralytics, raised the dead to life, and performed many other signs and wonders.' Culcianus asked: 'Was he not a common man? Surely he was not in the class of Plato.' Phileas replied: 'Indeed he was superior to Plato.' 'If you were one of the uncultured,' said Culcianus, 'I should not spare you. But now you possess such abundant resources that you can nourish and sustain not only yourself but a whole city. Therefore spare yourself and sacrifice.' 'I will not,' answered Phileas '. . . I have reflected many times and this is my decision.' Appeals to sacrifice for the sake of his wife and children left him constant. Soon after, he was led out to be beheaded. Feast: 4 February.

A.C.M., xlvi–xlviii and 319–53; F. Halkin, 'L' Apologie du martyr Philéas', *Anal. Boll.*, lxxxi (1963), 5–27; V. Martin, *Papyrus Bodmer XX: Apologie de Philéas évêque de Thmuis* (1964), 24–52; Eusebius, *H.E.*, viii. 10.

PHILEMON AND APPHIA (1st century), martyrs. Philemon, to whom *Paul's short epistle was sent at Colosse from Rome, was a Christian, whose slave Onesimus had run away. He had met Paul, who sent him back to his master with the letter which asked for Philemon's forgiveness. The tradition is that Philemon freed Onesimus and was later martyred at Colosse with his wife Apphia. Feast: 22 November in Roman Martyrology; 14 February or 6 July in the East.

J. Knox, *Philemon among the Letters of Paul* (1935, 1960); P. Benoit in *Dictionnaire de la Bible*, Suppl. vii (1966), 1204–11.

PHILIBERT (*c.*608–*c.*685), abbot, founder of Jumièges. Born in Gascony and educated by his father (who became a bishop) and by *Ouen, Philibert became a monk in St. Ouen's monastery of Rebais, was abbot for a short time, but resigned because of his inexperience and the monks' unruliness. He retired to Neustria, where Clovis II gave him land at Jumièges, where he founded the abbey in 654. Owing to his active opposition to Ebroin, Philibert was imprisoned at Rouen, and then retired to Poitiers and to the island of Heriou (Poitou), where he founded the monastery of Noirmoutier. Later he founded monasteries for monks at Quincay (near Poitiers) and Luçon and one for nuns at Pavilly. Philibert had died and been buried at Heriou; his relics, after various removals, rested at Tournus from 875. He was mentioned by Alcuin as a notable monastic founder. Feast: 20 August, kept by English monasteries connected with Jumièges after the Norman Conquest.

AA.SS. Aug. IV (1739), 66–95; R. Poupardin, *Monuments de l'histoire des abbayes de saint Philibert* (1905).

PHILIP (1st century), apostle. Nearly everything known about him is in the New Testament. He came from Bethsaida (Galilee); he became a disciple of Jesus early on, probably after following *John the Baptist; he then persuaded Nathanael (probably *Bartholomew) to follow Jesus. At the feeding of the 5,000 he remarked that two hundred pennyworth of bread would not be sufficient for each person to have even a little. Again, when the Greeks wanted to meet Jesus, they approached Philip first; at the last discourse Philip's request to Jesus to show them the Father elicited the reply: 'He that sees me, sees the Father.' (Cf. John 1: 43–51; 6: 5–7; 12: 21 f.; 14: 8 f.) Like the other apostles he was in the upper room awaiting the coming of the Spirit at Pentecost (Acts 1: 12–14), but after that there are only vague traditions. Some of these, which develop the role of Philip's supposed daughters in the early Church, are probably due to a confusion between him and Philip the Deacon (cf. Acts 8; 21: 8). Perhaps the most probable is the tradition which says that he preached the Gospel in Phrygia and died at Hierapolis, where he was also buried. His supposed relics were translated to Rome and placed in the basilica of the Twelve Apostles. But an ancient inscription there records that it was originally dedicated to SS. Philip and *James. In art Philip is represented either with a cross, on which he was believed to have suffered, or else with loaves of bread to recall his part in feeding the 5,000. Several screen paintings of him survive in Norfolk together with those of most or all the other Apostles (e.g. North Elmham, South Lynn, and Salle). It has also been suggested that the long cross which Philip holds (e.g. in the Malvern stained glass) may be a weapon with which in the *Golden Legend* he drove away a noxious dragon of the temple of Mars. Early manuscripts of the Martyrology of *Jerome place the feast of Philip alone on 1 May, which may indicate that James was joined to his feast after this dedication; both figure on this day in the early Roman sacramentaries. This traditional feast day of 1 May was altered in recent years because May Day was devoted to the feast of *Joseph 'the Worker' in 1955. In that year and after the feast of SS. Philip and James was transferred to 11 May, but in 1969 it was moved once more to 3 May. In the B.C.P. it has remained constant on 1 May, and the Eastern churches celebrate it on 14 November.

AA.SS. Maii I (1680), 7–34 with *C.M.H.*, pp. 222–3; B.T.A., ii. 203–5.

PHILIP BENIZI, see BENIZI.

PHILIP NERI, see NERI.

PHILOMENA, supposed virgin and martyr of early Rome. In 1802 a tomb (*loculus*) was discovered in the catacomb of Priscilla in Rome, closed with three tiles on which were painted the inscription LUMENA/PAXTE/CUMFI. This was soon emended to PAX TECUM FILUMENA ('Peace be with you, Philomena'), which was recognized as the original reading. Inside it were the bones of an adolescent girl of about fifteen, accompanied by a phial of blood which in those days, but not nowadays, was accepted, together with a palm symbol, as a sign of martyrdom. In 1805 the relics were given to the church of Mugnano, where they were enshrined; miracles and favours at her intercession were soon reported. The fame of Philomena spread through Italy aided by a nun's private revelations which asserted, among other things, that Philomena was a Latin name meaning 'daughter of light' when in reality it is a Greek one meaning 'beloved'. Fictitious Lives followed, which helped the cult spread among the credulous, but two other factors worked decisively in the same direction. One was the constant praise given to Philomena by J.-B. *Vianney (curé d'Ars), notably for the cures which he himself achieved; the other was the sudden recovery of Pauline Jaricot, foundress of the missionary Association for the Propagation of the Faith, at the shrine of Philomena, when almost dying. This cure in 1835 was one factor which led Gregory XVI to authorize the public cult of Philomena in several Italian dioceses including Rome. In 1855 Pius IX approved a proper Mass and Office.

Meanwhile critical scholars were not satisfied. Archaeological evidence pointed strongly to the bones discovered not being those of the original burial and to the tiles on the outside having been deliberately disarranged. The original burial may, but need not necessarily, have been those of a martyr, who was either Philomena or was the beloved of some unknown person. Her body may well have been translated to other Roman churches with those of other martyrs in the 8th or 9th centuries. Devout patrons of Philomena have often resented the attempts of scholars to establish the truth about her; to the relief of the latter and the indignation of the former (and those with vested interests in the cult and the shrine) the Holy See suppressed the cult of Philomena in 1960. The feast was formerly on 10 August. The story of the rise and fall of the cult of Philomena sheds light on a number of cults in earlier times, but differs from them in so far as it has been subjected to critical analysis from its starting-point in a scientific age.

O. Marucchi, 'Osservazioni archeologiche sulla iscrizione di S. Filomena' in *Miscellanea di Storia ecclesiastica e di Studi ausiliari*, ii (1904), 365–86; id., 'Studio archeologico sulla celebre iscrizione di Filumena scoperta nel cimitero di Priscilla', *Nuovo Bulletino di Archaeologia cristiana*, xii (1906), 253–300; F. Trochu, *La Petite sainte du Curé d' Ars* (1924): C. Hallack, *St. Philomena* (1936); B.T.A., iii. 299–301; arts. in *N.C.E.* and *Bibl. SS.*, v. 796–800.

PHOCAS OF SINOPE (4th century(?)), martyr. This saint is mentioned four times in the Martyrology of Jerome and occurs once in the OE Martyrology. He was a very famous martyr (but not bishop) of Sinope, on the Black Sea, and was a gardener. His praises were sung by St. Asterius (*c*.400); his relics were claimed by Vienne as well as by Antioch. It seems very probable that hagiographers have made one saint into three: Phocas of Antioch, Phocas the bishop of Sinope, and Phocas the gardener. Only the last seems authentic. According to the Legend Phocas was both a hermit and a very skilful gardener, who used his surplus produce to feed the visitors and pilgrims in his guest-house; any residue went to the poor. In a time of persecution Phocas was said to have been impeached as a Christian, condemned without trial, and soldiers were sent to kill him. Ignorant of his identity, they stayed the night at his guest-house and asked him where Phocas was. He answered that he knew the man they wanted and would help them in their search the next day. During the night Phocas dug a grave for himself and prepared for death. In the morning he divulged his identity; the soldiers, after recovering from their surprise and receiving his assurance that he regarded martyrdom as the greatest gain, killed him and buried him in the grave he had prepared. According to Asterius, his church drew pilgrims from far and wide and his relics were much sought after. Phocas became the patron of sailors in the Black Sea and the Eastern Mediterranean. This patronage may be connected with the resemblance of his name to the Greek word for a seal (*phoce*). Feast: on various dates, usually 22 September or 14 July (which may represent the translation feast to Vienne), but in the East the dates of 5, 6, 19 (dedication), and 22 July are found. In the OE Martyrology he is found on 14 July; his feast probably occurs through the dependence of this Martyrology on that of Ado, archbishop of Vienne.

C.M.H., pp. 374–5; B.T.A., iii. 617–19: G. Herzfeld, *An Old English Martyrology* (E.E.T.S., 1900).

PIALA, see FINGAR AND PIALA.

PIONIUS (d. *c.*250), martyr. This priest of Smyrna was arrested with several companions on the feast of *Polycarp. He was an eloquent preacher whose words are recorded in the contemporary Acts. Before his interrogation he placed a set of woven chains round his neck and those of Sabina and Asclepiades to prevent false claims being made that they had conformed. On the Saturday Polemon, the temple verger, came with his men to search out the Christians and drag them off to offer sacrifices and eat sacrificial food. They were led to the forum, where they were warned that it would be wise to obey the edict and sacrifice like everyone else.

Pionius made a long speech in his defence, which appealed to both Greeks and Jews. To the former he quoted Homer that it is not a holy thing to gloat over those who are to die (*Odyssey* 22. 412). To the Jews he cited biblical texts telling them not to rejoice when your enemy falls and not to be glad when he stumbles (Prov. 24: 17). The Christians are men who have been treated unjustly. They have not committed murder nor have they forced anyone to worship false gods or take part in sacrifices offered to the dead. Nor have they murmured against God, fornicated with pagan foreigners, or been ungrateful to their benefactors. Once he had visited the Holy Land and regarded its deserts and the Dead Sea and interpreted them as signs of divine displeasure. Similarly, the state of the Lydian decapolis, ruined by earthquakes and scorching, together with the volcanic fire of Sicily, remind us of the judgement by fire which is to come.

Attentive silence greeted his words. He ended: 'We do not worship your false gods, nor will we adore the golden idol.' Some advocates tried, as they believed, to save him from himself. They declared their love for him, they wanted him to live and to see the light. 'I too agree that life is good,' he answered, 'but the life that we long for is better; and so too of light, especially that one true light.' They then tried to persuade him to go into the temple of Nemesis, but he wished to persuade them to become Christians. His companion Sabina smiled at this and said: 'Those who believe in Christ will laugh unhesitatingly in everlasting joy.' They answered: 'You are going to suffer something you will not like: women who refuse to sacrifice are put into a brothel.' 'The God who is all-holy', she said, 'will take care of that.'

Again Polemon spoke to Pionius and urged him to sacrifice, but he replied that he was a Christian, who worshipped Almighty God who made the heavens and the earth and all things in them, who is known through Christ his Word. On being asked what church he belonged to, he replied 'The Catholic Church; with Christ there is no other.' Sabina and Asclepiades answered similarly.

All three were put in prison. When they refused the offerings of the believers, the gaolers were angry because they used to benefit from these offerings. So they were placed in the inmost prison where they praised God. Later they were examined again. Euctemon, a Christian leader, had offered sacrifice and attempts were made to force Pionius to do the same. He was carried into the temple kicking and struggling, but again he refused to sacrifice, making his faith even more explicit: 'The God (we worship) is he who made heaven and earth.' Lepidus asked if he meant the one who was crucified. Pionius answered: 'Yes, him whom God sent for the redemption of the world.' At this the officials guffawed loudly while Lepidus cursed Christ.

Repeated interrogation, torture by the fingernails, and sentence to be burnt alive all failed to change his mind. Pionius was finally burnt to death in company with a Marcionite called Metrodorus. Feast: 12 March, but 1 February in the Roman Martyrology.

A.C.M., xxviii–xxx, 137–67; H. Delehaye, *Les passions des martyrs* (1921), pp. 27–59; *Propylaeum*, p. 44; *AA.SS.*, Feb. I (1658), 37–46. B.T.A., i. 224–5.

PIRAN (Perran) (d. *c*.480), monk from Ireland or Wales who settled in north Cornwall, giving his name to Perranporth. He was the patron of Cornish tinners; pilgrimages were made to his shrine in the Middle Ages; his cult flourished also in Wales and Brittany; Exeter too claimed relics. In early medieval times his oratory and hermitage were completely covered by shifting sands. They were rediscovered in the 16th century and again in 1835, when an excavation was made. Three headless skeletons and three heads were found; since then the relics and considerable parts of the oratory have been destroyed by vandalism and other causes; what remains has been covered by an unsightly concrete structure. An ancient free-standing Celtic cross near by marks the site of the hermitage. The medieval identification of this saint with *Ciaran of Saighir must be rejected. Feast: 5 March.

C.S.P.; *N.L.A.*, ii. 320–7; G. H. Doble, *St. Perran, St. Keverne and St. Kerrian* (1931); P. Grosjean, 'Vita S. Ciarani', *Anal. Boll.*, lix (1941), 217—71; A. L. Rowse, 'Nicholas Roscarrock and his Lives of the Saints' in *Studies in Social History* (ed. J. H. Plumb, 1955).

PIRMIN (d. 753), abbot and bishop. Probably of Spanish origin and a refugee from the Moors, in 711 Pirmin rebuilt the abbey of Dissentis (Switzerland) after it was destroyed by the Avars, but is best known as abbot of Reichenau, which he founded in 724, acquiring fifty books for its library. Later he was exiled to Alsace for political reasons and founded monasteries at Murbach and Amorbach. The *Dicta Pirmini* was a popular book of theology and ethics against superstition, which enjoyed wide circulation in Carolingian times: it is very likely his work. Feast: 3 November.

M. L. W. Laistner, *Thought and Letters in Western Europe* (1966), pp. 179–80: B.T.A., iv. 248–9.

PIRO, see PYR.

PIUS V (1504–72), Dominican friar, bishop, and pope. Although his reign lasted only six years, he was one of the most important popes of the Counter-Reformation. Michael Ghislieri, who was born at Bosco, became a Dominican at the age of fourteen in the priory of Voghera. After his ordination he was lecturer in philosophy and theology for sixteen years, after which he held the offices of master of novices and prior. His reforming zeal led to his being chosen as Commissary General of the Inquisition by Cardinal Caraffa in 1551;

when Caraffa became pope, Ghislieri was appointed bishop of Nepi and Sutri in 1556; in 1557 he became inquisitor general and a cardinal. Later he was transferred to the ravaged diocese of Mondovi (Piedmont), which he restored to comparative peace and order, but was recalled to Rome by Pius IV who had succeeded the fiery Paul IV (Caraffa), but whose nepotism was as famous as the intransigence of his predecessor. Ghislieri's opposition to this abuse did not prevent him from being elected pope in 1565 on the death of Pius IV. He took the name of Pius V and made clear his intention of being a vigorous reformer by enforcing both the letter and the spirit of the decrees of the Council of Trent. His reform began at Rome. The largesse usually scattered among the crowd after the coronation was given instead to hospitals and those in real need; instead of a banquet for the magnates there was relief for the poorer convents. He transformed his household, helped in this necessary task by Charles *Borromeo, archbishop of Milan. His holiness was recognized by the Romans, who experienced his radical reform of the morals of the city by a drastic purge of the curia, the virtual elimination of brigandry and bull-fighting, and firm legislation against prostitution.

For the needs of the Church as a whole Pius V made important decisions. The Breviary (purged of many legends of the saints) was reformed, as was the Roman Missal, whose use was made obligatory except where there was a prescription of 200 years in favour of local rites. The Roman Catechism was completed and translated into many languages, and catachetical instruction of the young made obligatory for all parish priests. *Thomas Aquinas was declared a Doctor of the Church in 1567 and a new edition of his works published in 1570.

In international matters the two greatest forces which Pius V faced were the Ottoman Empire and the Protestant Reformation. Against the latter he used the Inquisition in Italy and Spain, but in England his intervention was more controversial and less effective. In answer to queries from various quarters about clarifying the situation of Roman Catholics in England with regard to Queen Elizabeth, he reissued the bull 'In Cena Domini' (1568), which claimed some papal suzerainty over secular rulers; after repeated attempts in various quarters to reconcile Elizabeth to the Church of Rome had failed, she was excommunicated by the bull 'Regnans in excelsis' of 1570 which absolved her subjects from allegiance to her. Although defended in some quarters, and the fact of its promulgation doubted in others, there can be no doubt that it reflected attitudes of the medieval papacy which were inapt in 1570. It proceeded from insufficient understanding of the situation of English Catholics; it made their position much more difficult; it gave their opponents in the government a wonderful opportunity, exploited to the full, of accusing them of disloyalty and treason. It was the last time that a pope would exercise anything like a 'deposing power'. In opposing the further penetration of the Turks into Europe Pius met with astounding success. A combined fleet of papal, Spanish, and Venetian ships under Don John of Austria decisively defeated the Turkish fleet at the battle of Lepanto. This broke their power in the Mediterranean. It was the last, but one of the more successful efforts by the papacy to contain and defeat the power of Islam in a new crusade. For its organization, coherence, and achievement Pius with his total commitment by frequent prayer, fasting, and other activity was largely responsible. His monastic austerity, personal devotion, and kindness to the poor and sick, his general reforming activities and his defence of Christendom against Islam must be set beside his misreading of the situation in England. He was canonized in 1712. A fine contemporary portrait survives at Rome and a bronze sculpture of 1697 decorates his tomb in the basilica of St. Mary Major. Feast: formerly 5 May, now 30 April.

AA.SS. Maii I (1680), 617–714; A. Van Ortroy, 'Le pape saint Pie V', *Anal Boll.*, xxxiii (1914),

187–215; Lives by G. Grente (1914), C. M. Antony (1911), and L. Browne-Olf (1943). See also L. Pastor, *The History of the Popes from the Close of the Middle Ages*, vols. xvii and xviii; P. Hughes, *The Reformation in England* (3 vols., 1950–4); A. G. Dickens, *The Counter-Reformation* (1968), *passim*; *O.D.P.*, pp. 268–9.

PIUS X (1835–1914), pope. Born at Riese (Venetia) of a poor family, he was ordained priest in 1858 and became archpriest of Salzano in 1867. In 1875 he became a canon of Treviso, chancellor of the diocese, and spiritual director of the seminary; in 1884 bishop of Mantua, and in 1893 patriarch of Venice and cardinal. At the conclave of 1903 he was elected pope in succession to Leo XIII: he took as his motto 'To restore all things in Christ' (Eph. 1: 10).

Many of his achievements realized this ideal: the encouragement of frequent communion and the admission to it of children from the age of about seven, the reform of Church music with the encouragement of Gregorian chant and (to a lesser degree) classical polyphony, the reform of Canon Law (promulgated by his successor Benedict XV), and the reorganization of the Roman Congregations. In a wider field he redirected and reinspired Catholic Action, giving it a deeper base than a merely socio-political one. In the field of Christian doctrine he condemned the error of Modernism in the encyclical *Pascendi* and the decree *Lamentabili:* regrettably this was the occasion for reactionary zealots to impugn the orthodoxy of a number of eminent Catholic scholars; it took years to recover from this crisis. In the field of Church–State relations in France, Pius sacrificed ecclesiastical property for the sake of independence from state control, asking the clergy and faithful for considerable material sacrifices for this purpose. Also in France he condemned the extremes of the 'liberal' movement called the *Sillon* and the extremes of right-wing political thought in the *Action Française* organization. It was perhaps unfortunate that the latter condemnation was not made public until some years after Pius' death.

He lived long enough to see his tireless efforts to avert a World War frustrated and he died on 20 August 1914 with a reputation for miracles, simplicity, and poverty, having written in his will 'I was born poor, I have lived poor, and I wish to die poor'. Certain aspects of wealth and ceremony in the Vatican were profoundly distasteful to him. There was a popular outcry in favour of his canonization immediately he died; but he was in fact canonized by Pius XII in 1954. Feast: formerly 3 September, now 21 August.

R. Merry del Val, *Memories of Pope Pius X* (1939); R. Bazin, *Pie X* (1928; Eng. tr. also 1928); H. Dal-Gal, *St. Pius the Tenth* (1954); *O.D.P.*, pp. 313–14.

PLACID (6th century), Benedictine monk. As a young boy he was entrusted to *Benedict at Subiaco to be educated and to become a monk. He once fell into the lake there and was rescued by *Maurus, according to *Gregory's *Dialogues*. A forgery of Peter the Deacon of Monte Cassino made him a martyr in Sicily with thirty companions, who in fact suffered before he was born—they were alleged to have been killed at Messina by Saracen pirates from Spain at a time long before the Moors had even reached Spain. However, this fantasy was 'confirmed' by the discovery of a deed of gift, purporting to be from Tertullus (Placid's father) to St. Benedict, giving him lands in Sicily; in 1588 relics were found at Messina which were believed to be those of the martyred Placid and companions. This led to the feast of Placid on 5 October being celebrated very widely and in particular by Benedictine monasteries, who regarded him as the patron of novices and customarily assigned this day to them as that on which they performed the liturgical functions usually reserved to the professed. In 1915, however, the Benedictine liturgical commission proposed to suppress this feast and to celebrate the boy Placid with Maurus. This, however, was refused until the next revision which took place about forty years later when the combined feast of Maurus and Placid was authorized for 5

October. Among the medieval calendars that of Abingdon kept Placid as 'abbot and martyr'.

E. Caspar, *Petrus Diaconus und die Monte Cassineser Falschungen* (1909); J. McCann, *St. Benedict* (1938), pp. 282–91; B.T.A., iv. 34–6.

PLASDEN, Polydore (alias Oliver Palmer) (1563–91), seminary priest and martyr. Born in London, the son of a craftsman, Plasden was educated at the English College, Douai (and Reims), and was ordained priest in Rome in 1586. He ministered in Sussex and in London from 1588 to 1591, when he was arrested with Edmund *Gennings in the house of Swithun *Wells in Gray's Inn Road. As priests ordained overseas, Plasden and Gennings were tried and condemned for treason, but they defended both their priesthood and their loyalty to the Queen. The execution at Tyburn on 10 December was supervised by Sir Walter Ralegh, who insisted that Plasden should be dead before being cut down. He was canonized by Paul VI in 1970 as one of the *Forty Martyrs of England and Wales. Feast: 25 October.

For bibliography see Edmund GENNINGS.

PLECHELM (Pechthelm, Pleghelm), a Northumbrian missionary of the 8th century, who with *Wiro and Otger went to Rome on pilgrimage, was consecrated bishop there, and evangelized the area of the Meuse valley in the Netherlands. They built a church and monastery at Roermond through endowments given by Pepin of Herstal, who was closely associated with both Plechelm and Wiro. There is some uncertainty about these saints, in so far as they have often, but wrongly, been claimed to be Irish; it is also possible that they were consecrated not at Rome but by *Willibrord. Plechelm died at Odilienberg and was buried there; later his relics were translated to Roermond. Feast: 16 July.

AA.SS. Iul. IV (1725), 50–60; W. Levison, *England and the Continent in the Eighth Century* (1946), pp. 82–3.

PLEGMUND (d. 914), archbishop of Canterbury. Mercian by birth, Plegmund lived as a hermit on an island near Chester, called after him Plegmundham and later Plemstall. He was called to the Wessex court by King Alfred for his scholarship and had probably been trained at a centre in western Mercia, comparatively unaffected by Danish invasions. He helped Alfred write the OE version of *Gregory's *Pastoral Care* and may have been partially responsible for the compilation of the *Anglo-Saxon Chronicle*. In 890 he was chosen archbishop of Canterbury and went to Rome to receive the pallium. He crowned Edward the Elder at Kingston in 901. In 908 he consecrated the New Minister at Winchester, in 909 he revisited Rome, and divided the Wessex dioceses of Winchester and Sherborne into Winchester, Ramsbury, Sherborne, Wells, and Crediton (later Exeter). He consecrated seven bishops on the same day (five for Wessex and two outside it) and brought with him from Rome some relics of *Blaise. More important than some archbishops both for promoting learning and developing Canterbury's metropolitan jurisdiction, the evidence for his cult is limited to one martyrology of Canterbury in the 13th century. Feast: 2 August.

D.N.B., s.v.; Stanton, p. 378; N. Brooks, *The Early History of the Church of Canterbury* (1984).

PLESSINGTON, John (alias William Scarisbrick) (*c.*1637–79), seminary priest and martyr. Born at Dimples, near Blackburn (Lancs.), of a recusant family, John was educated by Jesuits at Scarisbrick Hall and at Saint-Omer before he joined the English College at Valladolid (Spain). He was ordained priest in Segovia in 1662 and returned to England in 1663. He ministered to his co-religionists first at Holywell (Flintshire, now Clwyd), where the shrine of *Winefride was a place of pilgrimage throughout the penal times, and from 1670 onwards at Puddington Hall in the Wirral. His official function here was tutor to the Massey children; his real function that of missionary priest. In the scare following the 'Popish Plot' he was arrested and charged with being a priest. He was imprisoned at Chester castle and executed there on 19 July. His speech before execution was printed: he strongly asserted that he was condemned only for his priesthood, that it was not Catholic belief that the pope had power to 'give licence to murder princes', and asked God to 'bless the King, grant him a prosperous reign here and a crown of glory hereafter'. His quartered body was returned to Puddington to be placed on the four corners of the house, but the Masseys disobeyed this order and buried the body in Burton graveyard. The traditional grave there was opened in 1962, but did not contain remains which were certainly his. Plessington was canonized by Paul VI in 1970 as one of the *Forty Martyrs of England and Wales. Feast: 25 October.

R. Challoner, *Memoirs of Missionary Priests* (ed. J. H. Pollen, 1928), pp. 541–3; M. Waugh, *Blessed John Plessington* (pamphlet, 1961).

PLUNKET, Oliver (1629–81), archbishop of Armagh, martyr. Born of a noble, royalist family at Loughcrew (Co. Meath), he studied under Jesuit guidance at the Irish College, Rome, from 1645 at the expense of the Oratorian Pierfrancesco Scarampi, who had been a papal envoy to the Irish Confederate party. After brilliant academic success in theology and law, he was ordained priest in 1654, became professor of theology at the Propaganda College and procurator of the Irish bishops.

In 1669 he was appointed archbishop of Armagh, was consecrated at Ghent, and reached Dublin via London, where he was favourably received by Charles II's queen, Catherine of Braganza, whose influence he sought for mitigating the severity of the penal laws against Catholics. Oliver was one of only two Catholic bishops in Ireland: disorder and neglect had become the almost inevitable results of long-standing persecution. Even the sacrament of confirmation had been largely neglected owing to the shortage of bishops; within the first few months of his rule Plunket confirmed 10,000 people and also held a provincial synod. In face of these difficulties the Catholics were divided among themselves by long-standing disputes about the primacy of Armagh over Dublin, and later by some Franciscans who delated Oliver Plunket to Rome. He was, however, completely vindicated by the Holy See.

His policy was to promulgate the decrees of the Council of Trent, to maintain discipline among the diocesan clergy and better observance among the regulars, and to improve educational standards by the Jesuit College at Drogheda. The recognition of papal authority and jurisdiction made him liable to severe penalties, but he managed to remain on friendly terms with the Protestant clergy and gentry of Ulster; their high regard for him was a measure of the excellence of his character and achievements.

The panic caused by the false allegations of Titus Oates in 1678 resulted in the arrest of Plunket, who was charged at Dundalk with plotting to bring 20,000 French soldiers into Ireland and levying a tax on the poverty-stricken clergy to support 70,000 armed men. Such an absurd charge had no chance of sticking in Ireland; Plunket was moved to Newgate, where he was imprisoned until 1681. Although the court's jurisdiction over Irish affairs was doubtful, the false witness of two apostate Irish friars, together with the bias of the judge, resulted in a conviction for high treason. Sir Francis Pemberton, the judge, said that the foundation of his treason was setting up a false religion, which was the most dishonourable and derogatory to God of all religions and that a greater crime could not be committed against God than for a man to endeavour to propagate that religion.

The true reason for his condemnation being thus clearly stated, he was condemned to be hanged, drawn, and quartered. The sentence was executed at Tyburn on 1 July (Old Style). His body was taken to Lambspring Abbey (Westphalia) in 1684; it is now at Downside Abbey (Somerset), while his head is in the Oliver Plunket Memorial Church in Drogheda (Co. Louth). He was canonized in 1976. Feast: 1 July.

Contemporary accounts by Anon., *The Trial and Condemnation of Edward Fitzharris . . . and Oliver Plunket* (1681) and ed. P. F. Moran in *Spicilegium Ossoriense*, iii (1884), 102–8; modern Lives by P. F. Moran (1895), H. Concannon (1935), and E. Curtis (1963); see also A. Curtayne, *The Trial of Oliver Plunket* (1953); O. Plunket, *Letters* (1979).

POL-DE-LÉON, see PAUL AURELIAN.

POLYCARP (*c.*69–*c.*155), bishop and martyr. A disciple of *John the Apostle, he became bishop of Smyrna and one of the most important Christians in Roman Asia in the mid-2nd century. He defended orthodox Christian belief against the heresies of Marcion and Valentinus, the most influential of the Gnostics. The martyr *Ignatius, who met him on his last journey to Rome, recommended to him the care of his church at Antioch (*c.*107), while *Irenaeus of Lyons, who as a boy knew Polycarp, praised his gravity, holiness, and majesty of countenance. Polycarp's letter to the Philippians was so esteemed that it was read in churches of Asia during the lifetime of *Jerome. Near the end of his long life Polycarp visited Anicetus, bishop of Rome, to discuss a uniform date of celebrating Easter. Neither could accept the system of the other, so they agreed to differ in charity over their two traditions. Anicetus invited Polycarp to celebrate the Eucharist in the papal chapel on this occasion.

Soon after he had returned to Smyrna, a youth called Germanicus was killed at a pagan festival; the crowd called out: 'Away with the atheists. Fetch Polycarp.' He was found in a farm near by, neither provoking nor fleeing martyrdom, but calmly waiting. He invited his captors to eat a meal, while he prayed alone for an hour. At his interrogation, threats and promises did not shake his constancy. When ordered to execrate Christ, he answered: 'For 86 years I have been his servant and he has never done me wrong; how can I blaspheme my king who saved me? . . . I am a Christian; if you wish to study the Christian doctrine, choose a day and you will hear it.'

When the crowd at the games in the amphitheatre were told that Polycarp had confessed he was a Christian, they shouted first for the lions and then for him to be burnt at the stake. He was bound; an official killed him with the sword; his body was then burnt. Christians collected his bones and buried them. They also wrote an account of his trial and martyrdom, which is the earliest authentic example of its kind.

The traditional date of Polycarp's death (155) has been recently questioned; rival dates of 166 or 177 have been suggested, but there are still serious reasons for preferring the early date. His admitted age of 86 years as a Christian makes it certain that he was baptized in infancy or early childhood. He is a most important link between the time of the Apostles and the earliest Christian Fathers. The account of his martyrdom is precious evidence for the cult of saints as early as the 2nd century.

In England there are a few modern, but no ancient churches dedicated to him. But his feast was widely celebrated. Feast: 23 February, formerly 26 January.

AA.SS. Ian. II (1643), 691–707; texts of the contemporary documents in editions of the Apostolic Fathers by J. B. Lightfoot (1885), J. R. Harmer (1891), K. Lake (1932), *A.C.M.*, pp. 2–21; Eusebius, *H.E.*, iv. 14–15; H. Delehaye, *Les passions des martyrs et les genres littéraires* (1921), pp. 11–59; H. I. Marrou, 'La date du martyre de S. Polycarpe', *Anal. Boll.*, lxxi (1953), 5–20; P. Brind Amour, 'La date du martyre de saint Polycarpe (23 Fèv. 167)', *Anal. Boll.*, lxxxviii (1908), 456–62.

PORRES Martin de (1579–1639), Dominican lay brother. The illegitimate son of a Spanish grandee (John de Porres, knight of the Order of Alcantara) and of Anna Velasquez, a free negress of Lima, Peru, Martin apprenticed himself to a barber-surgeon. Some years later he joined the Dominicans as a lay-helper, but his life, especially his dedication to the poor, was so impressive that he was invited to make profession as a lay-brother.

He would spend his nights in prayer and penance, sometimes accompanied by visions and ecstasies, his days in nursing the sick and the plague-stricken, working for his monastery as barber, gardener, and counsellor; above all, caring for the poor, irrespective of race and colour. His cures seemed miraculous, his control of animals prodigious. His own community recognized his holiness to such an extent that they accepted his spiritual direction. They called him 'father of charity' but he called himself 'mulatto dog'.

At the age of sixty he died of a violent quatrain fever. His veneration by the faithful was immediate and spontaneous, miraculous cures were claimed at his tomb and a canonical inquiry began in 1660. This led eventually to his beatification in 1837 and his canonization by Pope John XXIII in 1962. His recognition as patron of race relations was due, not to any political or revolutionary activity but to his universal, caring charity to men of all races whom he served without counting the cost. Feast: 5 November.

G. Cavallini, *St. Martin de Porres: Apostle of Charity* (1963); *N.C.E.*, xi. 595–6; *Bibl. SS.*, viii. 1240–5.

POSSENTI, Gabriel (1838–62), Passionist cleric. A younger son of the governor of Assisi and his wife, he studied at the Jesuit college at Spoleto. There he was known for his love of clothes, dancing, and the theatre, and was called *Il Damerino* ('the ladies' man'). Twice during a serious illness he decided to enter a religious Order, twice he failed to do so. Later, in a procession of the miraculous ikon of Spoleto, he experienced an overpowering urge to become a religious and a priest. He achieved the first by joining the Passionist monastery at Morrovalle in 1856; the second was never fulfilled because he died young.

As a religious, he was noted for his cheerfulness (a characteristic which some portraits completely fail to reveal). He was committed to prayer and penance and specially devoted to the Sorrows of Mary, but the shadow of serious illness was never far away. He died at Isola del Gran Sasso of tuberculosis at the age of only twenty-four after a short but exemplary religious life.

Immense numbers of pilgrims have visited his shrine. He was canonized in 1920 and nominated patron of youth; later he was declared patron of the Abruzzi region. Some of his writings, mainly letters, have been published. He is also called Gabriele dell'Addolorata. Feast: 27 February.

B. Ceci, *Scritti di S. Gabriele dell'addolorata* (1963); F. Giorgini, *Fonti storico-biographice di S. Gabriele dell'Addolorata* (1965); Lives by C. Hollobough (1923); P. Gorla (1951); B.T.A., i. 429–31; *Bibl. SS.*, v. 1336–9.

POTAMIAENA AND BASILIDES (d. *c.*208), martyrs. Almost all we know of these martyrs comes from Eusebius, who stated that they were among the disciples of Origen. Potamiaena was much honoured among her people of Alexandria, both for the preservation of her chastity and for her torments and death for Christ. When interrogated by Aquila, prefect of Egypt, about her beliefs, she answered in a way that was contrary to the Roman religion, but her exact words have not been recorded. She was sentenced to death and was insulted by the crowd. A soldier called Basilides protected her, showing compassion and kindness. She thanked him, urged him to be of good heart, promised her prayers, and said she would soon repay him for his kindliness. She was then tortured by boiling pitch being poured over every part of her body: this is the first recorded example of this torment.

Basilides, now a Christian, declared it openly in spite of his fellow-soldiers' incredulous mockery, and was imprisoned. He told the other Christians who visited him that he had seen Potamiaena in a vision and that she had placed a crown on his head. He received the Eucharist and was beheaded the next day. Feast: 28 June.

Eusebius, *H.E.*, vi. 5; *A.C.M.*, pp. xxvii-xxviii, 132–5; Palladius, *Lausiac History*, c. 3; *AA.SS.*, Iun. V (1809), 355–7.

PRAEJECTUS (Projectus, Prix) (d. 676), bishop of Clermont, martyr. A native of the Auvergne, and educated by its bishop Genesius, he became a priest and, in 666, bishop. He founded monasteries, churches, and hospitals; his preaching revealed his learning and devotion. His death was due to intrigues and violence. Hector, ruler of Marseilles, was accused of outrages and misdemeanours. At the order of the emperor Childeric he was arrested and executed. Agritius believed this to be due to Praejectus and organized revenge. The bishop was stabbed and an assassin killed him with a sword, scattering his brains. Praejectus was venerated as a martyr. The cult spread to English monastic calendars of the 11th and 12th centuries. Feast: 25 January.

AA.SS. Ian. II (1643), 628–36; good contemporary Life by a monk of Volvic, ed. B. Krusch, *M.G.H.*, *Scriptores rerum merov.*, v. 212–48; *E.B.K. before 1100*; *E.B.K. after 1100*.

PRAXEDES, virgin of Rome (1st–2nd century), who was buried in the cemetery of Priscilla on the Salarian Way. The fine church of S. Prassede was built on the site of her house. Legend made her a sister of *Pudentiana and a daughter of the senator Pudens, supposedly converted to Christianity by *Peter. Benedict XIV said that the Acts were spurious and unworthy of credence: the cult of Praxedes is not one of the oldest in Rome. The most ancient reference to her may have been in Itineraries to the Catacombs of the 7th century. Feast: formerly 21 July, suppressed 1969.

O.D.C.C., s.v., *AA.SS.* Maii IV (1685), 296–301; R. Krautmeier, *Corpus Basilicarum Christianarum Romae*, iii (1967), 232–59.

PRIMUS AND FELICIAN (d. *c.*297), martyrs. These were Romans who suffered at Nomentum (12 miles from Rome) during the persecution of Diocletian and Maximian. A church was built over their tombs on the Via Nomentana. In 640 Pope Theodore brought their relics to the church of San Stefano Rotundo, and a mosaic, which still survives, was set up in the apse. Their legendary Acts make them patrician brothers who became Christians and whose commitment took the form of visiting the confessors in prison. After their arrest they were tortured and the judge tried to convince Felician that his brother, now eighty years old, had conformed. But Felician was not taken in, and the two brothers faced execution together. The translation of their relics from outside the walls of Rome to a church inside them is usually regarded as the first of its kind. Feast: 9 June.

AA.SS. Iun. II (1698), 149–54 with *C.M.H.*, p. 311; H. Delehaye, *Étude sur le légendier romain* (1936), pp. 14–31.

PRISCA, Roman lady of the early centuries who gave her name to the church on the Aventine hill since at least the 4th century. There was an early Roman cult of Prisca, whom the itineraries mention as a martyr. The Acts (10th century), which are historically almost valueless, identify her with a martyr whose relics had been translated to this church. From about the 9th century she had been also identified with the Priscilla in the Acts of the Apostles who was the wife of Aquila and the church became known as *titulus Aquilae et Priscae*, but this identification seems most unlikely. She is sometimes represented with two lions, who according to her Acts refused to attack her. Feast: 18 January, in sixteen English monastic calendars.

AA.SS., Ian. II (1643), 183–7; R. Krautheimer, *Corpus Basilicarum Christianarum Romae*, iii (1967), 260–76.

PRISCUS (Prix) (*c.*272), martyr. A citizen of Besançon, Priscus with some Christian friends fled during the persecution of Aurelian to Auxerre, where they were discovered and killed. The Martyrology of Jerome mentions him as a martyr and is witness to an early cult. The bodies were discovered by *Germanus of Auxerre, who built churches in their honour and helped to diffuse the cult. Feast: 26 May.

AA.SS. Maii VI (1688), 365–8; B.T.A., ii. 400.

PRISCUS OF CAPUA, martyr, named as such by the Martyrology of Jerome, the Gelasian Sacramentary, and the marble calendar of Naples. Nothing is known about him, and his fine ancient church at

Capua has been destroyed. Feast: 1 September in *R.M.* and thirteen medieval English monastic calendars.

Propylaeum, p. 374; *AA.SS.* Sept. I (1746), 99–108.

PRIX, see PRAEJECTUS, PRISCUS.

PROBUS, titular saint of the church of Probus (Cornwall), and reputedly made collegiate by Athelstan in 926. Mentioned as St. Probus by Domesday Book. Sherborne Abbey was formerly called Lamprobi or the church of Probus or else Propeschirche, but its calendar retains no memory of its former patron. Nothing is known of Probus and the *C.C.K.* lists him among those Cornish saints 'whose day is not certainly known'. If Probus ever existed and is not just a name meaning 'honest', he was probably a Celtic or British saint of the West Country of whom all is forgotten except his dedications.

Baring-Gould and Fisher, iv. 107; Stanton, p. 735.

PROCESSUS AND MARTINIAN, Roman martyrs of early date, who were publicly venerated in Rome from at least the 4th century and whose feast was in the early Roman sacramentaries. They were buried in the cemetery of *Damasus: in the 4th century a church was built over their tomb. Here *Gregory the Great preached a homily on their feast, in which he referred to the presence of their bodies, to the cures of the sick, to the harassment of perjurers, and the cure of demoniacs there. There is nothing left today of this church. The unreliable Acts make them the warders of *Peter and *Paul in the Mamertine prison, who were converted and baptized by Peter. A woman called Lucina is said to have buried them in her own cemetery, but Delehaye insists on the cemetery of Damasus as their resting-place. In the 9th century their relics were translated to St. Peter's, where they remain to this day under their altar in the south transept. Feast: 2 July, mentioned in OE martyrology, that of Bede, and the Sarum calendar.

C.M.H., pp. 347–8; B.T.A., iii. 7–8.

PROJECTUS, see PRAEJECTUS.

PROTASE, see GERVASE AND PROTASE.

PROTUS AND HYACINTH, Roman martyrs of unknown date, but mentioned in the 4th-century list of martyrs, in the early sacramentaries, and the Naples calendar of stone. This ancient cult received striking confirmation in 1845 when the tomb of Hyacinth was discovered in the cemetery of Basilla, with his name and the date of his burial (11 September); inside it were charred bones, indicating death by fire. Near it another inscription was found bearing the name of Protus M(artyr), but this tomb was empty, probably because the relics were translated into Rome by St. Leo IV. An inscription by *Damasus says they were brothers; the Martyrology of Jerome calls them 'teachers of the Christian law'. Their cult was early and widespread: the feast is mentioned in the OE Martyrology, the Martyrology of *Bede, and the Sarum calendar. A church in Blisland (Cornwall) called St. Pratts is probably dedicated to Protus. Feast: 11 September (9 September in OE Martyrology).

C.M.H., pp. 501–2; *AA.SS.* Sept. III (1750), 746–62 (fictitious Acts make them the household slaves of Eugenia, daughter of the prefect of Egypt, and join Basilla to them, converted by their persuasions); B.T.A., iii, 537–8.

PTOLOMAEUS AND LUCIUS (d. *c.*150), martyrs. Their early date, their Acts written by *Justin, and the circumstances of their deaths make these saints unusually interesting. Ptolomaeus converted to Christianity an unnamed married woman who with her husband had previously indulged in unspecified sexual sins. He, however, persisted in his evil ways and she wished to have a divorce. Her friends persuaded her to remain with him, hoping for his amendment, but hearing that in Alexandria he had behaved worse than before, she issued a *repudium* (declaration of dissolution) and left him. Before her conversion she had indulged in drunkenness and 'every sort of vice with servants and hirelings', but not for this but for her leaving him without consent did her husband file a complaint against her, alleging also that she was a Christian. He persuaded the centurion who had previously arrested Ptolomaeus for a crime for which he had been punished by Urbicus, the city-prefect of Rome, to ask Ptolomaeus whether he was a Christian. Being a truthful man, he admitted that he was; whereupon the centurion put him in chains and kept him in prison for a long time.

When he was brought to Urbicus, he was again asked simply if he were a Christian. 'Fully aware of the benefits he enjoyed because of Christ's doctrine', he confessed that he was indeed a Christian. So Urbicus ordered him to be executed. A Christian bystander called Lucius protested that Ptolomaeus had not been convicted of adultery, fornication, murder, clothes-stealing, or any crime whatsoever, but had been condemned only because he was a Christian. 'Your sentence, Urbicus, does not befit the Emperor (Antoninus) Pius nor his philosopher son (Marcus Aurelius) nor the holy senate.' Urbicus answered: 'I think you too are one of them.' Lucius responded: 'Indeed I am.' So he too was executed on the same charge. Feast: 19 October.

A.C.M., xvi–xvii, 38–41; *Propylaeum*, p. 462.

PUCCI, Antony Mary (1819–92), Servite priest. Born of a peasant family at Poggione de Vernio (Tuscany), he became a Servite friar at Florence in 1837. Imperturbable and prayerful, he studied at Monte Senario and was ordained in 1843. He then became curate and in 1844 parish priest of Viareggio. There he spent the rest of his life.

Unnattractive in looks and voice, taciturn and withdrawn by temperament, he was nevertheless an excellent organizer; but he often said that organization is the servant of charity, not its substitute. His care for the sick was outstanding in the epidemics of 1854 and 1866. He also pioneered the provision of seaside nursing-homes for children, and in a wider field worked also for the Association for the Propagation of the Faith. In 1883 he was appointed provincial of the Tuscan Province and held this office for seven years.

He died on 14 January, a model pastor, deeply mourned. Miracles were soon reported at his grave and he was canonized in 1962. Feast: 12 January.

Anon., *Un apostolo della carita* (1920); I. Felici, *Il curatino santo, B. Antonio M. Pucci* (1952); other Lives by P. M. Perroni (1953) and G. Papasogli (1962). See also B.T.A., i. 90–1; *N.C.E.*, xi. 1012; *Bibl. SS.*, Appendix.

PUDENTIANA, supposed Roman martyr of the 1st–2nd century. She is mentioned in the Itineraries of Rome of the early Middle Ages and in the Reichenau manuscript of the Martyrology of Jerome, but in no earlier known sources. In early Christian Rome a senator Pudens existed on whose land or house a church was built which was called *titulus Pudentis* or *ecclesia Pudentiana*; it seems likely that from this name came the supposition that it was dedicated to a 'St. Pudentiana'. Benedict XIV's commission for revising the breviary declared the Acts of *Praxedes and Pudentiana were spurious and unworthy of credence. Feast: formerly 19 May, in many English and other calendars, suppressed 1969.

AA.SS. Maii IV (1685), 296–301 with *C.M.H.*, p. 263; R. Krautmeier, *Corpus Basilicarum Christianarum Romae*, iii (1967), 277–302; B. Vanmaele, *L'Église pudentienne de Rome* (1965).

PYR (Piro), Welsh abbot of the 6th century. Caldey island was first called Llan Illtud after its founder *Illtud, but later it was called Ynys Pyr. What little we know of Pyr indicates that he was an unsuitable abbot and is one of those Celtic 'saints' who would never have been canonized by any formal process. Pyr got so drunk one night that on his way back to his cell he fell into a well and was dead when he was pulled out. *Samson was elected abbot in his place but found that the young monks had become ungovernable because Pyr's rule was so lax; he accordingly resigned the abbacy in disgust.

T. Taylor, *Life of St. Samson of Dol* (1925); Baring-Gould and Fisher, iv. 89–90.

Q

QUATTUOR CORONATI, see FOUR CROWNED MARTYRS.

QUAY, see KEA.

QUENBURGA (Coenburga) (d. *c*.735), nun, possibly abbess of Wimborne. *Cuthburga and Quenburga were daughters of Cenred, a Wessex sub-king, and brothers of Ina, later king of Wessex (688–*c*.726). Cuthburga married Aldfrith, king of Northumbria (685–704), but separated from him in order to become a nun at Barking under *Hildelith; later, with Quenburga, she founded Wimborne abbey, a double monastery, principally for nuns. The enclosure was so strict that not even bishops were allowed inside it. From this monastery came *Lioba and *Tecla, who helped *Boniface in his mission in Germany. The Life of Lioba by Rudolf also mentions this double monastery with fifty nuns; but by the time a letter in the Boniface collection was written (729–44) to the abbot of Glastonbury, Coengilsus, there were apparently three monasteries at Wimborne, i.e. one of men and two of nuns, ruled by Cuthburga and Quenburga, the abbesses. Cuthburga died on 31 August, Quenburga on an unknown date; their feast was often celebrated together on 31 August or 3 September.

M. Tangl, *Bonifatii et Lullae Epistolae (M.G.H.*, 1916), no. 55; *AA.SS.* Aug. VI (1743), 699–700; J. Mabillon, *AA.SS. O.S.B.*, III, saec. III, part 1, pp. 422–3; Stanton, pp. 431–2.

QUENTIGERNA, see KENTIGERNA.

QUENTIN (Quintin), martyr of unknown date, recorded by *Bede and some early martyrologies, mentioned by *Gregory of Tours as having a church dedicated to him. The place where he suffered, Augusta Veromanduorum, is now called Saint-Quentin (Aisne). These bare facts of his martyrdom were supplemented by an implausible legend. This makes him a Roman citizen who came to preach the Gospel in Gaul with *Lucian of Beauvais; Quentin preached at Amiens where the probably fictitious prefect Rictiovarus arrested and interrogated him, finally killing him by a series of fearsome tortures, graphically illustrated in the early medieval illustrated Life of the saint which survives at Saint-Quentin. His relics were translated in 835. Feast: 31 October, in the Sarum calendar, many English medieval monasteries and elsewhere.

AA.SS. Oct. XIII (1883), 725–820 with *Propylaeum*, p. 487; A. Poncelet, 'Carmina de S. Quintino', *Anal. Boll.*, xx (1901), 1–44.

QUERAN, see CIARAN OF CLONMACNOISE.

QUIRIAC (Quiricus), see CYRIAC.

QUIRICUS, see CYRICUS.

R

RADEGUND (518–87), queen. The daughter of Berthaire, king of Thuringia, she was brought up in an environment of violence and intrigue. At the age of twelve she was captured by the Franks; she became a Christian and, at eighteen, married King Clotaire, son of Clovis, whose nominal Christianity seemed to affect very little his native tendency to violence and immorality. Though Radegund united beauty with piety, Clotaire was repeatedly unfaithful, taunted her for her childlessness, and even murdered her brother. So, after six years of marriage, Radegund left the court, took the veil at Noyon, and became a deaconess. Later she founded the monastery of Holy Cross at Poitiers under the Rule of *Caesarius of Arles. The arrival of a relic of the cross there from Constantinople was the occasion for *Venantius Fortunatus composing the hymn 'Vexilla Regis prodeunt'. This monastery was a centre of scholarship (the nuns spent two hours a day in study), but also of Radegund's various peace-making activities.

Surrounded by her 200-strong community, she died on 13 August; miraculous cures were soon reported at her tomb; her feast was celebrated in France, especially Tours, from the 9th century or earlier; in England five ancient churches were dedicated to her, as well as the Cambridge College now known as Jesus. A late-15th-century Life, by Henry Bradshaw, provides additional evidence for English interest in her. Feast: 13 August.

Contemporary Lives by the nun Baudovinia and Venantius Fortunatus, with a later one, in *AA.SS.* Aug. III (1737), 67–92; Life by Henry Bradshaw (ed. F. Brittain, 1926); modern studies by F. Brittain (1925), R. Aigrain (1952), and L. Schmidt (1956).

RAGENER (Ragenerius) (d. *c.*870), soldier and martyr of Northampton. The only witness is a single manuscript of *N.L.A.* According to this, Bruning, the wealthy and devout parish priest of St. Peter, Northampton, in the mid-11th century, had a simple-minded manservant of Viking family, who set out on pilgrimage for Rome in honour of St. Peter, whom he called *drotinum* (i.e. 'lord'). But he was repeatedly admonished in visions to return. Once back, he saw the same celestial visitor as before, who now told him that the body of a friend of God lay buried under the floor of the church, and that the parish priest should be told where to find him. Bruning set about digging and found a grave just where he had been told. The news was made public but nobody knew who was buried there.

Alfgiva of Abingdon, who was severely crippled, was cured at the tomb during the Vigil on Easter Eve after seeing a miraculous light, and walked as she had never walked before. After three days of fasting, Bruning opened the tomb. In it he found bones with a scroll. This identified the body as that of Ragener, martyr of Christ, the nephew of King *Edmund: both had suffered for Christ in the same persecution.

Other miracles of healing followed; *Edward the Confessor enriched Northampton with many gifts; a fine shrine was made for the saint; Alfgiva became a nun in Northampton.

This account stands almost alone, but the existence of the feast on 21 November is proved by an entry in a Missal in the Bodleian Library, Oxford.

N.L.A., ii. 727–31.

RAINIER (Ranieri) **OF PISA** (1117–61), pilgrim, hermit, and preacher. Born in Pisa, the son of a prosperous merchant

Scacceri who had benefited from his town's growing trade with the East, Rainier learnt Latin as a youth. In 1140 he abandoned his wordly way of life through contact with a monk, and went on pilgrimage to the Holy Land where he stayed until 1153, having become a hermit. He then returned to his native town, lived as a monk at St. Andrew in Kinzica and then at San Vito. His early knowledge of Latin gave him access to the Bible and the Church Offices and enabled him to preach on occasion. He enjoyed a reputation for austerity, for accomplishing conversions, as well as healings. This brought popular acclaim on his death, which resulted in the significant burial of his body in Pisa cathedral, where it still remains. He was probably canonized by Alexander III, became patron of Pisa in the 13th century, and his name was entered in the Roman Martyrology in the 17th. A contemporary Life was written by his confidant and counsellor Canon Benincasa. Feast: 17 June.

AA.SS. Iun. III (1743), 421–69; *H.S.S.C.*, vi. 281; *Bibl. SS.*, xi. 37–44. Life by I. Felici (1961).

RAPHAEL, one of the three archangels mentioned in the Bible, notably in the Book of Tobit. The name means 'God has healed'. Raphael has been venerated from early times, especially in the East, as a healer, being sometimes identified with the angel who moved the waters of the healing pool in Jerusalem (John 5: 1–4). His name was in the Litany of Saints; he was depicted in art (in England as elsewhere) together with Michael and Gabriel, from whom he was distinguished by the presence of his companion Tobit with a fish. Although no churches were dedicated to him in England, Edmund Lacy, bishop of Exeter 1420–55, wrote an office in his honour. Various guilds of healing were placed under his patronage. Feast: formerly 24 October; now, with SS. Michael and Gabriel, 29 September.

I. Schuster, *The Sacramentary*, v. 189–91; E. F. Jacob, *Essays in the Conciliar Epoch* (1963), p. 160; G. McN. Rushforth, *Medieval Christian Imagery* (1936), pp. 393–4.

RAYMUND NONNATUS (1204–40), Mercedarian friar and cardinal. Everything known of him depends on late and not very reliable sources. According to these he was extracted from his mother's womb just after she had died (whence the name Nonnatus or 'not born') at Portello (Catalonia). He joined the Mercedarian Order under *Peter Nolasco at Barcelona. He was sent to Algeria where he redeemed many slaves and offered himself as a ransom for others' liberation. He obtained some success in the difficult task of converting Moslems to Christianity and was freed from prison. In 1239 he returned to Spain where he was nominated a cardinal by Pope Gregory IX. He died at Cardona, near Barcelona, on his way to Rome. Both in life and after death he had the reputation of a notable miracle-worker. Because of his own unusual birth he is invoked as patron of midwives. Feast: 31 August.

AA.SS. Aug. VI (1743), 737–46; *O.D.C.C.*, p. 1161; B.T.A., iii. 449–50; *Bibl. SS.*, xi. 12–16.

RAYMUND OF PENNAFORT (*c.*1180–1275), Dominican friar. Born in Catalonia of a family related to the kings of Aragon and the counts of Barcelona, Raymund was educated at Barcelona and later (from *c.*1210) at Bologna, where he took doctorates in civil and canon law. In 1219 he became archdeacon of Barcelona. In 1222 he joined the Dominican order. A lover of both solitude and the apostolate of reconciling heretics, Jews, and Moors, he was also a notable writer. His two principal works were his *Summa* of moral cases and his compilation of the Decretals of canon law, commissioned by Gregory IX, who had called him to Rome in 1230. For nearly 700 years this remained the standard collection. In 1235 Raymund was chosen by him as archbishop of Tarragona, but he refused the charge. In 1238, however, he was elected Master-General of the Dominicans; in spite of his reluctance, he eventually accepted.

One work which he completed during his generalate was the revision of the Dominican Constitutions; another was a systematic visitation of the rapidly growing Order. After only two years, however, he resigned and returned to Spain, from where he encouraged *Thomas Aquinas to write his *Summa Contra Gentes*.

He has often been claimed as the joint founder of the Mercedarian Order, whose main work was the redemption of captives from the Moors. But details of the story are suspect and it seems more accurate to attribute to him a less direct responsibility.

He died in extreme old age at Barcelona. He was canonized in 1601. Feast: 7 (formerly 23) January.

AA.SS. Ian. 1 (1643), 404–29; F. V. Taberner, *San Ramon de Penyafort* (1936); B.T.A., i. 149–52.

RAYNE (Regina), virgin, is recorded by William Worcestre as the titular of a church near Crewkerne (Somerset); St. Rayne's Hill, 2 miles west of the town, recalls this chapel today. She may have been a forgotten local saint, or else St. Regina, an early martyr of Autun, who occurs on 7 September in the Roman Martyrology and the Martyrology of Jerome. Her implausible Legend is based on that of *Margaret of Antioch.

C.M.H., pp. 492–3; F. Grignard, *La Vie de sainte Reine d'Alise* (1881, illustrated Legend); William Worcestre, pp. 122–3.

REGULUS, see RULE.

REMIGIUS (Remi) (d. 533), bishop, also called Apostle of the Franks. Of Gaulish parentage, Remigius became bishop of Reims at an early age. He is famous principally because he baptized Clovis I, king of the Franks (481–511). The queen, Clotild, was a Christian, but the king was converted after his sick infant son was restored to health and he himself won a spectacular victory over the Alemanni. Both these events were attributed to the power of Christ. Thus Clovis came, in Remigius' words, to 'adore what he had burnt and to burn what he had adored'. Remigius also baptized the king's family and followers, who were said to number 3,000. Under the protection of Clovis, Remigius preached the Gospel and founded bishoprics and churches. He died at Reims on 13 January.

Legends about him flourished. One attributed to him the power of touching for the King's Evil (transmitted by him to Clovis and claimed later by *Edward the Confessor and his Norman successors). Another asserted that the chrism for Clovis' baptism was miraculously provided by a dove; the remnant, called La Sainte Ampoule, was kept in Reims Cathedral until the Revolution.

In England six ancient churches were dedicated to Remigius. The translation feast of 1 October was celebrated by most English Benedictine monasteries, in the Sarum calendar, and, until recently, in the Roman calendar. The feast of 13 January survives at Reims.

AA.SS. Oct. 1 (1765), 59–187; letters and testament in *P.L.*, lxv. 963–76; see also Gregory of Tours, *Historia Francorum*, ii. 23 and B. Krusch in *M.G.H.*, *Scriptores rerum merov.*, iii (1896), 239–347; modern studies by R. Barroux (1947), F. Oppenheimer, *The Legend of the Sainte Ampoule* (1953), and M. Bloch, *Les Rois thaumaturges* (1924).

REYNOLDS, Richard (*c.*1492–1535), Bridgettine monk and martyr. Born of a Devonshire family, Reynolds read for an Arts degree at Christ's College, Cambridge, became a Fellow of Corpus Christi, and took a doctorate of Divinity. In 1515 he joined the community of Syon, Isleworth, a double monastery following the Rule of *Bridget of Sweden, the only one of its kind in England and notable for its holiness and learning. At least six Cambridge Fellows joined it during the last thirty years of its life: Reynolds left it ninety-four books. Well known to Erasmus, *More, *Fisher, and Pole (who praised him for his holiness as well as for his Latin, Greek, and Hebrew), Reynolds was soon sought after as a spiritual director by many and as a theological consultant by Fisher and More, especially over the king's proposed divorce from Catherine of Aragon. On this matter, Reynolds and his community were solidly in favour of the queen. The sources are silent about the sequence of events which led to his arrest in the spring of 1535. It is difficult to see how the community could have avoided taking the oath of Succession, but it was the oath of Supremacy which led to the final tragedy. This had declared Henry VIII to be the Supreme Head of the Church in England, and no effort was spared to induce Reynolds to take the oath acknowledging this new title. It was believed that if a religious of his eminent reputation conformed, many others would do the same. He refused and was committed to the Tower like John *Houghton and the other Carthusians. At his trial in Westminster Hall (28 April 1535) he claimed that he had 'all the rest of Christendom in my favour: I can even say that . . . the larger part of this kingdom is at heart of my opinion, although outwardly, partly from fear and partly from hope, they profess to be of yours. As to dead witnesses, I have in my favour all the General Councils, all historians, the holy doctors of the Church for the last fifteen hundred years, especially St. *Ambrose, St. *Jerome, St. *Augustine, and St. *Gregory.' He was sentenced to death and suffered at Tyburn with the three Carthusian priors on 4 May. He encouraged the others on the scaffold and was the last to suffer execution, promising a 'heavenly supper to follow their sharp breakfast taken for their Master's sake'. He was canonized by Paul VI in 1970 as one of the *Forty Martyrs of England and Wales. Feast: 25 October.

A. Hamilton, *The Angel of Sion* (1905); D. Knowles, *The Religious Orders in England*, iii (1961), 212–18.

RICCI, Catherine dei (1522–90), Dominican nun. She was born of a wealthy Florentine family and entered the Dominican convent at nearby Prato, founded under Savonarola's influence, in 1535. Here she made her profession and became in turn novice-mistress, subprioress, and in 1552 prioress. Unusually she was confirmed in this office for life. A good administrator, she also enjoyed nursing the sick. She became much admired outside her convent for her wisdom and exceptional 'psychological healthiness'. One of her admirers was Philip *Neri who not only corresponded with her but is claimed to have talked to her from Rome while she was at Prato.

She is specially famous for her extraordinary ecstasies experienced every week from 1542 to 1554. On Thursday and Friday the Passion of Christ was experienced by her not just passively, but her bodily movements conformed exactly to those of Christ whose passion she witnessed. Although unconscious, she stretched out her hands for the arrest, she stood majestically for the scourging, and bent her head to receive the crown of thorns. These visions were accompanied by the impression of the stigmata: news of them caused much talk and frequent visitors. In 1554 the nuns prayed efficaciously for them to cease. Another curious phenomenon was that a gold and diamond ring, given her, it was claimed, in an ecstasy by Christ, was visible to Catherine alone: others saw only a red 'lozenge' and a circlet round her finger. She died after a long illness, patiently suffered.

The canonization cause, in which the 'Devil's Advocate' was the future Pope Benedict XIV, critically examined all relevant claims. Catherine's own enduring admiration for Savonarola and the difficult psycho-physical phenomena were not insurmountable obstacles. As in the case of her younger contemporary, Mary Magdalene de' *Pazzi, canonization was granted in 1746 not for extraordinary phenomena but for heroic virtue and complete union with Christ. A striking portrait, attributed to Nardini, survives in the Pinacoteca of Montepulciano. Feast: 13 February.

Acta Canonizationis . . . Catharinae de Ricci (1749); Letters ed. by S. da Pisa (1912); G. di Agresti, *S. Caterina de'Ricci, Fonti* (1963), translated by J. Petrie (1986); Lives by F. M. Capes (1905), G. Bertini (1935), and S. Razzi in *Collana Ricciana Fonti* (1965); B.T.A., i. 328–31 and *Bibl. SS.*, iii. 1044–5.

RICHARD (d. 720), wrongly called 'King of the English'. The father of *Willibald,

*Winnibald, and *Walburga, Richard (the name apparently dates only from the 11th century) left his native Hampshire with his family on pilgrimage to the Holy Land, but died at Lucca and was buried in the Church of S. Frediano. Both at Eichstatt and at Lucca his relics were publicly venerated, at least from the 12th century. Although he is not mentioned in ancient Martyrologies, his feast was kept on 7 February, particularly at Lucca, where his supposed relics survive. A famous account of the pilgrimage on which he died was written by the nun Hugeburc; it is called the *Hodoeporicon.*

AA.SS. Feb. II (1658), 69–81; M. Coens, 'Légende et miracles du roi S. Richard', *Anal. Boll.*, xlix (1931), 353–97; W. Grothe, *Der hl. Richard und seine Kinder* (1908); see also C. H. Talbot, *The Anglo-Saxon Missionaries in Germany* (1954), pp. 153–77.

RICHARD OF CHICHESTER (Richard de Wych) (1197–1253), bishop. Born at Droitwich, the son of a yeoman farmer, Richard was a studious boy, but helped to restore the family fortune by working hard on the farm for several years. After refusing an advantageous offer of marriage, he studied at Oxford, Paris, and Bologna, where he gave seven years to canon law.

In 1235 he returned to Oxford and soon became Chancellor. His former tutor, *Edmund of Abingdon, had become archbishop of Canterbury and appointed Richard as his chancellor. He shared Edmund's ideals of clerical reform and resistance, where appropriate, to the secular power; he also shared his exile at Pontigny, and was with him when he died (1240). Richard now decided to become a priest and studied theology for two years with the Dominicans at Orleans.

After his ordination (1242), he was parish priest at Charing and at Deal, but was reappointed chancellor by archbishop Boniface of Savoy (1243–70). In 1244 Richard was elected bishop but King Henry III and part of the Chapter refused to accept him, while Boniface refused to confirm the rival election of Richard Passelew. Both sides appealed to the pope; the king confiscated the properties and revenues of the see, but Innocent IV confirmed the election of Richard de Wych and consecrated him bishop at Lyons (1245). Richard returned to Chichester, but the properties were not restored for two years, and then much dilapidated and only at the threat of excommunication. Meanwhile Richard lived at Tarring in the parish priest's house, visited his diocese on foot, and cultivated figs in his spare time.

Contemporaries reckoned Richard to be a model diocesan bishop. Charitable and accessible, both stern and merciful to sinners, extraordinarily generous to those stricken by famine, he was also a legislator for his diocese. The sacraments were to be administered without payment, Mass celebrated in dignified conditions; the clergy must observe celibacy, practise residence, and wear clerical dress. The laity were obliged to attend Mass on Sundays and holy days and to know by heart the Hail Mary as well as the Lord's Prayer and the Creed.

He was also prominent in preaching the Crusade near the end of his life. He saw this as a call to a new life, which would also reopen the Holy Land to pilgrims, not as a political expedition. He recruited numbers of Crusaders in Sussex and Kent, especially among unemployed sailors. But he fell mortally ill at Dover and died on 3 April. He was canonized in 1262 and his body was translated to a shrine behind the high altar of Chichester cathedral in 1276. This became a pilgrimage centre for the rest of the Middle Ages, until the shrine was despoiled in 1538 and the body buried secretly.

In art he is represented with a chalice at his feet, in memory of his having once at Mass dropped the chalice, which remained unspilt; murals also survive in Norwich cathedral and at Black Bourton (Oxon.). Unexpectedly, he is patron of the coachmen's guild at Milan, presumably because he drove carts on his family farm. He can also be seen as the type of the academic who is skilled in agriculture as well. One ancient English church is dedicated to him. He is also author of a famous prayer, recently set to popular music: 'Thanks be to thee, my Lord Jesus Christ for all the benefits thou hast given me, for all the pains and insults which thou hast borne for me. O most merciful redeemer, friend and brother, may I know thee more clearly, love thee more dearly and follow thee more nearly, day by day.' Feast: 3 April; translation 16 June.

Contemporary Life by Ralph Bocking in *AA.SS.* Apr. I (1675), 282–318; abridged Life in *N.L.A.*, ii. 328–38; Statutes in F. M. Powicke and C. R. Cheney, *Councils and Synods*, II (part i), 451–67 (1964); other studies by M. R. Capes (1913), C. M. Duncan-Jones (1953) and E. F. Jacob, 'St. Richard of Chichester', *J.E.H.*, vii (1956), 174–88.

RIGBY, John (d. 1600), martyr. He was born at Harrock (Lancs.) of an impoverished recusant family and went into service, first with a Protestant family and later with the recusant Huddlestons of Sawston Hall (Cambs.), where he met the Jesuits John Gerard and Nicholas *Owen, through whom he was reconciled to the R.C. Church. About two years later, when sent to the Middlesex Sessions to plead the illness of his master's daughter for her non-appearance on a recusancy charge, he was himself interrogated about his own religion. He answered bluntly that he had been reconciled to Catholicism. He was then sent to Newgate and after refusing liberty in exchange for conformity was sentenced to death. His fine physique and outstanding courage were remarked on by eye-witnesses of his execution, which took place at St. Thomas Waterings, Southwark on 21 June. He was canonized by Paul VI in 1970 as one of the *Forty Martyrs of England and Wales. Feast 25 October.

T. Worthington, *A Lancashire Man: the Martyrdom of John Rigby of Southwark* (ed. C. A. Newdigate, 1928); R. Challoner, *Memoirs of Missionary Priests* (ed. J. H. Pollen, 1928), pp. 238–45: J. E. Paul, *Blessed John Rigby* (pamphlet 1964).

RIQUIER (Richarius) (d. *c.*645), abbot. He was born at Celles, near Amiens; when a young man and still a pagan, he protected some Irish missionaries who were in danger from the local population. They then instructed him in the Christian faith; he became a priest and went to England for several years. On his return to France he founded a monastery at Celles, became famous as a preacher, and admonished King Dagobert and other magnates. Eventually he resigned his abbacy and became a hermit at Forest-Moûtier. There he died on 26 April.

This day is his usual feast, but there is also a translation feast on 9 October, when his relics were moved to the town now called Saint-Riquier (Somme), where a monastery was founded later. Riquier appears frequently in ancient calendars and litanies. One English church was dedicated to him at Aberford (W. Yorks.).

Two ancient Lives, one by Alcuin, are printed in *AA.SS.* Apr. III (1675), 441–62; verse Life by Hariulf in *M.G.H.*, *Scriptores rerum merov.*, vii. 438–53.

RITA OF CASCIA (1377–1447), widow, Augustinian nun, patron of desperate cases. Born at Roccaporena in Umbria, she wished in childhood to become a nun but married in deference to her parents' wishes a husband who subsequently became notoriously violent and unfaithful. They had two sons; Rita endured her husband's insults and infidelities for eighteen years; then one day he was brought home dead, murdered in a vendetta and covered with wounds. His sons wished to avenge him, but both died before this could be accomplished. Rita then became a nun (*c.*1407) at S. Maria Maddalena at Cascia. By constant prayer and mortification, accompanied by meditation on the Passion of Christ so intense that a wound appeared in her forehead, as though pierced by a crown of thorns, she became a mystic. The wound continued for fifteen years and could not be healed. Meanwhile she devoted herself especially to the care of sick nuns and to counselling sinners.

She died of tuberculosis and her reputation for holiness and miracles led to her incorrupt body being translated to an elaborate tomb which survives at the present time. Also contained in it is the local bishop's approbation of her cult in 1457. A verse Life with an early record of miracles survives too, as does an authentic portrait. She was beatified in 1626 and canonized in 1900. A new basilica with hospital, school, and orphanage was built in 1946. Her cult flourishes today, especially in Italy, Spain, France, South America, the Philippines, the United States, and Eire. While the baroque iconography stresses the aspect of a pathetic wife and mother consoled but also wounded by ecstasy, the recent popularity of her cult in Italy seems to be caused by her reputation (like that of *Jude) as patron of desperate cases. These, especially matrimonial difficulties (which have not been diminished by a lack of violent or unsatisfactory husbands) have made Rita a much-sought-after patron. According to an opinion poll in an Italian magazine, her popularity among its readers exceeds that of the Madonna herself. The English centre of her cult is at the Augustinian church of Honiton (Devon). Feast: 22 May.

AA.SS. Maii V (1685), 224–34; G. Bruni, *Vita de santa Rita de Cascia* (1941); other Lives by R. Connolly (1903) and M. J. Corcoran (1919); *N.C.E.*, xii. 541; *Bibl. SS.*, xi. 212–27.

ROBERT OF BURY ST. EDMUNDS (1171–81). He was alleged to have been crucified by Jews: as in the cases of *William of Norwich and 'little St. *Hugh' of Lincoln it is extremely likely that his death was due to other causes and that the cult was a popular expression of anti-Semitic hatred and suspicion. Robert was never canonized; the cult was unofficial, but it survived at least until the time of William Worcestre.

William Worcestre, P. 163; T. Arnold (ed.), *Memorials of St. Edmund's Abbey* (*R.S.*), i. 223; iii. 6.

ROBERT OF KNARESBOROUGH (1160–1218), hermit. The son of an important townsman of York, Robert became a cleric early in life. As a subdeacon he was a novice at the Cistercian abbey of Newminster, but he stayed only a few months. He then chose to live as a hermit at Knaresborough in a cave where another hermit, also in residence, was a knight in hiding from Richard I, on whose death (1199) he returned to his wife. Robert continued there for some years, until a wealthy widow offered him a cell and chapel at Rudfarlington, near by. A year later this hermitage was destroyed by bandits, so Robert lived at Spofforth under the church wall for a few months, then at Hedley (near Tadcaster), where he found the monks too easy-going, before returning to Rudfarlington. Here he had four servants and kept livestock, but was soon in trouble with William de Stuteville, constable of Knaresborough castle, for harbouring thieves and outlaws. The charge may have been true, for Robert was well known for charity to the destitute. The hermitage was destroyed by William; Robert returned to his cave at Knaresborough, where he lived for the rest of his life.

His benefactors included King John who gave him forty acres of land in 1216, which he eventually accepted for the poor and so refused to pay tithes on it. William de Stuteville also gave him land and cows. Robert had a companion called Yves, who remained with him for the rest of his life.

Robert's death, like much of his life, was controversial. Cistercian monks from Fountains tried unsuccessfully to aggregate him to their Order on his death-bed and, after his death on 24 September, to bury his body in their church. But he refused the first and foiled the second by arranging for his burial in the chapel beside his cave. Later the Trinitarian house at Knaresborough acquired the hermitage: papal records for 1252 offered an indulgence for 'Building the monastery of St. Robert at Gnaresbur, where that saint's body is buried'. This document followed his translation, but preceded any official process of canonization, for which a book of Lives and prayers was prepared. Official canonization never took place, but implicit approval was given to the cult. The chapel became a place of pilgrimage, where oil flowed from the tomb. Matthew Paris regarded *Edmund of Abingdon, *Elizabeth of Hungary, and Robert of Knaresborough as the outstanding saints of the early 13th century.

Churches at Knaresborough and Pannall (N. Yorkshire) were dedicated to Robert; seven stained-glass panels of his Life survive at Morley (Derbyshire), from Dale Abbey. The site of Robert's chapel can still be seen, overlooking the river Nidd. Feast: 24 September.

J. Bazire, *The Metrical Life of St. Robert of Knaresborough* (E.E.T.S., 1953); P. Grosjean, 'Vitae S. Roberti Knaresburgensis', *Anal. Boll.*, lvii (1939), 364–400; J. I. Cummins, *Legends, Saints, and Shrines of Knaresborough* (1928) see also R. M. Clay, *The Hermits and Anchorites of England* (1914).

ROBERT OF MOLESME (1027–1110), abbot, founder of Cîteaux. Born of a noble family in Champagne, Robert became a monk, and soon afterwards prior, at Moûtier-la-Celle. Later he became abbot of Tonnerre, but soon hermits of Collan asked him to teach them and eventually become their abbot. This was achieved through Roman intervention; Robert and his new community moved to Molesme *c.*1075. This reforming venture was, however, soon compromised by the access of wealth and the acceptance of unsuitable novices; so *Alberic and *Stephen Harding, both monks of Molesme, asked their abbot to lead them in yet another reform. Robert accordingly resigned his abbacy and joined these monks and their companions at Cîteaux (near Dijon) in 1098. The aim was to live strictly according to the letter of the Rule of St. Benedict, in poverty and seclusion. But in the absence of Robert, Molesme had deteriorated; so the monks petitioned the Holy See to restore their abbot. This request was granted; Robert left Cîteaux, not altogether reluctantly, and remained abbot of Molesme for the rest of his life. He died there on 21 March at the age of eighty-three. Not long after, *Bernard transformed the Cistercians into a monastic mass-movement. The traditional account of Cistercian origins including the role of Robert, has been rightly criticized in recent years: a number of documents seem to be about forty years later than their supposed date. Robert was canonized in 1222. Feast: 29 April.

AA.SS. Apr. III (1675), 668–78 and *P.L.*, clvii. 1269–94; M. Lefèvre, 'Que savons-nous du Cîteaux primitif', *R.H.E.*, li (1956) 5–41; id., 'Saint Robert de Molesme dans l'opinion monastique du XIIe et du XIIIe siecle', *Anal. Boll.*, lxxiv (1956), 50–83; J. Winandy, 'Les origines de Cîteaux et les travaux de M. Lefèvre', *Rev. Bén.*, lxvii (1957), 49–76; see also *M.O.*, pp. 208–26 and Additional Note C.

ROBERT OF NEWMINSTER (*c.*1100–59), Cistercian abbot. He was born at Gargrave (North Yorkshire), studied at Paris (where he wrote a lost treatise on the Psalms), was ordained priest, and became the rector in his home town. He then joined the Benedictines at Whitby, but became one of the founders of Fountains Abbey in 1132. In 1138 Robert was chosen as abbot of Newminster (Northumberland), a new foundation on land given by Ralph of Merly, lord of Morpeth. Newminster grew rapidly and founded dependencies at Pipewell (Northants.) in 1143, Roche (S. Yorkshire) in 1147, and Sawley (N. Yorkshire) in 1148.

Little is known of Robert: his biographer praised his singleness of purpose and his zeal for poverty and prayer; his collection of prayers and meditations survived him in the monastic library. Visions and diabolical encounters were also related of him. In 1147 some of his monks accused him of excessive familiarity with a pious woman; he cleared himself of the charge at Cîteaux and *Bernard, in token of his recognition of Robert's innocence, gave him a girdle, which was kept at Newminster for healing the sick. Robert also met Pope Eugenius III, who asked the bishop of Durham to give Newminster some land at Wolsingham. Robert was also a friend of *Godric of Finchale, who saw a vision of Robert's soul going up to heaven like a sphere of fire.

This was on the day of Robert's death, 7 June. He was buried in the chapter-house at Newminster, but was later translated to the church. Miracles reported at his tomb included one of a monk who fell to the ground from a ladder unharmed, while whitewashing the dormitory. The cult was Cistercian and local. Feast: 7 June.

AA.SS. Iun. II (1698), 47–9; P. Grosjean, 'Vita S. Roberti Novi Monasteri abbatis', *Anal. Boll.*, lvi (1936), 334–60; Reginald of Durham, *Vita S.Godrici* (ed. J. Stevenson, *S.S.* 1845); W. Williams, 'St. Robert of Newminster', *Downside Review*, lvii (1939), 137–49.

ROBERTS, John (*c.*1576–1610), Benedictine monk, priest and martyr. Born at Trawsynydd (Merioneth, now Gwynedd), Roberts was educated at St. John's College, Oxford, and at the Inns of Court (London). He joined the R.C. Church at Notre Dame, Paris, in 1598 and entered the English College, Valladolid, the same year. But he and five other students really wanted to be monks and joined the Benedictine monastery of St. Martin in the same town. This seemed like abandoning all prospect of apostolic activity in England, but in 1602 Pope Clement VIII authorized the Valladolid Benedictines to initiate just such a project. Roberts and one companion at once returned to England, in disguise. He so distinguished himself for his work in plague-stricken London that a contemporary commented: 'Among all the religious who have worked in that island this man may be almost reckoned the chief, both as regards labour and fruitfulness of preaching.' Within seven years he was arrested four times, banished twice and escaped from prison once. When in exile he helped to found the Benedictine monastery of St. Gregory, Douai (now Downside). In 1610 he returned to England and was arrested in early December at Holborn while saying Mass. Soon afterwards he was brought for trial before George Abbot, bishop of London, and Edward Coke, the Chief Justice. When accused of being a 'seducer of the people', he answered: 'If I am, then our ancestors were deceived by St. Augustine, the apostle of the English, who was sent here by the pope of Rome, St. Gregory the Great . . . I am sent here by the same Apostolic See that sent him before me.' Roberts was found guilty and condemned to death. On the night before his execution a Spanish lady, Donna Luisa de Carvajal, provided a fine feast in Newgate prison for twenty Catholic prisoners, at which she presided and John Roberts was the guest of honour. He was hanged, drawn, and quartered at Tyburn on 10 December 1610. He was canonized by Paul VI in 1970 as one of the *Forty Martyrs of England and Wales. Some autograph letters survive in the Public Record Office (London), as does one of his fingers at Downside Abbey. Feast: 25 October.

B. Camm, *A Benedictine Martyr in England: the Life and Times of Dom John Roberts* (1897); R. Challoner, Memoirs of Missionary Priests (ed. J. H. Pollen 1928), pp. 317–23; T. P. Ellis, *Catholic Martyrs of Wales* (1933), pp. 79–91; W. Phillipson, *Blessed John Roberts* (pamphlet, 1961).

ROCH (Rocco, Rock) (*c.*1350–*c.*1380), hermit. Born at Montpellier of a rich merchant family, Roch became a hermit and spent much of his life on pilgrimages. One of these was to Rome and included a stay there of three years (1368–71). While he was in Piacenza, he caught the plague and was fed in the woods by a dog, but was also reputed to have miraculously cured sufferers from the plague. One story relates that he returned to Montpellier, where his uncle refused to recognize him, and where he was imprisoned as an impostor. Another tradition, better based, says that he died at Angleria (Lombardy), imprisoned as a suspect spy. Miracles were claimed there at his tomb; his cult as patron of the plague-stricken spread quickly from there to Germany and France. Relics were claimed by Arles and Venice, where Tintoretto adorned his church with a cycle of paintings.

In England his memory is recalled by one Sussex place-name (St. Rokeshill) and by screen paintings in Devon and Norfolk. These depict him as a pilgrim with a sore on his leg, accompanied by a dog with a loaf of bread in its mouth.

His cult subsided during the 16th century, but was saved by the papal approval of his office for hermitages and churches dedicated to him. It revived in the 19th century during disastrous outbreaks of cholera. Feast: 16 August.

AA.SS. Aug. III (1737), 380–415; A. Fliche, 'Le problème de S. Roch', *Anal. Boll.*, lxviii (1950), 343–61; studies by G. Ceroni (1927) and A. Maurino (1936).

RODAN, see RUADHAN.

RODRIGUEZ, Alphonsus (1533–1617), Jesuit lay brother. The son of a wool merchant of Segovia, Alphonsus followed his father's profession. He married, but his wife and two children died young. He also failed in business. In 1571 he entered the Jesuit Order. He was sent to the college of Montesione (Majorca), where he was the hall-porter for the rest of his life. His prayer, self-sacrifice, and obedience were remarkable and bore fruit in his widespread influence as a counsellor. He also wrote a few ascetical works. A famous poem by Gerard Manley Hopkins praises him as an example of holiness realized in and through the duties of an unspectacular, humdrum life. He was canonized in 1888. Feast: 30 October.

AA.SS. Oct. XIII (1883), 585–657; J. Nonell, *Obras espirituales del beato Alonso Rodriguez* (1885–7); id., *Vida de San Alonso Rodriguez* (1888); M. Farnum, *The Wool Merchant of Segovia* (1945); W. Yeomans (tr.), *Autobiography of Alphonsus Rodriguez* (1964).

ROE, Alban Bartholomew (1583–1642), Benedictine monk, priest and martyr. Born in Suffolk, Roe was educated at Cambridge University and became an ardent and aggressive Protestant. It is said that a meeting at St. Albans with an imprisoned recusant whom Roe had undertaken to convert, resulted instead in his own discomfiture. After a period of study and of meeting several priests, Roe joined the R.C. Church in 1607 and was admitted to the English College, Douai, in 1608. Three years later, however, he was dismissed for insubordination during a period of crisis for the college. Nevertheless he became a Benedictine monk at Dieulouard, Lorraine (now at Ampleforth Abbey, N. Yorkshire), was professed in 1614 and ordained priest in 1615. The same year he helped to found the monastery of St. Edmund, Paris (now at Woolhampton, Berks.).

From Paris he returned to London, where he worked until 1618, when he was arrested and imprisoned for five years. Released through the influence of the Spanish ambassador, he was then banished, but returned to England a few months later. After two years he was again arrested and imprisoned at St. Albans. Friends procured his transfer to the Fleet, where he remained for a further fifteen years, during which he was often released on day parole. This enabled him to minister to many London recusants. Under the Long Parliament this lax arrangement ended: Roe was transferred to Newgate and tried in 1642 at the Old Bailey. He was accused of being a priest and a 'seducer of the people'. He was sentenced to be hanged, drawn, and quartered; the sentence was executed on 21 January. He was canonized by Paul VI in 1970 as one of the *Forty Martyrs of England and Wales. Feast 25 October.

J. McCann and C. Cary-Elwes, *Ampleforth and its Origins* (1952); J. Forbes, *Blessed Alban Roe* (pamphlet, 1960).

ROGER OF ELLANT (d. 1160), Cistercian abbot. English by birth, Roger became a Cistercian monk at Lorroy in Berry. Exemplary in his practice of poverty and other monastic observance, he was chosen as founding abbot of Ellant, near Reims. There he was well known for his care of the sick. After his death a chapel was dedicated in his honour and his relics enshrined. Feast: 4 January.

AA.SS. Ian. I (1643), 182–5; Stanton, pp. 2–4; B.T.A., i. 32.

ROGNVALD (Ronald) (d. 1158/9), earl of Orkney. The son of Kol, a chieftain in Norway, and a nephew of *Magnus, earl of

Orkney, Rognvald succeeded in regaining his earldom of which his kinsman, Earl Paul, had deprived him. In 1137, as a thank-offering, he began the building of the cathedral of Kirkwall, in which the relics of Magnus were enshrined. He went on pilgrimage to the Holy Land, but was absent from the Orkneys for three years. He was murdered in Caithness on 20 August, and was buried in St. Magnus Cathedral. *Orkneyinga Saga* (written *c.*1220) records that 'on the boulder where Earl Rognvald's blood had poured when he was killed we can still see it, as lovely as if it had been newly spilt'. He had the reputation of a saint and there was a popular cult. Chapel Ronald at Glenkindie (Aberdeenshire) was dedicated to him.

Orkneyinga Saga. The History of the Earls of Orkney, tr. and with introd. by H. Pálsson and P. Edwards (1978); J. M. Mackinlay, *Ancient Church Dedications in Scotland* (1914), pp. 298–303.

ROMANUS (1) (d. 258), Roman doorkeeper and martyr. The untrustworthy Acts of *Laurence said he was a soldier converted by this famous martyr. Romanus was buried by the road to Tivoli. Feast: 9 August, in the calendars of Rome, Sarum, and several English monasteries.

AA.SS. Aug. II (1735), 408–10; L. Duchesne, *Liber Pontificalis* i. 156.

ROMANUS (2) (d. *c.*640), bishop of Rouen. Educated at the court of Clotaire II, Romanus became a bishop in 630 and eliminated, as far as he could, all traces of idolatry from his diocese. The Rouen Chapter exercised a 'Privilege of St. Romanus' whereby a condemned criminal was released from the death sentence and carried the shrine of Romanus in procession. This custom survived until the French Revolution. Feast: 23 October in France, Rome, Sarum, and several English monasteries.

AA.SS. Oct. X (1861), 74–103; B.T.A., iv. 183.

ROMANUS (3), the name wrongly given by medieval hagiographers to *Ronan or *Rumon.

ROMUALD OF RAVENNA (*c.*950–1027), Benedictine abbot. Born of a noble Ravenna family, Romuald became a monk at the nearby Cluniac monastery of S. Apollinare-in-Classe after his father had killed a man in a duel. After prolonged study of the Desert Fathers, he aimed at restoring penance and solitude to contemporary monasticism and propagated the idea that monastic life, particularly in solitude, was the way of salvation for all. His most famous monasteries were Fonte Avellana, virtually refounded by his disciple *Peter Damian, and Camaldoli (on a wooded mountainside in Tuscany), which developed into a separate congregation after his death. His particular contribution to the Monastic Order was to provide for the hermit life, esteemed but rejected by Benedict, within the framework of the Benedictine Rule. The observance of Camaldoli influenced *Bruno and the Carthusian Order. Romuald was very austere in character; his Order has always been few in numbers, but it survives to this day. He died alone at Val-di-Castro on 29 June. His incorrupt body was translated to Fabriano on 7 February, thereafter kept as his feast. But now his feast is on 19 June.

Life by Peter Damian in *AA.SS.* Feb. II (1658), 101–44 and in *P.L.*, cxliv. 953–1008; modern Lives by T. Ciampelli (1927) and A. Pagnani (1967); see also *M.O.*, pp. 192–6; J. Leclercq, 'Saint Romuald et le monachisme missionaire', *Rev. Bén.*, lxxii (1962), 307–23; G. Tabacco, 'Romualdo di Ravenna e gli inizi dell'eremitismo camaldolese' in *L'eremitismo in occidente nei secoli XI e XII* (1965).

RONAN (1), Scottish hermit of the 7th century. Persistent tradition claims that he settled on the island of North Rona, where a fine oratory of that time survives, a unique relic of early Christianity in Scotland and similar to the Gallarus Oratory of Co. Kerry.

Legend relates that he was tormented by the evil tongues of the women in Eoroby (Lewis); that he was told in a dream to escape from them by sea; that a whale took him to North Rona, where he defeated various diabolical assaults on his person and his oratory. A later version related that his sister Brenhilda, exiled on a nearby island for some sin, died pining for her brother. A church at Eoroby is dedicated to him, as well as the chapel on North Rona.

H. C. Nisbet and R. A. Gailey, 'A survey of the Antiquities of North Rona', *Archaeol. Jnl.*, cxvii (1960), 88–115.

RONAN (2). Other saints of this name include:

(*a*) A bishop who died in Brittany after working in Cornwall; he is buried at Locronan. Feast: 1 June.

(*b*) A Scottish bishop of Kilmaronen in Lennox, implausibly identified with the Irish monk mentioned by *Bede as the defender of Roman calculation of Easter at the Synod of Whitby. St. Ronan's Well at Innerleithen (Peeblesshire) was popularized by Sir Walter Scott's novel of that name. According to tradition, the saint came to the valley and drove out the Devil and this is commemorated at the end of 'St. Ronan's Games', a week of festivities held every July, which comes to a climax when a schoolboy chosen to represent St. Ronan is given a pastoral Staff to 'cleek the Devil'. Feast: 7 February.

(*c*) A bishop, whose feast was kept at Canterbury on 19 November, and of whom the monastery possessed an arm relic. His identity is obscure, but he may be Romanus, deacon, and exorcist of Caesarea, whose feast is kept on 18 November.

K.S.S., pp. 441–2; Baring-Gould and Fisher, iv. 120–5; *E.B.K. after 1100*, i. 67.

ROSE OF LIMA (1586–1617), virgin. Born at Lima (Peru) of a Spanish family of moderate wealth, subsequently impoverished through unsuccessful speculation in the mines, she chose not to marry in spite of parental persuasion, but took a vow of virginity and joined the Third Order of St. *Dominic, taking as her model *Catherine of Siena. Extreme forms of penance, sometimes self-inflicted, matched the love of God which radiated from her presence to those who came into contact with her. She lived as a recluse in a hut in the garden and experienced both trials and consolations of an extraordinary kind. After a long illness which seems to have had psychological as well as physical elements, she died at the age of thirty-one. Perhaps her life is best understood as an attempt to make reparation for the widespread sin and corruption in contemporary society. She was canonized in 1671, the first saint of America, and was named patron of South America and the Philippine Islands. Feast: 23 August (formerly 30 August).

AA.SS. Aug. V (1741), 892–1029; *Compendium vitae, virtutum et miraculorum . . . B. Rosae de S. Maria* (1671); F. M. Capes, *The Flower of the New World* (1899); R. V. Ugarte, *Vida de Santa Rosa de Santa Maria* (1951); F. P. Keyes, *The Rose and the Lily* (1962).

RUADHAN (Ruadan, Rodan) (d. *c.*584), founder and abbot of Lothra (Co. Tipperary). Reputedly of royal Munster stock, he was educated at Clonard and is sometimes claimed as a bishop and one of the *Twelve Apostles of Ireland. His monastery is said to have numbered 150 monks. An ancient oratory, on to which the parish church of Lothra has been built, may be his. His Lives are all late and unreliable: one famous episode is that in which he indulged in a cursing match with the secular rulers of Tara so efficaciously that Tara was ruined and deserted. His hand was preserved in a silver shrine at Lothra until the Reformation. Feast: 15 April, mentioned in the Martyrology of *Oengus.

AA.SS. Apr. II (1675), 382–6; *V.S.H.*, ii. 240–52; *The Irish Saints*, pp. 280–1.

RUDESIND (Rosendo) (907–77), bishop and abbot. Born in Galicia of a noble family, he seems to have been consecrated bishop of Mondonedo (Dumium) at an early age. He founded Celanova abbey in 942, becoming a monk there and in 959 its abbot. Called on to administer the see of Compostella (960–7), he is said to have repelled in battle both Northmen and Saracens. He founded other abbeys, insisting on the Rule of St. *Benedict like other reformers of his time. He died at Celanova with a widespread reputation for wisdom.

In 1195 after the usual enquiry into his life and numerous miracles he was canonized. Feast: 1 March; translation, 1 November (recalling the event in 1601).

AA.SS. Martii I (1668), 102–19; J. Cardoso in *Studia Monastica*, iii (1961), 325–56; E. W. Kemp, *Canonization and Authority in the Western Church* (1948), pp. 89–98; *Bibl. SS.*, xi. 453–4.

RUFFIN, see WULFHAD AND RUFFIN.

RUFUS (Rufinus) of Capua, martyr. Nothing is known of this saint (who was not a bishop), but whose Legend made him the father of a girl raised to life by *Apollinaris of Ravenna. Feast: 27 August, in the Sarum calendar and in those of about fifteen English monasteries.

C.M.H., pp. 469–70; *AA.SS.* Aug. VI (1743), 9–11.

RULE (Regulus) (?4th century). This obscure Scottish saint commemorated in the Aberdeen breviary, was patron of Kylrewni, and supposedly the bearer of the relics of *Andrew to Scotland. This Legend, which is not entirely consistent, makes Rule a native of Patras in the 4th century, who was admonished in a dream by an angel to take part of the relics in his care to an unknown destination in the north-west. He kept on travelling until the same angel told him to stop at a place in Fife, where he built the church which housed Andrew's relics, and which was later called St. Andrews. The remainder of the relics had been taken to Constantinople. Feast: 17 October, but also, through confusion with St. Regulus of Senlis, on 30 March.

K.S.S., pp. 436–40.

RUMON, monk and bishop (?) of the (?) 6th century, patron of Tavistock and Romansleigh (Devon) and of Ruan Lanihorne, Ruan Major and Minor (Cornwall). William of Malmesbury visited his shrine at Tavistock *c.*1120, described him as a bishop, and regretted the complete absence of sources concerning his life. A West Country canon, possibly from Glasney (Penryn), made good this deficiency by providing a 'Life' for Rumon, which consisted simply of a transcript and abbreviation of the Life of the Breton *Ronan, but with 'Rumon' written for 'Ronan' throughout. This has caused confusion to scholars from the 12th century to the 20th.

Its most useful element is a description of the translation of Rumon's relics from Ruan Lanihorne, a Celtic monastery and the most ancient centre of his cult, to Tavistock. This was founded by Ordulph, count of Devon and Cornwall, in 981, and it was he who obtained the relics. There Rumon's body, but not (according to *C.S.P.*) his head, remained throughout the Middle Ages. The same source describes him as 'an Irish hermit who became a bishop, but left his country for Little Britain (i.e. Brittany), where he spent his life in abstinence and virtue'. Doble suggests that Rumon was a monk of Glastonbury who made a foundation in the Lizard peninsula of Cornwall. Glastonbury claimed relics of Rumon, who was venerated in the West of England, as well as at Norwich and Ramsey. His feast was on 30 August (with a fair at Tavistock from 1114); translation, 5 January. Various Irish and Scottish saints of the same or similar name are distinct.

G.P., pp. 202–4; P. Grosjean, 'Vie de S. Rumon', *Anal. Boll.*, lxxi (1953), 359–414; G. H. Doble, *The Saints of Cornwall*, ii (1962), 120–34; William Worcestre, 112–15; H. P. R. Finberg, *Tavistock Abbey* (1951).

RUMWOLD (Rumwald, Rumbald, Rumbold), supposedly a boy of the royal family of Mercia, buried at Buckingham, where there was a shrine before the Norman Conquest. His quite incredible Legend, a hagiographical curiosity, makes him a grandson of Penda, king of Mercia (d. 654), through his daughter, who had married a pagan prince of Northumbria. According to this, Rumwold was born at Sutton (thenceforth King's Sutton, Northants.) and died there only three days later, but not before repeating several times 'I am a Christian', making a profession of faith in the Holy Trinity, and asking for Baptism and Holy Communion from the priests Widerin and Edwold. He then preached a sermon on the Holy Trinity and the need for virtuous living, freely citing Scripture and the Athanasian Creed. After this he announced his imminent death and directed that he should be buried first at King's Sutton, then at Brackley, and finally at Buckingham. The prodigious infant then expired.

His cult was observed in these three places, and in at least six pre-Conquest monasteries of Mercia and Wessex, as well as in the Bosworth Psalter; but his name is not found in monastic calendars of after 1100. Churches were, however, dedicated to him in Kent, Essex, Northants., Lincolnshire, Dorset, and North Yorkshire, that in the last county being at Romaldkirk, which was named after him. A well also survives at Alstrop, Northants. At Boxley (Kent) a statue of him, formerly venerated, was burnt at the Reformation, but in Camden's time he was still invoked by the fishermen of Folkestone as their patron. The source of his Legend is not known; the saint's popularity, reflected also by street-names in various parts of the country, was unexpectedly persistent. Feast: 3 (or 2) November.

AA.SS. Nov. I (1887), 682–90; *N.L.A.*, ii. 345–50; *R.P.S.* R. H. Hagerty in *Records of Buckinghamshire*, xxx (1988), 103–110. For a somewhat similar prodigy see St. Theresa of Avila, *Book of the Foundations*, c. 20.

RUPERT, (d. *c.*710) bishop of Worms and Salzburg. Frankish or possibly Irish by birth, he founded the monastery of St. Peter at Salzburg and the nunnery at Nonnberg, where his sister Ermentrude became abbess. He then acted as a missionary bishop in the Danube area with notable success. Later he evangelized and preached the gospel at Regensburg (Bavaria). Near Salzburg he developed the salt-mines, for which reason his iconographical emblem is a barrel of salt. Many churches in this area are dedicated to him. Feast: 27 March.

AA.SS. Mart. III (1668), 699–706; B.T.A., i. 700–1; *Bibl. SS.*, xi. 506–8.

S

SAETHRITH (Saethryda), (7th century), abbess of Faremoutier-en-Brie. Mentioned by *Bede as a daughter (modern scholars make a stepdaughter) of Anna, king of the East Angles, Saethrith became a nun at Faremoutier like some other Anglo-Saxon princesses of her time. She did not return to England, but died at Faremoutier. Feast: 10 January.

AA.SS. Ian. I (1643), 626–7; Stanton, pp. 13–14.

SALOME, see JUDITH AND SALOME.

SALVIUS (7th century), bishop. The identity of a famous relic, presented to Canterbury Cathedral by William the Conqueror, when Lanfranc rebuilt it after the fire in 1069, is a matter of dispute. Some identify this Salvius with the bishop of Amiens, who flourished under Theodoric II and died in 625, and whose relics were transferred to Montreuil (Picardy). Feast: 12 January.

Another Salvius, a missionary bishop sometimes supposed to have come from Angoulême, arrived in Valenciennes *c.*768 and was soon murdered for the sake of his rich robes. He and a companion who shared his fate were buried at St. Vedast, Valenciennes. Feast: 26 June.

Yet a third Salvius was a Norman hermit in the forest of Bray with a reputation for miracles. He is believed to have flourished in the 6th century. Feast: 28 October.

It is perhaps ironical that Lanfranc, who questioned the cults of Anglo-Saxon saints, of whom many were reputable historical characters, should have introduced at least one set of dubious relics into the very rich Canterbury collection. Canterbury calendars place his feast on 26 June, thereby identifying him with Salvius of Valenciennes.

B.T.A., *s.v.*

SAMSON (d. 565), bishop of Dol, perhaps the most important British missionary of the 6th century. Scholarly opinion is divided about the authenticity of his Life and whether it was written in the 7th or the 9th century; the earliest manuscripts of it date from the 11th. Its most credible elements are the following. Samson was Welsh by birth: his father, Amon, being from Dyfed, and his mother from Gwent. As a child he was offered to *Illtud at Llantwit (South Glamorgan), where he was educated and ordained deacon and priest. After incurring the jealousy of Illtud's nephews in the community, Samson retired to Caldey (Ynys Byr). There he became cellarer and later abbot. He reformed an Irish monastery and then lived as a hermit near the river Severn. After becoming abbot of a nearby monastery and being consecrated bishop, he continued his missionary journeys, this time to Cornwall, where he stayed a considerable time; his disciples included *Austell, *Mewan, and *Winnoc. The places associated with him are Padstow, St. Kew, Southill, and Golant. One of the isles of Scilly is named after him, which possibly indicates a missionary journey at this time. But like many other Welsh monks, he made his final home in Brittany, which was the scene of much apostolic activity, including visits to the Channel Islands, where one town of Guernsey bears his name. He also founded monasteries at Dol (Brittany) and at Pental (Normandy). At Dol he exercised, it would seem, episcopal jurisdiction, although there was not a regular see there until some centuries later. The 'Samson peccator episcopus' who signed the acts of the Council of Paris in 557 is probably to be identified with him. He is an excellent example of the wandering Celtic monk-bishop.

Some of his relics, including an arm and a crozier, were acquired by Athelstan, king of Wessex 924–39, for his monastery at Milton Abbas (Dorset). This is one reason why his feast was kept in many English calendars. There are six ancient dedications in England: his cult was well established too in Wales and Brittany. His usual emblems are a cross or staff with a dove and a book. Through Usuard his name passed into the Roman Martyrology. Feast: 28 July.

AA.SS. Iul. VI (1729), 568–93; A. Plaine, 'Vita Antiqua S. Samsonis'; *Anal. Boll.*, vi (1887), 79–150; *R.P.S.*; R. Fawtier, *La Vie de S. Samson* (1912); T. Taylor, *The Life of St Samson of Dol* (1925); G. H. Doble, *The Saints of Cornwall*, v (1970), 80–103; A. W. Wade-Evans, *Welsh Christian Origins* (1934); F. C. Burkitt, 'St. Samson of Dol', *J.T.S.*, xxvii (1925–6), 42–57; E. G. Bowen, 'The Travels of St. Samson of Dol', *Aberystwyth Studies*, xiii (1934).

SAMTHANN (d. 739), Irish nun. This famous saint, included in both the litany and the canon of the Stowe missal, whose cult was introduced at Salzburg by *Virgil, was the founder of a convent at Clonbroney (Co. Longford). Her late Life says that she was fostered by the king of Cairbre Gabhra called Cridan, that the match arranged for her was prevented by a miracle and that she went to become a nun under St. Cognat at Ernaide (Donegal), from which she moved to Clonbroney. This source also preserves some of her supposed sayings: when a monk asked in what attitude should prayer be made, she answered in every position, standing, sitting, or lying. Another said he was going to give up study in order to pray more, but she answered that he would never be able to fix his mind and pray if he neglected study. When another said he was going on pilgrimage, she answered that the kingdom of heaven can be reached without crossing the sea and that God is near to all who call on him. She would not accept large estates for her convent, preferring to live in poverty, with but six cows to form the community herd. Feast: 18 December.

The Irish Saints, pp. 282–4.

SATIVOLA, see SIDWELL.

SAULI, Alexander (1534–92), bishop of Pavia. Born at Milan of a Genoese family, he joined the Barnabite Congregation in 1551, recently founded by Antony *Zaccharia. He studied in their college at Pavia and endowed it with a library. Ordained priest in 1556, he taught theology at the university and was known as an effective and challenging preacher. In 1567 he was elected provost-general of the Barnabites. About the same time Charles *Borromeo had become protector of the Humiliati with a mandate to reform them: he wished to merge them with the lively, observant Barnabites. This plan had the support of Pope *Pius V. Alexander however opposed them both because the plan would have reduced the quality of the Barnabites. In 1571 the attempted assassination of Borromeo by one of the Humiliati led to their suppression soon afterwards.

At this time priests of Sauli's seal and ability were rare: Pius V appointed him bishop of Aleria in Corsica. Their clergy were ignorant and the people irreligious; vendettas were rife and brigandage widespread. As Aleria was in ruins, he made Cervione the centre of the diocese. He visited it systematically, established new reforms, and promulgated the decrees of the council of Trent with due severity. After twenty years, his diocese was considered a model for its time, not least by his friend Philip *Neri. Sauli was offered the sees of Tortona and Genoa, but he refused them both; in 1591 however Gregory XIV insisted on his becoming bishop of Pavia. Only a year later he died while visiting Calozza.

A learned man with special skill in canon law, preaching, and catechesis, he was also believed to have the gift of prophecy, healing, and quelling storms at sea. Less famous than the more charismatic saints of the Counter-Reformation, Sauli is notable as an exemplary religious and pastor in an age of much abuse and corruption. He was canonized in 1904. Feast: 11 October.

AA.SS. Oct. V (1857), 806–34; Lives by F. Moltedo (1904), O. Premoli and others (1905); B.T.A., iv. 90–1; *Bibl. SS.*, i. 808–12.

SAVA (Sabas) **OF SERBIA** (1173–1236), first archbishop of the autocephalous Serbian church. Born in Tirnovo (Bulgaria), the third son of prince Stephen Nemanya (who achieved permanent independence from Byzantium for the Serbs), Sava became a monk at Mount Athos in 1191. In 1196 his father, having abdicated in favour of his son also called Stephen, became a monk there too and took the name of Simeon. Father and son then together founded another monastery at Mount Athos called Khilandari, which became a centre of Serbian religious and secular culture.

In 1206 Sava returned to Serbia and brought his father's relics to Studenica in 1208. He built the churches of Zica, where he became archbishop, Pec, and Milesevo. In 1219 he was consecrated bishop by the patriarch Germanus of Constantinople, then in exile at Nicea. Sava as metropolitan established both bishoprics and monasteries to complete the Christianization of the half-converted Serbs; he also built more churches with the help of his brother Stephen, who had been crowned king by papal legates in 1217. In 1230 Sava went on pilgrimage to the Holy Land and built the monastery of St. John at Jerusalem.

He was also important in the development of Serbian literature. He composed two *Typica* or Rules for his monastery, he wrote a Life and Office of his father Simeon (canonized in 1216), he wrote the *Law of Simeon and Sava*, important for our knowledge of the Serbian peasantry. He also commissioned translations of Greek religious works, which propounded doctrinal orthodoxy and refuted the errors of the Bogomils.

He died at Tirnovo and King Ladislaus translated his relics to Milesevo in 1237. There they were burnt by the Turks in 1594; but this did not prevent the spread of his cult, helped both by a rich iconographical tradition and by the revival of Serbian nationalism in the 19th and 20th centuries. Sava, as an exponent of vernacular religious culture closely associated with his family's political achievements, is a unique exemplar of Serbian identity. Although his life has sometimes been interpreted as though he deliberately separated Serbia from Rome, his feast is kept in Latin as well as Orthodox calendars, in Croatian and Serbian churches, on 14 January.

AA.SS. Ian. I (1647), 979–83; Lives by L. Mirkovic (1939), L. Skerl (1946), D. Pavlovic (1961); see also B.T.A., i. 86–7; *Bibl. SS.*, xi. 522–9; *H.S.S.C.*, vi. 233–4.

SAVIO, Dominic (1842–57). Born at Riva near Turin, Dominic was one of ten children of poor parents, a blacksmith and a seamstress. At the age of twelve he joined the famous school of John *Bosco at Turin; under his guidance he seems to have quickly developed a spiritual maturity beyond his years. The wisdom and moderation of Bosco prevented Savio becoming either a fanatic or a prig. Under his direction he was outstanding for cheerfulness and friendliness to all, the exact observance of discipline and the provision of sound advice. Once he was rapt in prayer for six hours continuously. Another time he had a vision of a bishop 'bringing light with a torch to the English people'. His health failed through tuberculosis, possibly aggravated by unsuitable treatment, and he died, apparently experiencing a vision of heaven, at the age of only fifteen. Soon afterwards John Bosco wrote his Life, which contributed substantially to his beatification in 1950 and canonization in 1954. As a child saint he could be compared to Aloysius *Gonzaga or Maria *Goretti. A few English churches and schools are dedicated to him. Feast: 9 March.

J. Bosco, *The Life of Dominic Savio*, tr. M. Russell (1934) and P. Aronica (1955); *N.C.E.*, xii. 1104–5; B.T.A., i. 539–41.

SCHOLASTICA (d. *c.*543), sister of *Benedict and first Benedictine nun. All that is known of her comes from the *Dialogues* of *Gregory the Great. Her nunnery was Plombariola, about five miles from Monte Cassino; Benedict and Scholastica used to meet once a year in a house at a distance from his monastery; on his last visit to her, she asked him in vain to stay longer to discuss 'the joys of heaven'. When he refused, she prayed for rain to such effect that a violent thunderstorm prevented him leaving and they spent the night as she had wished. She died three days later and was buried in the tomb Benedict had prepared for himself. Her relics were alleged to have been translated to Le Mans when Benedict's were supposed to have gone to Fleury. Feast: 10 February, in the Roman calendar with a high rank in Benedictine nunneries, of which she is the patron.

AA.SS. Feb. II (1658), 392–412; Gregory, *Dialogues*, bk. II, cc. 33–4 (ed. A. de Vogüé. *S.C.*, 1978); W. Goffart, 'Le Mans, St. Scholastica and the literary tradition of the translation of St. Benedict', *Rev. Bén.*, lxxvii (1967), 107–41.

SCILLITAN MARTYRS, see MARTYRS OF SCILLIUM.

SEBASTIAN, Roman martyr who suffered under Diocletian *c.*300. He was buried in a cemetery on the Appian Way close to the basilica which bears his name. His name is in the *Depositio Martyrum* (354). He was also connected with Milan, perhaps by birth or education. His Acts, wrongly ascribed to *Ambrose, are a fiction of the 5th century. According to this, Sebastian was a soldier who enlisted *c.*283 at Rome, strengthened the confessors *Mark and Marcellian in prison, and was created a captain of the pretorian guards by Diocletian, who did not know he was a Christian. After Sebastian had sustained other martyrs, Diocletian reproached him with ingratitude and ordered him to be shot to death with arrows. Sebastian recovered, confronted the emperor for his cruelty, and was beaten to death with clubs.

The earliest representations of Sebastian, as in mosaic in Ravenna and at the church of St. Peter's Chains, Rome (late 7th century) or in frescoes of St. Saba's church, Rome (early 8th century) depict him as an elderly bearded man holding a crown: there are also later examples of this type. But the more familiar one of his being pierced with arrows (notwithstanding the poor quality of the literary source) was extremely popular in the 15th century, supposedly because it gave Renaissance artists opportunities to portray a young and sometimes effeminate male nude in an ecclesiastical context. Sebastian was the patron of archers and, like *George and *Maurice, of soldiers; he also had a widespread patronage against the plague, due either to his invocation in a particular case of cessation of plague or to his courage in facing arrows which enabled him to immunize his devotees against it. He became one of the *Fourteen Holy Helpers. Feast: in the West (with *Fabian), 20 January; in the East, 18 December.

AA.SS. Ian. II (1643), 257–96; B. Pesci, 'Il culto di san Sebastiano a Roma nell' antichita e nel medioevo', *Antonianum*, xx (1945), 177–200; H. Delehaye, *Cinq leçons sur la méthode hagiographique*, pp. 35–7; A. Ferrua, *S. Sebastiano fuori le mura e la sua catacomba* (1968); *Bibl. SS.*, xi. 776–801.

SEBBI (Sebbe), king of East Saxons 664–94. After the apostacy of King Sighere, Sebbi sustained bishop Jaruman of Mercia in his conversion of the East Saxons (Essex, Hertfordshire, and London). Sebbi resigned his throne and became a monk shortly before his death, being notable for his prayer, penance, and lavish almsgiving. He was buried by the north wall of the old cathedral of St. Paul, London. There seems no trace of an ancient liturgical cult; his name was added to the Roman Martyrology, presumably through Bede's account of him, by Baronius. He was also reputed to have built the first monastery at Westminster. Feast: 29 August.

Bede, *H.E.*, iii. 30; iv. 11; *C.S.P.*; *Propylaeum*, p. 368.

SEIRIOL (6th century), abbot, founder of Penmon church (Anglesey) and its dependency Ynys Seiriol, now called Puffin Island. He and his friend *Cybi are Anglesey's principal saints. His well and ruined beehive cell survive at Penmon, as does a monastic settlement on nearby Puffin Island. Like many other Celtic saints he probably travelled by sea and settled near the coast on low-lying land, living first as a hermit and founding a community later. His well would have been used both for his own water supply and for baptism. The later monastic buildings at Penmon are a suitable memorial: they were inhabited by Austin Canons who frequently revived forgotten shrines. *Bede mentions Edwin of Northumbria's capture of Anglesey from Cadwallon, the Welsh king, but does not state that Edwin besieged him in Ynys Seiriol in 632. Matthew Arnold in the poem *East and West* repeats Celtic legends of Cybi and Seiriol, who lived in West and East Anglesey respectively. The only known dedications to Seiriol are at Penmon and Puffin Island: it seems that he was a saint of purely local cult. Feast: 1 February.

An Inventory of the Ancient Monuments in Anglesey (1937), pp. xci–xcii, 119–21, 141–4; Baring-Gould and Fisher, iv. 177–80.

SELEVAN (Selyv, Levan), patron of St. Levan (Cornwall) was probably a Welsh or Cornish saint of the 6th century. He may be the same as the Selevan or Selomon honoured in S. Brittany. A chapel on the cliff at St. Levan, believed to be his hermitage, and a well, survive in a ruined state. A bench-end there, carved with two fish, preserves the memory of his fishing from the rocks, when once he found two bream on the same hook. He removed them both and returned them to the sea. Again they both came to the hook and again were cast into the sea. The same thing happened the third time: Selevan took them home and found his sister *Breage had come to visit him with her two children. No date is provided for his feast by the Cornish Church Calendar. In Brittany, however, a King Selyf, often confused with Selevan, is venerated on 14 October.

G. H. Doble, *The Saints of Cornwall*, i (1960), pp. 3–9.

SENAN (d. *c.*544), Irish abbot, founder of monasteries. Born near Kilrush (Co. Clare), he first tended his father's cattle and later became a monk, studying first with Cassidan in Irrus, afterwards with Notal at Kilnamanagh (Kilkenny). His own foundations included Inniscarra (near Cork), Inis Mor (Canon Island), Mutton Island (Clare), but above all Scattery Island (near Kilrush), where there are still plenty of medieval ruins, of which none certainly date from Senan's time. The shrine of Senan's bell is in the Royal Irish Academy, Dublin. Feast: 8 March.

The patron of Sennen (Cornwall), often asserted to be Senan of Scattery, seems instead to have been an unknown Cornish woman saint, called Sanctae Sennanae in the Poll-tax rolls of 1377.

P. Grosjean, 'Trois pièces sur S. Senan', *Anal. Boll.*, lxvi (1948), 199–230; G. H. Doble, *The Saints of Cornwall*, i (1960), 145; *The Irish Saints*, pp. 285–7.

SENNEN, see ABDON AND SENNEN.

SERAPHIM OF SAROV (1759–1833), monk. Born at Kursk, the son of a builder, he studied hard as a boy and became a monk at Sarov, near Moscow, in 1779. The regime was austere: total abstinence from meat and only one meal a day (but none on Wednesdays and Fridays) seemed insufficient for the long hours of study of Scripture and the Fathers, choral prayer, and manual work in the bakehouse and carpenter's shop. In 1780 Seraphim fell ill and he remained bedridden for three years, during which time he was consoled by visions of the Blessed Virgin and the Apostles. When he recovered, he made an altar of cypress wood for the infirmary chapel.

Ordained priest in 1793, he celebrated the Eucharist every day, then a rare practice in Russia. In 1794, greatly saddened by his abbot's death, he became a hermit in a small wooden hut in the depths of the forest, two hours' walk from the monastery. His regime, not unlike that of *Godric, included woodcutting, cooking bread and home-grown vegetables, and caring for wild animals such as foxes, hares, wolves, and bears.

In 1804 he was attacked by brigands with his own axe: they left him for dead, but he managed to drag himself to the monastery. Five months later he returned to his hermitage, with a perpetual stoop and needing a stick for walking. In 1807 the abbot of Sarov died: Seraphim was offered his post but refused it. He submitted himself to the 'trial of silence'; speaking to nobody until 1810. He then returned to the monastery, living in a cell without bed, heat, or lighting. Another vision of the Virgin led him at this point to give up his solitary life and devote himself instead to the numerous visitors who came to see him and to the nuns of Diveiev, whom he directed with firmness and understanding.

On 14 January 1833 he was found dead in his cell, his clothes burnt by a candle which had fallen from his hands, his face turned towards an icon of the Virgin. His teaching was recorded during his life by Nicolas Motovilov but not published until seventy years later. In his emphasis on the Holy Spirit, source of light who transfigures the soul of the mystic, and on the importance of service and of poverty, Seraphim was a characteristic representative of Russian spirituality. He was canonized by the Council of the Russian Church after some opposition in 1903. Feast: 2 January.

C. de Grunwald, *Saints of Russia* (1960); V. Zander, *St. Seraphim of Sarov* (1975); G. P. Fedotov (ed.), *A Treasury of Russian Spirituality* (1950); I. Gorainov, *The Message of St. Seraphim* (1973).

SERF (Servanus) (6th century), Scottish bishop. All that can be safely asserted of him is that he was the apostle of western Fife of uncertain date. He is also sometimes claimed with less plausibility as the apostle of the Orkneys. The centre of his cult and probably of his activity was Culross. His Legend is a farrago of wild impossibilities. Feast: 1 July.

K.S.S., pp. 445–7; B.T.A., iii. 5.

SERGIUS OF RADONEZH (1315–92), monk. Born at Rostov of a noble family about 100 years after the Tartars conquered Russia, Sergius, when a boy, fled with his family to Radonezh, near Moscow. After the death of their parents, Sergius and his brother Stephen became monks together and restored the monastery of the Holy Trinity, thus re-establishing community life, which had ceased under the Tartars. This was achieved after two years' solitary life, but once accomplished it proved a permanent enrichment to the Russian Church. Sergius at one time or other acted as cook, baker, miller, tailor, and carpenter. He was chosen as superior by his twelve disciples in 1334. His insistence on the common life and prohibition of begging led to discontent; several monks wanted Stephen to be their abbot instead. So Sergius left to found another monastery in the remote forest. Later he was restored by the metropolitan Alexis.

With its wooden cells grouped round a wooden refectory and a stone church, the monastery resembled an early Charterhouse: the numerous visitors received an impression of great moral strength especially needed at this time. So deeply did they respect him that Sergius was invited to become metropolitan of Moscow, but he refused. He influenced events outside his monastery as a mediator and peacemaker in political matters, and the great military success of Dimitri of Moscow over the Tartars in 1380 was attributed in part to the prayers and advice of Sergius.

He founded about forty monasteries and after his death their number increased rapidly owing to his influence. Sergius had based his observance mainly on the teaching of *Theodore the Studite. In life and after death, Sergius was venerated as a saint. He was buried in his monastery church, now called Zagorsk, where numerous pilgrims have never been lacking. He was canonized before 1449 and his cult was approved by Rome. A mystic who favoured close co-operation with the State, Sergius became patron of Moscow and later of all Russia. His monastery and shrine were re-opened in 1945. Feast: 25 September.

G. P. Fedotov (ed.), *A Treasure of Russian Spirituality* (1981), pp. 50–83; abridged early Life in N. Zernov, *St. Sergius, builder of Russia* (1939); C. de Grunwald, *Saints of Russia* (1960); B.T.A., iii. 639–44; P. Kovalesky, *Saint Serge et la spiritualité russe* (1958).

SETON, Elizabeth (*née* Elizabeth Bayley), (1774–1821), widow and foundress. This first native saint of the USA was born of a devout and wealthy Episcopalian family; her father was a famous physician and the first health officer of the city of New York. At the age of nineteen she married a wealthy merchant William Magee Seton, and bore him five children; but at the age of twenty-eight she was left a widow. She then joined the R.C. Church on her return from Tuscany to Emmitsburg, near Baltimore. There she took vows and founded a sisterhood, the American Sisters of Charity, which was devoted to the relief of the poor and to teaching in parish schools. It was based on the rule of *Vincent de Paul. This order increased very considerably until today it is one of the most numerous and influential of its kind. Elizabeth Seton was beatified by John XXIII and canonized by Paul VI in 1975. Impressive cures claimed as miraculous include one from leukaemia and another from severe meningitis. In his canonization allocution, at which 1,000 nuns of her Order from N. and S. America, Italy, and missionary countries were present, the pope stressed her extraordinary contributions as wife, mother, widow, and consecrated nun, the example of her dynamic and authentic witness for future generations and the affirmation of 'that religious spirituality which your (i.e. American) temporal prosperity seemed to obscure and almost make impossible'. Feast: 4 January.

A. M. Melville, *Elizabeth Bayley Seton 1774–1821* (1960); J. I. Dirwin, *Mrs. Seton: Foundress of the American Sisters of Charity* (1962); J. B. Code (ed.), *Letters of Mother Seton to Mrs. Juliana Scott* (2nd edn. 1960); id. in *N.C.E.*, xiii. 136.

SEVEN APOSTLES OF BULGARIA (9–10th centuries). The Bulgar people, who occupied territory considerably larger in those times than modern Bulgaria, had intermarried with the denizens and adopted the Slav language. Their two first apostles are reckoned to be *Cyril and Methodius, although neither actually preached in Bulgaria. On the death of Methodius, Gorazd succeeded him in his missionary apostolate: although the extent of his territory is disputed, his relics are claimed by Berat (Albania).

Of the seven the most important for Bulgaria itself is Clement (Slovensky) of Okhrida. Born in 840, a Slav from southern Macedonia, he established a monastery at Okhrida and a bishopric at Velica not far away. He is regarded as the founder of this primatial see and the first Slav to become a bishop. His extensive apostolate took the form of education of the clergy and of the laity, to whom he preached a series of sermons in Slavonic, suitable for neophytes and explaining the principal feasts of the liturgical year. Clement died at Okhrida on 27 July 916.

His colleague Nahum succeeded him as bishop. Converted in Moravia by Cyril and Methodius, he journeyed with them to Rome and helped them with their translations into the vernacular: he is venerated in Russia as well as Bulgaria. Other companions of Clement called Sava and Angelar are also venerated with him. In different times and different places they all contributed to the fulfilment of the missionary plans of Cyril and Methodius. Feast: usually 27 July, but also in different places (17 July, 22 and 25 November).

Life of Clement in *P.G.*, cxxvi, 1193–1240; F. Dvornik, *Les Slaves, Byzance et Rome* (1926), pp. 312–18; B.T.A., iii. 130–1; *Bibl. SS.*, iv. 29–35.

SEVEN BROTHERS (2nd century), martyrs. Seven martyrs buried in different cemeteries of Rome were culted from early times on 10 July, but apart from their late and unreliable Acts, there is no evidence that they were brothers or, as is usually supposed, the sons of Felicity, martyr. The fact that one of them was buried near her tomb may well have been at the root of the legend, inspired perhaps by a desire to find a Christian equivalent to the story of the martyrdom of the *Machabees and their mother. The feast of the Seven Brothers was well attested in the early Roman sacramentaries and became general in Christendom (including England) from early times. The principal element of the Legend is that Felicity and the other martyrs refused to apostatize or to sacrifice to the pagan gods: each of them suffered the death penalty. Felicity, who had encouraged the others in turn, died last of all. Feast until 1969: 10 July.

AA.SS. Iul. III (1723), 5–28; *C.M.H.*, pp. 362–3; H. Delehaye, *Étude sur le légendier romain* (1936), pp. 116–23.

SEVEN SERVITE FOUNDERS (13th century). These devout Florentines, from some of the most famous families of the city, then prosperous but deeply affected both by the Cathar heresy and relaxed morality, joined a confraternity of the Blessed Virgin and later founded a new Order of Friars, called the Servites or Servants of Mary. Their names were Bonfilius Monaldi, John Bonaiuncta, Manettus dell' Antella, Amadeus degli Amidei, Hugh Uguccione, Sosthenes Sostegno, and Alexis Falconieri according to the received version, but there are some discrepancies with other accounts. They began by leading a life of prayer, austerity, and solitude on Monte Sennario, where they built a church and hermitage; for several years they refused to accept novices until an intervention by the bishop of Florence and Cardinal Castiglione. After this (1240) they adopted a stable way of life, based on the rule of St. Augustine and the Dominican Constitutions, becoming in fact friars instead of monks, wearing a black habit and living in towns. They made foundations early on at Siena, Pistoia and Arezzo, Carfaggio, and Lucca. Their most famous church is the Annunziata in Florence, still served by their order. The new order was recognized in 1259 and solemnly approved by Benedict XI in 1304; it has since spread into many parts of the world. There were no houses in England before the Reformation, but members of this Order came in the 19th century and there are several friaries today. A principal devotion fostered by the Servites is that of the Seven Sorrows of the Blessed Virgin, a development of the late medieval devotion to Our Lady of Pity, which offers a counterpart to the older one of the Seven Joys of Mary. Out of the Servite founders four became priors-general, two founded convents in France and Germany, while the last, Alexis, remained a lay brother all his life and outlived all the others. They were canonized in 1887. Feast: 17 February.

Propylaeum, pp. 59–60; F. A. dal Pino, *I prati servi di S. Maria dalle origini all'approvazione* (3 vols., 1972); B.T.A., i. 311–13.

SEVEN SLEEPERS OF EPHESUS were, according to 6th-century legend, early Christian Ephesians who were walled up in a cave near by, taking refuge from the persecution of Decius. God put them to sleep: 200 years later they awoke to find their city Christian. Soon after being discovered they died and were venerated as saints. The story was popularized by *Gregory of Tours and Jacob of Sarugh, but challenged by Baronius and many scholars since. It is sometimes called a Christianized pagan or Jewish legend akin to Rip Van Winkle. Feast: formerly 27 July.

B.T.A., iii. 193–6.

SEVERINUS, see BOETHIUS.

SEXBURGA (Sexburg), abbess of Ely 679–*c.*700. Daughter of King Anna of East Anglia, Sexburga married Erconbert, king of Kent, by whom she had two sons who succeeded their father as kings, and two daughters, *Erkengota and *Ermengild. While Sexburga was queen, she founded a nunnery at Minster-in-Sheppey, to which she retired as abbess after her husband's death in 664. In 679, on the death of her sister *Etheldreda, foundress of Ely, Sexburga became abbess there in her place. In

695 she translated Etheldreda's body, still incorrupt, into an old Roman sarcophagus from Grantchester, which was brought to the church at Ely. Sexburga died on 6 July. In 1106 the relics of saints Etheldreda, Sexburga, *Withburga, and Ermengild were again translated into new shrines at Ely, where they remained until the Reformation. Sexburga lay at the feet of Etheldreda, to her east. She is depicted with Etheldreda in a fine retable from Etheldreda's shrine, now at the Society of Antiquaries, London, and also figures in sculptured scenes of Etheldreda's life at Ely Cathedral. Feast: 6 July, translation, 17 October.

Bede, *H.E.*, iii. 8; iv. 19–21; *R.P.S.* E. O. Blake (ed.), *Liber Eliensis* (1962); J. Bentham, *The History and Antiquities of the Conventual and Cathedral Church of Ely* (1771), and W. Stevenson, *Supplement to Bentham's History* (1817).

SEZNI, see SITHNEY.

SHARBEL THE MARONITE (Sharbel Maklouf) (1828–98). Born in the village of Beqaa-Kafra (Lebanon), he was orphaned in early childhood and was brought up by an uncle. In 1851 he became a monk at the monastery of Our Lady of Mayfug, taking solemn vows in 1853. He was ordained priest in 1859. He lived in the monastery of St. Maro at Annaya (Gibail) for 15 years in all, delighting in singing the Office, working in the fields, and reading especially *The Imitation of Christ*. In 1866 he became a hermit in a purpose-built house owned by the monastery. The regime included fasting all the year round without meat, wine, or fruit: he slept on a mattress of leaves on the floor with a block of wood for a pillow. There, like *Antony and *Seraphim, he lived the regime of prayer and penance and experienced the temptations of the hermits of antiquity. This lasted for over thirty years.

In 1898, celebrating Mass in the Maronite rite, he suffered an attack of apoplexy just before the consecration. He was carried to his cell and died eight days later, on 24 December.

Some months after his burial, well-verified phenomena occurred. The body was fresh and incorrupt and was placed in a new coffin, where a reddish perspiration (sometimes called 'blood') flowed and caused the monks to change his clothes twice a week. In 1927 the Patriarch initiated an enquiry and the body was reburied. In 1950, after liquid was observed on the wall of the tomb, the body was found fresh and incorrupt again. Instantaneous cures and miraculous healings were claimed, some of the beneficiaries being non-Christian. The body was then reburied under concrete. This whole extraordinary story provides a modern, verifiable account of phenomena frequently claimed for medieval saints and frequently derided.

One of Sharbel's prayers may be quoted: 'Father of truth, behold your son who makes atoning sacrifice to you. Accept the offering: he died for me that I might have life.' Sharbel was beatified at the Second Vatican Council in 1965 and was canonized in 1977. Feast: 24 December.

P. Daher, *Vie, survie et prodiges de l'ermite Charbel Maklouf* (1953); other Lives by J. Eid (1955), M. Hayek (1962), and S. Garofalo (1965); see also D. Attwater, *Saints of the East* (1963), pp. 184–6; *Bibl. SS.*, viii. 568–9.

SHERWIN, Ralph (1550–81), seminary priest and martyr. Born at Roddesly (Derbyshire), he was educated at Exeter College, Oxford, where he obtained a Fellowship and, being considered 'an acute philosopher and an excellent Grecian and Hebrician', enjoyed the patronage of the Earl of Leicester. He was received into the R.C. Church in 1574 and joined the English College, Douai, where he was ordained priest in 1577. He next went to the English College, Rome, then deeply divided, and with a few others asked Pope Gregory XIII to place the College under Jesuit direction, which was eventually done.

In 1580 he gladly went to England with Edmund *Campion and Robert Persons. His apostolate lasted only a few months.

He was arrested at Nicholas Roscarrock's London house, imprisoned in chains at the Marshalsea, racked twice in the Tower and starved for several days to make him divulge the names of those he had reconciled to the Church. He is also said to have been offered a bishopric in the Church of England if he would conform. He was tried at Westminster Hall with Edmund Campion and suffered the same fate at Tyburn on 1 December. At his trial he had said: 'The plain reason for our standing here is religion, not treason.' A posthumous portrait survives at the English College, Rome, of which he was the protomartyr. He was canonized by Paul VI in 1970 as one of the *Forty Marytrs of England and Wales. Feast: 25 October.

B. Camm, *Lives of the English Martyrs* (1914), ii. 358–96; R. Challoner, *Memoirs of Missionary Priests* (ed. J. H. Pollen, 1928); M. Waugh, *Blessed Ralph Sherwin* (pamphlet, 1962).

SIDWELL (Sativola), virgin. This saint, possibly of British origin, has been culted at Exeter from early times; by 1000, pilgrims visited her shrine, which was also mentioned by William Worcestre and Leland. The late medieval catalogue of English saints (*C.S.P.*) describes her as follows: 'Born at Exeter, she was killed by her stepmother inciting the reapers to behead her. She was buried outside the city, where by her merits God heals the sick.' Sidwell's church just outside Exeter's east gate survives; formerly there was a well, where presumably the cures took place. There is a dedication at Laneast (Cornwall) with her sister Wulvella, where there was also a holy well. In art she is represented with a scythe and a well at her side, as in stained glass at Exeter Cathedral, All Souls College, Oxford, and Ashton, and on at least seven painted Devonshire rood-screens. It can scarcely be an accident that the legend of the jealous stepmother is also present in the Acts of *Juthwara, a supposed sister of Sidwell, nor that the emblems of Sidwell (scythe and well) correspond so closely to her name. Her historical existence must be considered doubtful. There is evidence for her feast being kept on 31 July (*C.S.P.* and Roscarrock), 1 August (Exeter calendar), and 2 August (a more substantial Exeter tradition, based on Grandisson's calendar and martyrology).

P. Grosjean, 'Legenda S. Sativolae Exoniensis', *Anal. Boll.*, liii (1935), 359–65; id., 'Codicis Gothani Appendix', *Anal. Boll.*, lviii (1940), 203–4; William Worcestre, p. 125 (an uncorrected copyist's blunder refers to the 'ecclesia sancti Volae'); J. Leland, *Itinerary*, 1. 228.

SIGEBERT (d. 635), king of East Anglia and martyr. Virtually all we know of him comes from *Bede. During the reign of his predecessor Redwald (who had attempted to combine the worship of Christ with that of the Germanic gods in the same church), Sigebert went into exile in Frankia and became a Christian. He returned as king in 630, a very learned man (*doctissimus*), and with the help of Honorius, archbishop of Canterbury, introduced *Felix as bishop of East Anglia, based at Dunwich (or possibly Felixstowe) and enabled with royal endowment *Fursey to establish his monastery at Burgh Castle. Felix under royal patronage also set up schools in East Anglia.

Sigebert did not reign for long: he resigned in favour of Ecgric and became a monk, possibly at Burgh Castle. Meanwhile Penda, king of Mercia, the scourge of other Anglo-Saxon kingdoms, made war on East Anglia. Sigebert's countrymen, fearful of the morale of the troops in battle, took him against his will out of his monastery and brought him to the army, hoping that the presence of one who had been a brave and famous general would allay their fears. He, however, refused to carry a weapon but only a staff. He was killed with Ecgric in the total defeat which followed. Sigebert, like some other Anglo-Saxon kings who died in battle, was venerated as a martyr. East Anglian liturgical books were destroyed in the Danish invasions and his feast has been variously assigned to 16 January and 27 September.

Bede, *H.E.*, ii. 15 and iii. 18; P. Hunter Blair, *The World of Bede* (1970), pp. 106–9; Stanton, pp. 35–6.

SIGFRID (1) (d. 688), abbot of Wearmouth. Nothing is known of his origins or early life, but in 686, while still a deacon, he was chosen to succeed *Eosterwine, the first abbot of Wearmouth appointed by the founder *Benedict Biscop to rule the community in his absence. Sigfrid was notable for his knowledge of Scripture, his temperance, and obedience. Unfortunately he also had a weak constitution and died of a lung disease after Benedict's return in 686, on 22 August, 688. *Bede is the authority for this date: a cult at Wearmouth and Jarrow is certain, following *Ceolfrith's translation of his relics.

Baedae Opera Historica (ed. C. Plummer, 1956), i. 364–404; ii. 355–77; J. F. Webb and D. H. Farmer, *The Age of Bede* (1983).

SIGFRID (2) (d. *c.*1045), bishop of Vaxjo, apostle of Sweden. Probably English and sent by King Ethelred to Olaf Tryggvason, king of Norway, Sigfrid, a monk of Glastonbury, took with him two fellow missionary bishops who planned to work in Sweden as well as Norway. Sigfrid baptized the king of Sweden, Olaf, built a church at Vaxjo, consecrated two bishops for East and West Gothland and left the district to evangelize the more remote areas. During his absence his principal helpers, his nephews, were murdered. On his return Sigfrid induced the king to spare the killers' lives: their punishment was commuted to that of a heavy fine. Sigfrid, however, refused to accept any of this money although, faced with the need to rebuild his cathedral, he was in considerable want. Later he worked also in Denmark. He died at Vaxjo. His cult is strongest in Sweden and Denmark, where metrical offices survive. He is represented in art as a bishop, carrying the heads of his dead nephews. These are sometimes misinterpreted as three loaves. Feast: 15 February.

The early Lives are in *Scriptores Rerum Suevicarum*, vol. ii, part i, 345–70; T. Schmid, 'Trois Légendes de S. Sigfrid', *Anal. Boll.*, lx (1942), 82–90; C. J. A. Oppermann, *English Missionaries in Sweden and Finland* (1937); M. Rydbeck, *Den helige Sigfrid* (1957).

SILAS (Silvanus) (1st century). He was the companion of *Paul chosen to take a letter from the council of Jerusalem to the Christians of Antioch (Acts 15). Afterwards he stayed with Paul at Antioch until Paul separated from *Barnabas; he then accompanied him to Syria, Cilicia, and eventually Macedonia. In his letters to the Thessalonians Paul associated Silas and Timothy with himself. Silas may also be identified with the scribe of 1 Peter (5: 12). Tradition relates that he died in Macedonia. Feast: 13 July, in the West; some Greek churches hold his feast on 26 November or 30 June and place him among the bishops of Corinth.

AA.SS. Iul. III (1723), 476–9 and *Propylaeum*, p. 285.

SILIN, see SULIAN.

SILVANUS, see SILAS.

SILVESTER, see SYLVESTER.

SIMEON STYLITES (390–459), hermit. He was the first and most famous of the pillar-hermits; even in his lifetime he was the object of pilgrimage and widespread veneration. He was the son of a shepherd on the Syrian border of Cilicia; following a vision in which he was exhorted to dig ever deeper in preparing the foundations of a house, he asked to be admitted to a neighbouring monastery as a servant. Here he remained for two years, after which he moved to the monastery ruled by Heliodorus at Eusebona (modern Tell'Ada, near Antioch). He increased his mortifications and feats of penance until he nearly died after wearing next to his skin a rope of twisted palm leaves which had eaten into his flesh. This was removed only by three days' treatment of being softened by liquids and then separated by incisions. On his recovery the abbot dismissed him.

He moved on again to Telanissos (Dair Sem'an), where he spent his first Lent without any food or drink. A priest, Bassus, who knew of his plans, left him ten loaves and some water in case of emergency. These were found untouched at Easter, but Simeon lay unconscious. He was revived by the Eucharist and by eating a few lettuce leaves. After three years in this hermitage he moved to the top of the mountain, where he made an enclosure and chained himself to the rock. The vicar of the patriarch of Antioch told him that a firm will, helped by divine grace, would enable him to remain in his chosen state without such artificial aids; so Simeon sent for a blacksmith to free him. But more and more visitors came, who interrupted his solitude and recollection.

This was the occasion of his adopting a new and singular way of life. He set himself up on a series of pillars where he spent the remainder of his life. The first one was about nine feet high, where he lived for four years; the second was eighteen feet high (for three years); the third, thirty-three feet high, was his home for ten years, while the fourth and last, built by the people, was sixty feet high. Here he lived for the last twenty years of his life. Lent was always a time of exceptional austerity: the first two weeks were spent praising God upright, the next two sitting, the last two in a horizontal position owing to increasing weakness from the total fast. Every day he repeatedly bowed his body in prayer: one visitor counted, it is said, 1,244 prostrations within the day. Twice daily he exhorted his numerous visitors, attracted by this unique prodigy. The solitude he had sought eluded him; it was replaced by throngs of sightseers, some Christian, some pagan, some converted by his example and miracles, some even were emperors, Theodosius, Leo, and Marcian. His preaching was practical, kindly, and free from fanaticism. He exhorted positively to sincerity, justice, and prayer and denounced swearing and usury with special energy. His fame spread far beyond the immediate neighbourhood: those from a distance who wished to consult him did so by letter. In an age of licentiousness and luxury he gave unique and abiding witness to the need for penance and prayer; his way of life provided a spectacle at once challenging, repulsive, and awesome.

Simon died on 1 September, bowing on his pillar which was only six feet wide, apparently in prayer. His body was buried at Antioch, accompanied by the bishops of the province and many of the faithful. There are ruins to this day of the church and monastery built near his pillar. The tradition of stylites was continued by *Daniel at Constantinople and later by another Simeon who lived to the west of Antioch in the 6th century. The stylites were in some respects the Christian equivalent of the Eastern fakirs, but their discourses revealed them as thoroughly Christian caring people of perfect orthodoxy and admirable charity. Simeon was a champion of the Doctrines of Chalcedon. Feast in the East: 1 September; in the West: 5 January.

AA.SS. Ian. I (1643), 261–86; Theodoret, *Historia Religiosa*, 26. There are also near-contemporary Greek and Syriac Lives in H. Lietzmann, *Das Leben des heiligen Simeon Stylites* (1908), for which see P. Peeters, 'S. Syméon Stylite et ses premiers biographes', *Anal. Boll.*, lxi (1943), 29–71 and A. Leroy-Molinghen, 'A propos de la Vie de Syméon Stylite', *Byzantion*, xxxiv (1964), 375–84; classic study of the whole movement in H. Delehaye, *Les Saints Stylites* (1923), resumed by H. Thurston in *Studies* (1923), 584–96; see also B.T.A., i. 34–7 and *Bibl. SS.*, xi. 1116–38.

SIMON (1st century), apostle. Called either the Canaanite or the Zealot by the Evangelists (the latter term may indicate former membership of a strict Jewish sect), Simon, like several other apostles, disappears from history after Pentecost, but there are various uncertain traditions about his subsequent preaching and martyrdom. One Eastern source gives Edessa as the place of his death, but Western tradition (as represented in the Roman Missal and Martyrology) says that he first preached in Egypt and then joined Jude (who had been in Mesopotamia); they went together to Persia, where they suffered martyrdom at Sufian (or at Siani). This tradition dates from the 6th century, but the cult goes back much further. In art Simon's usual attribute is a boat, as on East Anglian screens (with or without a book), or else a falchion, which according to the tradition reproduced by the *Golden Legend*, was the weapon with which the heathen priests hewed him to death. In the East the feast was kept on 1 July, the traditional date of their death, but in the West Simon and *Jude are culted together on 28 October, which possibly represents the day of their translation to St. Peter's, Rome.

AA.SS. Oct. XII (1867), 421–36 with *C.M.H.*, pp. 346, 575; G. McN. Rushforth, *Medieval Christian Imagery* (1936), pp. 101–2.

SIMON OF ATHERFIELD (Isle of Wight) is recorded as a martyr on 21 March 1211 in MS. Gonville and Caius, Cambridge, 111/205. This is confirmed by the Waverley Annals for the same year, which adds that miracles take place at his tomb very frequently. No other reference to him has yet been found; perhaps it is a case of a hermit or holy man undergoing a violent death at the hands of French invaders, as in the case of *Thomas of Hales.

H. R. Luard (ed.), *Annales Monastici* (*R.S.*, 1865), ii. 266.

SIMON STOCK (d. 1265), Carmelite friar. Little is known about his life before the year 1247, but it seems probable that Simon as a young man went on pilgrimage to the Holy Land, where he met some primitive Carmelites, then a hermit group, and joined them. When the Saracens made it impossible for them to remain there, they returned to Europe and Simon went to Aylesford (Kent); later (1254) he was elected superior-general of his Order at London. The years 1245–55 were crucial in the development of the Carmelites from a hermit order to one of mendicant friars, similar to the Franciscans and Dominicans. He founded houses in university towns, hoping to attract young graduates into the Order; he also founded other houses in various parts of England, Ireland, and Spain. A supposed vision of the Blessed Virgin to St. Simon, in which she is alleged to have promised that whoever died wearing the brown scapular of the Carmelites would be saved, has been the subject of much controversy. There is little or no contemporary or near-contemporary evidence for this story. It has, however, been extremely popular, as has the devotion of the brown scapular which came from it. It has been frequently propagated by Carmelite Friars. Although he was never formally canonized nor included in the Roman Martyrology, his feast was approved by the Holy See for the Carmelite Order in 1564 and some dioceses. Simon's relics were brought from Bordeaux, where he died, to Aylesford, his old home, in 1951. Feast: 16 May.

AA.SS. Maii III (1680), 650–1; A. Mombrun, *Vie de saint Simon de Stock* (1869); B. Zimmerman, *Monumenta Historica Carmelitana* (1907); F. M. Xiberta, *De Visione Sancti Simonis Stock* (1950).

SIMPLICIUS, FAUSTINUS, AND BEATRICE (Viatrix) (d. *c.*304), martyrs. The record of their martyrdoms at Rome on the road to Porto is known from the Martyrology of Jerome. In 1868 the cemetery of Generosa was discovered beside this road; it had a small church dating from the time of *Damasus, with contemporary frescoes and inscriptions. These list the martyrs as above and add Rufinianus, of whom nothing is known.

The unreliable Acts say that Simplicius and Faustinus were brothers, put to death for refusing to sacrifice to the pagan gods; Viatrix was their sister, who buried them, and who was later denounced by a neighbour who coveted her property. She was strangled in prison and buried with her brothers.

The relics of these martyrs were translated to the church of St. Bibiana and later to the basilica of St. Mary Major. Feast: formerly 29 July.

B.T.A., iii. 205.

SITHA, see ZITA.

SITHNEY (Sezni) is patron of Sithney, near Helston (Cornwall), where William Worcestre saw his tomb. There is still a cult of him at Guisséhy (formerly Ploesezny) in Britanny. The Life is an uninteresting plagiarism of that of *Ciaran of Saighir. According to a Breton folk legend, God one day revealed to him that he was to be the patron saint of girls. He was so alarmed that he asked to be excused the task because they would plague him for husbands and fine clothes and never leave him a moment's peace. He was then asked to look after mad dogs instead. He answered: 'I'd rather have mad dogs than women any day'; from that day onwards sick and mad dogs have been taken to drink the water of the well of St. Sezni. Feast: 4 August.

G. H. Doble, *The Saints of Cornwall*, ii (1962), 3–14; cf. *Anal. Boll.*, lix (1941), 220–1.

SIXTUS II (Xystus) (d. 258), pope and martyr. He became pope in 257 at a time when the controversy about the validity of baptism by heretics was acute. Like his predecessors and successors Sixtus upheld the Roman view that these baptisms were indeed valid; but unlike some of them he did so in such a way as to avoid giving offence. *Cyprian, who held the opposite view, told his fellow African bishops about the death of Sixtus: 'Valerian has sent an order to the senate to the effect that bishops, priests, and deacons should forthwith die. . . . Sixtus suffered in a cemetery on the sixth day of August, and with him four deacons. The Roman officers are very keen on this persecution: the people brought before them are certain to suffer and forfeit their estates. Please notify my colleagues of these details so that our brothers may be ready everywhere for their great conflict, that we all may think of immortality rather than death and derive joy rather than fear from this confession, in which the soldiers of Christ, as we know, are not so much killed as crowned.' The persecution was certainly severe: even if two deacons (instead of four) were actually taken with Sixtus, another one, *Laurence, followed them soon after. It seems that Sixtus was captured while addressing the Christian congregation and was killed by the sword. He was buried in the cemetery of Callistus on the Appian Way, very close to the cemetery of Praetextatus where he was captured. There is plenty of liturgical evidence for his early cult and he became one of the most popular of the Roman martyrs. The sayings of a pagan moralist, Sextus, were falsely ascribed to Sixtus in the Middle Ages. Feast: 6 August.

AA.SS. Aug. II (1735), 124–42 with *C.M.H.*, pp. 420–1; L. Duchesne, *Liber Pontificalis*, i (1886), 155–6.

SOCRATES AND STEPHEN, martyrs of unknown date, are placed by the Roman Martyrology on 17 September *in Britannia*. No martyrs of this name are known in England: the original entry most probably read *in Bithynia*.

Propylaeum, p. 402; H. Delehaye in *Proceedings of the British Academy*, xvii (1932), 3–21.

SOUTHWELL, Robert (1561–95), Jesuit, priest and martyr. Born at Horsham St. Faith (Norfolk), the son of Sir Robert Southwell, a recusant who later conformed, Robert was educated by the Jesuits, first at Douai, then at Paris. He wished to join the Society of Jesus at the age of seventeen. Refused because he was too young, he walked to Rome and was admitted there in 1578. He became prefect of Studies at the English College, Rome, was ordained priest in 1584, and left for England in 1586. He arrived in London at the time of the Babington Plot and narrowly escaped arrest; for most of his seven years apostolate he lived at Arundel House in the Strand, the home of Anne Dacres, whose husband Philip *Howard was imprisoned in the Tower. In 1592 Southwell was arrested by Topcliffe at Uxenden (Middx.), imprisoned in the Tower and at Newgate and was tortured at least nine times. After three years of this treatment he appealed to be either tried or set at liberty. He was then brought to trial at Westminster Hall, condemned for being a priest and was executed at Tyburn, aged thirty-three, on 21 February.

This event greatly shocked both the

court and the country: like *Campion, Southwell had a particularly acute mind and sensitive personality. He was, for example, a notable writer both of prose and of lyric poetry. His most famous works include: *An Epistle of Comfort* (letters addressed to Philip Howard), *An Humble Supplication to Her Majestie* (an exposure of the Babington Plot), *Mary Magdalen's Funeral Tears* (1594), *A short Rule of Good Life* (published posthumously in 1598) and *A Fourefold Meditation* (1606). His best-known poems are *The Burning Babe* and *St. Peter's Complaint* (a long narrative of the Life of Christ). A portrait in crayon, based on a lost oil painting, survives at Stonyhurst College (Lancs.). He was canonized by Paul VI in 1970 as one of the *Forty Martyrs of England and Wales. Feast: 25 October.

C. Devlin, *The Life of Robert Southwell, Poet and Martyr* (1956); P. Janelle, *Robert Southwell the Writer* (1935); R. Challoner, *Memoirs of Missionary Priests* (ed. J. H. Pollen, 1928); J. H. McDonald, *The Poems and Prose Writings of Robert Southwell* (Roxburghe Club, 1937); standard edition of his Prose Works by W. J. Walter (1827) and of his poems by J. H. McDonald and N. P. Brown (1967); modern editions of *Spiritual Exercises and Devotions* (ed. P. E. Hallett, 1931), of *An Humble Supplication to her Majestie* (ed. R. C. Bald, 1953), of *An Epistle of Comfort* (ed. M. Waugh, 1966), of *A short Rule of Good Life* (*E.R.L.*, lxxviii, 1971).

SOUTHWORTH, John (1592–1654), seminary priest and martyr. Born of the recusant family of Southworth of Samlesbury Hall (Lancs.), he entered the English College, Douai, in 1613 and was ordained priest in 1618. He returned to England the next year and worked mainly in London until 1623 and in Lancashire 1625–7. He was then imprisoned at Lancaster and condemned to death for his priesthood, but was released with fifteen other priests through the intervention of Queen Henrietta Maria. They were banished instead of being executed, but, in spite of the danger, Southworth returned to London a few years later and was very active with Henry *Morse in 1636–7 during the plague, when he ministered to its victims and organized relief for the recusant poor, especially in the Westminster area. Much of this work was accomplished while he was on daily parole as a prisoner in the Clink.

Little is known of his life in the subsequent years except for his name's occasional appearance on prison lists. In 1654 he was arrested once again, and after his own admission at his trial that he had exercised his priestly functions since his reprieve, he was condemned to death. The intervention of foreign ambassadors did not prevent him from being executed at Tyburn on 28 June, aged sixty-two. The Spanish ambassador bought his body from the hangman, had it stitched together, embalmed and sent to the English College, Douai. It is now in Westminster Cathedral. Southworth was canonized by Paul VI in 1970 as one of the *Forty Martyrs of England and Wales. Feast: 25 October.

R. Challoner, *Memoirs of Missionary Priests* (ed. J. H. Pollen, 1928), pp. 504–10; A. B. Purdie, *The Life of Blessed John Southworth* (1930); E. E. Reynolds, *John Southworth* (pamphlet, 1962).

STANISLAUS OF CRACOW (1010–79), bishop and martyr. Born of a noble family at Szczepanow, he was educated at Gnesen and perhaps at Paris, was ordained priest, and given a canonry at Cracow. He was consecrated bishop in 1072, became a zealous reformer, a tireless preacher, and a generous benefactor to the poor. A bitter quarrel with King Boleslaus II led eventually to the death of Stanislaus. The traditional account of the hagiographers is that Boleslaus perpetrated many acts of injustice and violence, in particular the abduction to the palace of a nobleman's wife, for which the bishop reproved him and threatened excommunication, which was pronounced when the king refused to repent. On his entry into the cathedral, the services were suspended, the king pursued the bishop to a chapel of St. Michael outside the town and told his guards to enter and kill him. This they were unwilling or unable to do, so the king killed the bishop with his own sword. Gregory VII placed an interdict on Poland; eventually Boleslaus fell from power. Some historians, however, maintain that Stanislaus was guilty of treason for plotting to dethrone the king, but this charge has been vigorously denied by others. Stanislaus was canonized in 1253. Feast: formerly 7 May, now 11 April in the latest Roman calendar. Stanislaus is patron of Poland; his cult is also in Lithuania, Byelorussia, and the Ukraine.

AA.SS. Maii II (1680), 200–80; early Lives also in W. Ketrzynski, *Monumenta Poloniae Historica*, iv (1884), 238–438; B.T.A., ii 244–6; *H.S.S.C.*, vi. 235–40.

STANISLAUS KOSTKA, see Kostka.

STEDIANA, see Stithian.

STEPHEN (1) (d. *c.*35), deacon and protomartyr of the Christian Church. All that we know of his life is in the Acts of the Apostles (6–7). He was one of the seven deacons, probably a Hellenistic Jew, appointed by the apostles to look after the distribution of alms to the faithful (especially the widows) and to help in the ministry of preaching. To judge by his famous discourse, even if it is somewhat 'retouched', Stephen was learned in the Scriptures and the history of Judaism, besides being eloquent and forceful. The gist of his defence of Christianity was that God does not depend on the Temple, in so far as, like the Mosaic Law, it was a temporary institution and destined to be fulfilled and superseded by Christ, who was the prophet designated by Moses and the Messiah whom the Jewish race had so long awaited. He finally attacked his hearers for resisting the Spirit and for killing the Christ as their fathers had killed the prophets. They then stoned him for blasphemy apparently without a formal trial, while he saw a vision of Christ on God's right hand. The witnesses placed their clothes at the feet of Saul (afterwards *Paul), who consented to his death.

At least from the 4th century (or earlier) his feast has been kept in both East and West. But the cult was given further popularity by the discovery of his supposed tomb by the priest Lucian at Kafr Gamala in 415. The translation of the relics, first to Constantinople and then to Rome, with some dismemberment and with the addition of the stones alleged to have been used at his martyrdom, contributed to the diffusion of his cult. From early times he was the patron of deacons, in the later Middle Ages he was invoked against headaches. By this time he was patron of innumerable churches, including several French cathedrals such as Bourges, Sens, and Toulouse. In England forty-six ancient churches are dedicated to him, most of them being built after the Norman Conquest. In art his usual attributes are a book of the Gospels with a stone and sometimes a palm of martyrdom. There are several splendid ancient examples of his representation; perhaps the most attractive one of the early Renaissance is that by Jean Fouquet at Berlin from a dipytch at Melun. There is a fine cycle by Fra Angelico at the Vatican. Feast: in the West, 26 December: in the East, 27 December; feast of the finding of his relics, formerly on 3 August, was widely celebrated in England and elsewhere. The event was described in the Golden Legend.

C.M.H., pp. 10–11; M. Simon, *St. Stephen and the Hellenists in the Primitive Church* (1958); M. H. Scharleman, *Stephen: a singular saint* (1968); F. M. Abel, 'Étienne (saint)', *Dict. Bibl.*, suppl. ii (1934), 1132–46; *Bibl. SS.*, xi 1376–92.

STEPHEN (2), see Socrates and Stephen.

STEPHEN I (d. 257), pope. Roman by birth and a priest when he succeeded Lucius I as bishop of Rome in 254, Stephen was invited to intervene in Gaul, where the bishop of Arles had become a Novatianist, by Faustinus, bishop of Lyons. Soon after this he became involved in a dispute in Spain. But the most important controversy of his short reign was that concerned with baptism administered by heretics, whose validity he defended with all his authority against *Cyprian and some African councils who had declared them null and void. His most famous sentence was 'No innovation must be introduced, but let that be observed which tradition has handed down.' He would not even meet a Carthaginian delegation in 256. Although traditionally venerated as a martyr, the early sources say nothing about this and the earliest Roman tradition seems to be that he died from natural causes. His later Acts, however, followed by the Roman Martyrology, say that he was captured while saying Mass in the persecution of Valerian. This and other details are borrowed from the Acts of *Sixtus II. Stephen's feast in the West is 2 August, but in the East 2 August or 7 September.

Letters of Stephen in *P.L.*, iii. 1033–44; Cyprian, *Epistolae*, lxvii–lxxv; Eusebius, *H.E.*, vii. 2–5; *AA.SS.* Aug. I (1733), 112–46 with *C.M.H.*, pp. 412–13; see also *O.D.P.*, pp. 20–1.

STEPHEN HARDING (d. 28 March 1134), third abbot of Cîteaux. He is generally believed to have been largely responsible for the *Carta Caritatis*, which established the influential Cistercian constitution, and for the introduction of lay brothers into the Cistercian regime. Modern research has emphasized that the development of the supposedly primitive Cistercian documents belongs to a date after Stephen's death, so his full importance in the history of early Cîteaux has yet to be evaluated. It is certain that he was abbot of the languishing Cîteaux when *Bernard arrived there with thirty other postulants, and it was he who appointed Bernard first abbot of Clairvaux.

Stephen was born in the south-west of England (his name possibly indicates an origin in a village near Porlock), and became a monk, or at least a student in the Benedictine monastery of Sherborne (Dorset). William of Malmesbury implied that he left the monastery to return to lay life, first in Scotland and then in France. After studying the liberal arts there for some years, he was converted and went to Rome, visiting various monasteries on the way and reciting daily the whole psalter. On his return to Burgundy he found Molesme and became a monk. But he became dissatisfied with observances which seemed to be based on neither reason nor authority and was one of a group of seven monks, including the abbot, *Robert of Molesme, who founded the new and austere monastery of Cîteaux. This was in 1098. Robert returned to Molesme, *Alberic was elected abbot and Stephen Harding prior. In 1109 Stephen was elected abbot. The final form of the Cistercian monastic family owes much to his influence, more than to Robert or Alberic. Stephen was probably the author of the original draft of the *Exordium Cisterciensis Cenobii* and the *Carta Caritatis*. The latter document, extremely influential in the constitutions of other monastic congregations as well as the Cistercian, provided a juridical framework which enabled Cîteaux, unlike many similar monastic endeavours of the same time, to achieve a permanent place in the life of the Church. Its two most important provisions were a yearly visitation of each abbey by the abbot of the founding house and the yearly assembly of all heads of houses for general chapter at Cîteaux. Its purpose was to safeguard permanently the original spirit and observance of Cîteaux. This also had been fostered by the rejection of all sources of luxury for personal and liturgical use and of feudal sources of income such as mills, fairs and serfs, and proprietary churches, tithes, and rights to customary church offerings for the community. Lay brothers, who came to live largely in the granges, exploited the lands of the monasteries, which were grouped together, as far as possible, near the monastery in large, contiguous areas. The choir monks devoted themselves to public and private prayer, *lectio divina*, and manual work (according to the letter of the Rule of St. Benedict), but not to systematic study at the beginning. Artistic work seems to have been discouraged later, but the Cîteaux Bible, regarded as the work of Stephen himself, shows marked affinities with contemporary English work.

The first Cistercian foundations, La Ferté, Pontigny, Clairvaux, and Morimond were made under Stephen's abbacy before he resigned in 1133, old and blind; these in their turn had made many foundations, including Waverley, Tintern, Rievaulx, and Fountains in England. He thus lived to see the future of the Cistercian Order assured. It is strange that he had to wait so long for equipollent canonization. He was mentioned in the *Compendium sanctorum Ordinis Cisterciensis* of John de Cireyo in 1491, but the Cistercian General Chapter prescribed his feast only in 1623 without recalling any evidence of public cult, miracles, or canonization. Their breviary of 1627 assigns the Office of the Common to him; the General Chapter of 1683 transferred his feast to 16 July from 17 April. The latter is his date in the Roman Martyrology, but it is uncertain how his name reached it.

AA.SS. Apr. II (1675), 496–501; *G.R.*, ii. 380–4; *P.L.*, clxvi. 1361–1510; J. B. Dalgairns, *Life of St. Stephen Harding* (revised by H. Thurston, 1898 and 1946); *M.O.*, pp. 197–200, 209–12, 752–3; D. Knowles, 'The Primitive Cistercian Documents' in *Great Historical Enterprises* (1963); C. Oursel, 'La Bible de Saint Étienne Harding et le Scriptorium de Cîteaux', *Cîteaux in de Nederlanden*, x (1959), pp. 34–43.

STEPHEN OF HUNGARY (Istvan) (*c*.975–1038), king. The son of Geza, duke of the Magyars who had settled in Hungary at the end of the 9th century and had become nominal Christians (at least in the upper ranks of society), Stephen married the sister of *Henry II in 995 and succeeded his father in 997. After successfully quelling insurrections of rival leaders, Stephen decided on a policy of both strengthening his own authority and establishing Christianity as the religion of his country. He obtained that Pope Silvester II gave him the title of king and also a crown, part of which is claimed to survive in the crown kept in Budapest. His coronation took place in 1001. By then Stephen had established various sees and monasteries, the most famous of which, Esztergom (the primatial see) and Pannonhalma (the principal monastery), both claim (with some others) to be founded by him. By introducing limited feudalism, by retaining control over the people as a whole through reducing the powers of nobles, by abolishing tribal divisions and setting up counties with governors appointed by him, he formed the Hungarians into a single kingdom. Much of his organization has lasted until recent times. In establishing Christianity as the religion of the nation he used the resources of the State by severely punishing superstitious customs derived from paganism; blasphemy and adultery were crimes like theft and murder; he both commanded all to marry (except churchmen), and forbade marriages between Christians and pagans. More pleasing elements in his character were his accessibility and just treatment for the poor and the oppressed. He also used to distribute alms, sometimes in disguise, which constituted a serious security risk, which once had almost fatal consequences. His son Emeric was prepared as his successor, but died before his father, in 1031. Part of Stephen's work was undone by his successors, but after his death at Buda miracles were claimed at his tomb and his relics were enshrined there in 1083. He has always been considered both a national hero and the most important of Hungary's many Christian kings. Feast: 16 August, formerly 2 September; translation on 20 August.

B. Homan, *Szent Istvan* (1938); G. Bonis, *Istvan kiraly* (1956); D. Sinor, *History of Hungary* (1959); B.T.A., iii. 466–9.

STEPHEN OF MURET (*c*.1047–1124), hermit and founder of the Order of Grandmont. Born at Thiers (Auvergne) of noble parents, he studied in the household of Milo, archbishop of Benevento. In 1076 he renounced his inheritance to become a hermit in the mountains of Ambazac at Muret (NE. of Limoges). There he led an austere life, with little food or sleep, for 46 years, remaining a deacon all his life. He also wore a metal breastplate instead of a hair-shirt, as is depicted by artists.

Towards the end of his life, disciples who had joined him in solitude established the Order of Grandmont and drew up a Rule based on his sayings. These are conspicuous for their intransigent insistence on total renunciation. He compared monastic life, as he understood it, to life in a prison. 'If you come here', he said, 'you will be fixed to the cross and you will lose your own power over your eyes, your mouth, and your other members' . . . 'if you go to a large monastery with fine buildings, you will find animals and vast estates; here, only poverty and the cross.'

Stephen died at Muret. The Rule of Grandmont was never widespread, but Henry II made several foundations, both in France and England, and petitioned the Holy See for Stephen's canonization. This was granted by Clement III in 1189. The austerity of Stephen inspired both Armand de Rancé and Charles de Foucauld. Feast: 8 February.

Life by the seventh prior of Grandmont in *P.L.*, cciv. 1065–72; J. Becquet in *Dict. de Spiritualité*, iv. 1504–14; J. Webster in *N.C.E.*, s.v.; *H.S.S.C.*, vi. 139–42.

STITHIAN (Stediana), Cornish saint, patron of Stithians. In medieval episcopal registers and taxation returns this is a woman saint; but nothing seems to be known of her.

STONE, John (d. 1539), Austin friar and martyr. Little is known of his early life, but in 1538 he was a priest and a doctor of theology at Canterbury when Richard Ingworth, Cromwell's Visitor, arrived to suppress the friary. All his community with the other secular and regular clergy of Canterbury, agreed to take the Oath of Supremacy, but Stone, alone of his Order, refused to do so, declaring forthrightly that 'the Kynge may not be hede of the Chyrche of Ynglonde, but yt must be a spyrytuall father adpoynted by God'. He was sent forthwith by Ingworth to Cromwell at London: Cromwell sent him down again for execution at Canterbury. It is not known how he had previously avoided taking the various oaths, nor how he had come to make his witness at the last hour to the faith in which he was brought up. His resistance seems to have been a surprise to all. He was hanged, drawn, and quartered at Canterbury on 27 December 1539 at the mound called the Dane John. The entry in the City Chamberlain's account book detailing the charge for the gallows, halter, and cauldron survives. He was one of the English martyrs depicted in Circiniani's murals at the English College, Rome, and was canonized as one of the *Forty Martyrs of England and Wales by Paul VI in 1970. Feast 25 October.

L. E. Whatmore, *Catholic Record Society Publications*, vol. 45 (1950).

STRAMBI, Vincent (1745–1824), bishop of Macerata and Tolentino. Born at Civitavecchia, the son of a pharmacist, he was educated for the local diocese and was ordained priest in 1767. On the advice of *Paul of the Cross, he joined the Passionist congregation in 1768. Once professed, he studied Scripture and the Fathers and lectured in theology and sacred eloquence. Later he was chosen for important offices, such as Provincial (1781) and Consultor (1784–96): he was also a renowned spiritual director.

In 1801 he was appointed bishop of Macerata and Tolentino in the Marches of Ancona. He improved standards in his diocese especially through the higher quality of its priests. He sold the old seminary and built a new one: he himself gave the students one conference each week, and insisted on their receiving two each week in Gregorian Chant. He also encouraged catechetics and founded a popular library. He generously helped both the school at Tolentino and the Somaschi orphanage.

In 1808, like many others, he refused to take the oath of allegiance to Napoleon and was expelled from his diocese, first to Novara, then to Milan. After Napoleon's defeat and subsequent escape from Elba, General Murat made Macerata his headquarters. Murat was defeated by the Austrians, to whom Vincent's personal appeal saved Macerata from being sacked. Other calamities however soon followed, such as an epidemic of typhoid and conditions of near-famine.

On the death of Pius VII Strambi resigned his see. He ended his days in Rome at the Quirinal, where he was the valued adviser of the conservative Pope Leo XII. He died on 1 January and his body was buried at Macerata. At various times in his life he wrote several books, especially on the priesthood. He was canonized in 1950. Feast: 25 September.

Lives by F. Cento (1951), Fr. Stanislaus (1925); see also B.T.A., iii. 664–5; *Bibl. SS.*, xii. 1178–80.

SUIDBERT, see SWITHBERT.

SULIAN (Silin) (6th century), founder but not patron of Luxulyan (Cornwall), abbot. Probably identical with Sulien, a Breton saint of Cornouaille and Domonée. Feast: 29 July.

Much confusion has arisen with another Breton saint Sulinus of East Brittany (feast: 1 October) and with a Welsh saint *Tysilio (or Suliau), whose feast is on 8 November, and whose Legend was pirated for a Breton saint. It is likely that the three feasts represent three different persons.

G. H. Doble, *The Saints of Cornwall*, v (1970), 104–26.

SULPICIUS (d. 647), bishop of Bourges. Sulpicius, later called Pius, came from a wealthy family, renounced marriage, and devoted himself from youth to good works. As bishop, he won great popular support for defending his people against tyranny as well as for his care of the poor and afflicted. He attended the council of Clichy in 627; towards the end of his life he obtained the appointment of another bishop to take his place. His death and funeral were remarkable for extraordinary manifestation of popular distress and sympathy. This is the saint who was the patron of the Paris seminary of that name which was famous for the piety and learning of many of its priests. Sulpicius has sometimes been confused with Sulpicius Severus, biographer of *Martin, who had died long before Sulpicius of Bourges was born. Feast: 17 January.

AA.SS. Ian. II (1643), 165–76, 967–9; critical edn. of the near-contemporary Life by B. Krusch in *M.G.H.*, *Scriptores rerum merov.*, iv. 364–80; L. Duchesne, *Fastes episcopaux de l'ancienne Gaule*, II, 28–9.

SUNNIVA (Synnöve), Irish princess and nun. Her story is legendary, like that of *Ursula. She is said to have embarked from Ireland with several companions in search of a haven to live consecrated lives in exile for Christ. They reached an uninhabited island called Selje (off the west coast of Norway, having travelled via Scotland). They settled into living the devout life, dwelling in caves and subsisting on fish. The neighbouring Jarl Haakon heard of their arrival and came to investigate: they fled to the caves and prayed to rest in God whenever and wherever they should die. Masses of rock crashed down and blocked all entrances to the caves. Much later the caves were explored and Sunniva's incorrupt body was discovered.

In 995 Olaf Tryggvason is said to have built a chapel in her honour. In 1170 her relics were moved to Bergen; Selje's church was given to Benedictine monks who dedicated it to St. *Alban. Five churches (some ruinous) still survive on this island. Feast: 7 July.

Latin Legend (11th century) in G. Storm, *Monumenta Historiae Norvegiae*, pp. 147–52; S. Undset, *Saga of Saints* (1934), pp. 68–86; B.T.A., iii. 42.

SUSANNA, see TIBURTIUS AND SUSANNA.

SWITHBERT (Suidbert) (d. 713), a Northumbrian monk and companion of *Willibrord in his apostolate in Frisia. Following the inspiration of *Wilfrid and *Egbert, Willibrord and his twelve companions set off in 690. Swithbert preached successfully in Brabant, Guelderland, and Cleves. In 693 he was sent back to England to be consecrated bishop by Wilfrid, then in Mercia. Swithbert left Friesland to become the apostle of the Boructuari in southern Westphalia. Heathen Saxons soon conquered this country: Swithbert withdrew to Frankish territory. Pepin and his wife Plectrudis gave him the island of Kaiserswerth, near Düsseldorf, where he founded a monastery and died soon afterwards. His name is recorded in the Calendar of St. Willibrord. His relics were found in a silver shrine at Kaiserswerth in 1626 and are still honoured there. A 5th-century manuscript of Livy at Vienna is sometimes said to have belonged to him because of an inscription in it 'Sutbertus episcopus de Dorostat', but it seems that this is just an attractive conjecture. Feast: 1 March.

Bede, *H.E.*, v. 9–11; Alcuin, *Carmen*, v. 1073; panegyric and hymn by Radbod of Utrecht in *P.L.*, cxxxii. 547–59; W. Levison, *England and the Continent in the Eighth Century* (1946), pp. 57–8, 62; F. Flaskamp, *Suidbercht* (1930).

SWITHUN (Swithin) (d. 862), bishop of Winchester. His cult was popular, but little is known of his life. Born in Wessex and educated at the Old Minster, Winchester, he was chosen by Egbert, king of Wessex 802–39, as his chaplain. He was also entrusted with the education of Ethelwulf, who succeeded to the throne in 839. Ethelwulf chose him in 852 as bishop of Winchester, the Wessex capital; during his ten years' episcopate Wessex consolidated its position as the most important kingdom of England and faced the first sporadic, but ominous, attacks by Vikings in the south of England. Swithun was famous for his charitable gifts and for his activity in building churches. He died on 2 July and asked to be buried in the cemetery; his grave, covered with a tomb-structure, was just outside the west door of the Old Minster.

After *Ethelwold became bishop of Winchester (964) and introduced monks to form the first monastic cathedral chapter in England, plans were made to translate Swithun's relics into the cathedral. This was accomplished on 15 July 971. The occasion was marked by many cures claimed as miraculous, which accounted for Swithun's high reputation as a healer, and also by very heavy rainfall, believed to be another manifestation of his power. Even today it is often said that if it rains on St. Swithun's Day, it will rain also for the following forty days. The translation was carried out as part of extensive building operations which included enlarging the Old Minster westwards, making Swithun's original tomb the centre of a 'shrine-church' with transepts on either side. Another translation in 974 involved some dismemberment, as there were now two shrines, one by the high altar and the other in the sacristy. Possibly the latter was the head-shrine taken by *Alphege, archbishop of Canterbury, when he was promoted from Winchester in 1005. After the Normans built a new cathedral at Winchester, Swithun's body was translated into it in 1093; this shrine remained a popular goal of pilgrims throughout the Middle Ages.

At the Reformation the shrine was demolished and Swithun probably buried under it, but the shrine was restored by the cathedral authorities in 1962. There are fifty-eight ancient dedications to Swithun in England and a few in Scandinavia. Feast: 2 July; translation, 15 July; ordination (at Winchester) 29 October.

AA.SS. Iul. I (1719), 321–37, completed by E. P. Sauvage, 'S. Swithuni translatio et miracula', *Anal. Boll.*, iv (1885), 367–410; Verse Life by Wulfstan in A. Campbell, *Frithegodi monachi breviloquium vitae B. Wilfredi et Wulstani cantoris narratio metrica de S. Swithuno* (1950); Life by Goscelin ed. E. P. Sauvage, *Anal. Boll.*, vii (1888), 373–80; Old English Life by Ælfric in W. W. Skeat, *Aelfric's Lives of Saints* (E.E.T.S.) i (1881), 440–71; G. H. Gerould, 'Aelfric's Legend of St. Swithun', *Anglia*, xxxii (1909), 347–57; see also M. Biddle, 'Felix Urbs Winthonia' in D. Parsons (ed.), *Tenth Century Studies* (1975), 123–40; M. Lapidge and M. Winterbottom, *Wolfstan of Winchester; Life of St Ethelwold* (1991); M. Lapide, *The Cult of St Swithun* (forthcoming).

SYLVESTER (Silvester) (d. 335), pope. The son of a Roman called Rufinus, Sylvester became bishop of Rome in 314, soon after the Edict of Milan recognized Christianity, ended persecution against it and tolerated all religions. Surprisingly little is known of him, but legends abound and were very influential in the Middle Ages. Sylvester was represented by legates at a synod of Arles against the Donatists and in 325 at the Council of Nicea. The Lateran palace was given to him by Constantine and this became the cathedral church of Rome; he also built other churches in Rome, probably the first churches at St. Peter's, Holy Cross, and St. Laurence-outside-the-walls. He was buried in a church which he built at the cemetery of Priscilla; but in 761 his relics were translated to the church of 'St. Silvester in capite' which is the church assigned to the English.

Some of the principal but unhistorical legends about Sylvester include his supposed baptism of Constantine (in reality Constantine was baptized only on his death-bed after the death of Sylvester), his curing him of leprosy at the Lateran Baptistery, and his receiving the forgery called the 'Donation of Constantine' which gave considerable temporal power to the papacy, especially in Italy, and purported to confer on him the primacy over other patriarchs. In the development of these legends the character of Constantine was also transformed into that of an ideal, but quite unhistorical, Christian emperor. These legends have considerably influenced the portrayal of Sylvester in art; his principal emblems are a chained dragon (or bull) and a tiara; the principal scene represented is that of the baptism of Constantine. Feast: in the West, 31 December; in the East, 2 January.

L. Duchesne, *Liber Pontificalis*, i. 170–201; W. Levison, 'Konstantinische Schenkung und Silvester-Legende' in *Miscellanea Francesca Ehrle*, ii (1924), 159–247; N. H. Baynes, *Constantine the Great and the Christian Church* (1929).

SYMPHORIAN, see TIMOTHY, HIPPOLYTUS, AND SYMPHORIAN.

T

TADWINUS, see TATWIN.

TANCRED, TORTHRED, AND TOVA, hermits of Thorney (Cambs.), killed by the Danes in 870. The first two were men, the third a woman, but nothing is known of them. The story of their martyrdom rests on the chronicle of Pseudo-Ingulph, which may include sources older than the 12th century. They were, however, venerated in their Thorney shrine by the year 1000, witnessed by *R.P.S.* and were among the many saints whose bodies were translated by *Ethelwold, but whose names William of Malmesbury was unwilling to write because they sounded so barbarous. Their feast was on 30 September at Thorney and Deeping.

R.P.S. and *C.S.P.*: William of Malmesbury, *G.P.*, pp. 327–9; *E.B.K. after 1100*, i. 129–44.

TARSICIUS, Roman martyr of 3rd–4th century. Although he is not in the Martyrology of Jerome, there was an early cult of this martyr, testified by the 4th-century verses of *Damasus. He was buried in the cemetery of Callistus; relics are claimed by the church of San Silvestro. According to Damasus, Tarsicius was carrying the sacrament of the Body of Christ when he was waylaid by a pagan mob who asked him what he was carrying. Rather than surrender his precious burden, he suffered death by stones and clubs. Later tradition locates the episode in the Appian Way and made Tarsicius an acolyte, although some scholars, impressed by a reference to Stephen in Damasus' verses, think he was a deacon. It is not certain whether he was carrying the sacrament to confessors in prison or from the papal Mass to the presbyters of other Roman churches. In more recent times his cult has been popularized by Nicholas Wiseman's novel *Fabiola* (1854) and by the presentation of him as a very young boy (not historically certain). This has led to his cult as patron of altar-boys and to the dedication of a few churches to his name. He is also patron of a confraternity of the Blessed Sacrament. Feast: 15 August.

AA.SS. Aug. III (1737), 201; A. Ferrua, *Epigrammata Damasiana* (1942), pp. 117–19; O. Marucchi, 'La questione del sepolcro del papa Zeffirino e del martire Tarsicio', *Nuovo Bulletino di Archaeologia cristiana*, xvi (1910), 205–25; B.T.A., iii. 335.

TATA, see ETHELBURGA (3).

TATHAI (Tathan, Tathar, Atheus) (5th–6th century). Of Irish origin, Tathai became a hermit in Wales and later founded the monastery of Llantathan (St. Athan). From here he came to Caerwent (Gwent), where he founded a monastic school. If we are to believe the Life, he was famous in the neighbourhood as a miracle-worker and as the 'Father of all Gwent, he was the defender of the woodland country . . . he was never angry . . . whatever was given to him, he gave to others . . . no-one was more generous in the West for receiving guests and giving them hospitality.' He probably died at Cearwent, but Llantathan also claimed to be his death-place. Feast: 26 December.

N.L.A., ii. 361–3; A. W. Wade-Evans, *Vitae Sanctorum Britanniae* (1944), 270–87; Baring-Gould and Fisher, iv. 211–14.

TATWIN (Tatuini, Tadwinus), archbishop of Canterbury 731–41. He was described by Bede as a man notable for his prudence, devotion, and learning. He was a priest of the monastery of Bredon in Mercia, to whose king, the powerful Ethelbald, he probably owed his promotion.

After receiving the pallium, he consecrated bishops for Lindsey (Lincs.) and

Selsey (West Sussex) in 733, the only recorded act of his short episcopate. His learning, however, is shown by two surviving manuscripts of his *Riddles* (*enigmata*) and four of his *Grammar*. The forty riddles, written with acrostic technique and influenced by *Aldhelm's works, treat of such diverse topics as philosophy, charity, the five senses, the alphabet, the book, the pen, scissors, anvils, and swords. The *Grammar*, called *Ars Tatwini*, is an expansion of Consentius', and owes something to Donatus, Priscian, and other sources.

Symeon of Durham records his death on 30 July 734. Like his predecessors he was buried in the abbey church of St. Augustine, Canterbury, and received an unofficial cult. His relics were translated with those of other Canterbury saints in 1091 when the church was enlarged. The epitaph on his tomb praised him for the same qualities described by Bede.

Bede, *H.E.*, v. 23; Symeon of Durham II, 31; Goscelin, *Historia Translationis S. Augustini*, *P.L.* 155, 15 *et seq.*; W. F. Bolton, *A History of Anglo-Latin Literature* (1967), i. 215–38; id., 'Tatwine's *De cruce Christi* and *The Dream of the Rood*' in *Archiv*, 200 (1963), 344–6.

TEATH, patron of St. Teath, Cornwall. Thirteenth-century documents refer to this saint as a woman, but nothing seems to be known of her.

E. Ekwall, *The Concise Oxford Dictionary of English Place-Names* (1960), p. 401.

TECLA (Thecla) **OF ENGLAND** (Thecla of Kitzingen) (d. *c.*790), Benedictine nun and abbess. English by birth and a relative of *Lioba, Tecla was a nun of Wimborne (Dorset) who was sent by the abbess Tetta to help *Boniface in his missionary work in Germany. For a time she was a nun under Lioba at Tauberbischofsheim until becoming abbess of Ochsenfurt and later Kitzingen. The year of her death is unknown, but her cult is testified by liturgical books which assign her feast, with the Roman Martyrology, to 15 October. Dates of 27 or 28 September are also found. Her shrine remained at Kitzingen until her relics and others' were scattered during the Peasants' War of the 16th century.

AA.SS., Oct. VII (1845), 59–64 with *Propylaeum*, p. 456; W. Levison, *England and the Continent in the Eighth Century* (1946), p. 77.

TEILO (Elidius, Eliud), an important 6th-century Welsh monk, and bishop, whose work and cult were centred on Llandeilo Fawr (Dyfed). There are ancient church dedications in the former counties of Carmarthenshire, Glamorgan, and Pembrokeshire, where he was born, probably at Penally. The *Gospels of St. Chad* (written in SW. Mercia *c.*700) became the property of a church of St. Teilo; marginal entries show that in the 9th century Teilo was venerated in S. Wales as the founder of a monastery called the *Familia Teliavi*. The book itself was regarded as belonging to Teilo; the curse of God and the saint is invoked on those who break the agreements it contains.

No Life of Teilo was written until *c.*1130, when Geoffrey of Llandaff composed a biographical sermon. Its elements include that he was the pupil of *Dyfrig and *Paul Aurelian. During the plague he went to Brittany for seven years, staying with *Samson at Dol. He then returned to Wales and died at Llandeilo Fawr. A dispute then arose between Llandeilo, Penally, and Llandaff about who should have his body. It was miraculously multiplied into three during the night so that each could have it! This was obviously an invention to explain the three different sets of relics. An omission of this author, duly supplied by the *Liber Landavensis*, was that he failed to make Teilo successor of Dyfrig in the 'see of Llandaff'. In the *Liber Landavensis* there are twenty-one places mentioned called *Llan Teliav*.

The tomb of Teilo, on which oaths were taken, is in Llandaff Cathedral. It was opened in 1850. Inside it was a record of another opening in 1736: 'the parson buried appear'd to be a bishop by his Pastorall Staffe and Crotcher.' The staff had dropped to pieces, but the 'crotcher' of pewter, still just held together. A large cup by his side had 'almost perished'. Another silver shrine in the Lady Chapel had his statue on it. At Penally there was a shrine of an unknown saint, who was later identified with Teilo. When the monastic community there dispersed, all trace of the cult was lost. Feast: 9 February, in Wales and Brittany.

G. H. Doble, *Lives of the Welsh Saints* (1971); J. G. Evans, *The Book of Llan Dav* (1893).

TELMO, see ERASMUS.

TENENAN (Tininor) (7th century), bishop. A native of Britain, he became a priest and then a hermit near Léon, Brittany. He then became bishop at Léon and probably died at Ploabennec, where he had built a forest hermitage and where his relics were long venerated. Feast: 16 July.

Stanton, pp. 341–2.

TESILIAN, see TYSILIO.

TEWDRIC (Theodoric) (5th–6th century), prince of Glamorgan, hermit. All that is known of him comes from the Book of Llan Dav. According to this late source, he resigned the rule of his people in old age to his son Meurig, and became a hermit at Tintern. In a chance invasion of Saxons he once again placed himself at the head of his people. The invaders were put to flight but Tewdrig was mortally injured by a lance. He died and was buried at Mathern, near Chepstow. This was formerly called Merthyr Tewdrig and the church is still dedicated to him. He is also said to have founded the churches of Bedwas, Llandow, and Merthyr Tydfil. Francis Godwin, bishop of Llandaff from 1601 to 1617, discovered in the church at Mathern a stone coffin containing the saint's skeleton, which had a badly fractured skull. Feast: according to William Worcestre and Stanton, 1 April; other late authorities give 3 January.

William Worcestre, pp. 74–5; Baring-Gould and Fisher, iv. 252–4; Stanton, p. 638.

THADDAEUS, see JUDE.

THECLA, see TECLA OF ENGLAND.

THECLA (Tecla) **OF ICONIUM** (1st century), virgin. This dubious saint, whose cult was suppressed in the Roman Church in 1969, enjoyed considerable popularity in the East and was commemorated for centuries in the West. Jerome said that the *Acts of Paul and Thecla* were apocryphal and Tertullian had long before exposed its author as a presbyter deposed from office who had falsely used Paul's name. In the 16th century Baronius tried to salvage part of these Acts as being historical, but modern Bollandists say that he laboured in vain. The story is a romance whose dialogue betrays Encratite influence. *Paul is supposed to have converted Thecla to Christianity and to the practice of virginity; Thecla broke off her engagement to a young man called Thamyris. Her parents and the magistrates had Paul scourged and expelled from Iconium for separating the betrothed and even husbands and wives from each other. Thecla was ordered to be burnt; a storm put out the fire; she was sent to the amphitheatre to be eaten by beasts; she baptized herself(!) in a ditch; the animals refused to attack her; she then escaped in men's clothes to rejoin Paul at Myra. He commissioned her to preach, but she retired to live in a cave at Seleucia for the next 72 years. She became famous as a miracle worker; but when some men came to kill (or ravish) her, she prayed to be delivered: the rocks opened and she was never seen again. Another account said that a secret passage led back to Rome, where she was buried close to St. Paul. According to Delehaye the fine basilica at Meriamlik (Seleucia) never contained her body, but it did become the centre of her cult; the absence of any burial tradition makes it likely that Thecla had no historical existence apart from the preposterous Acts. Thecla was never very popular in England, although she does figure in the Sarum calendar and a few monastic ones; there survives, however, a *Life and Miracles* of Thecla in Lambeth Palace MS. 94, which relates miracle stories connected with the church of Thecla at Llandegley (Powys). It is, however, not impossible that there is confusion with a Welsh Tecla or Tegla, otherwise unknown. Feast: 23 September; in the East, 24 September.

Propylaeum, pp. 412–14; *C.M.H.*, pp. 523–4; B.T.A., iii. 623–5; A. J. Festugière, *Collections grecques des miracles: S. Thècle* (1971), pp. 11–82; H. Delehaye, 'Les recueils antiques des miracles des saints', *Anal. Boll.*, xliii (1925), 49–57; J. Dagron, *Vie et miracles de sainte Thècle* (1978).

THEI, see DAY.

THEOBALD (Thibaut) **OF PROVINS** (d. 1066), hermit. Born at Provins (Brie) of the family of the counts of Champagne, Theobald with a companion called Walter opted for a hermit life in preference to a military one. They went first to St. Remi at Reims and then on to Pettingen (Luxembourg), where they built themselves two small cells. As they were untrained in crafts or agriculture, they hired themselves out by the day in the neighbouring villages, making a simple living by unskilled work for long hours; during the night they sang the Divine Office. They went on pilgrimage to Compostela, to Rome, and to other places in Italy; they eventually settled at Salanigo, near Vicenza, whose bishop ordained Theobald priest after his companion Walter had died. A small community gathered round Theobald, who was eventually professed as a Camaldolese monk; his mother settled near him at the end of his life. He died on 30 June, and was canonized in 1073 by Alexander III. He is patron of charcoal-burners. Several English medieval churches are dedicated to him, but he is sometimes confused with other saints of the same name such as Theobald of Alba (Piedmont), patron of cobblers and porters, whose feast is on 1 June. Theobald of Provins' feast is on 30 June or 1 July; his cult is centred on Provins and Saint-Thibault-en-Auxois (Côte d'Or), where the Cluniac priory had received important relics.

B.T.A., iii. 678–9 and 443; *AA.SS.* Iun. V (1715), 588–606.

THEODORE (4th century), martyr. One of the most famous soldier-martyrs of the East, whose cult was based on his shrine at Euchaita in Pontus, Theodore was also culted at Rome and in the West. Almost nothing is known of his life beyond the fact of his martyrdom. The panegyric, attributed to *Gregory of Nyssa, stresses his extreme efficacy as a wonder-worker. He was said to have refused idolatrous worship in the company of his fellow recruits, to have set fire to a pagan temple and to have died after a fearsome series of tortures. A church in Rome is dedicated to him and he figures in the Roman calendar on 9 November, also in the Sarum calendar and many medieval monastic ones. Relics were translated to both Venice and Chartres, which accounts for the presence of his Legend in the mosaics of St. Mark's and in 13th-century stained glass at Chartres. Already by the 10th century his Legend had become so complex that two Saints Theodore were posited, both soldiers, but one a recruit and the other a general.

H. Delehaye, *Les légendes grecques des saints militaires* (1909); *AA.SS.* Feb. II (1658), 23–37 and Nov. IV (1925), 11–89.

THEODORE OF CANTERBURY (d. 690), was probably the most important archbishop of Canterbury between *Augustine and Lanfranc both for his organization of the Church in England and as a scholar and teacher. There is no contemporary biography; nearly all we know of him comes from Bede. A Greek by birth (from Tarsus in Cilicia), who had been educated at Athens and was a monk by profession, Theodore, then resident in Italy, was introduced by *Adrian, an African abbot, to Pope Vitalian, who was then looking for a suitable candidate for the archbishopric of Canterbury in 666. This followed the death in Rome of Wighard, the archbishop elect and the choice of the kings of Northumbria and Kent in the crisis following the Synod of Whitby and an outbreak of plague. Adrian himself had been the pope's choice, but he had refused. Vitalian asked him instead to accompany and help Theodore; but Bede's assertion that this was because Theodore's orthodoxy was suspect seems unconvincing. Theodore was ordained subdeacon at the age of sixty-five; soon after, the other orders were conferred on him. He left Rome with Adrian and *Benedict Biscop, consulted *Agilbert, bishop of Paris and formerly bishop of Wessex on the way, and reached England in 669. He made a visitation of most of the country, filled vacant sees, set up an important school at Canterbury with Adrian, which soon became the source of several future bishops and attracted students even from Ireland, and held the first synod of the Anglo-Saxon church at Hertford in 672. Its ten decrees were based on canons approved by the Council of Chalcedon, adopted in the West, including Ireland. But they dealt admirably with the legacy of division in England between bishops trained by Roman and those trained by Irish masters; they also dealt with the respective rights of bishops and monasteries. A further decision was taken to create more dioceses, which was later implemented by Theodore in Northumbria (at the expense of *Wilfrid), in Mercia, East Anglia, and Wessex. Theodore's work was one of unification of disparate elements in the Church, of fusing the elements from Rome, Gaul, and Ireland into a single cohesive whole. Although he was high-handed in his division of the Northumbrian diocese, and the papacy upheld *Wilfrid against him, his policy, if not the way of implementing it, was sound. In pursuing it, he rightly respected the territorial limits of the regional kings' power by creating a second (or third) diocese within the kingdom, but avoided setting up dioceses with territory in different kingdoms. Towards the end of his long life he sought a reconciliation with Wilfrid and helped towards his partial restoration. According to Wilfrid's biographer alone, he also expressed a desire that Wilfrid should succeed him at Canterbury. This was never realized. Theodore's second synod, at Hatfield, produced a declaration of orthodoxy by the Church in England in the monothelite controversy. The synods later held at Clovesho were the direct result of Theodore inaugurating the series at Hertford which decreed that such yearly synods should be held.

Theodore's school at Canterbury taught not only Latin and Greek (very rare at this time), but also Roman Law, the rules of metre, computistics, music and biblical exegesis of the literal school of Antioch. Theodore is also known to have been interested in medicine. But the Penitential ascribed to him cannot be his work as it stands: some elements (e.g. on remarriage after divorce) are in plain contradiction to his known teaching, while others date from after Theodore's death. It is possible that certain elements may go back to Theodore's oral teaching, but the whole work has at least two editors and the original cannot be recovered. Some of his exegesis has been recently discovered.

Theodore died on 19 September at the age of about eighty-seven; he was buried close to St. Augustine in the monastery of SS. Peter and Paul, Canterbury. In 1091 his incorrupt body was translated. The oldest evidence of his cult is in the Calendar of St. Willibrord; later his feast is in the Leofric Missal. The fact that no biography of him was written until the late 11th century and the lack of any claim that he was a miracle-worker contributed to his lack of popularity. But Bede's judgement stands that the English churches prospered more than ever before in the episcopate of Theodore who was the first archbishop of Canterbury willingly obeyed by all Anglo-Saxon England. His great achievement was to give unity, organization, and scholarship to a divided church on the edge of the civilized world at an age when most men had reached retirement or infirmity. Feast: 19 September, but mainly at Canterbury, which also feasted his Ordination on 26 March.

AA.SS. Sept. VI (1757), 55–82; Bede, *H.E.*, iv. 1–3, 5–6, 12, 15, 19 and v. 8; *Eddius' Life of Wilfrid* (ed. B. Colgrave, 1927) cc. 15, 24, 43; F. M. Stenton, *Anglo-Saxon England* (1943), pp. 130–41, 180–3; H. Mayr-Harting, *The Coming of Christianity to Anglo-Saxon England* (1972);

P. Fournier, *Histoire des Collections canoniques en Occident* (1931–2); J. T. M. Neill and H. M. Garner, *Medieval Handbooks of Penance* (1938); N. Brooks, *The Early History of the Church of Canterbury* (1984).

THEODORE OF SYKEON (d. 613), monk and bishop of Anastasiopolis in Galatia. His mother, called Mary, kept an inn at Sykeon with her mother and sister; they were also prostitutes. Theodore's father was a circus artist, whose speciality was acrobatic camel-riding; he seems later to have had nothing to do with his son, whose upbringing was left to his mother. She had him baptized with the name of Theodore (= gift of God), and when he was only six wanted him to enter the service of the emperor at Constantinople, for which she had prepared him a gold belt and expensive clothes. Owing to a dream in which *George appeared to her, she abandoned this plan and had him taught his letters by a local teacher. At about this time the inn was transformed by the arrival of one Stephen, a wonderful cook. It became renowned for the quality of its food, which enabled the women to give up prostitution as an additional source of income. Stephen was elderly and devout; he encouraged Theodore to visit churches, receive the sacraments, and practise fasting and abstinence. After recovering from a nearly fatal attack of bubonic plague he developed the habit of visiting and watching in the nearby chapel of St. George, who admonished his mother in sleep after she had beaten her son soundly for going to the shrine in the early morning. Throughout his life Theodore propagated the cult of St. George. He became a hermit at Arkea, about eight miles away, living in a cave underneath a chapel. There his grandmother used to visit him and bring him fruit and vegetables. He was reputed to have accomplished exorcisms until he fled to a more complete solitude in the mountains, where he lived in a walled-up cave known only to a deacon in the vicinity. He was eventually rescued in a state of collapse: ill, dirty, and pest-ridden.

He was ordained priest very young (reputedly at the age of only eighteen) and went on pilgrimage to Jerusalem, where he visited the holy places and the hermits of the neighbourhood and where the bishop gave him the monk's habit. His mother meanwhile married a prominent business-man of Ancyra, his aunt and sister became nuns, and his grandmother, when he returned home, settled near him at Mossyna and helped in the treatment of girls believed to be troubled by unclean spirits. At his own request a wooden cage was made in which he passed the time from Christmas to Palm Sunday. He then moved into an iron cage, suspended on the face of the rock in mid-air above his cave; he ordered an iron breastplate to be made for him besides iron rings for his hands and feet and an iron collar and belt. The outfit was completed by an iron staff with a cross on it. His fasts were spectacular, bears and wolves were his friends, he enjoyed powers of healing and clairvoyance, which once included his deep suspicion of a finely wrought silver chalice which turned out to have been made out of a prostitute's chamber-pot. He was also outstanding in his practice of prolonged prayer. Near his hermitage he established a monastery for his followers who also took care of the many visitors who came seeking his counsel and prayer. Eventually a larger church was built. What had started as a hermit's cave had been transformed into a complex of larger buildings with church, monastery, and guest-house.

Supreme honour came on the death of Timothy, bishop of Anastasiopolis, when the clergy and landowners of the town asked archbishop Paul of Ancyra to appoint Theodore in his place. Predictably he first refused but then accepted. His episcopate, as depicted by his biographer, seems to have been notable for its long series of miracles. More interesting perhaps to the modern reader is his description of a notable African monk, Antiochus, who came to see him, on behalf of a town pillaged by barbarians. 'He had eyebrows that met each other . . . was about a hundred years old, the hair of his head was as white as wool and hung down to his loins; so too did his beard, and his nails were very long. It was sixty years since he had touched wine or oil, thirty since he had tasted bread. His food was uncooked vegetables with salt and vinegar; his drink water.' Theodore highly approved of him, consulted him about resigning his episcopate, helped him on his mission, gave him his own horse, and sent him on his way.

His desire to resign his bishopric arose from fear of the neglect of contemplation, the need for his presence in his monastery, and the constant trouble in villages which belonged to the Church. These had been entrusted to men of property in the towns who had oppressed the villagers unjustly. One called Theodosius was so persistent in his misrule that the peasants armed themselves with swords and catapults and threatened death if he would not leave. Theodosius confronted Theodore and alleged that they had risen at his instigation and that he had been absurdly prodigal; he finally kicked away the chair on which the bishop was sitting so that he fell on his back. Theodore then rose and said gently but solemnly that he would remain as bishop no longer. Often he had to break off his psalmody to settle details of administration. He was also disturbed by reports that his monks were leading 'careless and barren lives' in his absence. Accordingly he resigned his bishopric after ten years' rule, and settled in the oratory of St. Michael at Acrena (Akreina), close to Pidrum (Tchardak) near Heliopolis. Here he lived again as a monk and was conspicuous for the healings he accomplished.

At this time he was invited by the emperor and the patriarch to visit Constantinople, where he was much honoured by the emperor and empress who sat at table with him. Then it was decided that all the monasteries should have the power of sanctuary and that the appointment of abbots should be the care of the patriarch rather than the local bishops. His stay in Constantinople was marked by yet another series of miracles, one of which was the cure of the emperor's son of elephantiasis. After this he departed for his own monastery. Once again even more miracles are recorded, such as deliverance from pests of locusts, beetles, worms, or mice destroying the crops. He also had become a physician who would recommend without hesitation purges and hot-spring baths; he seemed to have the gift of reconciling married couples which led to barren wives having children. The date of his death was recorded by his biographer, but no details. His body was translated to Constantinople. Feast: 22 April.

Full, but excessively long, contemporary Life by Eleusius in *AA.SS.* April III (1675), 32–61 (tr. E. Dawes and N. H. Baynes, *Three Byzantine Saints* (1948), pp. 87–192); Encomium by Nicephorus Scevophylax, ed. J. Kirsch in *Anal. Boll.*, xx (1901), 249–72; *Propylaeum*, p. 152; B.T.A., ii. 146.

THEODORE THE STUDITE (759–826), abbot, monastic reformer, and theologian. Born at Costantinople, he became a monk in his uncle Plato's monastery at Saccudium (near Mount Olympus) in Bithynia. He was ordained priest in 787 and became abbot in 794. The Stusios community of Constantinople, revived by him in 799, became a model of Eastern monasticism. His teaching, notable for its fostering of community asceticism and for its delegation of authority, became known through his writings, which include conferences, letters, and regulations.

He also became a reformer in a wider context. Although the Emperor Constantine VI's adulterous marriage was tolerated by the patriarch of Constantinople, Theodore denounced it and suffered exile in 796 and again in 809. During a revival of the Iconoclast controversy (813–20) he was an eloquent defender of the images; for this he suffered both imprisonment and exile. Nevertheless, he continued to lead the Orthodox cause through his writings, which included appeals to Pope Paschal I. When the more tolerant Emperor Michael came to power, he also thought it best for Theodore to be away from Constantinople. For this reason he died on the island of Prinkipo. When Orthodoxy was restored in 844, his body was returned to Constantinople. Theodore's theological and liturgical works, as well as his poems and his syllogisms in favour of venerating images, are especially noteworthy. His monastic teaching has been very influential in all Eastern monasteries. Feast: 11 November.

Works in *P.G.*, xcix, also ed. A. Mai, *Nova Patrum Bibliotheca*, v (1849) and J. P. Cozza Luci, ibid., viii (1871) and ix (1888); studies by A. Gardner, *Theodore of Studium* (1905), I. Hauscherr, 'Saint Theodore Studite, l'homme et l'ascète', *Orientalia Christiana*, vi (1926), 1–87; E. Amann in *D.T.C.*, xv (part 1), 287–98; *N.C.E.*, xiv. 19–20; *O.D.C.C.*, pp. 1359–60.

THEODORIC, see TEWDRIC.

THEODOSIUS OF KIEV ('Of the Caves') (*c.*1002–74), abbot. Born at Vasil'evo (near Kiev) of a wealthy family in the service of the prince, he passed most of his early life at Koursk. When still very young, he unsuccessfully attempted a pilgrimage to the Holy Land. His father died when he was thirteen, but his dominating mother 'of muscular build with a voice like a man' tried hard to retain him in lay life and made a scene with the abbot when he became a monk. Theodosius fled to Kiev, taking refuge with the hermit Antony in a cave above the Dnieper. Here he received the tonsure and was ordained priest.

In 1062 he founded a monastery and built a church. He became abbot of the Caves monastery in 1063 and adopted the rule of *Theodore the Studite. His monasticism was marked neither by Palestinian excesses of mortification nor by Byzantine political activism, but resembled rather the ideals of *Basil. He stressed the importance of community life and charity to all, first to other monks but also to guests, the sick, prisoners (to whom he sent a cartload of food each week), and anyone of whatever class who sought spiritual counsel. Each monk had to study Scripture and the Fathers assiduously as well as practising exemplary poverty. Always accessible to all, he would perform tasks distasteful to young monks such as the personal care for two years of an old monk almost completely paralysed.

He cultivated friendly relations with the secular rulers: they in their turn lavishly endowed his monastery. This did not prevent him from defending the poor and the oppressed. He saw his monastery as wholly integrated with the society of his time, a City of God towards which the earthly city should tend. Inside Russia it enjoyed a very high reputation, but it was sacked by Tartars in 1240, 1299, and 1316. Later it was fortified by Peter the Great and in the 20th century it has suffered both from Bolsheviks and Nazis (who destroyed Theodosius's church). It became a historical museum and a centre of scientific research, but recently it has been restored to its original purpose.

Theodosius, who was the archetypal *staretz* or spiritual father, dwelt in by God and so able to bring light and comfort to all, left several striking sayings, such as: 'It is good for us to feed the hungry and the tramps with the fruits of our labour.' Again: 'Christ sought us out, found us, carried us on his shoulders and set us at the Father's right hand . . . It was not we who sought him, but he who sought us.'

He died at Eastertide and was buried in one of the original caves. In 1091 his body was translated to the principal church. In 1108 he was canonized by the bishops of the province of Kiev. His monastery is still a place of pilgrimage: among its attractions are incorrupt bodies of dead monks and skulls which (like *Walburga's and *Hugh's) exude oil used for anointing. His feast is widely celebrated among the Slavs, both Orthodox and Latin, on 3 May.

Early Life tr. by G. P. Fedotov, *Treasury of Russian Spirituality* (1950); C. de Grunwald, *Saints of Russia* (1960), D. Attwater, *Saints of the East* (1963); *H.S.S.C.*, vi. 241–4.

THEORIGITHA, see TORTGITH.

THERESA OF AVILA (1515–82), virgin, foundress of the reformed (Discalced) Carmelites. Born of an aristocratic

Castilian family at Avila, Theresa showed precocious piety by playing at hermitages with her younger brother and by once running away from home with him, hoping to go to Morocco and die as martyrs. She was brought up at home according to her rank until her mother died when she herself was only fourteen. An adolescent reaction followed with great interest in romances, fashion, and perfume: Theresa's father then sent her to be educated by Augustinian nuns in the town. A year and a half later she fell ill, but after reading *Jerome's Letters during convalescence, decided to become a nun. Her father, at first unwilling, gave his consent and Theresa entered the Carmelite convent of the Incarnation of Avila at the age of twenty. But a year later she fell ill again, possibly from malignant malaria; doctors treated her outside the convent within her family, but on her recovery she returned to it after three years. At this time the convent of the Incarnation was both large (140 nuns) and somewhat relaxed: its parlour was much frequented by ladies and gentlemen of the town and the nuns were able frequently to leave their enclosure. In this atmosphere, where solitude and poverty seem to have been lightly esteemed, Theresa first practised mental prayer, later abandoned it, and later still, after her father's death, resumed it, never again to give it up. Meanwhile her charm, affectionate exuberance, prudence, and charity were greatly appreciated, not least by the visitors to the convent. Little by little she was deepened by the practice of prayer until in 1555 she experienced an interior conversion; she identified herself with two penitents, *Mary Magdalene and *Augustine, whose *Confessions* deeply influenced her. She was helped by both Dominican and Jesuit directors, but unfortunately her visions and other experiences became known through indiscretion and led to much misunderstanding, ridicule, and even persecution. During the years up to 1560, however, she received strong support and encouragement from the austere *Peter of Alcantara.

After twenty-five years or more of unreformed Carmelite life she wished to found a house where the primitive rule would be strictly observed. This project met with much opposition from ecclesiastical and civil authorities; but her new house of St. *Joseph at Avila, founded in 1562 with thirteen nuns in conditions of poverty, hardship, and solitude, proved to be the prototype of sixteen others during her lifetime and provided inspiration and example of other reforms in other countries and centuries. Personal poverty, signified by the coarse brown wool habit and the leather sandals, was a characteristic. The regime of manual work, together with alms, provided their income for a very simple way of life which included perpetual abstinence from flesh meat. Theresa herself took her turn at sweeping, spinning, and other household tasks. The convents were small and poor, but were built in such a way that the needs of enclosure could be satisfied. Theresa's robust common sense, prudence, and trust in Providence allied with an extraordinary capacity for work and organization overcame all obstacles. In selecting candidates for this austere way of life, she insisted above all on intelligence and good judgement ('God preserve us from stupid nuns!') because she believed that intelligent people see their faults and allow themselves to be guided, while deficient and narrow-minded people fail to do so, but are pleased with themselves and never learn to do right.

During the late 1560s she was also active in reform of the Carmelite friars in association with *John of the Cross. This, like her own convents, met with much opposition from the Calced (or unreformed) Carmelites; but eventually they were recognized and accorded an independent juridical structure. Both in her lifetime and afterwards the Discalced Carmelite friars rendered invaluable service to the nuns by providing spiritual direction. In her teaching on prayer, Theresa's work was complemented by the more theological approach of John of the Cross; but her own writings in vivid vernacular stress among other things the existence of different kinds of prayer which are neither rudimentary nor properly mystical, but which can and do persist during a very long middle period which can last for half a lifetime or more. Fortunately for posterity she was commanded to write her books: these include her autobiography, the story of her Foundations, *The Way of Perfection* (written for nuns) and *The Interior Castle*, perhaps her most mature statement on prayer and contemplation. In 1582 she made her last foundation at Burgos, but died on her way back to Avila at Alba de Tormes on 4 October. Her body was buried and still rests there. In 1622 she was canonized; in 1970 she was declared a Doctor of the Church (the first woman saint to be so honoured). A contemporary portrait, painted in 1570 by Fray Juan de la Miseria, survives at Avila. Her usual emblems are a fiery arrow or a dove above her head; the most famous representation of her is Bernini's sculpture at the church of S. Maria della Vittoria, Rome, but it may be considered that its sensuality reveals Bernini more than Theresa. The ideals and way of life established by her survive in the numerous small communities of Carmelite nuns who witness to the importance of contemplation in the modern world, while her works are read by Christians of all denominations as well as by many who owe allegiance to none. Her feast is on 15 October because in 1582 on the very day after her death the Gregorian reform of the calendar was adopted and ten days were omitted from the month of October.

Works ed. Silverio de Santa Teresa (1915–19) and Letters in 3 vols. (1922–4); Eng. tr. by E. A. Peers (1946 and 1951), which had largely superseded earlier translations by D. Lewis, B. Zimmerman and the Benedictines of Stanbrook Abbey. The first Eng. tr. of her Autobiography was printed at Antwerp in 1611; Sir Tobie Mathew's version in 1623. There are very many Lives and Studies in most European languages: *AA.SS.* Oct. VII (1845), 109–790; F. de Ribera, *La vida de la madre Teresa de Jesus* (1590); Silverio de Santa Teresa, *Santa Teresa, sinthesis suprema de la raza* (1939, Eng. tr. 1947); R. Hooenaert, *Sainte Thérèse écrivain* (1922, Eng. tr. 1931); E. A. Peers, *Mother of Carmel* (1945); id., *Saint Theresa of Jesus and other Essays* (1953); id., *Handbook to the Life and Times of St. Teresa and St. John of the Cross* (1954); M. Auclair, *La vie de Sainte Thérèse d'Avila* (1950, Eng. tr. 1953); Fr. Thomas and Fr. Gabriel, *Saint Theresa of Avila: Studies in her Life, Doctrine and Times* (1963); see also V. Sackville-West, *The Eagle and the Dove* (1943); S. Clissold, *Saint Theresa of Avila* (1978).

THERESA OF LISIEUX (1873–97), virgin, Carmelite nun. Born at Alençon, the youngest daughter of Louis Martin, a watchmaker, and his wife, who died when Theresa was four years old, she was brought up in an atmosphere of traditional piety and separation from the world which was characteristic of a rather inward-looking, middle-class French Catholicism. In 1877 the family moved to Lisieux, where their aunt helped to look after the girls and where Theresa went to school with Benedictine nuns. One after the other her sisters became Carmelite nuns at Lisieux. Although she was the youngest out of the four who did so, she was the third to enter it, which she did at the age of fifteen. The exterior events of her short life are soon told. She never did anything extraordinary, but did perform every element of the austere Carmelite regime extraordinarily well. She never held important responsibility, but was assistant to the novice-mistress from 1893. In 1894 her father died after three years of near-insanity and her sister Céline joined her sisters in the convent. In 1895 she had a haemorrhage which was the first sign of the tuberculosis which was to kill her; because of this, she did not, as she had been inclined to do, offer herself as a volunteer to the Carmelites in the missionary foundation at Hanoi (Vietnam). Instead she stayed on in her convent, suffering sometimes heroically in silence. In June 1897 she was moved to the convent infirmary and on 30 September she died at the age of twenty-four. It is likely that she would have been unknown if she had not, under obedience, written a short spiritual autobiography called *L'Histoire d'une Âme*, edited (with certain alterations) by her sister. The popularity of this work, soon translated into most European languages and several Asiatic ones, together with a number of miraculous cures and an even larger number of 'favours', believed to be due to her intercession, caused the truly sensational spread of her cult. Beatified in 1923, canonized in 1925, she was declared patroness of the Missions in 1927 and of France in 1947. The special appeal of her cult lies in her extreme artless simplicity with her apparent sweetness (rendered somewhat saccharine by some of her devotees). To the more discerning, however, it is clear that her message is very close to that of the Gospels which she so frequently cited, and that, carried to its logical conclusion, it requires very great courage and self-sacrifice, in which she excelled, for its realization. The way of simple, self-forgetful but complete obedience which she recommended is a more taxing undertaking than that of the artificial use of exterior instruments of mortification which she rejected. The community which she joined was by no means free of limitation and imperfection: the influence of her life, in her convent, in her Order, and in the Church at large helped to lead many to a rediscovery of first principles and the primacy of the ordinary duties of the religious life over personal initiatives which frequently cloak self-will. In art Theresa is represented in a Carmelite habit holding a bunch of roses in memory of her promise to 'let fall a shower of roses' of miracles and other favours. Feast: 1 October.

Her autobiography was first published at Lisieux in 1899 (Eng. tr. in 1901 and 1927): facsimile of original manuscript, notes, and documents, 3 vols. (1956; Eng. tr. by R. A. Knox, 1958). Letters ed. A. Combes (1948, Eng. tr. 1948). Lives by H. Petitot (1922; Eng. tr. 1927), H. U. von Balthasar (1950; Eng. tr. 1953), I. F. Gorres (1958; Eng. tr. 1959), J. Norbury (1966). See also A. Combes, *Sainte Thérèse de Lisieux et sa mission* (1954; Eng. tr. 1956) and other works by the same author; V. Sackville-West, *The Eagle and the Dove* (1943). *Bibl. SS.*, xii. 379–94.

THIBAUT, see THEOBALD OF PROVINS.

THOMAS (1st century), apostle. Called Didymus (= the twin) in the Gospel of John but mentioned by all the evangelists, Thomas was impulsive enough to offer to die with Jesus on the way to Bethany, but dubious both about where Christ was going and the way there (John 11: 16 and 14: 5). Above all he is remembered as the apostle who refused to believe in the Resurrection unless he actually touched the wounds of the risen Christ (John 20: 25–8), an attitude for which the Fathers both blamed him for his lack of faith, and thanked him for his scepticism which was the occasion for reassuring future generations of believers by his confession of Christ's Divinity. There is much uncertainty about his missionary work after Pentecost. One tradition placed it among the Parthians, but another, more persistent, placed it in India, where the Syrian Christians of Malabar claim that they were evangelized by Thomas, who was killed by a spear and buried at Mylapore, near Madras. An ancient cross of stone marks the place where his body rested before its translation to Edessa in 394; but another tradition claims that he is still buried at the place in India now called San Tome. The Indian connection with St. Thomas was so well accepted in the 9th century that King Alfred of Wessex sent alms not only to Rome but also 'to India to St. Thomas and St. *Bartholomew'. When the Portuguese arrived in 1522, they found the tomb at Mylapore.

The translations of the relics of Thomas are a complex story and have left traces in the calendar. From Edessa they were supposed to have been moved to Chios in the Aegean Sea and from there to Ortona in the Abruzzi. Various writings such as the Acts of Thomas, the Apocalypse of Thomas, the Gospel of Thomas and the Infancy Gospel of Thomas are all apocryphal, dating from the 2nd to the 4th centuries; some of them are Gnostic or Manichean in origin. In art the most usual representation of him is the Incredulity of St. Thomas, but he is also depicted as one of the Twelve Apostles, when he holds the spear or lance with which he was martyred. But he is sometimes represented with a builder's T-square because in the Acts of Thomas (whence in the Golden Legend) he was said to have built a palace for an Indian king. Because of this he is the patron of architects and because of his earlier spiritual blindness he was invoked for sufferers from physical blindness. There were forty-six dedications of ancient churches to him in England. His life is represented on a 12th-century English bronze bowl in the British Museum (one of four surviving examples), in seven scenes which include one of the wedding-feast of the king's daughter. A feast of the translation was kept on 3 July as well as the traditional date of his death on 21 December. But in the Syrian churches and in Malabar, 3 July was believed to be the date of his death in the year 72. The latest revision of the Roman calendar adopts 3 July as his feast, although the B.C.P. retains the more usual western date of 21 December, while the Greeks celebrate his feast on 6 October.

C.M.H., pp. 658–9; *AA.SS.* Iul. I (1719), 632; G. E. Medlycott, *India and the Apostle Thomas* (1905); J. N. Farquhar, 'The Apostle Thomas in North India', *Bull. of John Rylands Library*, x (1926), 80–111; id., 'The Apostle Thomas in South India', ibid., xi (1927), 20–50; O. M. Dalton, 'On two medieval bronze bowls in the British Museum', *Archaeologia*, lxxii (1915), 12–18.

THOMAS AQUINAS (*c.*1225–74), Dominican friar and theologian. Born of a knightly family at Rocca Secca near Aquino, Thomas was educated from the age of five to thirteen at the monastery of Monte Cassino (founded by *Benedict), and later at the university of Naples for five years. There he met and was attracted by the Dominican friars; he planned to join their Order. This caused great indignation in his home, partly because the Dominicans were mendicants. Thomas, however, had set his heart on the intellectual apostolate of the friars. This did not prevent his family from pursuing, capturing, and imprisoning him for over a year at Rocca Secca; but he joined the Dominican Order in 1244. The rest of his life was divided between Paris and Italy, studying, lecturing, and writing incessantly until his death at the early age of forty-nine. His first master was *Albert the Great, who soon recognized his worth: he is said to have prophesied that although Thomas was called the 'dumb ox, his lowing would soon be heard all over the world'. Thomas was described by a contemporary as 'tall, erect, large and well-built, with a complexion like ripe wheat and whose head early grew bald'. His deep contemplative devotion at prayer, which was sometimes ecstatic, was matched by an intense power of concentration and an ability to dictate to four secretaries at once. His own handwriting survives; it is cramped and almost illegible, making very frequent use of abbreviations because the poverty of the friars obliged them to use parchment very sparingly. His first teaching appointment was at Paris in 1252, at the Dominican convent of S. Jacques. Here he wrote a spirited defence of the mendicant orders against William of St.-Amour, a Commentary on the Sentences of Peter Lombard, the *De Ente et Essentia*, and works on Isaiah and Matthew. In 1256 he became Master in Theology at the early age of thirty-one. Towards 1259 he began his *Summa contra Gentes*, i.e. a theological statement of the Christian faith argued partly by the use of pure reason without faith against Islam, Jewry, heretics, and pagans, probably not so much for the use of missionaries in foreign lands as for a university milieu where these opinions were well known. Islam had produced famous Aristotelian thinkers and Thomas's aim was to answer them from Aristotle himself.

But this work was set aside for some years because Thomas was sent to Italy in 1259, where he stayed for ten years, teaching at Anagni, Orvieto, Rome, and Viterbo and organizing the schools of his order. He completed the work *Contra Gentes* *c.*1264, and started the most important work of his life, the *Summa Theologica*, *c.*1266. This work which fills five substantial volumes is a comprehensive statement of his mature thought on all the Christian mysteries: it proceeds through objections and authoritative replies in each article to a concise summary of his view on the matter under discussion, after which the various objections are answered. Although in his own time there were several *summae* (others were composed by Franciscans such as Bonaventure), and in the later Middle Ages many of his positions were attacked, the emergence of a series of gifted Dominican commentators and the explicit approval of *Pius V and later of Leo XIII powerfully assisted its adoption as the standard theological text in many schools and universities. Its intrinsic excellence, its insistence on Aristotle combined with Platonist philosophy, its patristic learning and clear reasoning, have commended it to generations of theologians. But it remained unfinished.

In 1269 he was recalled to Paris for three years. The king, *Louis IX, highly esteemed him and consulted him; so also did the university of Paris. Once, as a guest at the king's table, he was absorbed in thought and quite oblivious of his surroundings. To the astonishment of all, this huge friar (who had grown very corpulent in middle age) banged his fist on the table and exclaimed: 'That's finished the heresy of the Manichees.' A gentle reproof from his prior was followed by the friar's apology and the immediate arrival of a scribe to take down his argument. In 1272 Thomas was recalled to Naples as regent of studies. Here on 6 December he experienced a revelation of God, after which he dictated no more, but said that all he had written in comparison to what he had then seen was like so much straw. He died on his way to the Council of Lyons on 7 March after a partial breakdown, caused no doubt by constant overwork. Quite apart from his oral teaching, his writings alone on theology, philosophy, and scripture with the study necessary to produce them would have taken several normal lifetimes. Throughout he was modest and unassuming and all his life a man of deep prayer and spiritual insight. His devotion in serving God through theological scholarship may be compared with that of Bede through historical and patristic work. He also met the needs of the faithful by writing commentaries on the Creed, the Our Father, and the Hail Mary, besides preaching on the commandments and the Creed. He was canonized in 1323; his body was translated to Saint-Sernin, Toulouse, in 1368 and thence to the Jacobins' church, Toulouse, in 1974. Pope Pius V declared him a Doctor of the Church in 1567; his *Summa Theologica* was accorded special honour at the Council of Trent. The substance of his work, but not all its details, remains as an authentic statement of Christian doctrine. Feast: formerly 7 March, but since 1970, 28 January.

Contemporary Lives by William da Tocco and Ptolemy of Lucca in *AA.SS.* Mar. I (1668), 655–747; K. Foster, *The Life of St. Thomas Aquinas* (1959; biographical documents, translated and edited); studies by M. Grabmann, *Thomas Aquinas, his personality and thought* (translated from the German, 1928); M. C. D'Arcy (1930); J. Maritain (1931) and A. Walz (Eng. tr. 1951). Works in Leonine edition (1882 ff.), Ottawa edition (1941 ff.), Eng. tr. by T. Gilby. See also: E. Gilson, *Le Thomisme* (Eng. tr.: *The Christian Philosophy of St. Thomas Aquinas*, 1957) and J. A. Weisheipl, *Friar Thomas D'Aquino: his Life, Thought and Works* (1975).

THOMAS OF CANTERBURY (Thomas Becket) (1118–70), archbishop and martyr. Born in London of a wealthy Norman family, Thomas was educated at Merton Abbey and at Paris. He was a financial clerk for a while and then joined the curia of Theobald, archbishop of Canterbury, notable for the quality of its personnel and the skill of their legal expertise. He was sent to study law at Bologna and Auxerre; after being ordained deacon, he became archdeacon of Canterbury in 1154. In this position of administration he was notably successful and was used by Theobald as a negotiator with the Crown. When Henry II succeeded to the throne of England in 1154 at the age of twenty-one, he chose Thomas, at Theobald's suggestion, as Chancellor of England in 1155. Thomas's close friendship with the young king, his employment on embassies such as that for the marriage of the infant prince Henry to Margaret, the French princess, and on military expeditions in which he actually led his troops into battle, apparently presaged a brilliant future in the political sphere. His personal efficiency, lavish entertainment and support for the king's interests even, on occasion, against those of the Church, made him a quite outstanding royal official.

In 1162, Henry, expecting the same relationship to continue, obtained his election as archbishop of Canterbury. But from this time Becket deliberately adopted an austere way of life and immediately, to the king's annoyance, resigned the chancellorship. However, the hairshirt, discipline, vigils, and maundies which he adopted did not end his previous magnificence or determination. In character he was sensitive and intransigent, ready in speech and thorough in action.

Now that he was archbishop, through no choice of his own, he was determined to carry through, at whatever cost, what he saw as the proper duties of his state. These included the paternal care of the soul of the king, tactlessly presented by his friend of yesterday, in a way which caused considerable annoyance. Thomas also opposed Henry in matters of taxation, on the claims of secular courts to punish ecclesiastics for offences already dealt with by church courts, also, and most important, on freedom to appeal to Rome. Henry for his part claimed to be acting according to the customs of his grandfather, Henry I, which he codified in the Constitutions of Clarendon. In the view of Henry's mother, Matilda, this codification was a mistake. It also failed to take into account developments in Church–State relations in the previous forty years caused by the Gregorian Reform and the Investiture controversy. Becket, however, first accepted these Constitutions (1164), but then seeing their implications, rejected them. A long and bitter struggle followed; neither king nor archbishop would give way. Henry demanded money which he claimed was owing to him from Becket's chancellorship. Petty persecution of his followers ensued. At a council in Northampton Becket, nearly alone, withstood the royal claims and appealed to the pope. He then escaped to France.

His exile lasted for over six years. He was befriended by the king of France, lived first in the Cistercian abbey of Pontigny and from 1166 at Sens. Both sides appealed to Pope Alexander III, who tried hard to find an acceptable solution. But the dispute grew in bitterness. The king was bent on Becket's ruin, while the archbishop used ecclesiastical censures against the king's supporters among the higher clergy and even attempted to obtain an interdict. His lands had been alienated and his supporters persecuted. But in exile he came to realize that Canon Law alone would never settle the issue and, under the influence of his more intransigent followers, appealed more and more to the deepest issues of principle which were, he believed, at stake. These were the claims of Church and State, ultimately of God and Caesar.

Although peace was eventually patched up in 1170 and Thomas returned to his diocese, the reconciliation was superficial. In defiance of the rights of Canterbury, Prince Henry had been crowned; Becket answered by excommunicating the bishops most concerned. In a rage Henry asked his courtiers who would rid him of this turbulent priest. Four barons took him at his word; after an altercation with Becket, they killed him in his own cathedral. Although he had not always lived like a saint, he certainly died like one, commending his cause to God and his saints, accepting death 'for the name of Jesus and for the Church'.

The news of his death shocked Christendom. Miracles were soon reported at his tomb: within ten years, they numbered 703. His faults were forgotten and he was hailed as a martyr for the cause of Christ and the liberty of the Church. He was canonized in 1173. Although the king did public penance for his death, and had to admit the freedom of appeals to Rome, in other ways he lost little in practice, accepting compromises, but retaining most of his real power. Becket's relics were translated in 1220.

Representations of Becket's martyrdom rapidly appeared all over Europe: early examples survive not only from France and Germany, but also from Iceland, Sicily, and even Armenia. Several fine caskets for relics made of Limoges enamel survive (e.g. at the British Museum and the Society of Antiquaries, London); there are notable cycles in manuscript books such as the Queen Mary Psalter and in stained-glass windows both at Canterbury and Chartres. English murals were also common. At Canterbury Thomas more or less displaced the following of the earlier local saints by the extreme popularity of the pilgrimage, which soon became one of the most important in Europe. The Pilgrims' Way, from London or Winchester to Canterbury, can still be traced; the stained-glass windows that depict it at Canterbury are a rich source for many details of medieval life; while Chaucer in the *Canterbury Tales* immortalized both its practice and its personnel. Erasmus later attacked several elements of the cult and Henry VIII destroyed the rich shrine, prohibited and defaced images of Thomas, and ordered all mention of his name in liturgical books to be erased. But eighty ancient English churches were dedicated to him. Feast: 29 December; translation, 7 July; there was also a local feast to commemorate his return from exile (1 December).

J. C. Robertson and J. B. Sheppard, *Materials for the History of Thomas Becket*, 7 volumes (*R.S.*, 1875–85); E. Magnusson, *Thomas Saga Erkibyscups* (*R.S.*, 1875); E. Walberg, *La Vie de saint Thomas le Martyr par Guernes de Pont Sainte Maxence* (1922); L. Halphen, 'Les Biographes de Thomas Becket', *Revue Historique*, cii (1909), pp. 35–45; E. Walberg, *La Tradition hagiographique de saint Thomas Becket avant la fin du douzième siècle* (1929); A. Duggan, *Thomas Becket: a textual history of his Letters* (1980); biographies by R. Winston (1967), D. Knowles (1970), F. Barlow (1986). Recent studies include C. Duggan, *Canon Law in Medieval England* (1982), R. Foreville, *L'Église et la Royauté en Angleterre sous Henri II* (1943), D. Knowles, 'Archbishop Thomas Becket: a Character Study' in *The Historian and Character* (1963); id., *The Episcopal Colleagues of Thomas Becket* (1951). For the cult and miracles see E. A. Abbott, *St. Thomas: his Death and Miracles* (1898) and R. Foreville, *Le Jubilé de S. Thomas Becket du xiii au xv siècles* (1958); for the iconography see T. Borenius, *St. Thomas Becket in Art* (1932) and 'Some further aspects of the Iconography of St. Thomas of Canterbury', *Archaeologia*, lxxxvii (1934), 1–86. See also W. L. Warren, *Henry II* (1973); B. Smalley, *The Becket Conflict and the Schools* (1973); R. Foreville, *Actes du Colloque internationale de Sédières* (1975).

THOMAS CANTELUPE, see THOMAS OF HEREFORD.

THOMAS OF HALES (OF DOVER), Benedictine monk, was killed by the French in a raid on the town on 2 August 1295. Some attempt was made to have him canonized, in view of a local, private cult which soon grew up round his tomb, and was encouraged by indulgences from the bishop of Winchester and the archbishop of Canterbury. A Life was soon written which gives no information about his birth, parentage, or place of origin, but concentrates on a conventional list of virtues and describes minutely the men of Calais guiding the soldiers to a secret place in the monks' dormitory at Dover opposite Thomas's bed, where chalices and charters were kept, and his violent death at their hands. King Richard II and 'several noble Englishmen' applied to Rome for his canonization; in 1380 Urban VI set up a commission to enquire into his life and miracles. Indulgences were given for visiting his tomb. The work was delegated to the priors of Christ Church, Canterbury, and St. Gregory's, Canterbury, but came to nothing. The prior and community of Dover seem to have been very reserved about it, through possible rivalry with Canterbury. An altar in the priory church, known popularly as that of 'the blessed Thomas de Halys', was probably that of Our Lady and St. Katherine, in front of which he was buried. Feast: locally, only, 2 August.

C.S.P.; P. Grosjean, 'Thomas de la Hale, moine

et martyr à Douvres en 1295', *Anal. Boll.*, lxxii (1954), 167–91 and 368; *N.L.A.*, ii. 555–8, translated by C. R. Haines, *Dover Priory* (1930), pp. 469–76; E. W. Kemp, *Canonization and Authority in the Western Church* (1948), pp. 123–4, 177.

THOMAS OF HEREFORD (Thomas Cantelupe) (1218–82), bishop. Born at Hambledon (Bucks.) of a noble and powerful Norman family related to the earls of Pembroke, Hereford, and Abergavenny, Thomas was the son of the steward of the royal household, while his mother was dowager countess of Evreux and Gloucester. An uncle Walter, bishop of Worcester 1236–66, was entrusted with his education, which prepared Thomas for the high offices he later held in both Church and State. He was sent first to Oxford in 1237, but his arrival coincided with a period of considerable student unrest caused by a conflict of jurisdiction following violent incidents. So Thomas and his brother Hugh went to Paris instead, where they lived in wealthy style as befitted their rank. Thomas was ordained priest when he took part in the Council of Lyons (1245) and obtained from the pope the useful dispensation of being able to hold several benefices at once (a practice often attacked by reformers), which he freely used, both during his prolonged period of study and afterwards. He read civil law at Orléans, obtained his licence in Paris in canon law (the subject usually chosen by curial career clerics), and returned to Oxford to lecture in it. But almost at once he became Chancellor of Oxford University (1261). He became known both as a firm disciplinarian and as a friend of poor students; he confiscated offensive weapons which were used by both northerners and southerners in riots and demonstrations. Thomas supported the barons against Henry III and was sufficiently important to be chosen for the delegation of spokesmen of their case, pleaded before *Louis IX at Amiens in 1264. When Henry III had lost the battle of Lewes, Thomas, from being Chancellor of Oxford, became Chancellor of England. But he held office for only a year, was replaced after the defeat of Simon de Montfort at Evesham, and retired to Paris as a lecturer.

An academic pluralist, with the advantages of high birth and considerable experience in politics, Thomas seemed destined for success in a worldly career rather than sainthood if he could overcome the enmities his previous actions had inevitably caused. Described by contemporaries as a redhead with a ruddy complexion, he also had a choleric temperament to match, which ensured that his remaining years would be both stormy and eventful. First he returned to Oxford, became a Doctor of Divinity and Chancellor for a second term in 1273. Meanwhile he continued to hold the precentorship of York, the archdeaconry of Stafford, four other canonries and several Herefordshire parishes. These he did not neglect, for he used to make unexpected visits to them to check up on his vicars' care for the parishioners, and the condition of the church fabric. Perhaps it was this contact with the diocese besides his family connections in the West and the favour of Edward I which led the canons of Hereford to elect him as their bishop in 1275. After the civil wars and two ineffective predecessors' reigns the diocese was in a reduced state owing to the aggression of local lay lords. Thomas noted with displeasure the absence of the Welsh bishop from his consecration and set to work to regain the lost rights of his see. Both lay and ecclesiastical magnates who had encroached on the rights of his diocese were confronted and generally defeated: the Earl's Ditch along the Malvern Hills was renewed by Gilbert of Clare, earl of Gloucester, to prevent his deer grazing on the bishop's lands. As a bishop, Thomas was also a changed character. He habitually wore a hairshirt, he was zealous in visiting his diocese and particularly in confirming children, he rebuked public sinners, especially the wealthy, and forbade unauthorized pluralism. As an energetic diocesan bishop he did much that was admirable; unfortunately his episcopate coincided with that of the angular John Pecham, archbishop of Canterbury 1279–92. The two men were destined to quarrel as certainly as were *Thomas of Canterbury, whom Thomas Cantelupe resembled in several ways, and Henry II. The conflict predictably was over metropolitan jurisdiction, especially in matters of wills and marriages which had been dealt with, or should have been, in the Hereford courts. These cases led to conflict over more general disputes about the nature and extent of metropolitan jurisdiction over local bishops; in this Thomas was the spokesman of the aggrieved bishops at Reading in 1279, and in due course Rome found largely in their favour. But in his personal quarrel with Pecham words and actions resulted in Thomas being excommunicated by his metropolitan. He went to the papal court at Orvieto in 1282, but died on 25 August at Montefiascone, worn out with asceticism and energetic involvement in many lawsuits, before judgment was pronounced. He was buried at Orvieto, but his heart and some bones were sent back to Hereford; Pecham tried unsuccessfully to have Christian burial refused.

At Hereford there was a sharp reaction against Pecham: Thomas's friend, Richard Swinfield, was elected bishop; a cult of Thomas rapidly grew, aided by more than 400 claimed miracles, which took place at his tomb; eventually Hereford became the most important pilgrimage centre in the west of England. The petition for canonization was supported by Edward I and by the bishop of Hereford and others; after the usual inquiry Thomas was canonized in 1320.

His relics were translated in 1287 and 1349. Thomas must surely have been the only canonized saint to have died while still excommunicated by the archbishop of Canterbury. His personal austerity, his zeal as a reforming diocesan bishop and an intrepid defender of the rights of his church, together with the numerous cures reported at his tomb enabled his contemporaries to overlook the less admirable elements of his character and activity. In a 14th-century stained-glass window of St. Mary's church, Credenhill (near Hereford), SS. Thomas of Canterbury and Thomas of Hereford are depicted together. Feast: 2 October.

AA.SS. Oct. I (1765), 539–705; R(obert) S(trange), *The Life and Jests of St. Thomas Cantilupe* (1674); Thomas' Register was edited by R. G. Griffiths and W. W. Capes (Canterbury and York Society, 1907); A. T. Bannister, *The Cathedral Church of Hereford* (1924); T. F. Tout in *D.N.B.*, s.v. Cantelupe, Thomas. See also D. L. Douie, *Archbishop Pecham* (1952); R. C. Finucane, *Miracles and Pilgrims* (1977); M. Jancey (ed.), *St. Thomas of Cantilupe, Bishop of Hereford* (1982).

THOMAS OF VILLANOVA, (1486–1555) archbishop of Valencia and reformer. Born at Fuentellana, he was educated at Villanueva de los Infantes, where his father was a miller. He studied both arts and theology at Alcala University, where he also lectured in philosophy. In 1516 he became an Austin Friar at Salamanca, was ordained priest in 1517 and elected prior in 1519. This office he held in several houses over a period of twenty-five years. He experienced ecstasies in prayer and was outstanding in his care for the sick. When he was provincial of Castile, he sent the first community of Austin Friars to Mexico in 1534. He became preacher at the court of Charles V; this led to his being consecrated bishop of the wealthy see of Valencia in 1544.

He accepted the charge reluctantly, but altered his way of life as little as possible. He wore a threadbare habit and spent many hours in prayer. He devoted much income as well as personal service to orphans, the sick, and the captives. He visited systematically his neglected diocese (without a resident bishop since 1427), held synods regularly, and corrected difficult clergy by combining tact with discretion, generally avoiding, in spite of criticism, heavy authoritarian methods. One of his special concerns was the care of convert Moors, whose commitment was sometimes superficial because of undue pressure or fear. He persuaded Charles V to support priests specially trained for this work, while he himself founded a college for the children of those recently converted. Because of the special needs of his diocese he was excused from attendance at the Council of Trent, although his reforming programme admirably exemplified its policy.

His many sermons influenced Spanish spiritual literature and his writings are notable in quantity and quality. Universities in the USA, Australia, and Cuba have been named after him. His complete dedication to works of charity made him the patron of a congregation of French Augustinian sisters. He was also called 'The Almsgiver'.

He was beatified in 1618 and canonized in 1658. Feast: 22 September.

AA.SS. Sept. V, 799–992; *Sermones de la Virgen y obras castellañas* (1952); P. Jobit, *L'Évêque des Pauvres* (1961); B.T.A., iii. 613–17; *N.C.E.*, xiv. 123–4; *Bibl. SS.*, xii. 591–5.

THORFINN (d. 1285), bishop of Hamar (Norway). Few details are known of his early life. He was born at Trondheim and may well have been a canon there before being chosen as bishop, as his name appears as a witness to the Agreement of Tonsberg (1277) in which King Magnus VI undertook to respect clerical privileges and allow freedom of elections. Some years later however the king repudiated this agreement: the archbishop of Trondheim and the bishops of Oslo and Hamar were outlawed and exiled.

Thorfinn journeyed to Rome to obtain help and returned to Ter Doest, a Cistercian abbey in Flanders, where he fell ill and died at a comparatively early age. Two documents concerning him survive: one is his will, which shows that he had little to bequeath. He left everything to his family, to churches in Hamar, and to the Cistercian abbey at Tautra, near Trondheim. The other is a verse written by a Cistercian monk of Ter Doest, which praised his patience, penance, and charity. This was hung up over his tomb. When this was opened 50 years after his death, unusual fragrance was noted and the poem publicized. His cult spread in Cistercian monasteries near Bruges and in Norway, where both ancient and modern churches were dedicated to him. Feast: 8 January.

AA.SS. Ian. I (1734), 548; S. Undset, *Saga of Saints* (1934), 200–79; B.T.A., i. 55–6; *Bibl. SS.*, xii. 460.

THORLAC (Þorlakr) **OF SKALHOLT** (1133–93), bishop and Iceland's first saint. Born of an aristocratic family, Thorlac became a priest in his early twenties and studied at Paris and Lincoln for about ten years. In 1161 he returned to Iceland and settled down to a life of devotion, study, and pastoral ministry. This was in contrast with the life-style of many other Icelandic priests who were married and owned their churches. He would begin the day by singing the Our Father, the creed, and a hymn, and would recite 50 psalms a day. In 1168 he was bequeathed a large farm, where he founded a community of Austin Canons; he was the abbot and his mother the housekeeper. In 1178 he was consecrated bishop of Skalholt, one of Iceland's two dioceses, by *Augustine, archbishop of Nidaros.

Thorlac followed the latter's reforming policies, for which his overseas education had prepared him. He tried to abolish clerical marriage, simony, and lay patronage, the usual targets of the Gregorian Reform bishops. He made some progress in these aims but did not achieve total success; he was however an influential spiritual guide. In his monastery of Thykkviboer it seems likely that at least some of the surviving Icelandic manuscripts were written which include ecclesiastical subjects such as Saints' Lives. There Thorlac died at the age of sixty. A saga of his life was written by a cleric of Skalholt and two books of miracles were recorded. He was canonized in 1198 by the bishops in the *althing* (assembly) of Iceland. The popular cult, which flourished until the Reformation, seems never to have been formally approved by Rome. Feast: 23 December.

Scriptores rerum Danicarum (ed. Langebek) iv. 624–30 (includes breviary fragments); H. Bekker

Nielsen and L. K. Shook, 'The Lives of the Saints in Old Norse Prose', *Medieval Studies*, xxv (1963), s.v. Þorlakr of Skalholt; B.T.A., iv. 602–3; *Bibl. SS.*, xii. 458–9.

THOUSAND MARTYRS OF LICHFIELD. Purely mythical collection of 999 companions of *Amphibalus, who supposedly escaped to Wales on the occasion of *Alban's martyrdom. On their way back they were martyred at a place believed to be Lichfield. Feast: 2 January.

W. Levison, 'St. Alban and St. Albans', *Antiquity*, xv (1942), 337–59.

THURKETYL (Thurcetel) (late 10th century), founder of Croyland abbey. Danish in origin and related to Oscetel, archbishop of York (d. 971), he first appears in the *A.S.C.* as abbot of Bedford, a house apparently unconnected with the 10th-century monastic reform. He was expelled from Bedford and admitted to the confraternity of St. Paul's. As 'a cleric of London' he refounded Croyland, the monastery of *Guthlac, and became abbot there. He owned considerable estates, those given by him to Croyland including Beeby (Lincs.), Wellingborough, Elmington and Wothorpe (Northants.), Cottenham and Oakington (Cambs.). It is not certain that there was a community at Croyland before him. His cult seems to have been limited to Croyland Abbey. Thurketyl is of interest as an example of some kind of continuity between the old and reformed monasticism of the 10th century: he seems to have had no official connection with either *Dunstan or *Ethelwold, but may perhaps have been drawn into the orbit of *Oswald's influence through a blood relationship and geographical proximity to Ramsey. Feast: 11 July.

A.S.C., *s.a.* 971; Orderic Vitalis, *Ecclesiastical History* (ed. M. Chibnall), ii (1969), xxvi–xxviii, 340–2; W. de Gray Birch, *The Chronicle of Croyland Abbey* (1883); D. Whitelock, 'The Conversion of the Eastern Danelaw', *Saga-Book of the Viking Society*, xii (1941); *M.O.*, pp. 51–2.

TIBBA (7th century), Anglo-Saxon nun. She seems to have been a solitary who lived at Ryhall (Leics.), where she was first buried. She may have been related to *Cyniburg and *Cyneswith; Abbot Aelfsige of Peterborough translated the relics of all three to Peterborough in 963. In the reign of Ethelred the Unready these relics were translated to Thorney, but they were restored to Peterborough in the reign of Henry I. Feast: 6 March.

A.S.C., *s.a.* 963; *R.P.S.;* Stanton, pp. 104–5; B.T.A., i. 500–1.

TIBURTIUS AND SUSANNA (3rd century), Roman martyrs. Originally they were culted separately. Tiburtius is known from an epitaph by *Damasus and he is mentioned in the early sacramentaries and pilgrim guides. He was buried on the Via Lavicana (3 miles from Rome) at a place called The Two Laurels. A church was later built here. Susanna, however, suffered at 'The Two Houses beside the Baths of Diocletian': the church here, formerly called *titulus Gaii*, was renamed the church of St. Susanna in the 6th century. A Legend of Susanna was written round the topographical data of the genuine martyrology entry, but invented, it would seem, various people and episodes with Pope Caius also having a part in the story. The reason for the common celebration of Tiburtius and Susanna together appears to be quite simply that their names are found on the same day in the martyrology. They did not necessarily suffer in the same year or even the same persecution. Feast: 11 August.

C.M.H., pp. 434–5; L. Duchesne in *Mélanges d'archéologie et d'histoire*, xxxvi (1916), 27–42; J. P. Kirsch, 'Die Martyrer der Katachombe ad duas lauras', *Ehrengabe deutscher Wissenschaft dargeboten von Katholischen Gelehrten* (1920), pp. 577–601; *AA.SS.* Aug. II (1735), 613–32.

TIBURTIUS, VALERIAN, AND MAXIMUS, Roman martyrs who were buried at the cemetery of Praetextatus on the Appian Way. Nothing more is known of them, but the writer of the fictitious Acts of *Cecilia used the names of the first two for the husband and brother-in-law of the saint. Feast: 14 April (since 1969 in local calendars only).

Propylaeum, pp. 137–8; H. Delehaye, *Étude sur le légendier romain* (1936), pp. 73–95.

TILBERT, bishop of Hexham 781–9. The successor of *Alcmund (1) and called saint and beloved father in the chronicles, he had, however, no known cult. His anniversary is 7 September.

Stanton, pp. 149.

TIMOTHY (d. 97), disciple of the apostle *Paul, bishop and martyr. Born at Lystra, the son of a Gentile father and a Jewish mother, Eunice, he studied Scripture as a young man, but was circumcised only by Paul, to make him acceptable to the Jewish Christians (Acts 16: 3). From then onwards he became the companion and sometimes the representative of Paul, for example to the Thessalonians, the Corinthians, and the Ephesians. The tradition recorded by Eusebius claimed him as first bishop of Ephesus: Paul's letters to Timothy direct him to correct innovators and teachers of false doctrine and to appoint 'bishops' and deacons.

The Acts of Timothy relate his martyrdom by pagans when he opposed pagan festivals (probably in honour of Dionysus, not Diana, as usually stated). He was killed by stones and clubs, ready to hand in the pagan festival of *Katagogia.* His supposed relics were translated to Constantinople in 356, where the cures at his shrine were mentioned by *Jerome and *John Chrysostom. Feast: in the East, 22 January (his traditional day of death); in the West, formerly 24 January, but since 1969 in the Roman calendar 26 January, with *Titus.

Acts of the Apostles and Paul's Letters to Timothy, *passim; Propylaeum*, p. 33; H. Delehaye, 'Les Actes de S. Timothée' in *Mélanges d'Hagiographie grecque et latine* (1966), pp. 408–15.

TIMOTHY AND APOLLINARIS, martyrs attributed to Reims on 23 August in some manuscripts of the Martyrology of Jerome, followed by the Sarum calendar. According to Duchesne and modern Bollandists, they are not martyrs of Reims at all, but quite simply the Roman martyr *Timothy (see next entry) of 22 August and *Apollinaris of Ravenna, culted at Reims on 22 August as well as on 23 July.

Propylaeum, p. 355; *C.M.H.*, p. 461.

TIMOTHY, HIPPOLYTUS, AND SYMPHORIAN (3rd–4th centuries), martyrs. These apparently unconnected martyrs were formerly culted together. There is considerable doubt about their identity. Timothy was a martyr at Rome under Diocletian, recorded in the *Depositio Martyrum* of 354. He was buried on the Ostian Way.

Hippolytus is said to have suffered at Porto or at Ostia; there may well have been confusion with *Hippolytus of Rome.

Symphorian was martyred at Autun *c.*200 for refusing to honour the pagan gods, notably Cybele, of whom there was a notable shrine. He was beheaded and buried in a cave, over which Euphronius, bishop of Autun, built a church in the 5th century. The village and church of Veryan (Cornwall) take their name from this martyr. Feast: formerly 22 August, suppressed in the Roman calendar in 1969: the Sarum calendar, however, gives 'Hippolytus and Companions' on 13 August and 'Timothy and Apollinaris' on 23 August.

B.T.A., iii. 380–1; G. H. Doble, *St. Symphorian* (1931).

TININOR, see TENENAN.

TITUS (1st century), bishop. A disciple of *Paul, who later became his companion and secretary, Titus was of gentile birth and for that reason was not circumcized when he became a Christian. He took part in the council of Jerusalem, was sent to Corinth on a difficult mission, and was later left by Paul to organize the church in Crete. Later still he was sent to Dalmatia, but he was believed to have returned ultimately to Crete, where he died and where he is venerated as its first bishop. Paul's epistle to Titus, whose authenticity has been much discussed, instructed him to ordain presbyters and to govern firmly the Cretans, whom Paul did not esteem highly.

Titus' body was supposed to be buried at Gortyna (Crete), until the head was taken to Venice in 823. His cult was mainly eastern: the Greeks and Syriacs keep his feast on 25 August; in the West he is commemorated in the Roman Martyrology on 4 January, but since Pius IX his feast was on 6 February; in the 1970 revision of the Roman Calendar Titus and *Timothy share a feast on 26 January.

Commentaries on the Pastoral Epistles by C. Spicq (Études Bibliques, 2 vols. 1969), J. N. D. Kelly (1963) and C. K. Barrett (1963); *AA.SS.* Ian. I (1643), 163–4.

TOLA, see OLAF.

TORTHRED, see TANCRED.

TORTGITH (Theorigitha) (d. 681), nun of Barking. Friend and companion of *Ethelburga, foundress of Barking, Tortgith, conspicuous for humility, zeal, and care for the young, became mistress of novices. After several years she became ill with paralysis for six years (669–75) and experienced a vision of Ethelburga just before the latter's death. Three years later, after losing her power of speech as well as the use of her limbs, she experienced another vision and this time conversed with her. Her words but not those of Ethelburga were recorded by witnesses and sent to *Bede. The conversation concerned the time of Tortgith's imminent death. Feast: 26 January.

Bede, *H.E.*, iv. 9; Stanton, p. 36.

TOVA, see TANCRED.

TRIDUANA (Tradwell, Trollhaena), virgin. Described variously as an abbess who came to Scotland either with a mythical Boniface or with *Rule, the supposed bearer of the relics of St. *Andrew to Scotland, Triduana is said to have lived a monastic life with two companions at Roscoby (Forfarshire); she died at Lestalryk (Lothian). Her relics were an important centre of pilgrimage at Restalrig, near Edinburgh: on 21 December 1560 it was ordained by the Scottish Reformers that 'the kirk of Restalrig, as a monument of idolatry, be raysit and utterlie cast down and destroyed'. Relics were also claimed by Aberdeen. She was invoked for curing diseases of the eyes because of the legend that when a local prince desired her because of her beautiful eyes, she had them taken out and given to him. She is patron of Kintradwell (Caithness). The site of her well at Restalrig (formerly believed to be a chapter-house) has been excavated; it had two stories, a chapel and piscina being built over the well itself. Some of the choir of the collegiate church built in 1487 and endowed by at least three kings of Scotland survives. A secondary shrine of Triduana was at Papa Westray in the Orkneys on a rock beside St. Tredwell's Loch. Feast: 8 October.

K.S.S., pp. 453–4; J. M. Mackinlay, *Ancient Church Dedications in Scotland* (1914), pp. 476–9.

TRILLO (?5th century), abbot. Nothing seems to be known of his life, but his memory is retained in the place-name Llandrillo (Denbighshire, now Gwynedd) and in the ancient oratory there built over a spring used for baptism, and whose structure resembles Irish examples. Another Llandrillo (Merionethshire, now Gwynedd) had a well where rheumatism was cured. A third church dedicated to him at Llandrygarn (Anglesey) has his feast on 15 June, which is in accordance with early Welsh calendars.

Baring-Gould and Fisher, iv. 263–4.

TRUMWIN (Tumma) (d. *c.*704), bishop of Abercorn 681–5. Nearly all that can be known about him comes from *Bede. When *Theodore of Canterbury divided the Northumbrian diocese of *Wilfrid into three, bishops were established for Deira, Bernicia, and Lindsey. Three years later two more were added for Hexham and the Pictish lands recently conquered by Northumbria. Trumwin was chosen for this see and consecrated by Theodore. He was also one of those who accompanied Theodore to Farne to persuade *Cuthbert to be consecrated bishop. Trumwin's episcopate was very short. He set up the see at Abercorn, and a monastery in Lothian on the Firth of Forth, but after the disastrous battle of Nechtansmere (685), when Egfrith, king of Northumbria, was killed, many of the English were either slain or enslaved or else escaped. Among the refugees were Trumwin and his monks, who fled to Whitby, where under abbess *Elfleda he lived 'a life of austerity to the benefit of many others beside himself'. His monks were dispersed among several monasteries. He died at Whitby and his relics were translated during the 12th century with those of King Oswiu and abbess Elfleda. There seems no early record of the date of his feast: Wilson's Martyrology gives 10 February.

Bede, *H.E.*, iv. 12, 26, 28; William of Malmesbury, *G.P.*, p. 254; Stanton, pp. 54–5.

TUDA (d. 664), bishop of Northumbria. According to Bede he was a 'servant of Christ, who had been educated by the southern Irish and consecrated bishop; he wore the ecclesiastical tonsure in the form of a crown [i.e. in the Roman way] and kept the catholic rules for the celebration of Easter'. He was appointed to the Northumbrian see just after the Synod of Whitby to replace *Colman of Lindisfarne who left for Ireland. No doubt it was hoped that he would be the person to unite the 'Irish' and 'Roman' factions in Northumbria, but this 'good and devout man' ruled for a very short time, as he died in the plague of 664 at the unidentified Paegnalaech, where he was buried. Unfortunately there is no firm record of his public cult as all the records of early Lindisfarne perished in the sack by the Vikings. His anniversary was 21 October.

Bede, *H.E.*, iii. 26–7; *AA.SS.* Oct. X (1861), 56.

TUDFUL, see Tydfil.

TUDWAL (Tugdual, Tual) (6th century), bishop. Of Welsh origin, this saint is known in Wales by place-names, but does not appear in ancient Welsh calendars. His cult, however, is strong in Brittany, especially round Léon, where Tudwal is reputed to have landed with his numerous family and monks. He settled at Lan Pabu, where he built a monastery. His cousin was the local ruler, but he obtained confirmation of his title to land from King Childebert I, who is said to have insisted that he become a bishop. This he did, and ruled at Tréguier for the rest of his life. Tudwal's name is found in three places on the Lleyn peninsula (Cardigan Bay); St. Tudwal's Island East (Ynys Tudwal) has a ruined chapel, dedicated to Tudwal and mentioned in the Taxation documents of 1291; originally his hermitage. By the time of William Worcestre and Leland it was abandoned. Tudwal's name appears in a Breton litany of the 10th century; in art he is depicted as a bishop, holding a dragon by his stole, like *Armel. Tréguier, Laval, and Chartres all claim part of his relics. Feast in most Breton calendars on 1 December, but 30 November and 2 December are also found.

A. de la Borderie, *Les trois anciennes Vies de S. Tudwal* (1887); Baring-Gould and Fisher, iv. 271–4; William Worcestre, pp. 136–7; J. Leland, *Itinerary*, iii. 88.

TUDY (Tudec) (6th century), monk and abbot. Of unknown place of origin, Tudy founded monasteries and worked as a missionary in Brittany. Place-names and dedications point to his activity or that of his disciples in both north and south Brittany: Île-Tudy on the mouth of the Odet (Finistère), not far from Quimper, with adjacent parishes which bear his name, probably represent the main centre of his activity. The parish of St. Tudy (Cornwall) represents a monastic foundation by Tudy or his disciples, possibly in concert with *Brioc, represented by the nearby parish of St. Breocke, and whose companion Tudy may have been. Feast: 11 May.

G. H. Doble, *The Saints of Cornwall*, iv (1965), 110–15; Baring-Gould and Fisher, iv. 276–9.

TUMMA, see Trumwin.

TURIBIUS OF MOGROVEIO (1538–1606), archbishop of Lima. Born at Mayorga (Spain), Turibius was a lay professor of Law at Salamanca University, from which Philip II appointed him principal judge in the court of the Inquisition at Granada. Very unexpectedly he was chosen as archbishop of Lima (Peru). Both these appointments were most unusual ones for a layman to hold; Turibius in vain pleaded his own incapacity and the enactments of canon law which forbade such promotions. All was in vain: he received orders and was consecrated bishop; he arrived in Lima in 1581. The vast diocese comprised some thousands of square miles, including coastline, mountains, and jungle: his first visitation took seven years. Abuses and scandals were notorious; lack of roads in Peru and the great distance from Spain made redress often impossible when officials were involved; there were immense numbers of baptized Indians who knew nothing of the Christian religion, partly because of the shortage of suitable clergy. Above all, the Spanish conquerors often gave appalling examples of tyranny, oppression, and cynical disregard for Christian moral teaching, as they were there to make their fortunes by any means in their power. Notorious offenders amongst the clergy were disciplined and the worst abuses were corrected. But Turibius also took positive steps to improve matters by building churches and founding institutions such as hospitals and religious houses. In 1591 he set up the first seminary or training college for priests in the New World, at Lima. He himself learnt the Indian dialects so that he could communicate directly with as many of the faithful as possible. His championship of their rights earned opposition and even persecution from the civil authorities, but by patient persistence he eventually overcame. He managed to visit every part of his diocese in spite of the dangers and the poor roads. His charity to the poor included not only the Indians but also those impoverished Spaniards who were too proud to ask for help: these he assisted without their knowing who had done so. He remained in harness right up to his death: he fell ill on a visitation at Pacasmayo, but died at Santa on 23 March. This is now his feast in the universal calendar. His cult has long been strong in the Americas with the feast formerly on 27 April; but he was recently selected for a world-wide cult both as a type of a pioneering missionary and reforming bishop and as a representative of South America, whose immense Christian population is often forgotten. He was canonized in 1726.

C. G. Irigoyen, *Nuevos estudios sobre la vida y gobierno de S. Toribio* (1906, 3 vols.); R. Levillier, *La organisation de la Iglesia, y Ordenes Religiosas en el Virrienato del Peru en el siglo xvi* (1919); B.T.A., ii. 176–8; *Bibl. SS.*, xxi. 712–15.

TWELVE APOSTLES OF IRELAND, a list of Irish saints supposedly trained by *Finnian at Clonard. In fact, some lived before his time, some were trained elsewhere, and Clonard did not have such a monopoly in producing important monks and apostles as this local tradition claimed. The saints in question are: *Brendan of Birr, *Brendan the Navigator, *Canice, *Ciaran of Clonmacnoise, *Ciaran of Saighir, *Columba, Colum of Tir da Glas, *Laserian, Mobi of Glasnevin, Ninnaid of Inismacsaint, *Ruadhan of Lothra, and Sinell of Cleenish.

The Irish Saints, pp. 165–9.

TYDFIL (Tudful), Welsh woman saint, patron of Merthyr Tydfil (Mid Glamorgan), where she was buried. Legend has it that she was one of the daughters of *Brychan, and was assassinated and buried here in 480. She is said to have met her death at the hands of pagans, probably British, but later called Saxons. Feast: 23 August.

Baring-Gould and Fisher, iv. 286–7.

TYSILIO, Welsh monastic saint of the 7th century, the centre of whose cult was at Meifod (Powys). Also in this country is the town called after him, Llandysilio, where he built his cell close to the Roman road. Besides the cluster of dedications to him here and in Clwyd, there is a chapel of his picturesquely sited in the Menai Straits, while dedications in former SW. Cardiganshire and another on the borders of former Pembrokeshire and Carmarthenshire (all now in Dyfed) suggest that as well as being a saint of Powys he also travelled to other parts of Wales as a *peregrinus*. A Tysilio or Suliau, of whom there is a cult in Brittany, is most probably a different person from the Welsh saint, although a Welsh origin is claimed for the Breton saint and a Breton Life makes a lively but unconvincing attempt to combine elements from the biographies of at least two men. Feast: 8 November.

G. H. Doble, *St. Sulian and St. Tysilio* (1936); E. G. Bowen, *Settlements of the Celtic Saints in Wales* (1954).

U

UGANDA, Martyrs of, see Lwanga.

ULFRICK, see Wulfric.

ULFRID (Wulfrid) (d. 1028), martyr. This Englishman was one of those who evangelized Sweden like *Sigfrid and others. After considerable success he met his end after attacking idolatry and breaking up a statue of Thor with an axe. He was then lynched by the crowd who witnessed this, and his body was thrown into a marsh. Feast: 18 January.

Stanton, pp. 24–5.

ULRIC, see Wulfric.

ULTAN OF ARDBRACCAN (d. 657). A learned man, who founded a school, educated and fed poor students, illuminated manuscripts, collected the writings of *Brigid, and wrote a Life of her, is also said to have been bishop and apostle of the Desi of Meath. No Life of Ultan has survived, but there is a long notice in the Martyrology of Oengus and a poem in his praise. Feast: 4 September.

E. Dummler, *Poetae Latini medii aevi*, i. 589; B.T.A., iii. 485–6.

UNCUMBER, see Wilgefortis.

UNY, see Euny.

URBAN (d. 230), pope and martyr. This pope, who was elected in 222, died a martyr and was buried in the cemetery of Callistus, has been confused with another Urban, who was buried on the Via Nomentana. Also the mistake was made of assuming that the Acts of St. *Cecilia were genuine and so the account in the *Liber Pontificalis* contains apocryphal material. It seems that we know virtually nothing about this pope beyond the fact of his martyrdom. Feast: 25 May, in the Roman calendar until 1969, in the Sarum missal and other medieval English calendars. The primitive date, however, is 9 August.

AA.SS. Maii VI (1688), 471–89 and *C.M.H.*, pp. 428, 262, and 273.

URITH OF CHITTLEHAMPTON (Erth, Heiritha), virgin, foundress of its church. Leland and *N.L.A.* do not mention her, Roscarrock knew of her existence, but said: 'What she was more, I know not. I would to God others would learne.' In fact there was a book of her life in the shrine, with a record of her miracles. The rhyming Latin poem about her in Trinity College, Cambridge (MS. 0.9.38), is probably based on this. Hence and from Camden we learn that she was born at East Stowford (Devon), that she was a maiden dedicated to the religious life and was killed by haymakers with their scythes at the instigation of a jealous, possibly pagan, stepmother. A stream sprang out of the ground from where she fell. These last details are the same as in the legends of *Sidwell and *Cyniburg. Urith is a Celtic name; she may have been a victim of the Saxons. Her date is unknown.

The offerings to her shrine were sufficient to build the tower of Chittlehampton, reputed the finest in Devon, and even in the last year of the pilgrimages there, the vicar's share of the offerings was £50, or three times his income from tithes and glebe. The removal of her statue in 1539–40 caused the loss of another £50 in offerings to the church. The pulpit of *c.*1500 survives with a figure of St. Urith holding a palm of martyrdom and the foundation stone of the church; her body may still be buried in the church. There is a 16th-century stained-glass window of her at Nettlecombe (Somerset). Urith is a

Christian name favoured in Devon to our own day. Feast: 8 July.

M. R. James, 'St. Urith of Chittlehampton', *Cambridge Ant. Soc. Proc.* 1902, 230–4; J. F. Chanter, 'St. Urith of Chittlehampton', *Rept. and Trans. Devon Association*, xlvi (1914), 290–308; G. McN. Rushforth, 'St. Urith', *Devon Notes and Queries*, xvii (1933), 290–1.

URSULA AND COMPANIONS (4th century(?)), virgins and martyrs. At the basis of the cult of these martyrs, whose Legend developed incredible additions, is a Latin inscription, carved in stone *c.*400, in the church of St. Ursula at Cologne. This records that Clematius restored a ruined church in honour of some local virgin-martyrs. Their names, number, and date, and circumstances of death were alike unrecorded. Posterity, however, was not content with such ignorance. A 9th-century sermon admitted that no authentic written account survived, but claimed to give the local tradition that they suffered under Maximian, that they were very numerous, that they had come to Cologne in the wake of *Maurice and the Theban Legion, and were probably British in origin. There is a disconcerting silence about them on the part of the martyrologies: a late 9th-century calendar gives the name of Ursula among a group of five, eight, or eleven martyrs. In the 10th century their number became fixed at 11,000, probably through the wrong expansion of an abbreviated text which read 'XI MV' into 'undecim millia virgines' (= 11,000 virgins) instead of 'undecim martyres virgines' (= eleven virgin-martyrs). However this may be, once launched, the Legend became popular and several writers invented details until it reached its final form in the *Golden Legend*. This may be summarized as follows. Ursula, daughter of a British Christian king, was betrothed to a pagan prince, but obtained a three-years delay because she really wished to remain a virgin. She spent this time of grace in a ship, cruising with ten noble companions, each of whom occupied a ship with a thousand companions on board. Winds drove them into the mouth of the Rhine; they sailed to Cologne and Basle, went on pilgrimage to Rome and returned to Cologne. There they were martyred by the Huns for their Christianity, Ursula having refused to marry their chief. The citizens of Cologne buried them and a church was built in their honour. There are other variants of the Legend, including one which gives Ursula a Cornish origin and makes her sail to Brittany for her marriage with 11,000 maidens and 60,000 serving-women.

In 1155 a vast collection of bones was found at Cologne, which were unhesitatingly identified with those of Ursula and her followers and were sent out as relics to many countries. The fact that some of these were of men and children (the collection probably came from a large hitherto unknown burial-ground) only gave impetus to the further development of the Legend. At the same time a number of forged inscriptions were 'discovered' of imaginary people alleged to have suffered with Ursula. Meanwhile further support was given to the cult by the revelations of Elizabeth of Schönau. This visionary, it is claimed, was fed with spurious information by two abbots of Deutz. The main areas of the cult of Ursula were the Rhineland, the Low Countries, Northern France, and Venice. But her supposed British origin does not seem to have made her particularly popular in England. Only two ancient churches were dedicated to her, but her feast occurs in the Sarum and other calendars on her usual day, 21 October.

Her late medieval iconography is extremely rich: about twenty-five cycles of her Life survive, painted from the 14th to the 16th centuries. Several of these are at Cologne, but there are also notable examples by Memling at Bruges and Carpaccio at Venice. The latter decorated the School of St. Ursula and includes elements dependent on the revelations of Elizabeth of Schönau such as the meeting between Ursula and Pope Cyriacus at Rome and the inclusion of a bishop and even a cardinal among the companions of Ursula in her martyrdom. In England there is a fine stained-glass window at Holy Trinity church, York, which depicts Ursula in the usual way, with crown and sceptre, and protecting under her cloak a group of her companions. Ursula was one of the saints affected by the Roman reform of the calendar in 1969: her feast is no longer in the universal calendar, but is permitted in certain localities.

AA.SS. Oct. IX (1885), 73–303; 'Historia SS. Ursulae et sociorum eius antiquior', *Anal. Boll.*, iii (1884), 5–20; W. Levison, *Das Werden der Ursula-Legende* (1928); M. Coens, 'Les Vierges martyres de Cologne', *Anal. Boll.*, xlvii (1920). 89–110; M. Tout, 'The Legend of St. Ursula and the Eleven Thousand Virgins' in *Historical Essays* (ed. T. F. Tout and J. Tait, 1902), pp. 17–56; J. Sozbacher and V. Hopmann, *Die Legende der hl. Ursula* (1964); F. Valcanover, *La leggenda di S. Orsola* (1963); G. de Tervarent, *La Légende de S. Ursule dans la littérature et l'art du moyen âge* (2 vols., 1931).

V

VALENTINE (3rd century), martyr. Two Valentines are listed in the Roman Martyrology on 14 February: one a Roman priest martyred on the Flaminian Way, supposedly under Claudius, the other a bishop of Terni who was martyred at Rome, but whose relics were translated to Terni. The Acts of both are unreliable and the Bollandists assert that these two Valentines were in fact one and the same. Neither of them seems to have any clear connection with lovers or courting couples. The reason for this famous patronage is that birds are supposed to pair on 14 February, a belief at least as old as Chaucer, just as the custom of choosing and calling oneself a Valentine is at least as old as the Paston Letters. On the other hand, some authorities see the custom of choosing a partner on St. Valentine's Day as the survival of elements of the Roman Lupercalia festival, which took place in the middle of February. Whatever the reason, the connection of lovers with St. Valentine, with all its consequences for the printing and retailing industries, is one of the less likely results of the cult of the Roman martyrs. No churches in England seem to be dedicated to Valentine, but from 1835 his relics are claimed by the Carmelite church in Dublin. Feast: 14 February.

Propylaeum, *s.d.* 14 Februarii, *AA.SS.* Feb. II (1658), 751–62; H. Grisar, *Geschichte Roms und der Papste im Mittelalter*, i (1901), 655–9; *Paston Letters* (ed. J. Gairdner 1904), no. 783.

VALERIA, see under VITALIS.

VALERIAN, see TIBURTIUS, VALERIAN, AND MAXIMUS.

VALERY, see WALARIC.

VAUBOURG, see WALBURGA.

VEDAST (Vaast, Foster) (d. 539), bishop of Arras. Famous as the priest who prepared Clovis for baptism by *Remigius, Vedast was then resident at Toul, where he had settled at some distance from his home, whose exact location is unknown. Clovis' conversion was occasioned by a victory over the Alemanni in 496, but four years before he had married Clotilde, who had prepared the way. Vedast was reputed to have cured a blind man, which strengthened the king in his resolve and converted some courtiers. He was appointed bishop of Arras in 499. The only vestige of Christianity was a ruined church, but during his long episcopate he restored religion in his diocese, to which Cambrai was added *c.*510. Roads, mountains, springs, and churches in Arras, Cambrai, and parts of Belgium bear his name: so do three ancient churches in England: one in London (Foster Lane, rebuilt by Wren 1695–1700), one in Norwich, and one in Tathwell (Lincs.). It is unlikely that Vedast ever visited England, but a limited and regional cult in England may well go back to the 10th century, when contacts with Arras and its neighbourhood were particularly marked. It was strengthened from the 12th century by the presence in England of Augustinian canons of the Arrouaise branch. Vedast's feast occurs in the Benedictional of St. *Ethelwold, the Missal of Robert of Jumièges, and the Leofric missal, also in the calendars of Sarum, York, and Hereford. Stained-glass pictures of him are in the churches of Long Melford and Blythburgh (Suffolk), which represent him with his traditional attribute, a wolf, with or without a goose in his mouth rescued by Vedast for its poor owners. Other attributes include a child at his feet or else a bear. Feast: 6 February (with *Amand), also at Arras 15 July and 1 October.

Ancient Lives by Jonas of Bobbio and by Alcuin in *AA.SS.* Feb. I (1658), 782–815, also in

M.G.H., Scriptores rerum merov., iii (1896), 399–427; see also G. and W. Sparrow Simpson, *Life and Legend of St. Vedast* (1896).

VEEP, see WENNAP.

VENANTIUS FORTUNATUS, (*c.*530–*c.*610), bishop of Poitiers. Born near Treviso and educated at Ravenna, he left Italy *c.*565 to visit the shrine of St. *Martin at Tours in thanksgiving for being cured of an illness of the eyes. In return for the hospitality he received he wrote laudatory poems in honour of his hosts. He visited Sigebert's court at Metz, where he stayed for two years earning his living by his varied talent as a writer, who brought something of Roman elegance and literary culture to a rather barbarous Merovingian court.

By this time the Lombards had invaded North Italy and Venantius settled at Poitiers, where he became steward and, after his ordination, chaplain to the nuns among whom were *Radegund and the abbess Agnes, to both of whom he wrote letters and poems. He was unusually sensitive to the hardships of women, who indeed played a considerable part in the development of Christian values in the Merovingian world. His letters to Radegund (much older than he) are rhetorically playful and affectionate: 'Even though the clouds are gone and the sky is serene, the day is sunless when you are absent.' When he could obtain them, he tells her that he will send her roses and lilies.

The best of his talents were stimulated by the arrival at Poitiers in 569 of relics of the True Cross, sent by the Emperor Justin II, which was the occasion for his fine hymn 'Vexilla regis prodeunt' ('The royal banners forward go'), used in the liturgy of Passiontide and especially Good Friday. At about the same time he composed 'Pange lingua gloriosi' ('Sing, my tongue, the glorious battle'), likewise for Passiontide and 'Salve festa dies' for Easter. These are all generally reckoned to be among the finest examples of Christian hymnody, combining as they do classical skill and Christian religious sentiment to a high degree.

Venantius' compositions were highly appreciated by contemporaries, among whom *Gregory of Tours encouraged him to collect and publish his poems, some of which were composed for great ecclesiastical occasions. Other bishops who befriended him were Felix of Nantes and Leontius of Bordeaux.

Venantius' other works include prose and verse Lives of Saints; in prose are Lives of *Hilary, *Radegund, and Severinus of Bordeaux as well as Albinus, Germanus of Paris, and *Paternus of Avranches; in verse those of *Martin and *Médard. His *In laudem Mariae* depicts the Virgin as queen of heaven, receiving homage, the object of respectful love, forestalling some of the elements of courtly love.

About the year 600 Venantius was elected bishop of Poitiers, but not much is known of his short term of office. Feast: 14 December.

Works edited by F. Leo and B. Krusch in *M.G.H., Auctores Antiquissimi*, iv (1881–5) also in *P.L.*, lxxxviii. 59–596; *B.T.A.*, iv. 558–9; J. M. Wallace-Hadrill, *The Frankish Church* (1983), pp. 82–8; B. de Gaiffier, 'S. Venance Fortunat, évêque de Poitiers: les témoignages de son culte', *Anal. Boll.*, lxx (1952), 262–84; F. J. E. Raby, *A History of Christian Latin Poetry from the Beginnings to the Close of the Middle Ages* (1953).

VÉNARD, Theophane (1829–61), martyr. A schoolmaster's son, born at Saint-Loup-sur-Thouet (Deux-Sèvres), he joined the Society of Foreign Missions of Paris as a young man, transferring to it from the seminary of Poitiers diocese. In 1852 he was ordained priest and in 1854 he was sent to Tonkin (Vietnam) in a time of severe persecution. Expelled from Namdiuh in 1856, he went to Hanoi, where however the renewed persecution obliged him to hide in caves and sampans. At last he was arrested, placed in a bamboo cage, and ultimately beheaded for the Christian faith. His letters and his example inspired the young *Theresa of Lisieux to volunteer for the Carmelite nunnery at Hanoi. In 1865 Vénard's body was translated to his Congregation's church in Paris, but his head remains in Tonkin. With 19 other martyrs from this area (see VIETNAM) he was beatified in 1909 and canonized in 1988. Feast: 2 February.

E. Vénard, *Vie et correspondance de J. Th. Vénard* (1864), selected letters republished in 1964; Life by F. Trochu (1929); J. Nanteuil, *L'épopée missionnaire de T. Vénard* (1950); *N.C.E.*, xiv. 594; *Bibl. SS.*, xii. 987–91.

VERGIL, see VIRGIL.

VERONICA, traditionally a pious woman who wiped the face of Christ when he fell under the weight of the cross on his way to Calvary. According to the legend, he left the image of his face on the cloth she used. A 'veil of Veronica' has been preserved at St. Peter's, Rome, since the 8th century and was much venerated in the 14th and 15th centuries. There has been much speculation about Veronica. Some identified her with the woman cured by Christ of an issue of blood, others with *Martha, the sister of *Lazarus, others with the wife of Zacchaeus or of a Roman officer. In reality the earliest version of the story comes in a late Latin interpolation to the so-called Gospel of Nicodemus (4th–5th century). Veronica is not mentioned in any early martyrology, nor in the Roman Martyrology; Charles *Borromeo suppressed her feast in the diocese of Milan. She has been ensured a place in popular devotion, if not in the Liturgy, by the addition of her story to the Stations of the Cross, an immensely widespread devotion of meditating on the Passion of Christ propagated by the Franciscans. Nevertheless this devotion with its fourteen stations only became standardized (with Veronica in it) in the 18th–19th centuries. Even the name Veronica has been the subject of critical enquiry. It was held by Gerald of Wales and others that her name really means *vera icon* (true image) among spurious representations of Christ, whence the Middle English 'vernicle'. But in the East the woman with the issue of blood was called Berenike long before she was associated with an image.

In sum, it seems likely that the story of Veronica is a delightful legend without any solid historical basis; that Veronica is a purely fictitious, not a historical character; and that the story was invented to explain the relic. It aroused great interest in the later Middle Ages in the general devotional context of increased concern with the humanity of Christ, especially the Holy Face, and the physical elements of his Passion.

Holy Year of Jubilee (1900) and *The Stations of the Cross* (1906); B.T.A., iii. 82–3; *N.C.E.* and *D.A.C.*, s.v.

VIANNEY, Jean-Baptise (1786–1859), curé d'Ars. Born at Dardilly (near Lyons) the son of a farmer, his early life was passed as a shepherd boy on his father's farm with little formal schooling. During some of these years the French Revolution with its attendant violence and outlawing of the loyal clergy also affected his upbringing. At the age of twenty he began studies for the priesthood, which were interrupted by a call to military service. He joined the colours as a conscript, but later, like many others, deserted; he continued his studies in secret, until the amnesty of 1810. He then received the tonsure and was admitted to the seminary at Verrières, from which he transferred to that of Lyons in 1813. He found his studies difficult throughout, especially Latin. He broke down at a *viva*, but was nevertheless admitted to orders (1815) because he was said to be the most devout, if also the most unlearned, student at Lyons; his vicar-general too stressed that the Church needed not only learned priests, but also holy ones. He became curate at Écully for two years until his parish priest, who was very austere and deeply appreciative of Vianney, died in 1817. Vianney was then appointed as parish priest of Ars-en-Dombes, a remote and unimportant village of about 250 inhabitants.

This was to be his home for the rest of his life. He lived mainly on potatoes, vigorously attacked blasphemy and obscenity, caused village inns to close for lack of custom, and waged ceaseless war against dancing and all immodesty. The more positive side of his apostolate included preaching and especially counselling, at which he excelled, both inside and outside confession. His insight into personal difficulties seems to have been helped by supernatural gifts of reading the secrets of hearts, by knowledge of events at a distance, and by prophecy. Poltergeist phenomena, which he attributed to the Devil, were also well attested. These included noises, personal violence, even the burning of his bed. Other marvels related of him included the miraculous multiplication of food, especially for the orphanage he had founded. Word of this was spread abroad; his attribution of them to the mythical *Philomena, of whom he set up a shrine, did not deceive his visitors. These came to number about 300 a day from 1830 until 1845, brought by trains from Lyons, where a special booking-office for Ars had been established.

Every day he preached at 11 o'clock and spent long hours in the confessional, sometimes as many as twelve in his earlier days, while just before his death, when visitors were reputed to number about 20,000 a year, he sometimes spent sixteen hours a day there. With the passing of time and the acquisition of greater experience and compassion he became less rigorous and more sympathetic to human frailty, although the recital of sins still brought him to tears. He also came to insist more and more on the love of God and the efficacy of the public liturgical prayer of the Church.

Three times he left Ars to become a monk, but three times he returned. He refused ecclesiastical promotion except for the canonry which he received against his desire, and whose robes he soon sold for the benefit of the poor. More surprising was the government's recognition of his work by a knighthood of the Imperial Order of the Legion of Honour. But he refused to be invested and never wore the decoration.

Worn out by his continued austerities and above all by the ceaseless stream of visitors who sought his counsel, he died at the age of seventy-three. He was canonized in 1925 and was named patron of the parochial clergy. His cult is now world-wide. Feast: 4 (formerly 9) August.

Sermons edited by M. A. Delaroche (4 vols., 1925); F. Trochu, *Le Curé d'Ars* (1925, Eng. tr. 1927); id., *L'Admirable Vie du Curé d'Ars* (1932, Eng. tr. 1934–6); H. Ghéon, *The Secret of the Curé d'Ars* (1928, Eng. tr. 1929); L. C. Sheppard, *The Curé d'Ars: portrait of a parish priest* (1958); other Lives by M. Trouncer (1959) and D. Pézeril (1959, Eng. tr. 1961); J. G. Genet, *L'Énigme des Sermons du Curé d'Ars* (1961).

VIATRIX, see SIMPLICIUS.

VICELIN (*c.*1086–1154), bishop of Oldenburg in Hostein and apostle of the Wends. Born at Hameln (Hanover) of a wealthy family, he studied at Paderborn (Detmold) and then directed a school at Bremen, becoming a canon there. Ordained priest by *Norbert at Magdeburg, he started his missionary apostolate to the western Wends in 1126. He preached and taught energetically, founded a church at Lübeck, but he had to move from this to Wippendorf (near Bremen) as his patron had died. To ensure permanence for his work, he founded a monastery of Austin Canons at Neumünster (Holstein), which made two foundations later. Obotrite pirates ravaged his churches and monasteries, but Christianity survived and grew. In 1149 Vicelin was appointed bishop of Oldenburg, but became paralysed and died a few years later. He was buried at Neumünster, but his relics were translated to Bordesholm in 1332. Feast: 12 December.

Helmold, 'Chronica Slavorum' in *M.G.H. Scriptores*, xxxii. 89–148; Life by F. Hestermann (1926); *Bibl. SS.*, xii. 1074–5.

VICTOR (1) (d. *c.*290), martyr. He was a soldier who was killed at Marseilles in the persecution of Maximian, having prepared and encouraged the local Christians to face death. He himself, it was claimed, suffered a variety of tortures. From early times his shrine at Marseilles became one of the most important pilgrimage centres of Gaul; his feast was kept in many parts of western

Europe, including England (from the 9th century). He is also depicted on at least two Devonshire screens (Tor Brian and Wolborough), dressed as a soldier, but holding a windmill. Feast: 21 July.

AA.SS. Iul. V (1727), 135–62; H. Delehaye, *Les Origines du culte des martyrs* (1933), 349–50; B.T.A., iii. 157–8.

VICTOR (2) (d. 303), martyr. Known as Victor Maurus, a Moor who was a soldier in the Praetorian Guard, he died for his faith at Milan under Maximian. Many churches, especially in the diocese of Milan, are dedicated to him, but his cult was extended to other centres of western Europe, including England (from the 9th century). Like his namesake of Marseilles, little is known of him, but hagiographers have invented fictitious details. Feast: 8 May.

AA.SS. Maii II (1680), 286–90; *C.M.H.*, pp. 238–254; B.T.A., ii. 250.

VICTORIA, Roman virgin martyr who suffered, according to R.M., under Decius, refusing both to marry her pagan fiancé Eugenius and to sacrifice to the gods. Her unreliable Acts were known to and used by *Aldhelm in his treatises on Virginity. Feast: 23 December.

Propylaeum, p. 597; B.T.A., iv. 599–600.

VIETNAM, MARTYRS OF (also called Martyrs of Indo-China or of Tonkin), died 1745–1862. These comprise a group of 117 martyrs in the three Vietnamese kingdoms of Tonkin, Annam, and Cochin China. They include both Europeans and Asians. There were 8 bishops, 50 priests, and 59 laymen, among whom were catechists and tertiaries. They were beatified in 1900, 1906, 1909, and 1951, and canonized in 1988.

During the first 200 years of Christianity in these parts it is believed that about 100,000 were martyred. Of most of these all historical record has been lost. The earliest martyrs of whom there is substantial documentation are the Spanish Dominicans Francisco Gil and Alonzo Lenziana: of these the first during nine years in prison directed a fruitful apostolate, while the latter, a fugitive for thirteen years, ministered faithfully but furtively to the native Christians. In 1773 two more Dominicans were beheaded, Hyacinth Casteneda, a Spaniard who had evangelized in the Philippines and China for several years before being deported to Vietnam, where he was imprisoned for three years. There he was joined by Vincent Liem, the first Indo-Chinese Dominican to be martyred, who had ministered to his countrymen for fourteen years before he was executed. In 1798 the first Vietnamese diocesan priests, John Dat and Emmanuel Nguyen, also suffered martyrdom.

During the first twenty years of the 19th century Christianity made steady progress, but this was dramatically interrupted by the persecutions under the Annamite kings Minh-Mang (1820–41) and Tu Duc (1847–83). From 1832 Minh excluded all foreign missionaries and ordered Vietnamese Christians to renounce Christianity by trampling on the crucifix: meanwhile churches were to be destroyed and teaching Christianity forbidden. Very many suffered death or extreme hardship. Once again Spanish Dominican bishops, Ignatius Delgado and Dominic Henarez, each of whom had worked for 50 years there, were arrested. The former died of hunger, thirst, and exposure in a cage before he could be beheaded (he was aged seventy-six), while Dominic and his Annamite catechist, Francis Chien, were both executed. Other Vietnamese priests who were martyred included Peter Tuan, Bernard Due, and Joseph Nien; a doctor Joseph Cahn and a tailor Thomas De suffered the same fate. Some of the victims seem to have been induced by drugs to make temporary retractations: others endured fearsome tortures, including cutting off the limbs joint by joint. A group of French missionaries, including Joseph Marchand and Charles Cornay, also suffered: the former, who was captured at Saigon, died (like *Bartholomew) while the flesh was torn from his body with red-hot tongs; the latter who was set up by weapons being buried in the plot of land he cultivated, was imprisoned in a series of cages: being young and endowed with a fine voice, was obliged to sing to his captors. Eventually on 20 September 1837 the sentence of the supreme tribunal 'that he is to be hewn in pieces and that his head, after being exposed for three days, is to be thrown into the river' was accomplished.

Persecutions were revived in 1847 when Christians were suspected of complicity in rebellion, while French and Spanish efforts to protect their nationals caused a xenophobic and anti-Christian ferocity. Once more foreign missionaries and native clergy and laity suffered death for Christianity. The most famous include Théophane *Vénard of the Paris Mission, Augustus Schoffler (from Lorraine), and John Louis Bonnard, who wrote a fine letter of farewell to his family before being executed on 1 May 1852. Also should be mentioned Stephen Cuénot, a bishop who had established three vicariates during twenty-five years' episcopate, was hidden by a pagan during persecution until he had to emerge for water, and died of dysentery just before the edict for his execution arrived.

Christians were marked on their faces with the words *ta dao* (= false religion); husbands were separated from their wives, and children from their parents. Christian villages were destroyed and their possessions distributed. Among those who suffered death in this persecution were Laurence Hung, Paul Lok, and John Hoan (priests), Andrew Nam-Thung (catechist), Michael Ho-Dinh-Hy (official), and Martha Wang, who carried letters from the confessors in prison.

In the persecution under Yu-Duk (1857–62) two more Spanish bishops were killed and a Vietnamese judge, Vincent Tuong, as well as two fishermen, Peter Thuan and Dominic Toai, who along with Peter Dai were burned alive in a bamboo hut. In June 1862 a treaty between France and Annam guaranteed religious freedom. This marked the beginning of the end of the persecutions, some of whose features recall the sufferings of the martyrs in the early ages of Christianity. Feasts: 2 February, 11 July, 6 November.

N.C.E., xiv. 199–9; B.T.A., iii. 77–80 and iv. 282–5.

VIGEAN, see FECHIN.

VIGOR (d. *c.*537), bishop of Bayeux. Born at Artois, Vigor was educated at Arras by *Vedast, became a preaching hermit at Ravière (nr. Bayeux), was ordained priest, and continued missionary work further afield. In 513 he became bishop, and distinguished himself for his assault on idolatry by demolishing a large and famous idol and building a church on the same site. He gave his name to Saint-Vigeur-le-Grand, a town near Bayeux where he founded a monastery; Vigor is also mentioned in the Life of *Paternus. Two ancient churches were dedicated to him in England, doubtless through Norman influence. Feast: 1 November, but often moved to one of the subsequent days owing to the feast of All Saints being also on 1 November.

AA.SS. Nov. I (1887), 287–306; B.T.A., iv. 238–9.

VINCENT OF SARAGOSSA (d. 304), deacon and proto-Martyr of Spain. Vincent, trained by Valerius, bishop of Saragossa, is known almost exclusively through his martyrdom. Of its fact there can be no doubt, but of its manner there is much room for speculation. The earliest witness was Prudentius; while *Augustine said, in a sermon in memory of the martyr, that his cult extended all over the Roman Empire and wherever the name of Christ was known. The Legend is old but not an eye-witness account. According to this, Vincent was a victim of the persecution caused by the edicts of Diocletian and Maximian. First he was imprisoned and weakened by semi-starvation. Then he was commanded to sacrifice, but he refused. Then he was racked, roasted on a gridiron, thrown into prison, and set in stocks. He died as a result of his sufferings.

Relics were claimed by Valencia and Saragossa, Lisbon, Paris, and Le Mans. While his cult in England is ancient, with mention in the OE Martyrology and plenty of pre-Conquest calendars for his usual feast, Abingdon (whose substantial relics of him were acquired in the 12th century by abbot Faricius), graded the feast extremely high with an octave. There are six ancient church dedications to him in England. In art he is often represented as a deacon holding a palm or else suffering the torture of the gridiron. This feature of his passion was afterwards appropriated to *Laurence. Feast: 22 January.

Prudentius, *Peristephanon*, v; Augustine, sermons, pp. 274–7, *P.L.*, xxxviii. 1252–68; Ps-Leo, Sermon XII, *P.L.*, liv. 501–6; *AA.SS.* Jan II (1643), 393–414; L. de Lagger, *S. Vincent de Saragosse* (1927); H. Delehaye, *Les Origines du culte des martyrs* (1933), pp. 367–8; *R.P.S.*; C.S.P.

VINCENT DE PAUL (more correctly Vincent Depaul) (1581–1660), founder of the Vincentian (or Lazarist) Congregation and of the Sisters of Charity. Born of a Gascon peasant family at Ranquine (now called Saint-Vincent-de-Paul, Landes), he was educated by the Franciscans at Dax, then at Toulouse University; he was ordained priest at the very early age of nineteen. It seems that the story of his enslavement at Marseilles, followed by two years in Tunisia with a subsequent escape to Avignon, is legendary. Early in life he was a court chaplain, drawing the revenues of a commendatory abbey until his conversion, occasioned by a false accusation of theft. In 1609 he was associated with Pierre (later cardinal) de Bérulle and became tutor to the children of the Gondi family and in 1617 parish priest of Châtillon-les-Dombes. Throughout his life he combined his apostolate among the rich and fashionable with utter devotion to the poor and oppressed. As chaplain to the Gondi family he was able to improve the lot of prisoners in the galleys and in 1622 gave missions to the convicts at Bordeaux.

In 1625 he founded a congregation of priests, who would live from a community fund, renounce all church preferment, and devote themselves to the faithful in smaller towns and villages. Its purpose was to re-establish a flexible apostolic life among the diocesan clergy. In 1633 they were given the Paris priory church of Saint-Lazare (hence the name Lazarists). In the same year Vincent founded the Sisters of Charity, the first congregation of 'unenclosed' women to be entirely devoted to the poor and the sick. In this he fulfilled the original plan of *Francis de Sales which had been transformed by the Roman Congregations into a more traditional type of religious life. In this venture Vincent was aided by Louise de *Marillac, the first superior; it was an immense success, especially in providing hospital care for the poor.

Even in his lifetime Vincent became a legend. Clergy and laity, rich and poor, outcasts and convicts all experienced the charisma and selfless devotion of a man entirely consumed by the love of God and his neighbour. Rich women collected funds and helped practically in his innumerable good works. He provided abundant alms for war-victims in Lorraine, sent his missionaries to Poland, Ireland, and Scotland (including the Hebrides); from 1643 he was influential at court during the regency of Anne of Austria, who highly esteemed him and valued his advice, except when he tried to persuade her to dismiss Cardinal Mazarin. Amidst all this activity he was sensitive to the dangers of Jansenism, which he actively opposed. He died at the age of nearly eighty and was canonized by Clement XII in 1737. He was most appropriately named by Leo XIII patron of all charitable societies, one of which is the widespread lay confraternity called the Society of St. Vincent de Paul, founded in 1833 by Frederick Ozanam. His congregations are widely diffused and highly esteemed through the English-speaking world, as elsewhere. Feast: formerly 19 July; now 27 September, the day of his death.

AA.SS. Sept. VII (1760), 374; earliest Life by L. Abelly, *La vie du vénérable servant de Dieu, Vincent de Paul* (1664); Letters ed. P. Coste (14 vols., 1920–5); Eng. tr. of selected letters by J.

Leonard, *St. Vincent de Paul and Mental Prayer* (1925), and *The Conferences of St. Vincent de Paul to the Sisters of Charity* (4 vols., 1938–40). Other Lives by P. Coste, *Le grand saint du Grand Siècle* (3 vols., 1932; Eng. tr. 3 vols., 1934–5); by J. Calvet (1948, Eng. tr. 1952), L. von Matt (Bruges 1959, Eng. tr. 1960), M. Purcell (1963). See also H. Bremond, *Hist. Littéraire du sentiment religieux en France*, iii (1921), 222–57.

VINCENT FERRER (1350–1419), Dominican friar. The son of an Englishman who had settled in Spain, Vincent was born at Valencia. He became a Dominican in 1367 and quickly distinguished himself both as a philosopher and a preacher, who had notable success in arousing Christians to repentance and converting Jews, including the Rabbi Paul who became bishop of Cartagena. The Avignonese pope of the Great Schism, Pedro de Luna, also called Benedict XIII, invited him to Avignon, where Vincent advised him without effect to achieve a reconciliation with the Roman Pope Urban VI.

Vincent left to devote himself entirely to preaching, which was to be his life's work. He met with extraordinary success in different parts of France, Spain, and Italy. One biographer said that he came also to England and Scotland. Some of his main topics were sin, the Last Judgement, and Eternity. Vincent's brother was prior of the Grande Chartreuse, which monastery received several notable subjects as a result of his preaching. In Spain he preached in the open air as no church was large enough to hold the crowds; again he converted many Jews.

In 1414 the Council of Constance attempted to end the Schism which had proliferated since 1409 with three, instead of two, claimants to the papal throne. Again Vincent tried to persuade Benedict to abdicate, but again he failed. He did, however, prevail upon Ferdinand, king of Aragon, to withdraw his allegiance. As a consequence Benedict's credibility collapsed and the schism was ultimately healed. The last three years of Vincent's life were spent in France, mainly in Normandy and Brittany. Worn out with his labours, he died at Vannes on 5 April. A spontaneous popular cult arose at once. The fact that most of his preaching had been in the territory of the Avignon obedience did not prevent the Roman Pope Callistus III canonizing him in 1455, the formal Bull being promulgated by Pius II in 1458. This authorized his feast on 6 April, but in fact it has always been held on 5 April.

Canonization Process and Works ed. P. H. D. Fages (1904 and 1909); *AA.SS.* Apr. I (1675), 477–529; M. M. Gorce, *Les bases de l'étude historique de Saint Vincent Ferrer* (1924); id., *Saint Vincent Ferrer* (1935); see also H. Finke in *Romische Quartalschrift*, xxxiii (1925), 150–8; H. Ghéon, *Saint Vincent Ferrier* (1940: Eng. tr. 1939); J. M. de Garganta and V. Forcada, *Biografia y escritos de San Vincente Ferrer* (1956); see also arts in *D.T.C.*, xv (1950), 3033–45 and *Bibl. SS.*, xii (1969), 1168–76.

VIRGIL (Vergil, Ferghil) (d. 784), bishop of Salzburg. An Irish monk, possibly educated by *Samthann, abbess of Colbroney, Virgil in the course of his exile for Christ came to the court of Pippin the Short and soon won his favour. He was sent to the defeated leader of a rising in Bavaria, Duke Odilo, to make peace; Odilo made him abbot of St. Peter's monastery and virtual ruler of the church in Salzburg without his becoming a bishop. The previous abbot of St. Peter's, John, had been appointed by *Boniface, who had a prolonged conflict with Virgil, mentioned in the correspondence to and from Rome. Boniface suspected Virgil, like some other Irish missionaries in the area, of heterodox teaching; probably the conflict between them was basically one of jurisdiction as in the conflict between 'Irish' and 'Romans' in 7th-century England. Virgil's cosmological speculations, also attacked by Boniface, can only be studied in Pope Zacharias's letter, which declared that Virgil would endanger his own (and others') salvation if he persisted in teaching the existence of another world under this one with other men and another sun and moon. It is not entirely clear whether Virgil really taught the existence of the Antipodes or that of the fairy world of Irish folklore.

Some time after Boniface's death (735), Virgil was consecrated bishop of Salzburg. He left a reputation for learning and missionary zeal to the Slavs in Carinthia. He also brought relics of *Brigid and Samthann to Salzburg and had some special interest also in Iona. He is patron of Salzburg and was formally canonized in 1233 (one of the rare Irish Saints to have attained this honour). Feast: 27 November.

Epitaph by Alcuin, *M.G.H.*, *Poetae*, i (1881), 340; Life (written in 12th century) ed. G. H. Pertz, *M.G.H.*, *Scriptores*, xi (1854) 86–95; F. S. Betton, *St. Boniface and St. Virgil* (Benedictine Historical Monographs, 1927); P. Grosjean, 'Virgile de Salzburg en Irlande', *Anal. Boll.*, lxxviii (1960), 92–123; H. Vander Linden, 'Virgile de Salzbourg et les théories cosmographiques au VIIIe siècle', *Bulletins de l'Académie royale de Belgique, Classe des Lettres* (1914), pp. 163–87.

VITALIS, martyr, died at Bologna, 3rd century. This titular saint of the famous basilica at Ravenna and of an early Roman church has been associated with two other martyrs through false identification. *Ambrose and Eusebius, bishop of Bologna, discovered the bodies of two martyrs who were afterwards said to be Vitalis and Agricola, supposedly a Bolognese gentleman and his Christian slave, who instructed him in the faith before they were both put to death. Feast: 27 November in Martyrology of Jerome, but 4 November from the 8th century at Bologna, and later in Roman Martyrology. The other ancient feast of Vitalis is 28 April, which marks the dedication of his church at Rome. This date is recorded by Bede and the OE Martyrology, Florus, and others. Sometimes on this day is found the entry Vitalis and Valeria, which comes from a purely fictitious identification of these two people with the parents of *Gervase and Protase. Valeria has no record outside these unreliable Acts. The casket which once contained her supposed relics is in the British Museum (Waddesdon Bequest).

Propylaeum s.d. 28 April and 27 November: *C.M.H.* on same days. Legends by Pseudo-Ambrose and others in *AA.SS.* Apr. III (1675), 562–5; *AA.SS.* Nov. II (part 1, 1894), 233–53; H. Delehaye, 'L'Hagiographie ancienne de Ravenne', *Anal. Boll.*, xlvii (1929), 5–30; id., 'Trois dates du calendrier romain', *Anal. Boll.*, xlvi (1928), 55–9.

VITUS (Guy), **MODESTUS, AND CRESCENTIA** (d. *c.*303), martyrs. Although the cult of these martyrs is extremely ancient, there has been much confusion over their identity and place of death. It is probable that there were two separate groups of saints: Vitus alone in Lucania (S. Italy) and Vitus, Modestus, and Crescentia in Sicily. What seems certain is that the cult of Vitus alone was the oldest, as in the Gelasian Sacramentary and an early South Italian Gospel book which assigns to his feast a pericope of the Gospel concerning cure from demonic possession and sickness. An ancient church on the Esquiline at Rome was dedicated to him. The Martyrology of *Bede and the OE Martyrology also list Vitus alone. His relics were claimed by Saint-Denis (Paris) and by Corvey (Saxony). He was invoked as the patron of those who suffered from epilepsy and nervous diseases, including St. Vitus's Dance (= Sydenham's chorea), and from the bites of mad dogs and snakes. By transference from 'St. Vitus's Dance' he is also the patron of dancers and actors; he was reckoned in Germany among the *Fourteen Holy Helpers. Modestus and Crescentia came to be attached to Vitus because their fictitious Acts made them his tutor and nurse respectively, responsible for his Christian education. Most of the medieval abbeys in England celebrated Vitus and Modestus without Crescentia, but five of them added her name (as did Sarum and *R.M.*) on their usual day: 15 June.

AA.SS. Iun. II (1698), 1013–42 and *C.M.H.*, pp. 319–20; B.T.A., iii. 545–6.

VLADIMIR (955–1015) prince of Kiev. Scandinavian in origin, a great-grandson of Rurik, traditional founder of the Russian state, Vladimir was brought up in the pagan Viking religion and before his baptism freely indulged in the violence, brutality, and lust often regarded (not least by the contemporary Arab chronicler Ibn-Foslan) as characteristic of the Varangians. He became Prince of Novgorod in 970; he had to flee to Scandinavia in 972 in the revolt of his brothers; but he soon returned victorious and consolidated his position as ruler of Kievan Russia by 980. In return for military aid from Byzantium he was converted in 989 and married Anne, daughter of the emperor, Basil II. The political and economic advantages of this marriage did not cancel his whole-hearted commitment to Christianity. He put away former wives and mistresses, he destroyed idols and supported the Greek missionaries who evangelized his people. Indeed, he sometimes tried to impose Christianity by force, but not all his people accepted it. It seems probable that the first converts were nobles and merchants and that, as elsewhere, Christianity penetrated slowly both in geographical and social terms. Kiev soon became a metropolitan see.

He was reluctant after his conversion to put to death murderers and robbers and was notable for lavish almsgiving, a practice hitherto unknown. He died on an expedition against one of his sons; before it he was reputed to have given away all his personal belongings. He and his successors fostered close relations with the Church in the West. His posthumous reputation was helped by a cycle of heroic poems; with his grandmother *Olga he was regarded as the Christian pioneer of all Russia. One of his descendants, Waldemar, king of Novgorod, married Gytha, the daughter of Harold II, king of England. Feast: 15 July.

S. H. Cross and O. P. Sherbovitz-Wetzor, *The Russian Primary Chronicle* (1953); N. de Baumgarten, *Saint Vladimir et la conversion de la Russie* (Orientalia Christiana, 1932); F. Dvornik, *The Making of Central and Eastern Europe* (1949); B.T.A., iii. 110–11; *Bibl. SS.*, xii. 1323–9; *N.C.E.*, xiv. 734–5.

VULMAR, see WULMAR.

W

WALARIC (Waleric, Valery) (d. 620), abbot. Details of his early life are uncertain: he was born in Auvergne of a peasant family; he learnt to read early in life; dissatisfied with his usual occupation of tending sheep, he became a monk to Autumo. Later he moved to the monastery of *Germanus near Auxerre and thence to Luxeuil under *Columbanus. Here he settled down and so distinguished himself at horticulture that the preservation of his vegetables and fruit against insects which destroyed most of the other crops was regarded as miraculous.

When King Theodoric expelled Columbanus with his Irish and Breton monks, Walaric with a monk called Waldolanus preached for a time very successfully in Neustria, but again he left this way of life and settled as a hermit near the mouth of the Somme. Here disciples gathered round him, so he became virtual founder of the monastery of Leuconaus, built by his successor Blitmund and later called Saint-Valéry-sur-Somme. He is also reputed to have evangelized the Pas-de-Calais area.

When Walaric died, cures were claimed at his tomb and a cult developed. This eventually spread to England through the Norman Conquest. William the Conqueror had his relics exposed for public veneration; he was invoked to provide a favourable wind for the expedition of 1066 which sailed from Saint-Valéry. Chester abbey kept his feasts on 1 April (with Croyland) and 12 December (translation). This latter might possibly commemorate the transfer of his relics by King Richard I to the Norman town of Saint-Valéry-en-Caux. His original abbey, however, later recovered them. A 12th-century chapel at Alnmouth was dedicated to Walaric, who also left his name in at least one village, Hinton Waldrist (Oxon.) which was held by Thomas de S. Walaric (Saint-Valéry) in the 12th century. Feast: 1 April; translation, 12 December.

AA.SS. Apr. I (1675), 14–30 and *Propylaeum*, pp. 120–1; 11th-century Life attributed wrongly to Raginbertus, ed. B. Krusch in *M.G.H.*, *Scriptores rerum merov.*, iv. 157–75; C. Brunel, 'Les actes faux de l'abbaye de Saint-Valéry', *Le Moyen Âge* (1909), pp. 94–116, 179–96; B.T.A., ii. 2–3.

WALBURGA (Walpurgis, Vaubourg) (d. 779), abbess of Heidenheim. The sister of *Winnibald and *Willibald, she was a notable example of the Anglo-Saxon monks and nuns who helped *Boniface in his missionary work in Germany. She was trained under Tatta at the double monastery of Wimborne (Dorset) from which she was sent to *Lioba, abbess of Bischofsheim. After two years there, now skilled in medicine, she became abbess of the double monastery of Heidenheim, established by Winnibald as the only known example of its kind in Germany: on his death she assumed full control. Owing to the lack of any contemporary biography practically nothing is known about her rule.

In 776 the relics of Winnibald were translated to Eichstatt; in 870 hers were laid to rest beside them. From the rock around her tomb medicinal oil flowed, to which miraculous cures were attributed. In 893 her relics were inspected and diffused, some to the Rhineland, others to Flanders, others to France. This spread her cult to these countries. One important centre was Attigny, where Charles the Simple established a shrine in his palace chapel and named her patron of his kingdom. Her feast of 1 May inappropriately coincided with a pagan feast for the beginning of summer and the revels of witches, whence the customs of Walpurgisnacht, which have no intrinsic connection with the saint. It is, however, not impossible that the protection of crops ascribed to her and represented by the three ears of corn in her images may have been transferred to her from Mother Earth (Walborg). Her more usual attributes are a crown and sceptre with a phial of oil. This still flows from her tomb. A modern abbess of Eichstatt was sufficiently important to be chosen to negotiate the surrender of the town to the Americans at the end of the last war. Her main feast is 25 February, translation feasts are 1 May, 12 October (Eichstatt), and 24 September (Zutphen).

AA.SS. Feb. III (1658), 511–72; W. Levison, *England and the Continent in the Eighth Century* (1956), pp. 79–81; M. Coens, 'Le séjour légendaire de sainte Walburge à Anvers d'après son office à la collégiale de Zutphen', *Anal. Boll.*, lxxx (1962), 345–60; F. M. Steele, *The Life of St. Walburga* (1921); B.T.A., i. 415–16; *Bibl. SS.*, xii. 876–7.

WALDEF (1) (Waltheof) (d. 1076), count of Northampton and Huntingdon. The son of Siward, earl of Northumbria, Waldef fought with distinction against the Normans both in 1066 and at the siege of York a few years later; but was pardoned by William the Conqueror, restored to his lands and given William's niece Judith in marriage. In 1075 he was involved in the rebellion of the Earls which was frustrated by the loyalty of *Wulfstan and Odo of Bayeux. Waldef revealed all to Lanfranc, on whose advice he went to Normandy and threw himself on the king's mercy. William, however, was not disposed to be merciful a second time: Waldef was imprisoned for a year and then beheaded for treason at Winchester. A fortnight later his body was buried in the chapter-house at Croyland (Lincs.), of which he was a notable benefactor.

There a cult grew up with strongly nationalist and political overtones: to Normans he was a traitor, to Anglo-Saxons a martyr. In 1092 his relics were translated to the church. The incorruption of his body was claimed, miraculous cures were reported on patients from the East Midlands, and a Norman monk who derided him was struck with sudden death. The Croyland tradition emphasized his regard for the Church, his repentance in prison, the faithlessness of his wife, the trickery which caused his involvement in the plot, and the story that he died reciting the Lord's Prayer, of which his severed head uttered the last petition. William of Malmesbury, though impressed by the miracles, was reserved about the cult: 'Our own times have found someone to declare a martyr . . . I hope it is not contrary to the truth.' The cult obtained local, but never national support: the feast of his beheading (*Decollatio*) was celebrated at Croyland on 31 August.

F. Michel (ed.), 'Vita et Passio Waldevi Comitis', *Chroniques Anglo-Normandes*, ii (1836), 111–23 with Miracles, ibid., 131–42; also in J. A. Giles, *Vitae quorumdam Anglo-Saxonum* (1854); Ordericus Vitalis, *Hist. Eccles.* (ed. Le Prévost), ii. 260–7, 287–9; *G.P.*, p. 321; F. S. Scott, 'Earl Waltheof of Northumbria', *Arch. Ael.*, xxx (1952), 149–213.

WALDEF (2) (Waltheof, Walden, Wallevus) (*c.*1100–60), Cistercian abbot of Melrose. Grandson of the Northumbrian patriot *Waldef and son of Simon, earl of Huntingdon, after whose death his mother Maud married *David I, king of Scotland, Waldef was brought up with *Ailred at the Scottish court. There he could have followed the life of a court cleric; instead, he became an Austin canon at Nostell (Yorks.) *c.*1130. In 1134 he was chosen as prior of Kirkham, recently founded, like Rievaulx, by Walter Espec. In 1140 Waldef was chosen by the canons of York as archbishop in succession to Thurstan, but King Stephen quashed the election because of Waldef's known Scottish sympathies. Strongly attracted to Cistercian ideals, Waldef tried to unite his community of Kirkham *en bloc* with Rievaulx, but met with effective opposition. The plan was not accepted; so Waldef became a Cistercian at Waldron (Beds.). The canons put every obstacle in his way; he also found the life very austere. But he persevered as a Cistercian and moved to Rievaulx, where Ailred had been elected abbot in 1148. In 1149 Waldef became abbot of Melrose, in succession to a man of ungovernable temper. He won his community by humility, simplicity, and kindness, preferring, with *Maieul of Cluny, to be damned for excessive mercy rather than for excessive justice. With the help of David he founded monasteries at Cultram and Kinross.

In 1159 he was elected bishop of St. Andrews, but refused the office because he realized that death was near. He was buried in the chapter house at Melrose. In 1207 his body was found to be incorrupt and was translated. In 1240 it was again translated, but this time it was no longer incorrupt. Waldef was never formally canonized but a popular cult continued until the Reformation. During his life many wonders had been recounted of him: Eucharistic visions of Christ in the form appropriate to the feasts of Christmas, Passiontide, and the Resurrection; visions of Heaven and Hell; miracles of multiplying food. Like other Cistercians such as Ailred and *Robert of Newminster, Waldef was more attractive in character than many monastic reformers. Feast: 3 August.

AA.SS. Aug. I (1733), 249–78 (abridged in *N.L.A.*, ii. 406–11); G. MacFadden, 'The Life of Waldef and its author, Jocelin of Furness', *Innes Review*, vi (1955), 5–13; J. B. Bulloch, 'Saint Waltheof', *Records of the Scottish Church History Society*, xi (1952), 105–32; D. H. Farmer, 'A Letter of St. Waldef of Melrose', *Analecta Monastica*, v (1958), 91–101; F. M. Powicke (ed.), *Life of Ailred of Rievaulx* (1950), pp. lxxi–lxxv; D. Baker, 'Legend and Reality: the case of Waldef of Melrose', *Studies in Church History*, xli (1975), 59–82.

WALL, John (alias Marsh) (1620–79), Franciscan priest and martyr. Born at Chingle Hall (Lancs.), the son of William Wall, a Norfolk recusant, John Wall was educated at the English College, Douai (1633–41), and at the English College, Rome (1642–5), where he was ordained priest. He returned to England in 1648, staying on his way at Douai at the friary of St. Bonaventure, where in 1651 he joined the Franciscan Order. In 1656 he returned to England, using the name Marsh, and worked for twenty-three years mainly in Warwickshire, based on Harvington Hall, which belonged to the Talbot family. In the anti-Catholic reaction caused by the 'Popish Plot' priests were sentenced to banishment, but Wall defied the proclamation. He was arrested at Rushock Court (Hereford and Worcester) and imprisoned at Worcester Castle, where he reconciled a number of prisoners to the Church of Rome. He was examined by the Privy Council and by Titus Oates, imprisoned at Newgate, and sent back to Worcester. Here on 17 August 1679 he was condemned, not for any involvement in a real or alleged plot, but simply for the fact of his priesthood. He was executed there five days later. In 1970 he was canonized by Paul VI as one of the *Forty Martyrs of England and Wales. Feast: 25 October.

R. Challoner, *Memoirs of Missionary Priests* (ed. J. H. Pollen, 1928), pp. 550–5; F. Davey, *Blessed John Wall* (pamphlet, 1961).

WALLEVUS, see WALDEF (2).

WALPOLE, Henry (1558–95), Jesuit, priest and martyr. Born at Docking (Norfolk), Walpole was educated at Norwich Grammar school, at Peterhouse, Cambridge, and at Gray's Inn. He is said to have joined the R.C. Church as a consequence of the martyrdom of Edmund *Campion, in whose honour he wrote and secretly printed a long narrative poem. He entered the English College, Rome, in 1583, but joined the Society of Jesus in 1584. In spite of poor health he was ordained priest at Paris in 1588, served as chaplain to the Spanish army in the Netherlands, and then taught in the English seminaries of Seville and Valladolid. From King Philip II of Spain he obtained a charter which authorized the establishment of the English College at Saint-Omer. In 1593 he returned to England, landing at Bridlington on 6 December, but was arrested the very next day at Kelham on suspicion of being a priest.

He was interrogated at York, transferred to the Tower of London where he was tortured fourteen times in two months, and as a result lost the use of his fingers. Indicted at York under the Act of 27 Elizabeth which made it high treason for an Englishman ordained abroad to minister in England, he was condemned to death. His plea that he was arrested before the thirty-six hours grace allowed by the Statute had elapsed was not allowed and he was executed at York on 7 April. He was canonized by Paul VI in 1970 as one of the *Forty Martyrs of England and Wales. Feast: 25 October.

A. Jessopp, *One Generation of a Norfolk House* (1879); P. Caraman, *Henry Garnet* (1964); J. Gerard, *Autobiography of a Hunted Priest* (ed. P. Caraman, 1952); *Documents relating to the English Martyrs* (Catholic Record Society, vol. v).

WALPURGIS, see WALBURGA.

WALSTAN OF BAWBURGH (date uncertain), confessor. This local saint of Norfolk, almost unknown elsewhere, is not mentioned in any known liturgical document, but there is plenty of evidence for an unofficial cult of some importance; both a Latin and an English Life survive. The former was written on a wooden triptych covered with vellum which hung over his shrine in the church of Bawburgh, near Norwich. As well as the vicar there were six chantry priests; the offerings at the shrine were so large that they paid for rebuilding the chancel in 1309 and were mainly due to the farmers and labourers of Norfolk who came once a year on 30 May to obtain a blessing on themselves and on their animals. The north chapel, which contained the shrine, was demolished at the Reformation. Bale recorded then that 'All mowers and sythe followers seek him once in the year.'

The Legend says he was born at Blythburgh, the son of a prince, but at an early age he left home and travelled north to dedicate himself to the poverty of the Gospel through seeking employment as a farm labourer. He took service with a farmer who was so pleased with him that he wished to make him his heir. Walstan refused, but asked instead for a cow in calf. This was given him; two calves were born and they eventually took his dead body to Bawburgh church, passing through a solid wall and leaving visible cart-tracks on the surface of the ford near Costessey. Walstan had died in a field, praying for all the sick and for cattle. The date given for his death is 1016, but this is incompatible with the claimed presence of the bishop and monks of Norwich at his funeral. There are various folkloric elements, especially in the English Life, which was written in verse in the late 15th century.

Whether or not Walstan really existed, his cult is interesting as an example of veneration by humble folk of one who shared the same round of agricultural pursuits as themselves and had attained sanctity in doing so. But the writers of the Lives could not resist the temptation of giving him an aristocratic pedigree and of bringing the bishop and monks to his funeral. Paintings of Walstan survive on at least five Norfolk screens; he is depicted crowned or with a sceptre, holding a scythe and sometimes accompanied by two calves.

M. R. James, 'Lives of St. Walstan', *Norfolk Archaeol. Soc. Papers*, xix (1917), 238–67; *N.L.A.*, ii. 412–15; F. Husenbeth, *Life of St. Walstan* (1859).

WALTER OF COWICK (Devon) (12th century), Benedictine monk. He is mentioned as a saint both by *C.S.P.* (ii) and by William Worcestre, from which two sources it may be inferred that he was born in Norwich, became a monk of the Order at Bec in Normandy, but led the religious life at Cowick, half a mile from Exeter, and was 'canonized'. *C.S.P.* adds that 'he was in Purgatory alive and saw the places of punishment; afterwards he wore a goatskin for the rest of his life'. Neither gives a date of any kind. Bec was founded in the 11th century and Cowick, founded *c.*1144 and dependent on Bec, was transferred to Tavistock in 1464, having presumably become denizenized under Henry V like the other alien priories. It is possible but unlikely that Walter was the object of a liturgical cult before the papal reserve of canonization became effective; it is more probable that William Worcestre is referring to canonization in a non-technical way and that he is simply recording the existence of a popular, unofficial cult.

C.S.P. (ii); William Worcestre, pp. 124–5; N. Orme, 'St. Walter of Cowick', *Anal. Boll.*, cviii (1990), 387–93.

WALTHEOF, see WALDEF (2).

WANDRILLE (Wandregisilus) (*c.*600–68), abbot. Born near Verdun, he was brought up at the Austrasian court and got married. But in 628 he and his wife separated by mutual consent to devote themselves to the monastic life. Wandrille was trained as a monk by St. Baudry at Montfaucon; afterwards he lived in complete solitude in a log hut near Saint-Ursanne in the Jura. His regime was basically that of the monks of *Colombanus, whose monastery at Bobbio he joined for a time. After this he spent ten years in the abbey of Romain-Moûtier and was ordained priest by *Ouen, bishop of Rouen. He finally settled at Fontenelle (Normandy), where he founded his own monastery. This, as a centre of asceticism, education, and agriculture, had considerable local influence. Its church was consecrated in 657; the place came to be called Saint-Wandrille.

Some time after his death the Rule of St. Benedict was adopted and for many centuries the abbey flourished. His relics were removed during the Viking invasions to Étaples, Chartres, Boulogne, and Mont-Blandin (Ghent). Through the latter centre his feast became known and was celebrated in southern England before the Norman Conquest. His abbey had at least three cells in England, the most important being Ecclesfield (South Yorkshire) and Upavon (Wilts.). His feast spread to other English centres, including York and Hereford.

A fine illustrated Life of Wandrille (11th century) survives at Saint-Omer; at least some of his relics were recovered by his abbey, which flourishes today. Feast: 22 July; translation, 3 March.

AA.SS. Iul. V (1727), 253–302; B. Krusch also edited the earliest Life in *M.G.H.*, *Scriptores rerum merov.*, v. 1–24; F. Lohier and J. Laporte, *Gesta sanctorum patrum Fontanellensis coenobii* (1936); *E.B.K. before 1100*, s.d.

WANNARD (Weonard, Wanner, Gwennarth) (date unknown). He was a Celtic monastic saint, possibly connected with *Dyfrig. He is the patron of St. Weonards (near Hereford) and probably of Llanwenarth (Gwent). He was depicted in a stained-glass window (now lost) of St. Weonards church as a bearded old man holding a book in one hand and an axe in the other and described as S. Wenardus Heremyta. There is no known feast.

T. Blount, *History of Herefordshire* (MS. in Hereford County Library, p. 230).

WARD, Margaret (d. 1588), martyr. Born at Congleton, Cheshire at an unknown date, she went into service from an early age, mainly with the Whittle family in London. She is known principally for her share in the escape of the priest William Watson from the Bridewell prison, accomplished through her smuggling a rope into his cell. Although injured by his fall from the roof, he got away, but the rope was traced to Margaret, who was soon arrested. She was severely tortured but refused to reveal Watson's hiding-place. She also rejected an offer of freedom as the price of conforming to the Church of England. She was tried at the Old Bailey on 29 August and was executed the next day, together with one priest and four laymen. Margaret Ward was canonized by Paul VI in 1970 as one of the *Forty Martyrs of England and Wales. Feast: 25 October.

Documents relating to the English Martyrs (Catholic Record Society, vol. v); L. E. Whatmore, *Blessed Margaret Ward* (pamphlet, 1961).

WEBSTER, Augustine (d. 1535), Carthusian monk and martyr. He became a monk at the Charterhouse of Sheen (the largest in England, founded in 1414), and soon after his profession was appointed prior of Axholme (Lincs.). In February 1535 he was on a visit to the London Charterhouse with his fellow prior, Robert *Lawrence of Beauvale to consult the prior of London,

John *Houghton about the attitude to be taken by the Carthusians with regard to the religious policies of Henry VIII, soon to be imposed on the country and consequently on all the religious, including monks. After the three priors' visit to Cromwell, their fate was exactly the same. Together they suffered martyrdom at Tyburn on 4 May and all three are among the *Forty Martyrs of England and Wales canonized by Paul VI in 1970. Feast: 25 October.

For further information and bibliography see Houghton John.

WELLS, Swithun (1536–91), martyr. Born at Bambridge (Hants) of a wealthy country family, Swithun Wells, a well-educated and travelled man, who was also poet, musician, and sportsman, lived a quiet country life until middle age. At one time he was tutor to the household of the earl of Southampton, later he married and founded his own school at Monkton Farleigh (Wilts.). In 1582 he came under suspicion for his popish sympathies and gave up his school. He actively supported priests, organizing their often dangerous journeys from one safe and friendly house to another. He and his wife, although they were impoverished, moved to Gray's Inn Fields in 1586 and made their house a centre of hospitality to recusants. Wells was twice arrested and interrogated, but released for lack of evidence. But in 1591 two priests, Edmund *Gennings and Polydore *Plasden, were arrested in his house while saying Mass. They were accused of high treason and later executed: Swithun Wells and his wife were both accused of harbouring priests and were also condemned to death. Mrs. Wells, who had given the priests hospitality, was reprieved but spent the remaining ten years of her life in prison; but Swithun Wells, who had been absent when the priests arrived, was executed at Gray's Inn Fields on 10 December. He used his last minutes of life praying for his executioners and expressing his forgiveness. He was canonized by Paul VI in 1970 as one of the *Forty Martyrs of England and Wales. Feast: 25 October.

R. Challoner, *Memoirs of Missionary Priests* (ed. J. H. Pollen, 1928), pp. 169–85; J. H. Pollen, *Acts of English Martyrs* (1891), pp. 98–127; *Documents relating to the English Martyrs* (Catholic Record Society), v. 131–3, 204–8.

WEM, see Gwen.

WENCESLAS (Wenzel) (907–29), duke of Bohemia and martyr. The son of Duke Wratislaw, Wenceslas was educated mainly by his grandmother Ludmilla, a devoted Christian, and became duke in 922. He often followed the advice of the clergy and worked for the religious and educational improvement of his people. This implied greater contact with the rest of the Christian world, particularly the German Empire, whose king, Henry the Fowler, Wenceslas recognized both as the successor of Charlemagne and as his own overlord. This policy, together with a pagan reaction against a determined Christian king, led to the death of Wenceslas at the hands of his brother's followers. Boleslav, his brother, who was implicated in his murder, nevertheless had the relics of Wenceslas translated to the church of St. *Vitus in Prague, where they became the centre of the cult and a place of pilgrimage. His feast was celebrated from 985; within another twenty or thirty years he became Bohemia's patron saint, his picture was engraved on the coins and the Crown of Wenceslas was regarded as a symbol of Czech nationalism and independence. Later, a series of wall paintings at the castle of Karlstein underlined his national as well as his religious importance.

There was no ancient cult of him in England, but his feast came in with the Roman Missal. J. M. Neale's famous carol 'Good King Wenceslas' made him a household word, but its contents are not based on any known incident in the saint's life; by its re-use of a 13th-century spring carol 'Tempus adest floridum' it successfully popularized Christian and Victorian ideals of social benevolence and practical almsgiving. Feast: 28 September.

AA.SS. Sept. VII (1760), 770–844 with *Propylaeum*, pp. 421–2; and P. Peeters in *Anal. Boll.*, xlviii (1930), 218–21; see also P. Devos, 'Le dossier de S. Wenceslas dans un manuscrit du XIIIe siècle', *Anal. Boll.*, lxxii (1964), 87–131; C. Parrott, 'St. Wenceslas of Bohemia', *History Today*, xvi (1966), 225–33; F. Dvornik, *St. Wenceslas* (Eng. tr. 1929); R. Turek and V. Rynes, 'Venceslao' in *Bibl. SS.*, xii. 991–1000.

WENDREDA (date unknown), obscure Anglo-Saxon female saint. She was presumably the foundress of a nunnery at March (Cambs.), where a 14th-century church (with magnificent angel-roof) is dedicated to her. This stood on the site of the Anglo-Saxon church. Wendreda's relics were removed by Elsin, abbot of Ely, in the 10th century to his own church, where they were enshrined in gold. Later, the story goes, these relics were carried into battle against Cnut at Ashingdon (1016), who captured them and later gave them to Canterbury. No trace has been found of a liturgical cult.

Liber Eliensis (ed. E. O. Blake, *C.S.* 1962), pp. 145–8.

WENEFRED, see WINEFRIDE.

WENNAP (Veep), obscure Cornish saint, eponym of the parish of Gwennap, also called in ancient deeds Lanwenep, i.e. the monastery of Wenep. The list of the children of *Brychan in the Life of *Nectan mentions one called Wynup, who has been identified unconvincingly with Wennap. His identity remains a mystery; there is no known feast.

G. H. Doble, *The Saints of Cornwall*, iii (1964), p. 139.

WENZEL, see WENCESLAS.

WEONARD, see WANNARD.

WERA, see WIRO.

WERBURGA (Werbyrgh) (d. *c.*700), abbess. Traditionally the daughter of Wulfhere, king of Mercia and his wife *Ermengild, Werburgh after her father's death became a nun at Ely under *Etheldreda, and possibly succeeded her mother as abbess. King Ethelred of Mercia, her uncle, recalled her to his kingdom and gave her charge of some nunneries in the Midlands. These, founded or reformed by her, included Weedon (Northants.), Hanbury (Staffs.), and Threckingham (Lincs.) where she died. She was buried at her own request at Hanbury, but her relics were translated to Chester in the late 9th or early 10th century, because of the danger from Danish armies. Another translation, at Chester in 1095, was the occasion for Goscelin writing her Life. Her shrine was a centre of pilgrimage until the Reformation; part of its stone base survives. There are twelve ancient English churches dedicated to her, including Hanbury and Chester. Her main emblem in art is a goose, which (in Goscelin's Life) she was supposed to have restored to life. This incident, however, is borrowed from the same writer's Life of the Flemish saint Amelburga. Feast: 3 February, translation (at Chester) 21 June.

The basic information is in Florence of Worcester, i. 32, amplified by the Ely tradition in *Liber Eliensis* (ed. E. O. Blake, *C.S.*, 1962) and later by Goscelin, for which see *AA.SS.* Feb. I (1658), 386–94; C. Horstman, *Henry Bradshaw's Life of St. Werburghe* (E.E.T.S., 1887); J. Tait, *The Chartulary or Register of the Abbey of St. Werburgh, Chester* I (Chetham Soc. vol. 79, 1920), pp. vii–xiv; see also H. P. R. Finberg, *The Early Charters of the West Midlands* (1961), and P. Grosjean, 'Codicis Gothani appendix,' *Anal. Boll.*, lviii (1940), 183–7; B.T.A., i. 241–2.

WHITE, Eustace (d. 1591), seminary priest and martyr. Born at Louth (Lincs.) of a well-known Protestant family, White joined the R.C. Church in 1584 and entered the English College, Rome, in 1586. He was ordained priest in 1589 and returned to England the same year to minister to Catholics in the West Country. He was arrested almost immediately at Blandford (Dorset), was imprisoned in the Bridewell, interrogated, and tortured. He was condemned to death for his priesthood and executed at Tyburn with Edmund *Gennings and others on 10 December. He was canonized by Paul VI in 1970 as one of the *Forty Martyrs of England and Wales. Feast: 25 October.

R. Challoner, *Memoirs of Missionary Priests* (ed. J. H. Pollen, 1928), pp. 169–85; *N.C.E.*, s.v.

WHYTE (White, Wite, Witta, Candida), female saint who gave her name to, and is buried at, Whitchurch Canonicorum (Dorset); her modest shrine, together with that of *Edward the Confessor at Westminster, are the only ones to survive intact in this country to this day. Various theories about her identity have been advanced: (1) that she was a West Saxon of whom no other record survives, (2) that she was a Welsh saint Gwen, whose relics were given by King Athelstan to this church, (3) that Whyte was a man, Albinus, bishop of Buraburg or a companion of *Boniface, martyred with him and then translated back to Wessex. William Worcestre and John Gerard both mentioned her relics: Thomas *More ironically referred to the custom of offering cakes or cheese to the saint on her feast, which was probably confined to this church alone. In 1900 her leaden coffin was opened. It was inscribed *Hic requiescunt reliquie sancte Wite*: the badly damaged reliquary contained the bones of a small woman, aged about forty. Feast: 1 June.

William Worcestre, pp. 73, 123; John Gerard, *Autobiography* (1950), p. 50; Baring-Gould and Fisher, ii. 68–9; B.T.A., ii. 438–9.

WIGBERT (d. *c*.738), abbot. English by birth, Wigbert was one of *Boniface's many English helpers in the evangelization of Germany. He became abbot of Fritzlar, near Cassel, where his most famous disciple was Sturm, the future abbot of Fulda. He also founded the monastery of Ohrdruf (Thuringia), but he died at Fritzlar. In 774 during the Saxon wars, his relics were translated to Buraburg and then to Hersfeld, whose patron he thus became. Feast: 13 August.

Life by Lupus, *Vita Wigberti* (ed. C. Holder-Egger), *M.G.H.*, *Scriptores*, xv. 37–43; W. Levison, *England and the Continent in the Eighth Century* (1946), pp. 76–9, 235–6; B.T.A., iii. 322.

WIGSTAN, see WISTAN.

WILFRID (Wilfrith) (*c*.633–709), bishop. Born in Northumbria, the son of a nobleman closely connected with the court, he was educated at Lindisfarne, the principal centre of Irish culture in the North. Dissatisfied, apparently with its insularity, but encouraged both by the queen, *Enfleda, and some of the monks, he went to Canterbury and then to Rome (653), where he studied under the archdeacon Boniface both Scripture and Canon Law. On his way back, he spent three years at Lyons, where he had previously been tonsured and had refused an offer of marriage. On his return to England, he became abbot of Ripon at the invitation of the sub-king Alcfrith. Here he introduced the Rule of St. Benedict and adopted the Roman (or Western) method of calculating Easter, introduced by Kentish missionaries like *Paulinus, but rejected by *Aidan and *Colman of Lindisfarne. At the Synod of Whitby (663/4) he became the articulate leader of the case for the Roman Easter calculation; his trenchant exposition won the day against the Iona system, which had been abandoned by the southern Irish some years before.

He was now chosen as bishop by Alcfrith; in the current dearth of respectable bishops in England, he went to France to receive episcopal consecration by twelve Frankish bishops at Compiègne. But he stayed there too long and found on his return in 666 that Alcfrith was dead (or exiled), and that his own place at York had been taken by *Chad, nominated by King Oswiu but dubiously consecrated. Wilfrid retired to Ripon, but was fully reinstated by *Theodore in 669. The years which followed were externally the most successful of his life. He enjoyed the favour of King Egfrith and his wife *Etheldreda; he obtained large endowments of land for his churches, especially Hexham, where he built a monastery and a church reckoned to be the finest north of the Alps; he adopted a life-style based on that of the Frankish bishops, with a large household, numerous retainers, and extensive patronage; he presided over a diocese co-terminous with the kingdom of Northumbria, extending from the Wash to the Forth at the time of its greatest expansion, with York as its centre. But this did not last. Wilfrid encouraged Queen Etheldreda to separate from her husband and become a nun in 672, while his power and wealth were the target of adverse criticism. In close collaboration with King Egfrith, Theodore in 678–81 divided the Northumbrian diocese into four over Wilfrid's head and without his consent. The substance of the decision was reasonable, but not the way it was executed. Wilfrid felt that he had been virtually deposed, quite unjustly and for no canonical cause; so, like many bishops from other parts of Christendom before him, he appealed to Rome for restoration. In doing so, he made history, as he was the first Anglo-Saxon to make such an appeal. On his way to Rome, he spent a year preaching in Frisia; by this example and later encouragement of disciples, he began the influential Anglo-Saxon Christian mission on the Continent.

The papacy, who had appointed Theodore to Canterbury, nevertheless ruled in favour of Wilfrid's restoration. But King Egfrith refused to obey it and imprisoned Wilfrid, only releasing him on condition that he left the kingdom. Wilfrid went to Sussex, the last stronghold of paganism in Anglo-Saxon England, preached there and in the Isle of Wight, and founded a monastery at Selsey. In 686 he was reinstated in Northumbria, but with reduced jurisdiction, by Theodore, and there he remained until 691. But a series of disputes broke out with the new king of Northumbria, Aldfrith, concerning endowments and the status of Ripon; Wilfrid retired to Mercia, where he acted as bishop in the Leicester area, and founded several monasteries. Their identification is not certain; but it seems that Peterborough, Brixworth, Evesham, and Wing all have some claim to be his foundations.

In 703 a synod of Austerfield (West Yorkshire), presided over by Bertwald, archbishop of Canterbury, decreed that he should resign his see of York, accept virtual deposition and confinement, and give up his monasteries. Once again, after an eloquent defence of his achievements, he appealed to the papacy; once again he was vindicated. His prolonged exile, widely believed to be unjust, was ended in 705 with a compromise at the Synod of the River Nidd. There he agreed to leave *John of Beverley as bishop of York, but he resumed full episcopal control of the diocese of Hexham and of his monasteries in various parts of the country in accordance with the papal privileges he had obtained for them. A few years later he died, aged seventy-six, at his monastery at or near Oundle (Northants), having bequeathed his considerable fortune to four causes: offerings to Roman churches, to the poor, to his followers who had shared his exile, and to his abbots 'so that they could purchase the friendship of kings and bishops'. He believed that this would be the best way to secure the monasteries' continuity.

The cult of Wilfrid was centred on Ripon, where he was buried, and on Hexham, where his disciple *Acca succeeded him as bishop and abbot. His widespread apostolate, and the translation of his relics, it was claimed, to both Canterbury and Worcester in the 10th century by *Oda and *Oswald respectively, led to a further diffusion of his cult, which became nationwide. Forty-eight ancient churches were dedicated to him. In art he is represented either preaching to, and baptizing the pagans, or else as a fully robed bishop with pastoral staff. The crypts of his churches at Hexham and Ripon survive.

As an apostolic pioneer, a monastic founder, a builder of churches and patron of art, and as a person of remarkable fortitude and persistence, inspired by grandiose ideals and imaginative vision, he deserves to be considered one of the most important men of the OE Church. Feast: 12 October; translation, 24 April.

B. Colgrave (ed.). *Eddius Stephanus' Life of St. Wilfrid* (1927); also ed. W. Levison, *M.G.H., Scriptores rerum merov.*, vi. 163–263 and J. F. Webb and D. H. Farmer (ed.), *The Age of Bede* (1983); Bede, *H.E.*, iii. 25, iv. 2, 12–16, 19, 23, v. 19; later Lives in A. Campbell, *Frithegodii Breviloquium* (1950) and J. Raine (ed.), *Historians of the Church of York* (*R.S.* 1879), vol. I. D. P. Kirby (ed.), *St. Wilfrid at Hexham* (1973), M. Gibbs, 'The Decrees of Agatho and the Gregorian Plan for York', *Speculum*, xviii (1973), 213–46; E. D. C.

Jackson and E. G. M. Fletcher, 'Excavations at Brixworth, 1958', *J.B.A.A.*, xxiv (1961), 1–15 and id., 'The Apse and Nave at Wing, Buckinghamshire', ibid., xxv (1962), 1–20. See also F. M. Stenton, *Anglo-Saxon England* (1946), pp. 123–45; E. S. Duckett, *Anglo-Saxon Saints and Scholars* (1947); D. H. Farmer, *The Rule of St. Benedict* (1968); D. P. Kirby, 'Bede, Eddius Stephanus and the Life of Wilfrid', *E.H.R.*, xcviii (1983), 101–14.

WILFRID II (d. 744), bishop of York. One of the five future bishops who was educated at Whitby under *Hilda, Wilfrid became the disciple of *John of Beverley, who on his retirement consecrated him as his successor. Little is known of his episcopate except his zeal for education. Like his predecessor he retired early, says Alcuin, in order to be free to serve God with his whole soul. Twelve years later he died at Ripon. From there in the 10th century two rival parties from Worcester and Canterbury both claimed to have taken the relics of the great St. Wilfrid. It seems likely that one or other of them may have taken the relics of Wilfrid II instead. His feast, on 29 April, is testified only by one calendar of Winchcombe (Glos.) and by some late martyrologies. There seems never to have been a widespread cult or popular interest in this saint.

Bede, *H.E.*, iv. 23; v. 6; Alcuin, *Carmen*, 1215–40; Stanton, pp. 185–6.

WILGEFORTIS (Uncumber; also called Liberata and Kummernis). The curious legend of Wilgefortis has its roots in a story recounted by *Gregory the Great. In its developed form, Wilgefortis was a septuplet of a pagan king of Portugal; together with her brothers and sisters she became a Christian and suffered martyrdom. Her father wanted her to marry the king of Sicily, but she had taken a vow of virginity. So she prayed to become unattractive: the result was that a moustache and beard grew on her face and her suitor withdrew. Her father accordingly had her crucified: while on the cross she prayed that all who remembered her passion should be liberated from all encumbrances and troubles. Her name is mentioned in several continental but no English martyrologies: there were, however, a hymn and a collect to her in the Salisbury *Enchiridion*. Images of her were to be found at Worstead, Norwich, and Boxford (Suffolk), which were despoiled in the reign of Edward VI, whose commissioners valued her clothes from two of them at 'xvj d' and 'xiv d' respectively. The English custom of offering oats at her statue was rightly derided by Thomas *More: 'Whereof I cannot perceive the reason, but if it be because she should provide a horse for an evil husband to ride to the devil upon, for that is the thing that she is so sought for, as they say. Insomuch that women have therefore changed her name and instead of Saint Wilgeforte call her Saint Uncumber, because that they reckon that for a peck of oats she will not fail to uncumber them of their husbands' (spelling modernized). There is no mention of this last point in the collect referred to above. A statue of Wilgefortis survives in Henry VII Chapel, Westminster Abbey. It seems that the cult originated in 14th-century Flanders, with feast on 20 July.

The legend of Wilgefortis is sometimes explained as an attempt to account for the clothed and bearded figure of Christ on the Cross. In our own day some doctors have speculated on the connection between anorexia nervosa in adolescent girls and the growth of hair in unusual parts of the body.

AA.SS. Iul. V (1727), 50–70; Gregory the Great, *Dialogi IV*, 13 (ed. A. de Vogüé, *S.C.* 1980); G. Schnurer and J. M. Ritz, *Sankt Kummernis und Volto Santo* (1934); J. Gessler, *La Vierge Barbue: la légende de sainte Wilgeforte ou Ontcommer* (1938); M. R. James, *Suffolk and Norfolk* (1930), pp. 152–3; B.T.A., iii. 151–2; *Bibl. SS.*, xxi. 1094–9; J. H. Lacey in *British Medical Jnl.*, cclxxxv (1982), 1816–17.

WILLEHAD (d. 789), bishop of Bremen. A Northumbrian, educated at York, and a friend of Alcuin, Willehad, like many of his countrymen before him, devoted his life to the spread of the Christian faith in western Europe. He landed in Frisia *c.*766 and started preaching at Dokkum, where

*Boniface was killed in 754. From there he passed on to Overyssel and Humsterland, where he narrowly escaped death, and then to the neighbourhood of Utrecht, where he consolidated the work of *Willibrord. In 780 he was sent by Charlemagne to evangelize the recently conquered Saxons, but a revolt by their king Widukind in 782 was the signal for the massacre or expulsion of the missionaries. Willehad went to Rome to consult Pope Adrian. While Charlemagne ruthlessly suppressed the revolt of the Saxons, Willehad copied manuscripts at Echternach. When peace was restored, he returned to his apostolate, was consecrated bishop in 787, and chose Bremen as his see. Here he built a cathedral of wood and dedicated it to St. Peter in 789, but died a few days later. Feast: 8 November.

AA.SS. Nov. III (1910), 835–51; L. Halphen, *Études critiques sur l'histoire de Charlemagne* (1921); W. Levison, *England and the Continent in the Eighth Century* (1946).

WILLIAM OF MALAVALLA (d. 1157), abbot. Little is known of his life. He seems to have been of French origin and to have been a dissolute soldier as a young adult. He was converted from this way of life, went to visit the Apostles' tombs at Rome, and asked Pope Eugenius III for both a pardon and a penance for his sins. He was told to undertake a pilgrimage to Jerusalem: in 1145 he returned, a changed man.

He became a hermit at Lupocavio (near Pisa), where he was joined by many followers. In 1155 he went in quest of greater solitude to Malavalla, a place of desolate squalor, in Sienese territory, where he lived in a cave. After some months of complete solitude living on herbs and fruit, he was discovered by the local lord who built him a cell above ground. Here he was joined by a disciple called Albert who wrote his Life, describing his hairshirts and manual work, his prayer, contemplation, and prophecy. Another disciple, a doctor called Rinaldo, joined them soon afterwards, but William died. His disciples buried his body in the garden, over which they later built a small church with a hermitage. Albert continued William's regime and his monks were called Gulielmites or Hermits of St. William. They subsequently spread into Italy, France, Flanders, and Germany. William was canonized by Innocent III in 1202: his relics were dispersed in the wars between Siena and Grosseto. Feast: 10 February.

AA.SS. Feb. II (1658), 433–91; *Vies des saints et des bienheureux*, ii. 234–7; *H.S.S.C.*, vi. 273.

WILLIAM OF MONTEVERGINE (1085–1142), abbot and monastic founder. Born at Vercelli of a noble Lombard family, he was early left an orphan. At the age of fourteen he went on pilgrimage to Compostella. In 1106 he became a hermit at Monte Solicoli (Basilicata), but still unsettled, started a pilgrimage to Jerusalem. After being attacked by robbers he returned. He now resumed the hermit life at Montevergine near Benevento. Here he built a cell and a church. He was joined by disciples whom he formed into a community. The regime was austere: meat, wine, butter, and cheese were forbidden, while on three days each week the only food was vegetables with dry bread. In 1124 the community found the regime too strict and demanded mitigation. This William refused; instead, he appointed a prior who eventually adopted the Rule of St. Benedict. William moved elsewhere in search of more complete solitude.

He tried again with a small community at Monte Laceno (Apulia), but physical conditions were too severe. A fire destroyed their huts, so they moved on to Monte Cognato (Basilicata). But once againt William appointed a prior and left, this time for Conza (Apulia), where he founded communities of monks and nuns. King Roger II of Naples invited him to Salerno and endowed William's other monasteries. To this period of his life belongs the legend of the prostitute sent from court to seduce him. He received her politely and then parted the coals in his fireplace with his bare hands and invited her to lie down with him among them. He was unscathed, she was converted, his traducers were discomfited.

William is an interesting example of the reformed monasticism of his time with its varied and sometimes incompatible commitment to solitude, austerity, and community life. He died at Golato, but his relics were translated to Montevergine, where a popular cult arose which was confirmed in 1728 and 1785. Montevergine is still a monastery, where a fine painting of the Madonna is the object of popular pilgrimage. Feast: 25 June; translation feast, 2 September.

AA.SS. Iun. V (1744), 112 ff. (critical ed. by G. Mongelli in *Samnium*, 1960–1); Life by G. Mongelli (1960); B.T.A., ii. 635–7; *Bibl. SS.*, vii. 487–9.

WILLIAM OF NORWICH, murdered in 1144, supposedly by Jews for ritual purposes. According to Thomas of Monmouth, a monk of Norwich, who wrote the Life *c.*1169, William, a boy of twelve apprenticed to a skinner at Norwich, was abducted by a strange man who promised he would become the archdeacon's kitchen-boy. Instead, he was gagged, shaved, lacerated with a crown of thorns, and crucified. His uncle Godwin asserted that he was murdered by Jews: this fitted in with the widespread, but quite erroneous, belief that the Jews sacrificed a Christian somewhere every year and that in 1144 it was the turn of Norwich. The cult started when William's body was discovered unburied in a wood. It was translated to the chapter-house and later to the Martyrs' Chapel (afterwards Jesus Chapel) in the cathedral.

The cult was popular but ephemeral. Visions and supposed miracles accompanied the translation in 1151; but by 1314 offerings at the shrine were worth only £1. 1*s.* 5*d.* and by 1343 they had dropped to only 4*d.* From the beginning there had been doubts and reservations about William among the Norwich community, and the papal letters of Innocent IV (1247) and Gregory X (1272), which vigorously refuted the accusations against the Jews of ritual murder, presumably had some effect on the cult, which was always merely local, the feast at Norwich being on 26 March. The chapel built on the site of his death became for a time a pilgrimage centre, but it fell into decay long before the Reformation.

Screen paintings of William survive in East Anglia at Loddon, Eye, and Worstead. He is usually depicted as a boy carrying three nails or being stabbed and crucified, while Jews look on. The cult has some importance as the first example in England of a particular kind of anti-Semitic propaganda: other examples occurred at Lincoln ('little St. *Hugh'), and elsewhere.

A. Jessopp and M. R. James, *Saint William of Norwich* (1896); M. D. Anderson, *A Saint at Stake* (1964); C. Roth, *The Ritual Murder Libel and the Jews* (1935); id., *History of the Jews in England* (1941).

WILLIAM OF ROCHESTER (William of Perth) (d. 1201). A native of Perth and a fisherman by trade, he experienced a conversion as a young man and devoted himself to the care of orphans and the poor, once saving from certain death an infant left at the door of the church. In accordance with a vow, he set off on pilgrimage to the Holy Land in 1201.

He took with him but one companion, a young man, who, after they reached Rochester, diverted him on a supposed short-cut and murdered him for his few possessions. His body was found by a madwoman, who garlanded it with honeysuckle and was cured of her madness through it. Other miracles were soon claimed. William was buried in Rochester cathedral, first in the crypt and then in the north-east transept, where offerings at his shrine contributed towards the rebuilding work of the cathedral.

In 1256 Laurence, bishop of Rochester, seems to have obtained some kind of papal approval of the cult. Recorded offerings at the shrine by King Edward I (1300) and Queen Philippa (1352) attest royal interest, while bequests of the 15th and 16th centuries are evidence for its continued local popularity.

St. William's hospital, on the road to Maidstone, marks the place of his death. Feast: (according to *C.S.P.*), 22 April; other authorities give 23 May.

AA.SS. Maii V (1685), 268–9; *N.L.A.*, ii. 457–9; W. H. St John Hope, *The Cathedral Church and Monastery of St. Andrew at Rochester* (1900).

WILLIAM OF ROSKILDE (d. 1070), bishop. An English priest who was chaplain to Canute, king of England (1016–35) and Denmark, he accompanied the king on his visits to Scandinavia. He was so shocked by the ignorance, idolatry, and superstition which he found that he decided to stay behind and help to preach the Gospel. Eventually he became bishop of Roskilde (Zeeland) and tirelessly laboured as a pastor. The few events recorded of him concern his attempts to improve the conduct of the king, Sweyn Estridsen. After the king had caused some supposed criminals to be killed without trial and in a church, violating sanctuary, William forbade him to enter this church next day until he was absolved from the guilt of shedding blood unjustly. Courtiers then drew their swords and William showed himself ready to die. Instead, Sweyn confessed his crime and donated land to Roskilde church as a peace-offering. Thenceforward until the king's death they worked together to foster and promote religion.

Sweyn's body was first buried at Ringsted abbey until the cathedral of Roskilde (the burial place of Danish kings) was sufficiently complete to receive it. William went out to meet the body, but died at its approach. So king and bishop were buried together at Roskilde. William appears in Danish calendars. Feast: 2 September.

B.T.A., iii. 470; *Bibl. SS.*, vii. 482.

WILLIAM OF YORK (d. 1154), archbishop. Of noble birth and with royal connections, William Fitzherbert became treasurer of York at an early age (*c.*1130) and a chaplain of King Stephen. In character he was kind, amiable, and easygoing. On the death of Thurstan, archbishop of York, in 1140 the canons of York, with royal support, chose William as his successor; but a disappointed minority, supported by *Bernard and the Yorkshire Cistercians, accused William of simony, unchastity, and intrusion. Both sides appealed to the pope, who ruled that the elect could be consecrated provided the dean of York could clear him of these charges and William purge himself of them by oath. After enquiry, Henry, bishop of Winchester and William's uncle, consecrated him. Meanwhile Bernard sent vituperative letters to popes and legates against both William and Henry. The premature death of Pope Lucius II deprived Henry of jurisdiction. The next pope was the Cistercian, Eugenius III, who heeded Bernard's intervention, suspended and deposed William, and appointed in his place the Cistercian abbot of Fountains, Henry Murdac.

William retired to Winchester and lived devoutly as a monk until 1153, when Bernard, Eugenius, and Henry Murdac all died. He was restored to his see and given the pallium. Soon after his triumphant return to York in 1154, he died suddenly, perhaps by poison. He was buried in his cathedral, miracles were reported at his tomb, and he was regarded both as the victim of injustice and as a saint. Honorius III appointed the Cistercian abbots of Fountains and Rievaulx to enquire into his life and miracles, and canonized him in 1227. In 1283 his relics were translated to a new shrine. In 1421 the famous St. William window was made; this depicts his life, death, translation, and miracles in sixty-two scenes.

The strong local cult at York filled a void caused by the early absence of any local saint's relics in contrast to the flourishing shrines of Durham and Beverley, but it had little support elsewhere. No ancient, but a few modern churches were dedicated to William. Feast: 8 June; translation, 8 January.

AA.SS. Iun. II (1698), 136–46; J. Raine (ed.), *Historians of the Church of York* (*R.S.*), ii. 270–91, 388–97; R. L. Poole, 'The Appointment and Deprivation of St. William of York', *E.H.R.*, xlv

(1930), 273–81; D. Knowles, 'The Case of St. William of York', *C.H.J.*, v (1936), 162–77, 212–14; C. H. Talbot, 'New Documents in the Case of St. William of York', ibid., x (1950), 1–15; A. Morey, 'Canonist Evidence in the Case of St. William of York', ibid., 352–4; F. Harrison, *The Painted Glass of York* (1927).

WILLIBALD (Willebald) (d. 786/7), bishop of Eichstatt. Brother of *Winnibald and *Walburga, Willibald was born in Wessex. He became a monk at Bishops Waltham (Hants.). Later he was one of the most travelled Anglo-Saxons of his time, by his journeys to Rome, Cyprus, Syria, and above all Palestine. Here he visited comprehensively both the Holy Places associated with Christ and numerous communities of monks and hermits. He dictated an account of these travels to Hugeburc, a nun of Heidenheim, who wrote it up under the title of *Hodoeporicon*. This was the first travel-book to be written by an Anglo-Saxon.

In 730 Willibald was back in Rome after a long stay in Constantinople. He chose to live at Monte Cassino; under his reforming influence, formed by his monastic experience in England and Palestine, *Benedict's own monastery, restored by Petronax in 717, entered on a new period of stable prosperity. At the request of *Boniface, Pope Gregory III sent Willibald into Germany. Boniface ordained him priest and later (742) bishop. His diocese was Eichstatt, the centre of his earlier preaching; at Heidenheim he founded a double monastery, whose observance was based on that of Monte Cassino. His brother Winnibald was abbot and, after his death, his sister Walburga abbess. This became an important centre, not only for the diocesan apostolate, but also for the diffusion and development of monasticism. Willibald was bishop for about forty-five years. He died at Eichstatt, where his relics are kept to this day. Feast, in *R.M.* and constantly elsewhere: 7 July.

AA.SS. Iul. II (1721), 485–519; the *Hodoeporicon* was edited by W. Holder-Egger, *M.G.H.*, *Scriptores*, xv. 80–117, with Eng. tr. in C. H. Talbot, *Anglo-Saxon Missionaries in Germany* (1954); see also M. Coens, 'Légende et Miracles du roi S. Richard', *Anal. Boll.*, xlix (1931), 353–97 and W. Levison, *England and the Continent in the Eighth Century* (1956).

WILLIBRORD (658–739), apostle of Frisia and archbishop of Utrecht. He was born in Yorkshire, where his father Wilgils became a hermit and was educated by *Wilfrid at Ripon. On Wilfrid's expulsion in 678 he went to Ireland both for study and voluntary exile; he stayed twelve years and was ordained priest. In 690 he returned to England; under *Egbert's inspiration he went with twelve companions as a missionary to Frisia. He made his way there through Frankish territory; he obtained strong support from Pippin II and began work in the area conquered and ruled by him. His mission prospered, especially after he had obtained support and encouragement from Pope Sergius when Willibrord visited Rome. During his absence one of his companions, *Swithbert, was consecrated bishop by Wilfrid in England and returned to preach to the Boructuarii (between the rivers Yssel and Ems). Willibrord returned to Frisia and continued as before. In 695 he went again to Rome, this time at Pippin's behest, to be consecrated bishop by Sergius, who gave him the additional name of Clement and sent him back with a definite mission to establish normal church organization with a metropolitan see at Utrecht, and suffragan bishoprics similar to the pattern at Canterbury and elsewhere. As at Canterbury, a cathedral of Christchurch was built and an old church of St. Martin restored to worship. Willibrord built churches and monasteries and consecrated bishops to new sees. In 698 he founded his largest monastery, at Echternach (now in Luxembourg), where he died more than forty years later, and which became an important pilgrimage centre.

In the area ruled by the Franks Willibrord's apostolate was permanently fruitful; in other districts it was more sporadic. Throughout his life he depended on the protection and patronage of the secular rulers. In 714, for example, he was driven out of Utrecht by Radbod, the pagan Frisian king; churches were destroyed and priests killed. Willibrord's work seemed largely destroyed. But in 719, on Radbod's death, Willibrord returned, not only to the western part of the country he had previously evangelized, but also to the east, where he had never penetrated. In these years he was joined for a time by *Boniface, whom he wished to be his successor, but Boniface went on to Germany instead. Willibrord penetrated into Denmark, where he bought thirty slave-boys and educated them as Christians. In Heligoland he baptized a number of the inhabitants, and killed some sacred cows which his followers needed for food. At Walcheren too he destroyed an idol at risk of his life. In these two instances the absence of any retribution on him considerably helped his apostolic activities.

Alcuin described his apostolate as based on energetic preaching and ministry, informed by prayer and sacred reading; Willibrord was always venerable, gracious, and full of joy. Even if the conversion of Holland and Luxembourg was neither so rapid nor so complete as some hagiographers claim, Willibrord's pioneering work, which inaugurated a hundred years of English Christian influence on the Continent, was of great importance and he thoroughly deserves his title of patron of Holland.

He died at the age of eighty-one and was immediately venerated as a saint. In connection with his shrine a sacred dance takes place to formalized steps, in which the bishops and clergy participate. Its origin is unknown, but it can be traced back at least as far as the 16th century. Perhaps the most interesting relic to survive is the Calendar of St. Willibrord, which was written for his own private use and contains a marginal entry in his own hand, which records his consecration at Rome and other biographical details. His cult has always been stronger in Holland and Luxembourg than in England. Feast: 7 November; translation, 10 November.

Bede, *H.E.*, iii. 13; v. 10–11, 19; Alcuin's Life in *AA.SS.* Nov. III (1910), 414–500 and, ed. W. Levison, in *M.G.H.*, *Scriptores merov.*, vii (1920), 81–141; *N.L.A.*, ii. 447–51; H. A. Wilson, *The Calendar of St. Willibrord* (H.B.S., 1918); W. Levison, *England and the Continent in the Eighth Century* (1956), pp. 53–69; id., 'St. Willibrord and his Place in History', *D.U.J.*, xxii (1940), 8–41; Modern Lives by A. Grieve (1923), K. Heeringa (1940), and C. Wampach (1953).

WILLIGIS (d. 1011), archbishop of Mainz. Born at Schoningen of humble origins, he soon showed ability and became a priest, then a canon of Hildesheim (near Hanover). Wolkold, precentor of Otto II who became archbishop of Meissen in 969, noticed Willigis and promoted him. He became chaplain to Otto and in 971 chancellor. Both before and after becoming archbishop of Mainz in 975 Willigis was prominent in promoting Christianity with great energy not only in the Empire but also in Schleswig, Holstein, Denmark, and Sweden. He also established or restored collegiate churches in Mainz and Halberstadt. His daily life included the constant study of the Bible and the organized relief of the poor.

On the death of Otto II Willigis became one of the most important and influential people in the Empire. Confirmed by Benedict VII in the right to crown emperors, Willigis crowned Otto III and later influenced him in favour of abandoning Italy and concentrating his resources north of the Alps. Otto III however died young in 1002. The disputed succession which followed was ended when Willigis crowned *Henry II and his wife *Cunegund at Paderborn. He then served this third monarch faithfully, now as an elder statesman and ecclesiastic. Like many others of his colleagues he was a notable art-patron: his motto was 'by art to the knowledge and service of God'.

He died in old age at Mainz and was buried in St. Stephen's church. The cult arose spontaneously at once. It is claimed that some of his Mass-vestments survive. Feast: 23 February.

Willigis is mentioned in the Chronicle of

Thietmar of Merseburg (976–1018) and in the Hildesheim annals; account of his office and miracles by W. Guerrier (1869); Life by A. Bruck (1962); see also B.T.A., i. 406–7; *Bibl. SS.*, xii. 1122–6.

WINEFRIDE (Wenefred, Gwenfrewi) (7th century), Welsh virgin. The principal interest of this saint lies not in the few known facts of her life, but in the ancient, widespread, and persistent character of her cult. The earliest Life was written in the 12th century and is a tissue of improbabilities. What seems certain is that the place where she lived was Holywell or Treffynnon (Flintshire, now Clwyd) and her cult was subsidiary to that of her uncle *Beuno. The Legend, written at Shrewsbury where her relics were translated in 1138, makes her a maiden who lived at home, whom Caradoc, the son of a neighbouring prince attempted unsuccessfully to seduce with a promise of marriage. In his rage at being refused, he pursued her and as she fled to a church, struck off her head. A fountain sprang up where her head touched the ground. Beuno raised her from the dead and for many years afterwards she was abbess of a nunnery at Holywell according to one account, but another said that when Beuno went to Clynnog, she went to Bodfari, then to Henllan and finally to Gwytherin where under St. Eleri's direction she became a nun in a remote mountain valley.

In the early Middle Ages her cult was confined to the Marches of North Wales and to Euias and Erging in the Southern ones. Evidence for this is certain from the 12th century, but this probably reflects a much earlier cult. In 1398 her feast was extended to the whole Canterbury province by Roger Walden, who was archbishop during the exile of Thomas Arundel; in 1415 his successor Henry Chichele, who, when bishop of St. Davids had been interested in Welsh saints, raised it to a higher rank. The development of both Holywell and Shrewsbury as pilgrimage centres to Winefride benefited from these liturgical alterations and from the important roads which passed through both, enabling pilgrims to visit several shrines in the neighbourhood on a single visit. A guest-house for them was built at Ludlow. The highest point came in the 15th century: Henry V made the pilgrimage on foot from Shrewsbury to Holywell in 1416; Edward IV is reputed to have done the same, while Lady Margaret Beaufort, mother of Henry VII, built the fine chapel still standing at Holywell after the battle of Bosworth Field (1485).

The pilgrimage and the cures at the spring of Holywell survived the Reformation: in 1629, it is claimed, 14,000 laity with their priests visited it on her feast. Although the number is almost certainly exaggerated, it is certain that Holywell became an important recusant centre with Jesuits and secular priests in more or less permanent residence and that the well continued to attract pilgrims. In 1774 Dr. Johnson saw people bathing there. In the 18th and 19th centuries the pilgrimages continued, as they do at the present day, in spite of the diversion of the original source of water through mining operations in 1917. The architectural complex of chapel and well forms the best-preserved medieval pilgrimage centre of its kind in Britain today. Six ancient churches are dedicated to her. Feast: 3 November; translation 22 June: some Welsh calendars commemorate her on 19/20 September or 4 November.

AA.SS. Nov. I (1887), 691–759; A. W. Wade-Evans, *Vitae Sanctorum Britanniae* (1944), pp. 288–309; C. De Smedt, 'Documenta de S. Wenefreda,' *Anal. Boll.*, vi (1887), 305–52; Baring-Gould and Fisher, iv. 185–96; P. Metcalf, *Life of St. Winifred* (1712; new edn. by H. Thurston, 1917); B.T.A., iv. 245–6; E. G. Bowen, *The Settlements of the Celtic Saints in Wales* (1956).

WINNIBALD (Winebald) (d. 761), abbot of Heidenheim (Würtemmburg). Brother of *Willibald and *Walburga, Winnibald made a pilgrimage with them to Rome, where he stayed on to study for seven years before returning to England. There he collected some companions and in 739 joined *Boniface in Thuringia. He was soon ordained priest and undertook missionary work in Thuringia and Bavaria. Later he rejoined his brother Willibald, now bishop of Eichstatt. Together they founded the monastery of Heidenheim. This followed the Rule of St. Benedict and became an important centre for its propagation. It was also the only double monastery among the 8th-century foundations in Germany, doubtless based on Anglo-Saxon models. The monastery was a centre of evangelism as well as of prayer and work; Winnibald narrowly escaped assassination from pagans in the neighbourhood. For long he suffered from ill-health: this prevented him from ending his life at Monte Cassino as he had hoped. He died at Heidenheim on 18 December 761. His sister Walburga ruled the double monastery after his death and his biographer was the nun Hugeburc, who also wrote Willibald's *Hodoeporicon.* Miracles were recorded at his tomb and his feast was kept on 18 December.

Life by a nun of Heidenheim edited by O. Holder-Egger in *M.G.H.*, *Scriptores*, xv. 106–17; W. Levison, *England and the Continent in the Eighth Century* (1946); C. H. Talbot, *Anglo-Saxon Missionaries in Germany* (1954); M. Coens, 'Légende et Miracles du roi S. Richard', *Anal. Boll.*, xlix (1931), 353–97.

WINNOC (Wunnoc, Winnow) (d. *c.*717), abbot. He was probably a Welsh monk who founded the Cornish church of St. Winnow and later joined the monastery of Sithiu (Saint-Omer) of which *Bertin was abbot. He founded the monastery of Wormhout (near Dunkirk), and built a church and hospital there. His zeal in manual work was famous: his supposedly miraculous grinding of corn is recorded in the OE Martyrology. His relics were translated to Bergues-Saint-Winnoc in 899/900. His feast is recorded in most English calendars of the 10th–11th centuries; this is partly due to the strong connection between Canterbury and Saint-Omer. Feast: 6 November; translation, 18 September.

AA.SS. Nov. III (1910), 253–80 and *Propylaeum*, pp. 500–1; G. H. Doble, *The Saints of Cornwall*, v (1970), 127–54; B.T.A., iv. 276.

WINNOL, see WINWALOE.

WINNOW, see WINNOC.

WINSTON, see WISTAN.

WINWALOE (Winnol, Onolaus, Guénolé) (6th century), Breton abbot. Trained by *Budoc on an island called 'Laurea', he became a hermit on the island of Tibidy, off the Breton coast, and practised the usual Celtic mortifications of reciting the psalter daily with arms outstretched and wearing clothes of goat-hair. He later founded the monastery of Landévennec, where he lived as abbot, died and was buried. His Life was written only in the 9th century. Some of his relics, when his monastery was destroyed by the Vikings in 914, were taken to Mont Blandin (Ghent), others to Château-du-Loir and thence to Montreuil-sur-Mer.

His widespread cult in England was due to two reasons: foundations in Cornwall from his monastery, and the diffusion of his relics. The churches of Landewednack and Gunwalloe (both in the Lizard) are dedicated to him, while his name occurs in English litanies of the 10th–11th centuries. Exeter, Glastonbury, Abingdon, and Waltham all claimed relics of him, and his name occurs frequently in English calendars of the same date. It is likely that this was due to *Dunstan's exile at Mont-Blandin and to later gifts of relics from the same source to Leofric, bishop of Exeter. Winwaloe was also known in East Anglia. His feast was celebrated at Norwich, where a street is named after him (recording the dedication of a church there) and his name occurs in a local weather jingle about the saints of the first three days of March:

First comes David, then comes Chad,
Then comes Winnol, roaring like mad.

In art Winwaloe is usually represented with a bell, at whose sound fishes would follow him; but on a screen at Portlemouth

(Devon) he is depicted carrying a church. Feast: 3 March, translation, 28 April (26 February at Barking).

A. De Smedt, 'Vita S. Winwaloei abbatis Landévennec', *Anal. Boll.*, vii (1888), 167–264; G. H. Doble, *The Saints of Cornwall*, ii (1962), 59–108; J. Le Jollec, *Guénolé, le saint de Landévennec* (1952).

WIRO (Wera) (d. *c.*753), monk and bishop of Utrecht. A Northumbrian who was, like *Willibrord, an apostle of Frisia, Wiro was appointed to the see of Utrecht by *Boniface *c.*741, but was not archbishop or metropolitan. It is possible that Wiro had been consecrated at Rome earlier, as his biographer claims. He also joined with Boniface in his letter of correction to Ethelbald, king of Mercia, in 746. The centre of his cult was Odilienberg, near Roermond, where he and his companions Pleghelm and Otger had built a church and monastery. Pepin of Herstall had given them the land for these and had encouraged their diffusion of Christianity in Frisia. Wiro was English and died in Holland, but some writers wrongly made him an Irishman who died in Ireland. In this latter they were followed by the Roman martyrology. Feast: 8 May.

AA.SS. Maii II (1680), 309–20 prints the unreliable Life which is no earlier than 858; L. van der Essen, *Étude critique et littéraire sur les Vitae des saints mérovingiens* (1907), pp. 105–9; W. Levison, *England and the Continent in the Eighth Century* (1956), pp. 82–3; I. Snieders, 'L'influence de l'hagiographie irlandaise', *R.H.E.*, xxiv (1928), 849–50.

WISTAN (Wynstan, Winston), prince of the royal family of Mercia, murdered 850. Grandson of Wiglaf, king of Mercia 827–40 and son of Wigmund who died in 839, Wistan was chosen as king in 840 on his grandfather's death, according to his Legend, but asked his mother Elfleda to rule as regent. Berhtric (Brifardus), Wistan's cousin, wished to marry her and seize power, but Wistan refused to allow the marriage, which he regarded as incestuous. Berhtric then murdered him at a place called Wistanstowe (probably Wistow, Leicestershire): three of Wistan's followers fell with him. Wistan's body was buried in the royal monastery of Repton with those of his father and grandfather.

In 1019 Alfwaerd, abbot of Evesham (later bishop of London) asked King Cnut to give him Wistan's relics. From then on Evesham was the centre of the cult. It is of special interest because some of Wistan's miracles were suspected and verified twice over. In Lanfranc's time, his former chaplain, Walter of Cerisy, was abbot of Evesham and subjected Wistan's relics, especially his head, to an ordeal by fire, from which it emerged unscathed. Over a century later, according to Thomas of Marleberge, the supposed miracle of 'hair' growing at Wistanstowe on the ground where the martyr fell, each year on his feast day, was verified by a commission sent by Baldwin, archbishop of Canterbury. Whatever the substance may have been, there was no doubt of the extraordinary phenomenon. Three ancient church dedications to Wistan are known, including Wistow and Wigston (Leics.). The Shropshire village of Wistanstow has a less convincing claim to be the site of the saint's death. Feast: 1 June.

Chronicon Abbatiae de Evesham (ed. W. D. Macray, *R.S.*, 1863), Appendix; D. J. Bott, 'The Murder of St. Wistan', *Trans. Leics. Arch. Society*, xxix (1953), 1–12; P. Grosjean, 'De Codice hagiographico Gothano', *Anal. Boll.*, lviii (1940), 90–103; J. C. Jennings, 'The Writings of prior Dominic of Evesham', *E.H.R.*, lxxvii (1962), 298–304; E. Gilbert, 'St. Wystan's, Repton', *Cahiers Archéologiques*, xvii (1967), 83–102; id., 'St. Wystan's, Repton; its date and significance', ibid., xxii (1972), 237 ff.; D. Rollason, *The Search for St. Wigstan* (1981).

WITE, see WHYTE.

WITHBURGA (1) (Witburh) (d. *c.*743), virgin. The youngest daughter of Anna, king of East Anglia and a sister of *Etheldreda, she lived as a solitary at Holkham (Norfolk), and later at East Dereham, where she is reputed to have founded a community and to have died before the buildings were completed. She was buried in the churchyard, but after fifty years her body was exhumed, found incorrupt and enshrined in the church.

In 974 Brithnoth, abbot of Ely, stole the body under the pretext that she would have wanted to be buried near her sisters. A band of his monks accompanied by soldiers went secretly by night to Dereham, having obtained the approval of King Edgar and *Ethelwold. They removed the body to their wagons, drove twenty miles to the river Brandun, on which they continued their journey by boat to the dismay of the men of Dereham, who had pursued them by land and could only watch helplessly while their treasure slipped away. The body was reburied at Ely where, however, the incorruption story was never exploited, as it might have detracted from Etheldreda's glory. In 1102 Withburga's relics were moved into the new part of the church; in 1106 they were joined by the bones of the other three Ely saints (Etheldreda, *Sexburga, and *Ermegild). The church at Holkham is dedicated to her; water in Withburga's well at Dereham churchyard was reputed to have sprung up when her body was first exhumed. Withburga's emblem in art, as on six Norfolk screens, is a tame doe, which William of Malmesbury described as her companion in solitude who provided her with milk. Feast: 17 March; translation 8 July; 18 April at Cambridge (*C.S.P.*).

E. O. Blake (ed.), *Liber Eliensis* (*C.S.*, 1962), pp. 120–3, 221–34; *A.S.C.* s.a. 798; *G.P.*, pp. 324–5; *N.L.A.*, ii. 468–70; M. R. James, *Suffolk and Norfolk* (1930).

WITHBURGA (2), mentioned in *R.P.S.* as resting at Ripon: otherwise unknown.

WITTA, see WHYTE.

WIVINA (d. 1170), abbess. A Fleming of noble birth, as a young woman she decided to be a nun: one of her suitors called Richard fell ill when she refused him. Restored to health by her prayers and counsel, he went his way, while at the age of twenty-three she became a hermit in a wood near Brussels called Grand-Bigard, with one companion. She also took her psalter with her, which survives at Orbais (Brabant). After a while her solitude was much disturbed by curious visitors, but one of them, Count Godfrey of Brabant, offered her land and endowment for a monastery. She ruled it as abbess, helped by monks from nearby Afflighem. The convent prospered in spite of accusations by some of her nuns that she lacked discretion in austerities. She refuted these accusations and died with a high reputation. Her tomb became a place of pilgrimage with many cures reported. A Life was written in the 13th century, but has little historical value. Her relics were translated to Notre Dame du Sablon, Brussels, in the 14th century and Urban VIII confirmed her cult in 1625. Feast: 19 December; translation, 25 September.

B.T.A., iv. 580–1; *Bibl. SS.*, xii. 1320–1.

WOLFEIUS (?11th century), according to William Worcestre, was the first hermit of St. Benet Hulme (Norfolk), and died on 9 December.

William Worcestre, pp. 232–3.

WOLFGANG OF REGENSBURG (*c.*924–94), bishop. Born in Swabia, Wolfgang was educated at Reichenau abbey (Lake Constance). Here Henry, brother of the bishop, persuaded him to set up a school at Wurzburg. In 956 Henry became archbishop of Trier and took Wolfgang with him; both were influenced by the reforming monk Ramuold. On Henry's death in 964 Wolfgang became a monk at Einsiedeln (Switzerland) where an Englishman called Gregory was abbot. Here he was given charge of the monastery school and was ordained priest. A missionary journey to Pannonia was not totally successful and in 972 he was appointed bishop of Regensburg.

His episcopate began with a thorough reform of the clergy. He restored the independence of the abbey of St. Emmeran over which he appointed Ramuold of Trier: he encouraged the regular canons to restore the common life and himself reformed two corrupt nunneries. Above all a man of prayer who never gave up his monastic habit or ways of thought, he was also an effective preacher and a generous almsgiver. Towards the end of his life Henry, duke of Bavaria, entrusted to him the education of his son, the future emperor *Henry II. Wolfgang died at Puppingen, near Linz, and was canonized in 1052. A lively and widespread cult, based on his relics at Regensburg, continues to the present day. Feast: 31 October.

AA.SS. Nov. II (i) (1894), 527–97; B.T.A., iv. 230–1: *N.C.E.* xiv. 987–8; I. Ziebermayr, *Die St. Wolfganglegende* (1924); *Bibl. SS.*, xii. 1334–42.

WOLFRAM, see WULFRAM.

WOOLOS, see GWYNLLYW.

WULFHAD AND RUFFIN (date unknown). They were traditionally brothers who were martyred at Stone (Staffs.), where their relics were kept. According to their Legend they were sons of Wulfhere, king of the Mercians, who put them to the sword after he had apostatized, killing them in the cell where they had been baptized by *Chad. At many points the Legend contradicts the known facts of history and can be rejected: the question remains whether or not there once were martyrs of this name, virtually unknown, who were given some kind of apparently respectable pedigree by this Legend. Feast: 24 July, mentioned in the Martyrologies of Altemps and Norwich and by Leland.

G. H. Gerould, 'The Legend of St. Wulfhad and St. Ruffin at Stone Priory', *Publ. Mod. Lang. Ass.*, xxxii (1917), 323–37; Stanton, pp. 354–7; P. Grosjean, 'Codicis Gothani appendix', *Anal. Boll.*, lviii (1946), 183–7.

WULFHILDA (Wulfhildis) (d. *c.*1000), abbess of Barking. Nearly all that we know of Wulfhilda comes from Goscelin, who wrote her Life in her monastery within sixty years of her death. She was brought up at the abbey of Wilton. When she was a novice, King Edgar wished to marry her, but she wished to remain a nun. Her aunt Wenfleda, abbess of Wherwell, deceptively invited her there to become her successor, but when she arrived, she found the king waiting for her and her aunt an accomplice to his desires. But she escaped through the drains in spite of chaperons inside and guards outside. Edgar pursued her at Wilton and seized her in the cloister; but she fled from his grasp and took refuge in the sanctuary among the altars and relics. After this Edgar renounced her and gave her Barking abbey, re-endowing it with the monastery of Horton (Dorset) and several churches in Wessex towns, and took her cousin Wulftrudis as his mistress instead. Her rule was neither peaceful nor uneventful. On the one hand she once miraculously multiplied drinks when Edgar, *Ethelwold, and a naval entourage from Sandwich visited her, but later, through intrigues of some of her nuns with Edgar's second wife, Ælfthryth, she was ejected from Barking and retired to Horton for twenty years. In *c.*993 she was reinstated, and for seven years was abbess both of Horton and Barking. Her principal feast was on the day of her death, 9 September; her translation took place on 2 September, *c.*1030 with that of *Hildelith and *Ethelburga. Both feasts were kept at Barking: the cult was local. There were additional feasts there on 7 March and 23 September.

M. Esposito, 'La vie de sainte Vulfilde par Goscelin de Cantorbéry', *Anal. Boll.*, xxxii (1913), 10–26; *G.P.*, p. 143 (but placing Wulfilda in an earlier reign); *N.L.A.*, ii. 506–10; *C.S.P.*

WULFRAM (Wolfram) (late 7th century), archbishop of Sens, and missionary. The son of a court official of King Dagobert, Wulfram became a monk and through his court connection was offered the archbishopric of Sens, which he accepted. He ruled his diocese for only two years, and resigned partly because a former archbishop was still alive, partly because he wished to evangelize the Frisians. For this purpose he went to Fontenelle and obtained monks to help him. They met with some success and made a few conversions, but as elsewhere in Europe at this time, the attitude of the king was likely to be decisive. They converted the son of King Radbod, but the king refused to interfere against the local custom of human sacrifices. In spite of himself he was impressed by both the missionaries and their miracles, but when at the point of baptism he asked where his ancestors were, Wulfram said that Hell was the lot of all idolators. Radbod answered that he would rather be in Hell with them than in Heaven without them, and so withdrew. Wulfram eventually returned to Fontenelle where he died.

His relics were translated to Abbeville, where they are still venerated. There are two ancient English churches dedicated to him, one of which is at Grantham. In Lincolnshire also the abbey of Croyland celebrated both his feasts, due probably to the fact that their abbot Ingulfph (1086–1109) was a monk of Fontenelle. But in Wulfram's own life there was probably some association with the English *Willibrord, the principal apostle of Frisia. Feast: 20 March; translation 15 October.

Life written at Fontenelle *c.*800 edited by W. Levison, *M.G.H.*, *Scriptores rerum merov.*, v. 657–73; *AA.SS.* Mar. III (1668), 143–65; W. Glaister, *The Life and Times of Saint Wulfran* (1878); B.T.A., i. 642–3; W. Levison, *England and the Continent in the Eighth Century* (1956), pp. 55–7; J. Laporte, *Inventio et Miracula S. Vulfrani* (1938).

WULFRIC (Ulric, Ulfrick) **OF HASELBURY** (Somerset) (*c.*1080–1154), priest and hermit. The near-contemporary Life by John, abbot of Ford, is accurate and informative. Wulfric was born at Compton Martin (Somerset), eight miles from Bristol. The lord of the manor was William Fitzwalter, also lord of Haselbury. Wulfric trained to be a priest and first exercised his ministry at Deverill, near Warminster. He was much addicted to hunting with hawks and dogs, but was converted to a more austere life in the early 1120s, reputedly through a chance conversation with a beggar. He then ministered at Compton Martin as parish priest until 1125, when he settled as an anchorite at Haselbury Plucknett (twenty miles from Exeter) in a cell on the north side of the chancel of the parish church. He had no official episcopal authorization, but was supported by the neighbouring Cluniac monks of Montacute. His penitential regime included rigorous fasting with prostrations, the wearing of chain-mail and frequent immersion in cold water. His gift of prophecy and second sight further increased his reputation for holiness.

Visitors to his cell, in which he was permanently enclosed, included Kings Henry I and Stephen. In 1130 Henry and Queen Adela obtained from him the healing of the knight Drogo de Munci from paralysis. In 1133 Wulfric prophesied the death of the king which took place in 1135. Stephen visited him with his brother, Henry of Blois, bishop of Winchester, when Wulfric greeted him as king even before his disputed accession; but on another occasion, Wulfric reproached him for misgovernment.

Wulfric worked at copying and binding books and made other articles for the services of the church. He persevered in his chosen calling until death, when the monks of Montacute unsuccessfully claimed his body, as did the Cistercians, for whom he had great affection, but to whose Order (in spite of contrary claims) he never belonged. They did, however, provide his biographer.

Wulfric's cult was slow to develop. Until 1169 no miracles were reported at his tomb, which, thanks to his disciple Osbern, was in his cell at Haselbury. But from 1185 till 1235 'innumerable' miracles were reported and Haselbury became a popular place of pilgrimage. Wulfric was mentioned with respectful admiration by Henry of Huntingdon, Roger of Wendover, and Matthew Paris. William Worcestre and John Leland also mention his tomb, and John Gerard in 1633 recorded that his cell was still standing and his memory by no means extinct. There seems to be no trace of an early feast in his honour, but Martyrologies of the 16th century record him on 20 February, as does a French Cistercian menology of the 17th.

M. Bell (ed.), *Wulfric of Haselbury* (1933, Somerset Record Society, t. xlvii); *N.L.A.*, ii. 511–18; T. Arnold (ed.), Henry of Huntingdon, *Historia Anglorum* (*R.S.*, 1879), Introduction, pp. xxix–xxx; D. M. Stenton, *English Society in the Early Middle Ages* (1965), pp. 214–17.

WULFRID, see ULFRID.

WULFSTAN (Wulstan) (*c.*1008–95), Benedictine monk, bishop of Worcester. Born of Anglo-Saxon parents at Itchington (Warwicks.), Wulfstan was educated at the abbeys of Evesham and Peterborough, where he excelled both in piety and in sport. In *c.*1033 he entered the household of Brihteah, bishop of Worcester. After he was ordained priest, he was offered a richly endowed church, but he refused it. Instead he became a Benedictine monk at Worcester cathedral priory. He soon became master of the boys, later cantor and sacristan. In *c.*1050 he became prior of this small community of only twelve monks: he regained lands which had been alienated, reformed the finances, and improved the monastic observance. He was specially zealous in preaching, baptizing, and counselling.

In 1062 the bishop of Worcester, Aldred, was promoted to the diocese of York. The papacy refused to allow him to hold the see of Worcester in plurality, as had been sometimes customary since the impoverishment of the York see through Viking action. Papal legates, then in England, recommended instead that Wulfstan should become the new bishop of Worcester. This choice was approved by King *Edward the Confessor and his council; Wulfstan was consecrated bishop by Aldred. He became one of the best examples of combining effectively the tasks of both monastic superior and diocesan bishop. He is the first English bishop known to have made systematic visitation of his diocese. He encouraged the building of churches on his own manors and on those of lay lords, he zealously promoted clerical celibacy, and insisted on the use of stone, instead of wooden, altars. Later he rebuilt his cathedral, of which his crypt remains, somewhat altered, today. He took his full share in the cathedral services and would comment in English on the Latin reading at his table. During his episcopate, indeed, Worcester became one of the most important centres of OE literature and culture. He was specially devoted to the English saints, notably *Bede, to whom he dedicated a church, *Dunstan, and *Oswald, his distant predecessor in his see, whose abstinence and generosity to the poor he imitated and surpassed.

Inevitably he was drawn into the political movements of his time. In 1066 King Harold sent him as his envoy to the Northumbrians to ensure their loyal support. Wulfstan was unsuccessful but not blameworthy. After the battle of Hastings, which he recognized as decisive, he was one of the first bishops to submit to William the Conqueror. He remained one of the few Englishmen to retain high office to the end of the Conqueror's reign and beyond. In the barons' risings of 1074 and 1088 he was loyal to the Crown and defended the strategic castle of Worcester against the insurgents.

Another notable achievement was his abolition of the trade in slaves from Bristol to Viking Ireland by his persistent and persuasive preaching. This was contemporary with the successful efforts of Lanfranc for the same end.

He supported Lanfranc's policy of reform. Worcester became a suffragan of Canterbury, ending its earlier ambivalent relation to York. Wulfstan sent his favourite disciple to Canterbury for further education and contact between the two communities was fostered by Eadmer. A late legend, implicitly contradicted by the confidence of contemporaries, was that he was poorly educated. In its crude form it can be safely rejected. He was probably neither more nor less learned than many of his Anglo-Saxon episcopal contemporaries.

He was described by his biographer, the monk Coleman, as 'of middle height . . .

always in good health . . . neither lavish nor niggardly in the choice of clothes and in his general standard of living'. He died at the age of eighty-seven, a venerable survivor of a past age.

His cult began almost at once and cures were reported at his tomb. William Rufus had it covered with gold and silver, but the relics were translated only in 1198. From 1200 full and detailed records of the cures were kept in preparation for the canonization, which was granted by Innocent III in 1203. King John held his memory in special esteem and was buried close by him. In 1216 his shrine was stripped to pay a levy of 300 marks made by Prince Louis of France, but a new translation was made to a shrine, more splendid than before, in 1218. On this occasion the abbot of St. Albans, William of Trumpington, took back to his abbey a rib of the saint and built an altar over it. In 1273 Edward I made thank-offerings at Wulfstan's shrine, after the Conquest of Wales.

Only one ancient church in England was dedicated to Wulfstan, but his feast was very widely celebrated in monastic and diocesan calendars. Feast: 19 January; translation, 7 June.

AA.SS. Ian. II (1643), 238–49; the lost OE Life by his chaplain Coleman was the basis of the admirable Latin Life by William of Malmesbury, ed. R. R. Darlington, *Vita Wulfstani* (*C.S.* 1928), Eng. tr. by J. H. F. Piele (1934); R. Flower, 'A Metrical Life of St. Wulfstan of Worcester', *Nat. Lib. of Wales Jnl.*, i (1940), 119–30. See also J. W. Lamb, *St. Wulfstan, Prelate and Patriot* (1933); *M.O.*, pp. 74–8, 159–63; D. H. Farmer, 'Two Biographies by William of Malmesbury', in *Latin Biography* (ed. T. A. Dorey, 1967), pp. 157–76; D. H. Turner, *The Portiforium of St. Wulfstan* (H.B.S., 1971).

WULGANUS (Wulgan), confessor. His body was claimed to rest at Christ Church, Canterbury 'in a chest on the beam beyond the altar of St. Stephen'. He has been identified as the patron of Lens, near Douai. According to *C.S.P.* he was born in Canterbury and went to Arras, where he died a holy death. Feast: 3 November.

E.B.K. after 1100, i. 66; *C.S.P.*

WULMAR (Vulmar) (d. *c.*700), abbot. Born in Boulogne, he was a married man who was separated from his wife and became a monk at Hautmont, where, although initially occupied in tending cattle and cutting wood, he became a priest and later a hermit. He founded two monasteries, one for monks at Samer near Calais, the other for nuns at Wierre-aux-Bois, about a mile away. His relics were translated to Boulogne and then to Ghent. Feast: 20 July, recorded in at least eight English Benedictine calendars and in a 10th-century addition to the Martyrology of Bede.

AA.SS. Iul. V (1727), 81–9; L. Van der Essen, *Étude critique sur les Vitae des saints mérovingiens de l'ancienne Belgique* (1907), pp. 412–14; B.T.A., iii. 154–5.

WULSIN (Wulfsin, Wulfsige) (d. 1002), first abbot of Westminster, bishop of Sherborne. Appointed by Edgar and *Dunstan first as superior of Westminster *c.*960, then as abbot in 980, he became bishop of Sherborne in 992, introduced a monastic chapter there in 993, but remained simultaneously abbot of Westminster. He is said to have rebuilt the church at Sherborne and improved the endowment. A few letters to or from Wulsin survive: one is from the scholar Aelfric (then abbot of Cerne), introducing his collection of canons for the instruction of priests. William of Malmesbury records that he warned his monks that having the bishop as their abbot would cause difficulty in the future. His pastoral staff and other *pontificalia* survived at Sherborne and were notable for their simplicity, which matched Wulsin's austerity of life. A relic not mentioned by William is the famous Sherborne Pontifical, which belonged to him and is a rich example of Winchester illumination. Wulsin died 8 January: his feast was kept at Sherborne, Westminster, Abbotsbury, and Worcester. His relics, together with those of *Juthwara, were translated at Sherborne *c.*1050. Feast: 8 January.

C. H. Talbot, 'The Life of St. Wulsin of Sherborne by Goscelin', *Rev. Bén.*, lxix (1951), 68–85 (cf. P. Grosjean in *Anal. Boll.*, lxxviii (1951), 197–206); W. Stubbs, *Memorials of St. Dunstan* (*R.S.*), pp. 406–9; *G.P.*, pp. 178–9; *N.L.A.*, ii. 520–2; *History of Westminster* (ed. J. A. Robinson), pp. 79–80.

WUNNOC, see WINNOC.

WYLLOW, according to William Worcestre, was a hermit born in Ireland, who was beheaded by Melyn ys Kynrede in the parish of Lanteglos, near Fowey (Cornwall). He was reputed to have carried his head for half a mile to St. Wyllow's bridge, where a church was built in his honour. This saint does not appear in the Cornish Church calendar.

William Worcestre, p. 107.

WYNSTAN, see WISTAN.

X

XAVIER, Francis (1506–51), Jesuit missionary. Born at the castle of Xavier (Javier) in Navarre, Francis, a Basque Spaniard, was educated at the University of Paris, where he met and eventually joined *Ignatius of Loyola, becoming one of the group of seven who took their vows at Montmartre in 1534, and were ordained priests in Venice three years later. From the very beginning preaching in the foreign missions was an integral part of the Jesuit ideal and vocation: Francis joined Simon Rodriguez at Lisbon and in 1541 sailed to Goa at the invitation of John III, king of Portugal, to evangelize the East Indies, fortified by a papal brief nominating him apostolic nuncio in the East. The journey took thirteen months.

Francis made this town his headquarters; his astonishing missionary achievements filled the remaining ten years of his life. He began by reforming Goa, which contained numerous relaxed Portuguese Catholics, notorious for cruelty to their slaves, open concubinage, and neglect of the poor. By example, preaching, and writing verses on Christian truths set to popular tunes, Francis did much to offset the apparent betrayal of Christ and the Church by bad Christians. For the next seven years he worked among the Paravas in southern India, in Ceylon, Malacca, the Molucca islands, and the Malay peninsula. He went among the poor as a poor man himself: sleeping on the ground in a hut and eating mainly rice and water. By and large he met with immense success among the low-caste but with almost none among the Brahmins. Wherever he went, he left after him numerous organized Christian communities: a good example of the permanence of his achievements is the persistent fidelity to Christianity of the Paravas, whom he also probably saved from extermination. From time to time he returned to his headquarters at Goa, but for long he had intended to go further east in spite of his propensity to seasickness and his difficulty in learning foreign languages.

In 1549 he went to Japan, translated an abridged statement of Christian belief, and made a hundred converts in a year at Kagoshima. He left them with his helpers and pressed on to Hirado, where he met with acclaim, to Yamaguchi, where a month's labour was fruitless, and lastly to the capital Miyako. Here he found he could not see the Mikado without offering a present which far exceeded his resources; the town was in a state of political turmoil, so he returned to Yamaguchi where he changed his tactics. He abandoned the external appearance of poverty, dressed in fine robes and gave presents of a clock and a musical box to the ruler as a representative of the king of Portugal. The result was that he obtained protection and the use of an empty Buddhist monastery. When he left, the total number of Japanese Christians was about 2,000: within 60 years they resisted fierce persecution, even to death (see MIKI AND COMPANIONS). In 1552 he was again at Goa, but left after a few months for China. On his way he fell ill and died almost alone on the island of Chang-Chuen-Shan. He had suffered extreme hardship, had worn himself out with ceaseless activity, yet enjoyed a high degree of union with God in prayer.

Some aspects of his apostolate have been criticized. Like most of his Catholic and Protestant contemporaries, he believed that all who died unbaptized would be damned. This gave both urgency to his activity and a lack of understanding of the great religions of the East. He is said to have used the government at Goa as a means of proselytizing, but this needs to be balanced by his frequent reproofs to, and habitual independence from, the Portuguese rulers. Again, like most other contemporary Christians, he believed that it was sometimes legitimate for the civil power to punish heresy. In these ways he was a man of his times: his pioneering techniques were not always followed by later generations of Jesuit missionaries.

After his death, his body was placed in quicklime and brought eventually to Goa, where it was enshrined and for long has been, in its incorrupt state, an object of popular pilgrimage. Recently, however, some corruption has set in, and it seems that it will not remain in this state for very much longer. His right arm was detached in 1615 and is preserved in the church of the Gesù at Rome. He was canonized by Gregory XV in 1622, and declared Patron of the Foreign Missions by Pius XI in 1927. His voluminous correspondence survives, which makes possible detailed and authentic study of the character of this saint. Feast: 3 December, the day after his death. Several religious missionary congregations bear his name: many churches and colleges have been dedicated to him in different parts of the world.

Letters in *Monumenta Xaveriana* (1899–1912), completed by G. Schurhammer and I. Wicki (1944–5) both in *Monumenta Historica Societatis Jesus:* biographies by A. Brou (1912), G. Schurhammer (1955, 3 volumes), and J. Broderick (1952); older Lives by E. A. Stewart (1917) and M. Yeo (1933). See also articles in *N.C.E.*, iv. 1059 ff. and *Bibl. SS.*, v. 1226–37.

XYSTUS, see SIXTUS.

Y

YSFAEL, see ISMAEL.

YTHAMAR, see ITHAMAR.

YVES, see IVES.

YWI, see IWI.

Z

ZACCARIA, Antony (1502–39), founder of the Barnabite Order. Born at Cremona, he studied medicine at Padua University and practised in his home town as a doctor. But he became a priest in 1528, having decided that he was called to exercise compassion by spiritual as well as physical healing. In 1530 he founded an order of priests bound by vows 'to regenerate and revive the love of divine worship and a properly Christian way of life by frequent preaching and faithful ministry of the sacraments'. The teaching of St. Paul and emphasis on the Eucharist were two characteristic devotions. He worked at Milan and Vicenza, but died prematurely at Cremona. His Order, like those founded by *Camillus of Lellis, Joseph *Calasanz, and *Jerome Emiliani, are examples of the revival of Christian life in Italy in times of notorious abuses. He was canonized in 1897. Feast: 5 July.

O. M. Premoli, *Storia dei Barnabiti nel Cinquecento* (1913); G. Chastel, *Saint Antoine-Marie Zaccaria, Barnabite* (1930); B.T.A., iii. 19–20, *Bibl. SS.*, ii. 216–20.

ZACHARIAS (d. 752), pope. By birth a Greek from Calabria, Zacharias became a deacon at Rome, and on the death of Gregory III was elected pope in 741. He persuaded the Lombard Liutprand to restore all the Roman territory he had occupied during thirty years, and to desist from besieging Ravenna. He attacked the iconoclastic policy of the Emperor Constantine Copronymus, but built up a cordial relationship with the Franks, largely through *Boniface, with whom he had a lively correspondence, part of which survives, over several years. These give the impression of great vigour and deep sympathy. He told Boniface to suspend polygamous and murderous priests, to abolish superstitious practices even if these were practised at Rome, to recognize the baptisms of those whose Latin was extremely inaccurate; with his synod of 745 he condemned the heretics Clement and Adalbert who had caused much trouble to Boniface. His share in the transfer of political power from the Merovingian to the Carolingian line, was important and significant. While he was pope, Zacharias translated the Dialogues of *Gregory the Great into Greek, which enjoyed a wide diffusion. Feast: 15 March (in the East, 5 September), but no really early evidence for the cult survives.

AA.SS. Mar. II (1668), 406–11; M. Tangl (ed.), *Bonifatii et Lullae Epistolae* (*M.G.H.*, 1916); W. Levison, *England and the Continent in the Eighth Century* (1956); C. H. Talbot, *Anglo-Saxon Missionaries in Germany* (1954). *O.D.P.*, pp. 89–90.

ZACHARY AND ELIZABETH (1st century), parents of *John the Baptist. All that we know about them for certain is contained in the Gospel of *Luke, chapter 1: their words recorded there have been used in the Christian liturgy daily (Zachary's canticle, the *Benedictus*) and less frequently (as in the Gospel for the feast of the Visitation). Eastern tradition, supported by *Basil and *Cyril of Alexandria, asserts that Zachary died as a martyr in the Temple by command of Herod. The Roman Martyrology, however, has nothing to say about Zachary's supposed martyrdom, but it joins Elizabeth to his cult. Feast of both: 5 November.

AA.SS. Nov. III (1910), 5–29; *Propylaeum*, p. 498; B.T.A., iv. 267.

ZENO (d. 371), bishop of Verona, confessor. An African by birth, he was consecrated bishop in 362 and has left a number of sermons as well as a reputation as a hardworking pastor who was zealous in building churches, in almsgiving and in purging his church from Arianism. He also founded nunneries and encouraged virgins living at home to be consecrated long before *Ambrose did the same in Milan. He denounced abuses connected with the *agape* and the interruption of Masses for the Dead by loud cries of lamentation. He was mentioned in St. Gregory's Dialogues as a martyr, but by error. He is usually represented with a fish, but whether this is a symbol of Baptism or a record of his addiction to angling is not entirely clear. Feast: 12 April.

AA.SS. Apr. II (1675), 69–78; sermons in *P.L.*, xi. 253–528 and in *C.C.* Series Latina, xxii (1971); B. Pesci, 'De Christianarum Antiquitatum Institutionibus in S. Zenonis Veronensis episcopi sermonibus', *Antonianum*, xxiii (1948), 33–42.

ZENO OF ROME, martyr and priest, titular of the basilica on the Appian Way. Feast (often with Vitalis and Felicula, whose connection with him is extremely slight); 14 February, in *R.M.* and at Barking and Malmesbury. William of Malmesbury mentioned his basilica. Some authorities make him a brother of *Valentine, but this seems to be an error.

AA.SS. Feb. II (1658), 751–4 with *C.M.H.*, p. 96.

ZENOBIUS OF FLORENCE (d. *c.*390), bishop. Not much is known about this patron of Florence, much depicted by early Renaissance painters. It seems that he was a member of the Geronimo family and became archdeacon of the town. His learning and piety won the attention of *Ambrose, who recommended him to Pope *Damasus. Zenobius served him first at Rome, then on a mission to Constantinople. On his return he became bishop of Florence, where his preaching, miracles, and austere life were notable. His 11th-century Life claims that he raised from the dead no fewer than five people including a child run over by a cart while playing in front of the Duomo. Zenobius is said to have lived until the age of eighty and to have been buried at San Lorenzo before being translated to the cathedral. Feast: 25 May.

He is mentioned in Paulinus' Life of Ambrose, ch. 50 (*c.*415) and his Lives are in *AA.SS.* Maii VI (1688), 49–69; see also *Bibl. SS.*, xii. 1467–70.

ZEPHYRINUS (d. 217), pope. He became bishop of Rome in 198, but as in the case of his successor, *Callistus, what little is known of him comes from his rival *Hippolytus, who described him as a simple man with little education. But, according to Eusebius, he excommunicated the two Theodoti and was called the principal defender of Christ's divinity. Often reputed to be a martyr perhaps because of suffering persecution, he nevertheless did not, it would seem, die a violent death. Feast (until 1969): 26 August.

AA.SS. Aug. V (1741), 783–9; L. Duchesne, *Le Liber Pontificalis* (1886), i. pp. clviii, 139–40; B. Capelle, 'Le cas du pape Zephyrin', *R. Ben.*, xxxviii (1926), 321–30; E. Amann in *D.T.C.*, xv (part 2; 1950), col. 3690 f.

ZITA (Sitha, Citha) (1218–72), a serving-maid of Lucca. Born at Monsagrati, she served the Fatinelli household from the age of twelve for the rest of her life. Often misunderstood and criticized by them, she eventually won their respect through her persevering devotion. Many miracle stories were told of her, including the attribution to angels of the baking of her loaves while she was rapt in ecstasy. Soon after her death a popular cult grew up round her tomb in the church of the Canons Regular of St. Frigdianus, shared in some degree by more prominent members of society. A liturgical cult was permitted in that church only by Leo X in the early 16th century, but it was solemnly confirmed as 'immemorial' in 1696; her name was added to the Roman Martyrology in 1748 by Benedict XIV.

Her popular cult had already spread to other countries in the later Middle Ages, testified by chapels in her honour as far afield as Palermo and Ely. In England she was known as Sitha and was invoked by housewives and domestic servants, especially when they lost their keys or were in danger from rivers or crossing bridges. She occurs in mural paintings (Shorthampton, Oxon.), in stained glass (Mells and Langport, Somerset), and on rood-screens in Norfolk (Barton Turf), Suffolk (Somerleyton), and Devon (Ashton). But her cult seems to have been popular and unofficial. No churches were dedicated to her, although St. Benet Shorehog (London), which had a chapel of St. Zita, was commonly known as St. Sithes. She appears in some English calendars, especially from Lincolnshire. Feast: 27 April.

AA.SS. Apr. III (1675), 497–527; *Propylaeum*, pp. 158–9; Benedict XIV, *Opus de servorum Dei canonizatione* (1787), lib. II, c. xxiv, no. 25; A. Guerra, *Istoria della vita di santa Zita vergine Lucchese* (1895); C. Woodforde, *Stained Glass in Somerset* (1946), pp. 181–2.

ZOILUS (d. *c.*304), martyr of Cordoba in Spain. He is believed to have suffered under the persecution of Diocletian; he was praised by Prudentius and his name is in the Roman Martyrology and that of Jerome. His feast was also kept at Chester for reasons unknown: he was wrongly called a pope there. At some time nineteen companions were added to his name, the first seven of which have the same names as those in the martyrdom of Symphorosa. Feast: 27 June, translation 4 November.

AA.SS. Iun. V (1709), 252–6 and *Propylaeum*, pp. 258–9; B. de Gaiffier, 'L'Inventio de S. Zoile de Cordoue', *Anal. Boll.*, lvi (1938), 361–9; B.T.A., ii. 527.

ZOSIMUS OF SYRACUSE (d. *c.*660), monk and bishop. The son of Sicilian landowners, Zosimus was offered to the monastery of St. *Lucy at the age of seven, where he was deputed to watch at the saint's relics. This was uncongenial to a boy accustomed to the open-air life of a farm and he ran away to his home. Brought back in disgrace, he experienced a menacing vision of Lucy, who, however, was appeased by the gracious Madonna who accepted his promise not to neglect his duty again. He settled down, became a good monk, and was forgotten for thirty years.

When the abbot died, the local bishop was invited to appoint his successor. In a scene reminiscent of Samuel's choice of David, the bishop asked for the missing monk to be sent for. He appointed Zosimus as abbot and ordained him priest: his rule became famous for wisdom and charity. When the bishop died, there was a disputed election; Pope Theodore appointed and consecrated Zosimus, who died at the age of ninety. These facts are drawn from a Life which purports to record contemporary information. Feast: 30 March.

AA.SS. Mart. III (1668), 837–43; B.T.A., i. 704–5.

APPENDIX I

PRINCIPAL PATRONAGES OF SAINTS

Accountants: Matthew
Actors: Genesius
Advertisers: Bernardino of Siena
Agricultural workers: Phocas, Walstan, Isidore the Farmer
Airmen and air passengers: Joseph of Copertino, B. V. M. (of Loreto)
Altar servers: Tarsicius
Animals and birds: Francis of Assisi
Animals (sick): Beuno
Apothecaries: Nicholas
Archaeologists: Damasus, Jerome
Archers: George, Sebastian
Architects: Thomas the Apostle, Barbara
Artists: Luke
Astronauts: Joseph of Copertino
Astronomers: Dominic
Athletes: Sebastian
Authors: Francis of Sales

Bakers: Elizabeth of Hungary, Zita
Bankers: Matthew
Basket-makers: Antony of Egypt
Bee-keepers: Ambrose, Bernard, Modomnoc
Beggars: Alexius, Martin of Tours, Benedict Labre
Bishops: Ambrose, Charles Borromeo
Blacksmiths: Dunstan, Eloi
Blind: Lucy, Dunstan, Raphael, Thomas the Apostle
Bookkeepers: Matthew
Booksellers: John of God
Boys: Nicholas, Aloysius
Bricklayers: Stephen
Bridgebuilders: John Nepomuk, Benezet
Broadcasters: Gabriel
Builders: Vincent Ferrer
Bursars: Joseph

Cab-drivers: Fiacre
Canonists: Raymund of Pennafort
Carpenters: Joseph
Charitable societies: Elizabeth of Hungary, Vincent de Paul
Children: Nicholas, Lambert
Clothworkers: Homobonus
Coachmen: Richard of Chichester
Cobblers: Crispin and Crispinian
Conservationists: Francis of Assisi
Cooks: Laurence, Martha
Clothworkers: Homobonus
Cripples: Giles, Gilbert of Sempringham

Dancers: Vitus
Dairymaids: Brigid
Deacons: Laurence, Stephen
Dentists: Apollonia
Desperate cases: Jude, Rita of Cascia
Diplomats: Gabriel
Doctors: Luke, Cosmas and Damian
Dogs (healthy): Hubert
Dogs (mad): Sithney
Dyers: Maurice
Dying: Barbara, Joseph, Margaret

Ecologists: Francis of Assisi
Ecumenists: Cyril and Methodius, Josaphat
Emigrants: Frances Cabrini
Engineers: Ferdinand
Epileptics: Dympna, Vitus
Eye-diseases: Lucy

Farriers: Eloi
Fathers: Joseph
Firefighters: Agatha, Laurence
Fishermen: Andrew, Peter, Simon, Zeno, Nicholas, Magnus
Florists: Dorothy, Rose of Lima
Funeral directors: Joseph of Arimathea

Gardeners: Fiacre, Phocas
Girls: Agnes, Catherine, Nicholas, Ursula
Goldsmiths: Dunstan, Eloi
Grocers: Michael
Gunners: Barbara

Hairdressers (ladies'): Mary Magdalen
Hairdressers (men's): Martin de Porres, Cosmas and Damian
Headache sufferers: Gereon, Stephen
Heart patients: John of God
Hermits: Antony, Giles, Hilarion
Holy death: Joseph
Homeless: Benedict Joseph Labre
Hopeless cases: Jude
Horses: Giles, Hippolytus
Hospitals: Camillus, John of God
Hoteliers: Amand, Julian, Martha
Housewives: Martha, Zita
Huntsmen: Eustace, Hubert

Husbandmen: George
Infantrymen: Maurice
Insane: Dympna
Intestinal disease sufferers: Erasmus
Invalids: Roch

Jewellers: Eloi
Journalists: Francis of Sales
Judges: Ivo of Brittany
Jurists: John of Capistrano

Kings: Edward, Louis, Henry
Knights: George, James the Great

Lawyers: Hilary, Thomas More, Ivo of Brittany
Lay-brothers: Gerard Majella
Lay-sisters: Martha
Leather workers: Crispin and Crispinian
Lepers: Giles
Librarians: Jerome
Lighthousemen: Clement
Lost articles: Antony of Padua
Lovers: Valentine

Married women: Monica
Mentally ill: Dympna
Merchants: Nicholas, Homobonus
Midwives: Pantaleon, Raymond Nonnatus
Miners: Barbara
Missionaries: Francis Xavier, Theresa of Lisieux, Leonard of Port Maurice
Missionary bishops: Paul, Turibius
Monks: John the Baptist, Antony, Benedict
Mothers: Blessed Virgin Mary, Giles, Monica
Motorists: Christopher, Frances of Rome
Mountaineers: Bernard of Aosta
Musicians: Cecilia, Gregory
Mystics and mystical theologians: John of the Cross

Negroes: Peter Claver
Nuns: Blessed Virgin Mary, Scholastica
Nurses: Camillus, Elizabeth of Hungary, John of God

Painters: Luke
Paralysed: Osmund
Parish priests: Jean-Baptiste Vianney
Pawnbrokers: Nicholas
Penitents: Mary Magdalene
Perfumiers: Nicholas
Philosophers: Justin, Catherine of Alexandria
Pilgrims: James, Mennas
Poets: Columba, John of the Cross
Poor: Antony of Padua, Martin Porres
Popes: Peter, Gregory the Great
Preachers: John Chrysostom, Bernardino of Siena
Pregnant women: Margaret of Antioch
Printers: Augustine, John of God
Prisoners: Dismas, Leonard, Roch
Publishers: John the Apostle

Race relations: Martin de Porres, Peter Claver
Radiologists: Michael
Repentant prostitutes: Mary Magdalen, Mary of Egypt, Margaret of Cortona
Retreatants: Ignatius of Loyola
Rheumatism sufferers: James the Great

Sailors: Nicholas, Francis of Paola, Phocas
Scholars: Bede, Jerome
Schoolboys: Nicholas, John Bosco
Schoolgirls: Catherine, Ursula
Scientists: Albert the Great
Secretaries: Mark, Genesius
Servants: Zita
Shepherds: Cuthbert, Bernadette
Sick people: Michael, Camillus, etc.
Singers: Cecilia, Gregory
Soldiers: George, Maurice, Oswald, James the Great
Speleologists: Benedict
Starving: Antony of Padua
Stonemasons: Four Crowned Martyrs
Students: Catherine of Alexandria, Thomas Aquinas
Surgeons: Cosmas and Damian, Luke
Syphilis sufferers: Fiacre, George

Tailors: Homobonus
Tax-collectors: Matthew
Taxi-drivers: Fiacre
Teachers: John Baptist de la Salle
Telecommunications: Gabriel
Television: Clare of Assisi
Theologians: Augustine, John the Apostle, Thomas Aquinas, Alphonsus
Thieves: Dismas
Throat sufferers: Blaise
Toothache sufferers: Apollonia, Medard, Osmund
Tramps: Benedict Joseph Labre
Travellers: Christopher, Julian, Magi

University Lecturers: John of Kanti, Thomas Aquinas

Virgins: Blessed Virgin Mary

Weavers: Maurice, Bernardino of Siena
Widows: Monica, Paula
Wine trade: Amand, Vincent
Women, unhappily married: Wilgefortis, Rita of Cascia
Workers: Joseph
Writers: John the Evangelist, Francis de Sales

Youth: Aloysius Gonzaga, John Bosco

APPENDIX II

PRINCIPAL ICONOGRAPHICAL EMBLEMS OF SAINTS

Anchor: Clement
Angel: Matthew, Cecilia
Apples: Dorothy
Arrows: Edmund of East Anglia, Sebastian
Axe: John the Baptist, Boniface, Magnus, Olaf, Winifred, Thomas More, John Fisher

Banner: George, James the Great, Maurice
Barrel of salt: Rupert
Battle-axe: Olaf
Basket of bread: Nicholas of Tolentino
Basket of fruit and flowers: Dorothy
Bear: Gall, Seraphim
Bees: Ambrose, John Chrysostom
Bell: Antony of Egypt, Winwaloe
Birds: Francis of Assisi
Blackbird: Kevin
Boat: Simon, Jude, Bertin
Book: Anne, Augustine, Bernard, etc.
Boys in tub: Nicholas
Breasts (on dish): Agatha
Broom: Martha, Petronilla, Zita
Bull: Luke, Frideswide, Thomas Aquinas

Camels: Mennas
Candle: Genevieve, Blaise, Gudule
Cannon: Barbara
Cardinal's hat: Bonaventure, Jerome, Robert Bellarmine
Cauldron of oil: John the Evangelist
Chalice: Richard, Hugh, etc.
Cheese: Juthwara, Brigid
Child on boar: Cyricus
Cloak: Martin of Tours
Club: Christopher, Jude, Magnus, Simon, James the less
Cock: Peter, Vitus
Comb (for wool): Blaise
Cow: Brigid, Perpetua
Cross: Helen, Philip
Cross saltire: Andrew
Cross upside down: Peter
Cross (T): Antony of Egypt
Crow: Antony, Paul the first hermit
Crown: Louis, Olaf, Wenceslas, etc.
Cruets: Joseph of Arimathea, Vincent of Saragossa
Crutch: Giles
Cup: John the Evangelist, Benedict

Dagger: Edward the Martyr, Peter the Martyr, Olaf, Wenceslas
Doe: Withburga
Dog: Dominic, Roch, Eustace, Hubert, Bernard of Aosta
Dove: Ambrose, David, Gregory, Samson
Dragon: Armel, George, Margaret of Antioch, Martha, Sylvester

Eagle: John the Evangelist
Eyes (on dish): Lucy

Fish: Neot, Zeno, Antony of Padua, Eanswyth

Globe: Henry, Louis
Globe of fire: Martin
Goose: Werburga, Brigid, Martin
Gridiron: Laurence, Vincent of Saragossa

Hammer: Apollonia, Eligius
Head held in hands: Denys, Oswald, Sidwell, Sigfrid, etc.
Hind or stag: Eustace, Giles, Hubert
Host in monstrance: Clare of Assisi

IHS tablet (monogram of Jesus): Bernardino of Siena
Intestines: Erasmus

Jar of ointment: Mary Magdalen, Mary of Egypt

Key(s): Peter, Petronilla, Martha, Zita
Knife: Bartholomew, Peter the Martyr, William of Norwich

Ladder: John Climacus
Ladle: Martha
Lamb: Agnes, John the Baptist
Lance: Jude, Thomas the Apostle, Gereon, Maurice
Lantern: Gudule, Lucy

Lily: Antony of Padua, Catherine of Siena, Dominic
Lion: Mark, Jerome
Loaves of bread: Philip, Nicholas of Tolentino

Mitres (three): Bernardino of Siena
Money bag (or box): Matthew, Nicholas
Monstrance: Clare, Norbert
Mountaineers' stick: Bernard of Aosta
Mouse: Gertrude of Nivelles

Nails: Joseph of Arimathea, Louis, William of Norwich
Necklace: Etheldreda
Net: Peter, Andrew, Blandina

Organ: Cecilia
Otters: Cuthbert
Ox-bone: Alphege

Phial of oil: Remigius, Januarius, Walburga
Pig: Antony of Egypt
Pilgrim's hat: James the Great
Pincers: Apollonia, Agatha, Dunstan, Eloi
Purse: Antoninus, Laurence, John the Almsgiver

Raven: Benedict, Oswald
Ring: Catherine of Alexandria, Catherine of Siena, Edward the Confessor
Roses: Theresa of Lisieux, Rose, Elizabeth of Hungary

Salmon with ring: Kentigern
Scales weighing souls: Blessed Virgin Mary, Michael
Scourge: Guthlac
Scythe: Juthwara, Sidwell, Walstan, Isidore the Farmer
Shamrock and snakes: Patrick
Shell: James the Great
Ship: Anselm, Bertin, Nicholas, Ursula
Shoes: Crispin and Crispinian
Shower of rain: Swithun
Spade: Fiacre, Phocas
Spear: Thomas the Apostle
Staff with Child Jesus: Christopher
Stag: Eustace, Giles, Hubert, Osyth
Star: Dominic, Thomas Aquinas, Vincent Ferrer, Nicholas of Tolentino
Stone: Stephen, Jerome
Surgical instruments: Cosmas and Damian, Luke
Swan: Hugh of Lincoln
Sword: Paul (and many martyrs)

Tongs: Dunstan, Eloi
Tower: Barbara
Tub: Nicholas

Vernicle: Veronica
Vine: Vincent of Saragossa

Well: Juthwara, Sidwell
Whale: Malo, Brendan
Wheel: Catherine of Alexandria, Christina
Wheelbarrow: Cuthman
Windlass: Erasmus
Wolf: Edmund of East Anglia, Francis of Assisi, Wolfgang
Women under cloak: Ursula
Wound in head: Peter the Martyr

INDEX OF PLACES

IN GREAT BRITAIN AND IRELAND ASSOCIATED WITH PARTICULAR SAINTS

CALENDAR

OF THE PRINCIPAL FEASTS OF SAINTS IN THIS VOLUME WHO ARE OR WERE VENERATED ON THESE DAYS

January

1: B.V.M., Odilo.
2: Basil and Gregory of Nazianzus, Munchin, Seraphim of Sarov, Gaspare del Bufalo.
3: Genevieve.
4: Roger of Ellant, Elizabeth Seton.
5: John Neumann, Simeon Stylites.
6: Peter of Canterbury.
7: Brannoc, Kentigerna, Lucian, Raymund of Pennafort, Canute Lavard.
8: Nathalan, Pega, Wulsin, Gudule, Thorfinn.
9: Berhtwald (1), Fillan.
10: Dermot, Paul the Hermit, Saethrith.
11:
12: Ailred, Benedict Biscop, Salvius, Antony Pucci.
13: Hilary, Kentigern, Antony Pucci.
14: Felix of Nola, Macrina the Elder, Sava of Serbia.
15: Ceolwulf, Ita, Macarius.
16: Fursey, Henry of Coquet Island, Marcellus, Sigebert.
17: Antony of Egypt, Mildgyth, Sulpicius.
18: Prisca, Ulfrid.
19: Branwalader, Canute, Henry of Finland, Wulfstan, Marguerite Bourgeoys.
20: Fabian and Sebastian, Fechin, Eustochium Calatato.
21: Agnes, Meinrad.
22: Berhtwald (2), Vincent of Saragossa, Anastasius, Vincent Pallotti.
23: Emerentiana, John the Almsgiver, Ildephonsus.
24: Babylas, Cadoc (2), Francis of Sales.
25: Dwyn, Paul, Praejectus.
26: Alberic, Bathild, Conan, Paula, Timothy and Titus, Tortgith, Augustine of Trondheim, Margaret of Hungary.
27: Angela, Julian of Le Mans.
28: John the Sage, Thomas Aquinas, Peter Nolasco.
29: Gildas, Julian the Hospitaller.
30:
31: John Bosco, Maedoc of Ferns.

February

1: Brigid of Ireland, Seiriol.
2: B.V.M., Jeanne de Lestonnac, Theophane Vénard.
3: Anskar, Blaise, Ia, Laurence of Canterbury, Margaret of England, Wereburga.
4: Gilbert of Sempringham, Phileas, John de Britto.
5: Agatha.
6: Amand, Dorothy, Mel, Paul Miki, Vedast.
7: Richard, Romuald, Ronan (2b).
8: Cuthman, Elfleda, Jerome Emiliani, Kew, Stephen of Muret.
9: Apollonia, Teilo.
10: Scholastica, Trumwine, William of Malavalla.
11: Caedmon, Gobnet, Gregory II, Benedict of Aniane.
12: Ethilwald (1).
13: Ermingild, Huna, Modomnoc, Catharine dei Ricci.
14: Conran, Cyril and Methodius, Valentine, Zeno of Rome, Sava of Serbia.
15: Sigfrid (2).
16: Juliana, Benedict Joseph Labre.
17: Finan of Lindisfarne, Fintan of Clonenagh, Loman, Seven Servite Founders.
18: Colman of Lindisfarne, Fra Angelico.
19:
20: Wulfric, Eustochium Calafato.
21: Peter Damian, Fructuosus.
22: Margaret of Cortona.
23: Jurmin, Milburga, Polycarp, Willigis.
24: Matthias.
25: Ethelbert of Kent, Walburga.
26:
27: Alnoth, Leander, Herefrith, Gabriel Possenti.
28: Herefrith, Oswald of Worcester.
29: Cassian

March

1: David of Wales, Swithbert, Rudesind.
2: Chad, Joavan.
3: Non, Winwaloe, Cunegund, Marinus.
4: Adrian of May, Casimir, Owin.
5: Ciaran of Saighir, Piran.
6: Baldred and Billfrith, Chrodegang, Cyneburg (1), Fridolin, Tibba, Conon, Colette.

7: Eosterwine, Perpetua and Felicitas.
8: Duthac, Felix of Dunwich, John of God, Senan.
9: Bosa, Constantine, Forty Martyrs of Sebaste, Frances of Rome, Gregory of Nyssa, Dominic Savio.
10: Kessog, John Ogilvie.
11: Oengus, Eulogius of Cordoba.
12: Alphege (2), Gregory, Mura, Paul Aurelian, Maximilian, Pionius.
13: Gerald of Mayo, Mochoemoc.
14:
15: Longinus, Louise de Marillac, Zacharias, Clement Hofbauer.
16: Finan Lobur, Abraham Kidunaia.
17: Patrick, Withburga, Gertrude of Nivelles.
18: Christian, Cyril of Jerusalem, Edward the Martyr, Finan of Aberdeen.
19: Alcmund, Joseph.
20: Cuthbert, Herbert of Derwentwater, Wulfram.
21: Benedict, Enda, Nicholas of Flue.
22:
23: Gwinear, Turibius.
24: Dunchad, Hildelith, Macartan.
25: B.V.M., Alfwold, Dismas.
26: Liudger, William of Norwich.
27: Rupert.
28: Alkelda of Middleham.
29: Gwynllyw and Gwladys.
30: John Climacus, Osburga, Zosimus of Syracuse, Leonard Murialdo.
31:

April

1: Agilbert, Gilbert of Caithness, Tewdric, Walaric, Hugh of Grenoble.
2: Francis of Paola, Mary of Egypt.
3: Pancras of Taormina, Richard of Chichester, Agape, Irene, and Chione.
4: Ambrose, Isidore.
5: Derfel, Vincent Ferrer.
6: Elstan, Irenaeus of Sirmium.
7: Celsus, Finan Cam, Goran, John Baptist de La Salle.
8:
9: Madrun, Mary of Egypt.
10: Beocca and Hethor, Hedda of Peterborough.
11: Guthlac, Stanislas.
12: Zeno of Verona.
13: Guinoch, Martin I, Carpus, Papylus, and Agathonice.
14: Caradoc, Tiburtius and Companions, Benezet.
15: Paternus of Wales, Ruadhan.
16: Bernadette, Magnus, Paternus of Avranches, Benedict Joseph Labre.
17: Donnan.
18: Laserian, Apollonius.
19: Alphege (1), Leo IX.
20: Caedwalla, Agnes of Montepulciano.
21: Anselm, Beuno, Ethilwald (2), Maelrubba.
22: Theodore of Sykeon.
23: George, Adalbert of Prague.
24: Egbert, Fidelis, Ives, Mellitus, Wilfrid.
25: Mark.
26: Cletus, Riquier.
27: Machalus, Zita.
28: Louis de Montfort, Vitalis, Peter Chanel.
29: Catherine of Siena, Endellion, Hugh of Cluny, Peter the Martyr, Robert of Molesme, Wilfrid II, Joseph Cottolengo.
30: Erkenwald, Pius V.

May

1: Asaph, Brioc, Corentin, Joseph, Marcoul, Philip and James.
2: Athanasius, Gennys, Mafalda, Theodosius.
3: Holy Cross, Glywys, Philip and James, Pellegrino Laziosi.
4:
5: Hydroc.
6: Edbert, Marian and James.
7: John of Beverley, Lindhard.
8: Indract, Odger, Victor (2), Wiro, Peter of Tarentaise.
9:
10: Catald, Conleth, Gordian and Epimachus, Antoninus, John of Avila.
11: Comgall, Credan (1), Tudy, Maieul, Ignatius of Laconi.
12: Ethelhard, Fremund, Nereus and Achilleus, Pancras of Rome.
13: Robert Bellarmine.
14: Matthias, Gemma Galgani, Maria Mazzarello.
15: Berchtun, Dympna, Hallvard, Pachomius, Isidore the Farmer.
16: Brendan the Navigator, Carantoc, Peregrine of Auxerre, Simon Stock, John of Nepomuk.
17: Madron, Paschal Baylon.
18: Elgiva, John I.
19: Dunstan, Peter Celestine, Pudentiana, Ivo.
20: Bernardino of Siena, Ethelbert of East Anglia.
21: Collen, Godric, Andrew Bobola.
22: Helen of Carnavon, Rita of Cascia.
23: William of Rochester, Montanus and Lucius, Alexander Nevski.
24: David of Scotland.
25: Madeleine Barat, Gregory VII, Urban, Zenobius.
26: Augustine of Canterbury, Philip Neri, Priscus.

27: Bede, Julius the Veteran.
28: Bernard of Aosta.
29: Alexander (1), M. Mag. de' Pazzi.
30: Hubert, Joan of Arc, Ferdinand.
31: B.V.M., Petronilla.

June

1: Gwen of Brittany, Justin, Nicomedes, Ronan (2a), Whyte, Wistan.
2: Erasmus, Marcellinus and Peter, Oda.
3: Genesius of Clermont, Kevin, Charles Lwanga and Companions.
4: Edfrith, Ninnoc, Petroc.
5: Boniface.
6: Gudwal, Jarlath, Norbert, Primus and Felician.
7: Meriasek, Robert of Newminster, Antonio Gianelli.
8: Medard, William of York.
9: Columba, Ephraem.
10: Ithamar.
11: Barnabas.
12: Basilides, Eskil, Leo II, Odulf.
13: Antony of Padua.
14: Dogmael.
15: Trillo, Vitus and Companions.
16: Cyricus, Ismael.
17: Adulf, Alban, Botulf, Briavel, Moling, Nectan, Rainier of Pisa.
18: Mark and Marcellian, Gregory Barbarigo.
19: Gervase and Protase, Juliana Falconieri, Romuald.
20: Alban, Edward the Martyr, Govan, Adalbert.
21: Aloysius Gonzaga, Leufred, Mewan.
22: Acacius, John Fisher and Thomas More, Paulinus of Nola.
23: Cyneburg, Etheldreda, Joseph Cafasso.
24: Bartholomew of Farne, John the Baptist.
25: Adalbert, William of Montevergine, Maximus of Turin.
26: John and Paul, Salvius.
27: Cyril of Alexandria, Zoilus.
28: Austell, Irenaeus, Potamiaena and Basilides.
29: Elwin, Judith and Salome, Peter and Paul.
30: Martyrs of Rome, Theobald of Provins, George the Hagiorite.

July

1: Julius and Aaron, Oliver Plunket, Serf.
2: B.V.M., Processus and Martinian, Oudoceus.
3: Germanus of Man, Thomas.
4: Elizabeth of Portugal, Andrew of Crete.
5: Modwenna, Morwenna, Antony Zaccaria, Athanasius the Athonite.
6: Maria Goretti, Monenna, Newlyn, Sexburga, Godeliva.
7: Boisil, Erkengota, Ethelburga (2), Hedda of Winchester, Maelruain, Merryn, Palladius, Thomas of Canterbury, Willibald, Sunniva.
8: Grimbald, Kilian, Urith.
9: Everild, Veronica Giuliani, Martyrs of Gorkum.
10: Alexander (2), Seven Brothers.
11: Benedict, Drostan, Thurketyl, Olga.
12: John Gualbert.
13: Henry the Emperor, Mildred, Silas.
14: Boniface of Savoy, Camillus, Deusdedit, Phocas of Sinope.
15: Bonaventure, David of Sweden, Donald, Swithun, Vladimir.
16: Helier, Plechtelm, Stephen Harding, Tenenan.
17: Alexis, Kenelm, Martyrs of Scillium.
18: Arnulf (1), Edburga of Bicester, Edburga of Winchester.
19: Macrina the Younger.
20: Arild, Margaret of Antioch, Wilgefortis, Wulmar.
21: Laurence of Brindisi, Praxedes, Victor.
22: Mary Magdalene, Wandrille.
23: Apollinaris, Bridget of Sweden, Cassian, Apollonius, Magi.
24: Christina, Wulfhad, and Ruffin, Boris and Gleb, Lewinna.
25: Christopher, James the Great.
26: Joachim and Anne.
27: Pantaleon, Seven Sleepers, Seven Apostles of Bulgaria.
28: Botvid, Samson.
29: Lupus, Martha, Olaf, Simplicius, Sulian.
30: Abdon and Sennen, Peter Chrysologus, Tatwin.
31: Germanus of Auxerre, Ignatius Loyola, Joseph of Arimathea, Neot, Justin de Jacobis, Helen of Skovde.

August

1: Alphonsus, Ethelwold, Kyned, Maccabees.
2: Etheldritha, Eusebius, Plegmund, Sidwell, Stephen I, Thomas of Hales.
3: Manaccus, Waldef.
4: Molua, Sithney, John Baptist Vianney.
5: Cassyon, Oswald of Northumbria.
6: Sixtus.
7: Cajetan.
8: Dominic, Lide.
9: Romanus (1).
10: Bettelin (2), Laurence.
11: Blane, Clare, Tiburtius and Susanna.
12: Jambert, Murtagh.
13: Hippolytus, Radegund, Wigbert, Benild, Maximus the Confessor.
14: Maximilian Kolbe.

15: B.V.M., Arnulf (2), Tarsicius.
16: Armel, Roch, Stephen of Hungary, Laurence Loricatus.
17: Hyacinth of Cracow, Clare of Montefalco.
18: Agapitus, Helena.
19: Credan (2), John Eudes, Mochta, Louis of Toulouse.
20: Bernard, Oswin, Philibert, Rognvald.
21: Pius X.
22: Alexander (3), Arnulf (3), Sigfrid (1).
23: Philip Benizi, Rose of Lima, Timothy and Companions, Tydfil.
24: Bartholomew, Ouen.
25: Joseph Calasanz, Ebbe, Genesius of Arles, Louis IX.
26: Bregwine, Ninian, Pandonia, Zephyrinus.
27: Decuman, Monica, Rufus, Caesarius of Arles.
28: Augustine of Hippo, Hermes, Julian of Brioude.
29: Edwold, John the Baptist, Sebbi.
30: Felix and Adauctus, Fiacre, Rumon.
31: Aidan, Cuthburga, Eanswith, Quenburga, Waldef (1), Raymund Nonnatus.

September

1: Drithelm, Giles, Priscus of Capua.
2: William of Roskilde.
3: Macanisius, Gregory.
4: Ultan.
5: Bertin, Laurence Giustiniani.
6:
7: Evurtius, Tilbert.
8: B.V.M., Disibod, Ethelburga (3), Kinemark.
9: Bettelin (1), Ciaran of Clonmacnoise, Peter Claver, Gorgonius, Omer, Wulfhilda.
10: Finnian of Moville, Frithestan, Nicholas of Tolentino.
11: Deiniol, Protus and Hyacinth.
12: Ailbe.
13: John Chrysostom.
14: Cornelius and Cyprian, Holy Cross.
15: Adam of Caithness, Catherine of Genoa, Mirin.
16: Cornelius and Cyprian, Edith, Geminianus.
17: Hildegard, Lambert, Robert Bellarmine.
18: Joseph of Copertino.
19: Januarius, Theodore of Canterbury.
20: Eustace, Korean Martyrs.
21: Matthew.
22: Laudus, Maurice, Thomas of Villanova.
23: Adomnan, Thecla.
24: Robert of Knaresborough, Gerard Sagredo.
25: Cadoc (1), Ceolfrith, Finbar, Firmin, Sergius, Albert of Jerusalem, Vincent Strambi, Wivina.
26: Cosmas and Damian, Cyprian and Justina, Nilus.
27: Barry, Florentius, Vincent de Paul.
28: Lioba, Machan, Wenceslas.
29: Michael and All Angels.
30: Honorius, Jerome, Tancred, Torthred and Tova.

October

1: Bavo, Mylor, Remigius, Theresa of Lisieux.
2: Guardian Angels, Leger, Thomas of Hereford.
3: Hewalds.
4: Francis of Assisi.
5: Maurus and Placid.
6: Bruno, Faith.
7: Helen of Cornwall, Osith, Justina of Padua.
8: Iwi, Keyne, Triduana, Pelagia.
9: Denys, John Leonardi, Luis Bertran.
10: Francis Borgia, Geron, Paulinus of York.
11: Canice, Ethelburga (1), Alexander Sauli.
12: Edwin, Wilfrid.
13: Comgan, Edward the Confessor, Gerald of Aurillac.
14: Burchard, Callistus, Manacca, Selevan.
15: Albert, Tecla, Theresa of Avila.
16: Gall, Hedwig, Lul, Gerard Majella.
17: Margaret-Mary Alacoque, Ethelred and Ethelbricht, Etheldreda, Ignatius of Antioch, Nothelm, Rule, John the Dwarf.
18: Gwen of Cornwall, John of Bridlington, Justus of Beauvais, Luke.
19: Jean de Brébeuf and Isaac Jogues, Ethbin, Frideswide, Paul of the Cross, Peter of Alcantara, Ptolomaeus and Lucius.
20: Acca, Maria Boscardin.
21: Fintan Munnu, Hilarion, Tuda, Ursula, Malchus.
22: Donatus, Mellon.
23: Ethelfleda, John of Capistrano, Romanus (2), Boethius.
24: Antony Claret, Maglorius, Felix of Thibiuca.
25: Crispin and Crispinian, Forty Martyrs of England and Wales.
26: Bean (2), Cedd, Eata.
27: Odran.
28: Simon and Jude, Salvius.
29: Colman of Kilmacduagh, Merewenna.
30: Alphonsus Rodriguez, Marcellus the Centurion, Clare of Montefalco.
31: Begu, Erc, Foillan, Quentin, Wolfgang.

November

1: All Saints, Benignus, Cadfan, Dingad, Gwythian, Vigor.

2: All Souls.
3: Clydog, Malachy, Pirmin, Martin de Porres, Rumwold, Winefride, Wulgan.
4: Birstan, Charles Borromeo, Clether.
5: Kea, Zachary and Elizabeth.
6: Illtud, Leonard, Melaine, Mennas, Winnoc, Vietnam Martyrs.
7: Congar (2), Willibrord.
8: Cybi, Four Crowned Martyrs, Gerardin, Tysilio, Willehad.
9: Theodore.
10: Aed, Justus, Leo, Andrew Avellino.
11: Martin of Tours, Theodore the Studite.
12: Cadwaladr, Josaphat, Lebuin, Machar.
13: Abbo, Brice, Stanislaus Kostka, Homobonus.
14: Dyfrig, Laurence O'Toole, Modan.
15: Albert the Great, Fintan of Rheinau, Malo.
16: Edmund of Abingdon, Gertrude, Margaret of Scotland, Giuseppe Moscati.
17: Gregory of Tours, Gregory the Wonder-worker, Hilda, Hugh of Lincoln, Martyrs of Paraguay, Philippine Duchesne.
18: Mabyn, Mawes, Odo.
19: Ermenburga, Ronan (2c).
20: Colman of Dromore, Edmund.
21: Condedus.
22: Cecilia, Philemon and Apphia.
23: Clement, Columbanus, Alexander Nevski.
24: Chrysogonus, Colman of Cloyne, Enfleda, Minver.
25: Catherine of Alexandria.
26: Leonard of Port Maurice.
27: Congar (1), Fergus, Virgil.
28: Juthwara, Gregory III, James of the Marches, Catherine Labouré.
29: Brendan of Birr.
30: Andrew.

December

1: Eloi, Tudwal.
2:
3: Birinus, Francis Xavier.
4: Barbara, John Damascene, Osmund.
5: Christina of Markyate, Justinian, Crispina, Galgano.
6: Nicholas.
7: Ambrose, Diuma.
8: B.V.M., Budoc.
9: Wolfeius.
10: Eulalia.
11: Damasus, Daniel the Stylite.
12: Finnian of Clonard, Jane Chantal, Vicelin.
13: Edburga of Minster, Judoc, Lucy.
14: Fingar, Hybald, John of the Cross, Nicasius, Venantius, Fortunatus.
15: Offa of Essex.
16: Bean (1).
17: Lazarus.
18: Flannan, Mawnan, Samthann, Winnibald.
19:
20: Dominic of Silos.
21: Peter Canisius, Thomas the Apostle, Beornwald.
22: Frances Cabrini.
23: Frithebert, Thorlac.
24: Mochua, Sharbel.
25: Alburga, Anastasia.
26: Stephen, Tathai.
27: John the Evangelist.
28: Holy Innocents.
29: Evroult, Thomas of Canterbury.
30: Egwin.
31: Sylvester.